AUSTRALIAN DICTIONARY

OF BIOGRAPHY

General Editor

DOUGLAS PIKE

CORRIGENDA
to accompany volume 5

Australian Dictionary of Biography
Volume 1: 1788-1850 A-H
Volume 2: 1788-1850 I-Z
Volume 3: 1851-1890 A-C
Volume 4: 1851-1890 D-J

This corrigenda cancels all previous corrigenda

CORRIGENDA
Australian Dictionary of Biography
Volume 1: 1788-1850 A-H

vii ACKNOWLEDGMENTS
line 9 *for* H. *read* W.
line 36 *read* O'Keeffe

5b ALLAN, D.
line 24 *for* About *read* In

6a ALLEN, G.
line 15 *delete* Moore's successor

7b ALLISON
line 44 *delete* [q.v.]

9b ALLPORT
line 28 *for* brother *read* son

11b ALT
line 13 *for* 1758 *read* 1757

14a ANDERSON, Joseph
line 12 *for* 1848 *read* 1841
line 13 *for* returned to England *read* had moved to India

32b ARTHUR, Sir George
lines 9-10 *delete* where . . . port
lines 19-20 *for* thanked . . . on *read* praised his gallantry in action.

33a lines 1-2 *for* his . . . and *read* On his return Arthur was given the freedom of the city of
line 46 *delete* improperly

39a ATKINS, R.
line 11 *for* 1791 *read* 1792

42b ATKINSON, J.
lines 17-18 *for* died in infancy. *read* lived to a ripe old age at Orange.

48a BAILEY
line 1 *for* 1873 *read* 1879.
line 6 *for* LL.B. *read* LL.D.

50b BALL
lines 37-40 *for* been . . . duty *read* sufficiently recovered to return to duty in December 1792 and in 1795 was promoted captain.

51a BALLOW
line 1 *for* 1809 *read* 1804
line 9 *for* 1837 . . . government *read* 1838 after serving as assistant surgeon at the Sydney general
line 43 *for* Thomson *read* Thompson

56a BANNISTER
line 64 *delete* re-em-

56b line 1 *for* ployment by *read* compensation from

57b BARKER, T.
line 9 *read* October

59b BARNES
line 16 *read* Paterson

64a BARTLEY
line 25 *read* nine

65a BASS
line 1 *for* filled *read* fitted

66b BATE
line 7 *for* His *read* A

74a BAUGHAN
line 5 *for* a pair of *read* five

83a BELLASIS
line 35 *for* [qq.v.] *read* [q.v.]

84a BENJAMIN, S.
lines 12-16 *for* The partnership . . . marriages. *read* On 15 April 1840 he married Julia, daughter of Abraham Moses.

92a BERRY
line 3 *for* seven *read* nine

99a BIGGE
line 4 *for* second *read* third
line 14 *for* 1814 *read* 1813
line 47 *read* weakening

103a BIRABAN
line 2 *for* Known . . . tribe *read* He returned to Lake Macquarie and
line 13 *for* 'Maggill' *read* 'Magill'

108a BISHOP, C.
line 33 *for* Nothing . . . him. *read* He appears to have died in 1810.

109b BLACKBURN
line 44 *for* where . . . 1846 *read* , which from 1843 became increasingly the main centre of his activities. From 1844 he
line 45 *for* as *read* was
     add later *after* and
line 49 *for* 20 *read* 16

110a line 5 *add* Fitzroy *before* Church
line 22 *for* 43 *read* 41
line 23 *for* 1839 *read* 1840
line 44 *delete* and court-house
line 62 *for* - *read*)
line 63 *delete* 40)

111b BLAIR
line 1 *for* 1889 *read* 1880

112a lines 51-54 *for* In 1883 . . . 1889. *read* On 11 June 1880 he died at his home, Greenmount, Toorak.

118b BLIGH, W.
line 4 *for* customs officer *read* boatman and land waiter in the customs service.

127b BOUCHER
line 1 *after* Frederick *add* (1801-1873)

128b lines 5-6 *delete* may ... who

132a BOURKE
line 18 *for* 2 *read* 4
line 26 *for* 4 *read* 7

132b line 63 *for* 1838 *read* 1837

138a BOWMAN, James
line 32 *for* Elizabeth *read* Mary

145a BRADLEY
line 7 *for* Mitchell *read* Witchell

153a BRISBANE
line 55 *for* Church *read* London

153b lines 10-13 *for* lifted . . . ending
read did not apply any censorship
when W. C. Wentworth's [q.v.]
Australian began publication, and
ended

157a BROOKS
line 9 *for* had to row *read* sailed

157b line 5 *delete* Richard

158b BROUGHTON, W.
line 11 *for* three *read* four

169b BROWNING
line 42 *for* Arthur *read* Franklin

172b BRUNY
line 1, bibliography *for* M. *read* E.

177a BUNCE
line 7, bibliography *read* Leich-hardt.

181b BURN
line 22 *read* Jemima

182a line 5 *read* Castle Town
line 43 *read* Jemima

189a BUSBY, John
line 63 *for* 1886 *read* 1887

195b CALLAGHAN
line 2 *for* 1851 *read* 1815

201b CAMPBELL, P. L.
line 1 *delete* (fl.
line 2 *read* (1826-1848)

202b line 46 *add* He died in London on
4 October 1848.

207b CAMPBELL, Robert junior
line 8 *read* Ramsay

215b CATCHPOLE
line 40 *add* on 13 May 1819.

223a CIMITIERE
line 18 *delete* [q.v.]

229a CLARK, W. J. T.
line 12 *for* Glenorchy *read* Campbell Town

229b line 29 *for* 15 *read* 13

238a COLLINS, D.
line 2 *delete* [q.v.]

247a CORDEAUX
line 19 *for* Cars *read* Caro
lines 62-64 *delete* Thomas Moore
... England,

247b line 1 *delete* and

248a COTTER
line 3 *read* Bantry

251b COVER
line 29 *read* Hassall

254b COWPER
line 53 *for* -29 *read* and 1829

255a line 30 *read* Frederic

257b COX, J. E.
lines 3-5 *for* England . . . Suffolk
read Suffolk, England. On 19 January 1821 he married Mary Ann
Halls at St James's, Bristol,

258a line 38 *read* Elliott

264a CROWDER
lines 23-24 *for* May 1793 *read*
January 1794

266a CUNNINGHAM
line 28 *for* 1829 *read* 1820

275a DACRE
line 19 *read* Bennet

277a DAMPIER
line 1 *for* 1652 *read* 1651
lines 2-3 *for* 8 June 1652 *read* 5
September 1651

278a line 26 *add* He died in London in
1715.
line 5, bibliography *add* L. R.
Marchant, 'William Dampier',
JRWAHS, 6 (1963).

279b DANA, J. D.
line 6 *for* efforts *read* effects

280a DANGAR
line 46 *read* Dartbrook

286a DARLING
line 58 *add* his wife, *after* by

288a DASHWOOD
line 6 *for* six *read* four
lines 8-9 *delete* until ... granted

289a DAVEY
line 44 *for* 1814 *read* 1815

9b DALLEY
line 14, bibliography *for* Angus *read* Augustus

38b DE BOOS
line 21 *for* 73 *read* 71

44b DENIEHY
line 32 *for* 1844 *read* 1845

45a line 19 *for* world *read* word

46a line 3 *for* Jamieson *read* Jameson

46b lines 11-12, bibliography delete *Bathurst* ... 1865;

83a DONAGHY
line 3 *for* After *read* Before
lines 4-5 *delete* John ... John
line 6 *for* were *read* had been
line 15 *for* 1868 *read* 1886

123a DYMOCK
lines 9-10 *delete* a councillor . . . University

132b EGGLESTON
line 14 *for* three *read* two *and for* one daughter *read* two daughters

137a ELLIOTT
line 12 *for* Westrip *read* Neestrip

155a FARNELL
line 13, bibliography *for* 1893 *read* 1883

155b FARR
line 40 *for* 95 *read* 96

182a FITZHARDINGE
line 11 *delete* erroneously

186b FLEMING, Joseph
line 18 *delete* [q.v.]

207b FOSTER, W. J.
line 14, bibliography *for* 1893 *read* 1883

216b FRASER, Sir Simon
line 46 *for* Anne *read* Anna

229b GARDINER
line 18 *for* after . . . leave *read* skipped bail

232a GARLICK
line 19 *for* 1874 *read* 1832?

240b GEOGHEGAN
line 10 *for* Easter . . . 1835 *read* 21 February 1830

241b GEORGE
line 44 *for* May *read* March

245a GILBERT, John
line 20 *for* Mann *read* Manns

245b line 14 *for* Wowingragang *read* Wowingragong
line 16 *delete* who ... them

253b GLADMAN
line 35 *for* 1882 *read* 1886

264a GOODLET
line 28 *for* 1903 *read* 1913
line 36 *for* Boys' School *read* Academy

269a GORDON, Alexander
line 2 *after* born *add* on 14 October 1815

282b GRAHAM, James
lines 42-43 *for* a founding *read* an early

294a GREGORY, A. C.
line 13 *for* Charles *read* Henry

294b lines 2-3 *for* 1863 ... 1879. *read* 1863, on 12 March 1875 was replaced as surveyor-general by W. A. Tully [q.v.], and became geological surveyor.

295a line 39 *for* Cantini *read* Catini
line 55 *for* Gascoigne *read* Gascoyne

306b GUERARD
line 39 *for* Wetterboro *read* Wetterbord

307a line 11, bibliography *for* ML *read* Dixson Lib

308b GUNTHER
line 3 *for* 28 *read* 25
line 21 *for* 1867 *read* 1868

311a GUTHRIE
line 6 *for* bought *read* leased

313a HACK
lines 7-8 *delete* by ... overland

347a HARGRAVES
line 8, bibliography *for* 10 *read* 38

355b HART, John
lines 46-47 *delete* where ... acres

358b HASSELL
line 6 *delete* [q.v.]

359b line 25 *for* Ethyl *read* Ethel

408b HOFFNUNG
line 29 *for* 1857 *read* 1858

416a HOLYMAN
line 37 *for* 1883 *read* 1882

428a HOSE
line 2 *after* born *add* on 24 September 1826
line 3 *delete* Rev.
line 16 *for* 1854 *read* 1855

429b HOSKINS
line 9, bibliography *for* 1893 *read* 1883

449a HUNTER, H.
lines 13-14 *for* but . . . raise *read* and raised

391b CHIRNSIDE
line 3 *for* Berwickshire *read* Cockburnspath, East Lothian
line 5 *for* Fairs *read* Fair
line 37 *add* later *before* building
lines 38-39 *delete* in the 1850s
line 42 *for* and *read* ; his son later acquired

392b line 8 *for* Bigbie *read* Begbie

395b CHRISTISON
line 28 *after* Mary *add* Woodward

399a CLARK, A. T.
line 21 *read* Alexandrina

403a CLARK, C.
line 1 *add* son of Daniel Clark and his wife Susanna, née Strudwicke.

404a CLARK, C. G. H. C.
line 44 *for* 3 *read* 30
for 1876 *read* 1877
line 49 *for* 15 *read* 16

411b CLARKE, G.
lines 5-6 *for* Blomfield *read* Clarke

415b CLARKE, Lady
lines 13-18 *for* In 1900 . . . president *read* In 1898-99 she was a member of the Women's Hospital Committee and in 1900 president of the Alliance Française,
line 19 *add* and *after* Children

417b CLARKE, M.
lines 48-50 *for* none . . . traced *read* at least two married in Victoria and survived him.

419b CLARKE, W.
line 1 *for* b. 1843 *read* 1843-1903

420a line 60 *add* He died at Cape Town on 9 March 1903 and in the same week his only son William Mortimer was killed in a riot.

420b CLARKE, W. B.
line 35 *read* Exequiale

426b CLIBBORN
line 46 *for* cousin *read* witness at the marriage

436b COHEN, Edward
line 7 *for* five *read* four *and for* three *read* four

439a COLE, E. W.
lines 53-54 *for* Jordan . . . Hobart *read* Jorden, of Lauderdale, New Town, Tasmania

443a COLLINS, R.
line 42 *read* Gwendoline

443b line 17 *read* Robert and William were
lines 18-19 *for* He was *read* They were
line 21 *read* They were
line 22 *for* his *read* the
line 2, bibliography *read* 1923

468b COTTEE
line 60 *read* civic

469a line 1, bibliography for One read A

473b COWIE
line 26 *read* in August

478b COWPER, Sir Charles
lines 13-14 *for* and . . . quarrel *read* . He had already quarrelled
line 19 *for* 1859 *read* 1858

489b CRACKNELL
line 3 *read* Salomons

493b CREWS
line 9, bibliography *read* 1859-69

495b CRISP
line 48 *delete* 8
lines 4-5, bibliography *for* 4 June . . . 1916 *read* 7 Dec 1889, 8 May 1897, 4 June, 23 July 1898, 5 Nov 1963, 7 July 1966

506b CUNINGHAM
line 7 *for* daughter *read* sister

509a CURRAN
line 1 *for* Julian *read* J. E. Tenison-

509b line 23 *for* Julian *read* Tenison-

511b CURRIE, J.
line 18 *for* built *read* leased

512b CUSTANCE
line 57 *for* Lawrie *read* Lowrie

291b DAVIES, R.
line 11 for IV read III

295a DAVY
line 5 add was a house surgeon at before Guy's

300a DAWSON
line 3 delete Belford,

301a DEANE
line 64 for violoncello read violin

301b line 1 for Morris . . . violin. read Charles Muzio the violoncello.
line 3 for Paine read Smith

306b DICKSON
lines 25-26 for and . . . England read He lost the case Brown v. Dickson and had to pay £333 in damages. He was also prosecuted for forgery and absconded to England while on bail.

327a DRUMMOND, John
line 20 read Marquis

332a DULHUNTY
line 41 delete [q.v.]

338a DUNLOP, E.
line 2, bibliography read Threlkeld

338b DUNLOP, J.
line 21 for life read list

343a EAGAR
line 15 for Richard read Robert

349b EASTY
line 9 delete [q.v.]

351a EDGE
line 1 add enlisted in the New South Wales Corps on 6 March 1790 and embarked in April. He
line 3 for some . . . March read in February
line 5 for comma read stop
lines 6-10 delete and . . . corps.

357b ENDERBY
line 39 for Gladwyn read Goodwyn

361a EWING
line 9 for the bishop of Tasmania read Bishop Broughton [q.v]
line 17 add He was priested by Bishop Nixon [q.v.] on 21 September 1843.

370a FAWKNER
line 51 for Dalhousie read Talbot

371a FENTON
line 35 for newly read new

378b FINNISS
lines 40-42 for became . . . 1881. read acted as auditor-general in 1876 and served on the Forest Board in 1875-81.

389b FLINDERS
lines 3-4 for parish . . . School read Grammar School and by the vicar of Horbling

413a FRANKLIN
line 40 for February read January

419a FROST
line 3 for Wales read England

419b line 54 for Port read Point

425b GARDINER
line 23 read business

437a GELLIBRAND
line 9 for Risby read Kerby

437b lines 44-47 for He was . . . Hesse. read He and his companion, G. B. L. Hesse, probably lost their horses and perished in the summer heat. The mystery was not solved.

453a GIPPS
line 10, bibliography for moments read comments

457b GOODWIN
line 34 read damages of £400

469b GRANT, John
lines 21-23 for and . . . voyage read . With Hayes, who joined him briefly in exile on the island that year,

498a HACKING
line 11 after European. add In 1794 he was granted thirty acres at Hunter's Hill.
lines 13-14 delete and . . . Hill

501b HALL, E. Smith
line 13 for George read William

502a HALL, E. Swarbreck
line 45 for 1831 read 1851

505b HALLER
line 1 for b. 1808 read 1808-1886

506a lines 24-25 delete is assumed to have
line 26 for daughter read two daughters; he died at East Melbourne on 29 March 1886

506a HALLORAN
lines 7-17 for Westminster . . . Aberdeen read Christ's Hospital. He entered the navy in 1781 but was

gaoled in 1783 for stabbing and killing a fellow midshipman. Acquitted in 1784, he married Mary Boutcher (d. 1792) and ran a school at Exeter until 1788 and then an academy at Alphington until he became insolvent in 1796. He was also charged with immorality. A professed Roman Catholic, he recanted in 1792 but never won the Anglican ordination he wanted. In 1797-98 he was in the navy posing as a chaplain. In 1800 he married Anna Hall and was awarded a doctorate in divinity at King's College, Aberdeen.

507a line 18 *after* son. *add* The Colonial Office advised Governor Darling of Halloran's shady career and rejected his appeal for a land grant for his establishment.
line 59 *for* first *read* second

507b bibliography *add* K. Grose, 'Dr. Halloran', *Aust J of Education*, Oct 1970

520b HARRISON
line 35 *read* Rocky

523b HASSALL, T.
line 45 *read* Queensland

524a HAWDON
line 58 *for* After . . . he *read* She died in 1854. In 1872 his son Arthur Joseph
line 61 *for* at Christchurch. *read* in Canterbury, New Zealand.

524b HAWKINS
line 36 *for* owned *read* leased

525a lines 18-19 *for* and . . . [qq.v.] *read* [q.v.]

526b HAYES, Sir Henry
lines 13-15 *for* defiant . . . and *read* defiance of Governor King earned Grant exile on Norfolk Island, Margarot and Hayes in

534b HEYDON
line 40 *for* 1838 *read* 1839

544b HOBSON, E. C.
lines 17-20 *delete* The . . . it.

549b HOLDEN
line 5 *for* 7 *read* 8

555a HOSKING
lines 25-27 *for* For a . . . with *read* His father was the London agent of Eagar [q.v.] & Forbes and John became the partner of

558b HOWE, G.
lines 20-21 *for* as . . . Horatio, *read* a son, Horatio Spencer Wills [q.v.],

562b HULL
line 18 *add* and *after* England

563b HUME, A. H.
line 15 *for* Barker *read* Barber

564b HUME, H.
line 60 *after* John *read* and

566b HUMPHREY
line 40 *delete* [q.v.]

573 HUON
read KERILLEAU *throughout*

573b line 48 *for* His *read* At Parramatta on 16 March 1812 his
line 52 *for* 1815 *read* 1811

574a HUTCHINS
line 49 *delete* [q.v.]

575a HUTCHINSON
line 62 *add* Forest *after* Sutton

577b HUXLEY
line 10 *delete* (M.B. London, 1845)

157a BEST, J.
line 7 read Vibilia

157b line 51 read Aidan's

177b BLACKMORE
line 1, bibliography before Early
add M. E. P. Sharp et al,

190b BONWICK
line 4 for child read son

195a BOOTHBY, B.
line 49 for 121 read 84

197b BOOTHBY, W.
line 32 for 1864 read 1861
line 47 for 1866 read 1864

207a BOWEN
line 3, bibliography read Carnarvon

208b BOWMAN
line 15 for Carey's read Cary's
[q.v.]

218b BRAIM
line 47 for 1867 read 1866
line 49 for Islington read Ilsington
line 53 for September read November

221b BRAZIER
line 3 delete McMillan
line 5 for Eliza, née Warren read
Mary, née McMillan

239a BRODRIBB
line 8 for 96 read 95 and for rector
read vicar

240b BROMBY
line 61 for 1863 read 1864

280a BRUNTON
line 44 read 1868

283b BUCHANAN, J.
line 24 read Southern

284a BUCHANAN, N.
line 28 for Thompson read Thomson

288a BUCKLAND, J.
line 16 read Frederic
line 18 for 13 read 3

297b BUNNY
line 29 read linguist

299b BURGESS
line 6 read civic

308b BURT
line 1, bibliography read Mc-
Clemans

315b BUTLER, H.
line 3 delete surgeon

320b BUZACOTT
line 3 for July read August

338b CAMERON, E. H.
line 13 for 1863 read 1860

341a CAMPBELL, Alexander
lines 28-29 for by 1850 read in
1843
line 48 after the read Sydney
branch of the

347b CAMPBELL, W.
lines 9-10 for Macarthur's . . .
Mountains read Macarthurs' Richlands station near Goulburn

348b CANI
line 8 read Ferretti

351a CANTERBURY
line 11 for 23 read 24
line 12 for Thomson read Tomson

357a CARR-BOYD
line 4 delete Dr
line 7 for There read At Campbell
Town

363a CARTER, G.
line 1 read 1830

363b line 36 delete aged 71

364a CARY
line 39 for 1839 read 1838

365a CASEY, J.
line 21 read Sandhurst
line 23 delete He . . . and
line 24 for in read In and after 80
add he

366a CASEY, R.
line 47 for 1892 read 1893

366b lines 15-16 delete remained . . . he
line 17 for sons read children

367b CASSELL
line 23 read Bruford

373b CHALLINOR
line 1 delete ?
line 2 add on 22 June 1814

375b CHALMERS, J.
line 59 for 1886 read 1885

376b CHALMERS, William
lines 2-3 for February read September

380b CHAPMAN, H.
line 3 add on 21 July 1803

382a line 8 for 1867 read 1868

CORRIGENDA

Australian Dictionary of Biography

Volume 3 : 1851-1890 A-C

10a à BECKETT, T. T.
line 11 *add* He left his estate to his surviving children and his second wife Laura Jane, née Stuckey.
line 8, bibliography *for* 1860-80 *read* 1859-69

15a ADAMS, F.
line 5, bibliography *read* Gavah

18a ADAMSON
line 1 *for* 1828 *read* 1827
line 3 *after* born *add* on 6 August 1827
line 49 *after* Stevenson. *add* She died in 1864 and on 26 August 1873 at Geelong he married Catherine Synnot.

18b AGNEW
line 1 *for* WILSON *read* WILLSON

20b ALDERSON
line 37 *for* Milford *read* Mitford

22a ALLAN, G.
line 40 *for* His son George *read* He

24a ALLAN, W.
line 3, bibliography *for* 1897 *read* 1891

31b ANDERSON, W.
lines 53-54 *for* by a radical candidate *read* and 1894
line 59 *for* Michael *read* Matthew

32a ANDERSON, W. A.
line 4 *after* only *read* surviving

37a ANGAS
line 38 *for* 1871 *read* 1876

39b APLIN
line 3 *for* Cowl, *read* Combe
line 7 *for* Burton *read* Bourton

43b ARCHIBALD
line 38 *for* 'ease' *read* 'case'

46b line 30 *for* Australia's *read* New South Wales's

49a ARMITAGE
line 14 *delete* at Madras

51a ARMSTRONG, bros
line 40 *for* Rupert *read* Robert
line 53 *add* -72 *after* 1871
line 58 *for* née Elliott, *read* Elliot, née Armstrong,

52a ARMYTAGE
line 47 *for* Geelong *read* the Diocesan
line 48 *after* was *add* part of

56a ASTLEY
line 6 *for* 1855 *read* 1859

58b ATKIN
line 9 *read* Shropshire
line 39 *for* March *read* January
line 41 *for* On 26 April *read* In

70b BADHAM
line 28 *read* Mnemosyne

71a lines 17-18 *for* the . . . Union *read* are the Badham Building, the Badham room in the union

72a BAGOT, R.
line 3 *read* Edwards
lines 3-4 *read* Sydney in 1849

72b lines 29-30 *read* Gregory.
line 32 *for* nineties *read* eighties

74a BAILEY
line 3, bibliography *for* 27 *read* 28

75a BAKER, E.
line 25 *read* Salomons

81a BALFOUR
line 39 *for* south *read* north

95a BARKLY
line 42 *for* 'Left' . . . Conservatives *read* radicals and ministerialists

109b BARRY
lines 33-34 *delete* and . . . off

111b BARRY, Z.
line 2 *after* born *add* on 1 February 1827
line 25 *for* 1862 *read* 1861

116a BASSETT
line 35 *read* in 1854

116b lines 60-61 *for* London . . . 1890) *read* Edinburgh (M.R.C.S.; M.D., 1880)

123b BEAN
lines 24-25 *delete* the . . . [q.v.],

124b line 2 *for* He was the *read* With J. L. Cuthbertson [q.v.] he was a

139b BENJAMIN
lines 12-15 *for* officially . . . [q.v.] *read* was present at the formal opening of Princes Bridge

147b BEOR
line 59 *for* July *read* June

150b BERRY, D.
line 8 *delete* [q.v.]

152b BERRY, G.
line 10 *for* 12 *read* 2

5a IRWIN
line 17 *for* 13th *read* 63rd
line 31 *read* five sons and four

5b line 49 *read* Stirling

17a JOHNSON, Richard
line 1 *for* 1753 *read* 1753?
line 11 *for* London *read* Oxford
and for 1786 *read* 1784

19a lines 38-40 *delete* Seven . . . Norfolk

19b JOHNSTON, E.
line 1 *for* 1771? *read* 1767
line 2 *for* about 15 *read* 20

32b KANE
line 57 *add* on 1 May 1883
line 58 *for* Lily *read* Alicia

35b KAY, W.
line 45 *for* 33 *read* 34

36b KELLY
lines 2-3 *read* 24 December

37b line 8, bibliography *for* Mar *read*
May

41b KEMP
line 39 *for* 1856 *read* 1854

46b KENT, W.
line 28 *for* principle *read* chief

51a KERR
line 24 *for* Charles *read* William
line 25 *delete* [q.v.]

52a KINCHELA
line 9 *for* 1831 *read* 1832

56a KING, P. G.
line 32 *add* 1788 *after* February

61b KING, P. P.
line 43 *for* 83 *read* 84

63a line 42 *for* 1834 *read* 1839

63b line 59 *add* stock *after* became
line 60 *for* 1854 *read* 1851

81a LANG, J. D.
line 27 *delete* In January 1859

85a LANGLANDS
line 10 *for* 1849 *read* 1848
line 5, bibliography *read* Nonconformists

91a LA TROBE
line 16 *for* 1846 *read* 1846-47

96b LAWSON
line 22 *delete* [q.v.]
lines 33-34 *delete* In 1828 . . . horses.

101b LEE
line 16 *delete* [q.v.]

108b LEVEY
line 1 *after* BARNETT *read*
(BERNARD)

119a LILLIE
lines 6-7, bibliography *for* Evening
. . . 3 *read* Lyttelton Times, 4

124a LOGAN
line 44 *read* Allan

143b LYTTLETON
line 22 *read* Lyttelton

144b MACARTHUR, A.
line 19 *for* , and . . . Jones *read*
Jones and his wife Fanny Edith

163b MACDOUGALL
line 60 *for* John *read* James

172a McKENZIE, A. K.
line 6 *for* sister *read* cousin

172b lines 5-6 *delete* and . . . Australia

190b MACQUARIE, L.
line 15 *for* along *read* among

194a line 26 *read* elegiac

196a MACQUEEN
line 34 *for* debtors *read* creditors

198a MAKINSON
line 12 *for* Bird *read* Sumner

207a MARRIOTT
line 10 *for* 1829 *read* 1833
line 11 *for* 1835 *read* 1836

207b line 14 *for* In December 1859 *read*
On 28 January 1860

213a MARTENS
line 43 *for* Church *read* cemetery

218a MEAGHER
line 11 *for* Confederate *read* Union

220a MEEHAN
line 24 *for* laid out *read* surveyed

226a MIDDLETON
lines 7-8 *for* his wife's death *read*
the death of his wife Mary Ann,
née Hull,

226b line 62 *for* Richard *read* Robert

231b MILLS, J. B.
line 25 *for* H *read* N

233b MINCHIN
line 54 *for* George *read* John

235a MITCHEL
line 58 *for* two *read* three

243b MOLLISON
lines 3-4 *for* overlanders . . . parliament *read* overlanders and pastoralists

244a line 28 *for* 1856 *read* 1858

251a MONTEFIORE
lines 27-30 *for* Early . . . London.
read After the depression the
Montefiore firm in Sydney went
bankrupt. The London firm had
suspended payment in 1841 and
Montefiore had returned to England.

254a MOORE, J. J.
line 1 *for* d. *read* 1790-

269a MURDOCH, P.
line 1 *delete* ? *after* 1795
lines 2-6 *for* descended . . . Wallaces
read born on 15 January 1795, son
of James Murdoch and his wife
Frances, daughter of John Wallace,

269b lines 21-24 *delete* in December . . .
He
line 32 *delete* whose Christian
names were
line 33 *add* whom he had married
on 5 February 1830 at Capelrig;
she *after* Brown,
line 34 *add* , survived by four
children. *after* later

274b MURRAY, T. A.
line 41 *for* 1840, *read* 1834

278a NAIRN
lines 47-48 *delete* where . . . 1829

280a NATHAN
line 25 *for* 1890 *read* 1898

280a NEALES
lines 4-5 *for* a sister of Jeremy *read*
née

285a NICHOLSON
line 57 *for* He . . . two *read* Of his
three

285b NIXON
line 30 *for* 1848 *read* 1847

288b NOBBS
lines 47-48 *delete* as a priest

290b OAKDEN
lines 3-4 *delete* (where . . . discoverer)
line 31 *for* Georgiana *read* Georgina

298b O'FLAHERTY
lines 60-63 *for* played . . . York
read appeared at theatres in New
York, Philadelphia and other cities.

299a bibliography *add* Bow Bells, 21
Dec 1864

311a PALMER, P.
line 18 *for* William Bryan *read*
Warrior

321b PEEL
line 3 *for* many *read* four
lines 4-5 *delete* , and . . . longer

325b PETRIE
line 3 *add* son of Walter Petrie and
Margaret, née Hutchinson.

326a line 47 *add* At Edinburgh in 1821
he had married Mary Cuthbertson;
they had nine sons and a daughter.
after fied.
line 49 *delete* lord

355b PUGH
line 10 *add* by a medical practitioner *after* first

364b RAVEN
line 54 *read* Squire [q.v.]

375b REID, A.
line 34 *for* 1836 *read* 1834

382b RITCHIE
line 24 *add* at Launceston *after* her

399a ROSS, Robert (minister)
line 7, bibliography *add* -Smith
after Lamb

404a RUMKER
lines 27-28 *delete* , through . . .
Brisbane,

411a RUTLEDGE
line 5 *read* Longford

412a line 17 *read* 1852

417b SAMSON
line 37 *add* He was a nominee in
the Western Australian Legislative
Council in 1849-56 and 1859-68.

419a SAVAGE, John
line 34 *for* John *read* Thomas

431b SCOTT, T. H.
line 17 *for* was . . . been *read* went
bankrupt as

436a SHARLAND
line 3 *delete* surgeon, *and* Mary
line 4 *delete* , née Culley
line 14 *for* Frederick *read* Frederic
lines 18-19 *delete* 1829 . . . and in
line 19 *add* he *after* 1835
lines 21-22 *delete* from practice,

436b line 32 *for* Sara *read* Sarah
line 35 *for* Nodd *read* Nod, Surrey
line 40 *for* Frederick *read* Frederic

444a SIDAWAY
line 1 *for* 1757? *read* 1759
line 4 *for* housebreaking *read* stealing

444b SIDDINS
line 30 *read* Siddins

445b SIMMONS
line 1 *for* 1880? *read* 1893

446b line 15 *add* He died in Sydney on 9 August 1893.

448a SIMPSON, S.
line 1 *for* 1792? *read* 1793
line 2 *for* born *read* baptized on 29 July 1793
line 23 *for* a woman *read* in 1838 Sophia Ann Simpson, a relation
lines 59-61 *for* substantial . . . standing, *read* cottage in Goodna, which

453a SMITH, T. W.
line 28 *for* the *read* an

467b SQUIRE
line 3 *add* for highway robbery

471a STANLEY, O.
line 49 *for* Harvey's *read* Hervey

480b STEPHENS, E.
line 1, bibliography *for* F *read* J

482a STEVENSON
line 14 *delete* , née Hutton,
line 17 *for* widow *read* daughter

495a STRZELECKI
line 12, bibliography *read* Havard

498b STURT
line 4, bibliography *for* 6 *read* 5

501b SWANSTON
line 21 *for* largely . . . for *read* an early subscriber to

505b TEGG
line 15 *for* W. *read* Gideon
line 16 *delete* Wilson

528b THOMSON, J.
line 61 *add* and *after* tions),
lines 62-64 *delete* and . . . spire),

531a THROSBY
lines 57-59 *for* and . . . and *read* arrived in the *Mangles* in August 1820 and at Liverpool in 1824 married Betsey, daughter of William Broughton [q.v.];

535a TORRENS
line 24 *read* Association

548b UNDERWOOD, Joseph
line 14 *for* Surgeon *read* the emancipist

550a VALE
line 8 *for* 1811 *read* 1812
line 11 *for* London *read* Ely

557b VON STIEGLITZ
line 34 *add* Bay District *after* Portland

569a WALSH, W. H.
line 3 *for* 12 *read* 10

569b line 6 *after* Ireland *add* Treherne

570a line 32 *for* March *read* February

575a WATLING
line 8, bibliography *for* N *read* M

576a WEDGE
lines 30-31 *for* by . . . government *read* as a Tasmanian parliamentary paper

585b WENTWORTH, W.C.
lines 42-45 *for* the . . . Wales *read* civilian juries were allowed in civil cases on the application of both parties and the approval of the Supreme Court.

597a WICKHAM
line 3 *for* December *read* November
line 4 *for* Captain *read* Lieutenant
line 18 *for* a *read* on 1 June 1843 Elizabeth, eldest

613a WILTON
line 3 *after* born *add* on 24 October 1795
line 48 *for* B *read* K

613b WINDER
line 18 *read* Leverton

616a WINDEYER
line 26 *reinstate* In July 1846

618a WITTENOOM
line 1 *for* 1789 *read* 1788
line 2 *after* born *add* on 24 October 1788

631a WYNYARD
line 29 *for* Cowe *read* Lowe

633b YOUNG
line 51 *for* [q.v.] *read* junior

AUSTRALIAN
DICTIONARY
OF BIOGRAPHY

VOLUME 5 : 1851-1890

K-Q

Section Editors

BEDE NAIRN
GEOFFREY SERLE
RUSSEL WARD

MELBOURNE UNIVERSITY PRESS

First published 1974
Printed in Australia by John Sands Pty Ltd,
Halstead Press Division, Artarmon, N.S.W. 2064, for
Melbourne University Press, Carlton, Victoria 3053
Overseas Agents: ISBS Inc., Portland, Oregon 97208, U.S.A.

ISBN 0 522 84061 2
Dewey Decimal Classification Number 920.094

Text set in 9 point Juliana type

PREFACE

This volume of the *Australian Dictionary of Biography* is the third of four for the 1851-1890 section. The first two volumes of this section and the two for 1788-1850 have already been published; six have been planned for the third section 1891-1939. This chronological division was designed to simplify production, for over six thousand articles are likely to be included. A general index volume will be prepared when the three sections are completed.

The placing of each individual's name in the appropriate section has been generally determined by when he did his most important work (*floruit*). For articles that overlap the chronological division, preference has usually been given to the earlier period, although most of the important Federationists will appear in the third section.

The selection of names for inclusion in the *Dictionary* has been the result of much consultation and co-operation. After quotas were estimated, Working Parties in each State prepared provisional lists, which were widely circulated and carefully amended. Many of the names were obviously significant and worthy of inclusion. Others, less notable, were chosen simply as samples of the Australian experience. Some had to be omitted through lack of material, and thereby joined the great anonymous mass whose members richly deserve a more honoured place; however, many thousands of these names are accumulating in a 'Biographical Register' at the *Dictionary* headquarters in the Australian National University.

Most authors were nominated by the Working Parties, and the burden of writing has been shared almost equally by university historians and by members of historical and genealogical societies and other specialists. Most of the unsigned entries were prepared in the *Dictionary* office.

The *Dictionary* is a project based on consultation and co-operation. The Australian National University has borne the cost of the headquarters staff, of much research and of some special contingencies, while other Australian universities have supported the project in various ways. Its policies have been determined by the National Committee, composed mainly of representatives from the Departments of History in each Australian university. At Canberra the Editorial Board has kept in touch with all these representatives and with the Working Parties, librarians, archivists and other local experts, as well as overseas correspondents and research assistants in each Australian capital. With such varied support the *Australian Dictionary of Biography* can truly be called a national project.

Canberra
1973   D.P.

ACKNOWLEDGMENTS

Special thanks are due to Professor J. A. La Nauze for his helpful guidance as Chairman of the Editorial Board and to Dr R. A. Gollan for acting in his absence. Those who helped in planning the shape of the work have been acknowledged in earlier volumes.

For this volume the *Dictionary* is grateful for many privileges extended by the Australian universities, especially the Australian National University.

For assistance overseas thanks are due to Peter Saunders and David Barron, Liaison Officers of the National Library of Australia in London; Dr T. I. Rae, National Library of Scotland; the Very Rev. J. B. Longmuir, Principal Clerk of Assembly, the Church of Scotland, Edinburgh; Institution of Royal Engineers, Chatham, Kent; Dr W. G. Baker, Edinburgh; the officials of the Public Record Office, Somerset House and the County Records Offices, and many clergy, archivists and others who have answered calls for help.

The *Dictionary* deeply regrets the death of such notable contributors as the Hon. Sir John Barry, Dr F. J. H. Blaess, Mrs M. Findlay, Rev. Dr F. Hambly, Sir Charles McDonald, A. D. Mickle, Miss J. E. Middleton and Fr O. Thorpe and of A. W. Bazley, Dr G. Buxton and Professor J. W. Davidson who, in their several capacities, greatly assisted the work of this and previous volumes.

Within Australia the *Dictionary* is greatly indebted to countless librarians and archivists in Canberra and each State, to the secretaries of many historical and genealogical societies, to the Registrars-General of Births, Deaths and Marriages, and of Probates, whose generous co-operation has solved many problems. Warm thanks for the free gift of their time and talents are due to all contributors and all members of the National Committee, Editorial Board and the Working Parties. For particular advice the *Dictionary* owes much to Dr C. A. Empis Wemans, Ambassador for Portugal, Mrs B. G. Brent, Miss Alexandra Cameron, Frank Cusack, F. M. Doherty, Mrs Vivienne Ellis, Professor B. Gandevia, Dr I. Getzler, D. J. Grant, A. J. and Nancy Gray, Mrs Dorothy Green, Dr N. Gunson, David Henshaw, Fr W. Kennedy, R. A. Littlejohn, C. Kimberley MacDonald, Miss Jill Roe, Assoc. Professor K. F. Russell, Dr Dorothy Shineberg, Dr F. B. Smith, Dr R. C. Thompson and many others. Grateful acknowledgment is also due to the Director and staff of Melbourne University Press; to the editorial staff: N. B. Nairn, H. J. Gibbney, Nan Phillips, Martha Campbell, Sally O'Neill, Suzanne Edgar and Deirdre Morris; to the painstaking assistance of Audrey Ferguson and Ruth Frappell in Sydney, Noeline Hall in Brisbane, E. Zalums in Adelaide, Wendy Birman in Perth, Mary Nicholls in Tasmania and Margery Walton in New Zealand and to the administrative staff, Dorothy Smith and Norma Gregson.

Late in 1973 the General Editor, Professor D. H. Pike, became seriously ill and was unable to see through to their final stages the proofs of the present volume or personally to write the above Acknowledgments. These tasks were completed by the other members of the editorial staff of the *Dictionary*. At the end of that year Professor Pike reached the normal University retiring age. A tribute to his great service will most fittingly appear in Volume 6, which will bring to the half-way mark the original scheme of the *Dictionary*, and, like the present volume, substantially reflect his own planning.

COMMITTEES

COMMITTEES

AUTHORS

ABBOTT, G. J.:
Lloyd, C.; Martindale; Merriman.
ALLARS, K. G.*:
Norton, J.
ANDREWS, B. G.:
Ledger; Marina.
AUCHMUTY, J. J.:
Pearson, J.
AUSTIN, K. A.:
Peck.
AVELING, Marion:
Purves, J.

BADCOCK, A. M.:
Kane.
BADGER, C. R.:
Lorimer, J.; Moorhouse, J.
BARKER, Theo:
Lee, G.; McPhillamy.
BARNARD, Alan:
Morris, A.; Mort; Nicolle.
BARRETT, John:
Osburne.
BARRY, John V.*:
Kelly, E.
BARTLETT, Geoffrey:
McCulloch, J., politician.
BATE, Weston:
Nicholls.
BEALE, Edgar:
Osborne, P.
BEALE, Howard:
Moresby.
BEARDWOOD, J. C.:
Pottie.
BEEVER, Margot:
Kerferd; Murphy, F.
BERGMAN, George F. J.:
Mocatta; Montefiore, E.
BIRMAN, Wendy:
MacDonald, C.; McNeil; O'Reilly, J.
BISHOP, D. F.:
Lardner.
BLAESS, F. J. H.*:
Oster.
BLAINEY, Geoffrey:
McArthur.
BLAKE, L. J.:
Langlands; Melville, F.
BODI, Leslie:
Püttmann.
BOLGER, Peter:
Morrison, Askin.
BOLTON, G. C.:
Leon; Mosman; Normanby; Palmerston; Pearse.
BOYCE, Peter:
Kennedy, A. E.; Ord.

* deceased

BRANAGAN, D. F.:
Keene; Murray, R.
BRAYBROOKE, E. K.:
Onslow, A. C.
BROWN, D. A.:
MacGillivray.
BRYAN, Harrison:
Macrossan.
BURMESTER, C. A.:
Petherick.
BURNS WOODS, Janice:
O'Grady, M.
BYRNES, Robert Steel:
McGavin.

CABLE, K. J.:
King, G., clergyman; King, R.; Linton; Macarthur, G.
CAMMILLERI, Cara:
Padbury.
CAMPBELL, Joan:
Mitchell, D.
CANNON, Michael:
Montez; Munro, D.
CARTER, M.:
King, H.; Mein.
CATO, Nancy:
Matthews, D.
CHAMBERLAIN, Cliff:
Mate.
CHAMBERS, Don:
Ormond.
CHISHOLM, A. H.:
O'Hea.
CLARKE, Jacqueline:
Longmore.
CLAUGHTON, S. G.:
Kelynack; Moulton.
CLOSE, Cecily:
McCarron.
COLLETT, Barry:
Mason.
COLLINS PERSSE, Michael D. de B.:
Persse.
CONNOLLY, C. N.:
Levy.
COOK, Peter:
Nicholson, W.; Patterson.
COOKSLEY, Jean:
Langton.
CORRIS, Margaret:
Laurens.
COWPER, Norman:
McCrae.
CRANFIELD, Louis R.:
Michel.
CROMBIE, A. C.:
Macdonald, A. R.

CRONIN, **Kathryn**:
  Leon.
CURRY, N. G.:
  MacCullagh.
CUTHBERT, D. D.:
  Primrose.

DALEY, Louise T.:
  Newton.
DAVIS, C.:
  McLean, A.
DAY, P. L.:
  Krause.
DIGNAN, Don:
  McIlwraith, T.
DOLLERY, E. M.:
  Legge.
DOUGAN, Alan:
  Kinross; McIntyre, W., clergyman;
  Mackie; Purves, W.
DOYLE, Alban:
  Laboureyas.
DUFFY, C. J.:
  Lanigan; McAlroy; O'Donovan, J.;
  O'Mahony.
DUNCAN, Ross:
  Playfair.
DUNLOP, E. W.:
  Marsh, M.
DURACK, Mary:
  Pumpkin.

EARNSHAW, John:
  Lang, J.
EDGAR, Suzanne:
  Laidlaw; Maclean, H.; Manning, J. A.;
  Mills; North; Pearce, H.
ENGLAND, George E.:
  Korff.
ERICKSEN, R. F.:
  Nobelius.
ERICKSON, Rica:
  Phillips.
EWERS, John K.:
  Moore, W. D.

FARROW, Fergus:
  McCombie.
FENDLEY, G. C.:
  McCoy.
FISCHER, G. L.:
  Kennedy, H.
FITZPATRICK, Dorothy:
  MacPherson, J.
FOLEY, C. J.:
  O'Neill.
FORSTER, Frank M. C.:
  Maund.
FOWLER, R. H.:
  Newbery.
FRANCIS, Charles:
  Moore, J., lawyer.

FREDMAN, L. E.:
  Levy; Levien.
FRENCH, E. L.:
  Morrison, Alexander.
FROST, Valerie:
  Lindt.
FYSH, Hudson:
  Kennedy, A.

GANDEVIA, Bryan:
  Neild.
GARRETT, John:
  Kirby.
GIBBNEY, H. J.:
  Lamb, E.; Lawes; Lilley; Lukin; Lumholtz;
  Macansh; Macartney, J.; McConnel; Mac-
  Devitt; Macfarlane; McIntyre, D.; Mac-
  kenzie, E.; McNab; Moreton; Morgan, F.;
  Mulligan;   Murray-Prior;   Musgrave;
  Newell; O'Connell; O'Donovan; O'Kane;
  O'Sullivan, P.; Quinn, J.
GITTINS, Jean:
  Kemble; Lewis; McGowan; McLachlan;
  Mathews, J.; Montgomery; Musgrove;
  Nettleton; Osborne, J. W.
GLASS, Frances Devlin:
  Moore, J. S.
GOODMAN, Rupert:
  MacDonnell, R.
GRIFFIN, James:
  Moore, J., bishop; O'Connor, M.
GRIFFITH, John:
  Osburn.
GRIMMETT, I. H.:
  Moore, W.
GROSS, Alan*:
  Palmer, J.; Panton.
GUNSON, Niel:
  Langham; Maitland; Morison; Moss;
  Poore.
GUNTHORPE, S. G.:
  O'Donovan, D.

HADGRAFT, Cecil:
  Lorimer, P.
HAGAN, J.:
  Murphy, W.
HALL, A. R.:
  Khull.
HALL, H. L.:
  Michie.
HALL, Noeline:
  Petrie, T.
HALLEY, E. M.:
  Maley.
HAMBLY, F.*:
  Maughan.
HARDIE, M. F.:
  Oliver, A.
HAYNES, Mark:
  Parry.
HENNING, G. R.:
  McMeckan; Paterson, J.

HENRY, David:
    Lord.
HENRY, Keith:
    Knipe.
HESELTINE, H. P.:
    May, P.
HILL, A. C.:
    Mead.
HILL, A. J.:
    Macarthur, E.
HIRST, J. B.:
    Martin, J., manufacturer; May, F.
HOARE, Michael:
    Macleay.
HOHNEN, Peter:
    McCaughey.
HOLROYD, J. P.:
    Mullen.
HOLT, H. T. E.:
    McFarland; Manning, C.; Milford; Owen.
HONE, J. Ann:
    Kimpton; Lang, M.; Luxton; MacBain; MacGregor, D.; McIlwraith, J.; McKinley; Mackinnon, D.; Macknight; Michaelis; Morton; Officer; Palmer, T.; Peppin.
HORN, K. A. R.:
    Morris, G.
HORNER, John:
    Linger.
HORNER, J. C.:
    Leakey.
HOSIE, John:
    Monnier; Poupinel.
HOWE, Renate:
    Powell; Quick.
HOWELL, P. A.:
    Lutwyche.

INGHAM, S. M.:
    Langridge; Mackay, A.; Mirams; O'Loghlen; O'Shanassy.

JECKELN, L. A.:
    McEvilly; O'Connor, R.
JOBSON, J. X.:
    Palmer, A.
JOHNSON, Ian:
    McDonnell, P.; Palmer, G.
JOHNSTON, Allan:
    McIntyre, J.; Owens.
JOHNSTON, W. Ross:
    Little; Pring.
JONES, P. I.:
    Lloyd, H.
JOYCE, R. B.:
    MacGregor, W.; Mackenzie, R.
JUKES, R. M.:
    Nicholson, M.

KEITH, B. R.:
    Morrison, G.
KIERNAN, Colm:
    Mitchell, J. E.

KING, C. J.:
    Moore, C., botanist.
KING, Hazel:
    King, G., clergyman; McLerie; Mayne.
KINGSTON, Beverley:
    Moffatt.
KNIGHT, J. L.:
    Krause.
KNOX, B. A.:
    Morgan, J.
KUNZ, E. F.:
    Makutz.

LACK, Clem*:
    Pugh.
LACK, John:
    Loder.
LAVERTY, John:
    Marshall, W.; Petrie, J.
LEA-SCARLETT, E. J.:
    Mei Quong Tart; Packer, C.
LEFROY, G. C.:
    Lefroy, A.
LEWIS, Miles:
    Oakden.
LOMAS, L.:
    McDougall, A.
LOWNDES, A. G.:
    Knox.
LOVE, J. H.:
    Loyau.
LYONS, Mark:
    Kidd; Leary; McGibbon; Moore, C., merchant: O'Connor, D. and J.; O'Farrell; O'Sullivan, R.

McBRIDE, Isabel:
    Mathews, R.
McCALLUM, Austin:
    Loughlin; Morey.
McCREDIE, Andrew D.:
    Paling.
McCULLOCH, Samuel Clyde:
    McCulloch, J., businessman, and W.
MACDONALD, Colin*:
    Macdonald, A. C.
McDONALD, C. G.*:
    Knaggs.
McDONALD, D. I.:
    Manning, F.; Penfold; Piddington.
McEVEY, Allan:
    Le Souef.
MACINTYRE, Stuart:
    McLellan.
MACKERRAS, Catherine:
    Marsh, S.; Nathan.
McLAREN, Ian F.:
    Power.
MACLAY, R. W. de M.-:
    Mikluho-Maklai.
McMINN, W. G.:
    Murray, J.

AUTHORS

McNICOLL, Ronald:
Nickle; Pasley; Pratt.
MAHER, J. T.:
Moriarty, A.
MANFORD, Toby:
Lilly.
MANHOOD, C. C.:
MacDonnell, R. G.
MANSFIELD, Bruce E.:
Melville, N.
MARGINSON, Julie:
Pigdon.
MARTIN, A. W.:
Parkes, H.
MEDCALF, M.:
Leake.
MELLOR, D. P.:
Liversidge.
MELLOR, Suzanne G.:
Lansell; Levey; Loureiro; Lyell; Mac-Mahon; Mansergh; Martin, A.; Miller, H.; Monahan; Moore, D. and H.; Nicholson, G.; O'Grady, T.; Permewan; Pohlman.
MICKLE, Alan D.*:
Lyall, W.
MIDDELMANN, Raoul F.:
Matheson; Parkes, E.
MIDDLETON, Emma E.*:
Middleton.
MILLER, J. S. C.:
Mendes.
MINCHIN, E. J.:
Minchin.
MITCHELL, Ann M.:
McCarthy; Munro, J.; Nimmo.
MITCHELL, Bruce:
McIntyre, W., school inspector; Matthews, W.; Morris, R.
MOORE, Michael T.:
Learmonth; Pasco.
MOOREHEAD, Alan:
King, J., explorer.
MORGAN, E. J. R.:
Morgan, W.
MORRIS, Christopher:
Murdoch.
MORRIS, Deirdre:
Miller, W.; Mueller; Pearson, W.
MORRISON, A. A.:
King, H.; Mein.
MORRISSEY, Sylvia:
McKenna.
MUECKE, D. C.:
Muecke.
MUIRDEN, Bruce:
Pitman.
MULVANEY, D. J.:
Mullagh.
MUNE, Marie:
Molineux.
MURRAY-SMITH, S.:
Kernot, C. and W.

NAIRN, Bede:
Lassetter; Long; Martin, J., politician; O'Farrell; Onslow, A. A.; Parker, H.
NELSON, H. N.:
Parker, E.
NILSSON, J. A.:
Mackay, J.

ODDIE, G. A.:
Oddie.
O'GRADY, Frank:
King, P.
O'KELLY, G. J.:
Kelly, W., priest; Kranewitter; McKillop, D.
OLDHAM, Ray:
Manning, J.
O'NEILL, Sally:
Kelly, D.; Knight; Krichauff; Kruse; Lee, D.; Lloyd, J.; Lyster; Mais; Manning, E.; Meredith; Murray, D.
O'REILLY, Neil:
O'Reilly, T.
ORLOVICH, Peter:
Mann.
O'SULLIVAN, David M.:
McCrea.

PARSONS, George:
Lennon; McCracken; McLean, W.; Morrow.
PARSONSON, G. S.:
Paton, J. G.
PASZKOWSKI, L. K.:
Kossak; Kubary.
PEEL, L. J.:
Plummer.
PENNAY, Bruce:
McCulloch, G.
PENNY, B. R.:
Labilliere.
PHILLIPS, A. A.:
Kingsley.
PHILLIPS, Walter:
Osborne, J.
PLAYFORD, Phillip E.:
Nicolay.
POLLARD, N. S.:
King, R.
POTTS, Annette:
Kelly, W., author.
POTTS, R. B.:
Lamb, H.
POWELL, Alan:
Moriarty, M.
POWELL, J. M.:
Ligar.
PRIDMORE, I.:
Nicolay.

QUAIFE, G. R.:
McDougall, R.; Pyke.

AUTHORS

RADIC, Maureen Thérèse:
  Lee, D.; Lyster; Palmer, R.
RAINER, Anthony R.:
  Moubray.
RATHBONE, R. W.:
  Lucas.
REED, T. T.:
  Kendall; Michael.
REEDMAN, L. A.:
  Menkens.
REFSHAUGE, Richard:
  Kintore; Moore, M.
REYNOLDS, John:
  Kayser; Latham.
RICHARDSON, G. D.:
  Mitchell, D. S.
ROBERTS, Kim:
  Keane.
ROBERTS, Philip J.:
  Nicholson, J.
ROBIN, A. de Q.:
  Macartney, H.; Perry.
ROE, Michael:
  Orton.
RODGERS, Dorothy A.:
  King, J. & W. E.
RUDE, G.:
  O'Doherty.
RUSSELL, K. F.:
  Macadam.
RUTLEDGE, Martha:
  Kater; King, G., merchant; Krefft; Lackey;
  Lee, B.; McElhone; Macintosh; Macleay;
  Manning, W.; Marks; Montefiore, J.;
  Oakes; Ogilvie; Patteson.

SELTH, P. A.:
  Pottinger.
SHAW, A. G. L.:
  Loch.
SHAW, Basil:
  McPherson, A.
SHEEHY, Thomas:
  Mair.
SHOLL, Reginald R.:
  Molesworth.
SMITH, C. E.:
  Merewether, E. and F.
STEPHENS, S. E.:
  Meston.
STEVENS, Robin S.:
  McBurney.
STOODLEY, June:
  Nash; O'Kane; Pattison; Plant.
STRAHAN, Frank:
  Massina.
SWAN, R. A.:
  Neumayer.
SWEENEY, Brian J.:
  Quinn, M.
TEALE, Ruth:
  Knaggs; McArthur, A.; Macarthur, W.;
  McLaurin; Marsden; Metcalfe; Pearce, S.

TEMPLETON, Jacqueline:
  Mackinnon, L.
THORN, Barbara:
  Pownall.
THORPE, Osmund*:
  McKillop, M.
TIBBITS, George:
  Kerr.
TIPPING, Marjorie J.:
  Macredie; Paterson, J. F.
TREGENZA, John M.:
  Pearson, C.
TURNER, Ian:
  Lalor.
TURNER, I. S.:
  Pell.

VALLANCE, T. G.:
  Keene; Murray, R.
VAN DER POORTEN, Helen M.:
  Kean; Oliver, M.
VAN DISSEL, Dirk:
  Lyall, J.; Milne; Parkin.

WALMSLEY, M. O.:
  Kingsford.
WALSH, G. P.:
  Kelly, T.; Kempt; King, W. F.; Lamb, J.
  and W.; Larnach; Leibius; Litchfield;
  Lloyd, G.; Love; Mitchell, J.; Montague;
  Murnin; Nichols; Nicoll; Paton, J.; Pitt;
  Pye.
WARD, John M.:
  Newcastle.
WARD, Russel:
  Marin la Meslée.
WARNER, J. R.:
  Kennion.
WATERSON, D. B.:
  Kates; McLean, J.; Miles; Perkins.
WESSELS, Sheila F.:
  Lascelles.
WETTENHALL, R. L.:
  Packer, F.
WHITLEY, G. P.:
  Krefft; Laporte; Masters.
WILSON, Paul D.:
  Macalister.
WOODHOUSE, Frank L.:
  Lindeman.
WOODHOUSE, Margaret:
  Kelly, J.
WRIGHT, R. P.:
  Monger.
WYKES, Olive:
  Morris, E.

YONG CHING FATT:
  Lowe.
YULE, Valerie:
  McColl; Murray, S.

REFERENCES

The following works of reference have been widely used but have not been listed in the sources at the foot of the articles:

D. Blair, *Cyclopaedia of Australasia* (Melbourne, 1881)

B. Burke, *A Genealogical and Heraldic History of the Colonial Gentry*, 1-2 (London, 1891-95)

J. A. Ferguson, *Bibliography of Australia*, 1-7 (Sydney, 1941-69)

H. M. Green, *A History of Australian Literature*, 1-2 (Sydney, 1961; 2nd ed 1971)

J. H. Heaton, *Australian Dictionary of Dates and Men of the Time* (London, 1879)

F. Johns, *An Australian Biographical Dictionary* (Melbourne, 1934)

P. Mennell, *The Dictionary of Australasian Biography* (London, 1892)

E. M. Miller, *Australian Literature . . . to 1935*, 1-2 (Melbourne, 1940) extended to 1950, by F. T. Macartney (Sydney, 1956)

Mitchell Library (NSW), *Dictionary Catalog of Printed Books* (Boston, 1968)

W. Moore, *The Story of Australian Art*, 1-2 (Sydney, 1934)

P. C. Mowle, *A Genealogical History of Pioneer Families in Australia* (Sydney, 1939)

P. Serle, *Dictionary of Australian Biography*, 1-2 (Sydney, 1949)

Australian Encyclopaedia, 1-2 (Sydney, 1925)

Australian Encyclopaedia, 1-10 (Sydney, 1958)

Dictionary of National Biography (London, 1885-1971)

ABBREVIATIONS

A.A.Co.	Australian Agricultural Company	Hist	History, Historical
Ac no	Accession number	HL	House of Lords
ACER	Australian Council for Educational Research	HO	Home Office, London
		Hob	Hobart
Adel	Adelaide	HRA	*Historical Records of Australia*
Adm	Admiralty	HRNSW	*Historical Records of New South Wales*
Agr	Agriculture, Agricultural		
ANU	Australian National University, Canberra	Inst	Institute, Institution
ANZAAS	Australian and New Zealand Association for the Advancement of Science	J	*Journal*
A'sian	Australasian	LA	Legislative Assembly
Assn	Association	LAN	Land Administration Board (Queensland State Archives)
Aust	Australia, Australian	LaT L	La Trobe Library, Melbourne
Battye Lib	J. Battye Library of West Australian History, Perth	LC	Legislative Council
		Lib	Library
BHP	Broken Hill Pty	LMS	London Missionary Society
bibliog	bibliography	LSD	Lands and Surveys Department (Tasmanian State Archives)
biog	biography, biographical		
BM	British Museum, London		
Brisb	Brisbane	Mag	*Magazine*
		Melb	Melbourne
CAO	Commonwealth Archives Office	MJA	*Medical Journal of Australia*
		ML	Mitchell Library, Sydney
cat	catalogue	MS	manuscript
Cmd	Command	mthly	monthly
CO	Colonial Office, London		
Col Sec	Colonial Secretary	nd	date of publication unknown
Com	Commission	NL	National Library of Australia, Canberra
CON	Convict records (Tasmanian State Archives)		
		no	number
CRS	Crown Solicitor's Office (Queensland State Archives)	np	place of publication unknown
		NSW	New South Wales
CSD	Chief Secretary's Department (Tasmanian State Archives)	NSWA	The Archives Authority of New South Wales, Sydney
CSIRO	Commonwealth Scientific and Industrial Research Organization	NT	Northern Territory
		OD	Outward Dispatches
CSO	Colonial Secretary's Office		
CSR	Colonial Secretary's Records (Battye Library, Perth)	p	page, pages
		PD	*Parliamentary Debates*
cttee	committee	PAH	see RPAH
Cwlth	Commonwealth	PLSA	State Library of South Australia
		PNGA	Archives Office of Papua and New Guinea, Port Moresby
ed	editor, edition		
encl	enclosure	PP	*Parliamentary Papers*
		PRGSSA	*Proceedings of the Royal Geographical Society of Australasia (South Australian Branch)*
Fr	Father (priest)		
		priv print	privately printed
G, Geog	Geographical	PRO	Public Record Office, London
GB	Great Britain	Procs	*Proceedings*
Gen	Genealogical, Genealogists	pt	part, parts
GO	Governor's Office	PTHRA	*Papers and Proceedings of the Tasmanian Historical Research Association*
HA	House of Assembly		
HC	House of Commons		

Q	Quarterly	SMH	Sydney Morning Herald
QA	Queensland State Archives, Brisbane	Soc	Society
		SPCK	Society for Promoting Christian Knowledge
Qld	Queensland		
[q.v.]*	cross reference	SPG	Society for the Propagation of the Gospel in Foreign Parts
RAHS	Royal Australian Historical Society (Sydney)	supp	supplement
		Syd	Sydney
rev	revised, revision		
RGS	Royal Geographical Society	TA	Tasmanian State Archives, Hobart
RHSQ	Royal Historical Society of Queensland (Brisbane)	Tas	Tasmania
RHSV	Royal Historical Society of Victoria (Melbourne)	tr	translated, translation
		Trans	Transactions
Roy	Royal		
RPAH	Royal Prince Alfred Hospital	Univ	University
RWAHS	Royal Western Australian Historical Society (Perth)	VA	Public Record Office, Melbourne
1st S	First Session	V&P	Votes and Proceedings
2nd S	Second Session	VDL	Van Diemen's Land
2nd s	second series	VHM	Victorian Historical Magazine
SA	South Australia	v, vol	volume
SAA	South Australian Archives, Adelaide	Vic	Victoria
SCT	Supreme Court (Queensland State Archives)	WA	Western Australia
		wkly	weekly
Sel	Select	WO	War Office

* The note [q.v.] accompanies the names of individuals, other than royal visitors, governors, lieut-governors and Colonial Office officials, who are the subjects of entries in the Dictionary.

K

KANE, BENJAMIN FRANCIS (1834-1872), educationist, was born in Kent, England, son of Benjamin Kane of the Royal Ordnance Department, Plymouth, and his wife Caroline, née Plow. He migrated to Van Diemen's Land in 1849 to complete his education and to become an assistant master at Launceston Church Grammar School under his brother Rev. H. P. Kane [q.v.]. He also edited a newspaper in Launceston before moving to Victoria, where on 10 February 1852 he was appointed to the Colonial Secretary's Office. On 15 March he was chosen from sixteen applicants as secretary and clerk in the new Board of National Education; his salary of £200 was raised in June to £300. Although by 1861 the National Board was educating only 14,000 children in its 187 schools compared with the rival Denominational Board's 77,500 children in 484 schools, Kane had responsible duties for his age and limited experience. He had become acting-inspector for National schools in 1853 and was responsible for setting up the emergency tent schools in gold-mining districts. Next year he became chief inspector and in 1855 a member of the Board for Teacher Training. As the gold fever waned friction between the two systems became more evident. The Denominational Board complained in 1861 that while the National Board was teaching only 20 per cent of the colony's children it was receiving 30 per cent of government funds. Kane, whose salary was £200 less than that of his counterpart in the Denominational Board, made out a case for equal pay to officers of the two boards, but without success. In 1862 the rival boards were abolished under Heales's [q.v.] Education Act. R. H. Budd [q.v.], head of the Denominational Board, was appointed inspector-general of the Common Schools Board at a salary of £1000 and Kane became secretary at £700. In 1872 he conducted a survey which revealed that religious instruction, the issue in dispute throughout the period, was being given in only 14 per cent of the schools under the Common Schools Board.

A bachelor, Kane boarded at Jolimont. With six friends, including Marcus Clarke and F. Haddon [qq.v.], he founded the Yorick Club in May 1868. Described as a 'highly popular and enthusiastic Yoricker', he was the club's first honorary treasurer and succeeded Clarke as secretary in October. In 1869 he was Clarke's best man. He died aged 38 at Jolimont on 8 December 1872 of acute hepatitis. After a service conducted by Rev. H. H. P. Handfield [q.v.] he was buried in the Anglican section of the Melbourne cemetery. Three weeks later the Common Schools Board was displaced by the Department of Education under ministerial control.

H. Mackinnon (ed), *The Marcus Clarke memorial volume* (Melb, 1884); *The Yorick Club, its origin and development* (Melb, 1911); *Government Gazette* (Vic), 10 Oct 1862; *Examiner* (Launceston), 21 Nov 1857; *Weekly Times* (Melb), 14, 28 Dec 1862; *Age*, 1 Oct, 9, 10 Dec 1872; *Argus*, 9, 24 Dec 1872; National Board of Education minutes 1851-61 (VA); Public Service Office lists, 1851, 1862, 1873 (VA).

A. M. BADCOCK

KATER, HENRY EDWARD (1841-1924), pastoralist and businessman, was born on 20 September 1841 at Bungarribee, near Penrith, eldest son of Henry Herman Kater (1813-1881) and his wife Eliza Charlotte (d. 1909), sister of J. B. Darvall [q.v.]. His father had arrived in Sydney on 23 December 1839 in the *Euphrates* with Durham cattle and six thoroughbred horses; he bought Bungarribee but after eighteen months faced bankruptcy and had to sell his stock. He moved to Caleula, started a cloth factory and later made enough as a flour-miller to retire to Sydney where he died in 1881.

Henry Edward was educated by his mother and for a year at Calder House, Redfern. He became a junior clerk in the Australian Joint Stock Bank at Mudgee. In 1861 he was held up by bushrangers when carrying bank-notes to Bathurst. In 1863 he acquired Gungalman, a cattle station on the Castlereagh. He established good relations with the Aboriginals and learnt bushcraft from them; he often used the local rain-maker. He sold Gungalman and set up as a flour-miller in Wellington. On 8 February 1870 at St Anne's Church of England, Ryde, he married Mary Eliza (d. 1935), daughter of William Forster [q.v.]. She had read the *Origin of Species* at 16 and studied Greek as a pastime at Wellington. In 1875 they visited Europe and Britain, where they earnestly looked at churches, art galleries and opera, and while visiting relations Henry saw and played his first lawn tennis.

In the 1870s Kater took up land in the Wellington District. With his brother Edward Harvey (d. 1903) he acquired Mumblebone on the Macquarie River near Warren. From John Smith [q.v.] in 1879 they bought merinos directly descended from Rev. Samuel Marsden's [q.v.] flock. In 1881 the brothers formed a partnership as Kater Bros; Henry had a third interest and attended to the city end of the business. Under Edward Mumblebone became one of the foremost studs in New South Wales; he developed strong-woolled, large-framed and plain-bodied sheep. Experiments with Vermont merinos proved unsuccessful.

In 1879 Henry had bought Mount Broughton near Moss Vale. He was a founder and president of the Bong Bong Picnic Race Club and sometime president of the Berrima District Agricultural, Horticultural and Industrial Society. In 1889 he was appointed to the Legislative Council on the recommendation of G. R. Dibbs [q.v.]. On 9 January 1908 the *Bulletin* complained that '19 years' research hasn't explained why [Dibbs] did it'. Despite such comments Kater proved a useful councillor, active on committees and interested in rural matters. In 1911 his opposition forced the government to modify the shires' bill. Edward Kavanagh, a Labor member, maintained that 'if one could satisfy Mr. Kater that a thing was in the interests of the State, then, irrespective of political party, one could rest assured of his support'.

In 1892-1924 Kater was a director of the Colonial Sugar Refining Co. and chairman in 1901-20. He was also vice-chairman of the Commercial Banking Co. of Sydney and a local director of the Liverpool and London and Globe Insurance Co. He represented Moss Vale in Anglican synods from the 1880s and his most charitable work was in connexion with the Royal Prince Alfred Hospital. A director from 1892, honorary treasurer in 1901-16 and chairman in 1920-24, he gave the hospital its first X-ray machine and £1000 to endow the H. E. Kater ward. In 1896 he had bought Egelabra, near Warren, and in 1906 when the partnership with Edward was dissolved his share was half the Mumblebone stud and Yanganbil About 1910 he took into partnership his son Norman who added Eenaweena. The three properties included 72,000 acres and, under the expert classer E. H. Wass, H. E. Kater & Son formed the well-known Egelabra stud. The Mumblebone stud continued to develop under E. H. Kater's descendants.

Henry Kater died on 23 September 1924 at his home, Headingley, Woollahra, and was buried in the Anglican section of the Sutton Forest cemetery. He was survived by his wife and younger son (Sir) Norman. Able in business and a shrewd judge of men, Kater left an estate sworn for probate at over £190,000.

NSW Sheepbreeders' Assn, *The Australian merino* (Syd, 1955); D. S. Macmillan, *The Kater family, 1750-1965* (Syd, 1966); *SMH*, 25 Sept 1924; *Illustrated Sydney News*, 1 Oct 1924; *New Nation Mag*, 15 Mar 1935; Kater family papers (NL); information from Mrs G. B. Kater, Sydney.
                                MARTHA RUTLEDGE

KATES, FRANCIS BENJAMIN (1830-1903), flour-miller and agrarian politician, was born on 1 July 1830 in Berlin, son of Benjamin Kates, miller, and his wife Henrietta. He graduated from Berlin University in 1852. In London he married Sarah Mathews in 1858 and soon afterwards migrated to Queensland. In 1859 he taught briefly at Rev. J. R. Moffatt's Collegiate School in Brisbane and then moved to Frederick Bracker's [q.v.] Warroo station on the Darling Downs. As tutor he was paid partly in sheep and accumulated much capital which he invested in store-keeping at Allora in 1863.

With his commission, store-keeping and money-lending profits Kates erected the Allora Flour Mills in 1871 and later built other mills at Warwick, Toowoomba, Ipswich and Roma. He prospered as selection accelerated on the Downs. He became a director of the Royal Bank of Queensland and the Queensland Mercantile Co. and acquired grazing farms at Allora, Richmond Downs (Roma) and Strath Elbess (Dalveen). However, his finances deteriorated after a European tour in 1888. Urban milling competition, poor harvests, colonial depression and unremunerative pastoral and closer settlement speculations nearly ruined him.

Kates represented the electorates of Darling Downs in 1878-81 and 1883-88 and Cunningham in 1899-1903. As a Griffith liberal, he had a close understanding of the selectors' predicament, and with his fertile technical mind he was an effective publicist of agrarian ideas. He pioneered such practical remedies as railway concessions, agricultural colleges, irrigation, conservation and government repurchase of freehold pastoral estates. In parliament he acted a double role : first, as a priest of the agrarian myths behind selection legislation; and second, as a cosmopolitan entrepreneur whose reason and talents could lead the farmers from subsistence slavery to financial independence.

As his hasty resignation in 1881 demonstrated, this slight, upright Prussian with a narrow, intelligent face dominated by long waxed moustaches was too impulsive and self-righteous to make an adroit politician. Despite his conviction, initiative and ideas he sometimes made the unforgivable colonial mistake of parading them. His practical efforts and milling enterprise later helped to make the agrarian dream a reality. Personal financial tragedy was concealed by public satisfaction with his part in creating a prototype of his ideal society of propertied yeomen. He died at Strath Elbess, Dalveen, on 26 September 1903 and left an estate of £2750 to his wife, a married daughter and his son Francis Henry.

D. B. Waterson, 'A Darling Downs quartet', *Qld Heritage*, Nov 1967; *Brisbane Courier*, 29 Sept 1903; *Warwick Argus*, 29 Sept 1903.

D. B. WATERSON

KAYSER, HEINRICH WILHELM FERDINAND (1833-1919), mining engineer, was born at Clausthal, Hanover, Germany, third son of Georg Andreas Kayser, mining engineer, and his wife Augusta, née Wisse. Educated at the Bergakademie Clausthal, he went to Adelaide in 1853 and to Melbourne in 1854. He worked on various goldfields, was naturalized in 1861 as a farmer and miner, and became a mining manager at Bendigo in 1863. In 1875 he was chosen from some ninety applicants to be manager of the Mount Bischoff Tin Mining Co. at Waratah, Tasmania.

In 1871 James (Philosopher) Smith [q.v.] had found tin deposits at Mount Bischoff and applied for a lease. His matchbox of samples aroused much local interest and next August Smith with a small party cut a rough track through the dense scrub from Burnie to the mount. Mining began in December and by June 1873 several tons of ore were sent to Launceston and Melbourne, causing such attention that a syndicate was formed to buy the mine. A mining expert was sent to the site and reported favourably but the project collapsed. However, in August the Mount Bischoff Tin Mining Co. was formed with 12,000 shares at £5. Smith sold the mine for £1500 in cash and 37 per cent of the company's shares. The first mining manager, William Crosby, spent £10,000 in forming fifty miles of road from Burnie to Waratah and battling against the incessant winter rain. At the mine Crosby's installations were primitive but by 1875 Waratah had a post office, a few houses and a well-patronized hotel.

Kayser took up duty at Mount Bischoff on 16 November. He first examined the lease and found much richer lodes: with difficulty he had them cleared of scrub and opened. Smith supplied him with sawyers for enlarging the ore-dressing sheds and the directors gave him an old 5-head battery which was installed in December 1876. He began damming creeks for water storage and increased the sluices. By August 1877 production had risen from 45 tons a month to 250 tons. By February 1878 he had spent some £90,000 and the company had an overdraft of £40,000 but shareholders received £12,000 as their first dividend. In March over 1500 tons of ore were piled at the mine waiting to be carted and the price of tin in London fell from £72 a ton to £55. The shareholders were irate but the directors allowed Kayser to install a 15-head battery in 1879 and to start an embankment 12 ft. high across Falls Creek. In that year with help from the Van Diemen's Land Co. a wooden tramway for horse-drawn trucks was completed from the mine to Burnie.

By 1881 the Falls Creek dam was completed, a supplementary 40-head battery had been installed, the mine was yielding over 220 tons of ore a week, three dividends of £6000 each had been declared and shares were selling at £62 10s. Eager to persuade his men to settle, Kayser built them good houses, a hospital and a grand temperance hotel at Waratah. In June 1883 he lit the town, mine and dressing sheds with hydroelectricity, the first in an Australian industrial plant, and in July 1884 held a banquet to celebrate the completion of an iron tramway to Burnie. In 1892 at Hobart he read a paper, published as *Mount Bischoff*, to the Australasian Association for the Advancement of Science, claiming that the company had built 6 reservoirs, installed 75 stampers for reworking the tailings, produced some 37,000 tons of ore valued at £2,300,000 and paid £1,113,500 in dividends.

In 1898 Kayser was succeeded as general mine manager by J. D. Millen but continued as consulting engineer to the company and lived in Launceston. As magistrate, coroner, registrar of births, marriages and deaths, almost sole employer in the Waratah district, owner of the *North-Western Advocate* and a humane despot, he was widely known as the 'Chief'. Large and impressive with his mutton-chop whiskers, heavy moustache, firm jaw and blue eyes he seemed more like a military officer than a mining engineer. In 1894-1905 he was an elected councillor of the Australasian Institute of Mining Engineers to which he read three papers and was president of its meeting at Launceston in 1898. He was also a member of the Institute of Mechanical Engineers and of the American Institute of Mining Engineers. In 1908 he moved to Victoria. He died at St Kilda on 12 October 1919, survived by his wife Mary Elizabeth, née Druce, whom he had married with Baptist rites in Melbourne on 4 March 1876, and by a son and seven daughters.

Cyclopedia of Tasmania, 1 (Hob, 1900); G. Blainey, *The rush that never ended* (Melb, 1963); *Argus*, 14 Oct 1919; *Examiner* (Launces-

ton), 14 Oct 1919; *Age*, 15 Oct 1919; James
Smith letters 1847-97 (TA).

JOHN REYNOLDS

KEAN, CHARLES JOHN (1811-1868),
actor-manager, was born on 18 January 1811
in Waterford, Ireland, son of Edmund Kean
(1787-1833), the celebrated tragedian, and
his wife Mary, née Chambers. Never intended for the stage he was educated at Eton,
but his father quickly acquired wealth, fell
into dissolute habits, became penniless and
deserted his wife. Charles left school to support his mother. After a humiliating début
on 10 October 1827 at Drury Lane, London,
he worked in the provinces, Holland, Germany and America, acquiring repute as a
meticulous actor, though performing in the
shadow of his father's fame.

In January 1838 Charles played Hamlet
at Covent Garden and his public success was
assured. On 29 January 1842 in Dublin he
married Ellen Tree (1805-1880), then one of
the most gifted and popular English actresses. Their married life was unmarred by
scandal and their respectability was confirmed in 1848 when Queen Victoria made
Charles director of her private theatricals at
Windsor Castle, a post he held for ten years.
Charles earned his place in English theatrical history through his management from
1850 of the Princess's Theatre, Oxford
Street, London. He brought exacting standards of rehearsal and performance to the
English stage and revolutionized lighting
techniques. His Shakespearian revivals were
renowned though sometimes ridiculed for
attention to historical detail in costuming
and scenery. In June 1857 he was proudly
elected a fellow of the Society of Anti-
quaries. In 1859 Charles and Ellen left the
Princess's Theatre, worn out and not well
off, too much having been spent on mounting their productions. Lacking sufficient
money for their anticipated retirement, they
toured the provinces extensively and then
turned to the colonies.

On 6 July 1863 Charles and Ellen with
their niece Patty Chapman (1830-1912), and
the actors James Cathcart [q.v.] and George
Everett (1824-1881), sailed for Melbourne
under contract to George Coppin [q.v.].
They opened at the Haymarket Theatre on
10 October but next day Charles lost his
voice and the company took a week off. From
19 October to 20 November they performed,
despite vicious opposition from Barry Sullivan [q.v.] at the rival Theatre Royal. On
26 November the Kean party arrived at
Sydney, which they liked better than Melbourne, and where they were often entertained by Governor Young. They had a
successful run from 2 December but on 18

January 1864 Charles became ill with a
stomach complaint. His death was widely
reported but he recovered and on 23 February they travelled to Ballarat and played
for ten nights to enthusiastic houses. Their
receipts were higher than elsewhere in the
tour: miners gave gold nuggets to Mrs
Kean and an old man walked over a hundred
miles to see them. Encouraged by this 'star'
treatment, they returned to Melbourne and
had a more successful season than before,
but bailiffs seized their costumes when the
Haymarket lessee fell behind with the rent.
Coppin and Kean had to assume management of the theatre. In May the Keans
played for two nights at Sandhurst and at
Geelong and at Melbourne. On 19 May Ellen
developed an abscess in her throat and they
abandoned a return to Ballarat and part of
a Sydney season. Charles estimated that
sickness had cost them three months of the
tour and Coppin complained that he had
spent £145 on medical expenses. The party
played their last Sydney engagement from
27 June to 4 July and the Keans gave readings at the Masonic Hall on 5-6 July. On
the 9th they left for California, Ellen re-
marking, 'I never left any place with so little
regret'.

Charles and Ellen returned to London
exhausted but performed in their major
roles. On 28 May 1867 Charles took ill in
Liverpool and died on 22 January 1868 of a
heart complaint. The Queen wrote an unusually personal note to Ellen sharing her
own grief for a loved husband. Ellen retired
from the stage and died on 20 August 1880,
survived by her only child, Mary (1843-
1898).

Although the Keans thought their colonial tour was not a success, the Australian
public received them with great warmth and
critics in the *Argus* and the *Age* abased
themselves before the Kean image. The sober
quality and meticulous performances of
Charles and Ellen were new to Australian
theatre lovers, who were seeing mature
English performers for the first time. As in
England, they helped to raise the social
standing of actors and the theatre.

J. Jefferson, *Autobiography* (Lond, 1890);
C. J. Kean, *Emigrant in motley*, J. M. Hardwick
ed (Lond, 1954); H. van der Poorten, Charles
and Ellen Kean in Australia, 1863-64 (B.A.
Hons thesis, Univ NSW, 1965); MS cat under
Kean (ML, Alexander Turnbull Lib, Wellington).   HELEN M. VAN DER POORTEN

KEANE, EDWARD VIVIEN HARVEY
(1844-1904), civil engineer, was born on 8
August 1844 at Birkenhead, Cheshire, England, son of Captain Edward Keane, R.N.;

he was related to the family of John Keane who was elevated to the peerage in 1839 for his services in Ghuznee, India. Educated at Christ's Hospital and privately, he was apprenticed to the railway contractors, William Dargan, Peto & Betts, and Lucas Brothers, and became a civil engineer. In 1876 he went to Melbourne but soon moved to South Australia where he worked as an engineer. As E. Keane & Co., railway contractors, he built many culverts, an engine shed at Naracoorte, reservoirs at Terowie and Orroroo, the 5 ft. 3 ins. line to Holdfast Bay and part of the 3 ft. 6 ins. line from Terowie to Pichi Richi. On 27 May 1879 he married Lilla Rebecca Wharton, daughter of Abraham White of Kapunda.

In 1882 the Keanes moved to Western Australia. Edward set up as a builder in Perth and made many influential friends, including John and Alexander Forrest. He also built several railways and in February 1886 won the contract for the first forty miles of the Midland Land Grant Railway Co.'s lines to be completed with rolling stock and other appliances in four years at an estimated cost of £1 million. The company failed to raise finance in London and Keane agreed to work at his own expense and accept part payment in land and company shares. He had lately finished a building at Fremantle for the National Bank and its manager gave Keane an overdraft of £20,000 which soon rose to £85,000. In 1888 he went to London where the company had called for debentures; despite their small success Keane borrowed £150,000 on their security. The bank recovered the overdraft which had enabled Keane to complete his contract but he was now burdened by his borrowing which he could not repay. With some government support but much strife and difficulty the railway was finished in eight years, and in 1895 his courage was rewarded with 80,000 acres and appointment as general manager of the Midland Railway Co.

Keane represented Geraldton in the Legislative Council from December 1886 to January 1889 and then Perth until December 1890. He was then elected for Perth to the new Legislative Assembly until December 1891 and was returned for Eastern Province to the council in May-June 1904. As a politician he was blunt and forthright, opposing the concentration of railways in the central districts and supporting free trade and Federation. He had been elected unopposed as mayor of Perth in 1891, but railway problems soon led to his resignation and he was given many glowing testimonials. Among his diverse interests he was a justice of the peace and a local director of the South British Insurance Co. He also built the Perth

Cathedral and the Fremantle Town Hall, in 1888 equipped the first party to go to the Yilgarn goldfields and later had a grazing property in the Eastern Districts where he imported well-bred stock. Laid low by pneumonia and a heart attack in an election campaign Keane died on 9 July 1904, survived by his wife and four of his five children. At his funeral flags in Perth were flown at half-mast. His large home, Cappoquon House, Keane's Point, Peppermint Grove, and its garden was a district show-piece. It was used as a rehabilitation centre for returned servicemen in World War I and later became the headquarters of the Royal Freshwater Bay Yacht Club.

W. B. Kimberly, *History of West Australia* (Melb, 1897); G. Blainey, *Gold and Paper: a history of the National Bank of Australasia Limited* (Melb, 1958); PD (WA) 1886-91; *Inquirer and Commercial News*, 19 Jan 1887; *Possum*, 22 Oct 1887; *Aust Advertiser*, 2 July 1890; *West Australian*, 31 Jan 1891, 8, 11 July 1904; *Morning Herald* (Perth), 11 July 1904; Perth City Council, Minute book 6.

KIM ROBERTS

KEENE, WILLIAM (1798-1872), geologist, was born in Bath, England, the sixth son of Thomas Keene, owner of the *Bath Journal*, and his wife Ann, née Buck. In 1821 he began to study medicine in London but became interested in geology and engineering and helped Goldsworthy Gurney (1793-1875) with chemical science lectures at the Surrey Institution. About 1823 at the British Embassy in Paris Keene married Sarah Charles (1804-1867), née Evans. In 1827 they moved to the Bayonne district in south-west France, where he soon engaged in mining salt and coal. In 1836 he was living at Bordeaux as a civil engineer. He gained wide experience of French coal-mines and oil shale deposits, and farmed on land near Bayonne and St Lon. In 1848 when revolution broke out in France he returned to England with his family. He probably worked in coalfields in Wales and near Manchester and developed a variety of maize for use in England. He also retained a financial interest in the *Bath Journal*. About 1850 his son William Thomas joined the California gold rush, went to Victoria in 1851 and later moved to New South Wales.

In 1852 Keene and family arrived in Sydney and in 1853 he made an appraisal of the geology around the Fitzroy iron-mines near Mittagong for the government. On 28 December 1854 he was appointed examiner of coalfields. From 1863 he was stationed in the Hunter valley with the additional duties of keeper of mining records. His geological work in Australia was mainly on the coal-bearing rocks of the Sydney basin in the Hunter River valley. In 1866-67 Keene prepared data about oil shale deposits there after development of the Hartley outcrops. Most of his geological work was published as government reports and some in newspapers. Two short papers dealing with aspects of the coal measures in New South Wales appeared in the *Quarterly Journal* of the Geological Society in London, of which he was elected a fellow in June 1865.

Keene's geology was practical and largely directed towards the economic exploitation of coal, but he was also involved with water supplies for Newcastle. Some of his broader geological concepts were rather out of date, but in the controversy on the age of the Australian coal measures he contributed data in support of Rev. W. B. Clarke against Professor F. McCoy [qq.v.]. In 1858 Keene opened a display of minerals and rocks that became a focal point for scientists visiting the district. He supplied geological collections for a number of institutions overseas and prepared displays of the colony's mineral wealth for exhibitions in London in 1862, Melbourne in 1866 and Paris in 1867, and won several medals.

Keene was a member of the Hunter River Vineyard Association and its president in 1865-66; his presidential addresses were published in 1867. He judged wine entries at many shows and constantly argued that the southern French treatment for wines was more suited to the New South Wales climate than the German. He also helped to form an association for widows and orphans of clergymen, and for some years was a magistrate. On 2 February 1872 he died aged 74 at his home in Raymond Terrace and was buried in the Anglican cemetery. He was survived by his only son and two of his seven daughters. A memorial window was erected by subscription in the Anglican Church at Raymond Terrace.

Newcastle Chronicle, 6 Feb 1872; *Town and Country J*, 9 Mar 1872; family records (held by Mrs A. Holloway, Dee Why, NSW).

D. F. BRANAGAN
T. G. VALLANCE

KELLY, DAVID FREDERICK (1847-1894), professor of classics, was born in Ireland, the eldest son of David Kelly, landowner of Castledawson, County Londonderry, Ireland. From Dungannon School he won a classical scholarship in 1869 to Trinity College, Dublin, was admitted to the Middle Temple on 23 April 1872 and moved to Clare College, Cambridge (B.A., 1875; M.A., 1879). He then taught the sixth form of Dulwich College but resigned at the end

of 1878 when he accepted an appointment as Hughes professor of classics and comparative philology and literature at the University of Adelaide. With his wife Louisa Jane, née d'Arenberg, and her brother, Frederick Augustus, he arrived at Adelaide in the *Assam* on 27 February 1879. Next day he was introduced to the university council.

The council had added evening classes to the regular day-time lectures but Kelly's expositions were not popular. In his address to the annual commemoration in December 1885 he criticized the growing emphasis on utilitarian subjects and strongly advocated the discipline of classics, especially the study of Greek which local educationists were trying to oust from South Australian schools and thereby from the university. He was more successful in his advocacy of sports. He had rowed at Cambridge and in Adelaide joined the University Rowing Club. He played tennis and was a member and sometime captain of the Adelaide Archery Club. He enjoyed carpentry, built a dogcart for himself and installed his own bells and lighting system.

From about 1886 Kelly began to suffer from locomotor ataxia. On 20 November 1886 his wife died at Oakbank, leaving a son, Ignatius George. Kelly later married her sister, Sophie Armstrong; their son, David Victor, was born at College Park on 14 September 1891. In October 1893 Kelly sailed in the *Oruba* with his wife and two children to spend Christmas in England. On 6 March 1894 he returned to Adelaide alone and in rapidly deteriorating health. Friends took him to hospital at North Adelaide where he died on 21 March, aged 46. He was buried at the North Road cemetery and the university was closed for the day. His will of 28 November 1890 bequeathed his estate of £750 to his wife but it was revoked and he died intestate. His son David (1891-1959) became a well-known British diplomat.

D. Kelly, *The ruling few* (Lond, 1952); *Register* (Adel), 27 Feb 1879, 3 May 1882, 2, 5 Nov 1886, 5 Oct 1893; *Observer* (Adel), 24 Mar 1894.

SALLY O'NEILL

KELLY, EDWARD (1855-1880), bushranger, was born in June 1855 at Beveridge, Victoria, the eldest son of John (Red) Kelly and his wife Ellen, née Quinn. His father was born in Tipperary, Ireland, in 1820 and sentenced in 1841 to seven years' transportation for stealing two pigs. He arrived in Van Diemen's Land in 1842. When his sentence expired in 1848 he went to the Port Phillip District, where on 18 November 1850 he married Ellen, the eighteen-year-old daughter of James and Mary Quinn; they had five daughters and three sons.

Ned attended school at Avenel until his father died on 27 December 1866. Left indigent, the widow and children moved to a hut at Eleven Mile Creek, about half-way between Greta and Glenrowan in northern Victoria, where James Quinn had taken up a cattle run of 25,000 acres of poor country in 1862. Well known in the district, the Quinns and two Lloyd brothers, who had married into the family, were suspected by the police in connexion with thefts of horses and cattle. In 1869 Ned was arrested for alleged assault on a Chinaman and held for ten days on remand but the charge was dismissed. Next year he was arrested and held in custody for seven weeks as a suspected accomplice of the bushranger, Harry Power [q.v.], but again the charge was dismissed.

In 1870 Kelly was convicted of summary offences and imprisoned for six months. Soon after release he was sentenced to three years' imprisonment for receiving a mare knowing it to have been stolen. In 1874 he was discharged from prison and his mother married George King. Kelly worked for two years at timber-getting but in 1876 joined his stepfather in stealing horses.

The Kelly family saw themselves as victims of police persecution, but as they grew up the boys were probably privy to the organized thefts of horses and cattle for which the district was notorious. Ned's younger brother, James (b. 1858), was sentenced to five years' imprisonment for cattle stealing in 1873; released in 1877 he went to Wagga Wagga where he was sentenced to ten years' imprisonment for stealing horses. He lived respectably after his release from gaol and died in 1946. His mother, always known as Mrs Kelly despite her second marriage, died in 1923. The third brother, Dan (1861-1880), had been sentenced to three months' imprisonment in 1877 for damaging property, and soon after his release in 1878 a warrant was issued for his arrest for stealing horses.

On 15 April a police trooper named Fitzpatrick went to Mrs Kelly's home, allegedly to arrest Dan. Fitzpatrick, a worthless and unreliable fellow, claimed that Ned Kelly shot him; although Ned was possibly not there, the true facts have never been satisfactorily established. Dan went into hiding; Mrs Kelly, her son-in-law, William Skillion, and a neighbour, William Williamson, were arrested and charged with aiding and abetting the attempted murder of Fitzpatrick. In October they were tried at Beechworth and convicted. The judge, Sir Redmond Barry [q.v.], sentenced her to imprisonment

for three years and the two males for six. Rewards of £100 were offered for the apprehension of Ned and Dan Kelly, who went into hiding in the Wombat Ranges near Mansfield. They were joined by Joe Byrne (b. 1857) from Beechworth, and Steve Hart (b. 1860), a daring horseman from Wangaratta.

Soon afterwards Sergeant Kennedy and Constables Lonigan, Scanlon and McIntyre set out to capture Ned and Dan, and on 25 October camped at Stringybark Creek where they were seen by Ned. Next day Kennedy and Scanlon went out on patrol, leaving Lonigan and McIntyre at the camp. The Kelly gang surprised the camp and when Lonigan drew his revolver Ned shot him dead. McIntyre surrendered. When Kennedy and Scanlon returned, they did not surrender when called on, and in an exchange of shots Ned killed Scanlon and mortally wounded Kennedy. Ned later shot him in the heart, claiming it was an act of mercy. McIntyre escaped to Mansfield and reported the killings.

On 15 November the Victorian government issued a proclamation of outlawry and offered rewards of £500 for each of the gang, alive or dead. Police were mobilized but their methods of pursuit and of obtaining information were crude and inept. On 9 December the Kelly gang took possession of a sheep station at Faithfull's Creek, about four miles out of Euroa, locking up twenty-two persons in a store-room. While Byrne guarded the captives, the other three went to Euroa where they held up the National Bank, taking £2000 in notes and gold. This crime resulted in a doubling of the reward, but on Saturday, 8 February 1879, the gang struck again, this time at Jerilderie, a town about thirty miles north of the Murray River. They locked up two policemen and took possession of the police station, remaining there until Monday morning. Wearing police uniforms, they held up the Bank of New South Wales for £2141 in notes and coin, and rounded up sixty persons in the Royal Hotel next door. Ned had given a written statement of over 8000 words to a bank-teller. What became of the original and of an earlier statement which Kelly sent to Donald Cameron, M.L.A. (1877-1880) is not known but, long after Kelly's death, copies made by a clerk in the Crown Law department became available. Known as the 'Cameron letter' and the 'Jerilderie letter', they are Kelly's explanation and justification of his conduct.

The reward for the outlaws was increased to £2000 a head and black trackers were brought from Queensland. Aaron Sherritt, a friend of Joe Byrne's, became an agent for the police, and on Saturday, 27 June 1880, was shot dead by Byrne in his own doorway near Beechworth, while the four constables assigned to guard Sherritt hid in a bedroom. Byrne and Dan then joined Ned and Hart at Glenrowan, where they took possession of the hotel run by Mrs Ann Jones and detained about sixty people. The outlaws foresaw that a special train would be sent from Melbourne on Sunday night, and would arrive at Glenrowan early on Monday, 29 June, and with the intention of wrecking it they compelled two railway workers to tear up some of the rails. The scheme came to nothing because a schoolmaster, Thomas Curnow, whom Ned had allowed to leave the hotel with his wife, child and sister, gave warning to the train crew. The other outlaws were equipped with armour made from plough mould-boards and Ned was protected by a cylindrical headpiece, breast and back plates and apron weighing about 90 lbs. Little sleep and much consumption of alcohol affected their judgment and, although the armour limited their movements and use of firearms, it gave them a false sense of invulnerability. Under Superintendent Hare, the police surrounded the hotel and shooting began. Hare was shot in the arm and Ned wounded in the foot, hand and arm. Dan, Byrne and Hart took refuge in the hotel and Ned went into the bush. The police continued to fire; Byrne was shot in the thigh as he stood at the hotel bar, and bled to death. About 5 a.m. Ned returned, still clad in armour, looking huge and grotesque in the early mist. He was brought down by bullet wounds in the legs.

Most of the captives in the hotel had succeeded in leaving the building, the last of them emerging about 10 a.m. An old man named Cherry was in a detached kitchen, fatally wounded by a police bullet; young John Jones, son of the hotel-keeper, was similarly shot in the abdomen and died in hospital. With Ned captured and Byrne dead, only Dan and Hart were not accounted for, but the police continued to fire sporadically until 3 p.m., when a policeman set the building on fire. Father Matthew Gibney went into the burning building to administer the last rites and reported three dead bodies were inside. One, Byrne's, was brought out by police. The other two were those of Dan and Hart, who had apparently taken poison and were burned beyond recognition. On 28-29 October 1880 at Melbourne Kelly was tried for the murder of Constable Thomas Lonigan at Stringybark Creek. He was found guilty and the judge, Redmond Barry, sentenced him to death.

Despite strong agitation for a reprieve Kelly was hanged at the Melbourne gaol on 11 November. He met his end without fear. His last words were 'Ah well, I suppose it has come to this', and by another version, 'Such is life'.

H. G. Turner [q.v.] described Ned Kelly as 'a shabby skulker', but observed 'It was a humiliating reflection . . . that the whole machinery of Government, the apparent zeal of a well-disciplined and costly police service, the stimulus of enormous rewards, and an expenditure of fully £100,000 were, for two whole years, insufficient to check the predatory career of these four reckless dare-devil boys'.

Beside Ned his three companions are shadowy figures and would have been soon forgotten without him. In the *Bulletin*, 31 December 1966, M. H. Ellis described Ned Kelly as 'one of the most cold-blooded, egotistical, and utterly self-centred criminals who ever decorated the end of a rope in an Australian jail'. As the outlaws were undoubtedly murderers and robbers, they should have excited public detestation. Yet it did not turn out that way, and the hold the Kelly legend has on Australian imagination is too clearly established to be disregarded. However deplorable, the popular estimate of Kelly's killings of the police at Stringybark Creek accords with his statement, 'I could not help shooting them, or else let them shoot me, which they would have done if their bullets had been directed as they intended', while elements of farce surrounding the bank robberies at Euroa and Jerilderie distract attention from the gravity of the crimes.

Clive Turnbull claims that 'Ned Kelly is the best known Australian, our only folk hero . . . Popular instinct has found in Kelly a type of manliness much to be esteemed — to reiterate: courage, resolution, independence, sympathy with the under-dog'. The legend brought into being the phrase, 'As game as Ned Kelly', for describing the ultimate in bravery, inspired numberless imaginative tales and folk-ballads, and has taken new life in Sidney Nolan's series of Kelly-gang paintings. The legend still persists and seemingly has a compelling quality that appeals to something deeply rooted in the character of the 'average' Australian.

The Kelly gang, or the outlaws of the Wombat Ranges (Mansfield, 1879); H. G. Turner, A history of the colony of Victoria, 2 (Lond, 1904); C. Turnbull (ed), Ned Kelly, being his own story of his life and crimes (Melb, 1942); M. M. Brown, Australian son; the story of Ned Kelly (Melb, 1948); F. Clune, The Kelly hunters (Syd, 1954); M. J. Jennings, Ned Kelly, the legend and the man (Melb, 1968); Ned Kelly, man and myth (Melb, 1968); V&P (LA Vic), 1880-81, 4 (85), 1881, 3 (22), (31), 1882-83, 3 (66); CON 14/11/33 (TA).   JOHN V. BARRY*

KELLY, JOHN EDWARD (1840-1896), businessman, was born on 17 June 1840 at Swan Reach, near Morpeth, New South Wales, son of James Kelly, settler, and his wife Mary, née O'Keefe. At 14 he worked in the Bourke district as a ration-carrier and store-keeper on a station, and four years later was head stockman for Vincent Dowling [q.v.], with whom he explored the west and north-west of New South Wales and to whom he was largely indebted 'for his early training and education'. In 1862 Kelly took up leases himself and built the Old Fort (Royal) Hotel in Bourke. On 26 August at West Maitland he married Margaret Agnes, née Tierney.

In 1868 he sold the hotel but continued to select land and became increasingly critical of government officials. In 1872 he was involved in a land dispute with James Tyson [q.v.] and after an 'altercation' with a lands official, Kelly had to pay damages of £30. In 1875 he moved to Ashfield and bought a bookselling and printing business at 426 George Street, Sydney. He continued as printer and publisher to the Council of Education and on 20 February began publication of the *Stockwhip*, a weekly devoted mainly to free-thought and critical of 'religious, social, commercial and political charlatans'. Politically it was pro-Parkes and anti-Robertson [qq.v.] and made libellous attacks on parliamentarians and other citizens. Although Parkes had encouraged Kelly, he begged him after five months to change the character of the *Stockwhip*, but Kelly refused. He became involved in court cases with his printer, with his tenant who objected to the noise of the printing machinery and with E. Greville [q.v.] for whom he printed Greville's *Official Post Office Directory of New South Wales*. A libel case with J. McElhone [q.v.] was dropped after Kelly apologized. Kelly had to pay damages of £250 to Robert Burgess of Tenterfield and lacking financial support had to sell the *Stockwhip* in September 1876. Over the years he was a frequent contributor to the press on public issues.

Kelly returned to his property at Weelongbar, Bourke, and in 1877 lent Parkes £500 but had difficulty in getting it back. In 1881 Kelly selected land near Trangie and adjoining blocks in the names of his son and daughter. He built Myalmundi, a fine homestead with gardens, dairy and a sawmill. Defeated for the Bogan in 1865, 1875 and 1885 when he narrowly lost to Sir Patrick Jennings [q.v.], Kelly held the seat in 1887-89. In the assembly he spoke up for men on the land, attacked the civil service and railway extension and was one of the eight Catholics who voted in favour of Sir Alfred Stephen's [q.v.] divorce bills. He

had mining interests, owned Copper Hill near Molong and was general manager of the Peak Hill Pty Co. In 1894 he was first mayor of Peak Hill but after three months resigned through ill health. He died from cancer of the throat at Peak Hill on 4 November 1896, survived by his wife, five sons and two daughters. He was buried in the Catholic section of the Peak Hill cemetery.

W. F. Morrison, *The Aldine centennial history of New South Wales*, 2 (Syd, 1888); M. Woodhouse, *An index to the Stockwhip, 1875-1877 with a life of John Edward Kelly* (Syd, 1969).   MARGARET WOODHOUSE

KELLY, THOMAS HUSSEY (1830-1901), wool-broker and businessman, was born in Athlone, County Westmeath, Ireland. He went to Sydney about 1860 and worked as a clerk and later wool-buyer for Gilchrist, Watt [q.v.] & Co. About 1874 he set up as a wool and produce broker and began to extend his business interests. He became a director of the Union Bank of Australia, the South British Insurance Co., the Perpetual Trustee Co. and the Australian Kerosene Oil and Mineral Co. He was also a large shareholder in such companies as Burns, Philp & Co. Ltd, Tooth & Co. Ltd, the Colonial Sugar Refining Co. Ltd and Aarons' Exchange Hotel Co. Ltd. His main interest was in the development of Australian mining in which he was prominent; by 1901 he was a shareholder in no fewer than twenty gold and copper mining companies. For many years he was managing director of the Sydney Smelting Co. and empowered his trustees to borrow up to £10,000 from his estate to continue it.

A quiet and popular businessman, Kelly was a familiar figure in aquatic circles; he was commodore of the Sydney Amateur Sailing Club and in 1900 donated the Carleton Cup to the Royal Sydney Yacht Squadron in memory of his son. In July 1894 he was present at a conservative rally in Sydney with Thomas Buckland, E. Vickery, T. A. Dibbs, G. H. Cox [qq.v.], E. W. Knox, J. H. Story, W. S. Buzacott and others who urged electors to return 'men of character and ability . . . [and] of known probity and business capacity' at the general elections. In 1898 he was strongly opposed to the Federation bill.

Kelly died at his residence, Glenyarrah, Double Bay, on 25 July 1901 and was buried in the Anglican section of Waverley cemetery. His estate was sworn for probate at under £259,000. He was survived by his wife Mary Ann Dick (d. 1902), whom he had married on 5 September 1864 according to Presbyterian rites, and by three sons and a daughter.

V&P (LA NSW), 1889, 2, 58; SMH, 7 July 1894, 27, 29 July 1901; Daily Telegraph (Syd), 27 Sept 1913.   G. P. WALSH

KELLY, WILLIAM (1813 ?-1872), author and barrister, was born in Ireland, son of Andrew Kelly, merchant of Camphill, Sligo County. Ownership of a large bleaching mill generously administered gave the family so favoured a position in the community that, when they lost their property during a financial setback, the local people applied a boycott to force the new owner to sell Camphill back. At some time after 1847 it passed into the hands of Andrew Kelly's brother-in-law, James Madden.

Perhaps this event decided William Kelly to break away from Sligo County, where he had practised as a magistrate and, according to a parish historian, his connexions promised an influential future. On 20 January 1849 he went in the Sarah Sands to America. He was among the first to cross the plains to golden California, and his account of the journey, An Excursion to California over the Prairie, Rocky Mountains, and the Great Sierra Nevada. With A Stroll through the Diggings and Ranches of that Country (London, 1851) is, according to Merrill J. Mattes, objective and 'more articulate than most', though sometimes overstated.

Stories of the Australian gold discoveries circulating in England on his return decided Kelly to sail to Port Phillip, where he arrived with his younger brother in the Cherusker on 30 April 1854. After touring the goldfields he expended his energies on a number of ill-fated ventures in Melbourne. He lost money building a stable and livery out of pisé, unsuccessfully entered a competition for the design of a new dock and in the early autumn of 1854 made an abortive attempt to establish a suburban parcels delivery service. According to his own account, he was then in Bendigo for more than a year and helped to work a quartz mill in which he held an interest, again without profit.

During his Victorian sojourn Kelly paid close attention to colonial politics. He wrote many letters to the Argus in support of the free entry of Chinese and in April 1857 fruitlessly stood for the Ovens against J. D. Wood [q.v.]. He eventually reverted to his earlier occupation of reporter, writing Life in Victoria or Victoria in 1853, and Victoria in 1858 (London, 1859). A reviewer in My Note Book, 13 April 1859, thought it 'an egregiously silly book, full of misrepresentations, lies, absurd self-laudations, and twaddle', but for all that his record of Victoria is very entertaining and of much interest.

Despite the title, Kelly left Melbourne in December 1857. London could not contain the fiery and eloquent Irishman for long, and before Life in Victoria was published he was off to the goldfields of British Columbia. His Canadian experiences, however, never got into print as his publishers, Chapman & Hall, did not receive a complete manuscript. Probably on the strength of his American travels, Kelly was elected a fellow of the Royal Geographical Society in June 1861, one of his proposers being Sir Richard Burton. On 5 February 1862 he obeyed his own dictum by taking a young wife, though vainly giving his age as 38. He married a 26-year-old Belgian widow, Marguerite Sidonie Mertens, née Durart, at Boulogne-sur-Mer, France, where he mostly resided until his death there on 4 March 1872. His epitaph recorded that he died 'Fortified by the Rites of the Holy Catholic Church'.

T. O'Rorke, History antiquities and present state of the parishes of Ballysadare and Kilvarnet in the county of Sligo (Dublin, 1878); M. J. Mattes, The great Platte River road (Lincoln, Nebraska, 1969); D. B. Smith, 'Bushby journal, 1858-59', British Columbia Hist Q, 21 (1957-58).   ANNETTE POTTS

KELLY, WILLIAM (1823-1909), Jesuit priest, was born on 21 October 1823 in Dublin, Ireland. After secondary education he entered Maynooth seminary but was expelled because of a poem he wrote in sympathy for the 'Young Ireland' movement. Later he applied for admission to the Society of Jesus and was accepted on 24 April 1850. On 21 September 1865 he arrived at Port Phillip with Joseph Lentaigne who became rector of St Patrick's College, East Melbourne; they were the first Irish Jesuits in the colony. For the next twelve years Kelly was officially master of the matriculation class at St Patrick's but was also appointed by his superior, Joseph Dalton [q.v.], to teach philosophy and theology to the students for the diocesan priesthood then housed at the college.

Kelly's repute as a versatile scholar did not rest simply on his classroom activities. He excelled as a polemicist and was the most celebrated Catholic preacher in Victoria from 1866 to 1877. Almost weekly the press carried reports of his Town Hall lectures and apologias. Dr Goold's [q.v.] diary for 1869 has him preaching at thirteen special functions all over Victoria, and Howard Willoughby [q.v.] claimed that 'Father Kelly is the orator chosen in Melbourne when the Church has to show that her right hand still possesses its cunning . . . He is the controversialist called upon to confute error in the lecture-hall, and win ringing applause from fiery partisans'. He was very popular and his speeches were often interrupted by 'deafening applause'. Perhaps his most celebrated doctrinal controversy was with Dr J. E. Bromby [q.v.] in several Town Hall lectures on the existence of hell. From 1869, although Kelly's most frequent topic was secular education, he also lectured in such diverse fields as history, zoology, literature, physics, astronomy and chemistry. In 1871 his paper on tests for arsenic to the Royal Society of Victoria won him election to its council in 1872-73. Optics and astronomy were his favourite fields and in 1882 the Royal Astronomical Society invited him to join the party which intended to observe the transit of Venus from the Blue Mountains.

In 1878 Dalton sent Kelly to Sydney as prefect of studies at St Kilda House, the forerunner to St Aloysius College. In Sydney he revealed himself less as a polemicist and more as a scholar, and so never attained the popularity that he had in Victoria. In 1888 he was recalled to Ireland to profess Greek and Hebrew to the Jesuit theological students at Milltown Park. At 80 he was credited with undertaking the study of Persian. He died on 30 January 1909 in Dublin.

H. Willoughby, *The critic in church* (Melb, 1872); *Age*, 1 Feb 1909; Jesuit and St Patrick's College records (Jesuit Provincial Archives, Hawthorn, Vic).   G. J. O'KELLY

KELYNACK, WILLIAM (1831-1891), Wesleyan minister, was born on 22 May 1831 at Newlyn, Cornwall, England, son of Nicholas Kelynack, sea captain, and his wife Jane Payne, née James. Educated at Penzance, he taught in a private school and then followed mercantile pursuits. Influenced by his uncle, Rev. John P. James, in 1849 he became a local preacher and in 1853 was recommended as a candidate for the Wesleyan ministry. He was sent by the Foreign Missionary Committee to Sydney and arrived on 23 May 1854.

Until 1856 Kelynack served in the Bathurst circuit but his health suffered. He was transferred to the Braidwood circuit in 1857-59 and in 1860 to Yass. At first he was content to work in sparsely populated areas and in churches with small congregations, but in 1861-64 was appointed in turn to the circuits of Chippendale, Parramatta and Wollongong. His years at York Street in 1865-67 and Surry Hills in 1868-70 were among his most active. He was coeditor of the *Christian Advocate and Wesleyan Record* in 1865-67 with Rev. William

Curnow and in 1868-70 with Rev. J. H. Fletcher [q.v.]; in 1865-70 he had served on the Missionary and Connexional Committees, the council of Newington College and the executive committee of the New South Wales Church Sustentation and Extension Society. He was also a member of the committees of Sydney City Mission and the New South Wales Political Association for the Suppression of Intemperance. He was transferred in 1871-73 to Goulburn where he was district chairman and in 1874-76 to Bathurst.

In 1877 Kelynack visited England to see his aged mother. He addressed the open session of the British Methodist Conference and succeeded in getting £3000 for Newington College, Sydney. Returning through the United States, he addressed the New York Preachers' Meeting and the Drew (Methodist) Theological Seminary, and preached to crowded congregations in New York, Baltimore and Chicago. He was awarded a doctorate in divinity by the University of New Orleans but refused the pastorate of a leading Methodist Church in America. He returned to Sydney in 1878 to serve the Bourke Street Church and in 1880 was elected president of the New South Wales and Queensland Annual Conference. In 1882-86 he was general secretary of Foreign Missions and visited most of Australia, New Zealand and Fiji, raising £6000 for the special fund. In 1887 he succeeded Fletcher as president of Newington College and in May 1890 was elected president of the Sixth General Conference of the Australasian Wesleyan Methodist Church. His eloquence in pulpit and on public platform and his ability in debate and administration were clearly recognized. 'His Christian catholicity combined with his rare public gifts caused him to be honourably known beyond the boundaries of his own church'.

Kelynack died from Bright's disease at Newington College on 1 November 1891 and was buried in Rookwood cemetery. He was survived by his wife Lucy Hannah (d. 1932), daughter of J. R. Houlding [q.v.], whom he had married on 9 April 1862, and by seven sons and four daughters. His estate was valued at £5600.

A portrait is in Newington College where Johnstone-Kelynack House commemorates his name.

M. Dyson (ed), *Australasian Methodist ministerial general index*, 1st ed (Melb, 1889); J. Colwell, *The illustrated history of Methodism* (Syd, 1904); J. E. Carruthers, *Lights in the southern sky* (Syd, 1924); D. S. Macmillan, *Newington College 1863-1963* (Syd, 1963); Lond Methodist Conference, *Minutes* (1853-54); A'sian Wesleyan Methodist Church, *Minutes* (1855-75); A'sian Wesleyan Methodist Church,

Minutes of the NSW and Qld conference (1874-89); *Newingtonian*, June 1888; *SMH*, 2 Feb, 2 May 1886, 4 Nov 1891; Council minutes, 1887-91 (Newington College, Stanmore); Parkes letters (ML); newspaper cuttings, 1874-91 (held by Mr A. Kelynack, Roseville).

S. G. CLAUGHTON

KEMBLE, MYRA (1857-1906), actress, was born on 17 November 1857 in Sligo, Ireland, only daughter of Pritchard Joseph Gill and his wife Teresa, née O'Donnell. She arrived in Victoria aged 7 and was educated at Geelong Convent School. In 1874 as Myra Kemble she made her stage début portraying Venus in a pantomime, *Twinkle twinkle little star*, at the Theatre Royal, Melbourne. She was described as 'phenomenally beautiful with gorgeous red hair, cream and peaches complexion and a superb figure'. Her next appearance, in a chorus at the Melbourne Opera House, was followed by several parts in Sandhurst under Heffernan's management. She then moved to Sydney where her striking looks won her a part as walking lady in *The Daisy Farm*, with which Samuel Lazar opened the new Theatre Royal on 11 December 1875. The next years brought many light comedy roles. She starred in Bland Holt's [q.v.] first production in Australia of *New Babylon* at the Victoria Theatre in 1877. Beauty, talent and natural charm combined to make her a favourite with the Sydney public. As Biddy in *Transported for Life*, May Meredith in *Our American Cousin* and in particular the fool in *King Lear*, she drew unstinted praise.

Back in Melbourne she was induced to appear at the Theatre Royal but declined permanent engagement because of commitments as Lazar's leading lady in Sydney. In March 1880 John Bennet engaged her for the Victoria and she moved from one show to another almost without losing a single night. Her popularity firmly established, she created a furore as Anne Catherick in *The Woman in White*, Lady Teazle in *School for Scandal*, Madame de Fontanges in *Plot and Passion* and Ophelia in *Hamlet*. She was the youngest Lady Macbeth to have appeared on the Australian stage. On 12 June she scored another success in Bland Holt's *New Babylon* at the Theatre Royal in Melbourne: audiences were enthralled; her speech was said to be exquisite and no rival could match her grace and charm. Her weekly salary was then £40.

At St Mary's Cathedral, Sydney, on 10 December 1878 Myra had married James David Whitehead, a widower born in England in 1846 and 'one of the straightest bookmakers in the colony'. In 1888 her portrait by Nerli attracted much attention at the Royal Art Society in Sydney. She and her husband planned a visit to Europe and her farewell benefit on 15 June 1889 at Sydney's Theatre Royal drew a packed house. She left Melbourne in the *Liguria* on 15 July with letters of introduction from many leading managers. In London the playwright, Robert Buchanan, wrote *Man and the Woman* specially for her, but the matinée performance at the Criterion did not achieve the success it deserved. She bought the colonial rights of *Dr. Bill* by Hamilton Aide and other pieces. An enthusiastic reception in Sydney on her return led to extensive tours of other cities in Australia and New Zealand. After her husband died she lived with her mother and died in the Melbourne Hospital on 27 October 1906. One of the best-loved actresses on the Australian stage, she was still remembered after fifty years.

N. Stewart, *My Life's story* (Syd, 1923); P. McGuire et al, *The Australian theatre* (Melb, 1948); *A'sian Sketcher*, 3 July 1880; *Table Talk*, 21 June 1889; *Argus*, 29 Oct 1906; *Bulletin*, 1 Nov 1906; *Age*, 5 Mar 1938.

JEAN GITTINS

KEMPT, JOHN FRANCIS (1805-1865), soldier, was born in England, younger son of Captain Francis Kempt, R.N., of Froxfield, Hampshire, and first cousin of General Sir James Kempt (1764-1854), soldier and in 1828-30 administrator of Canada. His father died on the North American station in 1815 and John was cared for by his father's relations. His father had wanted him to be 'placed to some profession or business ... either that of a Farmer or Land surveyor', but on 16 June 1830 he bought an ensign's commission in the 32nd Regiment. On 19 May 1837 he transferred to the 12th Regiment as a lieutenant. Promoted captain on 3 September 1850, he purchased a major's commission on 12 May 1854. He was appointed brevet lieut-colonel on 26 October 1858 and colonel on 5 January 1864. In 1855 he had received a legacy of £2500 from Sir James's estate.

In October 1854 Kempt arrived in Melbourne in the *Camperdown* from Ireland in command of part of the first battalion of the regiment. The rest of the battalion arrived in November and a detachment was sent to Eureka. In 1854-61 he commanded detachments on routine garrison duties in the Australian colonies. From 22 January to 22 March 1861, as the colony's senior military officer, he was administrator of New South Wales after Governor Denison left and before Sir John Young arrived. In these months the regiment was again used in support of the civil power at Lambing Flat.

Popular and urbane, Kempt's most notable work was in connexion with the second volunteer movement in New South Wales. In August 1860 Denison had consulted him on a scheme of management for a volunteer corps which would allow for expansion. Kempt's memorandum of 20 September set out the requirements and organization; he was appointed inspecting field officer for the volunteers with an allowance and salary. As a regular officer in charge of the volunteers Kempt was often in an unenviable position : on the one hand, the imperial authorities feared that he was being diverted from more legitimate duties; on the other, the colonial government wanted him to be more under their control. When the land-based naval brigade was formed and placed under his control, he incurred the undeserved enmity of Captain Hixson [q.v.]. In 1864 Kempt prepared several reports on the corps and in a letter to William Forster [q.v.] in April urged the government to allocate more funds to it. Kempt's work with the volunteers won him high repute and gratitude from both the Executive Council and the governor.

In 1865 Kempt was appointed to take command at the Queen's Redoubt, near Auckland, where a detachment of his regiment was stationed. He died there of a heart attack on 28 July and was buried with full military honours in the Symonds Street cemetery, Auckland. Probate of his effects was sworn in London at under £3000. His wife Mary Ann, who had accompanied him to New Zealand, died aged 90 at Kensington, London, on 25 March 1892; they had no children.

E. A. H. Webb, *History of the 12th Regiment, 1685-1913* (Lond, 1914); V&P (LA NSW), 1861, 1, 36; SMH, 23, 28, 29 Jan, 25, 26 Feb, 11, 18, 23 Mar 1861, 21 Aug 1865; *Daily Southern Cross* (Auckland), 29 July 1865; *New Zealand Herald,* 29 July, 2 Aug 1865; *Sydney Mail,* 12 Aug 1865; D. M. MacCallum, Essays in early colonial defence in New South Wales with particular reference to the volunteer movement (M.A. thesis, Univ Syd, 1961).

G. P. WALSH

KENDALL, THOMAS HENRY (1839-1882), poet, was born on 18 April 1839 at Ulladulla, New South Wales, the twin son of Basil Kendall and his wife Melinda, née McNally. His father was the son of Thomas Kendall [q.v.] and had been a Chilean naval officer, flour factor, farmer and shepherd and died aged 43 while conducting a school at Grafton in 1852; his widow and children then moved to her father's home at Wollongong.

Henry received some schooling before he joined the whaler *Waterwitch* in September

1855. On his return in March 1857 he rented a house for his mother, twin brother and sisters at Newtown, in Sydney. In 1859 he contributed poems to the *Month,* whose editor, J. S. Moore [q.v.], introduced him to other literary men including the solicitor, J. L. Michael [q.v.], who employed Kendall as a clerk at Grafton in 1861-63 and allowed him to use his extensive library. In August 1863 Kendall became a clerk in the Department of Lands with a salary of £150. In 1866 he transferred to the Colonial Secretary's Office with £200 a year. In 1859-69 Kendall won repute as a poet by regular contributions to newspapers and periodicals in Sydney and Melbourne and by the publication in 1862 of *Poems and Songs.* G. B. Barton [q.v.] praised him for 'his distinctly Australian poetry' and R. H. Horne [q.v.] compared him favourably with Wordsworth. In March 1868 he married Charlotte, 18-year-old daughter of John Yates Rutter.

Kendall was often in debt to friends and money-lenders through his sisters' extravagance and his brother's dishonesty. Fearing bankruptcy and dismissal he resigned from the civil service on 31 March 1869 and went to Melbourne where he was welcomed by members of the Yorick Club. In September George Robertson [q.v.] published his *Leaves from Australian Forests;* it was a financial failure despite favourable reviews. Unable to support his family on the meagre pay for poems and articles and lacking the flair and training for journalism, he was driven back to Sydney by poverty, ill health and drunkenness. Intervals of dogged literary effort alternated with lapses into melancholia. In December 1870 he was charged with forging and uttering a cheque; defended by W. B. Dalley [q.v.], he was found not guilty on the ground of insanity. His wife had to return to her mother and Kendall became a derelict; in April-July 1873 he was in the Gladesville Hospital for the Insane. Later that year he was befriended by William and Joseph Fagan and lived with their family at Gosford until his health was restored. In 1875 the brothers gave him work in their timber business at Camden Haven.

In May 1876 Kendall's wife and children rejoined him and he slowly supplemented his income by writing topical and political skits for the *Freeman's Journal,* and occasionally for the *Sydney Mail* and *Town and Country Journal.* In 1879 he wrote the words for the cantata and the hymn of praise sung at the Sydney International Exhibition and also won the *Sydney Morning Herald's* prize of 100 guineas for a poem on the exhibition. In December 1880 he published *Songs from the Mountains* which was an outstanding success. His reputation re-established, he sought help from Henry Parkes [q.v.] who in April 1881 had him appointed inspector of forests for which he was admirably fitted by his knowledge of native timbers. Unfortunately he could not cope with the long rides to inspect reserves in all weathers. In June 1882 he collapsed at Wagga Wagga and was taken to William Fagan's house in Bourke Street, Surry Hills. Survived by his wife, three sons and two daughters, Kendall died of phthisis on 1 August 1882. He was buried in Waverley cemetery where in 1886 a monument was erected to his memory.

Kendall was once regarded as the finest poet Australia had produced and he remains a true poet whose clarity and sweetness have not been excelled in the narrow lyrical field he made his own. As A. G. Stephens wrote 'His gift of melodious writing makes his verses memorable'. He was of middle height, spare and thin, with a pale face, dark hair and blue-grey eyes. An excellent swimmer and horseman, he loved the Australian bush.

G. B. Barton (ed), *The poets and prose writers of New South Wales* (Syd, 1866); F. C. Kendall, *Henry Kendall: his later years* (Syd, 1938); T. T. Reed, *Henry Kendall: a critical appreciation* (Adel, 1960); Aust Documentary Facsimile Soc, *Foreshadowings*, I. Burke ed (Syd, 1963); T. T. Reed (ed), *The poetical works of Henry Kendall* (Adel, 1966); G. G. McCrae, 'Henry Kendall', *Aust Woman's Mag*, Jan, Feb 1883; D. Clarke, 'New light on Henry Kendall', *Aust Literary Studies*, June 1966; T. T. Reed, The life of Henry Kendall (D. Litt. thesis, Univ Adel, 1954); Parkes letters (ML); Kendall papers (ML, NL and held by T. T. Reed).   T. T. REED

KENNEDY, ALEXANDER (1837-1936), pastoralist, was born on 11 November 1837 at Dunkeld, Scotland, son of John Kennedy, land steward, and his wife Christina, née Duff. While employed in Scottish pastoral pursuits he was attracted at 23 by the Queensland migrant scheme. He sailed from the Clyde in the *Persia* and arrived at Gladstone on 16 November 1861. His first post was at Rio on the Dawson, a sheep run leased by Peter MacIntosh. He then took charge at Wealwandangie on the Comet River where Kanakas were largely employed as station hands, but after the station was foreclosed during a depression in the wool industry, Kennedy returned to Rockhampton and bought 1400 acres which he named Cuena, and where he grew sugar. There in August 1871 he married Marion Murray. Cuena proved unsuitable for sugar-growing and the property was sold. Kennedy became manager of Lorne, near Tambo, another MacIntosh sheep property, where on 4 November 1873 their son John Peter was born, one of the first white children born on the Barcoo and without benefit of a doctor.

When Lorne was sold Kennedy bought Emmett, a small near-by property, but soon sold it and returned to Rockhampton. With a vision of unoccupied lands beyond the far western horizon he made two exploration trips on horseback. In 1878 he and his associates, James White Powell and Robert Currie, backed by a loan of £12,000 at 10 per cent interest from the Queensland National Bank, took up 398,400 acres on Sulieman Creek south of Cloncurry; the property became known as Buckingham Downs. Kennedy with his family and cattle trekked some 700 miles from Rockhampton and lived in a tent till a small hut was built. In the next years Kennedy and Powell took up land as far west as Calton Hills and stocked it with cattle and horses. Trouble was experienced with the Aboriginals, the warlike Kalkadoons, and in 1884 Powell was killed by them on Calton Hills. In 1888 Kennedy with Roger Hale Sheaffe as his partner worked the properties of Devoncourt, Bushy Park, Parkside and Calton Hills, depasturing 16,930 cattle and 520 horses. By 1892 the number of cattle estimated for mortgage had risen to 27,349, and at their peak these properties later carried over 50,000 cattle running on holdings which covered an area of over 1200 square miles. In 1879 300 bullocks had been overlanded to the Adelaide market where they brought £11 a head. About 1880 he sent 1000 head to Wodonga in Victoria but after paying the border tax of £1 a head they brought only £3 a head. In 1892 another 1000 went to the Townsville meatworks and 1000 to Wodonga.

In 1885 Kennedy became a member of Cloncurry's first council. For years his headquarters were at Devoncourt and then at Bushy Park. His association with the prolific mineral area of the Cloncurry and Mount Isa district began in 1897 when the Duchess copper lode was discovered by his son Jack; it was sold in 1906-07 for £15,000 to the Hampden-Cloncurry Copper Mines Ltd. In 1928 when the company's smelters were sold, the mine had produced £2 million worth of copper.

In 1908 Kennedy and his wife visited Scotland. On their return they settled at Cloncurry, then at Bushy Park and finally at Brisbane in 1919. In old age he became interested in aviation. He was an original provisional director of Qantas and was one of the guarantors for the young company's account. At 87 Kennedy was issued with the Qantas No. 1 ticket, and on 3 November 1922 flew from Longreach to Cloncurry, the first passenger to fly in a regular airline in eastern Australia. He died in Brisbane on

12 April 1936 and his wife died later that same year aged 89. Kennedy's ashes, together with the story of his life, were deposited in his memorial at Devoncourt.

W. H. Fysh, *Taming the north* (Syd, 1950); G. Blainey, *Mines in the spinifex* (Syd, 1960); *Graziers' Review*, 16 Mar 1922; LAN/N 30-33, 44-46, 138, SCT/CD 42, 52 (QA).

HUDSON FYSH

KENNEDY, SIR ARTHUR EDWARD (1810-1883), soldier and governor, was born on 9 April 1810 at Cultra, County Down, Ireland, the fourth son of Hugh Kennedy and his wife Grace Dorothea, née Hughes. After study at Trinity College, Dublin, he was gazetted an ensign in the 11th Regiment on 15 August 1827. He served in Corfu, bought a commission and later spent three years in Canada as a captain in the 68th Regiment. In 1846 he returned to Ireland and as a poor law inspector in County Clare saw much of the Irish famine. He sold his commission in 1848 and joined the colonial service, becoming governor of Gambia in 1851, Sierra Leone in 1852 and Western Australia in July 1855.

In Kennedy's seven-year term in Western Australia the colony's economy grew steadily and the population rose by 40 per cent largely because of the influx of convict labour. In the Legislative Council he was opposed by the elected members Lionel Samson and M. W. Clifton [qq.v.]. They were supported by the *Perth Gazette* and resigned within two years, alleging that Kennedy was riding roughshod over their proposal for a move towards self-government. The governor's rejection was endorsed by the Colonial Office but the acrimony continued until Kennedy left. However, his relations with the judiciary were reasonably amicable and his hand was strengthened when F. P. Barlee [q.v.], who had been his private secretary in Sierra Leone, was appointed colonial secretary.

Kennedy was early persuaded to use convict labour more intensively than his predecessor had allowed, and to concentrate on public works around Perth. The comptroller-general of convicts, Colonel E. Y. W. Henderson [q.v.], favoured dispersal of labour and sought to obstruct Kennedy's plans, but the depots at Albany in 1855, York and Toodyay in 1856 and Port Gregory in 1857 were closed and the number of ticket-of-leave men in government employment was reduced. Notable public works by convict labour were road clearance, swamp drainage around Perth and the first stages of Government House on St George's Terrace, Perth. To counter serious mismanage-

ment in the police and convict departments, Kennedy inquired into allegations of fraud involving the police commissioner and had him replaced. In 1859 a superintendent of convicts was suspended for embezzlement and another senior officer was dismissed for quarrelling with his superior.

Kennedy left the colony on 19 February 1862 for England where he was appointed C.B. in July. He was governor of Vancouver Island in 1863-67, governor-in-chief of the West African Settlements in 1868-72, governor of Hong Kong in 1872-77 and of Queensland in 1877-83. He was knighted in December 1867 and appointed K.C.M.G. in September 1871 and G.C.M.G. in May 1881.

In Queensland, with no constitutional problems, Kennedy was able to display his humanity and urbanity with good effect. His only unpopular action was to refuse the excited call of the working classes to dismiss the Chinese domestic staff which he had brought from Hong Kong. Sometimes he also complained that a few members appointed to the Legislative Council were unsuitable because of their unclear heads and unclean hands, but these were the comments of a strong-minded man and even the press declared them worthy of earnest attention. His last official act was to sanction the annexation of New Guinea by Queensland, subject to approval by the Colonial Office.

Kennedy had become very feeble and suffered severely from asthma. Attended by a devoted daughter he left Brisbane on 3 May 1883 farewelled by large crowds and many honours. He died at Aden on 3 June. Predeceased on 3 October 1874 by his wife Georgina Mildred, née Macartney, whom he had married in 1839, he was survived by a son and two daughters.

H. C. Gilliland, 'Arthur Kennedy's administration of the colony of Western Australia . . .', *British Columbia Hist Q*, 18 (1954); *Perth Gazette*, 18 Sept 1868; *Inquirer*, 20 June 1883; P. J. Boyce, The role of the governor in Western Australia, 1829-1890 (M.A. thesis, Univ WA, 1961); R. J. Eagleton, Governor Kennedy —governor of Western Australia 1855-1862 (RWAHS and Battye Lib, Perth).

PETER BOYCE

KENNEDY, HUGH (1829-1882), university registrar, was born on 19 September 1829, the second son of Hugh Kennedy of Cultra, County Down, Ireland, and his second wife Sophia, née Lowe. In 1847 he matriculated to Balliol College, Oxford, and studied divinity, classics, mathematics and logic. He left, probably without a degree, although he later claimed a B.A. Oxon. In 1852 Kennedy married Eliza Ann, née

Lloyd, and went to New South Wales. In January 1853 he became a clerk in the Colonial Secretary's Office and in March transferred to the Customs Department as seventh clerk. He resigned in September to become registrar and secretary of the University of Sydney. In 1855 he was also appointed assistant professor of classics and allowed a quarter of the lecture fees.

With less than a hundred students enrolled, Kennedy's duties as registrar were not onerous, but he was required to keep detailed minutes of senate and other meetings, registers (some in Latin) and deal with correspondence. These records, often in Kennedy's own handwriting, form the basis of the University of Sydney's official archives. His duties included keeping a watchful eye on the condition of student lodginghouses. His long term of office gave administrative stability to the university. Although his teaching of classics involved the centre of university education, his lecturing role had become purely nominal by the 1870s. To many students he was 'particularly handsome' but 'more ornamental than useful'. He was a member of the Linnean Society of New South Wales.

By 1880 Kennedy had become affected by mental illness and was granted leave of absence by the University Senate. The *Bulletin*, 8 January 1881, attributed his illness to unsuccessful land speculations. Kennedy died intestate at the Hospital for the Insane, Gladesville, on 26 May 1882 and was buried in the Anglican section of Rookwood cemetery. He was predeceased by his first wife, who had died on 1 September 1866, and survived by a daughter. He was also survived by his second wife Ellen, née Fitzpatrick, whom he had married on 26 September 1868, and by four children.

Univ Syd Archives.   G. L. FISCHER

KENNERLEY, ALFRED (1810-1897), premier and philanthropist, was born in Islington, London. In the *Vibilia* he arrived at Sydney in October 1831 by way of Hobart Town. With ample means he applied in December for land at Rooty Hill and in 1832 was assigned some male convict labour. By 1837 he had bought the Retreat, a large farm at Bringelly, and 4000 acres on the Cudgegong River in County Wellington and property in Parramatta. On 18 February 1834 at Windsor he had married Jane, daughter of Richard Rouse [q.v.]. When his father died Kennerley leased his land and sold his livestock, planning to return to England. He sailed with his wife for London in March 1842 and returned to Sydney in January 1845. He resumed farming at Bringelly, became a magistrate and, in trust for his wife, acquired from Rouse more property in Parramatta. Kennerley was not robust and found the climate very trying. In 1853 he returned to England with his wife.

In June 1857 the Kennerleys arrived at Hobart in the *Gloucester* and named their new home Rouseville. He became a magistrate in 1858, joined the city council and was elected alderman in 1861 and mayor in 1862-63 and in 1871-72. He had been elected to the Legislative Council in 1865 and on 4 August 1873 to 20 July 1876 was premier without office. With T. D. Chapman, F. M. Innes, W. R. Giblin [qq.v.], William Moore, P. O. Fysh and George Gilmore in his ministry, he was an active supporter of liberal legislation, advocating such bills as marriage to a deceased wife's sister, maintenance of deserted wives, children and indigent persons, public charity (1873), infants' custody and life assurance companies (1874), destitute children and juvenile offenders (1875) and building societies (1876). He also initiated a policy of extending public works but party strife hindered progress and he resigned from the Legislative Council in 1877.

Kennerley had served on the committee of the Benevolent Society in the 1860s and the board of the Public Library and the Education Department. In 1869 he was treasurer and a founder of the Boys' Home and Industrial School, which first admitted 30 boys and within six years had trained over 70 juveniles. In the 1870s he was on the committee of the General Hospital Board, a director of the Brickfields Invalid Depot and a commissioner for Charitable Institutions. A dedicated Anglican he had long given a large annual sum towards the incumbent's stipend; he became churchwarden of All Saints parish in 1876 and donated a new Sunday school building and many subscriptions towards improving the edifice.

His wife died on 4 May 1877 and soon afterwards Kennerley had a paralytic stroke. He recovered but was unable to continue his public activities. He died at his home in Elboden Place, Hobart, on 15 November 1897 in his 88th year. His estate included many shares in the Union Bank, government securities and much landed property in New South Wales and Tasmania. He left generous legacies to relations and friends in England, his church, his servants and many benevolent societies. His will was challenged by distant relations without success.

Cyclopedia of Tasmania, 1 (Hob, 1900); V&P (HA Tas), 1875 (64); *Weekly News* (Hob), 20 Feb 1869; *Mercury*, 16 Nov 1897; *Australasian*,

14 June 1898; Governor's dispatches 1832-33 (ML); correspondence file on Kennerley (TA).

KENNION, GEORGE WYNDHAM (1845-1922), Anglican bishop, was born on 5 September 1845 at Harrogate, Yorkshire, England, son of George Kennion (M.D. Edinb., 1837) and his wife Catherine Elfrida, daughter of T. J. Fordyce of Ayton Castle, Berwickshire; his grandfather Thomas was permanent curate of Harrogate from 1825 till he died in 1846. Kennion was educated at Eton and Oriel College, Oxford (B.A., 1867; M.A., 1871). Ordained deacon in 1869 he was chaplain to the bishop of Tuam in Ireland. In Yorkshire he was priested in 1870, diocesan inspector of schools in 1871-73, vicar of St Paul's, Sculcoates, in 1873-76 and vicar of All Saints, Bradford, in 1877-82.

At the request of the Adelaide synod a panel of English bishops selected Kennion to succeed Augustus Short [q.v.]. He was given an honorary doctorate of divinity at the University of Glasgow on 7 November 1882 and consecrated in Westminster Abbey on the 30th. On 5 December he married Henrietta, sister of Sir James Fergusson, governor of South Australia in 1869-73. On 7 March 1883 Kennion was enthroned in St Peter's Cathedral, Adelaide. He was soon at grips with the major problem of supplying a ministry to the growing suburbs of Adelaide. At his first synod in April he announced his plan for a voluntary society to finance this work, to help in country areas and to bring new clergymen into the diocese. An obscure subcommittee of synod for Home Missions became the Bishop's Home Mission Society, an imaginative move which not only raised the number of clergymen in the diocese from fifty to seventy-five but also provided a loan fund which helped to build sixty-two churches by 1894. Under Kennion's stimulus the numbers of communicants and lay readers doubled. With the paddle-boat *Etona* he initiated ministries serving the new settlers along the River Murray. He introduced the Sisters of the Church to the diocese in 1892, formed the Diocesan Board of Education and the Financial Board and organized the diocese into rural deaneries. He raised money for completing the cathedral and the foundation stone for the nave and towers was laid in 1890.

Kennion's relations with his clergy and synod were normally good and fruitful because he accepted readily the system of church government through voluntary synodal compact though it was new to him. He won repute for upholding constitutional forms but never quite understood the antipathy in South Australian society towards the established church. This misunderstanding, coupled with his firm Anglican convictions marred his relations with other denominations and frustrated his many attempts to have religious instruction introduced into state schools, and negated his tentative steps towards church unity.

Kennion had visited England in 1888-89 and in 1893. On the first trip he had refused appointment as coadjutor to the bishop of Durham. When Earl Rosebery, a contemporary at Eton and Oxford, offered him the bishopric of Bath and Wells some jealousy was aroused in English ecclesiastical circles, but Adelaide received his resignation on 1 September 1894 with equanimity. He did not take a leading part in church affairs in England on his return, but was remembered in his diocese as a true pastor and a just administrator, zealous for faith and order. At the University of Cambridge he lectured in pastoral theology in 1890 and was Ramsden Preacher in 1901. He had written the preface to *Wells Office Book* in 1896 and *The Teaching of the Wells Millenary* in 1909. His *Courage, Sincerity, Faith* (London, 1902) was a sermon preached at Christ Church, Mayfair, in commemoration of the death of General Gordon. After a serious illness he resigned his see in 1919 and died at Ayr on 19 May 1922.

Kennion was a popular figure, a hard worker and not a brilliant academic. He was a moderate high churchman and moderate in most things. He fitted the establishment, yet maintained a deep concern for the working man from his days at Bradford, preaching the Christian Socialism of men like Charles Gore. In Adelaide he founded Kennion Hall as a home for boys and had a special concern for newsboys. Vigour, humour and generosity marked the man: dignity, reaching to the austere, tempered with warm-hearted pastoral concern marked the bishop.

A portrait is in Bishop's Court, North Adelaide.

Australasian, 21 Apr, 17 Nov 1888, 13 May, 18 Nov 1893, 14 July, 10 Nov 1894; J. R. Warner, The episcopate of George Wyndham Kennion (B.A. Hons thesis, Univ Adel, 1958).
                                                    J. R. WARNER

KERFERD, GEORGE BRISCOE (1831-1889), premier and judge, was born on 21 January 1831 at Liverpool, England, son of Joseph Kerferd, member of a merchant family trading in South America and Mexico, and his wife Rachel, née Blundell. Although his own preference was law Kerferd was persuaded to enter the family business. After education at the Collegiate

Institute, Liverpool, and training in another merchant house, he was to have represented family interests in Mexico but when changing conditions made that trade uncertain he was sent instead to Victoria. In the *Albatross* he arrived at Melbourne in April 1853. Most accounts claim that he could not find premises so gave up the attempt to establish a branch of the family firm, a story which conflicts with his repute for persistence and may cover an unsuccessful speculation or trouble in the parent company. He spent most of the year mining at Bendigo, then worked with the merchants, W. M. Bell [q.v.] & Co., before setting up independently at Beechworth as a wine and spirits merchant late in 1854. With him was his wife Ann, daughter of William and Margaret Martindale of Salt Water River, whom he married on 17 December 1853 at St James's Cathedral, Melbourne.

In Beechworth Kerferd laid the foundations for his political and legal careers. Successful in business, particularly a brewery he started in 1855 and, confident that Beechworth could be the permanent centre of a thriving mining and farming district, he worked with energy and imagination for the development of the town. Spare hours he spent reading law and classics. First elected to the Municipal Council in May 1857, he was chairman for three terms between 1858 and 1864, and the driving spirit behind the establishment of the district hospital in 1856-57 and the benevolent asylum in 1861-63. He was largely responsible for the town's unusual water scheme which, though eventually successful and still in use, was not completed until 1874 because of engineering and funding problems. The storage area is known as Lake Kerferd.

Kerferd's entry into colonial politics seems to have been unplanned. An election campaign in spring 1864 brought complaints that Legislative Assembly members for the Ovens electorate spent their energies discussing political economy rather than demanding construction of roads and bridges. A representative was needed who had local interests at heart and was strong enough to win influence in government. Kerferd was an obvious choice and was persuaded to stand. Returned at the top of the poll in that first election, he held the confidence of Ovens voters until he retired twenty-two years later, a unique achievement in an era of turbulent and vindictive politics.

Such confidence was not misplaced. Though a free trader and constitutionalist, Kerferd was consistent in supporting progressive land laws on which success of settlement in his district ultimately depended, and in working for practicable local government legislation and decentralized

justice, particularly local insolvency courts. He fought skilfully for construction of the north-eastern railway, later for a Beechworth branch line, argued regularly for adequate funds for Beechworth institutions and probably secured the mental hospital begun in 1865. Less successful was his claim for an industrial school, disputed by Wangaratta interests to such effect that the proposed school was lost to the north-east altogether. Beechworth and district did not live up to Kerferd's expectations but declined as mining activity decreased and attempts at agricultural settlement failed. The town's survival may have been due to Kerferd's influence in establishing and maintaining its institutions.

Strongly-built with square, firm features, Kerferd was most notable for his calm purpose and solid good sense. These are qualities not usually associated with daring, yet when he moved to Melbourne he sold the Beechworth brewery and turned to law, the object of his youthful ambition. For two years a pupil of T. H. Fellows [q.v.], he took the examination required for entry to the Bar and was admitted on 12 December 1867. In 1871 with John Burnett Box he published *A digest of cases decided in the Supreme Court of Victoria from A.D. 1846 to A.D. 1871*, an abstract of 2136 decisions of local importance, particularly cases in mining and pastoral matters not discussed by contemporary authorities.

Kerferd's prominence as a jurist came not from his small practice but from his work in government. He refused the post of solicitor-general in the Sladen [q.v.] administration in May 1868, preferring then the roles of minister for mines and vice-president of the Board of Land and Works. He became chief law officer in five conservative governments: appointed solicitor-general in the Francis [q.v.] ministry formed in June 1872, he succeeded J. W. Stephen [q.v.] as attorney-general on 2 May 1874 and when Francis resigned in July assumed leadership as premier and attorney-general; he was again attorney-general under McCulloch [q.v.] in 1875-77, Service [q.v.] in 1880 and the Service-Berry [q.v.] coalition in 1883. In January 1886 he relinquished the office to become sixth judge of the Supreme Court.

In his one term as premier Kerferd's professed aim was to carry on the business of government following the virtual defeat of Francis's scheme for constitutional amendment and delays caused by the chief secretary's serious illness. He made no changes in the ministry except that James Service replaced the treasurer, Edward Langton [q.v.], who apparently wanted the leadership himself and would not join him. Apart from passing the Local Government Act very little was achieved in the face of constant obstruction. When a test vote on Service's budget was carried only by one in August 1875 Kerferd requested a dissolution but was refused by the acting governor, Stawell [q.v.], and resigned.

If unexceptional as leader Kerferd was highly regarded as a politician and, according to Service, more highly regarded within parliament than any other member. He rarely engaged in personal clashes, even during the most vituperative phases of the 1860s and 1870s, and despite strong views was rarely involved in ideological controversies. The core of his reputation was not the moderation of his conduct but his ability in shaping and handling legislation. Hardworking, quick to assimilate detail, smooth and lucid in debate, when in charge of a bill he was receptive to suggestions for amendment yet kept the House firmly to the task in hand. The even progress of the extensive legislative programme of the coalition in 1883-86 owed much to his skill in committee.

Kerferd also contributed effectively to moves towards Federation. A member of the 1870 select committees on intercolonial legislation and Federal union, he was appointed delegate to the Sydney Convention in 1883 and was one of the committee which drafted the constitution of the Federal Council. His judicial career ended his official share in the cause but in 1886 he privately accompanied Service and Berry to the Hobart session of the council.

Many objected to Kerferd's elevation to the bench in 1886. He was accused of political jobbery and the Bar refused him the welcoming courtesies usually offered a new judge. The press revived a controversy of 1869 when Kerferd had been suspected of bribing another parliamentarian to assist the passage of the infamous quieting of titles bill, although he was exonerated by the select committee which examined the charges. However, his performance as judge proved unfounded the fears and jealousies of those who believed he had insufficient knowledge of the law.

Kerferd died suddenly on 31 December 1889 at his holiday house at Sorrento and was buried in the Anglican section of St Kilda cemetery. His wife, three sons and five daughters survived him, inheriting an estate of £26,342, most of which was lost in the bank crashes of 1893.

J. L. Forde, *The story of the Bar of Victoria* (Melb, 1913); R. C. Harvey, *Background to Beechworth 1852-1964* (Beechworth, 1964); PD (Vic), 1864-85; V&P (Vic), 1869, 2 (D3); *Ovens and Murray Advertiser*, Sept-Oct 1864, 19 Apr 1884, Jan 1886, Jan 1890; *Age*, Jan 1886, Jan 1890; *Argus*, Jan 1886, Jan 1890; *Once a Month*, 1 Feb 1886; C. Woods, The early history of Beechworth (M.A. thesis, Monash Univ, 1970).

MARGOT BEEVER

KERNOT, CHARLES (1820-1882), chemist, stationer and politician, was born on 23 March 1820 at Rochford, Essex, England, eldest son of William Pearce Kernot and his wife Susannah, née White. He followed his father as a dispensing chemist in Rochford. A combination of financial and religious problems (he had abandoned the established church for Congregationalism) induced him to migrate and with two children, his wife and her sister he sailed in the *Duke of Wellington* and arrived at Melbourne in 1851.

The family soon moved to Geelong, while Kernot tried his luck in vain at the Ballarat and Mount Alexander diggings. He had brought a printer's outfit with him from England, and set up business in Geelong as a chemist, printer and stationer. In three years he accumulated comfortable wealth. In 1858-59 he built and occupied Milton House in the suburb of Newtown. In 1865 he retired from the chemist's business that he had run with his brother William Henry as partner.

Kernot entered municipal politics in 1859 as a representative of Barwon Ward on the Geelong Council; he was mayor in 1864 but retired from the council in 1866. As a member for Geelong East Kernot entered the Legislative Assembly in March 1868, pledged to support the McCulloch [q.v.] government on the question of the Darling grant, but turned against the administration and as one of the first 'Loyal Liberals' helped to remove it from office in September 1869. Although opposing that year's Land Act as too favourable to the squatters, Kernot later supported the MacPherson [q.v.] government, losing his seat in January 1871. Defeated again in 1874, Kernot re-entered the assembly in April 1876 and thereafter remained a reasonably consistent supporter of G. Berry [q.v.], approving his reform and fiscal policies but opposing him on payment of members. In February 1880 Kernot lost his seat as a Berry candidate on the platform of protection and constitutional reform, but regained it in July. He died in Geelong on 26 March 1882, survived by his wife Mary Wright (1824-1884) and by five sons and two daughters.

A Dissenter, something of a radical and strong on 'mutual improvement', Kernot also had a great taste for amateur engineering and a first-class home workshop; many of his descendants became distinguished in Australian engineering circles. He was active in business, organizing and promoting the affairs of the Geelong Gas Co., the Victoria Woollen and Clothing Mills, and the Geelong and Melbourne Railway Co.; he was also committed to the Geelong Mechanics' Institute and to local building and health and mutual benefit societies. He was an extreme opponent of state aid to religion, a supporter of the Education Act and a strong temperance advocate. He was regarded as 'one of the least talkative members who ever sat in the House, seldom speaking at all, and never for more than a very few minutes'.

W. R. Brownhill, The history of Geelong and Corio Bay (Melb, 1955); Argus, 27 Mar 1882; Geelong Advertiser, 27 Mar 1882; family papers (held by Mr M. H. Kernot, Melb).

                                    S. MURRAY-SMITH

KERNOT, WILLIAM CHARLES (1845-1909), engineer and educationist, was born on 16 June 1845 at Rochford, Essex, England, eldest son of Charles Kernot [q.v.]. Kernot subscribed to the tradition that the family was of Huguenot extraction, the name being a variant of the French 'Carnot' (although Kernot was not normally pronounced as a French word). He arrived with his family at Geelong in 1851 and attended Christ Church School and at the Flinders National School came under the influence of George Morrison [q.v.], to whom Kernot wrote 'I owe an untold debt of gratitude'. Admitted at 15 he had a 'happy and satisfactory' career in the University of Melbourne (B.A., 1864; M.A., 1866); by gaining the certificate of civil engineering in 1866 he became the first qualified engineer to be produced by the university, though he thought little of the course. He also gained a master of civil engineering in 1898.

Kernot's experience from 1865 to 1875 was to colour his approach to professional education. In 1865 through political influence he secured a post in the Department of Mines at a time of intense pressure of routine work checking land leases. His qualifications were 'as useless as a punkah would be at the South Pole', and after eighteen months he was dismissed. In 1867 he was appointed to water supply, in amiable surroundings but among men who 'as far as I could discern were perfectly unconscious even of the existence of physical laws'. When this office was disbanded he moved to the Department of Railways for some six months in 1870, finding there that the engineer-in-chief, T. Higinbotham [q.v.], 'never missed an opportunity of impressing upon me the uselessness and undesirability of University training for engineers', and

then returned to a reconstituted water-supply office, finally resigning from government service in 1875.

Kernot had been appointed part-time lecturer in surveying at the university in 1868, and next year received a similar appointment in civil engineering. Increasing classes at the university and growing returns from students' fees largely motivated his resignation from the public service. He claimed that 'at once' he discovered that, with consulting work, he could make several times his government pay. In 1882 the utilitarian 'schoolmaster' element on the university council succeeded in establishing four new chairs on the basis of 'favouring local men and appointing them without overseas competition'; in 1883 he became professor of engineering, the first in the university and the first graduate of the university to gain a chair there. Next year the first graduates in engineering, as distinct from holders of the 'certificate', appeared.

One of the earliest examples of Kernot's 'outside' work was his association for some years from 1876 with L. Brennan [q.v.] in developing early models of the steerable torpedo. In 1887 he sent Kernot £500 'as a slight expression of the inestimable service rendered by you' in the 'early and most trying stages of the invention'. In 1878 Kernot had visited Europe, inspected many engineering schools and industrial establishments and become acquainted with leading scientists and engineers. On his return to Melbourne he worked with assiduity as chairman of two juries, and member of another, at the International Exhibition of 1880; although handsomely thanked, Kernot refused to undertake similar duties at the 1888 exhibition, being convinced of 'the impossibility of arriving at thoroughly reliable and satisfactory awards'. In 1884 he accepted an invitation to join a New South Wales royal commission on railway bridges, thus involving himself in two years of part-time work. In 1888 he reported on railway bridges in the Derwent valley for the Tasmanian government and took part in a Victorian inquiry into the undergrounding of telephone and telegraph wires in the metropolitan area. In 1891 he again visited Europe and went on to North America, where he inspected many engineering schools and colleges, with a view to building an adequate engineering school for the University of Melbourne at his own expense; Kernot ruefully recalled that this project was negated by the 'great slump'. In 1892 he was chairman of an inquiry into the locomotive and rolling-stock branch of the Victorian railways, and later claimed, probably justly, that his advice on the balancing of locomotives was saving the government more than its annual subvention to the University of Melbourne. He published numerous scientific papers, his most important work being *On Some Common Errors in Iron Bridge Design* (1898). In 1901 he again travelled to England, France, Germany and South Africa. To the 1903 royal commission on the University of Melbourne he testified that he spent twenty-three hours a week in lecturing to, or close association with, his students.

To these public and academic duties Kernot added his broader concerns with engineering and education. He was president of the Royal Society of Victoria in 1885-1900 and virtually a permanent member of its council; he was active in the Victorian Institute of Engineers (president 1886, 1890, 1897-98 and 1906-07) and the Victorian Institute of Surveyors (president 1883-84). On F. Ormond's [q.v.] death in 1889 he became for ten very difficult years chairman of the council of the Working Men's College, an institution he once unfortunately referred to as 'University and water', but he fought fiercely for its independence. Kernot's *Address* to the college's annual demonstration in 1894 is, like many of his surviving speeches and lectures, noteworthy for its freedom from cant, its espousal of educational principles modern even eighty years later and its pungency. 'Payment by results' he termed 'a system admirably adapted to the cure of smoky chimneys, but most fatal in its effects on cloudy intellects'. On another occasion (but also with reference to the college) he remarked that the democratic atmosphere of a university 'altogether unfits men for submitting to the despotism either of a Russian Czar or a Victorian Education Department'. From his own funds he contributed generously to his institutions: in 1887 he provided £2000 for scholarships in physics and chemistry at the university; in 1893 he gave £300 for a foundry at the Working Men's College and in 1901 another £300 to that institution; in 1902 he donated £1000 towards a metallurgical laboratory at the university and in 1908 a further £200 for a scholarship in geology.

In areas of broader scientific and social concern, Kernot became in 1886 an inaugural member of the Australian Antarctic Committee, set up jointly by the Royal Society of Victoria and the Victorian branch of the Geographical Society of Australasia, the members of which, according to R. A. Swan, 'played a vital role as trail-blazers for the future exploration of the Antarctic continent'. In the same year Kernot was chairman of the board of arbitrators in the waterfront strike, his successful work being recognized by an address presented to him jointly by the Employers' Union and the Trades Hall Council, 'expressing the esteem and satisfaction of both bodies of his impartiality'. In 1903, while deploring 'the extreme Socialistic tendency' and even offering his and his students' services as strike-breakers during the railway engine-drivers strike, he firmly stated his sympathy 'with all the wants, ambitions and trials of the so-called workingman'. He was also an active member of the Baptist Union of Victoria (president 1902-03) and a staunch free trader.

Kernot was probably best known as what a later generation would call a 'stirrer'; indeed, his character and influence cannot be assessed without examining the stiff sense of professional dignity and ethics which led him into many disputes. His early humiliations in the public service made him a relentless scourge of bureaucratic incompetence and nourished a sense of self-righteousness in his many campaigns for safety, economy and the application of scientific principles in public works. He sternly lectured, in forthright categories, government and municipal engineers when he found faults in their designs, especially when these menaced public safety, and referred to the 'ordinary ignorant empiric who calls himself an engineer'. In the late 1880s he launched a long but successful campaign to have the railways admit the weaknesses in the important Moorabool viaduct near Geelong, and he had a lifelong interest in flood control on the Yarra and Barwon Rivers. Among many other battles he dedicated himself to a lengthy campaign against the anti-academic bias of the prestigious Institution of Civil Engineers in Britain, and to a similar fight against the unscientific and anti-theoretical approaches of government departments in appointing and promoting engineers and surveyors.

Kernot often told his students that 'I freely admit many mistakes and much weakness on my part, and . . . regret that my position was not held by some one of sturdier and less sensitive nature, better fitted than I for a career of continual conflict', but there seems little need to take this very seriously. By his autumn years he could point to honoured scars and draw comfort from many victories since the day when he was, in his own words, 'the first man that the University sent out to attack single handed the fortress of professional ignorance and prejudice'. He participated with immense energy in both social and professional life and believed strongly that material progress would lead to 'the evolution of a wiser, kinder, and more sympathetic race'. His disposition was benign, and his popularity considerable with students, colleagues and the public. However, his school of engineering was in some ways a disappointment; it lacked the munificent private backing of the Sydney school. Kernot had to battle deep-seated prejudice against the academically-trained engineer, and the depression of the 1890s, coming when he was at his peak, sadly affected his plans for development. He was criticized by some witnesses at the royal commission on the University of Melbourne (1902-04), and claims were made that his courses were 'superficial', purely descriptive and lacking in analytical and mathematical rigor. Perhaps more seriously, he threatened a member of his own staff who gave evidence critical of the school and secured his removal from academic employment, matters which properly angered the commissioners. However, degree courses in mining engineering (1901) and mechanical engineering (1907) were introduced before Kernot died, while electrical engineering (1912) had long been one of his ambitions. He can fairly be credited with laying sound foundations for the expansion of engineering in the University of Melbourne that took place after his death. More importantly, his spirited extramural sorties and his long campaign for the status of the engineer both within the profession and outside it were a necessary preliminary to the development of adequate academic courses at the university and elsewhere. Here lies his significance, and a large measure of justification for the claim made for him as 'the first Australian engineer'.

In 1880 Kernot had built a large and comfortable house, Firenze, on Royal Parade, Parkville, and there he lived out his life unwed but in company with others of his family. He was of comfortable means, mainly due to his consulting and industrial interests: in 1882 he, James Service [q.v.] and F. Pirani introduced electric light to Melbourne through the New Australian Electricity Co., with Kernot as chairman of directors (1882-1900). He was of pleasing eccentricity: he built a fabled 'velocipede', forerunner of the bicycle, about 1869 and claimed the record for a penny-farthing journey to Geelong; he was an enthusiast for ballooning; and in his later years he was still youthful enough to drive in a student procession his well-known steam car disguised as a locomotive. He died unexpectedly at his home on 14 March 1909. A younger brother, Wilfred Noyce, was professor of engineering at the University of Melbourne in 1932-36.

Deakin held Kernot eminent in his profession and known for 'his sense of justice and kindness'. Scott has written of his 'unruffled generosity and kindness', and Blainey has apostrophized him as 'Kindly and plump, wearer of the broadcloth'. In

My Life Story (1924) Arthur Lynch claims him as the only professor he knew at the University of Melbourne 'devoid of that detestable academic exclusiveness and starchiness', and tells how he stood for an hour under Kernot's old umbrella with him at a street corner while the rain poured, listening spellbound to a disquisition on the properties of iron.

E. Scott, *A history of the University of Melbourne* (Melb, 1936); G. Blainey, *A centenary history of the University of Melbourne* (Melb, 1957); Kernot papers (LaT L); family papers (held by Mr M. H. Kernot, Melb).

S. MURRAY-SMITH

KERR, PETER (1820-1912), architect, was born on 21 April 1820 in Aberdeen, Scotland, son of James Kerr (b. 1791), shipmaster and leather merchant, and his wife Helen, née Chesney. He served his articles with the Aberdeen architect, Archibald Simpson (1790-1847), and then worked with George Fowler Jones at York. In 1845 he was engaged by the duke of Sutherland to renovate and extend Dunrobin Castle. In 1848 he went to London and worked in the office of Sir Charles Barry (1795-1860), architect of the new Houses of Parliament at Westminster. Soon after they were opened by the Queen in February 1852 Kerr migrated to Melbourne.

Kerr joined the partnership of J. G. Knight [q.v.] & Thomas Kemp, architects and engineers. Kemp, who had worked in London under Barry, returned to England in 1855 but the firm of Knight & Kerr continued to about 1860 when Knight turned to other occupations. From the beginning the partners had a private practice but also designed and supervised government projects. In 1866-92 Kerr served in the Public Works Department as an architect, rising to first grade with a salary of £600 and taking charge of the 'principal Metropolitan Buildings'. His notable works included portions of the Law Courts, Government House, Post Office and Customs House. He was one of the able architects who enriched Melbourne with some of the finest classical public buildings in Australia but his reputation rests on the claim that he alone designed the impressive Houses of Parliament in Spring Street.

Kerr was associated with each of the four campaigns to complete the parliamentary buildings. Soon after he reached Melbourne a competition for designing the Houses of Parliament had been won by Smith & Pritchard but it was dropped. In a letter to the *Argus*, 15 January 1892, Kerr claimed that 'Our firm ... brought influence ... through our Mr. Knight and in the end the carrying out of the Houses of Parliament was entrusted to us. The designs for the Council and Assembly Chambers [built by 1858] and for the library [built in 1859] were prepared by me with my own hands and the drawings are still in existence [at the P.W.D.] to speak for themselves'. He also claimed that the building of these two projects were supervised by Knight and himself. In 1877 Kerr was appointed architect by the royal commission on extending accommodation in the parliamentary buildings. He designed and superintended the building of the Queen's Hall and the Vestibule, opened in 1879. He continued to work on the final scheme which included a massive dome and an overpowering Roman Doric façade round the entire building but only the west façade was completed by 1892. In June 1904 his paper on 'The Melbourne Houses of Parliament: The Ancient History' was read to the general meeting of the Royal Victorian Institute of Architects and published in the institute's journal.

Kerr served as a building referee in the administration of the Melbourne Building Act. His last work was as an honorary superintending architect for the memorial to Queen Victoria in the Alexandra Gardens, Melbourne. He died at South Melbourne on 31 March 1912, survived by his wife Harriette, née Bertrand, whom he had married in Melbourne on 8 August 1857, and by two sons and two daughters of their seven children.

Kerr was a fellow of the Royal Institute of British Architects. He also helped to found the Victorian Institute of Architects in August 1856, served on its first council and was made an honorary fellow when the institute received a royal charter in 1889.

G. H. Jenkins, *A short history and description of the Parliament House, Melbourne* (Melb, 1886); 'Peter Kerr (Hon. Fellow), F.R.I.B.A.', Roy Vic Inst of Architects, J, July 1905; D. S. Lyall, The architectural profession in Melbourne 1835 to 1860 (M. Arch. thesis, Univ Melb, 1966); N. Chlebnikowsky, Parliament House, Melbourne (B. Arch. research report, Univ Melb, 1970); Kerr papers (held privately by C. Kerr, Vic, and K. S. Kerr, Qld).

GEORGE TIBBITS

KHULL, EDWARD (1805-1884), stockbroker, was born in Glasgow, Scotland, son of Edward Khull, printer. He was trained as a printer in Glasgow and for some time employed James Harrison [q.v.]. About 1830 Khull married Catherine Dennistoun, a distant relation of Alexander Dennistoun who was a wealthy merchant. Encouraged by an introduction to Dennistoun's clients in the Port Phillip District and a 'power of a draft for £1000' on Dennistoun Brothers of Glasgow, Khull sailed with his wife and four children in the *John Gray* for Melbourne. He arrived in August 1848, stayed for two months with George Russell [q.v.] at Golfhill and was introduced to management of a sheep run. Embarrassed by the cost of his family's upkeep in Melbourne and unable to find suitable work for his son, he bought 6200 sheep on Tallygaroopna from the attorney of the absent licensee, Sherbourne Sheppard, and occupied the run. When Sheppard returned from England in 1849 he forcibly ejected Khull and repossessed the property. On 6 April 1852 the case, *Khull* v. *Sheppard*, was heard in the Supreme Court and the jury returned a verdict for the defendant.

In January 1851 Khull had been appointed government printer. Soon after gold was discovered at Ballarat he resigned and, with James Patterson as partner, set up as gold-brokers. From early 1852 Khull supplied the *Argus* with weekly reports on the gold market and with six annual statistical supplements on gold production, prices, exchange rates and other relevant matters. As one of the leading firms in the trade, Khull & Patterson were engaged by the Bank of Australasia to buy gold on commission. In 1853 the banks decided to bypass the brokers and to buy gold on their own account. In the *Argus* Khull used his weekly column to condemn this 'illegitimate' banking business, but he protested in vain and within a few years the banks controlled most of the trading in gold.

Late in 1852 as E. Khull & Co. he began to deal in stocks and shares. The appearance of his first share price list in the *Argus*, October 1852, marks the beginning of a share market in Victoria. As the banks took over gold dealing he gave more of his attention to sharebroking and became one of the leading figures in the industry. His regularly published share price list contributed to the gradual development of a wider market in stocks and shares. Although not prominent in the negotiations leading to the formation of Melbourne's first Stock Exchange in April 1861 he was one of its foundation members. However, he had already become a victim of the aftermath of Victoria's first speculative market in mining shares. He was involved in insolvency proceedings from May 1860 to February 1861. He had helped to found the *Stock and Share Journal* on 26 May 1860 which ceased publication in April 1861. His active business career did not long survive these experiences and he went into retirement. Predeceased by his wife, he died aged 79 at his home in

Collingwood on 5 May 1884. He was buried in St Kilda cemetery.

P. L. Brown (ed), *Clyde Company papers*, 4, 6 (Lond, 1959, 1968); A. R. Hall, *The Stock Exchange of Melbourne and the Victorian economy 1852-1900* (Canberra, 1968); *Argus*, 1851-61; *Australasian*, 10 May 1884.

A. R. HALL

KIDD, JOHN (1838-1919), store-keeper, dairy farmer and politician, was born at Brechin, Forfarshire, Scotland, son of John Kidd, boot manufacturer, and his wife Elizabeth, née Souter. He began work at an early age and sporadically attended parish and night schools. In 1857 he migrated to Sydney and set up as a baker. In November 1860 he married Sophie Collier, a native of Aberdeen.

After moving his business to Campbelltown Kidd soon won repute for honesty and tact, and expanded his business into a general store. By the 1870s further success had enabled him to acquire land and he became interested in the supply of milk to Sydney. He was an early champion of Ayrshire cattle and later a director of the Farmers' and Dairymen's Milk Co. Ltd. Increasingly important in the Campbelltown community, he was prominent in the Presbyterian Church and the temperance movement, a member of the local Public School Committee and an enthusiast for the School of Arts. He was appointed a magistrate in 1870.

Drawn by politics Kidd failed to win the seat of Narellan in 1877 but in 1880 was elected to the Legislative Assembly for Camden. Although a supporter of the Parkes-Robertson [qq.v.] ministry he aired his practical and independent views on a wide range of subjects and won some distinction for garrulity. About this time he gave up his store and retired to Blair Athol, his large home near Campbelltown. Over-confidence cost him his seat in 1882, but he was re-elected in 1885. He gave attention to the fiscal question and by a circuitous course came to favour protection. Defeated in 1887 he was re-elected in 1889 and in 1891 was appointed postmaster-general in Dibbs's [q.v.] protectionist ministry. Kidd was no bigot but his firm Presbyterianism led him to join the Loyal Orange Institution. Despite friendship with John Davies [q.v.], admiration for Parkes, and the predeliction of the Orange and temperance movement for free trade, Kidd firmly adhered to protection. His scornful denial of any connexion between protection and Catholicism often brought him into conflict with fellow Orangemen. However, it brought rewards:

his inclusion in Dibbs's ministry was more a consequence of the premier's desire to counter Orange criticism than from any particular virtue of Kidd. He proved to be a conscientious, unadventurous minister. He was a New South Wales commissioner at the Adelaide and Melbourne Exhibitions. Defeated in the 1895 election, he was returned in 1898 and was minister for mines and agriculture from April 1901 to June 1904 in a Progressive (Protectionist) ministry. An advocate of Federation since 1891, he was an unsuccessful government candidate in the 1901 Senate election, though he polled 43,000 votes. In 1904 Kidd was narrowly defeated and retired from politics. Gazetted honourable in 1904, he continued the business affairs that he acquired during twenty-five years in politics: trustee of the Savings' Bank of New South Wales and a director of the Australian Mutual Fire Insurance Society. Aged 81 he died on 8 April 1919 and was buried in the Presbyterian section of the Campbelltown cemetery. He was survived by two daughters.

Ex-M.L.A., *Our present parliament, what it is worth* (Syd, c1886); *Cyclopedia of N.S.W.* (Syd, 1907); W.A. Bayley, *History of Campbelltown* (Campbelltown, 1965); *SMH*, 6 Aug 1875; *Daily Telegraph* (Syd), 31 July 1894; *Campbelltown Herald*, 20 July, 3 Aug 1898; *Bulletin*, 20 Apr 1901, 7 Apr 1919; J. P. McGuanne, *Centenary of Campbelltown* (ML).

MARK LYONS

KIMPTON, WILLIAM STEPHEN (1832-1926), businessman, was born on 4 October 1832 at Litlington, Cambridgeshire, England, third son of Thomas Kimpton, farmer and grain merchant, and his wife Lucy Eleanor, née Sterne. He was apprenticed to a baker but loss of the family farm and rumours of riches in Victoria persuaded him and his brother Edward to migrate; they arrived at Melbourne in the *Melpomene* in November 1853. William worked on the wharf and then as a baker, gaining control of the business in return for wages owed him. He established a bakery in Brunswick Street, Fitzroy, prospered and in 1875 widened his activities by founding the Union Flour Mills. This step brought insolvency in 1877 but he recovered with Mortimer Rush as his partner and then Robert Chamberlain; by the mid-1880s Kimpton was on his own. After the Fitzroy plant was burnt down a new mill, equipped with the latest Hungarian roller-mill machinery, was built at Kensington in 1888. The fiscal policy of New South Wales ended Kimpton's weekly shipment there of one thousand bags of flour, so in that colony in 1892 he started a mill managed by his son.

In 1902 fire again destroyed the Melbourne mill but after reconstruction and incorporation with James Gillespie & Co. Kimpton owned the largest mill in Australia. He shipped flour to Queensland, Fiji and England besides having important trade connexions with South Africa and the East.

Kimpton was an excellent judge of draught horses and personally selected those he wanted for the business. He remained active in the firm though his sons took over increasing responsibility. His major interest outside the business was the Anglican Church and for twenty-six years he was a member of the Church Association and churchwarden of St Mark's, Fitzroy. On moving to Essendon he became churchwarden of St Thomas's to which he gave a pipe organ. He was also a councillor of the Old Colonists' Association. Kimpton had married Margaret Mason of Newcastle upon Tyne; after she died he married her sister, Isabella, in 1859. He died at his home, Milverton, Moonee Ponds, on 18 November 1926. Predeceased by his wife and one son, he was survived by four daughters and his son Albert Edward who, with his grandsons Victor and Charles, continued as directors of the firm.

J. Smith (ed), *Cyclopedia of Victoria*, 1 (Melb, 1903); *Weekly Times*, 13 July 1895; *Millers' J of A'sia*, 30 Oct 1915; *Argus*, 19 Nov 1926; *Essendon Gazette*, 25 Nov 1926; *A'sian Baker and Millers' J*, 30 Nov 1926; information from V. Y. Kimpton, Queen St, Melb.

J. ANN HONE

KING, GEORGE (1813-1899), Church of England clergyman, was born on 20 March 1813 at Fintona, County Tyrone, Ireland, second son of William King, linen merchant, and his wife Anne, née West. He was educated at Portora Royal School, Enniskillen, and Trinity College, Dublin (B.A., 1836; M.A., 1854; LL.D., 1885), made deacon in September 1836 and ordained priest in June 1837 by Bishop Mant of Down and Connor. After curacies at Larne and Portstewart, King became incumbent of Holywood in 1840. On 9 July he married a widow, Jane Stewart Mathewson (d. 1900).

Although his bishop was ready to forward King's interests, Mrs King's asthma prompted him to migrate to Western Australia, where he arrived with his family in October 1841 as an S.P.G. missionary. He settled at Fremantle and built a church in 1843, conducted day and Sunday schools and held services in the gaol and outlying districts. Unable to secure a government stipend or set up his projected district schools, he ran an institution for Aboriginal children and severely criticized the indifference of the settlers and the misguided policy of the government towards Aboriginals. Enthusiastic and hard-working, King already showed strong personal feelings and impatience with authority. In 1846 his health began to deteriorate and in 1847 he was permitted to leave the colony.

King hoped to serve in New Zealand under Bishop G. A. Selwyn, but on arrival at Sydney he was persuaded by Bishop Broughton [q.v.] to take temporary charge of St Andrew's parish. His appointment was made permanent in July 1848. King succeeded in restoring morale and in building up a loyal lay following, after the secession to Rome of his predecessor, R. K. Sconce [q.v.]. He became enthusiastically involved in the completion and the development of St Andrew's Cathedral. Episcopal opposition did not prevent him from helping to form the Anglican affiliated university college of St Paul in 1852-55. He was elected a fellow and served on the college council in 1855-93. At missionary meetings he pleaded the cause of Aboriginals in December 1853 and June 1856 and sent several to Selwyn's South Seas institution. With Augustus Morris [q.v.] King tried to found an Aboriginal establishment under Rev. William Ridley [q.v.].

In 1852 King had voted against the episcopal veto embodied in Broughton's scheme for a church constitution and renewed his opposition in November 1858 when Bishop Barker [q.v.] summoned a conference to prepare a draft constitution for submission to parliament. In 1859 King told a Legislative Council select committee that no legal enactment was needed and that episcopal powers were excessive. His personal interests had become entangled in these matters of principle. He resented the infringement of his rights as incumbent when in 1858 Barker appointed Rev. W. M. Cowper [q.v.] dean of St Andrew's Cathedral. In January 1860 his wardens, anxious to preserve the parochial character of the church, petitioned the Legislative Assembly. A select committee was sympathetic but inactive. In September, when told that he was not needed to assist at an ordination, he had the cathedral doors locked. This protest caused a public stir and, since the legal position of the Church of England was then under debate, he aroused some sympathy. He declined to recognize the episcopal tribunal of inquiry into the incident and appealed to the Supreme Court. In January 1861 the Banco Court upheld his appeal but ruled that the bishop could solely hear King's case. He then appeared under protest and his licence was revoked. Barker restored the licence and in 1863 King was appointed to St Peter's, Cook's River.

King did not figure in any further controversies but remained a loyal churchman. He travelled widely and continued to advocate his special interests. Although a staunch Ulsterman, he disapproved the growing activity of the Orange lodges. He was a founder and sometime president of the New South Wales Institution for the Deaf and Dumb and the Blind, and a director of the Society for the Relief of Destitute Children. In 1872 he moved to St Thomas's, Enfield, but resigned in 1879, retaining only the chaplaincy of the Anglican cemetery at Rookwood until 1886. In 1887 he published a pamphlet of his *Reminiscences.* He died at Homebush on 20 March 1899, survived by his wife, two of his five daughters and one of his two sons. He was buried in the churchyard of St Thomas's, Enfield. His estate was valued at £3200.

W. Norris, *Annals of the diocese of Adelaide* (Lond, 1852); J. G. Legge (ed), *A selection of Supreme Court cases in New South Wales,* 2 (Syd, 1896); R. Border, *Church and state in Australia 1788-1872* (Lond, 1962); S. M. Johnstone, *The book of St. Andrew's Cathedral, Sydney,* rev ed (Syd,1968); V&P (LA NSW), 1859-60, 3, 1205, (LC NSW), 1859-60, 1, 667; SMH, 12 June 1852, 10 Dec 1853, 20 June 1856, 20 July 1860; *Empire* (Syd), 8 Nov 1860; G. King, diary and papers (held by family); SPG records, diocese of Adelaide, Australia and Sydney (SPG Archives, Westminster); CSO records (Battye Lib, Perth).

HAZEL KING
K. J. CABLE

KING, GEORGE (1814-1894), merchant, pastoralist and politician, was born on 21 December 1814 in Riga, son of Robert King, a partner in the Baltic firm of Balfour & Co., and his wife Caroline, née Babat. Trained in London and on the Continent for a mercantile career, he spent five years in Riga and became a fluent linguist. In 1839 in London he married Jane, née Creighton; they arrived at Sydney on 25 July in the *Fergusson.* He set up as a merchant in George Street in the firms of Gordon & King and King & Moutry, but in 1843 was declared insolvent. He then became a general commission agent; in 1847 he was secretary to the Sydney Fire Insurance Co. and appointed official assignee. He joined Thacker, Daniell & Co., which in the 1860s became Daniell, King & Co. From the 1850s King served on the board of advice to the Australian Agricultural Co. and was a director of the Clarence and Richmond River Steam Navigation Co., the Commercial Banking Co. of Sydney, the London Chartered Bank and was chairman of the Australian Trust Co., the Southern Insurance Co., the Mel-

bourne Marine Insurance Co. and of the Australian Mutual Provident Society for fifteen years. He also served on the committee of the Sydney Chamber of Commerce and his firm was agent for several overseas insurance companies including one based in Canton.

In 1857 King was a founder and member of the first committee of the Union Club. In 1866 with Ernest and Oscar de Satgé [q.v.] he acquired Gowrie and Gonbungee stations on the Darling Downs. Gowrie, 103 square miles near Toowoomba, became the sole property of King and his sons. Nominated by J. L. Montefiore [q.v.] he won East Sydney in the New South Wales Legislative Assembly in 1869; he stood as a representative of commerce on a platform of free trade and the abolition of *ad valorem* duties. He was an independent supporter of Sir James Martin [q.v.] and retired in 1872. In 1865 King had been made consul for Italy, a position he took seriously, and tried to interest James Macarthur [q.v.] in cotton growing. He resigned in 1875 and was appointed a knight of the Crown by Victor Emanuel.

After a visit to England King settled in 1874 at Gowrie where he built a large homestead. He was a Queensland executive commissioner at the 1880 Melbourne International Exhibition. In London in 1881 he chaired the royal commission on the management of the agent-general's office and represented the Queensland government on the royal commission on the purchase of steel rails after Thomas McIlwraith's [q.v.] indictment by Samuel Griffith. On King's return in 1882 he was appointed to the Queensland Legislative Council. In 1885 he consulted Sir Henry Parkes [q.v.] on the New South Wales council's power to amend money bills when a similar clash occurred in Queensland. He resigned on 19 March 1890. About 1879 George King & Sons took up ten runs in the Warrego district near Cunnamulla, which were consolidated as Weelemurra in 1885. In the 1877-78 drought Gowrie was invaded by marsupials; some 40,000 wallabies were killed and their skins sold in Japan. While water-divining in 1887 he found coal and in 1889 the Gowrie colliery was opened.

A loyal Anglican, King was largely responsible for building St John's Church at Gowrie Junction. He was a lay reader and his wife gave an organ to the church. Disabled by a stroke in 1889, King died on 22 June 1894 from a cerebral haemorrhage and was buried in the Toowoomba cemetery. He was survived by his wife, to whom he left an annuity of £3000, and by seven sons and three daughters. His New South Wales estate was valued at almost £28,000. His eldest son Robert John represented Paddington in the New South Wales Legislative Assembly in 1889-91.

T. W. H. Leavitt (ed), *Australian representative men*, 3rd ed (Melb, 1888); SMH, 26, 30 Nov, 3, 4, 6 Dec 1869, 15 May 1871; *Brisbane Courier*, 27 June 1894; *Australasian*, 17 July 1894; MS cat under George King (ML); Insolvency file 648/1 (NSWA).

MARTHA RUTLEDGE

KING, HENRY EDWARD (1832-1910), barrister, public servant and parliamentarian, was born on 9 June 1832 at Kilmallock, Mount Coote, County Limerick, Ireland, son of John Wingfield King and his wife Alicia, née Coote. Educated at a collegiate school in Gloucester, he was attracted by the gold rush and went to Sydney in 1852. He soon moved to the Northern Districts (later Queensland) where some grazing licences were taken out in his name. He does not appear to have had any major part in grazing or gold-mining but he managed to acquire a working knowledge in these fields and it was later useful to him. At Brisbane in 1858 he married Harriette, sister of Dr William Armstrong of Toowoomba.

On 16 August 1862 King became a first-class surveyor and commissioner for crown lands in the Mitchell District. From 28 November 1867 to July 1870 he was gold commissioner in Wide Bay, which included Gympie. In the performance of his duties he became popular with the miners and, when Gilbert Eliott [q.v.] resigned in 1870, had little difficulty in winning the seat. He soon won repute for his tremendous industry and brilliant speeches, though his oratory sometimes obscured the subject matter and was marred by acidity and too great a tendency to personal attack. He was an active supporter of the Gold Fields Homestead Act. In politics generally he was a strong Liberal, with some interest in schemes for colonial federation and independence. During the political crisis in 1870-72 he played a leading part on the Liberal side, incurring especially the enmity of W. H. Walsh [q.v.]. In the 1871 election he was narrowly defeated by Walsh at Maryborough, but was immediately returned unopposed for Wide Bay holding the seat until November 1873.

When the Macalister [q.v.] ministry took office in January 1874 the treasurer, Hemmant [q.v.], succeeded in persuading King to take the secretaryship for public lands and mines, though he was not then a member of parliament. In November a safe seat was found for him at Ravenswood, another mining district. His administration of his department, though very successful, appeared too costly to Macalister and Hemmant, who also found King too sturdy at times for a colleague and too dangerous as an opponent. When Walsh resigned as Speaker in July 1876, all parties in the House combined to appoint King to the vacant post; he held it with dignity and success until November 1883. In 1884 he enrolled as a student in law and his experience, exact methods, knowledge of mining and command of language enabled him to pass his examinations brilliantly in September 1886, the first local candidate under new and severe rules.

King was interested in military affairs. On 25 March 1887 he was gazetted captain in the Queensland Irish Volunteer Corps but by March 1889 he was unattached and in 1892 was placed on the retired list. In 1888-89 he was one of the three royal commissioners who inquired into the general condition of the sugar industry in Queensland. On 30 July 1890 he was appointed crown prosecutor, District Court, Central Division, and in 1903 the Southern Division was added to his responsibilities. On 6 January 1910 he retired with a gratuity of six months' salary in lieu of extended leave, but on 5 February he died at South Brisbane. He was survived by his wife and by four sons and three daughters of their eleven children.

C. A. Bernays, *Queensland politics during sixty years* (Brisb, 1919); V&P (LA Qld), 1889, 4, 37; *Week*, 30 June 1877; *Brisbane Courier*, 6 Feb 1910.
A. A. MORRISON
M. CARTER

KING, JOHN (1820-1895), WILLIAM ESSINGTON (1821-1910), and ARTHUR SEPTIMUS (1827-1899), pastoralists, were born at Parramatta, the second, third and seventh sons of Commander Phillip Parker King [q.v.] and his wife Harriet, née Lethbridge. John and William went to England with their parents in 1822. In 1829 Harriet returned to Sydney with William and three other sons.

John (b. 9 January 1820) ended his schooling in England and at 17 returned to Sydney. He soon joined his brothers, Philip [q.v.] and William, at Gidleigh station which his father had bought in 1834 near Bungendore for about £600. In 1839 John took up a lease near Lake George and in 1841-43 held Ajamatong in the Maneroo district. From the high country he had glimpses of Gippsland which he described as an 'Australian paradise'. Among the first to settle there, he bought the rights of Fulham Park run (near Longford) in 1842. He sold out in 1846 and with Holt, Croft and Tooth formed John

King & Co. and bought the rights to Snake Ridge station. By 1854 the firm had acquired the Scarne and Rosedale runs, a total of 106,000 acres running 7000 cattle. King had started with sheep but turned to cattle, fattening them for the market in Van Diemen's Land.

In November 1855 John was elected for Gippsland to the Legislative Council and after responsible government to the Legislative Assembly until he resigned in September 1857. He was also one of the first magistrates on the bench at Alberton. At Rosedale on 20 January 1853 he had married Marianne Peck. She died on 1 August 1863 and he went to England where in London on 27 October 1864 he married Antoinette Stretanus, daughter of Rev. Dr Henry Geyle of the Dutch Church in Austin Friars. On their return to Victoria they lived at Nambrock, Rosedale, where in 1882 as 'Tanjil' he wrote his early reminiscences in *Our Trip to Gippsland Lakes and Rivers*.

At Rosedale John was a founder of the Mechanics' Institute, and a trustee and chairman of the Board of Guardians of St Mark's Church of England which was built in 1867 on land given by the family. In 1875-83 he served on the Rosedale Shire Council and was president in 1877-78. He also acquired the Mairburn property where he established a vineyard and lemon plantation, and with William gave land for a church at near-by Metung. His health failing in 1892 he made his home at Chislehurst, Hawksburn. He died there on 24 January 1895 and was buried in the St Kilda cemetery. He had two sons and three daughters by his first wife and a son and daughter by his second.

William Essington (b. 8 September 1821) was educated in Sydney. At 16 he worked at Gidleigh and then on the runs of John King & Co. In 1852-59 he was a gold commissioner on various fields in New South Wales. In 1859-63 he and Arthur ran a stock and station agency in Bourke Street, Melbourne; their first recorded sale was 176 bullocks from John King & Co. In 1864 Essington managed John's Sydney Cottage station. At Rosedale he was a trustee and secretary of the Board of Guardians at St Mark's. In 1869 he served on the first Rosedale Roads Board and when it became a Shire Council in 1871 he was elected president. He returned to Melbourne in 1872 and engaged in business pursuits, among them a directorship of the Colonial Mutual Fire Insurance Co. in 1891-1906. In 1895 he briefly managed Bayley's Reward Reef mine at Coolgardie. An active Anglican, he was a lay canon of St Paul's Cathedral in 1875-1908. On 27 April 1854 he had married Christiana Sarah, eldest daughter of William Edward Riley; they had eight sons and three daughters. Predeceased by his wife on 26 October 1886, he died at his home, Tregeare, Armadale, and was buried in the St Kilda cemetery.

Arthur Septimus (b. 9 February 1827) was educated in Sydney. In 1842-54 he worked with John in Gippsland and then returned to New South Wales. In 1859 he joined Essington in their stock and station agency in Melbourne. He leased properties in Gippsland and Hawkesview station near the Murray which he later bought and which was managed by his second son Baron Albert (1864-1936). In 1863 Essington was replaced in the agency by V. Cunningham. They leased some 150 acres at Ascot Vale, known later as King's paddock, where they agisted cattle from Queensland and Gippsland before sending them to Newmarket sale-yards. When Cunningham retired, Arthur's sons, Alan and Ernest, entered the firm which became A. S. King & Sons and later King Sons & Ballantine (now Australian Estates).

Always top-hatted when selling, Arthur was a notable figure and foremost among Victorian agents. For thirty years he was a local director of the Australian Mutual Provident Society, and in 1884-89 a director of the National Bank of Australasia. In New South Wales on 15 July 1857 he had married his cousin, Elizabeth Margaret Lethbridge (d. 1919); they had six sons and four daughters. From 1863 the family lived at Madford, Kew, and attended Holy Trinity where Arthur was for years a churchwarden. He died on 28 September 1899 and was buried in the family grave. Memorials to him and his wife are at Holy Trinity Church, Kew.

H. H. Peck, *Memoirs of a stockman* (Melb, 1942); A. E. Clark, *The church of our fathers* (Melb, 1947); C. Daley, *The story of Gippsland* (Melb, 1960); *Government Gazette* (NSW), 19 Feb, 1 July 1841; *Argus*, 25, 26 Jan 1895, 21 Nov 1910; *Rosedale Courier*, 31 Jan, 7, 21 Feb 1895; *Herald* (Melb), 15, 30 Nov 1910; Mrs T. L. F Rutledge, 'Bungendore', National Trust of Aust (NSW) Women's Cttee, Inspection no 127 (1968); Depasturing licence registers 1839-43 (NSWA); P. G. King family papers c1839 (ML) W. E. King journal (held by J. King, Kooyong), family papers (held privately).

DOROTHY A. ROGERS

KING, JOHN (1841-1872), explorer, wa born on 5 December 1841 in County Tyrone, Ireland, son of Henry King, soldier in the 95th Highlanders, and his wife Ellen née Orn. Educated at the Hibernian School Phoenix Park, Dublin, he joined the 70th Regiment at 14 and went with it to India The regiment was later involved in the mu tiny and King was present at some of th main engagements. While convalescent in 1859 he met George James Landells who was in India buying camels for R. O'H. Burke's [q.v.] expedition. King was discharged from the army and engaged by Landells to supervise the coolies in charge of the camels.

Burke's expedition, sponsored by the Royal Society of Victoria, was fêted as it left Melbourne on 20 August 1860. Early in October they reached Menindee where Landells resigned and King was put in charge of the camels. He was also chosen as one of the advance party which set out for Cooper's Creek. They reached it on 11 November and set up Camp LXV. The party split again; Burke, Wills [q.v.], King and Charley Gray, a sailor, were to make a dash to the Gulf of Carpentaria, 750 miles away, while the depot was left in charge of William Brahe who was expected to wait there for at least three months, as the rearguard with further supplies was expected to arrive in a few days.

The four men with six camels and a horse managed to travel some fourteen miles a day, reaching their goal on the tidewaters of the Albert River on 11 February 1861. Their return trip was disastrous. They lost their only horse and four of the six camels and ran low in rations. On 17 April Gray died. Four days later the exhausted men made a superhuman effort and in one day covered the remaining thirty miles to Camp LXV, arriving at 7.30 in the evening. The only human sign was the word DIG carved on a tree. They dug and found a box of rations and a message from Brahe that the rearguard had not arrived and that he had decided that very morning to return to Menindee with his men. King's surviving camels were too weak to pursue Brahe's party so Burke decided to make for Mount Hopeless, 150 miles away, and after two days rest they set out. For two months they struggled through inhospitable country, with their food diminishing, and growing weaker every day. Late in June Burke and Wills died, but incredibly King survived, kept alive by the kindness of Aboriginals until a relief expedition found him, half demented by starvation and loneliness, near to death himself.

King was taken back to Melbourne and given a public welcome. A royal commission of inquiry revealed the wretched mismanagement of the whole expedition but King's evidence was treated considerately. He was presented with a gold watch and an investment which yielded him £180 a year. He lived quietly with his sister until on 22 September 1871 he married his widowed cousin Mary Richmond, née Bunting. He never recovered from his privations on the expedition and died of tuberculosis on 15 January 1872 at his home in St Kilda.

A. M. Moorehead, *Cooper's Creek* (Lond, 1963); Burke and Wills Commission, Evidence, V&P (Vic), 1861-62, 3 (97).

ALAN MOOREHEAD

KING, PHILIP GIDLEY (1817-1904), pastoralist, was born on 31 October 1817 at Parramatta, eldest son of Captain Phillip Parker King [q.v.] and his wife Harriet, née Lethbridge. At 5 he went with his father to England and in 1824-25 he was at school at Bexley Place near Deptford. In 1826-30 he sailed with his father in the *Adventurer* to survey the southern coast of South America. In December 1831 King as a midshipman left in H.M.S. *Beagle* to continue the South American survey and became a lifelong friend of Charles Darwin [q.v.]. On 12 January 1836 he returned to Sydney and rejoined his parents at Parramatta. He went to the Murrumbidgee in 1837 and later to the Port Phillip District where he studied the handling of livestock. He then surveyed a road from Gloucester to New England and in 1842 entered the service of the Australian Agricultural Co. in charge of its cattle and horse studs at Stroud. In 1843 at St John's Church, Parramatta, he married Elizabeth (d. 1889), daughter of Hannibal Macarthur [q.v.].

In 1851 King was appointed superintendent of stock for the Australian Agricultural Co. and soon became assistant superintendent of the company's estates. In 1852 the discovery of gold in the bed of the Peel River and evidence that all the company's lands on the Peel could be auriferous induced the shareholders to form the Peel River Land and Mineral Co. King became New South Wales manager of the new company and moved with his family to Goonoo Goonoo, south of Tamworth, where he began a line of hereditary managers of the station which lasted until the 1920s.

King was plagued by difficulties: gold prospectors flocked into the company's property at Anderson's Flat, and when gold was found in the bed of the river itself, the company's boundary being the centre line of the river, chaos resulted. Eventually the company directors issued mining licences at 10s. a month and a system of river-bed licences was devised with the Crown, the directors each receiving half the fee. The gold rush denuded King of shepherds and stockmen but he managed the estate efficiently. He had a township laid out on the southern end of Goonoo Goonoo across the river from the Nundle goldfield. A sale of town lots was held on 1 July 1854, and Goonoo Goonoo itself became almost a village in the 1870s with its elaborate station homestead, post office, school, numerous cottages for em-

ployees, accommodation house and wool-
shed.

Although physically and mentally taxed
by his managerial duties King was prominent in local affairs. He promoted and encouraged the building of the Anglican
parsonage and school in West Tamworth,
persuading the company to contribute
£3600. In 1876-80 he was first mayor of Tamworth. By 1881 his son had taken over
management of Goonoo Goonoo although
stock matters were still referred to him. In
1879 he was a commissioner for the Sydney
International Exhibition. As a close friend
of Sir Henry Parkes [q.v.] whom he assisted
financially, King was appointed to the Legislative Council in 1880. He was president of
the Australian Club for years and in the
1880s a director of the Mercantile Bank of
Sydney. Still interested in marine surveying,
he published *Comments on Cook's Log
(H.M.S. Endeavour, 1770) with extracts,
charts and sketches* (1891). He died on 5
August 1904 at Double Bay and was buried
in the cemetery of St Mary Magdalene's
Church of England at St Marys. He was survived by two of his three sons and by a
daughter. His estate was valued at £41,691.

A. J. Prentice and C. B. Newling (eds), *Origin
and history of Tamworth and district* (Tam-
worth, 1918); W. A. Bayley, *Hills of gold*
(Nundle, 1953); V&P (LA NSW), 1881, 3, 389;
F. Odenheimer, *Reports* (ML); Peel River Land
and Mineral Co., *Reports* (ML, Soc Aust Gen);
P. G. and P. P. King papers (ML); Parkes letters
(ML); newspaper cuttings (ML).

FRANK O'GRADY

KING, ROBERT LETHBRIDGE (1823-
1897), Church of England clergyman, was
born in February 1823 at sea en route to
England, fourth son of Phillip Parker King
[q.v.] and his wife Harriet, daughter of
Christopher Lethbridge. He returned to live
at the family home, Dunheved, near Penrith, in 1829. In 1841, after some education
at The King's School, Parramatta, he entered
St John's College, Cambridge (B.A., 1846).

After a brief spell at Truro Grammar
School, King returned to Sydney and was
made deacon on 19 September 1847 and
ordained priest on 17 December 1848 by
Bishop Broughton [q.v.]. He served his
curacy under Archdeacon William Cowper
[q.v.] at St Phillip's, Church Hill, and on
30 December 1851 married Honoria Australia, daughter of James Raymond [q.v.] at
Denham Court, near Liverpool. In July 1855
King was appointed incumbent of St John's,
Parramatta. There he completed the rebuilding of the church and reorganized the parish
and Sunday schools. As a member of a land-

owning family, he remained interested in
agriculture and reported proudly to a select
committee of the Legislative Assembly of
his 'excellent experiment' in orange cultivation. Diocesan affairs soon claimed his
attention. He was active in the movement
which led to the inauguration of synodical
government and was a secretary to the conferences of 1865 and 1866. He had been
made an episcopal chaplain in 1858 and became a canon of the cathedral in 1867.

On 1 January 1868 King took office as
principal of Moore Theological College in
succession to Rev. William Hodgson [q.v.].
His nomination by Bishop Barker [q.v.] was
popular. King not only had scholarly and
scientific attainments; he was a representative of an Australian pioneer family and
would now train Australian clergymen.
During King's period, seventy-seven men,
more than in any of the next three decades,
were ordained from Moore College for seven
dioceses. Bishop Perry [q.v.] of Melbourne
continued to send students even after the
foundation of Trinity College and resisted
criticisms that King's notion of a proper educational standard was too low. King's
inability to improve the curriculum established by Hodgson was a reflection on
colonial education and the failure to attract
university graduates. He sought to overcome
the difficulties by a vigorous training in
pastoral care and public worship and by the
creation of a vital community spirit. He
built up fatherly relations with his students
and, as one of them, F. B. Boyce, later wrote,
influenced them greatly 'through the depth
and fervour of his spiritual life'. Until the
belated appointment of a vice-principal in
1877, King worked alone but by then his
health had so deteriorated that he resigned.

In June 1878 King returned to a parish
ministry. At Moore College he had retained
some parochial responsibility as titular incumbent of Holsworthy and from 1871
rural dean of Liverpool. He also took Gladesville and in 1880 moved to the city parish
of Holy Trinity. He acquired high diocesan
office as archdeacon of Cumberland in 1881,
an onerous position because of the frequent
episcopal absences and interregnums in the
1880s. He was also rural dean of Balmain in
1881-93 and a fellow of St Paul's College,
although he had resigned his canonry in
1877 and his bishop's chaplaincy in 1882.
King retained his interest in Moore College,
helped his successor with curriculum reforms and even returned as acting-principal
in 1884-85. He resigned his parish in 1893
and his archdeaconry in 1895. He retained
an active interest as secretary of the Church
of England Mission to Seamen until he died
at Stanmore on 24 July 1897. He was buried
in the Anglican section of Waverley ceme-

tery, leaving an estate of some £5000 to his
wife. He had three daughters and six sons,
of whom one had predeceased him and three
became Church of England clergymen.
When his wife died on 13 May 1902 the
estate was divided equally among the surviving children.

F. B. Boyce, *Fourscore years and seven* (Syd,
1934); M. L. Loane, *A centenary history of
Moore Theological College* (Syd, 1955); V&P
(LA NSW), 1865, 2, 599, 1866, 5, 755; *Church-
man*, 29 July 1897; *Town and Country J*, 31
July 1897.   K. J. CABLE

KING, WILLIAM FRANCIS (1807-1873),
pedestrian and street character, best known
as 'The Flying Pieman', was born in London,
the eldest son of Francis King, a paymaster
in the Treasury. Though intended for the
church, he had various jobs before becoming
a clerk in the Treasury where he met the
chaplain of the Tower, Rev. W. G. Broughton [q.v.]. He arrived at Sydney in 1829,
probably on a remittance, and through
Broughton was appointed schoolmaster at
Sutton Forest. After some years as a private
tutor to the Kern family at Campbelltown
and as a barman at the Hope and Anchor in
Sydney, he emerged as an athlete and extravagantly bedecked itinerant pieman: 'The
Ladies' Walking Flying Pieman'. An earlier
'Flying Pieman', the notorious and unfortunate Nathaniel McCulloch, had died in
May 1839.

King's pedestrian career seems to have
begun in 1842 reputedly after an unfortunate love affair. Among his many bizarre
walking feats were 1634 miles in 39 days
mainly in the wet, twice beating the mail
coach from Sydney to Windsor by several
minutes, Campbelltown to Sydney carrying
a 70 lb. dog between midnight and 9 a.m.,
1½ miles in 12 minutes carrying an 80 lb.
goat, and 192 miles around the Maitland
race-course in 46½ hours. In November
1847 at Singleton he walked 6 miles in 64
minutes 40 seconds. At the Fitzroy Hotel,
West Maitland, he undertook to walk 1000
quarter-miles in 1000 quarter-hours. At one
end of the measured ground was a shelter
tent where he rested for a few seconds every
half-hour, at the other 'King's death or glory
flag and coffin were mounted on a pile of
bricks'. On the ninth day he had himself
horsewhipped to spur him on and when he
had completed the feat he wagered £50 to
£40 to repeat the task starting that very
night but had no takers. After running,
walking, wheeling and jumping feats at
Maitland he went to Dungog where in
February 1848 he wagered to walk 500 half-
miles in 500 half-hours. Betting this time
favoured the clock, 'the Pieman having be-

come so corpulent', but King won. After
walking 60 miles in 12 hours 10 minutes at
Singleton he complained of sore ankles!
Later that year he took his 'unparalleled
feats of pedestrianism' to Moreton Bay
where carrying a heavy pole he beat the mail
coach from Brisbane to Ipswich by an hour.
After finishing his self-appointed tasks he
often gave a long speech to an admiring
audience. One of his last displays seems to
have been at Maitland in January 1851
when he announced in the press that he was
going to 'honour little Hexham with an
amusing pedestrian feat and an aquatic feat
on the river'. He returned to Sydney to
become one of its famous street characters
wandering about selling pies and issuing
rambling proclamations to passers-by.
Described as a sawyer, he died of paralysis
at the Liverpool asylum on 10 August 1873
and was buried in the Catholic cemetery,
Liverpool, a pauper, unremembered and
unmourned by those he had so often
entertained.

Contemporary sketches of 'The Flying Pieman' depict a well-built, athletic figure with
a somewhat distracted expression: one
shows him in an open shirt, blue jacket,
reddish breeches, white stockings and shoes,
wearing a top hat with coloured streamers
and carrying a long staff decorated with
ribbons.

J. C. L. Fitzpatrick, *Those were the days* (Syd,
1923); J. R. Tyrrell, *Old books, old friends, old
Sydney* (Syd, 1952); W. J. Goold, 'The ladies'
walking Flying Pieman', Newcastle and Hunter District Hist Soc, *Procs*, 3 (1948-49); *Sydney
Gazette*, 17, 20 June 1837, 14 May 1839; *SMH*,
29 Oct 1842, 17 Oct 1848; *Heads of the People*,
7 Aug 1847; *Maitland Mercury*, 13, 17, 20 Nov,
22, 29 Dec 1847, 22 Jan, 2, 16 Feb, 3, 10, 27
May, 17 Oct 1848; *Illustrated Sydney News*, 28
Apr 1855; *Sportsman* (Syd), 17 Oct 1900.
                                          G. P. WALSH

KINGSFORD, RICHARD ASH (1821-
1902), merchant, politician and landowner,
was born on 2 October 1821 in Canterbury,
Kent, England, son of John Kingsford, maltster, and his wife Mary, née Walker. He
arrived at Sydney in 1852 and went to Brisbane in 1854 as partner in a drapery business
in Queen Street with his brother John, who
later became pastor of the Jireh Baptist
Church in Fortitude Valley. While assisting
his brother as a lay preacher Kingsford became a fluent and sincere speaker. In May
1875 he was elected by a large majority
against the attorney-general, Ratcliffe Pring
[q.v.], for the South Brisbane seat in the
Legislative Assembly. He also served as an
alderman on the South Brisbane Municipal
Council in 1875-76 and was elected mayor

of Brisbane in 1876. As a supporter of Thomas McIlwraith [q.v.] he lost his seat in the 1883 election.

After an unsuccessful attempt at poultry farming at the Springs, Tingalpa, Kingsford left for Cairns where his son-in-law, William Charles Smith, was a bank manager. He bought property in the town and selected an area near Kuranda for growing fruit. In 1884 he was elected chairman of the Cairns Divisional Board and next year became president of the School of Arts, his keen love of reading ensuring the firm establishment of the town's first library. Cairns was proclaimed a municipality on 28 May 1885 and at the council's first meeting on 22 July he was unanimously elected mayor by his fellow aldermen; he was re-elected for a further term.

In 1888 Kingsford stood for the new Cairns seat in the Legislative Assembly, still an ardent supporter of McIlwraith. He was defeated after a bitter and costly fight by Frederick Thomas Wimble, founder and editor of the Cairns Post, who contested the seat because he had become a follower of Samuel Griffith. In 1890 Kingsford bought the Hambledon sugar plantation from Thomas Swallow [q.v.] and leased it to the sons, Swallow Bros; in 1897 it was acquired by the Colonial Sugar Refining Co.

In 1892-95 Kingsford had lived in Tasmania but on returning to Cairns he built his home, Fairview, some four miles from Cairns. In World War II it became well known as 'The House on the Hill', the experimental station for Z-force of the Inter-Allied Services Department. He was senior justice of the peace for North Queensland and for some years served on the Licensing Board. He died in Cairns on 2 January 1902 and was buried in the old McLeod Street cemetery. He was married twice: first, in 1852 at Bridge, Kent, to Sarah Southerden; they had one son and three daughters, of whom the eldest became the mother of the aviator, Sir Charles Edward Kingsford Smith; and second, on 31 August 1892 at St Paul's, Launceston, to Emma Jane Dexter who survived him with one daughter.

Kingsford was tall, heavily-bearded and dignified. His speeches in parliament show his liberal mind and generous understanding of others. He was widely read and his rich fund of apt quotations was used to good effect both in the pulpit and in parliament. He was devoutly religious and loyal to his colleagues.

R. S. Browne, A journalist's memories (Brisb, 1927); J. W. Collinson, Early days of Cairns (Brisb, 1939); J. W. Collinson, More about Cairns: the second decade (Brisb, 1942).

M. O. WALMSLEY

KINGSLEY, HENRY (1830-1876), novelist, was born on 2 January 1830 at Barnack, Northamptonshire, England, son of Rev. Charles Kingsley and his wife Mary, née Lucas; his older brothers were Charles (1819-1875), clergyman and novelist, Gerald (d. 1844), naval officer, and George (1826-1892), a doctor and travel writer. Henry's early years were mainly spent in Devon and Chelsea, settings which he used in his novels. Sensitive about his puny and ugly appearance, he was inclined to adulate more personable contemporaries, especially his brother Charles. He attended King's College School and in 1850 matriculated to Worcester College, Oxford, where he achieved considerable success as an athlete but none as a scholar. A legacy of £500 helped to pay his debts and he left Oxford without taking a degree in 1853.

He decided to migrate and arrived at Melbourne in the Gauntlet in December 1853. Little is securely known of his Australian years. He tried gold-mining on such fields as the Caledonia, Ararat and Omeo without success and there is fairly good evidence that he was briefly a police-trooper. A friendly squatter gave him house-room at Langi Willi station near Skipton before he returned to England in 1857.

Kingsley's first novel, The Recollections of Geoffry Hamlyn, was published in mid-1859 and was immediately successful. On this book continuing interest in his work is mainly based. It traces the adventures of the Buckleys and the Brentwoods, Devonshire county families whose dwindling incomes could not sustain their position, leading them to seek better fortune in Australia. According to W. K. Hancock, Kingsley probably saw Tubbutt station near Delegate for it strongly resembles the setting in which Major Buckley made his elegant home. Bushfires, bushrangers and cattle-branding scenes provide drama, and the more sympathetic characters marry beautiful and wealthy brides.

After his father died in 1860 Kingsley lived with his mother at Eversley. Ravenshoe, generally considered his best novel, ran as a serial in Macmillan's Magazine from January 1861 to July 1862 and was then published as a book. On 5 December 1862 Kingsley was admitted as a student to the Inner Temple, but he soon abandoned study. In The Hillyars and the Burtons, which was serialized in Macmillan's from November 1863 to April 1865 and then issued as a book, much of the action again takes place in Australia. A sub-plot is concerned with political life in 'Cookstown', an imaginary colony; for this purpose Kingsley used the issues and involvements of Victorian politics of the mid-1850s, introducing characters somewhat suggestive of Stawell, O'Shanassy and Duffy [qq.v.].

On 19 July 1864 he had married Sarah Maria Haselwood. They settled at Wargrave on the Thames but Sarah's health and their debts soon brought anxieties. Despite increasing difficulties Kingsley managed to produce another sixteen novels, most of them mediocre and written under stress. Of these later novels only *Reginald Hetherage* (1874) used Australia as part of its setting. He also wrote essays which included discussions of the explorations of Sturt and Eyre [qq.v.] and 'Travelling in Australia'. In 1869, harassed by debt, he accepted the editorship of the *Daily Review* at Edinburgh. In August 1870 he was in France as the *Review's* correspondent in the Franco-Prussian war and resumed his work as editor in October. He resigned early in 1871 and returned to London. Late in 1874 he moved with his wife to Cuckfield, Sussex, where, writing to the end, he died from cancer of the tongue on 24 May 1876.

Kingsley was a better-than-average Victorian romancer of conventional type. The general texture of his work is naturalistic, but spiced with melodramatic incidents and with emotional-moralistic characterizations of Dickensian type. He had no pretensions to depth of view or to imaginative largeness, but he had an easy liveliness and a beguiling geniality of tone. In picturing the new country Kingsley is most successful in treating the landscape and animal life. All the Kingsley brothers had a strong feeling for nature: Henry wrote of the bush with vividness, accuracy and a touch of lyrical delight. His treatment of the human conditions is often informing but limited by the prejudices natural to a man of his background. He assumes the superiority of upper-class Englishmen. Although he has given an admirably observed sketch of a station-hand (*Geoffry Hamlyn*, pp. 313-14), the nature of his prejudices may be judged by his comment on the lower-class migrants: 'A lazy independent class, with exaggerated ideas of their own importance in this new phase of their life, but without the worse vices of the convicts' (op. cit., p. 194).

Nevertheless Kingsley recorded his delight in the egalitarian good-fellowship of life on the diggings and gave a more favourable view of lower-class migrants in the following passage, despite its interesting proviso: 'A better set of fellows than the honest emigrants generally don't exist; but their superstitious respect for an old convict is almost pathetic' (*The Hillyars and the Burtons*, p. 61).

In general Kingsley gave an attractive migrant-encouraging picture of Australia.

He depicted it as the land of easy opportunity, despite his own failure to make a living there. The squatter pioneers of *Geoffry Hamlyn* make their way to fortune almost without hardship. One of them says, 'Money has come to me by mere accumulation; I have taken more pains to spend it than to make it' (*Geoffry Hamlyn*, p. 173).

One of Kingsley's indirect services to Australian letters came through his upper-class prejudices. His assumption that the English gentry could take the practical leadership of the Australian-born in conditions with which the latter were far more familiar so irritated Joseph Furphy that he wrote a rebuttal, one of his most vigorous passages of invective (*Such is Life*, p. 39). Kingsley might have been even more roughly treated if Miles Franklin had expressed her opinion of Gerty Hillyar, an Australian girl of great beauty, Victorian docility and exceptional silliness. Nevertheless Gerty is in many respects an interesting and probably accurately observed portrait of a squatter's daughter of the time, which has one notable value. Kingsley has endowed her with a mastery of the Australian argot of the period, and through her he has recorded some flavorsome samples of it for the benefit of posterity.

S. M. Ellis, *Henry Kingsley, 1830-1876. Towards a vindication* (Lond, 1931); J. Oldham and A. Stirling, *Victorian, a visitors book* (Melb, 1934); P. L. Brown (ed), *Clyde Company papers*, 6 (Lond, 1963); J. Barnes, *Henry Kingsley and colonial fiction* (Melb, 1971); W. K. Hancock, *Discovering Monaro* (Cambridge, 1972); B. Sutherland, 'Henry Kingsley and Australia', *Aust Q*, June 1945.

A. A. PHILLIPS

KINROSS, JOHN (1833-1908), Presbyterian minister, was born on 11 September 1833 at Ardoch, Perthshire, Scotland, son of James Kinross, farmer, and his wife Jessie, née Comrie. He was educated at the Free Church School of Muthill and Ardoch. At 15 he matriculated at the University of Edinburgh and, without completing a degree, entered New College, Edinburgh, for divinity studies. After further study in Berlin he was licensed as a probationer by the Free Church Presbytery of Auchterarder. He arrived in Sydney on 6 June 1858 and in December was ordained and inducted to Scots Church, Kiama, under the jurisdiction of the Synod of Eastern Australia which supported the Free Church of Scotland. On 9 December 1859 he married Elizabeth Johanna (d. 1895), daughter of Robert Menzies of Jamberoo, a retired naval surgeon.

Kinross spent seventeen years in Kiama, and pioneered church development in Win-

gecarribee, Sutton Forest, Moss Vale and
Kangaroo Valley. He was moderator in
1863. He believed in the Free Church principle that church and state must be separate
and was prominent in negotiations for the
union of the Synods of the Presbyterian
Church of New South Wales on 8 September 1865. He was admitted to the University of Sydney (B.A. *ad eund.*, 1869). In 1864
he had published a sermon, *The Church's
Warfare*, and in 1870 a *Lecture on the
Oecumenical Council.*

Kinross was elected first principal of St
Andrew's College, University of Sydney, in
February 1872, but withdrew when the
legality of the election was challenged by
Rev. J. D. Lang [q.v.]. Next year Kinross
became moderator of the General Assembly
of the Presbyterian Church of New South
Wales. In April 1875, after Rev. Adam
Thomson [q.v.] died, he was again elected
principal of St Andrew's. He lectured in the
Theological Hall within the college and after
his retirement on 24 October 1901 he was
appointed first Hunter Baillie professor of
apologetics and Christian ethics. He lived in
Stanmore for the short theological academic
year and for the rest of the year on his estate
at Jamberoo. He was a trusted leader in the
General Assembly and in 1880 represented
the Church at the Pan Presbyterian council
meetings in Philadelphia. He was chairman
of the council of the Presbyterian Ladies'
College, Croydon, in 1885-1906. In 1885 the
University of Edinburgh awarded him an
honorary doctorate. In 1897 he visited Edinburgh where he published *Dogma in Religion and Creeds in the Church.*

Kinross died on 16 October 1908 at Jamberoo where he was buried in a private cemetery, survived by two sons and three daughters. In a memorial address G. A. Wood,
professor of history in the University of
Sydney, said: 'I have lived in Balliol under
Jowett and I have lived in Andrew's under
the Doctor. Balliol was undoubtedly the
most respectable as well as the most distinguished of the Oxford Colleges. But of
the two Colleges, it was Andrew's that had
the greater measure of kindliness, good humour, harmony and charity. There was tri-
viality, and foolishness, and sometimes
(though seldom) the bad manners of high-
spirited thoughtlessness: but no unkind-
ness, no vice; nothing that disturbed the
Doctor in the serene possession of his own
Soul'.

Slight and spare with a trimmed beard,
Kinross's portrait by Ethel Stephens is in St
Andrew's College and a memorial window
in its chapel.

J. Cameron, *Centenary history of the Pres-
byterian Church in New South Wales* (Syd,
1905); C. A. White, *The challenge of the years*
(Syd, 1951); A. A. Dougan (ed), *The Andrew's
book* (Syd, 1964); *Australian Witness*, 31 Jan
1874, 1, 22 May, 12, 19 June 1875, 2 Dec 1876;
Presbyterian (NSW), 13 Jan, 20 Mar, 2 Aug, 25
Sept 1880, 24 Dec 1881, 25 Apr 1885; General
Assembly minutes 1865-1908 (NSW Presbyterian Lib, Assembly Hall, Syd); Scots Church,
Kiama, Kirk session minutes 1858-74 (NSW
Presbyterian Lib, Assembly Hall, Syd); private
papers (held by Miss Menzies Smith, Artar-
mon).   ALAN DOUGAN

KINTORE, SIR ALGERNON HAWKINS
THOMOND KEITH-FALCONER (1852-
1930), governor, was born on 12 August 1852
at Sixmount House, near Edinburgh, eldest
son of Francis Alexander, 8th earl of Kintore (1828-1880) and his wife Louisa Mada-
leine, née Hawkins. He was educated at Eton
and Trinity College, Cambridge (B.A.,
1874; M.A., 1877). On 14 August 1873 he
had married Lady Sydney Charlotte Montagu, second daughter of George, 6th earl of
Manchester. He succeeded his father as earl
in 1880 and was appointed to court and
other offices appropriate to a member of the
nobility. In 1885-86 he was a lord-in-waiting
to Queen Victoria and held minor appointments in the House of Lords. In 1886 he was
made a privy councillor and captain of the
Yeomen of the Guard. In 1889 he was appointed G.C.M.G. and governor of South
Australia. He arrived with his family at
Adelaide on 11 April in the *Orient* and was
formally welcomed by the administrator,
Chief Justice Way; the popular festivities
lasted the whole day.

Kintore's apointment, with many others,
indicated a change in British colonial policy;
in place of military and naval officers and
high civil officials, the government was
appointing members of the nobility to
governorships, an implied compliment and
an attempt to develop cordial relations between Britain and the colonies. Kintore took
a deep interest in the colony under his
charge, travelling more extensively than
any previous governor to make himself familiar with it. He was also interested in Federation and supported the Australasian
Federal Convention at Melbourne in 1890
but could not attend the convention at Sydney in 1891 because he had decided to cross
the continent from Port Darwin to Adelaide.
His aim was to 'learn what the continent
was like, and to satisfy the curiosity of the
Imperial Government as to the condition
and prospects of the wide tract of country'.
He delayed his departure to attend the funeral of David Bews and left for Melbourne
by train on 26 February, a week later travelling to Brisbane where he boarded the
Chingtu for Darwin. Accompanied by Dr

E. C. Stirling [q.v.], a telegraph operator, five other white men and three Aboriginals, he left Darwin on 9 April and followed the overland telegraph line through Katherine, Daly Waters, Tennant Creek and Alice Springs to Oodnadatta whence he completed the journey by train and reached Adelaide on 23 May. Apart from newspaper criticism about 'the privacy' of the trip and the lack of a 'correspondent', his journey aroused popular enthusiasm.

Although at Kintore's arrival the colony was emerging from severe depression, the ending of the boom in the eastern colonies, trouble with miners at Moonta in 1890 and the Broken Hill strike in 1892 delayed South Australia's recovery. He kept aloof from the unrest but had to deal with five changes of ministry before Kingston succeeded on 16 June 1893 in forming a government which lasted to December 1899. Kintore had always been impartial, though his friendship with Way caused him some trouble when he had him appointed lieut-governor without consulting the premier. Kintore resigned in 1895 and left Adelaide on 10 April. He resumed his post of lord-in-waiting at the court, serving Queen Victoria until her death and Edward VII until 1905. His court duties brought him the grand cordon of the Crown of Italy, the first class of the Prussian order of the Red Eagle and the Grand Cross of the Portuguese military order of Christ. In 1913 he was elected deputy-Speaker of the House of Lords.

Kintore was a prominent Mason; when he arrived in South Australia, Way resigned as grand master of the United Grand Lodge of South Australia in his favour, and he later became provincial grand master of the Kincardineshire Lodge. A fellow of the Royal Society of Edinburgh, he was awarded an honorary doctorate of laws by each of the Universities of Aberdeen and Adelaide. He died on 3 March 1930, survived by his wife, two sons and two daughters.

H. T. Burgess (ed), *Cyclopedia of South Australia*, 1 (Adel, 1908); *Australasian*, 13 Apr 1889, 25, 27 Feb, 25, 30 May, 6 June 1891; *Illustrated Sydney News*, 11 Apr, 9 May 1891; Parkes letters, vol 20 (ML).

RICHARD REFSHAUGE

KIRBY, JOSEPH COLES (1837-1924), Congregational minister and social reformer, was born on 10 June 1837 in Buckingham, England, son of John Kirby, flour-miller, and his wife Mary, née Coles. Educated at the Quaker boarding school in Sibford Ferris, near Banbury, he absorbed partly from his Quaker mother a lifelong concern for social reform. At 13 he entered his father's busi-ness but never lost his passion for reading and self-improvement. After his father's bankruptcy the family migrated to Sydney in 1854. Kirby worked in a flour-mill and, an Independent like his father, joined the Pitt Street Congregational Church where the members included such prominent men as David Jones, John Fairfax and Rev. John West [qq.v.]; their encouragement for Kirby cooled as he increasingly criticized the dominant social groups in New South Wales and advocated total abstinence. After abridged training by Rev. B. Quaife [q.v.] Kirby was called as an assistant minister at Ipswich in 1863. Ordained in February 1864 he became a pioneer Congregational minister on the Darling Downs. He was stationed at Dalby where he married Margaretta Hall (d. 1909).

In 1871-77 Kirby was pastor of the prosperous Congregational Church in Ocean Street, Woollahra, and active in the Public Schools League's successful campaign for free, compulsory and secular education. A militant and informed temperance reformer, his publications impressed Parkes [q.v.], who carried the 1880 Licensing Act that granted a measure of local option. In the seamen's strike of 1878-79 Kirby helped to persuade the Australasian Steam Navigation Co. to abandon the employment of Chinese labour. In September 1877 he took over the church extension work of the Congregational Union of New South Wales and was chairman of the union in 1879-80. He attacked academicism in the ministry and offended voluntarist opinion by advocating stronger central initiative in home missions and acceptance of land from the government to build new churches.

Kirby resigned in September 1880 and went to the depressed Congregational Church at Port Adelaide. An assiduous and successful pastor, he provided several youth organizations and induced a number of young men to enter the ministry. With their help he brought his denomination solidly behind temperance, women's rights and social reform. As secretary of the Social Purity Society in 1882 he spent his vacation advocating the cause in Melbourne and Sydney, and in 1885 won ecumenical support in a campaign to raise the age of consent from 13 to 16. On retirement he became a leader in the successful campaign in 1915 for 6 o'clock closing. He also sought religious instruction in state schools and helped to persuade the South Australian Congregational Union to abandon its insistence upon purely secular instruction. Later he became an advocate of an Aboriginal reserve in Arnhem land.

Kirby was chairman of the Congregational Union of South Australia in 1886 and 1906 and chairman of the Congregational Union of Australia and New Zealand in 1910-13. In 1891 he had been an Australian representative at the first International Congregational Council in London and travelled in Europe and India. In 1903 he visited the South Pacific, keenly observing the conditions of the peoples and race relations. An Evangelical, he was devoted to 'The Theology of the Glorious Blood' and steadfastly opposed to higher criticism of the Bible but managed to combine an open-mindedness towards Darwinism and eugenics with his staunch theological conservatism. In 1877-98 he published at least six pamphlets on social reform. Active and alert, he was a beloved patriarch but became increasingly eccentric. He died at Semaphore on 1 August 1924, survived by two sons and three daughters. His estate was valued at £5500.

L. Robjohns, *Three-quarters of a century* (Adel, 1912); E. S. Kiek, *An apostle in Australia* (Lond, 1927); J. A. Garrett and L. W. Farr, *Camden College, a centenary history* (Syd, 1964); *Congregational Year Book* (1863-70); *Echo*, 22 Aug 1878; Congregational Union of Aust records (Eastwood, NSW); Congregational Union records (Adel, SAA, ML).

JOHN GARRETT

KNAGGS, SAMUEL THOMAS (1842-1921), medical practitioner, was born in July 1842 at Tipperary, Ireland, son of Robert Corbet Knaggs (1809-1877) and his wife Phoebe, née Maiben. He arrived at Sydney in 1848 with his parents. In April 1855 his father was registered as a medical practitioner and settled in Newcastle as a chemist and druggist.

Knaggs was educated in Newcastle and studied medicine in Dublin (F.R.C.S., 1871) and Aberdeen (M.B., Ch.M., 1871; M.D., 1873). After service as resident medical officer at the Adelaide Hospital, Dublin, and visits to Paris and Vienna, he was registered on 8 January 1872 as a medical practitioner in New South Wales and practised in Newcastle until 1880. In July 1874 he had been appointed government medical officer and next year became salaried medical officer at Newcastle Hospital. He was interested in public health and often contributed to the *Newcastle Chronicle* and the *Newcastle Morning Herald and Miners' Advocate*. In 1875 he failed to establish a society similar to the Australian Health Society in Melbourne, but became editor of the *New South Wales Medical Gazette*. In October 1877 he started the short-lived quarterly, *Australian Practitioner*. A fellow of the Royal Society

of New South Wales from 1878 he was chairman of its medical section in 1888-89.

After a visit to Europe Knaggs began practising at Sydney about 1883. He was lecturer in clinical surgery at the University of Sydney and honorary surgeon at Prince Alfred Hospital until 1893. In August 1885 he was appointed to the New South Wales Board of Health and in 1887-92 examiner in anatomy and physiology for the Board of Technical Education. He was also active in the New South Wales branch of the British Medical Association and its president in 1887-88, and in 1892 joint honorary secretary with Professor T. P. Anderson Stuart of the third session of the Intercolonial Medical Congress of Australasia held in Sydney. He was sometime medical officer of the Department of Public Instruction, a member of the Railways Medical Board and a constant advocate for a ministry of public health. He edited the *Australasian Medical Gazette* from 1895 until 1901 when he visited Japan. He then gradually retired from practice. In the volunteer movement he had become surgeon to the naval brigade in 1872 and rose to the rank of fleet surgeon, retiring with a decoration for long service.

Knaggs crusaded against medical quacks and spiritualists. He cultivated his skill as a conjurer and gave public entertainments for charity at which he imitated 'sundry so-called spiritual feats, like levitation'. A prodigious pamphleteer he wrote on such subjects as phrenology, mediums and their dupes, his own recreations, and common complaints and their simple remedies. His best-known work was *Dr. de Lion, Clairvoyant. Confessions of a Vagabond Life in Australia, as narrated by Maiben Brook* (Sydney, 1895), a novel exposing how clairvoyants preyed upon human gullibility. He long insisted on the revision of legislation for the registration of deaths 'to prevent unqualified persons from amateur dabbling in medicine and surgery'. He continued to write articles for medical journals and in 1917 emerged from retirement to fight an outbreak of meningitis at Collarenebri. He died at Paddington on 6 April 1921 and was buried in the Anglican section of Waverley cemetery. He was survived by five of the seven daughters of his first wife Helena Charlotte, née Read, whom he had married in 1874, and by his second wife Amy Elfreda Bolekman whom he had married in 1899. An obituarist placed Knaggs among 'those who "toil terribly" in the daily "roast and boil" work of medicine and surgery'.

B. W. Champion, 'The Newcastle Hospital . . . 1815-1891', Newcastle and Hunter District Hist Soc, Procs, 6 (1951-52); W. J. Goold, 'Personalities of the past', Newcastle and Hunter

District Hist Soc, Procs, 10 (1955-56); MJA, 16 Apr 1921, p 320; 'Presidential address', Roy Soc NSW, Procs, 55 (1921); SMH, 7 Apr 1921.

RUTH TEALE
C. G. McDONALD*

KNIGHT, JOHN GEORGE (1826-1892), architect and administrator, was born in London, son of John Knight, stone and marble merchant. He took up engineering, joined his father's firm and in spare time studied architecture. In February 1852 he arrived in Melbourne and after a week on the goldfields joined the Public Works Department. While a government inspector at a salary of £1200, he joined the private practice of Thomas Kemp who returned to England in 1855. About 1853 Knight's design for Government House won the first prize of £500 but was not used. He later won prizes for designs of the Melbourne ship canal and docks. In 1856 when plans were resumed for the Houses of Parliament, the supervision was given to Knight and then handed to his partner, P. Kerr [q.v.]. Knight was a founder of the Victorian Institute of Architects and its first president in 1856-61. His paper on colonial building stones, read to the institute in 1859, was published in Melbourne and London in 1864. At St Paul's, Melbourne, on 21 April 1853 he had married Alice Bertrand.

Knight helped to organize the Victorian Exhibition of 1861 and designed a 'miniature Crystal Palace' to house the exhibits. Next January with his family he went to London as secretary for Victoria at the London International Exhibition. He won medals for his gilded pyramid representing the total amount of gold mined in the colony and for his collection of building stones. In 1864 he assembled the Victorian exhibits shown at the Dublin Exhibition.

In March 1865 Knight was appointed lecturer in civil engineering at the University of Melbourne at a salary of £100 with fees. In 1866 he had charge of the Melbourne Intercolonial Exhibition and in 1867 organized Victoria's contribution to the Paris Exhibition. In 1868 he was a founder and until 1871 first manager of the Athenaeum Club in Melbourne. He had compiled a pamphlet on the 1862 exhibition and in 1868 a souvenir booklet on the duke of Edinburgh's visit.

In the early 1870s Knight was attracted to the Northern Territory by reports of gold. In 1873 the South Australian government appointed him secretary and accountant to the resident, G. B. Scott, with extra duties as architect and supervisor of works. He sailed from Melbourne on 2 September, but the appointment of a Victorian annoyed Adelaide politicians. In November 1875 Knight was retrenched as supervisor of works and his salary as secretary and accountant was severely cut. He resigned and left for Melbourne in December, but in January 1876 accepted the post of goldfields warden. He returned to Port Darwin and on the goldfields promptly built a hospital, where he often tended sick miners himself. In April 1880 he became clerk of the Local Court, Palmerston, and was soon made deputy sheriff, clerk of the licensing bench, curator of the property of convicts, registrar, accountant and official receiver and returning officer. In 1887 he was granted leave to act as commissioner for the territory at the Adelaide Jubilee Exhibition and in 1888 commissioner at the Melbourne International Exhibition. He intended to resign in 1889 but was asked to act as government resident and judge. Next year he became government resident.

Knight was a fellow of the Royal Institute of British Architects, an associate of the Institution of Civil Engineers, and corresponding member of the Society of Arts, the Royal Dublin Society and the Royal Horticultural Society of London. In Palmerston he enjoyed a 'sort of patriarchal authority' but friends in Melbourne complained that his talents were wasted. Described as a 'very nice fellow, a real gentleman, and a jolly old chap', he was respected for his common sense and resource. He died at Palmerston on 10 January 1892, survived by three sons, two married daughters and by his wife, who was then living in London. She inherited most of his estate, valued at £800.

J. M. Freeland, The making of a profession (Syd, 1971); Argus, 21 Jan 1858, 12, 15 Jan 1892; Register (Adel), 18 Sept 1873; NT Times and Gazette, 6 Nov 1875, 12 Feb 1876, 15 Jan 1892; North Australian (NT), 10 Jan 1890; Advertiser (Adel), 12 Jan 1892.

SALLY O'NEILL

KNIPE, JOHN HANLON (1828-1895), auctioneer and estate agent, was born on 4 August 1828 in London, son of George Edward Knipe, silversmith, and his wife Mary Ann, née Hanlon. After apprenticeship he worked as a silversmith in London until he migrated to South Australia in 1853. He arrived at Adelaide on 29 March in the Sisters and joined the auctioneering firm of Sampson & Wickstead.

In January 1854 Knipe left Adelaide for the Bendigo goldfields. He had no luck as a digger and opened a store in Old Camp Street but soon joined a rush to Maryborough where he became an auctioneer in partnership with Henry Joseph Smith. He campaigned for the abolition of diggers'

licence fees and was a delegate to a conference at Ballarat, where he was taken prisoner at the riots. At Ballarat in 1855 Knipe
set up as an auctioneer and land speculator,
with branches at Creswick and Fiery Creek
but the depression in land values led to his
insolvency on 1 December. He returned to
Bendigo in 1857 and again set up as a general auctioneer and horse-dealer. He also
sold mining leases and became a founder of
the Johnson's Reef and Hustlers' Reef Gold
Mining companies and a prominent local
sharebroker.

In 1861 Knipe joined a rush to Otago but
in 1862 settled in Melbourne as an auctioneer, share-broker and estate agent, specializing in large suburban subdivisions, and in
1868 was managing the short-lived First
Practical Building Society of Victoria. He
was managing agent of the Royal Arcade in
1870-90 and an energetic founder of the
Victorian Manufacturers' and Exhibitors'
Association, serving as a director in 1877.
In March 1876 the association had 'demanded' construction of a permanent exhibition building, and in 1877 Knipe led a
deputation which prevailed on the government to build it in time for the International
Exhibition in 1880. Knipe had been a founder of the Victorian Humane Society in
1874 and served on its committee; he helped
to establish the Melbourne Tramway and
Omnibus Co. in 1883 and the Federal Stock
Exchange Co. Ltd in 1888. He also advocated
the formation of a Government Employment
Exchange and circulated about 23,000 copies
of his pamphlet on the subject, claiming that
Irish and Scottish colonists had the backing
of their national societies in gaining employment and left English migrants at a disadvantage.

In May 1866 Knipe had been elected
borough councillor of Prahran. Challenged
by rivals because of undischarged insolvencies in 1855, 1858 and 1862 he was removed
from office by a Supreme Court order.
However, Knipe soon obtained his discharge
and despite narrow defeat in the ensuing by-
election headed the poll in August. He
served two terms at Prahran and several
more as borough councillor of Hawthorn.
He was a strong advocate of land reform,
progressive land tax and tariff protection of
native industries. He often tried for election
to parliament but without success. In 1877,
after standing down in Boroondara in favour
of C. H. Pearson [q.v.], he contested East
Melbourne in May, and failed again in the
Boroondara by-election in December, East
Melbourne in 1886, and Jolimont and West
Richmond in 1889 and 1892.

Knipe died at his home in St Kilda on 31
August 1895 and was buried in the Methodist section of the Melbourne general cemetery. He was twice married: first, to Ellen,
née Crouch, in London on 18 January 1847;
and second, to Jane, née Munro, at Ballarat
on 29 June 1855. He was survived by two
sons and a daughter of his first marriage and
two sons and two daughters of the second.

H. M. Humphreys (ed), Men of the time in
Australia: Victorian series, 2nd ed (Melb,
1882); A. Sutherland et al, Victoria and its
metropolis, 2 (Melb, 1888); J. B. Cooper, The
history of Prahran (Melb, 1912); J. M. Tregenza,
The life and work of C. H. Pearson, 1830-1894
(Melb, 1968); Bendigo Advertiser, 1, 20 Feb
1858; Age, 16 Feb, 2, 15 Mar 1877, 2, 3 Sept
1895; Argus, 25 Dec 1877, 31 Aug 1883, 4, 6
Mar 1886; Table Talk, 19 July 1889; Parkes
letters (ML); information from Mrs E. M.
Checucci (Bendigo Hist Soc).   KEITH HENRY

KNOX, SIR EDWARD (1819-1901),
sugar-refiner and banker, was born on 6
June 1819 at Helsingör, Denmark, one of
eight children of George Knox, a Baltic merchant, and his wife Elizabeth Frances, née
Mullens. His father died in 1830 and Edward
was educated by his mother's family at a
Danish school and Soröe College. At 16,
after commercial training in Lübeck, he
entered his uncle's London merchant house
as a junior clerk. Promotion was slow and
he quarrelled with his uncle and decided to
seek fortune in Australia as a pastoralist.

Knox reached Sydney on 26 February
1840 in the Sophia. After some time at Bayly
Park, near St Marys, he joined the Australian Auction Co. and in 1843 became
manager. In August he transferred to the
Australasian Sugar Co. at a salary of £250
and 'more when times mended'. With two
associates he bought Bowden's refinery and
R. Cooper's [q.v.] distillery which he leased
to the Australasian Sugar Co. On 4 June
1844 at Hunter's Hill he married Martha,
sister of William Rutledge [q.v.]. Later that
year Knox was appointed official assignee.
He traded in real estate and accumulated
capital and recognition in the business community. He was a director of the Commercial Banking Co. of Sydney in 1845-1901 and
in his four absences overseas acted as a
London director. In July 1847, after the
managing director had been dismissed for
embezzling £10,700 out of capital of
£72,000, Knox became manager, with orders
to 'devote his whole time to the management' of the bank. In 1851 he resigned as
manager, became a director of the Sydney
Tramway and Railway Co. and helped to
found the Sydney Chamber of Commerce.

In 1854 the Australasian Sugar Co. went
into liquidation after dissension among the
partners. On 1 January 1855 Knox founded
the Colonial Sugar Refining Co., holding a

third of its capital of £150,000. The new company bought the refinery and distillery from Knox and his associates. He was its first chairman of directors and except when overseas held the post until 1901. For two years the company flourished and all raw sugar was imported. In 1856 a dividend of 50 per cent was declared. In 1857 the Victoria Sugar Co. was formed with half the capital subscribed by C.S.R. shareholders and half by Victorian merchants. As its superintendent and chairman Knox arranged for a refinery to be built at Sandridge. He sold his home and some shares in C.S.R. and went to England but world prices fell, leaving the company with costly stocks of sugar. Losses of £120,000 appeared probable and Knox faced ruin. He returned to Sydney to find that R. M. Robey [q.v.] planned to build a rival refinery. When the directors refused to sell his equity in C.S.R., Robey threatened legal proceedings to dissolve the company. Knox restored the confidence of some anxious partners, and gradually put the company's affairs in order. He determined that profits would never again be lavishly distributed but withheld to establish adequate reserves and to finance expansion. He discouraged competition by take-overs and fostered internal strength and efficiency. With shrewd judgment of world raw sugar markets he maintained a voluminous correspondence with overseas agents and kept abreast of technical developments in refining and milling. With a genuine interest in his employees he established one of the first staff provident funds and rarely had industrial trouble. Under his leadership refineries were established in other Australian colonies and New Zealand, and mills were built to crush cane from independent farmers in New South Wales, Queensland and later Fiji. In 1880 he handed over the general management of the company to his second son Edward William but remained chairman until 1901.

Knox had many other business and public interests. In the 1860s with M. C. Stephen [q.v.] he held Whiteside, 24 square miles in the Moreton Bay District, and six runs in the Burnett District. He served on the advisory committee of the Australian Agricultural Co. and as executor supervised the operations of other pastoral properties. In the early 1870s he was a director of the Sydney Exchange Co. and chairman and trustee of the local board of the Liverpool and London and Globe Insurance Co. In 1893 he had returned from England and been reappointed chairman of the Commercial Banking Co. of Sydney only two months before it suspended payment on 15 May. It reopened for business on 19 June after Knox had devised a scheme of reconstruction acceptable to both shareholders and depositors.

A devout Anglican, Knox had been a member of the Diocesan Committee in 1857 and a lay member of the Board of Missions. From 1866 he was a member of each Sydney, provincial and general synod, and active on many committees. He was associated with All Saints, Woollahra, and St Andrew's Cathedral. He was sometime a director of the Benevolent Society and the Sydney Infirmary and Dispensary, a founding director and chairman of the (Royal) Prince Alfred Hospital and vice-president of the Carrington Centennial Hospital for Convalescents, Camden. A friend described him as doing 'good by stealth in religious and charitable matters'. Knox was a member of the first Legislative Council in 1856-57 and was re-appointed in 1881, but resigned in 1894 through illness. Political life had no great appeal to him but in the 1880s he organized opposition in the council to Sir Alfred Stephen's [q.v.] divorce bills and gave painstaking attention to legislative details.

Knox was a founding member of the Union Club in 1857 and president in 1882-1901. In 1864 he had built a large Georgian-style house, Fiona, on New South Head Road, and later bought beautiful mirrors and Persian carpets in Paris. Devoted to his family, he took great pride in his sons and in 1894 celebrated his golden wedding and fifty years association with the 'sugar company'. In 1898 he was knighted. He died at his home on 7 January 1901 and was buried in Waverley cemetery, survived by his wife, four daughters and three of his four sons. His eldest son George (d. 1888) was a lawyer, Edward William succeeded his father as chairman of C.S.R., Thomas Forster became managing director of Dalgety & Co. Ltd and Adrian chief justice of the High Court of Australia. Fiona became part of Ascham Girls' School, Darling Point.

Portraits are in the Union Club, Colonial Sugar Refining Co. archives and Christiansborg Palace, Copenhagen, and a bronze bust by Lyndon Dadswell is in the Art Gallery of New South Wales. The east window in St Thomas's Church on Carwoola station was donated by Knox and his wife.

A. G. Lowndes (ed), *South Pacific enterprise* (Syd, 1956); Commercial Banking Co. of Sydney, *Half-yearly reports* (1845-1901); *Banking and Insurance Review*, 21 Jan 1901; M. Rutledge, Sir Alfred Stephen and divorce law reform in New South Wales, 1886-1892 (M.A. thesis, ANU, 1966); Knox papers (uncat MS, ML); Colonial Sugar Refining Co. Archives (Syd).

A. G. LOWNDES

KONG MENG; *see* LOWE KONG MENG

KORFF, JOHN (1799-1870), shipbuilder, was born on 9 September 1799 in London, son of John Conrad Korff, a German who migrated from Brunswick and became a haberdasher in Hackney. After sound schooling, he was apprenticed at the Royal Naval Dockyard in Deptford and qualified in shipbuilding and naval architecture. He opened a yard at Lowestoft where he built and repaired ships and prospered until some of his debtors failed and his business went into receivers' hands in 1833. After his affairs were settled he left his wife, three sons and a daughter with his mother and sailed for Sydney. He arrived in December 1835 with a letter of introduction to a leading merchant, Edye Manning [q.v.].

With Manning, Korff bought the wreck of a small steamer *Ceres* and with the aid of pontoons and a bullock team worked her ashore where he salvaged the timbers and from them built a 49-ton cutter *Rover's Bride*; the engines he proposed to install in a 270-ton paddle steamer he was building at the slipway on his farm at Miller's Forest on the Hunter. He was delighted with the long beams he was able to make from the giant flooded-gum trees. His new ship *Victoria* won great praise for the design which enabled her to cross the shallow Hunter River bar and for her strength and sailing qualities. Manning had financed the work and formed a company with Korff as superintendent. The *Victoria* carried passengers and cargo between Newcastle and Sydney for several years; she was sold for £16,000 when rivals, with iron ships and more powerful engines, took over the trade. Manning's company went bankrupt and Korff returned to shipbuilding as shipping was in great demand for linking the scattered settlements.

His wife Mary, née Gordon, whom he had married in London in 1820, arrived in 1840 with a thousand sovereigns strapped around her waist, and Korff was able to escape another bankruptcy. With his sons he built the 45-ton schooner *Sisters* in 1842 and in 1845 the 27-ton ketch *Brothers*. These two ships traded between Newcastle and Sydney carrying coal and general cargoes for many years. He also built the *Currency Lass* which ran for fifty-five years and the first clinker-built ketch *Kangaroo*, and designed the *Freak* built by the Chownes brothers on the Clarence. He became a marine surveyor to the underwriters of the Lloyds Insurance group and his surveys were often accepted in lawsuits. In 1864 he tried to rescue a ship caught on the Clarence River bar. With his son Frederick he established a ferry service to Balmain and another from Woolloomooloo Bay to Manly where he had acquired a water frontage for wharves. He did not complete his ambitious scheme to establish a shipping line to Auckland but acquired a large water frontage there. Survived by his wife and two sons, he died at his home in Hereford Street, Glebe, on 14 December 1870. Next day the Sydney papers reported that flags on various ships flew at half-mast in respect for his work.

In 1847 John Korff had sought refuge in a gale in a port which he called Korff's Harbour. In 1861 surveyors changed the name to Coff's but according to newspaper and family reports Korff's name continued to be used for many years.

Australian, 2 Jan, 2 Mar, 4 Nov 1841; *SMH*, 12 Nov 1844; letter from John Korff to his wife, 24 Apr 1840, document 362 (ML).
                                                    GEORGE E. ENGLAND

KOSSAK, LADISLAUS SYLVESTER (1828-1918), police inspector, was born at Wisnicz, South Poland, the youngest son of Michal Kossak, judge, and his wife Michalina, née Sobolewska. Educated at the Dominicans' College at Lvov, he entered the university. In 1848 when the revolution against Austria broke out in Hungary Kossak left the university and joined a regiment of lancers in the Polish Legion supporting the uprising. He was soon promoted sub-lieutenant and became an adjutant. After capitulation of the Hungarian army in 1849 Kossak and the remnants of the Polish Legion crossed the border and were interned in Turkey.

In 1851 Kossak landed at Southampton and in May 1852, with his friend Captain Leopold Kabat, sailed for Melbourne in the steamer *Chusan*. They prospected for gold without success and in October joined the Victoria Police Force as cadets. In August 1853 they were both naturalized, the first Poles to become British subjects in Victoria. On 17 September Kossack was promoted lieutenant and served in Castlemaine, Bendigo and Wedderburn as officer in charge of gold escorts. In 1854 he organized the police district of Avoca and in November was transferred to Ballarat. Listed as Cossack, he was one of the four sub-inspectors in charge of the seventy mounted police at the Eureka stockade. While a party of mounted police was held in reserve Kossak led a flanking movement, although many years later he was publicly named as one of the few officials in sympathy with the miners.

Kossak took over the district of Blackwood in 1855. Later he was transferred to Castlemaine where he became friendly with R. O'H. Burke [q.v.] who in 1860 invited him in vain to join the transcontinental expedition. In July Kossak was promoted inspector, but was later reduced and when his next promotion was due he was overlooked. His case came before the royal commission on the police force in 1862-63; he was then described as 'a most active and intelligent officer'. In April 1863 Kossak applied for twelve months' leave, planning to join the Polish uprising against Russia. He sailed in August for London in the *Yorkshire* and appears to have fought against the Russians and received a commission of captain from the Polish National Government. After the insurrection collapsed he went to England where on 2 September 1865 he married Eliza Scott, daughter of a captain in the Royal Marines; they had three daughters. Later he returned to Poland and for some time acted as insurance agent in Cracow. In 1872 he left Poland and by way of London and Liverpool reached Melbourne in October in the *Theophane*.

In September 1876 Kossak bought the Point Henry Tea Gardens near Geelong and spared no expense to make an attractive recreation centre. Despite his enthusiasm he was not successful and in 1878 he left Geelong, ruined and struggling to find employment. He could not rejoin the police since he had acted 'contrary to law as a British subject in participating in a rebellion, or taking arms against a friendly Power'. About 1880 he married a Pole, Mary Stelaski; they had three daughters and a son, but she died about 1893. Kossak went to the Western Australian goldfields. In 1904 he took part in the fiftieth anniversary of the Eureka stockade and the associated celebrations in Perth. With unusual vitality he stayed on the goldfields until 1914 but he made no fortune and rejoined his daughters in Melbourne. On 10 July 1918 he died aged 90 and was buried in the Springvale cemetery.

One brother, Juliusz, was a noted Polish painter, and another, Leon, was sent to Siberia for eight years for serving his country in 1863-64 against Russia.

H. B. Stoney, *Victoria* (Lond, 1856); T. McCombie, *The history of the colony of Victoria* (Melb, 1858); W. B. Withers, *The history of Ballarat*, 1st ed (Ballarat, 1870); A. L. Haydon, *The trooper police of Australia* (Lond, 1911); W. R. Brownhill, *The history of Geelong and Corio Bay* (Melb, 1955); L. Paszkowski, *Polacy w Australii i Oceanii 1790-1940* (Lond, 1962); E. F. Kunz, *Blood and gold; Hungarians in Australia* (Melb, 1969); PP (HC), 1851 (664); V&P (LA Vic), 1862-63, 2 (D36), 1881, 3 (31, appendix); *West Australian*, 5 Dec 1904; *Herald* (Melb), 12 July 1918; S. D. S. Huyghue, The Ballarat riots 1854 (ML); Police Department letters, 1852-63 (VA); family papers (held by author).   L. K. PASZKOWSKI

KRANEWITTER, ALOYSIUS (1817-1880), Jesuit priest, was born on 14 April 1817 in Innsbruck, Austria, and entered the Society of Jesus on 21 September 1836. He was ordained priest in 1847 but in the revolutions of 1848 the Jesuits were expelled from many of the German-speaking states. Opportunely, a wealthy Silesian farmer, Franz Weikert, asked for a chaplain to accompany German migrants whom he wished to settle in South Australia. Kranewitter and Maximilian Klinkowstroem, a Viennese Jesuit, volunteered. Weikert sold his properties to underwrite the passages of the group who were to work for him in forming a settlement near Clare, but dissensions split the party on the voyage and when they arrived at Port Adelaide in December 1848 only fourteen of the original eighty stayed with Weikert. The arrival of the two Jesuits was a welcome surprise to Bishop Murphy [q.v.]. The thinly-scattered and polyglot nature of the Catholic community presented many difficulties. Murphy asked Klinkowstroem to assist Dr Backhaus [q.v.] in the care of German Catholics around Adelaide, but ill health soon forced him to return to Europe. Kranewitter moved north with Weikert to Clare. In 1851 he bought a property some miles from Clare, named it Sevenhill and planted the first vines there.

Kranewitter's letters to Rome in these years are valuable accounts of pioneering in the mid-north of South Australia. In 1852 he accompanied a large group of diggers from the Clare district to the Victorian goldfields. On his return he established the settlement at Sevenhill on a European pattern, with houses and farms around a large church and college. Local German Catholics moved into the area to escape the bigotry to which they had been exposed at Tanunda but copper discoveries further north proved a strong attraction to many settlers. By 1856 four other Austrian Jesuits had joined Kranewitter and St Aloysius College was opened. In 1858 Kranewitter was recalled to Europe for his last year of Jesuit studies, and he returned next year with three more companions. In May 1870 he was sent to Richmond to minister to the German-speaking Catholics in and around Melbourne. For ten years he worked mainly in the semi-rural districts of Nunawading and of Heidelberg where he died suddenly on 15 August 1880.

Kranewitter was an affable priest, deeply dedicated to his people and receiving great devotion in return. His chief memorial was Sevenhill, which became a complex of boarding-school, seminary for diocesan students, Jesuit novitiate and scholasticate, wine cellars and the base from which the priests made their circuits of the mid-north. These journeys covered 25,000 square miles, from Morgan to Blinman, across to Wallaroo, Port Pirie, Port Augusta and even down to Port Lincoln. From Sevenhill more than forty stone churches and schools were built. Some 450 pupils passed through the college in 1856-86 and seminarians ordained to the priesthood included Julian Tenison-Woods, Christopher Reynolds [qq.v.] and Frederick Byrne (vicar-general). In 1882 the Daly River Mission in the Northern Territory was founded from Sevenhill and lasted till 1899. By 1901 some fifty-nine Austrian priests and brothers had worked in South Australia and the Northern Territory, a tribute to the initiator, Aloysius Krane-witter.

M. Watson, *The Society of Jesus in Australia* (Melb, 1910); P. Dalton, *A history of the Jesuits in South Australia and the Northern Territory* (ML); Aust Jesuit Provincial Archives (Hawthorn, Vic).

G. J. O'KELLY

KRAUSE, FERDINAND MORITZ (1841-1918), civil engineer and geologist, was born on 24 February 1841 at Cassel, Germany, the youngest son of Frederich Wilhelm Krausé, comptroller of the provincial treasury. At 16 he went to London where he qualified as a civil engineer and was later elected a fellow of the Linnean and Geological Societies. He arrived at Melbourne in the *Black Eagle* in January 1859 and was naturalized on 6 January 1868.

By 1863 Krausé was working at Daylesford with Ambrose Johnson, mining surveyor, on the scheme proposed by E. Wardle for the Castlemaine and Sandhurst water supply, and in 1865 Krausé supported it successfully before the select committee of inquiry. In December he was appointed engineer and surveyor in the Water Supply Department and in 1868 transferred to the Ballarat and Ballarat East Water Supply Committee. In March 1870 he became surveyor with the Geological Survey of Victoria at £1 15s. a day and was also mining registrar and inspector without additional salary. He reported on the black coal deposits of Westernport and Cape Paterson in 1871-72. In 1871 he and R. A. F. Murray [q.v.] laid the foundations of the Ballarat School of Mines Geological Museum collection, both being honorary curators. Krausé also took part in work for the Gong Gong and Stony Creek reservoirs and the planning of the Ballarat-Ararat and Stawell railway lines. His next major work was the survey of 600 square miles of rugged country between Jan Juc and Apollo Bay extending inland to Birregurra. He discovered similar rock se-

quences to the Westernport area but no workable coal seams. On transfer to the Ararat district in 1872 as mining surveyor he reported on the suitability of various quarries in the Grampians as sources of building stone. His meticulous survey of the Ararat goldfield was published in 1875. In November Krausé married Amy Augusta Dimock (1859-1933). Her fossil collection, still bearing her neat labels, is now in the Ballarat School of Mines. She often accompanied him on his field-work which took him to the Ovens, Creswick, Blackwood, Daylesford, Geelong and Upper Yarra areas and to Lal Lal where he reported on Victoria's only iron-smelting works in 1877. On Black Wednesday 1878 he was dismissed but was appointed in March 1879 as a surveyor with the Lands Department.

In June 1880 Krausé was appointed to the Ballarat School of Mines as lecturer in 'geology, palaeontology, mineralogy, electricity, magnetism, scientific mining, geological and topographical surveying' and as museum curator. In 1881 he was appointed professor of geology and in 1892 was elected president of the Staff Association. He was held in high repute by his students and also known as a keen musician. He resigned from the School of Mines to be lecturer in mining at the University of Melbourne from June 1895 to January 1897. Whilst at Ballarat in 1887-90 he had completed geological maps and reports on the parishes of Haddon, Carngham, Scarsdale, Lillerie, Smythesdale and Comeralghip; these were published in 1898. The Institute of Surveyors elected him a member in 1891. His *Introduction to the study of Mineralogy for Australian readers* was published in Melbourne in 1896. In January 1897 he became manager of the General Gordon mine near Kalgoorlie. In 1900 he contributed an article to the *Ballarat School of Mines Students' Magazine* on the mining geology of Kalgoorlie. Invited by a former student, George Denny, Krausé left for South Africa in 1901. His last work was a geological map of the Barberton area, Transvaal, published in March 1918. He died on 16 June, survived by his wife, three sons and a daughter.

D. H. Bowers (ed), *The Ballarat School of Mines: retrospect 1870-1970* (Ballarat, 1970); V&P (LA Vic), 1864-65, 2 (D19); W. Baragwanath, notes; information from Mr D. R. Krausé.

J. L. KNIGHT
P. L. DAY

KREFFT, JOHANN LUDWIG (LOUIS) GERARD (1830-1881), zoologist, was born on 17 February 1830 in the Duchy of Brunswick, son of William Krefft, confectioner, and his wife Johanna, née Buschhoff. He attended St Martin's College, Brunswick, in 1834-45 and then worked in a mercantile firm in Halberstadt. In 1850 he migrated to the United States and in November 1852 reached Victoria in the *Revenue*. He worked on various goldfields until 1857 when he went with William Blandowski's [q.v.] expedition to the Lower Murray and Darling Rivers. He made a large natural history collection and was employed by the National Museum, Melbourne, to catalogue it.

After his father died Krefft visited Germany in 1858. In 1860 he returned to Sydney with an introduction to Governor Denison and in June was appointed assistant curator of the Australian Museum on Denison's recommendation. The museum's trustees argued with the government about which authority should make the appointment and in May 1864 Krefft became curator. He had a broad knowledge of zoology and geology but specialized in snakes. He built up the museum's collections and won international repute as a scientist. Among his many correspondents were Charles Darwin [q.v.], Sir Richard Owen and A. C. L. Gunther of the British Museum, Professor Agassiz in America and many learned German scientists. Krefft was one of the few Australian scientists to accept Darwin's theory of evolution and disseminate his ideas in the 1860s. He became a councillor of the Royal Society of New South Wales, a fellow of the Linnean Society of London, a corresponding member of the Zoological Society of London and a member of several European scientific societies. In 1869 he was made a knight of the Crown of Italy.

In 1866 Krefft explored the Wellington caves and publicized their fossils. His most notable discovery was the Queensland lungfish, which he named *Ceratodus forsteri* after William Forster [q.v.]. He also named a giant devil ray after the duke of Edinburgh, for whose entertainment he staged a fight between a snake and a mongoose at the museum. In some 200 articles Krefft described many species. His more important publications include *The Snakes of Australia* (1869), his description of the lungfish in the *Proceedings* of the Zoological Society of London 1870 and *The Mammals of Australia* (1871). Some of his observations on animals have not been surpassed and can no longer be equalled because of the spread of settlement. A capable artist, he depicted scenery, Aboriginals and animals of the Murray River and wrote many illustrated articles for the *Sydney Mail*.

Devoted to the museum's interests, Krefft had clashes with some of the trustees, notably W. J. Macleay, Dr J. Cox, Captain A. Onslow [qq.v.], A. W. Scott and E. S.

Hill, most of whom were building up private collections sometimes at the expense of the museum. In December 1873 several specimens of gold were stolen from the museum and various rumours involved Krefft. In 1874 a Legislative Assembly select committee inquired into the working of the museum. The evidence was conflicting, but in its report the committee recommended the dismissal of Krefft. He appealed to Henry Parkes [q.v.] to send the attorney-general or another minister to the monthly meetings of trustees. On 16 June, at a special meeting with no ministerial trustees present, the trustees set up a subcommittee to inquire into Krefft's behaviour. The twelve charges ranged from drunkenness to disobeying the trustees' orders. Krefft sought help from Parkes who replied: 'You have been much to blame for indiscretion & in some cases disobedience . . . I have great respect for your undoubted ability & am truly sorry that you should be involved in such a disagreeable difficulty. I trust and believe you will be able to dispose of the charges preferred against you which as explained to me are in many respects frivolous. But you must learn to keep a cool temper & a respectful bearing even to gentlemen who may be opposed to you'.

Krefft refused to defend himself until shown the charges and evidence collected by the subcommittee. However, the trustees found Krefft unfit to be curator and dismissed him. He denied that they had such power and barricaded himself inside the museum. Late in August he was forcibly ejected by Hill for the trustees and some of his property taken. Krefft sued Hill and was awarded £250 damages; Judge Cheeke [q.v.] ruled that the trustees had no power to dismiss the curator. In 1875 Hill sought a retrial but the judges differed on the trustees' power of dismissal. Judge Hargrave [q.v.] criticized the trustees' behaviour as 'altogether illegal, harsh and unjust' while Judge Faucett [q.v.] believed Krefft's 'conduct justified his dismissal'. In 1876 parliament voted £1000 to Krefft for arrears of salary until July when his dismissal was finally confirmed by the governor-in-council. The Robertson [q.v.] government refused to pay unless Krefft signed a bond renouncing all claims against the government and trustees. In vain he appealed to the Supreme Court to compel the treasurer to pay. The *Cumberland Times* commented that, since the treasurer, attorney-general and chief justice were all trustees, 'unconscious prejudice, resulting from the circumstances of their position, must certainly have biassed their decision'. In 1877 Krefft sued the trustees for medals and property detained in the museum and was awarded £925 and refused to compromise when they offered to return his belongings with only £200.

The museum affair demoralized Krefft and destroyed his livelihood. Many of his research papers remained unpublished and his collections were damaged and muddled. His financial position was precarious and even a strong recommendation from Parkes could not win him employment. In 1880 his estate was sequestrated with liabilities of £1131. He died on 19 February 1881 from congestion of the lungs and was buried in the churchyard of St Jude's Church of England, Randwick. He was survived by his wife Annie, née McPhail, whom he had married on 6 February 1869, and by two sons. Two other children predeceased him. A great-nephew, Gerard Krefft, became a distinguished ichthyologist in Germany.

Supreme Court reports (NSW), 1874-75; V&P (LA NSW), 1870-71, 4, 1176, 1873-74, 5, 833, 930, 1875, 4, 243, 303, 1876-77, 5, 877, 1877-78, 2, 666; G. P. Whitley, 'The life and work of Gerard Krefft', Roy Zoological Soc NSW, Procs, 1958-59; G. P. Whitley, 'Gerard Krefft and his bibliography', Roy Zoological Soc NSW, Procs, 1967-68; Bulletin, 29 Jan, 26 Feb, 9 Apr 1881; Krefft letters (BM Natural History, and Zoological Soc, Lond); Krefft MS (ML and Aust Museum, Syd); Parkes letters (ML).
G. P. WHITLEY
MARTHA RUTLEDGE

KRICHAUFF, FRIEDRICH EDUARD HEINRICH WULF (1824-1904), politician, was born on 15 December 1824 in Schleswig, Denmark, son of Carl Krichauff, a Supreme Court judge, and his wife Julie, née von Bertouch. Educated at Husum, Schleswig, and the University of Kiel, he was apprenticed to Ludwig Fischer at the Kiel botanical gardens. In 1846 he matriculated to the University of Berlin and was reputedly one of the students who guarded the palace in March 1848. After the revolution in Schleswig-Holstein failed Krichauff decided to follow his friend F. Mueller [q.v.] to South Australia, and arrived in the Alfred on 6 December. He was naturalized on 13 July 1848 and, with the help of Samuel Davenport [q.v.], he and Mueller bought land in the Bugle Ranges between Strathalbyn and Mount Barker. Mueller soon returned to Adelaide but Krichauff farmed there till about 1866 when he set up as a land agent in Adelaide. On 10 May 1853 as a 'Protestant Dissenter' he married Dorothea Sophia Arivolina Fischer at her father's home near Macclesfield.

Krichauff was elected to the first District Council of Macclesfield in 1854 and of Strathalbyn in 1856; he was chairman of both for years. In February 1857 with John

Dunn [q.v.] he was elected to the House of Assembly seat of Mount Barker. He advocated payment of members but his motion failed. A strong supporter of R. R. Torrens [q.v.], he retired on 12 March 1858 after seeing the Real Property Act passed. He contested the assembly seat of Onkaparinga in 1868 but did not win it until April 1870. He was commissioner of public works in H. B. T. Strangways's [q.v.] ministry from 12 to 30 May. Krichauff resigned his seat in May 1882 to visit Europe and the United States. From April 1884 to March 1890 he held the seat of Victoria in the assembly and in June won a Southern District seat in the Legislative Council. He was defeated in 1893 and retired from politics.

Krichauff had a lifelong interest in scientific agriculture and made many experiments in his own garden. In parliament he spoke most often on subjects of land use. He became interested in the problem of re-afforestation and in September 1870 moved the appointment of a select committee to report on the establishment and replanting of forest reserves. In 1873 his Forestry Act was passed and in August 1875 he initiated the formation of a forest board. With Davenport and A. Molineux [q.v.] he was appointed to the Central Agricultural Bureau in April 1888 and was chairman till it was closed in 1902 : he and Molineux were made life members of the new Council of Agriculture. Krichauff also served on the council of Roseworthy Agricultural College.

Krichauff was an early member of the Volunteer Rifles and became a captain. He wrote articles for the Chronicle and published pamphlets in Adelaide on water supply by artesian and tube wells (1879), the dairy industry in Denmark (1895), the beet sugar industry (1896) and the wine industry (1899). He also wrote Fertilizing field and garden (Adelaide, 1901). He died on 29 September 1904 at his home at Norwood, survived by three of his four sons and by his wife (d. 1919), to whom he left his estate valued at £750. A mountain range in Central Australia bears his name.

E. Hodder, The history of South Australia, 1-2 (Lond, 1893); F. L. Parker (ed), Centenary history of South Australia (Adel, 1936); PD (SA), 1857-58, 2 Sept 1884; Advertiser (Adel), 29, 30 Sept 1904; Register (Adel), 29, 30 Sept 1904.
SALLY O'NEILL

KRUSE, JOHANN SECUNDUS (1859-1927), violinist, was born on 22 March 1859 at Melbourne, son of John August Kruse, analytical chemist, and his wife Johanna, née Schultz. He was educated at A. B. Tegethoff's school at St Kilda. He showed an early musical talent and from at least 1871 gave performances with his sister at concerts organized by the Melbourne German Liedertafel and the Metropolitan Liedertafel. In 1875 J. Herz [q.v.] and others organized a fund to send Kruse to study under Joseph Joachim (1831-1907) at the Berlin Hochschule of music; on 12 June he left in the *Northumberland* for Germany. He soon won repute as one of Joachim's foremost pupils and after a successful début was hailed as 'Joachim Secundus'. He also became principal violinist and sub-conductor of the Berlin Philharmonic Society.

In June 1885 Kruse returned to Melbourne in the *Rome*. On the afternoon of his arrival he was welcomed by members of the musical profession at Allan's [q.v.] music warehouse and at night was honoured with an impromptu serenade by the German Turn Verein and others at the Oriental Hotel. He was supported in his concerts by Nellie Melba (Mrs Armstrong). Descriptions of his performances in Melbourne were enthusiastic: the *Australasian* noted the 'rare excellence of his powers both as a poet-musician and as a perfect executant upon the violin' and the 'perfect sweetness, power, delicacy and rhythm' of his playing. He gave concerts at Sandhurst and at the Theatre Royal, Sydney, returning to Melbourne in late July. He was farewelled at a complimentary supper by the Musical Association of Victoria and left in the *Parramatta* on 11 August to become teacher of violin at the Hochschule in October.

In 1891 Krause left the Hochschule to go to Bremen as leader of the Philharmonic orchestra there. In 1892 he joined the famous Joachim Quartet as second violin. In July 1895 he returned briefly to Melbourne to visit his dying father. He brought with him his £1100 Stradivarius and gave four concerts in Melbourne, the last on 24 August. Critics spoke warmly of him as a 'matured artist whom it is a pleasure and privilege to listen to'; audiences were large and demonstrative.

In 1897 Kruse left the Joachim Quartet and settled in London, where he revived the Saturday and Monday popular concerts with 'conspicuous success'. He also formed his own quartet. With Australian artists he played in several London concerts including one at the Albert Hall in 1898. In 1902 he organized a series of orchestral concerts with Felix Weingartner (1863-1942) as conductor and in 1903 a Beethoven Festival of eight concerts. He then turned to teaching but in the war years was troubled by poor health and hostile attitudes to his German origin. In 1921 he emerged from retirement to play chamber concerts and in 1926 founded another quartet which gave a series of competent performances of Haydn, Mozart and Beethoven. Kruse died on 14 October 1927 in London, survived by his wife Christiane Dorothee, née Gildemeister, whom he had married on 12 September 1901 in London, and a brother who had carried on his father's business in Hawthorn.

W. A. Orchard, *Music in Australia* (Melb, 1952); *Australasian*, 17 Apr, 12, 14 June 1875, 27 June, 25 July 1885, 27 July, 10, 17 Aug 1895; *Argus*, 23, 24 June, 10 Aug 1885, 24, 26 Aug 1895, 18 Oct 1927; *The Times*, 18 Oct 1927; index to pieces performed (Roy Vic Liedertafel Lib).   SALLY O'NEILL

KUBARY, JOHN STANISLAW (1846-1896), naturalist and ethnographer, was born on 13 November 1846 in Warsaw, son of Stanislaw Kubary (d. 1852) and his wife Tekla, née Schur. He was brought up by his stepfather and after high school began to study medicine, but was persecuted by the Russian police for involvement in the Polish revolution in 1863-64 and fled to Germany. In 1868 he was appointed collector for Godeffroy's museum in Hamburg.

In September 1869 Kubary reached Apia, Samoa, and was briefly trained by Dr Graeffe. Attracted to ornithology he discovered an unknown type of gallinule and at least four sub-species of birds. In 1870 he visited various islands and in the Ebon Group collected material on ethnography and zoology and compiled a dictionary of the dialect. After some months at Yap he went in February 1871 to the Palaus where he successfully fought an influenza epidemic, winning the esteem and confidence of the natives; he was told many secrets and admitted to many rites. In 1873 he visited the Marshall and Caroline Groups and in August landed on Ponape, whence he explored ruins on Nanmatal Island and produced a map and description of the ancient 'basalt city'. In August 1874 he left in the *Alfred*, with a hundred crates of his collections. The ship was wrecked on Jaluit Island and only a few crates were salvaged. After collecting in Jaluit and Samoa he sent twenty-three crates to Hamburg. On 6 February 1875 he arrived in Sydney in the *Mikado* and successfully sought naturalization.

In May Kubary reached Hamburg. He visited Lvov and in the Second Congress of the Polish Physicians and Naturalists, as one of the Warsaw representatives, lectured on the classification of Polynesian, Melanesian and Micronesian languages. The Hamburg Geographical Society made him a corresponding member. In August he signed a five-year agreement with Godeffroy, and sailed for the Pacific. At Ponape he started a plantation and built permanent headquarters. In 1877-78 he collected in several islands and stayed at Truk for fourteen months. There he learnt that Godeffroy had released him from their contract, leaving him without a livelihood. He sailed with notable seamanship among the islands in a native canoe and corrected local maps. He then returned to Ponape and worked intensively on his plantation. There he married Anna Yelliott, daughter of an American missionary and his Micronesian wife.

Early in 1882 Kubary's plantation was destroyed by a hurricane. He worked at the Tokyo Museum and collected for the museum at Leiden and the Ethnographical Museum in Berlin, but won no permanent contract. Expert in Oceanic languages, he became interpreter on the German warship *Albatros*. In October 1885 he landed at Rabaul and took charge of a plantation at Matupit. Early in 1887 he signed an agreement with the Neu Guinea Kompagnie as manager of a trading post at Constantinhafen. He also collected ethnographical material and made a valuable collection of stuffed birds, shells and butterflies. In 1892 he left for Germany with his wife and only daughter, Izabella. Despite a flattering reception and a lecture at Lvov he found no employment and returned to New Guinea,

where he stayed till December 1895. He then went to Manila to clarify his rights to the plantation at Ponape. After months in hospital he returned to Ponape and found his plantation devastated in a native uprising. On 9 October 1896 he was found dead on the grave of his only son Bertram.

With little scientific training, Kubary proved his great ability and intelligence, winning the praise of many scholars for his contributions to natural history, ethnography, anthropology, cartography and linguistics as well as the love and veneration of the native people of the Western Pacific. He published at least two dozen scientific monographs, articles and papers in German, Polish and French. His most important work was *Ethnographische Beiträge zur Kenntnis des Karolinen Archipels* (Leiden, 1889-92). His name is commemorated in ornithology, entomology and conchology and by German geographers in a peak (often misspelt) in the Finisterre Range, New Guinea. A monument subscribed by forty-six German scientists and a few Poles was erected at Ponape.

L. Paszkowski, 'John Stanislaw Kubary—naturalist and ethnographer of the Pacific Islands', *Aust Zoologist*, 16 (1971) pt 2, and for bibliog.   L. K. PASZKOWSKI

L

LABILLIERE, FRANCIS PETER (1840-1895), author and imperialist, was born on 13 August 1840 in Melbourne, son of Charles Edgar de Labilliere (d. 1870), of Huguenot descent, and his wife Hannah, née Balle (d. 1880). His parents had migrated in the *Westminster* to Port Phillip in 1839 and bought the rights of Yallock Vale, a large sheep station near Bacchus Marsh, where his father served as a territorial magistrate; in 1856 he was returning officer for West Bourke at the first parliamentary elections under responsible government. An only son, Francis was tutored by his parents and often travelled with them. His upbringing spanned the years of the pastoral expansion and gold rushes. In 1859 the station was sold and the family returned to England, travelling for some time before settling in Westbourne Square, London. Francis was admitted to the Middle Temple on 7 November 1860, called to the Bar on 6 June 1863 and joined the south-eastern circuit. On 9 October 1867 at St Saviour's, Paddington, he married Adelaide, daughter of Rev. Edward Ravenshaw.

Disturbed by the apparent indifference of the mother-country to the separatism of her self-governing colonies, Labilliere joined imperial enthusiasts and others with colonial connexions or experience in a counter-thrust to unite the empire. He was honorary secretary to the conference on colonial questions in 1871 and in 1874-95 a fellow of the Royal Colonial Institute, founded in 1868 by private individuals as a nonpolitical force for 'promoting in England a better knowledge of the colonies and of India'. He was zealous in various aspects of the imperial cause. He assisted the honorary secretary of the new society, Sir Frederick Young, until it was able to maintain a paid staff, and served on its Library Committee in 1880. In 1878 he published a two-volume *Early History of the Colony of Victoria, from its discovery to its establishment as a self-governing province of the British Empire*, which added to the works in celebration of Victoria and Greater Britain. Nearly two-thirds of the book comprises documents which, with the contemporary writings of other Victorians such as James Bonwick and William Westgarth [qq.v.], drew attention to the wealth of documentation on the colonies' past in government offices in Britain. He was also an enthusiast for British migration to the colonies, and from 1874 urged the Colonial Office to annex eastern New Guinea.

Labilliere propagated the ideal of Greater Britain and sought to give it effective form by integrating the colonies with the centre through imperial federation, which he had proposed in 'The Future Relations of England and her Colonies' read at the Bristol Congress of the National Association for the Promotion of Social Science on 30 September 1869. He continued to advocate the cause at the Royal Colonial Institute and in discussion of the chairman's paper, 'On Unity of the Empire', in 1875 projected a truly imperial parliament, its members elected by the colonies as well as the United Kingdom. He raised the subject in more detail on 14 June 1881 in his paper 'The Political Organisation of the Empire'. As support grew he served with W. Westgarth and John Dennistoun Wood [q.v.] on a committee of six to draft the prospectus of the Imperial Federation League, founded in November 1884. Despite criticism he could claim growing success in his *Imperial Federation* (1886) and *Federal Britain: or, Unity and Federation of the Empire* (1894).

Labilliere died on 19 February 1895 at Mount Park, Harrow, Middlesex. He left an estate of over £5000 to his wife and surviving children. The Council of the Royal Colonial Institute sent condolences to the family and resolved that 'there is scarcely a man who will be more missed than he will be'. After his death the notion of imperial federation declined. A more lasting memorial is his *Early History of the Colony of Victoria*.

Roy Colonial Inst, *Procs*, 26 (1894-95), 164; *The Times*, 21 Feb 1895; *Australasian*, 13 Mar 1875, supp.

B. R. PENNY

LABOUREYAS, PIERRE (1842-1924), Marist Brother known as Ludovic, was born in November 1842 at Egliseneuve, Puy-de-Dôme, France, son of Jean Laboureyas and his wife Marie, née Pialloux. He joined the teaching congregation of the Marist Brothers founded in 1817 by Marcellin Champagnat in the Lyons diocese. After teaching in Britain he was chosen to lead the first four Marist Brothers to New South Wales at the invitation of the Catholic Education Association. They reached Sydney on 26 February 1872 and filled a void in Catholic education left by the forced departure of the Christian Brothers in the 1840s.

Repairs and alterations to a former Anglican school adjacent to St Patrick's, Church Hill, delayed the opening of a school until 8 April 1872. Brother Ludovic was faced with many problems among the clergy and laity and divisive national elements. The unruliness of his pupils was apparently improved by the inculcation of some religious practices. He had difficulties with Archbishop Polding [q.v.] who took control of the school away from the parish and gave it to a diocesan committee. Brother Ludovic was blamed for building debts and financial mismanagement. His careful and documented administration refuted these charges, but suspicions that large funds were being sent to France continued for years. Rumours were spread about his high-handed tyranny over his community and his personal luxury, but were dispelled by Polding on a canonical visit. Other rumours about the incompetence of his teachers were scotched by Brother Ludovic who welcomed an examination of the school by a panel of five priests and five laymen; this course was suggested by Polding in 1873 and at the behest of Archbishop Vaughan [q.v.] in 1874. The inspections showed that both teachers and pupils were doing satisfactory work. Increasing numbers of students and general dislike of the monitor system added to his worries, but the founding of a novitiate in July 1872 eased the teaching burden and filled the gaps when two of the original group defected and another suffered a long illness.

Brother Ludovic planned an evening school and began a school bank which was stopped by his superiors. Aware of the need for secondary education he encouraged his principal teacher, Brother Augustine, to found the Marist Brothers' High School in 1875 at St Patrick's, Church Hill. In cooperation with Vaughan, who foresaw the ending of state aid to denominational schools, he opened schools at Parramatta and St Benedict's in 1875. He bought a property at Parramatta and acquired another adjacent to the Marist Fathers at Villa Maria.

Brother Ludovic's leadership of the foundation ended with the arrival of Brother John (Denis Dullea) in January 1876 as provincial superior. As master of novices, Brother Ludovic acted as deputy for Brother John in his long absences. In 1880, with immense courage and vision but few resources, they undertook the building of the first stage of St Joseph's College, Hunter's Hill, finance being guaranteed by a friend of Brother Ludovic.

Brother Ludovic went to New Caledonia in 1884 but was soon summoned to Dumfries, Scotland, as novice master. He died in France in March 1924. By 1972 his small band of four brothers teaching in one school had grown to nearly a thousand Marist Brothers with 38,000 pupils in over ninety schools in the three provinces in Australia and New Zealand.

U. Corrigan, *Catholic education in New South Wales* (Syd, 1930); R. Fogarty, *Catholic education in Australia 1806-1950* (Melb, 1959); A. Barcan, *A short history of education in New South Wales* (Syd, 1965); T. L. Suttor, *Hierarchy and democracy in Australia 1788-1870* (Melb, 1965); P. J. O'Farrell (ed), *Documents in Australian Catholic history*, 1 (Lond, 1969); Marist Brothers Archives (Mittagong and Drummoyne, NSW, and General House, Rome).   ALBAN DOYLE

LACKEY, SIR JOHN (1830-1903), pastoralist and politician, was born on 6 October 1830 and baptized a Catholic on 18 January 1831 in Sydney, son of William Lackey and his second wife Mary, née O'Dowd. His father had been transported for inflicting a fatal blow and arrived in 1826 at Sydney in the *Sir Godfrey Webster*; he had a conditional pardon and a ticket-of-leave when he married on 7 December 1829. He was appointed bailiff at Parramatta in 1830, acquired land in the County of Cumberland and then held the licences of several hotels, one on the Dog Trap Road. He seems to have disposed of most of his property to the O'Dowds before he became insolvent in 1843 and in 1845 was gaoled for fourteen days for prevarication. In the 1850s he was manager of the Moorebank estate where he died on 8 September 1880.

John's grandfather, a wealthy publican, paid for his education at Parramatta at John Eyre's [q.v.] school and John Mills's Aldine House, and in Sydney at W. Cape's [q.v.] college. In 1849 John was a toll collector at the Lansdowne Bridge and camped in the old guard house. At Concord on 21 August 1851 at St John's Anglican Church he married Martha Anne Drummond Roberts, widowed daughter of W. Hutchinson [q.v.], thereby acquiring seven stepchildren. In 1852 he was appointed a magistrate and next year paid £254 for land near Concord. He took up grazing in the Parramatta district and as 'a jovial young farmer' bought and reared stock. In the early 1860s he took over the hotel on the Dog Trap Road and most of the adjoining land (Granville) which he laid out as a vineyard and farm. He also took up stations west of Peak Downs in Queensland. In the late 1870s he sold the farm and moved to Austermere near Bong Bong, once owned by his father-in-law.

Defeated for Central Cumberland in 1858, Lackey topped the poll for Parramatta in

1860. He faithfully supported John Robertson [q.v.], voted for his Land Acts and favoured land reform. In 1865 Lackey was defeated by the 'Byrnes-Farnell [qq.v.] racket' and retired to the country, but in 1867 won a by-election for Central Cumberland which he represented until 1885. He soon won repute for calmness, courtesy and iron self-control in the assembly. In 1874 he had 'never been known to say an offensive word even to his most bitter opponents' and was one of the few members who had 'never been called to order'. In 1870-72 his impartiality as chairman of committees increased his popularity and in 1872 when Sir James Martin [q.v.] was withdrawing from politics Lackey declined to lead the Opposition. Although he spoke rarely, he was fluent with an argumentative style full of pertinent information and experience. In 1874, with other native-born politicians, he advocated the release of the bushranger, Frank Gardiner [q.v.].

In 1875-77 Lackey was secretary for public works in Robertson's ministry. The Newcastle *Miners' Advocate* could not recall him 'ever doing anything' but thought he might 'assist the Government much by his elephantine gravity'. In 1877 he was minister of justice and public instruction in Robertson's ministry and in 1878-83 secretary for public works in the Parkes [q.v.] –Robertson coalition. A capable administrator, Lackey introduced bills for building many of the colony's railways and was responsible for beginning to supply Nepean water for Sydney. In October 1882 he resigned from the ministry for private reasons but was induced by Parkes to continue in office. In the *Freeman's Journal*, 15 July 1882, 'Cassius' described him as a 'gentlemanly machine for attaching a so-called responsible signature to the ideas and conceptions of your professional advisors' but had to commend him for 'never losing his temper'. 'Cassius' also criticized Lackey for nepotism: in 1875 he had appointed his second son time-keeper at Prospect reservoir and a stepson first superintendent of Sydney trams. In 1885 Lackey resigned from the assembly and was nominated to the Legislative Council. He suggested a parliamentary standing committee on public works and in August 1888 became its first chairman. In 1889 he was vice-president of the Executive Council in G. R. Dibbs's [q.v.] ministry.

With 'a keen eye for a clever two-year old', Lackey had long been interested in racing and in the 1850s was steward and treasurer of the Parramatta Turf Club. In the 1860s he was judge for the Australian Jockey Club and by 1873 was also handicapper and a steward. He helped to select and supervise the laying out of Randwick Race Course and became well known as a breeder and owner. A committee member of the Cumberland Agricultural Society, he became trustee, treasurer and a vice-president of the Agricultural Society of New South Wales in the 1860s. In August 1873 he read a paper to the society on the *History of Horses and Horsebreeding in New South Wales*. In 1888 he contributed 'Reminiscences of Horse Racing and Sporting in the Early Days' to the *Centennial Magazine*, August 1888. In the 1880s he was chairman of the Sydney Meat Preserving Co. and Lackey Street near Railway Square, where the firm had its premises, is named after him. He also acquired Buckwaroon, 108,000 acres near Cobar, and in 1891 bought the adjoining Amphitheatre run of 174,000 acres and the Mereworth estate at Moss Vale. In 1888 he was president of the Centennial Celebration Commission. He had been a member of the Union Club from 1869 and was president and vice-president of the Warrigal Club in Sydney where he lived when parliament was sitting.

In January 1892 Lackey succeeded Sir John Hay [q.v.] as president of the Legislative Council, where he became noted for the 'clearness of his decisions, delivered in a sonorous voice and with deliberate emphasis'. In 1894 he was appointed K.C.M.G. In his office he kept a portrait of Sir Robert Peel, with whom the *Bulletin* had once compared him. He resigned as president on 23 May 1903. In old age he represented 'the old-time Australian Squatter', full of dignity and geniality and enjoying 'universal reverence'. He died from senile decay on 11 November 1903 at Austermere and was buried in the Bong Bong Church of England cemetery. Predeceased by his wife on 5 August 1901 and by a daughter, he was survived by two sons.

D. M. Barrie, *The Australian bloodhorse* (Syd, 1956); V&P (LA NSW), 1883-84, 1, 78, 2, 102; *Illustrated Sydney News*, 17 Oct 1874; *Miners' Advocate* (Newcastle), 13 Feb 1875; *Bulletin*, 7 Aug 1880; *Freeman's J*, 15 July 1882; *Pastoral Review*, 15 Aug 1899, 15 Dec 1901, 16 June 1903; *Truth* (Syd), 31 Aug 1919; Parkes letters (ML); CO 201/577/539, 597/350.

MARTHA RUTLEDGE

LAIDLAW, THOMAS (1813-1876), businessman, was born on 23 September 1813 in Melrose, Roxburghshire, Scotland, eldest son of Alexander Laidlaw, merchant, and his first wife Helen, née Cochrane. He was related to William Laidlaw who was a friend of Sir Walter Scott. Trained as a banker in Scotland, Thomas Laidlaw arrived at Sydney in 1839. Next year he went to Yass and became a partner of C. B. Harrison, general store-keeper. Later they also trans-acted most of the banking business south of Goulburn.

Laidlaw became a trustee of the Yass Hospital in 1847, a member of the Yass District Council in 1848, a licensed spirits merchant and brewer in 1849, and postmaster in 1851. As he acquired social influence his probity earned him the nickname 'Honest Tom of Yass'. On Harrison's death the business passed to Laidlaw who made a fortune selling groceries, ironmongery, earthenware, liquor, drapery and ladies' clothing. He retired in 1866 and sold his substantial emporium to his manager, J. P. Ritchie.

In June 1859 Laidlaw was elected unopposed to represent Yass Plains in the Legislative Assembly, but in September his government contract as postmaster at Yass was discovered and he had to vacate his seat. He hastily resigned as postmaster and was re-elected to the assembly on the 15th. He supported Charles Cowper's [q.v.] government but declined the office of colonial treasurer. Too reticent to enjoy politics he retired on 10 November 1860 and could never be persuaded to contest another election although he used his influence in promoting local candidates. In 1866 he successfully supported the ministerial re-election of R. M. Isaacs [q.v.]. In the bitter elections of 1869-70, Laidlaw refused repeated requests to stand as the only local man with an independent outlook, but persuaded M. Fitzpatrick [q.v.] to contest the seat.

Laidlaw sat on Yass bench for many years and on his advice the Yass Courier was started in 1857. He took a benevolent interest in many local charities and was popular in the town and surrounding district. In retirement he acquired at least ten pastoral properties in New South Wales but in his last years was more often in Sydney than Yass. In 1841 he had married Catherine Galvin of Camden, who died of consumption the next year. He buried her in a specially consecrated corner of his estate and never remarried. As he prospered he brought out his stepmother Charlotte, née Haig, and three brothers and two sisters from Scotland to live with him at Yass; they all predeceased him.

Laidlaw died at Yass on 12 June 1876 after entering the Roman Catholic Church. He was buried beside his wife and their graves overlook that section of the main street of Yass which bears their name. His estate, valued at £175,000, was divided among friends in New South Wales, charities in Yass and relations in Scotland.

V&P (LA NSW), 1859-60, 1, 17, 71, 1870, 1, 431; *Empire*, 7 June 1859; *Town and Country J*, 24 June 1876; *Yass Courier*, 7 Feb 1866, 19 Nov 1869, 13, 16, 23 June 1876.   SUZANNE EDGAR

LALOR, PETER (1827-1889), Eureka stockade leader and politician, was born on 5 February 1827 in the parish of Raheen, Queen's County, Ireland, son of Patrick Lalor and his wife Ann, née Dillon. The family was descended from the O'Lalours, one of the Seven Septs of Leix who had fought against the English invasion of Ireland in the sixteenth century. The Lalors had leased the 700 acres of Tenakill since 1767 and remained fairly prosperous until the great famine of 1845. They were supporters of Ireland's freedom from British rule and of the rights of the Irish peasantry. In 1831 Patrick Lalor had led the resistance of the Leix peasants against the forcible collection of tithes for the established church and in 1832-35 represented Queen's County in the House of Commons where he was an ardent advocate for the repeal of the Act of Union. In 1853 he wrote: 'I have been for upwards of forty years struggling without ceasing in the cause of the people'.

The eldest of Patrick's eleven sons, James Fintan, became a leader of the Irish Confederation and the 'Young Ireland' movement of 1848. According to C. G. Duffy [q.v.], he was 'the most original and intense ... of all the men who have preached revolutionary politics in Ireland'. In the *Nation* he expounded his belief in 'Ireland her own, from the sod to the sky'. He became co-editor of the *Irish Felon* in 1848 but was in Newgate prison during the uprising. On his release, he plunged into a new unsuccessful revolutionary conspiracy. He died in December 1849. Fintan had urged his brother Richard in 1848 to form Confederate clubs and engage a blacksmith to make pikes for the peasants. Fintan's letters record only the suggestion that Peter should join the *Felon* club and that Richard should bring him to Dublin to take part in the rising.

Peter's early years were overshadowed by these dramatic events and by the famine but no evidence shows that he was actively involved. Later he commented that 'from what he had seen of the mode of conducting politics in [Ireland] he had ... no inclination to mix himself up with them'. Educated at Carlow College and in Dublin, he became a civil engineer. The years after the famine saw a great emigration from Ireland. Three of the Lalor brothers went to America while Peter and Richard migrated to Victoria attracted by the gold discoveries. They arrived at Melbourne in October 1852 and Peter found work on the construction of the Melbourne-Geelong railway; he and Richard also became partners with another Irishman as wine, spirits and provision merchants in Melbourne. In 1853 Peter left for the Ovens diggings. Early in 1854 he moved to Ballarat. Richard did not accompany him to the diggings and soon returned to Ireland where he became a member of parliament for Leix in 1880-92 and was an ardent Home Ruler and supporter of Parnell. Peter apparently saw himself as much merchant as digger, since he bought from the partnership over £800 worth of tobacco, spirits and other supplies; however, his departure for the goldfields ended his career as a city merchant.

At Ballarat Lalor staked a claim on the Eureka lead, where many Irish diggers were concentrated, although his own 'mate' was Duncan Gillies [q.v.], a Scot. He was reported to be among the shrinking minority of Ballarat diggers who were having 'fair luck' on their claims; he was involved, although not prominently, in the agitations over the miners' licence and 'digger-hunting'. Later Lalor wrote, perhaps thinking of the wrongs of Ireland, 'the people were dissatisfied with the laws, because they excluded them from the possession of the land, from being represented in the Legislative Council, and imposed on them an odious poll-tax' (licence fee) which an arbitrary officialdom sought to collect from diggers.

The Ballarat Reform League arose from the agitation against the imprisonment of three diggers charged with the burning of Bentley's Hotel. The league's programme reflected the radical beliefs of its leaders: it was overtly Chartist in its demands and, some said, covertly republican. Lalor was a member of the committee, although he must have had reservations about parts of its programme. On 29 November 1854 the league called its first mass meeting to hear the report of its deputation to the governor. Sir Charles Hotham had promised an inquiry into the diggers' grievances but refused to accede to the diggers' 'demand' for the release of their mates. The mood of the 12,000 diggers who gathered on Bakery Hill for the first time under their Southern Cross flag was for physical resistance. Resolutions were carried calling on the diggers to burn their licences and pledging the protection of the 'united people' for any digger arrested for non-possession of a licence. Lalor's first public appearance was at this meeting: he moved for a further league meeting on 3 December in order to elect a central committee.

On 30 November the troops had undertaken a 'digger hunt' on Bakery Hill. The news of the resulting clash spread rapidly through the diggings to the Eureka, where Lalor was working in his shaft, 140 ft. below ground, with Timothy Hayes, chairman of the league, at the windlass above. Diggers rushed to the scene and, as the troops withdrew with their prisoners, occupied the hill where the flag was again raised. The diggers dispersed to gather strength and resolved to reassemble at 4 p.m. None of the regular spokesmen was then present and Lalor 'mounted the stump and proclaimed "Liberty".' He called on the men to arm themselves and to organize for self-defence. Some hundreds were enrolled and Lalor, according to Raffaello Carboni [q.v.], 'knelt down, the head uncovered, and with the right hand pointing to the standard, exclaimed in a firm measured tone: "We swear by the Southern Cross to stand truly by each other to defend our rights and liberties". A universal well-rounded Amen, was the determined reply'. That night Lalor wrote to his fiancée, Alicia Dunne, a schoolteacher in Geelong: 'the diggers . . . in self-defence, have taken up arms and are *resolved to use them* . . . I am one amongst them. You must not be unhappy on this account. I would be unworthy of being called a man, I would be unworthy of myself, and, above all, I would be unworthy of you and of your love, were I base enough to desert my companions in danger'.

Next morning some 1500 diggers assembled on Bakery Hill and marched behind their flag to the Eureka. The leaders met and appointed Lalor commander. In response he said: 'I expected someone who is really well known to come forward and direct our movement. However, if you appoint me your commander-in-chief, I shall not shrink. I tell you, gentlemen, if once I pledge my hand to the diggers, I will neither defile it with treachery, nor render it contemptible with cowardice'.

In the next two days both sides continued their preparations. The diggers threw up a barricade of which Lalor wrote, 'it was nothing more than an enclosure to keep our own men together, and was never erected with an eye to military defence'; yet it closely resembled the fortified circular encampments planned by Fintan Lalor in 1848. Behind it, the men drilled and blacksmiths manufactured pikes. Lalor claimed no military expertise; he appointed a young American to look after the military side while he organized picketing and the procurement of arms, ammunition and other supplies. The government camp organized for action and infiltrated the stockade with spies.

Lalor did not expect an immediate attack and did not plan to confine defence to the stockade. By midnight on Saturday only about 120 men were left in the stockade, most of them Irish. Some hundreds had left to spend the night in their tents. At about 3 a.m., Sunday, 3 December, the troops and police attacked. They quickly stormed the flimsy stockade and its defences, killing thirty or more diggers and taking over a hundred prisoners. True to his pledge Lalor had stood his ground but was hit in the left arm and collapsed. He was hidden under logs and escaped the bayonets of the attackers. He was smuggled from the battlefield and eventually reached the home of Father Smyth, where his arm was amputated at the shoulder by a party of doctors. Legend has Lalor recovering consciousness during the operation and, seeing one doctor with signs of faintness, saying 'Courage! Courage! Take it off!'

Hotham offered a reward of £200 for information leading to the apprehension of a 'person of the name of Lawlor . . . height 5 ft. 11 in., age 35, hair dark brown, whiskers dark brown and shaved under the chin, no moustache, long face, rather good looking and . . . a well made man' who at Ballarat 'did . . . use certain TREASONABLE AND SEDITIOUS LANGUAGE, and incite Men to take up Arms, with a view to make war against Our Sovereign Lady the QUEEN'. There were no takers: public sympathy was overwhelmingly with the diggers. Lalor remained concealed in Ballarat for several weeks; from there he was taken by dray to Geelong, where he was cared for by Alicia Dunne and married her on 10 July 1855 at St Mary's Church.

Public subscriptions for the disabled Lalor raised enough money for him to buy '160 acres of very good land within 10 miles of Ballaarat'; he emerged from hiding to bid for the land and was not arrested. In March the reward had been revoked, and in April the thirteen diggers charged with treason were acquitted. The colonists generally shared Lalor's judgment of the stockade: 'neither anarchy, bloodshed, nor plunder, were the objects of those engaged . . . Stern necessity alone forced us to do it'. One eye-witness reports Lalor as saying that his object as leader was 'independence'; if this were so, it would seem that the independence he wanted was from arbitrary rule, from encroachments by the Crown on 'British Liberty', and that granted by access to the land, rather than the 'independence' of a republican democracy.

With the adoption of the recommendation of the commissioners appointed by Hotham to inquire into the condition of the goldfields that the Legislative Council be enlarged to include elected representatives of the goldfields, Lalor was one of two diggers' leaders returned unopposed in November 1855 to represent Ballarat. He told his electors: 'I am in favour of such a system of law reform as will enable the poor man to obtain equal justice with the rich'. When the first parliament was elected under the new Constitution in 1856 Lalor was returned unopposed to the Legislative Assembly for North Grenville, a Ballarat seat. He was appointed an inspector of railways at a salary of £600, but was soon debarred from this post when legislation was passed prohibiting civil servants from sitting in parliament.

In the assembly Lalor spoke out for the interests of the diggers: he successfully advocated compensation for the victims of Eureka, and unsuccessfully the right of miners to enter private property in search of gold; in vain he opposed the appropriation of funds for a memorial to Hotham, saying, 'There was sufficient monument already existing in the graves of the thirty individuals slain at Ballarat'. Yet he aroused hostility among his digger constituents by supporting plural voting on a property franchise and a six-months' residency qualification for the franchise, and land legislation which radicals held to favour the squatters. In defence he said that he would never consent to deprive a freeholder of his right to vote in virtue of his freehold, and that the danger inherent in conferring the franchise on 'an unsettled population' should be balanced 'by infusing into the people a conservative element by attaching them to the land'. He denied that he was a democrat if that meant 'Chartism, Communism, or Republicanism', but asserted that 'if democracy means opposition to a tyrannical press, a tyrannical people or a tyrannical government, then I have ever been, I am still, and will ever remain, a democrat'. The diggers were not convinced, and Lalor wisely stood for South Grant in 1859. He was elected and became chairman of committees at a salary of £800.

Lalor's stance in parliament appeared puzzlingly inconsistent. He was an early advocate of protection of local industry, believing that it would provide work for men no longer able to make a living on the gold-fields, but he also supported assisted immigration. Although a devout Roman Catholic, he opposed state aid to religion and supported a national education system provided that provision was made for religious teaching. He supported the 1860 and 1862 Land Acts providing for selection from the squatters' runs, but urged sale by auction of both freehold agricultural land and grazing leases, declaring that the creation of 'a middle class of landed proprietors' able to employ labourers at reasonable wages, was preferable to opening the land in small lots to men without capital. He supported reform of the Legislative Council but opposed payment to members. When the McCulloch [q.v.] government came into conflict with the council over the protectionist tariff and later the 'Darling grant', Lalor urged caution and abstained from voting on several of the government's vital measures, holding them to be unconstitutional.

Lalor's pursuit of his own judgment won him no friends in parliament, yet as a good local member with a strong personal following he topped the poll for South Grant in 1868. The ministry repaid his 'unsoundness' by refusing to reappoint him as chairman of committees. In the next three years Lalor virtually abandoned parliament for private business, attending only 31 of 174 divisions. He operated as a land and mining agent and was director of several mining companies, the most important being the New North Clunes. He was also chairman at a substantial salary of the Clunes Water Commission. On his initiative legislation was passed enabling the commission to borrow money for the construction of a water supply system for Clunes. The money was raised by the New North Clunes Mining Co. In 1873 the government bought the commission for £65,000, thus enabling New North Clunes to declare what the *Ballarat Star* described as the largest dividend ever paid by a mining company—£30 a share. It was also alleged that Lalor employed blacklegs to enforce a wage cut in one of his mines. Lalor was narrowly squeezed out of third place in the 1871 election by J. F. Levien [q.v.] whom he angrily described as 'a little jew boy' and against whom he pursued a vendetta.

The 1874 election was fought on the reform of the Legislative Council. Lalor was by now convinced that domination of the council by squatters made reform necessary, and that its powers should be limited to those enjoyed by the House of Lords. He was elected third member for South Grant. When Graham Berry [q.v.] formed his first government in 1875, Lalor became commissioner for customs. The government was defeated after a few months but Berry refused a dissolution by the governor and led his followers in a stonewalling campaign to disrupt the conduct of business. Lalor supported Berry's tactics wholeheartedly.

In the 1877 election Lalor again backed all Berry's policies, including payment of members. He won a landslide victory, and Lalor became postmaster-general and as commissioner for customs negotiated in vain with Henry Parkes [q.v.] to remove the border duties between Victoria and New South Wales. When the council refused to accept the payment of members, Berry retaliated by sacking the colony's senior public servants. *Melbourne Punch* laid this 'Black Wednesday' at the door of Lalor who had been outspoken in denouncing the 'arrogant power' of the council. However, Lalor twice

embarrassed the government and asserted his independence by voting against measures which Berry believed significant.

The Berry government was defeated in 1880 but Lalor topped the poll for South Grant as a Berryite. In a later election that year Berry won again and moved for the appointment of Lalor as Speaker. Although denounced by Thomas Bent [q.v.] as a 'rebel against the British crown' and as having been 'drunk on the floor of this House', Lalor was appointed unopposed. 'The first duty of a Speaker', he said, 'is to be a tyrant. Remove him if you like, but while he is in the chair obey him. The Speaker is the embodiment of the corporate honour of the House. He is above party. He is the greatest representative of the people'. Despite conservative fears that Lalor would lean towards his political friends he maintained the strength, dignity and impartiality of the chair, and was reappointed by successive parliaments until diabetes weakened his physique and impaired his judgment. The death of his only daughter and in May 1887 of his wife greatly affected him, and he resigned as Speaker in September.

The premier, Duncan Gillies, introduced a bill to grant Lalor £4000 to free him of financial worries in his last months. Despite party opposition in the assembly the bill was passed and later carried unanimously in the council. Earlier Lalor had refused the offer of a knighthood. In a bid to regain his health he took leave from parliament, but remained a member at the express wish of his constituents, and went by sea to San Francisco. On his return he became bedridden in the home of his only son, Joseph, where he died on 9 February 1889. Besides the requiem in Melbourne, flags were flown at half-mast and a special memorial service was held at Ballarat.

On entry into parliament Lalor had been described by the *Argus* as 'a bluff, straight forward gentleman who blurts out plain truths in a homely matter-of-fact style'. Certainly as diggers' leader and as parliamentarian he fought with courage, determination and often passion for the truth as he saw it. His loyalties were to principles rather than to individuals. The inconsistencies of his political stance can perhaps best be explained by the principles he consistently upheld : a well-ordered society based on a broad and prosperous land-holding class, governed by free men in the liberal institutions embodied in British constitutional procedures. Only when a class claimed exclusive and overbearing power and sought to impose its will arbitrarily was Lalor's anger aroused and turned him, however reluctantly, to action. Once committed to a course he did not waver from it. Neither a profound thinker nor a skilful politician, Lalor was a good fighter and a man of rectitude who came finally to earn the respect even of those whom he had most vehemently opposed on grounds of principle.

W. B. Withers, *The history of Ballarat*, 2nd ed (Ballarat, 1887); L. Fogarty (ed), *James Fintan Lalor* (Dublin, 1947); T. J. Kiernan, *The Irish exiles in Australia* (Melb, 1954); Historical Studies, *Eureka supplement*, 2nd ed (Melb, 1965); C. Turnbull, *Australian lives* (Melb, 1965); PD (Vic) 1856-87; *Australasian*, 19, 26 June 1880, 17, 24 Sept 1887, 16 Feb 1889; *Freeman's J* (Syd), 16 Feb 1889; J. Parnaby, The economic and political development of Victoria, 1877-1881 (Ph.D. thesis, Univ Melb, 1951); G. Robinson, The political activities of Peter Lalor (B.A. Hons thesis, Univ Melb, 1960); Lalor family papers (National Lib, Ireland).   IAN TURNER

LAMB, EDWARD WILLIAM (1828-1910), pastoralist, public servant and politician, was born on 6 February 1828 in London, second son of John Lamb [q.v.] and his wife Emma Trant, née Robinson. With his parents he arrived in the *Resource* at Sydney in May 1829. He was sent to England for education at the Royal Naval School and returned about 1846 to join the family firm, Lamb, Parbury & Co. In the next ten years he and his brother Walter [q.v.] managed stations for the firm near Boorowa and Harden. On 9 February 1854 he married Julia Clemence Fattorini, by whom he had two sons and three surviving daughters.

In 1858 Lamb and Thomas Skinner bought Dalgangal station in the Burnett District of Queensland. Four years later he took up five stations on Peak Downs with John Richard Black. Appointed chief commissioner of crown lands in November 1862, he held office until elected to the Legislative Assembly for Mitchell in July 1867. A month later he was appointed secretary for public lands in the Mackenzie [q.v.] ministry. Lamb confessed disillusion with the theories of E. G. Wakefield [q.v.], whom he had once known, and his main objective was a new land law. His bill was heavily amended by a select committee but in 1868 was passed as the Crown Land Alienation Act. His alleged maladministration of it led to his replacement in September and was one of the charges used to defeat the Mackenzie ministry in November.

Lamb resigned in December 1869 and next year failed to win the Clermont seat. He dissolved his partnership with Black in May 1874 and retired to Sydney. In 1880, on behalf of his son Edward Charles, he took up Alroy Downs in the Northern Territory.

Lamb lost heavily when the lease had to be abandoned in 1893. He wrote occasionally on development for the press until he died in a private hospital at Woolloomooloo on 18 October 1910.

Though well educated and intelligent, Lamb was unlucky in politics. Perhaps unfairly, a political lampoonist described him as

The fussy feckless silly bleating lamb
Condemned to drudge, to labor and take pains
Without an equal competence of brains.

M. J. Fox (ed), *The history of Queensland*, 2 (Brisb, 1921); PD (Qld), 1867, 316, 1868; SMH, 21 Oct 1910; H. M. Chester, Autobiography (ML); letter, MS 275 (Dixson Lib, Syd); Parkes letters (ML).   H. J. GIBBNEY

LAMB, SIR HORACE (1849-1934), mathematician, was born on 27 November 1849 at Stockport, Cheshire, England, son of John Lamb and his wife Elizabeth, née Rangeley. After his father died his mother remarried and Horace was brought up by her sister. He was educated at Stockport Grammar School where Rev. Charles Hamilton was headmaster and Frederick Slaney Poole a junior classics master. In 1867 Lamb won a classical scholarship at Queens' College, Cambridge, but was considered too young and went for a year to Owens College, Manchester, where he was influenced to study mathematics at Cambridge. In 1868 he was elected to a minor scholarship at Trinity College (B.A., 1872; M.A., 1875); in his first degree he was second wrangler in the Mathematical Tripos and was elected a fellow and lecturer of his college.

On 6 November 1874 the Act founding the University of Adelaide received the governor's assent and Thomas Elder [q.v.] donated £20,000 to the new university. The council decided to use this gift to found two professorships, one of them in mathematics. Meanwhile, Poole had migrated to South Australia and, knowing that Lamb was about to marry Elizabeth Foot, of Dublin, sister-in-law of Charles Hamilton, and would therefore have to resign his fellowship at Trinity, he wrote in 1875 to Lamb suggesting that he apply for the chair in Adelaide. Lamb was duly appointed and arrived with his wife in South Australia in March 1876 in time for the university's inauguration in April.

As one of the first four professors Lamb was prominent in establishing the academic and administrative structure of the university. He lectured in pure and applied mathematics as well as giving instruction in practical physics. The early experiment with evening lectures for students was not a success and the council arranged instead for the professors to give evening lectures to the general public on subjects which were to 'be handled in a manner at once scientific and popular'. Lamb's public lectures indicated his breadth and versatility, and included 'Sound and the Physical Basis of Music' and 'Optics with special reference to the Theory of Vision' in 1877, 'The Earth and our Knowledge of It' in 1878, 'Demonstrations in Physics' in 1879, 'The Scientific Principles involved in Electric Lighting and in the Electric Transmission of Power' in 1882 and 'Acoustics' in 1884. His *Treatise on the Motion of Fluids* had been published at Cambridge in 1879; retitled *Hydrodynamics* in 1895, it ran to many editions and was one of the masterly classics of applied mathematics. He was elected a fellow of the Royal Society in 1884.

In 1885 the University of Adelaide granted Lamb leave to enable him to visit England. He was farewelled from Adelaide by his colleagues and students who presented him with an address engrossed upon vellum: 'We who have enjoyed the rare privilege of sitting at the feet of so able an instructor as yourself gladly avail ourselves of the occasion . . . to express in some slight form our high appreciation of your ripe scholarship and the universal esteem in which you are held. The zeal displayed in the discharge of your arduous duties, and the interesting and happy manner in which you have delivered your able lectures will not soon be forgotten by those who have attended them. Your ready and generous assistance in times of difficulty, and the kind interest you have always shown in our welfare, have become bywords to us who in the pursuance of our studies have come under your care'. Lamb did not return to Adelaide but accepted appointment as professor of mathematics at Owens College and held that post until he retired in 1920. His last years were spent at Cambridge as an honorary fellow of Trinity College and as Rayleigh lecturer. After a brief illness he died at Cambridge on 4 December 1934.

The first six of Lamb's seven children were born in Adelaide. The eldest, Helen, became tutor in charge of Peele Hall, Newnham College, Cambridge; Ernest, the eldest son, became professor of engineering, Queen Mary College, University of London; the second son, Walter, was secretary of the Royal Academy of Arts, London, and was knighted; Henry became a fellow of the Royal Academy and was a well-known portrait painter and war artist.

Lamb won many honorary degrees and other academic distinctions. He served twice as vice-president of the Royal Society, received a royal medal in 1902 and in 1923 the Copley medal in recognition of his prominence and successful work in applied mathematics and was knighted in 1931. Later editions of *Hydrodynamics* incorporate the results of some of his many research papers, and among his other books, *Infinitesimal Calculus* (1897), *Dynamical Theory of Sound* (1910), *Statics* (1912), *Dynamics* (1913) and *Higher Mechanics* (1920), were adopted as texts in many English and Australian universities and greatly influenced progress in the teaching and research in applied mathematics. Lord Rutherford, when presenting Lamb's portrait to the University of Manchester in 1913, described Lamb as reaching 'more nearly my ideal of a university professor than anyone I have known'.

Univ Adelaide, *Calendar*, 1877; *Obituary notices of fellows of the Royal Society*, Dec 1935; *Register* (Adel), 30 July 1885; *The Times*, 5 Dec 1934.   R. B. POTTS

LAMB, JOHN DE VILLIERS (1833-1900), merchant, pastoralist and businessman, was born on 15 December 1833 at Millers Point, Sydney, fifth son of John Lamb [q.v.] and his wife Emma Trant, née Robinson. He joined his eldest brother Walter [q.v.] in Lamb, Parbury & Co. in January 1857 and took up a cattle run on the Bulloo River. He later joined P. Roberts as partner and manager of Murroo station near Mudgee where he established 'a high-class stud flock'. With Roberts he bought and occupied Coomoo Coomoo station in the Liverpool Plains district. By the mid-1860s Lamb had vast pastoral interests: Grevilia in the Port Curtis district, 7 runs totalling some 126,000 acres in the Burnett district, 18 runs totalling 972 square miles in the Warrego district and 13 runs in New South Wales mostly in the Albert and Warrego districts. His advice was often sought on pastoral matters; he was an examiner of applicants for inspecting sheep, chairman of the metropolitan sheep district, president of the Rabbit Destruction Commission, and in 1899 gave evidence to the royal commission on tuberculosis and other stock diseases.

Lamb's wide business interests included local directorships in English insurance companies and partnerships in pearling and mining ventures; he was also director of the North Shore Gas Co. and chairman of the Australian Kerosene Oil and Mineral Co. and the Australasian Mortgage and Agency Co. Ltd. In the 1890s he was a London director of the Commercial Banking Co. of Sydney. He imported Shorthorn cattle and trotting horses and was a well-known horse judge. Prominent in sporting circles, he helped to found the Royal Sydney Yacht Squadron in 1862, became a prominent official in the Australian Jockey Club and was renowned as an amateur whip and cross-country rider. A founding member of the Union Club, he was a councillor of the Agricultural Society of New South Wales and of the Church of England Grammar School, North Sydney. He was also an officer in the New South Wales Volunteer Corps. He lived for years at Maroomba, Chatswood, and died at Uralla, 22 Bayswater Road, Darlinghurst, on 25 March 1900. He was survived by his wife Henrietta Octavia (1839-1914), eighth daughter of Rev. Thomas Smith, whom he had married at St Mark's, Sydney, on 22 January 1859, and by two daughters and five sons, two of whom served in the South African war where one was killed. Lamb's estate was sworn for probate with assets of £7000 and debts amounting to £16,000; his debts were discharged and probate was granted on 11 March 1901.

SMH, 26 Mar 1900; *Pastoral Review*, 14 Apr 1900; Macarthur papers (ML).   G. P. WALSH

LAMB, WALTER (1825-1906), businessman and pastoralist, was born on 8 January 1825 in London, eldest son of John Lamb [q.v.] and his wife Emma Trant, née Robinson. He arrived in Sydney with his parents in the *Resource* on 6 May 1829 and was later educated at W. T. Cape's [q.v.] school and Sydney College. At 15 he became a clerk in his father's firm and at 22 a partner in Lamb, Spry & Co. On his return from a visit to England in February 1857 he, his brother John [q.v.] and Charles Parbury carried on as Lamb, Parbury & Co. In January 1855 Lamb had become an original shareholder and director of the Colonial Sugar Refining Co. and in 1880 chairman. By 1860 he was a director of the Commercial Banking Co. of Sydney, the Australian General Assurance Co. and the Sydney Exchange Co., and had served on the committees of the Sydney Chamber of Commerce and the Union Club.

In 1862-63 he revisited England. On his return he retired from the importing business. In the 1860s Lamb, Parbury & Lamb held 11 square miles on the Darling Downs and 10 stations totalling 238,000 acres in the Leichhardt district of Queensland. Lamb turned to grazing and farming, first at Greystanes near Liverpool, where he bred Shorthorn cattle, then at Merilong on the Liverpool Plains and Rooty Hill near Sydney. He claimed to be the first pastoralist to preserve native grass fodder on a large scale for dry seasons: in 1889 he had about 2000 tons of ensilage at Merilong. He visited

England again in 1882-83 and in 1884 decided to establish a cannery and fruit preserving works on his Woodstock estate at Plumpton (Rooty Hill). A £10,000 family company was formed and part of the estate leased to smallholders for the cultivation of stone fruits. Lamb studied the canning process in California and brought back R. Lister as his manager. The cannery opened late in 1887 and was successful until November 1893 when Lamb went bankrupt.

Lamb was a local director of several English insurance companies and the English, Scottish and Australian Chartered Bank. He was a director of the Sydney Infirmary and Dispensary, a trustee of the National Park in 1879 and president of the Union Club in 1878-82. He had been appointed a lieutenant in the Sydney Volunteer Rifles in September 1854 and was later a vice-president of the Rifle Association. A good judge of horses and a promoter of coursing, he introduced the new Plumpton system of coursing to the colonies at his Rooty Hill estate and later sold his grounds to the New South Wales Coursing Club. He twice refused Henry Parkes's [q.v.] offer of a seat in the Legislative Council before serving as a member in 1889-93. He claimed to have been a staunch protectionist since 1867 and favoured payment of members, early closing and was generally sympathetic towards labour interests. He protested against the proliferation of gambling, sweeps and totalisators, and advocated their proper control; in August 1891 he forecast that 'New South Wales will become the Monaco of the Australias and Sydney will be its Monte Carlo'.

Lamb died at Plumpton, Rooty Hill, on 13 November 1906 and was buried in the Anglican section of Rookwood cemetery. Probate was not granted until April 1918 when his estate was sworn at £10. He was survived by a daughter of his first wife, Jane (d. 1855), fourth daughter of William Cox, whom he had married in 1846, and by three sons and four daughters of his second wife Margaret Elizabeth (d. 1901), daughter of Henry Dangar [q.v.], whom he had married on 11 February 1858 at St Michael's Church, Surry Hills.

V&P (LA NSW), 1858, 3, 566, 580; *Town and Country J*, 22 Apr 1882, 15 Oct 1887, 23 Mar, 7 Sept 1889, 6 Feb 1892; SMH, 14 Nov 1906; *Pastoral Review*, 15 Dec 1906; Parkes letters (ML); MS cat under W. Lamb (ML).
G. P. WALSH

LANDSBOROUGH, WILLIAM (1825-1886), explorer, was born on 21 February 1825 at Stevenston, near Saltcoats, Ayrshire,

Scotland, son of Dr David Landsborough, clergyman, entomologist and artist, and his wife Margaret, née McLeish. Educated in Irvine, he migrated in 1841 to New South Wales where his elder brothers held two stations in New England. By 1850 an expert bushman he leased a near-by run and next year joined the gold rush to Bathurst with some success. In 1854 he followed his brothers north to Monduran, their station on the Kolan River, and with various partners applied for leases. He explored and named Mount Nebo in 1856 and later leased blocks in the area. He explored around Broad Sound in 1857, the Comet and Nogoa Rivers in 1858 and with Stewart examined the Bonar (Bowen) River in 1859. They reached Torrens Creek and looked carefully for traces of Leichhardt [q.v.]. From Rockhampton he then went with Nat Buchanan [q.v.] in search of new pastures, and traced Aramac Creek and the Thomson River. Their food ran out but they found good country. In 1861 Landsborough applied for 15 runs of 100 square miles each and with Buchanan and Edward Cornish formed the Landsborough River Co. to stock the new 'Plains of Promise', which he named Bowen Downs. To raise capital he sold all his stations except Glenprairie near Broad Sound. He also mortgaged Bowen Downs to the Scottish Australian Co. through its agents, R. A. A. Morehead [q.v.] and Matthew Young, thereby forfeiting his place in management of the stations, although he held a quarter of the shares until 1869.

In 1861 Landsborough was chosen by the Victorian and Queensland governments to lead a search for Burke and Wills [qq.v.] from the Gulf of Carpentaria southwards. In August the party left Brisbane in the brig *Firefly*, escorted by H.M.S. *Victoria*. In a cyclone the brig was driven on to a reef sixty miles south-east of Cape York. The frightened horses were unable to escape until Landsborough had the deck 'cut down to the water's edge'; all but one managed to swim to a near-by island. When the sea calmed, the *Victoria* pulled the *Firefly* off the reef. After makeshift repairs the brig was reloaded and in October arrived at Sweers Island in the Gulf of Carpentaria. A depot was formed on the Albert River at the site of Burketown and in November the party of 8, including 4 Aboriginals, and 25 horses started south. Landsborough followed the Gregory River and named the Barkly Tableland but near the site of Camooweal found desert with a network of dry channels. Realizing that rain could flood the country and isolate his starving party, Landsborough struggled back to the Burketown depot in January 1862.

With supplies from the *Victoria* he led his men south, 'hopping' from river to river. They encountered hostile Aboriginals on the Barcoo and on the Warrego their rations were reduced to boiled greenhide. On 21 May they reached Williams's station and learned that Burke and Wills had perished. With bulging tucker bags Landsborough continued his journey south and in October delivered the horses and gear to the authorities in Melbourne. He was fêted as the first explorer to cross the continent from north to south. He reported to the Royal Society on his route and the quality of land he had seen and at a reception in the Exhibition Building was presented with inscribed plate valued at £500. Critics in the Brisbane press had claimed that his search for Burke was a secondary objective because he had been commissioned by graziers to find good land. He emphatically denied these charges but *Journal of Landsborough's Expedition from Carpentaria* (Melbourne, 1862) and *Exploration of Australia from Carpentaria to Melbourne* (London, 1866) publicly revealed the locations of the best country he had traversed. In 1862 his second-in-command, George Bourne, also published his journal of the expedition in Melbourne. These reports led to a frenzied rush into the gulf country.

At a function in Sydney Landsborough had met Caroline Hollingworth Raine. They were married on 30 December 1862 and left for Britain where he was given a gold watch by the Royal Geographical Society in London and visited relations. He returned to Brisbane to find that he no longer owned Glenprairie; no record of its sale could be traced but rumour had his attorney losing the station on a throw of dice. Landsborough had been nominated for life to the Legislative Council. He took his seat on 2 May 1865 but resigned on the 11th. After a week he was reappointed but resigned again on 23 September. He then became police magistrate and commissioner of crown lands in Carpentaria. He found Burketown full of thieves and criminals fleeing from the law, and reprisals against Aboriginals for killing sheep and cattle were common. To keep order he recommended W. D. Uhr [q.v.] to lead a local band of native police. Appointed, he carried out his duties with zest but became truculent and even threatened to chain Landsborough to a tree like other law breakers. Other difficulties proliferated but the gulf townships prospered so rapidly that settlers began to boast that the area would soon become a separate colony. High officers in Brisbane proposed to appoint Landsborough government resident on the ground that he would then be able to make decisions without reference to the capital and thus prevent delays of at least three months. Unfortunately Landsborough and another magistrate made a mistake on the bench. Untrained and with no local lawyers to consult, they had decided a case against Uhr under the Masters and Servants Act instead of the Polynesian Labourers Act.

In September 1870 Landsborough was summarily dismissed as police magisrate and his name was struck off the roll of justices. Indignant residents in Carpentaria protested to the government on his behalf but in vain. On 24 March 1872 he left Burketown to defend himself in Brisbane but the quest was unsuccessful. He had lived too long in the bush to know any influential politicians. In 1872 the government appointed him to survey a road from St George to Cunnamulla and later commissioned him to clear the track. In sizzling heat twenty-three miles of the road had been cut but he was dismissed for 'paying his men the enormous high wage of 10 pence per hour'. He went to Stanthorpe where tin had been newly found in large quantities; he did well by mining alluvial tin.

Landsborough's wife had died of tuberculosis, leaving three daughters. Though friends cared for them he longed to be with them and to his joy he was made an inspector in the new Brands Office. He collected his daughters and made a home at Toowong. Worried about the girls being alone while he was at work, he sought an introduction to Maria Theresa Carr, née Carter, whom he had seen in church. A gifted musician but inefficient in business, she welcomed his proposal and they were married at Brisbane on 8 March 1873.

In 1877 Landsborough was restored to the Commission of the Peace. On 27 September 1882 the government rewarded him with £2000 for his explorations. He used the money to buy a property, which he named Loch Lamerough, at Caloundra. Hardships as an explorer made him a sufferer from chronic indigestion. He died on 16 March 1886 and was buried on his land, survived by three daughters and three sons. In 1913 his widow had his remains moved to the Toowong cemetery where a monument is over his grave; another is near his first grave. His journals are in the Oxley Library, Brisbane. His name is commemorated in Queensland by a town and an inlet near Burketown. In 1862 a gold-mining town in Victoria was named in his honour.

D. S. Macmillan (ed), *Bowen Downs, 1863-1963* (Syd, 1963); T. Welsby, 'William Landsborough—explorer', *JRHSQ*, 2 (1920-35); *Examiner* (Melb), 23 Aug, 6 Sept, 4 Oct, 15 Nov 1862; *Town and Country J*, 14 Apr 1877; *Brisbane Courier*, 17 Mar 1886.

GWEN TRUNDLE*

LANG, JOHN (1816-1864), barrister and novelist, was born on 19 December 1816 in Sydney, the second and posthumous son of Walter Lang, merchant adventurer, and his wife Elizabeth, née Harris, colonial-born 'niece' of James Larra [q.v.]. Elizabeth's second marriage was to Joseph Underwood [q.v.] of Ashfield Park, where Lang spent his boyhood and was guided in his early education by a family friend Dr William Bland [q.v.]. He later went to Sydney College under W. T. Cape [q.v.] and became one of its most outstanding scholars, publishing in 1835 a translation of *Horace's First Satire*, dedicated to Cape. In March 1837 Lang went to England and next year matriculated to Trinity College, Cambridge, but was soon sent down for composing a 'quaint litany' considered blasphemous. He then read law at the Middle Temple and was called to the Bar in May 1841. Accompanied by his wife Lucy, née Peterson, of Wakefield, Yorkshire, whom he had married in February 1839, he returned to New South Wales in the *Lady Kennaway* in October 1841 and was admitted a barrister to the Supreme Court. His second child and only son was born at Ashfield Park in November.

Lang briskly entered the social and political life of the colony, but his emancipist family connexions prevented his full acceptance in certain circles. From London James Sheen Dowling [q.v.] wrote to his father, the chief justice in Sydney, 'Young Lang proceeds to the colony . . . you will find him a clever fellow but somewhat troublesome. His family connexions will somewhat mar his fortune, they will be stumbling blocks in his path; he has married a lady of very good connexions and she may help him out of the mess'. Lang ineptly opposed representative government in a public speech in February 1842 and on 19 April with his wife and children he left Sydney in the *Nabob* for Calcutta. His departure may also be linked with strong evidence that Lang wrote the rare work of fiction, *Legends of Australia*, issued between January and March in Sydney anonymously in parts and incomplete.

Until 1845 Lang practised at the Calcutta Bar but next year went to Meerut where he founded the *Mofussilite*, becoming sole proprietor and editor in 1849. Under his guidance it became one of the most important newspapers in India. Two of his novels *Too Clever by Half* and *Too Much Alike; or, the Three Calendars* appeared serially in its columns in 1853-54. He also continued his legal practice and appeared for the army contractor Ajoodia Pershad and the Ranee of Jhansi, in both cases receiving large fees and rich presents. Lang visited England in 1852-53 and 1854-59. He devoted his time to literary work, travelled widely in Europe and enjoyed many friends in London theatrical and literary circles. His contributions to periodicals included Charles Dickens's [q.v.] *Household Words* and *All the Year Round*, and to *Fraser's Magazine* and *The Times* and *Globe* newspapers. He published nine novels, a volume of short stories and a travel book, *Wanderings in India* (London, 1859). Only two of the works have an Australian background: *The Forger's Wife* (1855) which is almost identical in plot to his 'Charles Frederick Howard' in *Legends of Australia*, while *Botany Bay; or, True Tales of Early Australia* (London, 1859) is thinly disguised fiction of events and people in the convict period and will always remain Lang's main contribution to Australian literature. Although his wife survived him and no record of a divorce has been found, Lang married Margaret Wetter at Mussoorie in May 1861. He died there on 20 August 1864 and his headstone is in the English cemetery.

Lang's talent as a novelist was melodramatic and indifferent, except when he wrote of the scenes of his youth. To his later contemporaries he had, despite some human failings, a wide intellect, remarkable memory and sparkling wit. Through narrow social sanction Australia lost one of its most brilliant sons and its first native-born novelist.

W. Forbes-Mitchell, *Reminiscences of the great mutiny, 1857-59* (Lond, 1893); Surendra Nath Sen, *Eighteen fifty seven* (Delhi, 1957); J. W. Earnshaw, 'Legends of Australia & John Lang', *Biblionews*, April 1958; C. Roderick, 'John Lang. First Australian-born novelist', *JRAHS*, 49 (1963-64); S. J. Routh, 'The Australian career of John Lang, novelist', *Aust Literary Studies*, June 1964; *Mofussilite*, 26 Aug 1864; Lang papers (held by author).

JOHN EARNSHAW

LANG, MATTHEW (1830-1893), wine and spirits merchant, was born on 6 May 1830 at Airdrie, Lanarkshire, Scotland, son of Matthew Lang, builder, and his wife Margaret, née London. He was educated locally and then joined Mackie, Gladstone & Co., wine and spirits merchants of Liverpool. He was sent to open a branch in Melbourne where he arrived in February 1854. He started business in Elizabeth Street but soon moved to larger premises and bought out his Liverpool sponsors. Lang sold only imported spirits and objected to the tariff as it tempted him to follow the current practice of mixing colonial with imported spirits. Lang had married Jane Scott in 1857 and in the early 1880s with his brother-in-law, Alexander Scott, as a partner he bought

Dixon & Co.'s aerated-water factory and built large cellars under his premises in Collins and Market Streets.

Lang did not confine himself to the wine and spirits trade and the large Mount Poole station near Milparinka, New South Wales, was only one of his many other interests. He was a director of Terry's West End and the Carlton breweries, the National Insurance Co., the Equity Trustees Executors and Agency Co., the National Fire Insurance Co., the Commercial Bank of Australia and Gillespie Bros.

In 1876 Lang was elected to the City Council but resigned in 1881 to visit Britain. In February 1889 he was re-elected and in October became mayor, an office he held for three consecutive terms: he was reputed to hear the Post Office chimes ringing out 'Return again Matthew Lang, thrice Mayor of Melbourne'. Lang arranged for the recruitment of some 2000 special constables during the maritime strike of 1890. He was active in building desiccators, installing food markets in Flinders Street and lighting the city by electricity, though these projects were not finished during his term. He advocated expansion of the rural population for 'at present the head of the colony is too large for the body'. He also struggled for the creation of the Metropolitan Board of Works, became its temporary chairman and in 1891 represented the City Council but declared that he would vote as a free agent or not at all. In 1892 the council celebrated its jubilee and Lang, ably assisted by his wife, a prominent charity organizer, gave a ball for 1700 and a lunch for the surviving citizens of 1842.

At the first annual meeting of the Australian Church in November 1886 Lang was elected to the committee of management. He was a Harbor Trust commissioner in 1886-93 and had a stormy year as president of the Royal Caledonian Society in 1891-92. He was also interested in politics but only entered parliament when it seemed ungracious to continue to refuse the deputation of influential electors for South Yarra Province. He was elected to the Legislative Council in November 1892 and 'quickly gained an insight into all [its] business'. His sudden death at his home in Sandringham on 2 March 1893 caused widespread regret and he was mourned as a 'strong man of sound ripe judgment, commercial knowledge', great integrity and 'warm hearted generosity'. He was buried in the Presbyterian section of the Boroondara cemetery; his estate of £52,800 was left mostly to his family.

A. Sutherland et al, *Victoria and its metropolis*, 2 (Melb, 1888); A. H. Chisholm, *Scots*

wha hae, history of the Royal Caledonian Society of Melbourne (Syd, 1950); *Argus*, 10 Oct, 10 Nov 1891, 9, 10 Nov 1892, 3 Mar 1893; *Age*, 3 Mar 1893; *Weekly Times* (Melb), 4 Mar 1893.
                                          J. ANN HONE

LANGHAM, FREDERICK (1833-1903), Wesleyan missionary, was born on 24 April 1833 at Launceston, Van Diemen's Land, son of Samuel Langham, builder, and his wife Eliza, née Robinson. Nurtured in a Methodist home he attended the Paterson Street Sunday school and was 'converted' under the ministry of Rev. William Butters [q.v.]. In 1847 the family moved to Victoria where Langham joined the Fitzroy Church. After two years training as a teacher in Britain he returned to Melbourne and on 16 November 1854 at Richmond married Ann Elizabeth Knight. In January 1855 Langham became headmaster of the Wesleyan Denominational School at Barker Street, Castlemaine, where he was a contemporary of S. W. Baker [q.v.] at the other Wesleyan school. Influenced by Rev. Thomas Raston to consider missionary work, Langham was prepared for the ministry by Rev. John Harcourt and in 1858 was received into the Victorian Conference. He was appointed to Fiji where he arrived in June.

Langham served at Lakemba in 1858-63, Bau in 1864-66 and Viwa in 1868-70. As one of the assertive 'colonial young men', he was resented at first by Rev. James Calvert [q.v.] and his colleagues, but Langham soon dominated the mission and was chairman of the Fiji district in 1869-94. From 1871 he lived at Bau where he won repute among Methodists as King Cakubau's adviser. Although his policies did not please all the missionaries, they accepted him as their spokesman. Believing himself the champion of the Fijians, he encouraged annexation by Britain, but often nettled the colonial administrators by his paternalism and lack of imagination. To his colleagues he was 'Father' Langham and Sir Arthur Gordon referred to him as 'The Cardinal'.

In 1874-75 and 1890 Langham and his wife visited Melbourne mainly for their health. They finally left Fiji in April 1895 and lived in Sydney where Langham worked on the revision of the Fijian Bible. Though always reluctant in Australia to travel on deputationary work, he identified himself with the Orange cause and was easily persuaded to give anti-Catholic missionary lectures, which involved him in public controversy with Cardinal Moran. In 1898 Langham went to England to see his New Testament through the press. The subsequent burning of some testaments at the Roman Catholic mission at Namosi received much publicity in Australia.

Langham's wife had helped his revision and was author of many Fijian hymns. Their adopted (European) daughter Annie Langham Lindsay died on 21 December 1901, just before the revised Old Testament was completed. His wife did not recover from this shock and died on 5 January 1902. Langham became a supernumerary in 1901 and travelled on deputationary work in Britain, mainly for the British and Foreign Bible Society, of which he was a life governor. He also shared in the 'simultaneous mission' of the Evangelical churches. In addition to the Fijian Bible he had published other works in Fijian, some in conjunction with other authors. Recommended by Sir William MacGregor, Langham was awarded a doctorate of divinity by the University of Glasgow. He died at Wilton Villa, Albion Grove, Hackney, on 21 June 1903 and was buried in Abney Park cemetery. Although he bequeathed a 'cannibal fork with human bone attached' to a sister in Melbourne, the rest of his Fijian collection was sold. He instructed his trustees to destroy his journals and correspondence but many of his original letters are in other collections.

Physically impressive with leonine hair and beard, Langham cut his missionary role in the cloth of the schoolmaster. As a disciplinarian his punishments were severe but tempered with justice; he once insisted on being caned by a wrongfully punished boy. His relentless energy and simple piety won him renown as a great missionary by his denomination and those of the religious public familiar with the romanticized version of his career.

C. F. G. Cumming, *At home in Fiji* (Lond, 1881); T. McCullagh, *Sir William McArthur* (Lond, 1891); A. H. Gordon, *Fiji: records of private and of public life, 1875-1880*, 1-4 (1897-1912); J. Colwell, *The illustrated history of Methodism* (Syd, 1904); C. F. G. Cumming, *Memories* (Lond, 1904); C. I. Benson (ed), *A century of Victorian Methodism* (Melb, 1935); *Methodist Recorder* (Lond), 23 Jan 1902, 3 July 1903; *Spectator and Methodist Chronicle*, 24 July 1903; *Bible Soc Mthly Reporter*, 1903; *British Mthly* (1903), 403; Methodist overseas mission papers (ML); MS and printed cats (ML and Dixson Lib, Syd).
                                       NIEL GUNSON

LANGLANDS, GEORGE (1803-1861), merchant and magistrate, was born at Dundee, Scotland, son of John Langlands, baker, and his wife Christian, née Thoms; he was a descendant of William Langlands (b. 1590) of Kilgraston. Educated at Dundee, he became a linen merchant at St Andrews and as a public-spirited citizen was elected mayor. In 1835 while chief magistrate he chaired the meeting of the Liberal and Re-forming Electors of St Andrews that sought Lord John Russell as the district's parliamentary candidate. He had married Betsy, daughter of Robert Ritchie; they had two sons and three daughters.

Encouraged by his brothers, Henry [q.v.] and Robert who had established a foundry in Melbourne, George sailed with his family in the *Lady Kennaway* and arrived at Port Phillip in December 1848. At the foundry he met the overlander, James Monckton Darlot, who had taken up the Brighton run in the Wimmera district, and who suggested that Langlands establish a store and post office on that station. For four weeks with three bullock drays laden with stores and household effects the family made a difficult journey north from Melbourne via Campbell's Creek and thence westerly till they camped on 30 June 1849 by the Wimmera River, where the teamsters' tracks from many stations met at the crossing. The tiny settlement of Horsham received official recognition in October when Langlands opened his log store and post office. The site later became the corner of Hamilton and Darlot Streets; near by was the family home also built of logs. This little outpost served squatters spreading west as far as the new colony's border, north beyond Lake Hindmarsh to the mallee country and south to the Glenelg River.

To ensure delivery of supplies for the stations Langlands set up a bullock dray service to Geelong and Melbourne and maintained it even when drivers charged £80 a ton as the gold discoveries increased costs. His early trading was mainly by barter: with the Aboriginals, sugar and clothing in exchange for wild game; with the settlers, station stores for wool, hides and tallow. While no local bank existed, rural produce was bought by tokens redeemable at Geelong. Although the lure of gold depleted the district's workforce Langlands benefited by trade with South Australians and other migrants overlanding to the diggings. His store, built in brick in 1854, became a focal centre for trading and for news and mail that took two weeks to arrive from Melbourne. In 1857 the district's first pack-horse mailman, Constantine Dougherty, future owner of the *Wimmera Star*, rode from the store to serve distant stations. Langlands also consigned regular shipments of rural products direct to England but suffered heavy loss when an entire cargo was lost at sea. He died aged 58 in Melbourne after a stroke on 9 February 1861.

However reticent, Langlands was a devout Presbyterian. He was described by Dougherty as 'the mentor of the town . . . a man of sterling character, and those who gained his confidence could always rely on his friendship and assistance'. Descendants are still highly respected in the city he founded.

H. Coulson, *Horsham centenary souvenir booklet* (Horsham, 1950); Langlands & Sons Pty Ltd, *A century of trading in Horsham, 1849-1949* (Horsham, 1951); L. J. Blake and K. H. Lovett, *Wimmera Shire centenary* (Horsham, 1962); papers held by the Langlands family.

                                    L. J. BLAKE

LANGRIDGE, GEORGE DAVID (1829-1891), politician, was born at Tunbridge Wells, Kent, England, son of William Langridge. Early left fatherless, he went to Banbury, Oxfordshire, where he became apprenticed to a carpenter and then went into partnership with his brother, a builder in London. In 1851 he married Maria Elizabeth, daughter of William Meade of Tunbridge Wells; they had nine sons and two daughters. The gold rushes brought Langridge to New South Wales where he spent three months before moving to Victoria in 1853. He was unsuccessful as a digger at Ballarat and Bendigo for six months but later recalled that he had been hunted for his licence. He settled at Collingwood and for two years worked as a carpenter on the building of Melbourne's military barracks before establishing his own contracting business. In 1869 he opened an auctioneering and estate agency firm; by 1881 he had established three building societies, the most important being the Langridge Mutual Permanent Building Society. In 1866 he had been elected to the Collingwood Town Council and was mayor in 1867 and 1872. On 18 February 1874 his wife died; on 13 December 1877 at the Wesleyan Chapel, Glebe, Sydney, he married Emily Judson, widowed daughter of John Holt, grocer, and his wife Betty, née Greenwood.

In 1874-91 Langridge represented Collingwood in the Legislative Assembly. His background and his urban working-class constituency were determining factors in his staunch and uncritical support of the Liberal leader, Graham Berry [q.v.]. He began by voting against payment of members but by 1877 decided 'to put myself right with my constituents, because it was against their wishes that I voted as I did'. He was an unspectacular back-bencher but in 1875 chaired the royal commission on friendly societies and in 1877 had a leading role in the relevant amending legislation. In 1878 Langridge served on the royal commission on closed roads and in 1885 was chairman of a select committee on the fire brigade system. From August 1880 to July 1881 he was commissioner of public works and vice-president of the Board of Land and Works in the third Berry ministry. His term of office was unremarkable save for the controversy over his decision to use 'Stawell' stone in the façade of the parliamentary buildings. He was a member of the 'Berryite' Opposition during the O'Loghlen [q.v.] ministry in 1881-83. From March 1883 to February 1886 Langridge was a competent commissioner of trade and customs in the Service [q.v.]-Berry coalition. Because of ill health he did not seek office in the Gillies [q.v.]-Deakin coalition in 1886-90 and left in July 1886 for a year's holiday in England. After his return he supported the ministry, but in October 1890 he criticized the government for its awkward handling of the maritime strike and acquiescence in Lieut-Colonel Price's provocative instructions during the crisis. Langridge was one of the seceding Coalition-Liberals who helped to defeat the government in early November 1890. He then became chief secretary, commissioner of customs and minister of health in the Liberal ministry of James Munro [q.v.]. He was acting premier in Munro's absence when he died suddenly on 24 March 1891 at his home in Clifton Hill, aged 62.

Langridge was a grand master of the Manchester Unity Independent Order of Odd Fellows, a Freemason and a member of the United Ancient Order of Druids. He was actively associated with various international trade exhibitions. He was a member of the Melbourne Water Supply Board and in 1891 treasurer of the Working Men's College. His unassuming ways and common sense in politics enabled him to retain the warm allegiance of working-class electors who were becoming dissatisfied with other Liberal representatives. His public meetings at Collingwood were gala occasions: he never lost the common touch, and artisans and labourers mourned his death in impressive numbers. Significantly, an early Labor politician, John Hancock, followed Langridge at Collingwood.

Federal Australian, 26 Apr 1883; *Imperial Review* (Melb), Oct 1887; *Argus*, 25 Mar 1891; *Leader* (Melb), 28 Mar 1891; *Observer* (Collingwood), 2 Apr 1891.   S. M. INGHAM

LANGTON, EDWARD (1828-1905), politician, was born on 2 January 1828 at Gravesend, Kent, England, youngest son of David Elland Langton, butcher, and his wife Mary, née Payne. Educated at a private school, he helped to establish schools and was secretary of the local Mechanics' Literary Institute before migrating to Melbourne at 24. On 7 March 1854 he married Jane

Eliza Pettifer. From about 1859-65 Langton was in partnership with his brother in a butcher's shop at Collingwood. He then made a career as accountant and average adjuster.

Langton first became involved in politics in the late 1850s, joining the committee which agitated for the separation of Fitzroy Ward from the City of Melbourne. When this was granted he served in 1859-60 as one of the new borough's first councillors. From 1859 he made several attempts to enter colonial politics and was elected for East Melbourne in January 1866 and in 1868 for West Melbourne. His initial political impetus was provided by the Free Trade League of which he was secretary from April 1865 to about March 1866. The league gave him a salary of £750 and paid his election expenses. A tireless worker he was also proprietor of the *Spectator*, a free-trade weekly which ran from July 1865 to March 1867.

In the constitutional crisis which ended in 1868 Langton led the conservatives in the assembly. When Sladen [q.v.] was asked to form a government, Langton became treasurer but the ministry lasted only from May to July. When Duffy [q.v.] became premier in June 1871 Langton was again offered a portfolio but refused. In 1872-74 he was treasurer and postmaster-general in the Francis [q.v.] administration and distinguished himself in a ministry that was often turbulent and inefficient. He was responsible for the reform of public book-keeping, the replacement of multiple loans by a single loan system and the change of the financial year from January-December to July-June. When Francis resigned in 1874 Langton hoped to become premier, but he had made many enemies. They included J. J. Casey [q.v.] who refused to serve under him. When G. B. Kerferd [q.v.] was chosen to lead the government Langton joined G. Berry and J. McCulloch [qq.v.] in the Opposition and contributed to Kerferd's defeat on his first budget. As the general election of 1877 approached, radical influence again dominated the political scene. West Melbourne had ceased to be a free-trade stronghold and despite a vigorous campaign and the revival in 1876 of the Free Trade League, Langton was defeated. Further attempts to re-enter parliament failed, chiefly because of his virulent tongue, his uncompromising attitude on free trade, his hatred of Gladstone and the legal battle which he initiated with the *Age* before the 1877 election. Although he had two victories in court, the publicity was politically ruinous.

In private life Langton had unostentatious but educated tastes. He was a director of several companies, a regular contributor to the press and sometime member of the literary staff and leader writer for the *Argus*. In 1874 he became an honorary member of the Cobden Club and for many years was vice-president of trustees of the Melbourne Public Library and Museum, and sometime president of the Institute of Accountants. Among his publications were *Bicentenary Celebration. The Act of Uniformity: its antecedents and results* (1862), *A Lecture on Free Trade* (1865) and *The Fiscal System of Victoria* (1880). He died of pneumonia at his home in Toorak on 5 October 1905, survived by a daughter and one of his two sons.

C. E. Sayers, *David Syme; a life* (Melb, 1965); *Ovens and Murray Advertiser*, 4 Apr 1874; *Age*, Jan-June 1877; *Argus*, Jan-June 1877, 25 Mar 1903, 5 Oct 1905, 7 Apr 1913; *Table Talk*, 14 Apr 1892; J. E. Parnaby, The economic and political development of Victoria, 1877-1881 (Ph.D. thesis, Univ Melb, 1951); G. R. Bartlett, Political organization and society in Victoria 1864-1883 (Ph.D. thesis, ANU, 1964); Haddon papers (LaT L). JEAN COOKSLEY

LANIGAN, WILLIAM (1820-1900), Roman Catholic bishop, was born in May 1820 at Lisdaleen, Tipperary, Ireland, son of Thomas Lanigan and his wife Brigid Anastasia, née Dauton. He studied at St Patrick's College, Thurles, and at Maynooth, where he was ordained on 8 April 1848. He worked mostly at Kilcummin and Bansha. In 1859 he applied for leave to go to Sydney at the invitation of Archdeacon McEncroe [q.v.], and was highly commended by his archbishop. He reached Sydney in December 1859, served under Father McAlroy [q.v.] in Goulburn and in 1861 made his headquarters at Berrima. On 19 April 1867 he was appointed to the vacant see of Goulburn in rather unexpected circumstances after Bishop Geoghegan [q.v.] had died in Ireland, Dean Hanly of Yass had declined and McAlroy was excluded as too implicated in the manoeuvring. Throughout his long episcopate Lanigan was a solid if dour and unexciting church ruler who had the advantage of an active team of priests including P. Dunne, P. Bermingham [qq.v.] and McAlroy and the guidance of Bishop Matthew Quinn [q.v.] of Bathurst.

Lanigan's main contribution to the evolution of Catholicity in Australia was made in helping to counter Archbishop Polding's [q.v.] policy of fusing English and Irish elements into a new Australian culture. In the early 1870s Rome was persuaded by Cardinal Cullen [q.v.], McEncroe, Bermingham and others that the future of the Church in Australia lay with the local Irish laity led

by bishops and priests, imported if possible direct from Ireland, where a supply of clergy and teachers was waiting to be tapped by leaders who would promise them missionary activity and freedom from English rule.

Advantage was taken of Polding's absence overseas to have Lanigan consecrated at Goulburn Cathedral on 2 June 1867 by Bishops J. and M. Quinn and J. Murray [qq.v.]. After the ceremony defiant speeches were made on the education question and the four prelates proffered advice to Rome on future policy. At a later farewell to the bishops on their way to the Vatican Council, Polding's proposal for a united Australian attitude in the Church was brusquely rejected by Lanigan. He also passed over the more experienced Hanly and chose McAlroy as his vicar-general. Four of his ten priests took the hint and returned to Sydney, but with habitual lack of humour he protested about Hanly's departure. The new authoritarian pattern of Irish Catholicism was beginning to prevail and the last vestiges of the old pioneer days were disappearing. At Bishop Lanigan's golden jubilee of ordination in 1898 the enormous growth of the diocese was described and it was noted that none of the clergy were native-born although the teaching orders were getting recruits.

Lanigan fully supported Archbishop Vaughan [q.v.] in his fight for Catholic education. Within his own diocese he introduced the Christian Brothers in 1874, the Patrician Brothers in 1886, the Presentation Sisters in 1874, the Brigidines in 1883 and the Passionist Fathers in 1890. He joined his fellow bishops in insisting on diocesan Josephite Sisters and took his first foundation from Perthville in 1882. Aged 80 Lanigan died at Goulburn from senile decay on 13 June 1900 and was buried in the sanctuary of Saints Peter's and Paul's Cathedral.

T. L. Suttor, *Hierarchy and democracy in Australia, 1788-1870* (Melb, 1965); J. O'Brien, 'In diebus illus', *A'sian Catholic Record*, 20-21 (1943-44); J. P. O'Malley, 'Bishop Lanigan', *A'sian Catholic Record*, 44 (1967); *Daily Telegraph* (Syd), 15, 16 June 1900; Roman Catholic Archives (Syd). C. J. DUFFY

LANSELL, GEORGE (1823-1906), mining entrepreneur, was born on 24 August 1823 at Margate, Kent, England, eldest son of Thomas Lansell, soap and candle maker, and his wife Elizabeth, née Budds. At 14 he entered his father's business where he worked until a younger brother, Wootten, who had been a sailor on convict ships to Australia, suggested that his brothers George and William migrate to Australia.

They went to South Australia in 1853. For six weeks George sought gold at Echunga but returned to Adelaide and worked at his trade. In 1854 the three brothers walked to Bendigo and set up as butchers and soap and candle manufacturers. The business prospered for three years although they had to move the boiling-down works to a less offensive position away from the developing town. In 1855 stockbrokers who met in his shop persuaded Lansell to invest in small quartz-mining companies. He lost heavily but worked and saved; he then put money into other claims and lost again. About 1860 he realized that the methods of quartz-mining were generally inefficient but he continued buying, increasing his own expertise and knowledge, though losing money through company crashes.

The tide turned in 1865, a disastrous year for Bendigo, when Lansell bought many shares in the old Advance Co. and the Cinderella mine. Now able to dictate policy he instructed his miners to 'keep sinking'; both mines rewarded his persistence with new-found reefs. Most of his large profits were returned to the mines which he pushed ever deeper, and though costs were crippling his determination, common sense and shrewdness usually paid off. In the early 1870s he won a fortune from the Garden Gully mine and then, for £30,000, bought the 180 mine which had already revealed a fortune in gold. He pushed the shafts down to over 3750 feet, found lode after rich lode and became a millionaire. Proud of being a 'Bendigonian', he was largely responsible for introducing the diamond drill to quartz mining in Australia. He was famous in Bendigo, not so much for his fortune but for his tireless efforts to maintain the mining industry and thereby to provide employment. Under his influence other companies expanded and he constantly urged his miners to invest in mining stock themselves. 'Buy into stock on a good line of reef when they are low-priced, pay calls and wait' was almost his total business philosophy. He was also very generous and a great helper of lame dogs. He enjoyed his paternalism but it was more than lip service and he created a fund for the widows and orphaned children of Bendigo miners.

Lansell was twice married: first, to Bedelia Jarvis Mulqueen; and second, in London on 12 August 1883 to Harriett Edith Bassford by whom he had five sons and a daughter. He had settled in London early in the 1880s but after seven years he was petitioned by Bendigo townsmen to return and help to restore the declining industry. On the tailings of the 180 mine and within hearing of its batteries, he remodelled his villa, Fortuna, a mansion of over forty rooms, lavishly furnished with pieces collected from around the globe. He designed the spacious gardens with walks, lakes and imported plants.

Commonly known as 'Australia's Quartz-King', he was director of thirty-eight mines and had some link with almost every mine in Bendigo. He gave liberal support to local charities but attributed his unwillingness to enter public life to the memory of his father's ruin by politics when fighting for corn law repeal. At his death on 18 March 1906 Lansell was mentioned in all the churches and flags were flown at half-mast. Bendigo's concern over the family's intentions towards mining were swiftly allayed as the eldest son, George Victor, continued his father's policies. In admiration and gratitude for Lansell's 'indomitable courage and persistent enterprise' the community raised a statue in his honour.

W. B. Kimberly, *Bendigo and vicinity* (Melb, 1895); E. J. Brady, *Australia unlimited* (Melb, 1918); *Punch* (Melb), 11 Feb 1904; *Argus*, 19 Mar 1906; *Bendigo Independent*, 19 Mar 1906.

SUZANNE G. MELLOR

LAPORTE, FRANCOIS LOUIS NOMPAR DE CAUMONT, COMTE DE CASTELNAU (1810-1880), naturalist and diplomat, was born on 25 December 1810 in London. Travel books by Captain Cook [q.v.] and Le Vaillant were his childhood reading. He studied natural science in Paris under Baron Cuvier, Geoffroy Saint-Hilaire and other noted zoologists. In 1837-41 he travelled in the United States, Texas and Canada; in 1843-47 he went from Rio de Janeiro to Lima in South America, collecting specimens from the River Amazon. After the 1848 revolution he became French consul at Bahia, Brazil. In 1856-58 he travelled in South Africa and then in Asia. In Siam he was French consul and the first European to study the country's fishes. He arrived at Melbourne in 1862 and became consul-general for France in 1864. He visited Sydney and Brisbane in 1876, was an active member of the Zoological and Acclimatisation Society of Victoria and of the Entomological Society of New South Wales. He died at his home, Apsley Place, East Melbourne, on 4 February 1880.

According to E. Marin La Meslée [q.v.], for a time his private secretary, the count lived with a Brazilian mistress and her young son. Tall and slightly stooped, Laporte was 'a man of simple tastes who perhaps neglected his appearance' and so was thought eccentric. To many he seemed mean and aloof but he was generous and warm-hearted to those who knew him well and a gifted raconteur.

Laporte's industry was amazing. His earlier works were lavishly produced but his later papers are marred by some inaccuracies, perhaps because written in English. As Laporte or Delaporte and later Castelnau he wrote about ninety books and papers, some jointly with colleagues, on a variety of scientific subjects: geography, palaeontology and anthropology, mammals, birds, reptiles and his favourite fishes and insects. His monographs on insects, written in his youth, were collected into a sumptuous *Histoire Naturelle*, published between 1835 and 1841. He described his 1843-47 journey as *Expédition dans les parties centrales de l'Amérique du Sud* (Paris, 1850-59). African and Asian studies followed and in the 1860s his 'Notes on Australian Coleoptera' were published in the *Proceedings of the Royal Society of Victoria*, 8 (1867-68). Then he turned to ichthyology and in the 1870s published several papers on Australian fishes in Melbourne, Paris and Sydney. The genus *Laportea* (tropical stinging tree) was named after him as were many insects and fishes. In 1879 a naturalist was sent by station hands a creature, part platypus, part lung fish and part eel. The naturalist described it to Castelnau, who reported it to the Linnean Society in Sydney as an archaic fish which he named *Ompax spatuloides*. The hoax was not discovered for years.

E. Marin La Meslée, *L'Australie nouvelle* (Paris, 1883); A. Musgrave, *Bibliography of Australian entomology 1775-1930* (Syd, 1932); G. P. Whitley, 'Francois Laporte, Count Castelnau', *Aust Zoologist*, 13 (1965); *Argus*, 5 Feb 1880.   G. P. WHITLEY

LARDNER, JOHN (1839-1931), surveyor, was born in April 1839 in Galway, Ireland, son of Thomas Lardner, farmer, and his wife Maria, née Cavanagh. Privately educated, he was for some years engaged in surveying in Ireland. In 1863 he went to New Zealand where he worked with the Government Survey Department in Auckland and Otago Provinces until his departure in 1866 for Victoria where he joined the Surveyor-General's Department on 26 November. In 1867-78 he worked under J. T. Harding in the Melbourne district, Otway Ranges and Mornington Peninsula, continuing in the first two areas in 1868-70 under M. Callanan who later became surveyor-general. On 4 January 1869 Lardner received his certificate as a contract surveyor from the Land Surveyors Board. Succeeding Callanan as head of the party in 1870, Lardner was engaged in laying out streets and blocks in Parkville, Albert Park, St Kilda Road and Queen's Road until 1873 when he went to Brandy Creek and Warragul, surveying 10,000 acres of scrub land. In 1874 Lardner cut up 11,000 acres in the Koo Wee Rup swamp and later surveyed the Moe swamp for drainage. After two years in Melbourne he was transferred to Gippsland in 1877 where he laid out new townships between Pakenham and Morwell along the Gippsland railway then being built, and connecting roads to the coast. In 1880 Lardner started surveying roads and improving gradients in the South Gippsland Hills from Poowong to Foster, including a survey of Whitelaw's Track cut in 1874-75. In 1881 he worked in the Drouin area and in 1883-84 in the Mirboo district. With the building of the Great Southern Line, Lardner was called upon to survey the town sites along it, including those now at Leongatha, Korumburra, Meeniyan and Tarwin. On completion of this work Lardner was appointed land officer to the Bairnsdale district and in 1896 the Sale district. In 1899 he became district surveyor of Gippsland with Bairnsdale as headquarters until he retired on 30 September 1903. He then lived in Leongatha, where he died on 25 October 1931. Predeceased by his wife Annie, née Cosgrove, a son and a daughter, he was survived by two sons and three daughters.

In Bairnsdale Lardner had been a member of the rowing and football clubs and the hospital committee. A founder and first president of the Leongatha bowling club, he was also a member of the Victorian Institute of Surveyors, a commissioner for taking affidavits and declarations, chairman of the land classification board and classifier under the Land Tax Act. Lardner's Track, the township and school of Lardner and the township of Nyora, named by him after the native cherry, serve as his memorials.

South Gippsland Pioneers' Assn, *The land of the lyrebird* (Melb, 1920); H. Copeland, *The path of progress* (Warragul, 1934); C. Daley, *The story of Gippsland* (Melb, 1960); *Bairnsdale Advertiser*, 1 Oct 1903; *Great Southern Star*, 27 Oct 1931; Lands Department records (VA); information from Miss M. M. Lardner, Leongatha.   D. F. BISHOP

LARNACH, DONALD (1817-1896), banker and financier, was born on 17 July 1817 in Caithness, Scotland, son of William Larnach (d. 1829), naval purser, and his wife Margaret, née Smith. He arrived at Sydney in the *Numa* on 22 November 1834 to join an elder brother, John [q.v.]. Larnach became manager of Barker & Hallen's [qq.v.] steam flour-mill and bought it in 1842. He engaged in mercantile pursuits and speculated in town lots in Bathurst and Sydney as well as a run on the Lachlan River near Gunning. On 3 September 1845 at Trinity Church, Sydney, he married Jane Elizabeth, eldest daughter of William Walker [q.v.]. In that year he was appointed an auditor of the Bank of New South Wales and on 20 August 1846 elected a director. As general manager he wound up the affairs of the 'old' bank in 1850. In 1852-53 he was president of the new bank which profited from gold-buying; Larnach claimed the credit for the bank's innovation of buying on the gold-fields. He had become a magistrate for Sydney in 1847.

Larnach arrived in London with a fortune on 16 June 1853 to organize a branch of the Bank of New South Wales and was appointed managing director on 23 May 1854 at a salary of £1200. Next year he offered to resign and return to Australia when his brother James was detected 'dealing privately in discounts for his own benefit'. Nothing came of it, though he put up over £2000 as surety for his brother. Energetic and efficient, Larnach's expertise in money matters was recognized in 1866 when he was appointed chairman of the committee of leading bankers dealing with matters arising out of the failure of the Agra & Masterman's Bank.

A close friend of Henry Parkes [q.v.] in the 1860s, Larnach constantly urged him to subsidize migration to New South Wales and, convinced that the Riverina would eventually be separated, advised the government to make what it could from selling all the crown lands in the area. He floated loans on the London market for the New South Wales government and sometimes for the other colonies. When New South Wales debentures fell he arrested the decline by his heavy purchases, from which he later profited greatly. In the fiercely competitive scramble for capital, he showed skilful organization and timing to prevent clashes of interest, although he often demanded greater powers of discretion from colonial treasurers whom he thought ignorant of London conditions. In the early 1870s while Charles Cowper [q.v.] was ill, Larnach virtually ran the New South Wales agent-general's office in addition to his own work. Conservative and often critical of radical colonial banking practices, he increasingly deplored the dangerous borrowing of the Australian colonies and re-emphasized the advantages of subsidized migration on the North American example. He also had a different view of the functions of the London branch of his bank from those of Shepherd Smith [q.v.], and signs of a rift in their good understanding began to appear in 1878 when the board decided to take deposits in

London against Larnach's advice. He hinted that he might resign at the end of June 1879 but loan-raising commitments caused him to postpone his trip to the colonies and he was appointed chairman of the London board.

Larnach was also a director and president of the London Joint Stock Bank, a director of the Indemnity Mutual Marine Insurance Co. and an investor in other colonial banks and the Colonial Sugar Refining Co. He kept close touch with Australasian conditions through correspondence and friendships with many politicians, businessmen and squatters such as G. A. Lloyd and William Forster [qq.v.], to all of whom he dispensed useful advice. He revisited Australia in 1880-81 and 1886. In 1885 he had contributed £500 to the patriotic fund for the Sudan contingent. He was a member of the Australian Club in Sydney.

Larnach was a colourful figure for a banker and had an enthusiastic, considerate and pleasant nature. The bank's historian, R. F. Holder, describes him as 'energetic, self-confident, and sure of his own rectitude; to those with whom he disagreed he was often querulous, sometimes impatient, but invariably willing to speak his own mind'. Larnach had bought a country seat, Brambletye, East Grinstead, Sussex, and was high sheriff of the county in 1883. He also owned much real estate in Suffolk as well as the colonies. He died at 21 Kensington Palace Gardens on 12 May 1896, survived by his wife (d. 1908), two sons and a daughter. His estate was sworn for probate at under £258,383 in New South Wales, £7450 in Victoria and personalty in England at £619,935.

N. Gunson, *The good country: Cranbourne shire* (Melb, 1968); R. F. Holder, *Bank of New South Wales: a history*, 1-2 (Syd, 1970); *A'sian Insurance and Banking Record*, 15 Sept 1888, 19 May 1896, 20 Mar 1897; *Australasian*, 1 Apr 1893, 11 July 1896; *SMH*, 4 Mar 1895; *Town and Country J*, 23 May, 11 July 1896; Col Sec land letters (NSWA); Parkes letters (ML).

G. P. WALSH

LASCELLES, EDWARD HAREWOOD (1847-1917), pastoralist and businessman, was born on 3 October 1847 in Bothwell, Van Diemen's Land, son of Edwin Lascelles and his wife Eliza, née Nicholas; he was a grandson of T. A. Lascelles [q.v.]. After his mother died he and his sister went to their uncle, C. J. Dennys [q.v.], a wool-broker in Geelong. At 16 Edward joined his uncle, became a partner at 21 and the firm became Dennys Lascelles & Co. in 1875. Lascelles became an expert wool-classer and broker, and as the chief wool-valuer and manager he extended the business in both Geelong and Melbourne. He also experimented in wool production at Ingleby, a lease near Winchelsea, and substantially improved both quality and clip.

In the 1870s Lascelles became interested in the mallee area of north-western Victoria. In December 1876 he took over the Lake Corrong sheep station on Yarriambiac Creek. He worked this lease in partnership with Arthur Mandeville and Alfred Douglas until 1883 when he became sole lessee under the provisions of the Mallee Pastoral Leases Act. By then the property included the Minapre and Wilhelmina runs, and he took over the Tyrrell Downs run on the eastern side of Lake Tyrrell. For some time he also leased 106 square miles in the far western mallee, planning experiments in reclamation and farming methods under desert conditions, but had to abandon the run after parliamentary opposition on the ground that his holdings were already adequate.

On all his mallee properties Lascelles faced the great problem of vermin eradication and succeeded with rabbit-proof fencing, methods of poisoning and clearing. In the late 1880s he began to plan the subdivision of Lake Corrong run into 480-acre allotments for wheat growing. The surveyor, George Murdoch, also drew up plans for the new service centre of Hopetoun. E. H. Lascelles & Co. was formed and subdivision began in 1891 when the first sale of farm allotments and township blocks was held. An irrigation and town water supply was set up largely financed by Lascelles. Near by an experimental farm was laid out with lucerne and wheat paddocks, a large orchard and a vegetable garden. The farm became a show place and Lascelles revelled in this proof of the district's prospects. After overcoming government opposition he began to build the Beulah-Hopetoun railway in 1893 but in the financial crisis the line was completed by the government.

Lascelles was the first to introduce into Victoria the system of share-farming whereby the tenant delivered a third of his harvest to the company, but when yields were very low the company did not take its share. In the early 1890s the Hopetoun settlement grew, attracting settlers from South Australia and Britain as well as Victoria. Lascelles was the first president of Karkarooc Shire in 1896-97, and as managing director of the Mallee Agricultural and Pastoral Co. Ltd opened up the Tyrrell Downs property on the Hopetoun model. Unfortunately the start of the venture coincided with severe drought in 1895-1902. The Hopetoun settlement was sufficiently established to survive, but the company ran into debt. However, a larger percentage of Lascelles's settlers survived than those on government subdivisions, and he encouraged them to remain on their holdings by extending credit with the local store-keepers, writing off debts and issuing a meat ration at weekly 'killing days'. Although the company's mallee settlements were not a financial success, many wheat farmers were firmly established and the mallee proved itself as an excellent wheat-growing region.

Lascelles was for several years a commissioner of the Geelong Harbor Trust and was prominent in local rowing, tennis and golf clubs. He was a Baptist. Before the long-term success of his settlements became apparent, he died at Geelong on 12 February 1917. He had married Ethel, daughter of C. J. Dennys, in 1887. Of their six children three daughters survived him.

Geelong Advertiser, 13 Feb 1917; M. Conran letters and E. H. Lascelles out-letters (Univ Melb Archives); Lascelles family papers.

SHEILA F. WESSELS

LASSETTER, FREDERIC (1828-1911), merchant, was born in December 1828 at Taunton, Somerset, England, son of Matthew Lassetter (d. 1887), Wesleyan minister, and his wife Elizabeth, née Bedford. In 1832 the family migrated to Sydney where Matthew became a confectioner and pastry-cook. In 1837 he accepted a call to Longford, Van Diemen's Land, and in 1842 opened a school in Launceston but after his wife died he left his family and went to America.

In 1845 Frederic moved to Melbourne and worked as a sales clerk for the auctioneer, William Easey. On a visit to Victoria, G. A. Lloyd [q.v.] was impressed by Lassetter and about 1848 invited him to join his Sydney firm. Lassetter became a first-class accountant and expert in commerce. On 10 June 1850 he joined L. Iredale & Co., a hardware and general merchant firm founded in George Street in 1820. Lassetter revitalized the business, beating its competitors to buy goods from incoming ships by arranging for early receipt of signals and having a horse and row-boat constantly ready. He also devised a novel system of advertising and in 1851-52 traded on the goldfields with large loads of goods. In 1852 he married Iredale's daughter, Charlotte Hannah.

On 7 September 1863 the firm became F. Lassetter & Co. and moved to large new premises in George Street with a gala opening attended by the governor, premier and other notables. An outstanding innovator, Lassetter formed a limited company in 1878 and by 1890 was the head of one of the biggest hardware firms in Australia, with warehouses in York and Clarence Streets. In 1894 he enlarged his George Street showrooms to occupy much of the western block between Market and King Streets, and transformed his firm into a general emporium. His *Monthly Commercial Review*, a 'complete general catalogue', circulated throughout Australia giving details of the vast array of goods in stock. In 1894-1906 he published the *Australian Field*, 'a journal for squatters, sportsmen, farm & fireside, etc'; his other publications included a pamphlet on the rules of lawn tennis. By 1910 Lassetter had one of the largest businesses in Sydney with nearly 1000 employees who had part in a profit-sharing scheme. Survived by his wife, four sons and two daughters, Lassetter died of a stroke on 5 September 1911 at Redleaf, Double Bay, and was buried in the Anglican section of South Head cemetery. His estate was valued at £231,311.

His son, HENRY BEAUCHAMP, was born at Edgecliff on 19 March 1860. Educated at Cheltenham, Eton and Sandhurst, he joined the 38th Regiment as second lieutenant in 1880; next year he became a lieutenant in the 80th Regiment and in 1884 was in the Nile expedition. A captain in 1887 he returned next year to New South Wales as a major and raised and trained the Mounted Rifle Brigade. Promoted lieut-colonel in 1894, he led a detachment to England for Queen Victoria's diamond jubilee and headed the colonial escort in the procession. In 1901-02 he commanded the New South Wales Mounted Rifles in the Boer war, was mentioned in dispatches and created C.B. Associated with his father's firm from 1891, he became managing director in 1911 and in 1915 returned to England and took command of a territorial brigade. Promoted brigadier-general, he was appointed C.M.G. in 1917. He returned to Sydney in 1924 and died on 17 February 1926, survived by his wife Elizabeth Ann, née Antill, whom he had married at Picton in 1891, and by one son. He was buried in the Anglican section of South Head cemetery and left an estate of £3240.

F. Lassetter & Co. Ltd, *Sixty years an employer* (Syd, 1910); Retail Traders' Assn of NSW, *J*, July 1923; *Town and Country J*, 22 June 1910; *SMH*, 6 Sept 1911, 18 Feb 1926.

BEDE NAIRN

LATHAM, EDWARD (1839-1905), brewer and businessman, was born in Liverpool, England, youngest of four sons of Henry Latham, contractor, and his wife Sarah, née Tatlock. His parents died when he was 5 and with two brothers he was sent to 'a boarding school' where he stayed for ten years. At 15 he joined a large soap-boiling establishment in Lancashire. In 1864 he migrated to Melbourne, on the voyage nursing his oldest brother who had consumption and died a day after they arrived. Latham soon moved to Hobart Town and was impressed by the beauty of the Derwent valley. On 1 February 1865 at All Saints Church, Hobart, he married a widow, Bertha Ashton, née Aitkins.

Unable to find a congenial business in Hobart Latham returned to Melbourne where his first child was born. The Carlton brewery was then on the market and he bought it with George, a brother of William Milne [q.v.]. With the help of an experienced brewer, Alfred Terry, they began to produce 50 hogsheads a week and gradually enlarged the output to 1200 hogsheads. By then Terry had died and Milne had resigned, leaving Latham in sole control. In 1880 he stood for the Carlton seat in the Legislative Assembly but without success. In 1883 he sold out to the Melbourne Brewing and Malting Co., but retained a large interest in the new firm and remained a director for some years. He bought for £6000 a holiday home at Queenscliff for the use of Anglican clergy of the Melbourne diocese. He also contributed generously to the building of St Paul's Cathedral. He had also helped to establish at the Carlton brewery one of the first volunteer fire brigades in Australia.

In 1884 Latham visited Europe and America with his wife, son and daughter, chiefly to study modern brewing methods. Plain and unpretentious despite his wealth he was drawn into the land speculation boom by William Lawrence Baillieu who on 7 December 1887 at St Jude's Church, Carlton, married Bertha Martha, daughter of Edward Latham. Baillieu was a founding director of the Real Estate Bank and in 1889 his father-in-law became a director of the Federal Bank. Latham also guaranteed Baillieu's overdraft at the Commercial Bank. Both lost heavily when these banks were suspended and were involved in the secret compositions of 1892. Latham took over the Richmond brewery but his finances did not recover. His wife and son died in 1894 and on 4 September 1895 at St John's Church, Camberwell, he married Emma Elizabeth, sister of W. L. Baillieu. Latham struggled as manager of the Richmond brewery until October 1901 when it was absorbed by the Carlton and United Breweries. Aged 65 he died at his home, Knowsley, Camberwell, on 3 July 1905 and was buried in Boroondara cemetery.

A. Sutherland et al, *Victoria and its metropolis*, 2 (Melb, 1888); M. Cannon, *The land boomers* (Melb, 1966); *Australasian*, 10 July

1880; *Argus*, 4 July 1905, 22 Nov 1911; *What's Brewing*, June 1965; History of the Carlton and United Breweries (NL and Univ Melb Archives).   JOHN REYNOLDS

LAURENS, JOHN (1821-1894), grocer and politician, was born on 23 April 1821 in St Heliers, Jersey, son of Jean Laurens and his wife Elizabeth, née Le Riche. At 19 he went to Canada where he worked as a blacksmith for most of thirteen years. In August 1853 he sailed from Nova Scotia for Melbourne, arriving in December with a store and dwelling house, which he erected in Spencer Street, West Melbourne. Six weeks later he opened a grocery business which proved so prosperous that by 1865 he was able to retire. He moved to the suburb of Hotham where he pursued a successful, if unspectacular, political career.

In 1870 Laurens was admitted to the Hotham Borough Council; he served on it until 1891 and was elected mayor in 1872 and in 1873. In 1877 as a fervent protectionist he contested the general election as a nominee of Berry's [q.v.] National Reform and Protection League and was returned for Hotham to the Victorian Legislative Assembly; thus the retired grocer joined the 'new men' controlling the Lower House and remained a loyal Berryite for the whole of his political career. He took his parliamentary duties seriously. He spoke often in the assembly, dividing his attention between major state or national issues and those pertaining more directly to his electorate. The attempts of the Berry government to reform the Upper House and to impose a land tax to break up the accumulation of large estates received Laurens's staunch support. He rose often to speak on the wider issue of electoral reform and to support payment of members. He was particularly concerned with public finances, and the lengthy speeches he devoted to the subject earned him repute as 'a man of facts and figures'. In 1887 he served on the royal commissions on banking laws and Melbourne's westward extension. Although most of his addresses were monumentally dull, they sometimes had effect: for instance, his careful and detailed investigation into the handling of the finances of the Victorian railways helped to bring about the suspension of the railways commissioners in 1891 and their subsequent dismissal.

While Laurens was an unwavering 'party man', he also saw himself as a true representative of his electorate. Hotham (its name was changed to North Melbourne in 1887 largely as a result of Laurens's urgings) was a populous inner suburb of Melbourne, largely working class in composition.

Laurens defended its 'interests' with characteristic doggedness but in the particular causes that he championed he demonstrated not so much a radical espousal of the working class and its aspirations as a concern for property values and the prosperous state of municipal finances. It was largely because he remained 'a consistent liberal', failing to respond to the new radical forces in his electorate, that he was defeated at the polls in 1892 by a Labor candidate, D. R. Wyllie.

Laurens had served his adopted land earnestly and consistently. His public and private life was unblemished by scandal or corruption. A Methodist, he supported churches and philanthropic bodies in his electorate and was a most involved member of the Melbourne Hospital Committee for over fourteen years. He died at his home in North Melbourne on 31 March 1894, predeceased by his wife Elizabeth Ann Spinks, née de la Cour, and survived by his adopted daughter Jane Helina.

H. M. Humphreys (ed), *Men of the time in Australia: Victorian series*, 1st ed (Melb, 1878); A. Sutherland et al, *Victoria and its metropolis*, 2 (Melb, 1888); V&P (Vic), 1877-92; *North Melbourne Advertiser*, 25 Mar, 8, 23 Apr, 20 May 1892, 6 Apr 1894; *Age*, 2 Apr 1894; *Argus*, 2 Apr 1894; *Table Talk*, 6 Apr, 1 June 1894; *Williamstown Advertiser*, 6 Apr 1894; J. E. Parnaby, The economic and political development of Victoria, 1877-1881 (Ph.D. thesis, Univ Melb, 1951).   MARGARET CORRIS

LAWES, WILLIAM GEORGE (1839-1907), missionary, was born on 1 July 1839 at Aldermaston, Berkshire, England, son of Richard Lawes, tailor, and his wife Mary, née Pickover. Educated in a village school at Mortimer West End, he was apprenticed for six years and in 1858 volunteered for service with the London Missionary Society. He was trained at Bedford and two weeks before ordination on 8 November 1860 he married Fanny Wickham; on 23 November they sailed for the Pacific.

Lawes was posted first to Savage Island (Niue), where in 1868 he was joined by his brother Frank. On 15 January 1872 he began a furlough during which he travelled thirteen thousand miles in Britain lecturing on the missions. In April 1874 he sailed for New Guinea and in November settled at Port Moresby with his wife and children as the first permanent European residents of Papua. Despite attacks of fever which decimated his Polynesian teaching staff and killed his youngest son, Lawes became an expert in the Motuan language and a respected friend of all the south coast tribes. His first European colleague, appointed in 1876, left when his wife became ill but in

1877 James Chalmers [q.v.] arrived, and early in 1878 Lawes left for England on furlough. In four years he had started eleven new mission stations and produced the first book in a Papuan language.

Lawes was then a public figure. Australian miners in Port Moresby in 1878 sought his return to smooth the relations with natives. From that time his unrivalled knowledge of Papua was in constant demand. Soon after his return in 1881 he helped the exploring parties of 1883, and in 1884 served as interpreter for the Protectorate proclamation by James Elphinstone Erskine [q.v.]. Lawes and his wife went to Sydney as Erskine's guests in H.M.S. Nelson and then toured Victoria and New South Wales. Since 1872 he had fought abuses of the Pacific labour trade and provided much of the ammunition for the work of Erskine's uncle on the subject in the House of Commons.

In 1885 Lawes travelled round the Papuan coast as unofficial adviser to Sir Peter Scratchley [q.v.]. Lawes's *Grammar and Vocabulary of Language spoken by Motu Tribe, New Guinea* was also published in 1885 and in May 1886 he went on furlough, returning in October 1887. Despite differences with the government secretary he was in demand as an adviser to the colonial government of Sir William MacGregor. Lawes had many helpers at his mission but its monopoly was soon eroded by the arrival of other sects and the delineation of spheres of influence.

In 1891 Lawes visited England and toured the Australian colonies as a lecturer in 1892. Soon after his return he decided to hand the administration of the mission to a younger colleague and to concentrate on a new training college at Vatorata where he served for ten years. In 1894 he was awarded a doctorate of divinity by the University of Glasgow on MacGregor's recommendation. The murder of Chalmers in 1901 was a serious blow and in 1906 Lawes retired. He left Port Moresby in March and settled at Sydney where he died on 6 August 1907. He was survived by his wife and three of their seven sons. His son Frank served as a government officer in the protectorate and colony; when he died in 1894 MacGregor described him as one who knew and sympathized with the natives.

Although Lawes travelled widely and understood his people he was more scholar and administrator than pioneer. His partnership with the adventurous Chalmers was almost an ideal combination.

J. King, W. G. *Lawes of Savage Island and New Guinea* (Lond, 1909); British New Guinea, *Annual reports 1888-1905*; LMS papers (NL); W. G. Lawes diary 1876-77, 1881-84 (ML); Protectorate and colony papers (PNGA).

H. J. GIBBNEY

LEAKE, GEORGE WALPOLE (1825-1895), barrister and magistrate, and SIR **LUKE SAMUEL** (1828-1886), merchant and Speaker, were born in Stoke Newington, Middlesex, England, the first and third sons of Luke Leake and his wife Mary Ann, née Walpole. Their father arrived in Western Australia in 1829 and in 1833 their mother followed in the *Cygnet* with the two sons.

George was sent to King's College, London, and returned briefly to the colony on his way to study law in Adelaide. After a visit to Perth in 1843 he spent some years in Melbourne before settling in Perth as a practising barrister. In 1852 he was admitted to practise as a notary public. Despite an earlier refusal he acted as crown solicitor in 1857 and again in 1858; his appointment was confirmed in 1860. He became acting police magistrate at Perth in 1863 and magistrate of the local court in 1864. Among other temporary posts he acted as chief justice in 1879, 1880 and 1887, as puisne judge in 1887 and 1889-90, and in 1872, 1874-75, 1879-80 and 1883 as attorney-general, an office which gave him a seat on the Legislative Council. In 1890-94 he was a nominee member of the first council under responsible government. He had been police magistrate for Perth in 1881-90 when he retired to practise as a Q.C. He had an interest in the *Inquirer* which he edited in 1865. In 1890 he compiled an index to the Western Australian statutes and advocated the establishment of a law library. He had been a foundation member of the Perth Town Trust in 1842 and vice-president of the Swan River Mechanics' Institute in 1864-65. Large, genial and charitable, he spoke well despite a slight hesitancy. He featured in many controversies. His eccentric wit and the justice he dispensed was not always conventional and his antipathy to the chief justice, A.P. Burt [q.v.], did not help his ambition for permanent elevation to the bench. In 1880 during an arbitration case he threw an inkstand at the defending counsel, Septimus Burt; he apologized next day but claimed that he had been annoyed by Burt for ten years. Leake's unreliability embarrassed the authorities and the Colonial Office soon resisted his promotion to higher office even for short terms. In July 1887 his appointment as acting judge led to a question in the House of Commons.

Meanwhile Luke was successful in commerce. By 1853 he was supplying tea, sugar and flour to the government and in 1854-64 his *Guyon* (146 tons) was plying between

Singapore, Calcutta and Mauritius, and bringing Indian and Chinese produce to Fremantle. He failed to win the Perth electorate in the Legislative Council in 1868 but succeeded in 1870. In his policy speech he favoured promotion of immigration, liberal land regulations, raising of loans and such public works as a sea jetty at Fremantle. At the opening session in December he was elected Speaker, a post he held with distinction until 1886. Though unable to be prominent in debate, he supported moves for free trade and opposed any increase of duties on necessities. Ultra conservative, he was against pensions for public services and any extravagance with the colony's funds. His strong opposition to the introduction of responsible government drew him into the group against the administration of Weld and Barlee [q.v.]. He was a director of the Western Australian Bank in 1854-86 and served as its chairman. In the Perth Town Trust he was briefly chairman in 1856 and then auditor. He was a vice-president of the Swan River Mechanics' Institute in 1863-64 and president in 1866-78. Appointed a magistrate in 1858 and visiting justice for Rottnest and Perth prisons in 1879, he served on the Central Board of Education in 1878-86. He was a commissioner for Australian and International Exhibitions in 1862, 1873, 1878, 1880 and 1886. He was the first captain of the Perth Volunteer Rifles from inception in August 1862 until he resigned in February 1872. In the Weld Club he was vice-president in 1878-82 and then president until 1886. On a visit to England in 1875 he was elected a fellow of the Royal Geographical Society, and zealously advocated what he believed the colony's best interest.

Luke was knighted in 1876 and next year granted arms. Conscientious and courteous, he gave much of his wealth to charity and £2000 in 1878 towards building St George's Cathedral. At Bromley, Kent, on 11 September 1855 he had married his cousin Louisa, daughter of Rev. Thomas Henry Walpole; they had no children. He died on 1 May 1886 near Malta on his way home from England, and was buried with a state funeral at East Perth cemetery, where a monument was erected in his honour. His widow married Dr Alfred Robert Waylen [q.v.] on 2 June 1887.

In 1886 G. W. Leake contested his brother's seat for Perth in the Legislative Council. During the election an opponent, John Horgan, published a daily manifesto in which an unnamed magistrate was accused of corruption. Leake sued him for libel and was awarded £100 damages. He died on 3 October 1895, predeceased in 1888 by his first wife Rose Ellen Gliddon whom he had married at Adelaide on 6 September

1850; he was survived by seven of their eight children, by his second wife Amy Mabel May, whom he had married in Perth on 7 January 1893, and by their infant daughter. His only son to reach manhood was George (1856-1902), who became a Q.C. and was premier of Western Australia in 1901-02.

W. E. Bold, *Souvenir of the centenary of the foundation of the city* (Perth, 1929); G. F. Wieck, *The volunteer movement in Western Australia, 1861-1903* (Perth, 1962); T. S. Louch, *The first fifty years . . . the Weld club 1871-1921* (Perth, 1964); PD (WA); *Government Gazette* (WA); *West Australian*, 5 May 1886, 28 June 1890, 4 Oct 1895; S. Burt letters to F. Barlee (RWAHS); Leake letters and papers (Battye Lib, Perth); Swan River Mechanics' Inst minutes (Battye Lib); CSO records and Governors' dispatches (Battye Lib).

M. Medcalf

LEAKEY, CAROLINE WOOLMER (1827-1881), author, was born on 8 March 1827 at Exeter, England, fourth daughter and sixth of the eleven children of James Leakey, painter of portraits, miniatures, landscapes and small interiors. She grew up in a deeply religious household and three of her surviving brothers became clergymen. Her schooling was restricted by delicate health, but she read avidly, particularly poetry. At 18 her health improved and she became involved in many charitable and religious activities including the Church Missionary Society and the Seamen's Society. In 1847 with a clergyman and his wife she sailed to Van Diemen's Land to help her sister Eliza, wife of Rev. James Gould Medland, who had migrated with his family to Hobart Town in 1844.

Within a year Caroline contracted fever, followed by hip disease and other complications, and for the next five years was an invalid. Though confined to the house she was able to observe the children and servants of the household, while a particular concern was the colony's medical and hospital care. By November 1851 her health was improving and she visited friends, Rev. T. B. Garlick and his wife, at Port Arthur. For some time she lived with Bishop Nixon [q.v.] and his wife at Boa Vista, where some of her poetry was written. Nixon encouraged her to publish her poems and in 1854 *Lyra Australis, or Attempts to Sing in a Strange Land* appeared in London and Hobart under her own name. These poems deal mainly with problems of sickness and death, infancy, youth and motherhood, and all have a strong religious theme. Two are addressed to her doctor, J. W. Agnew [q.v.], and his wife, who were family friends. The second part of the book is dedicated to Lady Denison.

In 1853 Caroline was urged to return to England as her only chance of life; she sailed in March and arrived in June after a voyage confined entirely to her cabin. Her health rapidly improved and she began preparing her poems for publication and writing articles for magazines and the Religious Tract Society. From October 1854 she acted as head of her deceased sister's school; in July 1855 her mother died and she returned to Exeter to look after her 80-year-old father; he died on 16 February 1865.

In March 1857 Caroline began writing a novel; under the name of Oliné Keese it was published in two volumes as *The Broad Arrow; Being Passages from the History of Maida Gwynnham, a Lifer* (London, 1859; Hobart, 1860). It ran to several editions. An important forerunner of Marcus Clarke's [q.v.] *For the Term of His Natural Life, The Broad Arrow* is one of the earliest novels with a convict as its chief character and written by a careful observer of convict society. As a novel it has major faults: sentimental, melodramatic and homiletic, the development of its plot is hindered by much extraneous exposition and the whole work is heavily loaded with what H. M. Green calls a 'priggish though not hypocritical religion'. In 1888 an Australian reviewer, unaware that the writer was a woman, found the incidents 'of a uniformly painful character' but the author 'forcible and effective' on abuses of the penal system. To Caroline the system was more humiliating than harsh, with brutality inflicted on convicts by their fellows and not by officials; such comments made her examination of the effects of transportation on Tasmanian society impressive. Not merely as the long-suffering woman of 'holy and guileless life' and 'still more lovely spiritual character' portrayed by her sister Emily, Caroline reveals her shrewd intelligence.

In the next years Caroline survived several acute attacks of fever but continued to write tracts and 'purely moral poems' for the *Girls' Own Paper*. In 1861 she also began to work for the Exeter Home for fallen women. From 1871 she devoted most of her strength to writing. After an illness of eighteen months she died on 12 July 1881.

E. Leakey, *Clear shining light: a memoir of Caroline W. Leakey* (Lond, 1882); J. E. Poole, 'The Broad Arrow: a reappraisal', *Southerly*, 1966, no 2; *Australasian*, 5 Feb 1887.

J. C. HORNER

LEARMONTH, WILLIAM (1815-1889) and PETER (1821-1893), pastoralists, were born in Scotland, the second and fourth sons of John Learmonth, army contractor, and his wife Margaret, née Watson.

William, born on 31 January 1815, was educated at the High School in Edinburgh and in 1834 arrived at Van Diemen's Land in the *Tamar*. At first engaged to a firm of solicitors, he turned to pastoral pursuits and developed Williamswood, a property near Evandale. By 1839 he had 14,000 sheep. Hard hit by the prevailing depression he visited Portland, Port Phillip District, in 1842 and, encouraged by an advertisement of cattle for sale at Port Fairy, left Tasmania in August 1844. He bought many cattle and decided to take up a run at Darlot's Creek despite warnings about hostile Aboriginals. He took up 39,000 acres near Portland and held the first licence for the property which he renamed Ettrick. In September 1845 he was joined by his wife Mary, née Ralston, whom he had married in April 1837, and their three children. He was then investing in sheep and by December had begun to pay off his debts. Although the commissioner of crown lands, F. Fyans [q.v.], urged him to withdraw because of troublesome Aboriginals, Learmonth stayed on. He prospered and was able to invest in several other runs. Ettrick became one of the best stations in the district and he held it until 1880.

In 1854-63 Learmonth lived in Portland, where he was partner of S. G. Henty [q.v.] in a mercantile business; they also held a 15,000-acre run near Hamilton. Learmonth was first mayor of the Portland Borough Council in 1863 and for years served on it and the Shire Council of which he was president many times. He also stood for the Legislative Council but without success. He was an enthusiast for the Volunteer Movement in which he became colonel. He was a keen sportsman and race-horse owner. He died at Ettrick on 7 July 1889, survived by his widow and three children.

Peter Learmonth was born on 9 February 1821 and worked on an uncle's farm until at 19 he decided to join his brother William in Tasmania. He worked on William's property near Evandale for two years and then started a sheep station on Tasman Peninsula. In 1848 he made a fruitless visit to the Californian goldfields but in 1851 gold again attracted him and he was successful at Forest Creek, near Castlemaine. He then decided to raise livestock and managed Francis Henty's [q.v.] Merino Downs station. In 1859 Learmonth turned to flour-milling, building or buying mills at Prestonholme, near Hamilton, and at Sandford, Byaduk and Penshurst. He also bought land at Prestonholme and Dunkeld for his merino flock and established a wool and finance business, P. Learmonth & Co., in Hamilton. His last big investment was to buy a third interest in the Nacimiento estate, Mexico, where he later gave his share of 82,000 acres to two of his sons. A practical citizen, he was an early member of Dundas Shire Council and often its president. He helped to establish the Hamilton Hospital and presided over its committee for years. He also raised capital for founding Hamilton College and Alexandra Ladies' College. He worked hard for temperance and helped to bring railway communication to the district. He died at Prestonholme on 19 July 1893, leaving an estate worth £54,000 and was survived by his wife Mary Jarvey (d. 1913), daughter of John Pearson, whom he had married on 18 December 1854; they had seven sons and three daughters.

William's eldest son, John Ralston (1838-1911), was born in Tasmania and educated by his parents at Ettrick. In 1855-56 he worked for the Bank of Australasia at Portland. From 1857 he managed some of his father's properties, becoming owner of Ellangowan station adjoining Ettrick. He was active in municipal affairs, became a justice of the peace in 1861 and was thrice president and eighteen years a member of the Minhamite Shire Council. He also gave long service as a Portland shire councillor. A crack shot, he was prominent as well in horse-racing and for years was a breeder, owner and judge at Hamilton and the Melbourne Show. He died at Ellangowan on 11 August 1911. He was survived by his wife Mary Jane Marshall, née Fulford, whom he had married in April 1875, by two of his three sons and a daughter, and by thirteen grandchildren.

A. Henderson (ed), *Australian families*, 1 Melb, 1941); N. F. Learmonth, *The Portland Bay settlement . . . 1800 to 1851* (Melb, 1934); *Portland Guardian*, 8 July 1889, 14 Aug 1911; *Hamilton Tribune*, 21 July 1893.

MICHAEL T. MOORE

LEARY, JOSEPH (1831-1881), solicitor and politician, was born at Campbelltown, New South Wales, son of John Leary and his wife Catherine, née Jones. Educated at St Mary's seminary and W. Cape's [q.v.] Sydney College, he studied at the University of Sydney for two years before returning to Campbelltown. In 1860 he won the Legislative Assembly seat of Narellan against the sitting member, John Hurley [q.v.]. His support for John Robertson's [q.v.] Land Acts together with his native birth and polished style proved his greatest assets in a bitter campaign. An able debater in parliament, Leary demonstrated that Catholicism was compatible with colonial liberalism by supporting not only the abolition of state aid

to religion and the establishment of the Irish National education system but also such radical causes as payment of members of parliament and divorce legislation. He argued that as a Catholic he would not practise divorce but it should be available for those who sought it. In the 1864 election he was denounced by Catholic clergy. He countered with denunciations of clerical interference in politics but was narrowly defeated by Hurley.

Leary took up law and after serving his articles under Richard Driver [q.v.] he was admitted as a solicitor on 22 December 1866. In one of his first cases he helped to defend the bushranging Clarke brothers [q.v.]. After failing to stay their execution, he joined the Society for Abolition of Capital Punishment and was later appointed to its executive. He maintained an interest in politics and supported Henry Parkes's [q.v.] 1866 Public Schools Act against the criticisms of many Catholics. Re-elected for Narellan in 1869, he lost the seat again to Hurley in 1872. In 1874 he contested Murrumbidgee without success but was elected unopposed at a by-election early in 1876, and held the seat against strong competition in 1877. He refused office in Parkes's 1877 ministry, but became minister of justice and public instruction in J. S. Farnell's [q.v.] 1878 'third party' government. By then Leary's views on public education had changed. In 1879-80 he condemned Parkes's public instruction bill although it did no more than introduce policies he himself had advocated in the 1860s. The Catholic-Liberal tradition he had represented had been an early victim of the sectarianism of the late 1860s and 1870s.

In 1880 Leary contested Camden in vain but he was already ill and on 20 October 1881 he died from heart and kidney disease at his home in Macquarie Street aged 49. Buried in Petersham cemetery, he was survived by his wife Catherine, née Keighran, whom he had married at Campbelltown on 6 September 1854, and by five sons and five daughters. He left goods valued at £200.

SMH, 19 Dec 1860, 16 Dec 1864, 16 Dec 1869, 16 Mar 1876, 21 Oct 1881; *Empire* (Syd), 2 Oct 1865; *Freeman's J* (Syd), 12 June 1869, 20 Oct 1881; J. P. McGuanne, Centenary of Campbelltown (ML); Parkes letters (ML).

MARK LYONS

LEDGER, CHARLES (1818-1905), adventurer, was born on 4 March 1818 in London, son of George Ledger, mercantile broker, and his wife Charlotte, née Warren. In 1836 he went to Peru, worked as a clerk for an English merchant firm, settled at Tacna and succeeded as a trader in wool, skins, bark and copper. In 1848 he began to breed alpacas at Chulluncayani and in 1852 was asked by British consular officials to supply some of the animals for New South Wales. He visited Sydney in 1853 to confer with Governor FitzRoy, E. Deas Thomson and T. S. Mort [qq.v.] and confirmed that the rewards would be satisfactory.

The export of alpacas from Peru was prohibited and Ledger was forced to drive them through Bolivia to Argentina and return across the Andes to Copiapo in Chile, where he arrived in April 1858 with a depleted flock. On 28 November Ledger, with South American shepherds and 256 alpacas, llamas and vicunas, disembarked from the *Salvadora* in Sydney. However, commercial interest had waned and plans to float a company to buy the flock were abandoned. The government paid £15,000 for the alpacas but this went to the Chilean merchants who had financed the project after Ledger's own funds were exhausted. In April 1859 he became superintendent at a salary of £300, later increased to £500, with £1000 a year for management expenses, but could get no further compensation. Disillusioned by the rejection of his claims for £7000 and by the failure of negotiations to repurchase the flock on liberal terms, he submitted his resignation three times in 1859-61. 'On the faith of promises made in this country', he complained, 'I undertook every risk—did succeed—and am ruined!' The government's decision to increase his salary to £800 and to grant him leave so that he could bring his children to Australia somewhat assuaged this bitterness but on 14 August 1862 he was suspended from office, apparently for misappropriating money given to him by the Acclimatisation Society of Victoria. In that year his display of stuffed alpacas won medals at the London International Exhibition.

Ledger vigorously defended his conduct and petitioned for a redress of his earlier grievances but decided in August 1864 to return to South America. He had intended to settle the alpacas at Nimmitabel, a region not unlike their natural habitat, but they had been depastured in turn at Liverpool, Camden and Arthursleigh station near Goulburn. Reserve prices were not reached at an auction in 1864 and most were then given away in small lots to graziers in New South Wales and Queensland.

On his return to Chile in 1865 Ledger began his second great adventure. In Bolivia his servant, Manuel Incra Manami, had spent four years collecting cinchona seeds, highly prized for their quinine but a prohibited export. Ledger managed to get some

seeds out; the British government refused to buy them but the Dutch government bought a small parcel, which was successfully cultivated in Java. Plantations of the species, later named *Cinchona ledgeriana*, provided much of the world's quinine from 1900 to 1940.

After living in America, Uruguay and Argentina Ledger returned to Australia in 1883. He died at Leichhardt on 19 May 1905 from senile decay and was buried in the Independent section of Rookwood cemetery according to Methodist rites. He was survived by three daughters; their mother, a South American, died in Peru in 1857 and Ledger's second wife, Charlotte Tooth, widow, whom he married in 1860, died in 1891. Although awarded a pension of 1200 guilders by the Dutch government in 1895, his estate was valued at only £2.

Ledger was sustained in his expeditions by great physical endurance, by expectation of personal reward and not least by a fervent desire to bring credit on the empire. His difficulties in Australia stemmed partly from his inability to account satisfactorily for his management of the alpacas, but he correctly believed that he had been deceived by verbal promises. A sketch-book of his adventures with the animals in 1849-58 is in the Mitchell Library.

G. Ledger, *The Alpaca: its introduction into Australia* . . . (Melb, 1861); N. Taylor, *Cinchona in Java; the story of quinine* (New York, 1945); P. Mander Jones, 'A sketch book found in Australia', *Inter-American Review of Bibliog*, 3 (1953); V&P (LC NSW), 1853, 2, 317, 1859-60, 5, 371, (LA NSW), 1861-62, 2, 1383, 1863-64, 1, 487, 770; *SMH*, 25 Nov 1850, 30 Nov 1858, 22, 30 Mar, 8 Apr 1859, 8 June 1860, 2 Oct 1861, 13 Nov 1862, 11, 25 Feb, 28 June 1864 20 May 1905; *Sydney Mail*, 6 Feb 1864, 29 July 1865; *Examiner* (Melb), 19 Nov 1859, 7 Jan 1860 26 Oct 1861; MS cat under Ledger (ML).

B. G. ANDREWS

LEE, BENJAMIN (1825-1917), shipowner politician and civil servant, was born on 5 November 1825 at Ampthill, Bedfordshire England, eldest son of Benjamin Lee and his wife Lucy Ann, née Poulton. His father had enlisted in 1804 in the 14th Regiment served in the Peninsular war and in 1828 retired with a pension of 1s. a day. Indentured to T. P. Macqueen [q.v.], he sailed as a bounty immigrant with his family in the *Mary* and arrived at Sydney in January 1829. He managed Segenhoe for a year and then moved to Parramatta where he bought town allotments. He was the licensee of several hotels and acquired land on the Paterson River. Aged 91 he died at Parra matta on 13 April 1879, leaving goods valued at £8000.

Lee was educated at The King's School, Parramatta, and in the early 1840s managed his father's farms. He went to England in 1854 and on his return married Sarah Amelia Stephens at Melbourne on 21 July 1856. Next year he moved to Maitland and with his brother John set up as general drapers. In 1861 Lee was chairman of the Hunter River New Steam Navigation Co. and gave evidence to the Legislative Assembly select committee on the Morpeth and Maitland Railway Co.'s incorporation bill. A magistrate from July he was excluded from James Martin's [q.v.] revised commission of the peace in 1864 but restored in July 1865. In the 1860s he held three runs in New South Wales and, with his father, two in Queensland.

In December 1864 Lee contested the Legislative Assembly seat of West Maitland as a free trader in an unusually violent campaign. The three candidates had almost identical policies but published abusive personal squibs. Lee denied such charges as seeking the local police magistracy, employing only Protestants and reducing wages on the company's wharf. He dispensed free grog and won by 116 votes after a riotous week. On 26 February 1868 in the assembly Lee, tormented by Allan Macpherson, punched his nose. It was the first blow in the House and government members cheered. Escorted outside by the serjeant-at-arms Lee was horse-whipped by Macpherson and a brawl ensued. After long debate the House resolved that both should be prosecuted. In May Lee pleaded guilty in the Central Court to assault 'in contempt of the said Assembly', but Macpherson entered a demurrer that he was not bound to answer the charge and Lee was not sentenced.

Lee, normally even-tempered and moderate, was re-elected for West Maitland in 1869 and 1872. A successful 'roads and bridges' member, he helped to organize Henry Parkes's [q.v.] Hunter River campaign in 1872 and invited him to stay if he did 'not mind the necessary annoyance of a house full of children'. Lee complained that the Morpeth election had been 'sadly bungled'. 'An uncompromising opponent' of Martin's second ministry he was rewarded by Parkes for his loyal support: after a long struggle Lee got a court-house for West Maitland and in October 1872 was appointed a commissioner to collect exhibits for the 1873 London International Exhibition. In 1874 he lost the chairmanship of the navigation company through financial difficulties and resigned his seat. Parkes had him appointed police magistrate at Bathurst with a salary of £500. The Bathurst Times criti-

cized such blatant political patronage but on 25 August Lee was given a silver tea and coffee service by his grateful electors.

Lee became visiting justice to Bathurst gaol, local mining warden in 1875, coroner in 1881 and later a guardian of minors. On 30 June 1889 he was transferred to the Water Police Office in Sydney and on 1 April 1890 became stipendiary magistrate with a salary of £800. On 14 March 1893 he retired with a pension of £247. In 1906 the Lees celebrated their golden wedding. He died from senility at his home in Johnston Street, Annandale, on 15 July 1917 and was buried in the Anglican section of the Gore Hill cemetery. Survived by his only son and eight daughters, he left an estate valued for probate at £5000.

NSW Supreme Court Reports, Cases at Law, 230, 7 (1869); R. H. Parsons, The fleets of the principal steamship owners registering vessels at Sydney . . . prior to 1900 (Adel, 1959); V&P (LA NSW), 1861, 2, 525, 1867-68, 1, 576, 579; Maitland Mercury, 8-17 Dec 1864, 16, 18 Dec 1869, 5 Mar 1872, 21-30 July, 6, 25, 27 Aug 1874; SMH, 27, 28 Feb, 2, 4 Mar, 12, 14 May, 9 June 1868; Sydney Mail, 19 Apr 1879; Town and Country J, 1 Aug 1906; Daily Telegraph (Syd), 5 Nov 1915; Parkes letters and MS cat (ML); Paterson River small settlers, 2/8014 (NSWA); Col Sec land letters, 2/7905 (NSWA).

MARTHA RUTLEDGE

LEE, DAVID (1837-1897), organist and conductor, was born on 20 March 1837 at Armagh, Ireland, son of James Lee, professor of music, and his wife Mary, née Scarlet. At 4 he entered the Armagh Cathedral School, at 7 became a chorister and at 12 was made deputy-organist of Armagh Cathedral. On leaving school he joined the Provincial Bank of Ireland as a clerk.

Lee arrived at Melbourne in the Morning Light on 26 July 1864. He was soon appointed organist at St Luke's Church, Emerald Hill, and opened its new organ in March 1865. He also founded the Emerald Hill Philharmonic Society. At various times he was organist at St Stephen's Church, Richmond, the Independent Church, Collins Street, where he led the choir for eight years, St Mark's, Fitzroy, and St Andrew's, Brighton. He opened organs in many city and suburban churches, notably St Patrick's Cathedral on 14 March 1880 and Chalmers Presbyterian Church, East Melbourne, on 30 April 1885. He was honorary organist of the Melbourne Philharmonic Society in 1866. In accord with the policy of choosing a choral rather than an orchestral conductor, Lee was appointed conductor from 1867 to 1874, when he visited America and Europe, and in 1877-88. He also taught music. In 1867 he joined the organist, Samuel Kaye, and set up a business importing pianos, harmoniums and organs. In 1875 the organbuilder, Robert Mackenzie, joined the firm and his factory was attached to Lee & Kaye's premises at 17 Collins Street. Three years later George Fincham [q.v.] bought the firm.

In October 1866 Lee played the organ at the inaugural ceremony of the Melbourne International Exhibition, with C. E. Horsley [q.v.] conducting. On 8 August 1872 he opened the new Town Hall organ. In 1877 he was appointed first city organist of Melbourne by the City Council. For some years his twice-weekly recitals in the Town Hall drew large audiences but they fell off partly because he 'seemed to have run through his repertoire and partly because he had a predilection for pieces that were scarcely adapted for organ playing'. He was invited to give the opening recital on the new organ of the Adelaide Town Hall in October 1877. He visited Europe again in 1887.

Lee's influence in the Philharmonic Society was later described by George Peake who claimed that Lee's 'keen business instinct possibly affected his musical judgement, while his bonhomie and personal popularity probably disarmed criticism, much to his own disadvantage as a public musician. His musical enterprise appeared to be influenced by a desire to please the public and win popularity, rather than promote the educational and progressive advance of musical art'. Lee's limitations as conductor of the society affected the musical life of Melbourne for many years; he was finally forced out of the society in 1888 after years of constant friction, especially because of his fruitless requests for payment of his salary. On 23 April 1877 at Christ Church, St Kilda, he had married Mary Mackenzie, eldest daughter of Archibald Johnson of Toorak House. She predeceased him without issue. Lee died of kidney disease at South Yarra on 12 May 1897 and was buried in the Anglican section of the Melbourne general cemetery. Pall-bearers included the mayor of Melbourne, G. L. Allan [q.v.], and G. Fincham.

G. Peake, *Melbourne Philharmonic Society diamond jubilee, 1853-1913* (Melb, 1913); E. N. Matthews, *Colonial organs and organbuilders* (Melb, 1969); *Argus*, 13 May 1897; *Australasian*, 15 May 1897.   SALLY O'NEILL
MAUREEN THERESA RADIC

LEE, GEORGE (1834-1912), pastoralist and stud-breeder, was born on 16 December 1834 at Claremont, a station near Kelso, the sixth son of William Lee and his wife Mary, née Dargin. Educated locally and at Sydney College, he managed stations for his father and settled at Wallaroy, near Bathurst. In 1870 his father died and he inherited land at Kelso and other stations including South Condobolin, later known as Merriwee. In 1872 he built Leeholme at Kelso, where he became well known as a stud-breeder of merinos and Shorthorn cattle. Devoted to the land Lee travelled widely in the management of his affairs.

With descendants of his father's grey mare, Sappho, Lee bred race-horses. Three times he recovered Sappho after she had been stolen by bushrangers. From a select number of high quality brood mares, the greatest of which was Etra Weenie, he bred some famous horses: The Barb, winner of the Melbourne and two Sydney Cups for John Tait [q.v.]; Kingsborough, winner of many races for Governor Robinson; and Merriwee, another Melbourne Cup winner and Savanaka, raced by Herbert Power of Melbourne. Although Lee leased or sold most of his horses, he raced Lecturer in his short unbeaten career and with him won the 1872 Sires' Produce Stakes. In 1897 he won the Debutant Stakes at Caulfield with Wigelmar. In 1906 Lee got the top price of 1600 guineas for his colt at William Inglis & Son's first yearling auction sale. Lee was a member and committeeman of the Australian Jockey Club and was prominent in the development of the race-course at Randwick.

A close friend of H. C. Dangar and F. B. Suttor [qq.v.], Lee resisted the persuasion of Suttor to stand for the Legislative Assembly in 1881. At Suttor's instigation, Sir Henry Parkes [q.v.] recommended his appointment to the Legislative Council and in December Lee reluctantly accepted nomination. Undistinguished as an orator and politician, he was a conscientious member and staunch free trader. Active in local affairs Lee was treasurer, president and later patron of the Bathurst show. He was also interested in the District Hospital, the local Turf Club and Agricultural Association. A prominent Anglican, he represented Bathurst in the Provincial Synod of New South Wales. A teetotaller and non-smoker, Lee abhorred bad language and reputedly never gambled.

Predeceased in 1904 by his wife Emily Louisa, née Kite, Lee died on 23 January 1912 at Leeholme and was buried in the Anglican cemetery at Kelso. He was survived by two sons and six daughters. His estate was valued for probate at nearly £153,000.

D. M. Barrie, *The Australian bloodhorse* (Syd, 1956); *100 Bathurst shows* (Bathurst, 1968); Bathurst Hist Soc Archives; Lee family records (held by Miss I. Traill, Bathurst).
THEO BARKER

LEFROY, ANTHONY O'GRADY (1816-1897), pastoralist and civil servant, was born on 14 March 1816 at Limerick, Ireland, the eldest son of Henry Lefroy, vicar of Santry near Dublin, and his wife Dorothea, daughter of John O'Grady of Kilballyowen. He was descended from Antoine Loffroy, a Huguenot refugee who left Flanders and settled at Canterbury about 1587. On 22 October 1832 Lefroy entered Trinity College, Dublin, and was followed on 2 July 1839 by his brother Gerald de Courcy. After graduation they decided to migrate to Western Australia. They sailed in the *Lady Grey* and arrived at Fremantle in January 1843. As they were being rowed ashore their belongings, including equipment and a bag containing 900 sovereigns, fell overboard; fortunately their possessions were soon recovered.

The brothers briefly visited their cousin Henry Maxwell Lefroy at York, before going to live with the Burges [q.v.] family to learn the essentials of colonial husbandry. Some months later they rented Springdale, near Northam, and a property at Bolgart. In 1846 they found a choice pastoral run at Walebing and took out a squatting licence. Faced with a dire shortage of labour when trying to develop Walebing and anxious to overcome the problem, Lefroy supported the settlers' petition to the Colonial Office for a penal establishment in Western Australia. Later he engaged several ticket-of-leave men to work on building projects at Walebing.

Men of his education and training were then rare in the colony and Lefroy was invited to join the civil service. He accepted and in 1849 became private secretary to Governor Fitzgerald. In 1856 he was appointed clerk of the Legislative and Executive Councils and colonial treasurer. He also served as chairman of the Board of Education, as paymaster of the Pensioners' Board and in 1875-77 as acting colonial secretary. Always amiable and tactful, Lefroy was nominated to the Legislative Council in 1856 and held office until responsible government in 1890. Before the elections in that year he announced his intention to retire on a pension after thirty-four years as colonial treasurer.

In the early 1850s Lefroy had dissolved his partnership with Gerald, who continued to manage the property at Walebing. Despite his landed interests 'it was not so much as a pastoralist that Lefroy was to have an enduring mark upon the history of the colony as his capacity as one of the oldest and most faithful servants of the Government'. On 3 June 1852 he married Mary, daughter of John Bruce [q.v.] and his wife Johannah Jacoba, née Herklotz; they had three daughters and two sons, one of whom,

Henry Bruce, became premier of Western Australia in 1917. Lefroy, already a fellow of the Royal Geographical Society, was appointed C.M.G. in 1878. He visited England and Ireland with his family in 1863 and died at his home, Cambray, in Perth on 20 January 1897.

W. B. Kimberly, *History of Western Australia* (Melb, 1897); J. S. Battye (ed), *Cyclopedia of Western Australia*, 1-2 (Adel, 1912-13); R. E. Cranfield, *From Ireland to Western Australia* (Perth, 1960); F. K. Crowley, *Forrest 1847-1918* (Brisb, 1971); *West Australian*, 30 Dec 1890; *Morning Herald* (Perth), 22 Jan 1897; CSO 1843-90 (Battye Lib, Perth).   G. C. LEFROY

LEFROY, SIR JOHN HENRY (1817-1890), soldier, governor and administrator, was born on 28 January 1817 at Ashe, Hampshire, England, son of Rev. John Henry George Lefroy (d. 1823) and his wife Sophia, née Cotterell. Educated at Alton, Richmond, and the Royal Military Academy, Woolwich, he was appointed second lieutenant in the Royal Artillery in December 1834, captain in 1842 and colonel in 1865. He had been director of the magnetical observatory at St Helena in 1840-42 and at Toronto, Canada, in 1842-53. He travelled widely in the north on magnetic and meteorological research, founded the Canadian Institute in 1849 and was awarded a doctorate by McGill University. In 1854 he became senior clerk at the War Office and scientific adviser on artillery and inventions in the Crimean war. In 1856 he prepared a detailed scheme of military training and was inspector-general of army schools in 1857-60. He served on the royal commission on defence in 1859 and in 1868-70 as director-general of ordnance he was made a C.B. In 1871 he became governor of Bermuda and before he left in 1877 was appointed a K.C.M.G. In 1846 he had married Emily Merry Robinson; she died in 1859 and in 1860 he married Charlotte Anna Dundas, widow of Colonel Mountain.

In August 1880 Lefroy was appointed administrator of Tasmania. He arrived at Hobart with his wife and daughter in October and was sworn in. Alert, cheerful and unobtrusive, he soon won immense popularity. He travelled throughout the colony and became well acquainted with its political and moral progress. He visited many mines, agricultural shows, concerts, art displays and particularly state schools where he went into each department, distributed pencils, shillings and lollies, listened to endless recitations and critically examined the outhouses. As president of the Royal Society of Tasmania he never missed a meeting, and his wife held regular fortnightly receptions at Government House. In Hobart and Launceston Lefroy also gave an erudite lecture on 'The Southern Skies', the proceeds going to the Young Men's Christian Association and the Risdon Home of Refuge. When he left the colony in November 1881 the Tasmanian Volunteer Artillery Corps presented him with an engraved plate for his constant support. The new governor, Sir George Strahan, arrived early in December.

Lefroy retired in 1882 as a colonel-commandant but gave occasional lectures and in 1885-88 served on the committee of the universities mission to Central Africa. He died at Lewarne, Cornwall, on 11 April 1890, survived by his second wife, two sons and two daughters. Lefroy was a fellow of many learned societies and his many publications included works on meteorology, astronomy, magnetic observations, antiquarian research and a much used textbook on artillery practice.

Australasian, 21 Aug 1880; *Mercury*, 11 July, 25 Nov 1881; *Argus*, 15 Apr 1890.

LEGGE, WILLIAM VINCENT (1841-1918), soldier and scientist, was born on 2 September 1841 at Cullenswood, near St Marys, Van Diemen's Land, son of Robert Vincent Legge (d. 1891) and his wife Eliza Graves, née de Lapenotierre; his grandfather was Michael Legge, barrister, of Dublin. His father had arrived in Tasmania on 12 August 1827 in the *Medway* with his five sisters, four of whom soon married; he was granted 1200 acres which he named Cullenswood after his home in Ireland.

As a child William was sent to England and educated at Bath and in France and Germany. He was commissioned in the Royal Artillery in 1862 and served with the imperial troops in Melbourne in 1867-68. He was then stationed in Ceylon where he pursued his studies of natural history, to which he had long been devoted. As secretary of the Royal Asiatic Society he reorganized the dilapidated museum at Colombo. He also continued the ornithological work begun by Edgar Layard and made an immense collection of birds. He left Ceylon in 1877 and returned to England, serving at Portsmouth till 1888. As an instructor in gunnery he had the task of mounting the heavy guns at Spithead. In his leisure he completed and published his *History of the Birds of Ceylon* (London, 1880).

Legge had early shown great interest in the defences of the River Derwent, and for this and a recommendation by Sir Peter Scratchley [q.v.] he was offered the command of the forces in Tasmania. He took up his new command on 6 December 1883, retiring from the imperial service with the rank of lieut-colonel. In April-May Legge had completed the torpedo course on H.M.S. *Vernon* at Portsmouth, and with advice from Scratchley and General Hardinge Steward ordered the new breech-loading guns for the colony from the Elswick Works at Newcastle upon Tyne. During his command the forces were entirely reorganized and the batteries defending Hobart were completed and armed with several of the latest types of guns, but many of his other recommendations went unheeded. He was twice re-engaged before his appointment ended in June 1890 through government retrenchment. When Colonel A. T. Cox retired in 1898 the command was again offered to Legge. He trained Tasmanian contingents for the Boer war and was in charge of the reception of the duke of Cornwall in 1900, and held his post until the forces were officially taken over by the Commonwealth in 1904.

Legge was a fellow of the Geographical Society and a member of the Zoological Society of London, the Linnean Society and the British and American Ornithologists' Unions and a founder and president of the Australasian Ornithologists' Union. As a member and vice-president of the Royal Society of Tasmania he read seventeen papers on various subjects including ornithology, flora and fauna, forestry and geology. Through him, the heights of certain peaks in the Ben Lomond Range were ascertained and in 1907 the highest point was named Legge Tor by the government. He was vice-president of the biological section at the Hobart congress of the Australasian Association for the Advancement of Science in 1902 and president of the same section at the Dunedin congress in 1904.

Legge was a lay-reader and Sunday school teacher, and restored the Church of England at Cullenswood, which had been built by his father. Legge was married first, on 1 December 1867 to Frances Anne Talbot (d. 1914), widowed daughter of Major W. Gray, of Avoca, Tasmania, and second, at Sydney on 3 August 1916 to Kathleen Louisa, daughter of Arthur Cunningham Douglas of Hobart. He died at Cullenswood on 25 March 1918 aged 78, survived by his wife and two sons of the first marriage; his only daughter died in 1906 aged 33 and his son Robert took over Cullenswood.

Cyclopedia of Tasmania, 1 (Hob, 1900); P. L. Brown (ed), *Clyde Company papers*, 1 (Lond, 1941); V&P (HA Tas), 1884 (162), 1887 (89); L. F. Giblin and E. L. Piesse, 'The Ben Lomond Range. Note on the height of the Legge Tor', Roy Soc Tas, *Papers*, 1907; 'Obituary', Roy Soc Tas, *Papers*, 1918; *Mercury*, 16 Aug 1916, 27 Mar 1918, 12 Aug 1927; *Examiner* (Launceston), 27 Mar 1918.   E. M. DOLLERY

LEIBIUS, CHARLES (CARL) ADOLPH (1833-1893), chemist and public servant, was born in Württemberg, Germany, son of Gottleib Leibius, merchant, and his wife Julie, née Boettinger. After studying science at the Universität Heidelberg (Ph.D., 1857), he went to London and studied analytical and assaying chemistry, working at the Royal College with Professor Hofmann. He arrived in Sydney in 1859 where on 31 March he was appointed assistant assayer at the branch Mint on a salary of £580. He was promoted senior assayer on 1 October 1870 at £700. In 1859 he had joined the Royal Society (Philosophical Society) of New South Wales. He was joint honorary secretary in 1875-86, a vice-president in 1886-87 and 1891-92 and president in 1890-91. His presidential address on 6 May 1891 dealt with the progress of some branches of applied science in the colony. In addition to his administrative work he delivered six short papers mainly on the identification and refining of gold and other ores. He was elected a fellow of the Chemical Society of London on 18 December 1879, and admitted to the University of Sydney (M.A. *ad eund.*, 1882).

Leibius's main interests were scientific. Enthusiasm, thoroughness and directness in all he did were strong features of his character. His genial and sincere disposition won him many friends, among the closest being Robert Hunt, deputy-master of the Mint. He was a director of the City and Suburban Building and Investment Society, and in 1885 contributed to the Patriotic Fund for the Sudan contingent. He died at his residence, Ithaca, Burwood, on 19 June 1893 and was buried in the Anglican cemetery, Rookwood. His estate was sworn for probate at under £11,500. He was survived by his wife Margaret, née Burnell (d. 1924), whom he had married on 31 October 1863 at St James's Church, Sydney, and by three daughters and a son, Gustav Hugo, who with Robert Garran published *Index of cases judicially noticed in the courts of New South Wales and on appeal therefrom, 1825-1895* (Sydney, 1896).

Chemical Soc, *J*, 65 (1894), 388; Roy Soc NSW, *Procs*, 28 (1894), 36; SMH, 20 June 1893.
G. P. WALSH

LENNON, HUGH (1833-1886), manufacturer, was born in County Armagh, Ireland, son of Michael Lennon, fish merchant, and his wife Mary, née Lennon. The family moved to Scotland when Hugh was young and at 15 he was apprenticed to R. Gray & Sons of Uddington as a ploughmaker. He accepted the 'hard discipline' at Grays and became a good tradesman. He then moved to Glasgow and decided to master engineering. After another apprenticeship he was employed first by John Caird & Co., second by Scott & Sinclair, and then by Walter Nelson's Hyde Park Engine Works, Glasgow, 'the college of Scotland for mechanics'. However, constant work undermined his health and in 1859 he migrated to Victoria 'with a broken down constitution and a good character'.

At the Hyde Park Engine Works Lennon had become interested in machine tools and invention. In Victoria, seeing the need for good agricultural machinery, he produced a plough suitable for dry farming on the northern plains. Among other innovations it was made of wrought-iron to minimize repairs and replaced the brittle English cast-iron mouldboard by a patented one in cast-steel. The technical superiority of his plough over imported rivals ensured it control of the market, and after August 1870 the sales of his single- and double-furrow ploughs were phenomenal. In 1871 he expanded his works, introduced a more sophisticated plant and developed a new reaping machine. By November demand exceeded supply and he was producing two machines a day. Mowers were also produced and in 1879 the 'New Imperial Stripper' was patented, the equal of any machine made in America and containing many of Lennon's innovations, including a revolutionary new method of gearing. In the late 1870s he also developed a winnower which, with the stripper, provided the best harvesting unit on the Victorian and indeed the Australian market. By the mid-1870s Lennon employed over a hundred men and operated such machines as steam hammers. The expansion continued in the 1880s and was financed by the reinvestment of profits. By 1884 the capital investment exceeded £25,000 and the firm was the largest of its kind in the Australian colonies, selling 700 ploughs, 224 reapers, 60 strippers and many winnowers, earth scoops, horse-works and harrows each year. The average profits of Hugh Lennon & Co. were about £1000 a year in the 1870s, rising to £2000 in the 1880s.

Lennon was active in local affairs. In 1882 he was elected to the west ward of the Hotham (North Melbourne) Borough Council but was defeated next year and took no further part in politics. From the early 1870s he was on the committee of the Agricultural Society of Victoria and its president in 1879-80. He was also active in his Presbyterian Church at North Melbourne and in the Royal Society of Victoria. Although he hungered for political success and social prestige he was never sure of his success. A brilliant innovator and entrepreneur with a flair for advertising and sales promotion, he was described by a contemporary as 'a great, rough man' but he had a deep love for Burns and Shakespeare. His papers reveal a complex character: he was very egotistical but fond of his family. Aged 52 he died on 22 July 1886 survived by his wife Isabella, née Don, a son and two daughters. He left an estate valued at £20,000.

Age, 23 July 1886; Argus, 23 July 1886; T. G. Parsons, Some aspects of the development of manufacturing in Melbourne 1870-1890 (Ph.D. thesis, Monash Univ, 1970); Hugh Lennon papers (Univ Melb Archives).

GEORGE PARSONS

LEON (LEE ON), ANDREW (1840?-1920), businessman, was born probably in China or in Hong Kong after the British annexation of 1841. After some experience of tropical agriculture in the West Indies, including two years in Cuba, he migrated in 1875 to Queensland where the Palmer gold rush was attracting many Chinese. Closely aligned with business interests established by several Hong Kong firms in Cooktown and Cairns, he managed the large store of On Lee in Cairns and then was a partner in the trading firm Sum Tung Lee in Cooktown and Sum Chung Lee in Cairns.

In 1881 through his contacts Leon was able to form a syndicate of a hundred Chinese in Cooktown and Hong Kong to take up land near Cairns for tropical agriculture. By 1885 they owned 2528 acres on which they had invested over £58,500 in improvements. After an unsuccessful attempt at cotton-growing the syndicate, somewhat ironically named the Hop Wah or 'Good Luck' Company, turned to sugar and in 1882 crushed the first cane processed in the Cairns district. The Hop Wah was run entirely as a Chinese co-operative, the only European being their engineer. With improved machinery, increasing skill and 500 acres under cane the Hop Wah's pioneer efforts won wide respect in North Queensland, but falling sugar prices and the lack of capital hit them and the rest of the industry in the mid-1880s. In 1886 the syndicate was forced to sell almost half of its land for £515,000 to the Charters Towers mining magnate, Thomas Mills, and its cane and machinery to a group of Cairns merchants who lost heavily in the speculation. The rest of the Hop Wah's land was used for fruit-growing until it too was mortgaged in 1894. In 1888 Leon bought a selection in the Barron Valley for fruit-growing where most of his energies were then directed, and he appeared to take only a cursory interest in the remaining Hop Wah land. Most of

the Chinese employed with the Hop Wah went into rice-growing, using their remaining capital to back the construction of a rice-mill by an Irish investor, Thomas Behan.

A convinced believer in tropical agriculture by small farmers, Leon had nearly succeeded in a venture which would have had implications for the future of the sugar industry and the concept of White Australia. His failure can be attributed to such incontestable forces as governmental inefficiency and natural calamities, but cognizance must also be taken of the defects in his planning. Like most of the early agriculturists in North Queensland, he overreached himself by investing in land of which only a small portion was suitable for cultivation. Even at the peak of the Hop Wah development, the returns barely covered the investments made. He later went to Hughenden where he was living in 1905, but was residing at Cairns when he died aged 80 of cancer on 27 June 1920.

As leader of a large group of Chinese in North Queensland and one of the five most prominent members of the whole Cairns community, Leon was able to combine the best of both cultures. A naturalized citizen he married a European woman and was immersed in the social and business life of the European community in Cairns. He also represented the Chinese community on municipal councils, acted as their legal interpreter and organized much of their business. His achievements and his social status posed great problems for anti-Chinese enthusiasts of the day.

Roy Com into the general conditions of the sugar industry, V&P (LA Qld), 1889, 4, 37; Queenslander, 2 May 1877; Cairns Post, 1884, Apr 1887; K. Cronin, The Chinese question in Queensland: a study of racial interaction (B.A. Hons thesis, Univ Qld, 1970); mortgage no 218, Hop Wah Plantation mortgage book 17 (QA); CRS/158 and LAN/AG 201, 212 (QA).

KATHRYN CRONIN
G. C. BOLTON

LE SOUEF, ALBERT ALEXANDER COCHRANE (1828-1902), pioneer and director of the Zoological Gardens, Melbourne, was born on 17 April 1828 at Sandgate, Kent, England, the fourth son of William Le Souef, later protector of Aborigines on the Goulburn River, and his wife Ann, née Wales. His family, descended from Huguenots who settled in Kent in the seventeenth century, bears the motto Souef sans foyblesse.

Educated at the Moravian Mission School in Neuwied, Germany, and privately, Albert arrived at Melbourne in 1840 in the Eagle. In 1841 he travelled with his tutor by bullock-dray to the protectorate station on the Goulburn where he spent three years, gained a lasting knowledge of the Aboriginals and learned bushcraft from them. His pastoral pursuits began about 1845 when he walked some eighty miles from Melbourne to Glenhope. He became overseer on Reedy Lake, Quambatook and Swan Hill stations, ran sheep and cattle in the north-east of Victoria and on Seven Creeks and Euroa stations, and overlanded stock to the Riverina, Tallygaroopna and Melbourne. His 'Personal Recollections of Early Victoria' reflect the hardship and danger he encountered; for example, he crossed the flooded flats of the Ovens on the day Joseph Docker's [q.v.] son drowned there. Occasionally the whimsical emerges, as in his impromptu employment of Bogong Jack the horse thief to care for his horses, and his experience with bullocks in mud, south of the Lachlan, that would 'bog a crow' and literally did. His interest in native fauna is shown in his recollections of local birds on the Yarra and of his first sight of bird species of the inland and the Murray River though he published only 'Notes on the fauna of Australia' in A. Sutherland et al, *Victoria and its Metropolis Past and Present*, 2 (Melbourne, 1888), and 'A Crow's Camp', *Australasian*, 6 June 1896. In 1863-93 he was usher of the Black Rod in the Legislative Council of Victoria. He gave long service to the Aborigines Protection Board, was a member of the Australasian Association for the Advancement of Science from 1888, and a corresponding member of the Zoological Society, London. In 1870 he became secretary and in 1882-1902 director of the Zoological Gardens (Zoological and Acclimatisation Society) at Royal Park at £300 a year.

Le Souef's appointment as director came at a time when, in contrast to his own and the society's aim to acclimatize animals, the need for a zoological collection to interest and educate the community was becoming recognized. His thirty-two years of administration achieved much in this direction. In 1880 he had toured Europe largely at his own expense to study zoological gardens and to gather specimens, and was inspired to make the collection in Melbourne of world standing. In 1870 the collection stood at 285 animals but by 1893 it had risen to about 1300 and the press justly claimed that his goal was being reached. Improved appearance of the grounds also emanated from his directorship, and his daily tour of inspection reflected his concern for his charges, a concern made more real by the continuing lack of financial support. He gave devoted interest, practical administrative ability and enthusiasm to the pursuit of his worthy and patriotic aim.

In 1853 Le Souef had married Caroline, the fourth daughter of John Cotton [q.v.]; born on 15 July 1834 in Barnstaple, Devon, she died at Royal Park, Melbourne, on 8 March 1915. A member of the Plymouth Brethren, Le Souef died at Royal Park on 7 May 1902 and was buried in Melbourne general cemetery. He was survived by four daughters and five sons, three of whom were associated with Australian zoological gardens.

J. Smith (ed), *Cyclopedia of Victoria*, 1 (Melb, 1903); A. Henderson (ed), *Early pioneer families of Victoria and Riverina* (Melb, 1936); H. M. Whittell, *The literature of Australian birds* (Perth, 1954); Zoological and Acclimatisation Soc of Vic, *Annual Report*, 1902; *Table Talk*, 31 Mar 1893, 30 Jan 1902; *Australasian*, 10, 17 May 1902; J. Seekamp, Some anecdotes from the past and present (Melb Zoological Gardens); papers and scrapbook (held by J. C. Le Souef, Vic).　　　　ALLAN McEVEY

LEVEY, GEORGE COLLINS (1835-1919), journalist and politician, was born on 13 April 1835 in London, son of George Levey. Educated in private schools and at University College, London, he sailed for Melbourne with his brothers Oliver and William and arrived in 1851. In May 1852 he was appointed clerk to the gold receiver at Forest Creek but stayed less than ten weeks. According to J. A. Panton [q.v.], Levey was 'very green' but he soon ventured into gold-buying with success and was among the first to use quartz-crushing machinery. In the mid-1850s he began contributing to Melbourne newspapers.

In 1858 Levey toured western Europe and Russia and wrote for the English press. On his return in 1860 he became sub-editor of the *Herald* and continued to write to English papers. By 1863 he was editor and chief proprietor of the *Herald* and reduced its price to 1d., thereby pioneering cheap newspapers. In 1868 he sold out to David Syme [q.v.] and until 1891 was a contributor and sometime editor of the *Age*. Among other business interests he maintained connexions with his brother William, who was a pioneer theatrical printer and proprietor of *Bell's Life*, then the only sporting journal in Melbourne; it started in January 1857 and was absorbed by the *Australasian* in January 1868. His brother Oliver was less successful as a printers' broker.

From August 1861 to December 1867 Levey held the Normanby seat in the Legislative Assembly. A fluent speaker and an excellent working member, he introduced in January 1862 the aliens' bill which was enacted in June. In the 1863 debates on Heales's [q.v.] amendments to the Duffy [q.v.] Selection Act of 1862, he advocated the reinstitution of public auction, claiming that 99 per cent of applications for land near Hamilton were made by speculators. By advocating protective duties to alleviate unemployment and encourage industry around Hamilton, he was returned unopposed in 1864 while near-by electorates were fiercely contested. However, he failed to win the Normanby seat in 1868 and Warrnambool in 1871.

In 1870 Levey had become secretary to the commissioners at the Sydney Exhibition. Later he represented Victoria and other colonies at exhibitions in Melbourne in 1872, 1875 and 1880-81, London and Vienna in 1873, Philadelphia in 1876, Paris (where with special permission he was awarded the *Légion d'honneur*) in 1878, Amsterdam in 1883 and the Crystal Palace in 1884. He was also secretary to the Tasmanian commission of the exhibition there in 1894 and to the colonial committee of the British royal commission to the Paris Exhibition in 1900. Experience gained from travel was augmented by his 'energy, zeal and powers of organizing', and in 1878 he was appointed C.M.G. for his services as an eminently successful emissary for his colonies.

Levey had continued writing for the international press: he published *The Handy Guide to Australia* (London, 1891) and *Hutchinson's Australasian Encyclopaedia* (1892), contributed to the *Encyclopaedia Britannica* and wrote some minor travel books. He had been an original member of the Yorick Club in 1868. In 1881-82 he served on the royal commission inquiring into the Kelly [q.v.] outbreak and performance of the police, and then returned to England. In 1885 he was examined in the Bankruptcy Court in London on a private engagement he had made in Melbourne with his creditors in 1866. He was appointed a member of the Board of Advice to the agent-general of Victoria in 1906 and joined the National Liberal Club. He was twice married: first, in 1863 to Euphemia Caulfield Dalton, daughter of C. W. Ligar [q.v.]; second, on 23 January 1877 at Washington to Mary Elizabeth, daughter of George Parker and widow of John Edward Bouligny (1824-1864), a congressional representative for Louisiana. Levey died in London on 13 April 1919.

H. M. Humphreys (ed), *Men of the time in Australia: Victorian series*, 1st ed (Melb, 1878); *Illustrated Aust News*, 9 Oct 1880; *The Times*, 15 Apr 1919; J. A. Panton, Memoirs (LaT L); J. M. C. Watson, Selectors and squatters in the Hamilton district in the 1860s (M.A. thesis, Univ Melb, 1957); L. C. Duly, The land selection acts in Victoria 1859-1869 (M.A. thesis, Univ Melb, 1959).   SUZANNE G. MELLOR

LEVI, NATHANIEL (1830-1908), politician and businessman, was born on 20 January 1830 in Liverpool, England, son of Joseph Levi, manufacturer, and his wife Sarah. He arrived at Hobson's Bay in April 1854 in the *Matilda Wattenbach* and in 1858 joined the firm of John Levey & Son who had stores in Melbourne and Maryborough.

After defeat in the 1859 election Levi represented Maryborough in the Legislative Assembly in 1860-65. He was the first Jew to sit in the Victorian parliament and was sworn in on the Old Testament with his head covered. He failed to win the Maryborough seat in 1866 but was promptly elected for East Melbourne in February. Perhaps his most notable speech was delivered when in January 1865 the treasurer, G. F. Verdon [q.v.], proposed new duties designed among other objects to give mild protection to local industries. On 24 January Levi led the attack on this proposal, claiming that the duties would raise prices and not benefit manufactures. In 1865-68, while the two Houses were locked in conflict over the tacking of the tariff and Darling grant bills to the annual appropriation bill, Levi voted persistently on the conservative or 'Upper House' side. However, he was a good local member, securing a railway link and attacking the gold export duty. He continued to contest East Melbourne in vain from 1868, but frankly changed his views, and as a Liberal candidate in 1881 advocated protection, Upper House reform, support for the Education Act and Chinese restriction. In the 1880s he again stood unsuccessfully for various seats. Elected to the Legislative Council for North Yarra Province in 1892-1904, he was very strongly opposed to income tax and wages boards. As a member of the royal commission on state banking in 1895 he accepted the bankers' evidence and opposed the majority recommendation to amalgamate the savings banks and establish a *Crédit Foncier* Land Mortgage Department.

Levi's changed fiscal views were probably affected by his own promotion of local industries. His interest in the Cape Paterson coalfield began in 1859 and lasted for many years. In 1864 his firm, Nathaniel Levi & Co., started a distillery at Footscray to manufacture spirits and sugar from beetroot. He won exhibition medals and compiled a handbook in 1870 explaining the techniques and benefits of the process, but the company had to sell the plant to pay the firm's debts. He then turned to auctioneering and agency business, and in 1884 took his two sons into the firm. He launched the short-lived *Daily News* in October 1885. For years he held the advertising concession from the Victorian railways. An early member of the Victorian

Manufacturers' and Exhibitors' Association, he was also a founder and trustee of the Chamber of Manufactures, serving as president in the depression years of 1893-95.

Prominent in the Jewish community, Levi was president of the Melbourne Hebrew Congregation in 1880-82 and 1904-05. Strong-willed, energetic and orthodox, he opposed concessions in observance and temporarily resigned from the congregation when the Jewish day school was closed in 1885. He died at St Kilda on 11 September 1908, predeceased in 1864 by his wife Sarah, and survived by two sons, Joseph and John.

T. W. H. Leavitt (ed), *Australian representative men* (Melb, 1887); L. M. Goldman, *The Jews in Victoria in the nineteenth century* (Melb, 1954); *Argus*, 12 Sept 1908; newspaper cuttings (held by Rabbi John Levi, Armadale, Vic).   L. E. FREDMAN

LEVIEN, JONAS FELIX AUSTRALIA (1840-1906), agriculturist and politician, was born on 28 March 1840 at Williamstown, Port Phillip, son of Benjamin Goldsmith Levien and his wife Eliza, née Lindo. His father's family was of French origin and his mother Portuguese. Educated in 1858-59 at a grammer school in Geelong, he was connected with that district all his life.

Levien entered politics as a conservative protectionist by defeating Peter Lalor [q.v.] for South Grant in 1871. At the elections of 1877 the supporters of Graham Berry [q.v.] won an overwhelming victory as an organized radical party. They were committed to a land tax which Levien, a nominal supporter, had opposed. Although the opposition capitulated, Levien, who had won the Barwon seat, joined four other members to vote against the bill. Meanwhile his opponent, John Ince, had submitted a petition to unseat him for engaging in the common practice of paying canvassers. The assembly ignored Levien's protest that Lalor, a member of the Elections and Qualifications Committee, bore him personal malice. By a party vote the committee issued a second report to rectify a loophole in the first which found Levien guilty of bribery, and declared the petitioner elected, awarding him costs. Levien represented Barwon in 1880-1906. As minister of mines and agriculture in the Service [q.v.]-Berry coalition in 1883-86 he introduced the bill which set up the Council of Agricultural Education, and became its first president. In the depressed 1890s he opposed new taxation and invariably voted on the conservative side.

Levien had early started a seed farm at Drysdale and later became a director of several companies in Melbourne, including the Colonial Mutual Life Assurance Society, the Colonial Mutual Fire Insurance Co., the Australian Mutual Livestock Insurance Co. and the Argus Permanent Building and Investment Society. He was appointed to several royal commissions on agricultural matters and was a member of the important shops and factories royal commission in 1901-03. One venture was less successful: in 1888 two years after he had opposed the scheme in parliament he had become chairman of Chaffey Bros Ltd, formed to promote an irrigation colony in north-western Victoria. Because of its huge debts and the complaints of the settlers, a royal commission inquired into the project in 1896. The commissioners criticized the Chaffeys for defective works and Levien for obtaining capital at excessive rates of interest. They added that Levien, 'who was believed to be possessed of large means, was induced to join the directorate in order to increase confidence'. Levien conceded that he had principal control of finance but claimed that the company owed him about £40,000 and that he had guaranteed large loans. His son, Harold, also gave evidence on behalf of the settlers.

Levien was one of the thirteen founders of the Australian Natives' Association, and was elected a vice-president and member of the first executive in July 1871, but he was not active in the years of the society's greatest influence. He died on 24 May 1906 at his home in St Kilda Road. On 15 March 1871 at Sydney he had married his first cousin, Clara Levien, and left a daughter and three sons, one of whom, Cecil James, became a prominent New Guinea pioneer. According to tradition Levien was the first Jewish child born in Victoria but his children were brought up as Anglicans.

A. Sutherland et al, *Victoria and its metropolis*, 2 (Melb, 1888); J. Smith (ed), *Cyclopedia of Victoria*, 1 (Melb, 1903); J. A. Alexander, *The life of George Chaffey* (Melb, 1928); L. M. Goldman, *The Jews in Victoria in the nineteenth century* (Melb, 1954); V&P (LA Vic), 1877-78, 1 (D15, 16), 1896, 3 (19); L. E. Fredman, 'Some Victorian Jewish politicians', Aust Jewish Hist Soc, J, 4 (1954-58); *Argus*, 25 May 1906; private information.   L. E. FREDMAN

LEVY, LEWIS WOLFE (1815-1885), businessman and politician, was born on 13 June 1815 in London, son of Benjamin Wolfe Levy, merchant, and his wife Martha, née Levy. In 1840 he migrated to Sydney and soon went into business at Maitland. In 1846 he moved to Tamworth where he bought land and established a flourishing general store. About this time he became a partner with his cousins, Samuel and David Cohen, in the Maitland mercantile firm, David Cohen & Co., and was the driving force behind the firm's expansion after he returned to Maitland in 1854. He moved to Sydney in 1862 but remained active in the firm's affairs. His business reputation grew steadily and from the mid-1870s he occupied an increasing number of commercial posts, becoming chairman of the Hunter River New Steam Navigation Co. and a director of the Newcastle Wallsend Coal Co., the Australian Gaslight Co., the United Insurance Co., the Commercial Banking Co. of Sydney and the Australasian Steam Navigation Co. He also acquired pastoral interests and by 1871 held Yarraman on the Liverpool Plains and was a partner in seven other runs.

In 1871 Levy was elected to the Legislative Assembly for Liverpool Plains. His disapproval of the Martin-Robertson [qq.v.] coalition led him into opposition until he retired early in 1872. In August 1874 he was returned for West Maitland, and with some reservations supported the government of Henry Parkes [q.v.] who had backed his candidacy and promised flood mitigation works in the district. However, Levy retired only three months later to devote more time to business matters. In parliament his chief concern had been to hold Parkes to his promise of flood works and, although he was a free trader with vague commitments to land and electoral reform, he displayed scant interest in matters of general policy. He had also advocated an elective Legislative Council but accepted appointment to it in 1880 as a representative of the Jewish community. He defended the council's rights and privileges and remained a member until 1885.

Levy's inability to give much time to politics stemmed partly from his active involvement with charitable, educational and religious institutions. He was a director of Prince Alfred Hospital and the Industrial Blind Institution, served on the board of the Sydney Hebrew School and was president of the Macquarie Street Synagogue in 1862-74 and from 1876 to 1877 when it closed. He then travelled overseas with his wife Julia, daughter of Samuel Solomon, whom he had married in 1845. He died on 25 January 1885, survived by his wife, eight sons and five of their seven daughters. He was buried in the Hebrew section of Rookwood cemetery. Although self-made, plain spoken and occasionally short tempered, he was widely respected and sincerely mourned. His estate, sworn for probate at over £245,000, was left mostly to his relations and friends and charitable institutions received £3875.

M. Macphail, *The Australian squatting directory* (Melb, 1871); D. J. Benjamin, 'The Macquarie Street Synagogue, 1859-1877', Aust Jewish Hist Soc, J, 3 (1953); 'Lewis Wolfe Levy', Aust Jewish Hist Soc, J, 6 (1970); *Maitland Mercury*, 1, 4 Aug, 5 Dec 1874; CO 201/592/313.
C. N. CONNOLLY

LEWIS, CHARLES FERRIS (1828-1900), mining entrepreneur and newspaper proprietor, was born on 4 April 1828 at Devizes, Wiltshire, England, son of Charles Lewis, farmer, and his wife Sarah, née Ferris. He went to London at 13 and probably joined the small-goods trade. He arrived at Sydney in July 1849 but soon joined the rush to the Californian goldfields. He reached San Francisco in February 1850 and for three years had some success near Sacramento. He returned to Sydney in 1853 and followed the rushes to Ballarat and Bendigo, spending some time at the Yam Holes near Beaufort. On 16 March 1855 he joined a prospectors' camp at New Bendigo (St Arnaud North). A good entertainer and full of energy, he won the esteem of the party's leader and was given a profitable 'golden hole'. One of the first at the Bell Rock diggings he took over the abandoned claim at Wilson's Hill, on which he and his friends made mining history when payable gold was brought up from a depth of 270 feet. When the Chrysolite Co. was formed he was a director and later as legal manager he steered it into the great dividend-paying Lord Nelson. He was also a pioneer of the Prince of Wales mine. He never sold a share for speculation but put his profits into redevelopment.

Lewis settled at New Bendigo in 1855 and devoted himself to promoting the district's welfare. He held an auctioneer's licence and opened estate and insurance agencies. When the town was surveyed in 1857 he and two others were asked to name the streets, one of which was called Lewis. He bought a site on Alma Street for £4 and built a weatherboard house, Wiltshire Cottage, which remained part of his home until 1900. In 1862 he topped the poll for borough councillors but resigned in 1867 to devote attention to the *St Arnaud Mercury* which he had bought. His sympathies were always with the independent and wage miner but every good cause was given the paper's support. He bound yearly volumes for presentation to the Borough Council of St Arnaud, the Shire of Kara Kara and the Mechanics' Institute.

In politics Lewis was an uncompromising Liberal and upheld his principles with no uncertain pen and voice. He was an active worker for the Church of England and helped to organize the building of Christ Church in 1866. In 1868 he married Jane, widow of Archibald Borthwick. He then carried on the Borthwick store until it was destroyed by fire in 1880. He was a director of the Country Press Association, the first representative of St Arnaud on the Maryborough Mining Board and a trustee of the local branch of the Australian Miners' Association. He held high office in the Manchester Unity Independent Order of Odd Fellows and was an active Freemason. He was appointed a justice of the peace in 1887 and gave evidence to the royal commission on gold mining in 1889-91.

Affectionately known as 'the Father of St. Arnaud', Lewis died suddenly on 3 May 1900 and was buried in the local cemetery, survived by his wife, two daughters and two sons, Charles Ferris and Thomas George, who carried on the *Mercury* until 1929.

J. Smith (ed), *Cyclopedia of Victoria*, 3 (Melb, 1905); Y. S. Palmer, *Track of the years* (Melb, 1955); *St Arnaud Mercury*, 5 May 1900; *Leader* (Melb), 12 May 1900.   JEAN GITTINS

LIGAR, CHARLES WHYBROW (1811-1881), surveyor, soldier and grazier, was born in Ceylon, where his father was stationed. Aged 13 years and 7 months he entered the Royal Military Academy, Sandhurst, on 8 February 1825. After four years he was reputedly commissioned in the Royal Engineers, but resigned to join the British Ordnance Survey which was then producing the famous one-inch topographical maps. He was mapping in Ireland until 1840 and gained experience in cartographic detail, particularly hill-shading techniques, to add to his military training in surveys.

Appointed surveyor-general of New Zealand, Ligar arrived at Wellington on 8 December 1841. His work was overshadowed by the excellence of some of his subordinates and he is mostly remembered as a land titles commissioner in the late 1840s. He was also a lieut-colonel in the Auckland Militia. He resigned from the New Zealand civil service in 1856 and went to Otago, hoping to obtain the post of provincial surveyor. However, he failed to dislodge John Turnbull Thomson (1821-1884), the capable incumbent, and made many enemies in the process. In his search for grazing country Ligar discovered gold in the Mataura River. He visited Victoria in 1857 as land commissioner for Otago, but incurred the wrath of his New Zealand neighbours when he tried to persuade Victorian pastoralists to buy large blocks in southern Otago. Despite these setbacks he retained influential connexions and was highly recommended to C. G. Duffy [q.v.] as the most competent officer to reform the Victorian survey system.

In 1858 Ligar became surveyor-general and for a time was impressive with his promises to reduce the cost of survey and open the land quickly for settlement. Within a few months he deliberately withheld large blocks of land from the market until they could be subdivided, claiming that the original scheme would surrender these areas to the squatters, 'a sacrifice of the public domain'. He took issue with A. J. Skene [q.v.] over appraising the quality of land in the colony and strongly protested that much larger areas were suitable for small-scale farming. At the same time he and his family were investing heavily in livestock and with Hugh Glass, R. S. H. Anderson and John O'Shanassy [qq.v.] as his partners Ligar leased three million acres in the Riverina. His plan for a geodetic survey was adopted in September 1858, a great improvement on the former magnetic surveys which were unreliable as legal documents and inadequate as a foundation for planning the expansion of settlement. The new survey adhered strictly to the true meridians and parallels, and despite much criticism provided an accurate framework for speeding local surveys. However, much of this achievement should be credited to R. L. J. Ellery [q.v.], who managed the new scheme in 1858-74.

Ligar's initial proposal to replace the entire staff of government surveyors by contractors was a major blunder and, since he had been appointed over the head of the experienced C. Hodgkinson [q.v.], his career in Victoria was doomed to failure from the first. He was always unpopular in the Lands Department and, because his promises to reduce expenditure and speed the surveys were not fulfilled by 1869, prominent politicians were demanding his removal. He resigned in September on a government pension of £500 and retired to Europe where he lived on the Mediterranean coast for some years before taking up a ranch in Texas.

On 12 March 1866 Ligar read a paper, 'Grass Tree', to the Royal Society of Victoria of which he was a councillor in 1859, 1860, 1863 and 1868, and vice-president in 1861 and 1865-67. In 1839 he had married Grace Hanyngton of Tyrone, Ireland. She died in April 1868 and he married Marie Williams of Auckland in 1869. He died in February 1881 in Texas and was buried at Willow Springs, Parker County. His diary from 22 November 1845 to 19 November 1846 is in the Auckland Public Library.

A. H. McLintock, *The history of Otago* (Dunedin, 1949); J. M. Powell, *The public lands of Australia Felix* (Melb, 1970); V&P (Otago Provincial Council), 1856 (5th S), appendix; V&P (LA Vic), 1858-59 (A9, A18), 1859-60, 4 (38); *New Zealand Gazette*, 29 Dec 1841, 5 Oct 1842, 9 Feb 1846, 8 Feb 1847; *New Zealand J*, 28 May 1842, 13 Mar 1847; *Nelson Examiner*, 6 Mar 1847; B. de Vries, The role of the land surveyor in the development of New Zealand, 1840-76 (M.A. thesis, Victoria Univ, Wellington, 1968); T. S. Hocken, MS notes 37 (Hocken Lib, Dunedin); information from Texas State Hist Assn.   J. M. POWELL

LILLEY, SIR CHARLES (1827-1897), politician and judge, was born on 27 August 1827 at Newcastle upon Tyne, son of Thomas Lilley and his wife Jane, née Shipley. Reared by his maternal grandfather and educated at St Nicholas Parish School, he was articled on 2 October 1849 to the Newcastle solicitor, William Lockey Harle, sent to his London office, and for two years studied at University College, London. On 3 December 1851 Lilley enlisted in the 1st Royal Dragoons as a private. On duty at Preston, Lancashire, he helped to start a free library and often lectured with moderation on temperance, adult education and industrial relations, but in 1853 he rashly fraternized with workers threatening a major strike. The military authorities thought him dangerous and gave him twenty-eight days in cells, nominally for absence without leave. Enraged, Lilley bought his discharge on 6 February 1854 and returned to the law. Advised in 1855 by James Wilson, founder of the *Economist*, he decided to migrate and on 6 July 1856 arrived at Sydney.

Lilley moved to Brisbane and on 10 November was articled to Robert Little [q.v.], but soon joined W. C. Belbridge in leasing the *Moreton Bay Courier* from James Swan [q.v.]. As editor he won popularity by advocating separation from New South Wales, but the paper was not a success and the lease was terminated. However, writing about politics had whetted his taste for participation. In 1859 he was active in forming the Liberal Association, which was widely criticized as a rigid machine geared for his own aggrandizement. On 10 April 1858 he had married Sarah Jane, daughter of Joshua Jeays, an architect with radical political views. To support his growing family Lilley returned to Little's office, completed his articles, was admitted to the Bar on 22 November 1861, joined J. F. Garrick [q.v.] as partner, and in December 1865 was appointed Q.C.

In May 1860 Lilley had been elected for Fortitude Valley to Queensland's first Legislative Assembly, defeating a squatter contestant by three votes. Known as 'Lilley of the Valley', his views harmonized with those of his radical constituents, many of

whom had been inspired to migrate by J. D. Lang [q.v.]. As an ex-soldier he became an enthusiastic officer of volunteers and in 1862, allegedly at Govenor Bowen's behest, he introduced a bill for a conscripted militia. The resultant uproar almost ended his parliamentary career. In a public meeting he sought to defend himself but was nearly lynched by his constituents and in June withdrew the bill.

From 11 September 1865 to 20 July 1866 Lilley was attorney-general in Macalister's [q.v.] ministry and again from 7 August 1866 to 15 August 1867. From 25 November 1868 to 12 November 1869 he was attorney-general in his own ministry. He was called as premier to solve an impasse caused by the almost equal strength of the parties but was plagued by the worst economic depression in Queensland's history and by his unstable coalition ministry.

Lilley's several cabinets included two other Liberals, four squatters, one northern separationist and the mercurial Macalister, and held within themselves all the strains and conflicts inherent in Queensland politics. Lilley was more impulsive than diplomatic and found his team difficult to manage. On 25 January Macalister, hoping to upset the government, resigned after a violent quarrel with Lilley and T. H. Fitzgerald [q.v.]. Lilley was able to secure Fitzgerald's resignation and persuaded Macalister to rejoin the ministry; James Taylor [q.v.] became secretary for lands, T. B. Stephens [q.v.] colonial treasurer and Arthur Hodgson [q.v.] colonial secretary, but Lilley's credit suffered from the reshuffle. In November 1869 when both John Douglas [q.v.] and Hodgson resigned, Ratcliffe Pring [q.v.] became attorney-general and Lilley colonial secretary. In these circumstances, his premiership was unimpressive. Only 17 of 39 bills introduced and only 3 of 10 introduced by Lilley were passed. Both his most important measures were lost in the second reading. Ironically, his one success was a comprehensive Pastoral Leases Act.

Lilley had resisted the extortionate claims made by the monopolistic Australasian Steam Navigation Co. for increase in its mail subsidies. In 1869 he visited Sydney with the governor and despite objections from his ministers signed a contract for three government steamers, an action which rapidly reduced the company's demands. On 1 January 1870 he abolished fees in government schools by ministerial directive, again without the approval of his colleagues. He was accused of arrogance and his parliamentary support began to evaporate. When the House met in April he had to move his own address-in-reply. In a bitter speech, J. P. Bell [q.v.] moved a no confidence motion and in the division Lilley was supported only by his cabinet and Henry Jordan [q.v.]. The *Courier* suggested that Lilley was defeated by the machinations of an Ipswich clique opposed to the Brisbane-Ipswich railway and to Bernays [q.v.] he was ahead of his time. His impulsive and domineering leadership of a patchwork cabinet and what the *Courier* called an unbecoming levity of manner were sufficient explanations.

When parliament met in November 1870, the new premier, Arthur Palmer [q.v.], with only sixteen supporters was saved from disaster when Macalister agreed to become Speaker. To Lilley this was treachery and, partly by a personal canvass, he secured Macalister's defeat in June 1871. As leader of the Opposition, Lilley was more effective than he had been as premier. A master of procedures, he virtually stopped government business from December 1870 to August 1871 by constant filibusters and adjournment motions; outside the House, he led public meetings and petitioned the governor for parliamentary reform. In August the administrator, Sir Maurice O'Connell [q.v.], dissolved parliament and in the following election Palmer secured a majority of six. Lilley refused to accept defeat. He claimed that the election had been won by inequitable electorates and continued the struggle until Palmer had passed his redistribution bill, the first significant reduction in the power of the squatting party. Despite the success of his struggle for democracy Lilley was ambivalent on the subject. Arrogant about his own brilliance, he described manhood suffrage as vicious because it allowed any shepherd or labourer to have the same influence as an educated professional or an employer who contributed heavily to the revenue.

Macalister returned to the assembly in June 1872 and soon became leader of the Opposition. Supplanted, Lilley claimed to have been so disgusted with his fellow members in 1870 that nothing would ever drag him back to the treasury. When the Palmer government fell on 8 January 1874, he rejected an invitation to join Macalister's ministry. He promised general support but continued to embarrass Macalister. In July he accepted the offer of an acting seat on the Supreme Court bench. On the retirement of Sir James Cockle [q.v.] in 1879 Lilley became chief justice. For a time he was influential in liberal councils but gradually drifted into the seclusion of the bench.

Lilley's flexible interpretation of radicalism was exemplified on 21 May 1881 when he was offered a knighthood. At first he sought permission to decline because the offer recognized not his personal qualities but his office. The Colonial Office believed that he was piqued because his political enemy, Palmer, had been knighted earlier and would thus have precedence, but when pressed, Lilley accepted on 28 October 1881. His principles occasionally caused other difficulties. His sentences on the crew of the blackbirder *Hopeful*, convicted for brutality and murder in 1883, polarized the colony. Advocates of coloured labour argued that the men had behaved in accordance with accepted custom and that the evidence against them was suspect. Their opponents saw Lilley's sentences as a salutary lesson but after a petition in 1888 the Morehead [q.v.] government released the men in spite of Lilley's objections.

With advancing age Lilley began to regret his detachment from active politics and to express outspoken support for extreme radical causes, often hinting that he would not stay permanently on the bench. In 1890 he became a hero to the socialist and republican movements by attacking politicians as a class, advocating an Australian republic and decrying the imperial connexion. By cultivating the growing Labor Party, he was invited in March 1891 to lay the foundation stone of the Brisbane Trades Hall and in 1892 he regretfully declined an invitation from the New South Wales Labor Electoral League to a public reception in Sydney.

Incautiously, Lilley left himself open to attack from those who objected to his views. The Supreme Court successes of his barrister son, Edwyn, became so frequent that they were once ascribed flippantly to 'the light of the son'. Because clients were quick to take advantage, Edwyn was said to receive more briefs than three other leading barristers together. The subject reached parliament in July 1890 when M. B. Gannon, a McIlwraith [q.v.] supporter, introduced the justices prevention bill to bar Edwyn from the Supreme Court, but the bill was opposed by legal members and vanished from the notice paper in November.

In 1891 Edwyn appeared for the Queensland Investment and Land Mortgage Co. of London in an action for fraud against its local directors including Sir Thomas McIlwraith and Sir Arthur Palmer. After thirty-seven days of hearing, he was permitted by his father to amend the pleadings and soon afterwards the chief justice decided to discharge the jury. He argued that no judge could accept a verdict against his own conscience and when the hearings closed after fifty-five days, he reserved judgment on 23 July 1892. Meanwhile Gannon had moved on 31 March in the House that no judge should sit alone or in chambers in any matter in which his son was counsel. Because the case was *sub judice*, the motion was deferred several times but on 21 July it was passed by 40 to 4. Lilley's judgment on 17 August gave substantial damages to the plaintiff and caused immediate uproar. McIlwraith is said to have sworn vengeance, and for the appeal in October a special arrangement was made with New South Wales for Sir William Windeyer [q.v.] to replace Lilley on the bench. The Full Court reversed Lilley's judgment.

For some time Lilley had contemplated retirement but announced it on 24 October and McIlwraith was rumoured to have had his revenge. Lilley immediately visited New Zealand on leave and returned to retire on 13 February 1893. In other colonies his views made him an embarrassing visitor to be practically ignored.

The apparent partisanship of Lilley's judicial swan song endeared him to the Labor Party. He saw a chance for a political comeback which would counterbalance his ignominious departure from the bench and at the same time injure those whom he saw as lineal descendants of old enemies. Rejecting invitations from republican supporters to contest northern seats, he announced in April 1893 his candidature for North Brisbane against McIlwraith. His running mate for the two-member seat was Thomas Glassey, the Labor leader. His thirteen point programme included repeal of the Land Grant Railway Act, abolition of coloured labour, a White Australia policy, radical electoral reform and a progressive land tax, but he foolishly insisted on his independence of the Labor machine. With an almost uniformly hostile press, Lilley and Glassey polled just over half the combined vote for McIlwraith and Kingsbury. Lilley died at his Brisbane home on 20 August 1897, survived by his wife, eight sons and five daughters.

After his knighthood, few Queenslanders could take Lilley's exaggerated radicalism seriously. Their distrust was reinforced by his rigid refusal to commit himself fully to the Labor Party. Rejected by his social equals, he was never quite accepted by those whom he sought to woo. He was more successful in his consistent pursuit of an educational ideal. Stimulated by the atmosphere of University College, London, he was instrumental before 1860 in establishing the Brisbane School of Arts and in 1869 helped to found the Brisbane Grammar School, serving later as its chairman of trustees. In 1870 his government fell partly over free education and in 1874 he chaired a royal commission which led to a free and secular education policy. This achieved, he began a campaign for a university and in 1891 chaired a royal commission on university establishment, but did not live to see it founded in 1909.

C. A. Bernays, *Queensland politics during sixty years* (Brisb, 1919); PD (Qld), 1868-69, 111, 1870, 257, 1873, 117; V&P (LA Qld), 1875, 2, 83, 1884, 2, 725, 1890, 1, 551, 1891, 3, 803, 1892, 1, 595; A. A. Morrison, 'Charles Lilley', JRAHS, 45 (1959-60); D. Anderson, 'Sir George Bowen and the problem of Queensland's defence 1859-1868', Qld Heritage, 2 (1970) no 3; *Brisbane Courier*, 27 Jan 1862, 19 Mar 1869, 18 July 1870, 27 Jan 1872, 20 Nov 1873, 14 June, 17 Aug, 29 Oct, 21 Nov 1892, 24 Aug 1897; *Town and Country J*, 10 July 1879; *Aust Republican*, 20 Sept 1890; *Pall Mall Gazette*, 12 Dec 1891; *Queenslander*, 29 Oct 1892, 28 Aug 1897; *Week*, 14 Apr, 5 May 1893; *Bulletin*, 28 Aug 1897; D. K. Dignan, Sir Thomas McIlwraith: a political portrait (B.A. Hons thesis, Univ Qld, 1951); J. C. Vockler, Sir Samuel Walker Griffith (B.A. Hons thesis, Univ Qld, 1953); Herbert letters, 17 Sept 1865 (Oxley Lib, Brisb); Barristers admission papers (QA); biog cuttings (Oxley Lib, Brisb); CO 448/1B/561; WO 12/482.   H. J. GIBBNEY

LILLY, JAMES (1845-1905), businessman and shipping agent, was born on 2 February 1845 at Launceston, Van Diemen's Land, son of James Lilly and his wife Hannah, née Dillon. In 1869 he went to Victoria and married Mary Hannah Field of Hawthorn. He soon formed a partnership with Charles V. Robinson, also of Launceston, and in 1871 they became established as shipping agents in Belfast (Port Fairy).

In 1876 Lilly entered into negotiations with the Western Australian government for a subsidy to run a coastal shipping service to replace the irregular sailings provided by the *Georgette*, which had foundered at Busselton. In 1877 with his family he left for Fremantle in the *Rob Roy*, which became the first steamer to ply the Western Australian coastal trade on a regular basis. The *Rob Roy* made monthly visits to Geraldton, Fremantle, Vasse and other intervening ports, connecting at Albany with Peninsular and Oriental Steam Navigation Co.'s steamers carrying mails to and from the colony. In 1879 the *Otway* was acquired from Victoria and brought into the service to provide the first direct link between Western Australia and the eastern colonies. Fortnightly sailings between Victoria, South Australia and Albany were arranged to coincide with the arrival of the *Rob Roy* from north-western ports. As trade expanded a third steamer, *Macedon*, was bought to increase the sailings but she was soon wrecked and replaced by the *Otway*. When the second government contract expired in 1882 Lilly sold his shipping interests to the Adelaide Steamship Co. for whom he became local manager. In 1894 Lilly owned the schooner *Bittern* on the Mauritius run. His company also handled the Western

Australian business of the Australasian Steam Navigation Co. Ltd, until its own agent was appointed in 1897. He had used his capital to acquire much property in Fremantle and in 1895 with George Swinburne was responsible for founding the Fremantle Gas and Coke Co. of which he was chairman until 1905.

The shipping service provided by James Lilly & Co. was often described in parliament as 'excellent' and from all accounts he was held in high regard by the Fremantle community. Fiery tempered but known as 'one of the old school', he earned the title of 'Father of Western Australian shipping'. A regular participant in local affairs, he was a justice of the peace and a member of the Fremantle Hospital Board from its inception. He died from an overdose of strychnine at Claremont on 18 April 1905 and was buried in the Church of England cemetery at Fremantle. He was survived by five daughters.

R. Osburne, *The history of Warrnambool, 1847-1886* (Prahran, 1887); J. K. Hitchcock, *The history of Fremantle . . . 1829-1929* (Fremantle, 1929); J. G. Wilson (ed), *Western Australia's centenary 1829-1929* (Perth, 1929); *Herald* (Fremantle), 7 Apr 1877; *Mail* (Fremantle), 19 Apr 1905; *West Australian*, 19, 20 Apr 1905; CSO records (Battye Lib, Perth).
                                                    TOBY MANFORD

LINDEMAN, HENRY JOHN (1811-1881), vigneron and surgeon, was born on 21 September 1811 at Egham, Surrey, England, son of John William Henry Lindeman, medical practitioner. Trained at St Bartholomew's Hospital (M.R.C.S., 1834), he was appointed surgeon in the naval hospital ship *Dreadnought* moored at Greenwich. In 1837 he became surgeon in the *Marquis of Camden* and went to India, Canton and other ports on a voyage lasting eighteen months. On 11 February 1840 at Southampton he married Eliza Harriet (d. 1900), daughter of Joseph Abraham Bramhall.

Dissatisfied with prospects at sea and in England, Lindeman migrated to Sydney with his wife and arrived in September 1840. He settled at Gresford on the Paterson River and opened a medical practice. In 1843 he acquired the Cawarra estate where he found the soil and climate suitable for successful wine-making and established a vineyard. He had visited the wine districts of France and Germany and learned much from their wines and production methods. He was soon making wine of excellent quality. In 1850 he became a member of the Hunter River Vineyard Association and regularly attended its meetings; he was president in 1863 and 1870. On 13 September 1851 a fire had destroyed his stores and cellars, equipment and 4000 gallons of wine, but he went to the Victorian goldfields, worked as a doctor and miner, and soon accumulated funds. He returned to Cawarra and rebuilt the winery, but for some years he had no wine sufficiently mature for sale.

In northern Victoria Lindeman had been impressed by the wines of the Rutherglen and adjoining districts. He continued his connexion with the area and by 1872 had a large wine trade at Corowa; later he bought vineyards in the district. In 1870 he transferred his business activities to Sydney because of the demands of cellar space and increased production. He set up bottling equipment at the Exchange Cellars, Pitt Street. In the 1870s he won high repute in Sydney for his colonial wines, with increasing production of fine table wines in the Hunter district and of sherries and muscats at Corowa. In 1879 he took three of his sons into partnership. He strongly advocated the consumption of light table wines in place of strong spirits, which he deemed harmful in the Australian climate. He established his firm on the sound basis of selling only mature wines of good quality.

Widely known and esteemed as a founder of the Australian wine industry, Lindeman died at Cawarra, Gresford, on 23 May 1881 and was buried there by Anglican rites. He was survived by his wife, five sons and five daughters.

E. Digby (ed), *Australian men of mark*, 2 (Syd, 1889); *Cyclopedia of N.S.W.* (Syd, 1907); M. Lake, *Hunter wine* (Brisb, 1964); M. Lake, *Vine and scalpel* (Brisb, 1967); H. P. Mollenhauer, *Hunter River wine industry* (np, nd); *Maitland Mercury*, 2 June 1881; *SMH*, 3 June 1881; *Town and Country J*, 4 June 1881; *Old Times*, Apr 1903.   FRANK L. WOODHOUSE

LINDT, JOHN WILLIAM (1845-1926), photographer, was born at Frankfurt on Main, Germany, son of Peter Joseph Lindt, excise officer, and his wife Justine, née Rambach. At 17 he ran away to sea and joined a Dutch sailing ship. He deserted at Brisbane; by 1863 he was at Grafton as a piano-tuner and then worked in a photographic studio. He visited Germany in 1867 and on his return bought the business. Using the wet-plate process he photographed the Clarence River district and its Aboriginals, producing albums in 1875 and 1876. He then sold out and went to Melbourne where he opened a studio in Collins Street. He soon won repute for his society, theatre and landscape photographs. In 1880 he photographed the capture of the Kelly [q.v.] gang at Glenrowan. When the first commercial dry plates arrived in Melbourne he went to Europe to seek agencies for the latest photographic equipment. On his return he worked in the studio and the Victorian countryside; many of his photographs were used in the railways. He also designed and modified cameras as well as 'advising in matters photographic'.

In 1885 Lindt went with Sir Peter Scratchley's [q.v.] expedition to the Protectorate of British New Guinea as official photographer. He presented an album of his New Guinea photographs to the Indian and Colonial Exhibition in London in 1886. He went to Europe to publish his *Picturesque New Guinea* (London, 1887), to visit the optical institutions and manufacturers which he represented and to seek more agencies. He was elected a judge at the international photographic exhibition at Frankfurt, received a gold medal from the Photographic Association of Vienna and became a member of the Royal Geographical Society, London. He had already won medals in exhibitions such as those at Amsterdam, Calcutta and Frankfurt. He was official photographer for the 1888 Melbourne International Exhibition but was not permitted to contest any awards.

Late in the 1880s Lindt photographed the Chaffey brothers' irrigation works on the River Murray. In 1890 he toured the New Hebrides and in June climbed the Tanna volcano. With a small grant from the Royal Geographical Society he toured Fiji where he photographed a fire-walking ceremony in 1892. He became a councillor of the Victorian branch of the Royal Geographical Society in 1893. He lost his clientele in the financial crisis and closed his studio in 1894. In 1895 he moved to the Hermitage, a new home that he had built at Blacks Spur. It became a well-known pleasure resort, with such attractions as three New Guinea-type tree houses in the garden designed by Ferdinand Mueller [q.v.]. Guests remembered Lindt's hospitality, his bush-walking, his flair for telling stories and showing lantern slides and his playing on the viola at musical evenings. He wrote articles and continued his photography and world-wide correspondence. One of his last exhibitions was of 'photograms' in the Albert Street Art Gallery in 1909.

At Grafton on 13 January 1872 Lindt had married Anna Maria Dorothea Wagner; she died on 27 May 1888 soon after delivering a stillborn child. On 10 July 1889 at Melbourne he married Catherine Elizabeth Cousens who had worked with him as a retoucher. Aged 81 he died during disastrous bushfires on 19 February 1926 at the Hermitage, survived by his wife.

J. J. Cato, *The story of the camera in Australia* (Melb, 1955); *Australasian*, 1 Nov 1884, 27 July 1889, 15 Nov 1890; M. McLardy, 'Our oldest living photographer', *A'sian Photo-Review*, Sept 1947; 'The great Lindt', *A'sian Photo-Review*, July, Aug 1952.

VALERIE FROST

LINGER, CARL FERDINAND AUGUST (1810-1862), musician and composer, was born on 15 March 1810 at Berlin, son of an engraver. His parents encouraged him to study music under notable teachers and he started his composing career with six sacred songs dedicated to the princess of Prussia. After visiting music schools in Italy, he won repute for composing operas, masses, symphonies, cantatas and other musical works. In the unsettled conditions of 1848 a Berlin Migration Society was formed by Richard Schomburgk [q.v.] and others. With a party of intellectual Germans, Linger and his wife Wilhelmine sailed from Hamburg in the *Princess Luise* and arrived at Port Adelaide on 7 August 1849; a daughter was born on the voyage.

On 30 August Linger applied for naturalization and received his certificate on 1 September. Unable to find work as a music teacher and unfamiliar with the English language, he was persuaded to buy eighty acres at Munno Para about eighteen miles from Adelaide. With his brother-in-law, Hermann Komoll, he built a house, cleared and fenced land and grew potatoes but after eighteen unhappy months he was in debt. He left his family on the farm and with two shillings in his pocket went to Adelaide. He found work tuning pianos and noting music scores, and three weeks later brought his wife and child to town. Helped by the wife of Andrew Murray [q.v.], he won access to the best Adelaide families as a music teacher and by 1852 had paid his debts, taken 'a beautiful house' on North Terrace and brought 'a magnificent instrument for 300 dollars'. In March he wrote to his mother about his good luck and respectable standing, and offered to pay her passage to Adelaide. His 'Ninety third Psalm' and 'Gloria' appeared in a printed programme of 1855, and his 'Concert Overture' is dated 1856. An undated manuscript of four songs for soprano and pianoforte has also been preserved. He had conducted Adelaide's first Philharmonic Orchestra and in 1859 its first performance of Handel's *Messiah* as well as helping to found a Liedertafel. He had often visited the Lutheran pastor, G. D. Fritzsche [q.v.], at Lobethal to attend his choir rehearsals. Linger was active in most of the musical and choral societies, often presiding or performing at their concerts. Extremely modest, especially when asked to publish more of his works, he invariably answered, 'Germany has plenty of better music than mine in manuscript'.

At the second anniversary of the Gawler Institute in October 1859 a 'Song of Australia' competition was held with prizes of ten guineas for the best words and the best music. Of the 96 poetic competitors, Mrs Caroline Carleton (1819-1874) won the prize for her five verses; in 1923 her admirers placed a granite memorial in the Wallaroo cemetery.

Linger won ten guineas for the music and the Song of Australia was sung in public for the first time on 12 December 1859. Although used widely in South Australia, it did not displace God Save the Queen as the national anthem or Advance Australia Fair first published in 1878 by W. H. Paling [q.v.] & Co. in Sydney. Linger's wife died of consumption in Adelaide on 7 April 1860. He then married Christiane Mathilde Hogrefe; their only child was born in Adelaide on 6 May 1861. Linger's health was then failing and, despite an intention to visit Berlin, he died from dropsy on 16 February 1862. He was buried in West Terrace cemetery and left an estate of £1200 to his wife. Although he had stimulated the taste for music in South Australia he was soon forgotten, but in the State's centenary year a subscription was raised for a sandstone monument, eight feet high, over his neglected grave. The memorial was unveiled by the premier before a thousand people and the 'Song of Australia' was sung.

E. H. Coombe (ed), History of Gawler 1837 to 1908 (Adel, 1910); L. A. Triebel (ed), 'A Carl Linger letter', South Australiana, 2 (1963); Register (Adel), 17, 18 Feb 1862, 28 Dec 1894; Observer (Adel), 23 July 1935; Advertiser (Adel), 21, 22, 26 Nov 1935, 17 June 1936, 16 May 1959; biog note on Mrs Carleton, 1047/5 (SAA).   JOHN HORNER

LINTON, SYDNEY (1841-1894), Church of England bishop, was born on 2 July 1841 at Diddington, Huntingdonshire, England, third son and fourth child of Rev. Henry Linton and his wife Charlotte, daughter of Rev. William Richardson. He was educated at Rugby School, where he excelled at football, and Wadham College, Oxford (B.A., 1864; M.A., 1870; D.D., 1884). A fine sportsman, he played in 1861 and 1862 for Oxford against Cambridge at Lord's. After several years as a private tutor and as a master at Haileybury College, he studied for holy orders and was made deacon in 1867 and priest in 1868 by the bishop of Gloucester and Bristol. Linton served his curacy at St Mark's, Cheltenham, and in 1870 became

vicar of Holy Trinity, Oxford, a poor parish that he developed successfully. In 1877 he was appointed to St Philip, Heigham, Norwich, and on 13 June married Jane Isabella, daughter of Rev. Dr Charles Heurtley, professor of divinity at Oxford. The vigour of Linton's ministry at Norwich resulted in the offer of the bishopric of the Riverina in November 1883. He raised £4000 for his new diocese and on 1 May 1884 was consecrated in St Paul's Cathedral, London. In March 1885 he arrived in the Parramatta at Sydney with his family and was enthroned in St Paul's Church, Hay, on the 18th.

Linton's new see had been made possible by a large benefaction from John Campbell [q.v.]. The diocese covered over a third of New South Wales but included few more than 20,000 Anglicans. Many of the landholders were absentees or non-Anglicans while the mines at Broken Hill were attracting increasing numbers of Methodists. In an effort to make his diocese an effective unit of the Church, Linton set up regular diocesan institutions. A Church Society was founded in 1885 to build up a central fund and promote the extension of work in the diocese. The first synod met in 1887 and by 1890 its constitution was in good order. A bishop's lodge, made of iron, was built at Hay, the episcopal centre. He recruited new clergy: the staff of six in 1885 increased to eighteen by 1893. Churches were built and new parishes formed and the diocese was enlarged by the accession of Wilcannia from Bathurst.

Linton worked unceasingly. An indefatigable traveller and missionary, he liked nothing better than to exercise a pastoral ministry in new areas. Only in Broken Hill did his experience fail him. Linton's energy masked the impermanence of much of his achievement. Fifty-one clergymen came but few stayed for long. The depression of the 1890s revealed the weakness of the finances and the extent of the reliance on Linton's private resources. For all his missionary zeal he kept rigidly to the traditional parish structure and did little to encourage a flexible ministry. Impatient with business routine, he did not nurture the diocesan institutions that he had founded. He was very popular, tolerant in his churchmanship and unwearying in his efforts but failed to adopt any systematic policy. Yet in such a sprawling diocese he did well to accomplish as much as he did. He died at Melbourne on 15 May 1894 and was buried in Kew cemetery. He was survived by three sons and three daughters.

W. C. Pritchard, Sydney Linton: first bishop of Riverina (Melb, 1896); R. T. Wyatt, The history of the diocese of Goulburn (Syd, 1937); Town and Country J, 10 May 1890; Riverine

Grazier, 2 Apr 1935; Riverina papers (Diocesan Registry, Narrandera); information from Miss Laurel Clyde.   K. J. CABLE

LITCHFIELD, JAMES (1825-1905), pastoralist and sheepbreeder, was born at Elmdon, Essex, England, son of James Litchfield, farmer, and his wife Mary, née Hayden. On 6 January 1852 at Great Chesterford, Essex, he married Anne Sherrin. They arrived at Sydney in May with mixed farming experience and good recommendations. After some months in Sydney and with W. Bradley's [q.v.] family at Landsdown, Goulburn, he accepted the post of overseer at Coolringdon, the headquarters of Bradley's stations in the Monaro, and some three years later as manager of Bradley's Myalla station. Like W. A. Brodribb [q.v.] he was encouraged and helped by Bradley to occupy land for himself. However, he decided to conserve his capital until the 1861 Land Act was passed and on 8 April 1862 selected 320 acres on Jillamatong Creek, Monaro.

Litchfield gradually built up his holdings by selection and purchase, and gave evidence how he did it to a parliamentary select committee on the administration of the land law in February 1874. He took up selections in the names of his children and employees because he approved of 'dummying' so long as it promoted settlement. He disliked the subterfuges that he and others had been practising but claimed that they would remain a necessary evil until the law was changed to conform with economic realities. He insisted that the minimum size for a viable pastoral freehold should be 2560 acres and not 320 acres. By 1884 he held over 20,000 acres in the Monaro and the value of his wool clip from 15,000 sheep was £3180. In March 1881 his evidence to the select committee on assisted immigration, which he favoured, gave details of the progress and problems of agriculture and grazing in the Monaro in 1851-81.

In 1865 Litchfield, with the aim of producing a strain well adapted to the hard Monaro environment, had established near Cooma the Hazeldean merino stud, which became famous not only in the colonies but also abroad. Starting with the progeny of Rambouillet ewes he began to import merinos, mostly of Saxon descent from Tasmanian studs in 1881, and in the early 1890s the famous Wanganella strain was introduced to his stud.

Intelligent and hard-working he established himself and his family by shrewdness and courage at a time and location where political, economic and environmental factors combined to spell ruin for the less skilful and resolute. He never entered politics but was keenly aware of the main issues and concerned about land and labour questions. Active in local associations, he was a member and spokesman for the Free Selectors' Association of Cooma, a president of the Cooma Pastoral and Agricultural Association and interested in the local Church of England and School of Arts. Though prominent in having the railway extended to Cooma he opposed the payment of parliamentarians and voted against Federation.

In 1891 Litchfield divided his estate, comprising Hazeldean, Woodstock, Springwell and Matong, among his four sons and retired to Sydney. He died at his residence, Havilah, Burlington Road, Homebush, on 20 August 1905, survived by his wife, four sons and three daughters. He was buried in the Anglican cemetery at Rookwood.

C. McIvor, *The history and development of sheep farming from antiquity to modern times* (Syd, 1893); F. F. Mitchell, 'Back to Cooma' celebrations (Syd, 1926); W. K. Hancock, *Discovering Monaro* (Cambridge, 1972); V&P (LA NSW), 1873-74, 3, 995, 1880-81, 3, 286; SMH, 22 Aug 1905; *Pastoral Review*, 15 Sept 1905; Perkins papers (NL); family papers (held by James Litchfield, Hazeldean, Cooma).
                                    G. P. WALSH

LITTLE, ROBERT (1822-1890), solicitor, was born on 17 November 1822 at Dungiven, Londonderry, Ireland, son of Patrick Little and his wife Mary Anne, née Boyle. Educated locally in private schools, he studied in 1844-45 for admission as an attorney and solicitor in various jurisdictions in Ireland. After practising in Ireland he sailed with his brother John in the *Ganges* to Sydney and arrived on 23 June 1846.

Robert was admitted to practice in New South Wales on 8 August and settled in Brisbane in December. He started a practice on his own, using his home at the corner of George and Adelaide Streets as his office. He tried to combine sheep-farming with legal work but soon gave up his pastoral ventures. When the New South Wales government expanded the judicial machinery of Moreton Bay in 1857 he was appointed on 1 April the first crown solicitor for civil and criminal causes. At first the volume of official work was small and he was allowed the right of private practice. In 1857 William Rawlins joined him, possibly as a partner, but left Brisbane after a few years. By 1861 Little had taken E.I.C. Browne [q.v.] as a partner and in 1880 H.L.E.R. Ruthning joined the firm. In 1867 the ministry ruled that the firm should conduct official civil actions as private solicitors; after 1868 they also carried out the railway conveyancing business of the government. In the 1870s Little was criticized in parliament for combining the crown solicitor's official work with private practice. In 1880 four politicians claimed that he was making private and public advantage out of the combination; in November a select committee exonerated him but recommended that the two sorts of legal business be separated. In 1882 the ministry decided that his official work required full-time attention. He retired from practice in 1885.

On 7 August 1873 Little chaired a meeting of attorneys that resolved to form the Queensland Law Society. He served on the committee for preparing the society's rules and at its first meeting on 8 September he was elected president, a position he held until 1880. An active citizen, Little was a good churchman and warden of St John's Cathedral; he was also vigorous in athletics and pair-oared rowing. He was a founder of the Queensland Turf Club and won the Breeder's Cup in 1866. Through his partnership with Browne he acquired a one-sixth interest in the *Brisbane Courier*. In politics he supported the squatters. Contemporaries described him as a patriarchal squire, 'tall, straight, distinguished looking' and 'a fine style of English lawyer'.

Little was married twice: first, on 15 September 1853 to Medora Anne, eldest daughter of Captain Geary, harbourmaster; and second, on 26 October 1875 to Eliza Harriet, sister of Sir John Bramston [q.v.]. In 1876 he moved into a spacious country house, Whytecliffe, at Albion Heights, built by A. Petrie [q.v.]. He visited Britain from November 1880 to April 1882. In 1889 he sailed for South Asia hoping to relieve his asthma, but contracted fever at Batavia and died at Mount Lavinia, Ceylon, on 17 January 1890. He was survived by nine children.

J. Bonwick, *Early struggles of the Australian press* (Lond, 1890); N. Bartley, *Australian pioneers and reminiscences*, J. J. Knight ed (Brisb, 1896); R. S. Browne, *A journalist's memories* (Brisb, 1927); V&P (LA Qld), 1860, 504, 1869, 1, 600, 1880, 1, 551; PD (Qld), 1875, 1880; *Brisbane Courier*, 25 Sept 1880, 21 Jan 1890; *Queenslander*, 11 Sept 1930; Qld Law Soc, files.   W. ROSS JOHNSTON

LIVERSIDGE, ARCHIBALD (1846-1927), scientist, was born on 17 November 1846 at Turnham Green, London, son of John Liversidge and his wife Caroline Sophia, née Jarratt. Educated privately, he entered the Royal School of Mines and the Royal College of Chemistry. In 1867 as a royal exhibitioner he became an instructor in chemistry at the Royal School of Naval Architecture. In 1870 he won a scholarship at Christ's College, Cambridge (M.A. *hon. causa*, 1887); in 1872 he became demonstrator in chemistry but resigned to take up appointment as 'Reader in Geology and Assistant in the Laboratory' at the University of Sydney. In 1874 he became professor of geology and mineralogy.

On arrival Liversidge had about ten students and two rooms in the main building. One of his first tasks was to secure proper recognition of science in both secondary and tertiary education. Science became a matriculation subject in New South Wales in 1873 but the teaching remained inadequate. In an address to the local Royal Society in 1900 he commented that 'It would be appropriate if the community turned over a new leaf with the new century by insisting on better provision for science teaching in schools'. He was an enthusiastic supporter of Henry Armstrong's heuristic method of teaching science, advocated technical education and was an original member of the Board of Technical Education. In 1880 he published his *Report upon certain Museums for Technology, Science and Art*. As a trustee of the Australian Museum he visited Europe in 1880 on a study tour. On his return he helped to establish the Industrial, Technological and Sanitary Museum and became a member of its first committee of management.

'After Homeric battles with the forces of Arts', Liversidge persuaded the senate to open a faculty of science and was its first dean in 1879-1907. He was one of the few who agreed to admit women to the university. In 1892 he founded a school of mines at the university and was a fellow of the senate in 1878-1904. In 1872 he had joined the local Royal Society, and as its honorary secretary in 1874-84 virtually re-established it, editing its *Journal and Proceedings* for many years. His fellow secretary, Dr C. A. Leibius [q.v.], said that 'We never got a move on until Liversidge came'. He was president in 1886, 1890 and 1901.

In the early 1880s Liversidge canvassed the idea of asking the British Association for the Advancement of Science to visit Australia but in vain. He then conceived an Australian association. Through his friends, Captain F. W. Hutton and Sir James Hector, he won the support of New Zealand and after much planning the Australasian Association for the Advancement of Science held its first congress in 1888. He was its honorary secretary until 1909 and president in 1898. In 1902 he founded the Sydney section of the Society of Chemical Industry. He also saw opportunities in Federation for introducing the decimal system for coinage and weights and measures, and for forming a national academy of science with headquarters in the federal capital. He also tried to start an Australian equivalent to the English journal *Nature* and had printed a prospectus for an Australian scientific journal.

Liversidge read papers to the Royal Society on 'The Deniliquin Meteorite' (December, 1872), 'Notes on the Bingara Diamond District' (October, 1874) and 'Iron and Coal at Wallerawang' and 'Nickel Minerals from New Caledonia' (December, 1874). In 1882 he became professor of mineralogy and chemistry. In 1876 he had first published *The Minerals of New South Wales*; a second and enlarged edition appeared in 1882 and the third, larger, edition coincided with the centenary of the colony in 1888. The book was widely reviewed and was his major contribution to science. He was mainly interested in the chemical composition of minerals but the absence of their detailed crystallography and optical properties reduced the usefulness of his book.

Liversidge was one of the first to detect gold and platinum metals in meteorites. He was also interested in dusts suspected to be of meteoritic origin, and an early demonstrator of the occurrence of gold in sea-water. He contributed over a hundred research papers to the Chemical Society, Royal Society of New South Wales and the Royal Society of London. His work was widely recognized and at least thirteen universities and scientific bodies gave him honorary degrees or memberships. He was a fellow of the Royal Society, the Chemical Society, the Royal Institute of Chemistry, the Geological Society, the Linnean Society and the Royal Geographical Society of London.

Liversidge was somewhat shy and retiring and never married. He was not a fluent speaker but as a lecturer at the university and in public gave successful and impressive practical demonstrations. He was quick to see the possibilities of liquid air for these purposes. When he retired in 1907 the chemistry department had seven lecturers and demonstrators and some 200 students. The university conferred on him the title of emeritus. He returned to London where he continued his interest in chemistry and worked in the Davy-Faraday research laboratory of the Royal Institution. In 1910-13 he served as vice-president of the Chemical Society, London. In his last years he lived at Fieldhouse, Kingston Hill, where he entertained many of his old colleagues and friends from overseas and enjoyed his motor cars. He died from a heart attack on 26 September 1927.

One of his old colleagues claimed that 'The late Professor Archibald Liversidge . . . was certainly the greatest organiser of science that Australia has seen and surely no-one in that country ever worked more unselfishly and with greater singleness of purpose than he to serve science for its own sake'. His estate was valued for probate at over £46,000. He made bequests to the University of Sydney, the Australasian Association for the Advancement of Science and the Royal Society of New South Wales to be used for encouraging research in chemistry by means of special lectures.

His portrait by John Collier, R.A., is in the University of Sydney.

R. J. W. Le Fèvre, 'The establishment of chemistry within Australian science', Roy Soc NSW, *A century of scientific progress* (Syd, 1961); T. W. E. David, 'Archibald Liversidge', Chemical Soc (Lond), *J* (1938), 598; D. P. Mellor, 'Founders of Australian chemistry: Archibald Liversidge', Roy Aust Chemical Inst, *Procs* (1957), 415.   D. P. MELLOR

LLOYD, CHARLES WILLIAM (1830-1919), grazier, was born at Acton Round, Shropshire, England, seventh son of Captain John Lloyd and his wife Mary, née Evans. He was educated in Bridgnorth and in 1839 entered Wenlock Grammar School. In 1843 because of his father's financial difficulties he went to live with a wealthy cousin, B. Duppa, who virtually adopted him. About 1850 Lloyd became manager of Duppa's woollen mill at Church Stretton, but left to control a friend's factory when he discovered Duppa's generosity would not be as great as he had hoped.

Lloyd's elder brother, John Charles (d. 1881), had migrated to Sydney in 1841 and became superintendent of Melville Plains for two brothers of Sir William Denison. About 1848 he managed W. C. Wentworth's [q.v.] Burburgate stations on the Liverpool Plains, which John bought in 1853. Another brother, Edward Henry (d. 1889), joined him in 1848 and became manager in 1853 when John went to England to recover his health. At his suggestion Charles joined Edward at Burburgate in September 1854.

Charles was assistant manager at Burburgate until 1858 when the brothers formed a partnership. He succeeded Edward as resident partner and general manager of Lloyd Bros. In 1856 he was one of the first to put up wire fences and to install steam-driven pumps for washing sheep. In 1860 he tried shearing unwashed sheep and scouring the wool on the station. In *Pages from the Journal of a Queensland Squatter* (London, 1901) Oscar de Satgé [q.v.], assistant manager at Burburgate in 1859-61, was impressed by the successful lambing arrangements and the Shorthorns bred from imported bulls and cows obtained from the Peel River Co. He also recorded that in 1860 one lot of wethers 'off the shears' sold in Homebush for the high price of 21s. 6d. each. Charles's most renowned innovation was his success in 1863 in dipping sheep to protect them against scab.

In 1863 Charles retired to Sydney; he had become a magistrate of the territory in 1858 and a member of the Australian Club. In January 1865 he withdrew from the partnership because of family quarrels and on 2 May married Rachel Eliza, second daughter of Alexander Campbell [q.v.]. They visited England and returned late in 1866. In that year Charles was listed as owning Dripping Rock and five runs with John as his partner. In 1871 Charles held Galathra West. Later in the 1870s at Sydney he became a councillor of the Agricultural Society and in 1875 a founding member of the Linnean Society. He had moved to Tarriaro, Gulligal, Namoi River, and in the late 1880s he lived at Elizabeth Farm, Parramatta. In 1893 he was recommended by leading colonists to the Cape Colony government as an adviser on the scab problem. Aged 89 he died on 8 September 1919 at a private hospital in Sydney and was buried in the Anglican section of Rookwood cemetery, survived by five sons and five daughters.

Lloyd papers (ML).

G. J. ABBOTT

LLOYD, GEORGE ALFRED (1815-1897), merchant, businessman and politician, was born on 14 November 1815 at Norwood, Surrey, England, eldest son of Joseph Lloyd, corn merchant and freeman of the City of London, and his wife Eleanor Sophia, née Lyne. Educated at Aske's Hospital School, London, he became a clerk to a shipping and insurance broker. When his father's health and business failed he migrated to Australia as clerk to a family friend and arrived in Sydney in 1833 with only 17s. 6d. In 1834 he was sent to open a store at Hinton on the Hunter River where he was also postmaster, and after his employer's failure farmed on the Williams River.

In 1840 he returned to Sydney and set up as an auctioneer in partnership with Ambrose Foss. In July 1843 Foss & Lloyd became insolvent with debts of over £3300; Lloyd's estate was not insolvent but he was liable for the deficiency in the partnership which paid 2s. in the £. Discharged in December 1843, Lloyd carried on business as auctioneer, tallow and hide merchant and later paid all his creditors in full. One of the first to buy Californian gold, he became

a pioneer buyer of Australian gold in 1851 and was soon contributing the authoritative 'Weekly Gold Circular' to the Sydney Morning Herald. He was a trustee and director of the Second Australian Benefit and Investment Building Society. In 1852 he was president of the Turon Golden Ridge Quartz Crushing Co. and the Sydney Gold Escort Co. He made a large fortune which he invested in steamships and in 1853 joined the Sydney and Melbourne Steam Packet Co. He had been secretary of the National School Society in 1842 and by 1851 was a director of the Sydney Infirmary and Dispensary and a committee member of the Benevolent Asylum, the Sydney Female Refuge Society, the British and Foreign Bible Society and the Australian Religious Tract Society.

In 1855 after a farewell banquet Lloyd returned to England where he became a liveryman in the Company of Haberdashers and freeman of the City of London by patrimony on 3 June 1856. In London his company, Lloyd, Beilby & Co., acted as commercial agents to the New South Wales government until 1859 when Lloyd lost heavily on his shipping ventures and went bankrupt in September. He returned to Sydney in 1860 and after his discharge in June resumed business as a general merchant importing wheat and flour from California and Chile. In the 1860s he became a director of the Cardiff Coal Co., the Bulli Coal Mining Co. and a local director of the London and Lancashire Fire and Life Assurance Co. Later he was agent for the Cornwall Fire and Marine Insurance Co. He also bought horses for the Indian government.

Advocating free trade, immigration, compulsory education, railway extension and a local harbour trust, Lloyd defeated James Martin [q.v.] for the Newcastle electorate in December 1869. A supporter, friend and admirer of Henry Parkes [q.v.], to whom he often gave sound advice on legislation and tactics in the House, he was postmaster-general in Parkes's first ministry from 14 May to 4 December 1872 and colonial treasurer to 8 February 1875. He introduced the penny postage to areas within ten miles of Sydney and abolished the duty on the postage of newspapers. In 1873 he suggested to Parkes that government funds could be invested more profitably in England and introduced the bill which abolished the ad valorem duties that had been in force for eight years. He reduced the interest rate on public loans from 5 to 4 per cent and was the first treasurer to create inscribed stock. He was also responsible for the abolition of tonnage dues at Newcastle, Wollongong and Kiama. In 1874 he wrote to Donald Larnach [q.v.] that if he secured a butt of sherry and some casks of brandy he would gain 'the lasting gratitude of the legislators of New South Wales, and if the Wine and Brandy are very superior they may go a long way to improve our legislation'. However, the Refreshment Committee repudiated the consignment and it was left in Lloyd's possession. He was secretary for mines in Parkes's 1877 ministry but in October was defeated in the general election.

In 1878 Lloyd suffered another business reversal. He wrote to Parkes on 16 July 1878 about heavy financial losses 'amounting up to over £10,000 in fourteen days by failure of other Houses and losses on our shipments to London', and went bankrupt in August. He again represented Newcastle from 1880 to 1882 when he visited Europe, but on his return was defeated in the general election. Lloyd was in England again in 1884-85 and on his return represented his old electorate from October 1885 to January 1887.

A frequent and good speaker in the assembly, Lloyd was as diverse in his political interests as in his business and private concerns. On 5 December 1879 he had praised Parkes's public instruction bill: 'If you had not done anything else this one Act will stamp your name indelibly upon the history of this Colony and send it down to posterity with a respect and veneration which could not be increased by a Statue of Bronze or Tablet of marble'. Lloyd was a founder and auditor of the Australian Mutual Provident Society and an original shareholder in the Sydney Exchange Co. in which he was a director in 1872-97. Widely travelled, he had visited California and New Zealand as well as Europe and was elected a fellow of the Royal Geographical Society, London, on 27 April 1857. In 1874 he became a member of the Royal Society of New South Wales. For over fifty years he was prominent in the Pitt Street Congregational Church.

In February 1887 Lloyd was appointed to the Legislative Council. Although active at first, he took little part after 1889 and rarely attended after October 1893 when he was given leave for six months because of ill health. He died at his home, Scotforth, Elizabeth Bay, on 25 December 1897 and was buried in the Congregational section of Rookwood cemetery. Probate of his estate was sworn at under £521. He was predeceased in 1887 by his wife Mary, third daughter of Rev. L. E. Threlkeld [q.v.], whom he had married in Sydney on 1 July 1841, and was survived by five sons and three daughters of their eleven children.

R. F. Holder, Bank of New South Wales: a history, 1 (Syd, 1970); V&P (LC NSW), 1852, 1, 1329, Sel cttees on Sydney Gold Escort Co. and NSW Coal and Intercolonial Steam Navigation Co. Bill, 1853, 2; V&P (LA NSW), 1873-74, 2, 863, 1875, 2, 771; SMH, 8 June, 8 July, 16 Nov, 14 Dec 1843, 21 Oct, 13 Dec 1844, 13 Aug 1850, 29 Mar 1855, 25, 26 Nov, 6 Dec 1869, 27 Dec 1897; Illustrated Sydney News, 31 Mar 1855; Town and Country J, 15 June 1872, 7 Apr 1877; Bulletin, 2 July 1881; Parkes letters (ML).

G. P. WALSH

LLOYD, HENRY GRANT (1830-1904), artist, was born on 6 January 1830 at Chester, England, son of Lieutenant Henry Lloyd, Bengal Native Infantry, and his wife Charlotte, née Williams. His father retired to Van Diemen's Land in 1840 and bought land at New Norfolk, which he named Bryn Estyn after the family home in Wales. Henry Grant became a divinity student at Christ's College, Bishopsbourne, Tasmania, but in 1851 Bishop Nixon [q.v.] decided that he was not a suitable ordinand. In 1846-57 Lloyd sketched in Tasmania and by 1858 was painting in New South Wales. He was influenced by Conrad Martens [q.v.] and was probably one of his pupils. Lloyd painted sporadically in Martens's style until the 1870s but could not subdue his own spontaneous vision. In artistic style and temperament he was perhaps closer to Samuel Elyard [q.v.] than to the accomplished Martens. Lloyd may also have been influenced by J. S. Prout [q.v.].

Much of Lloyd's early work is hasty and crude, with heavy over-painting and rather unpleasant colouring. In later years he sometimes used larger areas of clear wash, pale and delicate in tone, which with the white of the paper helped to achieve an air of simplicity and serenity. He also painted landscapes and rocks in deliberate contour patterns with stronger colours, but his figures and buildings are generally poor. Many of his sketches are landscapes, a number of which are of historical interest and include his lithograph 'Hobart Town from the New Wharf' about 1857 and his view of the Canberra plains in 1862. He was usually meticulous in giving each work a date and title; many even have compass directions. He travelled and sketched widely in New South Wales and Queensland until 1864, Tasmania in 1872-75 and New South Wales in 1875-80. He had probably visited Britain in the 1870s for he exhibited Welsh sketches in Dunedin where he lived in 1881-99 and was a member of the Otago Art Society; he visited Australia in 1887-88. In 1900 he settled in Tasmania and died at New Norfolk on 31 May 1904.

Some 1500 of Lloyd's sketches are in the Mitchell and Dixson Libraries, Sydney, and a collection of his work is in the Allport Library and Museum of Fine Arts, Hobart.

Otago Art Society, *Exhibition catalogue* (Dunedin, 1882, 1884, 1886-88, 1890-95, 1898-99, 1900-03); New Zealand Academy of Fine Arts, *Eighth annual exhibition* (1896); New Zealand and South Seas Exhibition 1889-90, *Official catalogue* (Dunedin, 1889); H. Allport, *Early art in Tasmania* (Hob, 1931); C. Craig, *Old Tasmanian prints* (Launceston, 1964), *Hobart Town Courier*, 27 Sept, 8, 11, 22 Oct 1851; *Mercury*, 1 May 1879, 27 Feb, 3 Dec 1892, 17 June 1897, 1 June 1904; D. J. Cross, Henry Grant Lloyd ... itineraries (ML); CSO 24/14/357, 48/1668 (TA).

P. I. JONES

LLOYD, JESSIE GEORGINA (1843-1885), author, best known as 'Silverleaf', was born on 4 June 1843 at Longford Farm, near Launceston, Van Diemen's Land, and baptized Jessy Georgianna, daughter of Joseph William Bell, auctioneer, and his wife Georgiana, née Ford. On leaving school she had sole charge of a large family of brothers and sisters but found time to teach a Sunday school class and play the church organ on Sundays.

On 6 September 1866 at the Wesleyan Chapel, Glenorchy, Jessie married George Alfred, son of G. A. Lloyd [q.v.]. They went to New South Wales and their first child, a daughter, was born in Sydney on 12 October 1867. For some years George had managed Goolhi station near Gunnedah. He then bought a share in Terembone station, near Coonamble, probably in partnership with G. W. Allen [q.v.], and the family moved into the slab and sawn timber homestead late in the 1860s. Their three sons were born there.

About 1878 Jessie began writing for Sydney periodicals under the name of 'Silverleaf'. From her earnings she was able to send her two elder children to boarding schools in Sydney. Her book, *The Wheel of Life: A Domestic Tale of Life in Australia*, was published in Sydney in 1880 and received favourable reviews. By then her short stories, essays and poems were appearing in the *Echo* and later in the monthly *Illustrated Sydney News* and the *Sydney Mail*. 'All Aboard. A Tale for Christmas' was serialized in the *Echo* in December 1879. In 1881-82 the 'Silverleaf Papers' appeared regularly in the *Illustrated Sydney News*, covering topics such as 'Glimpses of Station Life', 'Seasons of Drought', 'Town and Country Housekeeping', 'Squatters versus Selectors', 'Christmas in the Bush' and 'Natives'. Short stories and poems appeared in the *Sydney Mail* in 1882-83. Her novel 'Retribution' was serialized in the *Illustrated Sydney News* in 1884-85 and at her death she left an unfinished story, 'On Turbulent Waters'. Without being very original or revolutionary in her sentiments, 'Silverleaf' was popular as a

pleasant and cheerful narrator of outback life. A contemporary described her as a 'graphic and graceful writer, possessing the faculty of presenting her characters in a clear and unmistakeable light . . . The tone of her novels is always high and moral'.

Besides writing, Jessie enjoyed gardening, sketching and music: she was a pianist 'much above the average' and had a sweet contralto voice. She was a good chess player and an entertaining conversationalist. On 30 July 1885, after an illness of six weeks, she died at Terembone. She was buried on the station according to Anglican rites and her memorial service on 16 August at St Barnabas's Church, Coonamble, drew a large and sympathetic congregation. She left an estate worth £625, including mining shares and life insurance, and at her request about eighty volumes from her private library were given to the local Mechanics' Institute and St Barnabas's Church Sunday school. Not long after her death her husband left Terembone; he married again in Sydney in 1887, raised a second family and died on 8 February 1921.

Echo, 17 Jan 1880; *Coonamble Independent*, 22 Aug 1885; *Illustrated Sydney News*, 29 Aug 1885; information from L. H. Lloyd, Hastings, New Zealand.   SALLY O'NEILL

LOADER, THOMAS (1830-1901), businessman and politician, was born in London, son of Isaac Loader, merchant, and his wife Elizabeth, née Minifie. Educated at Christ's Hospital, he was employed in industry and with railway firms in England but overwork impaired his health. He decided to migrate and in 1852 arrived in Melbourne.

Loader set up as an ironmonger, wholesale saddler and importer of rolling stock. Calling for democratic reforms and an end to the squatters' land monopoly, he contested the Legislative Assembly seat of North Grant at the general election in 1856 but was defeated by J. B. Humffray [q.v.]. Later that year he helped to form the Victoria Land League and the Land Convention of 1857. In 1859 he was elected for West Melbourne as a Conventionist. In the Heales [q.v.] ministry, 1860-61, he served as commissioner of railways and then as postmaster-general but his appointment as commissioner of trade and customs raised objections that his seat was vacant because he had accepted a place of profit under the Crown. Loader promptly resigned but a parliamentary committee ruled in his favour. He was re-elected for West Melbourne, rejoined the ministry and received his salary as commissioner. He had moved successfully for a renewal of assisted immigration in May and published his own scheme in the pamphlet *Family Immigration for Victoria* (1861). He retired from parliament in August 1864 under pressure of private business. He was associated in the early 1870s with the West Melbourne Improvement League which advocated reclamation of the West Melbourne swamp and other improvements. He gave evidence to the commission on low lands in 1873 and to the 1887 royal commission on the extension of Melbourne westward. In 1877-96 he represented Melbourne's merchants and traders on the Harbor Trust Commission.

In 1872 Loader had founded the Apollo Stearine Candle Co. By 1882 the Footscray plant employed two hundred men and supplied raw materials to branch factories in Sydney and Brisbane. Intercolonial duties hampered the company's operations and, while Loader defended Victoria's protective duty on candles to the royal commission on the tariff in 1883, he favoured a uniform tariff for the Australian colonies and political union of New South Wales and Victoria. By 1884 he was calling on the politicians to recognize that commercial interests were silently making for Federation. He was president of the economy, trade and manufactures department at the 1880 Melbourne Social Science Congress and in his inaugural address argued that the empire should distribute its surplus population to the colonies to secure the great future of the English-speaking people and to prepare for the coming conflict with the 'hordes of the Asiatic races'.

Loader was a founder in 1873 of the City of Melbourne Bank and a director of the Squatting Investment Co., the Mutual Assurance Society of Victoria and the Perpetual Trustees and Agency Co. He suffered humiliation in Victoria's economic crisis of the 1890s. Allegations of reckless management led to an investigation in 1896 of the City of Melbourne Bank, of which Loader was chairman. At best he appeared incompetent. Alfred Deakin defended him when, with three other directors and two auditors, he was charged with concurring in the issuing of false balance sheets. All were acquitted. After a brief illness Loader died on 26 February 1901 at his home, Craigevar, Malvern, survived by his wife Anna Maria, née Hall, whom he had married in 1865, two sons and two of his four daughters.

B. Hoare, *Jubilee history of the Melbourne Harbor Trust* (Melb, 1927); G. Serle, *The golden age* (Melb, 1963); M. Cannon, *The land boomers* (Melb, 1966); V&P (LA Vic), 1860-61, 2 (D11); *Argus*, 13 Aug, 20 Oct, 1, 5, 12 Nov 1856, 6, 13 Aug 1861, 27 Feb 1901; *Age*, 14 Nov 1872, 10-13, 20 Mar 1896; *Federal Australian*, 10 Jan 1885; L. C. Duly, The land selection acts in Victoria 1859-69 (M.A. thesis, Univ Melb, 1959); G. R. Quaife, The nature of political conflict in Victoria 1856-57 (M.A. thesis, Univ Melb, 1964); Deakin papers (NL); Defunct trading companies papers (VSA).

JOHN LACK

LOCH, HENRY BROUGHAM, 1st BARON LOCH OF DRYLAW (1827-1900), public servant and governor, was born on 23 May 1827 in Edinburgh, the seventh son of James Loch, M.P., of Drylaw, and his wife Ann, née Orr. After service in 1840-42 as midshipman in the navy he was commissioned in the Bengal cavalry in 1844 and was A.D.C. to Lord Gough in the Sutlej campaign in 1845. In the Crimean war Loch helped to organize irregular Turkish cavalry, and in 1857-58 accompanied Lord Elgin's mission to China. In 1860 he returned as private secretary to Elgin on his second mission and negotiated the surrender of the Taku forts on the way to Peking, but Loch and his small party were then taken prisoner and suffered from ill treatment. Back in England he was appointed a C.B. and left the army but furthered his connexion with the Whigs by acting as private secretary to the Home secretary, Sir George Grey, in 1861-63, and marrying in 1862 Elizabeth, daughter of the Hon. Edward Villiers and niece of the earl of Clarendon and of C.P. Villiers. In 1863-82 he was lieut-governor of the Isle of Man, where he was popular but took little part in affairs outside his satrapy save for publishing in London a *Personal narrative of occurrences during Lord Elgin's second embassy to China* (1869), and a *Memorandum upon the present military resources of England, with suggestions as to the manner in which they may be strengthened* (1870). Created K.C.B. in 1880, he became a commissioner of woods and forests and land revenue in 1882 and was appointed governor of Victoria in 1884.

Like other governors, Loch took little part in political affairs, though his regular receptions were said to have helped to 'soften the asperity of political conflicts'. As a channel of communication with the Colonial Office he was replaced by the agent-general; with little confidential information at his disposal, his reports became somewhat infrequent and superficial. He was by-passed in the negotiations over the New Hebrides and New Guinea, and when Victoria's defence forces were being reorganized, Loch's support of the claims of the commandant, Colonel Disney [q.v.], for independence from the minister, F. T. Sargood [q.v.], was fruitless. However, Loch was more active and useful in discussions with Britain on naval affairs and Chinese immigration, though his influence on policy was slight. More important was his social success, particularly when irritation was aroused in some quarters by a variety of differences of opinion with Britain. He was favourably contrasted with his predecessor, the marquis of Normanby. Loch appears to have been esteemed by more than the few who normally heed activities at Government House. His wife was active in philanthropic works and in 1887 helped to organize the Queen's Jubilee fund for 'the relief of suffering womankind'.

On leave in England in 1889 Loch was appointed high commissioner for South Africa and governor of Cape Colony but before taking office he briefly returned to Melbourne. Promoted G.C.M.G. in 1887 and G.C.B. in 1892, he was appointed P.C. and created baron on his return to England in 1895. In the House of Lords he sat with the Liberal Unionists; he intervened in debates on African questions, and amongst other things demanded greater government control over chartered companies. He died on 20 June 1900 survived by a son and two daughters.

Loch was widely declared to have been the most popular and respected governor in Victoria. He and Lady Loch left behind nothing but pleasant memories, and received more than the usual quota of farewell addresses, mementos and presentations from the community.

W. Stebbing (ed), *Charles Henry Pearson . . . memorials by himself, his wife and his friends* (Lond, 1900); H. G. Turner, *A history of the colony of Victoria*, 2 (Lond, 1904); G. Serle, *The rush to be rich* (Melb, 1971); PD (HL), 1896-1900; *Age*, 12-14 Nov 1889; *The Times*, 21 June 1900.   A. G. L. Shaw

LOFTUS, Lord AUGUSTUS WILLIAM FREDERICK SPENCER (1817-1904), diplomat and governor, was born on 4 October 1817 at Bristol, England, fourth son of John Loftus, second marquis of Ely, and his wife Anna Maria, née Dashwood. Reared in aristocratic shelter and educated privately, he travelled on the Continent with his father in 1836-37 and met many notables. He was introduced to the court of William IV who undertook 'to look after him' in the diplomatic service and was appointed on 20 June 1837 on the king's death. He was an attaché to various British legations in Germany and at several European courts. He was chargé d'affaires at Berlin in 1853-58 and then became envoy extraordinary to the emperor of Austria. In 1866 he was sent to Berlin as ambassador and created G.C.B. In 1871-78 he was ambassador in St Petersburg. On 9

August 1845 in London he had married Emma Maria, eldest daughter of Admiral Henry Francis Greville; they had three sons and two daughters.

Early in 1879 Loftus sought a more genial climate and less arduous duties. He was appointed governor and commander-in-chief of New South Wales and its dependencies. Two sons came to Sydney with him, one as an aide-de-camp, and his wife joined him in 1880. His arrival in Sydney on 3 August 1879 was greeted with great enthusiasm. The press expatiated on the colony's honour in having so eminent a peer and forecast a refreshing change for New South Wales, but the honeymoon was short. Long years of professional diplomacy had given him self-effacing detachment and aversion to publicity. He knew nothing of colonies and parliamentary government but was expert in tact and ways of persuasion. With advancing years he suffered from increasing deafness and seldom left Government House after dark, withdrawing more often to the Blue Mountains and from 1882 to Hillview, the country house near Moss Vale that he had induced the government to buy for him.

Loftus was the communications link between the colony and the Colonial Office. He wrote on subjects ranging from prisons to sewerage but took care to seek advice from London on every contentious issue and on imperial-colonial relations. The Parkes-Robertson [qq.v.] coalition was in office when he arrived and it lasted until 4 January 1883. Loftus early tried to limit the days on which he signed documents but Parkes claimed that such a personal direction to the permanent heads of departments would overrule ministerial authority. Loftus thought that 'A Mountain has been made out of a Molehill' but accepted the rebuke. In one crisis between the two Houses he persuaded Parkes to wait for the Colonial Office's advice; when the Upper House insisted on amending the bill Loftus talked confidentially to individual councillors and persuaded them to concur. When the colony's divorce law was reserved for the third time, Loftus wrote privately to Hicks-Beach who persuaded the imperial government to modify its amendments; they were accepted in Sydney and became law.

After Alexander Stuart [q.v.] formed his ministry on 5 January 1883, letters between the cabinet and Loftus show growing friendship and close co-operation, the governor favouring the private note, tête-à-tête and dinner at Government House. When Stuart had a stroke and his deputy, Dalley [q.v.], was unwell and wanted to move to the assembly, Loftus tactfully rejected the proposal. Very confident on external affairs he was careful that 'protests' were changed into 'proposals'. In 1881 he insisted that a formal letter to the British minister in Washington be carried by Parkes when he visited America despite his commission from other Australian colonies. Under Stuart New South Wales faced more serious external affairs in New Guinea and Fiji. On 11 February 1885 news reached Sydney of General Gordon's death at Khartoum and next day Dalley offered military assistance to Britain. As commander-in-chief Loftus had a part in sending the Sudan contingent but spent most of his time at Moss Vale. He supported Federation, not for sweet reason but for fear of external attack or internal crisis, yet at heart remained an imperial federationist.

Loftus left Sydney in November with few cheers. Late in 1887 he was declared bankrupt with liabilities of £62,000. At Linden House, Leatherhead, he wrote four volumes of *Diplomatic Reminiscences*, which were published in London in two series, one for 1837-62 (1892), the other for 1862-79 (1894). Predeceased by his wife on 1 January 1902 and one daughter, he died on 7 March 1904 at Englemere Wood Cottage, near Ascot, and was buried at Frimley. He was survived by a daughter and three sons, one in the army, the others in the diplomatic service.

N. I. Graham, The role of the governors of New South Wales under responsible government, 1861-1890 (Ph.D. thesis, Macquarie Univ, 1973).

LONG, WILLIAM ALEXANDER (1839-1915), politician and race-horse owner, was born on 28 July 1839 in Sydney, son of William Long (1797-1876) and his second wife. His father and uncle, both sentenced to transportation for seven years, had arrived in Sydney, William on 7 September 1815 in the *Baring* described as a whitesmith, and Alexander (1802-1881) on 1 December 1819 in the *Earl St Vincent*, later becoming a publican. By 1828 William was licensee of the Saracen's Head at Millers Point and in 1831 took over the Commercial Tavern in George Street North, one of the most lucrative hostelries in Sydney. By 1835 he was a prosperous wine and spirits merchant and built Tusculum, a mansion at Potts Point. At Parramatta on 2 March 1827 he had married a widow, Mary Walker; after she died he married Isabella Walford (d. 1894) at Sydney on 2 September 1829. They had three daughters: Isabella (1832-1909) who married James Martin [q.v.]; Eleanor Jane (1842-1881) who married W. B. Dalley [q.v.]; and Selina (1844-1926) who married a nephew of A. Cheeke [q.v.]. William also invested in city property and left an estate of over £100,000.

Privately educated, Long studied law in England and was called to the Bar of the Inner Temple on 11 June 1862 and admitted to the New South Wales Bar on 22 December. He did not practise but on 30 June 1875 won the Central Cumberland seat in the Legislative Assembly. Although an undistinguished politician, he was colonial treasurer from August to December 1877 in John Robertson's [q.v.] ministry of which Dalley was also a member. In October he won Parramatta but lost it at the 1880 general election. In 1885, when he was a director of the Australian Joint Stock Bank, the Alexander Stuart [q.v.]-Dalley ministry had him appointed to the Legislative Council.

In parliament Long had revealed his interest in race-horses by arguing that the breeding of thoroughbreds had improved the quality of hackney, carriage, saddle and buggy horses. Opposed to totalizator betting, he observed that if the *Sydney Morning Herald* wanted to suppress gambling it should stop sending reporters to race meetings. Wealth acquired on his father's death had enabled him to increase his racing activities. In 1880-81 his Grand Flaneur won nine successive races, including the Australian Jockey Club Derby, the Victoria Derby and the Melbourne Cup, before he retired unbeaten. Among his many other horses Geraldine won the 1880 Australian Jockey Club Sires Produce Stakes, Dainty the 1880 Oaks, and Hopscotch the 1895 Epsom. By the mid-1890s, although a severe depression eroded his fortune, he was one of the best-known racing men in Australia. With Tom Brown as his trainer he had large stables and a private training track at Chipping Norton, and he planned the laying out of the near-by Warwick Farm race-course. Chairman of the Australian Jockey Club in 1898-1900, he encouraged increases in prize money. Long also bred horses, both at Chipping Norton and at the Hobartville stud, near Richmond, which he took over from Andrew Town [q.v.] at his death in 1890.

In 1901 Long went to England for several years and resigned from the Legislative Council in 1909. Leaving an estate of £250, he died unmarried in Lewisham Hospital on 30 November 1915. He was buried in the family vault at St Jude's Anglican Church, Randwick. Long was one of the many who lent their patronage and spent their money to enable the Australian thoroughbred industry to attain its high national prominence and international repute.

D. M. Barrie, *The Australian bloodhorse* (Syd, 1956); *Illustrated Sydney News*, 18 Aug 1877; *SMH*, 1 Dec 1915; newspaper cuttings, vols 92, 177 (ML).   BEDE NAIRN

LONG-INNES, *see* INNES, JOSEPH GEORGE LONG

LONGMORE, FRANCIS (1826-1898), politician and farmer, was born at Tullaree, County Monaghan, Ireland, fourth son of George Longmore (d. 1827), tenant farmer, and his wife Jane, neé Murdoch. He attended a local Presbyterian school and helped his mother and brothers until the family was evicted in the late 1830s. They migrated to Sydney and took up farming at Dapto. In 1851 they split up; Francis became a commission agent in Sydney and in 1852 followed the gold rush to Ballarat. Keen on temperance and a radical, he condemned his fellow diggers for drunkenness and political apathy, but also agreed with their common cause to break up control by the squatters and to open up land for small farmers. In 1857 Longmore settled on ninety acres he had bought at Lake Learmonth, near Creswick. In May 1859 he married Sarah Bankin, daughter of a wealthy neighbour; they had nine children.

In that year Longmore failed to win the Ripon and Hampden seat in the Victorian Legislative Assembly but held it in 1864-83. He advocated radical law reform to assist small selectors and soon won repute as their champion in the Lower House. As a member of the Liberal group he also fought for reform of the Constitution to effect the supremacy of the assembly and the introduction of protective tariffs. He was commissioner of railways and roads in MacPherson's [q.v.] ministry in 1869-70 and under Duffy [q.v.] in 1871-72 and for crown lands in Berry's [q.v.] ministries in 1875 and 1877-80. In his first portfolio he sought to help selectors by providing light and cheap lines to serve scattered farming districts, but delayed the building of a rail link to Hamilton, the squatting stronghold of the Western District. He also liberalized working conditions for railwaymen by supporting the adoption of the eight-hour day.

In 1875 Longmore had become chairman of the Melbourne Woollen Mills and president of the Permanent Building Association. He was also among the first liberals to realize the political potential of popular organizations and was a founder and president of the Victorian Protection League. In 1876 he helped to found the National Reform League. Amalgamated in 1877 they provided an effective bloc which, under Berry's leadership, helped the liberals to sweep the election. On taking the office of crown lands Longmore restricted borrowing by selectors because he was alarmed at the increased mortgaging of selections which he

claimed was only another way of transferring them to large landholders and capitalists. Despite worthy intentions he had not perceived the peculiar needs of selectors but public outcry forced him to amend the regulations. He was burnt in effigy by struggling Natimuk wheat-farmers who saw Longmore's restrictions as much a symbol of oppression as the continuance of squatting. At his instigation a royal commission inquired into land settlement and its report led to the Land Act, 1878, which liberalized earlier restrictions on selectors. The commission's final report was a triumph for Longmore as it recommended that existing squatting tenures be not renewed after 1880. He had criticized his predecessors in the Lands Department, but his own administration was not noticeably more effective. Hard-working and conscientious, he had to run an under-staffed department riven with graft and discontent. Reputedly an organizer of the Black Wednesday dismissals, he was dropped by Berry from the ministry in 1880.

In 1881-83 Longmore was chairman of the royal commission to inquire into the performance of the police during the Kelly [q.v.] outbreaks. His interest in Ireland's affairs was renewed and in 1882 he signed the Grattan 'Address' which sympathized with the Irish struggle for independence and encouraged opposition to the British government. The resulting furore led to his defeat at the 1883 elections though it won him acclaim as an Irish nationalist from the Irish Catholics in the colony. For the next ten years he farmed a selection at Lower Tarwin in South Gippsland but the land was difficult to develop and after two of his sons died he returned to Melbourne. In 1893 he challenged the premier, J. B, Patterson [q.v.], for the Castlemaine seat in vain but in 1894-97 he held the electorate of Dandenong and Berwick. Aged 72 he died at his home, Tullaree, Malvern, on 1 May 1898.

Throughout his career Longmore was the centre of controversy. Fiery, aggressive and uncompromising he made many enemies. He was not effective in translating radical policies into workable legislation, but is best remembered as a radical idealist who provided a conscience for contemporary liberals and the early Labor Party. He was 'a distinguished old democrat whose natural impulse was to take the side of the people'.

National Reform and Protection League, *Fifth anniversary, 1880* (Vic parliamentary pamphlets, 74/1349); A. Deakin, *The crisis in Victorian politics, 1879-1881,* J. A. La Nauze and R. M. Crawford eds (Melb, 1957); *Tocsin,* 12 July 1900; Berry-Bowen letters (LaT L); Lang papers (ML); Parkes letters (ML); J. J. Walsh papers (LaT L).   JACQUELINE CLARKE

F

LORD, GEORGE WILLIAM (1818-1880), pastoralist, businessman and politician, was born on 15 August 1818 at Macquarie Place, Sydney, youngest son of Simeon Lord [q.v.] and his wife Mary, née Black. At W. Cape's [q.v.] school he became head scholar and won a medal for general proficiency. At about 20 he went to the Wellington District and began acquiring squatting runs in partnership with his brother-in-law, Dr D. Ramsay [q.v.], and John McNevan. By 1850 in his own name he held Mulguthery in the Wellington District and Island in the Lachlan. In that year at Kelso he married Elizabeth, daughter of William Lee [q.v.].

A childhood friend of John Robertson [q.v.], Lord was elected for Bligh and Wellington to the first Legislative Assembly under responsible government; he held the seat until 1859 and then represented the Bogan until 1877. A supporter of James Martin [q.v.], he was colonial treasurer in Martin's third ministry in 1870-72. From lack of 'fluency of language' Lord was the first treasurer to read a written speech when introducing the budget, a practice followed by later treasurers with advantage. In 1871 the press criticized his budget for proposing 10 per cent *ad valorem* duties; they were soon reduced to 5 per cent by the assembly. He was a member of the delegation to the 1871 Intercolonial Conference on border duties. As treasurer he distinguished himself from his colleagues by his regular attendance in the House. Although not outstanding among contemporary politicians his knowledge of pastoral and financial affairs won him respect and by avoiding violent involvement in party tactics he was able to do much for his electors. In 1877 he was appointed to the Legislative Council on Robertson's recommendation.

In 1861 in the assembly's select committee on tendering for runs, Lord had complained bitterly of long delays in dealing with tenders, and advocated a return to the old system of 'first occupation'. In 1862 he won several silver and bronze medals at the Sydney Wool Exhibition and wrote to James Macarthur [q.v.] about exhibiting his wool in London. By 1865 he had nineteen runs amounting to 672,000 acres in the Riverina. He had disposed of them by 1871 but taken up fourteen runs in the Warrego and four in the Wellington Districts on which he paid rent of over £1100. Many of his land speculations were obscure but he also owned much real estate in Bathurst and Sydney including commercial premises in Macquarie Place. He was a director of the Commercial Banking Co. of Sydney in 1865-71 and 1875-80, and sometime of the Sydney Insurance Co., the Sydney Meat Preserving Co. and the Bowenfels Coal Mining and Copper Smelting

Co. In 1875 Lord refused to sell land at Botany to the Sewerage and Health Board to use as a dump for night soil, as he had bought it 'in order to keep people away from me'.

A territorial magistrate, Lord was also a founding member of the Union Club. He died from softening of the brain at his home, Kirketon, Darlinghurst, on 9 May 1880 and was buried in the family vault in the Anglican section of Botany cemetery. He was survived by his wife, two sons and two daughters. His goods were sworn for probate at £90,000.

V&P (LA NSW), 1861, 2, 922, 1866, 1, 738, 1875-76, 5, 355; Empire (Syd), 20, 29 Dec 1856; SMH, 15 Mar, 24 Apr 1871; Illustrated Syd News, 27 June 1874; Sydney Mail, 15 May 1880; Town and Country J, 22 May 1880; Truth (Syd), 17, 24 Mar 1912, 29 June 1919; MS cat and newspaper indexes (ML); CO 201/534, 563-65, 569, 584.   DAVID HENRY

LORIMER, SIR JAMES (1831-1889), politician and businessman, was born on 30 March 1831 in Dumfriesshire, Scotland, son of Thomas Lorimer, merchant, and his wife Catherine, née Walkin. Educated at Hatton Hall Academy, he was articled to a Liverpool softgoods firm trading with America and Africa. Advised for health reasons to take a long voyage, he arrived in Victoria in 1853 and decided to stay. Soon afterwards he founded the firm of Lorimer, Mackie & Co., merchants and shipping agents for the White Star Line. The firm later amalgamated with John Swyre & Son of London and Liverpool, set up a Sydney branch and after his partner retired became known as Lorimer, Rome & Co.

Lorimer was vice-president of the Melbourne Chamber of Commerce in 1864 and 1867-68 and president in 1868-70. A foundation member and first chairman of the Melbourne Harbor Trust, he supported the appointment of Sir John Coode [q.v.] to report on improvements to the port of Melbourne. Lorimer was dropped as chairman by Berry [q.v.] for party reasons but soon rejoined the trust as a representative for the merchants and traders of Melbourne. He succeeded Sir Francis Murphy [q.v.] as chairman of the local directors of the Bank of Australasia and helped to reorganize it. He was a director of the Bank of New South Wales and of the Northern and Southern Insurance companies. He had helped to form the Free Trade League; he became its president in 1865 but had little taste for political warfare and did not enter politics until 1878 when he was elected to the Legislative Council for Central Province.

After redistribution he was elected un-opposed in 1884 for Melbourne Province. He joined the Gillies [q.v.]-Deakin ministry in February 1886 as minister of defence. With Deakin and Berry he attended the Colonial Conference in London in 1887 but did not make any notable contribution to the discussion, although Deakin later claimed that Lorimer had mastered the details of the defence questions to be discussed 'more thoroughly than any one at the Conference'. He was appointed K.C.M.G. during the conference.

Lorimer was respected in parliament for his 'deliberate and mature judgment, ready commonsense and temperate demeanor'. He contributed to the work of the Harbor Trust and formation of the harbor battery for the defence of Melbourne. A member of the Committee of Management of Scots Church, Lorimer warmly supported the liberal Charles Strong [q.v.], especially in 1883, and the proposal for a legal separation of Scots Church from the Presbyterian Church of Victoria. However, he did not join the Australian Church when it was founded in 1885 but remained a nominal Presbyterian.

On 4 March 1858 Lorimer had married Eliza Kenworthy, daughter of the United States consul in Sydney. He died on 6 September 1889 of pleurisy and was buried in St Kilda cemetery, survived by his wife and ten of his eleven children. His estate was sworn for probate at £60,000.

B. Cowderoy (ed), *Melbourne's commercial jubilee* (Melb, 1901); B. Hoare, *Jubilee history of the Melbourne Harbor Trust* (Melb, 1927); A. Deakin, *The federal story*, J. A. La Nauze ed (Melb, 1963); C. R. Badger, *The Reverend Charles Strong* (Melb, 1971); *Argus*, 7 Sept 1889; *Table Talk*, 13 Sept 1889; *A'sian Sketcher*, 3 Oct 1889.   C. R. BADGER

LORIMER, PHILIP DURHAM (1843-1897), wanderer and poet, was born on 3 June 1843 in Madras, India, son of Alexander Lorimer, M.D., garrison assistant-surgeon, and his wife Charlotte (Phillipa), née Henderson. A sister Charlotte was born on 18 July 1841 and a brother Peter about 1844. Philip was educated at the Edinburgh Academy in 1854-59, attending classes 1-5 out of a seven-year course. His brother went to the same school in 1855-59 and took classes 1-4. A fellow-student was Andrew Lang. E. A. Petherick [q.v.], who had access to the Lorimer papers, states that Philip attended the University of Edinburgh; the university records do not mention him.

Although seemingly intended for the army, he migrated to Sydney in 1861. As a wanderer he went to the New England District first, then crossed the border into Queensland, and with about a dozen over-landers took 5000 sheep and 1000 cattle from Warwick to the gulf country. There he caught 'Gulf fever' early in 1866, moved to Port Denison, to Cloncurry and to Burke-town, where he saw two-thirds of the in-habitants die of fever. In mid-1867 on Bowen Downs he finally abandoned all hope of prospering in north Queensland and decided to return to New South Wales. There he composed the half-comic, half-satiric poem which begins:

Queensland: thou art a land of pest:
From flies and fleas we ne'er can rest.

It was frequently reprinted as a leaflet and sold for a few pence. Despite his decision he remained in Queensland for another three years, part of them on the Darling Downs.

In Sydney he wrote some poems addressed to real or imagined loves, was a vice-chair-man of the 'Excelsior' Loyal Orange Lodge in 1872 and wrote a poem for recitation at its meeting on 29 August, lost in un-fortunate business dealings some money remitted from England, and then set out in the early 1880s on his travels up and down the east coast, across the ranges, to diggings, stations, homesteads and townships. He was apparently welcomed by settlers, diggers, and even editors, and repaid the hospitality with verses that he could produce with no great difficulty. Sometimes he took odd jobs and occasionally may have settled for short periods. His life must have been most un-certain and much hardship slowed him down. Ill health attended his last years: he was occasionally in hospital, and at the end he probably became a little deranged. Un-married and intestate, he died of paraplegia in Rookwood Asylum on 5 November 1897. He was known to thousands as Old Phil the Poet; and perhaps he was, from some points of view, the only true bush poet of them all.

In 1859 Lorimer's sister Charlotte married (Sir) Peter Nicol Russell [q.v.], a benefactor of the University of Sydney. She com-missioned E. A. Petherick to edit a volume of Lorimer's poems and to provide a bio-graphical introduction. This was privately printed as Philip Durham Lorimer, *Songs and Verses* (London, 1901), with a biographi-cal sketch by E.A.P. Upon this volume any writer on Lorimer is heavily dependent.

H. A. Kellow, *Queensland poets* (Lond, 1930).
                                   CECIL HADGRAFT

LOUGHLIN, MARTIN (1833-1894), min-ing magnate, speculator and sportsman, was born on 3 November 1833 at Castlewarren, near Kilkenny, Ireland, son of Martin

Loughlin, farmer, and his wife Margaret. While still a boy he sailed for America; the ship was wrecked on Newfoundland but all hands were saved. In New York he worked briefly as a baker and then returned home. In 1855 Loughlin and his cousin, Patrick Brennan, migrated to Geelong and soon joined the gold rush to Pleasant Creek. Learning of new developments in deep-lead mining on the Ballarat field both men transferred their hopes to the co-operatives and companies which were forming to exploit the golden gutters of alluvial under the basalt plateau. Loughlin had remarkable good fortune. With Brennan he joined the Golden Gate Co-operative Co. as a working shareholder and by October 1856 also had shares in the Alston and Weardale Co. By March 1857 he was a working shareholder in the Kohinoor claim on the Golden Point lead which paid dividends of £304,460 after winning 147,570 ozs of gold; in the Melbourne share list of 3 June 1863 forty shares were quoted at £2800 each.

Loughlin rapidly extended his investments in company mines then discovering huge quantities of gold. His physical labour ended he moved into Craig's Hotel and divided his time drinking with other speculators and crossing the pavement to the 'Corner' where all local share transactions took place.

Between October 1874 and September 1876 Loughlin was one of the four members of a syndicate that owned the Egerton mine. They were much publicized defendants in court proceedings where the previous owners, Learmonth brothers [qq.v.] of Ercildoun, alleged conspiracy and fraud in connexion with its purchase by Loughlin for £13,500. On 19 September 1873, the day he took possession, the mine yielded rich gold. The profits after the syndicate took it over were £320,000. Final judgment was in favor of the defendants and although the Learmonths obtained leave to appeal to the Privy Council they accepted Loughlin's proposal that each side should pay its own costs and end the litigation.

The discovery of rich alluvial deposits near Creswick inspired Loughlin and others to exploit these buried rivers of gold. Almost the entire area was private property and the independent working miners could not afford to pay the royalty tax. Loughlin with seven other capitalists bought 6000 acres at £6 an acre from Alexander Wilson, brother of Sir Samuel [q.v.], who had bought Ercildoun from the Learmonths. In May 1881 the Seven Hills Estate Co. was registered in 10,000 shares of £20 but few of its original shares changed hands. Mining companies were soon formed to tap the gold. Loughlin took a hand in floating six of the richest mines in the district. They produced nearly 900,000 ozs of gold, paid £269,925 royalties and distributed £1,776,945 as dividends on an aggregate capital of £143,375. When the mines were exhausted the land was sold for £50,000.

Loughlin lost heavily in the financial crisis of the early 1890s 'more than £100,000', according to the Ballarat Star, 27 September 1894. Apart from mining he had a large interest in the Melbourne Tramway Co. and owned hotels and much land, including pastoral holdings in Queensland. He was a keen sportsman with a large racing stable : two of his horses, Sheet Anchor and Oakleigh, won for him the Melbourne and Caulfield cups double. A spectacular punter who wagered thousands on his string, he gave horses which had cost him £5000 to his friends when he gave up racing.

Unlike most of his business associates he shunned public life, although in 1891 he stood for Nelson Province in the Legislative Council and polled well. In August 1890 he donated three paintings by noted English artists, then valued at £4000, to the Ballarat Art Gallery. He was not a notable philanthropist but was generous to the Roman Catholic Church and its schools, and to the major Ballarat institutions.

After a lingering illness he died, unmarried, at Craig's Hotel on 22 September 1894 of cerebral paralysis. His estate was valued at £250,000. His brother Michael, a farmer of Kilkenny, and Michael's sons, Michael and Thomas, were the beneficiaries.

W. B. Withers, The history of Ballarat, 2nd ed (Ballarat, 1887); R. Gay, Some Ballarat pioneers (Mentone, 1935); J. H. W. McGeorge, Buried rivers of gold (Melb, 1966); Ballarat Courier, 24 Sept 1894; Ballarat Star, 25-27 Sept 1894; F. J. Fitzgerald, William Bailey and the Egerton mine (MS cat under Bailey, Ballarat Municipal Lib); Supreme Court transcript (held by Cuthbert, Morrow, Must & Shaw, solicitors, Ballarat).   AUSTIN McCALLUM

LOUREIRO, ARTUR JOSE (1853-1932), painter, was born on 11 February 1853 at Oporto, Portugal, son of Francisco José de Souza Loureiro and his wife Guilhermina. He studied painting at the Fine Arts Academy of Oporto and in 1873 competed for a state scholarship for study abroad. Though the committee was impressed he withdrew. In 1875 he sat for entrance to the Academy of Fine Arts in Lisbon where his talent was recognized by Count d'Almedina, under whose patronage Loureiro studied for two years at the academy and distinguished himself. He returned to Lisbon in 1879 and won the Portuguese government's art scholarship, given every five years to assist artists to study abroad. Living in the Latin quarter of Paris and studying at the Academie des Beaux Arts under Alexandre Cabanel (1823-1889), he exhibited at the salon in 1880, 1881 and 1882. He also met Marie Huybers, a Belgian girl related to Jessie Couvreur [q.v.], and despite the rules of his scholarship he married her; they had one son and one daughter. Illness prevented him from submitting the annual painting to the Lisbon Art Gallery and he lost the scholarship. He travelled to London where he exhibited and attracted attention from critics, but a warmer climate became essential. In 1884 he went to Melbourne, arriving as an almost helpless invalid. He was fluent in Italian and French but had little English.

The Victorian Academy of Art was early controlled by amateurs, but in 1885 after the return of T. Roberts a group of professional artists broke with the academy and formed the Australian Art Association; Loureiro with eight others were members. They held three exhibitions at the Buxton Gallery and successful smoke nights before amalgamating with the academy in 1888 to form the Victorian Artists' Society. Loureiro's portrait of James Cooper Stewart, mayor of Melbourne (1885-86), had been exhibited and bought for £200 by public subscription; according to the *Bulletin*, 19 March 1887, it was 'one of the best portraits ever painted in Australia'. For most of his time in Melbourne, Loureiro was 'Professor of Design' at the Presbyterian Ladies' College, constantly painted, sold pictures to wealthy Melbourne patrons and was said to have won prizes in all the exhibitions to which he submitted entries.

In 1899 Loureiro won a gold medal at London and in 1900 a third-class medal in Paris. His work was known for its broad, free handling and fresh out-of-doors feeling. In 1901 he returned to Oporto, set up a teaching studio and exhibited landscapes and seascapes of 'unexcelled technical perfection'. Some of his work was shown in 1920 at the National Society of Fine Arts Gallery and in 1923 at a commemorative exhibition on his artistic jubilee. In 1929 a collection of his best works was exhibited at the Salon of Silva Porto and the Uffizzi Gallery acquired a self-portrait. In April 1932 his colleagues, friends and admirers honoured him and he became a member of the Order of Santiago. Attracted by its beautiful landscapes, he went to Gerez, but he died suddenly on 7 July at Terras de Bouro. His paintings hang in Lisbon, Porto, Melbourne and Bendigo galleries. He was predeceased by his first wife and his only son Vasco was killed in World War I. Loureiro was survived by his second wife Eliza Fernanda de Sousa Pires (b. 1896) whom he had married on 19 June 1918.

Grande enciclopédia Portuguesa e Brasileira (Lisbon, 1936-1960); Bernard Smith, *Australian painting 1788-1960* (Melb, 1962); *Table Talk*, 19 Oct 1888; McCrae family papers (LaT L).
                                    SUZANNE G. MELLOR

LOVE, JAMES ROBINSON (1836-1914), merchant, was born on 22 June 1836 at Fintona, County Tyrone, Ireland, the younger son of William Love (1812-1885), shepherd, and his wife Ellen, née Robinson (1815-1882). In March 1841 he arrived in Sydney with his parents and brother as bounty immigrants in the *Brothers*. The family settled on the Coppabella run at Tumbarumba, New South Wales, owned by Love's father-in-law, James Robinson (d. 1868). His father failed on the land and in 1850 moved to Sydney, opened a retail grocery shop at 476 George Street and in 1860-64 represented West Sydney in the Legislative Assembly. James joined his business but in October 1866 Love & Son became insolvent and was finally wound up in 1875. On 1 September William was appointed police magistrate at Gundagai.

Meanwhile James, with £200 lent him by Frederick Lassetter [q.v.], had opened a wholesale grocery in a small warehouse near the corner of Park and George Streets, Sydney. He first concentrated on the city trade but in the 1870s sought country customers. In 1882 he took his eldest son Frederick into partnership, moved to new premises in Bathurst Street and appointed his first country traveller. In January 1888 he took his family to England, leaving the business in charge of Frederick. Love sent three of his sons to Dulwich College and Arthur, the second son, went on to Christ's College, Cambridge (M.A., 1904). In the early 1890s competition increased in the grocery trade and the firm had to employ more country travellers. In 1895 Love returned to Sydney to assume control. He visited England again in 1896 and returned permanently to Sydney in 1899 when his sons Arthur and Kenneth joined the business.

Love's firm had begun blending and marketing packet tea under the trade name Kinkara, a corruption of Kincora, a tea estate in Ceylon. In 1897 Kinkara tea and Mother's Choice flour were registered as brand names and became widely known. Love's reconstruction of the firm was seriously set back in 1900 when his warehouse, insured for only half its value of £44,000, was destroyed by fire. He suffered a further set-back when several employees left the firm and opened in opposition. In the drought of 1900-02 the firm had to close its branch offices in Newcastle and Brisbane. In 1907 J. R. Love & Co. became a limited company.

Like his father, Love was interested in charitable work: he was a board member and vice-president of the New South Wales Institution for the Deaf and Dumb and the Blind, a committee member of the City Night Refuge and Soup Kitchen and an energetic helper of the Boy's Brigade. He belonged to the Royal Sydney Yacht Squadron. From 1903 he acted as Greek consul in Sydney and consul-general for Greece in New South Wales. He died at his home, Theulda, Wahroonga, on 25 August 1914 and was buried in the Anglican section of South Head cemetery. Probate of his will was sworn at £33,200. Predeceased by his wife Kassie Louise (1841-1910), daughter of Launcelot Iredale, whom he had married at Surry Hills in 1863, he was survived by four sons and an only daughter.

R. Brampton, J. R. Love and Co. Pty. Ltd. a centenary history 1862-1962 (Syd, 1962); Government Gazette (NSW), 1866, 1875; SMH, 26 Aug 1914.   G. P. WALSH

LOWE KONG MENG (1831-1888), merchant and Chinese community leader, was born as a British subject in Penang, son of Lowe A Quee, merchant, and his wife Chew Tay. His forbears were natives of Sze Yap near Canton. He was educated at a high school in Penang and at 16 went to Mauritius to study English and French under private tutors. His command of these languages partly explains why he was readily recognized as a leader and accepted by both the Chinese and Australian communities.

Kong Meng entered the commercial field by trading extensively with merchants in Mauritius, Calcutta and Singapore and by travelling regularly between the Indian Ocean and the South China Sea as a supercargo. In 1853, hearing of the discovery of gold in Victoria, he went to Melbourne in his own ship. A year later he was established in Little Bourke Street as Kong Meng & Co., importers of tea and other delicacies. He was then the only Chinese in Australia to own a fleet of six ships; later some of them were engaged in procuring bêche-de-mer from the Torres Straits. In 1864 he was one of the first to attempt trade between Melbourne and Port Darwin. Among other lines of business he bought a gold mine at Majorca, Victoria, and speculated in many other mining ventures in the colony. He was also connected with banking and insur-

ance. With Louis Ah Mouy [q.v.] he served on the provisional committee of the new Commercial Bank of Australia in 1866 and they were amongst its most important shareholders. He represented the Chinese insurance companies, the On Tai and Man On, and had large interests in Hong Kong and Cairns, Queensland, where he helped to found the Hop Wah Sugar Co. which crushed its first sugar in 1882. Very successful in the variety and extent of his business he was probably the wealthiest Chinese resident in Melbourne as claimed by the *Mount Alexander Mail* in 1888.

A popular and enlightened leader in Melbourne's Chinese community, Kong Meng supervised Chinese clubs, settled disputes among his countrymen, helped them to find work and urged them to respect the British flag, law and justice. In 1859 he initiated a petition against the annual residence tax of £4 on every Chinese resident. He and two other Chinese leaders, Cheong Cheok Hong [q.v.] and Louis Ah Mouy, wrote a pamphlet in 1879 on *The Chinese Question in Australia, 1878-1879*, presenting the Chinese case on immigration restrictions. One of the main arguments was that the British government should apply the 1860 Peking Treaty to allow Chinese migrants to enter British territories as it gave reciprocal access to Britishers to enter China. In 1887 with other leading Chinese in Melbourne he helped to organize the Victorian Chinese petition to the two visiting Chinese commissioners, General Wong Yung Ho and U Tsing, against anti-Chinese immigration restriction laws. During the 1888 anti-Chinese campaigns in both New South Wales and Victoria, Kong Meng again took an active part in protesting against anti-Chinese legislation.

Despite his attitude towards the immigration issue, Kong Meng was far from unpopular and was elected by the Victorian government as a commissioner for the Melbourne Exhibitions in 1880 and 1888. Contemporary Australian writers described him as 'cultured', 'superior', 'influential' and 'highly esteemed', a gentleman with an 'exceedingly generous disposition' who 'gave liberally to churches and public charities, without respect to creed and denomination'. His leadership of the Chinese community in Victoria was also recognized by Emperor T'ung Ch'ih, who conferred on him the title of mandarin of the blue button, civil order, in 1863.

On 4 February 1860 in Melbourne Kong Meng married Mary Ann, daughter of William Prussia of Tasmania. He died on 22 October 1888 at his home in Malvern, survived by his widow and twelve children. The family later left Malvern and established a residential hotel at Fitzroy Street, St Kilda.

T. W. H. Leavitt (ed), *Australian representative men* (Melb, 1887); A. Sutherland et al, *Victoria and its metropolis*, 2 (Melb, 1888); I. Selby, *History of Melbourne* (Melb, 1924); V&P (LC Vic), 1856-57 (D19); *Age*, 31 May 1859; *Illustrated Aust News*, 20 Sept 1866; *Mount Alexander Mail*, 5 May 1888; *Argus*, 24 Oct 1888; *Leader* (Melb), 27 Oct 1888; *A'sian Sketcher*, 29 Nov 1888; G. A. Oddie, The Chinese in Victoria, 1870-1890 (M.A. thesis, Univ Melb, 1959).   YONG CHING FATT

LOYAU, GEORGE ETTIENNE (1835-1898), journalist and author, was born on 15 April 1835 in London, son of George Ettienne Loyau and his wife Catharine, née Chanson. His father died when he was a year old and his mother lived mostly on the Continent while he went to school in England. At 15 he took up clerical work. He sailed from Gravesend in the *Investigator* and arrived at Sydney on 4 August 1853. For seven years he travelled in New South Wales, Queensland and Victoria, his occupations including gold digger, shepherd, hutkeeper, shearer, overseer, stockman, cattle drover, cook, private tutor and press correspondent.

Loyau became editor of the *Burnett Argus* at Gayndah in 1861 but after four months transferred to the *Maryborough Chronicle* and in 1862 became parliamentary reporter and sub-editor on the *Queensland Daily Guardian* in Brisbane. In 1865 he moved to Sydney where he stayed for eleven years doing newspaper and clerical work between periods of unemployment. He also published three slim volumes of poetry: *The Australian Seasons* and *Australian Wild Flowers* in 1871 and *Colonial Lyrics* in 1872. After six months as editor of the *Gundagai Times* he moved in 1876 to Melbourne where he worked as a ticket writer and journalist. In April 1877 he moved to Adelaide and in August launched *The Australian Family Herald: a Weekly Magazine of Interesting Literature*, but only three issues seem to have appeared. He was editor of the *Gawler Bunyip* in 1878-79 and of the *Illustrated Adelaide News* in 1880-81. In South Australia he published *The Gawler Handbook* in 1880, *Representative Men of South Australia* and *The Personal Adventures of George E. Loyau* in 1883 and *Notable South Australians* in 1885. He also edited *The South Australian Annual: Australian tales by well known writers* in 1877. By 1895 he was back in Queensland where he wrote *The History of Maryborough* in 1897. He died of apoplexy at Bundaberg on 23 April 1898. He was predeceased by his first wife,

Eliza Ann, née Sharpe, whom he had married in Brisbane on 5 May 1862, and by his second wife Paulina, née Lynch, whom he had married in Sydney on 13 December 1865. He was survived by his third wife Eleanor Anne, née Parker, and by two sons and four daughters of his eight children.

Loyau had begun writing verses as early as 1854, and claimed to have contributed poems, novels, short stories and other articles to many newspapers. Despite this work he lived in poverty for much of his life, occasionally complaining about the lack of public appreciation of literature. Few of his poems have outlived nineteenth-century taste. He was capable of great variety in prose style, from flowery journalism and tedious descriptions to straightforward narrative and lively, whimsical anecdotes. His *Gawler Handbook* and *History of Maryborough* are valuable sources for local history, although the latter suffers from hasty compilation. His best and most consistent work is in the two volumes of short biographies of his South Australian contemporaries.

The poetical works of George Ettienne Loyau (ML); information from Mr W. H. Brown, South Casino, NSW.   J. H. LOVE

LUCAS, JOHN (1818-1902), politician, was born on 24 June 1818 at Kingston (Camperdown), Sydney, eldest son of John Lucas and his wife Mary, daughter of Thomas Rowley [q.v.]. His father had been born in the colony and was a miller, builder, publican and political activist. Educated at the Church of England school in Liverpool and Captain Beveridge's boarding school in Sydney, Lucas was apprenticed at 16 as a carpenter. On 4 January 1841 at Singleton he married Ann Sammons. About 1848 he returned to Camperdown where he was an innkeeper. Later he succeeded as a builder and contractor. In 1858 he became a magistrate and sat regularly in the Central Police Court.

In 1858 Lucas published a pamphlet, *Protection v. Free Trade*, in which he advocated protection in a young country to protect the labouring classes and the farmers. After several defeats he was elected to the Legislative Assembly for Canterbury in 1860. In 1864 he won both Canterbury and Hartley and sat for Hartley. In 1870-80 he again represented Canterbury. A first cousin of J. S. Farnell [q.v.], he supported liberal legislation, and in 1860 and 1861 twice unsuccessfully introduced a Chinese immigration regulation bill. After the Lambing Flat riots in 1861 the ministry adopted his proposed poll tax. A scathing critic of governments whatever their political complexion, he abhorred waste and bungling. Although he made many enemies by constantly trying to curb the perquisites of the public service, his political influence enabled him to establish three of his sons in the civil service. In 1866 he supported the Martin-Parkes [qq.v.] coalition, but after being ridiculed by Thomas Garrett [q.v.] as the 'off-side Minister', he deserted to the Opposition. By the end of the 1867 session he had acquired 'an unenviable notoriety for mischief and obstruction'. Lucas was hampered by his 'heavy lumbering way' and offensive 'bullying manner'. Although he detested dancing in public houses and failed to have the assembly's plush leather benches replaced by cane chairs, he saved Belmore Park in Sydney from subdivision and had land for parks set aside in every country town in New South Wales.

A prolific pamphleteer and compulsive correspondent of the Empire and Sydney Morning Herald, Lucas advocated free state schools, reformatories for wayward children, protection and many other causes. He was deeply interested in Sydney's water supply and advocated the damming of the George's and Warragamba Rivers. In 1875-77 he was secretary for mines in John Robertson's [q.v.] ministry and carried the Coal Mines Regulation Act and amendments to the Mining Act. The government fell before he could persuade his colleagues to spend a surplus of £1,750,000 on such impressive public buildings as the schools of mines and design. In 1880 he did not seek re-election, but was nominated to the Legislative Council. He strongly opposed Federation as premature and thought New South Wales had everything to lose; in 1890-91 he published two pamphlets on the question.

Lucas had been one of the first to visit the Jenolan caves in 1861 and described them in the Sydney Morning Herald, 5 June 1863. Through his efforts the caves were opened to the public and declared a reserve. One of the largest caverns was named after him. He was a director of the Botany Railway Co., the Bowenfels Coal Mining and Copper Smelting Co. and two mutual benefit building societies. He was also a trustee of the National Park. In 1882 he sued the government for £76,945 compensation for land resumed at Darling Harbour and valued by the government at £5676. The jury valued the land at only £4500. His appeal failed and, rankling at the verdict and criticism of the magnitude of his claim, he published his wrongs in the Darling Harbour Compensation Case (1883).

In 1888 Robertson pressed Parkes to allow one of the Lucas sons to resign from the public service as his dismissal was likely to have a 'very injurious effect on so kind and indulgent a father'. Lucas died from cardiac debility on 1 March 1902 and was buried in the Anglican section of Rookwood cemetery. Predeceased by his wife, he was survived by four sons and one daughter. His estate was valued for probate at over £11,000.

Supreme Court reports (NSW), 1882-83; V&P (LA NSW), 1855, 3, 407, 1862, 5, 558, 1869, 2, 476, 1878-79, 7, 12, 1883-84, 11, 755, 1885-86, 8, 804; Sydney Mail, 15 Oct 1864, 8 Mar 1902; Town and Country J, 27 Mar 1875, 8 Mar 1902; Illustrated Sydney News, 8 Apr 1875; Bulletin, 8 Mar 1902; Parkes letters (ML).

R. W. RATHBONE

LUCAS-TOOTH, SIR ROBERT LUCAS; see TOOTH

LUDOVIC, BROTHER; see LABOUREYAS

LUKIN, GRESLEY (1840-1916), editor, was born on 21 November 1840 at Launceston, Van Diemen's Land, son of George Lukin, brewer, and his wife Mary Anne, née Wilkins. He was educated in Carr-Boyd's College at Campbell Town, studied engineering for two years and then became an actor. In 1865 he joined his elder brother George Lionel in Queensland and on 1 September became recording clerk in his brother's Maranoa Land Office at Roma. On 8 January 1868 at Nurindoo on the Balonne he married Rebekah Hall from the Hunter River. In March he was transferred to the Lands Department in Brisbane and was soon promoted chief clerk possibly because of his work in drafting the Crown Land Sales Act of 1868. In November 1871 he became chief clerk of the Supreme Court.

Lukin had bought shares in the Brisbane Newspaper Co. and in 1873 he resigned his office to become editor of the Brisbane Courier and the Queenslander. He soon succeeded in improving both papers and in 1876 secured a major scoop by sending an expedition under Ernest Favenc [q.v.] to explore a proposed transcontinental railway route. He was popular with both Liberals and Conservatives and played a major part in forming the National Agricultural Association and the Johnsonian Club. In 1879 he was a commissioner for Queensland at the Sydney Intercolonial Exhibition but in February 1880 was bankrupted on his own petition because of unwise land and mining speculation. Soon afterwards he left Queensland.

Lukin was discharged from bankruptcy in March 1880. He was in Melbourne looking for a new paper in February 1881 and in February 1884 appeared in New South Wales as manager of a tin-mining company. However, journalism still called and in March 1890 he bought the *Boomerang* from William Lane. Maintenance of the paper's radical stance alienated middle-class support while advocacy of the Griffith policy on coloured workers alienated the Labor Party. Deepening financial depression came to a head and Lukin lost heavily when the paper was finally wound up in April 1892.

Anxious to improve his health, Lukin went to New Zealand in 1893 and took employment as a parliamentary reporter on the *Evening Post* in Wellington. In 1896 he succeeded E. T. Gillon as editor and remained in office until he died at Wellington on 12 September 1916. Predeceased by his wife in 1906, he was survived by one son and three daughters.

The cyclopedia of New Zealand, 1 (Christchurch, 1897); G. H. Scholefield (ed), *A dictionary of New Zealand biography*, 1 (Wellington, 1940); V&P (LA Qld), 1880, 2, 1387; *Illustrated Sydney News*, 29 Nov 1879; *Argus*, 13 Sept 1916; *Evening Post* (Wellington), 13 Sept 1916; A. G. Stephens papers (ML); Insolvency files (QA).   H. J. GIBBNEY

LUMHOLTZ, CARL SOPHUS (1851-1922), scientist and traveller, was born on 23 April 1851 near Lillehammer, Norway, son of a Norwegian army officer. He was educated at Lillehammer *Latin og Realskole* but objected to his father's idea of a clerical career and spent twelve months as a tutor in a country family. He then capitulated to his family and took a theological degree at the University of Christiania, but gradually became a zoological collector.

Lumholtz was encouraged by Professor R. Collett of the university, who in 1880 sent him on his first major expedition. He left Christiania in the sailing ship *Einar Tambarskjelver* and landed in South Australia on 1 September. He moved on to Rockhampton where early in 1881 he presented a letter of introduction to the Archer brothers [q.v.] of Gracemere, who had family connexions with Norway. For seven months he collected near Gracemere and from July 1881 to January 1882 made a long trip through western Queensland. Later in the year he went to Cardwell and established a new base at Herbert Vale. He decided that the best way to collect natural history specimens was to join the Aboriginals and for fourteen months lived and travelled with a tribe: he became the first scientist to describe the tree kangaroo which bears his name. He then visited Gracemere, left Bris-

bane in the steamer *Dacca* in April 1884 and returned to Norway with a large collection of zoological specimens for the University of Christiania. His *Among Cannibals* (London, 1889), in which he described his travels in Australia, was translated into four languages.

His Australian experience had fired his interest in primitive people and between 1890 and 1910 Lumholtz spent eight years on six expeditions into northern Mexico, the results of which were recorded in *Unknown Mexico* (London, 1912) and other minor works. In 1914 he planned an expedition to Dutch New Guinea with Norwegian support but because of World War 1 was diverted to Borneo where he spent two years, recorded in *Through Central Borneo* (London, 1920). In June 1921 he published a new plan for the exploration of New Guinea in an autobiographical article, 'My life of exploration', published in the New York journal *Natural History*, but before the plan matured he died at Saranac Lake, New York, on 5 May 1922.

Lumholtz was a perceptive observer but his observations were very unsystematic and sketchy. However, later research has confirmed some of his findings on tribal and territorial organization.

Natural History (New York), 22 (1922); 'A Norwegian naturalist in Australia', *Argus*, 14 Jan 1890; Archer papers (ML); information from Professor W. E. H. Stanner.   H. J. GIBBNEY

LUTWYCHE, ALFRED JAMES PETER (1810-1880), judge, was born on 26 February 1810 in London, eldest son of John Lutwyche, leather merchant, and his wife Jemima, née Holt. Educated at Charterhouse and Queen's College, Oxford (B.A., 1832; M.A., 1835), he was admitted to the Middle Temple in September 1831. After two years with a conveyancer he practised as a special pleader and from 1833 supplemented his income by reporting parliamentary debates for the *Morning Chronicle*, in which Charles Dickens [q.v.] was a colleague. At Gray's Inn he read law with J. J. Wilkinson, who encouraged him to write *An Inquiry into the Principles of Pleading the General Issue* (London, 1838). In it Lutwyche criticized the complex pleading rules adopted in 1834 because they had encouraged the use of technicalities. He censured the judiciary for inconsistent application of the new rules and championed the simplicity of the general issue, whose scope had been so restricted that a quarter of common law cases were decided on pleadings instead of merits.

Called to the Bar on 8 May 1840, Lutwyche joined the Oxford circuit. He also attended the county sessions in Staffordshire and Worcestershire, wrote law reports for *The Times* in 1840-52 and published in two volumes, *Reports of Cases . . . in the Court of Common Pleas, on appeal from the decisions of the Revising Barristers* (London, 1847, 1854). Early in 1853 his health broke down and he agreed to become the *Morning Chronicle's* correspondent in Sydney. In June he sailed in the *Meridian*, which was wrecked on Amsterdam Island on 24 August. Of the 108 on board 3 lost their lives and the others most of their possessions. His account of their experiences and rescue by Captain Isaac Ludlow of the Amercian whaler *Monmouth* appeared in the *Morning Chronicle* in December; in 1854 it was reprinted in London and a revised version published in Sydney. Ludlow took the survivors to Mauritius where the government found them passages to Sydney. Lutwyche arrived in the *Emma Colvin* on 30 December 1853. Admitted to the Bar, he obtained a practice and permitted E. K. Silvester to take the *Morning Chronicle* post. On 2 June 1855 at Christ Church St Laurence, he married a widow, Mary Ann Jane Morris.

Lutwyche was nominated to the Legislative Council by Governor Denison but on 1 May 1856 refused to 'take a seat in any House which was not an elective one'. On the 5th an anonymous writer in the *Sydney Morning Herald* alleged that he was the author of a *Morning Chronicle* report (written by Silvester) reflecting on Australian women. Though the *Herald* published his rebuttal, he sued John Fairfax [q.v.] for libel. A special jury found for Lutwyche but awarded him only £2 damages. Friendship with Robert Campbell [q.v.] had brought him to the notice of Charles Cowper [q.v.], who on 25 August asked him to serve as solicitor-general and government leader in the Legislative Council. He declined because Cowper's attorney-general, James Martin [q.v.], was not a barrister. However, Martin was admitted to the Bar on 11 September and next day Lutwyche accepted nomination to the Legislative Council and joined the ministry. Before the government fell on 2 October it sponsored the parliament's first statute, enabling the raising of certain loans, which he steered through the council stages in an hour.

In opposition while H. W. Parker [q.v.] was premier, Lutwyche consolidated his repute for vigorous, combative liberalism. A most vocal member, he had few regular supporters in the council and his partisan zeal antagonized the lawyers and pastoralists. Though not brilliant in debate, he had a sense of humour and his vigilance, shrewdness and forcefulness enabled him to hold

his own. Elected a vice-president of the Electoral Reform League in February 1857, he submitted a petition for manhood suffrage and equal electorates to a mass meeting in Hyde Park on 20 July. The crowd responded to his flair for demagogy and more than 4000 signatures were collected before he presented the petition to the Legislative Council.

On 7 September Lutwyche joined Cowper's second administration as solicitor-general and leader of the council. He carried the ministry's main reforms despite intense opposition, and his speech of 8 September 1858 on the electoral law amendment bill was printed and distributed as a democratic manifesto. He neglected private practice but took silk on becoming attorney-general in November. His policy that prosecutions for criminal libel be conducted by the Crown law officers, not private counsel, aroused hostility early in 1859 when Alexander Berry [q.v.] launched his first action against J. D. Lang [q.v.]. In the council Lutwyche was accused of political bias; badgered and baited beyond endurance, he lost his temper and walked out but apologized at the next sitting. In the trial the chief justice upheld his handling of the prosecution but the jury acquitted Lang.

On 21 February Lutwyche was appointed Supreme Court judge at Moreton Bay. He opened his court in Brisbane on 9 March, obtained authority to hold circuit courts and proceeded to fulfill Sir Alfred Stephen's [q.v.] prophecy that he would 'make a good Judge'. In November when the separation of Queensland was imminent, he claimed a seat on the Sydney bench, arguing that continued residence in Brisbane was incompatible with his post as a New South Wales judge. In Sydney, Forster's [q.v.] ministry ruled that he could either become judge of the Supreme Court of Queensland or resign. He denounced this decision but did not contest it as he chose to stay in Brisbane.

Lutwyche was appalled by the executive blunders accompanying separation. The first concerned the franchise. The imperial New South Wales Constitution Enabling Act had provided that the constitution of Queensland's legislature should resemble that of New South Wales at the time of separation. Advised by the Sydney judges, Denison interpreted the Order in Council establishing Queensland to mean that the new Legislative Assembly should be elected under the terms of the Constitution Act of 1853, not the Electoral Act of 1858. Queenslanders had exercised manhood suffrage in July 1859, and reversion to the 1853 provisions disfranchised a third of them. When the Order in Council was proclaimed in Brisbane, Lutwyche advised the new governor,

Sir George Bowen, that it could not over-ride the imperial statute and that the British government should rectify the illegality. Bowen claimed that the Queensland legis-lature should decide if manhood suffrage was to be restored. The Colonial Office agreed and overlooked the legal point raised in Lutwyche's memorandum. In July 1860 he told Bowen still more forcefully that the Acts of an invalidly constituted legislature must be void but Bowen and his ministers ignored the advice.

Meanwhile Sir Alfred Stephen's allegation that Lutwyche's wife was 'unfit . . . for the circle into which her husband's rank must place her' had led the Colonial Office to decide that Lutwyche could not be given a dormant commission to administer the government in the governor's absence. Thus arose the custom, peculiar to Queensland, of appointing the president of the Legislative Council as administrator. Lutwyche refused Bowen's offer of a seat in the Legislative Council because he wanted to confine him-self to his judicial duties. He was drawn from this neutrality when Sir Charles Nicholson [q.v.] assaulted his character and denounced his elevation to the bench as the 'political job' of an 'ultra-mobocratic' ministry. Nicholson convinced Bowen and many politicians that Lutwyche should not be made chief justice with such effect that Bowen asked the Colonial Office whether he could refuse to obey his Executive Council if it demanded Lutwyche's promotion.

Another flaw in the Order in Council was the reduction of Lutwyche's salary which the New South Wales Act (no 5, 1857) had fixed at £2000. In London Sir George Lewis advised that Lutwyche was entitled 'both in equity and law' to £2000 and that the imperial government would support his rights 'by all constitutional means' while his commission was in force. In response the Queensland parliament passed a Supreme Court bill cancelling the commission and substituting a new one carrying a salary of £1200. Bowen reserved the bill. Lutwyche petitioned the Queen to withhold assent and reasserted that the assembly had been elected unlawfully. While the constitutional issue was referred to the English law officers, the Colonial Office concluded that Lutwyche had been treated unjustly. The duke of Newcastle returned the bill to Bowen, observing that Queenslanders had been represented in the New South Wales parliament and inherited its engagement to maintain their judge's salary.

Lutwyche had further antagonized the Herbert [q.v.] ministry by questions about his precedence and status, and learnt that he had no prospect of becoming chief justice. In February 1861 he published extracts from his correspondence with the government in the *Moreton Bay Courier*, which presented him as a 'poor man's judge' championing democratic rights against irresponsible politicians. Large public meetings sympath-ized with him and petitioned parliament in praise of his judicial quality.

On 22 May Herbert tried to discredit Lutwyche by disclosing that he had impugned the Constitution's legality. In deference to Newcastle the Supreme Court bill was recommitted and passed, granting the judge £2000. However, both Houses carried resolutions against him for 'political partizanship, calculated seriously to impair confidence in the administration of justice', and for impugning the Constitution 'only after the close of the first session, and when a Supreme Court bill, drawn by Mr. Lut-wyche himself, securing certain personal advantages, had not been adopted'. The last charge was unfair: his doubts about the Constitution had been clearly stated in January 1860 and his draft bill, which was never presented to parliament made no reference to his commission, rank, salary and allowances. The *Courier* applauded his attempts to 'stand between the people and the Crown and do justice to both', and described the councillors as 'a pack of sycophantic nominees, who are destitute of Gentlemanly feelings, who lack common Christian charity, who have an utter dis-regard for truth, who have not the slightest acquaintance with the first principles of justice'. Without evidence Herbert and Nicholson alleged that the article was written by Lutwyche, but he seems to have only supplied some relevant documents. The council pronounced it a contempt of parlia-ment. When the attorney-general prosecuted the publisher, T. P. Pugh [q.v.], for seditious libel, Lutwyche told the jury that the charge must fail because the council was not part of the government. Pugh's acquittal was greeted with a great demonstration, bonfires and fireworks.

Without surrendering his old commission, on 14 August Lutwyche accepted a com-mission under the Supreme Court Act, 1861. However, he again petitioned the Queen about the local legislature's lack of authority, noting yet another *ultra vires* provision in the 1859 Order in Council. These doubts were resolved in October by the arrival of an imperial validating statute (24 & 25 Vic. c. 44), for the law officers in London had agreed that the legislature was illegally con-stituted.

Till August 1861 Lutwyche had been striving to maintain his independence from a legislature anxious to assert supremacy. For the next two years his quarrel, marred on both sides by obstinacy and animosity, was chiefly with the government. At each stage he gave full details to the press. In March 1862 he won a dispute over his travelling allowances on circuit by settling for £300 a year. In July he petitioned the Queen to disallow an Act which provided for a second judge but did not name him chief justice. He threatened refusal to execute all legislation of the session because two members of the assembly had taken their seats unlawfully. This prompted Bowen to inquire whether he could remove Lutwyche under Burke's Act (22 Geo. III, c. 75); the British law officers advised that he could.

The arrival in February 1863 of James Cockle [q.v.], who was sworn in as 'additional Judge and Chief Justice', relieved the government's anxiety only temporarily. On 25 May, during a general election, Lutwyche issued an address to his fellow-constituents in East Moreton, denouncing Herbert's administration as 'despotism cloaked in the guise of responsible government'. He attacked the ministry for encouraging 'large capitalists and companies' while restricting 'the enterprise of the man with moderate means', trying to 'gag the Press', creating 'new and unnecessary offices' and squandering public funds. He proclaimed his old faith in democratic institutions and demanded 'restoration of the franchise which was filched from us by the Order in Council of 1859'. In the Legislative Council a motion was listed on the notice paper for a select committee to examine his conduct since August 1861, with a view to addressing the Queen for his removal. Bowen, Herbert and Cockle feared that this proposal would produce a party fight over Lutwyche. On 10 August Cockle wrote to Lutwyche reporting rumours that public expression of his political opinions might affect his impartiality on the bench. Lutwyche replied with a defence of his judicial and personal freedom but agreed to restrain himself while a judge. Publication of these letters ended the controversy.

Lutwyche's attempts at self-aggrandizement had distracted the government from the essential justice of the causes he espoused. Puzzled 'that the child of Responsible Government in New South Wales should attempt to override Responsible Government in Queensland', Bowen privately acknowledged that Lutwyche was 'always punctilious in his behaviour towards me, and I have found him ready and able to do his work, and to render me any legal assistance which I might require'. After Pugh's trial, his judicial conduct was rarely questioned for, as Stephen observed, he had much 'aptitude and capacity'. In 1866-67 he collaborated with Cockle and Charles Lilley [q.v.] on a commission which

revised and consolidated 130 British and colonial statutes and much common law in 30 draft bills enacted in 1867. However, manhood suffrage was not restored until 1 January 1873. Lutwyche made firm friendships with Cockle and later judges who praised his perception and learning. He was acting chief justice in 1878-79 but, when Cockle resigned, did not seek promotion for he was crippled by gout. He remained a judge until his death on 12 June 1880.

In April 1859 Lutwyche had bought 94 acres near Kedron Brook. In 1860 he doubled his property and began building Kedron Lodge, designed by Christopher Potter in the style of an English manor house. An excellent host and 'most discriminating of gastronomes', he was a keen poultry fancier and patron of the turf, but apart from winning the Brisbane Cup with Dandy in 1870 had few successes with his horses. He wrote many nonpolitical articles for the press, the last in praise of the table-qualities of local fishes. He took pride in his early association with Dickens and in being claimed by pressmen as one of themselves.

Lutwyche and his wife were dedicated Anglicans. He often conducted services at settlements near Brisbane when clergy were scarce. In 1864 he bought the site for a church in the village near his property, and was instrumental in building St Andrew's Church and providing a parsonage and hall. He served as churchwarden until 1880 and gave the congregation an annual luncheon at his home. He encouraged his wife in raising funds for religious and charitable causes and, before visiting England in the 1870s, left a pillbox of half-sovereigns with the instruction: 'One to be taken by the wardens every Sunday until my return'. He drafted the constitution and canons of the Brisbane diocese, and a conference in September 1867 adopted his motions to establish a synod, founded by voluntary compact. He was a member of synod and the diocesan council from their inception. His wife had a granite Celtic cross erected over his grave at St Andrew's Church, and a suburb and parish bear his name.

A portrait is in the Supreme Court building, Brisbane.

Qld Supreme Court reports (1860-80); J (LC NSW), 1856-59; PP (Qld), 1860-63; Moreton Bay Courier, 1859-61; Brisbane Courier, 1861-80, 24 Oct 1931; Queenslander, 25 Oct 1879, 19 June 1880; W. R. Johnston, A study of the relationship between the law, the state and the community in colonial Queensland (M.A. thesis, Univ Qld, 1967); Executive Council minutes, 1-6 (Premier's Dept, Brisb); Lang and Macarthur papers (ML); Judges' letterbook 1856-78 (QA); CO 234/1-2, 4-8.

P. A. HOWELL

LUXTON, THOMAS (1850-1911), businessman, was born on 22 May 1850 at Bridgerule, Devon, England, son of James Luxton, farrier, and his wife Mary Ann, née Bassett. In 1852 the Luxtons sailed to Victoria. From Moonee Ponds they moved to the Bendigo goldfield where the father worked as a blacksmith and then opened a small grocery and a freighting business between Melbourne and Bendigo; he had some success but his intemperate habits left his family with very little when he died in 1866. Thomas left school at Ironbark to work in a Kangaroo Flat grocery for 30s. a week. A year later he joined W. D. Thomas in working a claim at Carshalton and within eighteen months their £1700 profit enabled Luxton to start as a mining speculator, helping to form the first Bendigo Stock Exchange. In 1872 Luxton married Sarah Schooling of Kyneton. He continued to live at Kangaroo Flat and was on the Marong Shire Council in 1874-77 and a guardian of St Mary's Church of England. As his stockbroking business grew Luxton gave more time and money to Bendigo's institutions. He became a life governor of the Bendigo Hospital and Asylum, a member of the United Cricket and Jockey clubs and the Agricultural and Horticultural Society and supported the Sustenation Fund founded by J. B. Watson [q.v.] for miners.

Luxton moved to Melbourne in the boom years describing them as a time when 'if a person only held out his hand money was placed in it'. He had bought a seat on the Melbourne Stock Exchange in 1887 and for a time was the only broker who was a member of the Melbourne, Ballarat and Bendigo Exchanges. In 1890 Luxton settled in East Prahran and in June 1893 was elected to the Prahran Council. The *Prahran Telegraph* claimed that Luxton answered the need for 'a cool, clear-headed man, one who had not been caught in the whirlpool of financial unrest'. On his election as mayor in 1894 *Melbourne Punch* praised him as one of the few 'who came through the disastrous "boom" unscathed' and with an improved bank balance. Known neither as a talker nor public speaker Luxton was thought unlikely by some to curb more voluble councillors, but all agreed that he, who in youth had excelled at boxing and horse-riding, would in occupying the mayoral chair fit it as well.

His years as mayor in 1894-97 were fruitful for Prahran's charitable institutions as Luxton and his wife worked tirelessly for the sick, poor and neglected. His special interest was for the blind and he was president of the Royal Victorian Blind Institute and the Victorian Association of Braille Writers. He was also chairman of the Prahran Mechanics' Institute, a commissioner of the Metropolitan Board of Works, a council member of the Melbourne Electrical Engineering School and Prahran's representative on the Prahran-Malvern Tramway Trust. He was concerned with the River Yarra improvements bill and induced Prahran to contribute £4000 for prevention of the Yarra floods. He was a firm believer in intercolonial free trade and as mayor publicly supported Federation, explaining that the saving on the consolidation of Australian loans would pay the loss on Victorian railways. In the 1890s he retained his interest in Bendigo, owning shares in gold and in the electric light and tramway companies. Indeed, most of his money was invested in the country districts and his faith in the future of agriculture led him to buy 2000 acres and lease 4000 acres at Barr Creek on the Murray River, irrigating 300 acres.

In 1901-02 Luxton was again mayor and then turned to politics which he had reputedly wanted for years to enter. In December 1903 he was elected to the Legislative Council for South Yarra Province and in 1904-10 represented Melbourne South. Speaking seldom and 'according to his conscience', he supported bills which helped miners. He also favoured the gaming suppression bill because betting on horses, unlike mining speculation, was of no benefit to the State. In every debate on the women's suffrage bill he sided with the ultra-conservatives.

Luxton bought the hardware businesses of McLean Bros [q.v.] & Rigg in 1907 and James McEwan & Co. in 1910. In the amalgamated company he was chairman and his four sons were directors. The manager proved incompetent and Luxton took over, vowing that if he were to be ruined at least he would be the cause. He soon mastered the hardware business but the strain probably affected his failing health and he died at his home, Royston, Malvern, on 5 September 1911, survived by his wife, four sons and three of his daughters.

J. Smith (ed), *Cyclopedia of Victoria*, 1 (Melb, 1903); *Prahran Telegraph*, June 1893, 9 Sept 1911; *Prahran Chronicle*, 1 Sept 1894; *Age*, 6 Sept 1911; *Argus*, 6 Sept 1911; *A'sian Hardware and Machinery*, 2 Oct 1911; James McEwan & Co. records (ANU Archives); Luxton scrapbook (held by Mrs R. Howard, Toorak).

J. ANN HONE

LYALL, JAMES (1827-1905), Presbyterian minister, was born on 9 April 1827 at Edinburgh, son of James Lyall, mason, and his wife Janet, née Pirrie. Educated at Edinburgh High School and the universities of Glasgow and Edinburgh, he trained for the ministry of the United Presbyterian Church at its Synod Hall in Edinburgh. His early aspirations to foreign missionary work had to be abandoned under medical advice, but while a student he engaged for ten years in mission work in Glasgow, Edinburgh and a colliery district near Alloa. After completing his studies he was licensed to preach by the Edinburgh Presbytery of the United Presbyterian Church. On 28 April 1857 he was ordained by the same presbytery in response to an appeal from the Gouger Street United Presbyterian Church seeking a replacement for Rev. Ralph Drummond [q.v.]. Next day Lyall married Helen Whitecross. He sailed with her for South Australia and arrived at Adelaide on 27 September.

Lyall devoted himself with zeal and enthusiasm to his ministerial duties, and in 1865 a new and larger church in Flinders Street was opened for the greatly increased congregation. In that year he played a part in reuniting the three branches of Presbyterianism represented in the colony after earlier attempts had failed. His ministry at Flinders Street was very successful and his congregation included such influential members as W. W. Hughes, John Duncan, David Murray [qq.v.] and John Gordon. Lyall and his wife were prominent in colonial affairs and devoted to evangelistic, social and missionary works. He was a founder of the inter-denominational City Mission, holding its early meetings in his vestry and acting as its first secretary. His wife was active in the Women's Christian Temperance Union and founding president of the Presbyterian Women's Missionary Union in South Australia; among her other activities she lectured and wrote a pamphlet on *The Duty and Privilege of Giving* (Adelaide, 1895).

For health reasons Lyall's congregation enabled him to visit Britain at the close of 1873; he also spent three months in Italy, opened a preaching station in connexion with the United Presbyterian Church at San Remo on the Riviera, and returned to Adelaide in March 1875. In January 1890 at Hobart he presided over the Federal Assembly of the Presbyterian Churches of Australia and Tasmania, the forerunner of the General Assembly of the Presbyterian Church of Australia. As moderator he visited Presbyterian missions in the New Hebrides and attended the annual meetings of the mission Synod at Aneityum. An account of this visit appeared in four letters in the *South Australian Register*, August 1890. In 1891 he visited Queensland to open the Federal Assembly, to report on the New Hebrides mission and to see the Kanakas on sugar plantations near Maryborough and Bundaberg. Mainly through his efforts the Presbyterian Church in South Australia undertook to support a mission of its own on the island of Tanna. He was also appointed convener of the foreign mission committee and of the Ministerial Association, and moderator of the South Australian Presbytery and Assembly in 1886-87 and 1897-98; for over twenty-five years he was foreign mission convener in the Presbyterian Church. Largely through his influence W. W. Hughes was persuaded to make his gift of £20,000 originally intended for Union College, of whose council Lyall was a member, available for founding the University of Adelaide.

In 1897 Lyall retired from the pastorate of the Flinders Street Church and was given £2000 as a token of esteem. He was representative elder in the South Australian Assembly for Wallaroo in 1898-1901, and for Goodwood in 1902-03. His wife died on 22 October 1902 aged 70 and he moved to Victoria, where he died at Mentone on 10 September 1905. He was buried in the West Terrace cemetery at Adelaide, survived by four sons and three of his five daughters.

Lyall was a devout and faithful minister of the older Presbyterian school and a powerful preacher. In his farewell sermon he claimed that he had 'availed himself of the principles of higher criticism in his interpretation of scripture', but his preaching and activities showed a more conservative outlook than any influence by the newer trends of thought.

Tablets to him and his wife in the Scots Church, North Terrace, Adelaide, were moved there when the Flinders Street Church was demolished.

Observer (Adel), 20 Nov 1897, 16 Sept 1905; W. Gray, The history of the Presbyterian Church in South Australia 1839-1938 (SAA).

                                    DIRK VAN DISSEL

LYALL, WILLIAM (1821-1888), farmer, was born at Foveran, Aberdeenshire, Scotland, fifth son of John Lyall and his wife Helen, née Webster. His father migrated to Van Diemen's Land in 1832, rented a farm and sent for his wife, six sons and two daughters; later he moved to Windermere on the River Tamar where he died in 1845.

William was early interested in farming: at 14 he was in charge of assigned servants minding sheep. He visited Port Phillip in November 1839 and in 1847 moved to Melbourne where he soon had a lucrative business shipping fat bullocks to Tasmania. Later he joined his brother-in-law John Mickle (husband of Margaret Lyall) and John Bakewell to start the firm of Mickle, Bakewell & Lyall. The firm engaged in pastoral pursuits and soon prospered. On 29 January 1849 at Launceston Lyall married Annabella Brown (b. Glasgow 1827); they had three sons and six daughters. In 1852-53 they lived at Tooradin station, one of the firm's properties in the Westernport Bay district. In 1854 Lyall took his family and his mother to Britain and began a lifelong study of agricultural chemistry. He returned in January 1856 and lived at Kew. In 1859 the firm of Mickle, Bakewell & Lyall was dissolved, the partners drawing lots for the three properties, Tooradin, Monomeith and Yallock. Lyall took over Yallock north of Westernport near Koo-wee-rup, where he built his permanent home, Harewood, but by arrangement with Bakewell he still occupied Tooradin. From 1859 he rented Tobin Yallock swamp on a 21-year improvement lease and started drainage schemes.

Lyall was well known as a stock breeder and for his experiments in acclimatization of animals and plants. From England in 1856 he had brought with him stud Herefords, Cotswold sheep, hares, pheasants and partridges. In 1858 he imported two Shetland stallions which his brother Andrew had chosen for him on Noss Island. He also bred Romney Marsh sheep and thoroughbred horses. He experimented with oyster culture and less wisely planted yellow gorse on his land. Over the years he collected a fine library of general history, Australian exploration literature and books on agricultural subjects; all his volumes were specially bound in leather. Successful at shows, he won fifteen prizes at the Mornington exhibition of the Port Phillip Farmer's Society in 1861. His private diaries reveal him as a very practical farmer.

Active in public life Lyall was for years a member and president of the Cranbourne Shire Council, first president of the Mornington Pastoral and Agricultural Society, and a founder of the Victorian Agricultural Society, the Zoological Society, the Acclimatisation Society and the Victoria Racing Club. In 1855-88 he was a member of the National Agricultural Society. He joined the Yeomanry Cavalry and sometimes took duty at the powder magazine. In 1859-61 he represented Mornington in the Legislative Assembly and was also a territorial magistrate. An invalid in his last years, Lyall died at Harewood on 20 January 1888 and was buried in Cranbourne cemetery.

R. V. Billis and A. S. Kenyon, Pastoral pioneers of Port Phillip (Melb, 1932); A. Henderson (ed), Early pioneer families of Victoria and Riverina (Melb, 1936); H. H. Peck, Memoirs of a stockman (Melb, 1942); N. Gunson, The good country: Cranbourne shire (Melb, 1968); Argus, 23 Jan 1888.

ALAN D. MICKLE*

LYELL, ANDREW (1836-1897), businessman, politician and conciliator, was born at Newburgh, Fife, Scotland, son of James Lyell, linen manufacturer, and his wife Margaret, née Haggart. Educated at Abdie Grange School near Newburgh, he joined Moon, Langlands & Co. of Dundee in 1849. He arrived at Melbourne in the Penola on 1 January 1853. He worked for Henry Langlands [q.v.], ironfounder, and in 1855 joined Langlands, Buick & Co., warehousemen. In 1861 the firm became Buick, Christie & Lyell, retail drapers and importers, with branches throughout Victoria. After five successful years, Lyell became a trade assignee with Gowan and in 1875 Ackroyd & Danky took over the accountancy and assignee side of the business, with Lyell's firm devoting itself to the public loans and large estates in which English investors were interested. He was also a large landowner in the north-east and Loddon plains. In 1881 Lyell & Gowan merged into the Mercantile Finance and Guarantee Co. Ltd, of which Lyell was manager and a director until 1888. By 1892 its successor, the Mercantile Finance Guarantee & Trustee Co., formed by B. J. Fink [q.v.] was bankrupt, and ironically Lyell and W. L. Baillieu were assigned to liquidate the existing companies.

In 1888 with Allard, Densham and later Butler as his partners, Lyell opened offices in Melbourne, Sydney and London. The company had its own steamers and investments in timber, slate and tin in Tasmania. In all his private business he had conspicuous success and was recognized as 'the best accountant Melbourne ever had'.

In Emerald Hill Lyell had been municipal councillor in 1865-67 and in 1877-80 he represented that seat as a free trader in the Legislative Assembly. His lucid pamphlet, Emerald Hill Election: Political Views of Mr. Andrew Lyell, revealed him as a follower of Bentham and J. S. Mill. He was opposed to the sale of crown lands, payment of members and excessive government expenditure. In the assembly he displayed marked debating ability, especially on financial subjects. In the political crisis in 1878 over payment of members, he was entrusted by the assembly to negotiate with the council and reached a successful compromise.

Lyell became known in the 1880s as the 'prince of negotiators' especially in conciliating. In the bootmakers' conflict in 1884-85 he arranged the preliminaries which led to a joint conference. In January 1886 he represented the Employers' Union in the wharf labourers and seamen's dispute, where his sincerity, lack of partisanship and 'consummate skill' in finding common ground prepared the way for a return to work and settlement by the arbitration of W. C.

Kernot [q.v.]. In this case Lyell suffered great loss through not attending to a business crisis of his firm in another colony. In 1886 he helped to draft the constitution of the voluntary Board of Conciliation, formed by the Employers' Union and the Trades Hall Council. In February 1888 the Tramway and Omnibus Co. rejected his offer to mediate in the strike over union membership but later, after a four-month strike by the Ironworkers' Union, the employers accepted his voluntary arbitration and the issue was resolved. He was insolvent in September-October 1890 but active and in great demand as conciliator in the maritime strike. In Sydney on 23 April 1891 he told the royal commission on strikes that he advocated voluntary arbitration because compulsion by legislation was not likely to suit both sides, but he agreed that compulsory conciliation was desirable because it could lead to a conference and settlement.

Lyell's capacity for work was enormous. In 1878 he assisted in negotiations by the Victorian government to acquire the Hobson's Bay United Railway. He was active in building societies and with W. Macredie [q.v.] founded the National Fire Insurance Co. In 1886 he was a founder and later president of the Incorporated Institute of Accountants and for years was auditor of several banks and public companies. He cheerfully devoted much time to public affairs and in both public and private business won repute for integrity which was then almost unrivalled. He visited Britain in 1861, 1868, 1873 and 1896 primarily for his health and he died on 18 December 1897 in Melbourne. He was twice married: first, in 1859 to Charlotte, née Owens, who bore him two sons and seven daughters; and second, to Janet, née Hamilton.

The history of capital and labour . . . (Syd, 1888); G. Serle, *The rush to be rich* (Melb, 1971); *Table Talk*, 28 Oct 1897; *Argus*, 20 Dec 1897.   SUZANNE G. MELLOR

LYSTER, WILLIAM SAURIN (1828-1880), operatic entrepreneur, was born on 21 March 1828 at Dublin, third son of Chaworth Lyster, army captain, and his wife Anne, née Keightly. William was named after his uncle, sometime attorney-general for Ireland. After a severe illness in his early teens he went on a sea voyage and visited Sydney and Melbourne in 1842. Reputedly he was then sent to Calcutta to become an indigo planter but returned about a year later. In 1847 he served as a volunteer in the Kaffir war under Sir Harry Smith. About 1848 he went to America and in Boston joined a theatre company. In 1855 he went with William Walker, 'soldier of fortune',

on his ill-fated expedition to Nicaragua. He fought in several battles as a captain but was in the United States on a recruiting tour when Walker's expedition collapsed.

In 1857 Lyster formed an opera troupe, with his brother Frederick as conductor and himself as musical director. The company had two prima donnas: Rosalie Durand who married Frederick; and Georgia Hodson, who had married first John Sharp, second John Robertson, and third William Lyster. In 1859 the company arrived in San Francisco. He engaged Lucy Escott and Henry Squires there and in 1861, with a full chorus and orchestra, the company travelled to Australia. On 25 March he opened at Melbourne's Theatre Royal with *Lucia di Lammermoor*, *Maritana* and *Lurline*. The company's repertoire was said to include over thirty operas. Despite good reviews the season ran at a loss, but encouraged by the brilliant success of the final nights Lyster returned for a second season in June. By the end of July Lyster's popularity was firmly established and after a month in Sydney he returned to Melbourne to make his headquarters. In the next six years he also toured the other colonies and New Zealand, presenting operas such as *Maritana*, *Il Trovatore*, *Lucrezia Borgia*, *Lucia di Lammermoor*, *La Traviata*, *Roberto il Diavolo* and *Faust*.

In 1868 Lyster decided to return with his troupe to the United States and on 29 August left for California in the *Alexander Duthie*. One of his tenors was E. A. Beaumont [q.v.] whom Lyster had accidentally shot in the face while hunting in 1867. The company was not successful in San Francisco. By 30 January their short season at the Metropolitan Theatre was closed and by March the troupe dispersed. Frederick Lyster joined the Metropolitan Theatre as musical director and conductor while William made arrangements with John Smith to form another company and then went on to Europe to engage singers. In Italy in September 1869 he engaged several singers including Lucia Baratti as prima donna, Lucy Chambers contralto, Mariano Neri tenor and Enrico Dondi bass. He bought music scores and the 'latest appliances, mechanical and otherwise' for his new productions. He returned to Melbourne on 20 January 1870 in the *Avoca*. Beaumont sailed from San Francisco to rejoin Lyster and the new company made its first appearance on 5 February with *Ernani*. In April the company went to Sydney for a short season. Lyster & Smith's contract with the Italian members of the company ended in January 1871 and most of them returned to Europe.

After the successes of 1870 Lyster had

leased the Princess's Theatre in Melbourne for another three years and began rehearsals for Offenbach's comic opera, *The Grand Duchess of Gerolstein*. He came to an agreement with an Italian opera company which, led by Cagli and Pompei, came to Australia by way of India. In May 1871 the combined companies gave a series of Italian operas. Later that year Lyster's English company toured Tasmania and in 1872 Victorian country towns. When the company of Madame Agatha States arrived in Melbourne Lyster provided a supporting band and chorus.

In February 1873 Lyster and others organized a small proprietary association to manage the new Prince of Wales Theatre. Lyster was manager with a salary of £1000, and held a sixth of the shares, equal in worth to his properties valued at £5000. In the next months Italian opera alternated with seasons of opera sung in English, the latter being more profitable to produce although Lyster himself preferred Italian opera. In May 1873 Cagli returned to Italy to engage more singers. By September 1874 Lyster was managing an Italian opera company in Adelaide and an English company in Sandhurst as well as arranging concert appearances for visiting artists in the Melbourne Town Hall and planning a Christmas pantomime.

In August 1877 Lyster produced Wagnerian opera in Melbourne for the first time, opening with *Lohengrin* on 18 August. *Aida* was also performed but the season was not a financial success. Lyster's health was declining and in July 1878 he left Sydney for America and Europe, accompanied by his wife and Beaumont. In March 1879 he reopened in Melbourne with a new company but his health did not improve. He planned to retire but on 27 November 1880 died at the Melbourne home of his friend, William Dean, survived by his wife. They had no children. He was buried in the Anglican section of the Melbourne general cemetery.

Lyster was a good conversationalist and widely-read. He was tall, black-bearded and, according to a nephew, had 'a fearsome temper'. However, he was popular with the public and the press described him as 'a liberal, pushing, energetic business man, personally liked . . . and possessed of that valuable quality, tact'. In 1867 he had bought land near Fern Tree Gully in the Monbulk area, known as Lysterfield from the mid-1870s when Lyster donated two acres for a school. At his home, Narre Warren Grange, he had a room acoustically fitted for the benefit of musical guests. He pioneered drainage improvements in the area and built up a prize-winning dairy stud. After his death friends commissioned his portrait by G. F. Folingsby [q.v.] and many tributes were paid to his part in establishing opera as a 'permanent institution' in Victoria.

J. B. Cooper, *The history of St Kilda . . . 1840 to 1930*, 1 (Melb, 1931); H. Coulson, *Story of the Dandenongs, 1838-1958* (Melb, 1959); *Examiner* (Melb), 30 Mar, 20 Apr, 27 July, 28 Sept 1861; *Australasian*, 2 Mar, 25 May 1867, 13 Mar, 10 Apr, 29 May, 25 Sept, 4, 25 Dec 1869, 11 Feb, 26 Aug 1871, 17 Feb 1872, 1, 15 Feb 1873, 19 Sept 1874, 25 Aug 1877, 4 Dec 1880; *Bulletin*, 12 June, 4, 18 Dec 1880; *Argus*, 29 Nov 1880, 26 Jan 1882; *Town and Country J*, 11 Dec 1880; *Table Talk*, 12 Aug 1926.

SALLY O'NEILL
MAUREEN THERESA RADIC

M

MACADAM, JOHN (1827-1865), analytical chemist, medical practitioner and politician, was born in May 1827 at Northbank, near Glasgow, Scotland, son of William Macadam and his wife Helen, née Stevenson. Privately educated in Glasgow, he began in 1842 to study chemistry at the Andersonian University. In 1844 he was appointed senior assistant, showing a flair for analytical chemistry. He then went to the University of Edinburgh for advanced study under Professor William Gregory and in 1846-47 assisted Dr George Wilson in his laboratory in Brown Square. Late in 1847 he returned to Glasgow and began teaching chemistry in class-rooms in High John Street. In that year he was elected a fellow of the Royal Scottish Society of Arts and in 1848 a member of the Glasgow Philosophical Society. He then turned to medicine at Glasgow (L.F.P.S., M.D., 1854; F.F.P.S.G., 1855).

Appointed lecturer in chemistry and natural science at Scotch College, Melbourne, Macadam arrived early in 1855 in the *Admiral*; he held this post until 1865. He was elected a member of the Philosophical Institute of Victoria in 1855 and served on its council; in 1857-59 he was honorary secretary and edited the *Transactions* in 1855-60. He was active in the move to obtain a royal charter for the society and in January 1860 when the Philosophical Institute became the Royal Society of Victoria he was appointed honorary secretary and in 1863 elected vice-president. As secretary of the Exploration Committee of the Burke and Wills [qq.v.] expedition he insisted on adequate provisions for their safety. He was admitted to the University of Melbourne (M.D. *ad eund.*, 1857). In 1858 he was appointed government analytical chemist and in 1860 became health officer to the City of Melbourne but apart from this work did not practise medicine. He was also a member of the Board of Agriculture.

Macadam was elected to the Legislative Assembly in 1859 for Castlemaine as a radical in sympathy with the Land Convention. He was postmaster-general in the Heales [q.v.] government from 26 April to 14 November 1861, lost his seat at the ministerial election in May but was re-elected in August and remained in parliament until he resigned in 1864. He had sponsored bills on medical practitioners and adulteration of food which became law in 1862 and 1863.

In 1861 he had acted as secretary to the Victorian Industrial Exhibition and begun a series of lectures on chemistry for medical students at the Analytical Laboratory, with Richard Eades [q.v.] lecturing on materia medica. Certainly these extramural classes hastened the formation of the Medical School at the university and when it opened in 1862 Macadam was appointed lecturer in chemistry.

Although in ill health in March 1865 he went to New Zealand to give evidence at the trial of Captain W. A. Jarvey, charged with the murder of his wife by poison. The jury failed to agree and on the voyage home Macadam fractured his ribs in rough weather. He developed pleurisy with effusion and on medical advice was prevented from attending the adjourned trial. Still sick and accompanied by John Drummond Kirkland, a medical student, he sailed in the *Alhambra* to attend the postponed trial but died at sea on 2 September 1865. Kirkland gave evidence at the trial and Jarvey was convicted. Macadam's body was brought back for burial in the Presbyterian section of the Melbourne general cemetery on 28 September. He was survived by his wife Elizabeth, née Clark, whom he had married in Melbourne on 18 September 1856, and by a son. Kirkland, who was appointed lecturer in chemistry, later became the first professor of chemistry at the university.

Tall, with long red hair, a flowing beard and powerful voice, Macadam always commanded attention. He was a skilled, popular and eloquent lecturer with an outstanding knowledge of analytical chemistry and always ready to hand on his knowledge. In Glasgow he had published several papers on analytical chemistry and in Melbourne wrote reports on public health, adulteration of food and soil analysis.

Trial of Captain Jarvey, on a charge of poisoning his wife (Dunedin, 1865); *Univ Melb Medical School Jubilee* (Melb, 1914); 'The late Dr. Macadam', *Aust Med J*, Oct 1865; *Illustrated Melb Post*, 25 Oct 1865; K. F. Russell, History of the Melbourne Medical School (held by author); Medical School letters (Univ Melb Archives).

K. F. RUSSELL

MACALISTER, ARTHUR (1818-1883), solicitor and politician, was born at Glasgow, Scotland, son of John Macalister, cabinet maker, and his wife Mary, née Scoullar. Educated in Glasgow, he qualified as a writer to the signet. At Edinburgh he married Elizabeth Wallace Tassie. He sailed with her in the *Abbotsford* and arrived at Sydney on 28 September 1839. He was appointed clerk of Petty Sessions and postmaster at Scone in June 1840. Dismissed in 1841 he opened a general store but his estate was sequestrated in 1842. By 1846 he was working for a Sydney solicitor. In 1850 he applied for admission to the Supreme Court as a solicitor, attorney and proctor and was admitted after passing an examination. He then started practice in Ipswich.

Active in the separationist movement Macalister stood in vain for the Stanley Boroughs seat in the Legislative Assembly in 1856. He lost again in 1858 when he challenged W. B. Tooth for the United Pastoral Districts seat of Moreton, Wide Bay, Burnett, Maranoa, Leichhardt and Port Curtis, but won the new seat of Ipswich on 14 June 1859. He ceased to sit on 10 December when the electorate was included in Queensland. He was given no place in the three-member provisional Executive Council chosen by Governor Bowen in December but won one of the three seats for Ipswich in Queensland's first Legislative Assembly. He joined the opponents of R. G. W. Herbert's [q.v.] ministry and was soon elected chairman of committees. In June 1861 he resigned in protest against Herbert's policies but changed his mind and was re-elected at the by-election he had caused. In March 1862 he joined Herbert's ministry as secretary for lands and works. In July he was temporarily appointed colonial secretary while Herbert was in England. R. R. Mackenzie [q.v.] resented this appointment and in August resigned from the ministry. When Herbert resigned in February 1866 Macalister formed an administration. He took the unusual course of retaining lands and works and appointed Mackenzie colonial secretary. The ministry continued Herbert's extravagant programme of works financed by loans. In July its financial guarantor, Agra & Masterman's Bank, failed and Macalister and his treasurer, J. P. Bell [q.v.], tried to introduce among other corrective measures a bill for issuing unsecured government notes. In advance the governor refused assent to any such bill and Macalister promptly resigned. Bowen then recalled Herbert who advised the governor to invite Macalister to form a new government, which he did on 7 August. His government was defeated in 1867 and he resigned on 15 August but his successor, Mackenzie, was in turn defeated with Macalister's help in November 1868.

Deserting Ipswich, Macalister stood for Eastern Downs and was elected unopposed on 25 September. In a new government led

by Lilley [q.v.], Macalister became secretary for public lands and works but in January 1869 resigned and crossed the floor, declaring that he had been unjustly accused of double-dealing in the ministerial negotiations by the colonial treasurer, T. H. Fitzgerald [q.v.]. The manoeuvre succeeded: Lilley obtained Fitzgerald's resignation and Macalister rejoined the ministry as secretary for public works and goldfields. When the Lilley government was defeated on 3 May 1870 Macalister was invited to form a ministry but failed. Palmer [q.v.] succeeded and when the assembly met, Macalister on 15 November accepted appointment as Speaker, thereby alienating many supporters. He was bitterly attacked by Lilley in the June 1871 election and after a hectic campaign lost his seat.

In October 1872 Macalister won a by-election for Ipswich. After the elections in 1873 Palmer was defeated on the choice of a Speaker in January 1874 and Macalister formed a government. It included Thomas McIlwraith [q.v.] and, after Lilley moved to the bench, S. W. Griffith. In 1875 Macalister visited Britain where at court he was appointed C.M.G. In Glasgow he was given a banquet by the lord provost. He returned to Queensland in April 1876 but announced the resignation of his ministry on 7 June. Three weeks later he was appointed agent-general for Queensland and travelled to Britain by way of America, where he acted as commissioner for Queensland at the Philadelphia International Exhibition.

Macalister was active in the Presbyterian Church and a founding trustee of St Stephen's, Ipswich. He served briefly on the Ipswich Municipal Council in 1862 and on the Board of Education from 1860 and was its chairman in 1862-67. He was a founding trustee of the Ipswich Grammar School, a member of the Caledonian and Prince of Wales Lodges and president of the Caledonian Society. As agent-general he was involved in the 'steel rails' controversy but a select committee and a later royal commission found him innocent of any misconduct. However, the commission criticized the efficiency of the London office and soon afterwards Macalister took six months sick leave. On 17 October 1881 the Queensland parliament granted him a pension of £500 and two days later he formally retired.

One of Macalister's notable legacies to Queensland was its narrow gauge railway system. As secretary for lands and works he enthusiastically approved the plans submitted in 1863 for the 3 ft. 6 ins. gauge line between Ipswich and Toowoomba. His uncritical acceptance of construction estimates later gave his opponents ample opportunities for attack as costs escalated, but his faith in a widespread railway system for Queensland never abated even when the Brisbane-Ipswich line led to loss of electoral support. In contrast, frequent changes in his land policy gave him, according to one opponent, a 'chameleon-like' character. Macalister used the land question to electoral advantage, varying his tactics to shifts in public opinion. He believed that agricultural settlement was necessary for prosperity but, as a townsman capable of losing himself on a well-worn bush track, he made little allowance for the Queensland environment. He ably administered the land laws in 1862-66 but had little success in implementing new legislation. While premier in 1875 he took a strong stand against pastoralists in the settled areas and authorized resumption of large quantities of pastoral land for agricultural settlement but by 1876 selectors were having difficulty in finding good farm land while the political manoeuvres of Macalister and his supporters were increasingly restricted.

Nicknamed 'Slippery Mac', Macalister frequently changed his attitudes, alliances, allegiances and colleagues, but not more often than some of his contemporaries. His methods of change earned criticism, not the changes themselves. To colleagues and electors he was an inveterate maker of promises but many were soon broken. He had remarkable political resilience and ability to survive and could usually restore confidence in those whom he had failed. He lost only one election between 1859 and 1876. He enjoyed political power and its privileges, and his shifts of allegiance and broken promises must be seen against the background of his ambition. The peaks in his career were the attainment of the premiership in 1866 and his successful comeback in 1874, after failure in 1871.

Macalister was handicapped by his health after 1867. In 1871, as Speaker in a Legislative Assembly bitterly split between Palmer and Lilley factions, he began to have difficulty with his speech. His absence from parliament in 1871-72 renewed his vigour, but in mid-1875 under pressure of office he collapsed. A skilled tactician and debater, he could still snap 'right and left with such certainty and force that very few care to receive a second bite at one encounter', but by 1876 his health increasingly prevented him from coping with changes in the political scene.

Macalister had many faults but commentators have over-emphasized them at the expense of his undoubted astuteness and administrative ability. Aged 64 he died bankrupt near Glasgow on 23 March 1883. His wife died in Brisbane on 14 September 1894, survived by two sons and three daughters of their nine children.

C. A. Bernays, Queensland politics during sixty years (Brisb, 1919); PD (Qld), 1864, 158, 1866, 519, 1867, 200, 1868-69, 108, 1870, 2, 1874, 16, 1881, 839; V&P (LA Qld), 1866, 949, 1880, 2, 311, 1881, 2, 121; Moreton Bay Free Press, 17 Mar 1856; Moreton Bay Courier, 22 Mar 1856; Brisbane Courier, 3 June 1861, 21 Mar, 29 July 1862, 18 July, 8 Aug 1866, 6 May 1867, 26 Jan 1869, 23 Mar 1874; Qld Daily Guardian, 4 Aug 1865, 8 Aug 1866, 15 Aug 1867; Warwick Examiner and Times, 16 Jan 1869, 2 July, 19 Nov 1870, 24 June 1871, 23 Mar 1883; Warwick Argus, 10 Mar 1869; Toowoomba Chronicle, 2 Nov 1872, 27 Mar 1883; Queenslander, 18 Mar 1876; B. R. Kingston, Land legislation and administration in Queensland, 1859-1876 (Ph.D. thesis, Monash Univ, 1970); A. A. Morrison, Town liberals and squatters (Freyer Lib, Univ Qld); CO 234/16.   PAUL D. WILSON

McALROY, MICHAEL (1823-1880), Roman Catholic priest, was born at Westmeath, Ireland, son of John McAlroy, farmer, and his wife née Ulyer. He was educated at Navan and at Maynooth where he became friends with Patrick Bermingham and Patrick Dunne [qq.v.] and was ordained in 1849. He became chaplain to Bishop Haly of Kildare and Leighlin, attached to the Carlow Cathedral, where he had leisure enough to study architecture. At the invitation of Dunne, seconded by Bishop Goold [q.v.] of Melbourne, he went to Melbourne with Bermingham in February 1855. Next year the three friends were posted to Geelong, but Goold soon became alarmed at their independence, criticism of himself and 'assertion of their personal and canonical rights'. He split up the three friends and McAlroy was given a 'roving commission' in the Ballarat area. Later unable to find enough parishioners in Gippsland, he returned but received no other offer.

McAlroy wrote to Archbishop Polding [q.v.] in Sydney, who was pleased to send him to Yass in 1857. In his four years there he enlarged the church and built others in Jugiong, Tumut, Gundagai, Wagga Wagga, Gunning and Binalong, all of solid construction and free of debt. A skilled horseman he averaged about 11,000 miles each year riding around his large parish. He won loyal support from the large number of Catholics in the district, some of whom he had helped to settle there. In 1861 he accompanied Charles Cowper [q.v.] to Lambing Flat after the riots. He was sent to Goulburn to build a convent for the Sisters of Mercy. He also built the bishop's residence there and churches at Taralga, Breadalbane and Grabben Gullen. In 1867 contrary to expectations he was passed over when Bishop Lanigan [q.v.] became bishop of Goulburn. McAlroy was made his vicar-general and in 1868 he was transferred to Albury, where he built the 'large and beautiful' Convent of Mercy and church, and also churches at Corowa, Howlong and Newtown. He helped to found St Patrick's College, Goulburn, in 1874 and brought the Sisters of Mercy to Yass in 1875. He died on 14 July 1880 from heart disease at Albury where he was buried.

F. Mackle, *The footprints of our Catholic pioneers* (Melb, 1924); T. L. Suttor, *Hierarchy and democracy in Australia, 1788-1870* (Melb, 1965); J. O'Brien, 'The apostle of the south', *A'sian Catholic Record*, 22 (1945) no 4; Dunne and Bermingham papers (Roman Catholic Archives, Syd).   C. J. DUFFY

MACANSH, JOHN DONALD (1820-1896), pastoralist and politician, was born on 31 May 1820 at Stirling, Scotland, son of John Macansh, naval surgeon, and his wife Ann, née White. Educated at Stirling Grammar School and Edinburgh High School, he migrated to Sydney in 1838 and worked in the Bank of Australasia. In 1840 he leased a property on the Hunter River from the Church and School Lands Corporation and in 1843 moved to Murrumburrah as a station manager for S. K. Salting [q.v.]. Together they established a merino stud at Bonyeo, near Murrumburrah, in 1845. Macansh occupied various properties in the Yass district, usually with members of the Salting family, until in 1867 he bought Gurley, near Narrabri, in partnership with two of Salting's sons. On 8 June 1849 he had married Sarah Jane, daughter of Archibald Windeyer [q.v.] of Raymond Terrace.

In Queensland Macansh bought Canning Downs and Albilah, near Warwick, in 1875. He settled on Canning Downs to raise stud dairy and beef cattle, became a magistrate and was elected to the Glengallan Divisional Board. In 1882 he leased Brunette Downs in the Northern Territory. After refusing appointment to the Legislative Council in 1886 because he disapproved its constitution, he accepted appointment in 1888 on a pledge to change the constitution. His liberal politics had little impact on the Legislative Council and when he died at a meeting of the Glengallan Divisional Board on 1 August 1896 he had done nothing to achieve his objective. He left an estate nominally worth £241,588, but it proved to be in some confusion. His six sons and five daughters agreed to carry on the business through a family trust, legalized by a private bill of 1910. Macansh Estate Ltd was still registered as late as 1957.

R. D. Barton, *Reminiscences of an Australian pioneer* (Syd, 1917); V&P (LA Qld), 1876, 3, 878, 1880, 2, 1001, 1910 (2nd S), 3, 1062; PD (LC Qld), 1890, 25; *Warwick Argus*, 4 Aug 1896; *Brisbane Courier*, 8 Aug 1896; *Pastoral Review*, 15 Aug 1896; *Qld Country Life*, 13 June 1957; Griffith papers (Dixson Lib, Syd).   H. J. GIBBNEY

McARTHUR, ALEXANDER (1814-1909), merchant, was born on 10 March 1814 at Enniskillen, County Fermanagh, Ireland, son of John McArthur, Wesleyan minister, and his wife Sarah, née Finlay. Educated privately, he was apprenticed in 1830 to a merchant in Omagh. After severe fevers he migrated to Sydney and arrived on 24 January 1842 in the *Margaret*. He began business with a consignment from his brother William (1809-1887) but soon became partner of William Little and James H. Atkinson. In 1848 he went to Ireland where in 1850 with his brother he formed W. and A. McArthur & Co., softgoods merchants. Alexander returned to Sydney in 1851 and profited handsomely as a shipping agent from the export of gold. His firm built a large Sydney warehouse and opened branches in Adelaide, Melbourne, Brisbane and Auckland. In August 1853 at Toxteth Park he married Maria Bowden, daughter of Rev. W. B. Boyce [q.v.]; they lived at Strathmore, Glebe Point, and had six sons and two daughters.

In 1854-55 McArthur visited England and on his return became a member of the Sydney Chamber of Commerce, a shareholder in the Australian Joint Stock Bank, director of many building societies and insurance and mining companies, and a justice of the peace. In June 1859 he was elected for Newtown to the Legislative Assembly as a free trader and an opponent of state aid to religion. On 11 October he moved the acceptance of the native chief's offer to cede Fiji to the Crown. Re-elected in December 1860, he resigned in June 1861 when nominated to the Legislative Council. He vacated his seat through absence in October 1865. In 1843 he had been elected to the committee of the Wesleyan Auxiliary Missionary Society of New South Wales; he was foundation treasurer of the Young Men's Christian Association of Sydney and a committee member of the Benevolent Asylum, the New South Wales Auxiliary Bible Society and other charities. He gave £2000 towards building Newington College.

In 1863 Alexander took over the London business and lived at Raleigh Hall, Brixton. In *Transportation to Western Australia. Three Letters to the Editor of the 'Daily News'* (London, 1864) he questioned 'the moral right [of the British Government] to poison the very atmosphere of four or five large and flourishing colonies' with convicts. In 1879 he and his brother gave £1000 to Ormond College in the University of Melbourne. In 1870-73 McArthur was a member of the first London School Board and in 1874-92 Liberal member for Leicester in the House of Commons, where he advocated the annexation of Fiji, stricter Sabbath observance and Home Rule for Ireland. He was a magistrate for Surrey, deputy-lieutenant for the City of London and a fellow of the Imperial Institute and from 1863 the Royal Geographical Society, and member of the Royal Colonial Institute in 1869, the Victoria Institute and the British Association. In 1898 his firm became a limited liability company with McArthur a director and in 1908 was reconstituted after liquidation. A devout Methodist, he died at Sydenham, London, on 1 August 1909.

E. Digby (ed), *Australian men of mark*, 2 (Syd, 1889); T. McCullagh, *Sir William McArthur* (Lond, 1891); J. Colwell, *The illustrated history of Methodism* (Syd, 1904); A. W. Martin, 'William McMillan—a merchant in politics', *JRAHS*, 40 (1954-55); *Empire* (Syd), 30 May 1859; *The Times*, 2 Aug 1909; *SMH*, 3 Aug 1909; *Town and Country J*, 11 Aug 1909; Macarthur papers (ML).   RUTH TEALE

McARTHUR, DAVID CHARTERIS (1810-1887), banker, was born in Gloucester, England, son of Captain Donald McArthur and his wife Elizabeth, née Wemyss. Educated in Scotland, he worked for an insurance firm in Edinburgh and then joined the Bank of Australasia when it opened in Sydney in December 1835. An able accountant, he went to Melbourne in a cutter with £3000 in coin, an armed guard and two bulldogs, and opened a branch of his bank in August 1838. He kept the government account and won so much private business that in three years his branch was nearly the size of the office in Sydney.

McArthur was often too good-natured; some of the early loans were unsound and probably delayed his promotion. He was nominated assistant superintendent of the entire bank in August 1843, but the London directors appointed instead J. J. Falconer, who was superintendent in 1849-67. McArthur remained as Melbourne manager, opened many new goldfields' branches in the 1850s and became general inspector of branches in 1862. He thrice visited New Zealand and spent much of 1867 pruning the bank's accounts in Christchurch before returning to Melbourne with charge of the entire bank. At 57 he was too old, according to the bank's historian, S. J. Butlin. He

was slow to interfere in the policies of branch managers and touchy when London interfered with his decisions. He was the brittle link in the chain of control from the London court to the remote branches. While most chiefs of the Anglo-Australian banks came to Australia as hand-picked executives and obedient servants of the London boards, McArthur had risen by his own merits and identified himself with his customers and his adopted country.

As a squire in the Heidelberg hills, leader of Melbourne's bankers, first chairman of the Associated Banks and commercial confidante of Melbourne politicians and merchants, McArthur was inclined to see Melbourne as the hub of the universe. He was sometimes lax in directing business in other colonies, and when his bank had trouble in Tasmania and New Zealand his reaction was to accept defeat. The London directors retired him in October 1876, gave him a free trip to England, an annuity of £1500 and later a seat on the bank's advisory board in Melbourne.

To his friends McArthur was kind, tactful, conscientious and honest. In Melbourne he was active in the Mechanics' Institute and many other movements; he was a member of the first lay committee to assist Bishop Perry [q.v.] in administering his diocese and in 1854 was on the committee which advised Governor Hotham on the colony's finances. He was chairman of the Heidelberg Road Board, one of the five original trustees of the Public Library of Victoria in 1853 and president of trustees of the Public Library, Museums and National Gallery of Victoria in 1880-83. At various times he was also chairman of the Austin Hospital, president of the Melbourne Cricket Club and Old Colonists' Association and chairman of the Trustees, Executors, & Agency Co. He died at his home Charterisville in East Ivanhoe on 15 November 1887, leaving an estate of £30,215 to his wife Caroline, née Wright.

A portrait is in the Melbourne boardroom of the Australia and New Zealand Bank and at St John's Church, Heidelberg, he is commemorated by a stained-glass window entitled 'King David'.

S. J. Butlin, *Australia and New Zealand Bank* (Melb, 1961); *A'sian Insurance and Banking Record*, Dec 1887, Mar 1900; *Argus*, 16, 17 Nov 1887; private information.
                                    GEOFFREY BLAINEY

MACARTHUR, SIR EDWARD (1789-1872), soldier, was born on 16 March 1789 at Bath, England, the eldest son of Captain John Macarthur and his wife Elizabeth [qq.v.]. He went to Sydney with his parents in 1790 and spent his boyhood there and at Elizabeth Farm, Parramatta. Sent to England in 1799 to be educated he returned to Sydney in 1806. With his father he took part in the deposition of Governor Bligh in 1808. He soon left for London taking his father's version of the rebellion and the first bale of merino wool to be exported from the colony. He obtained a commission in the 60th Regiment and served at Corunna and in Sicily. As a lieutenant in the 39th Regiment he took part in Wellington's campaigns of 1812-14 and was present at Vittoria, the Pyrénées and the battles in southern France. After brief service in Canada he joined the army of occupation in France.

In 1824 Macarthur went to New South Wales as the agent of T. P. Macqueen [q.v.]. He was impressed by the dispersion of the garrison from Moreton Bay to Hobart Town in the face of runaway convicts and 'hostile tribes'. In London he placed detailed proposals for a colonial militia before Under-Secretary Horton but the plan was rejected by Governor Darling in 1827. Macarthur competently represented Australian interests in London. He presented a petition from New South Wales in 1840. He advocated emigration in two small books, *Colonial Policy of 1840 and 1841, as illustrated by the Governor's despatches, and the proceedings of the Legislative Council of New South Wales* (London, 1841) and *Brief Remarks on Colonization* (London, 1846). He personally arranged the migration of German vinedressers to the Macarthur properties at Camden and also sought to develop coastal steamship services. After serving as secretary in the Lord Chamberlain's Office in 1843-46 he was on the military staff in Ireland. In 1851 he was posted to Sydney as deputy adjutant-general. Promoted colonel in 1854, he moved with the headquarters to Melbourne. He accompanied the commander-in-chief, Major-General Sir Robert Nickle [q.v.], to Eureka on 5 December. They talked freely with the miners and as a result of their investigations Nickle advised that martial law be withdrawn.

After Nickle died in May 1855 and Governor Hotham in December, Macarthur took over command of the forces and became administrator. He inherited a confused political situation and was coolly received by the press. However, his impartiality and his willingness to leave things to his ministers helped him, and when he handed over to Sir Henry Barkly on 23 December 1856 he had won the esteem of parliament and the people of Melbourne. Emily, wife of Hugh Childers [q.v.], described him as 'if not a brilliant statesman, an industrious, kind-hearted, Christian gentleman'. In 1858

Macarthur chaired a royal commission on the defences of the colony. In 1860 he returned to England and was appointed K.C.B. in 1862. In that year he married Sarah (d. 1889), daughter of Lieut-Colonel W. S. Neill. Promoted lieut-general in 1866, he died childless in London on 4 January 1872 and was buried in the Brompton cemetery. He was survived by his wife. His goods were valued for probate at £4000.

Macarthur's portrait by W. Strutt [q.v.] is in Parliament House, Melbourne, and his bust in St John's Church, Parramatta.

HRA (1), 11, 13; H. G. Turner, *A history of the colony of Victoria*, 1-2 (Lond, 1904); M. H. Ellis, *John Macarthur* (Syd, 1955); G. Serle, *The golden age* (Melb, 1963); V&P (LA Vic), 1858-59, 2 (40), 1859-60, 3 (18), 4 (41); *Argus*, 1, 7 Jan 1856, 17 Jan 1860; *SMH*, 4 Jan 1856; *Examiner* (Melb), 21 Jan 1860; *Town and Country J*, 30 Mar 1872; *The Times*, 20 July 1872; Macarthur papers (ML); CO 201/166.   A. J. HILL

MACARTHUR, GEORGE FAIRFOWL (1825-1890), Anglican clergyman and schoolmaster, was born on 19 January 1825 at The Vineyard, Parramatta, the third son of Hannibal Hawkins Macarthur [q.v.] and Anna Maria, daughter of Governor King. He was educated at The King's School, Parramatta, in 1832-39 and privately at Mulgoa but his father's financial troubles prevented him from going to an English university. Instead he entered the local theological hall, St James's College, and was well grounded in classics and divinity by its principal, Robert Allwood [q.v.]. He was made deacon on 19 March 1848, priested on 4 March 1849 by Bishop Broughton [q.v.] and appointed a curate at St James's Church. On 16 May 1849 Macarthur married Margaret Anne Priddle.

In February 1850 Macarthur was given temporary charge of Holy Trinity, Miller's Point, and in May 1851 the incumbency of St Mark's, Alexandria (Darling Point), where he opened the permanent church, enlarged the school and acquired a glebe. His family background made him sympathetic with the independent line in diocesan affairs taken by his congregation, which included many leading citizens. He disliked the assertion of episcopal authority and in 1852 led his parish in opposing Bishop Broughton's scheme of synodical government. Meanwhile he followed the policy of his predecessor, Rev. Henry Cary [q.v.], in taking pupils. By 1856 he had twelve students in 'St Mark's Collegiate School'.

In 1858 Macarthur was given leave and moved his school to Macquarie Fields House. He explained that ill health affected his preaching, but he was not in accord with

Bishop Barker [q.v.] over questions of churchmanship and his acceptance of a military chaplaincy, and next year he resigned the incumbency. Unable to pay his staff and repay loans from the Priddles and other supporters of the school, Macarthur was bankrupted in 1859 with debts of over £7000. The sale of his assets yielded a dividend of over 18s. in the £, and he was granted his certificate of discharge on 30 August. The school at Macquarie Fields later prospered and resident enrolments rose to more than eighty. Macarthur was an excellent schoolmaster and organizer. He built up a cadet corps, systematized the curriculum and enlisted the aid of university professors. An admirer of Professor Woolley [q.v.], he had adopted some of his theological liberalism and faith in national elementary education. In 1866 he published a sermon, *Memoriam*, a powerful defence of Woolley.

In 1864 The King's School had closed for lack of funds. To revive it, Macarthur was asked to become its head by Barker, who had come to admire his work at Macquarie Fields and had licensed him to the chapel there. Macarthur refused but, after W. H. Savigny and W. J. Stephens [qq.v.] had also declined, he accepted on conditions which gave him a virtual monopoly of authority. In July 1868 the school at Macquarie Fields officially became The King's School. With thirty-eight pupils Macarthur returned to the Parramatta building in February 1869. He worked hard to consolidate the school which increased in numbers and accommodation. Deliberately it remained largely a boarding school but socially it was more broadly based than the Macquarie Fields school had been. The King's School was sound rather than outstanding in academic work; as a teacher Macarthur was conventional but thorough and alert. He made much use of the cadet corps and created what was probably the best local version of the English public school at that time.

In 1884 Bishop Barry [q.v.] arrived, anxious for diocesan educational reform. He carried out a synod resolution of 1870 in favour of Church control of The King's School, which Macarthur had earlier frustrated. He resigned in June 1886 and became incumbent of Bodalla. He ministered at this parish and elsewhere until 1888. He died at Ashfield on 16 June 1890 and was buried in the Anglican section of Rookwood cemetery. He was survived by his wife, who died on 10 May 1904, by one of his three sons and by two daughters.

S. M. Johnstone, *The history of The King's School, Parramatta* (Syd, 1932); R. T. Wyatt,

The history of the diocese of Goulburn (Syd, 1937); H. W. A. Barder, *Wherein thine honour dwells* (Syd, 1949); *Church Sentinel*, Dec 1858; Church of England diocese of Sydney, *V&P of Synod* (1868, 1870, 1885, 1886); *Aust Churchman* (Syd), 23 Dec 1871, 20 June 1873; *The King's School Mag*, Dec 1887; *SMH*, 8 Apr 1852; Barker, Hassall and Macarthur papers (ML).

K. J. CABLE

MACARTHUR, SIR WILLIAM (1800-1882), landowner, was born in December 1800 at Parramatta, youngest son of John Macarthur and his wife Elizabeth [qq.v.]. At 9 he was 'a fine daring fellow' with 'the activity of a monkey' and a puckish sense of humour. He was educated by Huon de Kerilleau [q.v.] and from 1809 with his brother James [q.v.] in England. He returned to Sydney in September 1817 and for thirty years made the farm improvements his father had envisaged. An outstanding sheepbreeder he was the first to perfect the washing of wool for ensuring good presentation of the clip in London.

In 1822 William and James took up grants of 1150 acres each at Camden; they each added 2500 acres at Taralga in 1824 and soon afterwards an adjoining 4000 acres. In 1828 their father made over to them jointly half the livestock on the family estates. In 1834 William and James became partners with their brother Edward [q.v.] and in 1838 borrowed £10,000 in London to acquire the Belmont estate at Camden, where they built an inn, an Anglican Church and twenty cottages for selected immigrants from Kent and Dorsetshire. Most of the Macarthur sheep grazed on Richlands, Edward's 20,000 acres near Taralga. The brothers also bought land on the Abercrombie River and took up leases on the Lachlan and Murrumbidgee Rivers, including Nangus, 7500 acres near Wagga Wagga, where they ran cattle. Their sheep did not flourish and in 1849 were sold with the run. In June 1849 William and James held 28,000 acres at Camden, of which 3600 were tenanted, stock worth £47,500 and over 50,000 acres in Argyle and Georgiana Counties. In the early 1860s William was restrained by James from acquiring squatting runs in the west; they sold their Taralga estates and concentrated on the Camden properties.

William fostered horse-breeding, introduced the camellia, grew many fruit trees, vegetables and flowers and from 1843 published an annual catalogue of their plants. Later he built a hothouse and imported valuable orchids. He encouraged winemaking and brought out several families of German vignerons. By 1849 the twenty-five-acre vineyard at Camden was producing over

16,000 gallons of red and white table wines and brandies; 28,000 more gallons were stored in the cellars and improvements were valued at £2500. As 'Maro' he published *Letters on the Culture of the Vine, Fermentation, and the Management of Wine in the Cellar* (Sydney, 1844) and *Some account of the Vineyards at Camden* (London, 1849). Generous with advice and cuttings to vignerons in the Hunter Valley, Victoria and South Australia, he was president of the New South Wales Vineyard Association. In 1855 he was New South Wales commissioner at the International Exhibition in Paris, where his collection of Australian woods attracted attention. In October he toured the vineyards of the Pyrénées and Loire and next year those of Burgundy, the Rhine, northern Italy and Switzerland.

Macarthur disliked politics. In 1823 he had declined a magistracy but in February 1825 was appointed to the Camden bench. In July 1840 he helped to organize the association for promoting assisted immigration; he opposed change in the land regulations and the separation of Port Phillip. In July 1848 he was defeated by George Oakes [q.v.] for the Parramatta seat in the Legislative Council, but was elected in February 1849 for Port Phillip and in September 1851 for the Lachlan and Lower Darling. He vacated his seat in 1855. After a second visit to England as a commissioner at the London International Exhibition of 1862 he was appointed to the Legislative Council in October 1864 on the recommendation of James Martin [q.v.]. In August 1882 his seat was vacated by absence. In June 1836 Macarthur had joined the committee of the Australian Museum and from 1853 was a trustee; in November 1860 he became the first vice-president of the Acclimatisation Society of New South Wales and in 1870 a trustee of the Free Public Library. Vice-president of the Australian Club for many years, he was president in 1879, and president then senior vice-president of the Agricultural Society of New South Wales. In 1860-80 he was a member of the Senate of the University of Sydney. In his last years he suffered deafness and paralysis in the legs and from 1856 was troubled by a disagreement over his management of Edward's properties. 'Mild and unassuming' in manner, 'his countenance betokened good nature rather than depth of thought' and he was only 'anxious to pursue the even tenor of his way in peace'. He was much loved by younger members of his family. He was knighted in 1856, awarded the *Légion d'honneur* and in February 1861 was made an honorary member of the Société Impériale Zoologique d'Acclimatation. Macarthur died unmarried on 29 October 1882 and was interred in the family vault at Camden. His estate, valued at £38,000, was left to his niece Elizabeth, wife of A. A. W. Onslow [q.v.].

S. M. Onslow, *Some early records of the Macarthurs of Camden* (Syd, 1914); M. H. Ellis, *John Macarthur* (Syd, 1955); *SMH*, 31 Oct 1882; *Town and Country J*, 4 Nov 1882; Astley papers, Macarthur papers and Parkes letters (ML); Col Sec, In-letters 1819 and land papers (NSWA); newspaper indexes under James and William Macarthur (ML).   RUTH TEALE

MACARTNEY, HUSSEY BURGH (1799-1894), Church of England clergyman, was born on 10 April 1799 in Dublin, the youngest son of Sir John Macartney, baronet, and his wife Catherine, second daughter of Walter Hussey Burgh, lord chief baron of the exchequer. After private schooling, Macartney in 1816 entered Trinity College, Dublin (B.A., 1821; M.A., B.D., and D.D., 1847). Made deacon on 21 September 1822 and ordained priest on 14 September 1823, he served in curacies at Banagher, Killoe and Killashee, and was presented to the living of Creagh, County Cork, in 1831 by the marquess of Anglesea. On 7 March 1833 he married Jane, daughter of Edward Hardman and his wife Rebecca, née McLintock.

To better his health Macartney became rector of Kilcock, County Kildare, in 1843. His cousin, C. J. Griffith [q.v.], suggested that he migrate to Port Phillip and when Bishop Perry [q.v.] appealed for clergy to serve in the new diocese of Melbourne in 1847, Macartney's offer was accepted. He sailed in the *Stag* with his family and the bishop's party and arrived in Melbourne on 24 January 1848. For ten months he was in charge of the Heidelberg parish, holding services in the Presbyterian Church there and occasionally at Whittlesea, Broadmeadows and the Lower Plenty. In November 1848 Macartney was appointed archdeacon of Geelong, where he supervised the opening of new schools, extended the ministrations of the Church to surrounding localities and divided the parish of Geelong. Friction arose with the Christ Church trustees when a new vicarage was built at Ashby and the erection of St Paul's was started instead of extending Christ Church, but in 1852 Macartney left Geelong to become dean of Melbourne and incumbent of St James's Cathedral Church.

St James's was extended, repaired and on 30 December 1853 was consecrated, schools and services were established from Flemington to Bulla and by 1859 a parochial association was actively distributing funds to such charities as the Orphanage and Benevolent Asylum as well as the Melbourne Hospital, which the dean had helped to inaugurate. In 1855-56 Macartney administered the diocese whilst Perry was in England and in 1857 became archdeacon of Melbourne with responsibility for supervising deacons and lay readers not under a clergyman and for supplying ministrations to areas without resident clergy. This post he held for thirty years until he could no longer travel in country districts. In 1860 he resigned from St James's to devote himself to the work of the archdeaconry and assisting Perry with the growing administration. He was vicar-general in 1863-64 and again in 1874-77. When Perry resigned in 1876 the dean refused nomination as bishop of Melbourne, but continued to administer the diocese until Bishop Moorhouse [q.v.] arrived in 1877. Still vigorous at 84, he resumed charge of St James's in 1883 and administered the diocese between the departure of Moorhouse and the arrival of Bishop Goe in 1887.

In 1864 Macartney had been given a purse of sovereigns before he visited Britain with his family, and at his golden wedding he was presented with over a thousand sovereigns. In 1885 his health began to fail but he represented the diocese at every General Synod until 1886 and was active in founding St Paul's Cathedral. He died at the deanery, East Melbourne, on 8 October 1894, and after a service at St Paul's Cathedral was buried in the family vault in Melbourne general cemetery. Predeceased by his wife in January 1885 and by two daughters, he was survived by three daughters and three sons, two of whom were pastoralists and the third, named after his father, was incumbent of St Mary's, Caulfield, for thirty years until he died in 1898.

With decided opinions, natural eloquence and broad sympathies, Macartney was a thorough Irish Protestant in full sympathy with the Orangemen of Ulster. His evangelical attachment to the literal interpretation of the articles and liturgy of the Church of England and his administrative ability made him an ideal assistant to Bishop Perry who once described him as 'a willing horse who sometimes needed the rein but never the spur'. On only one point did Macartney publicly differ from his bishop: in 1856 his pamphlet State Aid to Religion and Education argued that it was the duty of the state to support the church and of the church to accept such assistance. As chairman of the Central Board of Education for the Anglican Church he firmly supported denominational schools and opposed the National education system. In Ireland he had published many books and pamphlets

and in Melbourne his printed works included a lecture on The Antichrist (1854), Education in Victoria for the future (1860), Marriage with a Deceased Wife's Sister (1872), Spiritism (1872) and Notes on the Book of Revelation (1894). Unable to appreciate advanced theological insights he did not always agree with Bishop Moorhouse, but his affection for Perry's successors and his loyalty to them was never in doubt, whilst his wide knowledge of the diocese made him an invaluable counsellor.

T. W. H. Leavitt (ed), Australian representative men, 1 (Melb, 1887); G. Goodman, The church in Victoria during the episcopate of the Rt. Rev. Charles Perry (Melb, 1892); E. C. Rickards, Bishop Moorhouse of Melbourne and Manchester (Lond, 1920); A. de Q. Robin, Charles Perry, bishop of Melbourne (Perth, 1967); V&P (LA Vic), 1867 (1st S), 4 (27); Vic Churchman, 12, 26 Oct 1894; Examiner (Melb), 9 June, 6 Oct 1860; Australasian, 18 Apr 1891; Table Talk, 3 Apr 1890, 24 June 1892, 13 Oct 1894; Bishop's letter-books 1850-94 (Diocesan Registry, Melb).   A. de Q. ROBIN

MACARTNEY, JOHN ARTHUR (1834-1917), pastoralist and horseman, was born on 5 April 1834 at Creagh, County Cork, Ireland, son of Rev. H. B. Macartney [q.v.] and his wife Jane, née Hardman. Educated at Lucan School and by private tutors in Dublin, he arrived at Melbourne in the Stag with his family in 1848.

Macartney continued his education with private tutors and then entered the legal office of Charles Sladen [q.v.] at Geelong. After twelve months he resigned and drifted around Victoria, spending some time on the goldfields. In 1852 he was appointed judge-associate to Redmond Barry [q.v.] but resigned after eighteen months to take up his first station at Wondilligong on the Ovens River. In 1857 he took Edward Graves Mayne of Beechworth as a partner and in September left for Queensland, where he took up Waverley run near Rockhampton early in 1859. He soon became a legend, both as a horseman and as a collector of runs. He is said to have regularly ridden the 125 miles from Waverley to Rockhampton in one day, carried out all necessary business and retraced the 125 miles next day. At various times he held twenty-five stations and four lesser properties in Queensland as well as four major runs in the Northern Territory. In long rides seeking land he explored much of Queensland and early in 1880 became a fellow of the Royal Geographical Society. His partnership with Mayne was dissolved in 1884 and in 1887 he joined forces with Hugh Louis Heber-Percy, nephew of the fifth duke of Northumberland.

Macartney took on a mail contract and, because of his passion for riding, neglected his stations to do the work himself. In 1893 the partners were in difficulties and lost many of their holdings. Macartney sought employment as a station manager. When told that he was too old, he is said to have vaulted over a table and thereby secured the job. He had returned to Melbourne in 1861 to marry on 4 January Anne Flora, daughter of A. C. Wallace-Dunlop, member of the Victorian Legislative Council in 1851-52. His autobiography *Rockhampton fifty years ago, reminiscences of a pioneer* was published in 1909. Predeceased by his wife, he died on 10 July 1917 at Ormiston House, Cleveland, survived by four daughters and two of his four sons.

M. J. Fox (ed), *The history of Queensland*, 1 (Brisb, 1909); Jack cutting book no 10 (Oxley Lib, Brisb); biog cuttings (Oxley Lib, Brisb).

H. J. GIBBNEY

MACBAIN, SIR JAMES (1828-1892), businessman and politician, was born on 19 April 1828 at Kinrives, Ross-shire, Scotland, son of Smith MacBain, farmer, and his wife Christina, née Taylor. The family later moved to Invergordon. A sickly child, James blamed a bad fall from a horse for his slight education. In 1845 he was indentured to an Inverness draper and in 1852 he became a commercial traveller with John Milligan, Son & Co. of Bradford, visiting much of Scotland and Northern Ireland. In May 1853 he married Jessie Smith of Forres and in October they arrived in the *Great Britain* at Melbourne. MacBain worked in the branch of the Bank of New South Wales. He visited Britain in 1857 and on his return became managing partner of the mercantile and pastoral agency, Gibbs, Ronald [q.v.] & Co. which in 1863 amalgamated with Richards Gibbs & Co. In 1865 the Australian Mortgage (Mercantile) Land and Finance Co. bought the business and MacBain continued as chairman and managing director for twenty-five years. He bought Glen Nevis station near Kilmore and by the late 1870s owned 40,183 freehold acres and leased 85,365 acres in the Murrumbidgee and Lachlan districts, but he rarely visited his northern runs.

In 1864 MacBain won the Wimmera seat in the Legislative Assembly. He consistently opposed the McCulloch [q.v.] ministry, the Darling grant and the extension of railways to Gippsland. He opposed the 1873 Land Act amendment bill because he 'had formed [his] opinions on the land question before

[he] ever became identified with pastoral pursuits'. The squatter, he claimed, must give way to the selector but must be justly compensated. MacBain was chairman of the Board for the Protection of Aborigines during a stormy period. He favoured the abolition of state aid but opposed the 1872 education bill and in the debate on payment of members displayed his conciliatory powers.

MacBain served on many finance committees and was a director of the Colonial Bank of Australasia, the Victorian Fire and Marine Insurance Co., the Australasian Fire, Marine and Life Assurance Co., the Australian Mutual Provident Society and at different times local director of the London Chartered and the English, Scottish and Australian Banks. He was a trustee of the Working Men's College and of the Public Library and National Gallery, a member of the Victorian Employers' Union, a founder and president of the Australian Club and president of the Kilmore Agricultural Society. In 1880 pressure of work obliged him to resign from the Legislative Assembly and in May he entered the Legislative Council as member for Central Province, which became South Yarra Province in 1882. From August 1881 to March 1883 he was member without portfolio of the O'Loghlen [q.v.] government, cajoled by Bent [q.v.] into accepting office, according to Deakin. MacBain was chairman of the Victorian Commission at the Amsterdam Exhibition in 1883 and next year succeeded Sir William Mitchell [q.v.] as council president. A surprise choice to some, MacBain's election was welcomed by the *Argus* for this citizen of 'credit and renown' had a legislative career unblemished by 'dereliction of duty' or unpleasantness. As president he had great social obligations and entertained Lord Rosebery and the earl of Carnarvon. MacBain was knighted in 1886 and appointed K.C.M.G. in 1889. He was also president of the executive commission of the 1888 Centennial Exhibition.

An ardent but tolerant Presbyterian, Sir James belonged to the Chalmers Church congregation, donated the site and funds for the Toorak Presbyterian Church and manse, and was a prominent member of the General Assembly; he attempted to mediate in the Charles Strong [q.v.] heresy case. He was a trustee of Scotch College and the Presbyterian Ladies' College, a councillor of Ormond College and an executor of Francis Ormond's [q.v.] will. MacBain was an enthusiastic member of the Royal Caledonian Society and as its president gave an inaugural celebration in the Town Hall to which he invited 1000 guests. He also loved weddings and parties and, though his leisure was restricted, he was a keen golfer, attending the formative meetings of the (Royal) Melbourne Golf Club.

At the height of his career Sir James suffered severe hepatitis from which he did not completely recover. He died on 4 November 1892 at his home, Scotsburn, Toorak. His funeral procession was two miles long and plans for a public memorial were discussed almost immediately. His estate was valued at £48,000. He was survived by his wife but was childless though he had adopted a nephew who took his name. Deakin described MacBain as a stolid, sturdy, honourable old Tory and the *Argus* wrote, 'if he was everywhere popular it was by no means because he was all things to all men . . . he had views of his own and a backbone of his own, only, as he never obtruded his ideas about racing, and about the amusements he considered dubious, he was respected when in a kind spirit he deemed it necessary to assert them'.

H. M. Humphreys (ed), *Men of the time in Australia*: *Victorian series*, 1st ed (Melb, 1878); T. W. H. Leavitt (ed), *Australian representative men* (Melb, 1887); A Sutherland et al, *Victoria and its metropolis*, 2 (Melb, 1888); J. D. Bailey, *A hundred years of pastoral banking* (Oxford, 1966); V&P (LA Vic), 1879-80, 3 (72); *Warrnambool Standard*, 17 Jan 1880; *Argus*, 6 Sept, 28 Nov 1884, 10 Nov 1891, 5, 8 Nov 1892; *Australasian*, 12 Nov, 17 Dec 1892; *A'sian Insurance and Banking Record*, 17 Nov 1892; J. E. Parnaby, The economic and political development of Victoria, 1877-1881 (Ph.D. thesis, Univ Melb, 1951).   J. ANN HONE

McBURNEY, SAMUEL (1847-1909), educationist and music teacher, was born on 30 April 1847 in Glasgow, Scotland, eldest of the five children of Isaiah McBurney, LL.D., and his wife Margaret, née Bonnar. His father was classics master at Glasgow Academy and later principal of a school at Douglas, Isle of Man; he published a work on Ovid in 1854 and was co-editor of the *Cyclopaedia of Universal History* (London, 1855); he went to Victoria about 1881 and died there on 5 July 1896.

Samuel's early education included musical training through the Tonic Sol-fa method. In 1864-66 he attended the University of Glasgow, becoming a prizeman in humanities. He migrated to Victoria in 1870 and taught classics and mathematics at schools in Kyneton, South Melbourne and Sale. He moved to Portland in 1875 and returned to England in 1876, intending to enter the Order of Benedicts, but a year later married Marie Louise Accleston. After a visit to Germany he returned to London to specialize in the Tonic Sol-fa method of teaching music, passing all the examinations of the Tonic Sol-fa College, London, and becoming a friend of the founder, John Curwen (1816-1880). McBurney returned to Victoria where in 1877 he was appointed principal of a Ladies' College in Geelong. During almost a decade at the college he was an active member of the local 'Shakspere' Society, published textbooks on English, geography and music theory and began his crusade to propagate the method in music education. In 1878 he founded the Victorian Tonic Sol-fa Association and in 1883 organized its first Intercolonial Conference at Geelong. From 1884 he began publishing articles on teaching the system in the *Australasian Schoolmaster* and writing letters to the press in an attempt to persuade the Education Department to recognize the method. In 1887 he toured the eastern colonies of Australia, conducting lecture-demonstrations and forming associations in New South Wales and Queensland. He also collected material on colonial peculiarities for Dr A. J. Ellis, *On Early English Pronunciation*, pt 5 (London, 1889). McBurney and his wife continued their lecture tour in New Zealand and North America, and then returned to England. To demonstrate the advantages of the system, McBurney passed examinations at the University of Dublin (Mus. Bac., Mus. Doc., 1890). Next year he was elected a fellow of the Tonic Sol-fa College, London.

On his return to Victoria in 1891 McBurney was given a temporary appointment as inspector of music with the Education Department and continued his advocacy of the system by giving lectures, offering postal courses and holding Tonic Sol-fa Summer Schools. Victoria's worsening economic situation led to retrenchments and McBurney's post in the Education Department was among those abolished. In 1894 with his wife he opened a Ladies' College at St Kilda and also began teaching music based on the Tonic Sol-fa system at the Blind Institute, St Kilda Road, using a Braille raised-type notation which he had devised. In 1898 he was appointed an examiner in the University of Melbourne (Mus. Doc., *ad eund.*, 1901). In 1902 he was appointed to the staff of the University Conservatorium of Music as teacher of sight singing and ear training.

McBurney was a prominent figure in education as scholar, teacher and author of many articles and books. He was widely travelled and interested in languages and dialects, serving for a time as secretary of the Esperanto Society in Melbourne. His compositions, although few and chiefly choral, include cantatas, part-songs and Australian patriotic songs. Aged 62 he died on 9 December 1909 at Melbourne, survived by his wife.

Register (Adel), 2, 3 May 1899; *Weekly Times* (Melb), 5 Aug 1899; R. S. Stevens, Samuel McBurney and the introduction of the Tonic Sol-fa method of teaching singing into Victorian state schools (B.Ed. Hons thesis, Univ Melb, 1971).   ROBIN S. STEVENS

McCALLUM, FRANK; see MELVILLE FRANCIS

McCARRON, JOHN FRANCIS (1848-1900), printer and publisher, was born on 2 August 1848 at Carronside, near Enniskillen, County Fermanagh, Ireland, son of Francis McCarron and his wife Sydney Frances. He arrived in Adelaide with his parents in 1854. Two years later the family moved to Melbourne where McCarron attended St James's School. In 1858 he joined the printing office of A. Goulding at St Kilda, and next year went to W. Goodhugh & Co. in Flinders Lane where he learnt the trade of compositor. He remained with the firm and its successor Fergusson & Moore until April 1872 when he established McCarron, Bird & Co. with Hermann Puttmann [q.v.], J. H. Bird (d. 1900) and Andrew Stewart as partners. The printing and publishing business at Flinders Lane grew rapidly; in 1877 the firm founded the monthly *Australasian Insurance and Banking Record*. In 1887 Bird retired and the firm moved to Collins Street, enlarging its business to include sections on lithography, engraving, bookbinding and stationery. In 1888 the firm published A. Sutherland's [q.v.] *Victoria and its Metropolis* and in 1891 the *Australasian Pastoralists' Review*. McCarron also bought the Sydney business of Gibbs, Shallard & Co.

McCarron's business interests were diverse. He speculated with success in mining and also took part in large financial transactions involving city and suburban properties. His venture into pastoral holdings in the late 1870s was less successful and in 1880 he disposed of his interest at some loss. He was a director of and prominent shareholder in several companies and building societies, including the New Northcote Brick Co. and D. Stratton & Co. Ltd, millers of Echuca, and from January 1896 was a director of the Foster Brewing Co. He took an interest in friendly societies and in the early 1870s was a promoter and first treasurer of the Emerald Hill Friendly Societies' dispensary. In November 1899 he was elected a member of the Melbourne City Council, representing Lonsdale Ward. He was a member of the Emerald Hill Artillery.

McCarron was an excellent raconteur and reciter. He had been an admirer and friend of G. V. Brooke [q.v.] and in the 1860s when Barry Sullivan [q.v.] managed the Melbourne Theatre Royal McCarron performed several times in charity productions such as the *Comedy of Errors*. On 13 April 1866 at the Presbyterian Church, Collins Street, he had married Ellen Bessie, daughter of Edward Teele of Emerald Hill; they had two sons and two daughters. He died suddenly from cerebral haemorrhage during a polka on 6 June 1900 at St Vincent's Hospital Ball, Melbourne Town Hall. He was buried in the Anglican section of Melbourne general cemetery.

Argus, 7, 9 June 1900.   CECILY CLOSE

McCARTHY, CHARLES (1814-1896), medical practitioner, was born in Blarney, County Cork, Ireland, son of Denis McCarthy, farmer, and his wife Ann. McCarthy qualified in Glasgow (L.F.P.S., 1846), married Rose Ann Patterson in 1849, migrated to Victoria in 1853 and was in general practice in Lonsdale Street, Melbourne, for twenty years. He was admitted to the University of Melbourne (M.B., M.D., *ad eund.*, 1862). In 1863-69 he was medical officer to the St Patrick's Society until dismissed for interference in its management. He was a member of the Medical Society of Victoria in 1862-70 and of the short-lived Victorian Medical Association in 1869-71.

From mid-1859 the *Argus* published correspondence from 'Medicus' who urged that treatment of alcoholism was a medical rather than a moral problem, and should be a government responsibility. Under pressure McCarthy admitted authorship in January 1866. He was concerned with the link between chronic alcoholism and insanity but opposed the incarceration of common drunkards with either lunatics or criminals. To assist dipsomaniacs to help themselves, he recommended controlled diet and exercise in the isolation of a special Inebriates' Retreat for periods of from one to three years. He did not believe in miracle cures.

McCarthy was described by Dr R. Youl [q.v.] as well-meaning but lacking 'the faculty of inducing people to like him'. However, he had the crusader's gift of persistence and could attract respect and influential support. In October 1866 James McCulloch's [q.v.] government resisted a request for funds for a retreat and legislation which would enable drunkards to be detained therein. But Attorney-General George Higinbotham [q.v.] put an appropriate clause into the Lunacy Act of 1867 and, though it proved useless, McCarthy in June 1868 had himself appointed a justice of the peace, which later facilitated the legal process of committal.

In September 1871 a new government promised limited financial support. In December 1872 a property of some 32 acres in Northcote was acquired and the inebriates treatment bill drafted by Dr Hearn [q.v.] became law. This bound an alcoholic to accept treatment for periods ranging from three to twelve months once the court gave an order for his restraint. McCarthy always claimed that this was the first Act of its kind in the world, though he was aware of experiments in the United States where a similar Act was operating in New York by about 1864.

McCarthy moved into residence as secretary and medical superintendent of the retreat which opened in October 1873. Public support was never strong; government money stopped after 1874 and McCarthy's salary was unpaid after the first year. He could only afford to take in paying patients. This frustrated the intention of the Act because compulsory orders for treatment could not be enforced on those who could not pay. Expense also inhibited long stay by patients and prevented McCarthy from producing convincing curative results. By 1877 the retreat trustees were embarrassed by failure and debt. They hastily and illegally agreed to McCarthy's offer to buy the property and continue to run it as a private venture. Scandal erupted in 1884 as a result of inquiries pursued by E. L. Zox [q.v.], who was chairman of the royal commission on asylums for the insane and inebriate, and an original supporter of the retreat as a charitable institution. McCarthy's behaviour was indiscreet but the commissioners' failure to acknowledge his pioneering efforts cannot be excused since they endorsed most of the principles advocated by him for decades.

In September 1885 McCarthy was ordered by Judge Molesworth [q.v.] to restore the retreat to a charitable trust, but he was not debarred from participation in the trust's affairs. No firm action was taken until December 1888 when the Inebriate Asylums Act repealed the 1872 measure, abolished private asylums with statutory powers, but accepted that the government did have a responsibility for inebriates. By a second Act in November 1889 the government took over the Northcote Retreat and its debt of £8500. McCarthy was employed to run it until a new superintendent was appointed in 1892. With the help of depression, the retreat quickly collapsed. McCarthy and his wife settled in Hawthorn where she died in 1894, and he on 29 February 1896; they had no children.

C. R. D. Brothers, *Early Victorian psychiatry 1835-1905* (Melb, 1962); *A'sian Medical Gazette*, 20 Mar 1896; *Argus*, 4 Jan, 26 Oct 1866; *Age*, 27 Apr 1872, 10 Jan 1874, 22, 28 Dec, 1881, 9 Sept 1885; A. M. Mitchell, Temperance and the liquor question in later nineteenth century Victoria (M.A. thesis, Univ Melb, 1966).

ANN M. MITCHELL

McCAUGHEY, SIR SAMUEL (1835-1919), pastoralist and philanthropist, was born on 1 July 1835 at Tullyneuh, near Ballymena, County Antrim, Ireland, eldest son of Francis McCaughey, farmer and merchant, and his wife Eliza, née Wilson. After formal schooling he learnt accounting and office management in his father's linen business and worked on the farm. Strongly influenced by his strict Presbyterian upbringing, he was persuaded by his uncle, Charles Wilson, to try his luck in Australia and in April 1856 reached Melbourne in the *Chamira*. To save money he walked 200 miles to the Wilson property near Horsham. McCaughey started as a general station hand but soon became overseer. His genial Irish humour and kindness helped him to get the best from his men and maintain their goodwill.

In 1860 McCaughey's relations backed his purchase of a third share of Coonong, 42,000 acres near Urana in the Riverina, in partnership with David Wilson and John Cochrane. Although they suffered such initial setbacks as the lack of water, McCaughey remained optimistic and in 1864 became sole owner. He brought water to Coonong by deepening Yanco Creek and building dams. In the 1860s he acquired Singorimba and Goolgumbla and by 1872 held 137,000 acres. In 1871 he visited his widowed mother in Ireland and in 1874 brought out his brother David (1848-1899) to help in managing his properties.

McCaughey founded his stud in 1860 by buying from James Cochrane of Widegewa old ewes descended from Tasmanian pure Saxon merinos. He later experimented with Silesian merinos from the flock of Prince Lichnowski and in 1866 with two Ercildoune rams from his uncle, Samuel Wilson [q.v.]. In 1873-75 McCaughey bought over 3000 rams from N. P. Bayly [q.v.] of Havilah, and some from Ercildoune and other well-known studs. To improve quality he spared no expense in fencing and subdividing his paddocks. By 1883 the Coonong stud was one of the best in the Riverina. In that year, anxious to increase the weight of his wool, he bought ten Californian merinos and was so satisfied with the results that he visited America in 1886 and secured 120 ewes and 92 of the finest rams in the state of Vermont;

six months later he selected 310 more Vermonts. The weight of the wool increased dramatically and for years the greasy, wrinkled Vermont sheep were invincible in shows. In 1879 only one of his stud rams had cut 16 lbs. of wool but by 1891 200 of them averaged 30 lbs. After severe losses in the 1902 drought McCaughey returned to Peppin [q.v.] blood from Wanganella, but Australian sheepbreeders have had great difficulty in eradicating the Vermont strain. For many years McCaughey was vice-president of the New South Wales Sheepbreeders' Association.

McCaughey had a flair for mechanical appliances and regretted that he had never taken an engineering course. Although he employed several blacksmiths, he did much of the experimental work himself and was responsible for the design and improvement of many farm implements. He pioneered in New South Wales the use of heavy machinery for ploughing and soil excavation. He acquired Coree in 1881, later owned by his brother David, and Toorale and Dunlop, 2,500,000 acres on the Darling from Samuel Wilson. He lived at Coonong where in 1876 he had built a large homestead with a garden and lake. At various times he owned or shared in twelve stations in New South Wales and three in Queensland with a total area of about 3,250,000 acres. From the mid-1880s Dunlop, Toorale and the Queensland stations were watered by artesian bores. In 1888 at Dunlop the shearing was done completely with Wolseley [q.v.] machines for the first time in Australia.

One of the first to see the advantages of widespread irrigation, McCaughey brought out Irish labourers who did not mind wet and boggy conditions. McCaughey was frustrated in his efforts to get more water for Coonong from dams on Colombo Creek when in 1898 he and his brother were sued in the Supreme Court by six down-stream graziers. In *Blackwood v. McCaughey* the jury awarded £2000 damages to the plaintiff and limited the height of the dams. On 15 June the other plaintiffs were compensated with £10,000 while McCaughey paid £17,000 in legal costs. In 1900 he bought North Yanco where he constructed a complex irrigation system with some 200 miles of channels and used two steam engines to pump water from the Murrumbidgee; his success persuaded the government to build the Burrinjuck dam which was completed in 1927. He built a magnificent mansion at North Yanco and was famed for his hospitality.

In 1899 George Reid appointed McCaughey and eleven others to the Legislative Council to secure the passage of the Federation enabling bill. He had no strong political leanings but his experience and knowledge of land were valued and he advocated large-scale immigration. He donated £10,000 to a fund for sending a bushmen's contingent to the Boer war. In 1905 he was knighted and visited Europe. He visited Louis Pasteur and tried in vain to obtain an efficient means of exterminating plagues of rabbits. After the federal Land Tax Act was passed in 1910 McCaughey started to dispose of his properties.

A great philanthropist, McCaughey was always ready to help people in trouble on the land. He contributed £10,000 to the Dreadnought Fund and another £10,000 to Dr Barnado's Homes. In World War I he gave liberally to the Red Cross and other war charities besides insuring 500 soldiers at £200 each. After long suffering from nephritis he died from heart failure on 25 July 1919. Unmarried he was buried in the churchyard of St John's Presbyterian Church, Narrandera. His estate was sworn for probate at over £1,600,000. Apart from bequests of £200,000 and all his motor vehicles to his brother John and legacies to his station managers and employees, he left £10,000 to increase the stipends of Presbyterian clergy, £20,000 to the Burnside Orphan Homes at Parramatta, £20,000 to Scots College in Sydney, £10,000 each to five other independent schools, £5000 to the Salvation Army and £5000 each to seven hospitals. Half the residue of his estate went to the Universities of Sydney and Queensland; the other half went to the relief of members of the Australian Military and Naval Expeditionary Forces and their widows and children.

A portrait by Sir John Longstaff is in the University of Sydney.

C. McIvor, *The history and development of sheep farming from antiquity to modern times* (Syd, 1893); H. H. Peck, *Memoirs of a stockman* (Melb, 1942); P. McCaughey, *Samuel McCaughey* (Syd, 1955); A. Crowley, 'The life and work of Sir Samuel McCaughey', *JRAHS*, 40 (1954); *Australasian*, 25 June 1898; private papers (held by Lady McCaughey, Syd).

                                        PETER HOHNEN

McCOLL, HUGH (1819-1885), irrigation promoter, was born on 22 January 1819 in Glasgow, Scotland, eldest son of James McColl and his wife Agnes, née Cowan. Reared in the highlands, he was apprenticed to a stationer in Glasgow and worked for fifteen years as a Tyneside bookseller. In 1843 he married Jane Hiers of South Shields, Durham. In 1852 they decided to migrate to Victoria and sailed in the *Emigrant* with five of their six children, but Jane died on

2 January 1853 as they entered Hobson's Bay. In 1856 he married Mary, sister of George Guthrie of the Bendigo pottery; they had one son and three daughters.

After working as printer, publisher of the short-lived *Banner* and *Diggers Advocate*, commercial traveller, mining manager, promoter of Bendigo district industries and legal manager for a Sandhurst gold-mining company, McColl became secretary in 1874 of the Grand Victorian North West Canal, Irrigation, Traffic and Motive Power Co. Ltd. This visionary project, evolved by Benjamin Hawkins Dods in 1871, was to supply water and provide transport for six million acres of Victoria's northern plains through a canal running westerly from the Goulburn River near Murchison to the Wimmera; in their enthusiasm the promoters saw it linking the Wimmera with the Murray and even the Gulf of Carpentaria.

McColl's 'water-on-the-brain' was apparent first in England while secretary of the Tyne Conservancy Committee which advocated navigation improvements and then in the goldfields of northern Victoria where he sought the building of dams for miners and farmers. From 1865 he was honorary secretary of the Sandhurst and Castlemaine Water Supply Committee which supported development of the Coliban River. His fame grew as he stumped the country seeking support for his canal company, preaching the need for water conservation and publicizing overseas projects. Public notice was mostly critical, often derisory. Support came mainly from only five country towns but the government rejected his plea for a grant of three million acres; protection of survey-pegs along the proposed canal-course was granted only in 1877. The promoters were over-optimistic in estimates of rainfall, river-flow and costs, and the canal project gradually fizzled out except for McColl's continued pressure for a canal across the northern plains, later the main feature of the Goulburn irrigation system.

Short, enthusiastic, irresistible and 'perpetually jolly', McColl was a Presbyterian of liberal-radical sentiments to whom 'nothing came amiss in the way of enterprise'. He was secretary of a Protectionists' Association, proposed a land lease league in 1875 which stopped the granting of large freeholds in the Mallee and had a vision of a temperance township that got only as far as its name, Longmore. Nevertheless his persistence and energy as an 'amiable but very visionary' hydraulic projector gave much impetus to public opinion.

At his fourth try in nine years McColl was elected in 1880 for Mandurang. He used parliament and, with Rev. E. C. De Garis, the Central Irrigation League to advance water conservation. Whatever the subject of debate, he spoke on 'watter' for the northern farmer, becoming a stock joke to many, but finally impressed Alfred Deakin and the Service and Berry [qq.v.] ministry. When a royal commission on water supply was granted in 1884, it investigated his arguments for government ownership of all watercourses and the development of water resources based on a hydrographic contour survey with canals on high ground irrigating by gravity. He was less of a prophet in dismissing the problem of drainage with irrigation. Although critical of rural waterworks trusts using diversions along effluent watercourses from unregulated rivers, he declared himself satisfied by Deakin's 1883 Water Act. The commission met first only a few days before he died at his home in St Kilda on 2 April 1885. The outcome was the Act of 1886 which laid the foundation for Victorian irrigation development a generation earlier than any other large-scale irrigation in Australia. Appropriately his son James Hiers (1844-1929) was minister of water supply in 1893-94 and later a Federal politician.

C. S. Martin, *Irrigation and closer settlement in the Shepparton district 1836-1906*, J. L. F. Woodburn ed (Melb, 1955); J. H. McColl, 'Hugh McColl and the water question in Northern Victoria', VHM, 5(1916-17); J. N. Churchyard, 'Pioneers of irrigation in Victoria', *Aqua*, 7 (1956) no 12; *Argus*, 4 Apr 1885; *Bendigo Advertiser*, 4 Apr 1885; N. W. Canal Co. press cuttings (LaT L).

VALERIE YULE

McCOMBIE, THOMAS (1819-1869), journalist, merchant and politician, was born in Tillyfour, Aberdeenshire, Scotland, son of Charles McCombie and his wife Anne, née Black. He arrived at Melbourne in March 1841 and tried his hand at squatting. In 1844-51 he was editor and part proprietor of the *Port Phillip Gazette* and on 1 January 1853 started the short-lived weekly *Reformer*. At Scots Church on 16 October 1844 he had married Elizabeth Willis.

In 1846-51 McCombie represented Bourke Ward in the Melbourne Town Council and served as chairman of the Health Committee. In June 1846 his motion was carried in the council for a humble petition to the Queen praying for the removal of Superintendent La Trobe. In August he chaired a large public meeting which adopted a similar resolution. In 1848 he was largely responsible for the election of Earl Grey as a Port Phillip representative to the Legislative Council in Sydney.

After gold was discovered McCombie

moved to the Mount Alexander diggings, where he drew public attention to the miners' grievances. On the separation of Port Phillip he contested the Kilmore electorate in vain but in 1856 he was elected to the Legislative Council for the Southern Province, and became minister without portfolio in the O'Shanassy [q.v.] ministry in March 1858. His parliamentary career was more solid than significant. Amongst other things, he argued for a comprehensive system of immigration with its cost a direct charge on the land instead of from public revenue. He proposed the introduction of Torrens's [q.v.] land titles into Victoria, and advocated uniform legislation in the colonies on such topics as the upset price of public lands, the abolition of transportation, the coinage and regulation of its value, postal matters, the naturalization of aliens, military establishments and lighthouses, railways, tariffs and excise. The ministry fell on 27 October 1859.

McCombie returned with his family to Britain where he was active on colonial affairs. He read a paper on the Aboriginals to the British Association at a meeting attended by the Prince Consort, and others on penal discipline, gold and colonization to the Social Science Association. He returned to Melbourne in the *Wellesley* in February 1866. He contested the Southern Province in the Legislative Council, but without success. In March 1868 he was elected for South Gippsland to the Legislative Assembly. A year later he sailed with his family in the *Talbot* for London. After great suffering he died in Scotland on 2 October 1869 aged 50, survived by his wife and two daughters of their four children.

McCombie had been connected with forming the Victorian Caledonian Society, the Melbourne Gas Co., the Commercial Bank of Australia and the Provident Institute of Victoria. Among his many publications were two descriptive novels: *Arabin, or The Adventures of a Colonist in New South Wales* (London, 1845); and *Frank Henly, or Honest Industry Will Conquer* (London, 1868). They were rather pedestrian accounts of contemporary Victorian life, but he has been credited with being 'one of the first Australian writers who addressed himself to the Australian rather than the English reader'. His enthusiasms for his adopted land and its problems were those of the journalist expounding ideas and novel proposals rather than practical action. 'Garryowen' [q.v. Finn] noted that he was known as 'Tammy Ass' and 'Silly Billy' and claimed that 'it would have been no mistake to call him so, but for the shrewdness and occasional snatches of ability that leavened his dullness'.

'The early printers of Melbourne, 1838-1858', *A'sian Typographical J*, 28 Sept 1897, 28 Jan 1898; H. G. Turner, 'The beginnings of literature in Victoria', *VHM*, 4 (1914); *Examiner* (Melb), 31 Jan 1863; *Argus*, 29, 30 Nov 1869.

FERGUS FARROW

McCONNEL, DAVID CANNON (1818-1885), grazier and farmer, was born on 14 January 1818 at Ardwick, Manchester, England, the eleventh child of James McConnel, cotton spinner, and his wife Margaret, née Houldsworth. He migrated to Sydney on 19 February 1840 and after investigating the Moruya and New England districts, decided to settle in Moreton Bay. In 1841 on the Upper Brisbane River he took up a run, naming it Cressbrook after a family home in Derbyshire; it was the first holding in the district to be stocked with sheep. His elder brother John had a run at Crows Nest for a time and then joined his brother. They soon found that Cressbrook was unsuitable for sheep. McConnel bought stud Shorthorn cows from the Australian Agricultural Co. in 1845 and later imported bulls from England, establishing a stud which became famous.

Leaving John in charge of Cressbrook, David returned to England in 1847 and at Old Grey Friars' Church in Edinburgh on 25 April 1848 married Mary McLeod. He intended to settle on a farm in Nottinghamshire but was recalled to Queensland because of financial difficulties at Cressbrook and arrived with his wife in the *Chaseley* in May 1849. The station did not suit his wife's health so McConnel settled near Brisbane. He took up land at Toogoolawah (Bulimba) where he built a large house in 1850, began farming on his own account and sold small blocks cheaply to deserving immigrants. In 1854 McConnel returned to England because his wife was seriously ill and for seven years travelled extensively throughout Europe. He published *Facts and traditions collected for A Family Record* (Edinburgh, 1861). On his return in 1862 he settled at Cressbrook. In 1868 half his run was resumed by the government but his petition failed to yield any compensation for his improvements. In 1873 he retired in favour of his son John. In 1885 he went to England and died after an operation in London on 16 June. His wife died on 4 January 1910. The Cressbrook property is still owned by the McConnel family.

Both McConnel and his wife were Presbyterians and deeply religious. Mrs McConnel worked actively for establishment of the Children's Hospital which was opened at Brisbane in 1876. As the wife of an Australian pioneer she published *Memories of days long gone by.* Her daughter, Mrs Mary Macleod Banks, published *Memories of pioneer days in Queensland* (London, 1931).

M. J. Fox (ed), *The history of Queensland,* 2 (Brisb, 1921); *V&P* (LA Qld), 1868-69, 145; *Queenslander,* 27 June 1885; *Graziers' Review,* 16 Jan 1922; *Telegraph* (Brisb), 22 Aug 1970.

H. J. GIBBNEY

McCOY, SIR FREDERICK (1817-1899), professor and museum director, was born in Dublin, son of Simon McCoy, physician and professor of materia medica, Queen's College, Galway (1849-73). He began medical studies in Dublin but soon turned to palaeontology and natural history. In 1841 his catalogues of the museum of the Dublin Geological Society and of the shells and organic remains of the Sirr collections in the Dublin Rotunda were published. He then worked for Sir Richard Griffith, classifying his collections which were embodied in *A synopsis of the characters of the Carboniferous Limestone Fossils of Ireland* in 1844 and *A synopsis of the Silurian Fossils of Ireland* in 1846. In 1845 McCoy joined the staff of the British Geological Survey. He worked on the Geological Map of Ireland until late in 1846 when he was chosen by Adam Sedgwick as his collaborator in the Woodwardian Museum, Cambridge. McCoy's 'enormous' and 'unremitting' labours in classifying the great collection of British fossils astonished Sedgwick who wrote of 'this excellent naturalist', 'incomparable and most philosophical palaeontologist'. In August 1849 McCoy became professor of geology and mineralogy and curator of the museum at Queen's College, Belfast. In vacations he worked at Cambridge and on excursions with Sedgwick and prepared *A Detailed Systematic Description of the British Palaeozoic Fossils in the Geological Museum of the University of Cambridge* which appeared serially from 1849. Professor Heinrich Bronn of Heidelberg greeted the work as 'one of the most important appearances in the literature of Palaeontology'. McCoy's prodigious flow of articles in learned journals had begun in 1838. In August 1854 he published *Contributions to British Palaeontology,* a reprint of contributions to the *Annals and Magazine of Natural History,* where twenty-eight of his articles appeared in 1845-54.

In August 1854 a committee of Sir William à Beckett, Robert Lowe [qq.v.], Professor Henry Malden, Sir John Herschel and G. B. Airey chose McCoy professor of natural science, one of the first four professors of the University of Melbourne

which opened in April 1855. He was offered £1000 a year and a house but no assurance of museum work. He lectured in the general laws of chemistry and, for the first time at an Australian university, in mineralogy, elements of botany, supervising a botanic garden at the university, comparative anatomy and physiology of animals, systematic zoology and 'Systematic and Practical Geology with some Palaeontology', in a three-year arts course. Students remained few. McCoy opposed his colleagues' utilitarian arguments against compulsory classics and became associated rather with the inadequacies of science teaching than the advocacy of its extension. Students in 1884 complained of 'botany in a lecture room and not in a garden', 'lectures in Zoology without practical demonstrations' and that 'no geology excursion is ever made'. Agitation produced a chair of chemistry in 1882 and of biology in 1887. McCoy continued after 1886 to teach 'systematic zoology and botany, physical and stratigraphical geology, mineralogy and palaeontology'.

A government museum collection had begun in 1853, but languished in storage in 1855. McCoy persuaded the governor to ask the university for accommodation. The university, pressing the government for completion of its buildings, agreed to allot rooms in the plan. From October the Philosophical Institute (later Royal Society) of Victoria and the press agitated against the museum's removal from town and probable control by the university. In July 1856 the institute ungraciously allowed McCoy to read part of a paper in which he advocated a museum for scientific research and education but not idle shows, and appointment of a director. In August, after a public meeting of protest and unsure of government resolve, McCoy boldly carried off the collection to the newly-completed university rooms. His *de facto* control ended in December 1857 when he was gazetted 'Director of the Museum of Natural and Applied Sciences', an office he held without salary until 1899. He had become government palaeontologist in May 1856 at a salary of £300. He fought to hold the museum at the university and in 1862 negotiated an agreement between the university and the government for a building in the university grounds. The National Museum, almost a facsimile of Ruskin's new Oxford Museum, with stone Gothic windows, a tower and a great hall 150 feet long and 60 feet wide, was opened in 1864.

McCoy's cavalier disregard of financial procedures exasperated governments. He built up an outstanding natural history and geological collection, including mining models, exploiting his knowledge of overseas sources. In 1870 the museum was placed under the Public Library trustees. The struggle to make him docile began. McCoy countered with pugnacity, soft answers or feigned obtuseness. Ever pestering for funds and uncovering trustees' plots to move the museum, he found his best defence and consolation in the popularity and scientific standing of the museum. Annual attendances averaged 53,000 in the 1860s, 95,000 in the 1870s, 110,000 in the 1880s and 108,000 in the 1890s. Painfully he acquired government money to publish serially his *Prodromus of the Zoology of Victoria* (1878-90) and *Prodromus of the Palaeontology of Victoria* (1874-82). McCoy was a naturalist who stayed indoors. His energies and curiosity were absorbed as sole scientific officer in classifying the museum's flood of acquisitions. Aboriginal artefacts he ignored.

McCoy became unfortunately associated with the ecological disruptions occasioned by exotic fauna. He was a leading member of the Acclimatisation Society (later Victorian Zoological Society) founded in 1861 to introduce mammals, fish and birds. In 1862 he urged the 'enlivening' of 'the present savage silence, or worse' of the bush with 'the varied, touching, joyous strains of those delightful reminders of our early home', the English song-birds; he also reported the release of a number of species, the origin of present flocks. Though not responsible for its introduction he rejoiced at the rabbit being 'so thoroughly acclimatized that it swarms in hundreds in some localities and can at any time be extended to others'. His defence of the introduced sparrow dismayed farmers.

In March 1856 McCoy told the select committee of the Legislative Council on gold that the search for deep reefs would prove vain. Later that year as chairman of a royal commission on aspects of the goldfields he visited the diggings and declared his 'Baconian method and general law by induction most completely proved'. Ignorant miners persisted and for years found profitable gold at 'heretical depths'. A royal commission on the University of Melbourne remembered this blot on geology in 1903, and his successor to the chair wrote a paper to prove McCoy was misunderstood, claiming that improved machines redefined 'profitable' reefs. Lesser community expectations of geological inquiry and more caution from McCoy would have saved him public and parliamentary disparagement. His discomfort became for the colony the *locus classicus* for the presumption of theorists and the vindication of practical men.

McCoy was a member of the Council of the University of Melbourne in 1882-87, but retired aware of growing disquiet at pro-fessors serving on council. He was not a university politician, reformer or student favourite. Advancing age, the demands of the museum, the growth of knowledge and his ardent anti-Darwinism decreased his influence, but lack of professional employment depressed growth in all science classes. McCoy was one of those 'experienced naturalists' Darwin [q.v.] 'by no means expected to convince, whose minds are stocked with a multitude of facts all viewed, during a long course of years, from a point of view directly opposite to mine'. In June 1869 McCoy delivered a popular lecture of three hours, and another in July 1870, both published as *The Order and Plan of Creation* (1870), denying 'authority, either in scripture or science, for belief in the gradual transmutation from one species into another' and finding geological confirmation for the *Genesis* phases of creation.

McCoy served on the Royal Society of Victoria Council in the 1860s and was president in 1864 and vice-president in 1861 and 1870. An increasingly acrimonious debate, mainly in the society's *Transactions*, between McCoy and W. B. Clarke [q.v.] on the age of the New South Wales coal deposits proved a well fought but unfortunately rear-guard action for McCoy. In June 1858 he was appointed to a Board of Science 'to advise the government on all matters wherein special scientific and technical knowledge is required' and later reported on subjects from mining machinery to the use of camels. He was a commissioner for the Victorian (1861), Intercolonial (1866) and International (1880) Exhibitions. In 1869-90 he served on the technological commission which fostered the slow beginnings of technical education in Victoria, by encouraging and subsidizing Schools of Mines and of Design, and supporting a Museum of Technology (1870) which McCoy publicly advocated in vain as a centre of research and formal education in technology. He served on the royal commission on the administration, organization and general condition of education in 1882-84 but dissented from the final report's opposition to state aid for church schools.

McCoy accumulated honours: fellow (1852) and Murchison medalist (1879) in the Geological Society, London; F. R. S., 1880; honorary member of learned societies in Cambridge, Edinburgh, London, Manchester, Moscow, New Zealand and Sydney; D.Sc. (Cantab.), 1886; C.M.G., 1886; K.C.M.G., 1891; and royal honours from Italy and Austria. From 1886 he suffered periods of protracted bronchial illness. Still taking his professorial classes and examining at matriculation he fell ill in April and died on 13 May 1899. He was buried in Brighton cemetery, predeceased by his wife Anna Maria, née Harrison, whom he had married at Dublin in 1843, and by their son and daughter. By July his museum was closed to reopen in December 1899 at Russell Street on the site he had opposed since the 1850s. The vacated building became the Student Union.

Fiery, impulsive, resilient, unsuited to collective enterprises, proud of his robustness, smart in dress, McCoy was of medium height with waved reddish hair, side whiskers and a determined chin. He retained in old age his verve, his jaunty step and his capacity for geniality.

W. Kelly, *Life in Victoria*, 1 (Lond, 1859); J. W. Clark and T. McK. Hughes, *The life and letters of the Reverend Adam Sedgwick* (Cambridge, 1890); E. W. Skeats, *Some founders of Australian geology* (Syd, 1934); J. S. Flett, *The first hundred years of the geological survey of Great Britain* (Lond, 1937); R. T. M. Pescott, *Collections of a century* (Melb, 1954); G. Blainey, *A centenary history of the University of Melbourne* (Melb, 1957); T. W. Moody and J. C. Beckett, *Queen's, Belfast 1845-1949* (Lond, 1959); G. Blainey, *The rush that never ended* (Melb, 1963); G. Serle, *The golden age* (Melb, 1963); *Alma Mater* (Univ Melb), Apr, June 1899; *Age*, 15 May 1899.   G. C. FENDLEY

McCRACKEN, ROBERT (1815-1885), brewer, was born in Ayrshire, Scotland, son of Robert McCracken, farmer, and his wife Martha, née Earle. He arrived at Melbourne in January 1841 with his brother Peter (1818-1892). With James Robertson as partner the brothers started the brewing firm of McCracken & Robertson in Little Collins Street West in 1851. The partners began with only two labourers and at first their output was four barrels of beer at a time, but they benefited from the increasing industrialization of brewing which resulted from the urban growth in the Melbourne area. From the start the firm 'tied' publicans and by 1870 it controlled a large share of the outlets for beer in the metropolis. The company also adopted the latest technology; when James Robertson retired in 1861 he was wealthy, although the firm had only just started its growth.

The 1860s were reasonably profitable but the success of the firm, then R. McCracken & Co., came in the 1870s. These boom years brought even greater demand for the company's product, especially as Robert had realized that Victorian drinkers wanted a light, bright-coloured beer. The new product sold well, and the tied house system gave the McCrackens a guaranteed market not only for beer but also for such things as wine, tobacco and sweets bought at a large discount and sold at an even larger profit. From the beginning the McCrackens had been interested in scientific brewing. Robert anticipated Pasteur by enforcing extremely high standards of cleanliness in the brewery. In 1873 the company secured the best available brewer, R. K. Montgomerie, a Tasmanian who was an early student of biochemistry; under his control 'bad' beer became a thing of the past. Montgomerie's brewing skill and McCracken's business acumen led to a quadrupling of output. By 1884 the firm was producing 500 barrels at a brew and its average annual output was between 90,000 and 100,000 barrels, and profits were extremely high. Montgomerie was paid on result and was reputed to earn as much as £12,000 a year in the early 1880s. This is probably an exaggeration but his income cannot have been less than £8000 when he left McCracken's in 1884 to open his own brewery.

Throughout the 1870s McCracken had improved his plant and increased the number of hotels tied to his firm. As a leader in labour conditions, he was the first brewer in Melbourne to introduce the eight-hour day in 1879. An avowed protectionist, he encouraged the malting industry and was reckoned one of its best customers. He was also one of the first brewers to realize that cane sugar could balance the instability of colonial malts, an innovation which was perhaps the greatest technical achievement of Victorian brewers.

McCracken showed little interest in public affairs but was widely recognized as a fair businessman, a good father and a generous employer. Aged 70 he died at his home in Ascot Vale on 17 February 1885, and was buried in the Melbourne general cemetery. He was survived by his wife Margaret, née Hannah, and by a daughter and four sons of their ten children. His estate was valued at £141,487. His firm continued under the control of his sons, Alexander and Collier, who had been admitted to partnership in June 1884. It retained independence until 8 May 1907 when it became a part of Carlton and United Breweries.

A. Sutherland et al, *Victoria and its metropolis*, 2 (Melb, 1888); *Aust Brewer's J*, 3 (1884); *Age*, 18 Feb 1885; *History of the Carlton and United Breweries* (Univ Melb Archives and NL).   GEORGE PARSONS

McCRAE, GEORGE GORDON (1833-1927), poet and man of letters, was born on 29 May 1833 in Leith, Scotland, eldest son of Andrew Murison McCrae, writer to the signet, and his wife Georgiana Huntly McCrae [q.v.]. Georgiana with her four sons landed on 1 March 1841 at Port Phillip, where her husband had migrated in 1839. After a short stay in Bourke Street, the family built Mayfield at Abbotsford on the River Yarra. In 1843 Andrew took up the Arthur's Seat cattle run, near Dromana, and on the north-western side of it overlooking the bay built a homestead now owned by the National Trust where the family lived in 1845-51.

George had attended a preparatory school in London, in 1841 he and his brothers were given lessons by their accomplished mother; and from 1842 they had the services as tutor of John McLure, a master of arts from the University of Aberdeen, from whom they received 'a regular and systematic course of instruction' and who proved a capable teacher and an ideal companion.

George became closely acquainted with the birds, animals, reptiles, trees and flowers with which the bush at Mayfield and Arthur's Seat then abounded, gained an understanding of and affection for the Aboriginals and learned fishing, shooting, riding and other arts of bushmanship. His fascination for the sea and ships and all things to do with them had begun at Leith, developed on the voyage to Australia, increased while he wandered round the wharves of Melbourne, and grew as he sailed and fished and watched the movement of ships from the shores of Dromana.

At 17 as a probationer with a surveying party in the Macedon district, McCrae escaped death on Black Thursday, 6 February 1851, when he and his companions straddled a log over a creek while the flames raged past them. Surveying did not attract him, and after a year with a Flinders Street merchant and a shorter time in the Melbourne Savings Bank, he joined the Victorian government service in 1854 and remained in it until as deputy-registrar-general he reached the retiring age in 1893. On leave in 1864 he travelled in England, Scotland and France, and in 1887 and 1894 made long visits to Mauritius and the Seychelles, for which he developed an abiding affection.

McCrae had a lively, interested, observant and romantic mind, and was impelled to commit to paper, in words or pictures, what he saw and what happened to him. Though he is not regarded as an artist, his paintings of ships were praised by Sir Oswald Brierly [q.v.]. Tom Roberts in a letter to Hugh McCrae mentioned 'a pen and ink of 2 vessels beautifully done', and the manuscript accounts of his travels and experiences are interleaved with sketches vividly illustrating the scenes and events he describes. However, he gave to writing most of his leisure before he retired and his whole time in the next thirty-four years.

His first published work was *Two Old Men's Tales of Love and War* (London, 1865). It was followed in 1867 by *The Story of Balladeädro* and *Mämba, 'the Bright-eyed'*, both based on Aboriginal legends. A long poem in blank verse, *The Man in the Iron Mask*, appeared in 1873. He contributed many short poems to the *Australasian* and other journals, and the *Melbourne Review* published as a serial, 'A Rosebud from the Garden of the Taj', in 1883. A novel, *John Rous*, a story of the reign of Queen Anne, was published in 1918 though written earlier. Extracts from a long poem, *Don Cesar*, were printed in the Sydney *Bulletin*. A small selection of his poems, *The Fleet and Convoy and Other Verses*, was published in 1915. His unpublished manuscripts include several volumes to which he gave the title 'Reminiscences—Experiences not Exploits'. Written after he retired, they contained remarkably detailed descriptions of the sights, sounds and incidents of his boyhood and early manhood. Though prolix, they are never dull and present a captivating picture of the countryside and people of early Melbourne.

McCrae, who has been called 'the Father of Victorian Poetry', had great facility in writing musical verse, which at times achieved the quality of poetry, but some critics found it too profuse and unpruned, and the modern ear is sometimes irritated by its 'poetical' wording and phrasing.

McCrae was an early member of the Yorick Club, which included R. H. Horne, Henry Kendall, Adam Lindsay Gordon, Marcus Clarke, Dr Patrick Moloney, and John Shillinglaw [qq.v.]. They met and talked together, encouraged and helped one another, and formed the only significant centre of literary interest and achievement in Victoria in the late 1860s and 1870s. They have been amusingly described by Hugh McCrae in *My Father and My Father's Friends*.

McCrae was tall and handsome, had an artistic temperament, a fine courtesy and 'a princely gift for friendship'. He was a gentle and kind man. He died at Hawthorn, Melbourne, on 15 August 1927, his mind alert to the end. Predeceased by his wife Augusta Helen, daughter of James Crago Brown, whom he had married in 1871, he was survived by their six children, including Hugh Raymond, a distinguished poet, and Dorothy Frances Perry, author of several books of verse.

R. G. Howarth, *Literary particles* (Syd, 1946); H. F. Chaplin, *A McCrae miscellany* (Syd, 1967); W. Dixson, 'Notes on Australian artists', *JRAHS*, 9 (1923); *Spinner*, July 1925; *Argus*, 11 July 1890, 16 Aug 1927; family papers.
                                    NORMAN COWPER

McCREA, WILLIAM (1814-1899), medical administrator and naval surgeon, was born on 14 October 1814 in County Tyrone, Ireland. His father died before William was 2 and at 13 he was apprenticed to his uncle, a medical practitioner in London. In 1830 McCrea began attending an extramural medical school in Soho and enrolled at St George's Hospital (L.S.A., M.R.C.S., 1834; M.B., 1851). In 1835 he had joined the navy as assistant surgeon and served for sixteen years, mostly on the coasts of North America and North Africa. In 1851 he sailed in the *Anna Maria* for Van Diemen's Land as surgeon in charge of 200 female convicts and arrived at Hobart Town in January 1852.

The gold rush was then producing great demands upon the administration to control health and maintain order in Victoria and McCrea was appointed assistant colonial surgeon. In charge of thirty imperial pensioners he was sent to the Forest Creek diggings as surgeon, coroner and magistrate. His naval training so suited him in this task that Lieut-Governor La Trobe petitioned for his retirement from the navy to stay on as colonial surgeon.

When Dr John Sullivan died in 1853 McCrea was appointed head of the Medical Department and as Victoria's first chief health officer was chairman of the newly-established Central Board of Health. He was an excellent administrator, and with naval discipline was firm but fair with his staff. He held these appointments for twenty-five years and firmly founded Victoria's health services. The Quarantine Department had been established in 1854 and next year the Vaccination Act was enacted. He was vitally concerned with the investigation and control of the epidemics of typhoid, dysentery, scarlet fever and diphtheria in Victoria. In Melbourne the establishment of the Yan Yean water supply, the application of sanitary reform and the opening of the Queen's Memorial Infectious Diseases Hospital were highlights of his term and reflect great credit on his administration. Among many duties he had charge of inmates in the Colonial Hospital, the Orphan Asylum and Lunatic Asylum and the Immigrants' Home. He also served on the Police Superannuation Board and the committee of the Austin Hospital for Invalids. He resigned as chairman of the Central Board of Health in 1879. He had been chairman of the royal commission on noxious trades in 1870-71 and next year the origin of typhoid. He served on the commission on foot and mouth disease in 1872 and the sanitary condition of Melbourne in 1888-90. His *Observations on Typhoid Fever* was published in Melbourne in 1879.

Described as tall, wiry and well built,

McCrea had an unmistakable north of Ireland accent. He died of hemiplegia and heart failure on 16 February 1899 at his home in Lennox Street, Richmond, and was buried in the Anglican section of the Melbourne general cemetery. He was survived by his wife Mary Jane, née Drew, whom he had married in 1846 at Milford, Wales, and by two daughters; a son had died in infancy.

Portraits are in the Archives of the Medical Society of Victoria and the Department of Mental Hygiene.

'Health administration in Victoria 1834-1934', *Health Bulletin* (Vic), 1935; Museum Archives (Medical Soc of Vic, Parkville).

DAVID M. O'SULLIVAN

MacCULLAGH, JOHN CHRISTIAN (1832-1917), Anglican priest, was born on 6 June 1832 at Johnstown, County Kildare, Ireland, son of James MacCullagh, land agent, and his wife Mary, née Holmes. Educated at Clontarf Crescent and Trinity College, Dublin, he entered the Islington Mission College but doctors warned him to give up study because it was affecting his sight. He arrived at Sydney in January 1863 and entered Moore College in May. Made deacon at St James's pro-Cathedral, Melbourne, on 18 December 1864, he was licensed to Lancefield and Romsey in 1865 and ordained priest at St James's on 27 May 1866. The first clergyman in the district, he opened in six years ten places for divine service and ten Sunday schools with a total of over 500 scholars. At Christ Church, Hawthorn, on 26 December 1865 he had married Elizabeth, who was born in Queen's County, daughter of John Ince, solicitor, and Caroline, née Cooke. His wife went with him on his tours but her health was a constant worry and she died on 22 October 1870 aged 27.

In November MacCullagh was inducted as incumbent of St Paul's, Sandhurst; he served there for forty-six years. His work resulted in the clearing of a large debt, the erection of a new tower, the installation of a peal of bells, a new gallery, organ and small chancel, and the building of a new vicarage, parish hall and three churches. Attendance at his Sunday schools rose to 1100 pupils, with nearly 100 teachers preparing classes in a course of lessons which he had drawn up. He was elected a canon of St James's and became a rural dean and in 1883 archdeacon of Bendigo. When the new diocese of Bendigo was established in 1902 many thought that he would be the first bishop, but advancing years and increasing obstinacy lost him the preference. At the first synod he argued strongly for St Paul's as the new pro-Cathedral but All Saints was chosen instead. He was reluctant to be its dean but was persuaded to accept the position of a cathedral dean while incumbent of another parish. He exercised authority at the cathedral only on diocesan occasions and parochial responsibilities at All Saints were left to him. In 1907 he was vicar-general of the diocese and acted as arch-deacon in 1909-14.

MacCullagh had contributed scientific and religious articles to the *Argus* and continued them in the *Bendigo Church News*. He also published Sunday school lesson material and notes for theological students. Active in the Christian Social Union he was chief spokesman in 1909 for a delegation which protested to the minister of mines on labour conditions in the Bendigo mines. At St Paul's he organized classes in English and scripture for members of the Chinese community. Friends knew him as an entertaining conversationalist, witty, quick at repartee and capable of deep indignation. He won repute throughout the whole district for his liberality and concern for those who suffered. A pronounced Evangelical, he returned each year to the text of his first sermon : 'For I determined not to know anything among you save Jesus Christ and Him crucified'.

Ill health marred the last years of Mac-Cullagh's ministry but he continued to hold the community's affection and respect. When he died at Hawksburn on 24 September 1917 he was almost penniless; for years he had given his income to those who needed it. He was buried in the Lancefield cemetery beside his wife.

Church of England Messenger (Vic), 20 Oct, 1, 29 Dec 1916, 26 Jan, 27 July, 5 Oct 1917; *Lancefield Chronicle*, 28 Oct, 4 Nov 1870; *Australasian*, 21 June 1902; *Argus*, 25 Sept 1917; *Bendigo Advertiser*, 25 Sept 1917; *Lancefield Mercury*, 28 Sept 1917; Registrar's book, Bishop Perry's letter-books (Melb Diocesan Registry).

N. G. CURRY

McCULLOCH, GEORGE (1848-1907), station manager, was born on 22 April 1848 in Glasgow, Scotland, son of James McCulloch, contractor. Educated at High School and at the Andersonian University, Glasgow, he followed pastoral pursuits in Mexico and elsewhere with little success before arriving at Sydney in the 1870s. His uncle, James McCulloch [q.v.], appointed him manager of McCulloch, Sellar & Co.'s Mount Gipps station, near Broken Hill, with an eighth share of the profits; it was a well-developed property of 540,000 acres with

71,000 sheep in 1877. In 1895 a report on the station criticized McCulloch's management but by then years of low rainfall had made the earlier optimism about country west of the Darling seem extravagant.

When Charles Rasp [q.v.] pegged a claim at Broken Hill in September 1883, McCulloch advised the formation of a syndicate and extension of the claim. Influenced by William Jamieson, a government surveyor who bought into the venture, McCulloch retained his share through tiresome months of uncertainty as the claim was explored. He once played euchre with a visiting Englishman to determine the price of a fourteenth share. McCulloch lost, parted with the share at £120 but later bought an equivalent one for £90. He dominated the small syndicate of station employees and adhered to the formalities of the mining regulations. As the syndicate widened he organized it into the Broken Hill Mining Co. and chose a manager. Favourable assay reports led to the need of more capital and the Broken Hill Proprietary Co. Ltd was floated in August 1885. McCulloch became a provisional director and was chairman of the local committee in 1886-88. In 1887 he went to London to float the British B.H.P. Co. with William Knox and again in 1890-91. He was a director of the B.H.P. Co. Ltd on the local, Melbourne and London boards, and of other mining companies including those associated with B.H.P. and the Mount Lyell Mining and Railway Co. Shrewd with shares, he won great wealth from the Western Australian goldfields. In 1892 he became chairman of directors of the B.H.P. Co. Ltd and was the uncompromising president of the Barrier Ranges Mining Association during the eighteen-week strike. When it ended he assured shareholders that they had all striven for the principles of 'freedom of contract and the right to manage the mine as we please, irrespective of unions and union agitators'. In 1893 McCulloch returned to London and on 11 May at the Strand Register Office married Mary Agnes Mayger, widowed daughter of William Smith, miner.

Strongwilled and straightforward, even blunt, McCulloch was large in build and had delighted in feats of strength and practical jokes when at Mount Gipps. At Broken Hill he had donated works to the Art Gallery and money to the hospital. In London he gathered a fine collection of pictures and sculpture which he displayed in four salons. He restricted himself to contemporary works and was especially attracted by the work of Millais. He also had a hall of sculptures including some by Rodin, but perhaps his art selection revealed prudent investment as much as taste. After a long illness he died at his home, 184 Queen's Gate, London, on

12 December 1907. He was survived by his wife to whom he left over £436,000. By his will of 5 January 1904 he directed that if she predeceased him the estate was to pass to her son Alexander McCulloch but should he die without issue it was to revert to the Crown for charitable, educational and national purposes.

R. Bridges, *From silver to steel* (Melb, 1920); G. Blainey, *The rise of Broken Hill* (Melb, 1968); B. Hardy, *West of the Darling* (Melb, 1969); *BHP Recreation Review*, 16 Dec 1925; *Barrier Miner*, 14 Dec 1907; BHP Co. reports, chairman's address 25 Jan 1893 (ML); Broken Hill Mining Co. minute books (ML).

BRUCE PENNAY

McCULLOCH, SIR JAMES (1819-1893), politician, was born at Glasgow, Scotland, son of George McCulloch. After primary education perhaps augmented in Germany, he entered the mercantile house of J. & A. Dennistoun. As junior partner he arrived at Melbourne in the *Adelaide* in 1853 to open a branch with Robert Sellar. When it closed in 1862 McCulloch, Sellar & Co. was formed in connexion with Leishman, Inglis & Co. of Leith. In 1856-57 and 1862-63 McCulloch was president of the Melbourne Chamber of Commerce; he was also a local director of the London Chartered Bank. In his last two years in Glasgow he had been collector of the Trades House, an influential educational and charitable institution, and in Melbourne he supported such charities and public causes as the Benevolent Asylum, the Melbourne Hospital and the St Kilda volunteers.

McCulloch was nominated to the Legislative Council in September 1854 and in 1856 was elected to the Legislative Assembly for Wimmera, after being defeated for Melbourne. He formed part of the liberal-mercantile group which helped to defeat W. C. Haines [q.v.] in March 1857 and J. O'Shanassy [q.v.] in April. McCulloch was invited to form the next ministry and attempted to unite all the leaders; O'Shanassy refused but Haines became chief secretary with McCulloch as commissioner for trade and customs. After the ministry fell in March 1858 he visited Britain, returning early in 1859. At that year's general elections he won East Melbourne in October, and became treasurer in the liberal-mercantile cabinet of W. Nicholson [q.v.]; after its defeat in November 1860 he again visited Britain. He returned in December 1861 and won the Mornington by-election next February. He also entered the St Kilda council, on which he served until 1864. Parties had been polarized at the 1861 general elections roughly along class lines with R. Heales's

[q.v.] radicals against the bourgeoisie and pastoralists. McCulloch supported the latter who were ruled by O'Shanassy. Early in 1863, however, he became restive at the fiasco of C. G. Duffy's [q.v.] 1862 Land Act which was too radical for his taste, perhaps at Duffy's personality and eventually at aspects of the ministry's financial policy. McCulloch regarded Duffy's proposed legislation to raise pastoral rents as 'repudiation'; moreover his firm was buying squattages in north-east Victoria as well as New South Wales. The ministry fell and in alliance with Heales, McCulloch became premier and chief secretary in June; in May 1864 he also became postmaster-general. Portfolios were divided equally between Healesites and liberal bourgeois, but the talent of the latter, who included G. Higinbotham, A. Michie and J. G. Francis [qq.v.], gave them the predominance. O'Shanassy refused to join, expecting the coalition to collapse, but it ruled almost continuously until 1871.

Land remained the major problem. The Legislative Council rejected Heales's bills in 1863 and early 1864 demanding a return to auction. McCulloch therefore made land policy the centre of the coming elections, followed by reform of the council. Before the poll in October-November he had to tackle two external problems. In 1863 a royal commission in London had recommended the increase of transportation to Western Australia and there were rumours of plans for new penal stations in Queensland and North Australia. McCulloch first tried moderation in a solemn parliamentary remonstrance but this was rejected. He then took vigorous action, deporting expirees arriving from the west, demanding total abolition and threatening to cancel the mail subsidy if steamers continued to call at Perth and arranging an intercolonial conference to try to concert measures. Britain gave way and thereby established him as a national leader in Victoria. A similar result emerged from the border duties question; although negotiations failed and customs houses reappeared along the Murray in September, to remain until 1867, he was again firm in asserting Victoria's interests. The border duties question, exacerbated by increasing differences between Victorian and neighbouring tariffs with the attendant risks of large-scale smuggling, led McCulloch to add 'tariff revision', which he had supported in 1859, to his platform. The Healesite commitment to it, and the protectionist views of Francis and several others of his more conservative supporters, increased the pressure. The element of protection was minimal and McCulloch rightly called it a revenue tariff, but it became the centre of a political battle which raised protection from the creed of the few to the policy of the many, by association with a struggle against the council.

The election was dominated by the land bill presented, Heales having died, by J. M. Grant [q.v.]. McCulloch won overwhelmingly and, although the council rejected his reform bill, it dared not refuse the land bill. When the tariff details were revealed in January 1865, the council prepared to stand firm. Businessmen denounced the tariff as ruinous and protectionist squatters wanted to defeat the ministry to stop Grant's vigorous administration of the Land Act. McCulloch followed a recent English precedent and tacked the tariff to the appropriation bill, which the council could not amend; it could, and did, reject it in July. Expedients had to be found for enforcing the new duties and making payments. For the latter the government borrowed money and confessed judgment when sued; as sole local director of the London Chartered Bank McCulloch's part was crucial for all other banks refused to lend the money.

The council had polarized politics and made McCulloch's preferred methods of compromise and consensus impossible. The basis of his support shifted rapidly leftwards. A new radical tone was set by the vigorous agitation of his supporters and Higinbotham's oratory. McCulloch began to use the radical device of the party caucus for management and discipline. When the council rejected an attempt to pass the tariff separately, McCulloch obtained a dissolution. In the election the free trade opposition was almost annihilated. The council still refused to pass the tacked measures and McCulloch resigned. As T. H. Fellows [q.v.] could not form a government and the expected imperial intervention was delayed, he resumed office and negotiated a compromise in April.

After a long recess McCulloch was confronted with difficulties in 1867. Several protectionists rebelled and his control of parliament weakened. However, the Darling grant crisis began in July and restored party discipline. Governor Sir Charles Darling had been recalled for becoming a ministerial partisan in 1866; the assembly had voted £20,000 to his wife but colonial regulations forbade acceptance. However, Darling had left the service and accepted the grant. McCulloch, committed politically and regarding it as a matter of honour, put it on the supplementary estimates. It was the least provocative method, and not a tack, but it could not be discussed coolly, still less separated out for the council to reject. The council therefore refused appropriations again in October. General elections followed in January-February 1868 on the inclusion of the grant in estimates. McCulloch's

victory was again overwhelming but in March he resigned because Downing Street had forbidden the governor to reintroduce the grant except as a separate measure. Charles Sladen [q.v.] eventually formed a minority ministry in May but, although some wavered, McCulloch's discipline held and his 'Loyal Liberals' or 'old hats' effectively halted parliamentary business. Others maintained the uproar and formed the powerful Loyal Liberal Reform Association, but the crisis collapsed in July because Darling had re-entered the colonial service and was granted an imperial pension.

McCulloch then formed his most radical cabinet but his choice angered many supporters whom he had not consulted. Some, like Higinbotham who joined the ministry reluctantly and was soon to leave it, resented the indecisive outcome of the crisis. Radical discontent increased in 1869 with land scandals and the continuation of squatting tenure in Grant's land bill; McCulloch's grasp suffered from being treasurer as well as chief secretary. He filled a vacant office from outside parliament and was defeated in September, but J. A. MacPherson's [q.v.] ministry lasted only until April 1870. As chief secretary again, McCulloch formed a moderate ministry which included MacPherson; radical disillusionment spread further. Symbolically, he had just become a K.B. Few opposed him actively, however. He at last achieved an old aim in abolishing state aid to religion, and although he had no time to pass his secular education bill he made it the main issue at the 1871 elections. However, falling revenue and the special appropriation of £200,000 from land revenue to railway construction which he had inserted in the 1869 Land Act, made increased taxation inevitable. Although Francis was treasurer the means were McCulloch's as much as his. The moderate increase in maximum duties to 12½ per cent affronted both protectionists and free traders, and a property tax alienated many of the uncommitted new members. His party split and McCulloch fell in June; he resigned his seat in March 1872 and left for England, where he acted as agent-general from January to April 1873 and was appointed K.C.M.G. in 1874. He returned to Victoria for the general election of March-April and won Warrnambool. Although his party, reunited soon after his departure to England, was now ruling in a coalition under Francis, he formed a private faction. When Francis was replaced by G. B. Kerferd [q.v.] and difficulties arose over financial policy he helped to defeat it. Immediately, however, he helped Kerferd to overthrow G. Berry's [q.v.] radical ministry on its land tax proposals and in October became treasurer and premier with half the

Kerferd cabinet. He tried in vain to settle the revenue question with a combination of direct taxes and was harassed by Berry's 'stonewall', overcome only by the 'iron hand' or closure. Berry, using McCulloch's former weapons of caucus and external organization against him, agitated for a progressive land tax, successfully but inaccurately branding McCulloch as a reactionary. In the elections of May 1877 he was crushed. He resigned office without meeting parliament, took little part in the constitutional crisis which Berry brought on and resigned his seat in May 1878.

McCulloch then concentrated on business, including directorships of several insurance and other companies, the Bank of New South Wales as well as the London Chartered, and was active in establishing the frozen meat trade. He also served as trustee of the Public Library, Museums and National Gallery in 1870-86. He left for Britain early in 1886 and lived at Garbrand Hall in Ewell, Surrey, until he died on 31 January 1893. He had no children, although twice married: first, in 1841 to Susan, daughter of Rev. James Renwick of Muirton, Scotland; and second, on 17 October 1867 to Margaret Boak, daughter of his associate, William Inglis of Dumbartonshire.

McCulloch was the merchant-politician *par excellence*, honest, vigorous and a capable financier who regarded Victoria as a business venture to be run by the most capable board of directors possible, whatever their politics, preferably under himself. His instinct for compromise was matched by his ferocious determination, both supported by great skill in manoeuvre and power in debate. His politics were always liberal, his policies remarkably consistent. He was instrumental in passing numerous reforms, notably on the land question, and in paving the way for protection, direct taxation and secular education. He was feared and admired rather than loved but had few peers as an effective politician.

C. G. Duffy, *My life in two hemispheres*, 2 (Lond, 1898); G. Serle, *The golden age* (Melb, 1963); G. M. Dow, *George Higinbotham: church and state* (Melb, 1964); M. Clarke, 'The Victorian political deadlocks',VHM, 13 (1928-29); W. T. Charles, 'The Victorian Protection Movement', VHM, 14 (1931-32); G. Bartlett, 'The political orders of Victoria and New South Wales 1856-1890', *Aust Economic Hist Review*, Mar 1968; *Argus*, 20 Aug 1859, 4 Feb 1893; *Leader* (Melb), 27 June 1863; *Weekly Times* (Melb), 4 Feb 1893; *Illustrated Aust News*, 1 Mar 1893; F. K. Crowley, Aspects of the constitutional conflicts . . . Victorian legislature 1864-1868 (M.A. thesis, Univ Melb, 1947); G. Bartlett, Political organization and society in Victoria 1864-1883 (Ph.D. thesis, ANU, 1964).   GEOFFREY BARTLETT

McCULLOCH, JAMES (1841-1904), businessman, was the third brother of William McCulloch [q.v.]. Educated at Douglas Academy, Newton-Stewart, he migrated to Melbourne in 1863 and joined the carrying company named after and directed by William. James worked first in Castlemaine but early in 1865 was sent to Echuca to open a branch of the firm. Although capital and guidance came from the Melbourne headquarters, James's energy, persuasiveness and diplomacy helped him to negotiate contracts with squatters for the carriage of their wool clips. He also acquired a small fleet of riverboats and barges. The company soon commanded most of the forwarding business from stores and offices opposite the wharf. On 27 February 1867 James married Alice Bolton, only daughter of Henry Hopwood [q.v.].

McCulloch visited Europe in 1873 and then settled in Melbourne to help his brother with the rapidly expanding company. He was a member of the board of directors and played a major role in its success. When business declined in the 1880s, James played a crucial role in attempting a merger with Wright, Heaton & Co. of Sydney and joined their board of directors. After William stepped down as director of his company in 1886, James carried on as the key member and was finally succcessful in merging with Wright, Heaton & Co. in 1898. The McCulloch Carrying Co. became the Victorian subsidiary, and James remained a director until 1904. He also had large interests in the Colonial Mutual Fire Insurance Co. and the Outtrim Coal Co., serving on their boards.

McCulloch drove into Melbourne each day from his home, Barholm, Oakleigh, where he bred Jersey cattle famous for the quantity and quality of their milk and for butter production. His pedigreed herd began with a bull and seven cows selected for him in 1888 by William in England and said to be the finest ever to leave the country. Three cows calved on the voyage to Melbourne. In 1889 McCulloch first showed his Jerseys in Melbourne and won first prize for a cow in milk. He later won many awards; for example, eight firsts and several other prizes at the Royal Melbourne Show in 1900. Descendants of his stock were scattered throughout Australasia. McCulloch was a member and sometime councillor of the Royal Agricultural Society and in municipal affairs at Oakleigh served as a shire councillor. Predeceased by his wife in 1895, he died on 9 June 1904; they had no children. A staunch member of the Australian Church, his funeral service was conducted by Dr Strong [q.v.].

J. Smith (ed), *Cyclopedia of Victoria*, 1 (Melb, 1903); I. Mudie, *Riverboats* (Melb, 1965); S. Priestley, *Echuca: a centenary history* (Brisb, 1965); A. Morris, *Rich river*, 2nd ed (Colac, 1970); McCulloch Carrying Co. papers (LaT L).   SAMUEL CLYDE McCULLOCH

McCULLOCH, WILLIAM (1832-1909), businessman, pastoralist and politician, was born on 22 October 1832 in Wigtonshire, Scotland, eldest son of Samuel McCulloch, laird of Chippermore, and his wife Helen, née McWhinnie. In 1852 he migrated to Victoria to try his luck at the Mount Alexander goldfields. He soon turned to store-keeping and later travelled for McEwan & Co., one of the largest importers in Melbourne. The slow growth of railways prompted him to become a carrier and forwarding agent and to found the firm which became the largest of its kind in Australia. In 1860 he went to Europe and in 1861 married Catherine Vance Agnew, younger daughter of Colin Christison of Barglass, Scotland.

McCulloch returned to Victoria and opened a carrying business at Woodend but soon moved the headquarters of the McCulloch Carrying Co. to Melbourne. Within fifteen years the company had twenty branch offices throughout Victoria, Riverina and South Australia, owned five Murray riverboats and was agent for about ten more and negotiated contracts with graziers on the Murray, Murrumbidgee and Darling Rivers. The Riverina trade was funnelled into Echuca, the company's biggest branch office, to be forwarded by rail to Melbourne. McCulloch was also a founder and director of the Moama-Deniliquin railway, opened in 1876. Railways later threatened to undermine his business and he relinquished leadership of the company in 1886. His younger brother James [q.v.] helped to direct the company until it merged with Wright, Heaton & Co. in 1898.

From 1870 William successively owned three properties close to Melbourne and invested heavily in stud cattle, sheep and horses imported from Europe. He specialized in Clydesdale horses, and his foundation stock of Shorthorns consisted of a dozen cows from the best herds in England. Later purchases were Pink 11th, one of whose calves brought 590 guineas, the bull Rapid bought from Lady Pigot for 1000 guineas in England, and Grand Duchess of Oxford bought for 2100 guineas in 1878. That year McCulloch spent £30,000 in England on prize and blood stock for seventeen animals. He claimed to have spent fully two years in 'a critical examination of the leading herds, and in attending every Shorthorn sale of importance'. In the 1880s he became interested in sheep and acquired Mertoun Park, a property near Colac. In 1886 he bought Warbreccan, 63,000 acres near Deniliquin, and in 1889 Woodlands, nearly 56,000 acres near Ararat and 'one of the most imposing country homes in Victoria', built in 1869 by John Wilson. A prominent supporter of coursing, he won the Victorian Waterloo Cup in 1874 with Royal Water. Ten years later he owned Monsoon, the runner-up, and Cumloden which won many matches. A great patron of the turf, he imported the best strains of English blood, amongst them Caiman and Pilgrim's Progress, sire of the Caulfield Cup winner, Lieutenant Bill, in 1902.

McCulloch represented Lonsdale Ward in the Melbourne City Council in 1872-76. Though pressed to accept the office of mayor, he declined since he wanted to visit Europe for health and business reasons. In 1880-1903 he represented Eastern (Gippsland) Province in the Legislative Council. He made few speeches but when debating argued quietly, briefly and yet diplomatically. He spoke his mind, was not afraid to make clear and positive recommendations and was especially knowledgeable about sheep, cattle, rabbits, railways, horse-racing, betting and women's suffrage. He was pro-Federation. A moderate in most issues, he was willing to listen cautiously to all sides but adamant when sure of his ground. In 1890 he was a prominent founder of the Pastoralists' Union in Victoria.

In 1895 McCulloch was appointed minister of defence in George Turner's first administration and as a cabinet member spoke more often, shepherding his share of bills through the chamber. When the Boer war broke out he organized and dispatched the first Victorian contingent. His loyal enthusiasm overrode all opposition. His transport work so impressed the governments of Tasmania, South Australia and Western Australia that they transferred all the transit arrangements of their contingents to the Victorian government. In 1901 he chaired the celebrations committee for the duke of York who opened the Federal parliament. He was minister of defence and health in the second Turner administration, and minister of public works and health in A. J. Peacock's cabinet until June 1902, when he was appointed to represent Victoria at Edward VII's coronation and to reorganize the office of the Victorian agent-general in London. In that year he was appointed C.M.G. He resigned from the Legislative Council in 1903 to run for the federal Senate but lost and retired to Woodlands, where he died on 4 April 1909. Predeceased by his wife in 1894, he was survived by three sons and three daughters.

Although delicate as a youth, McCulloch was tall and handsome, with very blue eyes and a well-clipped beard. Described in the press as accessible, genial and warm-hearted, he 'was always associated with integrity, honesty and probity' and 'charitable to a fault'. A staunch member of the Australian Church, he was one of the guarantors for its debt and Dr Strong [q.v.] preached at his funeral.

M. H. Ellis, *The beef shorthorn in Australia* (Syd, 1932); A. Henderson (ed), *Early pioneer families of Victoria and Riverina* (Melb, 1936); I. Mudie, *Riverboats* (Melb, 1965); S. Priestley, *Echuca: a centenary history* (Brisb, 1965); A. Morris, *Rich river*, 2nd ed (Colac, 1970); PD and V&P (LC Vic), 1880-1903; *Australasian*, 12 Feb 1881; *Argus*, 5 Apr 1909; McCulloch Carrying Co. papers (LaT L).

SAMUEL CLYDE MCCULLOCH

MACDEVITT, EDWARD O'DONNELL (1845-1898), barrister and politician, was born at Glenties, County Donegal, Ireland, son of Donald MacDevitt, barrister, and his wife Mary, née O'Donnell. He had some theological training but finished his education in law. Without being called to the Bar he left Ireland, probably invited by Bishop James Quinn [q.v.] with whom he arrived at Melbourne in the *Donald Mackay* on 20 March 1861. He soon moved to Brisbane, taught school for a time and probably on Quinn's behalf edited the *North Australian* at Ipswich. He was admitted a barrister in the Supreme Court on 20 February 1864 and built up a practice in Brisbane.

In 1864-65 MacDevitt was active in the campaign against secular education and in 1866-67 practised in Sydney. Soon after his return to Brisbane in 1868 he became a public figure by his unsuccessful defence of T. J. Griffin [q.v.] at Rockhampton. He practised mainly in northern courts and nominated for the Rockhampton seat in December 1869 but withdrew, seeing that only a local candidate could win. In September 1870 he was elected member for Kennedy on a northern separation platform. When the northern seats were redistributed MacDevitt won the new mining seat of Ravenswood on 29 December 1873. He had been prominent in the liberal obstruction campaign of 1872 and, probably on the advice of Charles Lilley [q.v.], was chosen by Arthur Macalister [q.v.] as attorney-general in preference to Samuel Griffith. Though a good speaker, MacDevitt was a poor administrator and was easily shown up by Griffith as a failure in office. He vainly

opposed the government's bill for abolishing denominational schools and in July 1874 sought appointment to the Supreme Court. When offered instead the bench of the Metropolitan District Court, he resigned his office and seat on 3 August and returned to Ireland.

While passing through America MacDevitt reported to the Queensland government on railways and in England served as a migration lecturer. In 1878 he was appointed one of three Queensland commissioners to the Paris Exhibition. He settled in Dublin to practise in land cases and after the Land Act was passed in 1881 published two technical pamphlets explaining it. He served as a legal assistant of the Irish Land Commission in 1881-89 and claimed to have been confidential emissary from the Irish government to the British cabinet. In Ireland he married Katie Power; they had one son and two daughters.

In 1890 MacDevitt returned to Australia and settled in Melbourne where he published a *Manual of the Melbourne and Metropolitan Board of Works Act* (1891). He went to Western Australia in 1896 and practised in Kalgoorlie, publishing his *Guide to the Goldfields' Act 1895* as a means of gaining attention. He was commissioned by the colonial government to edit a *Handbook of Western Australia* (1897). In August he was made secretary to a royal commission on mining but the appointment was inexplicably withdrawn a few days later. In January 1898 MacDevitt went to Melbourne for a holiday. During a heatwave he was learning to ride a bicycle but collapsed suddenly on 4 February and died in a Malvern street.

C. A. Bernays, *Queensland politics during sixty years* (Brisb, 1919); V&P (LA Qld), 1873, 185; PP (GB), 1882, 55, 287, 1889, 61, 679; *Brisbane Courier*, 18 Mar, 17 Sept 1864, 9-11 Jan 1865, 13 Dec 1869, 3 Sept 1870, 20 May 1872, 4 Aug 1874; *Port Denison Times*, 6, 13, 27 Aug, 10 Sept 1870; *Qld Times*, 11 Aug 1874; *Freeman's J* (Dublin), 8 Nov 1881, 11 Jan 1882; *Kalgoorlie Western Argus*, 10 Feb 1898; *Australasian*, 7 May 1898; *Daily Mail* (Brisb), 24 Aug 1907; S. W. Griffith diary, 8 Jan 1874 (Dixson Lib, Syd); Mines Dept 4458/97 (Battye Lib, Perth); Roll of Barristers (NSWA and QA).

H. J. GIBBNEY

MACDONALD, ALEXANDER CAMERON (1828-1917), accountant, surveyor and geographer, was born on 9 August 1828 at Campbelltown, New South Wales, third of the twelve children of Alexander Macdonald, grazier, and his wife Sarah, née Warby. At the local school he was awarded by Governor Gipps a set of mathematical instruments but soon left to help his father. In 1847-48 he made three trips to the Port

144

Phillip District with livestock and then had charge of 600 horses on Peechelba station near Wangaratta. In 1849 he joined Edward Barnett's survey party near Glenrowan and quickly mastered the craft. At Geelong in 1850 he became assistant and then partner of the surveyor, Charles Rowand, mostly in laying out the town. In the gold rush Macdonald went to Ballarat and had some success at Fryer's Creek but soon returned to Geelong. In 1852 he married Margaret Rainy, third daughter of Gilbert Robertson [q.v.].

Macdonald called himself an accountant but also practised as a surveyor, speculated in land and in his auction rooms sold many suburban subdivisions. In 1855 he helped to found the Geelong and Western District Agricultural and Horticultural Society and served for years as its honorary secretary and treasurer. He also helped to promote the Geelong Society of Architects, Surveyors and Civil Engineers, the Colonial Bank of Australasia in 1856 and the establishment of vineyards along the Barwon and Moorabool Rivers; later he became a trustee of the Geelong Vineyard Co. He was elected unopposed to the Geelong Town Council in 1857 and for a second term. He was involved in extending the railway to Colac and the Western District, and in 1870 became secretary of the local Railway League. He won wide repute for his energy and probity. His many agencies included the Provident Institute of Victoria, which was 'founded on a proprietary capital in shares'. In 1855 Macdonald discovered that no money had been subscribed and his correspondence with the managing director found its way into the press, with the result that the institute collapsed and at least one of its executives was convicted. In 1880 Macdonald drew public attention to two other bubble companies with similar effects. In 1871 and 1874 he had been persuaded to contest the seats of South Grant and Geelong East in the Victorian Legislative Assembly, but his free trade views were unpopular and he lost both elections.

In 1862 Macdonald had invested heavily in a company designed to search scientifically for gold in the Geelong district, and in 1860 became a director of the Fyansford Gold Mining Co. These and other speculations collapsed in the severe depression in the late 1860s. In 1876 he moved to Melbourne as a manager of companies, estate and financial agent and surveyor. Australian by birth, he wanted his country to know its origins and history. He was already recognized as an authority on Aboriginal place names and customs and had compiled a vocabulary of their words and meanings. He had also met such prominent Australian

explorers as Sturt and Mitchell [qq.v.] and enjoyed the friendship of Gregory, Landsborough, Giles, Tietkins [qq.v.] and Forrest. However, Macdonald became best known for his knowledge of Australian geography.

In October 1851 Macdonald had made a sketch map of the Ballarat goldfield, a copy of which is in the local School of Mines. He also compiled a large *Map of the Colony of New South Wales* (Melbourne, 1883). His wide travels took him sometimes far into central Australia. In 1886-98 he was active in promoting committees for exploring Antarctica, though the plans were premature. In 1896 his report on the Australian milk and butter industry had been translated and published in Cape Town. Probably his most important accomplishment was with the Victorian branch of the Royal Geographical Society of Australasia. Prompted by Sir Edward Strickland [q.v.] Macdonald helped to form the society in 1883 and served for twenty-three years as honorary secretary, treasurer and sometime editor and librarian. He played a part in instituting other branches of the society in New South Wales and South Australia, and organized interprovincial geographical conferences at Melbourne in 1884 and Adelaide in 1887. He read many papers on geographical science to the Australasian Association for the Advancement of Science and was president of the geography section at the Adelaide congress in 1893 and vice-president twice later. He had been elected a fellow of the Royal Geographical Society, London, in 1885, and later became a member of the Royal Scottish Geographical Society and the society in Lisbon. As a member of the Victorian branch of the British Astronomical Society he contributed two papers, one on the great comet he had witnessed in 1843. His many other memberships included scientific and historical societies, the Victorian Institute of Accountants and the Australasian Institute of Bankers. He was also a magistrate for Queensland.

At 72 Macdonald was described as 'a fine, stalwart specimen of an Australian' with 'a mind as bright as ever and his energy undiminished'. He continued to write extensively on Australian subjects until he died at his home, Erewhon, Prahran, on 18 June 1917. His burial in St Kilda cemetery was conducted by Rev. Charles Strong [q.v.] of the Australian Church in which Macdonald had been very prominent from the beginning.

H. M. Humphreys (ed), *Men of the time in Australia: Victorian series*, 1st ed (Melb, 1878); R. A. Swan, *Australia in the Antarctic* (Melb, 1961); Bankers Inst of A'sia, J, Dec 1900; *Vic Geog J*, 23-24 (1905-06), 33 (1917); *Argus*, 19 June 1917.   COLIN MACDONALD*

MACDONALD, ALEXANDER ROSE (1845-1931), civil servant, was born on 24 March 1845 in Inverness-shire, Scotland, son of Rev. Dr Donald Macdonald and his wife Ann, née Rose. He was educated at Inverness Academy and the Grammar Schools in the Old Town and New Town of Aberdeen. In 1860-64 he attended the University of Aberdeen, where he held a bursary of £10 a year, passed in 'classics' with a gold medal in Greek but did not take a degree. In 1870 he went to Queensland with his brother James and £5000 each from their father. The brothers invested in a 640-acre sugar plantation called Inverness, near Mackay. James broke down and in March 1875 they were declared insolvent, with debts of over £10,000. In July 1878 their certificate of discharge was granted and Alexander went droving on the Palmer. On 3 November 1880 at the Presbyterian Church, Mackay, he married Nancy Armitage.

In December 1881 Macdonald was appointed immigration agent at Mackay and inspector of Pacific Islanders. His sympathy for the Kanakas led to stories that he was twice shipwrecked taking them back to the islands. He certainly took every opportunity to send sick Kanakas to their island homes. In 1883 he inquired into charges made in the Melbourne *Leader* and *Age* by George Ernest Morrison against the captain and crew of the recruiting ship *Lavinia*. Macdonald questioned Morrison's veracity and concluded that 'a person of such very remarkable imaginative powers can, no doubt, with equal readiness and ease conjure up scenes that no eye has ever beheld outside of hell; and this record of the "Lavinia's" voyage must surely be one of those unhealthy visions'. He was backed by Samuel Griffith. Despite his acknowledged zeal, he was criticized by E. W. Docker in *The Blackbirders* (Sydney, 1970) for his failure to find any reason than change of climate for the death of twenty-five New Irelanders on the Colonial Sugar Refining Co.'s Homebush plantation.

In August 1888 Macdonald became police magistrate, assistant land agent and district registrar at Aramac. Next year he moved to Eidsvold where he was also gold warden and mineral lands commissioner. In 1891-93 he held the latter office for Palmer while police magistrate, acting land commissioner and assistant land agent at Maytown. In 1893-95 he was stationed at Herberton and was also visiting justice for the police gaol. In 1895 he was posted to Charters Towers and in 1896 to Georgetown.

On 1 November 1899 Macdonald became under-secretary for the Department of Mines and gold warden for Brisbane. His experience as a gold warden and mineral lands commissioner gave him a wide knowledge of mining in many parts of Queensland. With help from the parliamentary draftsman he drew up the Mining Act of 1901. Although amended, the Act has remained the basis of Queensland's mining legislation. He resigned on 24 March 1915. In his long retirement he often regaled his descendants with tales of the mining fields and the Pacific islands. He died on 21 December 1931 at Greenslopes and was buried in the Toowong cemetery, survived by four daughters and three of his five sons. His descendants live on both sides of the world.

V&P (LA Qld), 1883-84, 1435; Qld Government Mining J, 15 Jan 1932; Insolvency papers (QA); family information.   A. C. CROMBIE

MacDONALD, CHARLES (1851-1903) and WILLIAM NEIL (1860-1910), overlanders and pastoralists, were sons of Donald MacDonald and his wife Anne, née McAllum. Their father had migrated to Sydney from the Isle of Skye and their mother from Mull; they were married in the parish of Goulburn on 10 July 1849. Charles was born on 5 October 1851 and William Neil on 21 September 1860. The family moved to Clifford's Creek, Laggan, and the brothers became expert bushmen.

Inspired by Alexander Forrest's report in 1879 on the possibilities of the Kimberley district, the brothers were joined by two MacKenzie cousins, Peter Thomson, James McGeorge and Jasper Pickles. They set out from Laggan on 26 March 1883 with 500 cattle, 2 teams of bullocks and 50 horses on one of the longest droving trips across the continent. In north-western New South Wales the herd was increased by 500. Drought conditions delayed progress and most of the original party withdrew long before Cooper's Creek was reached. Stock losses were replaced, only to be reduced again by the continued drought. The brothers pushed on slowly into the Northern Territory and in 1885 arrived at the Katherine, where Charles became ill and had to be taken home via Darwin, leaving William to continue the journey with the remaining cattle. After eleven months of hardship and trouble with marauding Aboriginals, William arrived on 3 June 1886 at the junction of the Victoria and Margaret Rivers, where he took up land and named it Fossil Downs. Rejoined by Charles, the partnership developed into what was to become the largest privately-owned cattle station in Australia, over a million acres.

Charles died a bachelor at Goulburn on 30 August 1903 but requested that William's heir be called Kimberley after the district they had developed. At Goulburn on 30 April 1902 William married Ida Oliver and took her to live at Ingleside, Knox Street, Derby, Western Australia, where a son was born on 26 July 1903. William died on 16 July 1910 at the Waverley Hospital in Perth.

The two MacDonalds were noted for their kindness and hospitality and highly respected for their courage and endurance during the overlanding epic of 3500 miles and their pioneering work at Fossil Downs. The property was still held by the family in 1973.

C. McAlister, *Old pioneering days in the sunny south* (Goulburn, 1907); G. Buchanan, *Packhorse and waterhole* (Syd, 1933); M. Durack, *Kings in grass castles* (Lond, 1959); Goulburn & District Hist Soc, *Bulletin*, Sept 1972.   WENDY BIRMAN

McDONNELL, PERCY STANISLAUS (1860-1896), cricketer and broker, was born on 13 November 1860 in London, son of Morgan Augustus McDonnell (1824-1889), barrister, and his wife Frances Marie, née Bonham. In 1864 the family migrated to Melbourne and in 1868 Morgan was elected for Villiers and Heytesbury to the Legislative Assembly, serving as attorney-general under Sladen [q.v.] in 1868 and MacPherson [q.v.] in 1869-70.

McDonnell was educated at St Patrick's College, where he was a prodigy at cricket and a fine footballer. After an inauspicious début in intercolonial cricket in 1878, in which he got 'a pair' against New South Wales, he soon became one of the fastest scoring batsmen in Australian cricket. In 1878-85 he batted seventeen times for Victoria with an average of 30.31. For New South Wales from 1885 he batted fifteen times at 38.21. In 1886 at Melbourne he scored 236 of the New South Wales total of 363.

McDonnell toured England in 1880, 1882, 1884 and as captain in 1888. With 418 runs at 23.22 he was second to W. L. Murdoch [q.v.] in 1880 and again in 1884, with 1225 runs at 23.25. He headed the batting in 1888 with 1393 runs at 22.83. In nineteen tests against England he scored 958 runs at 29, with three centuries and a highest score of 147. One of his best innings was against the north of England in 1888 when, on a sticky wicket, he scored 82 in 55 minutes in a partnership of 86 with A. Bannerman [q.v.]. In 1884 against England at Adelaide he scored 124 and 83, his batting described 'as

unsurpassed for finish, power and complete command over the best of English bowling'. In all his first-class cricket he scored 6460 runs at an average of 23 and is reckoned one of the great Australian batsmen.

McDonnell died of cardiac failure at Brisbane on 24 September 1896 and was buried in the Roman Catholic section of Toowong cemetery. He was survived by two sons and his wife Grace, née McDonald, whom he had married at Sydney on 8 April 1891.

Town and Country J, 5 Oct 1889; *Australasian*, 26 Sept 1896.   IAN JOHNSON

MacDONNELL, RANDAL (1830-1877), educationist, was born in Dublin, son of Thomas MacDonnell, army officer, and his wife Frances, née Corry. Trained in Dublin at the National Model School, he arrived at Sydney in the *Telegraph* on 22 September 1853. For some months he taught in the National schools of Sydney but in 1854 established his own non-sectarian private high school in Paddington. He moved to Queensland in 1860 and was appointed by the Board of National Education as inspector of National schools on 26 June; after the Education Act was passed he became general inspector of primary schools in December. In 1870 his tasks were increased by the added duties as secretary of the Board of General Education after Robert Bourne died. He held both these offices until the State Education Act was passed in 1875. He was then appointed the first general inspector of the new Department of Public Instruction. In that year he made a tour of educational institutions in the southern colonies but little came of it because of disagreement about his duties with Samuel Griffith, the first secretary of the department.

MacDonnell resigned on 30 March 1876. As a justice of the peace, he was said to have been courteous, gentle and highly respected but always involved in controversy. Although a sincere Roman Catholic, he was noted for his anticlericalism and clashed openly on religious and educational issues with Archbishop Polding and Bishop Quinn [qq.v.]. In the turbulent early years of Queensland MacDonnell was prominent in the conflict between the denominations and the state over aid to non-vested schools and the place of religious teaching in education. He advocated the separation of religious and secular education, and never wavered from his stand that the Irish National system was the best compromise. Because of his Irish background and Catholic beliefs he was subject to bitter attacks by the Anglican bishop, E. W. Tufnell [q.v.]. He was also unfortunately identified with another Randal MacDonnell who published the pro-Quinn *North Australian*.

MacDonnell had served under three administrations as chief inspector and played a major role in the expansion of primary education from 4 schools and 493 pupils in 1860 to 263 schools and 36,271 pupils in 1876. Among other contributions were his development of teacher training, the commencement of the pupil-teacher system and establishment of the Normal School. In 1861 at Brisbane he had married Mary Sheehan of Brisbane; they had four sons and a daughter who died young. Aged 47 he died of consumption on 22 June 1877 and after a service at St Stephen's Cathedral was buried in the Brisbane general cemetery.

T. L. Suttor, *Hierarchy and democracy in Australia, 1788-1870* (Melb, 1965); V&P (LA Qld), 1861, 730, 1875, 2, 145, Board of General Education reports, 1861-76; *Brisbane Courier*, 23 June 1877; Board of General Education, Letterbooks 1860-63, 1 & 2 (QA); Board of National Education, Applications 1852-57 (QA); Education Dept, In-letter register 1875-76 (QA).

RUPERT GOODMAN

MacDONNELL, SIR RICHARD GRAVES (1814-1881), governor, was born on 3 September 1814 in Dublin, the eldest son of Dr Richard MacDonnell (1787-1867), fellow and from 1852 provost of Trinity College, and his wife Jane, second daughter of the dean of Ardagh, Richard Graves (1763-1829). Privately tutored, in 1829 he entered Trinity College (B.A., 1835; M.A., 1836; LL.B., 1845; LL.D., 1862). Called to the Irish Bar in 1838 and to Lincoln's Inn in 1841, he practised in London until he was appointed chief justice of Gambia on 20 July 1843. Despite the climate he was a competent judge. In October 1847 he became governor of the British settlements on the Gambia, where he organized several expeditions into the interior and among his adventures survived an assassination attempt. In 1852 he was transferred to St Lucia and in 1853 to St Vincent as administrator.

MacDonnell's next appointment was governor of South Australia, a surprising choice for a colony about to gain responsible government. With a reputation for severity he arrived at Port Adelaide on 9 June 1855 and took over from B. T. Finniss [q.v.], who had acted as governor since Sir Henry Fox Young had left in December 1854. MacDonnell was promptly active in the deliberations on the 1853 Constitution bill which the Colonial Office had returned to the

Legislative Council for reconsideration. His eagerness to show colonials that he knew what was best for them brought him into heated conflict with some of South Australia's reformers.

MacDonnell showed little respect for the cherished ideals of many in the community when he maintained that the colony was not ready for a bicameral legislature. He favoured a single-chamber parliament of thirty-six elected and four nominated members with whom he could maintain a balance between rival groups without stripping himself of all power and influence. His distrust of 'pure democracy' won him the support of conservatives but united the liberal and radical opposition against him. Once convinced that the colonists would not accept a unicameral legislature, he urged them to adopt a constitution similar to that of Tasmania. However, the Legislative Council elections in November 1855 returned a majority determined to make their own decisions. After acrimonious debate a compromise gave South Australia a Constitution with a democratically elected house of assembly and a property franchise for a legislative council with more than usual powers of review and revision. As a result the governor was blamed by disillusioned democrats, disappointed moderates and discontented officials for failing to ensure that the Constitution met the needs of all South Australians.

MacDonnell had difficulty in working with some colonial officials, particularly Finniss, and his efforts to find men who were both loyal and competent stirred up yet more trouble in a colony already wracked by political and personal rivalries. The governor's lack of diplomacy prevented any close liaison between himself and the new administration in the critical months after the Constitution was ratified and resulted in several unfortunate changes of government before the questions of power between governor and legislature were settled.

Powerful and hospitable, MacDonnell was fond of both outdoor and intellectual activities. He was an enthusiastic member of local rifle and archery clubs and keenly interested in the volunteer defence movement. He also identified himself with most of the literary, artistic and philanthropic organizations. At times his bustling energy dismayed Adelaide society but the governor saw himself as a leader and innovator. As a patron of South Australian culture he encouraged students who could not travel abroad to continue their post-primary schooling, and with his customary dash personally examined candidates and donated prizes, but his plan collapsed after he left the colony.

One of MacDonnell's main interests was the advancement of exploration and settlement of outback areas. He travelled widely in the colony and in 1859 led a small party to investigate country around the northern lakes and claypans, riding 1800 miles in three months. Maintaining that Sturt and Eyre [qq.v.] were overrated as explorers as they seemed 'generally to have a knack of getting into the most dismal places and finding barrenness from Dan to Beersheba', he urged the colonists to support J. M. Stuart's [q.v.] efforts to cross the continent. With little concern for the working class, he claimed that charity fostered sloth and pauperism. He encouraged the agricultural and pastoral industries. Particularly impressed by the settlers from Germany, he predicted that the colony had a great future for producing wine. In his seven-year term the acreage under wheat doubled in South Australia and he argued that farmers with capital would succeed so long as their methods did not rob the soil.

MacDonnell left South Australia on 4 March 1862. He returned to Ireland for a holiday before becoming lieut-governor of Nova Scotia. From October 1865 he served as governor in Hong Kong until he retired on a pension in 1872. In London he led a deputation of the Aborigines Protection Society to Lord Carnarvon in 1875. Predeceased by his wife Blanche Anne, daughter of Francis Skurray, whom he had married in 1847, he died at Hyères, France, on 5 February 1881 and was buried in London at Kensal Green cemetery. He had been appointed C.B. in 1852, K.B. in 1855 and K.C.M.G. in 1871.

Examiner (Melb), 3 Nov 1860, 27 Apr, 4 May 1861, 4 Jan, 22 Mar 1862; K. K. O'Donoghue, Constitutional and administrative development of South Australia from responsible government to Strangway's Act of 1868 (M.A. thesis, Univ Adel, 1950); Finniss papers (SAA); Govenor's dispatches 1855-62 (SAA).

C. C. MANHOOD

McDOUGALL, ARCHIBALD CAMPBELL (1818-1881), pastoralist, was born on the Isle of Islay, Scotland, the only son of Hugh McDougall, army captain, and his wife Jane, née Campbell. He arrived in Port Phillip in 1842. In 1845, with an Aboriginal and a mob of sheep, he camped on the present site of the Dunolly Court House, and later built his homestead in a forest of huge gums within view of Mount Bealiba. Neighbouring squatters held such large tracts of land that they did not dispute his claim. In 1851 he married Agnes Broadfoot, daughter of a family of shipowners and merchants; he had met her at Charlotte Plains, an adjoining run owned by the Simson family. Their son, Hugh, was the first white child born in the district.

McDougall's hopes for a permanent settlement were dashed in 1853 when his pastures were overrun by thousands of diggers seeking a share in rich alluvial gold. He referred to the gold rush as 'the fearful commotion of the infernal diggings' and, with men working at his very door, he sold his pre-emptive right section of 640 acres to H. N. Simson in 1854 and moved to Muskerry run on the Campaspe River near Axedale in the Bendigo district. Before offering McDougall's land for sale, Simson subdivided most of it into cultivation blocks and the rest into Goldsborough village, now a siding on the Melbourne-Mildura line.

McDougall returned to the Dunolly district in 1857 and formed a partnership with Simson to manage Archdale and Sandy Creek as well as his original Dunolly run. In 1861 he repurchased the remainder of his property at Goldsborough. In two dry summers McDougall just managed to save his homestead and flocks from fierce bushfires: in 1862 he was thankful for the help of a host of diggers who rushed to his aid following his frantic ride to Cochranes (Bealiba), and in 1863 he had all his clothes burnt when fighting fires in the same area.

For nearly twenty years McDougall worked to improve the services of his district. The town of Cochranes was largely the result of his persistent representations to the authorities to obtain one public institution after another. He was a member of the Road Board that preceded the Bet Bet Shire Council, a member of the Dunolly Hospital Committee and a vice-president of the Highland Society of the North West Province. Before he left the district, residents from Tarnagulla, Bealiba, Bet Bet, Natte Yallock, Eddington and Dunolly attended an evening in his honour. He took up land at Corner Inlet and also spent some time on the lower Murray.

McDougall retained his feeling for his Celtic ancestors. He was famous for his cordial hand-shake, his greetings in Gaelic, and for his regular appearances at Scottish gatherings in the garb of his clan and looking every inch a Highlander. When he judged the dancing and dress at the early meetings of the Maryborough Highland Society, he wore on his kilt a replica of a brooch taken by his ancestor, the lord of Lorne, from King Bruce in 1340. He died aged 62 at Spring Bank near Benalla on 14 May 1881. His wife, a devout Presbyterian, died on 14 June 1906 at Castlemaine aged 82. Of their two daughters and three sons, one son died

H

in infancy at Archdale and the last surviving son, John Lorne, died at Kilmore in 1944.

J. Flett, *Dunolly* (Glen Waverley, 1956); *Dunolly Express*, 25 July 1863, 20 May 1881; *Herald* (Melb), 8 June 1885; *Mount Alexander Mail*, 15 June 1906; *Kilmore Free Press*, 2 Jan 1944.   L. LOMAS

McDOUGALL, ROBERT (1813-1887), cattle breeder and agriculturist, was born on 16 April 1813 at Fortingall, Perthshire, Scotland, son of Alexander McDougall, sheep farmer, and his wife Grace, née Stewart. Attracted by outdoor life, he fished and hunted in the western isles in 1830 and from 1836 spent three years in Canada trapping beaver. He returned to Scotland but soon left for Port Phillip, where he arrived in November 1841. He was chosen by Thomas Learmonth [q.v.] to manage his Western District property. In the next years McDougall explored the lower Loddon and middle reaches of the Murray Rivers. In 1848 he rented land, bought stock and began to breed Shorthorn cattle, pigs and horses.

In the early 1850s he improved his Shorthorn herd by imports from Tasmania and rented property near Essendon to accommodate his growing activities. In November 1856 he was elected to the Legislative Assembly for West Bourke but retired in August 1857. In 1858 a committee of leading breeders, including Niel Black [q.v.], J. Ware and McDougall, was formed to compile and edit a herd book for the colony. A dispute over the status of locally bred stud, inflamed by personal animosities, ruined the plan and McDougall was left to edit those pedigrees made available. In 1859 he went to England to buy stud bulls and in the 1860s expanded his stud and refined his breeding techniques. An excellent showman and constant prize-winner, he was active in the Port Phillip Farming Society, a trustee of the National Agricultural Society and strongly supported the creation of a board of agriculture.

In 1870 McDougall bought Arundel farm at Keilor and went to England where he bought two prize Shorthorn bulls of the light-coloured Booth type which he was determined to propagate in the colony at the expense of the Bates strain favoured by his rival, Niel Black. His development of a fine herd contributed to the later expansion of the beef cattle industry but his uncompromising approach restricted his effect. In public controversy he was apt 'to urge with more force of language than those opposed to him liked'. Forthright and radical on contemporary issues, he supported democratic political reform, the abolition of state

aid to religion and the development of secular education. He had little time for squatters, insisting that they pay a fair price for their land and learn a few elements of their trade. McDougall was respected but not popular. Stern and severe, he spiced his conversation and public utterances with scriptural references and moral injunctions. His scruples made him troublesome in those organizations which he joined and the inflexible position he adopted on his own matters of principle often appeared to opponents as personal malice. He prided himself on his abhorrence of 'toadyism, trickery and tippling', and lawyers. He was a fine Gaelic scholar and a relentless Presbyterian.

In 1853 at Melbourne McDougall had married Margaret Rankin (1834-1913) of Hobart; they had one son and five daughters. After he died at Moonee Ponds on 25 June 1887, his estates Arundel and Warlaby were sold and his prize herds dispersed. They realized £40,000.

M. H. Ellis, *The beef shorthorn in Australia* (Syd, 1932); H. H. Peck, *Memoirs of a stockman* (Melb, 1942); M. L. Kiddle, *Men of yesterday* (Melb, 1961); *Age*, 28 June 1887; *Argus*, 29 June 1887.   G. R. QUAIFE

McELHONE, JOHN (1833-1898), merchant and politician, was born on 16 June 1833 in Sydney, son of Terence McElhone, milk vendor, and his wife Catherine, née Mallon. Educated at St Mary's Seminary School, he joined 'the Cabbage Tree mob' of wayward native-born youths. In 1851 he was an apprentice in Robert Towns's [q.v.] *Royal Saxon*. By 1859 he was a commission agent in Sydney. On 5 February 1862 at St Mary's Cathedral he married Mary Jane, daughter of John Browne, a wealthy squatter on the Liverpool Plains. In 1867-72 he was a broker and produce merchant in partnership with Richard Binnie, a saddler and brother-in-law of George Hill [q.v.]. In 1873 McElhone advertised as a stock, station and wool agent but soon set up as a hide and tallow merchant and exporter of colonial produce.

In August 1875 he contested the Legislative Assembly seat of Upper Hunter; defeated by Thomas Hungerford [q.v.] McElhone had the election declared null and void, and as the free selectors' champion won the second ballot after a bitter fight. He survived Hungerford's allegations of bribery and corruption but was later censured by the press for inciting the selectors to violence against the squatters, whom he described as 'the biggest thieves in creation'. In 1876 he was banquetted by the selectors of Jindera for helping to open the Colombo and Yanco reserves for selection. In the 1877 elections he told his constituents that 'I pride myself on having been the chief obstructionist in the Assembly'. He railed against 'the roguery, the corruption, the jobbery' of parliament and so viciously attacked land agents in parliament that he was sued by Thomas Garrett [q.v.] for £5000 damages.

In 1878-82 McElhone represented Fitzroy Ward in the Sydney Municipal Council. In 1880 with his penknife he exposed defective work in the foundations of the Town Hall and the ensuing 'corporation frauds' stirred up so much scandal that the government architect resigned. In February at the Town Hall he was called 'a servile lickspittle' by Daniel O'Connor [q.v.] and promptly punched him below the left eye and drew blood; an aldermanic scuffle followed. McElhone's impetuosity sometimes led him into 'serious violations of fairness and propriety'. In November 1882 his speech attacking Sir John Robertson's [q.v.] land bill was followed by the division on which the Parkes [q.v.]-Robertson government fell. McElhone was credited with 'one of those rare speeches which affect votes'. Elated at his success, in December he challenged Parkes in East Sydney and with the help of the Catholic vote was elected ahead of Parkes. On the hustings he argued the necessity of providing work for the colony's children; when a woman interjected, 'What if you haven't any children?', he roared back, 'Change the bull!'. He also won the Upper Hunter and boasted that 'his friend', W. B. Dalley [q.v.], had written 'every word' of his electoral address.

McElhone's support of Alexander Stuart's [q.v.] ministry was short-lived but he 'repeatedly obstructed the business of the House' and was criticized by Governor Loftus for 'violent and abusive language'. In March 1883 after a dispute with A. G. Taylor [q.v.] McElhone challenged him to resign and contest Mudgee with him. Both resigned their seats; McElhone lost but was again returned for the Upper Hunter. In February 1884 O'Connor denounced him in the House as 'an illiterate mountebank', 'a commercial Shylock', 'an unscrupulous vulture' and 'a political Quilp'. Repute as a boxer usually saved McElhone from such attacks but in 1888 he was beaten in a fight with George Matheson, member for Glen Innes, in the parliamentary smoking room.

In 1881 his father-in-law had died and excluded three of his daughters from an estate valued at over £110,000. McElhone entered a caveat against probate being granted. Although his case was pleaded by Julian Salomons [q.v.] from 9 to 29 August 1882, he was unable to prove in Browne v. McElhone that the testator had been senile. He offered to forgo any claim if his sisters-in-law benefited but was criticized for exposing scandals in the Browne family and for making his 19-year-old daughter give evidence. In 1884 a Legislative Assembly select committee found that McElhone had three times recommended J. T. Handsaker for government employment. Handsaker was not only in his debt but also a notorious drunkard, and after he was given employment his salary went to McElhone. Denounced by the Evening News for corruption, McElhone unsuccessfully sued the proprietors for libel. In 1885 although nominated by supporters he did not canvass his electorate and was defeated. He visited England and in February 1887 regained the Upper Hunter.

McElhone had been repeatedly forced by the Speaker to apologize and in 1888 was taken into custody by the serjeant-at-arms. Incurably litigious he successfully sued Alderman James Poole for infringing the 1879 Sydney Corporation Act but failed to get a Supreme Court injunction restraining the Australian Mutual Provident Society from using £25,000 of its funds to create a superannuation fund for its staff. He did not stand in the 1889 elections and in 1891 ascribed his defeat to his views of the shearing strike. An advocate for freedom of contract, he had denounced the union leaders from the hustings as 'scoundrels'. In turn he had been castigated as 'a traitor to the free selectors and working men'. In 1894 he was defeated for the Fitzroy division of East Sydney but won the seat as an independent free trader in 1895. He could not adapt to the changed politics of the 1890s: he dismissed Federation as 'a cuckoo cry taken up by a lot of scheming politicians' and thought the payment of members 'pernicious' and that the 'self-styled labour members' had done nothing for the country.

Honest, hot-tempered, ribald and at times scurrilous, McElhone was more than a mere rough-neck. His endless questions in parliament exposed many public wrongs, and his vitality and purpose were respected. His driver, Bill Inglis, an ex-prize-fighter, was often useful in the rough and tumble of electioneering. About 1881 McElhone had built a four-storied house in Rockwell Crescent, Potts Point, near the Woolloomooloo steps named after him. He died on 6 May 1898 from heart disease and was buried in the Catholic section of Waverley cemetery. Predeceased in 1894 by his wife, he was survived by six sons and three daughters to whom he left an estate valued at over £42,000.

Supreme Court Reports, cases at law, 2 (1881), 6 (1885), 9 (1888), cases in equity, 10 (1889); A. B. Piddington, *Worshipful masters* (Syd, 1929); V&P (LA NSW), 1875, 2, 283, 1875-76, 1, 16, 769, 1877-78, 1, 267, 1880-81, 1, 104, 1883-84, 3, 196, 1887-88, 1, 374, 479, 3, 982, 1889, 1, 660; F. MacDonnell, 'John McElhone, the inquisitive alderman', RAHS *Newsletter*, June 1970; *Maitland Mercury*, 1-5 June, 10, 24, 31 July, 3-7 Aug 1875, 20 Oct, 8 Nov 1877, 16, 20, 25 Nov 1880, 2 June 1881, 7-12 Dec 1882; *SMH*, 12 Dec 1877, 9, 10, 12, 15-19, 22-26, 29 Aug 1882, 8 Mar, 29 June 1883, 30 June, 3, 10, 18 July 1894, 28 Nov 1898; *Australasian*, 26 Apr 1879, 14 Mar 1885; *Bulletin*, 7 Feb 1880, 16 July, 24 Sept 1881, 27 May, 2 Sept 1882, 27 Oct 1883; *Pastoral Review*, 16 July 1891; Parkes letters (ML); newspaper cuttings (ML); information from F. E. McElhone, Syd; CO 201/584, 598, 600, 608.   MARTHA RUTLEDGE

McEVILLY, WALTER O'MALLEY (1820-1867), parliamentary librarian, was born in County Mayo, Ireland. As a labourer who could read and write he was tried on 24 March 1840 at Tipperary for forgery and sentenced to seven years' transportation. He reached Sydney on 17 August in the *King William*. On 23 February 1841 he was transferred from the Hyde Park barracks to the Legislative Council offices as door-keeper and paid the usual rate of 1s. 9d. a day. He petitioned for a ticket-of-leave; granted on 25 January 1844 it was replaced by a government ticket on 22 March. In that year he signed a petition to the Queen against the exclusion of 63 Catholics from the special jury list and all Catholics from the jury impanelled for the state trials in Dublin.

In 1843 Richard O'Connor [q.v.] was appointed as librarian of the Legislative Council library. McEvilly was assistant librarian from 1 July 1850 at a salary of £109 and on 20 May 1856 was promoted librarian with a residence in the parliamentary premises. He was reported to have 'zealously and well discharged the duties of Librarian'. After his appointment the library more than doubled its 6990 volumes and important administrative changes were made. In May 1860 the library committees of the council and assembly recommended one general parliamentary library and reading rooms for each House in place of separate libraries. The proposal was adopted and in 1862 the management of the parliamentary library was entrusted to a joint committee from both Houses; the duties of McEvilly and future librarians were also set down. In February 1859 McEvilly was a leader in a meeting of Roman Catholics protesting the appointment of Dr W. F. Bassett [q.v.] to the board of the Parramatta Catholic Orphanage. Threatened with excommunication by Archbishop Polding [q.v.] he

withdrew but the case went to Rome on appeal.

On 4 August 1863 a long-standing disagreement between McEvilly and his assistant, Francis Robinson, led to a fight in which both were hurt. A testimonial from 63 of the 72 members of the assembly attested to McEvilly's 'zeal, efficiency, uniform quiet and obliging and peaceful disposition'. Robinson was later dismissed.

McEvilly was fond of field sports and a sound judge and breeder of thoroughbred bloodstock. As 'Mr. O'Malley', his mother's maiden name, he owned and trained such successful horses as Yattenden, winner of the first Sydney Cup in 1866. His first offspring, Yatterina, bred by McEvilly in 1865, was reputed one of the best thoroughbred mares exported to New Zealand. Yattenden also sired Dagworth, one of the best performers of the 1870s, and two Melbourne Cup winners.

A sporting challenge to a fellow guest of J. Morrice, M.L.A., at Moss Vale to race up and down a railway embankment resulted in a broken leg and brain injury to McEvilly. He died intestate four days later on 16 October 1867 at his residence at Parliament House and was buried in the Roman Catholic cemetery, Sydney. He was survived by his wife Mary Anne, née Farrell (d. 1907), whom he had married in St Mary's Cathedral on 6 November 1847, and by three sons and four daughters.

D. M. Barrie, *The Australian bloodhorse* (Syd, 1956); V&P (LA NSW) 1867-68, 1, 949; *Bell's Life in Sydney*, 19 Oct 1867; *Freeman's J* (Syd), 19 Oct 1867; LC letters (LC NSW).

L. A. JECKELN

McFARLAND, ALFRED (1824-1901), judge and author, was born on 24 April 1824 at Coleraine, County Londonderry, Ireland, son of John McFarland, merchant linen-bleacher, and his wife Anne, née Heuston. Educated at Foyle and Belfast Colleges, Trinity College, Dublin, and Lincoln's Inn, London, he was called to the Irish Bar in 1847. For ten years he practised in the Dublin courts and as a conveyancer and real property lawyer. He also wrote *Treatise on Equity Pleading, Ireland* (1848) and *Observations on the Act to Regulate the Proceedings in the High Court of Chancery in Ireland* (1850). In 1856 at Dublin he married Janetta Jeffreys. In 1857, nominated by the lord chancellor of Ireland, he was appointed sole judge of the principal civil and criminal courts of Western Australia; despite his resignation in July 1859 he stayed in office until his successor arrived early in 1861.

McFarland was admitted to the Bar of

New South Wales on 8 April 1861 and acted as a judge of the District Court until his appointment as chief commissioner of insolvent estates. He became judge of the District Court and chairman of Quarter Sessions for the metropolitan district on 14 December 1865 but, preferring a country circuit, later went to the southern district until he returned to the metropolitan district in 1888. He was also a law reader in jurisprudence at the University of Sydney, a member of the board of law examiners and a frequent contributor to the literary columns of leading Sydney journals. He published several books including *Illawarra and Manaro: Districts of New South Wales* (1872) and *Mutiny in the 'Bounty!' and Story of the Pitcairn Islanders* (1884). His manuscript of a history of 'Australia and the New Hebrides from 1606 to 1804', to which he devoted many years, was destroyed by fire before it could be published.

In 1878 delays in the enactment of legislation drafted by McFarland and others induced him to stress acceleration in law reform. He proposed the re-establishment of the office of solicitor-general as a permanent crown law officer to supervise all government bills. In 1886 he offered his services as minister of justice to Sir Henry Parkes [q.v.] who refused. In 1889 he defied the Legislative Council when it ordered the production of his notes in a criminal trial to a select committee into the severity of a sentence he had imposed on a Chinese; the matter had already been decided by the government in the judge's favour.

In 1891 McFarland briefly resumed practice as a barrister and continued his historical research. He claimed that he had to retire from the bench because he was forced to petition to sequestrate his estate as two judgment creditors levied execution and, without his knowledge that the sale was to take place, the sheriff sold his possessions at a very low figure. His debts were £5191. He died at his home in Neutral Bay on 11 March 1901, survived by his wife, two sons and four daughters. He was buried in the cemetery of St Thomas's Church of England, North Sydney. He was reputed a careful judge and noted for the clear and orderly way in which he marshalled the facts of intricate cases and in his masterly charges to juries.

Australian, 1878-79; *SMH*, 16 Aug, 27 Sept 1889; Parkes letters (ML); A. McFarland notebook, WA 1858 (ML); CO 18/99, 105, 111.

H. T. E. HOLT

MACFARLANE, SAMUEL (1837-1911), missionary, was born on 18 February 1837 at Johnstone, near Glasgow, Scotland, a son of poor parents with a large family. He had little schooling and after apprenticeship became a railway mechanic. In 1853 when his family moved to Manchester he joined the Oldham Road Congregational Chapel and soon decided to be a missionary. Despite his scanty education, he prepared himself, was accepted by the London Missionary Society, trained at Bedford and ordained on 11 November 1858. Soon afterwards he married Elizabeth Ursula Joyce, sister of a colleague, and sailed with her on 6 January 1859 for the Loyalty Islands; he reached Lifu on 30 October.

The island had been annexed by France in 1853 and French Marist priests had arrived in 1858. Tribal jealousies, sectarian conflict and French fear of British influence complicated his task and from May 1864, when his mission was destroyed by a punitive expedition, he waged a masterly paper war with the administration. His ruthless professionalism, which alienated some of his colleagues and French officialdom, helped to maintain the position of the mission in the island but later led to diplomatic demands by the French government for his removal.

Macfarlane toured eastern Australia as a mission delegate from December 1867 to March 1868. After his removal from Lifu was decided on 14 June 1869 he began planning a mission in New Guinea. In December 1870 Rev. A. W. Murray arrived to replace him. On 30 May 1871 they sailed in the *Surprise* to reconnoitre New Guinea. They returned to Lifu on 2 November. Leaving Murray in temporary charge of New Guinea, Macfarlane left with his wife and four sons for England. He published *The Story of the Lifu Mission* (London, 1873) and had his plans for New Guinea approved by the society.

Macfarlane returned to Sydney on 26 June 1874 and relieved Murray at Somerset, Cape York, on 29 July. In the next four years he made 23 voyages, visited over 80 villages, established 12 mission stations, learned something of 6 languages and published translations in 2 of them. In 1877 he moved his headquarters to Murray Island to implement a policy of supervising coloured teachers resident on the mainland. His objection to the preference of his colleagues, W. G. Lawes and James Chalmers [qq.v.], for residing among their congregations caused much dissension; the estrangement was deepened by Macfarlane's sometimes arrogant assumption of seniority. In the steamer *Ellengowan* he explored between 28 August and 28 December 1875, named the Baxter River and took H. M. Chester and Luigi D'Albertis [qq.v.] seventy miles up the Fly River. He was widely criticized over a shooting incident on the second voyage.

For the benefit of his family Macfarlane returned to England in June 1886 and published *Among The Cannibals of New Guinea* (London, 1888). He received an honorary doctorate from the University of St Andrews in February 1887 and served as an officer of the London Missionary Society until he retired in 1894. He died at Southport, Lancashire, on 27 January 1911, survived by his wife who died on 28 October 1913, aged 76. Two sons later became missionaries in China.

A. W. Murray, *Forty years' mission work in Polynesia and New Guinea, from 1835 to 1875* (Lond, 1876); L. M. D'Albertis, *New Guinea: what I did and what I saw* (Lond, 1880); O. C. Stone, *A few months in New Guinea* (Lond, 1880); A. Wichmann, *Nova Guinea*, 2 (Leiden, 1910), pt 1; J. Sibree (ed), *LMS: a register of missionaries, deputations, etc. from 1796 to 1923* (Lond, 1923); R. Leenhardt, *Au vent de la Grande Terre* (Paris, 1957); W. P. Morrell, *Britain in the Pacific Islands* (Oxford, 1960); *Australasian*, 9 Oct 1875, 29 Jan, 5 Feb, 29 Apr supp, 3 June 1876; P. A. Prendergast, *A history of the London Missionary Society in British New Guinea, 1871-1901* (Ph.D. thesis, Univ Hawaii, 1968, copy ANU, NL); J. M. Douglas, *The Loyalty Islands and S. Macfarlane 1859-1869* (B.A. Hons thesis, ANU, 1971); LMS papers (NL).   H. J. GIBBNEY

McGAVIN, MATTHEW (1807-1874), Presbyterian minister, was born in Irvine, Ayrshire, Scotland, son of Robert McGavin, grocer, and his wife Mary, née Reid. Trained at the United Presbyterian Church's Synod Hall (M.A., 1830), he was ordained on 15 June 1831 at Stonehouse. The parish had apparently been depleted because the call was signed by only 94 members and 66 adherents, small numbers for Scotland. Under his ministry at Stonehouse, however, the church made numerical progress, many members joining from Glassford, Dalserf and Lesmahagow.

McGavin accepted a call to the church, known as Wellwynd, at Airdrie in Lanarkshire and was inducted there on 2 March 1841. A new church was built, opened and dedicated in 1847, and surrounding districts, Chapelhall, Coatdyke, Cadder and Rawyards, were drawn within the bounds of the parish. A gifted musician, he composed a Psalm tune known as 'Clydesdale', still used in some Presbyterian churches, and with Andrew Thomson, organist at Paisley, published *The Precentor's Guide to the Selection of Tunes* (1853). After a record period of 'unbroken peace' he resigned his parish at Airdrie in February 1863. A deputation of the congregation asked him to delay this step, but he told them that their only course was to acquiesce because his mind was made up.

McGavin arrived in Brisbane in August 1863 and immediately took over the work based on the Creek Street Church, vacant for some time following the ministry of Rev. Thomas Bell. Under McGavin's vigorous ministry the work grew and prospered. He was moderator of synod in 1868. The building of a more enduring church than the earlier wooden structure had been started but the funds ran out and the new church was never completed. For some years the congregation worshipped in the composite building, part Gothic in style, having a nave without transepts. In aid of the Queensland Presbyterian Sabbath School Union McGavin gave and published two lectures on *The Claims of Popery* (Brisbane, 1874). Soon afterwards he suffered a serious illness and went to Sydney for treatment. He died at Milson's Point on 16 December and was buried in the Presbyterian section of Willoughby cemetery. He was married twice in Scotland : first, in 1830 to Elizabeth, née Cluff, who bore him three sons and four daughters; and second, in 1856 to a widow, Grace Drummond, who survived him.

The Creek Street parish later sold its property for a large sum to the neighbouring National Bank of Australasia Ltd, and transferred its work to Leichhardt Street (St Paul's Terrace), on that hill building the fine Gothic church which remains one of the architectural adornments in Brisbane.

A. Hay, *Jubilee memorial of the Presbyterian Church of Queensland* (Brisb, 1900); R. Small, *History of the congregations of the United Presbyterian Church from 1733 to 1900* (Edinburgh, 1904); R. Bardon, *Centenary history of the Presbyterian Church of Queensland 1849-1949* (Brisb, 1949); V&P (LA Qld), 1875, 2, 232; Church of Scotland records (Church Offices, 121 George St, Edinburgh).

ROBERT STEEL BYRNES

McGIBBON, JOHN (1828-1882), Presbyterian minister, was born on 14 June 1828 at Glasgow, Scotland, son of George McGibbon and his wife Mary, née Calder. Educated at Edinburgh in parish and night schools, he was recruited by Rev. J. D. Lang [q.v.] for the Australian ministry in 1849. He arrived in Sydney with Lang early in 1850 and in December was licensed by his Synod of New South Wales. He assisted Lang at the Scots Church. In 1853 the committee of management tried to have McGibbon appointed co-pastor but Lang objected. Some of the committee and congregation withdrew and formed a new congregation under McGibbon at Woolloomooloo. A successful minister, he was liked by his congregation who, led by John Frazer [q.v.], had by 1860 built and largely paid off a substantial stone church and manse in Palmer Street. McGibbon had been ordained by the Synod of Australia and was active in it. In 1865 he was its clerk when it dissolved connexion with the established Church of Scotland and united with the General Synod of New South Wales. He was moderator of the Sydney Presbytery in 1871 and of the Presbyterian General Assembly in 1874. He studied at the University of Sydney (B.A., 1863; LL.B., 1868; LL.D., 1870) and in 1873-82 was a member of the theological faculty of St Andrew's College.

McGibbon championed what his supporters called Evangelical and others ultra-Protestantism. For him a central tenet of Protestantism was its opposition to Rome. He first achieved prominence in 1865 when he attacked Governor Young for supporting an appeal for funds to rebuild St Mary's Cathedral after its destruction by fire. Several long controversies with Catholic apologists followed and introduced into colonial life a level of sectarian debate absent since the early 1840s. In 1866 Catholic attempts to prevent him lecturing on a theme that 'Rome was the anti-Christ' resulted in the 'Battle of York Street'. In 1868, after more serious sectarianism sparked off by H. J. O'Farrell's [q.v.] attempt to assassinate the duke of Edinburgh, McGibbon with Revs Zachary Barry, Barzillai Quaife, Wazir Beg [qq.v.] and John Sharpe founded the *Australian Protestant Banner*, a weekly that exposed and attacked the errors of Rome and 'accomodating' Protestants. In 1869, after a dispute with Beg, McGibbon began the *Protestant Standard* and edited it with increasing assistance from Barry until 1881; it was the organ of the Orange lodges in the colony until 1895.

In the early 1870s McGibbon had been the chief publicist for the Loyal Orange Institution of New South Wales which was rejuvenated in 1868. His iteration that Orangeism was simply Evangelical Protestantism did much to break down English prejudice against its Irish associations and helped the institution to reach its peak of 25,000 members in the early 1880s. In great demand as a speaker he often preached from the pulpits of other Protestant denominations and often visited the country. In October 1870 he began the Protestant Institute to combat the new Catholic Truth Society. In the late 1860s and early 1870s he had strongly supported the movement to build a Protestant Hall. He had helped to win Presbyterian support for Henry Parkes's [q.v.] 1866 Public Schools Act and in 1874-75 he and Barry championed Rev. James Greenwood's [q.v.] Public School League, ensuring that it adopted a moderate interpretation of 'secular'. Although not a total abstainer he campaigned energetically for temperance. In 1877-80 he appeared seventeen times before the licensing bench to prevent the opening of a public house opposite his church. His comments on the case took him twice to another court to answer libel charges. He also stressed Sunday observance and condemned dancing, theatre, race-going and gambling.

McGibbon's energetic advocacy undermined his health. In 1876 heart disease was detected. A world trip provided only temporary respite and in 1881 he gave up all editorial duties. On 22 June 1882 he died at the Palmer Street manse, survived by his wife Margaret, née Ferguson, whom he had married in 1855, and by four sons and three daughters. His estate was valued at £7510. Orangemen erected a large obelisk over his grave in Rookwood cemetery.

J. D. Lang, *The case of the Scots Church, Church Hill* (Syd, 1853); J. Cameron, *Centenary history of the Presbyterian Church in New South Wales* (Syd, 1905); J. E. Carruthers, *Memories of an Australian ministry 1868-1921* (Lond, 1922); A. D. Gilchrist (ed), *John Dunmore Lang*, 1-2 (Melb, 1951); C. A. White, *The challenge of the years* (Syd, 1951); *Presbyterian and Australian Witness*, 1 July 1882; *Protestant Standard*, 1 July 1882; *Bulletin*, 1 July 1882; *Town and Country J*, 1 July 1882; M. Lyons, *Aspects of sectarianism in New South Wales circa 1865-1880* (Ph.D. thesis, ANU, 1972).

MARK LYONS

MacGILLIVRAY, PAUL HOWARD (1834-1895), scientist and medical practitioner, was born at Edinburgh, son of William MacGillivray and his wife Marion, née Askill. His eldest brother John [q.v.] became a notable naturalist. Paul was educated at Marischal College in the University of Aberdeen (M.A., 1851), where his father had been appointed professor of natural history in 1841. While still a student Paul, with some help from his father, published *A Catalogue of the Flowering Plants and Ferns growing in the neighbourhood of Aberdeen* (1853). When his father died in September 1852 MacGillivray relinquished his study of science and turned to medicine in London (M.R.C.S., 1855). Later that year he migrated to Melbourne.

MacGillivray began to practise at Williamstown and joined the local volunteer naval brigade as a medical officer. In 1862-73 he was resident surgeon of the hospital in Bendigo and then took up private practice there. Although his great love was still natural science, MacGillivray revealed an aptitude for surgery. His many papers on surgical matters included three works in 1865-72 on the management and treatment of hydatid cysts. In 1874 he was elected president of the Medical Society of Victoria.

MacGillivray was also well known as one of the foremost naturalists in Australia. In 1857 he was elected a member of the Philosophical Institute (later Royal Society) of Victoria and from 1859 began to publish in the society's Transactions a series of important illustrated papers on the Australian and related representatives of the Phylum Polyzoa (Bryozoa), commonly known as 'sea-mosses'. The fine descriptions and figures from his own hand in Professor McCoy's [q.v.] Prodromus of the Zoology of Victoria (Melbourne, 1878-90) are models of precision and clarity and remain, together with MacGillivray's 'The Tertiary Polyzoa of Victoria' (Transactions of the Royal Society of Victoria, 4, 1895), standard bases for any research on Cainozoic Polyzoa. For the Royal Society of South Australia he also wrote on the fossil polyzoans of that colony.

On 2 December 1880 MacGillivray was elected a fellow of the Linnean Society of London. On 20 June 1881 he gave the inaugural address to the Bendigo School of Mines Science Society on the objects worth accomplishment. He was an energetic member of the Field Naturalists' Club of Victoria and other institutions. Although modest and 'habitually silent and reserved with strangers', he was respected for his probity and sincerity in advocating educational and scientific progress.

For publication by the Royal Society of Victoria he had nearly finished a large monograph on the 'Polyzoa of Victoria' when he died on 9 July 1895 at his home in Bendigo. He was survived by his wife Elizabeth, née Shields, five daughters and a son who had served in the South African Mounted Police before settling in Western Australia. MacGillivray's collections and valuable library were bought by the government for the National Museum of Victoria.

A. Sutherland et al, Victoria and its metropolis, 2 (Melb, 1888); R. T. M. Pescott, Collections of a century (Melb, 1954); V&P (LA Vic), 1872, 3 (57) 147; Aust Medical J, 20 July 1895; H. B. Graham, 'The fruits of Lister's labours', MJA, 20 June 1953; Argus, 10 July 1895.   D. A. BROWN

McGOWAN, SAMUEL WALKER (1829-1887), scientist and administrator, was born on 4 January 1829 in Londonderry, Ireland, eldest son of Samuel McGowan and his wife Eliza, née Walker. Educated at Midland District Grammar School, Kingston, Canada, he studied law in Toronto. After his father died in 1847 McGowan turned to telegraphy in which he had experimented. Taught by Professor Samuel Morse, he gained practical experience with several telegraph companies in North America.

Encouraged by news of gold discoveries in Australia McGowan decided to migrate to Victoria. Early in 1853 he arrived in the Glance at Melbourne, intending to form a private company to provide telegraphic linkage between Melbourne, Sydney and Adelaide as well as the goldfields. He soon captured the interest of capitalists but the government decided to make all telegraph lines a public monopoly. In September tenders were called for the construction of an experimental line between Melbourne and Williamstown and McGowan's was accepted. On 1 March 1854 he was appointed general superintendent of the Electric Telegraph Department of Victoria and two days later the first telegraph service south of the equator was opened. By December the experimental line had been extended to Geelong. In 1857 all main centres were connected and lines radiated from Melbourne westwards to Portland and northwards to the Murray River, and by the end of October telegraph communication between the three capital cities flowed freely.

McGowan represented the Victorian government in the Victoria when she laid the cable to Tasmania in 1859 although satisfactory communication with the island was not effected for another ten years. In March 1869 the postal and telegraph departments were amalgamated and McGowan became inspector of postal and telegraph service. Early in 1885 he was appointed deputy postmaster-general.

At St James's Old Cathedral, Melbourne, on 30 June 1857 McGowan married Annie, eldest daughter of H. W. Benton of Kingston; they had two sons and two daughters, the younger of whom, Henrietta Celeste, became a journalist on the staff of the Age. The McGowans lived in Hotham Street, St Kilda, and visited the beach daily in summer. McGowan also enjoyed walks in the Dandenongs with Ferdinand Mueller [q.v.]. He served on the Council of the Royal Society of Victoria at various times from 1862 and was a captain in the Torpedo Corps formed for the defence of Port Phillip Bay. In 1886 he was granted leave for twelve months on full salary to investigate developments in telegraphy overseas. In London he opposed J. H. Heaton's [q.v.] proposal for a penny postal service between England and the colonies as a scheme which would only increase the postal department's annual deficit. He also discussed overseas cable services with the chairman of the Eastern Extension Co. In Canada talks were held with the president of the Canadian Pacific Railway for a proposed shipping line between Vancouver and Australia. He sailed for Melbourne, armed with copious notes for a report to government, but became ill and died on 18 April 1887, nine days after his return. He was buried at Oakleigh cemetery, survived by his wife and their four children.

Proud of his achievement in introducing electric telegraphy to Victoria, McGowan had a dinner service made in England, decorated with elaborate cable and Morse motifs and a compass centred on each plate. His only public memorial appears to be a stained glass window set in the Anglican Holy Trinity Church, Balaclava, a tribute from his colleagues.

R. H. Vetch, *Life of Lieut.-General the Hon. Sir Andrew Clarke* (Lond, 1905); Roy Soc Vic, *Procs*, 24 (1887), 179; F. R. Bradley, 'History of the electric telegraph in Australia', *JRAHS*, 20 (1934); *Argus*, 12, 19 Apr 1887; *Leader* (Melb), 23 Apr 1887; *Herald* (Melb), 20 Feb 1954.
                                              JEAN GITTINS

McGREGOR, ALEXANDER (1821-1896), shipowner and merchant, and JOHN GIBSON (1830-1902), shipbuilder, were the first and third sons of James McGregor (b. 1782) and his wife Janet (1798-1862), née Smith. Alexander was born at Paisley, Scotland, sailed from Leith with his parents in the *Dunmore* and arrived at Hobart Town in February 1831. John Gibson was born at sea and christened at the Cape of Good Hope. The family lived in a cottage in Bathurst Street. The brothers served apprenticeships under the shipwright, John Watson, and then started building small boats on their own account. By 1855 Alexander had acquired the Domain shipyard. He sold it in 1869 to John who had been his foreman.

On 24 June 1847 Alexander had married Harriet Bayley at her home according to the rites of the Church of Scotland. Her brothers were engaged in the whaling trade and Alexander bought shares in their venture. He had a whaling fleet of eight ships by 1857 and maintained them even after whaling declined, claiming that they served as the Reformatories of the Colony'. He also started the firm of McGregor, Piesse & Co., general merchants in Elizabeth Street. With business acumen, they bought many ships for exporting whale oil, bluegum timber and wool. Their 'Red Iron' fleet became known in every Australian port as

well as London, and was reputed to earn the firm some £8000 a year. By 1875 in Hobart they also had a large warehouse in Salamanca Place and New Wharf.

McGregor represented Hobart in the Legislative Council in 1880-96. Though not very active in debates, he was an acknowledged authority on maritime matters and his advice was respected. Among other subjects he criticized the absence of shipowners on the Marine Board and its method of election, and claimed that the harbourmaster was too arbitrary in making rules. In 1883-84 McGregor, Piesse & Co. had a long correspondence with the premier, W. R. Giblin [q.v.], for stimulating migration to Tasmania by subsidies to British shipping companies; the government rejected McGregor as the negotiator but his proposal doubled the number of migrants arriving from Britain in the next decade. In his last years McGregor suffered from bouts of dementia, speculating wildly in country land and mining. In 1894 he authorized his agent to sell the Anchor tin mine to English investors for £10,000. He retired next year and transferred the business to his head clerk, Samuel Thomas Kirby. He died on 4 August 1896 at his home, Lenna, Battery Point, leaving an estate of £4364 to his relations.

John Gibson ran the Domain shipyard until he retired in 1890. Among the many ships he built were the *Petrel, Helen, Hally Bayley* and *Loongana*, all well known in intercolonial trade. His *Harriet McGregor* was noted for fast passages on the Hobart-London run. He was also a director of the Tasmanian Fire and Life Insurance Co. for many years and a justice of the peace from 1886. He died on 5 October 1902 at his home in Cross Street, Battery Point, where he had lived for half a century. He was survived by his wife Christina, née Stewart, who died on 21 November 1903, and by two sons and two daughters.

Cyclopedia of Tasmania, 1 (Hob, 1900); *V&P* (HA Tas), 1879 (105), 1882 (132), 1884 (42); *Bulletin*, 3 Apr 1880; *Mercury*, 6 Aug 1896, 6 Oct 1903; information from Captain J. B. Haly, Bexhill-on-Sea, England.

MacGREGOR, DUNCAN (1835-1916), pastoralist, was born near Learan, Perthshire, Scotland, son of John MacGregor, tenant farmer, and his wife Janet, née Sinclair. He sailed from Liverpool on 7 June 1857 in the *Marco Polo* and soon after arrival in Victoria went to New South Wales, where he managed Mount Murchison and Donald MacRae's Culpauline station on the Darling River. He also explored much of south-west Queensland. In 1868 he returned to Victoria and on 25 February married Margaret, daughter of Donald and Christina MacRae.

The MacGregors lived at Glengyle, Moors Road, Coburg, and held Clunie, a property near Chintin in the Romsey district. There in 1869 MacGregor formed the basis of his famous studs of pure Booth Shorthorns and Leicester sheep. The latter he founded with twenty-five ewes from W. Field's stud in Tasmania and a ram bred by Mathew Wait of progeny from Steel's Deep Creek stud. He added more ewes from Field in 1887 and six rams from Branxholme Park, Southland, New Zealand. He believed that 'the essential for success in breeding animals is the gifted faculty that recognises the kind of animals that ought to be selected . . . the real fundamental principle of breeding is hereditary'. His cattle and sheep studs testified to his possession of this 'gifted faculty' as did his development of the Clydesdale horse. Although a strong pleader for reliable stud-books, he resented government attempts to interfere with the importing of horses, arguing that 'protective measures are at all times to be avoided when they interfere with the freedom of the individual'.

By 1874 MacGregor was able to move into south-west Queensland. With his widowed mother-in-law he increased the MacRae holdings in the Gregory South and Warrego Districts, and with other partners and through agents took up many of the runs comprising Durham Downs on Cooper's Creek. Most of these leases were applied for and granted between 1874 and 1879, and others not till 1884. By then he was in partnership with James MacBain [q.v.], Alex McEdward and John Bell as Mac-Gregor & Co. By 1893 Durham Downs carried 96,000 sheep, 26,000 cattle and 4000 horses, all mortgaged in June 1894. Mac-Gregor acquired leases of the twenty-one runs of Glengyle in Gregory North in the late 1870s and early 1880s and also the leases of Melba Downs, Miranda, Yanko and Mimosa. Glengyle carried 14,113 cattle and 180 horses, the other stations 42,500 sheep, 364 horses and 11,257 cattle. All were mortgaged in 1895.

MacGregor's Victorian concerns fared better. In 1875 he had bought 3928 acres for between 25s. and 43s. an acre of Koo-wee-rup swamp. Two years later his drainage scheme was operating; 3871 acres were drained by 1880 at a cost of £1754 and 200 acres cleared of tea-tree, and the Dalmore studs of Shorthorns and Leicesters were in residence there. Enterprising though Mac-Gregor's drainage activities were, they flooded his neighbours' properties, and caused two protracted legal cases, stimulating his love of litigation and incurring for him the temporary hostility of the

Berwick and Cranbourne Shire Councils. Reports of the richness of this area, the 'Garden of Victoria' aroused interest and in 1889 the government began to drain Koo-wee-rup. By then he had acquired a second Pakenham property, Gowanlea, near Tooradin. In 1891 he turned over the management of this estate and Dalmore to his sons Donald and John, and at Chintin founded the Clunie Border Leicester stud with Scottish ewes and rams bought at Harper's Avondale sale.

MacGregor was a Presbyterian. Aged 81 he died at Clunie on 28 January 1916, survived by his wife and six children. Dour and sturdily built, he was remembered as an intrepid explorer, bushman, conqueror of swamp land and judge of stud stock.

W. T. Wright, The live stock annual of Australia (Melb, 1903); H. H. Peck, Memoirs of a stockman (Melb, 1942); Berwick (Vic) Shire Council, From bullock track to bitumen (Berwick, 1962); N. Gunson, The good country: Cranbourne shire (Melb, 1968); Aust Law Times, 9 Aug 1902, p15; Daily Telegraph (Melb), 27, 29 Apr 1880; Age, 29 Jan 1916; Argus, 29 Jan 1916; Pakenham Gazette, 18 Sept 1959; L. M. Key, Historical geography of the Kooweerup district (M.A. thesis, Univ Melb, 1967); pastoral holdings records (QA); papers held by B. D. MacGregor, Armadale, Vic.

J. ANN HONE

MACGREGOR, SIR WILLIAM (1846-1919), medical practitioner and colonial administrator, was born on 20 October 1846 at Hillockhead, parish of Towie, Aberdeenshire, Scotland, eldest son of John Mac-Gregor, crofter, and his wife Agnes, daughter of William Smith of Pitprone. The family was large and poor so William worked as a farm labourer. However, his intellectual promise was fostered by his schoolmaster, the minister and the local doctor. With their help and his own perseverance he entered Aberdeen Grammar School in April 1866 and enrolled at the University of Aberdeen in October next year. Intending to enter the church he began arts but turned to medicine when his future wife Mary Thomson became pregnant. They were married on 4 October 1868 and their son was born next January. MacGregor studied at Anderson's Medical College (L.F.P.S.) and the Universities of Aberdeen (M.B.) and of Edinburgh (L.R.C.P.) and was registered on 9 May 1872. He became a medical assistant at the Royal Lunatic Asylum, Aberdeen, but left to join the colonial service as assistant medical officer in the Seychelles, probably attracted by the salary of £250.

MacGregor arrived at the Seychelles with

his wife in February 1873. There and in Mauritius he was encouraged by the governor, Sir Arthur Gordon (1829-1912), to take on administrative tasks as well as medical work, and as inspector of schools and liberated Africans he became interested in the problems of labour and under-privileged people. His first daughter was born on Curieuse Island in 1874. That year Gordon was appointed governor of Fiji and on his advice MacGregor became chief medical and health officer at Levuka in June 1875. As his administrative duties grew he practised less as a doctor and despite over-work and discouragement refused tempting offers to practise in New South Wales. As receiver-general (treasurer) from 1877 he carried out detailed financial work for the colony: he was colonial secretary from 1884 and acting-governor from January to August 1885 and December 1887 to February 1888. In early 1885 he had supported the proposal of a trade treaty with Victoria but the Colonial Office received it coldly. In 1886 he represented Fiji at the Federal Council in Tasmania where he began a lifelong friend-ship with Sir Samuel Griffith. His wife had died of dysentery on 9 February 1877 and in November 1883 he married Mary Jane, daughter of Captain Cocks, harbourmaster at Suva; their two daughters were born in Fiji.

Recommended highly by Gordon and Griffith, MacGregor was appointed adminis-trator of British New Guinea in 1887 to succeed John Douglas [q.v.]. He reached Port Moresby on 4 September 1888 and was sworn in after formally proclaiming British sovereignty. After leave in 1894-95 he returned for a second term, this time as lieut-governor in 1895-98. He had to report to the governor of Queensland and consult him on all important matters, while New South Wales and Victoria had the right to inter-vene. With this restricted power and a budget of some £15,000 he tried to protect the Papuans and develop the country. He resisted all attempts, even those supported by the Australian colonies, to exploit Papuan land or labour, clashing in particular with Sir Thomas McIlwraith [q.v.]. To supplement the power of his Executive and Legislative Councils and officials MacGregor appointed Papuan village constables, and recruited Papuans into the armed con-stabulary. He also encouraged such European enterprises as coconut plantations and gold-mining, and encouraged Papuans to share in similar ventures. To establish government contact with the Papuans he often made visits of inspection and in the process explored some six hundred miles up the Fly River and climbed Mount Vic-toria. In spare time he continued his interest

in classics and literature, kept up his French and German and learnt Italian, reading cur-rent works of biography and history and subscribing to French and German period-icals, but rarely saw his family in New Guinea.

In 1898 MacGregor was appointed governor of Lagos. He found difficulties in applying his humanitarian paternalism but maintained his concern for sanitation and health, assisting Sir Ronald Ross (1857-1932) in confirming his theories about the trans-mission of malaria by mosquitoes. In his memoirs Ross described MacGregor as 'wise, grave, but humorous, bearded, thickset . . . his low voice and kindly manner filled all with trust in him . . . a mathematician, a practiced surveyor, a lapidary, and a master of many arts, but always proud of his medical upbringing and of his nationality'.

MacGregor left Lagos almost in disgrace in 1902 for his public criticism of the Crown agents and for his policies towards the in-land protectorates. In 1904 he was appointed governor of Newfoundland. His handling of the clash between the local government and the British government over American fishing rights off the Newfoundland coast won him praise as 'the model of what a colonial governor should be'.

In 1909 MacGregor was appointed governor of Queensland. He accepted the limits of responsible government and al-though critical of some of his ministers' policies did not openly censure his advisers. However, in confidential dispatches to the Colonial Office he criticized the treatment of the Aboriginals and the limited support given to scientific research, particularly in primary industry. He travelled widely through Queensland, often accompanied by his wife. In March 1910 he became first chancellor of the University of Queensland. Active in its administration, he supported the provision of a suitable site but more importantly fought to retain language qualifications, preferably Greek or Latin, for matriculation in arts, engineering and science to conform with standards in other British universities. He was president of the Royal Geographical Society of Queensland and encouraged progress in the Queensland Museum to which he had sent many valuable artefacts while in New Guinea.

Appointed K.C.M.G. in 1889, G.C.M.G. in 1907 and privy councillor in 1914, MacGregor retired and left Queensland in July. He bought Chapel-on-Leader in Roxburghshire, Scotland, and in World War I advised the Colonial Office on Pacific problems. His observation of Sir Hubert Murray's rule in Papua had convinced him that Australia could be trusted with primitive people and he had become a strong advocate of Australia expanding her interests in the Pacific.

MacGregor had become estranged from both the children of his first marriage. His favourite elder daughter of the second marriage, who had married Sir Alfred Paget, died in 1918. After an operation for intestinal adhesions and gall-stones MacGregor died on 3 July 1919 and was buried at Towie, Aberdeenshire. His wife survived him by less than three months. His estate was valued at some £35,000.

The embitterments and frustrations of MacGregor's personal and official life left him unsatisfied. Yet his achievements were considerable and his humanitarian concern for the people he ruled and his scientific approach to problems remain of relevance.

R. B. Joyce, *Sir William MacGregor* (Melb, 1971) and for bibliog.   R. B. JOYCE

McILWRAITH, JOHN (1828-1902), manufacturer and shipowner, was born on 26 May 1828 at Ayr, Scotland, eldest son of John McIlwraith, plumber, and his wife Janet, née Howat. Educated at Watson's School and the Wallacetown Academy, he entered his father's plumbing business. An industrious worker, he still found time for helping to found the Ayr Musical Association. In January 1853 he arrived in Victoria. He tried the goldfields and in November joined Alexander and Francis Graham in a plumbing, painting and glazing business. He soon left them and opened a shop in Melbourne with zinc and lead pipes sent by his father. In September 1855 he moved his store to the back of his Collingwood home; with continual shipments from his father he gradually built up his business despite strong competition. He mainly supplied the plumbing trade but did profitable work on the new water supply scheme and in 1858 fitted up the Melbourne Hospital's hot water supply. With his father's help and in partnership with his brother Thomas [q.v.] he planned the construction of a lead mill. In September 1860 he went to Britain to buy the 'most powerful and best machinery used there for manufacturing sheet lead'. He returned with it in July 1861 and by mid-1862 the mill was working. In the next years he consolidated his business position but relationships with his father worsened as his advice and help were less and less required.

After an unsuccessful bid McIlwraith, 'an out and out Protectionist', was elected in 1870 to the Melbourne City Council for the new and dominately free trade Albert Ward. In 1873-74 he was mayor but his term was clouded by the death of a son and

his wife's illness. In 1874 he became a magistrate and was pressed to stand for parliament but refused, for 'once go into politics and there is no end to it'. He was a member of the Australian and European Bank's provisional committee and a Harbor Trust commissioner in 1877-82. In 1875 he began to manufacture block tin tubes with hydraulic machinery at his Melbourne lead works and won medals in Melbourne and the United States. His tubes were in great demand by the gas companies. In 1876 he was Victorian commissioner at the Philadelphia Exhibition. He had leadrolling machinery built in Ayr to American specifications and for many years imported his lead from Western Australia.

In 1875-78 McIlwraith was Melbourne agent for his brother Andrew who became the partner of M. D. McEacharn in a shipping business. McIlwraith also joined John Carson in a line of coastal coal and wool steamers and in 1877 commissioned the *Kerangie* which was wrecked in February 1879. In 1882 John McIlwraith and his brother Thomas made a triumphal return to Ayr; they received the freedom of the city in 1884. McIlwraith returned to Victoria in 1886 but left again at the end of the decade confident that his eldest son could manage the business. The first news of the depression failed to hurry his return. He was more concerned when John Danks [q.v.] set up in Sydney, and advised his Sydney branch to build a shot tower. On returning to Melbourne in 1893 he found a grim situation and compared it to plague panic. Of the thirty-four companies whose shares he held, half had suspended payment and he had to keep a supply of gold ready to meet current accounts. The continuing slump wore down his optimism and made him long for Scotland.

Andrew McIlwraith's shipping firm survived the crash but after an acrimonious row in 1895 John made him buy him out and when this was settled late in 1896 he felt 'as if [he] had got a new lease of life'. However, he remained unreconciled to the colony, attributing the continuing depression to radicalism and trade unionism. Business affairs and a bad fall in 1898 kept him in Victoria until April 1901. He died in Ayr on 9 September 1902, survived by his wife Mary, née Whannell (d. 1915), three daughters and three sons, John, Thomas and David who continued to run the Melbourne and Sydney lead works and the *Flinders*, bought in 1894 for the Western District trade. McIlwraith left an estate valued at £21,840.

H. M. Humphreys (ed), *Men of the time in Australia: Victorian series*, 1st ed (Melb, 1878);

Argus, 10 Oct 1873, 2 Oct, 7 Nov 1874; *Age*, 20 May, 3, 5 June 1893, 11 Sept 1902; *Ayr Advertiser*, 11 Sept 1902; *Warrnambool Stanard*, 12 Sept 1902; *Australasian*, 13 Sept 1902; *Bulletin*, 20 Sept 1902; John McIlwraith & Co. records (ANU Archives).

J. ANN HONE

McILWRAITH, SIR THOMAS (1835-1900), premier and capitalist, was born on 17 May 1835 at Ayr, Scotland, brother of John McIlwraith [q.v.]. Thomas's education was fuller than that of John and included a term in arts at the University of Glasgow. He had intended to enter a learned profession but John's success in Melbourne persuaded him to migrate to Victoria in 1854. After mining at Bendigo he was a partner in Cornish & Bruce [qq.v.] and profited from the Melbourne-Bendigo railway. In the railway department he worked as a surveyor and engineer on the Melbourne-Port and Geelong-Ballarat lines. In 1860 he was engaged by the contractor, J. V. A. Bruce [q.v.], on the Melbourne-Bendigo railway which included the Big Hill tunnel. In a dispute with the Victorian government he represented his employers and attracted public attention. In 1864 he contested the Sandhurst seat in the Victorian Legislative Assembly but won few votes as a free trader. Meanwhile he had taken up eight runs in the Maranoa district of Queensland with his lifelong managing partner, Joseph C. Smyth.

Thomas retained close relations with John, invested £3000 in John's business and on 6 June 1863 married Margaret Whannell, sister of John's wife. When Thomas finally settled in Queensland, Margaret was reluctant to live on Merivale station far from Brisbane. In 1871 she visited Merivale with her two daughters but soon returned to Melbourne for the birth of a third. In 1874 they decided to live in Brisbane but Thomas found that his wife was drinking heavily and sent her to Scotland. Her daughters, Jessie (b. 1866) and Mary (b. 1868), went to expensive boarding schools in Edinburgh, but Blanche (b. 1872) lived with her mother. McIlwraith tried to separate his wife from her children but his father rejected the proposal because, despite her bitterness, Margaret's behaviour had been exemplary. She died in Scotland on 14 October 1877.

McIlwraith's ethics displayed the harsh double standards of many Calvinists. He once reproached a politician for reading a newspaper on Sunday although he himself drank to excess, fathered an illegitimate daughter in Victoria and did not emerge blameless from the three largest financial scandals in Queensland history. Despite his success in Victoria and assets of £11,543 19s. 5d., the easy land terms offered by Queensland attracted him and at 28 he diverted his capital and energy to the new colony. Though at first he lived only partly in Queensland, the threat to his new investments from financial depression and pastoral recession in 1866-75 helped to commit him fully to the colony. The collapse of an English financial house ended the reckless expansion of 1860-66 and while southern flocks expanded Queensland's sheep numbers fell by 15 per cent by 1878.

McIlwraith & Smyth, troubled by drought, breeding problems and low prices, lost some of their runs. In April 1869 his father urged him to transfer his investments to the family shipping business, but McIlwraith preferred to solve his problems by exchanging his sheep stations for cattle runs and by seeking more British and Melbourne capital. In 1870 he declared his faith in the meat producing potential of Queensland and, encouraged by his father, saw a major market developing among British workers. It was thus no accident that McIlwraith in 1879-80 provided some of the capital for the *Strathleven* experiment in shipping refrigerated meat and butter to Britain, or that the ship was chartered by his brother Andrew of McIlwraith McEacharn Ltd.

McIlwraith's final departure from Victoria in the early 1870s was dictated by the need to supervise his Queensland investments and his entry into Queensland politics. He advocated developmental railways and in 1869 told a sceptical audience in Roma that the west could not prosper without a railway to Roma. He was returned for Warrego in January 1870 in a by-election, resigned on 9 September 1871 because of business problems and was returned again for Maranoa on 25 November 1873. His campaign for a trunk railway to Roma led to his appointment as secretary for public works and mines on 8 January 1874. Soon afterwards Samuel Griffith became attorney-general; their disagreement about railway, land and education policies foreshadowed a rivalry which dominated Queensland politics till 1892.

The parliament that McIlwraith entered was still divided between a squatter majority and a minority of Liberal townsmen. Cutting across this division were changing factions designed to secure expenditure in particular areas. He found his cherished line to Roma blocked by a combination of Ipswich townsmen and West Moreton squatters, both objecting to the cost of extended railways. At the same time northern members sought extension of the short Rockhampton railway which hardly paid for its axle grease. McIlwraith vainly advocated an overall plan in which railways would bring the maximum traffic to the best port in the cheapest way. Parliamentary log-rolling and opposition to these piecemeal programmes encouraged him to stress electoral redistribution and payment of members. While approving liberal plans for government-sponsored immigration and railways to develop closer settlement he maintained that a franchise based on population and the voting strength of settled areas could inhibit works expenditure needed in the interior. The colony's vacant lands were, he believed, a sacred trust from the imperial government to be used for accommodating the surplus population of Britain. Taught by his Liberal father, he believed that parliamentarians should have sufficient pay to devote all their time to politics but he feared the professional politician who thought more about the needs of his constituents than those of the whole colony.

In his maiden speech McIlwraith had explained that he was not one to describe squatters as necessarily unprogressive; indeed, they were among the most enterprising colonists. Since the policies of the Palmer [q.v.] ministry represented the static and sentimental side of squatting, McIlwraith sat at first with the Liberals, but despite his faith in heavy immigration and land settlement he never shared the Liberal dream of the interior as a cornucopia of smallholders like the American mid-west. What later became the sacred cow of a living area was anathema to McIlwraith who claimed that closer settlement without increased production was an illusion. He saw no conflict between grazing and agriculture since both used different types of land and each must be put to its most profitable use. To him squatting was a business enterprise, not a way of life, and squatters must retire before closer settlement. In the early 1880s he incorporated all but one of his many stations in the Darling Downs and Western Land Co., the North Australian Pastoral Co. and the Queensland Investment and Land Mortgage Co. to live as a financier and deploy his capital more flexibly.

McIlwraith first proposed a land-grant railway from Roma to the Gulf of Carpentaria when minister for works in the 1874 Macalister [q.v.] government and elaborated it when premier in 1881. The first enabled Griffith to force him out of office and the second antagonized his squatting supporters who preferred the secure perpetual leases and extended government railways offered by Griffith to dispossession by land-grant companies. McIlwraith also underestimated the political power of the

northern electorates whose seaport residents objected to their hinterlands being drained into Brisbane, while working-class voters feared that land-grant railways would be built by coolies.

McIlwraith's ideas on public finance were adopted within five years but he lost the works portfolio in 1874. In the Opposition he campaigned for an overall plan of major public works and for a comprehensive local government bill which would relieve the central government of responsibility for roads and bridges, thereby minimizing log-rolling and regional factions. Supported by many businessmen attracted from the Liberal party by this policy, McIlwraith was able in 1875-78 to establish the first cohesive political party in Queensland. The squatters, their power broken by the redistribution of 1876, preferred his policies to the run-busting legislation of the Liberals.

All McIlwraith's economic theories depended on massive intakes of overseas capital either by government loans or land-grant railways. In 1871 he startled the Legislative Assembly by advocating a £3,000,000 loan in London, thus leading the colony into one of the highest *per capita* debts in the empire. To avoid loan charges he wanted to use the land-grant principle but admitted that this meant alienating large tracts of land before the building of the railway had realized their potential value. He argued, however, that the land-grant principle was not primarily a means of building railways but of promoting land settlement.

In the general election of November 1878 McIlwraith won the new seat of Mulgrave and as colonial treasurer formed his first government on 21 January 1879. He promised to raise capital for trunk lines west from Brisbane, Rockhampton and Townsville. In January 1882 when Palmer resigned as colonial secretary, McIlwraith passed the Treasury to Archibald Archer [q.v.] and became colonial secretary himself. His Divisional Boards Act of 1879, the most comprehensive in Australia, gave local governments unparalleled autonomy but forced rural areas to assume the financial burden of local works. When critics complained that western graziers had government railways while the agricultural community had to finance its transport through heavy rates, he was forced to build some uneconomic branch lines in agricultural areas. However, his railway policy meant that Queensland built more trunk lines than any other colony.

These developments, pursued both by the government and the adventurous Queensland National Bank in which McIlwraith was deeply involved, helped to attract

£12,500,000 of private investment as well as large government loans and 26,685 immigrants in 1883. Even the seasons smiled on him and when he visited London from October 1879 to June 1880 he was lionized. His objects were to investigate the agent-general's office, to fix a loan figure, to negotiate with a cable company and to finalize railway and shipping contracts. Early in 1880 a select committee investigated allegations by William Hemmant [q.v.] of corrupt dealing between McIlwraith and his brother Andrew in some of the contracts. In 1881 a travelling royal commission examined the charge in England and exonerated the McIlwraiths but suspicion remained. He was appointed K.C.M.G. in 1882 and his repute revived in the nationalist fervour generated by his abortive annexation of eastern New Guinea in 1883.

At the height of his popularity and success McIlwraith committed political suicide. He lost his squatting supporters in the 1883 election by insisting on a land-grant railway from Charleville to the Gulf of Carpentaria and antagonized the working class by proposing to introduce Indian coolies for sugar plantations. His following was reduced to eighteen and Griffith became premier in November. McIlwraith then revisited England. In his absence the boom generated by his development policies began to collapse. The primary staples were again suffering from successive droughts and the downward trend in world prices while McIlwraith and a host of imitators had turned to speculation in real estate and mining. Faced by temporary business difficulties, he retired from politics in June 1886.

At the general election of May 1888 McIlwraith won North Brisbane and led a new National party to victory. He sought in vain to discredit the first Labor member, Thomas Glassey, and in September emerged victorious from a constitutional battle with Governor Musgrave over the prerogative of mercy. By November ill health had forced him to resign the premiership to B. D. Morehead [q.v.]. After a trip to Japan he quarrelled with his colleagues about William Pattison's [q.v.] undue influence and on 14 September 1889 resigned from the ministry. Unable to remain long on the back benches, he astounded everyone in August 1890 by joining his old enemy Griffith as colonial treasurer in what was called 'the Griffilwraith' coalition. His influence became obvious when Griffith, the erstwhile champion of white labour, broke the great strike of 1891 by military force and in 1892 revoked his 1885 prohibition of Kanaka recruitment for the sugar industry. Even the land-grant principle received legislative endorsement although no concessionaire

could be found to use it. McIlwraith represented Queensland at the National Convention in 1891 but he favoured only a limited form of Federation and in 1900 advised Queensland without success to abstain.

McIlwraith's Queensland Investment and Land Mortgage Co. was already in difficulties. Since 1888 the London directors had complained that the local board made advances not only on flimsy security but on illegal titles secured by dummying. In 1892 they charged McIlwraith, Palmer and two others with fraud. After fifty-five days in the Supreme Court the chief justice, Sir Charles Lilley [q.v.], discharged the jury and gave judgment for the plaintiffs. An appeal reversed the judgment and McIlwraith was alleged to have applied pressures which forced Lilley to resign. Griffith took his place and McIlwraith became premier in March 1893. He resigned in October and served as chief secretary and secretary for railways until 29 March 1895 although he had left for England on 15 January.

McIlwraith ended his political career under a cloud. Despite his absence and lack of a seat, he was appointed minister without portfolio in the hope that his health would permit his return, but his financial position was already insecure. Until 1879 he had been a director of the Queensland National Bank and had used its resources for his large speculations in 1884-90. In 1893 the bank had been saved from collapse only by government assistance. After the Queensland National Bank Agreement Act was passed in 1896, a committee investigated its affairs. The report, delayed for three months by McIlwraith's refusal because of ill health to return for examination, revealed a degree of mismanagement amounting almost to corruption. He was alleged to have debts to the bank of over £251,000, covered by security of only £60,700 while a further £77,000 owed by him had been written off as irrecoverable. He claimed that he and E. R. Drury [q.v.] had been partners in speculation but asserted that many of his apparent debts were incurred as an agent of the bank. He complained bitterly that the report had been published without his defence but his financial repute was ruined and even the conservative *Brisbane Courier* condemned him. On 25 November 1897 the Labor Party with government support succeeded in passing a resolution that he should retire from the ministry. On 9 December he resigned from the Executive Council. He died in London on 17 July 1900 and was buried at Ayr. His second wife Harriette Ann, née Mosman, whom he had married in 1879, was Palmer's sister-in-law;

she survived him with a fourth legitimate daughter born in 1881.

Although McIlwraith's economic ideas grew with experience they remained remarkably consistent throughout his career but by the 1890s they made him almost an anachronism. In 1918 T. A. Coghlan wrote that by 1893 the peculiar liberalism of Griffith had expunged any impression made by McIlwraith. Francis Adams [q.v.] saw him as 'the only public man in Australia who, by any stretch of imagination, one could call great'. More practical, Sir William MacGregor saw him as 'an able bully with a face like a dugong and a temper like a buffalo'. Nevertheless McIlwraith certainly had a vision of Queensland outrivalling her neighbours and a grand political style appropriate to his physical stature.

C. A. Bernays, Queensland politics during sixty years (Brisb, 1919); V&P (LA Qld), 1880, 1, 471, 2, 711, 1882, 2, 693, 1888, 1, 679, 1889, 1, 293, 1897, 2, 699; PD (Qld), 1897, 1652; Sydney Mail, 1 Feb 1879; Town and Country J, 15 Feb 1879; Australasian, 5 Mar 1898; Brisbane Courier, 19 July 1900; Bulletin, 28 July 1900; D. K. Dignan, Sir Thomas McIlwraith: a political portrait (B.A. Hons thesis, Univ Qld, 1951); J. C. Vockler, Sir Samuel Walker Griffith (B.A. Hons thesis, Univ Qld, 1953); Palmer-McIlwraith papers (Oxley Lib, Brisb).

DON DIGNAN

MACINTOSH, JOHN (1821-1911), ironmonger, alderman and politician, was born on 8 July 1821 at Auldearn, Nairn, Scotland, son of James Macintosh, farm manager, and his wife Barbara, née Watson. Educated at the local parish school, he was orphaned at 10 and worked as a farm labourer for 2s. 6d. a month. In September 1838 he sailed with his sister and brother-in-law in the Asia as bounty immigrants and reached Sydney on 10 May 1839. He went up country and worked at fencing, splitting, tobacco planting and whatever else was available; employed in a store on the Paterson River for five years, he used his spare time to educate himself. In 1846 he set up in Sydney as an ironmonger and soon had twelve employees making nails, hinges and other hardware. With 'an inventive turn of mind' and 'always anxious to be a manufacturer', he was looking for suitable premises for a factory when the gold rush lured all his men. On 10 May 1849 at St Andrew's Presbyterian Church he had married Caroline Alway; although blind she 'was of great use' to him in building up a flourishing business.

From December 1861 to November 1877 Macintosh represented Macquarie Ward in the Sydney City Council. For years he advocated an increased water supply and improved sewerage in the belief that cleanliness and plenty of pure water were the best means of ensuring the city's health. In 1867 he proposed a scheme for diverting sewerage from Sydney Harbour to Bondi, and it was later carried out. In 1869 he chaired Henry Parkes's [q.v.] testimonial fund, but in 1872 was elected to the Legislative Assembly for East Sydney as a supporter of James Martin [q.v.]. He sought larger funds for municipalities and in 1873 successfully moved for a select committee on their operation; as chairman he stressed that their inadequate endowments prevented them from carrying out improvements. In 1874 he criticized Governor Robinson's minute on the Gardiner [q.v.] case and voted against Parkes's ministry on the issue.

As an alderman Macintosh was perturbed by the condition of the unemployed and recommended numbers of the destitute to the commissioner of railways for free passes to the country where many found work. In June 1877 in the estimates debate he argued that before £100,000 was voted for assisted immigration proper arrangements should be made for the migrants' reception in the interior. In July he carried a resolution that all reports relevant to immigration be tabled in the House. In 1880 he told a select committee that the creation of local boards in the country was urgent if work was to be found for migrants. Regular in attending parliament, Macintosh introduced unsuccessful bills on patents and copyright. In 1880 he did not seek re-election after his wife died but in 1881 was appointed to the Legislative Council where he served on many committees.

Macintosh was a Freemason and in 1865 treasurer of the Robert Burns Chapter. An early supporter of the Sydney Mechanics' School of Arts, he served on its committee from 1863 and as vice-president in 1875, later helping to found Sydney Technical College. A magistrate from 1868, he was a director and treasurer of the Australian Permanent Building and Investment Society and a trustee and sometime president of the Second Industrial Benefit Building and Investment Society. In the 1870s he made his two elder sons partners in his business as J. Macintosh & Sons. In 1879 the firm supplied the government with £352 worth of iron and hardware for the Exhibition Building. By the mid-1880s he had over forty employees and each month was distributing and selling over 500 tons of hardware. Although a total abstainer and member of the local Temperance Alliance, Macintosh's appointment in 1882-84 as a licensing magistrate was approved by publicans. In 1883 he was a New South Wales commissioner for the Amsterdam Exhibition and in 1890-91 served on the royal commission into the city and suburban railways.

About 1870 Macintosh had bought Lindsay, Darling Point, and later acquired an estate at Burradoo. Survived by three sons and four daughters, he died at Lindsay on 6 July 1911 and was buried in the Presbyterian section of Rookwood cemetery. His estate was valued for probate at £49,000. His home was later bequeathed to the Women's Committee of the New South Wales branch of the National Trust of Australia.

E. Digby (ed), *Australian men of mark*, 2 (Syd, 1888); V&P (LA NSW), 1873-74, 5, 154, 1878-79, 1, 492, 7, 661, 1879-80, 5, 796; SMH, 5 June 1869, 7 July 1911; *Illustrated Sydney News*, 29 May 1875; *Daily Telegraph* (Syd), 29 May 1894; *Old Times*, April 1903; CO 201/577, 583, 597; MS cat (ML).   MARTHA RUTLEDGE

McINTYRE, DUNCAN (1831-1866), pastoralist and explorer, was born in Argyle, Scotland, son of James McIntyre, farmer, and his wife Mary, née MacDougall. He was probably orphaned when young and adopted by a relation, Archibald McIntyre, whose son Donald was often supposed to be Duncan's brother. McIntyre arrived in Port Phillip about 1849 with his foster parents and worked as station superintendent at Bullock Creek, Glengower, near Castlemaine, with another relation, Donald Campbell. On 5 March 1862 at St James's Cathedral, Melbourne, he married Mary Clyde Morris.

In mid-1863 Duncan and Donald McIntyre decided to seek a run in the new country round the Gulf of Carpentaria. Travelling overland, they found the Upper Darling in flood in January 1864 and learned that Queensland had imposed a quarantine restriction on stock imports. While awaiting an entry permit McIntyre spent five months exploring the Paroo, Bulloo and Barcoo Rivers, then took a small party to Cooper's Creek. As his permit had not arrived he took one European and three Aboriginals on an exploring trip to the Gulf. On his way he found two very old horses and two trees marked with 'L' many years earlier. In December 1864 he left Donald to take up the station and returned to Victoria where he reported that he had found traces of the long-lost Leichhardt [q.v.].

Although sceptics suggested that both trees and horses may have been connected with William Landsborough [q.v.] rather than with Leichhardt, his report convinced Ferdinand Mueller [q.v.] who organized a committee of wealthy ladies, raised finance

in both Melbourne and Europe, and commissioned McIntyre to lead the Ladies' Leichhardt Search Expedition for a fee of £1500.

Leaving final arrangements to his second-in-command, Dr James P. Murray, McIntyre left for the north and on 21 August 1865 at Mount Murchison took over seven men, forty-two horses and seven camels from Murray. After a long dry stage they reached Cooper's Creek on 26 November but found it dry and had to return to the previous camp in some distress. While McIntyre searched for water, Murray lost his head, served medicinal brandy to the men and lost most of the horses and much equipment. On his return McIntyre discharged Murray and other culprits. After a long rest he left for the Gulf on 9 February 1866 reaching Gibson's station in the Gilliat River late in March. From 20 April to 4 May he camped sixteen miles from Burketown and often visited the township where an epidemic of a peculiarly virulent fever was raging. He reported on 4 May that he was following rumours of a white man among the Aboriginals but on 23 May fell ill while on his way to a base camp on the Gilliat River. He died on 4 June 1866 and was buried on what later became Dalgonally station, held by Donald McIntyre till 1907.

McIntyre was accused of using the search committee to finance his own search for land and David Blair [q.v.] in his *Cyclopaedia of Australia* compared him with Robert O'Hara Burke [q.v.]. Neither of these views is fair. McIntyre was thoroughly honest and a far better bushman than Burke.

J. N. McIntyre, *White Australia; the empty north* (Syd, 1920); *Petermanns Geographische Mitteilungen*, 1865, 1866; *Age*, 23 Dec 1864, 3 Jan 1865; *Pastoral Times*, 31 Dec 1864; *Brisbane Courier*, 12 Jan 1865, supp; *Illustrated Melb Post*, 18 July 1865; *Aust News for Home Readers*, 25 July 1865, 25 Apr 1866; *Weekly Herald* (Brisb), 2 June 1866; *Australasian*, 21, 25 July, 22 Sept, 8 Dec 1866; CO 234/15/257.   H. J. GIBBNEY

McINTYRE, SIR JOHN (1832-1904), politician and businessman, was born on 24 April 1832 in Glasgow, Scotland, son of Malcolm McIntyre and his wife, née McGuinness. Educated at South End Academy, he began a medical course at the University of Glasgow but was attracted to Victoria by reports of gold discoveries and in 1852 arrived at Portland in the *Runnymede*. He worked various mining claims with success and settled at Bendigo where in 1855 he set up business as apothecary and gold-buyer in partnership with Dr James Eadie but continued his mining pursuits, especially quartz-crushing.

In the early 1850s McIntyre supported the Red Ribbon Movement against conditions on the goldfields. He was prominent in the agitation for unlocking the lands and treasurer of the local land league. In 1857 he offered to lead the diggers to Melbourne 'to prevent the robbery and spoliation of the patrimony of the people'. In 1856 he had been elected to the Sandhurst Court which dealt with mining matters and in 1858 to its successor, the mining board. As its chairman he was a leader in framing the first code of local mining by-laws and president of the first conference of mining board representatives in Melbourne. His many investments in mining were profitable and he travelled overseas several times to procure foreign capital for local mines, notably in 1887 when he formed a company in London to introduce British capital into the Maldon mines.

In 1859 McIntyre was elected to the Sandhurst Municipal Council but went to Europe with his family. On his return in 1862 he rejoined the council, becoming chairman in 1863 and then first mayor before he resigned in 1868. As mayor he was host to the duke of Edinburgh when he visited Bendigo in December 1867. In 1876 he represented Victoria at the Philadelphia Centennial Exhibition, partly to observe the arrangements so that he could make recommendations for the Victorian celebrations a decade later. In Bendigo he took a special interest in the local hospital, giving long service as honorary secretary and later as a trustee. He was a territorial magistrate and a guardian of minors for the Bendigo district.

McIntyre tried several times to enter parliament, contesting Mandurang in 1866 and Sandhurst in 1871 and 1874. In 1877 he was persuaded to stand again and won Sandhurst. An outspoken free trader, he actively opposed protection and lost his seat in June 1880, but early in 1881 won Maldon in the by-election which followed J. Service's [q.v.] resignation from the seat. From 23 January 1893 to 27 September 1894 in the J. B. Patterson [q.v.] ministry he was president of the Board of Lands and Works and commissioner of crown lands and survey. He was a member of the royal commissions on the tariff in 1881 and gold-mining in 1889 and served on the railway standing committee in 1890. He lost his seat in September 1902.

Described as 'grand company', McIntyre was a popular and energetic administrator. He was appointed a K.B. in 1895. A Presbyterian, he was honorary colonel of the Scottish Regiment. He had married in 1853 Jeanne Grant, sister-in-law of Dr Eadie. She died in 1861, leaving three sons; in 1875 he married her sister Isabella who died in 1902. McIntyre's health broke down after his exhausting but vain campaign for election to the Senate in December 1903. He died at his home in Brighton on 18 January 1904 and was buried at the Back Creek cemetery, Bendigo.

A. Sutherland et al, *Victoria and its metropolis*, 2 (Melb, 1888); *Australasian*, 21 Dec 1867, 28 Jan 1893, 5 Jan 1895, 28 Nov 1903, 23 Jan 1904; *Sydney Mail*, 10 May 1884; M. G. Finlayson, Groups in Victorian politics, 1889-94 (M.A. thesis, Univ Melb, 1964).

ALLAN JOHNSTON

McINTYRE, WILLIAM (1805-1870), Presbyterian minister, was born in March 1805 at Kilmonivaig, Inverness-shire, Scotland, the fifth son of Duncan McIntyre, sheep farmer, and his wife Catherine, née Kennedy. Educated at the parish school, he went to the University of Glasgow (A.M., 1829). After teaching in Glasgow, he entered the Divinity Hall to study for the ministry and was licensed as a probationer by the Presbytery of Dunoon. J. D. Lang [q.v.] was impressed by his preaching and enlisted him 'for New South Wales'. McIntyre probably needed little persuading as his cousin Peter McIntyre [q.v.] had much land in the Hunter Valley and New England and had been followed to the colony by other cousins.

In the *Midlothian*, with 250 devout Gaelic-speaking Highlanders, McIntyre reached Sydney on 13 December 1837. Four days later he held the first Gaelic service in the colony. He acted as assistant to Lang until 1840 as editor of the Protestant *Colonist* and as 'Professor' of theology in the Australian College. He regularly visited Gaelic-speaking settlers in the Hunter Valley. In 1841 he was inducted to Maitland and was moderator of the Synod of Australia and his address, *The Weakness and Power of the Christian Ministry* was published in Sydney in 1842. At his own instigation he was appointed chairman of a committee to investigate the possibility of training ministers in Australia. In 1844, after he had sought to dispense with banns, McIntyre married his cousin Mary, nearly twenty years his senior, sister of Peter McIntyre. She owned three large stations in the New England district as well as other property. The *Colonial Observer* termed the marriage a 'monstrous irregularity'.

On 10 October 1846 McIntyre and most of his congregation withdrew from the Synod of the Established Church of Scotland and with Tait, Stewart and others established the first Synod of Eastern Australia in connexion with the Free Church of Scotland. McIntyre was elected its first moderator. In 1860 he advertised a lecture on 'The Heathenism of Popery, Proved and Illustrated', which upset Irish Catholics and led to the famous Maitland riots, said to have involved over 1000 people. McIntyre was injured and seventeen prosecutions followed. In February 1862 he became minister of St George's, Sydney. The congregation was in dire financial straits with a building debt of over £10,000. He proved not only a faithful pastor but also ministered without stipend and succeeded in paying off the debt.

McIntyre allied himself with those committed to Calvinistic theology, strongly advocating Free Church principles and disclaiming indiscriminate endowment. He maintained that his fellow presbyters never understood the position in Australia, 'in reference to the disruption'. He totally rejected Lang's 'voluntaryism'. With the congregation of St George's he remained outside the Union of the Synods of Eastern Australia and of New South Wales in 1864 and its final union with the Synod of Australia and the United Presbyterians who created the Presbyterian Church in New South Wales in 1865.

Lang denounced McIntyre but admitted that he 'was one of the honestest men in New South Wales . . . although dogmatical and fond of power to an inordinate degree, Mr. McIntyre was nevertheless apt to become the dupe of far inferior men'. Outside his own church he supported the Benevolent Society, the Bible Society and Church Extension. He was commissioned by the Free Church to visit Scotland and recruit ministers, and returned in 1854 with his nephew, James McCulloch and his own brother Allan, who became minister of the Manning River Free Church Congregation and was succeeded there by the youngest of the family, Duncan Kennedy, who died in 1899.

While serving a further term as moderator, McIntyre died at his manse in Roslyn Terrace, Macleay Street, Sydney, on 12 July 1870. A massive monument with a Latin inscription by Professor Badham [q.v.] marks his grave in Rookwood cemetery. His wife died on 31 March 1872; they had no children.

J. D. Lang, The dead fly (Syd, 1861); J. Cameron, Centenary history of the Presbyterian Church in New South Wales (Syd, 1905); J. C. Robinson, The Free Presbyterian Church in Australia (Melb, 1947); A. D. Gilchrist (ed), John Dunmore Lang, 1-2 (Melb, 1951); C. A. White, The challenge of the years (Syd, 1951); SMH, 31 Mar, 4, 10, 13, 16, 18 Apr 1860, 14 July, 10 Aug 1870; McIntyre papers (Presbyterian Lib, Assembly Hall, Syd); family papers (held by Miss Joanna McIntyre, ML).   ALAN DOUGAN

McINTYRE, WILLIAM (1830-1911), school inspector, was born on 29 January 1830 in County Antrim, Ireland, son of William McIntyre (1802-1867), farmer. and his wife Margaret, née McGrath. Educated at the Normal Training College, Dublin, he married Sarah Humphrey in County Antrim in 1851.

McIntyre had become an organizing master by 1856 when the New South Wales Board of National Education induced him to migrate with free passages and half-pay on the voyage. On arrival he became inspector for the Hunter River district. In 1859-60 he was principal teacher of the Fort Street Girls' School and in 1861 was appointed district inspector of the northern district which included all the colony north of the Hunter Valley. Travelling by way of the north coast he established several schools. Soon after reaching his headquarters at Armidale he enlisted the support of 'many of the gentlemen of the town most distinguished for talent and liberal views'; four months later a National school was opened there. He helped to establish 45 new schools so that 55 were functioning when he left the district in 1868.

McIntyre had normally travelled some 3500 miles a year in his large district and tried to visit each school twice a year. In 1863 he almost drowned when his horses were swept away while trying to cross a flooded river. From 1867 he was also required to inspect the denominational schools under the Council of Education; his report criticized the low standards of classrooms, school organization and teaching ability compared with the public schools.

In 1868 McIntyre was transferred to the Goulburn district which had twice as many schools and included Mittagong, Yass, Adaminaby and Eden. In 1869 he wrote that he had 'grown grey in the service' and that his constitution had been 'partially ruined by hardship, exposure and slavery'. He also claimed to have been responsible for the half-time schools which enabled more children to receive schooling from an itinerant teacher. He was given a testimonial from grateful parents when he left in 1872. In 1873-77 he served in the Camden district and, apart from six months' leave in Britain, again in Goulburn in 1878-81.

In 1867 William Wilkins [q.v.] had deferred McIntyre's promotion and in 1869 charged him with inadequacy in performing his duties as inspector. In spite of a spirited defence, McIntyre was not advanced as quickly as many younger men. In 1881 he was demoted and for two years had roving commissions around the colony. From 1884, when Wilkins retired, McIntyre was stationed in Sydney as an inspector in the metropolitan area. In 1890 he became deputy chief inspector with a salary of £650. He was apparently so well established that the Public Service Board did not demand his retirement at 65 but let him continue until 1902.

While in Armidale McIntyre had bought a farm of 320 acres which he called Antrim Park. He spent £30 on a slab hut and £233 on fencing, and with the aid of contract labour was soon selling bags of potatoes. He also bought horses and cattle. By the 1880s he was leasing out small farms at low rental on condition that they were cleared and fenced. He kept careful records of his expenses on inspection tours and when the department substituted a daily allowance he was delighted by his profit. He had a good eye for a bargain and by the 1890s was buying cases of whisky for himself and other departmental officials. He also bought regular tickets in consultations on Sydney and Melbourne races. He died on 9 December 1911 at his home in Glebe and was buried in the Presbyterian section of Rookwood cemetery. He was survived by his wife, to whom he left most of his estate of £7549, and by three sons and four daughters. Fourteen volumes of his diaries are in the Mitchell Library.

Council of Education, *Annual reports* (Syd, 1866-69); *Armidale Express*, 1861-64; Board of National Education, Fair minute book 1854-58 and miscellaneous in-letters 1848-66 (NSWA); Council of Education, Inspectors' itineraries and weekly diaries 1867-72 (NSWA).

                                    BRUCE MITCHELL

MACKAY, ANGUS (1824-1886), newspaper proprietor and politician, was born on 26 January 1824 in Aberdeen, Scotland, son of Murdoch Mackay, soldier, and his wife Elizabeth, née McLeod. His father took the family to Sydney in 1827 and became a private in the Veteran Corps at Parramatta. Intending to join the Presbyterian ministry, Angus attended J. D. Lang's [q.v.] Australian College and later taught there. For some time he was headmaster of a Sydney Presbyterian school but abandoned his theological predilections in favour of journalism and involvement in the anti-transportation movement. In 1847 he was editor of the *Atlas* founded by Robert Lowe [q.v.]. In 1850 he managed a business at Geelong for Henry Parkes [q.v.] but

returned to Sydney to join the staff of the *People's Advocate*.

In May 1851 Mackay visited the Ophir and other goldfields as a special correspondent to the *Empire* and in 1852 was its parliamentary reporter. From March to October 1853 he was a digger and special correspondent to the *Empire* on the Ovens fields where he spoke at a meeting on miners' grievances. In October Mackay appeared as a miners' delegate before the select committee on the goldfields and spoke strongly against the licence fee. He then moved to Bendigo where, for a year as special correspondent to the *Argus*, he reported the many rushes in the district. In 1854 at Melbourne he married Margaret O'Shannasy; they had three sons and three daughters.

In 1855 Mackay and two others bought the *Bendigo Advertiser* and in 1863 they established the *McIvor Times*; after its sale the firm bought the *Riverine Herald*. As a newspaper editor and proprietor at Bendigo, Mackay took a keen interest in local affairs. In 1855 he was one of three who formed the Working Miners' Protection Society which supported the 'co-operative association of working miners' against 'monopolists'. He was active in the miners' eight-hour movement and in the campaign to obtain an adequate water supply for Bendigo; in 1867 he was president of the Mechanics' Institute.

In 1868 Mackay was elected for Sandhurst Boroughs to the Legislative Assembly and appointed a member of the Board of Education. From April 1870 to June 1871 he was minister for mines in the McCulloch [q.v.] ministry. He held the same office in the Francis and Kerferd [qq.v.] ministries from June 1872 to August 1875; he was also minister for public instruction from July 1874 to August 1875. Defeated in the 1877 election he was returned after a successful petition unseated his opponent. In July 1879 he was prominent in a syndicate which started the Sydney *Daily Telegraph*. Editorial duties in Sydney prevented him from contesting the elections in 1880 and 1883, but he again represented Sandhurst after winning a by-election in May. Three years later he was defeated at the polls.

Partly because of his free trade opinions Mackay was a 'moderate' Liberal in Victorian politics. In 1853 he assured the select committee on the goldfields that 'you need not fear going too far in extending the franchise as much as possible'. In 1868 he opposed the Darling grant but supported the assembly in its constitutional conflict with the council. Mackay advocated secular and compulsory education which would be free only to the poor. As minister for mines he introduced in 1872 a bill for mining on private property but it was rejected by the council; three of his later bills met the same fate. While opposed to 'Berryite' policies, he had reservations about the increasing conservatism of the McCulloch ministry in 1875-77. In his last years he was a critic of the Service-Berry [qq.v.] coalition.

Mackay won well-deserved repute as an efficient administrator. He was mainly responsible for the 1873 Regulation of Mines Act which legalized the eight-hour system and enforced important safety standards in the mines. In the Board of Education he advocated the secular solution which parliament later adopted. Indeed the education bill introduced by the McCulloch ministry in 1870 and drafted by Mackay and the solicitor-general, H. J. Wrixon [q.v.], was remarkably similar to the main provisions of the Education Act of 1872. He was regarded as an efficient second minister for public instruction in a difficult year of transition.

Mackay was a good example of those attracted to the goldfields who did modestly well in later decades. Besides newspaper interests he invested in mining ventures and left an estate valued at £6722. Although an unimpressive speaker, his contributions to debates were usually well prepared and constructive. His reputation for dourness was belied in part by his great interest in theatricals and cricket. Mackay's first wife died in 1874, survived by two sons and three daughters. In Melbourne on 15 July 1875 he married Annie Leslie Anderson. He died at his home in Sandhurst on 5 July 1886.

R. L. Knight, *Illiberal Liberal: Robert Lowe in New South Wales, 1842-1850* (Melb, 1966); *Argus*, 6 July 1886; D. F. C. Johanson, The development of Bendigo from a goldfield into a community (B.A. Hons thesis, Univ Melb, 1959); D. Grundy, The politics of church-state relations in Victoria, 1868-1872 (Ph.D. thesis, Univ Melb, 1972).

S. M. INGHAM

MACKAY, JOHN (1839-1914), explorer, sailor and harbourmaster, was born on 26 March 1839 in Inverness, Scotland, son of George Mackay, farmer, and his wife Ann, née Munro. Educated at the Free Church Academy in Inverness, he went with his parents to Melbourne in the *Australia* in 1854 and next year to the New England district, New South Wales. His father took up Ness Farm, a sheep run between Armidale and Uralla. John lived there mostly but made one South Pacific voyage as purser.

In 1859 Mackay joined the gold rush on the Rocky River near Armidale. His claim was almost worked out next year when he was persuaded by pastoralist friends to lead an expedition in search of northern grazing land. His qualifications for the enterprise included some surveying for landowners and overlanding with his friend, Nat Buchanan [q.v.]. In his party were John Macrossin, who contributed largely to its finances; Hamilton Robinson, a grazier from Bendemere; Giovanni Barberi (John Barber), an Italian and former ship's carpenter; Duke, an Aboriginal, the only one to lose his life on the expedition; and J. Muldoon and D. Cameron, who left the expedition before it was completed. They left Armidale in January 1860 and travelling inland reached Rockhampton on 2 March. The exploration began after they left the settlement at Marlborough some sixty miles north of Rockhampton on 22 March. Mackay led his party along the banks of the Isaacs River but tree markings and a deserted camp indicated they were following the track of G. E. Dalrymple [q.v.], whose expedition had left Rockhampton before Mackay's arrival. The party retraced their steps for some distance and then turned east into *terra incognita* between the Burdekin and the watershed of the Isaacs River which Leichhardt [q.v.] had noted. Their discovery of this area on 16 May became known as the Mackay district.

Mackay's association with the district after its discovery was brief. His tender for a run was accepted by the Queensland government early in 1861. The proviso that runs be stocked within nine months led him into partnership with James Starr, a New England squatter. Unaware of his partner's financial difficulties, Mackay had stocked his lease, Greenmount, with 1200 cattle by January 1862 but Starr's insolvency forced him to sell out in 1863. With Dick Spencer, Mackay discovered a better pass through the Clarke Range than the one he had used earlier.

Mackay's labours won him little recognition. Since Governor Bowen had promised in 1864 that the government would remunerate him if his discovery ever became important, Mackay petitioned the Crown Lands Office in 1874 seeking recognition of his find. He also included his soundings and geographical sketch of the bar and mouth of the Pioneer River at Mackay, and work he had done in 1860 in the cutter *Presto* chartered at his own expense. His petition resulted in the river being gazetted a port of entry, and two months later his sketch is said to have appeared in Buxton's *Map of Queensland*. In 1882 from Fiji Mackay petitioned for 'consideration as his discovery had proved highly beneficial to the colony'. On 30 October John Stevenson, member for Normanby, successfully moved an address to the governor praying him to grant Mackay a thousand agricultural acres. However, the Executive Council threw the address back to the Legislative Assembly on the grounds that the governor had no power to act on a motion. Stevenson promptly proposed to amend the resolution by turning it into a bill for Mackay's land grant, but the premier insisted on postponing the bill and before it could be introduced a new and hostile ministry had been formed.

After leaving Greenmount Mackay had become interested in exploring New Guinea but it came to nothing. He gained his master's certificate in 1865 and for eighteen years commanded ships under various flags in the South Pacific. In 1883-89 he was harbourmaster at Cooktown and in 1892-1902 at Brisbane. He was chairman of the Queensland Marine Board in 1902 until appointed portmaster in 1912. He died at St Helen's Hospital, South Brisbane, on 11 March 1914. He was survived by his wife Marion, née McLennon, whom he had married at Cooktown in 1883, and by their two sons and two daughters.

H. L. Roth, *The discovery and settlement of Port Mackay* (Halifax, 1908); G. C. Bolton, *A thousand miles away* (Brisb, 1963); PD (Qld), 1882 (2); *Morning Bulletin*, 11 Apr 1914; *Daily Mercury*, 6 Apr 1962; John Mackay papers (ML); Hugo Strong papers (ML).

J. A. NILSSON

McKENNA, MARTIN (1832-1907), brewer and pastoralist, was born on 11 November 1832 at Carrahill, Kilkenny, Ireland, son of Patrick McKenna, a Catholic farmer, and his wife Anastasia, née Feehan. After working for a Quaker firm of millers he migrated to Victoria in 1854. He mined on such goldfields as Ballarat, Ararat, Blackwood and Forest Creek but caught typhoid.

McKenna then went to Kyneton where he joined his cousin Michael McKenna in business. By 1858 he was able to join a friend, Jowett, in building the Campaspe brewery in Beauchamp Street, Kyneton, and twenty years later combined with Johnson & Cock's brewery on the Campaspe. McKenna became chairman of the Kyneton Brewing Co., Jowett retiring from the business. In 1879 the malt house was built in Ebden Street.

In 1861 McKenna and others including C. & M. Lyons took up occupation licences at Baynton, and the basis of McKenna's Glen Erin estate was formed. He also owned properties at Tylden and Katunga. In 1883 he told the royal commission on the tariff that he had between 4000 and 5000 acres, with 120 acres under crop and the rest grazing Lincoln sheep, cattle and horses.

McKenna's business interests included membership of the Board of Union Trustees and Executors Co. and shares in the Tram-

ways Co. His tall upright figure was well known in Kyneton and in Melbourne where he wore a silk top hat and frock coat. He was a splendid host and enjoyed the respect of his contemporaries as an impartial and forceful leader in local affairs. His local offices included membership of the Land Board in the early days and presidency of the Kyneton Hospital and Racing Club. He was a sergeant in the volunteer Prince of Wales Light Horse in the 1860s. In 1864, after two years as a councillor, he was elected mayor of the borough of Kyneton. When Kyneton became a shire in 1865 he was its first president and remained a councillor till 1907. He was elected to the Legislative Assembly for the Kyneton Boroughs in March 1868, and held the seat as a moderate protectionist until he retired in March 1874. In the Legislative Council he contested the North-Western Province in 1881 without success. He later held the post of returning officer for elections to the Legislative Assembly. He was also a justice of the peace.

In 1865 McKenna had married Catherine, daughter of Bartholomew Wheeler of Carlsruhe; they had eleven children. One of their six sons became a Catholic priest and others carried on his civic interests. After two years of illness McKenna died on 7 May 1907.

A. Sutherland et al, *Victoria and its metropolis*, 2 (Melb, 1888); *History of Kyneton 1901-1935*, 2 (Kyneton, 1935); V&P (LA Vic), 1883, 4 (10); *Aust Brewer's J*, 20 Mar 1905, 20 May 1907; *Table Talk*, 2 Jan 1902; *Argus*, 9 May 1907; *Kyneton Observer*, 9 May 1907.

SYLVIA MORRISSEY

MACKENZIE, SIR EVAN (1816-1883), soldier and pastoralist, was born on 5 August 1816 at Portobello, Edinburgh, son of Colin Mackenzie and his wife Isabella, née Cameron. Educated mainly in Europe he learnt to speak French, German and some Greek. On 17 April 1837 he volunteered as a cadet in the 1st Kaiser Ferdinand Hussar Regiment of the Austrian army. He served on garrison duty at Ujécs in Hungary, was promoted second lieutenant on 1 April 1838 and resigned on 31 April 1840.

In September Mackenzie sailed with his brother Colin for Sydney and in 1842 took up a station at Kilcoy, near Brisbane. He was appointed a justice of the peace, built the first house in Ipswich and in 1844 bought land at Kangaroo Point where he started a boiling-down works and established a village. He was prominent in various public meetings of squatters and a friend of Ludwig Leichhardt [q.v.]. On 2 November 1844 he married Sarah Anna Philomena, daughter of James Parks of Londonderry.

Mackenzie's father was created baronet in 1836 and when he died in 1845 Evan succeeded to the title. He sold his Queensland interests and retired to Scotland in April 1846. He became a magistrate and deputy lieutenant of Ross and Cromarty County but continued to travel. He spent some time in America and was not resident at his home, Belmaduthy House, when the 1881 census was taken. He died in London on 12 December 1883, survived by four daughters. His only son Colin Charles (b. 1848) predeceased him and the title became extinct.

After Mackenzie left Queensland stories of a mass poisoning of Aboriginals by arsenic on Kilcoy during his tenure started to circulate. Though never confirmed, the rumours were mentioned in a select committee in 1861 and repeated by W. Coote [q.v.] in 1867. They became part of the Australian legend but no suggestion of participation by Mackenzie was ever made.

J. D. Lang, Cooksland in north-eastern Australia (Lond, 1847); W. Coote, The history of the colony of Queensland (Brisb, 1867); M. Aurousseau (ed), The letters of F. W. Ludwig Leichhardt (Cambridge, 1968); V&P (LA Qld), 1861, 477; Town and Country J, 23 Feb 1884; Osterreicher Staatsarchiv, Kriegsarchiv, Vienna.
                                               H. J. GIBBNEY

MACKENZIE, SIR ROBERT RAMSAY, (1811-1873), squatter and politician, was born on 21 July 1811 at Coul, Ross-shire, Scotland, the fourth son of Sir George Steuart Mackenzie, 7th baronet, and his wife Mary, fifth daughter of Donald Macleod of Geanies, Ross-shire. With £750 Mackenzie arrived in the Wave at Sydney in April 1832 and joined his brother James. He soon paid H. H. Macarthur [q.v.] £500 for sheep which he depastured at Riddlesdale, near Dungog, and the brothers began to speculate in land. In 1837 Mackenzie bought Salisbury station in the New England district and separated from his brother, promising him £3000. By 1839 he was heavily in debt and borrowed £8000 from his family in Scotland. He continued to buy stock and take up runs in New England; at different times he held Bolivia, Furracabad, Ballindean, Turracabal and Tenterfield stations, which were left in the charge of managers while he lived in Sydney. By December 1840 he was £19,000 in debt, but claimed that he 'could work it out'. He sold Salisbury to M. H. Marsh [q.v.] and Bolivia to S. A. Donaldson [q.v.] with whom he had a kind of partnership. In April 1841 under the Insolvency Act he took out a letter of licence

and his affairs were put in the hands of Donaldson & Dawes as agents. His accounts failed to improve and in 1844 he became bankrupt with debts of over £27,000. An absentee squatter who allegedly lived extravagantly in Sydney, Mackenzie's financial methods were slipshod and he kept 'no book of accounts showing . . . receipts of the wool'. His speculations were deliberately obscure and his creditors suspected that people held sheep and properties for him. After the crash he managed Tenterfield for Donaldson. In 1846 Mackenzie got his certificate of discharge and married Louisa Alexandrina (d. 1906), daughter of Richard Jones [q.v.]. In 1847 he was appointed a magistrate and lived at Clifton, New England.

In 1856 Mackenzie was part-lessee of fifty-two runs with a total area of 1536 square miles in the Leichhardt and Burnett Districts, on the upper Dawson River, in the Carnarvon and Expedition Ranges and on Barambah Creek. His average tenure was about three years, but this time his transactions were profitable and he had disposed of all his interests by the depression of 1867. He was a trustee of the Trust and Agency Co. of Australasia and lived in New Farm, Brisbane.

On the separation of Queensland Mackenzie entered politics. He was chosen on 18 December 1859 by Governor Bowen, who described him as a pastoralist 'of high honour and integrity, of methodical habits of business', as colonial treasurer in Herbert's [q.v.] first ministry. From May 1860 to April 1869 he represented the Burnett in the Legislative Assembly. While treasurer he described G. E. Dalrymple's [q.v.] proposed expedition to the Burdekin as land speculation and influenced the government to countermand the proclamation opening the Kennedy district. From December 1859 he had served on the Board of National Education and as chairman of the Board of General Education set up under the 1860 Act, but resigned in 1861 after being rebuked in parliament for his opposition to subsidies for denominational schools and left the board in 1862.

Mackenzie resigned as treasurer when Arthur Macalister [q.v.] was preferred as acting head of the administration when Herbert went to England in 1862. Bitterly disappointed, Mackenzie published in the Guardian his correspondence with Herbert, interpreting it as a promise of succession. He put even more blame on Macalister and joined those who opposed him. However, the offer of the colonial secretaryship induced Mackenzie in February 1866 to serve under Macalister, who resigned on 18 July in the financial crisis. After Herbert's brief premiership, Macalister formed another ministry but without Mackenzie whom he alleged had made a written offer to join him. Mackenzie led the attacks on Macalister, partly on the extent of free selection envisaged in a land bill. He defended the alienation of land to squatters and asserted that 'a great deal of balderdash had been talked about squatters and "cormorants".' Macalister resigned on 15 August 1867 and Mackenzie formed the next government as premier and colonial treasurer.

His ministry, dominated by squatting members including Arthur Palmer [q.v.], passed land legislation guaranteeing graziers in the settled areas ten-year leases of half their existing runs with extensive rights of pre-emption, and in the outside areas twenty-one-year leases. Mackenzie's Crown Land Alienation Act seemed to encourage agriculture but led to much dummying and speculation by the squatters. His ministry passed forty-eight measures, including several innocuous legal bills, but his position as leader was never assured. Though defeated by two votes in August 1868 during the address-in-reply debate, his resignation was refused by Governor Blackall who granted him a dissolution. When parliament met in November he won the vote on the address-in-reply only by the casting vote of the Speaker and resigned.

On 21 December 1868 his brother William died and Mackenzie succeeded as 10th baronet. Despite his organizing ability he did not seek re-election in 1869. In 1871 he returned to Scotland where he died on 19 September 1873, survived by his wife, a son and four daughters, two of whom married into the Archer family [q.v.] of Queensland.

Mackenzie was not an outstanding squatter or politician. As an absentee squatter he could justly be described as a cormorant who left no roots in the land. Although premier and leader of the Opposition in Queensland he had no firm support and was dominated by other politicians. Physically large, he was limited intellectually and as a leader.

C. A. Bernays, *Queensland politics during sixty years* (Brisb, 1919); J. F. Campbell, 'Discovery and early pastoral settlement of New England', *JRAHS*, 8 (1922); *Brisbane Courier*, 28 July 1862; *The Times*, 24 Sept 1873; P. D. Wilson, The political career of Hon. A. Macalister (B.A. Hons thesis, Univ Qld, 1969); Bankruptcy papers, 1250 (NSWA); Land and Col Sec files (QA).   R. B. JOYCE

MACKIE, GEORGE (1823-1871), Presbyterian minister, was born at Fettercairn, Kincardineshire, near Montrose, Angus, Scotland, son of John Mackie, farmer, and his wife Elizabeth, née Sheriffs. Educated at the local school, he engaged in commerce for some years and matriculated at the University of St Andrews, where he read classics and philosophy, but did not take a degree. He also attended the divinity course of the Free Church at New College, Edinburgh. He became a good scholar and was later said to be fluent in French, German, Italian and Spanish. He was licensed by the Free Church Presbytery of Brechin in 1848 and sent by its Colonial Committee to Australia. He sailed in the *Lysander* to Melbourne where he preached his first colonial sermon and in the *Shamrock* arrived at Sydney on 25 March 1849.

Mackie ministered briefly to the Pitt Street Congregation of the Free Church (later part of St Stephen's, Macquarie Street) which was awaiting the arrival of Rev. Alex Salmon from Barrhead, Scotland. On Salmon's arrival Mackie was ordained by the Free Church Presbytery at Jamberoo and became minister of Illawarra and Shoalhaven. Soon afterwards he married Barbara, fourth daughter of William Smith of Montrose, who came from Scotland with her father to join him. He served this large area from Kiama until 1857, when he went to Lake Learmonth and Burrumbeet in Victoria and was succeeded by John Kinross [q.v.]. His parents and other members of the family had settled in the Burrumbeet district, and Mrs Mackie's sister Jane was the wife of a neighbouring minister, Rev. Thomas Hastie of Buninyong.

Mackie's ministry at Learmonth and Burrumbeet was very active. He built a manse at Lake Learmonth and established churches at Miners Rest, Creswick and Clunes. He helped to create the Presbytery of Ballarat and ministered over a wide area. While in Sydney on church business in 1860 he heard that Elizabeth, youngest of his three daughters, had contracted diphtheria. He hurried home to discover that his wife, aged 30, and daughter, aged 19 months, had died of the disease on 13 August. Soon afterwards he moved to the parish of Horsham where in December 1860 he married Margaret Lyon. In May 1862 he was called to South Yarra and exercised a singularly successful ministry until 1871.

Mackie was small and slightly built but had great energy. As an earnest pastor he inspired much affection and became a public figure in Melbourne. He was convener of the Presbyterian Church's Chinese and Aborigines Mission Committee in Victoria; he also took a keen interest in evangelism in the Melbourne gaol. He strongly favoured the union of the Synod of Victoria and the Free Presbyterian Church of Victoria, which took place on 7 April 1857. Among many causes he supported the Deaf and Dumb Institute and the temperance movement. He was also a member of the Independent Order of Rechabites, the Loyal Orange Lodge, the Grand United Order of Gardeners, the Manchester Unity Oddfellows and the Young Men's Christian Association. He was elected moderator of the Presbyterian Church of Victoria and installed on 14 November 1871. Three weeks later he was taken ill during divine service in South Yarra Church and died on 12 December aged 48, survived by his second wife and two daughters. His funeral was well attended by his fellow ministers and many other dignatories in Melbourne, and Governor Manners-Sutton sent his carriage.

R. Sutherland, *The history of the Presbyterian Church of Victoria* (Lond, 1877); J. Cameron, *Centenary history of the Presbyterian Church in New South Wales* (Syd, 1905); D. M. Stewart, *Jubilee history of the Presbyterian Church in Victoria* (Melb, 1909); C. A. White, *The challenge of the years* (Syd, 1951); *Argus*, 13 Dec 1871; papers written by D. G. Walton, Ballarat (held by author).

ALAN DOUGAN

McKILLOP, DONALD (1853-1924), Jesuit priest, was born on 27 April 1853 in Portland, Victoria, brother of Mary [q.v.] who founded the Josephite Sisters, the largest Australian congregation of nuns. He was educated at St Aloysius College, Sevenhill, South Australia, where he entered the Society of Jesus in June 1872 and did his noviceship and studies in rhetoric and philosophy until 1877. He then taught at the college until 1882 when he was sent for theological studies to Innsbruck in 1883, to north Wales in 1884-85 where he was ordained priest and to Roehampton for his Jesuit studies. With two Jesuit companions he returned to Adelaide on 14 October 1886, all three destined for the mission to the Aboriginals in the Northern Territory. This mission, conducted in 1882-90 by the Austrian Jesuits from Sevenhill, involved nineteen Jesuits and had the largest number of Aboriginals of any in the Northern Territory. Anthropologists such as W. E. H. Stanner and R. M. Berndt single it out for its insights and appreciation of Aboriginal culture.

The policy adopted on the mission stations followed the model of the Jesuit Reductions in eighteenth-century Paraguay, and McKillop became its most forthright exponent. In 1887-89 he was attached to the Rapid Creek station, near Palmerston, to work and study the Mulluk Mulluk dialect, the lingua franca of the Daly region. Late in 1889 he was sent by Fr Anton Strele [q.v.] to found a new station at Serpentine Lagoon on the Daly. With four companions he laboured for a year among the Madngella and other tribes who had never seen whites, but with little effect.

In December 1890 McKillop was made Superior of the whole mission which then had three stations and a residence in Darwin. He was responsible for the whole venture but the financial upkeep bore heavily on him since the assistance promised by the bishops did not materialize. Deeming the stations had failed, he closed them and in August 1891 concentrated his eleven Jesuits in one new station on the Daly. Despite some successes the policy of small, self-supporting agricultural townships did not attract the Aboriginals and most converts were inconstant. The station was struck by severe poverty and his begging tours in the south and east in 1892-93 were unsuccessful because of the depression and apathy.

The continuing decimation of the tribes made the Jesuits seriously doubt the survival of the Aboriginals. McKillop clung to his policies of preserving the native culture but outside factors crowded in to produce a tragic desperation as he foresaw the end of 'the daydream of my life'. In vivid prose he often lashed out in the press at 'blood-stained Australia', at the white and Chinese population and at the government, whom he castigated for pusillanimity in granting land and finance to missions in tribal territories. Worn-out and seriously ill he was ordered south in October 1897. Leadership of the mission then became mediocre and after floods in 1898-99 the station was closed.

McKillop's direction had been realistic but his criticism of official policy probably lost him co-operation from the government. In intermittent good health he worked in Jesuit parishes in Norwood, South Australia (1898-1901), in Victoria at Hawthorn (1902-03) and Richmond (1904-10), Sevenhill (1911-13) and Norwood from 1914 until he died on 2 February 1924. His 'Anthropological Notes on the Aboriginal Tribes of the Daly River, North Australia' had been published in the *Transactions* of the Royal Society of South Australia, 1892-93. The evidence of J. L. Parsons and Charles J. Dashwood to the select committee on the proposed Aborigines' bill of 1899 suggests that the failure of the Jesuit enterprise in the territory helped to confirm the negative character of government legislation on Aboriginals for the next decades.

V. L. Solomon, N. T. *Times almanac and directory* (Palmerston, 1886-90); Roman Catholic mission reports, PP (SA), 1886-89, 1891-94,

I

1896-99; R. M. Berndt, 'Surviving influence of mission contact on the Daly River . . . ', *Neue Zeitschrift für Missionswissenschaft*, 8 (1952); G. J. O'Kelly, The Jesuit mission stations in the Northern Territory, 1882-1899 (B.A. Hons thesis, Monash Univ, 1967); Aust Jesuit Provincial Archives (Hawthorn, Vic).

G. J. O'KELLY

McKILLOP, MARY HELEN (1842-1909), best known as Mother Mary of the Cross, was born on 15 January 1842 in Fitzroy, Melbourne, the eldest of eight children of Alexander McKillop and his wife Flora, née McDonald. Her parents had migrated from the Lochaber area in Inverness-shire and married soon after they reached Melbourne. After a prosperous start the family became impoverished.

Mary was educated at private schools but chiefly by her father who had studied for the priesthood at Rome. To help her family Mary became in turn a shopgirl, a governess, and at Portland a teacher in the Catholic Denominational School and proprietress of a small boarding school for girls. As she grew to womanhood Mary was probably influenced by an early friend of the family, Father P. B. Geoghegan [q.v.], and began to yearn for a strictly penitential form of religious life. Concluding she would have to go to Europe to execute her plan, she placed herself under the direction of Father J. E. Tenison-Woods [q.v.] who, as parish priest of Penola in South Australia sometimes visiting Melbourne and Portland, wanted to found a religious society, 'The Sisters of St Joseph of the Sacred Heart'; they were to live in poverty and dedicate themselves to educating poor children. With Mary its first member and Superior the society was founded at Penola on 19 March 1866 with the approval of Bishop Sheil [q.v.]. The Sisterhood spread to Adelaide and other parts of South Australia, and increased rapidly in membership but ran into difficulties. Tenison-Woods had become director of Catholic schools and conflicted with some of the clergy over educational matters. One priest with influence over the bishop declared publicly he would ruin the director through the Sisterhood. The result was that Mary was excommunicated by Bishop Sheil on 22 September 1871 for alleged insubordination; most of the schools were closed and the Sisterhood almost disbanded. The excommunication was removed on 21 February 1872 by order of the bishop nine days before he died.

In 1873 at Rome Mary obtained papal approval of the Sisterhood but the Rule of Life laid down by Tenison-Woods and sanctioned by the bishop on 17 December 1868 was discarded and another drawn up. Tenison-Woods blamed her for not doing enough to have his Rule accepted and this caused a permanent breach between them. She travelled widely in Europe visiting schools and observing methods of teaching, and returned to Adelaide on 4 January 1875. In March she was elected Superior-General of the Sisterhood. In journeys throughout Australasia she established schools, convents and charitable institutions but came into conflict with those bishops who preferred diocesan control of the Sisterhood rather than central control from Adelaide. In 1883 Bishop Reynolds [q.v.], misunderstanding the extent of his jurisdiction over the Sisterhood, told her to leave his diocese. She then transferred the headquarters of the Sisterhood to Sydney. On 11 May 1901 she suffered a stroke at Rotorua, New Zealand. Although retaining her mental faculties, she was an invalid until she died in Sydney on 8 August 1909.

Mary's finest feature was her large blue eyes. Affectionate but determined, her virtues were multitudinous with charity towards her neighbour outshining all. Always regarded as holy, she was put forward in 1972 as a candidate for the honour of beatification and canonization and on 1 February 1973 the Cause was formally introduced.

Life of Mother Mary, foundress of the Sacred Heart, Westmead (Syd, 1916); O. Thorpe, *Mary McKillop* (Lond, 1957); Archives, Archdiocese of Adelaide, Congregation for the Propagation of the Faith (Rome), Sisters of St Joseph (North Sydney).

OSMUND THORPE*

McKINLAY, JOHN (1819-1872), explorer, was born on 16 August 1819 at Sandbank on Holy Loch, Argyllshire, Scotland, third son of Dugald McKinlay, merchant and feuar, and his wife Mary, née McKellar. Educated at Dalinlongart School, he migrated to New South Wales with his brother Alexander in 1836. They worked with their uncle who held land near Goulburn until he became bankrupt in 1840. Strong, energetic and 6 ft. 4 ins. tall, John turned to outback districts and learned much bushcraft from the Aboriginals. He also made money by taking up squatting leases on the River Darling and selling them. By 1851 he held occupation licences in South Australia, some in partnership with James Pile of Gawler and others near Port Augusta. By then McKinlay was thoroughly self-reliant, an accurate shot and equal to almost any situation except public speaking.

In August 1861 McKinlay was chosen by the House of Assembly to lead the South

Australian Burke [q.v.] Relief Expedition. Eight of the party assembled at Kapunda with 26 horses, 4 camels and a loaded cart. Further north he bought 12 cattle and recruited a bullock driver. At Blanchewater station he collected six months' stores sent up from Port Augusta and a hundred sheep. The party reached Cooper's Creek in mid-October and made a depot at Lake Buchanan. McKinlay made many excursions and found what he thought was the grave of William Gray. On the assumption that all Burke's party had perished, W. O. Hodgkinson [q.v.] was sent to Blanchewater to report and bring up fresh supplies; after a month he returned with a cook and newspapers announcing the rescue of John King by A. W. Howitt [qq.v.] and the deaths of Burke and Wills [q.v.]. On 7 December McKinlay found the tree marked by Howitt near Burke's grave and buried a document showing his intention to proceed to the Gulf of Carpentaria in hope of meeting H.M.V.S. *Victoria*.

McKinlay returned to the depot and following his instructions examined the country north-west of Lake Eyre. After finding many lakes and much pastoral land he turned north. Heavy rain in February 1862 transformed Sturt's [q.v.] Stony Desert into 'running streams and blossoming meadows'. The stores had been depleted and the cart abandoned but for some time the party lived well on plentiful fish and meat. However, the leader never relaxed his strict discipline and good relations with the Aboriginals. He shaped the course accurately and on 20 May arrived near the mouth of the Albert River but mangrove swamps prevented sight of the Gulf of Carpentaria.

Unhappily the *Victoria* had sailed for Melbourne and the party was bitterly disappointed. With his usual determination McKinlay decided to make for Port Denison (Bowen) six hundred miles away on the east coast of Queensland. His watch had become useless for calculating the distance travelled, his bullocks were reduced to two, his remaining horses were in bad shape, his camels were lame and had to be fitted with leather boots, and his last four pounds of flour were reserved for making gruel in case of sickness. By 20 June his men were rationed to twenty ounces of salt meat a day and by 31 July all the livestock except ten horses had been eaten. On 2 August McKinlay saw fresh cattle tracks and soon the herd with two men came in sight. Within an hour the party was 'pitching in to roast beef and damper', but for weeks the men suffered great pains after meals.

McKinlay led his men slowly over the last eighty miles to Bowen, where he was given a complimentary dinner and a hand-some testimonial on the eve of sailing for Rockhampton on 22 August. A month later he reached Melbourne. The Royal Society of Victoria welcomed him, and with Landsborough [q.v.] he was given an enthusiastic reception in the Exhibition Building. In October McKinlay arrived in Adelaide, handed his journal and charts to the government and was awarded £1000; the five men who returned with him were given six months' pay. He was banquetted by the mayor and given a silver tea and coffee service. At Gawler he was welcomed as 'a conquering hero' but demurred from making speeches. Although he had summed up the actions of each day before he slept, he had no talent for talking or writing about his own exploits. Described as 'the knight-errant of explorers', he went his own way and ignored critics. His party was the second to cross the continent from south to north and, like J. M. Stuart [q.v.], he never lost any of his men.

In 1865 McKinlay was chosen to lead an expedition to determine a better site for settlement than Adam Bay in the Northern Territory. He sailed from Port Adelaide in September and arrived at the bay in November. He denounced it as worthless for a port and city, and went in search of better country. He favoured Port Darwin for a port and its hinterland, and found scattered patches of good country on the Victoria and Roper Rivers. He then turned north to the East Alligator River but was hemmed in by floods. In June 1866 he killed his horses, dried the meat, bound the skins to saplings and made a raft on which he took his party safely to Adam Bay. In July he joined the *Pioneer* and by way of Timor returned to South Australia. He revisited the Northern Territory in 1870 to select sites for holders of land orders and then offered to survey the route for the overland telegraph from Darwin but his terms were rejected by the government.

Between his explorations McKinlay continued to take up new runs. On 17 January 1863 at St George's Church, Gawler, he married Jane Pile. Worn out by hardships he died on 17 January 1872 and was buried at Willaston cemetery with a very large funeral. An impressive monument was erected in his honour at Gawler, its foundation laid by John Forrest on 14 November 1874. A portrait of McKinlay is in the Gawler Institute.

J. Davis, *Tracks of McKinlay and party across Australia*, W. Westgarth ed (Lond, 1863); B. Threadgill, *South Australian land exploration 1856 to 1880*, 1 (Adel, 1922); V&P (SA), 1861 (147, 185), 1862 (12, 218), 1865-66 (131), 1866-67 (80, 82), 1870-71 (36); *Examiner* (Melb), 7 Sept, 7 Dec 1861, 19 July 1862, 10

Jan 1863; *Observer* (Adel), 15, 22 Nov 1862, 4 Jan 1873; *Town and Country J*, 11 Jan 1873.

McKINLEY, ALEXANDER (1848-1927), newspaper proprietor, was born in London, son of James McKinley, publisher, and his wife Mary, née Loughrey. The family migrated to Melbourne about 1857. In 1869 Alexander and his older brother James bought the *Talbot Leader*. In April 1871 they sold it, returned to Melbourne, bought the Melbourne *Punch* and with the help of F. T. D. Carrington's [q.v.] cartoons made it a formidable opponent of Berry's [q.v.] political party. Alexander also published *Saturday Night*, first for an American and then as owner, renaming it *Once a Week* and improving it with news covering Sydney and Melbourne. In 1881 he bought out James and Carrington from *Punch* and also acquired the *Melbourne Bulletin* which they had run from the *Punch* office. James later had a share in the *Daily Telegraph* and briefly controlled the *Herald*. In 1886 Alexander amalgamated *Punch* and the *Bulletin* and as publisher also of the *Jewish Herald* and the *Australasian Schoolmaster* acquired larger premises by 1889.

McKinley made money from his newspapers but more from his part in the land speculation of the 1880s, selling a Queen Street site, bought for £135 a foot, for £750 a foot. The 1893 collapse of the banks hit him severely. *Once a Week* ceased publication and McKinley concentrated on saving *Punch*. James sold the *Herald*, became editor of *Punch* and retained that post until he died in 1908. In 1892, determined to restore good government and prosperity, Alexander won the Toorak seat in the Legislative Assembly. He favoured Federation and retrenchment in the public service, opposed the principle of one man one vote and thought income tax an inquisitorial institution. He also advocated the opening of co-operative fruit canneries, the export of dried fruits and the building of irrigation works by experts. He was declared 'a very sensible and level-headed M.P. notwithstanding his intimate connection with comic journalism'. However, he did not seek re-election in September 1894 and his 1904 and 1913 bids for Legislative Council election were unsuccessful.

In 1885 McKinley was elected to the Malvern Council. He was president in 1890-93 and mayor in 1901, 1910-11 and 1918-19. He maintained that the mayor should make the Town Hall his home and 'exercise his hospitality exactly as he would in his own home'. He gave the tower clock in 1891. He was even more attentive to children's wel-

fare, legislation for which he had fought in parliament. In 1907 he became a special magistrate for the Children's Court, serving as its chairman for twenty years. He was also president of the Children's Welfare Association. His addresses 'Crime and the Child' and 'The Child and its Pitfalls' expounded his views that every child was capable of good; environment and the collapse of family protection were the main offenders. He advocated a farm home for wayward boys and the 1917 Children's Court Amending Act was largely his work.

McKinley gave himself unsparingly to the project in hand. An active Presbyterian, he joined the Chalmers Church Bible class at 16, taught Sunday school in Talbot and was connected with the La Trobe Street Mission School for twelve years. He was on the St George's Church (East St Kilda) Committee and later on the Malvern Church Committee. A devoted father, McKinley took his family overseas in 1889 and 1904 and gave his daughter Ethel a university education. He steered *Punch* through the difficulties of World War I selling it in 1920 when he also retired from municipal life. His last years were spent at his home, Yallambie, Tooronga Road, where he died on 18 April 1927, survived by his wife Emma, née Firman, and two daughters.

J. B. Cooper, *A history of Malvern* (Melb, 1935); *Alexander McKinley, his work and service* (Melb, nd); *Prahran Telegraph*, 8 Sept 1888, 29 July 1893, 9 Sept 1911; *Argus*, 19 Apr 1927; family scrapbooks.   J. ANN HONE

MACKINNON, DANIEL (1818-1889), pastoralist, was born at Lagg, Isle of Arran, Scotland, son of John Mackinnon, farmer, and his wife Mary, née Curdie. At 21 he abandoned his theological studies at the University of Glasgow and migrated to Port Phillip in the *Caledonia*, arriving in September 1839. For a few months he lived with John Aitken [q.v.] at Sunbury and then with Major Fraser took up a run at Mordialloc. This proved a disastrous venture and Mackinnon lost most of his capital. An uncle and grand-uncle came to his assistance and with another uncle, Daniel Curdie, Mackinnon moved to the Western District in search of land. They took up Lovely Banks and continued as partners until 1843, when Curdie took Tandorook and Mackinnon, in partnership with Hugh Scott, kept the Jancourt portion of 10,000 acres. In 1852 Mackinnon & Scott bought the rights to Marida Yallock; the partnership was divided and Mackinnon took Marida Yallock. By 1857 he had bought 7000 acres and had also invested in New Zealand property. In 1858 he visited Scotland where he married Jane Kinross.

In 1859-85 Mackinnon was a member of the Hampden Road Board and its successor, the Hampden and Heytesbury Shire Council, and was president for six years. He was also acting trustee in the long drawn-out settlement of the important Hastie estate. Finding more than half his time devoted to the affairs of others, he refused to be gazetted a justice of the peace.

Marida Yallock was originally sour country but years of hard work made it one of the most famous fattening properties in Victoria. Mackinnon specialized in Shorthorn cattle. He also bred hacks and carriage horses and supplied the Victorian Police Department. In the early 1870s he invested in sheep and by 1875 was running some 12,000.

Mackinnon was an active supporter of the Zoological and Acclimatisation Society; he established Californian quail at Marida Yallock but English song birds died. A keen horticulturist, he won prizes at the Camperdown Horticultural Show for his flowers and successfully planted elms, bluegums and Tasmanian and Japanese trees. At Marida Yallock the Mackinnons entertained their friends, including Niel Black and Professor H. A. Strong [qq.v.]. In 1874 Mackinnon, Black and others, angered by the views of the *Hampden Guardian*, established the *Camperdown Chronicle* with James Allen as editor and a capital of £1500. With Mackinnon as treasurer and other strong backing the *Chronicle* thrived and in 1877 he bought out the *Guardian*. He also supported the Camperdown branch of the Free Trade League of Victoria.

In the 1870s Mackinnon became interested in Queensland investment. He made a trip north and with Andrew Tobin bought Marion Downs, a cattle run in the North Gregory district, and later became sole owner; the station remained in the family until 1934. In 1884 William Kinross, Mackinnon's second son, took over the management of Marida Yallock. In 1885 Mackinnon resigned from the council and revisited Scotland. His last term as president in 1882-83 had not been altogether happy but his advocacy of railway extension had earned the gratitude of the whole shire.

Mackinnon's letters reveal his care for relations, neighbours and friends and his concern for the simple things of life. A devoted Presbyterian, he was active in the management of the Camperdown and Terang Churches, helped the Cobden Church and gave money to various church causes. In 1884 he donated to the scholarship fund of Ormond College and served on its council from 1885 until he died on 19 February

1889. He was survived by his wife, two daughters and four sons who were educated at Geelong Grammar School: the eldest, Donald, entered New College, Oxford, (B.A., 1883) and was admitted to the Bar of the Middle Temple (1883); James Curdie went to Trinity Hall, Cambridge, in 1886 and became a pastoralist; and Kenneth John also went to Trinity Hall, Cambridge (B.A., 1891).

A. Henderson (ed), *Early pioneer families of Victoria and Riverina* (Melb, 1936); *Presbyterian Monthly*, 1 Mar 1889; *Camperdown Chronicle*, 22 Sept 1883, 21 Feb 1889; Mackinnon papers (LaT L).   J. ANN HONE

MACKINNON, LAUCHLAN (1817-1888), pastoralist and newspaper proprietor, was born on 26 February 1817 at Kilbride, Isle of Skye, Scotland, second son of John Mackinnon, Presbyterian minister of Strath, and his wife Ann, daughter of Lauchlan Mackinnon of Curry. Educated privately and at Broadford School, Skye, he worked with his uncle, Lauchlan Mackinnon, a writer to the signet in Glasgow. He migrated to Van Diemen's Land in 1838 and then to Sydney whence he overlanded stock to Adelaide for Campbell & Co. About 1840 he took stock from Sydney to Port Phillip where he decided to settle. He took up the Tarrangower run in 1839-41, Ovens River in 1841 and, with Webster & Co., Mount Fyans in the Western District in 1841-53 and Mount Battery in 1858-66.

Mackinnon contested a Port Phillip seat in the New South Wales Legislative Council in 1848, supported by many Western District squatters. Calling themselves the 'constitutional party' and accepting separation from New South Wales as imminent, they fought with determination against those who sought renewed transportation and were attempting to force immediate separation by boycotting the election. Successful in 'thrash[ing] old Curr [q.v.] and his party off the stage', Mackinnon struggled for justice for Port Phillip against exploitation by Sydney, demanding that all moneys raised in the district be spent there. He vacated his seat in June 1849 but won it again in July and held it until June 1850.

Mackinnon was member for Warrnambool and Belfast in the squatter-dominated Victorian Legislative Council from December 1852 till he resigned in May 1853. At a protest meeting in 1852 he had stood alone among squatters in opposing their more extreme claims. He recognized the importance of squatting and was prepared to meet what he called the pastoralists' 'just claims', but he opposed the long leases and pre-emptive rights of purchase which they demanded under the 1847 Order in Council, the spirit of which he denounced, declaring himself in favour of 'free trade in land'. In the bitter anti-transportation controversy he championed the colonists' right to refuse to take convicts. Inflammatory speeches, even threatening secession from Britain, at the monster protest meetings in 1849 and 1850, which petitioned the Queen and parliament and the vacillating council in Sydney against the renewal of transportation, earned him repute as a fiery and outspoken orator. His friend, William Westgarth [q.v.], who went with him in 1852 to lead the Anti-Transportation League's delegation in support of the cause in Tasmania, describes the ingenious means by which Mackinnon was persuaded to temper his immoderate speechmaking by friends who feared, in sensitive Launceston, the 'straightforward honesty' of the 'vigorous Highlander . . . who could never take a subject of deep interest to himself quietly'.

In that year Mackinnon became a partner in the Argus with Edward Wilson [q.v.] and took over the business side of the paper which, despite its enormous increase in circulation and influence under Wilson's management, was near financial collapse. Persuading Wilson that he was charging 2d. for a paper that cost 5½d. to produce, Mackinnon insisted on doubling the price and adding 25 per cent to the charge for advertisements, thereby ensuring the journal's prosperity. Allan Spowers joined them as junior partner in 1857.

Mackinnon retired to England in 1868 and settled at Elfordleigh, Devonshire, to enjoy the pleasures of English country life. For a time he lived at Arundel, Sussex, often visiting his estate at Duisdale, Isle of Skye, and offering hospitality on the grand scale. Always delighted to entertain his friends' sons who went to England to finish their schooling, he undertook responsibility for the education and training of his cousin, Lauchlan Charles Mackinnon, his intended successor in the Argus.

While expressing confidence in the local board and anxious to leave its members a free hand in managing the Argus, Mackinnon continued to follow its affairs closely and offer advice. Unlike Wilson he refused to be alarmed when Syme's [q.v.] Age outstripped the Argus in circulation. He deplored Wilson's 'proneness to panic' and with Spowers always outvoted any move to disturb the paper's prosperity. An extensive tour of North America in 1869 to observe the practices there left him confident of the 'impregnable strength' of the Argus.

When the telegraph link between Britain and Australia became imminent, Mackinnon was convinced of the importance of an independent news service and in 1870 attempted to form a press association embracing all colonial newspapers which could receive news telegrams direct from London, thus avoiding dependence for foreign news on Reuter. By 1872 when the link with Britain was established, he had succeeded in achieving a cable partnership between the Argus, Sydney Morning Herald and South Australian Register, whose London representatives selected and cabled the news at their discretion, dispensing foreign news to associated papers outside the 'ring'. Opposed to 'stinting, false economies', Mackinnon fought for 'free expenditure' on the special news service, despite its high cost of some £8500 a year until a special press rate was introduced in 1886.

Mackinnon did not write for the Argus but his business ability was chiefly responsible for its financial success. His letters to his representative, J. S. Johnston [q.v.], reveal his assurance and liberal vision in business; with enterprise, energy and no fear of 'bold action', he constantly exhorted his colleagues, impatient of the timidity and narrow vision which led to short-sighted policies. He was just but stern with employees, intolerant of incompetence and claimed that sentiment was a 'fatal error' in business.

Mackinnon was a vigorous, forthright Presbyterian, respected by his friends for his courage and integrity. A Liberal in politics he had profound faith in education 'without which Religion and Morals must give place to every species of public and private depravity'. He was a member of the original Council of the University of Melbourne. He died at Malpas Lodge, Torquay, Devon, on 21 March 1888 leaving a vast estate. He was twice married: first, to Jane Montgomery who died in Sydney on 13 June 1849; and second, at Parramatta on 9 May 1850 to Emily Bundock who died at Malpas Lodge on 17 June 1893 survived by two adopted children.

Garryowen (E. Finn), The chronicles of early Melbourne, 1-2 (Melb, 1888); W. Westgarth, Personal recollections of early Melbourne and Victoria (Melb, 1888); R. V. Billis and A. S. Kenyon, Pastoral pioneers of Port Phillip (Melb, 1932); M. L. Kiddle, Men of yesterday (Melb, 1961); Argus, 23 Mar 1888; The Times, 24 Mar 1888; Niel Black papers (LaT L); Haddon papers (LaT L); J. S. Johnston papers (Univ Melb Archives).   JACQUELINE TEMPLETON

MACKNIGHT, CHARLES HAMILTON (1819-1873), pastoralist, was born in Edinburgh, son of Rev. Dr Thomas Macknight and his wife Christian Crawfurd, née Macknight, a cousin. Educated at the High School and the University of Edinburgh, he attended the Scottish Naval and Military Academy for a year before sailing to Port Phillip where he arrived on 1 March 1841. James Hamilton Irvine and William Campbell went with him, the three men having agreed to combine resources. In May the partners took up the 25,000-acre Strathlodden run and Bough Yards, 22,400 acres near Castlemaine, but left the district in 1842 and acquired 47,228 acres between Macarthur and Port Fairy in the Western District. They overlanded 600 head of cattle and horses from their old stations to the new run which they called Dunmore. They had some trouble at first with Aboriginals who maimed stock and stole station stores. Once or twice Macknight was a member of punitive expeditions, but he won repute for just dealing and gained the confidence of the Aboriginals.

Macknight was determined to develop the run, even pondering the possibilities of emu oil. Dunmore was soon regarded as the most improved homestead in the district. It had three substantial slab huts with great stone chimneys and a pisé dairy with a large milking shed. Macknight also constructed dams.

Campbell sold his share in the property in 1847, disheartened by years of toil and small reward. Macknight and Irvine stayed and were amply repaid after 1851 when the gold rushes created a heavy demand for meat. Macknight blamed the Victorian government for insecurity of tenure which he claimed had prevented the sinking of capital in the subdivision of runs with the result that scab went largely unchecked and production potential was far from being realized. The royal commission, appointed by Sir Charles Hotham to inquire into squatting tenure, published its report in 1855. Outraged, Macknight published *A Review of The Report of The Squatting Commission*, in which he upheld the services of the squatters to the country. When the opportunity came to buy land he did so with fervour, but like many others he over-extended himself. A friend and admirer, Rolf Boldrewood [q.v. T. A. Browne], records that Macknight tackled the land question with his usual unflinching moral courage.

In 1863 Dunmore was divided. Macknight and Irvine retained one portion while Dunmore West was acquired by the Trust and Agency Co. Irvine continued as Macknight's partner till the early 1870s. At Dunmore Macknight specialized in the breeding of Shorthorn cattle. His purchases in 1843 at the sale of the Boldens' [q.v.] stud served as a foundation for one of the finest herds in the district. In 1875 the Dunmore stud was dispersed at the peak of the cattle boom and thirty-nine animals realized an average of £672 a head. Macknight also bred racehorses but his greatest interest became the breeding of pure merinos. He bought half the Camden flock from Griffith & Greene [qq.v.], convinced that Camden blood was more important than any other in the colonies and must be preserved at all costs. This he did for years in spite of the black soil and heavy country of Dunmore and the continual outbreaks of fluke and footrot in the flock. Finally he decided sheep could not thrive at Dunmore and sold them all, but not before he had established himself as one of the greatest authorities on sheepbreeding. He believed in inbreeding and wrote many long argumentative letters to the Melbourne *Economist*, the *Australasian* and other papers. With Dr Henry Madden he wrote *On the True Principles of Breeding* which was published in Melbourne in 1865. Macknight maintained that long experience and observation were needed to make a great breeder but he also believed that such men were born with the ability.

Macknight served for years as a member of the Belfast (Port Fairy) Shire Council and magistrate for the Belfast General Sessions District. He was a foundation member and president of the Minhamite Shire Council. With a strong interest in education he was president of the Belfast Young Men's Improvement Society and lectured on literary and scientific subjects to various societies in the Western District. Boldrewood records that his manner of speaking was logically clear and trenchant. Macknight supported the movement for total abstinence and was on the committee of management of the Belfast Hospital and Benevolent Asylum.

Macknight was struck by a falling tree during a bush fire and died three days later on 9 March 1873, leaving little for his family. He was survived by his wife Everina Isabella, née Heatley, whom he had married in 1856, and by four sons and two daughters. The sons were educated at Melbourne Grammar; three became doctors and the other an architect.

R. Boldrewood, *Old Melbourne memories*, 2nd ed (Melb, 1896); A. Henderson (ed), *Australian families*, 1 (Melb, 1941); *Temperance News*, April 1873; *Australasian*, 15 Mar, 10 May 1873; Kiddle papers (Univ Melb Archives).

J. ANN HONE

McLACHLAN, LACHLAN (1810-1885), civil servant, was born in Argyllshire, Scotland, son of Kenneth McLachlan, laird of

Killanohauah and captain in the 64th Regiment, and his wife Mary, née Bruce. After rudimentary education at home, he was sent to school at Fort William, went to High School in Edinburgh and entered the university to study law. Following family tradition he attended Sandhurst Military College before returning to Edinburgh to be articled to a writer to the signet.

In December 1840 McLachlan was appointed agent for a company which had taken up large tracts of land in New Zealand. He left Glasgow in the *Brilliant* and arrived at Melbourne in July 1841. He visited Hobart Town where he appears to have spent his time between visits to Governor Franklin and the penal settlements. The knowledge he gained of criminals was to serve him well in his later work as police magistrate. He went to New Zealand in September but the newly-formed government would not recognize his company's claims. He spent the next decade holding 'some office in the judicial department of that Colony', and visited Scotland early in 1852.

McLachlan returned to New Zealand as resident magistrate but soon went to Melbourne. He almost died from asphyxiation at a fire in the Shakespeare Hotel in January 1853 but on 9 February was appointed police magistrate at Castlemaine. The attorney-general, William Stawell [q.v.], called on him and he was rushed under trooper escort to the neighbouring goldfields of Bendigo 'to restore order in a most turbulent area'. He was appointed stipendiary magistrate on 29 March at a salary of £500. Since forceful administration of the law was necessary and urgent, McLachlan carried out his duties with speed, rigour and conscientiousness. The police court at Bendigo was a canvas tent on a wooden frame lined with green baize. McLachlan's predecessor had sat on a ten-gallon whisky keg and his clerk of court on a smaller one. The prisoner stood in front of the bench between two policemen.

McLachlan was soon a local identity and many tales were told of 'Bendigo Mac' as he came to be known. His humour amused his court but business always proceeded with decorum. His chief detective officer, Simon O'Neil, visited the magistrate each evening and, over a glass of wine, would give him foreknowledge of the culprits to appear next morning. In court McLachlan would ask the prisoner his name, study him from every angle with monocle firmly fixed and then, feigning sudden recognition, exclaim: 'Now Sir, you can't deceive me Sir, you are so-and-so, alias so-and-so. You were at Norfolk Island in such-and-such a year. You were one of the Point Puer boys!' He administered justice with equity and criminals learned to shun the district. A gag might be ordered for an abusive prisoner but McLachlan was lenient with mild offenders, often expressing sympathy when forced to impose fines on diggers too poor to pay the heavy licensing fees. With drunks his 'Fined 40/-; take him away' became a byword as in one of Thatcher's contemporary ballads. With a detective's zest he had the sagacity to understand complicated cases but his determination to put down crime and rowdyism led to a rigid interpretation of his duties and brought censure from some quarters. McLachlan declined to support Governor Hotham's impolitic instructions to collect licensing fees at bayonet point and thereby won the support of the commissioner, J. A. Panton [q.v.], who understood the temper of the diggers. Largely through the tact and forbearance of these two men, Bendigo was spared the riots which enforcement of similar laws in Ballarat provoked.

In 1855 McLachlan's transfer to Fiery Creek was rumoured and the news was received with 'sorrow and concern' by respectable members of the community. But the rumour was false and in 1856 his court was reported to be so quiet as to cause comment in the Melbourne press. In 1858 he gave evidence to a select committee inquiring into charges against the chief police commissioner, Captain C. MacMahon [q.v.]. McLachlan's description of conditions at the Bendigo lock-up, a structure 'with floor, roof, wall and all of sheet iron like a steam boiler', and the account of his impulsive discharge of its prisoners on a suffocating Sunday morning showed genuine concern for the people. Bendigonians saw him as a rectifier of their grievances.

McLachlan lived in a cottage on the hillside facing the Town Hall and Market Square, with a pleasant view of the camp. He did not associate much with the 'newly risen, vulgar rich of camp and town' but according to Panton 'he was a great favourite in our little circle'. In community life he was a director of the Sandhurst branch of the Bank of Victoria, laid the foundation stone of the first Presbyterian Church at Eaglehawk in 1859 and as a founding member of the Bendigo Caledonian Society was usually judge at annual gatherings because of his proficiency in bagpipe music. On 31 May 1871 he sat on the bench for the last time. The court was filled and many eulogies followed its proceedings. On 5 June the Executive Council granted him leave for a year. On the 14th a banquet in the Town Hall celebrated the first reunion of the Society of Old Bendigonians and honoured 'Bendigo Mac'. On 10 July he was presented with a purse of 700 sovereigns, a testimonial from the people of Bendigo. He moved to Melbourne but failing sight darkened his last years. Aged 76 he died on 6 August 1885, survived by his wife Mary, née Smith, and five daughters.

G. Mackay, The history of Bendigo (Melb, 1891); W. B. Kimberly, Bendigo and vicinity (Melb, 1895); G. Mackay, Annals of Bendigo, 1-2 (Bendigo, 1916, 1926); V&P (LA Vic), 1857-58, 1 (D27) 77; Argus, 16 Oct 1855, 17 Oct 1856, 7 Aug 1885; Bendigo Advertiser, 7 Aug 1885; Bendigo Independent, 7 Aug 1885; W. H. Manwaring diaries, 1857-70 (LaT L); J. A. Panton memoirs (LaT L).   JEAN GITTINS

MACLANACHAN, JAMES (1799?-1884), settler and politician, was born near Muirkirk, County Ayr, Scotland. He was 'respectably educated' and early acquired a complete knowledge of livestock. Indentured to James Robertson whom he had known in Scotland, he sailed for Hobart Town in the Lusitania and arrived on 29 October 1821. Maclanachan's agreement ended in 1824 and he was granted 100 acres of summer marsh at Hollow Tree near Black (Abyssinia) Tier, but sold it when he became manager of a property at Salt Pan Plains near Ross. At St David's Church, Hobart, on 9 March 1826 he married a widow, Sarah Reddenbury; they had no children.

On 5 November 1827 he was sworn in as a division constable of Methven parish and later appointed poundkeeper. After Maclanachan's house was robbed in 1828 and many of his sheep were stolen at York Plains, he retaliated by bringing several runaway convicts to justice. He broke up the gang of the notorious villain, Samuel Hillary, who escaped but his shepherd was executed for felony and two accomplices were sent to Macquarie Harbour. When Maclanachan's home was raided by hostile Aboriginals in his absence, his wife 'purely by her resolution' fought them off. In 1830 he applied for another land grant but was refused because he had sold his original grant. With support from some landowners, he petitioned Lieut-Governor Arthur to reconsider the decision, claiming that 'by economy approaching to parsimony he had saved sufficient to put him into possession of a flock of 1800 improved sheep, 3 horses, 75 cattle and a set of agricultural implements'. Arthur was not impressed but in January 1831 rewarded Maclanachan's fearless conduct as a constable by allowing him 500 acres on conditions of residence. Maclanachan resigned his official duties in February 1835 and selected 500 acres near Tunbridge, calling his property Ballochmyle after an area in Ayrshire famous for its association with Robert Burns. By 1842 he

had cut a drain to carry water from Tunbridge town to Ballochmyle and bought more land at Salt Pan Plains. He was appointed a justice of the peace in September 1843 and later became chairman of the Court of General Sessions at Oatlands and of the Great Lake Road District. He represented Oatlands in the Tasmanian House of Assembly in 1859-62 and Jordan in the Legislative Council in 1868-83. He attended regularly but sat on only one select committee and introduced only one bill, protection of land against trespassers, which did not reach the council. His major role was presenting petitions, most of them against state aid to religion.

As a youth Maclanachan had been attracted by the prize-winning black-faced sheep of the Muirkirk area exhibited at the Highland Society's shows. In 1836 he fought an absurd battle with James and Edmund Bryant, stockbreeders of Sandhill near Jericho, who had allegedly challenged him to show against them but then refused. However, his zeal for exhibiting livestock was not abated and in September 1838 he helped to found the Midland Agricultural Association; he was its first secretary and treasurer until 1875 and patron until 1883, winning many valuable prizes. At Ballochmyle he built many aviaries and claimed to have introduced to Tasmania hares and pheasants as well as sixty varieties of singing birds. In his last years he was threatened by an apoplectic stroke and lived quietly.

A staunch supporter of the Free Church of Scotland, Maclanachan had served as an elder of the church at Campbell Town and treasurer of synod's funds; on his retirement he was presented with an address and a purse of sovereigns. He died from paralysis at his home on 22 January 1884. Predeceased by his wife, he was buried in her vault near Kirklands, Campbell Town. His death was given on his tombstone as 1881 but his death registration and his probate gave 1884. He left an estate valued at £5428 and bequeathed his prize cups, plated ware, candelabra, tea and coffee services, books and pictures to the six sons of Dr William Crooke, £1000 to his niece in Scotland and £100 for building a Presbyterian Church at Tunbridge and £400 for its first minister.

J. Heyer, The Presbyterian pioneers of Van Diemen's Land (Hob, 1935); P. L. Brown (ed), Clyde Company papers, 2 (Lond, 1952); Examiner (Launceston), 12 Mar 1859; CSO 1/353/8053; correspondence file on Maclanachan (TA).

McLAURIN, JAMES (1821-1891), grazier, was born on 23 July 1821 at Dunoon, Argyllshire, Scotland, the second son of

James McLaurin (1771-1864), farmer, and his wife Mary, née McGibbon (1783-1856). On 2 January 1838 he arrived at Sydney in the *Brilliant* with twenty-seven members of his family and went to Singleton, where his father was manager of James Bowman's [q.v.] station. In October 1839 he and his brother Alexander (1823-1872) overlanded cattle to Adelaide for Edward and George Howe. Next year on a similar trip he had many skirmishes with Aboriginals and discovered and named the Edward River. After cattle dealing on the Melbourne market, he formed Allanvale station in the Westernport district with his brother Alexander and John Webster as partners.

About 1843 McLaurin worked on the Howes's Murray runs and made many trips with stock to Melbourne. When the Howes went bankrupt he took cattle for wages and by 1845 with his father and three brothers had occupied an abandoned run near Deniliquin, renaming it Cornalla. His unpublished 'Memories of Early Australia' (in the Mitchell Library) records that he and Archibald 'had to milk twenty cows before breakfast, split posts all day and thresh wheat by candlelight . . . and it was not uncommon to see the milk cows coming home with spears sticking in them'. In the early 1850s the five partners bought Derulamein for £3000 on the breakup of Benjamin Boyd's [q.v.] Deniliquin run and in November 1855 paid a record £24,000 for the near-by 50,000-acre run of Moroco; later they acquired the 64,000-acre cattle run of Billabong in the Murrumbidgee district. By 1866 the family held over 203,000 acres in the Riverina.

In 1852 James had been attracted to the Victorian goldfields but within three months went to Albury where he built the Fanny Ceres flour-mill. In 1859 he was appointed a magistrate and in 1859-60 served on the first town council. In 1861 he sold the mill to George Day [q.v.] in exchange for the 90,000-acre Yarra Yarra run, near Germanton (Holbrook). When their father died in 1864 the brothers dissolved the partnership and James took Yarra Yarra and Billabong. When Yarra Yarra was threatened by the bushranger Daniel Morgan, McLaurin led his sons and station hands in a raid on Morgan's camp, only to find it deserted; in his absence the homestead was plundered by the bushranger. In 1862 McLaurin petitioned parliament for pecuniary relief after 6305 cattle worth £20,132 had been compulsorily slaughtered in an outbreak of pleuro-pneumonia. By the 1870s he had restocked with sheep and was growing wheat. An elder of the Presbyterian Church, he liberally supported its local causes. In March 1872 he was elected to the Legislative Assembly for the Hume; a petition against his return was dismissed as 'frivolous and vexatious'. He resigned in February 1873 and refused nomination to the Legislative Council. In February 1891 he sold his holdings to his four eldest sons. He died on 10 November at Yarra Yarra and was buried in the Germanton cemetery. Predeceased by his first wife Ann, née Sparrow, who died in 1853 without issue, and by his second wife Isabella McDonald (d. 1887), née Rankin, he was survived by five sons and three daughters of his second wife.

E. W. O'Sullivan, *Under the Southern Cross* (Syd, 1906); J. Webster, *Reminiscences of an old settler* (Christchurch, 1908); Pastoral Review Pty Ltd, *The pastoral homes of Australia — NSW* (Melb, 1910); C. Fetherstonhaugh, *After many days* (Syd, 1918); A. Henderson (ed), *Australian families*, 1 (Melb, 1941); W. A. Bayley, *Border city* (Albury, 1954); R. B. Ronald, *The Riverina: people and progress* (Melb, 1960); *Albury Daily News*, 11 Nov 1891; *SMH*, 11 Nov 1891; *Border Post* (Albury), 13 Nov 1891; J. D. Lang papers (ML).

RUTH TEALE

MACLAY *see* MIKLUHO-MAKLAI

McLEAN, ALEXANDER GRANT (1824-1862), surveyor-general, was born in Scotland, the second son of Captain John Leyburn Maclean, principal superintendent of convicts (1837-55), and his wife Jane Eliza, née Grant. He arrived in Sydney with his family in the *Earl Durham* on 31 August 1837. In April 1842 Governor Gipps was asked by Surveyor-General Sir Thomas Mitchell [q.v.] to fill a vacancy in his department by appointing McLean who had long been studying plan drawing and doing useful work. He was appointed on 11 May, became chief draftsman in 1856 and was secretary to the Court of Claims in 1854-59. In 1855 he told the commission into the Surveyor-General's Department of drafting and surveying procedures and his objection to the large number of temporary staff. At the 1859 select committee on the Survey Department he attributed the department's inefficiency to lack of supervision and the dual system of staff and licensed surveyors.

In August the minister for lands, John Robertson [q.v.], reorganized the Survey Department and made McLean acting surveyor-general on 12 August. Robertson believed that although McLean lacked field experience he had ability and long departmental experience. Instructed to propose reforms, McLean argued that an efficient and energetic administration was required, not radical changes. He rearranged the duties of his staff, transferred some to the Department of Lands and appointed district surveyors to supervise licensed surveyors. In January 1861 Governor Denison severely criticized the unprofessionalism of the surveyors-general and the inaccuracy of their methods. He strongly advocated a trigonometrical survey but McLean believed that cost outweighed its merits. He authorized the compilation of a map of New South Wales which was published in 1861. His work facilitated the introduction of Robertson's Land Acts. On 1 November 1861 he was appointed surveyor-general.

An original member of the volunteer movements of 1854 and 1860 McLean attained the rank of captain. On 6 April 1861 at St Anne's Church, Ryde, he married Catherine, daughter of Captain John Woore. For some time he had suffered from Bright's disease aggravated by overwork. On medical advice he took leave in August 1862 to stay with E. K. Cox [q.v.] at Fernhill, Mulgoa. His condition worsened and he died on 28 September at Fernhill aged 38 and was buried in St Thomas's Anglican churchyard. He was survived by his wife and an infant daughter. He had failed to establish efficiency or to overcome the arrears of work, but his energy, attention to detail and obliging manner raised the department in popular esteem, something his more qualified predecessors had failed to achieve.

A town near Grafton is named after him. Portraits are in the Mitchell Library and the Department of Lands.

Returns of the colony of NSW, 1842-62; V&P (LC NSW), 1855, 2, 43, (LA NSW), 1858-59, 2, 10; SMH, 4 Sept 1837, 10 Apr 1861, 29 Sept-7 Oct 1862; *Sydney Mail,* 27 Sept-11 Oct 1862; Col Sec in-letters 42/3549 (NSWA); Executive Council NSW minutes 1 Aug 1859, 29 Oct 1861 (NSWA); Lands Dept in-letters 59/3466, 61/4087, surveyor-general 1859-62 (NSWA); Lands Dept out-letters, surveyor-general 1859-61 (NSWA); Woore papers (ML); MS cat (ML); CO 201/517.   C. DAVIS

MACLEAN, HAROLD (1828-1889), public servant, was born on 14 May 1828 at Lakefield, Inverness, Scotland, third son of Captain John Leyburn Maclean, 43rd Regiment, and his wife Jane Eliza, née Grant. In August 1837 he arrived with his family at Sydney. At 16 he became a clerk in the Colonial Secretary's Office. On 3 January 1852 he became assistant commissioner for the goldfields at Sofala and in 1856 at Tambaroora. In 1858-64 he was senior gold commissioner on the western goldfields.

Widely trusted, Maclean settled miners' disputes on the spot and later sat in the Appeals Court. He often advised the government and was responsible for changes in goldfields legislation and regulations, which he believed were the main factors affecting the miners' well-being. In 1858 he told a Legislative Assembly select committee of the civic virtues of the Chinese on the goldfields. The report of the 1870 royal commission into the goldfields leaned heavily on his evidence.

In August 1864 Maclean became sheriff of New South Wales. Determined to reform the inhuman conditions of the colony's prisons, he began by inspecting the recently improved gaols of Victoria in 1865. He hoped to implement classification, uniform management for all gaols and systematic employment for inmates. In 1867 his new regulations for the remission of gaol sentences were more lenient than England's, and against British advice he banned the treadmill. In 1869 he studied prison management in Britain and confirmed his ideals of separate treatment and productive labour. In 1871 his initiation of prison photography for identifying criminals was followed in other Australian colonies. He also ordered modern equipment to make prisons self-supporting by more useful hard labour.

In 1874 Maclean was promoted sheriff and comptroller-general of prisons. In 1875 he and the engineer-in-chief for harbours promoted a plan for an open prison, where prisoners would have increasing wages, leave passes and outside accommodation, for building a breakwater at Trial Bay near Smoky Cape: 'the most important departure that has been made by any country'. The system began but was not fully operative until 1886. In 1878 at a royal commission into alleged torture at Berrima Gaol, he defended occasional, recorded and brief use of the gag and chaining men to the cell wall but denied any spread-eagling. The commissioners recommended reforms and exonerated Maclean, praising his 'intelligence, experience, zeal and enlightened humanity'.

Maclean personally investigated prisoners' complaints, acted as a 'protector', reprimanded officers on prisoners' evidence and took pride in the decreasing number of second offenders during his régime. Despite insufficient funds, he worked to end indiscriminate herding together of all prisoners. Though at first in solitary confinement, they could progress towards more lenient treatment and training. On leaving gaol they received clothing, money, tools and passage to a place of employment. He carefully selected and trained warders and demanded better salaries and conditions for them. He argued that the prisons should be industrious hives of labour, and allowed prisoners schooling, choir practice and visits by authorized outsiders. He was sometimes painfully conscious of his difficult position, open to misinterpretation as too lenient or too harsh, but ex-prisoners often visited him.

In 1875 Maclean was a founding member of the Linnean Society of New South Wales. In October 1889 he took leave to recruit his health but died of typhoid fever in Sydney on 6 November intestate. He was buried in the Anglican section of Waverley cemetery. To one obituarist he was a 'judicious, large-hearted, kind and merciful friend' to convicts. He was survived by a son and a daughter of his first wife Emily Strong, (d. 1860), whom he had married on 16 May 1856, and by his second wife Agnes Helen, née Campbell, whom he had married on 26 February 1862, and by their two daughters.

V&P (LA NSW), Reports on the goldfields, 1856-57 to 1864, Reports on the prisons, 1870-89; V&P (LA NSW), 1858, 3, 467, 1871-72, 2, 135, 373, 1877-78, 3, 289, 1878-79, 3, 1033, 1887-88, 7, 144, (LC NSW), 1867-68, 1, 899; PD (LA NSW), 1879-80, 3, 2663, 1883-84, 979; *Sydney Herald*, 4 Sept 1837; SMH, 15 Apr 1878, 1 Sept 1886; *Town and Country J*, 16 Nov 1889; *Sydney Mail*, 23 Nov 1889; A. W. Powell, The Trial Bay project: politics and penal reform 1861-1903 (B.A. Hons thesis, Univ New England, 1970); Parkes letters (ML); MS cat under Maclean (ML).   SUZANNE EDGAR

McLEAN, JOHN DONALD (1820-1866), squatter and politician, was born at Condrae House, Kilmuir, Isle of Skye, Scotland, youngest son of Donald McLean, land-owner, and his wife Flora, née Nicholson. His father became a founding director of the Australian Agricultural Co. in 1824.

Educated at Kilmuir Parish School, McLean migrated to Sydney with his brother and sister in 1837. After pastoral experience on the Clarence River he moved to the Darling Downs in 1848 and bought Westbrook station in 1853. By 1868 he had acquired partnerships in some fifty southern and western Queensland runs, 'more than any other private individual in the country'. He also had extensive shipping and mercantile interests in New South Wales. On 13 September 1855 at St Phillip's Church, Sydney, he had married Mary Strutt and for three years they toured Europe. In 1860 he leased Hawthornden House, Sydney, and in 1865 built the mansion, Quiraing, at Edge-cliff for £16,000.

A friend of Hodgson, Watts [qq.v.] and other 'Pure Merinos', McLean represented Eastern Downs in the Queensland Legislative Assembly from May 1862 to Decem-

ber 1866. At first he was described as 'more likely to be influenced by his interests than his intellect' and 'a flunkey unable to speak, much less think for himself'. His sober influence grew slowly, but his land order and family purchases on the Drayton Agricultural Reserve displayed little care for legislative intentions or popular feeling. In a classic statement he scorned free selection as 'subversive of the true principles of civilization', disastrous for the revenue, productive of 'hordes of thieves and robbers' and economically fallacious. Realizing the force of the urban political threat, he claimed that while the squatters 'had run a race and won it, that was no reason why they should be prevented from running any more'.

A member of the select committee in the financial emergency of 1866, McLean became treasurer on 21 July after opposition by Governor Bowen and the banks against Macalister's [q.v.] legal tender note issue proposals had led to the collapse of the ministry. McLean's managerial experience and financial success had unexpectedly carried him into an office which he claimed to be 'a *duty* which I owe to my adopted country ... to protect [its] credit'. Certainly his respectability, shrewdness and soundness helped to stabilize the interim Herbert [q.v.] ministry and ensured public confidence at a critical time. However, the price was high. The Leasing Act of 1866 which then 'typified all that was wrong with land policy' was the Pure Merinos price for inclusion of their representatives in the succeeding Macalister government. Before his policies could be seriously criticized McLean fell from his horse and died from concussion of the brain on 16 December 1866. He was buried at Westbrook. A parish near Toowoomba is named after him.

McLean was survived by his wife and seven children. His probate was sworn at £69,000 in Queensland and £30,000 in New South Wales. He left substantial legacies to relations and most of his estate to his wife. In a significant decision of the Supreme Court of New South Wales, affirmed by the Privy Council in 1878, his legatees were exempted from Queensland stamp duties because his family lived in Sydney and his own sojourn at the Queensland Club and Westbrook in 1862-66 did not determine residence.

PD (Qld), 1866, 365-69, 571; *Darling Downs Gazette*, 8 May 1862, 18 Dec 1866; *Toowoomba Chronicle*, 8 Apr 1876; *Brisbane Courier*, 3 May 1878.   D. B. WATERSON

McLEAN, WILLIAM (1845-1905), merchant, was born on 12 January 1845 in Dumfries, Scotland, son of Peter McLean, cabinet maker, and his wife Jane, née Strong. The family arrived in Melbourne in 1853 and William completed his education. He was employed first by John McTier and later by the hardware firm, E. Keep & Co. After seven years McLean was ready to open his own hardware business and in 1870 he went into partnership with T. E. White. In 1872 the partnership was dissolved and McLean was joined by his brother Joseph and William Rigg as McLean Bros & Rigg which specialized in wholesale and retail iron-mongery, general hardware and machinery importing.

The new company grew quickly into one of the successes of 'Marvellous Melbourne'. In 1876 the partners opened an office in London; branches were established at Adelaide in 1879 and Sydney in 1884 and an office in New York in 1886. In 1887 the firm became a limited liability company with the partners holding a controlling interest and McLean as general manager. The company was very prosperous. In 1887 the 'emporium' in Elizabeth Street, Melbourne, was claimed to be 'second to none in Victoria'; it specialized in hardware and machinery but furniture, silverware, clocks and marble and bronze statuary were also featured. At the rear McLean Bros & Rigg built a four-storied wholesale warehouse in Collins Place, and had an iron yard and bond store in Bourke Street. Imported machinery was assembled in a large blue-stone factory at Port Melbourne. McLean had many overseas agencies and with patent rights to many local inventions was able to diversify his business. In the 1880s Victoria's protectionist policy opened a profitable field for investment and McLean, though a moderate free trader, was quick to exploit the new opportunities, taking large con-tracts from the Victorian railways, Melbourne Tramway Trust, Telegraph Department and Public Works Department. He described himself as a follower of the 'Conservative Party' but twice resisted pressure to contest safe Legislative Council seats. In 1883 he argued cogently before the royal commission on the tariff, supporting the infant industry argument but detailing many anomalies of the tariff structure.

McLean was appointed a justice of the peace for the Central Bailiwick and in 1884 a commissioner of the Savings Banks of Victoria. He served on the Melbourne Hos-pital Committee in 1882-94, and was chair-man of the Melbourne Permanent Building Society, a director of the Federal Bank and chairman of the Melbourne Coffee Taverns Co. A strong advocate for temperance he was treasurer of the Victorian Alliance and a supporter of the Northcote Inebriate

Retreat. He was also active in the Young Men's Christian Association and as a leading member of the Collins Street Baptist Church helped to engage Rev. Samuel Chapman [q.v.] for its pastor in 1887 and S. P. Carey in 1897. McLean organized the Victorian Baptist Fund and was well known for his generosity.

McLean could afford his philanthropy while the land boom lasted. He was promi-nent in the Real Estate Bank, the Centennial Land Bank, the United Property Co. and the Union Finance Co. He used his chair-manship of the board of the Federal Bank to lend £20,000 to the Melbourne Permanent Building Society, but his overdraft of about £100,000 with the Federal was concealed from the shareholders by 'floating' balances before each settlement day to put the directors' accounts in credit. This was accomplished by borrowing from the City of Melbourne Bank. The collapse of the boom made McLean's insolvency inevitable. In 1894 he resigned his public offices and filed his schedule for £200,000, most of which was owed to the Federal and Real Estate Banks. He was allowed to retain his general managership in McLean Bros & Rigg and was finally released from sequestration in 1898. In 1900 he resigned from the firm which was bought by T. Luxton [q.v.] in 1907.

After retirement McLean made the last of his eight visits to Europe and in 1901 set up as a manufacturers' agent in Little Flinders Street. His health was failing and he was ordered to rest but would not follow medical advice. On 6 February 1905 he was found drowned off the Middle Brighton pier. In 1869 he had married Margaret, daughter of Andrew Arnot. Of their eleven children, Oliver was active for some years in the firm's management.

A. Sutherland et al, *Victoria and its metro-polis*, 2 (Melb, 1888); J. Smith (ed), *Cyclopedia of Victoria*, 1 (Melb, 1903); M. Cannon, *Land boom and bust* (Melb, 1972); *Bulletin* (Melb), 22 Dec 1882; *Argus*, 9, 19 Oct 1886, 4, 6 Feb 1905; *Age*, 9 Dec 1893, 24 Feb, 14 Nov 1894; insolvency papers 90/2005 (VA).

GEORGE PARSONS

MACLEAY, SIR WILLIAM JOHN (1820-1891), pastoralist, politician and patron of science, was born on 13 June 1820 at Wick, Caithness, Scotland, second son of Kenneth Macleay of Keiss and his wife Barbara, née Horne. Educated at the Edinburgh Academy in 1834-36 he entered the medical school of the University of Edinburgh. Orphaned in 1837 he was left with little money and two younger brothers to educate. Though fascinated by medical and scientific studies, he accepted the advice of his uncle Alexander McLeay [q.v.] to migrate and arrived in Sydney in March 1839 in the *Royal George* with his brother Walter. He found the company of his uncle and cousins William Sharpe and George Macleay [qq.v.] congenial and under their influence acquired an increasing interest in natural history. In 1840 Macleay joined George on the family's runs first at Goulburn, then on the Murrumbidgee. A magistrate from 1841, he sat on the Wagga Wagga bench from 1847. He served on the local National school board and in 1852 was a founder of the Murrumbidgee Turf Club. By 1848 he had taken over Mulberrygong, 90,000 acres on the Murrumbidgee, and soon acquired Kerarbury in which he held a share until the 1870s. A Freemason he had become grand warden of the Provincial Grand Lodge of Scotland in 1855 and in 1861-66 he was a captain in the Sydney Volunteer Artillery. At St James's Church in 1857 he had married Susan Emmeline, 18-year-old daughter of E. D. Thomson [q.v.]. They lived in Macquarie Street until he leased Elizabeth Bay House from George in 1865.

In 1855 Macleay had been elected to the Legislative Council for the Lachlan and Lower Darling Pastoral District. After responsible government he represented the Lachlan and Lower Darling in the Legislative Assembly in 1856-58 and the Murrumbidgee in 1859-74. In 1860 he was a member of the general committee of the New South Wales Constitutional Association which failed in its aim of securing for parliament 'the services of gentlemen of standing and education' in the elections during ferment over the land laws. A protectionist from the 1860s, he pressed his own views by the unusual tactic of moving for select committees which he then chaired. In 1863 as chairman of the select committee on harbour defences he recommended batteries on North and South Heads. In November 1866 he used the report of the select committee on the unemployed to advocate the imposition of 20 per cent *ad valorem* duties on all timber imports and manufactures to protect local cabinet makers. Although described in James Gormly's [q.v.] *Reminiscences* as an able politician who 'always took an independent stand', his hostility to Henry Parkes [q.v.], whom he regarded as a radical upstart, led him to support John Robertson [q.v.]. In December 1868 after the attempt to kill the duke of Edinburgh, malice towards Parkes as much as a desire for truth led Macleay to move for and chair a select committee to inquire into 'the existence of a conspiracy for purposes of treason'. Although the committee found no Fenian conspiracy, the

report was rejected by the assembly and Parkes later carried resolutions expunging it from the parliamentary records. In February 1870 as chairman of a select committee on railway extension Macleay proposed horse-drawn railways instead of main trunk lines. In 1870-91 he was a trustee of the Free Public Library and a member of the commission on defence from foreign aggression.

Macleay built up large pastoral holdings in New South Wales usually with working partners. While travelling to the Murrumbidgee he beat off an attack by Ben Hall's [q.v.] gang and was later awarded one of the gold medals struck to honour those who helped to suppress bushranging. Attracted by viticulture he had a forty-acre vineyard at Lake Albert near Wagga Wagga in the 1870s. He did not withdraw from politics completely and in 1877 was appointed to the Legislative Council on the recommendation of Robertson. That year he was president of the royal commission on oyster culture and in 1880-83 the fisheries commission. He was also a commissioner for the exhibitions in Philadelphia in 1875, Melbourne in 1876 and 1880, Sydney in 1879 and Amsterdam in 1883. He was elected to the Senate of the University of Sydney in 1875 and knighted in 1889. Active in moves to form a Protectionist party, he was president of the National Club and as chairman of its political committee attended the first National Protection Conference in October. However, by then he had won repute for his scientific achievements.

Although scientific opportunities in the colony were meagre in the 1840s and 1850s Macleay was fortunate to have the support of his cousin in studying insects and inland fishes. His active scientific career did not begin until, frustrated by the lack of a regular outlet for workers in the biological sciences, he helped to found the Entomological Society of New South Wales in 1862; within a year the society gave 'an impetus ... to collecting ... hitherto unknown in the colony'. Macleay sent George Masters [q.v.] to Queensland to collect insects and in 1863-66 thousands of his specimens were exhibited by the society. In 1865 Macleay had inherited his cousin's collections at Elizabeth Bay House; Captain A. A. W. Onslow and Dr James Cox [qq.v.] were frequent visitors. Early attracted by the Australian Museum, Macleay became a trustee and was involved in the dismissal of its curator, Gerard Krefft [q.v.]. Although an interested party Macleay served on the select committee on the museum in 1874 and gave evidence. He denied imputations that he had added to his private collections at the museum's expense but admitted that he had offered a higher salary to the assistant curator, Masters, to care for his large collections at Elizabeth Bay.

Well read in zoological literature, Macleay demanded the highest standards of taxonomic and analytical writing for the Entomological Society. Despite support from R. L. King, A. W. Scott and F. L. N. Laporte [qq.v.] the society's enthusiasm waned. Macleay's home and collections at Elizabeth Bay became a centre for naturalists, scientists and interested amateurs. He employed collectors of specimens throughout the continent and began to adopt the role of patron of Australian science by extending the scope of his own work in all fields of zoology and encouraging botany, geology and the marine sciences. He accepted the first presidency of the Linnean Society of New South Wales, formed in October 1874. From this office he castigated the local Royal Society for tolerating papers 'not of a scientific character' and promoted the Linnean Society as the colonial institution for independent pursuit of zoology, botany and geology. In June he had entertained the *Challenger's* scientists at Elizabeth Bay and in February 1875 at his own expense bought and fitted out the barque *Chevert* for a scientific expedition to New Guinea. His team included many scientists and collectors but from May to September the expedition was beset by dissension and dogged by fever, native hostility and contrary weather, and failed to enter the Fly River. They returned to Sydney with many scientific specimens, papers and reports but Macleay was harshly criticized for disavowing the potential of New Guinea as a site for European colonization. Thereafter his interest in science centred on his own work and collections, and patronizing the work of others.

Macleay was more than a dilettante and patron of science. He wrote over seventy reports and papers on entomology, ichthyology and other areas of zoology and was among the first colonials to publish most of his work in Australian journals. Though not always above scientific jealousy and often dependent on pupil assistants, he became the resident 'Sir Joseph Banks' [q.v.] of Australian science. His major works include the two-volume *Descriptive Catalogue of Australian Fishes* (Sydney, 1881) and *Census of Australian Snakes* (1884).

Survived by his wife, Macleay died without legal issue at Elizabeth Bay House on 7 December 1891 and was buried in the Anglican section of Waverley cemetery. His estate was valued for probate at over £81,000. The Macleay collections, valued at some £25,000, passed to the University of Sydney with £6000 to pay the curator. He also left £12,000 to found a chair of bacteriology but the university senate rejected his conditions and the money went to the Linnean Society. In 1956 the society and the university agreed to use the income from the bequest for part of the salary of the Linnean Macleay lectureship in microbiology. The society had already been given £14,000 from Macleay's estate and, after his wife died in August 1903, received £35,000 to endow four 'Linnean Macleay Fellowships' and an additional £6000.

Linnean Soc of NSW, *Macleay memorial volume*, J. J. Fletcher ed (Syd, 1893); Entomological Soc of NSW, *Trans*, 1864-73; J. J. Fletcher, 'The Society's heritage from the Macleays', Linnean Soc of NSW, *Procs*, 45 (1920); *SMH*, 2 Feb 1876; *Town and Country J*, 12 Dec 1891; M. Lyons, Aspects of sectarianism in New South Wales circa 1865-1880 (Ph.D. thesis, ANU, 1972); Macarthur papers, Macleay family papers (ML); Log of the *Chevert* (Univ Syd Archives); Macleay diaries (Linnean Soc of NSW Archives).   MICHAEL HOARE
MARTHA RUTLEDGE

McLELLAN, WILLIAM (1831-1906), mining agent and politician, was born on 12 August 1831 in Crieff, Perthshire, Scotland, son of Peter McLellan and his wife Margaret, née Sim. Educated at local schools, he worked as a carpenter before migrating to Victoria. He arrived in Melbourne on 11 November 1850. Next year he started prospecting for gold which took him to many fields in New South Wales and Victoria. He moved to Ararat in 1857 when the Canton lead was discovered, and was elected a member of the local Mining Board.

In 1859 Ararat was created a two-member constituency of the Legislative Assembly and McLellan was elected a representative in October. He was then a popular radical, specially interested in unlocking the land. The election at Ararat attracted five candidates and caused some heat; McLellan's three opponents survived a show of hands but after declaration of the poll they were alleged to have 'found it discreet to make themselves scarce during the afternoon'. McLellan himself was described as being a 'mild mannered man as ever scuttled a ship or cut a throat'. Egalitarian radicalism characterized his attitude in his first decade in the Legislative Assembly. As a member of the Land Convention he also championed manhood suffrage in his successful campaign for re-election in 1861. He created a stir in 1863 when he formally moved that steps be taken 'to insure the representatives of the people against the undue influence exercised by bankers, squatters, agents of secret and corrupt associations and others'. Throughout his career he assiduously cultivated his constituency and his most notable achievements were the establishment of the Mental Hospital in Ararat and the decision to route the Melbourne-Adelaide railway through Ararat rather than Hamilton.

McLellan continued to represent Ararat until it became a single-member constituency in 1877. Like other politicians associated with mining and finance, his initial democratic antagonism to the squatters moderated. He held office in J. A. MacPherson's [q.v.] ministry as commissioner of public works from January and vice-president of the Board of Land and Works from February to April 1870, and under C. G. Duffy [q.v.] from June 1871 to June 1872 and Sir James McCulloch [q.v.] from October 1875 to May 1877 as minister of mines. He had accumulated some wealth as a director of mining companies and his politics became increasingly dexterous even toward squatters. Although he retained the declamatory and ebullient style that earned him the ironical sobriquet of the 'dove of Ararat', his increasingly rare declarations of radical sentiment had little substance. After at least three unsuccessful contests he was again elected for Ararat in February 1883. He served on over twenty select committees and was chairman of committees in 1889-92. His attitude in 1886 may be inferred from his advice to parliamentary dissidents: 'I don't object to the Opposition coming into power, but I ask them to have patience, and to bide their right time for taking the reins, when who knows but that I may be sitting behind them . . . and supporting them in a right cause'.

After 1892 McLellan crossed the floor several times but was not given a portfolio, though in 1897-98 he served as a member of the royal commission on old age pensions. He was defeated in the 1897 election by R. F. Toutcher, a member of the Australian Natives Association. McLellan died of heart failure on 12 April 1906, survived by his wife Mary Eliza, née Moodie; they had no children.

L. L. Banfield, *Like the ark: the story of Ararat* (Melb, 1955); PD (Vic), 1886, 968; J. E. Jenkins, 'Early Ararat', VHM, 8 (1920-21); *Ararat Advertiser*, 23 Aug 1859; 23 July 1861, 13 Apr 1906; S. M. Ingham, Some aspects of Victorian liberalism 1880-1900 (M.A. thesis, Univ Melb, 1950); M. G. Finlayson, Victorian politics 1889-94 (M.A. thesis, Univ Melb, 1964).
STUART MACINTYRE

McLERIE, JOHN (1809-1874), soldier and police officer, was born in Ayrshire, Scotland, and educated in Caithness. He enlisted early as a private in the Scots Fusilier Guards. Dilligent, intelligent and literate he became an orderly clerk at the War Office, London. Commissioned in 1838 as ensign and adjutant of the 58th Regiment, he was promoted lieutenant on 27 June 1841.

In October 1844 McLerie arrived at Hobart Town in the transport *Emily*. He soon transferred to the regimental headquarters in Sydney. In 1845-47 he served with his regiment in the first Maori war in New Zealand, and on his return to Sydney was appointed adjutant and paymaster of the New South Wales Mounted Police Force on 1 May with an extra salary of £109 10s. In 1848 the press and the Legislative Council criticized the mounted police as a military force no longer suited to the character of the colony. McLerie's post was reduced. On 24 September 1849 he became principal gaoler in Sydney and, after his retirement from the army, superintendent of police on 1 October 1850. He faced many problems: the Sydney police were inadequate in numbers and training and their repute had been tarnished by the ignominious removal of several of their former heads after much public scandal. In Sydney gangs of hooligans roamed the streets at will and on 1 January the police had failed to quell a serious riot. A select committee of the Legislative Council recommended a thorough reorganization of the police. The Police Regulation Act unified the force under an inspector-general and McLerie, who had already improved the Sydney police, was appointed provincial inspector for the city and suburbs of Sydney. He was also visiting magistrate at Darlinghurst gaol and Cockatoo Island; his salary totalled £500.

Reorganization of the police was interrupted by the discovery of gold and further delayed when the Police Act was disallowed in London on a technicality. In 1852 an amendment Act reduced control by the inspector-general, but McLerie took over the office on 28 October 1856 at a salary of £800 and a house. He was also captain and commandant of the Yeomanry Cavalry. The 1862 Police Regulation Act again brought the force under the centralized control of the inspector-general and increased his executive powers. By 1874, mainly because of his efforts, the police had gained public confidence by controlling most bushranging. He had been ill when H. O'Farrell [q.v.] attempted to assassinate the duke of Edinburgh, but believed that O'Farrell had accomplices in America or Ireland. McLerie had risen from the ranks and won the respect and affection of his men who familiarly called him 'the General'.

A prominent Freemason, McLerie was substitute provincial grand master of St

Andrew's Lodge. He was a founder of the Society for the Relief of Destitute Children, a committee member of the Benevolent Asylum and the Sydney Female Refuge and a trustee of the Savings' Bank of New South Wales. In spare time he had built up a noted numismatic collection. He died from chronic bronchitis at Pitt Street South on 6 October 1874 and was buried in the Camperdown cemetery after a service at Christ Church St Laurence conducted by the bishop of Sydney. He was survived by his wife Jemima, née Dillinger, whom he had married in England, and by four sons and a daughter. His goods were sworn for probate at £1000. Posthumously he was awarded one of the special medals struck to honour those who had helped to suppress bushranging. A granite monument designed by the colonial architect, James Barnet [q.v.], was erected over his grave by his men.

Sel cttee on destitute children, V&P (LC NSW), 1854, 2, 1; V&P (LA NSW), 1861, 1, 919, 1234, 1868-69, 1, 797, 897, 1872-73, 3, 1528, Public Charities Com, 1873-74, 6, 2nd report, 236, 3rd report 47; H. King, 'Some aspects of police administration in New South Wales, 1825-1851', JRAHS, 42 (1956); SMH, 7 Oct 1874; Illustrated Sydney News, 17 Oct 1874; Town and Country J, 24 Oct 1874; Bulletin, 4 June 1881; MS cat under J. McLerie (ML).

HAZEL KING

MacMAHON, SIR CHARLES (1824-1891), police commissioner and politician, was born on 10 July 1824 at Fecarry House, Omagh, County Tyrone, Ireland, son of Sir William MacMahon, baronet and master of the rolls, and his second wife Charlotte, née Shaw. He served in Canada as an ensign with the 71st Regiment, transferred to the 10th Hussars and retired with the rank of captain after service in India. He joined the Royal Irish Constabulary in 1851. In India he had taken on extra duties as veterinary surgeon, for which he had a diploma.

MacMahon arrived in Melbourne in October 1852 with large capital and many letters of introduction which he did not present because, as he declared, he meant to make his own way. In January 1853 he applied for the sinecure of stud-master to the new police force but was persuaded by the chief commissioner, W. H. F. Mitchell [q.v.], to become assistant commissioner. With Mitchell he reorganized the force by dispensing with chief constables and abolishing magistrates' control over police. While Mitchell was in England MacMahon became acting chief police commissioner in 1854. He was chief commissioner in 1856-58 and proved himself to be a diligent, painstaking officer and a 'high-minded and honourable public servant'. His military experience was invaluable in organization, though he was not good at delegating authority. During his administration he compiled the first police code for guidance of members, and the force was in a promising condition on his resignation.

On 19 February 1858 a select committee on 'Captain MacMahon's Case' was appointed to inquire into the management of police funds, the general conduct of the force since 1853 and the charge that MacMahon had profited personally from police contracts. Specifically also, a prisoner had died from lack of ventilation in the Sandhurst lock-up which was made to MacMahon's design and of iron purchased from him, and murder by negligence was imputed. The committee's report in June 1858 stated that the irregularities uncovered were rendered necessary by the peculiarities of the time and sanctioned by the government of the day, and that there was not the slightest evidence to substantiate the charges made against MacMahon. On 12 October copies of 'all Papers relating to the Retirement of Captain MacMahon from the Government Service' were submitted to the Legislative Assembly, because of the dispute between MacMahon and his ministerial head, J. O'Shanassy [q.v.], over the district inspector, William, brother of H. E. P. Dana [q.v.]. O'Shanassy demanded that Dana be granted a transfer to Bourke and MacMahon, referring to Dana as 'impatient of control' and believing such interference detrimental to the force, offered his resignation which was accepted on 17 July.

MacMahon had been a member of the Executive and Legislative Councils in 1853-56. From August 1861 to August 1864 he represented West Bourke in the Legislative Assembly and was minister without portfolio in the O'Shanassy ministry till June 1863. From 1866 to 1878 he represented West Melbourne, strongly supported by the Irish Catholic community. In 1875 he was appointed K.B. for his services as Speaker from April 1871 during the troublesome period until the election of the new Berry [q.v.] ministry in 1877. MacMahon was in general sympathy with the landowning and mercantile groups, a 'staunch' free trader and therefore opposed to Berry, who at the general elections accused MacMahon of being a corrupt Speaker, giving decisions contrary both to parliamentary law and practice, and to the facts before him. MacMahon wavered between horse-whipping his critic and suing him for libel, but was dissuaded from both courses and could only emphatically deny the aspersion.

MacMahon was a member of the 1870 royal commissions on Federal union and on penal and prison discipline. He again represented West Melbourne in 1880-86 in the assembly and then retired from politics. He had broad business interests and was director of the Melbourne Banking Co. and the Australian Alliance Assurance Co. in the 1860s.

MacMahon was twice married; first, to Sophie Campbell, sister of a Canadian barrister who became a magistrate at Beechworth, Victoria; and second, to Clara Ann, daughter of C. J. Webster of Yea. He had no children. He died at his East Melbourne home on 28 August 1891 and was buried according to Anglican rites in the Melbourne cemetery.

J. Sadleir, *Recollections of a Victorian police officer* (Melb, 1913); P. S. Cleary, *Australia's debt to Irish nation-builders* (Syd, 1933); V&P (LA Vic), 1857-58 (D27); *Age*, 31 Aug 1891; J. E. Parnaby, The economic and political development of Victoria, 1877-1881 (Ph.D. thesis, Univ Melb, 1951).   SUZANNE G. MELLOR

McMECKAN, JAMES (1809-1890), master mariner, shipowner and pastoralist, was born in Wigtonshire, Scotland, son of James McMeckan, farmer, and his wife Grace, née Carth. The family had owned the larger part of the parish of Kirkcolm for over 300 years. Appropriately educated, James at 14 sought a maritime career. In 1829 he was apprenticed to a London shipping firm, Brocklebank & Rolt. He became a thoroughly practical seaman, typical of the sailing age. For twenty years he led a varied career in the merchant marine and the navy. His experience included convict transportation, the London-Hobart run and the Australian coastal trade. In 1840 he had become a master and in 1849 transferred to the new Tasmanian-built barque *Mary Brock* engaged in a regular Melbourne-Adelaide service. He was in command when she was wrecked on the South Australian coast in 1852.

McMeckan did not return to the sea and as the Victorian goldfields had been opened he grasped the opportunity to enter business. In 1853 with J. H. Blackwood [q.v.] as junior partner he established McMeckan, Blackwood & Co. and commenced operations as shipping agents and general merchants. McMeckan had exclusive control over the shipping side of the business and Blackwood handled the rest. The goldfields' demand for wheat and flour soon gave the new firm trading links with the South Australian miller, Samuel White. The company helped to establish a regular steamship service between Melbourne and Adelaide in 1854 when they obtained the agency for the new 301-ton steamer *Havilah*, which was com-

manded and part-owned by McMeckan's younger brother Hugh. The success of the weekly service brought a mail contract from the two colonial governments and further tonnage was added to the agency. The partners bought the *Queen*, the first steamer on their own account, in 1856.

During the 1860s the firm successfully controlled the Melbourne-Adelaide trade. They added another four steamers either by outright purchase or together with their Adelaide associates. They branched out into New Zealand services commencing with passengers, general cargo, mail and livestock to Dunedin in 1860. A year later the Otago gold rush offered enormous opportunities for the direct Melbourne-Port Chalmers traffic and within three months 15,500 prospectors had been landed. Late in 1864 gold was discovered at Hokitika on the west coast of the South Island, and the Australasian trade received another great stimulus. The ships which the firm bought or chartered in order to exploit the expanding commerce gave them pre-eminence in the trans-Tasman trades.

The firm retained its hold over the Melbourne-Adelaide trade till the mid-1870s. It had dominated the Northern Territory trade carrying supplies for the overland telegraph construction in 1871-72 and the later gold and copper miners. However, the Adelaide Steamship Co. was formed in 1875 and it created serious competition in the Melbourne-Adelaide trade; in 1877 the partners sold two steamships and their interests in this run to the Adelaide company. Unfortunately several company ships were wrecked in the 1870s and the partners were faced with buying ships equal to those of their other new opponent, the enterprising Union Steam Ship Co. of New Zealand. In 1878 McMeckan, Blackwood & Co. sold the New Zealand business and the four most modern ships to Union Steam and thereafter acted as its agent. As a shipping agency the firm was wound up in 1883 and the principals concentrated on their pastoral properties in the Riverina, and the Charlton district, Victoria.

McMeckan had refused various civic and public positions because of deafness and inability to serve two masters despite his sanguine temperament. He gave the business undivided attention and his shrewdness, integrity and punctiliousness won him high esteem from a large circle of friends and acquaintances. Unmarried, he died at Corsewell, Hawthorn, on 23 May 1890, aged 81, and was survived by several relations in the colony. In his honour two nephews and two nieces gave £10,000 to Scotch College in 1922 for building McMeckan House for boarders.

H. M. Franklyn, *A glance at Australia in 1880* (Melb, 1881); T. W. H. Leavitt and W. D. Lilburn (eds), *The jubilee history of Victoria and Melbourne*, 1 (Melb, 1888); W. A. Laxon, 'The Blue Emu at sea', *Sea Breezes*, 41 (1967); *Age*, 26 May 1890; *Argus*, 26 May 1890; *Australasian*, 14 June, 31 Dec 1890, 18, 25 July, 1, 8 Aug 1891.

G. R. HENNING

McMINN, GILBERT ROTHERDALE (1841-1924), surveyor and public servant, and **WILLIAM** (1844-1884), surveyor and architect, were born at Newry, County Down, Ireland, sons of Joseph McMinn, bank manager, and his wife Martha, née Hamill. After Joseph died, Martha sailed with her eight children in the *Albatross* and arrived at Port Adelaide in September 1850. On leaving school Gilbert took up surveying and William was apprenticed to the architect, James Macgeorge (d. 1918).

In June 1864 William sailed for the Northern Territory in the *Henry Ellis* as a chainman for the expedition of B. T. Finniss [q.v.] and Gilbert followed in the *South Australian* as a labourer in October. William was appointed a surveyor on 17 August 1865 at 16s. 6d. a day and mapped some 15,000 acres around the Adelaide River but suffered from the steamy heat and quarrelsome colleagues. The expedition became so desperate that a group of thirty took passage in a ship bound for Singapore while William and five others bought from another ship a 23-foot boat, named it the *Forlorn Hope* and sailed 2000 miles to Champion Bay (Geraldton). At Adelaide in March 1866 he gave damning evidence to the commission inquiring into Finniss's expedition.

William had joined the public service as a draftsman on his return but resigned in 1867 to practise as an architect. Among other work he helped to prepare the plans for Prince Alfred College and the successful competition design for the General Post Office in 1867 and alterations to the Supreme Court in 1869. Next year John McKinlay [q.v.] offered to mark a route for the overland telegraph from Port Darwin to Port Augusta, and nominated William as his surveyor. The government rejected the proposal but appointed him surveyor and overseer of works for the northern part of the telegraph. The section contractors, Joseph Darwent and William Trevett Dalwood, arrived at Darwin on 9 September and completed ninety miles of line before the rainy season set in on 8 November. Despite bogged vehicles and a strike, another hundred miles had been cleared and poles erected by mid-March 1871. McMinn warned the contractors that their progress was unsatis-

factory and although the 'wet' had ended annulled the contract on 3 May. The remaining eighty-three miles of the section were finished by government parties, but McMinn's action was ill judged. On his return to Adelaide in July he was dismissed and after long inquiry Dalwood was compensated with £11,000.

Meanwhile in the central section of the overland telegraph Gilbert had become leader of a subsection from Marchant Springs to the Alice River. On his surveys in February 1871 he discovered Simson's Gap and thereby a practical route east of J. M. Stuart's [q.v.] track through the MacDonnell Ranges. He completed his subsection on 15 November and took over the next northern subsection from W. W. Mills, finishing it on 29 December. He then started building the telegraph station at Alice Springs and in July 1872 left for Adelaide, a month before the first transcontinental message came through.

In Adelaide William had taken an office in the Register Building and practised as an architect, sometimes with partners but mostly by himself. He designed and built several dignified houses with elegant entrances, some hotels and the original wing of the Children's Hospital. He also won second place for his design of a bridge over the Torrens. While in partnership with Edward John Woods in 1877-78 McMinn's greatest triumph was the first building of the University of Adelaide. At Glenelg on 14 March 1877 he married Mary Frances Muirhead; they had two daughters. He died in North Adelaide on 14 February 1884 aged 40.

On 18 June 1873 Gilbert had been appointed senior surveyor and supervisor of works in the Northern Territory at a salary of £350. He wrote a section of the chapter on the territory in *South Australia: its history, resources and productions*, edited by W. Harcus [q.v.] in 1876. Until J. L. Parsons arrived at Palmerston in May 1884 McMinn acted as government resident for fourteen months; his quarterly reports were succinct and practical, and he was also responsible for finding the tree marked by Stuart when he reached the north coast. In 1884 Gilbert took leave in the south and after his return was appointed resident magistrate and customs officer in 1886 at Borroloola near the Gulf of Carpentaria and the Queensland border. Resigning on 26 May 1888, he went to Adelaide and in 1890 to Sydney, where he became a justice of the peace and in 1894 published a paper on drainage in the *Agricultural Gazette*. Next year he moved to Adelaide and worked in the education department but resigned in August 1896 to try his fortune in Western

Australia. By August 1899 he was in Adelaide planning with two others to undertake hydraulic mining in the Northern Territory, but in a few years the project dwindled and died. By 1907 he was settled in Melbourne and on 2 July read a paper on the Northern Territory to the Hawthorn Literary Society.

At Palmerston McMinn was twice married: first, on 28 November 1874 to Anna Grove; and second, on 15 November 1884 to Madge Fleetwood Marsh. He lived for some years at Hawthorn and then St Kilda with his daughter Beulah, a nurse. Aged 83 he died from sudden heart failure on 18 October 1924 and was buried privately in the Box Hill cemetery. Predeceased by his wives and two daughters, he was survived by one son of his first marriage and two sons and two daughters of his second.

W. H. Bagot, *Some nineteenth century Adelaide architects* (Adel, 1958); Inst of Engineers (Aust) and Aust Post Office, *The centenary of the Adelaide-Darwin overland telegraph line* (Syd, 1972); PP (SA), 1865 (89), 1865-66 (131), 1866-67 (17), 1870-71 (36), 1875 (122), 1877 (103); *Advertiser* (Adel), 15, 16 Feb 1884; *Register* (Adel), 8 Aug 1899; *Argus*, 21 Oct 1924; *Centralian Advocate*, 29 Oct 1970, 11 Feb 1971; McMinn papers (SAA); Univ Adel Archives.

McNAB, DUNCAN (1820-1896), Catholic missionary, was born on 11 May 1820 at Achrinich, parish of Morven, Argyllshire, Scotland, son of Patric McNab and his wife Cirsty. In 1832 he went to Blair College, a seminary near Aberdeen, and in June 1835 to the Scots College in Rome but left on 8 August 1840 before taking his oath as a missionary. He returned to Scotland and was admitted a priest on 8 March 1845. Inspired perhaps by his kinship with Mary McKillop [q.v.], he dreamed of a mission to the Australian Aboriginals but was refused by a bishop perpetually short of priests, and spent twenty years in parish work. He dabbled in Gaelic literature and at Airdrie in 1862 fell foul of Irish parishioners, probably by arguing the Scottish birth of St Patrick.

Given leave to migrate McNab arrived at Melbourne in the *Chariot of Fame* on 29 July 1867. For eight years he was tied to parish work in Geelong, Portland and Bendigo. In March 1870 he was refused permission to join the New Norcia Benedictines in Western Australia, but in September 1875 he was permitted to start a personal mission in Queensland. At Mackay he began to see that the one hope for Aboriginals was to treat them not as 'a problem'. He therefore sought for them the right to own land and to be treated as responsible adults by

law and as individuals. His dour common sense did not appeal to either the government or his clerical superiors, while his fervent and mystical Catholicism made him suspect in the Protestant majority. In March 1876 he became ill and went south to recuperate. On his return he began raising money for work among tribes at Gympie, Kilcoy, Durundur and Bribie Island. He was gazetted a commissioner for Aboriginals but became unpopular with other commissioners by advocating individual homesteads rather than reserves. He quarrelled with Bishop James Quinn [q.v.] who considered him a tool of government and refused help, while Tom Petrie [q.v.] believed that he was the dupe of supposed converts. In June 1878 he wrote a long appeal to Rome for help but received no reply and decided to appeal in person. In August 1879 he sailed in the *Kent* and next year induced Pope Leo XIII to authorize a Jesuit mission to the Aboriginals, vainly importuned the Colonial Office in London, travelled through the United States and returned to Victoria. After persuading the South Australian Jesuits assigned to Aboriginal missions to select the Northern Territory rather than Queensland, he turned his attention to Western Australia.

McNab arrived at Perth early in 1883 and became a chaplain to Aboriginal prisoners on Rottnest Island. His recommendations on vocational training to the 1883 commission on Aboriginals were implemented halfheartedly. He then made a reconnaissance to the north and in April 1884 settled alone at Goodenough Bay, near Derby. For two years he laboured patiently with little success but in April 1886 he was joined by Fr William Treacy. In August he visited Derby and was diverted to the pastoral care of miners at Hall's Creek. In his absence Treacy had been struck down by fever and went south, and the mission buildings were destroyed by fire. This was the last straw. According to Aboriginal tradition, McNab, tired and old, rode from Derby to Albany accompanied by one faithful Aboriginal. He took ship for Melbourne where he lived in a Jesuit house at Richmond and worked quietly as a parish priest until he died on 11 September 1896.

McNab's curious mixture of Celtic mysticism and Scottish common sense antagonized many but his proposals for native welfare would, if adopted, have saved much agony. His name is still revered in the tribal traditions of the north-west.

P. F. Moran, *History of the Catholic Church in Australasia* (Syd, 1895); J. E. Handley, *The Irish in modern Scotland* (Cork, 1947); M. Durack, *The rock and the sand* (Lond, 1971); V&P (LA Qld), 1876, 3, 161, 1878, 2, 66, (LC WA), 1883, 2nd S (16); M. Durack, 'The priest vho rode away', *Westerly*, Nov 1962; R. L. Evans, 'Queensland's first Aboriginal reserve', pt 2, *Qld Heritage*, Nov 1971; *Advocate* (Melb), 9 Sept 1896; McNab to Propaganda, Rome, 10 July 1878 (Jesuit Provincial Archives, Hawthorn, Vic); information from Melb Diocesan Hist Com; CO 234/40/597, 621.

H. J. GIBBNEY

McNAUGHTAN, ALEXANDER (1815-1884), merchant, was born on 28 November 1815 at Milngavie, Dumbartonshire, Scotland, son of Alexander McNaughtan, United Presbyterian minister, and his wife Janet, née Blackwood. Well educated, he was trained in a firm engaged in the North American trade. At 26 he joined Kerr, Alexander & Co. and was sent to Van Diemen's Land for experience in the Launceston branch. The firm bought wool, whale bone, bark, kangaroo skins, hides and other raw products, in association with Kerr, Bogle & Co., which had started in Launceston in 1834 but soon made its headquarters at Hobart Town. In 1842 Kerr, Alexander & Co. was dissolved and McNaughtan became a partner in Kerr, Bogle & Co. John Bogle had returned to Glasgow in 1839 and Robert Kerr died in Hobart on 15 January 1846 aged 37. McNaughtan took charge in Hobart and on 29 March 1847 married Margaret, the sister of Robert Kerr.

By 1856 McNaughtan had carefully wound up the firm. In the next two years he became a justice of the peace, director of the Union Bank, trustee of St Mary's Hospital and chairman of the Chamber of Commerce. He helped to form the Gaslight Co., arranged the survey of water reticulation in Hobart, organized extensive searches for coal and promoted steamship services on the Derwent River and the east coast. He also made liberal gifts to the High School, Hutchins School, Royal Society, Public Library and Botanical Gardens, and helped to form groups for sponsoring migration from Scotland. When he left Hobart late in 1858 leading citizens held a meeting to honour him and decided to found scholarship fund named after him.

In Launceston he founded McNaughtan & Co. with Thomas Brown and John Dunn junior as his partners. On 10 February 1859 the firm contracted to lay a submarine telegraph cable across Bass Strait for £50,000, a third of which was paid by Victoria. The sections from Cape Otway to King Island and from Circular Head to the River Tamar were successful, but unfortunately, storms and rockbeds south of King Island broke the cable soon after it was laid, despite many attempts to find a sandy bottom. A few messages came through late in 1859 but the cable problem was not solved until 1868 when an English company contracted to lay a new cable from Low Head to Cape Schanck for £70,000 and to run and maintain the telegraph until 1888 for £7000 a year, paying the Tasmanian government any excess.

A select committee in Hobart exonerated McNaughtan from any fault and he was paid for his work, but his health was undermined by exposure and worry. He helped to form the Launceston Gas Co. in 1863 and presented a neat conservatory to the Northern Horticultural Gardens. Many landowners sought his help in introducing exotic plants and animals. For some years he was a warden of the Launceston Marine Board and in 1863 gave wise counsel to the select committee on the Deloraine railway. In the depression of 1864 he went bankrupt but managed to pay 19s. 6d. in the £.

Eulogized as a public benefactor and fine citizen, McNaughtan returned to Hobart where he had built a pleasing and unostentatious home in beautiful grounds stretching from Montpelier Street to De Witt Street. He lived there happily with his wife until she died on 20 December 1868. She was buried in the old Presbyterian cemetery in Church Street and given an inscription on one face of the monument to her brother. With no children and his energy spent, McNaughtan returned to his birthplace where he died from heart disease on 6 August 1884.

V&P (HA Tas), 1856 (35), 1859 (92), 1863 (26, 42), 1864 (92), 1868 (24); *Examiner* (Launceston), 26, 30 Sept 1884; A. Rowntree, 'Three good men', *Saturday Evening Mercury*, 19 Jan 1957.

McNEIL, NEIL (1857-1927), railway contractor, timber merchant and landowner, was born on 30 December 1857 at Dingwell, Inverness-shire, Scotland, second son of Neil McNeil (1827-1915), railway contractor, and his wife Elizabeth, née Urquhart. He migrated to Victoria with his parents about 1860 and settled at Ballarat. Educated at Ballarat College, he joined his father's firm and soon became superintendent. Later he set up as a contractor and won government contracts for railways from Hamley Bridge to Balaklava in South Australia, Colac-Camperdown and Lilydale-Healesville in Victoria and Fingal-St Mary's in Tasmania. In Hobart he was also responsible for constructing large works for the metropolitan water supply scheme.

In 1882 McNeil went to Western Australia where he built the Jarrahdale-Bunbury and Geraldton-Mullewa railways. In 1889 he was involved in promoting and constructing the Victoria reservoir in the Darling Range and the Perth water supply scheme, initially a private venture. In that year the 'Neil McNeil Company, Jarrah Timber Station' was incorporated in Victoria and as managing director McNeil successfully negotiated the sale of Western Australian timber in London. Through his efforts English capital was later invested in the company, which in 1897 became Jarrahdale Jarrah Forests and Railways Ltd. Activities expanded greatly in the next two years: the concession was extended for forty years, three hundred men were employed on the mills, and Jarrahdale was described as 'a community of happiness and contentment'. In 1902 the company amalgamated with Millar Brothers to become Millars' Karri and Jarrah Co. Ltd.

For some time McNeil lived in Melbourne but made regular trips by sea to Albany and overland to Jarrahdale to supervise the mills. On a visit to Britain in 1890 he married Jessie Alexandra, daughter of Hugh Laurie, in Ayr, Scotland, and on his return to Western Australia he acquired ten acres of choice land between Claremont and Cottesloe. He soon built The Cliffe, a large home constructed mainly of jarrah, to demonstrate his faith in the quality of local timber for building purposes.

From the early 1890s to the turn of the century his interests rapidly widened. An early visitor to Kalgoorlie in the gold rush, he acquired shares in the Star of the East Mine in the Murchison, the Wealth of Nations and Londonderry mines. He also bought such properties as Surrey Chambers and McNeil Buildings in Perth and Phillimore Chambers in Fremantle. In 1908 he bought 9000 acres in the Blackwood district and the Mount Barker estate, one of the finest orchards in the south-west, where he concentrated on pioneering the export trade of apples and pears as well as producing large quantities of stone fruits for commercial purposes. He also imported stock and bred excellent carriage horses.

A staunch Presbyterian, he donated £1000 towards the building of St Andrew's Presbyterian Church in Perth. He also gave generous support to the Young Men's Christian Association and to the victims of the earthquake disaster at Messina in 1908. Respected for his business acumen and honesty, he was appointed a justice of the peace for Western Australia in 1902. He died without issue on 8 May 1927 at The Cliffe and was buried in the Presbyterian section of Karrakatta cemetery.

J. S. Battye (ed), Cyclopedia of Western Australia, 2 (Perth, 1913); V. G. Fall, The mills of Jarrahdale (Perth, 1972); V&P (LC WA) 1887-88 (AI, 14); Inquirer, 17 Mar 1886; West Australian, 10 May 1927; Western Mail, 6 Apr 1939.
                                        WENDY BIRMAN

McPHERSON, (JAMES) ALPIN (1842-1895), bushranger best known as the 'Wild Scotchman', was born in Inverness-shire, Scotland, eldest of the eight children of John McPherson, farmer, and his wife Elspeth, née Bruce. The family migrated in the William Miles and arrived at Moreton Bay on 19 January 1855. The father worked as a farm labourer for D. C. McConnel [q.v.] of Cressbrook. Alpin went to a Brisbane school where his diligence pleased the teachers; he learnt some French and German, and became a fluent and entertaining speaker. Apprenticed to the builder, John Petrie [q.v.], he attended the Brisbane Mechanics' School at night and achieved prominence in its debating class.

In 1863 McPherson ran away and worked on various stations, becoming an excellent horseman and an accurate shot. His first recorded law-breaking activity was early in 1865 near Bowen, where at gunpoint he held up a publican who owed him back wages. The government offered a £50 reward for his apprehension. He went to New South Wales and is alleged to have stuck up several parties on the Northern Road. According to the Sydney Morning Herald, 23-24 February, he assumed the name of John Bruce, stole a horse from Wowingragong but failed to find his hero Ben Hall [q.v.]. The Scotchman lost his horse and ammunition and, in his only clash with the police, was shot in the arm by Sir Frederick Pottinger [q.v.]; in return he had only blank cartridges to fire. He took to the scrub and was reading quietly by the Lachlan River when the police surrounded him. He was taken to Forbes and remanded from week to week until he was sent to Sydney to be tried for shooting at Pottinger. The charge was dropped when that officer died in April.

McPherson was remanded for holding up the publican near Bowen, where he was committed to the October Assizes at Rockhampton. He escaped from the ship at Mackay, stole a horse and began to rob mail coaches on the roads between Maryborough, Gayndah and Gladstone, sometimes sending the stolen cheques to Governor Bowen. The government raised the price on McPherson's head to £250 and the police commissioner, David Thompson Seymour, lamented the appearance of bushranging in Queensland while the parliament debated the felons apprehension bill. On 31 March 1866 the Scotchman was waiting for the mailman near Gin Gin station when he was recognized by John Walsh who quickly organized an armed party of four. McPherson's horse was too fatigued to outpace his pursuers and when they fired he surrendered. He was taken to Maryborough and remanded to the criminal sittings in Brisbane for holding up the publican but was found not guilty, much to the disgust of officialdom. He was then taken to Maryborough to face charges of robbing the mails, found guilty and sentenced by Chief Justice Cockle [q.v.] to twenty-five years in the penal settlement on St Helena Island, Moreton Bay.

McPherson entered St Helena on 13 September 1866 and remained there until his sentence was remitted on 22 December 1874, following a petition presented by Brisbane citizens at the instigation of Rev. B. G. Wilson. While on St Helena he again aroused public imagination with a spectacular though unsuccessful escape attempt. On his release he worked on McConnel's property at Cressbrook as a stockman and later overseer of an outstation. The manager of another outstation was Sylvester Browne, brother of the novelist, T. A. Browne [q.v.], author of Robbery Under Arms. Legend has some of McPherson's exploits adapted for use in the novel by Browne who was familiar with the Scotchman's story through correspondence with his brother. In his last years he was known for his anecdotes and ready wit, regaling listeners with stories of the bushranging days. Aged 53 he died on 23 August 1895 at Burketown, North Queensland, survived by his wife Elizabeth Annie, née Hasfeldt, whom he had married in 1878 at Blackall, and by four sons and two daughters.

P. W. McNally, The life and adventures of the wild Scotchman (Brisb, 1899); G. E. Boxall, The story of the Australian bushrangers (Lond, 1902); J. T. S. Bird, The early history of Rockhampton (Rockhampton, 1904); D. Dignan, The story of Kolan (Brisb, 1964); Maryborough Chronicle, Apr-Sept 1866; Morning Bulletin, Apr-Sept 1866; Weekly Herald (Brisb), 14 Apr 1866; N. W. Broun, Memoirs of a Queensland pioneer (Oxley Lib, Brisb); N. M. Mullett, The history of the wild Scotchman (Oxley Lib, Brisb); Monduran station records (Gin Gin, Qld).   BASIL SHAW

MacPHERSON, JOHN ALEXANDER (1833-1894), politician, was born on 10 October 1833 at Springbank, Limestone Plains, second son of John MacPherson (1798-1875), landowner and squatter, and his wife Helen, née Watson. His grandfather, Peter MacPherson (1760-1844) of Skye, had brought his family in the Triton to Sydney in 1825 and settled near Bathurst.

John Alexander was probably the first European boy born on the site of Canberra. About 1840 he moved with his family to Melbourne, where he went to school. His early experience was mostly pastoral but in 1853-54 he attended the University of Edinburgh for a term, and after 1861 studied law at the University of Melbourne. In 1866 he was admitted to the Victorian Bar, but unlike his brother James (1842-1891) he did not practise, although he was treated as a 'learned' member of parliament and sat on the royal commission on intercolonial legislation in 1870.

For some time before 1861 MacPherson lived in the Western District and for four years managed Croxton, one of his father's stations. On 8 July 1858 he married Louisa Elizabeth, daughter of Cuthbert Fetherstonhaugh, police magistrate at Hamilton. In 1861 he nominated for Dundas, a large electorate round Hamilton, opposing 'the mobocracy of Melbourne, Geelong and the goldfields' as a local candidate in favour of planned land settlement, but withdrew in favour of W. Mollison [q.v.] and returned to Melbourne. 'Not wealthy' in 1864, and 'with no personal interest in squatting' in 1869, he owned some 2000 acres of the Croxton estate by 1877 and shared in Nerrin-Nerrin, a station of 62,000 acres which was managed by his brother William (1837-1901). He joined the Melbourne Club in 1871, the Australian Club in 1878 and in 1870-80 was a trustee of the Public Library, Museums and National Gallery.

MacPherson entered the Legislative Assembly in November 1864 for Portland, defeating W. Haines [q.v.]. From February 1866 to July 1878 he was member for Dundas. An independent with liberal sympathies, he accepted the need for some form of tariff and land selection, and for most of his career followed Sir James McCulloch [q.v.]. Although some resented the 'Roman virtue' which failed to win Hamilton an early railway or to organize its land sales well, his seat was one of the safest.

His ministry from 20 September 1869 to 8 April 1870 falls somewhat outside this pattern. Five years of increasingly assiduous parliamentary work left him frustrated at being judged by McCulloch 'no fit companion for a Casey, a Sullivan and a pair of Smiths' [qq.v.] and he helped defeat him on Robert Byrne's motion condemning the appointment of an outside party organizer to the ministry. The new mixed majority would accept no established leader and MacPherson at 35 became chief secretary. His ministry, more dissident Liberal than Constitutionalist, had no clear policy and was weakened by two defeats in ministerial elections yet it completed such important outstanding business as the lands bill, already before council, which became law after some concessions to squatters. Much business was done in the short recess but new appointments, particularly that of Graham Berry [q.v.] as treasurer, made his cabinet more radical and harder to control, and most Constitutionalist support was lost. After rejecting an adverse vote against Berry's largely protectionist budget Mac-Pherson could not ignore the majority assembled against him on 29 March 1870. Distrusting his more radical colleagues he did not seek a dissolution but resigned on 8 April.

MacPherson's acceptance of the lands portfolio in McCulloch's succeeding ministry was approved in Dundas but brought him a storm of recrimination from his ex-colleagues and the press, leaving him shaken, half-convinced of his unfitness for high office and dependent on McCulloch, then attacked as a squatter monopolist. He strove to make his lands administration exemplary, and with some success, but was no match for Berry, Duffy [q.v.] and the Age. Under fire, after McCulloch lost office in June 1871, MacPherson's reputation remained dubious at least till 1872 when his main critics lost power and were themselves subjected to acrimonious criticism.

When Francis [q.v.] became premier MacPherson supported the Education Act in 1872 but grew more critical, specially after McCulloch returned from London in 1874. He voted against the Constitution bill on which Francis resigned and, after supporting Kerferd's [q.v.] reconstruction, joined McCulloch and Berry in destroying it. Though laid up by a hunting accident for the early weeks of Berry's first ministry he helped McCulloch to destroy that government in 1875.

Under McCulloch as premier, MacPherson was chief secretary and administered with care his department's lepers, lunatics, police, prisons, culture and Aboriginals. When Berry, denied his dissolution, obstructed parliamentary business, MacPherson acted as deputy to his leader, seconding the gag and sending police against demonstrations.

After Berry's landslide victory in 1877 a conservative improver of MacPherson's type was without honour in the new radical-dominated parliament. His arguments against the land tax and its discrimination against joint estates and criticism of Berry's crisis measures went unheeded. In October MacPherson said his day of usefulness was over and foreshadowed his retirement, in practice from 19 February 1878, technically

from July. He embarked later that year on a long tour and settled in England, where his son was educated at Harrow and Cambridge, and his six daughters married. He died on 17 February 1894 at Thorpe, Chertsey, Surrey, still part-owner of Nerrin-Nerrin, but almost forgotten in Victoria.

C. G. Duffy, My life in two hemispheres, 2 (Lond, 1898); A. Henderson (ed), Australian families, 1 (Melb, 1941); PD (Vic), 29 Nov 1864-8 Aug 1878; I. P. MacPherson, 'MacPherson family history', Canberra District Hist Soc, J, Dec 1969; Hamilton Spectator, 10, 17 Aug 1861, 13-22 Sept 1864, 22 Sept 1869, 1 Jan, 13-20 Apr, 6 July 1870, 1 May, 11 Aug, 14, 18 Oct, 3 Nov 1875, 20 June, 1, 9, 11 July 1878; Argus, 2 Sept-19 Oct 1869, 21 Feb 1894; Illustrated Aust News, 1 Nov 1869; Age, 1 Mar 1879, 21 Feb 1894; J. E. Parnaby, The economic and political development of Victoria, 1877-1881 (Ph.D. thesis, Univ Melb, 1951); G. A. Bartlett, Political organization and society in Victoria 1864-1883 (Ph.D. thesis, ANU, 1964).

DOROTHY FITZPATRICK

McPHILLAMY, JOHN SMITH (1825-1887), grazier, was born on 15 September 1825 at Windsor, New South Wales, the fourth son of William McPhillamy and Mary Scott, who were both sentenced to transportation for seven years at the Ayr Court of Justiciary on 27 April 1816. Mary arrived at Sydney in February 1817 in the Lord Melville and William in March in the Sir William Bensley. McPhillamy became overseer for Robert Smith at Bathurst and died in 1828. Mary later married Smith whose home station was Mount Tamar. He acquired other runs before he died on 15 December 1851. Childless he left his estate to the McPhillamy children.

John worked for his stepfather as a station manager. On 5 March 1849 at Mount Tamar he married Maria Sophia, née Dargin. They lived at Bellevue until he inherited Mount Tamar and moved there. With prosperity McPhillamy devoted himself to grazing and to civic affairs. He leased part of Mount Tamar to tenant farmers and in times of adversity he not only reduced their rents but also advanced provisions, thereby winning repute for generosity. He helped found the Agricultural Association at Bathurst and won prizes for his fine-woolled rams at the first show in 1860. Interested in politics he supported Thomas Mort [q.v.] for election to the Legislative Assembly in 1856. Another candidate, W. H. Suttor [q.v.], carried the hostilities aroused by the election into the public life of Bathurst and virtually wrecked the Agricultural Association. In June 1859 McPhillamy won the West Macquarie seat but resigned on 6 December.

McPhillamy slowly withdrew to concentrate on his pastoral activities which continued to prosper. By 1871 he held eight runs in the Wellington District. At Mount Tamar he built a private race-course where the Bathurst Picnic Race Club held its first meeting in 1882. He died at Mount Tamar on 18 July 1887 and after a large funeral procession was buried in the Presbyterian section of the Bathurst cemetery although he had been baptized an Anglican. He was survived by four sons and three daughters. He left an estate valued for probate at over £80,000.

100 Bathurst shows (Bathurst, 1968); Town and Country J, 20 Aug 1887; McPhillamy papers (McIntosh, McPhillamy & Co., Bathurst); Parish records (St Matthew's Church, Windsor); Bathurst Hist Soc Archives; family papers. THEO BARKER

MACREDIE, WILLIAM (1813-1891), insurance manager and philanthropist, was born on the Isle of Arran, Scotland, son of Robert Macredie, sailor, and his wife Elizabeth, née Cunningham. He visited Canada in his late teens and in his early twenties was sent by the Phoenix Fire Insurance Co. of London to establish the first successful insurance agency in Trinidad. He lived there for sixteen years and travelled widely in both North and South America. He went to Victoria in the early 1850s, joining his four brothers who were early squatters. In 1855-56 he was in partnership with Matthew Lang [q.v.], wine and spirits merchant, in Elizabeth Street. With business acumen, he looked after the extensive interests of his cousin Archibald Cuninghame (d. 1856), a barrister who had returned to England as agent for the Victorian colonists in their plea for separation and had remained there as Victoria's first unofficial agent-general.

In 1857 Macredie became manager of the Australasian Insurance Co. but in 1863, after building up the business so that shares rose from 20s. to 55s., he resigned and became a partner of Hastings Cuningham [q.v.]. The formation of Cuningham & Macredie as wool-brokers, woolstore owners and stock and station agents was a turning point for Australia in wool marketing. The company conducted sales in Melbourne and imported many high-grade rams from Germany and elsewhere. It provided finance for those who wished to buy through the local market. Later it became the Australasian Mortgage & Agency Co. Ltd. In addition the Macredie family held interests in several pastoral properties and engaged in extensive and remunerative quartz-crushing operations. Cuningham &

Macredie lasted until 1868 when Macredie became secretary of the Pastoral Association of Victoria. He was also made secretary of the National Insurance Co. which had headquarters in Melbourne with branches throughout Victoria and in other colonies. The success of mutual life assurance in America suggested to Macredie that the idea would be successful in Victoria. In 1869 he helped to merge his company in the new National Mutual Life Association of Australia and served as its first secretary until 1872. He also negotiated the take-over of several smaller insurance companies.

In 1856 Macredie had published two pamphlets: Roads for Victoria: How to Make them cheaply, efficiently, and quickly under the pseudonym 'An old Backwoodsman'; and State aid to Religion in Victoria. His amusing and invaluable paper, 'Personal Reminiscences on Insurance Business', was delivered to the Insurance Institute of Victoria in October 1886. Many big businessmen were then becoming involved in shady speculations but Macredie retained his integrity and social conscience. His philanthropic work in Melbourne included the Women's Hospital, which he helped to found and served as honorary secretary for many years. He was also active in establishing the Society for Assisting Persons of Education and remained on its committee until 1891. A shrewd investor and wise administrator, he had a lively and inquiring mind and often commented on current events and social problems in the Argus and elsewhere. A noted raconteur, he used to tell stories of Melbourne's early fires fought with primitive appliances and hampered by the slowness of carting water from the Yarra.

Macredie and his wife Anne Fuller, née Stone, were closely associated with the Church of England. They had many friends and in 1858 built Elm Tree House at the corner of Domain Road and Walsh Street, South Yarra. There Macredie died of pneumonia on 27 April 1891 and was buried in the Melbourne general cemetery with the mayor, Matthew Lang, as his chief pall-bearer. He was survived by his wife and their only daughter Alice, who retained the family home for many years.

Macredie's brothers were well-known Victorian pastoral pioneers. Robert Reid arrived in 1838 and in the early 1840s went searching for runs in the Wimmera. He was given licence to 80,000 acres at Avoca and Wycheproof in 1846-48 and held Banyenong West in 1846-55 and Laen in 1846-58. His brother Andrew, an artist of merit, arrived in 1848 and was Robert's partner at Banyenong West in 1855-61, took over Laen in 1858-61 and held Watchem in 1859-64 jointly with Robert who, however, died in 1859 at Stuttgart, Germany. The property remained in their joint names until their brother George (1826-1883) bought out the interest. When Banyenong West was sub-divided in 1861 William took over part of the run. George and his brother John arrived in August 1840 as cabin passengers in the *Culdee*. They were in partnership at Lillirice station on Mount Emu Creek near Portland from 1845 until John sold his interest and returned to Scotland in 1853. In 1844 George had been an active member of the committee formed at the separation meeting in Mel-bourne. Like Robert, George had been appointed a territorial magistrate by Lieut-Governor La Trobe in 1852. George held Watchem station in 1864-70 and for some time was a member of the firm of Cuning-ham & Macredie.

T. F. Bride (ed), *Letters from Victorian pioneers* (Melb, 1898); R. V. Billis and A. S. Ken-yon, *Pastoral pioneers of Port Phillip* (Melb, 1932); P. L. Brown (ed), *Clyde Company papers*, 4-5 (Lond, 1959-63); National Mutual Life Assn of A'sia, *A century of life* (Melb, 1969); *A'sian Insurance and Banking Record*, 15 Nov 1886, 18 May 1891; *Argus*, 4 Apr 1891; Cuninghame papers, 1-3 (ML).   MARJORIE J. TIPPING

MACROSSAN, JOHN MURTAGH (1833-1891), politician, was born at Crees-lough, Donegal, Ireland, son of Neil Macrossan, farmer, and his wife Agnes, née Murtagh. He was educated in private and Catholic schools in Ireland and Glasgow. He arrived at Melbourne in 1853 and was a miner in Victoria and probably in New South Wales and New Zealand before 1865 when he was certainly located on the North Queensland goldfields. By the early 1870s he had emerged as a leading figure among the North Queensland miners. In 1871 he organized the Ravenswood Miners' Pro-tection Association which petitioned the minister for removal of the field warden. In that year Macrossan was convicted in the Townsville court of having assaulted the warden, T. R. Hackett, whom he had publicly horsewhipped. In November 1873 Macrossan was returned to the Queensland Legislative Assembly for one of the newly-constituted seats for the Kennedy electorate. After some years as an independent, he threw in his lot with Thomas McIlwraith [q.v.]. In the 1878 elections, which brought the Conservatives to office, Macrossan swung the northern electorates solidly behind McIlwraith, but was himself defeated by making a last-minute decision to contest a doubtful seat. However, he was given the portfolio of works and mines on 21 January

1879 and in March was elected for Towns-ville; he retained this seat until 1891.

Macrossan resigned from the ministry in March 1883 but returned to office in June 1888 under McIlwraith. In January 1890 he added the portfolio of colonial secretary to that of mines. As a minister Macrossan was able and hard-working. His first actions in 1879 had been to introduce economy and order into the railways, though the Opposition asserted that his wholesale dis-missals from the Ipswich railway workshops could be shown to have a sectarian bias. He was responsible for two mining Acts which were well received and clearly repre-sented many reforms. In particular the 1888 Act emphasized employer liability in cases of accident and included such radical measures as inspection by workers' repre-sentatives.

As a politician Macrossan was used, both in and out of office, as the major debating strength of the Conservative Party: good examples are the no confidence motion of 1876, the Ipswich dismissals of 1879, and especially in 1880 the steel rails scandal, the mail contract and the Douglas [q.v.] libel. They all show a lack of restraint which came out most strongly on other occasions affecting him personally: for example, the debate on Griffith's education bill in 1875; the judgment of Sir Charles Lilley [q.v.] in the case of *McSharry* v. *O'Rourke* in 1886; and perhaps the bitterness surrounding the election of W. H. Groom [q.v.] as Speaker in 1883. Ironically enough, this fierce lack of restraint probably caused him to be passed over twice when the leadership fell vacant. In 1886 when McIlwraith first retired he was succeeded as leader of the Opposition, not by Macrossan his obvious lieutenant but by Albert Norton [q.v.]. Again, in November 1888 when McIlwraith resigned as premier, the party chose B. D. Morehead [q.v.].

In February 1890 Macrossan and Sir Samuel Griffith attended the conference on Federation called by Sir Henry Parkes [q.v.] in Melbourne. Although the government resigned in August Macrossan was chosen to accompany Griffith to the Australasian National Convention at Sydney in 1891. Macrossan had been suffering from heart disease for some years but he had an attack of bronchitis and died during the convention on 30 March. He was buried in Nudgee, Queensland. He was survived by his wife Bridget, née Queely, whom he had married at St Joseph's Church, Townsville, on 1 October 1874, and by a daughter and five of their seven sons. Hugh Denis (1881-1940) and Neal (1889-1955) became chief justices of Queensland, and Vincent was one of Brisbane's leading solicitors. Not the least of the paradoxes associated with Macrossan is that he founded a Queensland legal tradition despite his oft-expressed contempt for those who lived on the law.

Some mystery surrounds the source of Macrossan's income, but he must have had some substance to remain an unpaid member of parliament for twelve years. He certainly controlled the *Northern Advocate* and *Miners' Journal* for some time and was rumoured to have other newspaper interests in the north. He also appears to have invested in lead mining and was involved in railway construction contracts in New South Wales and perhaps in Queensland.

Macrossan was physically small and slight, pale-complexioned and almost delicate in appearance. His deep-set eyes and heavy beard, jet black in his earlier years, attracted attention and hinted at a depth of feeling and a strength of expression to which his contemporaries all attest. Solitary by nature, he was known to miners as 'Jack the Hatter', and he seems not to have made friends easily. This difficulty must have been enhanced by his intense vigour in party politics, the bitterness and passion of the speeches in and outside the House, the strength of his insistence on his Catholic religion and a clear determination not to conciliate or to suffer fools gladly.

Macrossan's early loyalty to the Conservative Party must have shocked his original electors, the northern miners, but the suggestion that he had betrayed his constituents as a price for future office seems ill-based. Whatever his changes of attitude, a consistency can be distinguished in his actions on issues he thought vital, but his vacillation on such matters as payment of members of parliament cannot be freed completely from the suggestion of opportunism. On some subjects, however, he stood firm, irrespective of party policy or personal advantage. Committed to the interests of working miners, he legislated for their safety and was much more consistent in opposing Chinese coolie immigration to the goldfields than he was on Kanakas or Indians in agriculture. A fervent advocate for North Queensland, he complained that its interests were ill-served by 'Queen Street Ministries'. While still in opposition in 1876, he secured the appointment of a Financial Separation Commission. In 1886 he came out openly for complete separation for the North and in the assembly made one of Australia's great statements for local self-government. Though supported only by the balance of his 'Northern Nine', he tried again in 1890 and came as close as 26 votes to 32 to carrying the House. On religious questions he was always consistent and arguably affected his personal prospects thereby. Contem-poraries regarded him as the lay leader of Catholicism in Queensland. Rumour persists that he had been intended for the priesthood.

Finally, Macrossan emerged as one of the earliest and ablest of the apostles of Federation. Contemporaries have recorded his fervent, infectious enthusiasm and clear grasp of principles. In the convention debates he stands out for his knowledge and admiration of American precedent. Wise and Deakin recorded that he was a quiet speaker but stress the detail and incisiveness of his argument. To Queensland journalists he was ever the fiery demagogue, and to his long-time enemy Thadeus O'Kane [q.v.] his oratory was 'raw and bloody bones'. Undoubtedly a Statesman Macrossan lay behind the Politician Macrossan.

H. Bryan, *John Murtagh Macrossan: his life and career* (Brisb, 1958); V&P (LA Qld), 1891, 1, 271, 296, 312; H. Bryan, 'John Murtagh Macrossan and the genesis of the White Australia policy', *JRHSQ*, 5 (1953-57); *Australasian*, 15 May 1886; *Brisbane Courier*, 31 Mar 1891; *Daily Mail* (Brisb), 28 Sept, 5 Oct 1907; H. Bryan, The political career of John Murtagh Macrossan (M.A. thesis, Univ Qld, 1954).

HARRISON BRYAN

MAIR, WILLIAM (1806-1904), soldier and civil servant, was born on 31 August 1806 at Glasgow, Scotland, son of Hugh Mair of the 42nd 'Black Watch' Regiment and his wife, née Woodburn. Educated at Inverness, Glasgow and Londonderry, he was commissioned in November 1830 in the 99th Regiment which he joined in Ireland next June. He served in Mauritius from 1831 to 1836, when he was promoted lieutenant, and in Ireland in 1837-41.

Mair was ordered to escort 200 convicts to Van Diemen's Land and sailed in October from Dublin in the *Richard Webb*. He arrived at Hobart Town in March 1842 and soon sailed for Sydney. The rest of the regiment arrived later by detachments. Mair was paymaster to the regiment and for some time quartermaster. In February 1843 he became adjutant of the mounted police. With light duties in Sydney he went to such outlying stations as Maitland, Penrith, Bathurst, Berrima, Goulburn and Yass. On 7 December 1843 he went to Melbourne and visited stations in the Port Phillip District. With La Trobe's permission he rode as far as Port Fairy and returned overland to Sydney through Albury and Goulburn in January 1844.

In October 1846 La Trobe sought more mounted police to control riots between Orange and Catholic factions in Melbourne and asked Mair to take command of the Port

Phillip mounted force. Mair resigned as
adjutant in Sydney and rode to Melbourne,
recruiting on the way. He remained commandant of the force until it was recalled
to Sydney in 1849 and disbanded. Appointed
a magistrate of the town of Melbourne in
1846, he was made a commissioner in
December 1849 to examine and report on
disputed boundaries of squatting leases in
Gippsland. He was accompanied by William,
brother of H. E. P. Dana [q.v.], and within
a few weeks had successfully completed the
assignment. In January 1851 La Trobe
appointed him police magistrate for Port
Fairy with instructions to form police
benches at Belfast, Warrnambool and
Horsham. In October he was police magistrate for Buninyong and Ballarat, and commissioner in charge of those new goldfields
until 31 December. In 1852 he was asked
to enrol, equip and drill a mounted police
force for escort and other duties on the
goldfields, and at a depot in Melbourne he
recruited 12 officers, 18 gentlemen and 250
troopers, the first cadet corps raised in the
colony. On 1 January 1853 the various police
groups, including Mair's Gold Mounted
Police Force, were amalgamated and Mair
became paymaster of the new force under
W. H. F. Mitchell [q.v.] at a salary of £700.
He had remained in the army but in May
1855 sold his commission, assuming that by
an Act of parliament his future working
conditions and retiring allowance were
secure, but the Act was repealed and he lost
many of the privileges he had held in the
civil service while still in the army. He
remained in the police force until 1 January
1875.

In the Russian scare of 1860 Mair enrolled
and commanded a volunteer rifle corps at
Brighton. In 1862 he was promoted lieut-
colonel of the volunteer force and in 1867
commanded the St Kilda district. In 1875
he was promoted to the Melbourne district
and in 1884 became a lieut-colonel of the
defence force. He retired from the Victorian
militia with the honorary rank of colonel
in January 1886. Active in civic affairs Mair
was a founder of the Moorabbin Roads
Board and its chairman for five years. He
retired to Nyora, Gippsland, where he died
on 1 January 1904. By his marriage to
Catherine, née Lyons, he had four sons and
six daughters.

Port Phillip Government Gazette, 16 Jan, 1
Oct 1851; *Sabretache*, Oct 1968; *Argus*, 21-31
July, 21, 25 Aug, 4 Sept 1846; *Brighton
Southern Cross*, 23 Jan 1904; biog notes under
Mair (LaTL).   THOMAS SHEEHY

MAIS, HENRY COATHUPE (1827-1916),
engineer, was born on 14 May 1827 at
Westbury-on-Trym, near Bristol, England,
son of Henry Mais, engineer, and his wife
Amelia Jane, née Coathupe. Educated at
Bishop's College, Bristol, he was articled for
seven years to W. M. Peniston, one of J. K.
Brunel's chief engineers, and worked on
English railways. For some months at Birmingham he made steam engines, superintended the building of locomotives at
Swindon and in 1850 worked on the Hull
docks.

In December Mais arrived in Sydney
with machinery for a foundry and engineering works but found conditions too unsettled and joined the Sydney Railway Co.
as acting engineer. He resigned in March
1852 and among other work supervised the
building of a steam sawmill at Brisbane
Water. He returned to Sydney and in 1855
joined the City Commissioners' Department
as assistant engineer on the water and
sewerage works. Later that year a select
committee into the department's handling
of the sewerage works accused him with
other city engineers of 'negligence, ignorance or corruption'. Though his dismissal
was recommended, the city commissioners
strongly opposed the committee and protected him. After government pressure Mais
resigned in May 1856 but for five months
was given a temporary post in the railways
and then practised privately. In January
1857 another select committee accused him
of 'gross misconduct' and inexcusable errors
while working on the sewerage project.

Mais went to Victoria and in 1859-61
worked for Cornish & Bruce [qq.v.], with
charge of the Gisborne, Black Forest and
Woodend section of the Sandhurst-Mel-
bourne line. As engineer and general manager of the Melbourne Railway Co. for three
years, he won praise as a 'first class man in
every sense of the word'. In December 1863
the Colonial Bank of Australia awarded him
£25 for his conduct of the Melbourne railway during the floods. When the suburban
railways were taken over by the government in 1866 he joined the Water Supply
Department.

With high professional and personal
references Mais applied on 19 February 1867
for the post of engineer and architect to the
South Australian government. After interviews he was offered £750 as engineer-in-
chief and appointed on 27 March. His post
included the general managership of railways and charge of all public works except
buildings, but his duties were eased by the
appointments of an engineer of harbours
and jetties in March 1876 and a hydraulic
engineer in April 1878. In the late 1870s he
was well known in Adelaide as a 'splendid
host'; at his home in Rundle Street, Kent
Town, he gave musical evenings with

dances to follow and lavish suppers. On 30 September 1882 his wife Jane Amelia, née Weaver, died in Adelaide aged 49. Soon afterwards he toured railways and other works in Europe and America. His lengthy report with many detailed illustrations was printed in 1884 as a parliamentary paper.

In 1887 Mais became involved with the private Silverton Tramway Co. over building a connexion from the Barrier Ranges to the transcontinental railway in South Australia. In parliament he was accused of accepting private work and using government draftsmen to prepare plans for the company; Mais conceded that he had acted in an unusual manner but contended that the circumstances were exceptional and would greatly benefit the colony. However, his resignation was accepted and six-months' leave granted in March 1888 only after he agreed to pay his fees from the Silverton Tramway Co. into the treasury.

Mais left Adelaide and went into private practice as a consulting engineer in Melbourne. As an arbitrator he acted in important disputes between railway contractors and the governments of Victoria, New South Wales, Queensland and Tasmania. For sixteen years he was chairman of the Victorian Advisory Committee of the Institute of Civil Engineers. He was a member of the Institution of Civil Engineers, London, of the Society of Engineers, London, and the American Society of Civil Engineers. He was a Freemason. He retired in 1912 and on 25 February 1916 died at his home in South Yarra, survived by three sons and two daughters.

V&P (LC NSW), 1855, 3, 475, (LA NSW), 1856-57, 3, 182, 220, (HA SA), 1868-69 (45), 1883-84 (27, 230), 1887 (82), 1888 (65), (HA Tas), 1889 (94), (LA Vic), 1896, 3 (19); PD (SA), 1868, 1887; *Register* (Adel), 17 Nov 1887, 15 Mar 1888, 1 Mar 1916; *Argus*, 28 Feb 1916; *Advertiser* (Adel), 1 Mar 1916; Research note 158 (SAA).   SALLY O'NEILL

MAITLAND, EDWARD (1824-1897), public servant and novelist, was born on 27 October 1824 at Ipswich, England, son of Charles David Maitland, Evangelical curate of St James's Chapel, Brighton. Through descent from the Berties (dukes of Ancaster) he was connected with distinguished scholars and politicians. His clergymen brothers, Charles and Brownlow, were prominent writers. Intended also for the church he entered Caius College, Cambridge (B.A., 1847), but, reacting against his father's uncompromising Calvinism, he took a year's leave from England to resolve his views. He went to Mexico, moved to the

Californian goldfields in 1849 and extended his trial period indefinitely.

Maitland next visited New South Wales where his connexion, Sir Charles FitzRoy, was governor-general. He was appointed commissioner of crown lands and police magistrate at Wellington in 1854. On 3 May 1855 at Darling Point he married Esther Charlotte (1834-1856), the second daughter of William Bradley [q.v.] of Goulburn Plains, and granddaughter of the explorer, W. H. Hovell [q.v.], whom he succeeded as commissioner of crown lands at Goulburn in that month. He became president of the Goulburn School of Arts and was active in stimulating public discussion. He believed that Australians were in danger of becoming hidebound by 'worn out and cast off traditions' and that they leaned too far ' towards class privileges and class prohibitions'. He strongly criticized Bourke's Church Act and the religious certificate required by the University of Sydney in 1854 'in direct violation of the charter'. He decided to return to England and gave his farewell lecture at the School of Arts, Sydney, on 9 January 1858.

In England he devoted his time to writing. His novel, *The Pilgrim and the Shrine* (1867), is largely set in Australia; though mainly an account of his spiritual pilgrimage it gives intimate glimpses of life at the goldfields and on the land, besides airing his political views. His character, Captain Travers of Yarradale, was almost certainly based on Hovell. The character of Mary was drawn largely from Mary Margaret, née Turner, the wife of John Woolley [q.v.]. Maitland's later novels were based on mystical themes and the future of society, envisaging Australia as a powerful nation in *By and By* (1873). In *England and Islam* (1877) he showed much foresight and originality, anticipating some ideas later held by the psychiatrist C. G. Jung and the damaging consequences for civilization of the exclusively masculine nature of the Christian God. Though a successful writer for the *Spectator* and the *Examiner* he jeopardized his career by his friendship with the eccentric Dr Anna Kingsford and by his claim to possess 'spiritual sensitiveness' which enabled him to see the spiritual condition of people and to remember his own past lives as a prince of Thebes, Daniel, St John the Divine and Marcus Aurelius. He campaigned against vivisection and meat eating and helped to found the Theosophical Society of which he became vice-president. With Mrs Kingsford he started the Hermetic Society in 1884. After her death he founded the Esoteric Christian Union in 1891. He wrote profusely but was lamented by his literary colleagues as 'a great natural talent gone to waste'. He died at Tonbridge, Kent, on 2 October 1897. His two-volume *Anna Kingsford: her life, letters, diary, and work* had been published in London in 1896.

With his gigantic frame and sensitive nature Maitland entered easily into 'platonic relationships' with intellectual married women. His son Charles, brought up in England, became a lieut-colonel in the Bombay medical service.

R. T. Wyatt, *The history of Goulburn, N.S.W.* (Goulburn, 1941); *Athenaeum* (Lond), 16 Oct 1897.   NIEL GUNSON

MAKUTZ, BELA (1857-1923), safemaker and manufacturer, was born on 29 September 1857 at Felsöbánya, Hungary. At 12 he was apprenticed to a cousin as a cobbler. After five years Makutz had learned the trade and left for Galatz in Rumania, where he joined his uncle, an ironfounder. After seven years in this trade he was urged to move again; he went to Turkey and then to Alexandria where he worked in an iron-foundry. Ever on the go and carrying little more than his growing experience, Makutz arrived in Melbourne in 1882 where within a few months he launched a safemaking firm first with H. Ehret and later with T. Barke as partners. The partnership was dissolved when the banks failed in the eastern colonies and Makutz moved to the Murchison gold-fields in Western Australia, where he started a blacksmith shop and followed the mining industry, but with little success. In 1895 he opened his safemaking workshop in Perth. It soon grew : by 1912 he was natural-ized and was employing a staff of about fifty and had also bought a wheat-growing property of 7000 acres at Nugadong.

An outstanding example of the self-made man, an expert at his trade, with little formal education but much courage and industry, Makutz prospered. In 1885 he had married Cecilia Albers of Melbourne; their two sons, Ernest and Rudolph, both took part in the management of the business. Makutz died in Perth on 10 August 1923 but his firm survived him. With over seventy years behind it the company is almost an institution in Western Australia. Its workshops are at Belmont, a suburb of Perth.

J. E. Battye (ed), *Cyclopedia of Western Australia*, 1 (Adel, 1912); E. F. Kunz, *Blood and gold: Hungarians in Australia* (Melb, 1969).
                                                     E. F. KUNZ

MALEY, JOHN STEPHEN (1839-1910), engineer, was born on 5 April 1839 in Albany, Western Australia, son of Kennedy Maley from northern Ireland and his wife Martha Mary from Hampshire, England. He spent his early years in Albany and on the Murray River. Apprenticed to Solomon Cook [q.v.] of Perth he became a mechanical expert on the steam ferries on the Swan River and worked on the reconditioning of the Causeway over the Swan River.

In the 1860s Maley went to Greenough Flats, the colony's wheat centre, where he was granted blocks of some ten acres each, on which with the help of convict labour he built houses. He engineered the building of the first bridge over the Greenough River. He planted wheat, built a three-storied mill of stone and beside it, Home Cottage, his two-storied residence, both still standing in 1973. Another of his enterprises was the Golden Sheaf Hotel which he later sold to William Wilson; it was demolished after severe damage in the great flood of 1888. He ground all the flour needed at Greenough Flats, Geraldton and Northhampton. His mill was the first to use silk dressing machin-ery, and with Charles Crowther in 1872 he shipped fifty tons of silk dressed flour to England, where it was much admired.

Maley was a vestryman of St Catherine's Anglican Church, chairman of the Green-ough Roads Board, and for several years president of the Geraldton Agricultural Society. Kind, benevolent and given to hospitality, he applied progressive methods to his business. His inherited Irish vivacity is illustrated by his escapade immediately after Governor Hampton had declared the new Perth Bridge and Causeway open for traffic, in galloping ahead before he could be stopped, determined to be the first across it. His health declined in later years and he died at Greenough on 28 December 1910. On 27 August 1862 he had married Eliza-beth Keniest (b. 1841), eldest daughter of Frederic Waldeck; they had nine sons and five daughters. Two sons volunteered for service in the South African war, others established a farming property at Three Springs and two entered the Western Aus-tralian parliament.

Western Mail (Perth), 7 Jan 1911; family information and records.   E. M. HALLEY

MANN, JOHN FREDERICK (1819-1907), explorer and surveyor, was born on 16 December 1819 at Lewisham, London, son of Cornelius Mann, lieut-colonel in the Royal Engineers, and his wife Sarah, née Fyers; both his grandfathers were generals. Educated at Gibraltar where his father was stationed, he entered the Royal Military College, Sandhurst, in August 1834. After nearly four years he abandoned a military career in favour of serving in the Trigonometrical Survey of Britain. In 1841 he sailed in the *Palestine* and arrived at Sydney on 6 March 1842.

At the instigation of H. W. Parker [q.v.], Mann began early in 1846 to prepare for an expedition in search of Ludwig Leichhardt [q.v.], whose unexpected return to Sydney in March thwarted the plan. In October Mann joined as second-in-command another expedition led by Leichhardt, who now intended to go from Brisbane direct to Peak Range and after reconnoitring there to follow a westerly course to the Swan River. In August 1847 Mann returned to Sydney after the expedition had been aborted mainly by illness. In 1888 his *Eight Months with Dr. Leichhardt, in the years 1846-47* revealed much personal animosity between Leichhardt and himself and other members of the expedition and attempted to vindicate his own role and that of his companions.

Appointed a licensed surveyor on 20 March 1848 in the Surveyor-General's Department, Mann was posted to the Counties of Murray, St Vincent and Argyle, where in addition to the Counties of King and Camden he worked on surveys until 1880. On 14 September 1848 he tendered his resignation because of 'circumstances of a private nature' but withdrew it a week later. On 7 October 1853 he resigned from his survey of the Counties of Murray and St Vincent on account of 'the numerous applications which are at present made for the purchase of small farms, and the increased difficulty I find in being able to perform the survey of them'. However, he continued in the Survey Department after his area was reduced. On 16 April 1857 at St Mark's Church, Darling Point, he married Camilla Victoria (d. 1863), daughter of Sir Thomas Mitchell [q.v.]. In 1863 Mann was licensed as a surveyor under the 1862 Real Property Act. Paid by the government on a scale according to the area surveyed, his earnings ranged from £482 in 1862 to £773 in 1866. In the early 1870s he was given charge of the Mudgee district. In September 1874 he was transferred to Corowa to carry out new mining regulations, but ascribed his move to insinuations that he had given unfair priority to work for N. P. Bayly [q.v.]. The Corowa district did not pay and he found the work unpleasant. By 1879 he was still a licensed surveyor but no longer in government employ.

On 22 October 1884 he sailed for New Guinea in the flagship H.M.S. *Nelson* as a representative of the Geographical Society of Australasia at the proclamation of a Protectorate over the south-east of the island by Commodore James E. Erskine [q.v.]. He

returned to Sydney on 2 December. His reports in the society's *Proceedings* in 1889 and 1894 predicted that 'a great future is in store for this fine country, though that future may be far distant'.

Mann had often corresponded with the Sydney press on such subjects as Australian history and the Aboriginals. A pensioner, he died on 7 September 1907 at his home Carthona, Neutral Bay, and was buried in the cemetery of St Thomas's Church, North Sydney. He was survived by two sons and a daughter.

Sel cttee on crown lands, V&P (LC NSW), 1854, 2, (LA NSW), 1878-79, 4, 183; *SMH*, 9 Sept 1907; J. F. and G. V. F. Mann papers (ML).
                                              PETER ORLOVICH

MANNERS-SUTTON; see CANTERBURY

MANNING, CHARLES JAMES (1841-1898), judge, was born on 10 July 1841 at Balmain, Sydney, the second son of Edye Manning [q.v.] and his wife Fanny Elizabeth, née Turner. In 1847 he went to England with his parents and was educated in Devonshire and in 1855-61 at Winchester College; he matriculated and entered Corpus Christi College, Oxford (B.A., 1864). He was called to the Bar of Lincoln's Inn on 17 November 1865 and practised on the western circuit before returning to Sydney where he was admitted to the Supreme Court on 22 December 1866. In 1870-74 he was a parliamentary draftsman with Alexander Oliver [q.v.] and at times he acted as a crown prosecutor and law reporter. At the Bar he built up an extensive practice in all jurisdictions. He was standing counsel for the Bank of New South Wales, an official visitor to the Hospitals for the Insane at Gladesville and Callan Park, executor and trustee of the will of T. S. Mort [q.v.], attorney for Benjamin Buchanan [q.v.] and a director of the New South Wales Fresh Food and Ice Co. and the Illawarra Steam Navigation Co.

In 1883 Manning had a severe illness and went to England. On his return in 1886 he confined his practice to Equity and became leader of the Equity Bar. He occasionally acted as a Supreme Court judge and was appointed a puisne judge on 13 November 1889. He became a judge in bankruptcy, where he originated a practice which proved most satisfactory and helped to elucidate the bankruptcy law. He also became an assistant equity judge and in 1891 the first probate judge.

In 1890-98 Manning was a member of the Council of The King's School and in

1892-98 a fellow of the Senate of the University of Sydney. Religious and philanthropic, he was a member of the Church of England Provincial Synod. In the 1893 depression his clear decisions helped to pilot banks, companies and building societies through surrounding shoals. In 1896 he became chief judge in Equity. A stickler for court etiquette despite his unjudicial-looking moustache, he was popular with the Bar and his careful judgments were commended several times and often upheld by the judicial committee of the Privy Council.

Manning died at Hunter's Hill, Sydney, on 8 August 1898 from phthisis pulmonaris against which he had courageously and uncomplainingly struggled for fifteen years. He was buried in the churchyard of St Anne's Church of England, Ryde. He had been held in affectionate regard by both branches of the legal profession, and Chief Justice Darley [q.v.] referred to him as 'a refined, courteous and kindly gentleman, a learned, able, hardworking and conscientious judge with a keen insight into human nature'. Manning was survived by a daughter of his first wife Clara Isabella, née Athorpe, whom he had married on 26 May 1870 at St Mark's, Darling Point, and by his second wife Emily Urania Camden, née Goodridge, whom he had married on 9 January 1879 and by three of their five sons and a daughter. Both his marriages had been witnessed by his uncle, W. M. Manning [q.v.]. His estate, valued at £21,000, was left to his wife 'in perfect trust that she will deal with it wisely'.

Cyclopedia of N.S.W. (Syd, 1907); Government Gazette (NSW), 13 Nov 1889, supp; 'Memoranda', NSW Law Reports, 1896, 1898; D. J. Quinn, 'Puisne judges of New South Wales', Review of Reviews (Lond), 20 Dec 1894, Aust ed; SMH, 23 Sept 1878, 14, 15 Nov 1889, 9, 10, 12 Aug 1898; Parkes letters (ML); Register of deeds, no 331, book 321 (Registrar-General's Dept).   H. T. E. HOLT

MANNING, EMILY MATILDA (1845-1890), writer and journalist best known as 'Australie', was born on 13 May 1845 in Sydney, daughter of (Sir) William Manning [q.v.] and his first wife Emily Anne, née Wise. Educated at a private school in Sydney, she was encouraged to take an interest in literature by Professor Woolley [q.v.]. From 1860 Emily lived in the family home, Wallaroy, and her friends included the children of Sir Alfred Stephen's [q.v.] second marriage; balls, picnics, croquet matches, music and amateur theatricals at Government House were part of her busy and happy social life. In 1864 an exchange of light-hearted poems with D. S. Mitchell [q.v.] suggests a romance between him and Emily, but she soon went to England and contributed to such periodicals as Miss C. F. Yonge's Monthly Packet, which provided 'attractive reading of a high and refined type' for teenage girls. After return to Australia she wrote for the Town and Country Journal, Sydney Morning Herald and Sydney Mail, either anonymously or using the pen-name 'Australie'. She later joined the staff of the Illustrated Sydney News. On 22 December 1873 at St John's, Darlinghurst, she married the solicitor Henry Heron (Hiron); they had six sons and a daughter.

Emily published The Balance of Pain and Other Poems (London, 1877). It included eight hymns and over twenty-five poems, one of which 'The Emigrants' was set to music and produced as a dramatic cantata in October 1880 by the Petersham Musical Society. Reviewers acclaimed her poems as 'characterised by great purity of tone and loftiness of purpose', with many pieces breathing sympathy for the suffering and trials of humanity. Able and thoughtful, she wrote on art and taste as well as questions of the day, ranging from problems of sanitation, prison discipline and forestry to the domestic matters 'which might be expected to come within a woman's province'. She read widely, wrote a book review column for the Sydney Mail in 1880 and was noted for 'incisiveness and earnestness'. Interested in the higher education of women, she started a class for studying French language and literature. Survived by her husband (d. 1912) and six children, she died of pneumonia on 25 August 1890 at Blandville; she was buried in the Anglican section of Waverley cemetery.

Her husband had been in financial difficulty from the early 1880s and at Emily's death discreet reference was made to the 'weary burden of trouble' which enforced her withdrawal from society. The family was dependent on the kindness of her father and stepmother whose loving care for Emily and her children was gratefully recognized in 1895 by Sir William's will.

R. M. Bedford, Think of Stephen (Syd, 1954); G. D. Richardson, 'David Scott Mitchell', Descent, 1 (1961) pt 2; Illustrated Sydney News, 18 Aug 1877; SMH, 26 Aug 1890; Bulletin, 30 Aug 1890; Sydney Mail, 30 Aug 1890; Town and Country J, 30 Aug 1890.
                                        SALLY O'NEILL

MANNING, FREDERIC NORTON (1839-1903), medical practitioner, was born on 25 February 1839 at Rothersthorpe, Northamptonshire, England, son of John

Manning, farmer, and his wife Eliza, née Norton. He studied at St George's Hospital, London (M.R.C.S., L.S.A., 1860) and the University of St Andrews (M.D., 1862). Joining the navy as a surgeon he saw active service in New Zealand.

On a visit to Sydney in June 1867 Manning was invited by Henry Parkes [q.v.] to become medical superintendent of the Tarban Creek Lunatic Asylum. Before accepting, Manning went overseas and studied methods of patient care and administration of asylums; on his return to Sydney he submitted a notable report. He was appointed to Tarban Creek on 15 October 1868 and immediately reported on the isolation of patients from their relations in accommodation best described as 'prison-like and gloomy', the inadequate facilities for their gainful employment and recreation and the monotonous diets deficient in both quantity and quality. In January 1869 the asylum's name was changed to the Hospital for the Insane, Gladesville, wherein patients were to receive treatment rather than be confined in a 'cemetery for diseased intellects'. By 1879 radical changes in patient care and accommodation had been made. Gladesville was extended and modernized and an asylum for imbeciles set up in Newcastle and a temporary asylum at Cooma. Manning minimized the use of restraint and provided for patient activities.

On 1 July 1876 Manning was appointed inspector of the insane with responsibility for all mental institutions except the Parramatta asylum for criminals. At the colonial secretary's request he reported on the accommodation at Parramatta condemning it as 'a prison and a bad prison into the bargain'. One of his first tasks after appointment as inspector-general of the insane in 1879 was to introduce a series of reforms to correct the cumulative evils at Parramatta. The 1878 Lunacy Act gave legislative backing to what he had long sought: procedures for admission and discharge, the responsibilities of medical practitioners defined and control of all institutions placed under a centralized administration. To break down indifference and deep-rooted prejudices he encouraged visitors to the asylums and organized public discussions on the causes and treatment of insanity. The problem of overcrowding was beyond his control while governments refused to plan for the future. After much agitation by Manning new hospitals were opened at Callan Park and Goulburn and additions made to the Darlinghurst reception house. Manning believed that staff should be competent and encouraged in-service training for nurses and attendants. He often criticized the accommodation and low wages. He supported the creation of the Austra-

lasian Trained Nurses' Association and in 1899-1902 was its first president.

Manning had become a trustee of Prince Alfred Hospital in 1873 and was a member of the New South Wales branch of the British Medical Association. In 1876 he was elected to the Royal Society of New South Wales and in 1883-84 was chairman of its medical section. In 1883-96 he was an examiner and in 1886-88 the first lecturer in psychological medicine at the University of Sydney. In 1882 he had been appointed to the Board of Health and in 1889-92 was medical advisor to the government, president of the Board of Health and health and emigration officer for Port Jackson. He was prominent in the proceedings of the second (1889) and third (1892) sessions of the Intercolonial Medical Congress of Australasia.

Manning had served on an inquiry into the Hospital for the Insane at New Norfolk, Tasmania, in 1884 and on another at the Bay View Lunatic Asylum in 1894. In 1895 he served on the royal commission on the notorious poisoner, George Dean. He agreed with Dr P. S. Jones [q.v.] that the evidence was compatible with attempted suicide and secured Dean's release. On 12 February 1898 ill health forced Manning to retire. A tribute to his administration was that the hospitals for the insane had not attracted unfavourable publicity during his thirty years. He set up as a consultant in mental health. In February 1899 he was appointed to the royal commission on public charities. In 1901 he became a trustee of the National Art Gallery of New South Wales. Unmarried he died from a stomach ulcer on 18 June 1903 at his rooms in Phillip Street and at his wish was buried in the cemetery at Gladesville Hospital. Some of his papers are in the National Library of Australia.

D. I. McDonald, 'Frederic Norton Manning (1839-1903)', *JRAHS*, 58 (1972), and for bibliog.

D. I. McDONALD

MANNING, JAMES (1814-1893), architect and builder, was born on 17 August 1814 at Burdrop, near Banbury, England. After qualifying as a civil engineer he worked in London with charge of the houses of many peers. In the Ordnance Department he served in the remodelling of Tilbury fort in 1847-49. Appointed clerk of works in Western Australia he sailed with Captain E. Y. W. Henderson [q.v.] in the *Scindian* and arrived on 1 June 1850. He played an active part in the building programme initiated in the colony by the convict establishment. The precise contribution of Manning and others is difficult to assess because some designs were by officers of the Royal

Engineers and such important public buildings as Government House, Pensioners Barracks and Perth Town Hall were constructed jointly by the imperial and colonial Public Works Departments. Most records of the imperial department left the colony after transportation ended but the remainder indicate that Manning had special ability in the use of timber. The fine jarrah hammer-beam ceiling of Perth Town Hall was probably his design although the main structure was designed by R. R. Jewell [q.v.].

Plans bearing Manning's signature include the convict depot (1856, 1859) at Mount Eliza, the commissariat stores (1856) and guard-house at Fremantle, the residency (1866) at Albany, the first stage of the customs house, bonded store, post office (1868) and gaol additions (1866, 1870) at Geraldton, the court-house, bonded stores (both 1866), Toodyay gaol (1868) and police stations at Northampton and Williams (both 1867), Kojonup and Lower Blackwood (both 1868) and the second stage of Government House at Rottnest. He also constructed the wooden jetties at Albany, Vasse, Bunbury, Fremantle and Champion Bay, bridges over the Upper Canning, several on the Albany Road, the King and Kalgan Rivers, the Avon at York, Northam and Newcastle (Toodyay), the most notable being the Fremantle Traffic Bridge (1864-66) known as Hampton's Folly. The colony's roads, iron lighthouse at Point Moore and the two leading lights at Champion Bay were monuments to his supervision.

A justice of the peace, Manning retired from the imperial department with a pension of £300 in 1872 but continued to design and build. He died on 22 July 1893 at his home Burdrop, Fremantle. The pall-bearers at his funeral were distinguished citizens. Predeceased on 26 October 1877 by his wife Jane, née Yeldham, he was survived by a son and two married daughters.

Possum, 21 Jan 1888; *West Australian*, 24 July 1893; Public Works Dept, Plans no 64, 65, 77, 77/9, 77/12, 79, 81, 137, 141, 143-45, 147, 183, 196, 206.   RAY OLDHAM

MANNING, JAMES ALEXANDER LOUIS (1814-1887), pastoralist, was born on 9 April 1814 in Exeter, England, third surviving son of John Edye Manning [q.v.] and his wife Matilda Jorden, née Cooke. Educated in France and Exeter, he travelled in Europe. In 1830-33 he attended Hohenheim Agricultural College near Stuttgart and visited Goethe nine months before he died and discussed foreign missions.

In 1834 Manning arrived at Sydney and next year settled on Cumbamarra, near Yass. He established rapport with the Aboriginals, whom he called 'nature's gentlemen', and gathered details of their religious beliefs which he later published. He became a magistrate in 1836. In 1840-41 he capitalized on the Port Phillip District's need for meat by sending overland large drafts of cattle but the value of his own property was diminished by catarrh which attacked his sheep for five successive seasons after 1848. In 1853 he joined his brothers Edye and William Montagu, T. S. Mort, E. and R. Tooth [qq.v.] and John Croft to form the Twofold Bay Pastoral Association which held 400,000 acres in three stations on the Monaro and three in the Bega district. From 1854 Manning, as managing partner, lived on the central estate Kameruka. Enterprising and energetic, he overcame a labour shortage by introducing German families and cleared a road route from the Monaro to the coast at Merimbula, making that port the trade outlet for the southern Bega Valley.

As part of their vigorous efforts to hinder free selection the partnership was dissolved in 1860. Manning retained Wolumla and Towamba and bought Kameruka in 1861, but John Robertson's [q.v.] Land Acts, combined with floods and disease, broke up their huge holdings. In 1862, after losing 7000 cattle through pleuro-pneumonia, Manning sold Kameruka. Assisted by his brother William, he began again at Wanagabra, 2000 acres near Bega in 1864. An enthusiastic innovator, he planted thriving vineyards, introduced maize to the district, initiated scientific American methods of cheese making and agitated for a telegraph between Bega and Sydney, sending the first message in 1868. In 1870 he moved to Queensland, where with Mort he spent huge sums experimenting with freezing and preserving meat. From 1871 Manning lived in Sydney, keeping an interest in Wanagabra, managed by his son Albert after 1869, and Black Flat in the Bombala district.

In 1873 Manning joined the Royal Society of New South Wales and read papers which were published in its *Proceedings* and as pamphlets *Our Coal and Coal Ports* (1874), *Sydney water supply by gravitation* (1874) and *Notes on the Aborigines of New Holland* (1882). He promoted plans for a railway linking Illawarra and Sydney and, at the government's invitation, in 1873 guided the engineer surveying this difficult route. On the trip he made plans for a water supply by gravitation for Sydney which he persistently but unsuccessfully advocated for three years in pamphlets, letters and the press; it was an excellent and professional feasibility study which he effectively developed on a smaller scale on his own property. Manning can well be described in the words he used for his uncle James, 'a man of most versatile information and learning'.

In 1845 at Melbourne Manning had married Mary Mehitabel, eldest daughter of Major Firebrace. He died at Double Bay on 26 October 1887 and was buried in Waverley cemetery, survived by his wife, to whom he left £15,000, and three sons and three daughters.

J. Gormly, *Exploration and settlement in Australia* (Syd, 1921); W. A. Bayley, *The story of the settlement and development of Bega* (Bega, 1942); V&P (LA NSW), 1877-78, 4, 400, 1878-79, 7, 6; B. Ryan, 'Kameruka Estate, New South Wales, 1864-1964', *New Zealand Geographer*, 20 (1964) no 2; *Illawarra Mercury*, 3 Jan 1860; *SMH*, 27 Oct 1887; *Bega Standard*, 29 Oct 1887; *Town and Country J*, 29 Oct 1887; K. B. Ryan, Towns and settlement of the south coast, New South Wales (Ph.D. thesis, ANU, 1965); Macarthur and Deas Thomson papers (ML); Parkes letters (ML).　　SUZANNE EDGAR

MANNING, Sir WILLIAM MONTAGU (1811-1895), barrister and politician, was born on 20 June 1811 at Alphington, Devon, England, son of John Edye Manning [q.v.] and his wife Matilda Jorden, née Cooke. Educated in Tavistock, Southampton, he went to University College, London. He worked for his uncle, Serjeant Manning, and entered Lincoln's Inn in 1827. Called to the Bar in 1832 he practised on the Western Circuit. With S. Neville in London he published in three volumes, *Reports of Cases Relating to the Duty and Office of Magistrates Determined in the Court of King's Bench* (1834-38) and *Proceedings in Courts of Revision in the Isle of Wight* (1836). On 16 August in Paris he married Emily Anne, sister of Judge Edward Wise [q.v.]. In 1837 they decided to join his family in Sydney and arrived on 31 August in the *City of Edinburgh*. Manning was soon appointed a magistrate and chairman of the Quarter Sessions with a salary of £800. Annually re-elected by the magistrates, he was also commissioner of the Courts of Requests in 1841-43 and became solicitor-general in 1844, the office being confirmed in 1845 through the influence of Lord Brougham. In 1848-49 he acted on the Supreme Court bench and relieved Chief Justice Stephen [q.v.] of the Equity work. His wife had died on 16 November 1846 leaving three children; on 7 June 1849 at St Saviour's, Argyle, he married Eliza Anne, daughter of Rev. W. Sowerby [q.v.].

From 1837 Manning had acquired real estate: 1200 acres at Mulgoa, some 50 town allotments at Kiama and 1000 acres in the Illawarra. Possibly his father's defalcations led Manning to seek a larger fortune than was possible from the Bar. In 1848 he held 63,000 acres in the Lachlan District. He joined his brothers Edye and James [qq.v.] and with them E. and R. Tooth and T. S. Mort [qq.v.] was a partner in the Twofold Bay Pastoral Association which held over 400,000 acres in the Monaro and Bega districts. With Mort he financed the Maizena Co. at Merimbula. He shared in shipping ventures with Edye but had severe losses in 1851 when their uninsured *Phoenix* was wrecked. As solicitor-general he was allowed private practice but derived only £200 from it.

In October 1851 Manning was nominated to the Legislative Council by Governor FitzRoy. In debates on the new constitution, despite his friend James Macarthur [q.v.], he admired the American Constitution and asserted that a colonial hereditary House of Lords was inapplicable in the colony. The council was dissolved on 29 February 1856 but he remained solicitor-general until 5 June when he was given a pension of £800. He advised Governor Denison on the interim administration and refused to join Stuart Donaldson [q.v.] in a temporary ministry before the elections were held. He topped the poll for the South Riding of Cumberland as an 'independent liberal' conservative and was appointed to the interim Executive Council. On 6 June he became attorney-general in Donaldson's ministry and paid £3000 towards the discharge of his father's debts. Manning cautioned against too hasty administrative changes but the ministry was uneasy and he complained that 'electioneering interests are leading both Donaldson & Darvall [q.v.] to break faith with me'. The government fell in August but in October Manning took office under H. W. Parker [q.v.], introducing twenty-two bills and carrying seventeen.

The arduous work of setting up the administrative machinery of responsible government affected Manning's health and he resigned on 25 May 1857 and was made Q.C. He sold the furniture at Orwell House for £1000 and after a farewell banquet, a testimonial, a purse of £1000 for a portrait and a piece of plate he sailed for England with his family. He found himself 'particularly blessed, in finding scarce one missing of the many friends whose memory I had cherished during an absence of 20 years'. On 23 February 1858 he was knighted by the Queen and in January 1859 at his uncle's house was given an ornate silver epergne and four dessert stands. He returned to Sydney in November 1859 and advised Denison on the arrangements for Queensland's separation, drafting the inaugural proclamation. In February 1860 he refused a temporary seat in the Supreme Court but reluctantly agreed to act as attorney-general under W. Forster [q.v.] on condition that he would 'be in no way identified with the general policy of the Government, nor expected to enter either House of Parliament'. After three weeks the ministry fell and he refused to continue under John Robertson [q.v.]. In June 1861 he accepted nomination to the Legislative Council 'if permitted to enter the House unfettered by any pledge or conditions' but indicated that he would not oppose Robertson's land legislation. In 1862 when opposing the Legislative Council bill he argued that the nominee principle should have a longer trial and despite objections to the late swamping of the House 'he upheld the right of it being done under proper circumstances'.

Manning had returned with a fortune of £30,000 and when the Twofold Bay Pastoral Association was dissolved in 1860 he was paid £22,000 by Robert Tooth. In 1859-60 he built Wallaroy, Edgecliff, for £10,000 and paid Andrew Lenehan £250 for furniture. He took pride in an extensive garden with rare trees, shrubs and masses of flowers as well as tennis and croquet lawns and an archery ground. In 1861 he contributed £2600 to a partnership with Thomas Hood and his brother in Langton station (Peak Downs), Queensland, and next year joined Mort and J. T. Allan [q.v.] in squatting ventures; in 1867 they held six runs totalling over 500 square miles in the Mitchell District. He also held runs in New South Wales with Mort. By 1867 Langton station had debts of £25,000; it was sold to Harden, Wood & Manning. He was a director of the Moruya Silver Mining Co. and in 1866-67 and 1868-70 of the Australian Joint Stock Bank. He also had interests in mineral lands.

From 1863 Manning was counsel for the Australian Mutual Provident Society. A lover of literature and music, he was vice-patron of the Orpheonist Society and in the 1880s president of the University Music Club. He was an early member, trustee and later vice-president of the Australian Club, vice-president of the Civil Service Club, a steward of the Australian Jockey Club, member of the Royal Sydney Yacht Squadron and active in charitable institutions. He was founding president of the New South Wales Rifle Association in 1860-95, elected to the Senate of the University of Sydney in 1861 and vice-president of the Horticultural Society of New South Wales in the 1870s.

In August 1865 Manning refused to serve as attorney-general under C. Cowper [q.v.].

On 12 August 1868 as president of the Sydney Sailors' Home he invited the duke of Edinburgh to picnic at Clontarf to raise funds for the home. Manning was walking beside him when the duke was shot and believed that he had saved the prince's life by diving for O'Farrell's [q.v.] pistol. He claimed his own escape from death 'almost to have been miraculous'.

In October 1868 Manning became attorney-general under Robertson but refused to sit in cabinet or represent the government in the Legislative Council. In January-December 1870 he served under Cowper. He had to deal with the complex and unsuccessful criminal proceedings for slave-trading against the master of the *Daphne* in the Vice-Admiralty Court. The prosecutor, Captain Palmer, attacked Manning but Governor Belmore declared that his conduct of the case 'so far from meriting censure was most disinterested'. He also advised Belmore on other imperial questions and served on the Law Reform Commission. By August his finances were precarious. He had heavy losses when the Queensland Steam Navigation Co. was liquidated and ' "Esprit de corps" de famille' had led him to incur 'imprudent responsibilities' for two brothers and a nephew, but the mortgaged Peak Downs station caused his worst losses. He owed about £20,000, two-thirds of it to the Bank of New South Wales. He wrote to Shepherd Smith [q.v.], the general manager, that he could not cope with his difficulties which were increased when his Peak Downs's partners sequestered their estate in Queensland. Though humiliated by his name appearing in the Queensland Insolvency Court he managed to compound some debts and helped by Edward Knox [q.v.] secured his release from the Bank of New South Wales in November 1871. Wallaroy had to be let but, according to Shepherd Smith, he 'improperly' managed to keep some mineral lands near the Peak Downs copper mine which in 1872 began to pay dividends. Thenceforth he confined himself to his 'own proper work' and was back in Wallaroy by 1874.

In 1873 Manning served on a select committee on a new Legislative Council bill and drew up resolutions as the basis for legislation. No longer a conservative he proposed that the council be elected in the same way as the assembly but with only four electorates, 'cumulative' voting to represent minorities and retirement of a third of the members every three years. In February 1875 Governor Robinson asked him to form a ministry. He failed because Robertson and his followers would not join a ministry led from the council. More conservative elements praised Manning for his attempt because he said that the prerogatives of the Crown were threatened and constitutional advantages might accrue from recognition of the Legislative Council in the choice of a premier.

On 28 April 1876 Manning became a puisne judge of the Supreme Court, thereby losing his pension and earnings at the Bar. On accepting office he wrote to the attorney-general, W. B. Dalley [q.v.], advocating recent law reforms in England: 'I have always been disposed to look at the Law . . . from a public, rather than from a professional point of view'. His 'struggle to prevent suffering to suitors' and extra duties affected his health. He wrote in 1879 to Parkes [q.v.] asking in vain for relief. By 1882 G. Long Innes [q.v.] could comment: 'Manning is as mournful as ever — the poor old boy is gouty, doleful and disappointed'. In 1883 he visited England with his wife and three daughters. On returning in March 1884 he resumed his duties as primary judge in Equity. In October 1887 he resigned from the bench and was reappointed to the Legislative Council.

In April 1878 Manning was elected chancellor of the University of Sydney. He claimed that 'the teachings of the Faculty of Arts are the very essence of University education and the chief source of culture'. The university expanded rapidly under his guidance and in the 1880s faculties of law, medicine, science and engineering were established. In 1881 he gained the admission of women to all university privileges on 'an equal footing with men'; the women students' union, Manning House, was named in tribute. He acquired the organ for the Great Hall and hoped to endow a chair of music. He won increased government grants to the university and was responsible for freeing the £200,000 bequest of J. H. Challis [q.v.] from English estate duty; in 1890 the income was used to found new chairs. In 1893-94 he successfully fought the university's case for retention of government grants in commemoration addresses and the press.

In 1892 Manning was appointed K.C.M.G. He died at Wallaroy, Edgecliff Road, on 27 February 1895 and was buried in the cemetery of St Jude's Church of England, Randwick. He was survived by a son and a daughter of his first marriage and by his second wife and their son and three daughters. His daughter Emily [q.v.] was a well-known writer. His estate was valued for probate at £14,623.

A portrait by Sir John Watson-Gordon, R.A., in 1858 is in the University of Sydney.

V&P (LA NSW), 1869, 1, 343, 1871-72, 1, 511; SMH, 7 June 1856, 22 Dec 1873, 19 Mar 1874, 3-6, 10 Feb 1875, 28 Feb 1895; Illustrated London News, 19 Mar 1859; Empire (Syd), 12 Sept 1862; P. Loveday, Parliamentary government in New South Wales, 1856-1870 (Ph.D. thesis, Univ Syd, 1962); Earl of Belmore letters, Cowper papers, S. A. Donaldson ministry letters, Manning papers no 246, 1107, Parkes letters, Stephen papers MS777, MS and printed cats (ML); Bank of NSW Archives; CO 201/493-94, 504, 508, 517, 522-23, 532-33, 536, 546, 548, 551, 557-59, 565, 581, 584, 587.

MARTHA RUTLEDGE

MANSERGH, JAMES (1834-1905), civil engineer, was born on 29 April 1834 at Lancaster, England, second son of John Burkitt Mansergh, draper. Educated locally and at Preston, in 1847 he entered Queenwood College, Hampshire, an advanced institution reputed for mathematics. He was first apprenticed to McKie & Lawson in 1849 and by 1866 was in partnership with his brother-in-law, John Lawson, after whose death he practised alone until his sons joined him. His first works were railways, particularly in Wales and Brazil, and he then specialized in waterworks and sewerage. He designed the scheme which cost £6,000,000 and was to supply Birmingham with over 100,000,000 gallons of water a day. He also designed and constructed water supply and sewerage plans for other major English cities and was a consultant on hundreds of parliamentary and municipal committees. He was president of the Institution of Civil Engineers, a councillor of the Institution of Mechanical Engineers and a fellow of the Royal Society.

In 1889 after the appalling reports of the royal commission on Melbourne's sanitary conditions and a vigorous press campaign with public protest demanding reform, Mansergh was invited to advise on a deep-sewerage scheme for Greater Melbourne. He arrived with his son Ernest as assistant on 18 October and left on 13 December. The contour plans of the whole area which he had requested did not arrive in England until April 1890. His figures were provided by H. H. Hayter [q.v.], government statistician, who from the population of 427,200 in 1889 estimated a total over 1,680,000 by 1934. This growth seemed reasonable to Mansergh and induced him to propose the high figure of seventy-five gallons of water a head each day for sewerage and domestic use because of 'the almost universal and very free use of baths'.

Mansergh found the level of pollution in Melbourne disgraceful. 'Open gutters conveying chamber slops and other foul liquids in the open' into the Yarra and Hobson's Bay were standard. Heavy rain often overflowed from gutters into low-lying houses and yards, while the subsoil was 'permanently besodden and stinking' from this overflow and from disused cesspits. He was also disgusted by industrial waste from tanneries and other factories and by the disposal methods for domestic refuse. His aim was 'to remove all human refuse from the proximity of human habitations without the assistance of human labour': all cesspits and pails were to be replaced by water closets which were to drain into underground channels; street gutters were to carry only rain water to the rivers and all other water was to be carried by pipes to two land treatment plants to be installed at Werribee and Mordialloc. These plans, submitted in August 1890, were to cost over £7,000,000. The press attacked his high estimates and the plan was modified but as implemented was 'substantially his', though at a greatly reduced estimate and without the Mordialloc plant.

Mansergh's later projects included waterworks for Toronto and sewerage schemes for Colombo and the Lower Thames valley. He married twice: first, in July 1859 to Mary, daughter of Robert Lawson of Skerton, Lancashire, by whom he had two sons and two daughters; and second, in September 1898 to Harriet, née Branford, widow of Nelson Irons of Tunbridge Wells. He died in Hampstead on 15 June 1905.

G. Serle, *The rush to be rich* (Melb, 1971); V&P (LA Vic), 1890, 4 (182); *Age*, 17 June 1905.   SUZANNE G. MELLOR

MARIN LA MESLEE, EDMOND MARIE (1852-1893), public servant, geographer and writer, was born in France, son of Colonel Edmond la Meslée. Educated for the navy, he served on land at the battle of Sedan in September 1870. After the débâcle he left the forces and taught French in the Jesuit College at Mauritius. On 16 January 1876 he sailed in the *Alphington* for Melbourne, where he became private secretary to the French consul-general for Australia, the comte de Castelnau, F. Laporte [q.v.]. Marin la Meslée accompanied de Castelnau and his party by train and road to Sydney, by sea to Brisbane and on a short tour of the Darling Downs. In 1878 he became a temporary draftsman in the Department of Lands and worked in the Surveyor-General's Office. In 1879 he became a member of the Royal Society of New South Wales. On 17 January 1880 at St Michael's Catholic Church he married Clara Louisa Cooper. In that year with Russell Barton [q.v.] he made an extensive tour of north-western New South Wales including visits to Dubbo, Cobar and Bourke.

In 1882 Marin la Meslée visited France where he read a paper to the Société de Géographie, Paris, and arranged for the publication by E. Plon & Cie of his *L'Australie Nouvelle* (1883). It describes in lively style his travels in the outback and his impressions of Australian life and society. It seems to have been well received in France but no English translation was published until 1972. Back in Sydney he was primarily responsible for founding the Geographical Society of Australasia. As honorary secretary at its inaugural meeting in Sydney on 22 June 1883 he read to an audience of some 750 people his paper on *Past Explorations of New Guinea and a Scheme for the Scientific Exploration of the Great Island* (Sydney, 1883). In 1884 he organized the first Australian Geographical Conference in Melbourne and with A. C. Macdonald [q.v.] edited the society's *Proceedings*. In August 1886 he became a compiler in the office of the chief government statistician, T. A. Coghlan, and in 1890 was appointed to the International Exchange Board. Active in cultural circles he was a propagandist for Australia in France and became more interested than many native or British-born colonists in the growth of Australian nationality. He contributed regularly to the *Nouvelle Revue*, *Le Temps* and *Le Courier Australien* and on 15 May 1892 published a long article on Henry Parkes [q.v.] and the Federation movement in the *Revue des Deux Mondes*. He was friendly with Parkes and did much research for him in European books and journals.

On 17 December 1893 Marin la Meslée and his wife were accidentally drowned when the *Ripple* capsized in Sydney Harbour near South Head. On the 19th after an inquest they were buried in the Roman Catholic section of Rookwood cemetery. Coghlan was among the mourners at the funeral. They were survived by three sons, Athol, Raymond and Rennie. Urbane, intelligent and civilized, Marin la Meslée was endowed with tact, zest for life and common sense enough to make him acceptable to all sorts of people in his adopted country.

E. Marin la Meslée, *L'Australie nouvelle*, R. Ward tr and ed (Lond, 1972); RGS of A'sia (Vic), *Trans*, 11 (1894); *SMH*, 18 Dec 1892; Parkes letters (ML).   RUSSEL WARD

MARINA, CARLO (1832-1909), pastoralist, was born at Piacenza, Duchy of Parma, son of Johan Marina, merchant and farmer, and his wife Judita, née Itory. After some years as an engineering apprentice he left home at 15 for musical training in the

Milan College of Music but joined the Piedmontese army and served in the Lombardy campaign of 1848. In 1849 he fought at the battle of Novara, became a prisoner in Tuscany, escaped, was with Garibaldi at the siege of Rome and again taken prisoner. On his release he visited Malta, returned to Italy and in 1855 received a contract from the British government to supply meat to troops in the Crimean war. In 1856 he arrived in Melbourne.

By 1861 Marina was at the Burrangong goldfields in New South Wales, where he set up as the 'Real Diggers' Butcher' until his marriage at Yass on 18 August 1861 to a widow Eliza Tout (1821-1902), née Harcombe. In 1862 they leased the Moppity run near Young and gradually acquired a freehold estate which by 1892 covered 11,255 acres. Although known as a vigneron, orchardist and cattle exhibitor, his main interest was sheepbreeding. The Moppity flocks were descended from those of John Macarthur [q.v.] but Marina improved their quality by introducing new blood. His most prized ram was Mount Victoria which was mated with 1000 stud ewes purchased from the breeder, E. K. Cox [q.v.], of Rawden. Mount Victoria was grand champion ram at the Young, Grenfell and Yass Shows in 1876, and in 1879 Marina took first prize for washed combing wool at the Agricultural Society's Show in Sydney, where he regularly attended the sheep sales. In the 1880s and 1890s he never ran less than 12,000 sheep. He was also a successful breeder of horses: in 1890 he won first prize for blood stallions at the Young Show and in 1892 he had at stud Stratagem, a half-brother to the champion Cremorne. Two years later Stratagem was shot by an assailant who remained unknown despite rewards offered by Marina and the government.

An early pioneer and a generous bene-factor of local charities, Marina was prominent in Young society for years. His estate was a showplace; its entrance gates were bedecked with flowers which spelt the word 'welcome'; once inside, itinerant journalists and visiting celebrities were shown over Eliza's gardens, the spacious homestead, dairy, vineyards and wine cellars, then entertained over dinner by Marina's repertoire of songs and stories; later they were driven back to town in a sulky pulled by three ponies named Charge, Light and Brigade. Lord Carrington, Sir Henry Parkes and Alexander Oliver [qq.v.] at different times enjoyed his hospitality and in 1899 local enthusiasts suggested that the Moppity area should become the site for the federal capital.

A typical immigrant of the gold rush years, Marina succeeded as a pastoralist by

a combination of diligence, flexibility and luck. He died at his home on 30 September 1909. He was buried in the Anglican cemetery, Young, survived by his son C. W. C. 'Willie' Marina (1862-1911) and by a daughter; his estate was valued at £17,544. Although he never forgot his exciting youth in Italy, he and his family became completely assimilated into Australian society. His brother Camillo married the widow of a police sergeant shot by bushrangers and became a hotelier in Young, Murrumburrah and Kiama; his daughter-in-law Helen (1860-1940), known as the 'digger's friend', was made M.B.E. for her charity work during and after World War 1, and his grandson Bertie was president of the Returned Service-men's League in Young before he died in 1920 from wounds received at Gallipoli. Part of Carlo's original property is still owned by descendants.

W. F. Morrison, *The Aldine centennial history of New South Wales*, 2 (Syd, 1888); W. A. Bayley, *Rich earth* (Young, 1956); *Miner and General Advertiser*, 3, 7, 13 July, 31 Aug, 7 Sept 1861; *Burrangong Courier*, 6 Aug 1862; *Burrangong Chronicle*, 21 Mar, 18 Aug 1877, 13 Jan 1883, 2 July, 23 Aug 1890, 13, 27 Aug, 2 Nov 1892, 11 Aug, 22 Sept, 6 Oct 1894; *Sydney Mail*, 21 June 1884; *Burrangong Argus*, 16 Nov 1887, 15 Oct 1902; *Bulletin*, 14 Jan 1904; *Young Chronicle*, 2 Oct 1909, 16 Sept 1920, 12 Feb 1940; Registers of payments of rents for runs, 1856-62 (NSWA); information from Mr D. Marina, Young.   B. G. ANDREWS

MARKS, JOHN (1827-1885), agriculturist and politician, was born on 24 November 1827 at Coagh, County Tyrone, Ireland, eldest son of James Marks and his wife Elizabeth, sister of Samuel Charles [q.v.]. In January 1828 he reached Sydney in the *North Britain* with his parents. They settled in the Illawarra, where the five Marks brothers became well known.

Educated at the Sydney Normal Institution under Henry Gordon, John returned to the Kiama district and became a 'practical Agriculturist'. In 1856 he was elected as a Liberal for East Camden to the first Legislative Assembly after responsible government and held his seat until the 1859 dissolution. A supporter of Charles Cowper [q.v.], he unsuccessfully moved that a break-water was necessary at Kiama. He later refused to stand and in 1861 declined nomination to the reconstructed Legislative Council. In 1858 he built a two-storied Georgian house, Terragong, on his Jamberoo farm, where he bred Ayrshire cattle. In 1866 he helped to reorganize the Kiama Agricultural and Horticultural Society and was president in 1866-73. A magistrate, he was an alderman of the Kiama Municipal Council in 1868-74 and mayor in 1870.

In 1876 Marks moved to Sydney where he had acquired much real estate and lived at Glenrock, Darling Point; his brother Samuel moved to Terragong, where his descendants still live. On 14 January 1878 John accepted nomination to the Legislative Council and under J. S. Farnell [q.v.] was vice-president of the Executive Council and government representative. His infrequent speeches were noted for their moderation and 'gentlemanly style'. A generous subscriber to public charities, he took the platform at a meeting in 1880 to raise funds for Irish famine relief. He was honorary treasurer of the Aborigines Protection Association and on the committee of the Industrial Blind Institution. He financed the Presbyterian Church at Jamberoo and, as a councillor of St Andrew's College, University of Sydney, gave it a scholarship. In 1879 he was an elector for the university senate. 'An insatiable reader', Marks conversed 'with facility and fluency upon a great diversity of subjects'. President of the Eastern Suburbs Amateur Athletic Club, he was a lover of sport; an excellent rifle-shot and clay pigeon shooter, he was also a good cricketer and played for parliament against the press.

On 1 February 1860 at St James's Church, Sydney, Marks had married the widow Elizabeth Preston Little (d. 1908), daughter of William Moffitt [q.v.]. His brother James who married her sister Sarah Jane, was also well known in the Illawarra, built Culwalla House at Jamberoo, was an alderman for Piper Ward in the Woollahra Municipal Council and in 1891-94 represented Paddington in the Legislative Assembly. John Marks died at Glenrock on 3 March 1885 from cirrhosis and was buried in the Presbyterian section of Waverley cemetery, survived by his wife, to whom he left his estate valued at £19,000, and by two sons and three daughters. His eldest son Theodore, a leading architect, was prominent in Sydney racing circles, known to the 'ring' as a heavy punter; the Sydney Turf Club's Theo Marks Quality Handicap at the Rosehill autumn meeting was named after him. Glenrock became part of Ascham School.

E. Digby (ed), *Australian men of mark*, 1 (Syd, 1889); F. McCaffrey, *History of Illawarra and its pioneers* (Syd, 1922); *Empire* (Syd), 16 Apr 1856; *SMH*, 5 Mar 1885; *Illawarra Mercury*, 7 Mar 1885; MS cat (ML); information from Miss P. Watson, Syd.   MARTHA RUTLEDGE

MARSDEN, SAMUEL EDWARD (1832-1912), Anglican bishop, was born on 1 February 1832 at O'Connell Plains, son of

Thomas Marsden, merchant, and his wife Jane Catherine, fourth daughter of Rev. Samuel Marsden [q.v.]. Samuel left The King's School, Parramatta, went to England with his mother and was educated at Gloucestershire and at Trinity College, Cambridge (B.A., 1855; M.A., 1858; D.D., 1870). In December 1855 he had been made deacon and next year ordained priest by the bishop of Hereford. After serving as curate at St Peter's, Hereford, in 1855-58 and Lilleshall, Shropshire, in 1861, he was perpetual curate at Bengeworth, Worcestershire. He was dominated by his mother and the legend of his grandfather whose biography he wrote about 1857 but never published.

Recommended by Bishop Barker [q.v.], Marsden accepted the new see of Bathurst in New South Wales and on 29 June 1869 was consecrated in Westminster Abbey. In January 1870 at Cheltenham he married Beatrice McLaren. Installed at Bathurst on 5 May he found that his diocese reached the South Australian and Queensland borders but contained only 13 parishes, 15 clergy and no railways. He relied on Barker's counsel in forming a Church Society and in May 1873 a synod. In 1876-77 he visited England in a vain attempt to attract men and money but in his absence his influence was undermined by Rev. Thomas Smith [q.v.]. Marsden was criticized for failing to recruit clergy, for ordaining ill-educated men, for administering his diocese by himself and his clerical registrar, and for disregarding a fractious and infrequent synod.

In September 1879 Smith's closure of the Bathurst denominational school brought to a head the dissension between parishioners led by James Rutherford [q.v.] and the bishop and many of his clergy. Rev. John Thomas Marriott was created dean of All Saints Cathedral by synod and Marsden assented in May 1882. Marriott later claimed that as dean he had precedence over Marsden's choice of a vicar-general and aired the issue in many letters to church leaders in England and Australia. The diocese was stigmatized as 'a by-word for division and trouble' and the bishop as a 'gossip and too much given to flattery'. Marsden offered to resign and left for England in November 1884. On 10 May 1885 his mother died in Bathurst and he returned briefly to relinquish the see.

Generous with his private means, Marsden built his own Bishopscourt. He had formed 19 new parishes and introduced 67 clergymen. He toured extensively despite a skin complaint. Without pretence to scholarship, his Evangelicalism dominated the diocese. 'One of the kindest and most conscientious of men', he was an irresolute administrator yet adamant when opposed.

Marsden assisted in the dioceses of Canterbury, Winchester and Norwich, and settled at Dyrham Lodge, Clifton Park, Bristol. Assistant bishop of Gloucester and Bristol in 1892-97 and Bristol in 1898, he was created honorary canon of Gloucester in 1900 and Bristol in 1905. In 1906 he gave £1000 toward the bishopric of Sheffield. Predeceased by his wife in 1909, he died of diabetes at his home on 15 October 1912. His estate of £16,065 was divided among his two sons and two daughters.

G. S. Oakes, *Jubilee of the diocese of Bathurst, 1870-1920* (Bathurst, 1920); F. B. Boyce, *Fourscore years and seven* (Syd, 1934); G. S. Oakes, 'Bush memories', *JRAHS*, 7 (1921); *Bathurst Times*, 12 Feb 1890, 22 Oct 1912; R. M. Teale, The Anglican diocese of Bathurst, 1870-1911 (M.A. thesis, Univ Syd, 1968); S. E. Marsden papers (ML).   RUTH TEALE

MARSH, MATTHEW HENRY (1810-1881), barrister, pastoralist and parliamentarian, was born in Wiltshire, England, eldest son of Rev. Matthew Marsh, canon and chancellor of the diocese of Salisbury, and his wife Margaret, née Brodie. Educated at Westminster School and Christ Church, Oxford (B.A., 1833; M.A., 1835), he was called to the Bar of the Inner Temple in 1836 and practised on the Western Circuit and the Wiltshire Assizes. He had few briefs and on the advice of his uncle, B. C. Brodie, migrated to New South Wales. He reached Sydney in the *Broxbornebury* on 24 June 1840 and bought a 34,000-acre property in New England from R. R. Mackenzie [q.v.] which he called Salisbury Plains. He later acquired Boorolong, another New England run of 175,000 acres and Maryland, 200,000 acres on the Darling Downs. A magistrate from 1841, he was an early member of the Australian Club.

Joined by his brother Charles whom he left to manage his stations, Marsh visited England where he married Elizabeth Mary, sister of E. C. Merewether [q.v.] in 1844. They returned in 1845 and lived in a canvas-lined slab hut known as Old Sarum until Salisbury Court was finished in 1846. Charles continued to manage Boorolong. A believer in cheap labour, Marsh found English immigrants 'discontented and troublesome' and in 1852 imported Chinese shepherds from Amoy whom he paid £7 4s. a year. In 1849 he successfully sued his superintendent for neglect and damages and next year won a Supreme Court action refusing a new trial. In September 1851 he was elected unopposed as a 'Liberal Whig' to the Legislative Council for the districts of New England and Macleay. He took part in the debates on W. C. Wentworth's [q.v.] constitution bill and derided American 'mobocracy', opposed an elected Upper House and denied the value of representation according to population. In 1854 he was a member of the commission to send exhibits to the Paris Exhibition. In August 1855 he vacated his seat in the council and returned to England with his family, leaving Charles to run his stations.

In 1857 Marsh was elected to the House of Commons in the liberal interest for Salisbury; his fellow representative was E. W. T. Hamilton [q.v.]. In parliament Marsh supported separation of the Moreton Bay District though regretting that the new colony did not include New England. Appointed honorary representative in England for the Queensland government he was the principal commissioner for Queensland at the London Exhibition in 1862. From June to December 1865 he visited Australia and his support for Queensland separation was recognized at a public banquet in Brisbane. On his return he published *Overland from Southampton to Queensland* (London, 1867). In the House of Commons he had brief notoriety as a leading Adullamite with Robert Lowe [q.v.] against the reform bill of 1866 and cited his colonial experience as proof of the destructiveness of democratic politics. He retired from parliament in 1868 and was defeated for Salisbury next year.

A fellow of the Royal Geographical Society, Marsh revisited his Australian estates in 1873. A magistrate for Wiltshire and Hampshire and a deputy-lieutenant of Wiltshire, Marsh lived at Mansion House, Ramridge, Hampshire. He died on 26 January 1881 at Bournemouth, survived by his wife and three daughters. His eldest daughter Georgina Eliza Lucy married Sir Herbert Croft and descendants still live at Salisbury Court. Marsh's goods were valued for probate at £38,000.

G. N. Griffiths, *Some northern homes of N.S.W.* (Syd, 1954); R. B. Walker, *Old New England* (Syd, 1966); V&P (LC NSW), 1841-52; *The Times*, 31 Jan 1881; A. Gardner, Northern and western districts, N.S.W., 1842-54, 1 (ML); Sir Bernard Croft papers (Salisbury Court); Macarthur and Elizabeth Marsh papers (ML).
E. W. DUNLOP

MARSH, STEPHEN HALE ALONZO (1805-1888), musician, was born on 4 January 1805 in Kensington, London, only son of Henry Marsh. His widowed mother kept 'a finishing school for young ladies' near Kensington Palace. He later gave concerts throughout Britain under the patronage of the duchess of Kent and the harpist,

Nicholas Bochsa [q.v.], offered to teach him. In Paris Marsh was given an Erard harp, which he took everywhere, even carrying it on a camel in Egypt.

In February 1842 Marsh arrived in Sydney with his wife in the *Sir Edward Paget*. Ludwig Leichhardt [q.v.] was a fellow passenger and recorded that Marsh often gave recitals to the passengers. He rented a house 'for the enormous sum of 100 thalers [£150]' and asked Leichhardt to occupy 'his little spare room' and 'share some of the expense', which he did for six months. Soon after arrival Marsh was asked by Isaac Nathan [q.v.] to take part in a 'mixed concert' at the Sydney College. He engaged the two Nathan girls to sing at his proposed series of chamber concerts but their father refused and the two musicians became rivals. By 1845 Marsh was able to give a concert 'under the most distinguished patronage' with an orchestra of forty-five supplemented by the band of the 99th Regiment, and 'enraptured his audience by his delightful harp-playing'.

When Nathan wrote *Hail Star of the South! Australasia Advance!*, Marsh produced *Advance Australia*, 'dedicated to its inhabitants', describing it as 'The Australian National Anthem'. When Nathan celebrated Leichhardt's unexpected return from Port Essington with *The Greeting Home Again: A Paean on Leichhardt's Return*, to words by E. K. Sylvester, Marsh immediately set the same verses with a harp accompaniment, which Leichhardt thought 'extraordinarily beautiful'. He capped it with *Dr. Leichhardt's March*, written 'on the successful termination of his expedition, by his friend S. H. Marsh'.

Nathan's *Don John of Austria* (1847), was described as the 'first opera wholly produced in Australia'. Marsh followed with *A Gentleman in Black*, also claiming it as 'Australia's first opera'. In 1859 his cantata for solo soprano, *In Thee Oh Lord Do I Put My Trust*, was first sung in Sydney by Madame Anna Bishop. Later he went to Melbourne where in 1861 his opera was again performed. His wife had died and he married the 18-year-old Harriet Turner. He left Australia with his family in 1872 and after two years in Japan settled in San Francisco where he continued teaching till 1878. Marsh died there on 21 January 1888, survived by his wife, two of his five sons and a daughter. Most of his manuscripts were destroyed by the great fire and earthquake in San Francisco in 1906.

A. H. Chisholm, *Strange new world* (Syd, 1941); C. Mackerras, *The Hebrew melodist* (Syd, 1963); SMH, 25 May, 1 June 1842, 5 May 1843, 23 May, 8 Aug, 2 Oct 1844; J. L. Hall,

'New light on Stephen Hale Marsh', SMH, June 1955; *Australian*, 30 Nov, 3 Dec 1845; Letters relating to Marsh and Leichhardt and Report on Leichhardt papers in ML and Dixson Lib (ML).   CATHERINE MACKERRAS

MARSHALL, JAMES WADDELL (1845-1925), merchant, was born on 2 June 1845 at Falkirk, Stirling, Scotland, son of William Marshall and his wife Agnes Aitken, née Waddell. His father died in 1847 and the family estate was swallowed up in legal costs. At 12 Marshall had to go to work. At 14 he joined the Falkirk drapery of P. & J. Gentleman & Co. His apprenticeship ended, he moved to a drapery in Dundee and then to London, where he was employed by James Spence & Co., retail drapers in St Paul's Churchyard; he was there for a year and worked seventy-five hours a week. Through the London agency of David Murray [q.v.] Marshall was offered a job with J. A. Northmore, an Adelaide draper. As James Waddell he arrived at Port Adelaide on 21 November 1867 in the *Saint Vincent* and as James Waddell Marshall married Annie Walters on 24 September 1872; thereafter he dropped the name Waddell.

With a fellow assistant, William Taylor, Marshall began saving and in 1874 set up a store in Hindley Street. When John Hodgkiss, warehouseman, retired in 1881, they bought his business in Rundle Street and set up as James Marshall & Co., drapers and importers, with a furniture warehouse in Stephens Place. Soon afterwards they were burnt out but insurance covered the stock and they rebuilt. They bought adjoining premises and the business grew to the largest of its kind in South Australia with some 800 employees. From the start Marshall followed a policy of vigorous advertising. His influence on Adelaide business was great and from successful experience his advice was 'Stick to your business and put your heart and soul into it; Mind your own business . . . See that you do enough to satisfy yourself . . . Do everything you are asked to do, and do it promptly; study your employer before studying self. . . Make yourself indispensable . . . Do everything with a good heart'.

Marshall avoided politics and shrank from personal publicity. Always liberal towards deserving philanthropic causes, he served on the boards of the North Adelaide Children's Hospital, the Memorial Hospital, the Home for Incurables, the Royal Institution for the Blind, the Queen's Home at Rose Park, the Adelaide Benevolent and Strangers' Friend Society and the State Children's Council. He was a founder and member of the board of the Young Men's Christian Association for which he bought W. R. Fletcher's [q.v.] library. He was a member of the Flinders Street Presbyterian Church and superintendent of its Sunday school but later attended the Kent Town Methodist Church. He was an energetic member of the Adelaide City Mission. He was fond of cricket and football and regularly attended the Adelaide Oval. In his youth he had been active in such sports as tennis, cycling, boxing, fencing, skating and swimming even though they often meant rising at 4 a.m. He made about ten visits to Britain.

After his wife died Marshall married Florence Emma Stacey on 7 October 1913. For many years he lived at Payneham, and in the early 1900s bought a home with a lovely garden at Mount Lofty. After World War I he lived in Victoria Avenue, Unley Park, where he died on 10 March 1925 survived by his wife, three sons and four daughters. He was buried in Payneham cemetery after a service at Kent Town Methodist Church, and Marshall's store was closed for the day as a mark of respect. He left an estate valued at £26,000.

Register (Adel), 11 Mar 1925.

MARSHALL, WILLIAM HENRY GEORGE (1850-1920), town clerk, was born on 12 September 1850 at Brisbane, son of William Henry Marshall, carpenter and builder, and his wife Emma, née Fairfax. His parents had been selected for migration to Moreton Bay by J. D. Lang [q.v.] and arrived in the *Lima* in 1849. Marshall was educated at the Normal School in Brisbane and at 15 as office boy entered the Brisbane Municipal Council where his father represented Valley Ward. Ability and devotion to duty soon brought Marshall to the notice of the aldermen and, when the town clerk was dismissed for neglect of duties in 1873, the mayor, James Swan [q.v.], appointed Marshall acting town clerk despite his youth. On 24 February 1874 he was chosen from a number of applicants to fill the permanent office of town clerk, a position he occupied with distinction for forty-six years.

Marshall was town clerk while the population of the municipality (city after 1902) and the functions of the corporation grew substantially. An extensive and complex system of committees developed, the permanent staff grew from 7 in 1874 to 24 in 1920 and 8 separate departments emerged within the civic administration. In order to ensure the effective co-ordination of departments Marshall, as town clerk, was made chief administrative officer of the municipality in 1899. Pressure of work later induced him to resign from the Commission of the Peace to which he had been appointed in 1882.

In 1896 the Queensland government appointed Marshall to the royal commission on local government in the colony. In a rider to its report he revealed strong liberal views, objecting vigorously to recommendations for restricting the ratepayers' rights and franchise. He helped to form the Local Authorities Association of Queensland in 1896 and actively supported the Local Government Clerks' Association of Queensland, formed in 1914. Though retiring, modest and courteous by habit, his tact, administrative ability and trustworthiness enabled him to secure the co-operation of the municipal staff and to win the respect and confidence of the aldermen and the community.

Marshall was a member of the Church of England. He died in hospital on 28 December 1920, survived by his wife Jane, née Saint, whom he had married in Brisbane on 9 December 1874, and by three sons and three of their four daughters. He was buried in Bulimba cemetery. The Brisbane City Council decided to provide a 'lasting memorial' within the Town Hall in memory of one who had served the city so well over more than half a century.

Portraits are in the Brisbane City Council and the Oxley Library.

W. F. Morrison, *The Aldine history of Queensland*, 2 (Syd, 1888); G. Greenwood and J. Laverty, *Brisbane 1859-1959* (Brisb, 1959); V&P (LA Qld), 1896, 2, 525; *Brisbane Courier*, 29 Dec 1920; Municipal Council minutes 1865-1902 and City Council minutes 1903-1920 (Town Hall, Brisb).   JOHN LAVERTY

MARTIN, ARTHUR PATCHETT (1851-1902), writer, was born on 18 February 1851 at Woolwich, Kent, England, son of George Martin and his wife Eleanor, née Hill. In December 1852 the family arrived at Melbourne where Martin was educated at St Mark's School, Fitzroy, and matriculated at the University of Melbourne in February 1868. He worked in the post office from November 1865 to 1883, but for most of these years was a casual writer, prominent in giving papers and debating in the Eclectic Society where he succeeded H. K. Rusden [q.v.] as secretary. For six years Martin edited the *Melbourne Review*, which he and H. G. Turner [q.v.] established in 1876. Martin's lifelong belief was that Australian literature could best develop with an Australian school of criticism beside it; only then would it adjust its perspectives. He published *Sweet Girl Graduate* (1876), which included short poems and a sentimental novelette. More verses followed: *Lays of To-day: Verses in Jest and Earnest* (1878), and *Fernshawe: Sketches in Prose and Verse* (1882), collected from the *Melbourne Review* and other journals. He was closely associated with the theatre through his brother-in-law, Arthur Garner. A. D. Mickle describes Martin as a 'born Bohemian', and recalls the regular walks his father took with the 'brilliant talkers' Patchett Martin and Alfred Deakin. Walter Murdoch refers to Martin's light mockery, wit and indolence.

In 1883 Martin left Australia under a cloud, as co-respondent in a divorce case, and remained embittered by friends shunning him. However, he soon became established in London journalism, writing regularly for the *Pall Mall Gazette*. He was the satirist of the 'Australasian Group' who regarded themselves as exiles but retained a keen interest in Australian affairs, particularly literature. He wrote an introduction to the 18th edition of the poems of Adam Lindsay Gordon [q.v.] and was his advocate in many articles. In *Literature* he hailed the first volumes of Lawson and Paterson with pride and triumph, avowing that 'the un-English, thorough Australian style and character of these new bush bards' appealed to 'the rising native population'. In 1889 he published *Australia and the Empire*, a patchwork of essays on Australian affairs and prominent men, and in 1893 *True Stories from Australasian History*. His major work, *Life and Letters of the Right Honourable Robert Lowe, Viscount Sherbrooke* (1893), was a clearly-structured, dignified work and generally accurate, with information from Lowe's friends and relations. He also wrote the entries on Sir Henry Parkes, W. C. Wentworth and Sir William Windeyer [qq.v.] in the *Dictionary of National Biography*.

On 11 January 1886 in London Martin had married a widow, Harriete Anne Bullen, daughter of Dr John Moore Cookesley. Together they wrote verse and arranged the publications of expatriate Australians in various periodicals. The *Bulletin*, 7 March 1896, described his talent as rather thin, claiming that his verse was 'deficient in wit and poignancy, but with sufficient fluency and sentiment to be readable'. He was a minor poet, at best remembered for his literary criticism and journalism. Though reputedly influential in promoting Australia's broader interests, he was, according to Deakin in May 1889, 'ill-informed on public affairs' and 'did not pretend to follow them' before leaving Australia. His influence in Britain seems illusory despite his activities in Liberal Union politics. His health collapsed and his wife sought help from friends in Britain and Australia. By their aid he went to Tenerife where he died on 15 February 1902.

W. Murdoch, *Alfred Deakin* (Lond, 1923); A. D. Mickle, *Many a mickle* (Melb, 1953); J. Manifold, *Who wrote the ballads?* (Syd, 1964); Deakin letters, 1540/5483, 7499, 8080

SUZANNE G. MELLOR

MARTIN, SIR JAMES (1820-1886), politician and chief justice, was born on 14 May 1820 at Midleton, Cork, Ireland, eldest child of John Martin, castle steward, and his wife Mary, née Hennessey (1795-1876), who were married on 5 July 1819 at Glanmire, Cork. Offered employment by Governor Brisbane, John sailed with his family in the *John Barry*, reached Sydney on 6 November 1821, and worked as a groom at Parramatta. Reputedly baptized at St Mary's by J. J. Therry [q.v.], James was educated at Parramatta at a dame's school and by others including D. Thurston and Rev. W. Walker [q.v.]. His parents made sacrifices to send him to W. T. Cape's [q.v.] school in 1833-36, where he brilliantly fulfilled his juvenile promise. He had contributed to newspapers including the *Australian* on which he became a journalist; influenced by its editor G. R. Nichols [q.v.], Martin became firmly committed to the aspirations of the native-born. In 1838 as 'Hirundo' he wrote a bitter article on the ignorance of the Molesworth committee on convict transportation, and published *The Australian Sketch Book*, fifteen essays full of youthful self-consciousness but exhibiting intense patriotic feelings. With Henry Parkes [q.v.] he wrote for W. A. Duncan's [q.v.] *Australasian Chronicle* and in 1839 he was acting editor of the *Australian*.

By 1840 Martin had taken a keen interest and some part in the stirring constitutional and social issues confronting New South Wales, but lively and partisan debate had exposed in him a polemical and snobbish streak reflecting awareness of his humble background and intellectual potential. Thrustful and capable, he was determined to prove that he had the qualities necessary for social and material success. Law attracted him as a career that would give his ambitions and talents full play and produce commensurate rewards irrespective of his origins. At 20 he was articled to Nichols and continued to speak and write, sometimes as 'Junius', on the need for representative government. In 1843, attracted by the conservative native-born strand, he was on the committee of W. C. Wentworth and W.

Bland [qq.v.] at the colony's first elections. Sharpening his vision of a new type of colonial upper class based on merit and patriotism rather than family eminence, he campaigned resentfully against William Bowman, a low-brow exclusive candidate for Cumberland Boroughs, but Martin could envisage no useful role for ex-convicts. When admitted a solicitor on 10 May 1845 he was probably the outstanding young member of the native-born group.

Influenced by Robert Lowe's [q.v.] lordly liberalism Martin wrote for the *Atlas* in 1844 and from May 1845 was its manager and editor for two years. He intensified the newspaper's violent attacks on Governor Gipps's land policy and began to censure Governor FitzRoy's private life. Martin's developing hauteur was reinforced by his increasing income as one of the most successful practitioners in the police courts but his drive remained unabated for educational improvement and further constitutional reform. Meanwhile his enemies diversified, repelled by his rare combination of lowly birth, pugnacity, colonial patriotism, ability and growing wealth. He added to his opponents by strong support for fiscal protection in 1848 and backed by Wentworth and Robert Fitzgerald [q.v.], won the Legislative Council seat of Cook and Westmoreland, but was unseated in June 1849 because he lacked the necessary property qualification. Next month he regained the seat and was one of the most active councillors, seeking reform of the city corporation, helping to found the university and revealing his favour for renewed transportation.

Martin's family was strongly Catholic but his own denominational faith weakened as he matured. Catholicism was the religion of the Irish and their offspring, a large proportion of the colonial lower orders, but it jarred with Martin's dream of personal advancement, though he retained warm family links. Lowe influenced Martin's religious doubts and they were aggravated by an attack on him in 1850 by Fr J. McEncroe [q.v.] as 'a living example of the effects of an education not based upon religion'. Next year many Catholics unsuccessfully supported A. Longmore against him in the contest for Cook and Westmoreland. On 20 January 1853 at St Peter's Anglican Church, Cook's River, he married Isabella, sister of W. A. Long [q.v.] and daughter of a wealthy ex-convict wine and spirits merchant. He did not formally join the Anglican Church but remained convinced of the strong need for a society based on Christian principles. On this ground in 1854 he disapproved payment to Jewish ministers though he was always tolerant.

The discovery of gold in February 1851

accelerated forces shaping constitutional change. Martin actively supported legislation to control the goldfields and sponsored the establishment of a mint. In April he was a member of Wentworth's select committee to prepare 'a Declaration and Remonstrance' against British constitutional proposals and in November he helped to prepare a petition to the Queen and parliament. The pressure persuaded the British government to allow the colonists to draw up their own constitution and in 1852 Martin was an active member of the committee. In the transitions of the early 1850s his conservatism was modifying but he opposed manhood suffrage and sought an upper house composed 'of representatives who are large landed proprietors'. In a notable council speech in August 1853 he effectively defended the draft constitution and revealed that Edmund Burke remained his chief inspiration but Disraeli rather than Wentworth was looming as his political exemplar. As amended, the constitution still displeased the liberals with its restricted franchise and nominated second chamber. Martin did not agree wholeheartedly with them but perceived that the old colonial conservatism, based on a landholding ascendancy, had to be curbed. His leading role in constitution-making and his legislative record had brought him to the forefront of politics; he was asked to run for Sydney at the first responsible government elections in April 1856 but he won his old seat.

Martin had hoped in vain to be the first premier of New South Wales but in August became attorney-general in the second ministry led by C. Cowper [q.v.]. This honour soon showed that Martin's rise through merit had aroused ire and envy in politicians and lawyers, and wrecked his hopes of joining the old upper class. He was not a barrister and his appointment was opposed strongly in the assembly and by the Bar. Embittered by the political opposition, he accepted the legal objections and was admitted to the Bar on 11 September and made Q.C. in 1857; but the government fell. In October 1856 P. G. King wrote to James Macarthur [qq.v.] 'I am much pleased to see the "Cowper cum Martin" ministry upset—what a vulgar fellow the latter is. I should think no decent person would ever cross his threshold again or send their cards. I was amused at the use he tried to make [in the assembly] of your having once put your feet under his mahogany'. While advancing in the new form of Sydney society, Martin had become secretary of the Sydney College committee in 1848 and the Sydney Choral Society in 1854; in 1855 he was appointed to the National Board of Education and in 1858-59 was on the committee of the Sydney Club. In 1853 he bought Clarens on a site overlooking Sydney Harbour in Wylde Street, Potts Point, and as his income and family increased he improved its grounds to make it one of the most imposing mansions in Sydney. A younger group of able native-born, notably W. B. Dalley [q.v.], disagreed largely with his politics but recognized his patriotic achievements and mounting legal eminence.

By 1860 Martin was one of the great colonists, but he had difficulty in coming to terms with the liberal ascendancy in politics in 1858-60 although he was Cowper's attorney-general again in 1857-58. He opposed manhood suffrage in 1858, land reform in 1861 and abolition of grants to religion in 1862; his protectionist views remained unpopular. In early 1863 his social liberalism dominated his defence of three members of Frank Gardiner's [q.v.] bushranging gang and especially his attempt with Dalley to save one from the gallows. By then a new cluster of political problems had emerged, related to economic management, education reform, relations with Victoria over the Riverina and the menace of bushranging. The liberals under Cowper and John Robertson [q.v.] had few answers, but Martin had adjusted to the situation and as attorney-general formed his first ministry on 16 October. With an uncertain following and a weak cabinet Martin's strong policy included *ad valorem* duties and border tariffs, but he could not carry it and lost the 1864-65 general election on the fiscal issue.

Cowper's new government, formed partly from liberal remnants, had to implement Martin's financial policy but lasted less than a year. Parkes had perceived Martin's new political stature and sounded him out on an alliance. Martin had written for Parkes's *Empire* in 1851 but had been temperamentally and politically opposed to him for the rest of the 1850s; on 8 January 1866 he told him 'There is no further occasion ... to refer to our past misunderstandings'. On 22 January they formed the strongest ministry to that time, with Martin attorney-general and premier. His control complemented Parkes's social flair in the important 1866 Public Schools Act and in measures to help neglected children. They reformed the Municipalities Act, reached an agreement with Victoria on the border duties and pacified the Riverina. By early 1868 the government's resolution had flagged and was shaken on 12 March by the attempted assassination of the duke of Edinburgh by H. J. O'Farrell [q.v.]. This incident shocked Martin's sense of decorum and social responsibility and he forced the treason felony bill through parliament in one day. Looking back in 1870 on the episode Martin rightly reminded Parkes that at an agitated and possibly perilous time they had done their utmost 'to preserve the public peace and act impartially to all parties'. But the ministry had lost its cohesion and Parkes's withdrawal on 17 September 1868 was followed by Martin's resignation on 26 October. He was knighted next year.

In 1861 Martin had been elected as a fellow of the University of Sydney and was on the committee of the Victoria Club; in 1864-65 he was a committeeman of the Hyde Park Improvement Society and in 1871 vice-president of the Civil Service Club. He had taken some interest in business and by 1870 held three directorships. In 1872 he was appointed to the Commission of Defence from foreign aggression. An examiner of the university's faculty of law he was at the top of his profession. In 1856-68 he had reputedly spent £20,000 on beautifying Clarens, including the erection in its grounds of a replica of the Choragic Monument of Lysicrates (now in the Sydney Botanical Gardens). But he remained in politics and on 16 December 1870 returned as premier with a cabinet including one of his most durable opponents, Robertson, as colonial secretary. This liaison marked both the dissolution of the post-1855 liberal combinations and the end of Martin's attempt to provide an effective conservative political strand. He rejected Gavan Duffy's [q.v.] proposals for federation, but his government was moribund and fell in 1872 when no agreement could be reached with Victoria on renewing the scheme to obviate border duties.

As early as the mid-1860s Martin had reflected on succeeding Sir Alfred Stephen [q.v.] as chief justice and in 1872 he sat with Stephen on the Law Reform Commission. Parkes's proposal in 1873 to promote Edward Butler [q.v.] aroused a political and sectarian storm that did not obscure Martin's pre-eminent qualifications for the position and his appointment in November was not only the greatest triumph of the native-born in the nineteenth century but also realized his own personal dream of status through talent and hard work. With the help of Dalley, who had become his brother-in-law in 1872, Martin consolidated his position as a leader of Sydney society, stressing intellectual and artistic leadership and brilliant conversation with fine food and wine. He built a grand holiday house, Numantia, in the Blue Mountains in 1877 and was followed there by other notables.

In 1872 Parkes noted that Martin 'loved power for power's sake', and wrote perceptively that 'There is no man in these Australian colonies of a more imperious nature than Sir James Martin', and that while he was neither strong-willed nor vindictive he was protected from himself by 'the sanctities of the constitutional freedom under which he lives and his professional respect for the principles of law'. These qualities conditioned paradoxical elements in Martin's personality: an egalitarianism with snobbish overtones; a respect for the British lifestyle tempered by strong Australian patriotism that concentrated on New South Wales, conditioned affection and respect for the bushland and produced antipathy to those colonists who put their homeland before their adopted country or who did not acknowledge the primacy of the mother colony. As chief justice he detected in Governor Robinson some of the corrupting defects of power he had discovered earlier in Gipps and FitzRoy, and in 1874 protested to Parkes when he was not made administrator when the governor was in Fiji. Next year his resentment led to an explosive exchange of letters with Robinson in the *Sydney Morning Herald*: the correspondence was ostensibly about the respective roles of governor and chief justice but reflected Robinson's easy British assumption of superiority and tutelage, and Martin's Australian rejection of the trappings of imperial patronage.

By the middle 1870s Lady Martin had borne eight sons and seven daughters. Wealthy in her own right she grew dissatisfied with Martin's constant circuit tours, his obsession with Numantia and his insensitive response to her complaints about the inadequacies of Clarens for a large family. Fearful of typhoid fever she also developed a distaste for the nauseous and toxic smells emanating from Rushcutters Bay that often swept Clarens with the east winds. Their domestic misery was increased in 1880-81 by the death of two children and of her sister, Dalley's wife, and by Martin's ill health. In 1882 Lady Martin moved to Vaucluse. Dalley sided with her: 'Although Clarens is one of the loveliest of residences', he wrote to Martin, 'and your genius has made it a dream of beauty I am entirely of her opinion that it is neither large enough for the family nor for your station with its necessary social liabilities'. But there was no reconciliation.

Martin proved a notable chief justice. On his appointment he acknowledged that previously he may have been offensive to many colonists but begged them 'kindly and generously to forget'. His profound professionalism facilitated his efficient exercise of the duties of the office and his acceptance of its responsibilities. J. A. Froude [q.v.] saw Martin in 1885 as 'a stout, round-faced, remarkable old man, with a fine classical

training', who, 'if [he] had been Chief Justice of England . . . would have passed as among the most distinguished occupants of that high position'. A sordid murder case in 1884 reflected his mastery when he reminded the jury that they and not newspapers had to decide the verdict. Several times he pointed out that his salary of £2600 was insufficient and in 1881 told Parkes that at least seven barristers received more. He maintained his right to speak on important issues and in 1878 at a public meeting congratulated Disraeli on the Berlin settlement. In 1885 he told the Christian Evidence Society that colonial laws were based on Christianity and he was happy to join 'those who wish again to call to mind the proofs of its truth'. Archbishop Vaughan [q.v.] wrote him a warm letter in 1881 but he did not return to the Catholic Church. When he died on 4 November 1886 of heart disease he was buried at St Jude's, Randwick, by Dr A. Barry [q.v.], Anglican primate of Australia. His death marked the inevitable failure of the first generation of the New South Wales native-born to generate an Australian patriotism. He was survived by his wife, six sons and six daughters. In 1909 Lady Martin died and his remains were transferred to her grave in Waverley cemetery. Martin Place in Sydney is named after him, Lady Martin's Beach at Point Piper after her.

J. A. Froude, *Oceana, or England and her colonies* (Lond, 1886); R. L. Knight, *Illiberal Liberal* (Melb, 1966); J. M. Bennett (ed), *A history of the New South Wales Bar* (Syd, 1969); I. Getzler, *Neither toleration nor favour* (Melb, 1970); E. Grainger, *Martin of Martin Place* (Syd, 1970); J. N. Molony, *An architect of freedom* (Canberra, 1973); M. Rutledge, 'Edward Butler and the chief justiceship, 1873', *Hist Studies*, no 50, Apr 1968; *Empire* (Syd), 17 Apr 1856, 29 May 1860; *Town and Country J*, 25 Mar 1871; *Illustrated Sydney News*, 30 Jan 1874; *Syd Q Mag*, Mar 1886; Belmore, Cowper, Macarthur, Martin papers and Parkes letters (ML).

BEDE NAIRN

MARTIN, JAMES (1821-1899), manufacturer and politician, was born on 23 April 1821 in Foundry, Cornwall, England. His father, who died before his birth, had run the foundry which gave the village its name. Martin had little schooling but early developed his mechanical bent. He worked first for a millwright and then at the Tresavean mine, where he built a working model of a 'man engine' or lift for the engineer who pioneered the adoption of this device in Cornish mines.

Seeking relief from asthma, Martin migrated in the *Belle Alliance* and in July

1847 arrived in South Australia. After working in Adelaide for John Ridley [q.v.] and others, he moved to Gawler in June 1848 and set up as a blacksmith and wheelwright. He soon became a manufacturer, making bullock drays, agricultural implements and other ironwork; in the 1870s branches were opened at Gladstone and Quorn. In 1874-85 he had as a partner Frederick May [q.v.] whose engineering skill greatly expanded production of mining machinery. Martin added railway rolling-stock and in 1888, as the final seal of success, won a government contract for constructing forty-seven railway locomotives at a cost of £167,000; the first was delivered in April 1890 and by December 1894 he could celebrate the delivery of a hundred locomotives.

Martin was several times mayor of Gawler and a leading member and patron of most of the town's organizations. He was an Anglican but did not confine his financial support to his denomination. He represented Barossa in the House of Assembly in 1865-68 and North-Eastern Province in the Legislative Council in 1885-99. In 1865 he had supported Goyder's [q.v.] valuations of the pastoral runs and in 1885 a protective tariff, both popular causes, but by 1894 he had moved to the right. On the hustings he criticized the Labor Party and favoured the programme of the conservative National Defence League which endorsed his candidature. His greatest parliamentary achievement was to secure the construction of the Barossa reservoir which supplied Gawler with water from 1902. In 1903 a statue with the inscription 'A tribute to his public worth' was placed in the town's main street; it now stands in a park on the banks of the South Para River.

Martin had visited Britain in 1879 to gather information about modern machinery. His firm reached peak production with 700 men and works of 18 acres by 15 June 1898 when he celebrated the jubilee of his arrival in Gawler; despite rain the event was attended by some 1500 people. He died a widower on 27 December 1899 and was buried with much mourning in Willaston cemetery. He had been married three times: first, on 28 March 1848 at Trinity Church to Christiana Fox (d. 1852) who bore him two children; second, on 6 March 1853 at Gawler to Ann Lock (d. 1853); and third, on 2 August 1858 at North Adelaide to Charlotte Vickerstaff Brad(l)ey (d. 1894). His estate of £27,000 included landed property which was left to his son John, a farmer; the business went to a nephew, John Felix Martin.

After 1900 demand for mining machinery lessened and government railway workshops took business away from Gawler.

Agricultural expansion outside Gawler's hinterland widened the market for agricultural machinery and competition became keener. In 1907 Martin & Co. went into liquidation. The general engineering business was bought by Henry Dutton of Anlaby and the Gawler Implement Co. was formed to carry on the manufacture of agricultural machinery.

E. H. Coombe (ed), *History of Gawler 1837 to 1908* (Adel, 1910); M. Williams, 'Gawler: the changing geography of a South Australian country town', *Aust Geographer*, 9 (1964); *Observer* (Adel), 6 Oct 1889, 30 Dec 1899; *Register* (Adel), 15 June 1898.   J. B. HIRST

MARTINDALE, BEN HAY (1824-1904), engineer and public servant, was born on 1 October 1824 in London, son of Benjamin Martindale, of Martindale, Westmorland. Educated at Rugby and the Royal Military Academy, Woolwich, he was commissioned second lieutenant in the Royal Engineers in June 1843. After a year at Chatham he was posted to Woolwich. Service at Gibraltar, Corfu and Dover followed and in September 1856 as a captain he joined the staff of the inspector-general of fortifications, London.

Martindale refused the offer of the New South Wales Executive Council to superintend the building and running of the colony's railways but reconsidered his decision at the request of Governor Denison and arrived at Sydney in July 1857 as chief commissioner of railways. He had also been appointed superintendent of the electric telegraph and commissioner of roads. After the Government Railway Act in December 1858 he became commissioner of railways. Early in 1859 his title was changed to commissioner of internal communications but in October the Department of Lands and Works was separated into two parts and he became under-secretary for public works and commissioner of railways, losing some of his independent powers as he came under direct control of the parliamentary secretary of public works.

In three years Martindale had served under six ministries and carried much responsibility yet he was blamed in the press and parliament for any inadequacies in roads or railway services. These attacks might have been parried by pointing to the paltry sums approved by parliament for public works but he generally adopted an unconciliatory stand. A select committee into railway construction had vindicated him in 1859 but some parliamentarians still harassed him. Convinced that he could not efficiently fulfil his duties without the 'proper respect' of the assembly, he resigned in November 1860 and sailed for England. Deputations from parliament and the Public Works Department presented him with tokens of their esteem. One testimonial summed up his contribution: 'On your arrival in the colony railway communication was in a crude and unformed condition; under your administration . . . it has assumed a distinct and firmly established character. Electric telegraphs . . . have extended throughout the length and breadth of the land, affording facilities of intercourse and conducing to the public prosperity'.

A far-sighted and capable administrator, Martindale aimed at providing indispensable communications on a rational basis, unlike the politicians who saw roads and railways only in terms of votes and thereby brought his New South Wales career to an abrupt conclusion. In England he was appointed deputy inspector-general of fortifications. In 1862 he became director of the Barrack Department and later served on committees for army sanitation and military allowances. His rapid promotion and appointment of C.B. in 1871 show how highly the army esteemed him. As a colonel he resigned in June 1873 to become general manager of the London and St Katherine Docks Co.; he was made a director in 1889. Predeceased in 1902 by his wife Mary Elizabeth, née Knocker, he died on 26 May 1904 at Weston Lodge, Albury, Surrey. He was survived by at least two sons.

NSW Railway and Tramway Mag, 1 Dec 1920; *SMH*, 15 Jan 1861; *The Times*, 20 May 1904; information from Inst of Roy Engineers, Chatham, Kent.   G. J. ABBOTT

MASON, FRANCIS CONWAY (1843-1915), politician, was born on 21 February 1843 in County Fermanagh, Ireland, fourth son of John Mason, farmer, and his wife Ann, née Conway. Educated in Ireland and at St John's Wood, London, he was employed at the East India docks before he migrated to Melbourne about 1863. He was a schoolmaster, probably in a naval training ship, and living at Lygon Street when at the Church of St Francis on 30 July 1868 he married Henrietta Emily (1847-1936), daughter of William Dove; she was born in Hobart Town.

For some time Mason was an official visitor of metropolitan lunatic asylums and then turned to politics. He unsuccessfully contested the Avoca by-election in July 1870, and next February opposed the attorney-general, Archibald Michie [q.v.], for the seat of South Gippsland. The young newcomer spent six weeks in 'prosecuting his canvass energetically'; handsome and charm-

ing, he carefully made personal contact with many voters. He stressed that, unlike Michie, he would be able to devote 'the whole of his time' to representing South Gippslanders and knew the needs of the electorate for which he advocated specific and detailed proposals. He defeated the attorney-general by 180 votes to 150. He was defeated in 1877 but returned next year. Defeated again in 1886 he was re-elected in 1889. He supported Sir Graham Berry's [q.v.] policies on protection and the Constitution, voting with him in the crisis of 1878, and the attack on the constitutional reforms of the Service [q.v.] government. Mason also advocated legislative and financial assistance for selectors in difficult country, for whose problems he had much understanding. He kept in close touch with his constituents and often performed small errands for them in the metropolis.

Venal in a genial way, Mason was subject to rumours about his private life and criticism for failure to pay gambling debts. For the sake of both the electorate and himself he traded votes for public works with Thomas Bent [q.v.]; on 17 September 1894 the deal was exposed by the *Age* to defeat Bent. Mason did everything in his power to have the railway in South Gippsland extended and managed to have it routed beside his property. As a vice-president of the 1889-91 royal commission on coal, he spent excessive time on the possibilities of the meagre Foster coal deposits. He supported the Gillies [q.v.] government's railway bill of 1890, but when it was laid aside he crossed the floor to support Munro and Shiels. When Shiels formed a government in April 1892 Mason became chairman of committees by 'judicious canvassing'. He excelled in his new post. His capacity for exact analysis, concise expression, knowledge of parliamentary procedures and great tact enabled him to expedite the business of the bitterly contested tariff reform bill with a skill that earned admiration even from his opponents. Meanwhile he made it his business to 'feel his way among the members', and gained sufficient support to win election as Speaker after Berry lost his seat in October 1897.

Mason enjoyed immensely the eminence and the execution of his office. The House was in a period of decorum and he could look forward to the customary knighthood. Beatrice Webb described him as a 'worthy but vulgar individual' who had 'tried on three different occasions to entice Sidney to have a drink'. As Speaker he read the prorogation of 10 September 1902 after the unexpected defeat of the Irvine government. This formality was his 'political death warrant' as it was for many country members. While Speaker he had neglected his electorate and was defeated in the ensuing election. Although an active Catholic he was only slightly affected by his religion in parliament. He retired from politics and engaged in minor public works. He was not knighted, the first Speaker not to be so honoured, but was given a State funeral after he died at his home in South Yarra on 19 June 1915. He was buried in the Melbourne general cemetery with Roman Catholic rites. His wife, two sons and two married daughters survived him.

B. Webb, *The Webbs' Australian diary, 1898*, A. G. Austin ed (Melb, 1965); V&P (LA Vic), 1869, 2 (D8-10), 1890, 4 (168, 213), 1892-93, 1 (D2, D5); *Avoca Mail*, 23, 30 July 1870; *Gippsland Times*, 10 Jan 1871; *Federal Australian*, 10 May 1883, supp; *Table Talk*, 7 Oct 1892; *Herald* (Melb), 19 June 1915; *Age*, 21 June 1915; *Argus*, 21 June 1915.

BARRY COLLETT

MASSINA, ALFRED HENRY (1834-1917), printer, was born on 3 November 1834 at Stepney, London, son of Charles Edward Massina, artist, and his wife Susan. In April 1850 he was apprenticed to the London printing firm of Sydney Waterlow. In 1854 he married Frances Hemming, née Bridges, sailed with her for Victoria in the *George Marshall* and arrived at Port Phillip on 5 April 1855. Almost penniless he left his wife working in Melbourne to support herself and their baby son and made a luckless foray to the goldfields. He returned to Melbourne and was employed by W. H. Williams, printer. A fellow employee was Samuel V. Winter [q.v.] with whom Massina was later associated on the board of directors of the *Herald*, Melbourne.

In 1859 Massina joined with William Clarson, Joseph Shallard and Joseph T. Gibb to form the printing firm of Clarson, Shallard & Co. In 1866 Clarson and Gibb went to Sydney and the firm became Clarson, Massina & Co. Massina's son, Alfred Lionel, was admitted to partnership in 1868. After Shallard withdrew his financial interest in 1876 Richard John Foster and William Smith Mitchell were admitted as partners and the firm reconstructed as A. H. Massina & Co., which is still its name.

The firm engaged in publishing as well as printing. Its most famous publication was the *Australian Journal*, which gained overseas sales as well as finding its way to bush shanties and city homes throughout Australasia. The first issue, 2 September 1865, announced that 'the ablest COLONIAL pens of the day will be engaged on our staff. Historical Romances and Legendary Narratives of the old country will be mingled with tales of Venture and Daring in the new'. Adam Lindsay Gordon, Henry Kendall and Marcus Clarke [qq.v.] were 'able pens' who contributed to this magazine, which outlived Massina by many decades. His imprint on the firm was energetic application of sound business judgment rather than editorial work; he left the running of the *Australian Journal* to George Walstab [q.v.] and later to William Smith Wilson. However, Massina is credited with the decision to fund Marcus Clarke, then only 23, for visiting Tasmania in 1869 to gather material on the early convict days. In 1870 the *Australian Journal* commenced serialized publication of Clarke's powerful and brooding convict story, *His Natural Life*. Massina met deadlines and expected others to do so. He locked the brilliant and erratic author in an office, with sustaining drams of whisky, to force production of instalments for the magazine. Massina later gave this experience as his reason for disregarding business acumen and allowing a rival, George Robertson [q.v.], to take the profitable opportunity to publish the work in book form.

Massina's financial management ensured the firm's steady growth. Along with job printing it was sustained by popular publications which had originated in the 1860s. These included the *Australian Melodist*, a series of booklets of words of popular songs, and *Clarson, Massina & Co.'s Weather Almanac and General Guide and Handbook for Victoria*, to which a medical section was added and led to publication of *Dr. L. L. Smith's* [q.v.] *Medical Almanac*. The *Colonial Monthly* was a notable short-lived magazine issued in 1867 as a revamped version of the newly-acquired *Australian Monthly Magazine*. Clarke was again a contributor, as were Kendall and R. H. Horne [q.v.]. The magazine was sold in 1868 but the firm continued to print it. A notable later success was the collected poems of Adam Lindsay Gordon, published by A. H. Massina & Co. in 1877. It is known that Gordon owed the firm money for costs of printing his book *Ashtaroth* and Massina refused him a loan on the day of Gordon's suicide on 24 June 1870. Debate continues as to circumstances of Massina having rights to publish the poems.

In the early 1880s Massina's sons, William and Henry, joined the partnership. The decade saw a miscellany of new publications, ranging from *The Australian Merino* to *Men and How to Manage Them*. In addition the firm printed the *Sportsman*, then owned by Massina's friend S. V. Winter, and acquired by Massina in 1896. The lightweight *Massina's Penny Weekly* was issued from 1899 to 12 February 1901.

In 1891 Massina visited the United States and England. His observations led to A. H. Massina & Co. installing Victoria's first linotype machine in 1894. Its worth being proven, the machine was introduced to the *Herald* in 1895. By then he had released management of A. H. Massina & Co. to his son Alfred Lionel, and had given increasing attention to the *Herald*. Winter's Melbourne Newspaper Co. had obtained control of the *Herald* in the early 1870s and Massina is reputed to have given periodic financial support. He and W. L. Baillieu were directors who saw the *Herald* through the financial crisis of the early 1890s, and Massina was chairman by 1902.

In 1909 Massina retired from business, styled as 'hale, energetic and hearty', of 'frank bonhomie', yet one who 'has not . . . mingled in public life'. In 1864 he joined the Richmond Rifles Volunteer Corps, attaining the rank of captain, and later was a member of the Lillydale Shire Council. Overall he appears as a man who set wheels turning yet preferred to see that others ran them. His home was in Richmond, Melbourne: his retreat at Wandin.

Massina was an Anglican and a Mason. His first wife died in 1893. On 15 October 1898 he married Edith Elizabeth, née Hicks. He died on 4 February 1917 at Richmond. He had seven children, all by the first marriage. He was survived by his second wife, a son Henry and daughters, Fanny and Alice. He was buried in Boroondara cemetery. His estate was probated at £33,438.

R. G. Campbell, *The first ninety years: the printing house of Massina Melbourne 1859 to 1949* (Melb, 1949); *Cowans: the A'sian Printing and Stationery Mag*, Apr 1909; *Argus*, 5 Feb 1917; Affidavits and recognizances, newspaper registrations, Companies Branch (Registrar-General's Dept, Melb).   FRANK STRAHAN

MASTERS, GEORGE (1837-1912), entomologist, was born in July 1837 in Maidstone, Kent, England, son of George Masters, gardener, and his wife Matilda, née Terry. He became a gardener and about 1856 migrated to Melbourne. Interested in natural history, he was employed by Dr Godfrey Howitt [q.v.] for some two years. He collected insects in Tasmania and sold them to W. J. Macleay [q.v.]. By 1860 he was a gardener at Shepherd's Darling Nursery in Sydney. Recommended by Gerard Krefft [q.v.], Masters was sent by Macleay to Queensland to collect insects for him. In 1863-66 he exhibited thousands of insects before the new Entomological Society of New South Wales.

On 2 June 1864 Masters was appointed assistant curator and collector to the Australian Museum at a salary of £200, on condition that he sold his private collection and made no new one, an agreement he ignored. In the 1860s he travelled extensively in Queensland, New South Wales, South Australia, Lord Howe Island, Tasmania and Western Australia and in 1870 in the Snowy Mountains area and Queensland. He was a splendid shot, caught venomous snakes with his bare hands and was fearless in the bush and with Aboriginals. Masters made large collections which included a series of the newly-found Queensland lungfish, 'the preserved skin of a black gin', such rarities as the western bristle-bird and the noisy scrub bird, venomous snakes for Krefft and many thousand insects and invertebrates. At one stage he had collected more than half the natural history specimens in the museum. He also continued to collect for William Macleay and increased his own collection. In 1874 Masters testified against Krefft before the Legislative Assembly select committee inquiring into the Australian Museum. However, his evidence was inconsistent and he was embarrassed by questions about the woman whom he had taken on his Western Australian trip and represented as his wife.

Lured by a salary rise of £100 Masters became curator of the Macleay museum in January 1874. He travelled widely in New South Wales, beachcombed round Port Jackson and in the *Pea Hen* dredged up and down the coast for specimens. In 1875 he went on Macleay's *Chevert* expedition to New Guinea, where he found the first-known egg of the bird of paradise. In 1871-74 he published his *Catalogue of described Coleoptera of Australia* in parts and they were continued in 1885-87 in the *Proceedings of the Linnean Society of New South Wales* where he often exhibited his specimens. When the Macleay museum was transferred to the University of Sydney, Masters remained its curator until 1912. His unrivalled knowledge of the habits and life histories of Australian animals largely went unrecorded as he disliked writing.

Full-bearded and energetic, Masters had strong likes and dislikes. With age he suffered ill health and failing sight. After an accident in a cab on his way to Government House he died at Elizabeth Bay on 23 June 1912 and was buried in the Anglican section of Waverley cemetery. Predeceased by his first wife Matilda Elizabeth, née Hodges, on 20 May 1903 and their only child, he was survived by his second wife, a widow, Mary Jane Howard, née Franklin. Although reputed to own much property, he left an estate sworn for probate at £3300.

V&P (LA NSW), 1873-74, 5, 849, 876, 1875, 4, 276; G. P. Whitley, 'George Masters, naturalist', *Aust Zoologist*, 16 (1971) pt 2, and for bibliog.
                                                                  G. P. WHITLEY

MATE, THOMAS HODGES (1810-1894), grazier and store-keeper, was born on 5 April 1810 at Canterbury, England, son of Thomas Mate. At 23 he migrated to Sydney where he stayed for some months and then moved to the country to gain pastoral experience. On 8 February 1836 at St James's Church, Sydney, he married Maria Bardwell.

Mate bought a few sheep from H. H. Macarthur [q.v.] and in 1837 took up a run on Tarcutta Creek. His primitive homestead was half-way on the track between Sydney and Melbourne so he added an inn and store for travellers. Though the Aboriginals were then very numerous he avoided conflict by his kindness and faithful promises. By 1849 the Tarcutta school had sixteen children, four of them Mate's, and the station was well stocked with sheep and cattle. In 1850 he decided to open a general store at Albury. The town was then very small but it grew rapidly after gold was discovered and river transport was opened. As his emporium prospered he expanded as a wholesaler and had a bonded store. At first his store housed the post office and after 1858 a telegraph office but both moved to other premises in 1862.

Prominent in Albury's growth, Mate served on the Albury Hospital Committee and chaired a banquet to celebrate the opening of the bridge across the Murray on 2 September 1861. In 1859 he had contested the Hume electorate; as a squatters' candidate holding land on the Murrumbidgee and near Albury as well as Tarcutta he was beaten by three votes chiefly because floods prevented many country electors from voting. He won the seat in December 1860 and held it until November 1869. He sought in vain to confine John Robertson's [q.v.] free selection to settled areas instead of the whole colony but in 1866 succeeded in initiating a bill for preventing the careless use of fire which became law in April. As a supporter of the Martin [q.v.] ministry he helped to pass the Public Schools Act in December and was gazetted a magistrate of the territory.

From 1864 Mate was involved in much litigation mostly over land. His major holdings were Kulki near Urana and the Tumberumba and Brae's Springs runs near Albury and Tarcutta, which were managed by his sons. His store continued to expand and as mayor in November 1888 he was chosen to open the Albury market yards which soon attracted store cattle from all north-eastern Australia, especially after Victoria raised its stock tax. Predeceased by his first wife, Mate died at Manly from pneumonia on 22 July 1894 and was buried in the Anglican section of Waverley cemetery. He was survived by his second wife Florence, née Brown, whom he had married at Albury in 1882, and by three sons and four daughters of the first marriage and one daughter of the second. His probate was sworn at over £13,000. His firm is still the largest in Albury.

H. H. Peck, *Memoirs of a stockman* (Melb, 1942); G. L. Buxton, *The Riverina 1861-1891* (Melb, 1967); V&P (LA NSW), 1876-77, 3, 418, 1881, 3, 649; *Australasian*, 9 May 1868, 24 June 1876; *Pastoral Review*, 15 Aug 1894.
                                                                  CLIFF CHAMBERLAIN

MATHESON, JOHN (1821-1882), businessman, was born at Lairg, Sutherlandshire, Scotland, son of William Matheson, crofter, and his wife Anne. Two uncles who had been indigo planters in India and settled in Van Diemen's Land for health reasons invited John to visit them; in 1835 he went by fishing smack from Cromarty to London where he embarked for Tasmania. Until 1838 he worked in a merchant's office in Hobart Town. He then joined the Union Bank of Australia at its new Hobart branch as an accountant. One of the tellers he met was James Blackwood [q.v.]. In 1845 Matheson became the manager of the Geelong branch of the Union Bank and in 1851 was appointed to Melbourne.

Early in 1853 Matheson became first manager of the Bank of Victoria. As the new bank was the first with almost exclusively Victorian shareholders, he wrote to the government arguing that the existing banks in Melbourne were 'merely Branches of Banking Houses whose interests are not identical with those of the Colonists'. He asked for his bank to be given not only a share of government deposits but to be made the sole depository. The new bank wanted to manage the public debt and accept measures for the regulation of the issue of bank-notes 'under similar arrangements to those which characterize the relation between the Bank of England and the British Government'. Matheson did not achieve this high position for his bank but was soon made its first general manager. He held this position until his retirement in 1881, except when he visited England in 1859-61 to establish the bank's London office. In 1870-73 he had been a member of the royal commission inquiring into the state of the Victorian public service.

Matheson held several properties, the

most prominent being Moranghurk at Lethbridge, between Geelong and Ballarat, which
he acquired in stages after 1857; his
descendants held the property until 1953.
Matheson also held interests in Mount
Napier near Hamilton, Maryvale near
Casterton with his brother Robert, and
Kilfera in the Riverina. At St Kilda he
owned the stately home, St Leonards, which
became a fashionable boarding house early
in the twentieth century. A staunch Presbyterian, John was married to Flora Macdonald; they had four sons and four
daughters. Two sons died young and the
eldest son inherited Moranghurk. Matheson
died in Melbourne on 10 July 1882, leaving
an estate worth £250,000.

Self-educated, Matheson's success depended heavily on his skill in combining
banking with squatting when these pursuits
were probably the most profitable in Victoria. It was his good luck that he died
before the bursting in 1891 of the boom,
which had depended so heavily on lending
of short-term local and foreign funds on
long-term mortgage security. The bearers at
his funeral included not only his children
and Henry Miller [q.v.], the biggest shareholder of the Bank of Victoria, but also
James [q.v.] and Donald Munro who
suffered heavily when the bubble burst.

H. M. Humphreys (ed), *Men of the time in
Australia: Victorian series*, 1st ed (Melb, 1878);
P. L. Brown (ed), *Clyde Company papers*, 2-7
(Lond, 1952-71); G. Blainey, *Gold and paper:
a history of the National Bank of Australasia*
(Melb, 1958); V&P (LC Vic), 1853-54, 3 (D12);
Argus, 11 July 1882; *A'sian Insurance and
Banking Record*, 10 Aug 1882; *Australasian*,
7 Oct 1882; *Pastoral Review*, 15 Oct 1909; in-
formation from N. M. Matheson, Toorak.

RAOUL F. MIDDELMANN

MATHEWS, ROBERT HAMILTON
(1841-1918), surveyor and anthropologist,
was born on 21 April 1841 at Narellan, New
South Wales, son of William Mathews and
his wife Jane, née Holmes. His early years
were spent at Narellan and from 1850 on
his father's property south of Goulburn. He
was educated by a tutor and later by his
father who was a classicist. Against his own
inclinations towards the university and a
profession, he remained on the land. His
introduction to surveying came when he
assisted Deering's party on the main South
Road in 1866-67, and worked with Kennedy
and Jamieson on the northern rail route to
Tamworth in 1867-69. In July 1870 he
topped his examinations as a licensed
surveyor.

Mathews worked in northern New South
Wales, surveying in the far west and in

New England for twenty years. On 4 July
1872 at Tamworth he married Mary Sylvester Bartlett. In the 1880s they lived at
Singleton and in 1882-83 visited America,
Britain and Europe. Mathews became a
justice of the peace for Queensland, South
Australia in 1875 and New South Wales
in 1883 and was coroner at Singleton. He
lived at Parramatta after 1889 where he
acted as deputy coroner, and wrote *Handbook to Magisterial Inquiries and Coroners'
Inquests*, which was issued in several
editions.

As a surveyor in northern New South
Wales Mathews had an unrivalled oppor-
tunity to observe the remnants of traditional
Aboriginal life and customs in areas rapidly
opening to settlement; his curiosity soon
developed into close observation and record.
In the 1890s he first published his studies,
with work on Aboriginal rock art in the
Singleton district. Encouraged by W. D.
Campbell, he prepared a paper on rock art
which was awarded the medal of the Royal
Society of New South Wales in 1894.
Retiring from surveying in the early 1890s
he devoted his last years to anthropology and
hoped eventually to complete a full-scale
work on the Aboriginals. His field investigations produced research data on linguistics,
social structure, ceremonial life, customs and
art. He travelled widely to interview informants and also had a full correspondence
in Australia and beyond. By character
reticent, methodical and independent, he
prided himself on ascertaining his facts from
the Aboriginals themselves, and testing all
accepted theories. Although he was a
member of the Presbyterian Church and
versed in biblical literature, his interest in
Aboriginal beliefs and ceremonial seem to
have been inspired by anthropology.

Mathews was one of many enthusiasts,
mostly with little or no formal training in
anthropology, concerned with recording
Aboriginal culture. His reports on ceremonial life and language are invaluable,
often the only record for large areas of
northern New South Wales. He also studied
and wrote on the tribes of the Northern
Territory and Central Australia. He published some two hundred papers, with an
impressive range of overseas publications,
at a time of immense national and international interest in the Australian
Aboriginals. A corresponding member of
the Anthropological Society of Paris, he was
awarded its Godard silver medal.

Mathews's views on the social structure,
descent systems and marriage laws in
Aboriginal society differed from those
accepted by Alfred Howitt, Lorimer Fison
[qq.v.] and Baldwin Spencer. They
questioned his field methods and his inter-

pretation of data. Some of these controversies cannot now be resolved for lack of evidence, while in other areas his ideas are now more readily acceptable to anthropologists, for example his use of the term 'section' and his conclusions on marriage laws. His work remains a vital contribution to knowledge.

The large-scale work he planned was not completed when he died at Parramatta on 22 May 1918, but his papers remain sufficient tribute to his enthusiasm for his self-imposed task. Survived by his wife, four sons and a daughter, he was buried in the Presbyterian section of the Parramatta cemetery.

J. Greenway, *Bibliography of the Australian Aborigines* (Syd, 1963); A. P. Elkin, 'The development of scientific knowledge of the Aborigines', *Australian Aboriginal studies*, H. Shiels ed (Melb, 1963); W. S. Dun, 'Presidential address', Roy Soc NSW, *Procs*, 53 (1919); information from Professor D. J. Mulvaney, ANU, and Mr and Mrs F. M. Mathews, Bayview, NSW.   ISABEL MCBRYDE

MATTHEWS, DANIEL (1837-1902), missionary, was born on 28 February 1837 at Truro, Cornwall, England, fifth child of John Matthews, master mariner, and his wife Honor, née Williams. He was educated at church schools in Truro and St Ives and the Wesleyan College, Taunton. With his mother and brother William he joined his father on the Victorian goldfields in 1853. After some success at the Bendigo diggings they moved to South Melbourne. Daniel became a temperance worker. After teaching at Geelong he moved to Echuca with his brother in 1864 and opened a store to provision river steamers. He championed detribalized Aboriginals living about the town and across the Murray River in Moama. With William he selected three blocks with an 800-acre river frontage on John O'Shanassy's [q.v.] Moira lease in 1865-68. In 1869 Matthews visited England but failed to get financial help for the mission from his eldest brother John.

In 1870 Daniel and William gave twenty acres for an Aboriginal village and school which they called Maloga. In June 1872 at Port Melbourne Daniel married Janet, daughter of Rev. Kerr Johnston. The Maloga Mission School was started in 1874 and Janet became its chief voluntary worker. It was nonsectarian and received limited help from private persons, some rations from the Victorian Board for the Protection of the Aborigines and a few grants from the New South Wales government. Matthews publicized the plight of the Aboriginals by visiting Sydney, constant lobbying, writing to the press and addressing meetings. In 1880 he helped to form the New South Wales Aborigines Protection Association. From 1883 the new Aborigines Protection Board provided funds for Maloga but Matthews received no salary until 1885. In 1883, through petitions signed by educated Aboriginals from Maloga, he had 1800 acres of river frontage near Barmah declared an Aboriginal reserve, Cumeroogunga.

Unpopular with the younger generation because of his insistence on early rising, daily prayer and no alcohol, Matthews also faced hostility from local squatters and later from the Victorian Board for the Protection of the Aborigines and a faction of the New South Wales Aborigines Protection Association. The trouble culminated when the association removed the Maloga buildings to Cumeroogunga, three miles upstream, and put its own officers in charge. After a visit to England with two Aboriginal converts Matthews was the victim of a determined smear campaign in 1890. Though the Maloga property and homestead reverted to his elder brother in 1895 Matthews carried on the mission; the number of inmates had varied from fifty to two. From 1876 he had published annual reports, including excerpts from his daily diaries. For a time his base was Beulah House on the southern side of the Murray, where he took in displaced half-castes. In 1900 the last Maloga report was issued from Barry Parade, Carlton. It was succeeded by the *Australian Aborigines' Friend*, a monthly which appeared until 1902.

In 1899 Janet began the Metco and Manunka Missions near Mannum, South Australia. One of Matthews's last acts was to obtain the near-by 40-acre Forster reserve on behalf of the Aboriginals. With great courage Matthews could not be intimidated and made bitter enemies among officials. In his last decade he found every door closed against him besides suffering unfounded imputations against his honesty. As an itinerant preacher he travelled widely in Queensland, New South Wales, Victoria and South Australia in an old Cobb & Co. coach with two horses, carrying the 'Maloga Quartette', an Aboriginal singer and three of his children. Matthews died at Mannum on 17 February 1902 from entero-colitis and was buried in the Mannum cemetery, survived by his wife, one son and three daughters. Janet carried on the Mannum mission until 1911 and died in Adelaide on 25 September 1939.

J. B. Gribble, *Black but comely* (Lond, 1884); E. R. Gribble, *Forty years with the Aborigines* (Syd, 1930); R. R. Morgan, *Reminiscences of the Aboriginal station at Cummeragunga*

(Melb, 1952); E. G. Docker, *Simply human beings* (Brisb, 1964); S. Priestley, *Echuca: a centenary history* (Brisb, 1965); Board for the Protection of the Aborigines, Letters 1878-98 (held by Aborigines' Welfare Board, Melb); Matthews papers and Parkes letters (ML); Aust hist records cat under Coronderrk (LaTL); newspaper cuttings under Aboriginal Affairs (ML); J. Matthews papers (SAA); Norman family papers (held by Miss R. Norman, Adel).

NANCY CATO

MAT(T)HEWS, JULIA (1842-1876), actress, was born on 14 December 1842 in London, daughter of James Mathews, sailor and artificial flower maker, and his wife Sarah, née Irviner, music teacher. Julia was taught dancing by her mother and went with her parents to Sydney, where on 28 August 1854 she made her début at the Royal Victoria Theatre, impersonating Little Pickles in *Spoiled Child*. After some training as a singer she joined a light opera company to tour the Victorian goldfields. At Beechworth she is said to have attracted R. O'H. Burke [q.v.].

Julia made a most successful entrance to the Melbourne stage in the second of two plays shown at Coppin's [q.v.] Olympic Theatre on 24 August 1855. In the farce *Old and Young* she impersonated four characters of widely diverse temperaments: in the first affectionate and engaging; in the next boisterous; in the third a self-willed young gourmand; and an exquisitely provoking precocity in the last. Coppin had made a find. In October she was Arthur in his production *King John*, playing a difficult part with propriety and pathos. By January 1856 she had become a favourite with Melbourne audiences, surpassing herself as the duke of York in a burlesque *Richard ye Third*. Still little more than a child she was said to have exhibited surprising versatility, and a golden future was predicted. In 1858 she made a second appearance on the goldfields.

Julia was playing at the Princess Theatre in Melbourne in August 1860 when Burke proposed marriage to her. She was then well known as a soprano singer 'whose auburn curls and charming voice captured his heart'. Burke was about to start on his disastrous expedition to cross the continent. Julia refused him but on hearing that the expedition was in difficulty she was one of the first to approach the *Argus* to agitate for a search party.

On 17 September 1863 Julia was given a benefit by the Melbourne Garrick and Orpheus Clubs at the Princess before she left for New Zealand. Warmly received by a crowded house she was presented with an illuminated address and a handsome gold bracelet; at the end she spoke her lines of farewell, specially written for the occasion by W. M. Akhurst. At Dunedin on 23 April 1864 she married her New Zealand manager, William Mumford; they had three children.

In 1867 Coppin presented her at Sydney's Prince of Wales Theatre under vice-regal patronage and also at a command performance for the duke of Edinburgh. With her parents and family she left for England and on 18 November won distinction as the first Australian-trained singer to appear at Covent Garden Opera House. She played the part of the duchess in an English version of Offenbach's *La Grande-Duchesse de Gerolstein*. Australian papers reported high tributes from the London press but one review described her as 'a lady newly-arrived from Australia whose vocal powers are not at all remarkable but who is lively and clever as an actress'.

The only value that Mumford placed on his wife was as 'a machine for grinding out golden sovereigns for him to waste in drink and debauchery'. She bore with his failings till patience wore out and in 1870 obtained a judicial separation. Her father was careful to save sufficient money to keep her children from want, but he died in 1874, leaving his wife to sustain the family while Julia toured Europe and America under various managers mostly in *opéra bouffe*. She was devoted to her father and became a devout Catholic after his death. At St Louis, Missouri, she contracted a malarial disease and died in Mullanphy Hospital on 19 May 1876.

A. Bagot, *Coppin the great* (Melb, 1965); *Empire*, 29 Aug 1854; *Illustrated Sydney News*, 23 Sept 1854; *Argus*, 25 Aug, 9 Oct 1855, 21 Jan 1856, 17 Sept 1863, 21 June 1876; *Illustrated London News*, 23 Nov 1867; *The Times*, 20 Nov 1867; *Aust J*, 1 Feb 1868; *St Louis Despatch*, 20 May 1876; *St Louis Daily Globe Democrat*, 21 May 1876; *Era* (Lond), 28 May 1876; *Entr'acte*, 3 June 1876.

JEAN GITTINS

MATTHEWS, WILLIAM (1833-1890), schoolteacher, was born in November 1833 in Devon, England, son of William Veale Matthews and his wife Margaret, née Kiddle. He arrived in Sydney about 1855 and married Margaret McLeod at Carcoar in 1856. In 1860 he began teaching under the Board of National Education and by 1864 was in the Hunter Valley as headmaster of the Maitland Model School.

In the 1860s and 1870s Matthews was prominent in short-lived teachers' organizations to which the board gave limited tolerance and encouragement. In 1864-65 he was secretary of the Hunter River National

Teachers' Mutual Improvement Society and in 1874 secretary of the new Teachers' Association of New South Wales, the most vigorous of the teachers' associations before the late 1890s. The association's journal published unsubstantiated charges of prejudice and injustice against inspectors, and the Council of Education decided to punish four teachers: the president, Frederick Bridges [q.v.]; the vice-president; the author of the charges; and Matthews who was to be suspended for three months and transferred to a country school. The punishments were reduced to three-week suspensions after abject apologies were made. The association soon disappeared, partly because teachers were frightened of official displeasure but mainly because they would not accept the official definition of their role and were only encouraged to discuss scholastic matters but not salaries and conditions of work.

Matthews was not cowed by this experience and after a few months as headmaster at Glebe explained to Wilkins [q.v.] that he could not hold the usual school exhibition because he did not have the money. His salary of £150 was supplemented by over £200 from pupils' fees but changes in regulations and the scale of fees had reduced his total income by almost £150. In March 1875 he was forced to sequestrate his estate which was not released until 1889. For a time he was less prominent in teachers' affairs but became secretary to a large meeting of teachers called in 1883 to protest about new regulations under the 1880 Public Instruction Act.

Although the Act stabilized and increased teachers' incomes, they remained unprotected against administrative authority, and in 1887 Matthews was blamed for the falling attendance at his school. The inspectors alleged that he was an unpopular and inefficient teacher, but he asserted that reductions were caused by the opening of new schools, departure of Catholic pupils, bad weather and economic recessions. He pleaded against demotion to a smaller school: he had a good record, was in bad health, had sunk his savings in a property at Fairfield and had not received a fair hearing in the dispute. He found that the 1884 Civil Service Act did not apply to teachers, but in September 1887 he was moved to Macquarie Street South with his salary reduced from £400 to £336 a year. His health deteriorated and next year he was granted early retirement. A Freemason, he died on 28 December 1890 and was buried in the Anglican section of Rookwood cemetery. He was survived by his wife, two daughters and five of their seven sons. His estate was valued at £967.

Aust J of Education, 1868-70; *J of Primary Education*, 1871-73; Teachers' Assn of NSW, *J of Primary Education*, 1873-74; B. Mitchell, A history of public school teachers' organisations in New South Wales, 1855 to 1945 (Ph.D. thesis, ANU, 1969); Council of Education, minute book and out-letter book 1874 (NSWA); William Street School files 1887 (NSWA).

BRUCE MITCHELL

MAUGHAN, JAMES (1826-1871), Methodist New Connexion minister, was born on 25 October 1826 at Hebburn, County Durham, England, son of James Maughan and his wife Isabella. He was still an infant when his father died and his mother remarried. They moved to Seaton, north of Newcastle upon Tyne, where in 1838 James enjoyed a year's schooling under an Anglican minister. Next year he resolved to go to work and study at night school. Insufficient sleep led to poor health and in 1840 he contracted rheumatic fever. In 1842 he joined the Methodist New Connexion and in 1844 became a local preacher. In 1847 when the minister in the Mossley circuit, Lancashire, became ill Maughan took his place and at the next conference was made a minister on probation. He served in the Bradford, Macclesfield, Derby and Dewsbury circuits before being received into the full ministry in 1852. For two years in London his intelligent preaching doubled the membership and led to the building of a second New Connexion Chapel. He then served for two years in Leeds and three in Dudley where he worked with the Wesleyans and other Methodist groups in a united Sunday school and helped to raise funds for enlarging the building. In 1859 he was appointed to Castle Green Church, Bristol, where he attracted prominent notice by preaching on such subjects as a local fire disaster, the appearance of a comet and against sham war-making at voluntary reviews. At Stockport on 8 March 1854 he had married Catherine Moss.

In May 1862 Maughan was dedicated for service in Australia and with his wife and four children he left Liverpool in the *Blanche Moore*. For his Sunday services and scientific lectures fellow passengers presented him with a piece of scientific equipment when the ship reached Melbourne on 1 September. He found the cost of living too high in Melbourne and Ballarat so decided to make his headquarters in Adelaide where he found the largest number of his denomination. He held his first services on 21 December and continued to preach in public rooms until a new church was opened on 12 December 1864 in Franklin Street. Two other chapels were built outside Adelaide and a new mission house was built in Whitmore Square on land provided by G. F. Angas [q.v.]. Maughan won great respect by his paper, 'The Drainage of Adelaide', read to the Adelaide Philosophical Society on 15 August 1865 and by his public lecture in 1866 on 'Mr. Baxter, Louis Napoleon, the coming struggle, and Christ's second advent'. However, his health was undermined and to recuperate he decided to visit England. He left in April 1869 with his friend, Samuel Way, who was eminent in Bible Christian circles. In England they tried to amalgamate the two denominations but without immediate success. While under treatment for congested lungs Maughan ignored the advice of his doctors and insisted on preaching often and in widely separated places on his Australian work. Although he greatly helped the cause in South Australia he damaged his health. He returned to Adelaide in October 1870 but within four months a bronchial attack prevented him from preaching. He died on 8 March 1871 and was buried in West Terrace cemetery, leaving an estate of less than £900. His wife died at Malvern on 2 August 1911, after long and unobtrusive work for philanthropy. She was survived by a daughter and three sons.

A tablet in his memory was subscribed by his congregation and was erected at the church named after him.

W. Cooke, *The man of all work* (Lond, 1872); B. Gregory, *Side lights on the conflicts of Methodism . . . 1827-1852* (Lond, 1899); J. M. Witherow, *Church rebels and pioneers* (Lond, 1928); *Observer* (Adel), 31 Jan 1863; *Register* (Adel), 9-12 Mar 1871.   F. HAMBLY*

MAULT, ALFRED (1829-1902), engineer and civil servant, was born in South India. Exceptionally well educated, he became a competent linguist and acquired some knowledge of public health, arts and mathematics. As a civil engineer he helped to build part of the Glasgow and south-west railway near Kilmarnock, the Neilston and Barrhead branch and the Caledonian railway near Rutherglen. For some time he lived at Coventry, designing and building waterworks, and wrote a textbook for Macmillans on *Natural Geometry* (London, 1877). He then moved to France and as chief engineer designed and built railways for the *Compagnie Anglaise* which also held the concession for the sewerage of Paris.

With high testimonials Mault applied to the Tasmanian government for engineering work in November 1882 and was appointed to undertake the 'parliamentary' survey for the Derwent Valley railway, the route of which had been a subject of local acrimony since 1880. He arrived in 1883 and soon made a satisfactory survey. In November he was appointed to undertake the engineering survey and in December to superintend the works. In 1886 a royal commission on railways and public works criticized his quantity surveys 'as inefficiently performed'; despite his zest for economy some piers and abutments had to be rebuilt. In July Mault was appointed to the Central Board of Health as engineering inspector at a salary of £350. He soon condemned the sanitation of Hobart and submitted two plans, one for open drainage to cost £20,000 with annual maintenance of £16,300, the other for closed underground drainage to cost £60,000 with maintenance of £7000. He then made plans on the sanitation of Launceston. In 1889 he planned water supplies for several northern towns and sanitation for New Norfolk.

In December 1890 Mault heard that the seventh International Congress of Hygiene and Demography was to be held in London in August 1891, and recommended Tasmania be represented. The premier was not impressed but when he learnt of Mault's 'eminent service with English and Parisian Drainage Works' he submitted Mault's name to the agent-general who passed it on to the organizing committee of the congress. On 23 March 1891 Mault was invited to attend the congress and as a vice-president in the engineering section to send a copy of his paper. Meanwhile he had gone to the mining areas of Strahan and Mount Zeehan. On his return he accepted the invitation on 16 May and submitted his report, 'Sanitation of a mining settlement, Mount Zeehan'. The government agreed to give him leave and £300 under the Public Health Act. He left Hobart on 27 June and in Melbourne and Adelaide talked to officers of the boards of health and public works. He arrived in London on 3 August and returned in June 1892, with many papers on the congress and the latest developments in Europe.

From July 1886 Mault had acted as secretary to the Central Board of Health without salary but with one clerk. Among other things he had to report on outbreaks of smallpox, diphtheria and even one case of leprosy. In April 1888 his salary as engineering inspector was reduced to £300. On 6 October 1891 he asked for more pay, submitting that much of his work was unpleasant, that local boards absorbed most of his time and that he was paid at the same rate as second clerks in other departments. The government replied that the financial position and his unofficial duties justified the reduction; later his salary was raised to £325. At the Australasian Association for the Advancement of Science Congress at Hobart in 1892 he lectured on 'Sewage of a Seaside Town' to the section on sanitary science and hygiene, at the 1893 congress in Adelaide as president of the section he lectured on 'Urban Sanitation' and at the 1902 congress served as secretary to the section.

Mault had been elected a member of the Royal Society of Tasmania on 8 September 1884 and his first paper, read on 13 October, described his careful observations of the Derwent River. He presented papers on 'Natural Geometry' and Hobart's drainage in 1886, and in 1889 Hobart's tides, 'Detention of Flinders at Mauritius' and 'Notes on Charts of the coast of Tasmania', copied from the Hydrographical Department in Paris. His later papers ranged from Tasman's charts, which he had copied at the British Museum in 1892, to Antarctic exploration and practical forestry. He was elected to the society's council in 1901. He died of cancer at his home in Holebrook Place, Hobart, on 16 November 1902 and his funeral service at All Saints Church was well attended, the chief secretary ordering by telegraph from Launceston a handsome wreath.

V&P (HA Tas), 1886 (64, 139), 1887 (136), 1889 (83, 114, 130, 137), 1891 (54, 86a); *Mercury*, 17 Dec 1902; CSD 16/29/491, 19/10/75, 22/26/182.

MAUND, JOHN (1823-1858), physician and analytical chemist, was born on 12 March 1823 at Bromsgrove, Worcestershire, England, eldest son of Benjamin Maund (1790-1863) and his wife Sarah. Benjamin was a chemist, botanist, fellow of the Linnean Society (1827) and author and publisher of such periodicals as the *Botanic Garden*.

Never physically robust, Maund's early education was largely private. He chose a career in medicine and began his training as a surgical apprentice at Prescot, Lancashire. He then studied at the University of Glasgow with academic distinction and was appointed assistant surgeon to the St Pancras Infirmary, London. He gained the qualifying diploma of the Royal College of Surgeons on 7 August 1845 and spent most of the next year attending hospitals and lectures in Paris. On his return he obtained by examination the licentiate of the Society of Apothecaries of London. He practised briefly at Brecon, Wales, and on his father's urging from 1848 at Harlow, Essex. In August 1849 he was awarded a doctorate in medicine at the University of St Andrews. Finding his health affected by the climate and type of work, he decided in 1851 to migrate to Victoria and practise there as an analytical chemist. He sold his practice, studied chemistry in London in 1852 and received certificates from the Royal College of Chemistry and the Polytechnic Chemical School.

Maund sailed with his sister in the *Janet Mitchell* and arrived at Melbourne on 3 January 1853. The sickness on board and ashore provided enough work to induce him to recommence a medical practice. He rented a house at 189 Lonsdale Street East until May 1857 when he built a house at 53 La Trobe Street East. His practice grew rapidly because he added professional skill and knowledge to his kindliness and devotion.

Maund was admitted to the University of Melbourne (M.D., *ad eund*, 1857). He had become a member of the Victoria Medical Association and helped to achieve its union on 18 July 1855 with the rival Medico-Chirurgical Society of Victoria to form the Medical Society of Victoria. He served on the committee and as a secretary of the society, and on 25 August was first to propose its journal. He and Joseph Black were appointed founding editors of the *Australian Medical Journal* which was published next year. In 1856 Maund initiated and convened a strong sub-committee to promote the society's views on medical registration and the establishment of a medical board. Moved by the desperate plight in childbirth of many poor women, he and R. T. Tracy [q.v.] determined to establish an institution for their care. They leased a house in August 1856 at 41 Albert Street, East Melbourne, and, supported by a committee of women headed by Frances, wife of Bishop Perry [q.v.], founded the Melbourne Lying-in Hospital (later Royal Women's Hospital). Maund presented the first statistical report of the hospital in the *Australian Medical Journal* in 1857, one of several medical papers which he published.

Maund was appointed by the government to the new office of analytical chemist. His most important work was water analysis on the Yan Yean scheme. In July 1854 he was a founding councillor of the Victorian Institute for the Advancement of Science and read and had published papers on the deterioration of grain and flour, on the mineral water of Victoria and on the water of the Plenty River. In 1855 he was active in amalgamating this society with the Philosophical Society to form the Philosophical Institute. He died from acute enteritis on 3 April 1858 and was buried in the Melbourne general cemetery. He was not married and the sister who had cared for him returned to England. His house was sold to Edward Barker [q.v.] and his practice taken over by J. G. Beaney [q.v.]. A staunch Anglican, he was also a Freemason of the Meridian Lodge of St John. F. Mueller [q.v.] made a graceful tribute to his friend Maund in his *Fragmenta Phytographiae Australiae* (Melbourne, 1858-64) and named after him a new genus of the rush family, *Juncaginaceae Maundia*.

A memorial window is in the parish church at Bromsgrove, Worcester, and a portrait, commissioned posthumously by the Medical Society of Victoria and painted by Nicholas Chevalier [q.v.], is in the Royal Women's Hospital.

C. E. Sayers, *The Women's* (Melb, 1956); *Aust Medical J*, July 1858, p194; H. B. Graham, 'Happenings of the now long past: the centenary of the Medical Society of Victoria', *MJA*, 16 Aug 1952; *Age*, 5 Apr 1858; *Argus*, 6 Apr 1858.   FRANK M. C. FORSTER

MAURICE, PRICE (1818-1894), pastoralist, was born at Wrexham, Denbighshire, Wales. Well educated, he was offered a post in the East India Co. but declined. He migrated to South Australia, paying his passage in the *Caleb Angas*, and arrived at Port Adelaide on 9 August 1840. The province was then entering depression and he bought a horse to look around cautiously. In 1843 he took up an occupation licence on the River Gilbert and bought lambing ewes. As his flock multiplied he turned north and acquired the leases of Pekina and Oladdie, 671 square miles near Tarcowie. In New South Wales he bought breeding cattle and overlanded them to Pekina, his head station. He also leased the runs of Warrow, Lake Hamilton and Bramfield, 943 square miles on the Port Lincoln Peninsula. By 1865 he had 215,000 sheep and over 3500 bales of wool but within ten years the best parts of his leases were resumed for agricultural selection. In 1874 he took up the 5358 square miles of Mount Eba station, 270 miles north of Port Augusta. The run was isolated and the rainfall very uncertain but despite high cost he sank 83 wells of which 36 yielded water. He also held an annual race meeting partly to attract shearers.

At Mount Barker on 1 January 1849 Maurice married Matilda Brown; they had four sons and a daughter. In 1854 his wife's sister Hannah (b. 1844) was taken into the home and adopted. In 1862 Maurice and family toured Europe. In 1870 he bought the Castambul estate, 5300 acres in the Adelaide Hills near Morialta, and stocked it with Angora goats from Turkey. His wife died in 1881 and Hannah looked after him. Overwork and anxiety broke his health and he returned to Britain, leaving his leases in the hands of an agent. For £18,000 Maurice bought Mauriceville, Eaton Gardens, West Brighton, which he left to Hannah with £20,000 in bonds of a Queensland bank and an annuity of £500 when he died aged 76 on 10 May 1894. Apart from his South Australian land and livestock valued at over £250,000, he left £80,000. His will was

proved on 14 July by the High Court of the United Kingdom and sent to South Australia for resealing. In England his children contested the payment of dues to the colonial government before the estate was sold and the proceeds divided, but pleaded in vain. His third son Richard Thelwall won repute as an explorer and his only daughter Laura Matilda married Baron de Montimart.

R. Cockburn, *Pastoral pioneers of South Australia*, 1 (Adel, 1925); *75 Law Times* 415; *Observer* (Adel), 19 May 1894, 11 Apr 1896.

MAY, FREDERICK (1840-1897), engineer and manufacturer, was born in Perranzabuloe, Cornwall, England, eldest son of Henry May, copper miner, and his wife Mary Ann. His formal education was meagre and he worked in the mines from an early age. He sailed with his parents, four brothers and a sister for South Australia in the *Melbourne* and arrived on 6 December 1858. The family settled at Burra, a copper-mining centre, but moved to Wallaroo soon after copper was discovered there in 1860. May was employed at both places on the construction and installation of mining machinery. At Wallaroo he was appointed engineer of the smelting works and at 23 superintending engineer at the Moonta mine. This mine became one of the most efficient and technically sophisticated in Australia, a tribute to May's ability as well as the intelligent management of the company and Captain Hancock [q.v.].

In February 1874 May became a partner in James Martin [q.v.] & Co. at Gawler. The firm's expansion into mining machinery and general engineering owed much to May's skill. In March 1885 the partnership was dissolved and he started his own business with his brother Alfred as manufacturers of agricultural implements, but specialized in mining and smelting machinery, the demand for which rose rapidly with the discovery of Broken Hill and Western Australian mines. In the 1890s the firm employed up to 250 men. May devoted himself to improving machinery for separating the sulphide ores mined at Broken Hill and his concentration machinery with its patent plunger jigs was widely adopted. After extensive trials Broken Hill Proprietary Co. Ltd chose May's machinery for its new concentration plant in 1896. His firm also supplied much of the machinery and equipment for B.H.P.'s smelters at Port Pirie where a branch factory was established.

May had a keen interest in technical education and served on the council of the Gawler School of Mines. He was also a councillor in the Gawler Corporation and a vice-president of the Gawler Agricultural Society. He was twice married: first, at Bingo mines on 14 September 1862 to Mary Ann Mitchell (d. 1896) by whom he had five sons and three daughters; and second, at Laura on 14 October 1897 to Margaret Maxwell Diek. May relaxed from oversight of his works but died of a heart attack at Semaphore on 15 December aged 57. He was given an impressive burial in Willaston cemetery.

E. H. Coombe (ed), *History of Gawler 1837 to 1908* (Adel, 1910); M. Williams, 'Gawler: the changing geography of a South Australian country town', *Aust Geographer*, 9 (1964); *Bunyip* (Gawler), 24 Dec 1897; *Observer* (Adel), 30 Dec 1897.   J. B. HIRST

MAY, PHILIP WILLIAM (1864-1903), black and white artist, was born on 27 April 1864 at New Wortley, Leeds, England, second son of Philip May (d. 1873), brass-founder, and his wife Sarah Jane (d. 1912), née Macarthy. His grandfather, Charles Hugh May, was a landowner and squire of Whittington, Derbyshire. His father had been apprenticed to the engineers, George and Robert Stephenson, and his mother came from a family with theatrical connexions.

Phil was educated in Leeds at St George's School in 1872-75, the Oxford Lane School in 1876-77 and the Park Lane Board School in 1877. At 13 he was forced by his father's reduced finances to work in a solicitor's office which he soon found uncongenial. He also worked for an estate agent, in a music store and as time-keeper in an ironfoundry. At 14 he was invited to do some drawings for the Yorkshire *Gossip*, a short-lived comic weekly, and later for the *Yorkshire Busy Bee*. In 1877 he joined a touring theatrical company managed by Fred Stimpson. His main duty was to provide six posters at 12s. a week. He also had to play small parts and made his first professional appearance at the Spa Theatre, Scarborough. In 1883 he was again in Leeds designing costumes for the Christmas pantomime at the Grand Theatre.

Early in 1884 May went to London where he led a precarious and impoverished existence. On 21 April the proprietor of a photo shop near Charing Cross published a print of May's drawing of the actors Irving, Toole, and Bancroft; the winter number of *Society* carried a double page drawing by May, entitled 'The Seven Ages of Society'. Disheartened by his lack of success May had returned to Leeds when William Allison, editor of the *St Stephen's Review*, commissioned him to illustrate the special Christmas number. From the spring number

of 1885 the magazine regularly used illustrations, and May was taken on to the staff at £8 a week. About this time he married Lilian, widow of Charles Farrer. May's drawings were appearing in the *Penny Illustrated Paper*, the *Pictorial World* and the *St Stephen's Review* when in the autumn he met W. H. Traill [q.v.], who was seeking new artists in England for the Sydney *Bulletin*. May accepted a contract for £20 a week and sailed with his wife in the *Orient*, reaching Sydney on 29 December.

In Sydney May manifested a Bohemian pattern of life with many friends in theatrical and artistic circles. His drawings first appeared in the *Bulletin* in January 1886 and continued regularly until late in 1888 and spasmodically thereafter until 1894. Many were of a political character, often aimed at such well-known personalities as John Robertson, Henry Parkes [qq.v.] and George Reid. Others depended on the observation of social types, as in the series entitled 'Things We See When We Go Out without our Gun'. At their best they combined satire, sympathy and accurate detail. Altogether May produced over 800 drawings for the *Bulletin*.

May's Australian sojourn was no more than a transitory episode. In late 1888 his contract with the *Bulletin* expired and he decided to return to England despite offers of a renewed contract at a substantially increased salary. With his fare subsidized by £1000 from Theodore Fink of Melbourne, May and his wife sailed in the *Orizaba*, disembarking at Naples. After a brief stay in Rome he returned to England but soon moved to Paris, where he shared a studio with Henry Thompson, and numbered among his friends William Rothenstein, Charles Conder [q.v.], and John Longstaff. He settled in London in 1890 and renewed connexion with the *St Stephen's Review*. Probably his importance for it were the illustrations to the series, 'The Parson and the Painter'; in 1891 they were published in book form and the rapid sale of 30,000 copies assured May's fame and reputation.

May's first drawings for the weekly *Graphic* had already appeared on 12 November 1890. On 10 October 1891 it printed his sketch of Arthur Roberts in *Joan of Arc* at the Gaiety Theatre, and in 1893 sent May and E. S. Grew on a world tour to make travel notes and sketches. But May refused to travel beyond Chicago and returned to London on 6 May. In February 1895 he joined *Punch* and by 1896 was its chief pictorial humorist.

May firmly established himself as the leading black and white artist and his work appeared in most of the illustrated publications. In a number of interviews he ascribed the development of his style to the inadequacies of the *Bulletin's* printing machines; A. G. Stephens contested the justice of these comments, but in Australia May first developed the economic and vigorous mastery of penmanship which was his special trademark, and black and white pen drawing remained his real *métier*. In 1892 some of his work was collected in the first *Phil May's Illustrated Winter Annual*. Through thirteen winter editions and three extra summer numbers, the annuals appeared until 1905. In 1895 he published *Phil May's Sketch Book*, in 1896 *Phil May's Guttersnipes*, in 1897 *Phil May's A.B.C.*, and in 1904 the album, *Phil May in Australia*, appeared with an introduction by A. G. Stephens.

In January 1903 May fell ill and died childless of phthisis on 5 August at his home in Melina Place, St John's Wood. On his deathbed he was given the last rites of the Roman Catholic Church. Buried in the cemetery of St Mary's Church, Kensal Green, he was survived by his wife who later remarried.

J. H. Thorpe, *Phil May: master-draughtsman & humorist, 1864-1903* (Lond, 1932); *Town and Country J*, 12 Aug 1903; newspaper cuttings and notes under Phil May (ML).

H. P. HESELTINE

MAYNE, WILLIAM COLBURN (1808-1902), soldier and public servant, was born on 22 July 1808 in Dublin, youngest child of Captain John Mayne of Lattin, County Tipperary, Ireland, and his wife Theodosia, née Colburn. Educated at Feinaiglien School and Trinity College, Dublin, he was gazetted ensign in the 5th Regiment on 11 August 1825 and promoted lieutenant in 1826. In December 1831 he finished a course in the senior section of the Royal Military College and won a first-class certificate, becoming a captain on 10 May 1833. In 1838 he retired for health reasons, sailed in the *Hero of Malown* and arrived at Sydney in April 1839.

After some years on stations in different areas Mayne rented the Toongabbie estate from Major Wentworth. In 1845 he was nonsuited in the Supreme Court when he sued his attorney George Turner for the recovery of £600 lent to Gilbert Champagne. In December 1846 he became commissioner of crown lands for the Wellington District. He took a lively and humane interest in the well-being of local Aboriginals and at his suggestion an area was reserved for them on the Barwon River where they had established a permanent fishery. He also urged the colonial government to introduce a clause into run leases which would reserve hunting and fishing rights to the Aboriginals but the plan was not legally possible.

In 1850 Mayne submitted a report to the Legislative Council select committee on the divided state of the police. He stressed that unity of action, centralized information and a single executive head of police for the whole colony were necessary for efficiency and recommended a system modelled on the Royal Irish Constabulary. He also suggested that the existing police forces be disbanded and replaced by a whole new force recruited in Ireland, together with wives and children. Apart from his last suggestion, Mayne's recommendations for reorganizing the force were adopted by the legislature.

On 1 January 1852 Mayne was appointed inspector-general of police in place of W. Spain [q.v.], but the 1850 Police Regulation Act was disallowed by the British government on a legal technicality. An amended Act in 1853 reduced the powers of the inspector-general. His title was retained and his office remained the channel of communication for all police business but his executive control included only those police within the County of Cumberland and the Mounted Road Patrols. As inspector-general he was an official member of the Legislative Council from 14 May 1852 until February 1856 when it was reconstituted under responsible government. He was reappointed by the Donaldson [q.v.] ministry on 4 August to represent the government in the new council but resigned three weeks later. On 18 September 1856 he was appointed auditor-general by the Cowper [q.v.] ministry.

On 10 November 1864 Mayne became the first agent-general for New South Wales in London and in 1867 he also acted as head of the New South Wales commission for the Paris Exhibition and spent some time in France. He retained his office as agent-general until 1871 when he was granted a colonial pension. Except for a four-year visit to Europe he spent his last years in retirement at his home in Burwood. In the 1860s and 1870s he had held two stations in the Darling District and five in the Leichhardt District. In 1891 he was a special guest at a luncheon arranged by Sir Henry Parkes [q.v.] 'to the contemporaries of the advent of constitutional government'. Noted for his remarkable memory, Mayne died on 1 September 1902. Predeceased by his wife Mary Ellen, née Turner, whom he had married in Scotland in 1831, he was survived by two sons and five daughters. He was buried in the Anglican section of the Enfield cemetery and left an estate valued for probate at over £76,500.

HRA (1), 22, 23, 26; *Returns of the colony of NSW* (1846-56); Police Establishment report, V&P (LC NSW), 1850, 1; Sel cttee on Police, Report, V&P (LC NSW), 1850, 2; SMH, 2 June 1845, 2 Sept 1902; H. King, Police organization and administration in NSW 1825-1851 (M.A. thesis, Univ Syd, 1956).   HAZEL KING

MEAD, SILAS (1834-1909), Baptist minister, was born on 16 August 1834 at Curry Mallet, Somerset, England, youngest son of Thomas Mead and his wife Honor, née Uttermare. Descended from generations of farmers, he was baptized at 15 and joined local Baptists in building a chapel where he served as a lay preacher. Eager to do more, he decided to secure an education and after work walked to Taunton to attend night school. He entered Stepney College (B.A., 1857) and studied philosophy, theology and law at the Dissenters' Regent's Park College (M.A., 1859; LL.B., 1860). At the University of London he worked on eastern languages for a doctorate of divinity, but London then had no power to grant such a degree; when the restriction was abolished in 1900 the university rejected such a long-deferred award.

Mead applied in vain for acceptance by the Baptist Missionary Society. However, a group of Baptists in Adelaide, after unsuccessful attempts to establish a central church, decided to secure a minister from England. G. F. Angas [q.v.] wrote to Regent's Park College asking the principal to nominate a suitable minister. The letter was sent to Mead and challenged him. On arrival at Port Adelaide in the *Parisian* on 13 July 1861 he preached at chapels in Adelaide and North Adelaide. Regular services began at White's Rooms and within a month a Baptist Church was constituted with twenty-six members. Inspired by Mead's enthusiastic leadership, the congregation decided to build a large church in Flinders Street; it was opened on 19 May 1863. When its cost of £7000 was cleared by 1864 he established at Furreedpore, India, the first constituted Australian Baptist Foreign Mission and later helped to found similar societies in other Australian colonies.

By 1871 Mead had 410 active members and the Flinders Street Church was often called the 'cathedral' of the South Australian Baptist Union, in which he became three times president and four times honorary secretary. Solidly Evangelical, he formed the Christian Endeavour Society of South Australia. He also published tracts on salvation and holiness, and his *Scripture Immersion* (1867) was also published in German. As a founder of Union College for training ministers of three denominations, he was a tutor in exegesis for fourteen years. In 1877-78 he visited England and in 1882 told the South Australian commission on the working of the Education Acts that he doubted the value of reading the Bible in British schools and advocated 'distinct separation of church and state'. Active in the wider community he became president of the Young Men's Christian Association in 1893. By 1896 he could claim that he had trained over thirty ministers and that the South Australian Baptist Union had 4270 active members and over 600 teachers for the 6500 children in its Sunday schools. He preached his last sermon at Flinders Street Church on 10 January 1897. He had married twice in South Australia: first, at Gumeracha on 25 May 1864 to Anne Staple by whom he had six children; and second, at Flinders Street on 22 October 1878 to Mary Leighton.

Mead returned to England where he became principal of Harley College, London. In 1901 he went to Western Australia and was co-pastor with his son-in-law, Rev. A. S. Wilson, of the Baptist Church in Museum Street, Perth. When Wilson moved to New Zealand, Mead lived with his daughter Gertrude, a medical practitioner. He died of pneumonia at Perth on 13 September 1909. He was survived by three daughters and a son, Cecil Silas, who after graduating at the University of Adelaide (B.A., 1887; M.B., B.S., 1891) served as a medical missionary in eastern Bengal for twenty-nine years, returned to Adelaide to teach anatomy in 1923-39 and died in June 1940.

Among Mead's many memorials is a little chapel in Rajbari, East Pakistan, built by Australians who followed his lead in establishing Baptist missions in India.

H. E. Hughes, *Our first hundred years: the Baptist Church of South Australia* (Adel, 1937); *Observer* (Adel), 21 Dec 1861, 7 Sept 1895; *Register* (Adel), 14 Sept 1909, 5 Aug 1911; Flinders Street Baptist Church minutes.

A. C. HILL

MEI QUONG TART (1850-1903), merchant and philanthropist, was born at Hsinning (Sun-ning), Canton Province, China, son of Quong Tart, dealer in ornamental wares. At 9 he went to New South Wales with an uncle who had charge of a shipload of coolies for the Braidwood goldfields. He lived in Thomas Forsyth's store at Bell's Creek and soon joined the family of Robert Percy Simpson whose wife Alice, née Want, taught him English and converted him to Christianity. Encouraged by his guardians to acquire shares in gold claims, he was wealthy at 18. After the Simpsons moved to Sydney he built a cottage at Bell's Creek and lived a gay and leisured life, friendly with both Chinese and Europeans. At Braidwood and Araluen he was prominent in sporting, cultural and religious affairs and organized a series of popular Chinese horse-races at Jembaicumbene. In 1871 he was naturalized on 11 July, joined a lodge of Oddfellows and in 1885 became a Freemason; in 1877 he had been appointed to the board of the public school at Bell's Creek.

Quong visited his family in China in 1881 and on his return opened in Sydney a tea and silk store, followed by a tea shop which was intended to provide customers with samples of China tea, but proved so successful that he began a chain of them. He also agitated for the suppression of opium imports and in 1883 accompanied Sub-Inspector Martin Brennan on an investigation of the Chinese camps in southern New South Wales. Their report revealed widespread opium addiction and on 24 April 1884 Quong presented to Alexander Stuart [q.v.], colonial secretary, a petition seeking the ban of opium imports. On a visit to Victoria in June he tried to win support for his anti-opium crusade in Melbourne and Ballarat.

On 30 August 1886 Quong married a young Englishwoman, Margaret Scarlett. In 1885-88 he provided a series of free feasts for the inmates of destitute asylums. In 1887 he revived the anti-opium campaign with a second petition to parliament and published a pamphlet, A Plea for the Abolition of the Importation of Opium, but in that year anti-Chinese sentiment flared and he spent much time defending his countrymen and often acted as an interpreter. In January 1888 he was appointed a mandarin of the fifth degree by the Chinese Emperor and again visited China. On his third Chinese tour in 1894 he was advanced in rank to a mandarin of the fourth degree.

In December 1889 Quong opened an elaborate restaurant in King Street; it was followed in December 1898 by a dining hall in the new Queen Victoria Markets which became one of the most popular social centres in Sydney. His employees, mostly Europeans, benefited from his enlightened policy with time off for shopping and sick leave with pay. After August 1890 when he opened a bazaar at Jesmond near Newcastle he was in constant demand as a speaker at charitable and social functions; his Scottish songs and recitations mingled with quaint wit guaranteed full attendances. A zealous Anglican, he had his children baptized and educated in different Christian denominations to avoid charges of prejudice. On 19 August 1902 he was savagely assaulted by an intruder in his office in the Queen Victoria Markets. After a partial recovery he

died from pleurisy at his home, Gallop House, Ashfield, on 26 July 1903 and was buried in the Rookwood cemetery. He was survived by his wife, two sons and four daughters.

Quong was the only Chinese who succeeded in being accepted fully by the New South Wales community, but the popular view of him as a Chinese leader was not that of the Chinese community which was split by factions and separated from him by a wide social and cultural gap.

M. Tart, Quong Tart, or how a foreigner succeeded in a British community (Syd, 1911); Quong Tart papers (Soc Aust Gen, Syd).

E. J. LEA-SCARLETT

MEIN, CHARLES STUART (1841-1890), barrister, politician and judge, was born on 14 June 1841 in Maitland, New South Wales, son of John Stuart Mein, bank manager, and his wife Mary, née Hall. Educated at Cape's [q.v.] school and Sydney Grammar School, he entered the University of Sydney (B.A., 1863; M.A., 1865), where he met S. W. Griffith who was to be his lifelong friend. Mein taught for some years at Sydney Grammar School. As private secretary to the attorney-general of New South Wales he went to Queensland in 1867 and in 1870 was entered on the roll of solicitors. He attracted attention by his advocacy in the courts and the lucidity of his opinions. In 1873 at the Presbyterian Church, Brisbane, he married Annie Theresa McCarthy; they had no children.

In July 1876 Mein was appointed to the Legislative Council and made postmaster-general in George Thorn's [q.v.] ministry, also holding the post under John Douglas [q.v.] until 21 January 1879. In the Opposition during the McIlwraith [q.v.] ministry in 1879-83 he led the Liberals in the Legislative Council with an old-time distrust of Gladstonian innovations. In June 1884 he became postmaster-general under Griffith and in January 1885 secretary for public instruction. In April he was offered appointment as judge. At first he was strongly opposed by the barristers who had objected to the Legal Practitioners' Act which made possible the raising of a solicitor to the bench. At his installation the Bar was conspicuous by its absence, but his skill and general demeanour enabled him to overcome the obstacle. Well read and an interesting conversationalist, he had a most kindly and generous nature.

Like many other leading citizens he was interested in the voluntary forces. Commissioned major in the 1st Infantry Regiment on 5 July 1880, he became lieut-colonel of the 1st Queensland (Moreton) Regiment on 24 February 1885 and commanded the Easter encampment but retired when appointed to the bench. He died of kidney disease at his home, Lauraville, Elizabeth Bay, Sydney, on 30 June 1890, and was buried in Toowong cemetery, Brisbane.

V&P (LA NSW), 1866, 2, 638, 663; *Brisbane Courier*, 1 July 1890; *Queenslander*, 5 July 1890; Griffith papers Q186 (Dixson Lib, Syd).

A. A. MORRISON
M. CARTER

MELVILLE, FRANCIS (1822-1857), bushranger, was born probably Francis McNeiss McNiel McCallum in Inverness, Scotland. He had some schooling but about 12 became a thief. In the Perth Court of Judiciary he admitted to serving four sentences totalling twenty-two months before 3 October 1836 when at 15 he was sentenced to seven years' transportation for housebreaking. As Edward Melville (Mulvell) he served for twenty months in English gaols and was then sent to Hobart Town in the *Minerva*. He arrived on 29 September 1838 and in October was placed at Port Arthur in the Point Puer institution for juvenile convicts. In 1839-48 he came before the police magistrate twenty-five times. In 1841 his sentence was extended by two years for felony in February and to life for burglary in July; in September he was sent to Port Arthur for five years. Recommended in 1846 for a year's probation, he absconded and lived with the Aboriginals for a year. After recapture he was given nine months' hard labour in chains, an experience repeated in January and August 1850.

Calling himself Captain Francis Melville and posing as a gentleman, he reached Victoria about October 1851 and by December had turned bushranger. He claimed leadership of the Mount Macedon gang that waylaid travellers in the Black Forest. In 1852 he held up Alfred Joyce [q.v.] at Norwood station and watched for travellers along the western track from the central goldfields across the Wimmera. Legend claims that police almost trapped him near Mount Arapiles where he had a cave. During shearing at Wonwondah he ordered and paid in lordly fashion for having his lost horse found and breakfast prepared. Charles Carter [q.v.] and his sons, travelling with drays on Fiery Creek Plains, encountered Melville and two companions 'with hard-set faces like hawks ready to pounce on their quarry'; the bushrangers found the Carters' weapons too much to stomach and rode off. They held up teamsters at Rokewood. In early November Melville trailed a digger to Mary-

vale station where he robbed him and captured the manager.

Early in December Melville moved into the Western District. At Marida Yallock he ordered the Mackinnon girls to entertain him; he sang and played the piano before leaving. On the 18th with William Roberts he held up sixteen men in Woady Yallock shearing shed and robbed the owner and three others. Next day at Bruce's Creek the bushrangers robbed Thomas Warren and William Madden of £37 but gave them £10 for travelling expenses. On the 24th they held up two bush workers at Fyansford. In Geelong they put up at Christy's inn, dined and visited a brothel. Melville's boasting and £100 reward for his capture induced a woman to warn the police. Alerted, Melville smashed a window and climbed into the street. He knocked down a policeman, ran toward the Ballarat Road but was met by Henry Guy on a fine horse. As he tossed Guy from the saddle the horse escaped; Guy grappled with him until two policemen arrived. Roberts had already been arrested and the bushrangers spent Christmas in South Geelong gaol.

Captain Foster Fyans [q.v.] committed them on 3 January 1852 for trial before Judge Redmond Barry [q.v.] on 3 February. On three charges of highway robbery Melville was sentenced to twelve years' hard labour. Imprisoned in the hulk *President*, Melville attempted on 4 June to bite off a sergeant's nose; he was beaten by the warders' 'neddies' and given twenty days' solitary. On 20 January 1854 he had another month solitary for 'inciting the prisoners to mutiny'. In mid-year John Price [q.v.] had him transferred to the hulk *Success* and allowed him to work ashore in the Point Gellibrand quarry. Melville behaved and was allowed to spend three days a week allegedly translating the Bible into the Aboriginal language; in fact he was planning with a former ship's captain, Billy Stevens, to seize a cutter and sail to Gippsland; their eight accomplices included Harry Power [q.v.]. They captured the tow boat, took Constable Owens as hostage and rowed down Hobson's Bay with Melville yelling 'Goodbye at last to Victoria'. As the water police and guard boats closed in Stevens smashed Owens's skull and leapt into the sea to his death. When captured Melville is credited with saying: 'I would sooner die than suffer what I have been subjected to in these hulks in the past four years'.

A Citizens' Committee engaged Dr Mackay to plead the convicts' case but Melville conducted his own defence before Judge Robert Molesworth [q.v.] on 19 November 1855. He was charged as Thomas Smith, alias Frank McCallum, alias Captain Melville and in cross-examination upset police claims that he had murdered Owens but Molesworth ruled that all were guilty when a man died while attempting to escape custody. Melville argued that he had been charged as Thomas Smith (a name he had never used), that he was sentenced to work on the roads not imprisoned in a hulk, that a warrant for custody in a hulk did not extend to a quarry and that treatment in the hulks was degrading. He and two other conspirators were sentenced to death but the case was referred to the Full Court. For the trials the Citizens' Committee briefed R. D. Ireland [q.v.], who called the three condemned men as witnesses and secured acquittal of the six. At a public meeting the committee demanded an inquiry into the Penal Department and Melville's acquittal.

On 4 December the Full Court concluded that the Crown had not produced a warrant for Melville's transfer from the *President* to the *Success* and thus failed to prove that he had tried to escape from legal custody; the death sentence was respited. The Melville case made legal history; in 1964 Sir John Barry asserted that it was 'good law'. Melville was transferred to Melbourne gaol where he had outbursts of fury and warders were warned not to excite him. At dawn on 12 August 1857 a warder found him strangled by a red-spotted blue scarf; whether he committed suicide or was murdered has never been decided.

Melville created a legend of the cultured gentleman of good address and scholarship turned highwayman, considerate to those whom he robbed, courteous and charming to women, and a nineteenth-century Robin Hood. Yet he was a swaggerer courageous behind a brace of pistols and a skilful confidence man destroyed by the penal system and his unbalanced character.

S. Carter, *Reminiscences of the early days of the Wimmera* (Melb, 1911); J. C. Hamilton, *Pioneering days in Western Victoria* (Melb, 1923); B. Cronin and A. Russell, *Bushranging silhouettes* (Syd, 1932); G. E. Boxall, *The history of the Australian bushrangers* (Syd, 1935); C. Phillips, *Cry of the dingo* (Lond, 1956); J. V. Barry, *The life and death of John Price* (Melb, 1964); CSO papers, 1852 (SAA).   L. J. BLAKE

MELVILLE, NINIAN (1843-1897), cabinet maker, undertaker and politician, was born on 29 December 1843 in Sydney, son of Ninian Melville and his wife Catherine, née Hayes. His father came from Aberdeen and was sentenced on 20 April 1833 at the Perth Court of Judiciary to seven years transportation for stealing clothes; he reached Sydney in the *Fairlie* in February 1834, received a ticket-of-leave in 1838 and set up as a cabinet maker in the 1840s. Educated in Sydney, young Melville was apprenticed to the cabinet makers, John Hill & Sons. Early interested in public affairs he spoke with his father from platforms in the Domain. In 1862 he married Martha Heaton who died in September 1865.

After competition from foreign furniture had destroyed the Melvilles' business they organized the unemployed in 1866 to demand a protective tariff. In evidence before W. J. Macleay's [q.v.] select committee on the unemployed young Melville boasted that 'the whole of the unemployed movement lies in my hands'. In 1867 he went to Melbourne and worked as an undertaker at Brunswick and cabinet maker at Richmond. He tried in vain for election to the Legislative Assembly as a radical candidate. At Hawthorn on 29 December 1868 he married Mary Brooks.

Melville returned to Sydney about 1874 and plied his trade in Newtown. Defeated for East Sydney in the general elections of October 1877, he was chairman of the Working Men's Defence Association and failed to unite it with the Free Selectors' Association in a programme of protection, political reform and opposition to assisted immigration. In May 1880 he was elected to the Legislative Assembly for Northumberland and held the seat until 1894. In 1881-83 he was president of the Protection and Political Reform League. In the first edition of *Songs from the Mountains* in December 1880 Henry Kendall [q.v.] had included 'The Song of Ninian Melville', presenting him as the epitome of democratic politics (which the poet detested) and of 'that immense impostor that they call the "working man"'. Kendall also accused him of making a name by attacking religion, despite Melville's demands for sabbatarian and temperance legislation.

Melville was also connected with the Orange movement and as a Freemason was worshipful master of the Southern Cross Lodge. An alderman of Newtown from 1879, he was elected mayor in 1882. In 1883 he became whip for Alexander Stuart's [q.v.] ministry. In November 1885 a select committee inquired into Melville's receipt of £25 from a bottle manufacturer for allegedly winning concessions from a member of the government. Melville claimed that it was a business debt connected with his agency in Wallsend and in February 1886 the committee reported that the allegations were not proven. In that year he made the Speaker's chair.

In the heated elections of 1887 Henry Parkes [q.v.], denounced him as 'the veriest charlatan that ever lived'. He was secretary to the parliamentary protectionist party and with E. W. O'Sullivan organized its election campaigns. G. R. Dibbs [q.v.] offered Melville a portfolio in January 1889 but he preferred to serve the party and the country in other ways. In April 1889 he was elected chairman of committees and in troubled times showed himself more than the excitable partisan. His brushes were usually with the wilder members of his own side. In 1892 he was sued without success in the Supreme Court by J. M. Toohey [q.v.] for £2000 for forcible ejection from the House.

Melville welcomed the return of the first Labor members to parliament in 1891 but soon condemned their refusal to support protection. Redistribution forced him to contest the new seat of Waratah in the 1894 elections but he was defeated by a Labor candidate. In financial difficulties from 1886 when his friends at Lambton paid his debts, he missed his parliamentary salary and pressure from the *Mont de Piété* in 1894 sent him bankrupt in October with debts of £1800. His estate was released in January 1895. An alderman of Ashfield and Summer Hill in 1895-97, he was mayor in 1896.

Although a member of temperance orders, 'Ninny' with his large pipe and long black coat and topper was often seen in public houses telling audacious stories. He died suddenly on 26 June 1897 at his home, Northumbria, Summer Hill, and was buried according to Primitive Methodist and Good Templar rites in the Balmain cemetery. He was survived by his wife, two sons and two daughters.

Ex-M.L.A., *Our present parliament, what it is worth* (Syd, c1886); W. Chubb, *Jubilee souvenir of the municipality of Newtown, 1862-1912* (Syd, 1912); T. T. Reed (ed), *The political works of Henry Kendall* (Adel, 1966); V&P (LA NSW), 1866, 5, 631, 1885, 2nd S, 1, 33, 115, 1885-86, 1, 60, 68, 79, 120, 2, 138, 1887-88, 1, 335; PD (NSW), 1880-94; *NSW Law Reports*, 1892; B. Atkins, 'Antecedents of the N.S.W. Protection Party, 1881-1891', *JRAHS*, 44 (1958); *Australasian*, 28 Aug 1886, 11 June 1892; *SMH*, 28 June 1897.   BRUCE E. MANSFIELD

MENDES DA COSTA, BENJAMIN (1803-1868), merchant and philanthropist, was born on 17 July 1803 at Enfield, London, first of two children of Benjamin Mendes da Costa and his second wife Louisa, daughter of Edward Naylor of Ponders End. Benjamin was baptized on 9 February 1804 at Enfield Parish Church, where his parents had been married on 21 September 1802 according to the ceremonies and rites of the established Church. The marriage register discloses that Louisa was a minor and married with her father's consent. Their second child was a girl, Louisa, born in 1806. Neither Benjamin nor Louisa married. Their father came of a Portuguese Jewish family that settled in England in the eighteenth century. By his father's first marriage to Esther Machoro, recorded in the London Synagogue Register, they had two children, Hananel and Jacob Joseph; they were brought up as Jews but the children of the second marriage were members of the Church of England.

Da Costa and his sister arrived in South Australia on 7 July 1840 in the *Fairlie*. He set up as a merchant in Hindley Street and in 1843 moved to Grenfell Street. The reasons for his migration to Adelaide are obscure but other Jews, such as the Montefiore [q.v.] brothers, had played an important role in founding and developing South Australia and may have influenced him to settle in the new province. He weathered the depression and as his business prospered he acquired six town acres and fifteen country sections. He was also elected to the committee of the Mechanics' Institute. In the 1850s he visited the Victorian goldfields with Adolph Heinrich Frederick Bartels (1821-1879), a tobacconist who won repute for his authority on many kinds of business. Soon after his return to Adelaide da Costa sailed for London. At first he lived at 53 Gower Street, and then retired to 8 Bedford Square, Brighton, where he died of lung cancer on 26 November 1868.

In Adelaide da Costa had become friendly with the second colonial chaplain, Rev. James Farrell, who ministered at Trinity Church where da Costa was a regular worshipper. The only personal legacy in his will was a bequest to Farrell 'as a mark of esteem'. Da Costa had also become friendly with Bishop Augustus Short [q.v.] who with Farrell was closely connected with the founding of the Collegiate School of St Peter, which had started in 1847 at Trinity Church. Their interest in this school undoubtedly influenced da Costa to bequeath his real estate in South Australia to the Council of the Collegiate School of St Peter, subject to the life interests of ten relations, one of whom was his sister Louisa who died in 1898. The last surviving relation died in 1910 and in 1912 the property was vested in the school. The Da Costa Building is now on the site where he had lived in Grenfell Street, and at the school a hall, house and scholarship are named after him.

J. Stephens, *The land of promise* (Lond, 1839); *South Aust Almanack and General Directory*, 1841-43; *Register* (Adel), 11 July 1840; *SA Mag*, Sept 1842; *Australasian*, 20 Mar 1869.
J. S. C. MILLER

MENKENS, FREDERICK BURNHARDT (1855-1910), architect, was born at Varelin, Oldenburg, Germany, son of Herman Heinrich Menkens, and his wife Anna Margaret. Educated at home until 13, he worked for five years at practical trades and attended building academies in Nienburg and Holzminden. He attended the Royal Polytechnicum at Hanover (Dip. Arch., 1876), toured Europe in 1877 and migrated to Adelaide in 1878. After a few months in the Colonial Architect's Office he moved to Melbourne. A slump in the building industry caused him to work as a tradesman along the Murray River, at Echuca and at Sandhurst. In 1881 he set up an architectural practice in Maitland, New South Wales, and in 1882 moved to Newcastle. In 1884 he completed the interior of the temporary pro-Cathedral designed by J. H. Hunt [q.v.]. Menkens was a staunch friend until they argued over Newcastle Cathedral in the early 1890s. He achieved early success with his work on the School of Arts, Newcastle, the Deaf and Dumb Institute, Waratah, and the Mechanics' Institute, Hamilton. By 1888 'he had been successful and had obtained more than his share of public support'; he also won a competition for the building of the main Presbyterian Church, St Andrews, and in 1891 for a new Town Hall in Newcastle. After a stormy meeting the aldermen of the council awarded the £100 prize to Menkens but later disagreements brought an end to the scheme.

In June 1895 Menkens was sued in the Supreme Court for slander and £1000 damages by H. Kingsbury, an electrical contractor, whom he had accused of installing a lightning conductor made of cheaper metal than specified and of trying to deceive his client. Kingsbury was awarded 40s. damages and £126 costs but Menkens refused to pay and was imprisoned for debt. At first in the Maitland lock-up, he was feasted by his friends, who also supplied him with comfortable furniture, his drawing equipment and commissions until he was moved to Darlinghurst Gaol. In October his estate was sequestrated; apart from what he owed to Kingsbury he admitted moneys marked cash in his cheque book were winnings at the races and items drawn to self were losses; in October 1894 he had borrowed £40 from William Rouse to cover losses on the Caulfield Cup. His only assets were a block of land at Auburn and his wearing apparel. On 9 August 1896 his estate was released and he was discharged from prison.

More successful than ever Menkens designed many commercial buildings in Newcastle including five city warehouses. He worked for such notable citizens as Bishop Murray [q.v.]. Always strongly pro-fessional he was sometimes feared by local builders, but he combined a thorough understanding of architecture with a practical knowledge of the building trades. In 1907 he took F. G. Casteleden into partnership and visited his aged mother in Germany. He returned to live in Sydney in his newly-built house in Avoca Street, Randwick.

Aged 55 Menkens died childless at Randwick from cirrhosis on 10 March 1910 and was buried in the Anglican section of Waverley cemetery. His estate was valued for probate at over £6500. On 16 November 1885 at St Patrick's Church, Sydney, he had married a widow Margaret Downey, née Brennan, according to Roman Catholic rites. The marriage was dissolved in the Supreme Court on 25 February 1891 on the petition of Menkens; costs went against the co-respondent.

J. M. Freeland, *Architect extraordinary* (Melb, 1971); *Newcastle Morning Herald*, 12 Dec 1884; *SMH*, 4, 5 June, 7 Aug 1895; Bankruptcy papers 10218/7 (NSWA).

L. A. REEDMAN

MEREDITH, CHARLES (1811-1880), politician, and LOUISA ANN (1812-1895), author, were born in Britain, Charles on 29 May 1811 in Pembrokeshire, son of George Meredith [q.v.], and his cousin Louisa on 20 July 1812 at Birmingham, daughter of Thomas Twamley and his wife Louisa Ann, née Meredith.

Charles sailed with his father and other children for Van Diemen's Land and arrived in March 1821. Denied a land grant by Lieut-Governor Arthur, Charles moved to New South Wales in 1834 and bought sheep which he placed upon terms with pastoralists in the Murrumbidgee area. He also took up shares with W. A. Brodribb [q.v.] in a cattle run in the Maneroo district and in 1838 went to England. On 18 April 1839 he married Louisa at Old Edgbaston Church, Birmingham. They sailed for Sydney in the *Letitia* and arrived in September. While Charles inspected sheep stations on the Murrumbidgee Louisa stayed at Bathurst. After a few weeks in Sydney they moved to Homebush.

In 1840 Charles, Louisa and a young son went to Oyster Bay, Tasmania, where his father owned Cambria. They bought an adjoining estate, Springvale, and in August 1842 moved to their newly-built house. Meanwhile news reached them of insolvencies in Sydney which involved the loss of 'all we owned in that colony'. Unable to pay the interest on their mortgages, Charles was appointed police magistrate at Port Sorell in 1844 through the patronage of

Lieut-Governor Eardley-Wilmot. In 1848 Meredith resigned and with his wife and three young sons returned to Cambria where he rented part of his father's property. In 1858 he moved to Malunnah in Orford and from July 1879 acted as police magistrate at Launceston.

In the first House of Assembly Meredith won the Glamorgan seat and held it until September 1860 when he obtained leave because of ill health. He represented Hobart Town in 1861-62, Glamorgan in 1862-66, Kingborough in 1866-70, West Devon in 1871-75, Norfolk Plains in 1876-77 and West Devon again in 1877-79. He was colonial treasurer from February to April 1857 in Gregson's [q.v.] ministry and under Whyte [q.v.] from January 1863 to November 1866; from November 1872 to August 1873 he was minister of lands and works under Innes [q.v.] and from 20 July 1876 to 9 August 1877 colonial treasurer under Reibey [q.v.]. He was chairman of committees in 1875-76. In June 1879 he resigned because of heart disease. An advocate of free trade, he was also active in preserving native flora and fauna and introduced a bill to protect the black swan from extinction. He died at Launceston on 2 March 1880. A mountain range in north-east Tasmania and a public fountain in the Hobart Domain commemorate him.

Louisa was educated mainly by her mother. She grew up in Birmingham and in the agitation leading to the 1832 Reform Act she learnt 'to think independently and express herself fearlessly on religious and social issues'; later she published several newspaper articles in support of the Chartists. Her first book in 1832 was a collection of poems, with illustrations designed and etched by herself. Undaunted by the pioneering of her first years of marriage, she continued to write and sketch, turning to the observation of colonial life and the study of bush flora and fauna. She published in London Notes and Sketches of New South Wales (1844); her frank comments provoked angry reviews in Sydney but the book was widely read as one of Murray's Colonial and Home Library series. In February 1850 she completed a companion account in two volumes, again in diary form: My Home in Tasmania, during a residence of nine years. Over the Straits: a visit to Victoria followed in 1861. She also wrote some fiction. Phoebe's Mother, 2 volumes (1869) was first serialized as 'Ebba' in the Australasian in 1866-67, and Tasmanian Friends and Foes, Feathered, Furred and Finned: A Family Chronicle of Country Life (1880) included coloured plates from her own drawings. Nellie, or Seeking Goodly Pearls appeared in 1882. She produced seven books of poems between 1842

and 1891 and for her Bush Friends in Tasmania: Last Series, went to London to see it through the press. Her wildflower drawings won medals in exhibitions in Australia and overseas, notably in the Melbourne Exhibition of 1866. The Tasmanian government granted her a pension of £100 in 1884 for 'distinguished literary and artistic services' to the colony.

In her last years Louisa was lamed by chronic sciatica and became blind in one eye. She also lost much of her small income in the bank failures of the early 1890s and in June 1893 wrote bitterly to Sir Henry Parkes [q.v.] : 'I have made a mess of my life in many ways—my retrospects are mainly regrets'. But by the public she was remembered for her great vivacity and cheerfulness. She had been a devoted housekeeper and for years sewed all her family's clothes. As well as writing, she studied plants, insects, seaweeds and fish of Tasmania's east coast and was an active member of the Society for the Prevention of Cruelty to Animals and an honorary member of the Tasmanian Royal Society. An 'omnivorous reader', she was an excellent conversationalist; J. Jefferson [q.v.], who saw her in theatricals at Government House, Hobart, remarked that she was capable of 'rivalling Fanny Kemble on the stage and as an interpreter of Shakespeare on the platform'. In her books she was most successful as a 'shrewd and cultivated' observer of colonial life. Her descriptions, particularly those of domestic conditions and of the natural environment, were praised by many contemporaries as among the most reliable and practical, and remain a valuable source for social historians. 'A poet in feeling, an artist by instinct, a naturalist by force of circumstances, a keen botanist, and an ardent lover of landscape scenery', Louisa died at Collingwood, Victoria, on 21 October 1895, survived by two sons.

M. Swann, 'Mrs Meredith and Miss Atkinson, writers and naturalists', JRAHS, 15 (1929); SMH, 1 Mar 1845, 13 May 1856; Examiner (Launceston), 4 Mar 1880, 22 Oct 1895; Bulletin, 13 Mar 1880; Town and Country J, 3 Apr 1880; Once a Month, Mar, Apr 1886; Illustrated Sydney News, 4 June 1892; Argus, 22 Oct 1895; Australasian, 26 Oct 1895; The Times, 4 Dec 1895; Parkes letters (ML).

SALLY O'NEILL

MEREWETHER, EDWARD CHRISTOPHER (1820-1893), public servant and company superintendent, was born on 20 February 1820 in London, fifth son of Serjeant Henry Alworth Merewether, K.C., town clerk of London and recorder of Reading, and his wife Elizabeth Maria, née Lockyer. Educated at Charterhouse in 1830 and Westminster in 1834-37, he entered University College, Oxford, in 1838 intending to take holy orders but left without a degree.

In the *Stratheden* Merewether arrived at Sydney in September 1841 and became aide-de-camp to Governor Gipps next January. He also served as aide-de-camp to Sir Maurice O'Connell [q.v.] and Governor FitzRoy. In 1846 he resigned to become colonial secretary in the Port Curtis colony which lasted for only a few months in 1847. At Earl Grey's direction the New South Wales government made him commissioner for crown lands in the Lower Darling district. Merewether disliked the heat but fortunately served only two months in 1848 before he was moved to the Macleay River district. Stationed at Belgrave, near Kempsey, he was sent to Sydney in 1854 as acting agent of the Church and School Corporation's estates and acting chief inspector of distilleries. In 1856 he resumed duty as commissioner of crown lands for the New England and Macleay districts with headquarters at Armidale. He was soon recalled to Sydney as clerk of the Executive Council and in 1858-59 was in England to negotiate for steam postal communication from London to Sydney via Panama. The chairman of the committee assisting him was E. W. T. Hamilton [q.v.]. In 1860 he married Augusta Maria, elder daughter of Dr James Mitchell [q.v.].

In 1861 Merewether accepted Hamilton's offer to become general superintendent of the Australian Agricultural Co. and moved to Newcastle where he built The Ridge on the Burwood estate. His good management restored the company's fortunes. He overcame labour troubles in coal-mining and with James Fletcher [q.v.] helped to arrange the 'vend' system. Merewether closely supervised the company's large stations. On Warrah he had a sheep-washing pool and pump installed at a cost of over £4000 and in 1868-75 the run was subdivided with wire fencing for £13,500. His superintendency was distinguished by meticulous attention to detail and full reports to the directors in London. At the half-yearly meeting in February 1874 a group of shareholders insinuated 'that his administration of the Company's affairs was influenced by his private business interests'. He resigned but was mollified by the court of directors and presentation of £1000 for his services and remained until 31 December 1875. Coal and agricultural workers gave him testimonials referring to his fairness, integrity and considerateness.

Merewether had become increasingly in-

volved with management of the Burwood estate. In 1869 he assisted the family's counsel in litigation that eventually wrested control of Mitchell's estate from the confidence trickster, William Ernest Wolfskehl. Later as owner of the estate he had to negotiate with himself when the company wanted to mine under it. In 1876 he left the management of the estate to Robert Scott junior, and moved his family to Sydney where he built Castlefield at Bondi and Dennarque at Mount Wilson, alternating between them for winter and summer. For some years he was a local director of the London Chartered Bank and occasionally visited Newcastle. He was president of the New South Wales branch of the Royal Geographical Society and in 1889 published his presidential address. In 1887 he had generously financed exploration in New Guinea by T. F. Bevan [q.v.] who gave his name to the Merewether River. He became president of the Australian Club, the Sydney Lawn Tennis Club, and vice-president of the Belvedere Cricket Club in Sydney. He was also a fellow of the Imperial Institute and a member of the Linnean Society. Unobtrusively he was a benefactor of schools, schools of arts and St Paul's College, University of Sydney. He paid for building St Augustine's Church of England in the suburb named after him at Newcastle. He died on 30 October 1893 and was buried in the Anglican section of Waverley cemetery. He was survived by his wife, six sons and three daughters, to whom he left his estate valued for probate at almost £235,000.

V&P (LA NSW), 1858, 3, 268, 1858-59, 2, 490, 1875, 3, 519, 536, 1881, 3, 406, 1885-86, 1, 141, 284, 5, 1059; J. R. Robertson, Warrah: the genesis of a pastoral property (M.A. thesis, ANU, 1960); C. W. Lloyd papers (ML); A.A. Co. papers (ANU Archives); Merewether estate archives (Newcastle Public Lib).

C. E. SMITH

MEREWETHER, FRANCIS LEWIS SHAW (1811-1899), public servant and university chancellor, was born on 18 March 1811 in England, eldest son of Francis Merewether, rector of Haverhill, Sussex, and his wife Frances Elizabeth, née Way; he was a first cousin of E. C. Merewether [q.v.]. Educated at Eton and Trinity College, Cambridge (B.A., 1835), he arrived at Sydney in 1838 and worked in the Treasury. He joined the Australian Club and became its secretary. In 1841 he married Kate Amelia, sister of J. H. Plunkett [q.v.]; they lived in Cumberland Street, Sydney, where three of their five children were born.

In 1841 Merewether became immigration

agent and for two months was acting colonial treasurer. Although appointed deputy registrar of the Supreme Court at Port Phillip, he remained in Sydney. In 1842-43 he was clerk of the Legislative Council and of the Executive Council in 1843-51. As immigration agent he helped to bring out Irish orphans and winemakers to the Hunter Valley. He was also a trustee of the Savings Bank of New South Wales. Nominated to the Legislative Council in 1851 he became postmaster-general. Next year he became auditor-general and joined the Executive Council. He was a director and chairman of the Sydney Tramway and Railway Co. In 1854-56 he relieved C. D. Riddell [q.v.] as colonial treasurer. Nominated to the new Legislative Council on 24 June 1856 he strongly protested in 1858 against applying the Increased Assessment and Rent Act to runs already taken up. He resigned on 10 May 1861 in support of Sir William Burton [q.v.] but was one of the few reappointed to the council as a life member in June.

In 1849 Dr H. G. Douglass [q.v.] had sought Merewether's political influence for the establishment of a university. He referred Douglass to W. C. Wentworth [q.v.] who led the agitation culminating in an Act of incorporation and endowment. Merewether was a member of the original Senate of the University of Sydney and his far-sighted work for it earned him the nickname 'Futurity'. He successfully proposed that the 180-acre Grose Farm be accepted as an alternative site to the inadequate Sydney College. In his reminiscences of the University of Sydney (1898) he recalled that 'my good friend, the Colonial Secretary, a cautious Scotchman, stared at me in amazement at the audacity of my proposal', but agreed when he learnt that the plan envisaged four affiliated colleges as well as parkland. Merewether battled over the plans for the university buildings. As a member of the building committee he claimed that Edmund Blacket's [q.v.] plan was 'much too insignificant for the site, and prospectively inadequate'. Dissatisfied also with the next plan submitted, he was overruled by his colleagues and had to content himself with the thought that he had at least 'got the grand Hall'. In 1854 he became vice-chancellor. While acting chancellor in the absence of Sir Charles Nicholson [q.v.], he proposed a coat of arms and motto for the university. A modified version of his suggestion and his second proposal for a motto *Sidere mens eadem mutato* were accepted. In 1862 he became chancellor. He was a member of the Philosophical Society (Royal Society) of New South Wales.

Merewether visited England in 1863 and

his father's death in 1864 was possibly responsible for his failure to return. In 1865 his seat in the Legislative Council was vacated. He lived at Ingatestone Hall, Essex, until he died on 27 December 1899. He left his estate to his son Charles and daughter Lavinia.

C. E. Smith, 'F.L.S. Merewether', *JRAHS*, 59 (1973) pt 1, and for bibliog.   C. E. SMITH

MERRIMAN, JAMES (1816-1883), ship-owner and alderman, was born on 23 October 1816 at Parramatta, son of George Merriman and Mary, a convict. Orphaned as an infant, his guardians had him educated. In 1828 he and his sister Mary were lodging with J. G. Raphael [q.v.], an emancipist dealer in Pitt Street. Merriman served his indentures as a cooper, practised his trade and sailed in a whaler for four years. On returning to Sydney about 1850 he became licensee of the Whaler's Arms at Millers Point and later the Grafton Hotel and the Gladstone Hotel.

About 1852 Merriman was in partnership with William Andrews running regular shipping services between Sydney and Wellington, Nelson and Lyttelton in New Zealand. Soon afterwards with Captain Fairclough he prospered as an organizer of whaling. In 1861 as a 'captain and owner' he complained to a Legislative Assembly select committee of the difficulty of engaging a crew at the Shipping Office, and by the mid-1860s was engaged extensively in the bêche-de-mer trade in Torres Strait. He lived in Osborne House, Argyle Place. By 1866 he had bought an interest in the *Telegraph* for his eldest son William, was reputed to own the *Metaris* and in 1869 the *Blue Bell*, both for the bêche-de-mer fishery. In 1869 he told the royal commission on the alleged kidnapping of natives from the Loyalty Islands that he had never visited the islands or employed any islanders at his wharf but in Sydney had engaged about twenty islanders at the Shipping Office for a whaling voyage in the *Blue Bell*. He had always refused offers to take Kanakas to Queensland but for a time he had a man-servant from Lifou. He was also a founder of the pearl-shell industry in Torres Strait which he continued till about 1880. In 1875 he had the steamship *Pearl* built but sold her in 1877.

On 25 October 1867 Merriman had been elected to the Sydney City Council for Gipps Ward and represented it until 1883. He was mayor in 1873, 1877 and 1878 and had to contend with the weakness of the council's finances. In October 1877 as a free trader he topped the poll for West Sydney in the Legislative Assembly even though illness had prevented his campaigning. He advocated reform of the land law, extension of the railways, a municipal bill which would provide increased endowment for the city and a building act. He supported the 1866 Public Schools Act but opposed the payment of members of parliament. In 1878 he became a commissioner at the Sydney International Exhibition of 1879. He also served as a trustee of Hyde, Phillip and Cook Parks and as a transit commissioner. His unsparing exertions as treasurer of the Indian Famine Relief Fund in 1879 led to the illness which caused his death.

Quietly energetic, sensible and persevering, Merriman was credited with giving Sydney mercantile life stability. He died on 13 May 1883 from heart disease and dropsy at his home in Argyle Street and was buried in Rookwood cemetery. He was survived by his wife Anne, née Thompson, whom he had married in 1843, and by two sons and three daughters. His estate was valued for probate at over £51,000.

Roy Com on alleged kidnapping of natives of the Loyalty Islands (Syd, 1869. Microfilm under Misc. Documents, ML and G1819 Roy Navy Aust Station, NL); E. Digby (ed), *Australian men of mark*, 1 (Syd, 1889); V&P (LA NSW), 1861, 2, 1317, 1873-74, 5, 1884; *Town and Country J*, 30 Dec 1876; *SMH*, 24 Oct 1877; *Bulletin*, 20 Mar 1880; *Sydney Mail*, 19 May 1883.
                                    G. J. ABBOTT

MESTON, ARCHIBALD (1851-1924), journalist, civil servant and explorer, was born at Donside, Aberdeen, Scotland, son of Alexander Meston and his wife Margaret, née Clark; his grandfather was Sir William Meston, last governor of Dunnottar Castle. In the *Saldhana* he went with his parents to Sydney in 1859 and lived at Ulmarra on the Clarence River where his father taught him the rudiments of farming. At 19 he spent six months in Queensland rambling through the country districts; he returned to New South Wales and at Sydney married Margaret Frances Prowse Shaw. They went to the Clarence River district and in 1874 to Queensland where he managed the Pearlwell plantation of Dr Waugh on the Brisbane River. From December 1875 he was editor of the *Ipswich Observer* until 1881 when its office was moved to Brisbane as the *Daily Observer and East Moreton Advocate*.

From November 1878 to July 1882 Meston represented Rosewood in the Queensland Legislative Assembly, serving for two years as party whip. The German settlers in his electorate supported him but he was censured by the *Nord Australische Zeitung* for defecting from his party in the 'steel rails' controversy. He contested the seat of Cook in 1907 without success.

From February to August 1881 Meston edited the *Townsville Herald* but became insolvent in November and was not discharged until 1885. By then he had moved to Cairns where he managed the sugar cane plantation of Horace Brinsmead & Co. on the Barron River until 1889. He also served on the Cairns Divisional Board and was its chairman from February 1883 to July 1884. Involved with the Cairns Railway League, he advocated that port as the coastal terminus of the proposed line to the western mines. Rival leagues claimed Port Douglas and Mourilyan but Cairns was chosen.

Early interested in exploration, Meston had climbed Mount Kosciusko in 1860. This pastime brought him into contact with the Aboriginals whose customs, habits and languages he studied. An observer of natural history, he led a government party in January 1889 to the Bellenden Ker Range and explored its summit, finding a new plant of the mangosteen family; it was named *Garcinia mestonii* in his honour. The report on this exploration was published and his successful journey led to other official engagements. In 1894 he was commissioned by Horace Tozer, colonial secretary in the Nelson ministry, to prepare plans for improving the lot of Queensland Aboriginals. His proposals were embodied in the Aboriginals Protection Act of 1897. He was made a justice of the peace and from January 1898 to December 1903 was protector of Aboriginals for southern Queensland which later included the central division.

In 1910 Meston was appointed director of the Queensland Government Tourist Bureau in Sydney and continued free-lance journalism. A picturesque figure, he was caricatured by Will Donald in the *Bulletin*. On retiring from the public service he returned to Brisbane. His writings on early Queensland and on the Aboriginals and their lore were very readable although embellished with rhetoric. A student of Greek mythology, he was reputed to keep parliamentary reporters in turmoil with obscure legendary references. In 1895 his *Geographic History of Queensland* had been published in Brisbane.

Meston had some success in such sports as swimming, running, rowing, boxing, hammer-throwing and weight-lifting. He was also a good marksman and learned to throw the spear and boomerang from his Aboriginal acquaintances. Aged 73 he died at the Brisbane General Hospital on 11 March 1924, survived by his wife and by four sons and one daughter of their seven children.

R. S. Browne, *A journalist's memories* (Brisb, 1927); Griffith papers (Dixson Lib, Syd); family information.   S. E. STEPHENS

METCALFE, MICHAEL (1813-1890), merchant and customs agent, was born on 4 October 1813 at Tranby, Yorkshire, England, son of Michael Metcalfe, shipowner, and his wife Ann, née Bell. Educated for commerce, he went to sea and by 1831 was working at St Katherine Docks, London. In July 1837 he arrived in the *Achilles* at Sydney, where he became a customs agent and later a partner of James Powell. About 1857 he formed Michael Metcalfe & Co., shipping and insurance agents, and in 1862 was manager of Metcalfe's Marine Assurance Co. In 1864 he took over the shipping agency of his brother John Bell, and in 1869 was joined by Joseph Henry Storey as partner. In 1839 Metcalfe had helped to form the Australasian Steam Navigation Co., being auditor and later a director till 1881.

In 1853 as a provisional director of the Sydney Dry Dock Co. Metcalfe gave evidence to the parliamentary select committee on its operations. In 1858 he promoted the Newcastle Wallsend Coal Co. of which he was a major shareholder and in 1861-90 its chairman. He was a director of the Clarence and Richmond River Steam Navigation Co. and in 1863-90 of the Illawarra Steam Navigation Co. He helped to establish the Sydney Exchange Co. and was auditor and a director. In 1862-90 he was a director and after 1874 chairman of the Australian Gaslight Co. A trustee and director of several building societies, he served on the committee of the Sydney Chamber of Commerce, the first committee of the Union Club and as treasurer of the Australian Library.

An active High Church Anglican, Metcalfe in 1838 became a foundation churchwarden of Christ Church St Laurence, patron and trustee of its schools and long a parochial nominator. He joined the committees of the Church of England Lay Association and the Australian Board of Missions (1850), and was for years treasurer of the Melanesian Mission. As a member of the Diocesan Committee, he gave to the building fund of St Andrew's Cathedral and in 1868 belonged to its first chapter. He helped to endow the dioceses of Grafton-Armidale in 1867 and Bathurst in 1869; at St Paul's College, University of Sydney, he was bursar and a fellow in 1860-85. In 1866-89 he represented the college on the synod of the Diocese of Sydney. He was sometime a committee member of the Benevolent Society and the Society for the Relief of Destitute Children and a director

of Sydney Infirmary and Dispensary. In 1875 he was appointed by Parkes [q.v.] to the public charities commission. Metcalfe died of heart failure on 27 October 1890, leaving an estate of £24,982 to his wife Agnes Georgianna, née Robinson, whom he had married in 1845 at Christ Church, and to four sons and four daughters.

E. Digby (ed), *Australian men of mark*, 2, 3rd ed (Syd, 1889); L. M. Allen, *A history of Christ Church S. Laurence Sydney* (Syd, 1940); *SMH*, 20 Oct 1890; V&P Synod 1866-90 (Syd Diocesan Registry); MS cat under M. Metcalfe.
                                                    RUTH TEALE

MICHAEL, JAMES LIONEL (1824-1868), poet, was born at Red Lion Square, London, second son of Jacob Michael, solicitor, and his wife Rose Lemon, née Hart. He left school at 15 and was privately tutored in English, French, Italian and drawing. After visiting Europe he was articled to his father with whom he later practised as a solicitor. He became associated with the Pre-Raphaelites in whose defence he is said to have written a pamphlet which was well received by Millais, Turner, and Ruskin. In May 1853 he arrived in Sydney and on 30 July was admitted a solicitor. He went into partnership with David Lawrence Levy and later practised on his own account. On 13 February 1854 in Scots Church he married Eleanor Grubin; their only child, James, was born at Burwood on 16 October.

Late in 1855 Michael met J. S. Moore [q.v.], who introduced him to other literary men. He regularly contributed verse, essays, and criticism to the *Month*, edited by Moore, and the *Southern Cross*, edited by D. H. Deniehy [q.v.]. In November 1857 Michael published *Songs without Music*, a collection of lyrics, *Isle of Vines: A Fairy Tale for Old and Young* in 1858 and in April 1860, *John Cumberland*, a narrative poem partly autobiographical. A long romantic poem, 'Sir Archibald Yelverton', which he had contributed to the *Month* in September 1858, was not published separately. His guests at literary dinners in his Burwood home included Henry Kendall [q.v.]. Bankrupt in 1858 Michael transferred his legal practice to Grafton in October 1861. He became a member of the committee and secretary of the local School of Arts. The only lawyer in the district, he had a busy practice but found time to contribute leading articles, poems, essays and practical advice to farmers in the *Clarence & Richmond Examiner*. He read widely and studied plants, ferns, mosses and insects. He also dabbled in chemistry and theology. In 1862-63 his clerk was Kendall who described him as an elegant verse writer, an able essayist and a brilliant talker rather than a poet.

In 1864 Michael was legally separated from his wife and given custody of their son. Michael developed chronic bronchitis and later asthma after an accident forced him to spend two nights in the bush in wet clothes without food or shelter. In May 1866 he wrote to his father 'God help those, who with the habits and education of London, the recollection of intelligent society, and the tastes of a gentleman are doomed to settle in a place like this'. In 1868 he suffered from gastric fever and his doctor advised him to curtail his work and studies. On 26 April he went for a walk dressed in a great-coat, galoshes and a cap with ear muffs. His body was found two days later in the Clarence River; an open verdict was returned at the inquest and he was buried in the Grafton cemetery with no minister present.

Michael was of medium height with a swarthy complexion and a self-possessed manner. He was a sparkling conversationalist, lecturer and advocate but diffuse as a writer and without originality; he lacked the capacity to be more than a competent writer of smooth and graceful verses. He had little capacity for administration and by improvidence died heavily in debt.

J. S. Moore, *The life and genius of James Lionel Michael* (Syd, 1868); *Clarence & Richmond Examiner*, 28 Apr, 5 May 1868; *SMH*, 11 May 1868; *Australasian*, 2 Apr 1870; Bowden lectures (Clarence River Hist Soc records, Grafton City Council); Michael papers (ML); private information.   T. T. REED

MICHAELIS, MORITZ (1820-1902), businessman, was born on 8 November 1820 at Lügde, near Bad Pyrmont, Hanover, son of Reuben Michaelis and his wife Sara. His parents, though financially struggling, sent him to a private school and in 1835 to Holzminden to study medicine. After a brilliant year the money ran out and he had to begin a four-year apprenticeship with a Brakel firm. He then worked for a Cologne linen merchant and was soon manager. In 1843 he joined a Manchester firm, Sampson & Leppoc, and won rapid promotion. He visited Germany in 1848 and on his return considered Australia as the remedy for his ill health which Manchester only aggravated. The offer of a higher salary prevailed but when the gold rush began the firm decided to send Michaelis and Adolphus Boyd to Victoria. On a farewell visit to Germany Michaelis met Rahel Gotthelf, daughter of his sister's husband. They married on 14 April 1853 and in August arrived at Port Phillip in the *Falcon*.

Surrounded by gold mania Michaelis set himself the limited ambition of being 'a well to-do man' in ten years and with Boyd began business in Richmond. Within a year Michaelis had to return to England for more goods, of which he was to sell £25,000 worth at one auction. In 1855 Michaelis and Boyd broke with Sampson & Leppoc, moved to Collins Street and with a capital of £15,000 drew up a five-year partnership agreement. Boyd returned to England to manage the fortnightly shipment of goods and, except for £10,000 lost through a dishonest employee, the firm prospered; in 1860 the agreement was renewed. In 1864 Michaelis visited Europe but on his return faced ruin. The end of the American civil war lowered the price of cotton goods and a shipment of elastic-sided boots proved faulty. In May 1866 the partners' creditors accepted a composition of 14s. in the £ and in March 1867 the partnership was dissolved. Michaelis had already joined his nephew, Isaac Hallenstein, who in 1864 had bought a tannery at Footscray.

Michaelis, Hallenstein & Co. grew rapidly; in 1873 Isaac established a London branch and in Melbourne 780 hides were turned out a week; in 1876 the Sydney branch, Farleigh, Nettheim & Co., started and in 1879 Michaelis, Hallenstein & Farquhar was established in New Zealand. The firm won awards in Melbourne, Sydney, London, Paris, Amsterdam and Calcutta. It also pioneered the Australian glue industry and processed gelatine. To Michaelis, the success was due to his management and Isaac's hard work. In 1883 he was able to pay his creditors. In 1884 he took his family to Europe for a two-year visit marred for him by rheumatism. The crash of the 1890s was not entirely unexpected by Michaelis and the firm kept down its overdraft and survived. Michaelis maintained that business would recover 'when once the mercantile world has got clear of its speculative and weakened members, when I doubt not we shall reap the reward of my caution'.

Michaelis had wide interests and though never seeking public office vigorously supported the liberal reform movement and for years was acting consul for Prussia. In 1860 he had acted as special auditor for the National Bank. Fascinated by mechanical inventions he financed several and was also involved in salvage operations. He loved music and plays and frequented Melbourne's early theatre. A Jew by birth, he did not continue to practise the orthodoxy of his childhood and often visited the Unitarian Chapel where the minister was 'a very clever preacher'. Michaelis was treasurer of the Melbourne and East Melbourne Hebrew congregation, founded the St Kilda congre-

M

gation in 1871 and gave large sums to both. Though a committee member of the Melbourne Hebrew School he sent his sons to Wesley College. He was a member of the Sabbath Observance and Jewish Aid Society Committees and a founder of the *Australian Israelite* which he later boycotted. He supported many charities, gave £500 to the Melbourne Hospital and with his sons gave £1000 to the Alfred Hospital in memory of his wife who died in 1901. His greatest interest was his family whose unity he maintained by personal and written contact and an implacable will. Only sons and sons-in-law of partners became shareholders but Michaelis advised them to acquire financial independence. He published *Chapters from the story of my life* (Melbourne, 1899).

In old age Michaelis spent increasing time at Romawi, the 4000-acre property on Lake Victoria, Gippsland, bought in 1889. There, after an unsuccessful attempt to produce wattle bark, he bred cattle and sheep and enjoyed visits from his family. In 1901 his health declined and his rheumatism worsened. He died at Linden, St Kilda, on 26 November 1902, survived by seven daughters and four sons. He was widely mourned as a man of great honour 'who would do good by stealth and blush to find it fame'.

L. M. Goldman, *The Jews in Victoria in the nineteenth century* (Melb, 1954); *The Michaelis, Hallenstein story 1864-1964* (Syd, 1964); *Table Talk*, 11 Dec 1902; *Aust Leather J*, 15 Dec 1902, 16 Jan, 15 Feb 1956; Michaelis, Hallenstein Pty Ltd records (ANU Archives).

J. ANN HONE

MICHEL, LOUIS JOHN (1825-1904), gold discoverer, was born on 5 July 1825 at Walworth, Surrey, England, son of Louis Michel and his wife Elizabeth, née Watts; his parents were of French origin and came to England in the seventeenth century. He migrated in 1840 to Melbourne with his uncle. He worked as an assistant in a Collins Street grocery, saved diligently and after a few years bought the licence of the Rainbow Hotel in Swanston Street.

In 1849 a youth named Chapman showed the proprietor of the Waterman's Arms Hotel in Melbourne a nugget of gold measuring 2 in. by 3 in. Michel was one of many who went to see the find and though nothing came of the incident it served to whet his interest in finding gold. In April 1851 when the news of the discovery of gold at Summerhill Creek in New South Wales created excitement in Melbourne, Michel formed a party with William Habberlin, James Furnival, James Melville, James Headin and Benjamin Greenig to search for gold in the Upper Yarra districts and Plenty Ranges. For some weeks they had no success but on 30 June found likely quartz on the banks of either Deep Creek or Anderson Creek near Warrandyte. The party returned to Melbourne and Michel showed the quartz to Lieut-Governor La Trobe.

Michel's party disbanded. He soon proposed to Habberlin that the search should continue and offered to provide all expenses. Habberlin agreed and this time they kept much closer to the Yarra River than before. About 13 July the two men found a small quantity of alluvial gold in the bed of Anderson Creek about half a mile from its junction with the Yarra. They returned to Melbourne and put in a claim for the £200 reward offered for the discovery of a goldmine within two hundred miles of Melbourne, but this reward was never paid. Michel also offered to take any party to the scene of his discovery, and on 6 August he conducted an official party to the site. Some satisfactory finds were made and within a week three hundred people were prospecting along the banks of the creek. However, the discoveries at Ballarat soon caused the Anderson Creek goldfield to be abandoned though it was reopened about 1854 and worked with tolerable success for over sixty years.

In 1853 the select committee of the Legislative Council on the claims for the discovery of gold in Victoria decided to reward J. Hiscock of Ballarat, J. W. Esmond [q.v.] and Michel with £1000 each. However, the committee found that 'Michel and his party have . . . established their claim to be held as the first publishers of the discovery of a goldfield in the Colony of Victoria'.

Michel sold the Rainbow Hotel soon after visiting the Ballarat goldfields and bought the Ship Inn at Williamstown. He lived mostly in Lygon Street, Carlton, and in 1862-77 was licensee of the Duke of Wellington Hotel on the corner of Russell and Flinders Streets. Appointed rate collector for the Victoria Ward of the Melbourne City Council in 1883, he held the post until a few months before he died on 24 September 1904. Predeceased in 1875 by his wife Alicia, née Bell, whom he had married at St James Old Cathedral on 21 October 1844, he was survived by six of their eight children.

A. Sutherland et al, *Victoria and its metropolis*, 2 (Melb, 1888); J. Flett, *The history of gold discovery in Victoria* (Melb, 1970); L. R. Cranfield, 'Discovery of gold in Victoria', *VHM*, 31 (1960).

LOUIS R. CRANFIELD

MICHIE, SIR ARCHIBALD (1813-1899), lawyer and politician, was born at Maida

Vale, London, son of Archibald Michie, merchant. Educated at Westminster School, he was admitted to the Middle Temple in 1834 and called to the Bar in 1838. In London he had helped to form the Abolition of Taxes on Knowledge Committee in 1836. He migrated to Sydney and in 1840 married Mary, daughter of Dr John Richardson. On 29 May 1841 he was admitted to the New South Wales barrister roll. His practice flourished despite his other activities. He bought two lots in Brisbane and wrote for the *Atlas* when it was founded in November 1844. An enthusiastic speaker, he often lectured with immense popularity at the School of Arts but was troubled by a throat affection. To relieve it in 1847 he visited South Australia by sea. Though endorsed by the Anti-transportation League for the Legislative Council seat of Cumberland County he was defeated, but in 1849 was a prominent speaker at the rally against the landing of *Hashemy* convicts at Sydney. He returned to England but soon afterwards migrated to Canada, then to Sydney and in 1852 to Melbourne.

Admitted to practise in the Supreme Court Michie became an associate of T. T. à Beckett [q.v.]. He was appointed to the Legislative Council in November but resigned in August 1853 to concentrate on his own practice. In 1855 he was one of the barristers who defended the Eureka rebels. He had bought a share in the *Melbourne Herald*, edited by G. S. Evans [q.v.], but lost so heavily that he sold out despite his year's earnings of £8000 at the Bar.

In 1856 Michie was elected to the new Legislative Assembly, second of the five members for Melbourne. He worked with such Protestant liberals as R. Heales, J. McCulloch, F. T. Sargood and J. Service [qq.v.]. In March 1857 Michie helped O'Shanassy [q.v.] to bring down the Haines [q.v.] ministry but refused to enter O'Shanassy's government because J. L. V. F. Foster [q.v.] had joined it; instead Michie became attorney-general in the reconstructed Haines ministry from 29 April 1857 to 10 March 1858. In a determined effort in 1857 to abolish state aid to church schools, he explained that his support for it in 1852 had been due to 'the transition crisis of social history through which Victoria was then passing'. His bill was passed in the assembly but defeated in the council by one vote; he failed again in 1858 and 1859. He won a St Kilda seat in October and supported Nicholson's [q.v.] land bill, claiming that without it much of the goldfields population would leave Victoria. He lost his seat in 1861 because, according to C. G. Duffy [q.v.], he neglected the electorate. In 1860 his *Victoria Suffering a Recovery* had been published but

its attack on the idea of 'protection to native industry' did not help his election. He certainly seems to have been an influential spokesman for free trade.

In 1863 Michie became Victoria's first Q.C. In July when the member for Polwarth and South Grenville retired, he won the by-election and in November 1864 recaptured a St Kilda seat. From 4 August 1863 to 18 July 1866 he was minister of justice in the McCulloch ministry although not a member after December 1865. Prominent in debates on the tariff bill and the deadlock over protection, he denied that a tariff with low duties could be called protection; quoting J. S. Mill he asserted that in a new country and new conditions 'a certain measure of protection might not only be necessary but justifiable'. As the appropriation and the tariff bills 'were not unrelated and incongruous matters', he contended that the government's action did not constitute a tack.

Michie was returned as member for Ballarat West and from 8 April 1870 to 19 June 1871 was attorney-general in the third McCulloch ministry. Although he had lost his seat in the January elections, he again stayed in office despite protest by F. Longmore [q.v.]. In August he was sworn in as a Legislative Council member for Central Province, but in May 1872 was given six months' leave because he had lost his voice. In 1873-79 he was agent-general in London for Victoria and was appointed K.C.M.G. in 1878. He returned to Victoria and practised as a barrister but with 'no flashes of the old fire'. He had antagonized solicitors by his attitude to the proposed amalgamation of the legal profession. In four select committees on federal union he had supported Federation. He served on the royal commission on penal and prison discipline in 1870 and was appointed chairman of a royal commission on public instruction in 1881 but resigned. He was also active in the Acclimatisation Society of Victoria.

In 1875 Michie supported C. G. Duffy's suggestion that if Britain became involved in war, Australia should be allowed neutrality, and in 1889 he opposed the notion of Imperial Federation. He lectured at length to a big audience in the Melbourne Town Hall in 1885, strongly advocating the annexation of all New Guinea. Interested in the economic well-being of Victoria he had advocated a Central Bank in 1860 and strongly favoured encouraging immigration in 1870. When the economy collapsed after the land boom, he condemned James Munro [q.v.] for 'bolting' to the safety of the Agent-General's Office in London while his companies went into liquidation. In May 1893 Michie wrote to the *Age* applauding the efforts of the solicitor-general, Isaac Isaacs, to compel the premier, J. B. Patterson [q.v.], and the attorney-general, Sir Bryan O'Loghlen [q.v.], to prosecute Sir Matthew Davies [q.v.] on a charge of issuing a false balance sheet for the Mercantile Bank.

A successful barrister, Michie in about 1858 had bought 73 Chancery Lane where a number of barristers were soon established. He continued to write for the *Melbourne Herald* and *Punch*, and for many years was Victorian correspondent for *The Times*. He continued to lecture on various subjects from Shakespeare to ghosts and published many pamphlets, some of which were reprinted in *Readings in Melbourne* (London, 1879).

References to his brilliance abound but he never attained the political prominence of some contemporaries, partly because of his large legal practice and partly because his political convictions were not very strong. With 'rare personal honour and . . . high integrity', he was often too uncompromising and outspoken. A superb parliamentarian, Duffy compared him with Disraeli, and Dr Evans exclaimed in 1857, 'Would to God his judgment and consistency were equal to his genius'. Aged 87 Michie died on 21 June 1899 at St Kilda, survived by his wife, three sons and two daughters. His estate was sworn for probate at £19,700.

C. G. Duffy, *My life in two hemispheres*, 2 (Lond, 1898); A. G. Austin, *Australian education, 1788-1900* (Melb, 1961); G. Serle, *The golden age* (Melb, 1963); M. Cannon, *The land boomers* (Melb, 1966); C. D. W. Goodwin, *Economic enquiry in Australia* (Durham, N. C., 1966); R. L. Knight, *Illiberal Liberal* (Melb, 1966); A. de Q. Robin, *Charles Perry, bishop of Melbourne* (Perth, 1967); A. Dean, *A multitude of counsellors* (Melb, 1968); *My Note Book*, Feb-Dec 1857; *Argus*, 8 Jan 1885, 23 June 1899; *Age*, 23 June 1899; *The Times*, 23 June 1899; G. R. Quaife, The nature of political conflict in Victoria 1856-57 (M.A. thesis, Univ Melb, 1964); Michie papers (LaTL); Thomas à Beckett, Memoirs (held by E. L. à Beckett, Toorak).

H. L. HALL

MIDDLETON, JOHN (1825-1894), policeman, was born in Foulsham, Norfolk, England, son of Michael Middleton, labourer, and his wife Mary Ann, née Phillips. In 1841 he worked in a Foulsham bakery and in 1843 enlisted in the 5th Regiment. He served in Ireland and later in Mauritius, where in 1848 at Port Louis he married Ellen, née Hartley of Lancashire. They sailed with two children in the *Alecto* as steerage passengers and arrived at Melbourne on 13 October 1852.

Middleton became a baker in Melbourne and later at Diamond Swamp, New South Wales, before he joined the Western Road Patrol in November 1854 as a trooper. Keen and ambitious, he daily recorded his movements and those of other officers. He served at Diamond Swamp from 1855 where he was promoted sergeant, at Blackheath from 1857 and Hartley from 1860. In 1861 he was sent to Tuena, close to the hide-outs of 'highwaymen' in the Abercrombie Ranges. In May-June 1861 with Constable Hosie he looked for the bushranger, Johnny Peisley. On 15 July they rode to Bigga and next day went to Fogg's sly-grog shop where they surprised Frank Gardiner [q.v.]. Without mentioning Gardiner, Middleton recorded in his diary: 'Middleton and Hosie [went] to Fogg's. Middleton shot in four places, returned to Bigga. Hosie slightly wounded returned after'. Although Middleton arrested Gardiner, Hosie allegedly allowed him to escape. In December Middleton received a gold ring from Captain Edward Battye, superintendent of the Western Road Patrol, 'in admiration of the indomitable courage displayed by him in attacking and eventually capturing (after being severely wounded) the outlaw "Gardiner" with a single barrelled Pistol, knowing him at the same time to be armed with a brace of Revolvers'. In 1864 Middleton was a main witness for the Crown in the trials of Gardiner but contradicted himself in evidence. In 1875 he was awarded one of the silver medals issued by the government for gallant and faithful services in resisting or capturing bushrangers.

Middleton served as inspector of slaughterhouses at Tuena, Stoney Creek, Orange and Bungendore before he retired in 1876 with a gratuity of £136 10s. In 1865 he had made his home in Orange and became an alderman and mayor in 1891. For years he had suffered from paralysis and cancer of the lip, the result of injuries and exposure. Aged 68 he died on 6 November 1894 at Orange and was buried in the Anglican cemetery. He was survived by five sons and four daughters.

C. White, *History of Australian bushranging*, 1 (Syd 1900); *Orange Leader*, 10 Nov 1894; *Western Advocate* (Orange), 10 Nov 1894; J. Middleton diary and family papers (ML); information from NSW Police Dept.

EMMA E. MIDDLETON*

MIKLUHO-MAKLAI, NICHOLAIEVICH (1846-1888), scientist and explorer usually known as Nicholas Maclay, was born on 17 July 1846 at Rozhdestvenskoye, Russia, second son of Nicholai Hijtch Mikluho-Maklai, hereditary nobleman, and his wife Ekaterina Semenovna, née Bekker.

Educated in St Petersburg at a secondary school, he briefly studied law and philosophy at the university and in 1864 moved to Heidelberg. He studied medicine at Leipzig in 1866 and palaeontology, zoology and comparative anatomy at Jena. On vacation travels he became a competent linguist, and in the Canary Islands examined sponges and shark brains, on which he published important papers. Marine biology drew him to the Red Sea and after a bout of malaria to the Volga. His attention was drawn to New Guinea as a promising field for anthropological and ethnological studies. Aided by the Imperial Russian Geographical Society he visited European museums and met leading scientists. In October 1870 he sailed in the Russian corvette *Vitiaz* and by way of South America and the Pacific Islands reached Astrolabe Bay in September 1871.

From his hut at Garagassi Point, Maclay visited many villages, collected specimens, drew faces and scenery and named mountain peaks. With patience, courage and medical skill he won the confidence and co-operation of the inhabitants. He found them far from long-headed as earlier reported and studied their languages and characteristics. His necessities were running out when the corvette *Isumrud* arrived in December 1872. He named the Maclay Coast from Isumrud to Vitiaz Straits and in the corvette went to the Halmaheras and Philippines where he found primitive tribes similar to those he had seen in New Guinea. In 1873 at Batavia he published his anthropological observations, sent specimens and comments to his European teachers and recuperated for six months at Buitenzorg in the mountains. He then visited the Celebes and Moluccas, and at Papua-Koviai in west New Guinea found ethnological traits similar to those on the Philippines and Maclay Coast. After local exploration he returned to Papua-Koviai and found that raiders had smashed his hut, stolen his equipment and killed some local supporters. With skill he captured the chief offender and brought him to justice, but the experience contrasted so strongly with the goodwill of the more isolated natives of the Maclay Coast that he determined to preserve their cultures.

In April 1874 Maclay went to Amboina, where in June he was found seriously ill by Captain John Moresby [q.v.] who had been sent to look for him. By July Maclay was at Buitenzorg resting and preparing publications. In November he went to Singapore and for 176 days travelled in Malaya where he found more primitive tribes whose ethnological characteristics were akin to those in the Philippines and New Guinea. In December he returned to Buitenzorg and published four papers suggesting a relation

between the natives of the regions he had investigated.

In January 1876 Maclay sailed to the Halmaheras and Carolines, and on the Admiralty Islands established that the natives' enlarged teeth were not a racial trait but resulted from chewing betel nut with lime. He returned to Astrolabe Bay in June and with material from Singapore built a new home at Bugarlom near Bougu village. Renewed friendships and greater facility with dialects enabled him to visit many villages in the mountains and on the coast and islands. He prevented violence which threatened to erupt from superstition and warned his native friends against slave traders. He also made drawings and collections of local animals but confined his diaries to anthropological matters. In November 1877 he sailed north among the islands and reached Singapore in January 1878. He went to Hong Kong in June and in July arrived at Sydney with large collections.

On 26 August Maclay addressed the local Linnean Society on the need for a laboratory of marine studies on Sydney Harbour. The lecture was one of his thirty-four research papers and notes published by the society; he was made an honorary member in 1879. He also became closely associated with W. J. Macleay [q.v.], sharing common interests particularly in the study of sharks. In November 1878 the Dutch government informed him that on his recommendations it was checking the slave traffic at Ternate and Tidore. In January 1879 he wrote to Sir Arthur Gordon, high commissioner for the Western Pacific, on protecting the land rights of his friends on the Maclay Coast, and ending the traffic in arms and intoxicants in the South Pacific. In March, after continuing his campaign for the laboratory, Maclay sailed in the *Sadie F. Caller* for the islands north-east of Queensland. He expected the ship to return to Sydney with his collections but half of them were lost when she went elsewhere. With James Chalmers [q.v.] he visited villages on the south coast of New Guinea but found no evidence to upset his conviction that the people were of common origin. In April 1880 he went to Somerset, Queensland, and thence to Brisbane, where he resumed his studies on the comparative anatomy of the brains of Aboriginal, Malayan, Chinese and Polynesian origin. He inspected Aboriginals on the Darling Downs and palaeontological excavations of extinct mammals at Stanthorpe and Glen Innes. Meanwhile he continued to send notes and specimens to his former teacher, Rudolph Virchow (1821-1902).

Maclay returned to Sydney in January

1881. With help from the government and scientific societies in Sydney and Melbourne his ambition for a marine laboratory was at last realized. While it was being built at Watsons Bay he worked in Sydney museums and collected evidence for his campaign against the exploitation of natives. In August he went to New Guinea in hope of providing guidance at the trial of the murderers of native missionaries and their families at Kalo. He returned in October and found the laboratory almost complete. When the Russian Pacific fleet visited Melbourne in February 1882 Maclay joined the *Vestnik* and arrived at Krondstadt, Russia, in September.

Maclay lectured to the Russian Geographical Society and each morning explained his collections and drawings to enthusiastic visitors. He was awarded a gold medal by the society and a certificate of honour by the Czar but failed to raise funds. He visited Virchow in Berlin, Turgenev in Paris and T. H. Huxley [q.v.] in London. In 1883 he joined the *Chyebassa* at Port Said. His luggage went to Sydney while he sailed to Batavia. A Russian corvette took him to Astrolabe Bay in March, where the natives reported favourably on European visitors, and thence to Hong Kong. In April he sailed for Sydney and was joined at Thursday Island by Chalmers. Together they sought recognition from the Colonial Office of the land rights of natives in eastern New Guinea, their freedom from forced labour and protection from intoxicants. In London Moresby supported their petition but action was too slow to prevent the German annexation of north-east New Guinea on 16 November 1884. Meanwhile Maclay had reached Sydney on 11 June 1883 to find many of his records and collections had been destroyed nine months earlier in the Exhibition Building fire. In August he worked at the marine laboratory and prepared papers for publication. On 27 February 1884 he married Margaret Emma Clark, widowed daughter of Sir John Robertson [q.v.] at her father's home, Clovelly, Watsons Bay.

Maclay wrote to Bismarck in October seeking protection of Pacific islanders from white exploitation and later protested against the German annexation. Early in 1886 he returned to Russia with his family and twenty-two boxes of specimens. He arranged some publications, lectured in St Petersburg and on his travels visited the family estates and scientists. At Vienna he and his wife were married by rites of the Russian Orthodox Church. He intended to return to Sydney but his health deteriorated and he died on 2 April 1888 in his wife's arms. Her income from his estate ended in

1917 and she died in Sydney on 1 January 1936 survived by their two sons.

A portrait by Corsuchin is among his records at the Library of New South Wales.

E. S. Thomassen, *A biographical sketch of Nicholas de Miklouho Maclay, the explorer* (Brisb, 1882); F. S. Greenop, *Who travels alone* (Syd, 1944); S. Markov, *Nikolai Miklukho-Maclay* (Moscow, 1946); N. N. Miklukho-Maklai. *Sobranie sochinenii*, 1-5 (Moscow, Akademii nauk SSSR, 1950-54); D. Fischer, *Unter Südsee-Insulanern* (Leipzig, 1955); *Na Bregu Maklaya* (Moscow, Akademii nauk SSSR, 1961); N. A. Butinov, N. N. *Miklukho-Maklai-velikii ruskii uchenyi-guamanist* (Leningrad, 1971); Miklouho-Maclay papers and M. de Miklouho-Maclay diary, 1888 (Fisher Lib, Univ Syd); relics (ML).

R. W. de M.-MACLAY

MILES, WILLIAM (1817-1887), squatter and politician, was born on 5 May 1817 at Kingsknowe, Edinburgh, son of William Miles, farmer, and his wife Alison, née Wilson. Educated at Colinton Parish School, he moved about 1831 to Glasgow and became an ironworker. At Colinton in 1838 he married Mary Taylor. They sailed in the *Duncan* as assisted migrants and arrived at Sydney on 30 June.

Miles found work with W. H. Chapman as a 'general useful' on his Macleay River station. He was soon an overseer and in 1844 became manager for Captain Charles Steele at Towal Creek. Later Miles supervised several of John Maclean's New England properties. With David Bell he overlanded stock from New England to the Dawson River, Queensland, in 1852 and later rented Kinoul station. In 1857 Miles acquired Dulacca on the Western Downs and in the Queensland pastoral expansion of the 1860s took up more runs in the Leichhardt, Warrego, Maranoa and Gregory North Districts. His final acquisition was Park Head, a freehold estate on the Condamine River near Dalby, where he lived until retiring in the 1870s to his home, Raceview, in Toowoomba.

Miles was shrewd and cautious as a pastoralist. He was one of the few Queensland pioneers to profit from this hazardous activity and his investments later proved to be more soundly based than those of most contemporaries. His practical knowledge of sheep-farming was invaluable and he prospered largely by continuous speculation, moving west when closer settlement threatened and perspicaciously selling out before drought or depression struck. His profits were invested, particularly in the Royal Bank of Queensland which he founded in 1885 and of which he was chairman of directors, and the Metropolitan Building Society. He also held politically-useful shares in several Queensland newspapers.

In 1864 Miles entered the Queensland Legislative Assembly for Maranoa. Defeated by McIlwraith [q.v.] in 1873, he held Carnarvon in 1874-75, Northern Downs in 1876-78 and Darling Downs in 1878-87. After visiting the Philadelphia Exhibition in 1876 he joined John Douglas's [q.v.] ministry as colonial secretary on 15 March 1877 and held the post until appointed secretary for public works in November. He resigned in November 1878 before the Douglas group began to disintegrate. On the victory of the Griffith Liberals in 1883 Miles returned to the public works portfolio, coupling it with that of mines, and holding both until 1887 despite increasing deafness.

As a colourful politician with blunt vigour, definite commitments and strong personal hates and allegiances, Miles was no orator but he tried to dominate his audience by a combination of conviction, common sense, lung-power and steam-roller debating tactics and mannerisms. Unswervingly loyal at a time when devotion to principles or leaders was not characteristic of colonial politicians, he quarrelled with his friend McIlwraith in 1871 and later conducted a bitter legal and political battle with his countryman, whose flamboyant financial and public schemes he suspected and distrusted. Although a thoroughgoing squatter until 1874, he became known for his advocacy of liberal principles. This conversion coincided with the transfer of his investments from pastoral paddocks to urban streets. Like most of his group, property was his God and self-improvement the way to salvation, but unlike many of his pastoral fellows he believed that opportunities to acquire riches should be enlarged and that the government should underwrite developmental schemes and foster agricultural settlement.

Miles favoured heavy borrowing and was responsible for great, if not always wise or lucrative, expenditure between 1884 and 1887. Successful in the Works Department he was not happy as secretary of mines since he lacked the special knowledge, vision and patience necessary for success. The very qualities which served him well in one office handicapped him in the other, and he was never in the first rank as a politician. He was tenacious, outspoken, unusually honest and hard-working, and his rough manners and picturesque profanities made him a valuable workhorse of the Griffith ministry but his faults and virtues counterbalanced in smaller measure the cool caution of his leader. A Presbyterian, Miles died at Toowoomba on 22 August 1887 and was buried in Toowong

cemetery, survived by his wife and two daughters. His probate was sworn at an unexpectedly low £60,708. A town in Queensland is named after him.

Toowoomba Chronicle, 25 Aug 1887; *Queenslander*, 27 Aug 1887.   D. B. WATERSON

MILFORD, SAMUEL FREDERICK (1797-1865), judge, was born on 16 September 1797 in Exeter, England, eldest son of Samuel Frederick Milford of Heavitree, magistrate and deputy lieutenant of Devon and Sussex, and his wife Jane, née Foskett. Educated at the High School, Exeter, he entered St John's College, Cambridge (B.A., 1819; M.A., 1822). Called to the Bar at Lincoln's Inn on 10 May 1822, he practised at Bristol and became a judge in the Diocesan Ecclesiastical Court. In 1842 illness induced him to seek better health in Australia; recommended by his cousin Sir William Follett, attorney-general, he was appointed master in Equity in New South Wales with a proposed salary of £1000.

Milford arrived in Sydney on 1 January 1843 in the *Hamlet* with his wife Eliza, née Butler, whom he had married in 1825, and their six children. Admitted to the colonial Bar on 23 January 1843 he was sworn in next day as master in Equity. He also became chief commissioner of insolvent estates and deputy-commissary and surrogate of the Vice-Admiralty Court. The Legislative Council reduced his salary but Governor Gipps charged the difference to Crown revenue.

Milford ably discharged the office of master in Equity but was refused a salary rise in 1848. On 1 January 1856 he was appointed an additional judge of the Supreme Court and deputy-judge and commissary of the Vice-Admiralty Court in New South Wales. He also presided at Brisbane Circuit Courts and in other jurisdictions of the New South Wales Supreme Court but claimed the right, when the two colonies were separated, to be recalled to the New South Wales bench. On 1 April 1857 he became first resident judge at Moreton Bay but sought return to Sydney. He strongly disagreed with W. M. Manning, attorney-general, and J. B. Darvall [qq.v.], solicitor-general, who held the opinion that on separation Milford would cease to be a judge of the New South Wales Supreme Court. However, he helped with court arrears in Sydney and, supported by Chief Justice Stephen and Judge Therry [qq.v.], was reappointed to the New South Wales Supreme Court on 21 February 1859.

As primary Equity judge and judge of the

Vice-Admiralty Court Milford continued to preside in all jurisdictions though his talents lay chiefly in Equity, where his hard work, courtesy and kindly disposition won general esteem. His expeditious judgments were generally upheld on appeal. In 1865 against medical advice he attended the Assizes at Maitland where he died on 19 May. He was buried in the Anglican section of Camperdown cemetery with a state funeral. He was survived by his wife, four sons and two daughters, to whom he left goods valued at £4000. A stained glass window in St Andrew's Cathedral, Sydney, was erected by members of the legal profession in appreciation of his services and those of Judge Wise [q.v.] who had also died that year.

His eldest son Charles Sussex served with the army in India, retired as major-general and visited Sydney, where in 1877 he placed a mural tablet in St Mary's Cathedral to the memory of his mother who had worshipped there for thirty years. The second son Herman, a barrister, was a surrogate to the Vice-Admiralty Court of New South Wales from 1859 until he died in 1865. His third son Frederick, a surgeon on the teaching staff of St Vincent's Hospital, Sydney, wrote extensively on medical subjects, and was a keen and fearless yachtsman. His youngest son Henry John Bede became a solicitor in Sydney in 1855 and as an independent in 1864 defeated Henry Parkes [q.v.] for Braidwood in the Legislative Assembly. He practised in Sydney until 1867 and then at Rockhampton, where in 1869 he won a by-election in the Queensland parliament but resigned in April 1870 without taking his seat. From 1885 he practised at Charters Towers where he died on 29 February 1888, survived by his wife Katherine Charlotte, née Dick, whom he had married at Sydney in 1856, and by two sons and a daughter.

HRA (1), 25; J. T. S. Bird, *The early history of Rockhampton* (Rockhampton, 1904); V&P (LC NSW), 1855, 1, 693, 729, 1859-60, 5, 251, (LA NSW), 1858, 1, 10, 1203, 1859-60, 2, 511, 1865, 2, 890; J. A. Dowling, 'The judiciary', *JRAHS*, 2 (1906-09); *MJA*, 13 Mar 1926; *SMH*, 2 Jan 1843, 23 Feb 1859, 21 June 1865, 30 Nov 1868; *Sydney Mail*, 6 Feb 1864; Governor's despatches 1842-43 (ML); Milford notebooks (NSWA); Attorney-General's Dept papers, v 1 (NSWA); CO 201/508.   H. T. E. HOLT

MILLER, HENRY (1809-1888), financier and politician, was born on 31 December 1809 at Londonderry, Ireland, son of Henry Miller (Millar), captain in the 40th Regiment, and his wife Jane, née Morpeth. In 1823 his father, a veteran of the Peninsular war and Waterloo, took his family to Sydney with a detachment of his regiment in charge of convicts and in August 1824 he became the first commandant at Moreton Bay; transferred to Van Diemen's Land in 1826 he had charge of the ordnance store until the regiment went to India in 1829; he retired in 1832 and returned to Hobart Town where he died in 1866, predeceased by his wife in 1841.

Henry travelled with his family and was educated in Paris and Glasgow. In 1828 he became a clerk in the Tasmanian Audit Office. After a visit to Port Phillip in 1839 he resigned his post and settled in Melbourne. He soon began business as a financier and in 1845 as a merchant. In 1849 he founded the Victorian Fire and Marine Insurance Co., of which he was chairman, and in 1850 the first of a 'Union Terminating' series of building societies and was president of six of the seven he established. The leading promoter of the Bank of Victoria, incorporated in October 1852, he was chairman of directors until 1888. In 1859 he founded the Victorian Life and General Assurance Co. Claiming that speculation was not in his blood, he steered clear of mining companies though his many pastoral holdings and city properties were gamble enough.

In 1851-56 Miller represented South Bourke, Evelyn and Mornington in Victoria's first Legislative Council. In July 1852 he induced it to petition for a branch of the Mint in Melbourne. In November 1854 he unsuccessfully introduced a bill for a general system of education. In six years he served on fifty-three select committees, including one that framed the new Constitution. In the new Legislative Council he represented Central District from November 1856 to March 1858 and then Western District until January 1867. In 1857 he had supported the government's railway scheme but opposed in vain the creation of a new insurance company. Few believed that his opposition centred on the concept of limited liability status which he had previously championed, but rather that his monopoly would be broken by the proposed company. His priorities began to appear questionable. Under O'Shanassy [q.v.] he was made minister for trade and customs from March 1858 to October 1859. In July 1866 he became vice-president of the Board of Land and Works, commissioner of railways and roads, and representative of the McCulloch [q.v.] ministry in the Legislative Council. Public comment was adverse on this 'about face'. No longer trusted by his electorate he failed at the polls in January 1867 and retired from politics.

Miller was an opportunist: the *Imperial Review*, July 1888, lamented that no illegality could be pinned on him because he always observed the law. While minister of customs he was alleged to issue permits readily to his own firms but tardily to all others. After Duffy's [q.v.] 1862 Land Act he had founded a Free Selection Land Investment Society to help those who joined for 15s. to pay off a mortgage by monthly instalment; however, fines for non-payments and resumption were the penalty for two months' default or a debt of £6. Miller acquired a fortune through this one venture. A brilliant investor he continued to amass city properties and pastoral holdings. From his great wealth he took up four-fifths of the £50,000 loan floated by the Corporation of Melbourne for public works in 1868 and gave £5000 to St Paul's building fund in 1881. The press was convinced that he gained political influence by such moves. Generally reticent, some said secretive, he dedicated himself to making wealth, thereby earning the nickname of 'Money Miller'.

After paralysis in 1887 his health was uncertain. He died on 7 February 1888 at his thirty-acre property Findon at Kew and was buried in the Melbourne general cemetery. At Trinity Church, Hobart, on 11 November 1834 he had married Eliza, daughter of Captain Mattinson. She died on 5 April 1892, survived by four sons and three married daughters. A son, Edward (1848-1932), served for twenty years in the Legislative Council and in 1917 was knighted. Henry Miller's real and personal estate was eventually sworn for probate in New South Wales at £163,817, and at £1,456,680 in Victoria where it was taxed at 5 per cent.

HRA (1), 16, (3), 6; G. Serle, The golden age (Melb, 1963); Argus, 16 Nov 1857, 8 Feb 1888; Daily Telegraph (Melb), 8 Feb 1888; Australasian, 9, 23 June, 13, 20 Oct, 8 Dec 1888; 9 Apr 1892; CSO 50/7 (TA).

SUZANNE G. MELLOR

MILLER, MAXWELL (1832-1867), journalist, politician and author, was born in London, third son of Robert Miller, barrister, and his wife Jane Matilde, née Montmorini. For nine years he attended St Paul's School and then won the Camden exhibition to Worcester College, Oxford, in October 1850 and as Fitzgerald scholar transferred to Queen's College in 1851. Attracted to Victoria by reports from his elder brother William and by an offer from Bishop Perry [q.v.] of an inspectorship of Church of England schools, Miller migrated to Melbourne in 1852. He claimed that he had 'made Education a study from inclination' but disorder caused by the gold rush upset

his plans. He became a sub-editor of the Argus and in 1855 was invited to Hobart Town with his brother to start the Tasmanian Daily News. It began on 14 March but ran at a loss until 2 June 1858 when it was incorporated in the Hobarton Mercury.

On 17 September 1856 Miller was elected a member for Hobart in the House of Assembly and from 26 February to 25 April 1857 served under T. G. Gregson [q.v.] as a minister without portfolio. When Francis Smith [q.v.] became premier in May Miller energetically supported his bill for creating the Tasmanian Council of Education with control over superior schools and endowment of scholarships. Miller criticized existing schools and argued that 'above all, we must render the masters careless of the whims or caprices of parents' but claimed that honours and prizes would induce practical Tasmanian youths to prolong their scholastic careers and 'learn to submit to discipline as do English boys'. Smith's bill, passed in 1858, had much influence on the colony's education system and was amended and re-enacted three times before the University of Tasmania was established in 1890. Miller often asked awkward questions in the assembly but in 1860 submitted a useful list of the Grammar Schools of England and the reigns in which they were founded.

Miller resigned from parliament in 1860 but was re-elected for Hobart on 28 May 1862. He resigned again in 1864 and on 29 July was appointed assistant clerk and librarian in the assembly. He had published The Tasmanian House of Assembly. A Metrical Catalogue, full of witty verses in 1860, and Financial Condition of Tasmania, a lecture to the Hobart Mechanics' Institute on 27 January 1862. As librarian he collated a useful Catalogue of The Blue Books in possession of the Parliament of Tasmania in May 1865. He continued as assistant clerk until he died in the Hobart General Hospital on 10 April 1867 aged 34.

V&P (HA Tas), 1860 (28, 71), 1862, 25.

MILLER, ROBERT BYRON (1825-1902), lawyer and politician, and GRANVILLE GEORGE (1847-1910), judge, were born in London, the eldest and youngest of four sons of Robert Miller and his wife Jane Matilde, née Montmorini. Their father had entered Trinity College, Dublin (B.A., 1822; M.A., 1827), and was called to the Bar of the Middle Temple on 10 November 1826; he practised on the Midland circuit, became serjeant-at-law on 7 November 1850 and from January 1856 was a circuit judge in Leicester and Rutland until he died on 5 August 1876.

Robert was born on 19 April 1825 and educated at private schools and King's College, London. He was trained in his father's chambers, admitted to the Middle Temple in 1843 and called to the Bar on 28 January 1848. After practising in London he decided to migrate, arrived at Hobart Town in January 1855 and was admitted a barrister in the Supreme Court of Tasmania. On 11 April he married Emily, daughter of George Berkeley Harrison of London. They settled in Launceston where Miller was a partner of Adye Douglas [q.v.] for five years. He is credited with finding 'some primitive customs in . . . Tasmanian courts' and risking the displeasure of those in power by successfully introducing 'changes more in accordance with justice and freedom'.

In 1861 Miller was elected a member for Launceston in the House of Assembly and soon started to propose bills for legal reform. He was appointed solicitor-general in 1862 and in January 1863 attorney-general in James Whyte's [q.v.] ministry. With the premier he tried in vain to persuade the Victorian government to share in the cost of the submarine telegraph cable from Cape Schanck to Low Head. At the general elections in October 1866 he clashed with his independent constituents who abhorred the ministry's proposal for *ad valorem* duties and income tax. He therefore contested a Hobart seat and won, but the ministry was defeated in November and soon afterwards he resigned from politics. For three years he practised in Melbourne and then returned to Launceston. Criminal actions were his speciality. His cases were thoroughly prepared and his eloquence, experience and quick perception magnetized juries, often turning defeat into victory. According to the press, he was 'the cleverest of his class that Tasmania has known'. In 1871-76 Joseph Powell was his partner and then his eldest son Ernest Granville. For years he was president of the Mechanics' Institute and as an alderman strongly supported improved drainage and sanitation. Increasing deafness made him withdraw from the practice which passed to his son. He died at his home in Elphin Road, Launceston, on 5 October 1902, survived by his wife, three sons and several daughters. He left an estate of £1982 to his family.

Granville George was educated at Trinity Hall, Cambridge (B.A., 1874) and called to the Bar of the Inner Temple on 3 November 1873. He migrated to Queensland in 1877 and was admitted to practise in the Supreme Court on 4 December. He was briefly crown prosecutor and in 1879 became master of titles. In November 1882 he was appointed a district court judge, his duties taking him as far as Normanton and other remote parts of north and west Queensland. From close acquaintance Sir Arthur Rutledge described him as 'a most careful, able, painstaking, and just Judge'. Miller was always ready to take the place of a colleague temporarily and was 'merciful to a degree in sentencing wrongdoers'. With a retiring disposition he made few close friends and on circuit his favourite exercise was walking. In his last years he presided over the Land Appeal Court. He died from chest trouble at his home, Clonmyle, Bowen Terrace, New Farm, on 6 July 1910 and was buried in Toowong cemetery. Predeceased by his first wife Clara Theresa Daly whom he had married in 1882, he was survived by his second wife Frances Georgina O'Reilly whom he had married in 1905.

Examiner (Launceston), 6, 7 Oct 1902; *Mercury*, 6 Oct 1902; *Brisbane Courier*, 7, 8, 9 July 1910.

MILLER, WILLIAM (1846-1939), athlete, was born on 16 December 1846 at Liscard, Cheshire, England, son of Alexander Miller, wine and spirits merchant, and his wife Sarah Anne, née Hatton. At 5 he arrived in Victoria with his family and in 1862-69 worked for the Melbourne and Hobson's Bay Railway Co. as station-master and telegraph instructor. In fencing, boxing and gymnastics he showed singular proficiency and in 1872 won the Australian broadsword championship by defeating a sergeant of the Light Hussars. In America from 1874 to 1880 he defeated cosmopolitan champions in boxing and wrestling, winning 55 out of 72 matches with 11 draws. In 1879 he defeated the walker Duncan Ross over 102 miles in 24 hours and drew with the champion weight-lifter Richard Pennell, both lifting 1550 lbs. of solid iron. In Melbourne an eight-hour wrestling match in 1880 with his former pupil William Muldoon ended in a draw. He defeated the Scottish wrestler and weight-lifter Donald Dinnie in dumb-bell contests and later drew with him in a wrestling match despite a broken leg.

In 1883 Miller opened a gymnasium in Liverpool Street, Sydney, and in May challenged the champion boxer L. Foley [q.v.] to fight with gloves for a stake of £500. Spectators broke up the fight after forty rounds and it was called a draw though Foley conceded the fight. In Melbourne he coached at the Olympic Club in 1884-89 and later at his gymnasium in Elizabeth Street. He competed in Graeco-Roman wrestling matches with Whistler and T. Cannon and defeated Sali and Christol combined. He appeared on the stage in a Shakespearian wrestling scene and lectured on physical culture in the Hibernian Hall. In 1886 he retired from competitive sport but in America issued challenges in 1889 for boxing, wrestling, fencing and weight-lifting, none of which was taken up.

In Melbourne from 1889 to 1903 Miller, nicknamed professor, continued wrestling and defeated R. Ross in April 1890 at the Melbourne Athletic Club of which Miller was manager. The only athlete to hold the Australian championships for boxing, fencing, wrestling and weight-lifting, he weighed 14 stone, was 5 ft. 9¾ ins. tall, had 17 ins. biceps, 17 ins. calves and a 46 ins. chest. In 1895 he published *Health, Exercise and Amusement* in Melbourne.

In 1903 Miller returned to America and was manager of the San Francisco Athletic Club and later athletic instructor with the New York police. On 2 March 1872 at Emerald Hill, Melbourne, he had married Lizzie Margery (d. 1929), née Trible, daughter of an American Baptist minister; they had no children. From 1917 Miller lived in Baltimore where he died on 11 March 1939. He was buried in the Greenmount cemetery, and the Baltimore *Sun* described him as 'one of the greatest all-round athletes in the world'.

J. E. Tonkin (ed), *The English, Australian & American sporting calendar* (Syd, 1884); 'Vigilant' (ed), *Australian sporting celebrities* (Melb, 1887); *New York Times*, 13 Mar 1939; *Bulletin*, 14 Aug 1880, 26 Feb 1881, 17 Feb 1937, 26 Apr 1939; *Australasian*, 3 Oct 1885, 25 Sept, 25 Dec 1886, 12 Oct 1889, 8 Mar, 12 Apr 1890.
DEIRDRE MORRIS

MILLS, CHARLES (1832-1916), sheepbreeder, was born at Horsburgh Castle, Peebleshire, Scotland, son of George Mills, a sheep farmer from one of the oldest lowland families, and his wife Jean, née Purves. Educated at the Edinburgh Institution, he found office work distasteful and for eight years worked with Border Leicester sheep at Gilmanscleuch, a farm his father leased for him in Selkirkshire. He migrated to Melbourne in 1863 and worked on the McKenzie family's Mount Pleasant station in north Gippsland. With J. J. Smart and Andrew Neilson he later took up two large leaseholds, Watchem and Morton Plains, on the fringe of the Mallee in north-western Victoria. Successful, he sold his share in the stations in 1872 and went to Scotland, where in December 1874 he married Margaret, daughter of John Ainslie, a sheepbreeder of Fairfield, near Edinburgh, and returned to Australia with her.

In 1875, with Neilson and William Smith, Mills bought Uardry, 70,000 acres on the northern bank of the Murrumbidgee near Hay. They were fortunate in acquiring a small flock of pure Peppin [q.v.] merinos. Mills managed the property and made the stud flock his personal care. By careful selection, mating and avoiding outside blood, he established a first-class merino flock with 'a bold combing wool of medium to strong quality'. From the 1880s Uardry sheep were exhibited at the Hay show, where they won 104 champions and firsts, and 60 second prizes. Experts agreed that 'no bettershaped or better conditioned merino sheep' had been bred.

When his partners died Mills bought their shares and continued to control Uardry until 1900, when his eldest son Ainslie, and then his third son Neilson, took over the practical management; they later formed a family company, Charles Mills (Uardry) Ltd. Mills continued to advise what was one of the most highly improved and intensively irrigated studs in Australia. By 1917 Uardry had 38 ground tanks, 11 wells and 15 subartesian bores equipped with windmills, tanks and troughs.

In 1870-79 Mills served on the Board of Sheep Directors for the Hay District, and was appointed a magistrate on 2 August 1883. 'One of the most noted merino sheep breeders of Australia', he was unpretentious, kindly and given to 'quaint humour and droll sayings'. In his last years he lived at Fyan's Lodge, Toorak, Melbourne, where he died on 20 May 1916, survived by his wife, three sons and two daughters; he was buried in the Boroondara cemetery. A Uardry ram adorned the reverse side of the one shilling piece and the stud remained the property of the company until it was sold in April 1973.

Pastoral Review Pty Ltd, *The pastoral homes of Australia—N.S.W.* (Melb, 1910); E. J. Brady, *Australia unlimited* (Melb, 1918); NSW Sheepbreeders' Assn, *The Australian merino* (Syd, 1955); R. B. Ronald, *The Riverina: people and properties* (Melb, 1960); *Government Gazette* (NSW), 1879 (1), 1883 (3); *Pastoral Review*, 15 Oct 1907, 16 June 1916; *Argus*, 22 May 1916; *Australasian*, 3 June 1916.
SUZANNE EDGAR

MILNE, SIR WILLIAM (1822-1895), wine and spirits merchant and politician, was born on 17 May 1822 at Glasgow, Scotland, eldest son of William Milne, merchant, and his wife Elizabeth, née McMillan. Educated at Glasgow High School, he was trained in commerce. With a free passage as a farm servant he arrived at Port Adelaide on 29 October 1839 in the *Palmyra*. The family had intended to join him but their plans were changed when the father died. At Trinity Church on 4 March 1842 Milne married

Eliza Disher (1818-1912) whose family also had free passages in the *Palmyra* and had settled near Nairne. Milne went to Van Diemen's Land but returned in 1845 and with his brother-in-law, John Disher of Oakbank, as partner set up as wine and spirits merchants. In 1846 they took over the business of Patrick Auld [q.v.].

Successful in his distillery, Milne sold it in 1857 and represented Onkaparinga in the House of Assembly. He was commissioner of crown lands and immigration in the Baker [q.v.] ministry from 21 August to 1 September 1857, under Hanson [q.v.] from 5 July 1859 to 9 May 1860, under Ayers [q.v.] from 22 July to 4 August 1864 and under Boucaut [q.v.] from 28 March 1866 to 3 May 1867. He served as commissioner for public works in the Waterhouse [q.v.] ministry from 19 February 1862 to 4 July 1863, and under Blyth [q.v.] from 4 August 1864 to 22 March 1865. In 1868 he resigned from the assembly and in 1869 was elected to the Legislative Council. He served as chief secretary in the Hart [q.v.] ministry from 30 May 1870 to 10 November 1871 and under Blyth from 10 November 1871 to 22 January 1872.

While with the Crown Lands Department Milne ruled that before any land was put up for sale, a hundred be first declared so that every buyer could secure commonage rights. Under former ministers the best land outside the limits of hundreds had often been surveyed and put up for auction, thus placing agriculturists at such disadvantage that sections were usually bought by the squatter on whose run the land was situated. Milne's regulation thus encouraged land settlement by farmers. In 1863 he introduced an amendment to the Scab in Sheep Act which helped to extirpate the disease. He had cuttings made in the South-East to drain large tracts for agricultural purposes; 100,000 acres of rich alluvial soil were thus reclaimed and one section was named Milne's Gap. In 1866 he introduced the scrub lands bill which induced settlers to take up country covered with mallee and other scrub, hitherto regarded as valueless. In 1857-58 he helped to pass the Real Property Act and R. R. Torrens [q.v.] always referred to him as 'an early and warm supporter of the cause'.

In June 1870 the Hart government initiated the construction of the overland telegraph to Port Darwin and Milne carried the bill authorizing it through the Legislative Council; he was responsible for carrying out the work. By surmounting the difficulties which arose through the failure of contractors to complete their sections, he enabled the line to be completed within the specified time. He was associated with other public works such as telegraphs to Sydney,

Mount Gambier, Port Augusta, Moonta and Milang, the extension of waterworks to Port Adelaide and Port Augusta, the erection of lighthouses at Cape Jaffa and Cape Jervois and the building of many railways. He was also responsible for many bills and in 1859 alone initiated eight Acts relating to statute law consolidation and two more for establishing militia and volunteer forces. On 25 July 1873 he was nominated president of the council by William Morgan [q.v.], who drew attention to Milne's social standing and influence, the respect he commanded in the colony, his parliamentary experience and his firmness to 'guard carefully the privileges and rights of the council'. For his services to the colony he was appointed K.B. on 12 October 1876 but in 1878 recommendation by Governor Jervois failed to win him a K.C.M.G. He retired from politics in 1881 and visited Britain in 1884.

Milne was agent of several absentee colonists, a director of the Moonta Mine Co. from 1873 and chairman in 1888-90. After the amalgamated Wallaroo and Moonta Mining and Smelting Co. was formed he was chairman of its board in 1890-95. He was also a trustee of the Savings Bank, a councillor of the Zoological and Acclimatization Society and served on the committee of the Institution of the Blind and the Central Roads Board in 1858-59. Prominent in the volunteer movement, he became a captain in the mounted and foot forces. After a short illness he died at his home, Sunnyside, Glen Osmond, on 23 April 1895, survived by his wife, three of their four sons and three of their five daughters. His funeral service at St Andrew's Presbyterian Church, Adelaide, was well attended and his estate of £53,000 was left to his family.

J. J. Pascoe, *History of Adelaide and vicinity* (Adel, 1901); H. T. Burgess (ed), *Cyclopedia of South Australia* (Adel, 1909); *Observer* (Adel), 27 Apr 1895; Musgrave to Carnarvon, 14 May 1875, Jervois to Hicks-Beach, 26 Oct, Dec 1878 (Confidential dispatches, SAA).

DIRK VAN DISSEL

MINCHIN, RICHARD ERNEST (1831-1893), zoological director, was born on 5 March 1831 at Greenhills, Tipperary, Ireland, thirteenth of the nineteen children of William Minchin, B.A., owner of Greenhills and rector of Dunkerrin, and his wife MaryAnn, daughter and coheiress of Corker Wright of Rutland, King's County. His father's family had moved from Gloucestershire to Ireland in the seventeenth century and acquired estates in Tipperary and adjoining counties. In 1852 Greenhills was sold and the family migrated to various countries, some settling near Christchurch, New Zealand; a brother, John Birch, became an early geographer in the Andes.

Minchin was educated at Dr Baillie's School and migrated to South Australia in the *Stag* with a brother, Henry Paul (1826-1909), in 1851. Henry had studied law in Dublin and for a decade was stipendiary magistrate and protector of Aborigines at Mount Remarkable, later turning to coffee planting in South India. The brothers had letters of introduction to the sheriff, Charles Burton Newenham, and to Captain C. H. Bagot [q.v.] on whose station Minchin worked for a time. He then moved to Victoria about 1854 and joined another brother, Corker Wright (1829-1926), who in 1858 became clerk of courts at Raglan, near Beaufort. On 19 September 1854 Minchin had married Ellen Rebecca, daughter of Richard Ocock, solicitor of Ballan; their first son Ernest William was born at Geelong in 1856.

With his wife and young family Minchin moved to South Australia where he was appointed a third-class clerk in the civil service on 14 January 1857. In 1859-69 he worked in the new Land Titles Registration Department as second draftsman, his salary rising to £260. From 1870 to about 1884 he was a contractor for the department, taking charge of the section when the senior draftsman was absent.

As an honorary member and secretary, Minchin was a prime mover in establishing the South Australian Acclimatization Society, founded in July 1878 to replace an earlier effort which had lapsed. The new president was the chief justice, S. J. Way, and largely through Minchin's work its name was changed to the South Australian Zoological and Acclimatization Society. In July 1881 as honorary secretary he wrote to the governors of the Botanic Gardens asking for part of their land for the preservation of animals. When the governors refused, a deputation from the society called on the chief secretary, J. C. Bray [q.v.], who favoured the project but refused support because residents of North Terrace feared that the animals would break out or keep them awake. In February 1882 a second deputation to Bray was led by Way with similar results. In March the society sent a memorial with 830 signatures to the governors of the Botanic Gardens renewing the request for land. The reply was obdurate and a third deputation to Bray asked for land near the Lunatic Asylum. The press suggested other sites and slated the governors: 'It was well known that Dr Schomburgk [q.v.] did not love animals in his garden'. In April another memorial with 1520 signatures was sent to the Botanic

Gardens and the governors suggested a site on the north side of the River Torrens, promising their hearty co-operation. In August a motion was carried in the House of Assembly for a zoo near Albert Bridge to be run by the Zoological and Acclimatization Society.

Minchin was appointed director of the Zoological Gardens in November. He had it fenced substantially and started to build a keeper's cottage. He visited the Melbourne zoo and Le Souef [q.v.] sent one of his keepers to serve the society. From his own collection in North Adelaide Minchin transferred a large aviary and other enclosures to the zoo and specimens were brought from the Botanic Gardens. With a 'special faculty for collecting' and a keen eye for a bargain he built up a large variety of birds and beasts without getting into debt. Through the society he received trout ova from Tasmania for hatching and gave publicity to the laws for the protection of animals and fish. In 1879-80 the society imported and freed English thrushes, skylarks, goldfinches and other birds.

In 1883 the zoo was formally opened on 23 May and Sir Thomas Elder [q.v.] became president of the society. He provided funds for a rotunda and the purchase and transport of the first elephant, Miss Siam. The first lions were donated in 1884 by Sir James Fergusson, then governor of Bombay, and J. H. Angas [q.v.] presented the first lioness. Minchin also acquired 2 tigers, 2 Tasmanian tigers and a large variety of birds. In 1885 the society sent him to South East Asia where he collected a rhinoceros, 2 white buffaloes, a black panther, 2 leopards, a sun bear, 10 tiger cats, 2 alligators, many monkeys and sundry 'curious creatures' from the royal menagerie in Siam and from Java, Ceylon, Malaya and the Northern Territory. On this tour Minchin was elected a corresponding member of the Zoological Society of London. In 1887 he visited Europe and with help from South Australian expatriates acquired more specimens for the zoo. In 1889 he was elected an honorary life member of the society and moved into the director's new residence at the zoo.

Minchin had little training for his mammoth task but his good judgment in collecting specimens was matched by the architectural elegance of the buildings for his animals. According to Governor Kintore, the society's gardens were more excellently managed than any outside London, the credit being due to Minchin's untiring care. In 1890 he was given leave and went to Hong Kong where he caught a wasting disease. He returned to Adelaide but was confined to his home. Minchin moved with his family to

Mount Barker where he died on 4 January 1893. After a large funeral he was buried in North Road cemetery. Predeceased by his first wife on 6 July 1882 he was survived by two sons and three daughters, and by his second wife Ellison Barbara Christina, daughter of Robert Forsyth Macgeorge, whom he had married in Adelaide on 16 August 1883. He left an estate of £1190. His second son Alfred Corker (1857-1934) had acted as honorary director in his father's absence and served as director for forty-one years.

PP (SA), 1860 (165) 18, 1866-67 (22) 28, 1882 (93); PD (SA), 1882, 1883-84; *Government Gazette* (SA), 1857, 44, 68, 666, 1858, 43, 484, 1859, 24; SA Acclimatization Soc, *Annual Report*, 1878-79; SA Zoological and Acclimatization Soc, *Annual Report*, 1880-1893; *Advertiser* (Adel), 5 Jan 1893, 21 Sept 1934.

E. J. MINCHIN

MIRAMS, JAMES (1839-1916), promoter and politician, was born on 2 January 1839 at Lambeth, London, third son of James Mirams, Congregational minister, and his wife Elizabeth, née Cole. Educated at a Congregational school at Chishall, he trained as an ironmonger and worked at Royston. When his father accepted the position of minister at the Independent Church, Collins Street, Melbourne, Mirams sailed with the family and arrived in June 1857. He tried dairy farming at Braybrook until all his cattle died, and then became a teacher at the National school in Fitzroy and in 1863-74 a bookseller, stationer and newsagent at Collingwood.

In 1874 Mirams was the promoter and secretary of the Premier Permanent Building, Land, and Investment Association, which had a flourishing business by the mid-1880s. In that decade he became involved in numerous speculations, such as the Freehold Farms Co. and the Essendon Land and Tramway Co. Ltd. A Sabbatarian and a leading temperance advocate, he was also the promoter of the flamboyantly designed Federal Coffee Palace which was opened in time for the 1888 Exhibition.

Between 1871 and 1875 Mirams had made four unsuccessful attempts to enter the Legislative Assembly, but represented Collingwood from February 1876 to February 1886 and Williamstown from November 1887 to March 1889. Politically he was a staunch Liberal and at first a committed follower of Graham Berry [q.v.]. A founder of the Liberal party, he was secretary of the Central Council of the Victorian Protection League in 1875-76 and of the National Reform and Protection League in 1877. The Sydney *Bulletin* described him as one of the most 'uncompromising democrats' of the 1880s. No doubt his long political association with the distinctly working-class suburb of Collingwood helped to shape his views. A consistent critic of the Legislative Council during the constitutional crisis in 1877-80, he opposed plural voting and supported payment of members and uniform electorates. He was an ardent protectionist and sought to improve the new system of state schools. He advocated the leasing of remaining crown lands (a principle partly accepted in 1884) and the establishment of a national bank of issue. In 1885, a time of rampant 'jingoism', he opposed aid to the British government in the Sudan and in 1886, with the apparent success of Parnell at Westminster, he was one of the few Protestant politicians openly to favour Home Rule.

Yet apart from appointment as chairman of the royal commission on the tariff in 1881-83 Mirams's political fortunes did not prosper. Perhaps he was too doctrinaire to be trusted in a Liberal party which represented a coalition of interests. He quarrelled with Berry over the compromise settlement of the constitutional question, and condemned the formation of the coalition Conservative-Liberal ministry in 1883. He hoped to succeed Berry as party leader but Alfred Deakin was preferred in 1885. The election of 1886 revealed his frustrations and was a portent of his later political affiliations. Under the auspices of a hastily-formed National Liberal League, Mirams and F. H. Bromley, president of the Trades Hall Council, ran on the same ticket for Collingwood but both were defeated.

Mirams's political reverses coincided with his frenetic role as one of the pace-makers of the land boom. In 1887 £300,000 was placed on deposit with the Premier Building Association; the amount doubled next year when its affairs were in utter disorder; the society had borrowed more than the legal limit of three times its paid-up capital. Much of the new money was borrowed on the security of the society's own loans to borrowers. In November he resigned as secretary; the first signs of the 'pricking' of the land boom, his mismanagement of the society's finances and his embarrassing involvement in other speculations forced the issue. The society closed its doors in December 1889. Meanwhile Mirams had invested £1 million in land purchases; in March 1890 he filed his application for liquidation by arrangement, the schedule showing debts of £373,485. His estate eventually paid 2d. in the £1. In November 1890 he was convicted of issuing a false balance sheet with intent to defraud on behalf of the Premier Building Association, and was sentenced to a year's imprisonment.

After his release Mirams continually protested his innocence; in 1896 he lost a protracted libel action against the *Argus*. For a time he was a milkman and then an accountant. In 1900 he published *A Generation of Victorian Politics* in Melbourne; in 1901 he failed dismally in the first elections for the House of Representatives. In 1911 he was the unsuccessful Labor candidate for the state seat of Evelyn. He died on 21 June 1916, survived by his wife Mary Ann, née Paterson, whom he had married in 1859, and by seven sons and three daughters.

In passing sentence in 1890, Chief Justice Higinbotham [q.v.] had summed up Mirams's main failing: 'you are in the position of a man who will not look at the facts, and who is determined not to consider that it may be possible that he has done wrong'. With strong opinions and inflexible views, he was less fortunate than other leading 'boomers' during Victoria's economic débâcle of the early 1890s.

M. Cannon, *The land boomers* (Melb, 1966); G. Serle, *The rush to be rich* (Melb, 1971); *Argus*, 24 Oct, 27 Dec 1890, 18 Apr, 8 May 1896.
                                    S. M. INGHAM

MITCHELL, DAVID (1829-1916), builder, contractor and businessman, was born on 16 February 1829 in Forfarshire, Scotland, son of William Mitchell, tenant farmer, and his wife Anne. In 1846 he was apprenticed to a master mason and on completing his indenture sailed from Liverpool on 6 April 1852 in the *Anna*, ariving at Melbourne on 24 July.

Mitchell worked as a mason and saved money to build a shanty on a lot in Burnley Street, Richmond. Next year he visited Bendigo and near-by goldfields but returned to set up as a building contractor at his Richmond site, which became the centre of his business operations. In 1856 he married Isabella (b. 1833), daughter of James Dow, an engineer at Langlands [q.v.] Iron Foundry, and built a new home, Doonside, to replace his shanty.

The next forty-five years saw his active and successful participation in a variety of business ventures. Work had been started in 1850 on rebuilding St Patrick's Cathedral, Eastern Hill, and in April 1856 Mitchell won the tender for the masonry work for £7760. By mid-1858 he had completed this work on the first stage of the building but it was then decided to demolish the existing structure and to start again with W. W. Wardell [q.v.] as architect.

By 1859 Mitchell had a factory for steam-made and pressed bricks at Burnley Street. In 1874 he became a shareholder in the Melbourne Builders' Lime and Cement Co., formed to break the monopoly of the Geelong limeburners. By 1878 he had bought Cave Hill farm at Lilydale and began working its limestone deposits, later also handling the distribution. In 1888 his extensive workshops at Richmond were destroyed by fire. He rebuilt the works and added two new ventures, the production of 'Adamant' plaster and in 1890, with R. D. Langley as partner, a Portland cement factory at Burnley using materials from Lilydale.

In 1890 Mitchell formed a company to mine a channel and tunnel on the Yarra River at Pound Bend, Warrandyte, and employed gangs of Chinese to work three miles of riverbed for gold. By 1894 he had cheese, butter, bacon, ham and soap factories at Cave Hill, housing them in a complex of well-designed brick buildings. In 1888 his dairy had operated the colony's first mechanical milking device. By 1900 he owned vineyards and wineries at Yeringberg, Coldstream and St Hubert's. He acquired several large stations in various districts, including the Bethanga estate on the upper Murray, Jancourt in the Western District, Gooramadda, Dueran, Barjarg and Colbinabbin, most of which were subdivided and sold.

Among his many large structures Mitchell built the Menzies Hotel in William Street (1857), the Paterson, Laing & Bruce [q.v.] warehouse, Flinders Lane (1871), Scots Church, Collins Street (1873-74), the Presbyterian Ladies' College, East Melbourne (1874), Prell's Buildings (1887), the Masonic Hall, Collins Street (1888), the Equitable Insurance Building (1893), the National Bank and the New Zealand Loan Co.'s wool and grain warehouses at Kensington. His grandest venture was the Exhibition Building, which employed 400 men and was opened in 1880. He retired from building in 1899 and concentrated on his other business interests.

Mitchell had given support to the eight-hour movement in 1856 but was not very active in public affairs. He was a member of the Council of the (Royal) Agricultural Society and of the Builders' and Contractors' Association. As a Presbyterian he was a long-time member of Scots Church choir. His musical interests included playing the violin at home and encouraging the talents of his daughter Helen, later Dame Nellie Melba, but even when she became world famous his natural reticence prevented him from openly praising her singing. Predeceased by his wife in 1881, he died on 25 March 1916. Of his ten children, he was survived by Frank, Charles and Ernest, Dame Nellie Melba who travelled extensively after 1886, and three married daughters living in Melbourne.

A portrait is held by the David Mitchell Estate Ltd., and another by Hugh Ramsay is in the Castlemaine Art Gallery.

J. Smith (ed), *Cyclopedia of Victoria*, 1 (Melb, 1903); *Illustrated Aust News*, 9 Oct 1880; *Argus*, 19 Oct 1888, 27 Mar 1916; *Australasian*, 9 May 1903; *Age*, 27 Mar 1916; J. Mitchell, David Mitchell, builder, 1852-1899 (thesis, Architecture Lib, Univ Melb, 1968).

JOAN CAMPBELL

MITCHELL, DAVID SCOTT (1836-1907), book collector and national benefactor, was born on 19 March 1836 in Sydney, only son of Dr James Mitchell [q.v.] and his wife Augusta Maria Frederick, née Scott. In October 1852 he became one of the first undergraduates of the University of Sydney (B.A., 1856; M.A., 1859), where he won scholarships in mathematics, with prizes also in physics and chemistry; he also played cricket outside the university. In December 1858 he was admitted to the Bar but never practised though he is said to have later declined appointment as attorney-general.

With independent means Mitchell shared in the diversions of Sydney society and won renown especially for prowess at whist. On slight evidence he is alleged to have had a broken romance with Emily, daughter of Sir William Manning [qq.v.], thereby changing the course of his life. Probably more significant was the death of his father in February 1869; his will was successfully contested by the family on the grounds that his mind had been failing and he was under an outsider's undue influence. The notoriety of the case was humiliating to the refined and sensitive Mitchell. His mother died in 1871 and he moved from the family home in Cumberland Street to Darlinghurst Road, where he lived in increasing seclusion as a bibliophile.

Mitchell had been reared in a cultivated household; never robust, he preferred books and intellectual interests to business or politics. By 1866 he had won some repute for scholarship in English literature and for the next twenty years he collected mainly English literary works, including many fine editions, which in 1900 exceeded 10,000 volumes. From about 1886, probably encouraged by George Robertson [q.v.], he turned almost solely to the record of Australia and its surrounding region. Book-collecting, which had been an intellectual pastime in youth and a scholarly vocation in maturity, became his all-absorbing purpose. His aim, not merely comprehensive but exhaustive, was to gather a copy of every document he could that related to Australia and also to the Pacific, the East Indies and Antarctica.

In this aim Mitchell was favoured: he had wealth, leisure and position, with useful social connexions yet was free from outside distractions. His scholarly knowledge of books, coupled with education, experience and a talent for book-collecting, approached genius. Moreover his predecessors and competitors were few and less fortunate. He was also well served by the booksellers, especially Robertson and his assistant, F. Wymark, who had vision besides bibliopolical skill. After 1895 he was aided and encouraged by H. C. L. Anderson, the principal librarian, who had seen Mitchell as the chief rival of the Public Library of New South Wales and set out to combine forces.

His association with Anderson, and perhaps with Dr James Norton [q.v.], Mitchell's solicitor and president of the library trustees, probably most influenced the disposition of his collection. Apart from Mitchell, the library had the best Australasian collection and had demonstrated a capacity and will to develop it. Mitchell was ageing and in poor health, with no relations of like interests to his own. On 17 October 1898 he offered to bequeath his collection to the library trustees. The offer was immediately accepted and eventually his conditions were met: the trustees were incorporated in 1899 and after the intervention of the premier, J. H. Carruthers, the Mitchell wing of the new library building was begun in 1906.

Mitchell had been baptized in St James's Church, Sydney, but became an agnostic. In all other matters he was a conservative. He was of spare build and delicate constitution although having nothing of doctors. Reserved and modest, he was a good conversationalist with a touch of wit and humour. He remained unmarried and lived meagrely and unostentatiously in a comfortless house, declining honours and any infringement on his privacy. His cousin, Rose Scott, was his nearest approach to a personal friend though he readily helped deserving scholars. He had a name for parsimony except in his collecting, where he spent liberally but with the collector's ethics that had no place for sentiment. He was also a good landlord though he did little to develop his estates of more than 42,000 acres, mainly in the Hunter Valley, leaving their management to agents.

Mitchell died on 24 July 1907 and bequeathed to the library trustees his entire collection with an endowment of £70,000. After some minor bequests the residue of his estate of £261,000 went to his sister Augusta, wife of James Merewether. Despite his fine memory and erudition he wrote nothing and left as his one main memorial the Mitchell Library in Sydney. When opened on 8 March 1910 it had some 60,000 volumes and much other material. It remains unrivalled in its field and is one of the great national collections in the world.

J. R. Tyrrell, *David Scott Mitchell: a reminiscence* (Syd, 1936); A. H. Spencer, *The hill of content* (Syd, 1959); C. E. Smith, *Dr. James Mitchell* (Newcastle, 1966); B. Stevens, 'David Scott Mitchell', *Lone Hand*, Oct 1907; G. D. Richardson, 'David Scott Mitchell', *Descent*, 1 (1961); H. C. L. Anderson, David Scott Mitchell, some reminiscences (ML); F. V. G. Wymark, Reminiscences of D. S. Mitchell (ML); D. S. Mitchell and Rose Scott papers (ML).

G. D. RICHARDSON

MITCHELL, JAMES (1835-1914), pastoralist, was born on 29 May 1835 at Brisbane Meadows, Bungonia, fourth and youngest son of Captain William Mitchell (1786-1837), grazier, and his wife Elizabeth, née Huon de Kerilleau. Her brother Charles had bought Mungabareena station (on the present site of Albury) from C. H. Ebden [q.v.] in 1836 and gave it to his widowed sister who moved there with her sons about 1841. Among the first white children on the Murray, the boys roamed with the Woradgery tribe and learned much Aboriginal lore and language. One brother, Thomas (d. 1887), managed Mungabareena for his mother for some years before taking up Tangambalanga on the Kiewa River and later Bringenbrong.

Trained as a pastoralist by his brothers, James took over Table Top (Mungabareena) in 1859 and in twenty-five years enlarged it from 3000 to 50,000 acres. With surplus timber removed, rabbits exterminated and netting-fences and dams constructed, the station became a model property famous for its fine Devon cattle, blood horses and merino sheep whose wool often topped the market. In 1884 Table Top carried 49,000 sheep, 129 cattle and 96 horses. A noted rider in his youth and sportsman, Mitchell was patron of the Albury Racing Club, the Albury Licensed Victuallers' Race Club and his colours were a popular sight on Sydney, Melbourne and country race-courses. His most successful horse was Cremorne whose wins included the Doncaster Handicap (1893) and the Caulfield Cup (1896).

Mitchell was genial with liberal instincts and generous impulses. He died at Table Top on 3 April 1914 and was buried in the Church of England cemetery, Albury. He was survived by his wife Sarah Jane, née Huon, whom he had married at Wodonga about 1862, and by three sons and five daughters of their nine children. His estate was sworn for probate at over £143,000. A generous benefactor to Albury, he had given £2000 towards the new hospital in 1913-14. In his will he set aside £4000 for St Matthew's Church of England, £2000 to the clergy superannuation fund for the Goulburn diocese and smaller amounts to other churches and charities; all his employees were remembered by small legacies.

E. J. Brady, *Australia unlimited* (Melb, 1918); W. A. Bayley, *Border city* (Albury, 1954); *Sydney Mail*, 5 July 1884; *Albury Daily News*, 3 Apr 1914; *Evening News* (Syd), 3 Apr 1914; *Wagga Express*, 4 Apr 1914; *SMH*, 2 June 1914.

G. P. WALSH

MITCHELL, JOSEPH EARL CHERRY (1840-1897), shipowner, politician and steel manufacturer, was born on 22 July 1840 in Cheshire, England, son of Richard Mitchell, shipbuilder, and his wife Margaret, née Cherry. After apprenticeship to his father he migrated to Sydney in 1859. He set up as a coal merchant in Newtown and later extended his interests to collieries and shipping, sending his colliers as far afield as China. Elected to the New South Wales Legislative Assembly he represented Newtown in 1881-82, 1883-85 and 1888, and Illawarra in 1889-91. A staunch free trader, he supported Henry Parkes [q.v.].

Mitchell, who held a major interest in the South Bulli mine and was associated with the adjoining Bellambi colliery, made the first positive move in New South Wales to establish an iron and steel industry when he visited England in December 1889 to increase his capital. English aid was offered, conditional on government support and the outcome of an investigation into iron ore resources near the Illawarra by the Scottish metallurgist, Ormiston.

Soon after Ormiston's favourable report G. & C. Hoskins emerged to challenge Mitchell. Protectionists supported the Hoskins's claims for a tariff of at least 15 per cent and a substantial government subsidy to compete with British steel. Mitchell ably put the free-trade case that neither tariff nor subsidy was necessary. On his side, he requested a contract to supply the government with steel rails. After several more visits to England Mitchell was assured of financial support and the issue was contested in parliament and the press. On 27 September 1897 cabinet accepted his terms but before parliament could ratify the decision Mitchell died from cancer on 22 October at his home, Milton House, Bellambi. He was buried in the Wesleyan section of Rookwood cemetery, survived by his wife Charlotte, née Harrison, of Bowral, whom he had married in 1866, and by three sons and five daughters. Charlotte died on 13 March 1919 at Milton House. Before Mitchell built the Methodist Church still in use at Bellambi, a monthly service was held at Milton House. Mitchell Street, Alexandria, was named after him.

SMH, 8, 9, 18 Jan 1885, 23 Oct 1897; *Daily Telegraph* (Syd), 16 Jan, 18, 19 Feb, 28, 30 Sept 1897; Mitchell papers (Wollongong City Lib and ML); Parkes papers (ML).

COLM KIERNAN

MITCHELL, WILLIAM (1834-1915), businessman and civic leader, was born on 18 June 1834 at Aberdeen, Scotland, son of David Mitchell and his wife Margaret, née Annand. With his parents, two brothers and three sisters he sailed from London in the *Thetis* and arrived at Port Phillip in February 1849. Apprenticed to a Melbourne baker, he broke his indentures in 1851 to visit the diggings at Castlemaine, where in six weeks he won gold worth £120. On his next visit he was joined by his father and they made £400 in about seven weeks. After equal success on a third trip William set up as a baker in Flemington but moved the business to Footscray in 1854. At St James's Church, Melbourne, on 19 August 1857 he married Margaret Powell.

In 1864 Mitchell sold the bakery to his brother David (1837-1919) and set up as a building contractor. The business thrived and soon became a major enterprise. With others he successfully floated the Footscray Gas Co. in 1874 and was a director for twenty years. Later he helped to start the Australian Woollen Mills in Footscray. With prosperity he turned to civic affairs. He won a seat in the Footscray Municipal Council in 1866; contesting each election he served as a councillor until 1893 and was mayor in 1885 and 1890. He was a member of the Melbourne Harbor Trust in 1884-86 and served on the Melbourne and Metropolitan Board of Works. He was appointed a justice of the peace in January 1876 and perhaps his greatest achievement was as chairman of the local bench from 1885 to 1915; his varied magisterial work involved an estimated 30,000 cases and despite his few peculiarities won him repute for his fairness and sincerity.

Mitchell was fond of sport. He was elected a member of the Victoria and Caulfield Racing Clubs in 1882 and the first president of the Footscray Bowling Club in 1901. On 19 August 1907 he celebrated his golden wedding. Serving on the bench to the end, he died of heart failure at his home Lynd-hurst in Footscray on 21 June 1915 and was buried privately in the Melbourne general cemetery. He was survived by his wife, nine children and thirty grandchildren.

J. Smith (ed), *Cyclopedia of Victoria*, 1 (Melb, 1903); H. Michell (ed), *Footscray's first fifty years* (Footscray, 1909); *Argus*, 22 June 1915; *Advertiser* (Footscray), 26 June 1915; *Independent* (Footscray), 26 June 1915.

MITCHELL, SIR WILLIAM HENRY FANCOURT (1811-1884), public servant, was born at Leicester, England, second son of George Barkley Mitchell, vicar of St Mary's Church, and his wife Penelope, daughter of William Fancourt. He was appointed writer in the Van Diemen's Land Executive Council's Office and arrived in the *Clyde* at Hobart Town in June 1833. Under Lieut-Governor Franklin he acted in several other offices. In May 1841 his visit to Flinders Island to inquire into costs of maintaining the Aboriginals induced Franklin to write to the Colonial Office recommending an increase of salary for Mitchell because of his responsible duties and faithful service. On 21 August at St John's Church of England, New Town, he married Christina, daughter of Andrew Templeton of Glasgow. On 21 March 1842 he resigned his appointment and in April they sailed for Port Phillip where he acquired Barfold station near Kyneton.

Mitchell was the first territorial magistrate sworn in by Judge William Jeffcott [q.v.]; in 1848 he was asked to choose the site for the town of Kyneton. Lieut-Governor La Trobe appointed him chief commissioner of police with orders to stamp out bushranging. When Mitchell began duty on 1 January 1853, the police force was disrupted by defections to the goldfields but he organized the amalgamation of the various police groups in the colony and within a year built up the force from 700 to over 2000. In a few months bushranging had been almost eradicated, and with help from Captain Charles MacMahon [q.v.], whom he had nominated as superintendent of city police, Mitchell reorganized the force in Melbourne, dividing it into sections each with its own beats and patrols. From August to November 1853 he was an official nominee in the Legislative Council.

After a visit to England in 1854-55 Mitchell resigned from the police and was succeeded by MacMahon. In the transition to the new Constitution in November 1855, he joined Haines's [q.v.] first ministry as an honorary minister, though not a member of the Legislative Council, and was sworn in as a member of the Executive Council. In November 1856 he was elected as one of the five original members for the North-Western Province in the council. From April 1857 to March 1858 he was postmaster-general in Haines's second ministry. Defeated at the council election in November 1858, he was returned at a by-election in August 1859 and from December 1861 to June 1863 was minister for railways and roads. In 1869 he was elected chairman of committees and in 1870 president of the Legislative Council, holding that office until 1884. For a quarter of a century he had been one of the staunchest conservatives and active defenders of the council. In 1875 he was appointed K.B. He was chairman of the Australasian Agency and Banking Corporation and in 1881, on its formation as a company, became chairman of directors of R. Goldsbrough [q.v.] & Co. He died suddenly at Barfold on 24 February 1884 and was given a public funeral. Of his nine children, the younger son Edward was knighted and for years was a leader of the Victorian Bar.

V&P (LC Vic), 1853-54, 3 (D18), (LA Vic), 1857-58, 1 (D27), 1861-62, 2 (D57); Australasian, 29 Nov 1884.

MOCATTA, GEORGE GERSHON (1815-1893), pastoralist and merchant, was born on 21 March 1815 in London, youngest child of Daniel Mocatta, a broker who helped to found the West London Synagogue, and his wife Nancy, née Goldsmid. Equipped with an adequate education, he arrived on 22 February 1829 at Sydney in the *Jupiter* with the family of his brother-in-law, J. B. Montefiore [q.v.]. In 1835 he served on the Mudgee committee of the Patriotic Fund and was sent to help in managing Montefiore's large holdings near Wellington. After a visit to Van Diemen's Land Mocatta returned to Wellington and asked the government for protection by mounted police. In 1839 he was a proprietor of the Australian Subscription Library. When Montefiore's empire began to decline, Mocatta branched out on his own. In 1839 he held leases of nearly 18,000 acres in the Counties of Bathurst, Westmorland and Georgiana. About 1840 he settled briefly at Blackdown near Bathurst but next year decided to dispose of the lease.

Unable in the depressed times to sell his stock profitably, he overlanded 1600 head of cattle belonging to himself, Suttor [q.v.] and Lee to the Moreton Bay District where he arrived on 17 September 1842 after a 'fortunate' journey of twelve weeks. He took up Grantham station on the Darling Downs and refused to accompany H. S. Russell on an expedition up the coast in a whale boat. By 1848 Mocatta had moved into the Burnett District where he was one of the earliest squatters. His first lease, Wigton station, was followed by Aranbanga, Johnboon, Malmaison and Mount Debatable, giving him a total of 96,000 acres, but reluctant shepherds and depredations by Aboriginals, scab and catarrh decided him to sell Wigton in 1851. In 1855 he sold his other stations to Montefiore, Graham & Co.

Mocatta returned to Sydney where in 1857 he married a rich widow, Lydia Harriet Voss. In July he established George Mocatta & Co., produce merchants. The firm opened a store on Circular Quay where it sold agricultural products in connexion with its branch at Liverpool. He was treasurer of the Cumberland Agricultural Society and a member of the Liverpool Turf Club. In the early 1860s he took his family to Europe and reputedly spent many years in France. In Sydney by 1875 he set up as a ship-broker with B. P. Campbell. By 1883 he had acquired Tauranga station near Auckland in New Zealand but in 1888 returned with his family to Sydney. He died on 21 March 1893 and was buried in the Congregational section of the Gore Hill cemetery without the presence of clergy. He was survived by his wife, three sons and a daughter. His estate was valued for probate at £143.

J. Campbell, *The early settlement of Queensland* (Ipswich, 1875); H. S. Russell, *The genesis of Queensland* (Syd, 1888); J. E. Murphy and E. W. Easton, *Wilderness to wealth* (Nanango, 1950); *Government Gazette* (NSW), 1840; *Australian*, 12 June 1835, 2 Nov 1841; H. S. Bloxome, The discovery, exploration . . . of the Burnett River district in Queensland (Oxley Lib, Brisb); H. S. Bloxome, The early settlement of the Burnett River district . . . (ML); Col Sec papers, petition A1278 (ML); run registers (QA).   GEORGE F. J. BERGMAN

MOFFATT, THOMAS DE LACY (1826-1864), squatter and politician, was born at Athlone, County Westmeath, Ireland, son of James Robert Moffatt, rector of Athlone, and his wife Elizabeth, née Kellett. Educated in Athlone, he went to Sydney in 1844 to gain experience with his uncle, Captain R. G. Moffatt, at Parramatta. In 1846 he joined the squatters moving north and took up Callandoon station on the Darling Downs; he sold the station in 1849 and settled at Drayton. At Parramatta in 1850 he married Mary Isabella, widowed daughter of Thomas Bell.

With his brother-in-law, J. P. Bell [q.v.], Moffatt became a partner in Cumkillenbar run near Dalby. He also leased two other runs, Wyanga and Goondiwindi, but continued to live at Drayton until 1861 when he moved his family to Ipswich. On 9 May 1860 he had been elected for Eastern Downs in Queensland's first Legislative Assembly. On 4 August 1862 he succeeded R. R. Mackenzie [q.v.] as colonial treasurer. His policy in office was not specially noteworthy, although a minor crisis over the auditing procedures of his department made changes necessary. Aged 38 he died at Waterstown, Ipswich, on 2 October 1864. He was buried in Ipswich with an Anglican ceremony, survived by his wife and two sons and two daughters of their eight children.

Of Moffatt it had been said that 'whatever his principles may be . . . they give him little trouble'. He had won repute as the 'heaviest and best got up man in the Assembly', the 'Queensland Chesterfield' and for the kind of pragmatism which seemed to characterize the successful squatters of the 1850s in Queensland.

PD (Qld), 1867; Qld *Guardian*, 25 Mar 1862; Brisbane Courier, 4 Oct 1864; *Darling Downs Gazette*, 6 Oct 1864; Qld *Times*, 6 Oct 1864.

BEVERLEY KINGSTON

MOLESWORTH, Sir ROBERT (1806-1890), judge, was born on 3 November 1806 in Dublin, only son of Hickman Blayney Molesworth, solicitor, and his wife Wilhelmina Dorothea, née Hone. The family claimed descent from Sir Walter de Molesworth who accompanied Edward I to the Holy Land and was sheriff of Bedfordshire and Buckinghamshire in 1298-1308. Robert was descended from the first Viscount Molesworth, created in 1716, and in 1821 he won a scholarship to Trinity College, Dublin (B.A., 1826; M.A., 1833). Called to the Irish Bar in 1828, he joined the Munster Circuit and practised in Ireland until 1852. In 1838 he had published An *Essay on the Registration of Deeds and Conveyances in Ireland*, and *Receivers in Chancery in Ireland*. On 6 January 1840 he married Henrietta, daughter of Rev. Joseph England-Johnson.

In 1852 the Molesworths migrated to Adelaide and next year to Melbourne, where he was at once admitted to the Victorian Bar. He soon had a large practice and on 27 October 1853 was appointed acting chief justice for a term when Sir William à Beckett [q.v.] was ill. From 4 January 1854 he served as solicitor-general while James Croke was absent, and on 15 April was appointed a nominee in the Legislative Council. In succession to Croke he was solicitor-general under W. C. Haines [q.v.] from 25 November 1855 to 17 June 1856 when he became the fourth appointment to

the Supreme Court bench. In March the Administration of Justice Act (19 Vic. no 13) had authorized the sittings of a single judge in the Equity, Insolvency and Ecclesiastical jurisdictions, and he discharged those duties for nearly thirty years.

Though Molesworth sometimes sat in the Criminal Court most of his work was on the Equity side. An admirable judge, he was noted for his industry, courtesy, learning and expedition; very few of his decisions were successfully challenged. His most remarkable achievement was as chief judge of the Court of Mines. In dealing with this new province he established a code of precedent which gave much satisfaction to the legal profession and the mining industry and became a guide in other Australian colonies and overseas. Apart from a short visit to New Zealand he never left the colony, and took no leave except the Court vacations. He had a strong constitution and his only sick leave was five weeks in 1881. The profession complained of his habit of sitting through the luncheon hour and of his later occasional irascibility, but appreciated his dispatch and dry humour. On 1 July 1885 he was appointed acting chief justice and sat as such until 1 May 1886 when he retired. He was given an ovation at a farewell ceremony in the Court and knighted by patent on 9 July.

Molesworth's judicial achievements were the more remarkable because of domestic unhappiness, which culminated in an extraordinary matrimonial suit in the Supreme Court from 1861 to 1864. His wife petitioned for judicial separation on the ground of cruelty, and he counter-petitioned for similar relief on the ground of her alleged adultery in 1855 with R. D. Ireland [q.v.] and in 1861 and 1862 with some person unknown, resulting in the birth of an illegitimate child in England. On an interlocutory application for alimony *pendente lite* in 1862, Mrs Molesworth was represented by G. Higinbotham [q.v.].

The trial, which attracted much attention, took place before Chief Justice Stawell [q.v.] and a jury in November 1864. The jury absolved Molesworth (who had personally given evidence) of cruelty, and Mrs Molesworth of adultery with Ireland, but found against her on the charge of adultery with a person unknown. In December her appeal to the Full Court failed; her petition was dismissed and the judge's counter-petition succeeded. She died in 1879 aged 56. At his own request Molesworth never sat in a matrimonial case after the trial.

Molesworth had long been a prominent member of the Church of England Assembly. He lived quietly in Melbourne until he died on 18 October 1890 and was buried in the

Kew cemetery. He was survived by a married daughter and two sons, Hickman who became a judge and Robert a pastoralist.

V&P (LA Vic), 1864-65, 2 (C2); *Government Gazette* (Vic), 1853, 1653, 1854, 37, 182, 1599, 1855, 3125, 1856, 1019; *Vic Law Reports*, Insolvency, Ecclesiastical and Matrimonial cases, 1 (1861-62), 57; *Argus*, 18-23 Nov, 15-18, 26 Dec 1864, 20 Oct 1890.   REGINALD R. SHOLL

MOLINEUX, ALBERT (1832-1909), farmer, editor and promoter of agriculture, was born on 11 July 1832 in Brighton, Sussex, England, eldest of the four sons of Edward Molineux, shoemaker and farmer, and his wife Martha. With free passages the family sailed for South Australia in the *Resource* and arrived on 23 January 1839. His father suffered from tuberculosis and became a turnkey at Adelaide jail. Albert went to school and then worked on a farm at Klemzig but left to become a printer's apprentice. In 1851 he joined the gold rush to Victoria and returned in 1855 with modest success. He worked with his father on a farm at Gilbert River and then became a compositor with the Adelaide firm, Vardon & Pritchard. On 7 March 1861 at Adelaide he married Mary Ann Harris; they had one son.

In 1875 Molineux decided to produce an agricultural journal and with a fellow compositor, Samuel Richards, as his partner borrowed type from Vardon & Pritchard and on 10 August produced the first edition of the *Garden and Field*. Richards resigned after six months but Molineux continued the journal in his spare time. He also wrote for the *Observer* in 1875 and was later its agricultural editor. With these positions and his own journal he exerted great influence on South Australian agriculture.

From 1875 in the *Garden and Field* Molineux had advocated the establishment of experimental farms, the appointment of a professor of agriculture and the creation of a department of agriculture. To the select committee on vegetable products in 1887 he outlined a proposal which with little variation became the Agricultural Bureaux system with a Central Bureau of nine members and branches limited to twelve members. The bureaux were not only recipients of information; they kept data on crops and fodder, supplied insects and weeds for identification and established experimental plots. In 1888-1902 Molineux was secretary of the Central Bureau. In 1894 he incorporated the *Garden and Field* with the *Journal of the Bureau of Agriculture*; this connexion was severed in 1897 when the *South Australian Journal of Agriculture* was published for the bureaux.

In private enterprise Molineux was managing director of the South Australian Fishing Co. until it failed and as the chief advocate for settlement of the Ninety Mile Desert was involved in the financial disaster of the Emu Flat settlement. He was more successful with voluntary organizations. Through the *Garden and Field* he published material from the Chamber of Manufactures, the Royal Agricultural and Horticultural Society as well as various specialist groups. As a committee member of the Field Naturalists Society he was indefatigable in seeking specimens, made the first trawling nets and obtained many specimens of fish hitherto unknown. He acquired a pygmy whale skeleton for the Adelaide Museum and examined a specimen of marsupial mole (*notoryctes typhlops*) discovered by his nephew. For these services he was nominated to the Linnean Society by Ferdinand Mueller [q.v.] and Charles French and elected a fellow. He also wrote pamphlets on bees, forest culture and *Handbook for farmers and gardeners in Australia* (Adelaide, 1893).

Molineux insisted that the exploitive wheat monoculture in South Australia be displaced by diversifying agriculture with scientific methods. He focused on the need for improved fertilizers and was an early protagonist for the use of superphosphate. He was also responsible for spreading information to fruitgrowers about insecticide and fungicide sprays. Seeking to diversify agriculture, he advocated experiments with a wide variety of products, including such wildly optimistic suggestions as growing taro in the Port River and sowing *agave americana* in the Ninety Mile Desert. As new crops grew, their manufacture became important and he was instrumental in establishing butter factories, obtaining information and encouraging the pickling, canning and drying of fruit and vegetables. Above all he wanted to increase communication between farmer and scientist. The bureaux system was ideal for this need and changed only when the Department of Agriculture professionalized many of its functions and dispensed advice.

After Molineux retired as secretary of the Central Bureau he became a life member of the Council of Agriculture which in 1902 replaced it. He died of peritonitis on 6 June 1909 at Semaphore, survived by his second wife Eliza, née Ingham, whom he had married at Norwood on 21 August 1897. From investments in land he left her over £5500.

PP (SA), 1887 (90), 1890 (96); *J of Agr* (SA), July 1909; *Garden and Field*, 1 May, 1 Aug 1870, 1 Aug 1891, Dec 1893; *Register* (Adel), 7

June 1909; *Observer* (Adel), 10 June 1909; M. E. Mune, Information and extension services among farmers of the partially developed lands of the upper south east of South Australia (M.A. thesis, Univ Adel, 1962).

MARIE MUNE

MOLONEY, PATRICK (1843-1904), physician and writer, was born in Ireland, son of James Moloney and his wife Catherine, née Kelly. The family migrated to Port Phillip. Educated at St Patrick's College, Patrick entered the University of Melbourne in 1862, one of the three students who began their studies in the new medical school. In 1867 Moloney and William Carey Rees were the first students in Australia to graduate in medicine. In his first year Moloney had also studied arts, winning second-class honours as well as the classics and logic exhibition, but did not complete the arts course. In 1866 he won the Vice-Chancellor's Prize for an English essay and obtained first-class honours in the third and fourth years of the medical course. In 1868-73 he was resident medical officer at the Melbourne Hospital. He set up in private practice in Lonsdale Street in 1874 and later moved to 106 Collins Street East. In 1875-98 he was honorary physician to the Melbourne Hospital, elected by the subscribers as was the custom before 1910. He was closely associated with the Medical Society of Victoria and its president in 1885. Appointed in 1887 one of the university lecturers in clinical medicine at the hospital, he was also physician to such institutions as the St Vincent de Paul Boys' Orphanage.

Moloney was tall, bearded and handsome with a twinkling eye and a distinct personality. According to a contemporary, 'he was hopeless as a teacher of students, but to his fortunate house physician he was a liberal education'. One autumn day Moloney arrived at the hospital and said 'Do you know what I should like to be doing today? A drive into the country behind a good spanking horse, a good cigar in my mouth, a bottle of whisky under the seat, and that girl in red from the Gaiety by my side'.

John Madden, a fellow student at St Patrick's College, later described Moloney's more serious side: 'His inmost instinct . . . was towards poetic gentleness, and abstract philosophy, and, as he grew older, his leisure and recreation were sought in these directions to the exclusion of the more active and material pursuit of his profession . . . and in no way was this more displayed than in detecting the philosophy underlying extravagances of human character by the light of humour . . . He was gentle and generous always and so free from any

egotism that I think the successes of his friends gladdened him more than his own great ones'.

Well known as a popular physician Moloney was even better known as a writer, poet and littérateur. For a time he edited the *Australian Medical Journal* and often contributed to Melbourne *Punch*. Under the pseudonym of 'Australis' in the *Australasian* he wrote many sonnets and verses as well as a series of papers entitled 'Under the Greenwood Tree' but perhaps his best contribution was his *Sonnets: ad Innuptam*. His verses, often anonymous, appeared in the *Vagabond Annual*, *Hash* (1877) and *Booke of ye olde English Fayre* (1881); one of his poems, 'A Matin Song' was set to music by Dr G. W. Torrance [q.v.]. In 1879 he had published in the *Humbug*, and in *An Easter Omelette* presented seventeen of his sonnets, which have appealed to later anthologists of Australian verse. A great conversationalist, he was a friend of such literary lions as Marcus Clarke [q.v.], whom he attended in his last illness, Henry Kendall and Adam Lindsay Gordon [qq.v.]. They used to meet at Dwight's [q.v.] bookshop near the White Hart to discuss artistic and literary problems. Moloney was elected to the Yorick Club in 1868.

On 11 May 1876 at St Patrick's Cathedral, Melbourne, Moloney married Ellen, daughter of James Quirk of Carlton. In 1898 he sailed for England where he spent his last years. He died at Ulverston, Lancashire, on 21 September 1904. His only daughter was married in England to John Boland, M.P. for Kerry and an Oxford graduate who practised at the English Bar.

A. P. Martin (ed), *An Easter omelette* (Melb, 1879); *Univ Melb Medical School Jubilee* (Melb, 1914); H. McCrae, *My father and my father's friends* (Syd, 1935); B. Gandevia, *The Melbourne medical students 1862-1942* (Melb, 1948); *Intercolonial Medical J of A'sia*, 9 (1904); *Table Talk*, 29 Jan 1892; *Age* (Melb), 24 Sept 1904; *Argus*, 24 Sept 1904; *Catholic Advocate*, 1 Oct 1904; G. T. Howard, Early medical Melbourne, D. M. Morton, High road and hazards in medical practice, D. M. O'Sullivan, Interview with Mr James Moloney (typescripts, Vic Medical Soc, Melb).

MONAHAN, THOMAS (1812-1889), businessman, was born in Dublin, son of John Monahan, farmer, and his wife Elizabeth, née Dunn. After schooling he worked as an assistant at Kildare Hospital for seven years and left with written recommendations from local notables. As a coachman he was given a free passage in the *North Britain* which sailed from Kingstown in August

1839 with 285 migrants. Twenty died of typhus on the voyage and on arrival at Sydney the ship was quarantined on 14 December; when the last of the migrants were released on 1 February 1840, six more adults and four children had died. Monahan, who had worked hard during the epidemic, was given a testimonial by the ship's surgeon and appointed a hospital attendant in Sydney. On 22 February 1841 at St Mary's Church he married Mary Timms, a bounty immigrant who had arrived at Sydney in 1832, aged 25. Soon afterwards they sailed for Melbourne.

Monahan's first transaction was to buy the Flinders Street building where the Port Phillip Club held its inaugural dinner on 17 March 1841. The club soon ran short of funds and approached the Melbourne Club for amalgamation in February 1843. Many members joined their former rival and the Port Phillip Club was closed by mid-1843 but Monahan retained the stables for some years. In 1845 he built the Queen's Arms Hotel and from then favoured hotel properties, often acting as his own publican. He had large properties, both lands and buildings, in the city, St Kilda, Sandridge, Emerald Hill and later in New South Wales, and usually collected his own rents. He became one of Melbourne's largest property owners and very wealthy.

Monahan speculated in only one mining venture, the Evelyn Tunnel and Red Jacket at Buckland, where his son-in-law, John Alston Wallace [q.v.], made a fortune; Monahan lost £7000 and never again trespassed outside building. He was proud that he always paid in cash and that his fortune had been won by hard work, forethought, his wife's deft handling of the books and the frugality of their household. He never took part in municipal or parliamentary affairs, though his wealth made him well known. When the foundation stone of the Melbourne Hospital was laid on 20 March 1846 in Little Lonsdale Street, he was one of the first subscribers, with £20; he also became one of its first life-governors. Otherwise he was not known for philanthropy, even to the church, and was sometimes criticized for his miserly gifts for which it was always necessary to canvass him.

Predeceased by his wife, Monahan died on 25 May 1889 at his home, Erindale, St Kilda. He was survived by one daughter, Mrs Keogh, a widow with four children, and by his son-in-law and executor, J. A. Wallace, a widower with six children. The estate of more than £950,000 after tax was left to his family but led to litigation in September 1898 despite Monahan's deathbed admonition to Wallace, 'John, be strong but be merciful'.

HRA (1), 20; J. B. Cooper, *The history of St Kilda . . . 1840 to 1930* (Melb, 1931); *Argus*, 27, 28 Mar 1889.   SUZANNE G. MELLOR

MONGER, JOHN HENRY (1831-1892), merchant and agriculturist, was born on 25 January 1831, son of John Henry Monger, overseer at Lake Monger, and his wife Mary. His parents had sailed in 1829 under Colonel Lautour's emigration scheme to the Swan River, where their son was one of the first Europeans born. The family left their home near Perth and in 1836 trekked eastward toward the newly-discovered Avon Valley where his father took up land, opened a small hotel built of wattle and daub at York, and farmed in a small way until he died on 8 October 1867. Lake Monger and a street in Perth are named after him.

Young Monger spent some years of his early life in England but returned to the colony in 1853. He married Henrietta Joaquina, daughter of Charles Alexander Manning, a Fremantle merchant; they had four sons and four daughters. He set up as a merchant with a head office in Perth and branches at Fremantle, York and later on the goldfields, finally sharing with John Bateman in Fremantle and George Shenton [qq.v.] in Perth in the wholesale and retail trading business. Monger's wholesale warehouse was in William Street and the retail business opened in 1872 in Hay Street. He was fortunate in commanding a large capital and in being able to obtain almost any credit he desired in London. Despite the colony's recurring currency problem an order on Monger of York was accepted more readily than a sovereign. He had inherited his father's estate and with efficient management enlarged it, acquiring some of the colony's richest soil. He also invested in station property and held land in nearly every part of the country.

With Shenton Monger owned the barque *Helena Mena*, named after the owners' eldest daughters. With the sister ship *Charlotte Padbury* the barque regularly voyaged between Perth and London. For years Monger was the leading exporter of sandalwood which then ranked second among the colony's exports. His pastoral innovations amounted to a managerial revolution. When shepherds were scarce he turned to fencing and his example led to its widespread adoption. He imported large quantities of fencing wire which he supplied to pastoralists on long and easy terms of credit. He was one of the first to introduce ring-barking which increased the carrying capacity of the York country. A progressive farmer, he imported first-class stock for breeding purposes, exhibited extensively at the agricultural shows and carried off many prizes.

When representative government gave the franchise to property owners in 1870 Monger was elected a member for York in the Legislative Council. He held his seat until June 1875 when business prevented him from giving time and attention to politics. As one of the largest farmers in the Eastern Districts he was one of the first nominees of the Legislative Council under the new Constitution from December 1890 to February 1892. Chairman of the Town Council of York, a justice of the peace, a member of the Roads Board and active in the York Agricultural Society, he gave generous support to many public enterprises and worked unsparingly for the Methodist Church, taking particular interest in the welfare of its younger members. He died at the family home, Faversham, York, on 23 February 1892 and was buried beside his father in the Wesleyan cemetery in Perth.

W. B. Kimberly, *History of West Australia* (Melb, 1897); J. T. Reilly, *Reminiscences of fifty years' residence in Western Australia* (Perth, 1903); *Possum*, 3 Dec 1887; *Daily News* (Perth), 23 Feb 1892; York Agr Soc, Minute book 1858-94 (Battye Lib, Perth).   R. P. WRIGHT

MONNIER, JOSEPH (1825-1874), Marist Father, was born on 15 March 1825 at Amathay-Vesigneux in the Jura Mountains, France, son of Xavier Monnier and his wife Agnès, née Perrenet. Educated in a seminary at La Consolation, the philosophy seminary at Vesoul and from 1845 at the theologate at Besançon, he joined the Marist novitiate at Lyon in 1847, took vows as a Marist on 22 December 1848 and was ordained on 18 February 1849 at Belley. A clear thinker, he revealed notable gifts as a public speaker especially by simplicity and lucid explanation. For five years in the parishes of southern France he conducted missions of religious renewal until 1856 when his superiors acceded to his requests to go to the Pacific missions of the order. He worked for eight years on Tonga in the central Oceania vicariate of Bishop Pierre Marie Bataillon.

In 1864 Monnier moved to New South Wales and joined the staff of the college at Clydesdale, near Richmond, founded by Bataillon to train a Polynesian priesthood. The attempt failed through the unsuitable, lonely location and a series of floods. Finding that the school was progressing satisfactorily in 1865, Monnier began to help in the parishes at Penrith and then Campbelltown. As his grasp of English improved, the demand for his preaching grew. Requests to preach missions in parishes and retreats to

nuns and priests drew him further afield. From 1866 he was continually on the move through the dioceses of New South Wales and Queensland. James Murray [q.v.], bishop of Maitland, praised the effect of his missions, particularly upon men. He was about to start a new mission at Wellington, New South Wales, when he was recalled to Sydney by Father Poupinel [q.v.] in September 1868. After Archdeacon McEncroe [q.v.] died, Archbishop Polding [q.v.] had offered his city parish of St Patrick's, Church Hill, to the care of the Marist Fathers, and Monnier was nominated parish priest. The church was built beside the home of William Davis, one of the earliest known centres in the colony at which Mass was said, and revered as a shrine by Irish-Australian Catholics. Monnier's unsparing work and genuine love of the Irish melted their opposition to the transfer of the parish to French priests. In 1872 he welcomed Brother Ludovic Laboureyas [q.v.] and the first Marist Brothers to open St Patrick's Boys' School.

Monnier's kindness to others was in marked contrast to the rigorous severity with which he treated his own body. He died from angina maligna on 15 September 1874 and was buried at St Charles's Church, Ryde. After the widely-attended funeral, ardent followers stripped his room of any personal belongings which could be kept as mementos. In 1967 his headstone with those of other Marists was moved to the Villa Maria, Hunter's Hill.

Memoir of the late Reverend Joseph Monnier, S.M., tr by W. A. Duncan (Syd, 1876); J. Hosie, The French Mission: an Australian base for the Marists in the Pacific, to 1874 (M.A. Hons thesis, Macquarie Univ, 1971); Monnier letters (Marist Archives, Rome, microfilm ML and NL).   JOHN HOSIE

MONTAGUE, ALEXANDER (1815-1898), store-keeper, pastoralist and politician, was born at Cloughlin, County Tyrone, Ireland, son of James Montague, farmer, and his wife Mary, née Montague. Educated at a county school and a private seminary, he worked on his father's farm. He arrived in Sydney in 1841 and worked for the merchants Cooper & Holt [qq.v.] until 1848 when he set up as a general store-keeper at Cooma cattle station in the Monaro district. One of the first to petition for the survey of the township he bought many town lots and built the first stores in Cooma. Business flourished and he acquired the Cooma run which he sold in 1857 at a profit. Later he took up Numarella and Mowle's Gully near Cooma, and Dooloodondoo in the Moruya district. In 1861 he buil the first steam flour-mill at Cooma and formed a partnership to work a coal mine at Myalla. He was appointed a magistrate on 11 August 1864.

At first Montague mainly ran cattle and in 1864 sent three boatloads to New Zealand, but bad weather, pleuro-pneumonia and quarantine restrictions resulted in costly failure. He also sold stock in Victoria. In the 1870s his eldest son, James Hugh (1850-1924), took over the management of the properties. In 1884 Numarella's 15,400 acres carried 10,200 sheep, 600 cattle and 120 horses; the property was also known as Green Hills and when sold to W. A. Lang in the late 1890s was renamed Carlaminda.

Nominated as a candidate for Monaro in the Legislative Assembly at a meeting on 22 June 1859, Montague received the largest show of hands but declined to contest the poll. For years he declined to stand for parliament because of business commitments but remained politicially active: an early advocate of closer settlement and a supporter of Daniel Egan, James Martin and Thomas Garrett [qq.v.], he chaired a number of political meetings. He represented Monaro in the Legislative Assembly of New South Wales in 1875-77. Regularly attending the House he showed himself to be liberal, progressive, in favour of free trade and, not surprisingly, the extension of the railway from Goulburn to Cooma. He was defeated at the next election by John Murphy (1821-1883), another Monaro grazier.

Montague was a founder of the *Manaro Mercury* and the Cooma Hospital. A keen horse fancier, he was president of the local agricultural society and for years a judge for the Monaro Jockey Club. Though kind, straightforward and honest he was also firm and strong-willed. He died at the Mill House, Vale Street, Cooma, on 7 October 1898 and was buried in the Catholic cemetery at Cooma. He was predeceased in 1876 by his wife Rosina (Rose), youngest daughter of Hugh O'Hare of Nimithy Vale, Monaro, whom he had married on 4 February 1850, and by three daughters; two sons survived him.

W. F. Morrison, *The Aldine centennial history of New South Wales*, 2 (Syd, 1888); F. F. Mitchell, 'Back to Cooma' celebrations (Syd, 1926); V&P (LA NSW), 1875-76, 1, 18, 4, 964; SMH, 18 Feb 1850, 30 June 1859, 29 Dec 1874, 7 Jan 1875, 11, 14 Oct 1898; *Illustrated Sydney News*, 18 Sept 1875; Perkins papers (NL).

G. P. WALSH

MONTEFIORE, ELIEZER LEVI (1820-1894), businessman, etcher and gallery director, was born in the West Indies, son of Isaac Levi, merchant of Barbados and Brussels, and his wife Hanna, a cousin of the philanthropist, Sir Moses Montefiore. Like his brother Jacob [q.v.], Eliezer adopted the name of Levi Montefiore. Educated in England, he migrated in 1843 to Adelaide where he became a commission and shipping agent. On 3 May 1848 in Adelaide he married his cousin Esther Hannah Barrow Montefiore.

In 1849 Montefiore went to Melbourne as manager of the Victorian branch of J. B. Montefiore [q.v.] Graham & Co. but resigned and became secretary of the Australian Insurance Co. Though appointed a justice of the peace he was mainly interested in literature and the arts. In 1861 he was a member of the committee to arrange a celebration for the 300th anniversary of Shakespeare's birth. In 1870 he helped to found the Victorian Academy of Art and on its behalf presented the prizes at the International Colonial Exhibition in Sydney. In February he became a trustee of the Melbourne Public Library, Museums and National Gallery but resigned early in 1871 and settled in Sydney.

Montefiore managed the Pacific Fire and Marine Insurance Co. in 1871-91, but with T. S. Mort [q.v.] and other friends he formed the New South Wales Academy of Art. In 1874 he became one of the original trustees for administering the funds voted by parliament towards forming the National Art Gallery of New South Wales; it was opened on 22 September 1880. A talented black and white artist, Montefiore illustrated the catalogues of the gallery with his etchings of the principal pictures in 1883-93. Elected a member of the Royal Society of New South Wales in 1875, he contributed to its journal such essays as 'Etchings and Etchers' (1876) and 'Art Criticism' (1879). His 'Agnosticism among the poets' was published in the *Sydney Quarterly Magazine*, 1890. In 1889-91 he was president of the Board of Trustees and served as director of the gallery in 1892-94. In August he went to Melbourne and Adelaide to select pictures for exchange with the Sydney gallery. Soon afterwards he died at Woollahra on 22 October, aged 74, lamented by many friends, not only as a leading patron of the arts but also for his personality. Predeceased by his wife on 10 July 1882, he was survived by six daughters.

A sculpture in marble by Theodora Cowan was placed in the Art Gallery of New South Wales in 1898.

H. Munz, *Jews in South Australia, 1836-1936* (Adel, 1936); L. M. Goldman, *The Jews in Victoria in the nineteenth century* (Melb, 1954); *Cosmos Mag*, 1894; SMH, 23 Oct 1894; *Bridge* (Syd), Aug 1972.

GEORGE F. J. BERGMAN

N

MONTEFIORE, JACOB LEVI (1819-1885), merchant and financier, was born on 11 January 1819 at Bridgetown, Barbados, son of Isaac Levi and his wife Esther Hannah; a member of a notable Sephardi family, she was a first cousin of Sir Moses Montefiore and connected to the Rothschilds by marriage. Jacob and his brothers adopted the name of Montefiore. After his father died in 1837 Jacob decided to join his uncle, J. B. Montefiore [q.v.], in New South Wales and reached Sydney in the *Lord William Bentinck* in October. Jacob soon started trading on his own account. Well educated, he wrote plays including *The Duel* which he translated from the French; it was performed at the Theatre Royal in 1843. His operatic libretto, *John of Austria*, was set to music by Isaac Nathan [q.v.] and performed in 1847. In 1844 he visited England and on his return in 1845 became a partner of the wealthy Scot, Robert Graham. Montefiore, Graham & Co. soon opened a branch in Brisbane and in 1849 another in Melbourne where Jacob's brother Eliezer [q.v.] took charge. The firm also acquired a total of 270,000 acres of leasehold in the districts of Gwydir, New England, Moreton Bay, Wellington and in 1855 George Mocatta's [q.v.] runs in the Burnett; they were all transferred to Montefiore in 1861 when the partnership was dissolved.

Fascinated by political economy, Montefiore in 1853 was chairman of the committee which opposed Wentworth's [q.v.] constitution, thereby becoming a lifelong friend and sometimes creditor of Henry Parkes [q.v.]. In May 1856 Montefiore was nominated to the Legislative Council. In his pamphlet, *A Few Words upon the Finance of New South Wales, addressed to the members of the first Parliament*, he advocated a tax on unproductive land to encourage farming, reduce land speculation and provide revenue; he also recommended a central or national bank and a railway from Sydney to Melbourne. In 1861 he published *Catechism of the Rudiments of Political Economy*, 'an unanswerable defence' of free trade.

By 1855 Montefiore was a director of the Bank of Australasia, a committee member of the Chamber of Commerce in 1856 and a director of the New South Wales Marine Assurance Co. from 1857. In 1858 he arranged in London for Baron Rothschild to finance railway construction in the colony but Charles Cowper [q.v.] delayed in submitting the scheme to parliament. Montefiore was one of Sydney's foremost businessmen. He had become a magistrate in 1857, joined the Royal Sydney Yacht Squadron, and from 1863 was the Belgian Consul. Chairman of the Chamber of Commerce in

1866-69 and 1874-75, he led its campaign for extending electric telegraphs and for a Pacific mail service. He was a founder of the City Bank and chairman in 1863-70, founding chairman of the Pacific Fire and Marine Insurance Co. formed with colonial capital in 1862, a director of the Sydney Exchange Co., the Australian Gaslight Co., the Moruya Silver Mining Co., the Tomago Coal Mining Co., the Glanmire Gold Mining Co. and the Northern Rivers' Sugar Co. In the 1870s he was chairman of the New Wallsend Coal Co. and a director of the Mutual Life Association of Australasia. In 1862-65 he traded on his own and lived at Birchgrove House, Balmain, with his brother Octavius and a cousin Herbert, whose firm was Montefiore & Montefiore. In 1866 he joined them in Montefiores & Te Kloot but in 1867 with S. A. Joseph [q.v.] established Montefiore, Joseph & Co. In the 1870s they were agents for the Aberdeen Clipper Line. In 1864-72 Montefiore held 82,000 acres in the Leichhardt District and in 1870-82 Montefiore, Joseph & Co. held 135 square miles in the South Kennedy District. With J. B. Young and J. B. Rundle [q.v.] he held over 100 square miles on the Darling Downs.

In 1864 Montefiore had addressed a public meeting in support of free trade and dissolution of the assembly over the fiscal policy. Next year he was president of the Free Trade Association. A director of the Sydney Sailors Home, he served on the commission to plan the public reception of the duke of Edinburgh in 1867. He condemned Geoffrey Eagar [q.v.], colonial treasurer, for ruining the colony's credit by mismanaging the sale of debentures. In 1869 he sat on the royal commission on alleged kidnapping of natives of the Loyalty Islands. Disgusted by the Opposition he nominated George King [q.v.] for East Sydney in the mercantile interest, a seat that Parkes was contesting. Montefiore told Parkes that they were unlikely ever to 'think alike in politics', but in the 1872 elections he decided to abstain from any political action and offered Parkes 'to aid the cause with my purse'. Later that year he visited North America and Europe. In October 1873 he advised Parkes not to appoint Edward Butler [q.v.] chief justice, fearful that 'giving to the Roman Catholics the *majority* on the Bench will raise all churchmen throughout the country'. In 1874 Montefiore was appointed to the Legislative Council on Parkes's recommendation but resigned in 1877.

A member of the Jewish congregation from his arrival in the colony, Montefiore had advocated the claims of the Jewish community for a share in state aid to religion in 1845. In 1868 he secured official recognition by the Council of Education of the Sydney Hebrew Certified Denominational School despite opposition from James Martin [q.v.]. In 1876 he was a representative commissioner for Philadelphia and Melbourne Exhibitions. After a farewell banquet organized by the Chamber of Commerce and a 'handsome money testimonial', he returned to London.

In London Montefiore was a director of the Queensland National Bank and the Queensland Investment and Land Mortgage Co. In 1878 he joined a syndicate that offered to lay a submarine cable between Java and Cape York, the profits to be divided between the syndicate and the New South Wales government. Despite repeated appeals to Parkes the government took the advice of Sir Daniel Cooper [q.v.] who rejected the plan as 'absurd' and too costly. Montefiore was also a member of the Australian Transcontinental Railway Syndicate which planned a railway from Roma to the Gulf of Carpentaria in return for a land grant of 10,000 acres per mile. However, the railway bill, introduced by Thomas McIlwraith [q.v.], was defeated in the Queensland parliament on its second reading in 1883. Montefiore repeatedly asked Parkes in vain to appoint him agent-general for New South Wales and advised Parkes to take advantage of cheap money and consolidate all 'the debts of New South Wales into a permanent funded stock'. In 1880 Montefiore served on the London Commission for the Sydney International Exhibition which he had promoted.

A fellow of the Royal Colonial Institute from 1877, Montefiore missed 'that country of my adoption' but in 1881 wrote to Parkes that 'It may be you are right that I could have been more useful out there than I can be here but I am afraid that the callings of ambition are in some degree the prompters for here I am lost among the millions and to court public favour is rather too costly an experiment'. He died from heart disease at his home Keir Bank, Upper Norwood, on 24 January 1885, leaving his estate to his wife Caroline Antonine Gerardine Louyet, whom he had married in London on 9 July 1851.

D. J. Benjamin, 'The Sydney Hebrew Certified Denominational School', M. Z. Forbes, 'Jewish personalities in the movement for responsible government in New South Wales', Aust Jewish Hist Soc, J, 4 (1954-58); V&P (LA NSW), 1858-59, 1, 93, 2, 905, 1861, 1, 833, (LA QLD), 1862, 5, 789, 1879-80, 5, 590; *Sydney Mail*, 13 Feb 1864; *SMH*, 30 Mar 1876, 28 Jan 1885; Parkes letters (ML); CO 201/503, 522, 526, 577, 584.

MARTHA RUTLEDGE

MONTEZ, LOLA (1818-1861), dancer and courtesan, was born in Limerick, Ireland, and christened Maria Dolores Eliza Rosanna, daughter of Ensign Edward Gilbert and his fourteen-year-old wife who claimed descent from Spanish nobility. Her father died in 1824 and her mother married Major John Craigie, later adjutant-general of the British army in India. Educated at boarding schools in Britain and France, Lola was ordered by her mother at 19 to marry an aged judge; instead she eloped with Lieutenant Thomas James whom she married in Ireland on 23 July 1837. In 1839 James took her to Simla, India, but eloped with another woman. Lola returned to England in 1842 and James won a judicial separation on the ground of her adultery on shipboard.

Lola visited Spain and trained as a dancer, calling herself Donna Lola Montez. She made her début before royalty at Her Majesty's Theatre, London, on 3 June 1843; although beautiful and accomplished she was hissed off the stage when recognized as James's wife. Penniless she fled to Europe, giving performances which were then considered suggestive in Warsaw, Paris and elsewhere. In turn she became the mistress of Franz Liszt, Alexandre Dumas, and Alexandre Dujarier, part-owner of *La Presse*. After Dujarier was killed in a duel on 11 March 1845, Lola went to Munich posing as a Spanish noblewoman. The ageing King Ludwig I of Bavaria fell in love with her, buying a large house and settling an annuity on her. Lola exerted great political influence for a time; ministries rose and fell at her bidding and she won support from radical university students. On 25 August 1847 Ludwig created her Countess Marie von Landsfeld but the Bavarian aristocracy and middle class refused to acknowledge her. On 7 February 1848 street riots broke out against her influence and on the 10th thousands of burghers marched on the palace to demand her expulsion. Presented with proof of her background and infidelities, Ludwig gave way but also insisted on abdicating the throne. Lola fled to Switzerland when her Bavarian rights were annulled.

In April 1849 Lola returned to London, going through the form of marriage with a young Guards officer, George Trafford Heald, on 19 July. On 6 August she was arrested on a charge of bigamy but released on bail. She fled with Heald to Spain, where he drowned next year. Lola returned to the stage, touring Europe and America, carrying a cowhide whip and often a pistol, and becoming involved in innumerable assaults, scandals and legal actions. In gold-rush San Francisco, she gave the first performances of her notorious 'Spider Dance'. On 1 July 1853 she went through the form of marriage with Patrick Purdy Hull, owner of the *San Fran-*

cisco Whig. He soon sued for divorce, naming a German doctor as co-respondent: a few days later the doctor was found shot dead in near-by hills.

In May 1855 Lola appointed a young actor Noel Follin as her manager. In June they sailed for Sydney in the *Fanny Major* with their own company. They arrived on 16 August and opened with local actors at the Royal Victoria Theatre on the 23rd in a farrago entitled 'Lola Montez in Bavaria'. Two weeks later Lola and Follin (who had changed his name to Folland) decamped from Sydney. A sheriff's officer followed them on board the *Waratah* with a debtor's warrant of arrest; Lola undressed in her cabin and dared the officer to seize her but he left on the pilot boat without her. Lola opened at the Theatre Royal, Melbourne, on 13 September in her Bavarian role; when audiences diminished she began to perform the 'Spider Dance'. She was denounced by the press but the mayor of Melbourne, sitting as a magistrate, refused an application for her arrest. From 26 November to 31 December she played to full houses in Adelaide, returning to a 'rapturous welcome' at Sydney in January 1856. She opened at Ballarat on 16 February in a series of sketches; greeted by packed houses she invited miners to shower nuggets at her feet as she danced. The *Ballarat Times* attacked her notoriety; Lola retaliated by publicly horsewhipping the editor, Henry Seekamp, at the United States Hotel. On 21 February he published another critical article; she swore a warrant for his arrest on a charge of criminal libel but failed to appear when the case came up for trial. She had meanwhile been assaulted by the wife of her goldfields impresario and took a full month to recover. From 1 April Lola successfully toured Bendigo, Castlemaine and other Victorian towns, then sailed with Folland for San Francisco. Near Fiji on the night of 8 July he was lost overboard: no official investigation seems to have followed.

Rapidly ageing, Lola failed in attempts at a theatrical comeback in various American cities. She arranged in 1857 to deliver a series of moral lectures in Britain and America written by Rev. Charles Chauncy Burr. She seems to have been genuinely repentant but then was showing the tertiary effects of syphilis and her body began to waste away. Aged 42 she died on 17 January 1861 and was buried in Greenwood cemetery, Brooklyn, as Mrs Eliza Gilbert.

C. C. Burr, *Autobiography and lectures of Lola Montez* (Lond, 1858); *Illustrated London News*, 20 Mar 1847, 26 Jan 1856; *New York Herald*, 20 Jan 1861; SMH, 10 July 1865; *Table Talk*, 13 Aug 1886; J. A. Panton memoirs (LaTL).
                                    MICHAEL CANNON

MONTGOMERY, WALTER (1827-1871), actor, was born on 25 August 1827 at Long Island, United States of America, and named Richard Tomlinson. As a youth he went to England. While working with a shawl manufacturer in London he took part in amateur entertainments, appearing at the Soho Theatre in *Othello*. Engaged to play in provincial towns, he gained most favour in Nottingham. His first professional appearance in London was as *Othello* at the Princess Theatre on 20 June 1863. He gave readings of Shakespeare, Tennyson and Macaulay, and appeared in Shakespearian drama on the London stage but seems to have inspired little interest until July 1865 when at the Haymarket he won recognition for his interpretation of *Hamlet*. In November 1866 he played Orlando to Helen Fawcet's Rosalind at Drury Lane. He then toured America before turning to Australia.

Melbourne in the early 1860s had revelled in Shakespearian productions. In 1867 they were sustained by two newcomers: James Anderson, brought out by G. Coppin [q.v.], was playing to appreciative audiences when Montgomery's arrival was advertised a week before he was due. He was to succeed T. B. Sullivan [q.v.] at the Royal and had a genius for exploiting publicity. His *première* of *Hamlet* on 20 July attracted a full house and enthralled his audience. According to one critic, 'His acting is so new, so fresh, so pre-eminently natural that it occasions in the mind a curious blending of surprise and delight'. Production followed production, each hailed with enthusiasm. Each portrayal, *Macbeth*, *Othello*, *Shylock* or *King John*, was pronounced equally impressive. Anderson also won support and the rivalry added interest.

With two such actors Melbourne became a centre for discussion and partisanship. Hardly a day passed without dispute over their merits. *Richard the Third* was shown to full houses in both theatres on the same evening. Anderson was said to be more traditional and less accomplished but Montgomery evoked the greater controversy, the major issue being whether Hamlet was indeed mad. His own sanity also became a matter for debate.

With pale complexion, graceful figure and general appearance Montgomery was well suited to his favourite role as tragedian. However ardent his admirers, opponents disliked his flamboyant nature, despised his vanity and were nauseated by his shameless exploitation of acquaintanceship with the duke of Edinburgh during his visit in 1867-68.

Montgomery toured New Zealand with Marion Dunn, followed by an equally satisfying reappearance in Melbourne in 1868.

He tried to persuade her to go with him to America and England, but instead she married Marcus Clarke [q.v.]. He returned to London in 1871 and on 31 July began a season at the Gaiety Theatre. On 30 August at St George's Church, Hanover Square, he married Laleah Burpee Bigelow, an American who was later reputed to have a husband still living. They were to have left for America but on 1 September he shot himself. This echoed an incident on the eve of his departure for Australia when he sent for his favourite horse, Tudor, and shot him through the head. The inquest returned a verdict of suicide while of unsound mind.

A. Sutherland et al, *Victoria and its metropolis*, 2 (Melb, 1888); H. McCrae, *Story-book only* (Syd, 1948); P. McGuire et al, *The Australian theatre* (Melb, 1948); B. Elliott, *Marcus Clarke* (Oxford, 1958); *Argus*, 13, 22, 27 July 1867; *The Times*, 4 Sept 1871. JEAN GITTINS

MOONDYNE, JOE; *see* JOHNS, JOSEPH BOLITHO

MOONLITE, CAPTAIN; *see* SCOTT, ANDREW GEORGE

MOORE, CHARLES (1820-1895), merchant, auctioneer and alderman, was born on 29 August 1820 at Ballymacarne, County Cavan, Ireland, son of James Moore, farmer, and his wife Catherine, née Rogers. Educated at Drumkeen School, Fermanagh, Ireland, he was apprenticed at 12 to an elder brother, a Cavan draper. His indentures finished, he worked at his trade in Dublin and London. In September 1849 he sailed for South Australia with a shipment of drapery which he sold at a good price in Adelaide. After visiting Melbourne he settled in Sydney in 1850 and opened a drapery which prospered in the gold rushes. He soon bought Charles Newton's auctioneering business.

In 1860 Moore built a substantial house, Baden-Baden at Coogee, and was elected to the Randwick Municipal Council, where he often led the minority Coogee faction in protests against the actions of S. H. Pearce [q.v.] of Randwick. A councillor until 1886, Moore was elected mayor in 1863. He was also a member of the Botany-Randwick-Coogee Roads Trust. In December 1865 he was elected to the Sydney City Council for Bourke Ward and was mayor in 1867-69. With R. Driver [q.v.] Moore won repute as an improver. In his mayoralty the site for the Town Hall was acquired, plans drawn and the foundation stone laid. He successfully championed earlier plans for making dams to improve the capacity of the Botany swamps, Sydney's main water source. He had the Tank stream covered, Macquarie Street extended to Circular Quay and the Tarpeian Way formed. His most famous improvement involved the Sydney Common. Of some 1000 acres this sandy waste was generally believed to be crown land but in 1866 he traced documents proving that in 1811 it had been vested in Sydney's inhabitants. He planned to improve and sell part of it to provide funds to improve half of the rest; the remainder was to be gazetted as a water reserve. The scheme was supported in parliament by the colonial secretary, Henry Parkes [q.v.], and the secretary for lands, J. B. Wilson [q.v.]. Early in 1867 work began on levelling the sand hills and planting them with grass and trees, and the council renamed the common 'Moore Park'. Moore Street (Martin Place) was also named after him.

Moore had a prickly personality and despite his improvements and refusal to accept a mayoral salary he was often criticized by opposing councillors. In May 1869 he resigned and visited Europe. On his return in 1871 he was re-elected to the council and held his seat until 1886. Still an improver, he had plans drafted for an underground railway to Circular Quay. From July to October 1874 he represented East Sydney in the Legislative Assembly; in 1880-95 he served in the Legislative Council. He was a supporter, friend and sometimes creditor of Parkes. In 1880 he moved to Moore Court, a mansion he had built at Springwood.

In January 1854 Moore had married Sarah Jane Wilcox, who died without issue. In 1882 he again visited Europe and in 1883 at Kingston, Ireland, married a widow Annie Hill Montgomery. Evangelical in outlook, he was an active Anglican and, despite contrary assertions by the *Freeman's Journal*, eschewed the sectarianism that marred municipal politics, although he made a legacy to a niece conditional on her not marrying a Catholic. He was vice-president of the Church of England Defence Association formed in 1886 to combat growing ritualism. Childless, he died of senile decay and heart failure on 4 July 1895 and was buried in the Emu Plains cemetery. His estate was valued at £17,755.

E. Digby (ed), *Australian men of mark*, 1 (Syd, 1889); I. Moore, *Glimpses of old Sydney and N.S.W.* (Syd, 1945); W. B. Lynch and F. A. Larcombe, *Randwick, 1859-1959* (Syd, 1959); V&P (LA NSW), 1866, 5, 1009, 1867-68, 4, 974, 1869, 2, 423; W. A. B. Greaves, 'Recollections of old Sydney', JRAHS, 3 (1915-17); SMH, 27 June 1867, 21 Apr 1869; *Illustrated Sydney News*, 25 July 1874; *Sydney Mail*, 13 July 1895; G. Gerathy, The role of the Sydney City Council in the development of the metropolitan area 1842-1912 (M.A. thesis, Univ Syd, 1970); Parkes letters (ML).   MARK LYONS

MOORE, CHARLES (1820-1905), botanist, was born on 10 May 1820 at Dundee, Scotland, son of Charles Muir and his wife Helen, née Rattray. He was educated in Dundee and Dublin, where his brother David became director of the Glasnevin Botanic Garden in 1838; the family name was changed to Moore when they went to Ireland. Charles worked as a botanist on the Ordnance Survey of Ireland and trained at Kew and Regent's Park. On the recommendation of Professors Lindley and Henslow he was appointed 'government botanist and director of the Botanic Gardens in Sydney' by the Colonial Office.

Moore reached Sydney in the *Medway* on 14 January 1848. He roused local resentment by displacing J. C. Bidwill [q.v.], a colonial appointment, and was obstructed by some members of the Committee of Management. Moore found the gardens badly neglected and was instructed to restore their scientific character, without destroying their value for recreation. He labelled plants 'showing the Natural Order, Scientific Name and Authority, English name and Native Country of each Plant', a system still followed. He avidly collected for the gardens and corresponded widely for exchanges of seeds and plants. In 1850 he gathered specimens from the New Hebrides, Solomon Islands and New Caledonia.

Moore established a medicinal plant garden and herbarium. To increase attention to economic botany he started a library and added a room where he lectured to university students until 1882. Governor FitzRoy had abolished the Committee of Management in 1851 but amateur scientists and disgruntled nurserymen secured a select committee on the management of the Botanic Gardens. Chaired by G. R. Nichols [q.v.] it included Moore's old antagonists. He was subjected to a searching examination, his qualifications were challenged and 'no effort was spared to embarrass him and condemn his administration'. The committee reported that although Moore had acted with ability and industry much had been left undone, but Governor Denison ignored their plea that the director should henceforth be merely the curator.

In 1857 Moore visited the Blue Mountains and in 1861 the Richmond and Clarence Rivers to collect timber specimens for the London Exhibition of 1862 and published A *Catalogue of Northern Timbers*, which he later revised several times. He continued to improve the gardens, reclaimed land in Farm Cove and secured a water supply. In 1864 he advised the Colonial Office that none of the valuable timber trees of New South Wales were hardy enough to cultivate in Britain but would grow in Cape Colony.

Appointed commissioner for the Paris Exhibition in 1867, he was relieved of his duties for arriving too late with his exhibits by visiting the gardens of the governor's residence at Kandy. He also toured France and Spain on behalf of the citrus industry. In 1869 he visited Lord Howe Island and in 1874 attended the Botanical Congress and the International Horticultural Exhibition in Florence.

Moore landscaped and planted the grounds of the Garden Palace built in 1879 for Sydney's International Exhibition. In 1882 he was involved in the dismissal of Captain R. R. Armstrong [q.v.] and next year had J. C. Dunlop and his wife removed because they displayed 'uxorious affection' in the gardens. Dunlop successfully sued Moore in the Water Police Court but in June the magistrate's decision was reversed by the colonial secretary, Alexander Stuart [q.v.].

Moore was a commissioner for the Philadelphia and Melbourne Exhibitions of 1876. A member of the Hyde Park Improvement Committee, he became a trustee for Hyde, Phillip and Cook Parks in 1878, a founding trustee of the National Park and an elective trustee of the Australian Museum in 1879 and chairman of the Vine Diseases Board and planner of Centennial Park in 1887. He was a fellow of the Linnean and Royal Horticultural Societies and an associate of the Royal Botanic Society in London. From 1856 he had served on the council of the Philosophical Society (Royal Society of New South Wales after 1866), was president in 1880 and published four papers in its *Proceedings*. In New South Wales he was a councillor of the (Royal) Zoological, Agricultural and Acclimatisation societies. Moore published A *Census of the Plants of New South Wales* (Sydney, 1884) but his major work was *Handbook of the Flora of New South Wales* (1893) in which he was helped by Betche [q.v.]. He retired as director on 5 May 1896 and visited Europe.

Moore's successor at the Botanic Gardens, J. H. Maiden, regretted that Moore 'did not commit to paper the horticultural and botanical reminiscences of his long official career . . . His dislike of writing extended even to letter writing'. Predeceased on 10 October 1891 by his wife Elizabeth Bennett, née Edwards, Moore died childless on 30 April 1905 in Paddington and was buried beside his wife in the Anglican section of Rookwood cemetery. His estate was valued for probate at over £5300. Nineteen species were named after him by F. Mueller [q.v.].

V&P (LC NSW), 1852, 1, 1175, 1855, 1, 1155, 1176, (LA NSW), 1866, 5, 745, 1867-68, 1, 93, 3, 153, 4, 1073, 1870, 1, 640, 1873-74, 1, 365, 1883, 1, 566, 1883-84, 1, 287, 2, 749; SMH, 28

June 1883; L. A. Gilbert, Botanical investigation of New South Wales 1811-1880 (Ph.D. thesis, Univ New England, 1971); CO 201/530.

C. J. KING

MOORE, DAVID (1824-1898), business-man, was born on 4 February 1824 in Sydney, son of Captain Joseph Moore and his wife Ann, née Bailey. Captain Moore was merchant partner in W. Walker [q.v.] & Co. which was interested mainly in whaling. After schooling David entered the office of Walker & Co. and won distinction as a shrewd businessman. In 1851 he moved to Port Phillip where his reputation from Sydney aided his quick acceptance in mer-cantile circles. In 1853 he set up in Flinders Lane and in 1855-59 in Bourke Street. He was a founding member of the Melbourne Chamber of Commerce in 1851, a general committee member from 1855 and president in 1857-58, 1873-75 and 1878-79.

At the first Legislative Assembly elections in 1856 Moore was asked to stand for one of the five seats in the Melbourne con-stituency. All factions supported him be-cause it was important 'that the commercial interests of this young but important city should be represented in the New Parlia-ment', and he was the Chamber of Com-merce candidate. Surprisingly he topped the poll. A staunch free trader, he was allied with other liberal-mercantile members like J. McCulloch and J. Service [qq.v.] and was a member in 1856-58 of the 'Responsible Reformers' faction with G. S. Evans, Robert McDougall, A. Michie [qq.v.], J. McCulloch and G. S. Horne who were holding the balance of power. With these men and three others Moore voted to overthrow both the first Haines and O'Shanassy [qq.v.] govern-ments.

On 29 April 1857 Moore was appointed president of the Board of Land and Works in the second Haines government. He introduced the Haines land bill in May and in June moved the second reading, maintain-ing that no new provisions were needed for the sale of agricultural land since that already released was often left unused. Like many others he argued that removal of the squatters was impractical but insisted that they should pay more heavily for their privilege of leasing. The vociferous oppo-sition to the bill centred around the Land Convention constituted in July. Genuine land reformers like Service and R. Heales [q.v.] rejected some of the convention's extreme policies and forced amendments pro-viding cheap rentals for farming land, but the bill was rejected by the Legislative Council in September. By early 1858 when the Haines 'party' fell into disarray, Moore,

Michie and McCulloch returned to their private affairs, disillusioned by the chaos to which they themselves had contributed. Moore was remembered later as one of the 'old venerables' but no politician. His last public duty was service on the royal com-mission on the Public Works Department of 1873.

Financially Moore was successful, acquir-ing large pastoral properties in New South Wales and Victoria. He was a local director of the Bank of New South Wales for forty-two years and served on the London board when he visited England in 1860-61. He was also chairman of the Southern Insurance Co. and had been a director of the Victoria Sugar Co., later merged with the Colonial Sugar Refining Co. Ltd, in which he also held big interests. A firm Anglican, he was warden of Christ Church, St Kilda, for twenty years. He died on 11 July 1898, sur-vived by his wife Isabella, née Barass, four daughters and a son Charles, who for years was associated with the family business.

G. Serle, The golden age (Melb, 1963); Argus, 12 July 1898; G. R. Quaife, The nature of political conflict in Victoria 1856-57 (M.A. thesis, Univ Melb, 1964).

SUZANNE G. MELLOR

MOORE, HENRY BYRON (1839-1925), public servant and businessman, was born on 11 February 1839 in Surrey, England, son of Frederick Farmer Moore, businessman and later head of the Victorian Government Store Department, and his wife Emily, née Coe. After practical education mostly at Stratford-le-Bow, he sailed for Victoria and arrived at Corio Bay in November 1852. He hoped to be an engraver but at 14 he became a field-clerk and draftsman in the Survey Department at Geelong, where he added crescents to relieve the monotony of the town's streets. In 1861 he was appointed district surveyor and was in the party which surveyed the route for the Cape Otway-Geelong telegraph line. In 1862 he went to England for his health, taking the Burke and Wills [qq.v.] diaries with him; he was also elected a member of the Royal Geographical Society.

On his return in 1863 he worked on maps, plans and photolithography for the Lands Department. In 1865 he was given charge of selection procedures in the eastern half of the colony under Grant's [q.v.] Act and composed his parody of Tennyson, 'The Charge of the Dirty Three Hundred' (squatters' dummies), but again the travel-ling taxed his strength. In 1866 he was land commissioner in Gippsland and in 1870 assistant surveyor-general.

A.D.B.

In 1873 after a public outcry against dummying Moore toured Victoria collecting evidence. In 1874-77 he reorganized the Survey and Lands Department, where he simplified and streamlined the occupation branch by dividing it into territorial divisions at headquarters. In 1878 he gave important evidence defending his impartiality to the lands commission of inquiry.

Moore was one of the permanent classified officers 'dismissed without distinction' on Black Wednesday, January 1878. He soon received offers from other colonies but refused and set up as a surveyor and financial agent. When R. J. Jeffray built the Exchange for £20,000 Moore leased it and housed there his brokerage business and financial newspaper. Moore spared no efforts to induce the mercantile community to make the Exchange its rendezvous, providing club amenities and such facilities as a telephone exchange, reading rooms with overseas newspapers, an innovatory wool circular distributed throughout the world, an intercolonial and international telegraph service and shipping registers and cargo loadings for major ports. Many stockbrokers carried out most of their business at Moore's Exchange but he became insolvent when B. J. Fink [q.v.] persuaded brokers to build their own exchange, completed in 1891. Moore was heavily involved in speculative land companies, like the Beaumaris Park Estate Co. Ltd which collapsed, and Moore crashed for over £66,000, paying 3d. in the £.

Moore always had a wide range of interests and a knack for realizing the use of inventions. In 1880 he founded the Melbourne Electric Light Co., was its manager and lit up the Eastern Market on 1 July 1881, a memorable night for Melbourne though the movement was premature. He also established the Melbourne Telephone Exchange Co. which gave the city a telephone service two years before London. By 1882 the government had realized its mistake but the company was in a strong position and in 1886 asked £78,750 for a transfer. Commerce was demanding a more efficient and less costly service and was hostile when the company settled in August 1887 for £40,000, still a handsome profit, and the 1100 subscribers were transferred.

On 17 June 1881 Moore became secretary of the Victoria Racing Club, retaining the post until 1925. He saw the value of acquiring land at the back of Flemington, bought it himself when the committee refused, and willingly resold some at his purchase price when later required. His surveying knowledge helped the club to plan four new grandstands and create spacious lawns and gardens, especially of roses, making Flemington a world-class course. He developed the

club in Australian racing eyes, made the Melbourne Cup a major annual occasion with complimentary tickets to entice celebrities, and helped racing generally by suggesting the registering of bookmakers. Seeing himself as a manager only, he missed no meetings but rarely watched a race and never placed a bet.

Moore was active in charitable work all his life. In World War 1 the V.R.C. raised £102,019 for war funds and he himself chose the comforts sent overseas. The V.R.C. Benevolent Fund 'for racing men in necessitous circumstances' was his idea. He helped to raise money for the Talbot Colony for Epileptics, and the Children's Hospital gained money from the sale of his musical chants and a fairy-tale. He wrote for an hour at dawn almost every day; a gifted musician and enthusiastic gardener, he loved cooking despite his various fads about food.

On 20 September 1877 Moore had married Mary Jane, daughter of Charles Samuel Morrow of Melbourne; they had three daughters and two sons. The last surviving member of the 'literary coterie that formed the Yorick Club', he died at his home in Collins Street on 22 June 1925, and after a funeral service with rites of the Anglican Church, of which he had long been a senior member, was buried in Brighton cemetery attended by 500 mourners.

M. Cannon, *The land boomers* (Melb, 1966); *Punch* (Melb), 5 Nov 1908, 16 June 1921, 15 Jan 1925; *Argus*, 22, 23 June 1925.

Suzanne G. Mellor

MOORE, JAMES (1807-1895), lawyer, pastoralist and banker, was born in January 1807 in Dublin, son of George Moore, Q.C., LL.D., of Kilbride, County Wicklow, and his wife Elizabeth, daughter of James Armstrong. In 1826-31 his father represented Dublin City in parliament and was a descendant of Garrett, first Viscount Moore of Drogheda, whose ancestry traced from the union of John of Gaunt and Katherine Swynford. At 16 James entered Trinity College, Dublin (LL.M., 1827; B.A., 1828; M.A., 1832). For twelve years he studied and travelled extensively in Europe, on his last trips accompanied by his friends, Redmond Barry and W. F. Stawell [qq.v.]. In 1840 Moore was admitted to the English Bar but did not practise and later that year migrated to Melbourne. He bought land on the St Kilda Esplanade and in partnership with C. J. Griffith [q.v.] took up Glenmore station near Melton. In 1842 Moore married Harriet Maria, daughter of Dr John Watton who had arrived at Melbourne in 1839 and practised medicine before taking up Mount

Rouse station. The marriage was blessed with five sons and eight daughters.

From the first Moore was enthusiastic at prospects in the colony and his letters home encouraged many Irish contemporaries including Stawell to migrate to Port Phillip. In 1843 Moore, Griffith and Molesworth Greene [q.v.] went overland on horseback to Portland Bay to study the pastoral possibilities of the Western District. In June 1848 Moore sold his interest in Glenmore to Greene and in 1849 acquired Barjarg station near Benalla. Like many early colonists he was troubled by the vast changes after gold was discovered but, believing that the solution lay in religion rather than politics, he returned to Britain in 1853. He studied arts and theology at Caius College, Cambridge (M.A., 1854), but difficulties with some of the Thirty-nine Articles induced him not to be ordained. In 1856 he returned to Victoria where he developed Warrenbayne near Wangaratta and other stations. By 1863 he had sold them all and made his home in Lonsdale Street, Melbourne.

In 1864 Moore acquired a farm at Moonee Ponds, Melbourne. He sat regularly as a justice of the peace, served on the committee of the Melbourne Hospital, was prominent in the Anglican community and assisted many charitable institutions. In 1867 he became comptroller of the Melbourne Savings Bank. Despite lack of experience in this field his appointment proved fortunate. A strong believer in hard work and thrift, his conservatism in lending lost him some popularity but the policies he helped to promote increased public confidence in the bank and kept it aloof from the rise and collapse of the hysterical land boom. Numerous branches of the bank were opened in Melbourne suburbs and it became one of the world's great savings banks. When Moore retired in 1892 savings deposits with the bank amounted to almost £3,750,000. He died on 6 October 1895 at Richmond and was buried in the old Melbourne cemetery.

Although a conservative Anglo-Irish patrician and perhaps too conscious of his aristocratic ancestry, Moore was learned, high principled, deeply religious and kind. Many descendants live in Melbourne; a plaque depicting him late in life and papers are held by the family.

T. F. Bride (ed), *Letters from Victorian pioneers* (Melb, 1898); M. F. E. Stawell, *My recollections* (Lond, 1911); T. Craddock and M. Cavanough, *125 years: the story of the State Savings Bank of Victoria* (Melb, 1967); *Argus*, 7 Oct 1895.   CHARLES FRANCIS

MOORE, JAMES (1834-1904), Roman Catholic bishop, was born on 29 June 1834 at Listowel, County Kerry, Ireland, where his uncle was a priest and guided him towards the Church. After three years at a 'classical' school in Tralee he entered All Hallows Missionary College in 1852 but showed little aptitude for studies. Ordained a priest for Melbourne he volunteered as chaplain in the *Annie Wilson*. Beginning as curate of St Francis's, he was soon promoted to parish priest because of his zeal. Ill health in 1862 led Bishop Goold [q.v.] to give him a roving commission to collect money for the cathedral; within six months he showed great talent for collecting funds for bluestone and mortar.

Appointed to Ballarat in 1866, Moore found too few churches for the growing population and listed his priorities as churches, schools and societies. He soon paid the debt on St Patrick's and built the bluestone Church of St Alipius, Ballarat East. Made dean in 1869, he went in 1873 to Rome with Goold to make arrangements for a Ballarat diocese. Michael O'Connor [q.v.] was preferred as bishop but Moore was awarded an honorary doctorate of divinity and became vicar-general, business manager and 'Guardian Angel' of the diocese. He was made a monsignor in 1882 and administered the diocese after O'Connor died. At his silver jubilee in 1883 the laity honoured him with a golden chalice and the wish that he succeed to the throne. He was consecrated by Goold on 27 April 1884.

Moore was gracelessly conscious of the dignity and power of his office, more than any bishop in Australia, according to his friend Dean Goidanich. In 1875 he had bought a twelve-acre site near Lake Wendouree for the bishop's palace. Quicktempered, vigilant and ruthless he was feared by his priests. Punctilious in canonical visitations he relished confirmations as an occasion for homilies. With no pretence of oratory he told 'practical truths' though 'a verbatim report of his words would not always have looked well in print'.

Moore was a resolute and fearless builder. He had briefly studied church ornament and furniture, and for St Patrick's Cathedral he brought sumptuous equipment and decorations from all parts of Europe. Pleased to be a citizen 'of no mean city', he adorned it with buildings which stimulated employment and trade, including a Nazareth House for orphans and the aged, staffing it with the Poor Sisters. He raised some £300,000 from a flock of less than 35,000 and spent half of it in Ballarat. St Patrick's was the first Catholic Cathedral in Australia cleared of debt; its consecration on 19 November 1891 was the peak of Moore's episcopate and was attended by Cardinal Moran and the archbishop of Wellington among others. He squeezed taxes from his priests to recruit 'young levites', doubling their numbers from 27 to 54, and he brought out Redemptorists and Brigidines.

Moore readily believed that secularists wanted to Protestantize state schools and in 1884 threatened to withdraw Catholics from those schools if the Bible was taught. In 1875-84 the diocese had spent £67,291 on education alone and by 1904 had 11 boarding schools, 13 high schools for both girls and boys, and 60 primary schools in 35 parishes. Moore was a sedulous Roman rather than Gallican-Irish. Liberal in public spirit he made gifts to bodies outside his Church and sat on the committees of the hospital, benevolent asylum and art gallery, finally winning praise from the Anglican bishop for 'refraining from making public attacks upon Christian bodies outside the R.C. Church'. A diabetic, Moore died on 26 June 1904 after long illness. At his funeral the Anglican bishop was represented as well as Presbyterians and Jews.

T. W. H. Leavitt and W. D. Lilburn (eds), The jubilee history of Victoria and Melbourne (Melb, 1888); P. F. Moran, History of the Catholic Church in Australasia (Syd, 1895); R. Fogarty, Catholic education in Australia 1806-1950 (Melb, 1959); G. Serle, The rush to be rich (Melb, 1971); E. O'S. Goidanich, 'James Moore, Bishop of Ballarat', Austral Light, Aug-Oct 1904; Advocate (Melb), 26 Apr 1884, 2 July 1904; Ballarat Star, 28 Apr 1884, 27 June 1904; A'sian Sketcher, 2 June 1884; Ballarat Courier, 27 June 1904; Bishop Goold letters, 3 Apr 1856 (Roman Catholic Archives, Melb); Bishop Geoghegan letters, 14 Oct 1858 (Roman Catholic Archives, Adel).   JAMES GRIFFIN

MOORE, JOSEPH SHERIDAN (1828-1891), teacher, publicist and man of letters, was born in Grafton Street, Dublin, son of Luke Moore, solicitor, and his wife Bride Marion, née Sheridan. Educated by the Jesuits at Stonyhurst College, Lancashire, he migrated to Sydney in 1847, became a Benedictine monk and headmaster of Lynd-hurst College, Glebe. Always a transplanted Irishman, he had many disagreements and dissatisfactions with Archbishop Polding and Abbot Gregory [qq.v.]. He left Lynd-hurst on 1 April 1856 and on 3 October 1857 married Flora Macdonald Harris (b. 1832) at the Ashfield district registry. Although he did not rejoin the Church until 1872 he had been editor of the Catholic Freeman's Journal in 1856-57.

Moore was well known in literary circles, specially in the coterie centred around N. D. Stenhouse [q.v.] and included J. L. Michael, Professor Woolley, D. Deniehy, W. B. Dalley and Henry Kendall [qq.v.]. Moore was esteemed by some but condemned as a charlatan by the native-born members who distrusted him and F. E. T. Fowler [q.v.] because of their snobbish emigré valuation of literature propounded in the Month. Moore criticized the poetry of Henry Parkes and Charles Harpur [qq.v.] not only for its inferior literary quality but also for its self-conscious nationalism.

Moore's literary output supplemented his teaching and coaching of aspirants for university honours in his own City College and in Randwick College and University Hall. He specialized in classics but also taught a liberal-progressive syllabus ranging from modern languages to geography and science. His writings were prolific: his Spring Life Lyrics (1864) was an anthology of light Romantic verse on conventional themes, and his essays in The Ethics of the Irish Under the Pentarchy (1872) aimed to recreate Irish prehistory and customs for Irish-Australians; his strange combination of the Romantic excesses of contemporary German and Irish writers sometimes shows a delicate touch and feeling that is more than mere sentiment. In the 1870s and 1880s he wrote many pamphlets and articles for such different publications as Archbishop Vaughan's [q.v.] Express and the Bulletin. In 1873 he had been declared bankrupt with debts of over £1000; his estate was not released until May 1874.

Claiming to be an orator, Moore lectured at Mechanics' Schools of Arts and other institutions with a high moral sense of his listeners' need for intellectual, literary and social improvement. On 12 July 1865 in one of his most constructive lectures, published as University Reform, Its Urgency & Reasonableness, he argued against exclusiveness in the local university and advocated introduction of evening and 'extern' students, liberalizing of courses to include a modern language and creating medical, civil engineering and architecture schools. In demand as a speaker, his bumptious posings often irritated his audiences, although his handbook on Elocution (1855), prepared for his students at Lyndhurst College, showed that his theories on oratory were clear, moderate and restrained.

Moore died at his home in Elizabeth Street, Redfern, on 17 October 1891 and was buried in the Catholic section of Waverley cemetery. His wife, who survived him with two sons and two daughters, was a prominent concert and oratorio singer in 1852-82; on her death in 1910 she was vice-president of the Sydney Philharmonic Society.

J. R. Tyrrell, Postscript (Syd, 1957); T. L. Suttor, Hierarchy and democracy in Australia,

1788-1870 (Melb, 1965); M. Shanahan, *Out of time, out of place* (Canberra, 1970); *Freeman's J* (Syd), 14, 21, 28 Nov 1868, 10 Feb, 29 July 1871, 24 Nov 1891; *SMH*, 17 Nov 1891; *Bulletin*, 24 Nov 1891; *Town and Country J*, 24 Nov 1891; A. M. Williams, Nicol Drysdale Stenhouse: a study of a literary patron in a colonial milieu (M.A. thesis, Univ Syd, 1963); Moore, Kendall and Stenhouse letters (ML).

FRANCES DEVLIN GLASS

MOORE, MAGGIE (1851-1926), actress, was born on 10 April 1851 as Margaret Virginia Sullivan in San Francisco, of Irish parents who had migrated to Sydney and then to California. Starting early as an actress, she became a local favourite. At 20 she met J. C. Williamson [q.v.]. Together they were earning up to £200 a week, and married on 2 February 1873 at St Mary's Cathedral, San Francisco.

In September G. Coppin [q.v.] engaged them for an Australian tour. They sailed in the *Mikado* on 27 May 1874 with a new play *Struck oil*, in which they had succeeded in California. The Williamsons, Maggie's brother Jim and a whole company played in Honolulu and Fiji, and arrived in Sydney on 1 July and Melbourne on the 8th. On 1 August they opened with *Struck oil* with Williamson as John Stofel and Maggie as Lizzie at the Theatre Royal, supported by *The fool of the family*. The critics were lyrical, specially praising Maggie. The season included other plays and ended on 21 December, *Struck oil* having played for fifty-seven nights. The Williamsons' share of the profits was £6000.

After success at Ballarat, Geelong, Castlemaine and Sandhurst the company left on 1 March 1875 for Sydney. Opening at the Queen's Theatre with *Struck oil* on the 10th, it drew large crowds and played for forty-four nights. In Adelaide from 28 August they had 'crowded houses and enthusiastic applause'. After the season closed on 2 October they played in India, Egypt, Italy, France and Germany, opening in London with *Struck oil* at the Adelphi Theatre on Easter Monday 1876. Critics praised the Williamsons' acting and the season ran for a hundred nights. They had added to their repertoire Boucicault's [q.v.] *Arrah na Pogue*, which with Maggie in the title role was almost as successful as *Struck oil*. After two years in America they returned to Melbourne on 15 August 1879 with the sole Australian rights to the Gilbert & Sullivan comic operas.

Threat of legal action prevented piracy of the Gilbert & Sullivan operas and, as the first authorized performances of a Savoy opera, the Williamsons presented *H.M.S.* *Pinafore* in Sydney on 15 November, Melbourne on 14 February 1880 and Adelaide on 15 May. Maggie created the role of Little Buttercup but her favourite part was Josephine. Among other operas Maggie played Ruth and sometimes Mabel in *The pirates of Penzance*, Lady Jane in *Patience*, Katisha in *The Mikado*, Fairy Queen in *Iolanthe* and the duchess of Plaza Toro in *The Gondoliers*. On 24 November 1883 she created perhaps her best operatic role as Bettina in *La Mascotte*, in which Nellie Stewart [q.v.] played Fiametta. In 1890 Maggie was brilliant as Meg in *Meg, the castaway*. In 1887 on a visit to her mother in San Francisco she won great success in her performances; with Williamson in 1891 she toured India but he was then turning to organization.

Relations between Williamson and Maggie became strained, and she formed her own company. In 1894 she defeated an injunction by Williamson who tried to prevent her production of *Struck oil*. From May 1897 Williamson lived with Mary Weir and on 29 May 1899 Maggie divorced him. She continued to travel but her 1900 season in San Francisco failed. On 12 April 1902 in New York she married Harry R. Roberts.

In 1903-08 Maggie travelled in North America and Britain. She returned to Sydney and under J. C. Williamson Ltd starred in seasons from 1908 to 1912, sometimes reviving *Struck oil* with Roberts. In 1915 she joined the Royal Comic Opera Company as Mrs Pitt in *After the girl*, and toured Australia with it, crowning her career as Mrs Karl Pfeiffer in *Friendly enemies* in 1918; she also played Lizzie Stofel in the Pugliese Enterprises film of *Struck oil*, with Roberts as Stofel. In July 1920 she had success with Roberts in Gregan McMahon's production of Charles Kenyon's *Kindling* at the King's Theatre, Melbourne.

For the fiftieth anniversary of her first Australian appearance, a lavish testimonial jubilee was staged at Her Majesty's Theatre, Sydney, on 1 August 1924. Maggie played the second act of *Struck oil*, Nellie Stewart appeared and Dame Nellie Melba attended; the proceeds exceeded £1500. Next year she retired to California to live with her sister. On 16 March 1926 she was run over by a cable car in San Francisco. Her leg was amputated but she died at noon.

Vivacious and ebullient, Maggie was a national favourite. Her acting was better than Williamson's and is reputed to have made his fortune. Extremely versatile, she had a fine voice, a perfect sense of comedy, much skill at dancing and a charming personality. An animal lover, she kept a menagerie at her Rose Bay home. Most significantly she retained her popularity with audiences to the end of her theatrical life.

F. C. Brewer, *The drama and music in New South Wales* (Syd, 1892); E. Soldene, *My theatrical and musical recollections* (Lond, 1897); N. Stewart, *My life's story* (Syd, 1923); J. B. Fowler, *Stars in my backyard* (Ilfracombe, 1962); A. Bagot, *Coppin the great* (Melb, 1965); V. Tait, *A family of brothers* (Melb, 1971); P. J. F. Newton, 'The firm. The story of J. C. Williamson and his firm', *Masque* (Syd, 1969), no 8; *Australasian*, 8 Aug, 26 Sept, 26 Dec 1874, 23 Jan, 6 Feb, 6, 27 Mar, 1 May, 28 Aug, 9 Oct 1875, 15 Jan 1876, 9, 23, 30 Aug, 27 Sept, 25 Oct, 22 Nov 1879, 21 Feb, 10 Apr, 22 May 1880, 26 July 1890, 12 Dec 1891, 31 Mar 1894, 18 Mar, 3 June 1899, 31 May 1902, 10 July 1920, 19 July, 9 Aug 1924, 20 Mar 1926; *Advertiser* (Adel), 30 Aug 1875; *The Times*, 24 Apr 1876; *Argus*, 26 Mar 1894, 30 May 1899, 2 Aug 1924; *New York Times*, 17 Mar 1926; *SMH*, 17 Mar 1926; Maggie Moore's MS (ML).

RICHARD REFSHAUGE

MOORE, WILLIAM (1821-1893), Methodist missionary, was born on 24 March 1821 at Parramatta, son of John Moore, veterinary surgeon, and his wife Sarah, née Cooper. About 1831 he went to Richmond where he was brought up as a Wesleyan and trained as a tanner and currier by his uncle. Influenced by Rev. Samuel Wilkinson, he experienced a religious conversion in 1838. A year later he began to preach and soon became an accredited local preacher. On 3 June 1842 at the Wesleyan Chapel he married Mary Ann, eldest daughter of John Ducker of Richmond.

In 1847 Moore offered for missionary work in Fiji but assent was not immediately possible. Instead Rev. W. B. Boyce [q.v.] sent him and William Lightbody to investigate the religious situation in the Moreton Bay District. They reported after returning to Sydney and Moore was appointed a home missionary at Brisbane, where he arrived with his wife on 17 October. Local residents were already conducting religious meetings and a Sunday school. Moore expanded this work, forming congregations and building churches at Burnett Lane, Brisbane, and at Limestone (Ipswich), preaching also at South Brisbane. At Zion's Hill (Nundah) he conducted a preaching ministry to the German mission community established by Schmidt and Eipper [qq.v.], influencing some of the missioners to become preachers in the Moreton Bay circuit. As the founder of Wesleyan Methodism in Queensland Moore covered his extensive circuit by horseback except when travelling to Ipswich by river steamer.

In 1849 Moore received his call to Fiji and arrived in the islands in January 1850. He was finally examined for the ministry in 1853. In Fiji he laboured with conspicuous success for nineteen years, showing exceptional ability to understand and influence the people. He became an apt Fijian scholar and translator. He served chiefly at Rewa, which he reopened as a mission station in 1854, but also at Bua, Nadi, Kadavu, Bau and Ovalau. He had visited Australia only in 1861 and 1865 but ill health caused his permanent return in 1869. With health restored he served the New South Wales Conference for fifteen years at Armidale, Wollongong, Kiama, Balmain and Windsor. The conference elected him chairman of his district three times and president of the conference in 1883. He supported the building of Newington College at Stanmore and helped to inaugurate its fund. He also played a significant part in founding the Wesleyan Ladies' College opened at Burwood in 1886.

Superannuated in 1885, Moore lived at Stanmore until he died on 12 September 1893; he was buried at Rookwood, survived by ten of his sixteen children. As a missionary Moore was much criticized for speculating in land, probably on behalf of his large family. Though not a great preacher or administrator, he was esteemed for his pioneering qualities and dedication. His colleague, Rev. J. Waterhouse [q.v.], referred to him as 'a fine fellow — one of the most useful — tho' perhaps most humble of our number'. Lorimer Fison [q.v.] described him as one of the greatest Australian missionaries.

B. C. Seemann, *Viti* (Cambridge, 1862); S. M. Smythe, *Ten months in the Fiji Islands* (Lond, 1864); J. Blacket, *Missionary triumphs among the settlers in Australia and the savages of the south seas* (Lond, 1914); R. A. Derrick, *A history of Fiji* (Suva, 1946); R. S. C. Dingle (ed), *Annals of achievement: a review of Queensland Methodism, 1847-1947* (Brisb, 1947); MS A2814, A2815 (ML).   I. H. GRIMMETT

MOORE, WILLIAM DALGETY (1835-1910), pastoralist and businessman, was born on 30 August 1835 at Oakover on the Upper Swan River, eldest son of Samuel Moore and his wife Dorothy, née Dalgety. His father, a brother of G. F. Moore [q.v.], had arrived in Western Australia in 1833. At 15 William entered the office of the surveyor-general, J. S. Roe [q.v.], but resigned in 1854 to take a position on a station held by Hamersley & Co. in the Irwin River District, later becoming its manager. In 1858 he joined a party led by F. T. Gregory [q.v.] to explore the Murchison and Gascoyne areas. In 1862 Moore abandoned pastoral activities and moved to Fremantle, where he went into partnership with J. H. Monger [q.v.]. In

1867 he established the firm of W. D. Moore & Co. which still carries on business under that name, his active association with it lasting until 1900. On 19 July 1860 he had married Susanna Dora Monger and after her death he married Ann Gallop on 20 February 1879; he had twelve children by the first marriage and six by the second.

Moore was active in political and civic affairs as well as commerce. He represented Fremantle in the colony's Legislative Council from August 1870 to May 1872, and in 1890-94 was a nominee in the first Legislative Council under responsible government. He was briefly treasurer of the Fremantle Town Council which replaced the Town Trust in 1871. In that year he served on the committee formed to investigate the construction of a deep-water jetty at Fremantle, and in 1892 was a Legislative Council representative on another committee set up to study C. Y. O'Connor's proposals for an inner harbour.

While manager of W. D. Moore & Co. he conducted pearl-fishing at Shark Bay in 1877-87, built a flour-mill at Fremantle known as the Phoenix because it 'rose from the ashes' of one that had been burned down, established mercantile houses at Cossack and Roebourne under the name of the North-west Australian Mercantile Co., owned a timber-mill at Quindalup in the south-west and later bought the Osborne Hotel. He was a member of the Chamber of Commerce and its president for ten years, and a director of a number of companies. For many years he owned Cheriton, a station property near Gingin, the vineyard Millenden in the Upper Swan and near-by Oakover, where he had been born. He died at Fremantle on 22 April 1910, survived by five sons and nine daughters.

His youngest brother Samuel Joseph Fortescue was born on 3 April 1846. After service under the surveyor-general he was a grazier and store-keeper at Dongara in 1867-1901. He retired to Claremont and represented Irwin in the Legislative Assembly in 1904-14 as well as holding several civic posts. He died at Claremont on 9 May 1921.

W. B. Kimberly, *History of West Australia* (Melb, 1897); J. K. Ewers, *The western gateway* (Fremantle, 1948); R. Oldham, 'The reminiscences of William Wade', *JRWAHS*, 6 (1962); *West Australian*, 23 May 1910.

JOHN K. EWERS

MOORHOUSE, JAMES (1826-1915), Church of England bishop, was born on 19 November 1826 at Sheffield, England, only son of James Moorhouse, master-cutler, and his wife Jane Frances, née Bowman. Educated in a private school, he entered St John's College, Cambridge (B.A., 1853; M.A., 1860;

D.D., 1876). At Ely Cathedral he was made a deacon in 1853 and ordained priest on 12 November 1854. He was curate at St Neot's in 1853-55, Sheffield in 1855-59, Hornsey in 1859-61 and perpetual curate at St John's, Fitzroy Square, London, in 1862-67. While vicar of St James's, Paddington, in 1867-76 he was appointed chaplain in ordinary to the Queen and prebendary canon of St Paul's in 1874-76. At Cambridge he had been appointed select preacher in 1861 and Hulsean lecturer in 1864; at Lincoln's Inn he was Warburton lecturer in 1876. His distinguished record and many notable publications led to an offer of the see of Melbourne vacated by Charles Perry [q.v.], and then of the see of Calcutta. Despite pressure to stay in England he accepted Melbourne. Consecrated at Westminster Abbey on 22 October, he arrived in Victoria, was installed at St James's Cathedral, William Street, on 11 January 1877 and on the 15th publicly welcomed at the Town Hall.

Almost the antithesis of his predecessor Perry, the second bishop of Melbourne had intellectual distinction, administrative skill, eloquence and leadership; he also smoked a pipe and walked with a bulldog. He accepted the challenge of a large diocese with no episcopal colleague other than at Ballarat. From arrival he loved the brash, exciting Victoria, and Melbourne responded to his lively and vocal affection. His immediate tasks were the building of a suitable cathedral and the provision of an educated clergy. At an inaugural meeting on 19 April 1877 in the Town Hall to discuss the cathedral committees were appointed for raising funds and building. In July the problem of site was debated and continued till 20 October when the corner of Swanston and Flinders Streets, favoured by Moorhouse, was accepted. He also chose the architect, William Butterfield. The foundation stone was laid on 13 April 1880 and the building was completed, excepting the central and western towers, in January 1891. By then £100,000 had been raised for it. Moorhouse also wanted to recruit and train a local ministry 'so adequate in number and so approved in qualification that we shall become independent of assistance from home'. His younger clergy were so poorly qualified 'that complaints among the educated laity are loud and almost universal'. In the University of Melbourne he started a new building for Trinity College, opened in 1878, founded a new theological faculty and began theological studentships towards which he donated £1000. Despite these efforts complaints about the clergy's education continued and in his time the diocese was never wholly independent of clerical assistance from England.

Moorhouse's major contribution to the Melbourne public was a series of annual lectures, beginning with 'Messianic Prophecies' in 1877 and ending with 'The Galatian Lapse' in 1885. Large numbers attended and the last lectures filled the Town Hall. His sermons and addresses were always well received since, like Rev. Charles Strong [q.v.], he was a leader of liberal religious thought. Unafraid of controversy he argued with Marcus Clarke [q.v.] with some success in 1897, and with the Roman Catholic archdeacon, Patrick Slattery [q.v.], and other clerics and secularists on his refusal to offer special prayers to end the drought; instead he told the people of Kerang 'to agitate, combine, cry out' for water conservation and irrigation. In 1883 his permission to Canon Bromby [q.v.] for an exchange of pulpits with Strong sparked off another controversy. He refused to join the clamour against Judge Higinbotham [q.v.] for his *Science and Religion* (1883) but castigated Judge Williams [q.v.] for his *Religion and Superstition* (1885). Moorhouse was quick to defend what he deemed spiritual truths, the essentials of Christianity. He had no interest in denominational quarrels and little in disputed points of theology, claiming that 'Nothing will prevail to detatch men from error but a candid and charitable method of proclaiming the truth', and again, 'Nothing will induce me to join in the bigoted howl' against Rome.

Moorhouse took his pastoral oversight seriously. He professed to love teaching more than administration but never neglected his duty. Each year he spent two and sometimes three months in difficult travel. He encouraged church building in country centres, concerned himself with the education and licensing of stipendary lay readers and instituted a system whereby rural deans had importance in the church's government. He recognized the need for further division of the diocese and was prepared to give generous aid to a diocese of Sandhurst for which plans were discussed in 1885. He won the respect of all kinds of men, including A. W. Howitt [q.v.] who could barely tolerate Perry. His correspondence with the clergy receals a clear, decisive mind. Never afraid to exercise episcopal discipline, he was certain and sympathetic; men always knew where they stood with Moorhouse.

In education Moorhouse reversed Perry's opposition to the 1872 Act. With other denominations he fought hard for non-dogmatic, scripturally-based religious instruction in state schools and supported the Catholic claim for state aid in their separate school system. In an important address on education to the Melbourne Social Science Congress in 1880 he deprecated the narrow curriculum of the colony's state schools. He pointed to the press, theatre and political life as educational forces, to the need for science, poetry, drama, object lessons and school museums to enrich the curriculum even at primary level. He advocated citizen participation, school boards, decentralized administration and payment of fees. In 1881 he had little part in the agitation for admission of women to the University of Melbourne, where he was elected chancellor in 1884, opposed the founding of a women's college but strongly proposed an Anglican girls secondary school. He supported the opening of the Public Library and Art Gallery to the public on Sundays and patronized some stage plays to the consternation of some of his followers. Failing to introduce religious instruction into the schools, he encouraged Saturday and Sunday schools with success though recognizing their limitations.

Active in the broader aspect of church politics, Moorhouse began to work for an Australian Church Congress in 1877, saw it convened in Melbourne in 1882 and gave the inaugural address on 14 November. He was active in the negotiations to give a constitution to the whole Australian Church and with the question of the primacy. Although not a noted social reformer, he was alert to social problems. He castigated Graham Berry [q.v.] for dismissing civil servants in the crisis of January 1878, warmly espoused the opening of clubs for working men, welcomed the Salvation Army and formed the first Church of England Mission to the streets and lanes of Melbourne in 1885. He continued to publish on religious subjects as well as such topics as water conservation, irrigation and Federation.

News of his translation to Manchester was received in Melbourne with surprise and consternation. The only precedent for translating a colonial bishop to an English see was that of George Selwyn of New Zealand. Moorhouse said that the change was desirable because the burden in Victoria was becoming too heavy and Manchester offered some relief. He left Melbourne on 10 March 1886 and was enthroned as the third bishop of Manchester on 18 May. He ruled his new diocese wisely and well, displaying the same liberality of mind, tolerance and indifference to trifles which marked his Melbourne episcopate. He retired in 1903 to Taunton, Devon, where he died on 9 April 1915. Predeceased in 1906 by his wife Mary, née Sale, whom he had married in 1861, he left an estate worth over £54,000, of which he bequeathed £40,000 to a niece and the rest to relations.

By nature and training Moorhouse was a

broad churchman, reasonable and sceptical. His religious faith was based on an early mystical experience, about which he was reticent. His religious opinions changed little throughout his life, even though his first published lectures were an attack on Baden Powell, an author of the *Essays and Reviews*. He attached no label to himself but clearly belonged to the school of F. D. Maurice, Dean Stanley and Benjamin Jowett. Not an original thinker or a profound scholar he made no distinctive contribution to theology, although his Hulsean Lectures in 1865 show that he anticipated the Kenotic theory of the *Lux Mundi* group in 1890. His greatest talent lay in explaining the bearing of contemporary biblical scholarship on religious thought and practice. His principal guides on matters biblical were Lightfoot, Westcott, Hort and later Professor Sanday. He read no German but knew the standard German works on bible and church history in translation. He rejected the verbal infallibility of scripture and welcomed scholarly investigation into its text and history. He welcomed all scientific discovery and refused to reject any seeming conflict with biblical teaching. He held that the miracles of the New Testament were unique and divinely appointed for a sufficient reason: in the post-apostolic age natural laws held invariable sway. He held firmly to the orthodox creeds and had no wish to amend or vary the Thirty-nine Articles or the Athanasian Creed, and asserted: 'we may not change our creed, but we do change our understanding of it, as age succeeds to age'.

E. C. Rickards, *Bishop Moorhouse of Melbourne and Manchester* (Lond, 1920); H. W. Nunn, *A short history of the Church of England in Victoria 1847-1947* (Melb, 1947); A. de Q. Robin, *Charles Perry, bishop of Melbourne* (Perth, 1967); C. R. Badger, *The Reverend Charles Strong* (Melb, 1971); G. Serle, *The rush to be rich* (Melb, 1971); *Church of England Year-book*, 1877, 1886; *Church of England Messenger* (Vic), 1877-1887; *Argus*, 12 Apr 1915; F. B. Smith, Religion and freethought in Melbourne, 1870 to 1890 (M.A. thesis, Univ Melb, 1960).   C. R. BADGER

MOORHOUSE, MATTHEW (1813-1876), medical practitioner, civil servant and pastoralist, studied medicine in London (M.R.C.S., 1836). He was practising in Hanley, Staffordshire, when appointed by the Crown as the first permanent protector of Aborigines in South Australia. Acquainted with the Congregationalist minister, R. W. Newland [q.v.], at Hanley, Moorhouse joined his party in the *Sir Charles Forbes* and arrived at Holdfast Bay in June 1839. He chose a section near Newland's settlement at Encounter Bay where he was one of the first to cultivate land.

Official duties as protector involved Moorhouse in many activities. He had to safeguard native interests in land and see that agreements between settlers and Aboriginals were fulfilled, to mediate in disputes and bring offenders to justice, to find the number and location of the tribes, to learn their languages and customs, and to train them in the arts of civilization, specially reading, writing and cultivation. Above all he was to give them a knowledge of the Christian religion. His work demanded arduous travel to investigate sheep stealing and attacks on settlers. Although he centred attention on the Adelaide tribe his protection extended to tribes in the River Murray district and on Eyre Peninsula. He accompanied the commissioner of police, T. S. O'Halloran [q.v.], on expeditions and was present at the summary execution of several natives after the massacre of survivors of the wreck *Maria* in 1840. He co-operated with members of the Dresden Missionary Society and the Anglican archdeacon, M. B. Hale [q.v.], in opening Aboriginal mission stations near Port Lincoln. An enthusiastic believer in educating Aboriginal children, he built a school in Adelaide where he tried to teach them in their own language but without success. At Governor Grey's request he published *A Vocabulary and Outline of the Grammatical Structure of the River Murray Language* (Adelaide, 1846).

In defending Aboriginal rights Moorhouse sometimes conflicted with the government and hostile colonists while his methods were often criticized by the press. He saw the worst aspects of assimilation but his patient efforts did much to alleviate some of the harshness. Later deterioration of native and European relations and decline of the Aboriginal population made his efforts fruitless but his concern for Aboriginal welfare and justice won him respect from many settlers and affection from the natives.

Active in colonial affairs, Moorhouse joined the Adelaide Philosophical Society and was a vice-president in 1853. He lectured to the Literary Association on various topics and was a member of the Statistical Society. Appointed a justice of the peace in 1841, he was an able and diligent magistrate. In 1849 he served on provisional committees for the proposed railway to Port Adelaide. In June 1851 he was returning officer for the Yatala electoral district and in July was appointed to the Destitute Board, later serving as secretary. On 4 January 1842 at Trinity Church, Adelaide, he had married Mary Ruth Kilner; they had three children.

In 1856 Moorhouse went to England

where he lectured on South Australia and promoted migration. He then visited North America where he travelled over 5000 miles by railroad and investigated various systems of education. On his return he resigned as protector and was elected a representative of the City of Adelaide in the House of Assembly in 1860 and in October 1861 served as commissioner of Crown Lands and Immigration in the ten-day ministry of G. M. Waterhouse [q.v.]. In October 1862 he resigned and became a pastoralist. He bought shares in properties near Riverton and Saddleworth but soon sold out and with Joseph Fisher [q.v.] and others bought 27,700 acres near the Hummocks. Moorhouse managed the station until R. Barr Smith [q.v.] bought it in 1870. He worked other holdings near Saltia, but settled at Bartagunyah near Melrose where he often gave his professional services to settlers. After a brief illness he died at Bartagunyah on 29 March 1876, survived by his wife, two sons and a daughter. His estate of £7000 was left to his family.

R. Cockburn, *Pastoral pioneers of South Australia*, 1 (Adel, 1925); J. B. Cleland, *Pioneer medical men in South Australia* (Adel, 1941); PP (SA), 1860 (165), 1861 (131), 1862 (88); A. A. Lendon, Matthew Moorhouse (SAA).

MOREHEAD, BOYD DUNLOP (1843-1905), pastoralist, businessman and politician, was born on 24 August 1843 at Sydney, son of Robert Archibald Alison Morehead [q.v.] and his wife Helen Buchanan, née Dunlop. Educated at Cape's [q.v.] school, in Scotland for eighteen months and Sydney Grammar School, he matriculated at the University of Sydney in 1860 but left after two terms. He tried various gold and sapphire diggings and in 1862 as a clerk joined the Bank of New South Wales but was dismissed for insubordination in 1864. After acquiring pastoral experience on several stations he was manager of the Scottish Australian Investment Co.'s Bowen Downs in 1866-81, often acting as an inspector of the company's other stations. In 1870 a thousand cattle were stolen from Bowen Downs and driven to South Australia. Morehead went to Adelaide to recover them and trace the thieves who were later indicted in Queensland without success. With A. B. Buchanan in 1873 he founded B. D. Morehead & Co. which had two branches: a mercantile and trading business, and a stock and station agency. By 1877 he had thirteen stations in the Mitchell District.

In the Queensland Legislative Assembly Morehead represented Mitchell from September 1871 to December 1880 and Balonne from October 1883 to April 1886. In the Legislative Council he served as postmaster-general and ministerial representative from December 1880 to August 1883, colonial secretary from June to November 1888, premier, chief secretary and colonial secretary from November 1888 to August 1890, and a councillor from June 1896 to October 1905. While holding office he was competent and decorous but without it seemed to scorn the townee politicians who did not share his advocacy for squatting, conservatism and self-help. Well read, he revelled in sarcastic quotations ranging from Cornewall Lewis's *Government of Dependencies* to Edward Gibbon's account of Mohammed's iron coffin suspended in mid-air. He called the *Brisbane Courier* 'a mendacious paper edited by a hireling', insisted on points of order and a proper quorum in the House and described the premier as 'the biggest show in the colony and might be seen in parliament every evening'. When taunted as a squatter he replied, 'Wasn't Nebuchadnezzar sent grazing for his sins'. Morehead's wit, vivacity and undaunted pluck won him the title of 'guerrilla debater'.

In 1879 when given no office under Thomas McIlwraith [q.v.] Morehead organized a subsection of seven young bloods to harass the premier by playing cards till midnight unless called to carry a division. In 1881 rumour had Morehead auctioning some 9000 acres of country lands for £1 an acre. In 1882 a select committee of the assembly investigated the rumour. Samuel Griffith claimed that the land was auctioned at 10s. an acre by Morehead Ltd for the 2½ per cent brokerage but refused to name his informants. Summoned by the committee Morehead claimed that 'it would not be consistent with my honour, nor with my dignity, to rebut charges against me and my firm', and declined to answer Griffith's unsubstantiated rumours.

Morehead was at his best defending the pioneers who developed the colony's prosperity and quoted 'God made the country, but the devil made the towns'. He admitted to employing Kanakas on his stations but 'thought it cowardice to say that white labor could be put down by black labor'. Yet his tender feelings were near the surface when trouble came to his friends and employees. In January 1881 he attended the Intercolonial Conference on massacres in the Pacific and seconded the motion by A. H. Palmer [q.v.] that the Queen 'cause such action to be taken as will prevent the recurrence of such outrages against life and property'. In 1889 Sir Henry Parkes [q.v.] visited Brisbane to put his Federation scheme to Queensland leaders but Morehead was 'ill in bed'. In 1896 he refused an offer to represent the colony as agent-general in London but in 1901 served on the royal commission on liquor laws.

Morehead suffered disaster in the 1893 crisis. He had been a director of the Queensland National Bank for some years and invested heavily in share stock which long remained valueless owing to calls on liabilities. Despite many visits to Britain his health continued to deteriorate. Predeceased by his first wife Annabella Campbell, née Ranken, whom he had married at Lockyersleigh, Goulburn, on 4 June 1873, he died from a cerebral haemorrhage on 30 October 1905 at a private hospital in Gregory Terrace, Brisbane. He was survived by his second wife Ethel, née Seymour, whom he had married at Brisbane on 3 April 1895, by seven daughters of his first marriage and by one daughter of the second. His estate outside Scotland was sworn for probate at £713.

PD (Qld), 1871-1904; V&P (LA Qld), 1882, 659; Queenslander, 4 Nov 1881, 8 Oct 1892; C. Verney, 'Reminiscences', Daily Mail (Brisb), 31 Aug 1907; Univ Syd and Bank of NSW Archives; CO 201/595, 610.

MORESBY, JOHN (1830-1922), admiral, hydrographer and explorer, was born on 15 March 1830 at Allerford, Somerset, England, second surviving son of Captain Fairfax Moresby (1786-1877) and his wife Eliza Louisa, née Williams. Educated locally, he joined the navy at 12 as a cadet. In 1845-49 he served as a midshipman on the American and Mediterranean Stations and then took a gunnery course. Promoted lieutenant in 1851, he served in South American waters and the Baltic during the Crimean war. On half-pay as a commander from 1858, he served on the China Station in 1861-64. Promoted post captain on 1 January 1865, he was on half-pay but worked as a marine surveyor in Ireland for five years.

In January 1871 Moresby was sent to the Australian Station in command of the 'old-fashioned paddler' H.M.S. Basilisk. Four months out of Plymouth she put into Melbourne for repairs but was immediately ordered to Sydney and nearly wrecked in Bass Strait. After a refit Moresby was sent to New Zealand and returned to Sydney in 1872. He was then ordered to Torres Strait to suppress kidnapping from the South Sea Islands. On the way north he rescued thirteen surviving natives from the disabled Peri. Before leaving England Moresby had hoped to survey the waters off northern

Australia and New Guinea and had acquired some survey instruments. From Cape York he sailed through the imperfectly charted waters of Torres Strait and sighted Saibai Island and Warrior Reefs south of the Papuan coast. He returned to Sydney and in April reported the results of his hydrographic surveys to Commodore Stirling and the Admiralty.

After a cruise to Norfolk Island and the South Seas Moresby was sent to Torres Strait. He was lent a survey officer by the Queensland government and on his way north captured the 'black-birding' Melanie and Challenger, which he sent to Sydney and had their masters successfully prosecuted in the Vice-Admiralty Court under the 1872 Kidnapping Act. By 31 January 1873 he was again in Torres Strait. Hoping to land in New Guinea but uncertain of official support, he used the pretext of searching for Mikluho-Maklai [q.v.]. He found the deep-water channel near Jervis Island, sailed across the Gulf of Papua to Redscar Bay and further down the coast found an opening in the reef. Moresby personally conned the Basilisk into Fairfax Harbour, Port Moresby, naming both after his father. Time forced him to return to Cape York. Two months later he sailed to Yule Island, named Robert Hall Sound, then turned east and explored and charted the coast. He claimed New Guinea for Britain at Possession Island and then charted Milne Bay, where he defined the eastern extremity at East Cape.

Moresby returned to Sydney in July; although the government and press in Sydney and Brisbane hailed his work Stirling condemned his actions and referred them to the Admiralty, which approved Moresby's work and found that he had not disobeyed orders. In January 1874 he was ordered to England and on the way sailed to Port Moresby, around East Cape to the D'Entrecasteaux Islands and up the north coast to Astrolabe Bay. This laborious and meticulous work completed, he sailed for Amboina where he found Maclay. Moresby arrived in England on 15 December 1874 and described his Australian service as 'the most notable part of my naval career'. He was applauded for his work but the Admiralty failed to recognize its quality and significance. A large part of the area charted by Moresby later became a German protectorate.

In 1876 Moresby published Discoveries and Surveys in New Guinea. From 1878 he had charge of the dockyard and naval establishments in Bermuda. Promoted rear-admiral in 1881, he became assessor to the Board of Trade and the Court of Appeal. He retired in 1888 as vice-admiral. In 1909 he published Two Admirals, an autobiography with a short account of his father's career. Moresby died at Fareham, Hampshire, on 12 July 1922. In 1859 he had married Jane Willis Scott (d.1876); they had one son and four daughters. In 1914 a destroyer was named after him. A gifted artist, he had presented two pictures to the Australian navy.

M. A. Lewis, *The navy in transition, 1814-1864* (Lond, 1965); *Geog J*, 60 (1922); G. C. Ingleton, 'A brief history of marine surveying in Australia', *JRAHS*, 30 (1944); *The Times*, 13 July 1922; *SMH*, 25 Apr 1925; CO 201/574.

HOWARD BEALE

MORETON, BERKELEY BASIL (1834-1924), pastoralist and politician, was born on 18 July 1834 at Woodchester, Gloucestershire, England, fourth of the ten sons of Henry George Francis Moreton, second earl of Ducie, and his wife Elizabeth, daughter of Lord Sherborne. Educated at Rugby, Magdalen College, Oxford, and the Royal Agricultural College, Cirencester, he sailed for Sydney in the *Waterloo*, arriving on 27 November 1855. After two years of colonial experience at Ugoble station on the Murrumbidgee, he formed a partnership with Esmond de Preux Brock; they bought Wetheron station, near Maryborough, Queensland, in May 1859. On 13 October 1862 Moreton was married by a Baptist minister to Emily Eleanor, daughter of John Kent, commissioner of crown lands; they had two sons and eight daughters.

Moreton's brother Seymour (b. 1841) arrived in 1859 and when Brock sold out in the early 1860s the two brothers became partners. On 30 August 1870 Berkeley was elected to the Legislative Assembly for Burnett but resigned on 24 October 1871. On 7 November 1873 he was elected for Maryborough but resigned again in March 1875 to provide a seat for John Douglas [q.v.]. He was re-elected for Burnett on 1 October 1883; in March-April 1885 he was postmaster-general in the Griffith ministry, secretary for public instruction until April 1886 and combined the post with that of colonial secretary until June 1888. He spoke rarely and in May 1888 was defeated in a general election but appointed to the Legislative Council. He resigned from the council in 1891 to contest Burnett. Defeated he stayed out of politics until 1901 when he was appointed to the council by the Philp ministry, holding his seat until March 1922. He was a member of the Rawbelle Divisional Board, a magistrate and a trustee of the Queensland Museum.

When his brother, the third earl, died on 28 February 1920, Moreton succeeded to the

title and left Queensland on 14 July 1922 to take his seat in the House of Lords but died on 7 August 1924 at Tortworth, Gloucester. His brother Seymour married Mary Ellen, a sister of Berkeley's wife, and died in Brisbane on 8 April 1905, survived by two sons and two daughters. A younger brother, Matthew Henry (1847-1909), failed on a sugar plantation near Maryborough in 1885 and became a resident magistrate in British New Guinea.

N. M. Brown, Memoirs of a Queensland pioneer (Oxley Lib, Brisb); biographical cutting book (Oxley Lib, Brisb).

H. J. GIBBNEY

MOREY, EDWARD (1832-1907), mining and civic leader, was born on 27 March 1832 at Frindsbury, Kent, England. Apprenticed in the merchant navy at 13, he served in ships trading on the English coast and the Mediterranean. In 1852 he signed on for Hobart Town in the *Columbus*, went to Mauritius and in the *Sir Walter Scott* to Adelaide where he worked as a supervising stevedore before commanding a brig on the Yarra in Melbourne for two months. At Geelong in 1853 he joined a party of gold-seeking sailors from the *Bournehuf* and *Stelonheath*. They went to Ballarat where as a co-operative they had astonishing success for three years. By quickly changing claims from Prince Regent Gully to Sailors' Gully, New Chum Gully, Dalton's Flat, Red Hill, Gum Tree Flat and the Jewellers' Shops where a claim 24 feet square yielded a ton of gold, the sailors became wealthy enough to go their own ways.

Morey witnessed the attack on Eureka Stockade on 3 December 1854 and was one of the first to tend the wounded diggers; later he declared that the affair savoured of a massacre. In 1855 he began to furnish ill-equipped miners with tools and gear, taking in payment a share in their claims. He extended his mining interests to Buninyong, Carngham, Linton and Happy Valley. He followed the gold rush of 1861 to Otago where he was moderately successful and returned to Ballarat to become its most spectacular investor and landowner. By the late 1860s he had a large share in the rich quartz mines of Sebastopol and was founder and director of many companies working deep leads. He was a member of Loughlin's [q.v.] syndicate of eight which in 1875 formed the Seven Hills estate to mine near Creswick.

Very wealthy, Morey began to invest in land. He bought properties at Linton, Skipton, Pitfield and Maryborough, mined gold from them and profited from stud sheep and dairy cattle. By 1880 he had formed more mining companies and held more leases than any other investor in the colony. Until 1883, when he handed over to a son, he was in business as a machinery merchant. He imported engines and heavy equipment for the deep-lead mines when companies could afford machinery manufactured in England and Germany. He was also a director of the Phoenix Foundry and the Ballarat Woollen Mills. On two notable explorations outside Victoria he was commissioned in 1869 by the directors of Stanley Copper Mines north of Blinman, South Australia, to report on their operations and in 1888 with Henry Gore he reported extensive tracts of rich minerals in northern Queensland.

In 1884 Morey became patron of the new Ballarat Fine Art Gallery Public Association and later served on the gallery council, the committees of the School of Mines and Old Colonists' Association. In 1888 he was elected to the Ballarat City Council and mayor in 1894. In 1889 he became a member for Wellington in the Legislative Council but in 1904 and 1907 contested the seat in vain. He had served on the council's select committee on railways in 1891 and was nominated by the Munro [q.v.] government to the first Country Fire Brigades' Board. A cricketer and footballer, he helped to found the Ballarat Yacht Club in 1877 and was commodore in 1881-91.

At St Paul's Church, Ballarat East, on 25 June 1855 Morey had married Mary Ann, only daughter of Alexander Frickett of Manchester. In 1882 with his wife and a daughter Morey went abroad in search of his mother who had gone to America after her eight children had separated; he discovered that she had died in England just before his arrival. He died on 4 October 1907 from a clot on the brain, predeceased by his wife and five of their six daughters and nine sons, the eldest of whom was Edward, a cricketer who played for Australia against a visiting English team.

Generous and hearty, Morey earned the admiration and respect of his local community. Impressive and convincing, he was often commended for his faith in the nation's mineral potential and played an important role in Ballarat's rise to a large provincial centre. Inability to read and write never hindered him because his daughter looked after his correspondence and he could scrawl a signature.

His monuments are the stone lions in the Ballarat Botanic Gardens and the ornamental cast-iron gates at the main entrance.

W. B. Withers, *The history of Ballarat*, 2nd ed (Ballarat, 1887); W. B. Kimberly (ed), *Ballarat and vicinity* (Ballarat, 1894); R. Gay, *Some Ballarat pioneers* (Mentone, 1935);

Ballarat Courier, 5 Oct 1907; *Ballarat Star*, 5 Oct 1907; information from E. L. Morey, Mount Eliza, and Mrs S. W. Wiencke, Box Hill North.   AUSTIN McCALLUM

MORGAN, FREDERICK AUGUSTUS (1837-1894), publican and mining investor, was born on 20 June 1837 in Sydney, eldest of four sons of Frederick Augustus Morgan, tailor, and his wife Emma Martha, née Woodward. He spent his early years round Bathurst where he always claimed to have found gold before Hargraves [q.v.]. On 11 October 1864 he married Mary Jane Wheatley at Tenterfield. In 1866 they moved to Warwick, Queensland, where he engaged in mining, kept a hotel, butcher's shop and racing stables. In December 1879 he took over the Criterion Hotel at Rockhampton and was soon joined by his brothers Thomas, Edwin and Alex. His wife did most of the hotel management while Morgan and his brothers prospected and developed small mines.

In the 1860s William Mackinlay, a stockman on Calliungal run, found rich gold on a hill then known as Ironstone Mountain and worked it secretly for years. His daughter married Sandy, one of the two sons of John Gordon who held a 640-acre selection on the northern boundary of Calliungal. She revealed the secret to her husband and Sandy and his brother Donald made ineffective attempts to investigate the deposit in 1881. Donald moved to the Peak Downs district as a station overseer and Sandy settled in Rockhampton as a paid mine-worker.

Early in 1882 Sandy went to work for the Morgan brothers at the Galawa mine and agreed to show them the mineral deposits on Gordon's selection. In July 1882 he took Thomas and Edwin Morgan to the spot where after three days of prospecting they realized that the mine was very rich. Despite an ambiguous agreement to share with Gordon, the Morgan brothers pegged out claims in their own names and a few days later sold a half share to William Knox D'Arcy, a Rockhampton solicitor, Thomas Skarrett Hall, branch manager of the Queensland National Bank, and William Pattison [q.v.], a local butcher. As the syndicate proceeded to develop the mine its phenomenal riches became apparent. Aware of an old Australian tradition of mines deteriorating with depth, the Morgan brothers became nervous. Edwin sold his share to Frederick Augustus, who then sold out to Hall, D'Arcy and Pattison for £62,000, and in October 1863 the last brother, Thomas, sold his share for £31,000. Although aware that he had lost the chance of an enormous fortune, F. A. Morgan retired to live in comparative affluence at Rockhampton. He invested in local business ventures, held Canal Creek and Targinie runs and built a boiling-down works and jetty but remained at heart a miner. After an abortive attempt to enter the Queensland parliament in support of Samuel Griffith he confined himself to local politics and in 1891-93 was mayor of Rockhampton. He died there on 8 November 1894, survived by his wife and one son. His brother Edwin died in Brisbane on 18 September 1916.

W. G. C., *Some account of the Mount Morgan gold mine* (Rockhampton, 1885); F. W. Sykes, *The Mount Morgan gold mine* (Syd, 1893); W. H. Dick, *A mountain of gold* (Brisb, 1889); J. G. Pattison, *'Battler's' tales of early Rockhampton* (Melb, 1939); V&P (LA Qld), 1886, 3, 115; B. G. Patterson, 'The story of the discovery of Mount Morgan retold', JRHSQ, 4 (1948), and 'The story of the Mount Morgan mine', *Qld Government Mining J*, 20 June 1950; *Morning Bulletin*, 9 Nov 1894; B. G. Patterson, The Mount Morgan mine, MS446 (NL).   H. J. GIBBNEY

MORGAN, JAMES (1816-1878), newspaper proprietor and politician, was born on 29 September 1816 in Longford, Ireland, son of Michael Morgan, a farmer descended from an Anglican family. Educated at Miss Edgeworth's private school, he followed agricultural pursuits and in 1835-38 was a surveyor in Wales. He sailed in the *Palestine* and reached Sydney on 14 March 1841. He went north to Broken Bay, hoping to join the squatting boom, and by 1845 was manager of a property on the Namoi. This experience enabled him to continue north to the Darling Downs where in 1849 he managed the Gammie brothers' Talgai station. In 1854 Morgan leased Crow's Nest station but failed within the year and returned to management in 1855. At Sydney in 1848 he had married Kate Barton, also from Ireland.

Morgan never succeeded as an independent squatter. In 1860 he bought a small property, Summerhill, near Warwick, and entered the civil service as inspector of stock for the Darling Downs. His chief task was to prevent the importation of diseased stock, but he antagonized squatters of the kind that he presumably had wished to be. They forced his resignation in 1867, an event which completed Morgan's severance from pastoral ambition. It also precipitated him into a career of journalism and politics in which he advocated a land policy favouring the small agricultural selector. He was mayor of Warwick in 1867-68 when he bought the *Warwick Argus* in opposition to the *Warwick Examiner and Times*.

Morgan's editorials were sharp and aggressive. His principal target was the dummying which many large squatters practised after the 1868 Land Act, but bitterness led him often into intemperance. He was more persuasive when advocating the need to elect for Warwick constituency a member who would seek protection for agriculture and such public works as would benefit the increasing population of farmers and shopkeepers. This programme won him the seat in 1870 against G. J. E. Clark [q.v.]. Next year Morgan, a Freemason, seriously offended many Roman Catholics and was beaten by Clark's brother, Charles [q.v.], after a close contest.

Morgan returned to the legislature unopposed in 1873 but soon showed that attacks on property had no place in his agrarianism. He strongly opposed free selection before survey and supported the fairly conservative Land Act of 1876. He was chairman of committees in 1874-78 but as member for Warwick was disappointing. He added to his failures by helping to form the Darling Downs Farmers' Co-operative Association which lasted but two years. Though weakened by a severe liver disease he contested Warwick again in 1878, but his record and personality were against him and so was the increased urban population of Warwick; he lost heavily to Jacob Horwitz, store-keeper and miller. In June he had transferred the *Argus* to his sons. He died on 29 December from the effects of a fall from a steamer in Brisbane, survived by his wife, six daughters and five sons, including Arthur, later premier of Queensland. He was paid tribute at his funeral in Warwick by 1200 locals and by the premier and government officials.

D. B. Waterson, 'A Darling Downs quartet', *Qld Heritage*, Nov 1967; *Warwick Argus*, 5 Dec 1878.   B. A. KNOX

MORGAN, SIR WILLIAM (1828-1883), merchant and politician, was born on 12 September 1828 at Wilshamstead, Bedfordshire, England, son of George Morgan, farmer, and his wife Sarah, née Horne. He reached Port Adelaide in the *Glenelg* on 13 February 1849. He worked first on land near the River Murray and his life was saved by an Aboriginal, Ranembe, whose name Morgan later gave to one of his sons. Morgan was next employed by Board Bros, grocers, of Hindley Street, Adelaide, until he left for the Victorian gold diggings in 1851. He had modest success and on returning to Adelaide bought Boords' business and established

William Morgan & Co., wholesale and retail grocers in Hindley Street. By 1865 the retail business was closed and the firm had become merchants in Currie Street but retained the premises in Hindley Street for about five years.

Morgan was elected a member of the Legislative Council in August 1867, coming second in the poll; re-elected in 1877, he headed the poll despite his refusal to have a committee working for him and retained his seat until 1883. He became chief secretary in the second Boucaut [q.v.] ministry on 3 June 1875 but resigned on 25 March 1876 because personal business was too pressing. He served again as chief secretary in the fourth Boucaut ministry from 26 October 1877 to 27 September 1878. When Boucaut was elevated to the bench of the Supreme Court Morgan became premier and chief secretary on 27 September 1878. He resigned office on 24 June 1881 because his financial affairs had become involved, particularly through unfortunate investments in copper and nickel mines in New Caledonia. Among many other business interests he was a founder in 1865 of the Bank of Adelaide. In politics he was a free trader, claiming that direct taxation should be levied mainly on individuals according to their incomes rather than indirect taxes on what they spent, which to Morgan was the general effect of customs duties. During his periods in office public works were greatly extended: a town, named after him, was made at the railhead of the line connecting Adelaide with the north-west bend of the River Murray; Adelaide's deep-drainage sewage system, the first in an Australian capital, was begun; and much building in Adelaide, including the first parts of the University of Adelaide, the Public Library and in 1881 the National Gallery. He had been a delegate to the 1871 and 1880 Intercolonial Conferences in Melbourne and in a much-quoted speech in 1877 strongly advocated Federation of the Australian colonies.

Morgan was far-seeing, imaginative and energetic; he crammed much, probably too much, publicly and privately into his fifty-five years. He declined the offer of a baronetcy because he believed that Australia was too young a country to be burdened with hereditary titles, but in May 1883 he accepted appointment to the order of K.C.M.G. On 8 July 1854 he had married Harriett, daughter of Thomas Matthews of Hurd's Hill, Coromandel Valley; they had nine children. In June 1883 he left for England on a business trip. He died on 2 November at Brighton, and after a well-attended Anglican service was buried beside his parents at Wilshamstead.

E. Hodder, *The history of South Australia*, 2 (Lond, 1893); G. D. Combe, *Responsible government in South Australia* (Adel, 1957); PP (SA), 1872 (2), 1880 (56, 102, 183), 1881 (74); *Register* (Adel), 3 Nov 1883; *The Times*, 3 Nov 1883; *Australasian*, 10 Nov 1883.

E. J. R. MORGAN

MORIARTY, ABRAM ORPEN (1830-1918), public servant, was born in County Cork, Ireland, son of Merion Marshall Moriarty [q.v.] and his wife Anne, née Orpen. In the *St George* he reached Sydney with his family in January 1843. At 16 he became a clerk in the Colonial Secretary's Department; by 1853 he was chief clerk in the Department of Lands and in 1857 commissioner of crown lands for New England and Macleay, and police magistrate, Armidale. In February 1858 he was elected to the Legislative Assembly for New England and Macleay. T. G. Rusden petitioned that Moriarty's return was unconstitutional because he was receiving money from the Crown but the assembly rejected the plea. On 13 October Moriarty resigned and became clerk of the Executive Council on 8 November.

Strongly recommended by Governor Denison, Moriarty accompanied Sir George Bowen to Brisbane as his private secretary. They arrived on 10 December 1859 and Bowen signed the proclamation drafted by Moriarty notifying his assumption of office as 'Captain-General and Governor-in-chief of the Colony of Queensland and its Dependencies'. Moriarty read the proclamation to the assembled public and the colony of Queensland came into being. A week later Bowen appointed him clerk to the Executive Council and colonial under-secretary, fully using his 'ability and experience' in the difficult months after separation. He helped to establish the civil service and was also secretary to its board of examiners and a member of the board to open tenders for runs of crown lands. In September 1860 he returned to Sydney and on 17 September was appointed chief commissioner of crown lands with a salary of £800 and helped John Robertson [q.v.] to draft his land legislation. He was a member of the Royal Sydney Yacht Squadron in 1862 and in the Volunteer Rifles was an ensign in 1865, lieutenant in 1868, captain in 1870 and quartermaster in 1875-77.

Because of the Cowper [q.v.]–Robertson's government's retrenchment policy, Moriarty was also under-secretary for lands from 29 December 1869 with no extra salary. In June 1870 the colonial treasurer, Saul Samuel [q.v.], ordered an inquiry into Moriarty's accounts by the inspector of public revenue. He revealed that although Moriarty was a legally constituted collector of public moneys he kept no proper accounts and 'very great irregularity has existed'; Moriarty had paid public moneys into his own account at the Union Bank until transactions were completed, thus delaying payment of the money into the Treasury. The inspector later found another £771 had been allegedly paid into Moriarty's private account during the inquiry. In a minute for the Executive Council Cowper noted that 'the loose and highly reprehensible practice . . . led to the painful conviction that grave suspicion attaches to Mr. Moriarty of appropriating public monies to his private uses'. Incredulous that after twenty-four years of faithful service his probity could be impugned, Moriarty denied the charge and claimed that gross overwork had affected his health. The auditor-general, C. Rolleston [q.v.], could not deny the irregularities but pointed to three extenuating circumstances. First, 'the system . . . has grown up with the department' and had never before been condemned. Second, Moriarty's physical depression was derived from overwork and inability to give proper attention to either department. Third, 'no loss to the Revenue, or to any person concerned, has been discovered, or . . . even suspected'. He regretted that Moriarty would not produce his passbook, but his account at the Union Bank was for fiduciary matters while his private account was at the Australian Joint Stock Bank. Although Moriarty produced a letter from his bank manager showing that the money had always been covered, Cowper was not satisfied and Moriarty was dismissed on 8 September.

In May 1872 Sir Alfred Stephen [q.v.], while administrator of the colony, employed Moriarty as his private secretary and aide-de-camp and recommended his reinstatement. In July 1873 Moriarty warmly thanked Parkes [q.v.] for acceding to his request for the chief clerkship in the Lands Department. In October the Parkes government survived a censure motion over Moriarty's reinstatement after a stormy debate. In 1875 the Robertson government appointed him chief commissioner of conditional purchases at £600 a year. From 1878 he divided the duties of the department with the under-secretary, W. W. Stephen [q.v.], and was also chief commissioner for conditional sales. In 1879 his salary was raised to £800. After Alexander Stuart's [q.v.] 1884 Land Act was passed Moriarty became chairman of the Goulburn Land Board from 1 January 1885 with a salary of £830. In October 1888 he applied to Parkes for the vacant under-secretaryship for lands but pleaded in vain.

In 1895 Moriarty bought part of the Gundary subdivision near Goulburn and later part of the Ashbury estate at Bungendore. He retired as chairman of the local land board in 1896 and lived at Iveragh, Goulburn. Always a stern father, he became ill-tempered in old age. Aged 88 he died on 22 May 1918 and was buried in the Anglican cemetery at Tirrana, near Goulburn. Predeceased by his wife Harriett Christiana, née Powell, whom he had married at Bungendore on 24 April 1856, he was survived by four sons and four daughters of their thirteen children. His estate was valued for probate at £1652.

V&P (LA NSW), 1858, 1, 493, 885, 945, 1861, 2, 932, 1865-66, 3, 107, 162, 1870-71, 3, 781, 1872-73, 2, 926, 1878-79, 4, 85, (LA Qld), 1860, 365, 421; SMH, 31 Oct 1873; Daily Telegraph (Syd), 24 May 1918; Aust Worker, 30 May 1918; Parkes letters (ML); CO 234/1/118; information from W. A. Gordon, Nimmitabel, NSW.
                                                        J. T. MAHER

MORIARTY, MERION MARSHALL (1794-1864), portmaster and politician, was born in County Cork, Ireland, fifth son of Vice-Admiral Sylverius Moriarty and his wife Lydia, née Hinton. He joined the navy in 1807, serving at Copenhagen and on the Mediterranean and West Indian Stations. In 1814 he was promoted lieutenant but ill health forced his return to England and in 1815 he retired on half-pay. On 15 October 1816 in County Kerry he married Anne (d. 1877), daughter of Edward Orpen of Killowen. He attended the University of Edinburgh (M.D., 1821) and practised in Dublin but was later employed by the St George's Channel Steam Navigation Co., commanding steamers on the Cork-Bristol run.

In 1842 Moriarty was appointed portmaster in New South Wales and harbourmaster in Sydney by the British government. He reached Sydney with his family in the St George on 23 January 1843. As portmaster he displaced Thomas Watson and aroused local resentment. His duties included the control of ports, lighthouses and pilot services in the colony. His career as harbourmaster was uneventful until 1847 when he piloted H.M.S. Inflexible aground in Sydney Harbour. Though an investigating committee recommended his dismissal, he held his post until 1857 when he was pensioned by H. W. Parker's [q.v.] ministry. He was a director of the Second Australian Benefit, Investment and Building Society.

In 1855 Moriarty had been defeated by Stuart Donaldson [q.v.] in the Legislative Council by-election for Sydney Hamlets and failed again in 1856, but from August 1860 he represented Braidwood in the Legislative Assembly. He died from a diseased spleen on 10 January 1864 and was buried in the Anglican cemetery at St Leonards. He was survived by his wife, six daughters and three sons, one of whom Abram Orpen [q.v.] became under-secretary for lands.

The eldest son EDWARD ORPEN (1825-1896) was born in County Kerry and educated at Trinity College, Dublin. Moriarty worked briefly as a cadet on constructing the breakwater on the Isle of Portland. He reached Sydney with his family and set up as a consulting engineer and surveyor. On 1 June 1849 he became an assistant in the Surveyor-General's Department. In 1853-55 he was engineer and surveyor (later chairman) for the Steam Navigation Board and in 1855-58 engineer for Hunter River improvements. In October 1858 he became engineer-in-chief for harbours and river navigation in the Department of Works with a salary of £1100. In January-October 1862 he was commissioner and engineer-in-chief for roads and in 1865 a superannuation fund commissioner. He controlled the building of water supply schemes for Wollongong, Bathurst, Wagga Wagga, Albury and Hunter Valley towns. In 1867 he was a commissioner for Sydney's water supply and in 1869-70 president of the Hunter River Floods Commission.

Moriarty was a lieutenant in the Volunteer Artillery and as captain from 1869 served on the commission on defence from foreign aggression and on the board for inspecting and maintaining the supply of colonial warlike stores. In 1871-73 he was captain of the Engineers Corps, Volunteer Rifles. Permitted to engage in private projects, he supervised the building of two bridges for the Penrith Nepean Bridge Co. in the 1850s and Pyrmont Bridge in 1865-66. In 1869 he confessed his 'habit of receiving private pupils for instruction' and in 1874 investigated the Grey River entrance for the New Zealand government.

In 1875 Moriarty became a member of the Public Works Tender Board and the Sewerage and Health Board. To the government he suggested plans for a haven at Trial Bay by using prison labour to build a mile-long breakwater across the entrance. Work began in 1877 but stopped in 1903 after over £160,000 had been spent. From 1877 he had an extra £300 a year as engineer of Sydney's water supply. In 1878 he studied such works in England and North America as docks, breakwaters and river-locks.

Moriarty was a councillor of the Philosophical Society and a member of the Royal Sydney Yacht Squadron and the Linnean Society of New South Wales. In 1852

he had published a pamphlet *A few Practical Hints upon Roads, and Roads Systems*. He retired on 31 December 1888 with a pension of £791 13s. and went to England. He died at Southsea, Hampshire, on 18 September 1896 and was survived by his wife Leila Helen, née Geary, whom he had married in Brisbane on 18 May 1853. He left her his estate valued at £5800.

Sel cttee on pilots' duties regulations, V&P (LC NSW), 1850, 2, week 10, 138; V&P (LA NSW), 1869, 1, 96, 1870-71, 3, 913, 1885-86, 1, 537, 656, v 2, 481, 1887-88, 2, 1156; SMH, 24, 31 Jan 1843, 9 Feb 1844, 11 Jan 1864; *Moreton Bay Courier*, 19 May 1853; *Sydney Mail*, 16 Jan 1864, 22 June 1878; A. W. Powell, The Trial Bay project: politics and penal reform 1861-1903 (B.A. Hons thesis, Univ New England, 1970); S. A. Donaldson ministry letters (ML); Governor's dispatches 1846-48 (ML); Moriarty family press cuttings (ML).   ALAN POWELL

MORISON, ALEXANDER (1813-1887), Congregational minister, was born on 22 February 1813 at Kilkenny, Ireland, said to be son of a Scottish Highlander 'whose settlement in Ireland was due to his being wrecked upon its coast'. Morison arrived at Hobart Town in the ministry of Rev. Frederick Miller [q.v.] whose Brisbane Street Chapel he joined in August 1832. His promise as a preacher and layworker led him to consider the Congregational ministry and he returned to Europe early in 1834 to enter Highbury College, London. He was probably in Dublin in 1838 when he responded to the appeal of the Colonial Missionary Society and returned to Hobart in December with Rev. John West [q.v.]. Morison was appointed to Pittwater by the Van Diemen's Land Home Missionary Society with a commission to preach 'anywhere in general'; he itinerated widely from Tasman Peninsula to Deloraine, preaching in forty-two stations at least three times each year and opening chapels at Cambridge and Carlton. The chapel at Richmond was completed after he left. In all, six churches looked to him as their founder.

When Rev. William Waterfield [q.v.] resigned from Collins Street Independent Church in 1843 Miller recommended Morison to supply the vacant pulpit for two months. He arrived in Melbourne in July and was soon called to the pastorate, where he ministered vigorously for twenty-one years, clearing the church debt almost immediately and building up the membership from 21 to 586. As the only Congregational minister in Port Phillip and secretary of the newly-formed Port Phillip Colonial Missionary and Christian Instruction Society, he attempted to extend his parish but had little support until Rev. Benjamin Cuzens arrived at Geelong in 1849, Rev. Thomas Odell at West Melbourne and William Moss [q.v.] at Prahran in 1850. He became the first chairman of the first Congregational Union of Victoria in June 1852 and was a leading figure in its affairs until its dissolution in 1856. Although Morison took the position of English Dissenters against state aid, some of the views derived from his Irish Congregational background were regarded as Tory by his more radical colleagues. In 1851-52 he applied to La Trobe for land grants for church sites, a measure leading to friction with the union which interpreted his action as a 'gross violation of the voluntary principle'. Though he travelled widely on horseback and preached at the goldfields much of this work was given up after the arrival of Rev. J. L. Poore [q.v.] and the founding of the Congregational Home Mission in 1854. In 1860, when the new Congregational Union and Home Mission was founded by Poore and others, representatives from the Collins Street Church were conspicuously absent. Morison would not accept the union's authority, particularly over land, and this stand led him to resign his pastorate in 1864.

Recognized for his intellectual qualities, Morison was a popular lecturer, a constant contributor to the local journals and author of several pamphlets. In 1853 he was appointed to the first council of the University of Melbourne where he exercised a liberalizing influence, supporting such privileges as the admission of women. In 1865 he was admitted to the Presbyterian ministry and 'passed several weary years' at Clunes in 1869-72, 'cut off from all the congenial society to which he had been accustomed'. On resignation he returned to Melbourne, rejoined the Congregational Church and was appointed professor of Hebrew, church history, philosophy and apologetics in the Congregational College. He held that post until he died at South Yarra on 14 April 1887. On 27 November 1851 he had married Salome, daughter of Philip Pitt of Cliftonvale Hunting Grounds, Van Diemen's Land, and granddaughter of Richard Pitt [q.v.]; of their eight children, five survived their parents.

Congregational Union, *Jubilee volume of Victorian Congregationalism 1888* (Melb, 1889); D. M. Stewart, *Jubilee history of the Presbyterian Church in Victoria* (Melb, 1909); A. C. Nelson, *History of the effective establishment of Congregationalism in the Australian colonies and New Zealand* (Hob, 1930); E. Scott, *A history of the University of Melbourne* (Melb, 1936); W. Moss, 'Independency in the Australian colonies, especially in Victoria', *The principles and history of In-*
dependency, A. Gosman et al (Melb, 1879); *Vic Congregational year book*, 1888; *Argus*, 16 Apr 1887; R. I. Cashman, Nonconformists in Victoria in the 1850's (M.A. thesis, Monash Univ, 1963); Congregational Union of Vic, Minute books and Church records (Independent Hall, Melb).   NIEL GUNSON

MORRIS, AUGUSTUS (1820?-1895), pastoralist and politician, was born in Van Diemen's Land, son of Augustus Morris and his wife Constantia, daughter of Thomas Hibbins [q.v.]. In 1820 Morris senior, a former convict, occupied grazing land under licence at Hanging Sugar Loaf near Ross, and owned the inn, punt and a farm at Cove Point.

In 1835 Morris interrupted his schooling at the Hobart Town Academy to accompany John Aitken [q.v.] and Henry Thompson on their five-week exploration around Port Phillip, where in 1837 he joined Hugh Murray junior on his Lake Colac station to learn sheep-raising. Resale to the Royal Bank of a station he had bought on the northern end of the lake brought Morris into contact with Benjamin Boyd [q.v.] in 1842. On his behalf Morris explored the salt bush country of the Riverina, from Urana and Deniliquin along the Edward and Billabong to the Murrumbidgee junction, and took up runs. He was one of the early advocates of the value of salt bush country for sheep. He was later employed by W. C. Wentworth [q.v.] in the management of Tala, Yangar, Nap Nap and Paika stations that he had taken up for Wentworth. A syndicate consisting of Morris, T. S. Mort, Thomas Holt and T. W. Smart [qq.v.] acquired those properties from Wentworth in 1853; within months Morris bought out the rest of the syndicate at a price 30 per cent above what it had paid. In 1849 he bought Callandoon station in Queensland; there he used only Aboriginals as stockmen and Chinese as hut-keepers. In the decade from 1853 Morris greatly increased his pastoral and other assets, using credit liberally. The decline in the meat market and drought in 1864-65 led to forced sale of his stations. He was bankrupted in 1866 but released next year.

Morris was member of the New South Wales Legislative Council in 1851-56 for the pastoral districts of Liverpool Plains and Gwydir, and in 1859-64 represented Balranald in the Legislative Assembly. Though most financial business connected with his stations was done in Melbourne after the late 1850s, he did not support the squatter-led movement for Riverina's independence or its union with Victoria. His legislative interests were narrowly pastoral. He advocated formation of a native police force, eradication of noxious weeds and native dogs and in 1863-64 introduced the Prevention and Cure of Scab in Sheep Act.

In 1857, when James Harrison [q.v.] of Geelong was taking out his second patent for ice-making, Morris tried to persuade Victorian stockowners to raise a £100,000 prize to encourage the use of artificial cold to preserve fresh meat for transport to Europe. Though ridiculed he persisted in this eccentricity. In 1865 he met E. D. Nicolle [q.v.], who within a year produced drawings of refrigeration equipment thought to be adequate. Morris tried unsuccessfully to launch a public subscription to finance construction of an experimental model, but it was not until T. S. Mort backed them in the summer of 1866-67 that work began. Morris's belief in preservation by cold was vindicated by successful trials of the machine in September 1867 and he soon left for England to investigate competing methods and popularize the idea of frozen meat. An English patent for the process was taken out in the names of Mort and Nicolle by William Mort. Although Morris remained a publicist for refrigeration he took no further direct part in the long search for a system suited to ocean transport.

Morris was an executive commissioner for New South Wales at the 1876 Philadelphia Centennial Exhibition. He used the position imaginatively and diligently to promote trade between the two countries, writing numerous pamphlets and newspaper articles on subjects ranging from tobacco culture and railway operation to the administration of schools. He became the Sydney agent for the Edge-Moor Iron Co. of Wilmington, Delaware, and obtained for it the contract for a long bridge over the Shoalhaven River in which it used techniques new to Australia. He was also agent for the Baldwyn Locomotive Co. and procured rolling stock for the government. In 1879 he was secretary for the Sydney International Exhibition and in 1884 was honorary secretary for New South Wales for the Bordeaux Wine Exhibition and a member of the Calcutta Exhibition Commission.

In the ferment accompanying the first major review of the colony's land laws since the 1861 Land Acts, Morris and George Ranken [q.v.] were appointed by the Alexander Stuart [q.v.] ministry to inquire into the situation. Their report, printed as a parliamentary paper in May 1883, condemned indiscriminate free selection and proposed reforms along lines earlier suggested by Stuart and later embodied in the 1884 Crown Lands Act. From 1886 he was official assignee. He died from heart disease at Manly on 29 August 1895 and was buried in the Anglican cemetery. He

was survived by two sons from his marriage to Sarah Merciana Charlotte Bailey, two other sons having died.

In the House of Lords, between W. C. Went-worth . . . and J. C. Lloyd . . . (np, c1862, copy ML); E. Digby (ed), *Australian men of mark*, 2 (Syd, 1889); V&P (LA NSW), 1883, 2, 77; *SMH*, 14 Sept 1875.   ALAN BARNARD

MORRIS, EDWARD ELLIS (1843-1902), headmaster and professor, was born on 25 December 1843 in Madras, fourteenth child of John Carnac Morris of Madras and his wife Rosanna Curtis, daughter of Peter Cherry, senior judge of the Indian Central Division. According to family tradition, his grandfather John Morris, a director of the East India Co., was the illegitimate son of the younger brother of George III. Morris was educated at Temple Grove Preparatory School in East Sheen, Victoria College in Jersey and Rugby in 1859-62. As an exhibitioner in 1862 he studied classics, law and modern history at Lincoln College, Oxford (B.A., 1866; M.A., 1869). In 1867-71 he taught at noted schools in England and Berlin, studying French and German during vacations. Appointed headmaster of Melbourne Church of England Grammar School, he arrived in the colony in April 1875 to succeed Dr J. E. Bromby [q.v.]. On 1 January 1879 he married Edith Sarah Catherine, daughter of George Higinbotham [q.v.].

Morris had early successes in developing the school along English public school lines. The number of boys attending the school increased rapidly and he built Witherby Tower, Wadhurst, a science block and the library that bears his name. In 1876 he instituted the prefect system and the school magazine, *Melburnian*, to which he often contributed. He produced the first *Liber Melburniensis* in 1879, changed the school colours to Oxford blue and designed the school flag and coat of arms used until 1909. He instituted the first school concert and exhibition of hobbies. Although fearful that physical activities were deemed more important than the intellectual, he laid down the cricket pitch in 1875, launched the first school boat in 1876 and introduced drill classes in 1877.

From 1879 financial difficulties beset the school. The number of pupils decreased, partly because of economic conditions and partly because of Morris's disciplinary measures. He refused to truckle to parents who removed their sons because of his forthright reports and strict interpretation of regulations. Claiming that he had failed in running the school on English lines, Morris resigned in March 1882 intending to return

O

to England. However, in November he was appointed Hughes [q.v.] professor of English at the University of Adelaide. The University of Melbourne had been talking of a similar chair since 1870 but now promptly advertised it and invited Morris. He accepted and became professor of modern languages and literatures from January 1884. He introduced pass courses of two years in English and one year of both French and German, and the final honours course and master of arts degree, lecturing single-handed in all three subjects. The university awarded him its first doctorate of letters in 1899. He was chairman of the Professorial Board in 1888 and 1890-93, a founder and committee member of the University Union and chairman of the University Extension Board's Committee in 1894.

A devout Anglican, Morris was a member and treasurer of the Council of Trinity College. Known as the 'philanthropic professor', he served on the Visiting Committee for Industrial Schools and Jika Reformatory in 1879 and as founding president of the Charity Organization Society in 1887 presided over the first two Australian Conferences on Charity in 1891-92. He was founding editor of *Australasian Schoolmaster* in 1879-82, president of the Educational Section of the Social Sciences Congress in 1880, trustee of the Public Library in 1879, a promoter of the Australasian Library Foundation in 1896, president of the Victorian Section of the Home Reading Union in 1892 and foundation president of the Melbourne Shakespeare Society in 1884-88. He supported all these causes in his many contributions to the *Argus* and *Melbourne Review* and sometimes corresponded with the *Manchester Guardian* and *Calcutta Englishman*. His articles reveal him as a liberal who supported academic freedom, higher education of women, church unity and extension of educational opportunity. Predeceased by his wife in 1896 he died on 1 January 1902 on leave in England, survived by three daughters and a son.

Most of Morris's works appeared first in London and include A *memoir of George Higinbotham* (1895) and *Austral English: a dictionary of Australasian words, phrases and usages* (1898). In 1874-89 he edited Longmans's *Epochs of Modern History*, writing *The Early Hanoverians* (1874) and *The Age of Anne* (1878). He also edited the four volumes of *Cassell's Picturesque Australasians* (1887-89) but later turned to excerpts from poets, novelists and explorers with tracts on education and the charity movement.

G. Blainey, A *centenary history of the University of Melbourne* (Melb, 1957); H. S. Morris,

Back view (Lond, 1960); *Argus*, 1875-1902; *Australasian*, 11 Nov 1882, 4 Jan, 17 May 1902; *Illustrated Sydney News*, 7 June 1890; *Table Talk*, 16 Sept 1892; *Bulletin*, 18 Dec 1897; O. Wykes, The teaching of French in New South Wales and Victoria, 1850-1958 (M.Ed. thesis, Univ Melb, 1958); Morris papers (held by family); Univ Melb Archives.

OLIVE WYKES

MORRIS, GEORGE FRANCIS (1834-1910), vigneron, was born in Warrington, Lancashire, England, son of William Gregg Morris, draper and Quaker, and his wife Emma, née Francis. He arrived in Melbourne, probably on 10 September 1852 in the *John Taylor*, and went to the Ovens River goldfields where he was moderately successful. He moved to the Buckland diggings as a store-keeper and thence to Beechworth where he bought into Scott & Co., general merchants. The firm prospered but in 1858 he sold his own share to it and visited Europe. Returning to Victoria he bought 220 acres of Gooramadda station near Wahgunyah and Rutherglen at an auction in April 1859 and added to this property until he became the largest landowner in the district. He used his land for cropping and grazing and later bred horses. He also owned four steam-threshing machines which he hired throughout his district and far into New South Wales. He became a noted pioneer of farm mechanization but is chiefly remembered as a vigneron.

In 1860 Morris had planted a few vines to test the suitability of his land for wine growing. The experiment was so successful that he bought more land and planted more vines until he was harvesting grapes from 700 acres. These he supplemented by buying the produce of 1250 acres owned by smaller vignerons of the district. In the early 1860s Morris built a fine home called Fairfield and under the ballroom established his first cellar. Soon it was too small and by 1892 he had built another cellar of 39,000 square feet above ground; it was fitted up with the most modern machinery driven by steam and held 750,000 gallons. He travelled several times to Europe in the interests of Australian wines. In 1886 he was commissioner for Victoria at the Colonial and Indian Exhibition in London. On this and other visits he increased his own knowledge of wine-making to the advantage of the whole Victorian industry. At the same time he vigorously promoted the sale of Australian wines in London, where from his own vineyard he supplied as much as 100,000 gallons in one year.

Morris had an enviable record of service

to local government. He was one of the nine original members elected to the Rutherglen Road Board on 8 October 1862. He served two separate three-year terms on the board but when it became the Rutherglen Shire Council in 1871 he was not elected. He served on the council in 1876-78 and 1881-98, when he left the district to live at Arral, Clendon Road, Toorak. He was five times president of the shire and appointed a justice of the peace on 16 September 1878.

Morris maintained his interest in the vineyard, and as late as 1906 he paid a visit to Europe, partly for the benefit of his health but more particularly to procure disease resistant vines to replace the ravages of phylloxera since 1897. On 1 January 1910 he had a cerebral haemorrhage from which he failed to rally. He died on the 8th and was buried in Brighton cemetery. He married three times: first, Sarah Anne Hughes of Melbourne; second, Lydia Irving; and third, Ellen Francis. He was survived by three sons and two daughters of the eleven children of his first wife.

North Eastern Hist Soc, *Rutherglen and its history* (Rutherglen, 1968); *Federal Standard* (Chiltern), 1862-98; *Chiltern Leader*, 7 Apr 1894; *Age*, 11 Jan 1910; *Argus*, 11 Jan 1910; *Rutherglen Sun*, 11 Jan 1910; *Wine and Spirit News*, 21 (1910); papers held by C. T. G. Morris, Mia Mia Vineyard, Rutherglen.

K. A. R. HORN

MORRIS, ROBERT NEWTON (1844-1931), educationist, was born on 28 March 1844 at Jamberoo, New South Wales, son of Robert Morris, farmer, and his wife Elizabeth, née Aldridge. After some education at Illawarra House Academy, Kiama, he was in business for about five years until 1864 when he became one of the first six pupils at Camden College, Newtown, the Congregational Theological College and Grammar School. At the University of Sydney (B.A., 1870) he had an outstanding record; in his final year he was the most distinguished student in the school of chemistry and experimental physics, and worked temporarily in these fields after Professor A. M. Thomson [q.v.] died and before Archibald Liversidge [q.v.] was appointed in 1872.

Morris entered the Congregational ministry and in September 1872 became the second principal of Camden College. In May 1874 he resigned, ostensibly because of ill health, but the college was suffering financial troubles and losing pupils. He followed his ministry in South Australia before returning to New South Wales to conduct a grammar school at Yass and in 1879 a Presbyterian school at Goulburn, where in 1880 he

strongly opposed the opening of the Mechanics' Institute Library on Sunday afternoons.

In 1881 Morris was appointed a public school inspector for the Maitland district, an unusual appointment from outside the service. He resumed his studies and won a prize at the University of Sydney (LL.B., 1884; LL.D., 1886). He was an inspector in the metropolitan area in 1885-89 and from 1890 to his retirement in 1911 was examiner of teachers, trainees, and secondary and technical students. In 1896-1901 he was also superintendent of technical education. In 1903-04 he introduced wider courses and higher standards in the examinations for teachers and for applicants for posts as pupil-teachers.

In December 1927 Morris's estate was sequestrated when he was unable to honour promissory notes made to W. J. Allen [q.v.] for the purchase of four pianos. His assets were fifteen acres at Tempe and shares in the Rotary Brick Press Co. Ltd. He had no occupation and depended on relations for support. Predeceased by his wife Elizabeth Anne, née Tucker, whom he had married at West Maitland on 27 September 1879, Morris died at Sydney Hospital on 30 July 1931 after being accidentally knocked down by a car. He was survived by two sons and a daughter.

Report of the minister of public instruction (Syd, 1881-1911); *Cyclopedia of N.S.W.* (Syd, 1907); J. A. Garrett and L. W. Farr, *Camden College, a centenary history* (Syd, 1964); Bankruptcy papers, 26823/15 (NSWA).

BRUCE MITCHELL

MORRISON, ALEXANDER (1829-1903), schoolmaster, was born on 3 February 1829 at Edinkillie, Morayshire, Scotland, sixth son of Donald Morrison, farmer, and his wife Catherine, née Fraser. Educated at the parish school, Elgin Academy and King's College, Aberdeen (M.A., 1851), he began teaching at Elgin Academy but soon became rector of St John's Grammar School, Hamilton, Lanarkshire, where he increased the enrolment in four years from 194 to 397. His eldest brother was a minister and others held teaching positions; they were well known to the Free Church's Colonial Committee which in 1857 was asked by the Free Church Presbytery of Victoria to select a principal for Scotch College, Melbourne, where the first head, Robert Lawson, had resigned. The committee approached two of Alexander's brothers in vain but Alexander accepted. In 1855 he had married Christina, daughter of Alexander Fraser. In the *Essex* he sailed with her, a son, a younger brother

Robert and a female relation, arriving at Melbourne on 25 July 1857. His brother George [q.v.] later became first headmaster of Geelong College and Robert a master at Scotch College and vice-principal in 1869-1904.

The presbytery was embarrassed by a claim from the Colonial Committee for £1000 for travelling expenses, but Morrison paid them himself. Within three years the college enrolment rose from 56 to 284; it had passed 300 by 1870 and remained steadily above that number until 1892, when the depression cut it by a third, before recovering. For most of this time Scotch College was the largest church school in Australia. By his appointment terms Morrison collected all fees, paid running costs and remitted 5 per cent of the gross revenue in the first year and 10 per cent thereafter to the Presbytery's Education Committee for an improvement fund. The fund was inadequate for his plans and he made several personal loans for new buildings in 1858-73, a cricket ground in 1879 and tennis courts in 1901. In 1878 he advanced money at 7 per cent to permit renewal of an £8000 mortgage and in 1893-97 met all deficits. A director of the National Mutual Life Association of Australasia Ltd in 1897-1903, he had helped in its amalgamation with the Mutual Assurance Society of Victoria in 1896. He had interests in Goldsbrough Mort [qq.v.] and argued for its reconstruction in 1893. Victorian Scots were awed by the resounding success of the magisterial figure who backed his judgment with money.

Moves to alter the pervasive classicism of colonial secondary schools had been tentative in the 1850s; Morrison wanted change and set about making Scotch College in the image of Elgin Academy. He appointed qualified teachers of French and German, offered in 1859 to endow a modern languages exhibition at the University of Melbourne and succeeded in having French and German made matriculation subjects in 1862. He detached the teaching of English from classical studies, introducing in 1859 J. D. Morell's method of analysis of sentences and in 1860, for the first time in Australia, the study of English literature. He engaged Dr John Macadam [q.v.] to teach chemistry by practical demonstration and in 1873 the college had the first science laboratory in an Australian school. Between 1858 and 1865 Morrison made such 'extras' as book-keeping, drawing and music regular subjects. Despite his persistence the university did not make science a matriculation subject until 1881, music until 1892 and drawing until 1899. In the 1860s debate on liberal education he stood with the Taunton commissioners, arguing that mental faculties were 'better cultivated by variety than exclusiveness', contrasting the 'critical' scholarship demanded by classics and the descriptive discipline of modern studies, and warning against 'ministering to the ends of a vulgar and material utility'. A visit to Britain in 1875 convinced him that Victorian schools were as well adapted to the times as English grammar schools. Firm and compassionate, he found corporal punishment necessary, though his diaries attest that it distressed him. He taught classics with success and published A First Latin Course, which was revised in association with W. F. Ingram and republished in 1903. For him the college was a public not a sectarian school so in 1862 he organized classes in Hebrew for a large Jewish enrolment. In 1866 he served on the royal commission into public education; in 1873 he was awarded an honorary doctorate of laws by the University of Aberdeen and in 1877 LL.D, ad eund., University of Melbourne.

In 1878 Dr J. E. Bromby [q.v.] moved successfully for Morrison to become a member of council. He agreed with the professors' claim to control of academic matters but was impatient with their toleration of irresponsibility and their conservatism. Exasperated at delay in publishing matriculation results in January 1882, he persuaded the vice-chancellor to publish them within twenty-four hours on his own authority and publicly blamed the delay on Professor J. S. Elkington, who protested but got no support. Morrison opposed J. D. Kirkland's appointment to the chair of chemistry, and criticized the high standard of first year Greek which he claimed with justice was 'killing' the subject while the professors refused to replace Greek with a modern language. He opposed the appointment of local men to chairs without advertising overseas. In 1898 he moved Marshall Hall's dismissal from the chair of music for publishing opinions 'incompatible with the University's neutrality on moral and religious questions'. For Professor Baldwin Spencer he could not do enough, pressing the council to allow him to join the Horn expedition to the Macdonnell Ranges in 1894 and securing £1000 from David Syme [q.v.] for Aboriginal research. On the finance committee he persuaded the government to modify reductions in its grant in the 1890s, negotiated the Wyselaskie [q.v.] bequest in 1885 and secured Francis Ormond's [q.v.] gift of £20,000 for a chair of music in 1887. In favour of admitting women to degrees, he opposed a request from female medical students for concessions. Fearing government resumption of Presbyterian land in the university reserve, he took the lead in the foundation of Ormond College in 1881.

Though a firm believer in the necessity of the 1843 Disruption, Morrison welcomed the union of Victorian Presbyterians in 1859. When the Presbytery of Melbourne proceeded against Dr Charles Strong [q.v.] in 1881 his Evangelical loyalty conflicted with his desire for some freedom of doctrinal interpretation. He opposed the presbytery's procedure as irregular. Strong later accused him of equivocation. When Strong's assistant, Rev. George Dods, was called to Scots Church in 1886 Morrison opposed it successfully in presbytery on the grounds of Dods's inadequacy for a prominent pulpit, his weak adherence to certain doctrines and his complicity in the congregation's abortive secession in 1883. The *Argus* denounced Morrison and he was threatened with legal action.

Morrison's public interests were the Aborigines Protection Board of which he was vice-chairman in 1887-89, the Blind Asylum, the Teachers Training College and Federation for which he prayed earnestly. He encouraged games but did not play himself; he relaxed at his Mount Martha home, 'Craigie Lea', and later at the Australian Club. Though prone to conjunctivitis he was a voracious reader. Predeceased by his wife on 13 April 1883, he died from heart failure on 31 May 1903, survived by all but one of his children.

A portrait by R. H. Dowling [q.v.] in 1885 is at Ormond College.

J. Mitchell, *Spoils of opportunity* (Lond, 1938); N. Adams, *Family Fresco* (Melb, 1966); National Mutual Life Assn of A'sia, *A century of life* (Melb, 1969); V&P (LA Vic), 1867, 4 (27), 1901, 3 (36), 1903, 2 (20), 1904, 2 (13); Aborigines Protection Board reports, V&P (LA Vic), 1881-1903; *Evening Mail* (Melb), 23, 27 Jan 1882; *Argus*, 16 Feb, 3, 25 Mar 1886, 17 Aug 1894; *Australasian*, 30 Jan 1892; *Table Talk*, 1 Apr 1892; E. L. French, Secondary education in the Australian social order 1788-1898 (Ph.D. thesis, Univ Melb, 1957); Morrison diaries 1875, 1883-86, 1894-96, 1898-1901 (Ormond College Archives); Council, Professorial Board and Senate minutes (Univ Melb Archives); Presbyterian Church blue books 1869-1903 and Scotch College minute books (Presbyterian Assembly Hall, Melb).   E. L. FRENCH

MORRISON, ASKIN (1800-1876), merchant, was born of Scottish ancestry on the family estate of Gortmore at Augher, County Tyrone, Ireland. He joined the *Orelia* in London for Hobart Town, landed with his merchandise on 9 May 1829 and soon made a handsome profit from the speculation. After selecting land at St Peter's Pass, near Oatlands, he continued his trading and developed lucrative connexions between the colonies, China and Britain. Two of his best-known voyages were those in the *Cleopatra* from Dublin and the brig *Resource* from Canton. He was reputed to have made a profit of £10,000 from a cargo of tea he brought from China in the brig *Caroline*. By 1835 he had given up sailing with cargoes and was settled as a Hobart merchant, owning and chartering ships for whaling, exporting wool and oil, and importing China tea and Mauritius sugar.

Morrison applied his profits in land ownership; he bought the beautiful property of Runneymede in an isolated but fertile valley twenty miles east of Hobart and another at Rosny on the Derwent estuary. He acquired other farming land in the colony to the extent of not less than 12,000 acres, sharing with various partners such as John Walker, G. C. Clark [qq.v.] and Duncan McPherson. His other speculations proved less successful than shipping and land ownership. His ferry *Twins* (sometimes called *Kangaroo* or *Double Guts*), a powerful but noisy double-engined steamer, ran across the Derwent at a loss for four years before he gave it to Captain Taylor in 1863. He also suffered loss from his part in the Mersey-Deloraine Tramway project, and a share in Peter Barnard & Co. of Launceston was said to have cost him £78,000. He was engaged in such varied business as the Sorell Steam Navigation Co. which intended to run a steam-powered barge up the shallow Coal River to near Richmond in 1854, the Hobart Town Gas Co., the Domain shipyard, the Union Bank, the Hobart Savings Bank, and the Hobart and Launceston Marine Insurance Co. His tender for the construction of the first Sorell Causeway was accepted by the government and he completed this valuable link between Hobart and the Tasmanian east coast.

Money and property brought their train of honour and office. Morrison was made a justice of the peace in 1837, was nominated by Lieut-Governor Denison to the Legislative Council, and after responsible government in 1856 represented Sorell in the House of Assembly until 1860. A leading figure in Hobart's business coterie and member of the 1846 commission for lighting and paving the streets, Morrison helped to form the Tasmanian Club, was a director of the Chamber of Commerce and treasurer of the Royal Exchange Association. Long prominent in Hobart he was neither voluble nor outstanding as an organizer, and though co-opted to serve as a councillor on the Royal Hobart Regatta Committee, the Acclimatization Society, the Art Treasures Exhibition, the Gardeners' and Amateurs' Horticultural Society and St Mary's Subscription Hospital, he was generally passive and retiring. His interests were widely dispersed but his special enthusiasm outside business was the breeding of fine horses. He lived partly at Runneymede and at times in his town house near his business on the New Wharf where the thoroughfare is named after him. In 1871 he sold his city business to Macfarlane Bros. He died in his town house on 29 May 1876, aged 76 and unmarried. From his lands at St Peter's Pass he left an annuity of £100 to his cousin Andrew Morrison, and legacies to other relations. He signed his will with a mark.

Cyclopedia of Tasmania, 1 (Hob, 1900); F. C. Green, *The Tasmanian Club, 1861-1961* (Hob, 1961); A. Rowntree, *Battery Point today and yesterday* (Hob, 1968); *Mercury*, 31 May, 10 June 1876; W. Sorell papers NP 332/136 (TA).

PETER BOLGER

MORRISON, GEORGE (1830-1898), educationist, was born on 11 December 1830 at Morayshire, Scotland, son of Donald Morrison, farmer, and his wife Catherine, née Fraser. He attended the Elgin Academy and won a scholarship to the University of Aberdeen where, after an outstanding course in classics, mathematics and natural philosophy, he graduated with a master's degree. He had been president of the university debating society. His first appointment was as mathematics master at the Naval and Military Academy, Gosport, England. Later he taught at the Dollar Academy, Scotland.

On the advice of his brother Alexander [q.v.], George migrated to Melbourne in 1858 and taught mathematics at Scotch College for six months before accepting the headmastership of Flinders National School, Geelong. An elder of the Presbyterian Church, he was soon marked down by his minister, Rev. A. J. Campbell [q.v.], to direct a new church school which he was promoting. Geelong College opened on 8 July 1861 with Morrison as headmaster and a church committee in business control. Like many other schools, Geelong College early ran into difficulties. Morrison insisted on efficient management and a permanent site, matters not easily encompassed by the pastoralists on the committee, and by 1864 this body was ready to abandon the college to him on condition that he paid all liabilities. As a private school the college was, according to Morrison, 'condemned to outer darkness and phenomenal success'. In 1871 at Newtown he opened a fine new building which remains his memorial. He earned repute for uprightness and excellence of scholarship. His students won many exhibitions at the matriculation examin-

ations and he also presented candidates for the first year of arts at the University of Melbourne with notable success.

Morrison early insisted on scholarship and character, through religion, as the only essentials of education, but later conceded the value of sports and military training. In a time of stern discipline, his canings were feared less than his carpet lectures on the rewards of unrighteousness. The ultimate testimonial to his work and character was the respect of alumni and the public for the college which he personified, even though it was a private business.

Morrison's work was recognized by the University of Aberdeen which awarded him an honorary doctorate of laws in 1891. He was then still teaching but gradually handed over administration to his third son. While taking a class he felt faint and died within a few minutes on 15 February 1898. On 7 December 1859 at Scotch College he had married Rebecca Greenwood whom he had met in Scotland. Of their five sons and three daughters, the eldest, George Ernest, became famous as 'Chinese' Morrison, Reginald was known internationally as an amateur athlete and Norman succeeded his father as headmaster of the college.

A posthumous portrait by Sir John Longstaff is in the Norman Morrison Memorial Hall at the Geelong College.

G. McL. Redmond, *Geelong College, history, register and records* (Melb, 1911); B. R. Keith (ed), *The Geelong College 1861-1961* (Geelong, 1961); *Argus*, 7 Oct 1911; Annual reports and records, 1863-90 (Geelong College).

B. R. KEITH

MORROW, JAMES (1843-1910), inventor and manufacturer, was born in County Tyrone, Ireland, youngest son of Robert Morrow and his wife Ann, née Milligan. The family arrived in Melbourne in 1852 and his father opened a livery stable in Spencer Street. They moved to Fitzroy, where James and his brother Tom attended the Bell Street school and later the famous model school. James was then apprenticed to James Madders, who had a small engineering business in Melbourne. He also met Hugh Lennon [q.v.]. After completing his apprenticeship in 1860 Morrow became a foreman in the Carlton firm of Joseph Nicholson & Co., manufacturers of agricultural implements, drays and wagons. In the early 1860s the firm had economic difficulties and James suggested that a mower of new design be produced. The success of this machine was largely responsible for improving the firm's financial position.

Morrow also developed a double-speed

reaper, which could be converted into a mower by the operation of a lever, and a combination reaper and horse-works. These and later inventions were patented in the name of James Nicholson, who gave Morrow a portable threshing plant and a team of horses valued at £300. In the industry's off-season Morrow toured the country as a contract thresher which in the late 1860s provided a welcome supplement to his income.

By 1872 Morrow had married Catherine Treahy and rented a small cottage at Carlton. He selected 320 acres at Shepparton, where his wife moved to fulfil the residential obligations. The selection was later increased to 1000 acres and controlled mainly by his wife; James visited the property on weekends. In 1879 Nicholson died and Morrow began to take out patents under his own name. In 1880 he patented a spur-gear stripper with immediate success. He refused the Soho Foundry's offer of £6000 for the patent rights, and used the patent to buy a half-share in Nicholson & Co. which then became Nicholson & Morrow. He seems to have taken a major part in the control of the firm, which achieved high profits in the 1880s.

In 1883 the Victorian government offered a prize for a successful harvester. Morrow had long been interested in such a machine; he patented a prize-winning stripper with a threshing attachment in August 1883, but the machine was not a combination harvester. Although other patents for harvesters followed that year, the most important was Morrow's patent of a stripper harvester in January 1884. With the same machine he had won £75 in the Dookie field trials in December 1883, and it was in operation two months before H. V. McKay completed his machine. The harvester patented (V3649) by Morrow in January 1884 was the first successful machine of this type.

Nicholson & Morrow's 'Union' harvester was a success but sold slowly. Farmers were wary of the new invention, and in 1901 McKay and Nicholson & Morrow each sold only fifty machines a year although both machines had proved themselves in operation at the Victorian government trials. At Jung Jung and Numurkah in December 1885 Morrow's machine was awarded £110 and McKay's machine £100. Morrow continued to push the harvester even when his family advised him to abandon it, and much of the firm's profits from other sources seem to have been sunk into the venture.

Aged 67 Morrow died on 3 September 1910 at Ascot Vale and the Nicholson family withdrew its capital from the partnership. Robert Morrow tried to continue the business, but his five brothers and three sisters could not agree and the firm was declared

an inessential industry and closed in 1914. Despite attempts to revive the firm after World War 1 the market had been won by McKay.

Age, 21 Aug 1937; C. R. Crocker, The combination harvester: inventions, patents and trials in Australia 1879-1886 (Inst of Applied Science, Melb); family and business papers (held by R. B. Morrow, Ashburton).

GEORGE PARSONS

MORT, THOMAS SUTCLIFFE (1816-1878), businessman, was born on 23 December 1816 at Bolton, Lancashire, England, second son of Jonathan Mort and his wife Mary, née Sutcliffe. Brought up in a close family circle in Manchester in aspiring middle class ideals and comfort, he received a sound and practical education. However, his father did not succeed in Manchester and when he died in 1834 his estate was not sufficient to give his sons the start in life that they expected. For many years the eldest son William met outstanding demands on the estate from his clerk's salary. Thomas too had become a clerk with no prospects when he was offered a position in Sydney which he saw as a way to restore the family fortunes. In February 1838 he arrived at Sydney in the *Superb* and was later followed by his younger brothers Henry (1818-1900) and James (d. 1879).

Mort became a clerk in Aspinall, Browne & Co., later Gosling, Browne & Co., and gained extensive experience in local and international commerce with an eventual salary of £500. At Christ Church St Laurence on 27 October 1841 he married Theresa Shepheard, daughter of James Laidley [q.v.]. In September 1843 he set up as an auctioneer and soon prospered in general and wool sales. He was not the first to auction wool in Sydney but innovated regular sales where wool alone was offered, drawing specialized sellers and buyers together in an orderly manner. In the late 1840s he auctioned livestock and pastoral property at specialized sales, gave credit to selected purchasers and later provided finance for running expenses. In the 1850s he provided facilities for growers to consign wool through him for sale in London. These additions completed an integrated set of services to pastoralists that formed the pattern for later wool-broking firms.

Meanwhile in 1848 Mort was associated with the Australian Mutual Provident Society and in 1849 he joined a committee to found a company to promote sugar growing at Moreton Bay and next year was a member of the Sydney Exchange Co., a director of the Sydney Railway Co. in 1851, floated the Great Nugget Vein Mining Co. in 1852, helped to finance Henry Parkes's [q.v.] *Empire*, and subscribed to the Sydney Gold Escort Co. By 1850 Mort had become the premier auctioneer in Sydney and was already wealthy enough to satisfy his early ambition. He experimented with partnership arrangements hoping eventually to retire from active business. In 1850-51 he was in partnership with Alexander Campbell Brown as Mort & Brown. In 1855 Mort & Co. was formed to run the wool sales and consignments which were handled in London by his brother William; its partners originally included his brother Henry and J. V. Gorman and in 1860 Benjamin Buchanan [q.v.]. Mort & Co. was reformed in 1867 with Mort, his son Laidley, Henry and Buchanan as partners. In 1856-67 pastoral financing was undertaken by T. S. Mort & Co. in which his partner was Ewan W. Cameron [q.v.]. Mort's wealth was multiplied many times in the 1850s as a result of inflation and successful speculation in pastoral properties.

In March 1855 Mort's dry dock at Waterview Bay (Balmain) opened for business; by 1856 he had sunk some £80,000 into it. Built to accommodate the largest vessels then expected to enter the port, it provided facilities sufficient to induce the companies operating the regular overseas mail services to put steamers on the Australian run and make Sydney their terminus. However, for many years profits were disappointing. The dock was grossly over capitalized; its scale reflected Mort's misplaced faith in the future demand promised by the pressure on ship-repairing services by the peak gold rush traffic. Owned until 1861 by a partnership that included Captain T. S. Rowntree [q.v.], the dock was leased to various shipping companies, ship-repairers and engineers.

In 1860 Mort somewhat unwillingly had acquired the Bodalla, originally Boat Alley, estate near the mouth of the Tuross River. Still recovering from long ill health and debilitating hypochondria started by a riding accident in 1855 and intensified on his visit to England in 1857-59, he saw in Bodalla both a potential country estate for his retirement and a challenge to his concept of the productive purposes of capital. He planned to make it into a model of land utilization and rural settlement: a tenanted dairy estate run as an integrated whole. He had the beef cattle on Bodalla removed, land cleared, river swamps drained, fences erected, farms laid out, imported grasses sown, provided milking sheds and cheese- and butter-making equipment and selected tenants. Butter and cheese of steadily improving quality were produced for the Sydney market. Within a decade tenants

were not prospering as share-farmers and Mort chafed under their right to make production decisions. In the early 1870s the whole estate was back in Mort's hands, run as three farms with hired labour. Specialized labour, first-class facilities, efficient stock control, careful stock-breeding programmes and controlled blending of milk from different breeds and farms all paid off in higher quality products.

In 1862 Mort was a founding director of the Peak Downs Copper Mining Co. in Queensland and the Waratah Coal Mining Co. at Newcastle. In 1866 he decided to make direct use of the dock himself partly for reasons of profit, partly to generate more business for William his agent in London and partly to develop an operating business that he could leave to one of his sons. He put in even more capital, added iron and brassfoundries, a patent slip and new facilities for boiler-making, blacksmithing and engineering. He brought in Thomas Macarthur, a marine engineer, as working partner and renamed the firm Macarthur & Co. The emphasis on marine engineering was still misplaced and when Macarthur died in 1869 Mort developed the general engineering side. His dock manager was James Peter Franki whose experience in railway and mining engineering drew orders to build bridges, crushing machinery and retorts. They assembled imported railway locomotives and in 1870 put into service the first wholly locally produced locomotive. As sole owner of the dock, Mort offered his employees in 1870 a half-share in it to improve labour relations. Some agreed to buy shares and for two years the dock's affairs were managed by a committee of Mort, Buchanan, Franki and four leading hands. The arrangement was made formal in 1872 by the creation of Mort's Dock and Engineering Co. with those men as shareholders and in 1875 the company was incorporated with limited liability. In 1874 he had become a director of the new Sydney Exchange Co. and built a tin-smelting works at Balmain.

In the mid-1860s Mort began to look to refrigeration as a possible solution to three main problems: as a pastoral financier he was vulnerable to falling wool prices on the value of pastoral assets; as owner of a large engineering plant, he was anxious for manufacturing orders; and as a milk and butter producer he wanted better access to the Sydney market. From 1866 until 1878 he financed experiments by E. D. Nicolle [q.v.] to design and produce refrigeration machinery suitable for use in ships, trains and cold-storage depots. Successful land trials prompted a premature public subscription to finance a trial shipment of frozen meat to London in 1868; another subscription was opened in 1875 for a shipment that was loaded in the *Northam* in 1877 but removed before sailing because of a mechanical defect. Although their machinery was never used in the frozen meat trade, Mort and Nicolle developed commercially viable systems for domestic trade which were brought together in the New South Wales Fresh Food & Ice Co. formed in 1875. They included a slaughtering and chilling works at Bowenfels in the Blue Mountains, a cold store at Darling Harbour, milk depots in the Southern Tablelands, and refrigerated railway vans for meat and milk. The refrigeration venture, on which Mort spent over £100,000 and from which his return was negligible, points up more sharply than any other the business judgments and character of the mature Mort. Like the dock and Bodalla, the investment was a community service that could not be justified after the event by normal economic criteria.

Mort enjoyed his wealth and it gave rein to a natural flamboyance which, often hidden in his personal dealings, was epitomized in his house Greenoaks, Darling Point, where it flowered in Gothic extravagances. In 1846 he had bought the land and built the house. In his 1857-59 visit to England Mort attended a sale at the earl of Shrewsbury's Alton Towers. Among other acquisitions were Elizabethan armour, old English coats of mail, a cabinet that had belonged to Marie Antoinette, antique oak furniture and about 120 pictures. On his return he engaged Edmund Blacket [q.v.] to make additions to the house including an art gallery which with his gardens were open to the public. A keen gardener, he won many prizes at the flower shows in the 1840s and 1850s. In 1851 he served on the committee of management of the Australasian Botanical and Horticultural Society and in the 1870s became president of the Horticultural Society of New South Wales. He was also a vice-president of the Agricultural Society in 1861-78. He was a commissioner for the 1873 London International Exhibition and in 1876 for the Philadelphia and Melbourne Exhibitions.

A strong High Churchman, Mort was one of the most prominent Anglican laymen in Sydney. He gave the land for St Mark's Church, Darling Point, commissioned Blacket to design it and contributed generously to its building and upkeep as well as to the building of St Andrew's Cathedral and St Paul's College, University of Sydney. He was a founding fellow of the college and a warden of St Mark's. He was also the founder of Christ Church School in Pitt Street and a friend of Bishop Patteson [q.v.].

Mort died on 9 May 1878 from pleuropneumonia at Bodalla where he was buried; he was survived by five sons and two daughters of his first wife and by his second wife Marianne Elizabeth Macauley, whom he had married at St Mark's on 30 January 1874, and by their two sons. His goods were valued for probate at £200,000 but the income and capital realizations distributed to his beneficiaries totalled some £600,000. On 14 May a meeting of working men in Sydney resolved to show the esteem and respect in which they held his memory; as a result his statue, sculpted by Pierce Connolly, stands in Macquarie Place.

Mort's brother Henry, company director and pastoralist, represented West Moreton in the New South Wales Legislative Assembly until the separation of Queensland and West Macquarie in 1859-60. In 1881-1900 he was a member of the Legislative Council.

A. Barnard, *Visions and profits. Studies in the business career of T. S. Mort* (Melb, 1961).
ALAN BARNARD

MORTLOCK, WILLIAM RANSON (1821-1884), grazier, was born at Moat House, Melbourn, Cambridgeshire, England, son of a banking family. In 1843 he sailed from Plymouth in the *Imaum of Muscat*. In the crossing-the-line celebration he wore a heavy money-belt and was thrown overboard and with difficulty rejoined the ship. He arrived at Port Adelaide on 9 November. He sailed for Sydney in the *Dorset* on 17 December and returned with a quantity of mixed merchandise to Adelaide. He set up as a maltster with interests in flour-milling. In 1850 at Port Lincoln he married Margaret, 18-year-old daughter of John Tennant who had arrived in South Australia from Scotland in 1839.

Mortlock was appointed an inspector of sheep under the 1852 Scab Act at a salary of £350, but resigned on 28 April 1853. His first pastoral venture was an occupation licence near Port Lincoln in 1847; with additional leases and purchases it became Yalluna station and was held by the family for a century.

Prudent and pragmatic, Mortlock was a far-sighted pioneer who not only gained much reward but whose thrusting restless spirit led to the success of grazing in low-rainfall areas of South Australia. Most of his undertakings were successful and he built up a large fortune. After a visit to England in 1864 he greatly extended his holdings by acquiring in 1867-68 the Pichi Richi, Mount Arden and Yudnapinna leases. Their combined carrying capacity was prodigious, Yudnapinna alone shearing over 100,000 sheep. He was also keen on horse-racing. Considerate but firm with Aboriginals, he once saved the life of a boy who became his devoted attendant. Mortlock represented Flinders in the House of Assembly from 7 May 1868 to 2 March 1870, 27 December 1871 to 14 January 1875, and from 30 April 1878 to 19 March 1884. He spoke with force and his pithy comment enlivened debate. He also achieved some notoriety in November 1872 when with J. Riddoch he burst open the locked door of the assembly while the Speaker was in the chair. Aged 63 he died at Avenel House, Medindie, on 10 May 1884, survived by his wife, son and three married daughters. His probate was sworn at nearly £100,000.

His son William Tennant (1858-1913) was educated at the Collegiate School of St Peter, Adelaide, and Jesus College, Cambridge. Though admitted to the Inner Temple on 24 October 1878 he did not practise in South Australia but joined his father and succeeded to his estates. He represented Flinders in the House of Assembly in 1896-99 and 1901-02. In 1892 he bought Martindale Hall, a Georgian-style mansion built in 1879-80 near Mintaro, where he continued the hospitality established by its previous owner, Edmund Bowman, attended to his fine merino flock, developed the gardens and orchards and pursued his racing interests. He died on 17 August 1913 at Martindale. He was survived by his wife Rosina, née Tennant, who with one of her two sons, John, founded the Ranson Mortlock Trust which provided for research by the Waite Research Institute into soil erosion and plant regeneration at Yudnapinna station in 1952. With help from the J. T. Mortlock estate and Mrs Dorothy Mortlock, the Mortlock Experimental Station was later established at Martindale for research into animal production.

R. Cockburn, *Pastoral pioneers of South Australia*, 1 (Adel, 1925); J. Melville, 'The Mortlock Experimental Station', Adel Univ Graduates' Union, *Gazette*, June 1967; *Observer* (Adel), 17 May 1884; *Register* (Adel), 18 Aug 1913.

MORTON, WILLIAM LOCKHART (1820-1898), pastoralist, explorer and inventor, was born on 19 December 1820 at Cambusnethan, Lanarkshire, Scotland. His engineering studies at the University of Glasgow were curtailed and he migrated to Port Phillip, arriving in August 1841 during the depression. He was first employed in a boiling-down works on Saltwater River. He then moved around and was working for Anne Drysdale [q.v.] when he first won

repute for ingenuity. He constructed an efficient pump and more importantly, a dip for dressing scab in sheep.

In 1845 Morton managed Sutton Grange station, east of Mount Alexander. Late in 1846 he took up a share in Morton Plains (near Birchip), fell out with his partner and for twelve months managed a station at Kyneton before taking up Plains of Thalia where he ran sheep. In 1853 he acquired the adjoining Salisbury Plains but after drought and disease he abandoned both stations in 1855 and moved to Melbourne. At Morton Plains he had invented the swing gate for drafting sheep; on 14 January 1848 he explained the principle of the gate and race in a letter to the *Argus*.

In July 1859 Morton invited twenty businessmen to invest in a Queensland expedition to the Burdekin in hope of a government reward for finding a good port and harbour. This scheme fell through but later that year Morton and two others explored country north of Rockhampton. His account of the trip was given to the Philosophical Institute of Victoria and published in 1860 as *Notes of a recent personal visit to the unoccupied portions of Northern Queensland*. To the Royal Society of Victoria he proposed the settlement of the Victoria River district in North Australia, claiming that conditions were suitable though labour would have to be imported. His address was published in 1861 as *Suggestions for the Formation of a New Settlement in Australia*. He then travelled through Victoria's Mallee district in search of water and pastures and in 1864 explored in Gippsland, returning with rich specimens of copper ore and great expectations. Keen on acclimatization, he had helped to found the *Yeoman and Australian Acclimatiser* in 1861 and was also active in the Port Phillip Farmers' Society. In 1864 he raised the question of patent rights for his two inventions and so began a press controversy. Some pastoralists claimed to have used the swing gate before 1847 but in 1886 a parliamentary inquiry found Morton the inventor of both the sheep dip and the swing gate.

Morton's journeys to New South Wales and Queensland brought him little reward and he tried for years to acquire land leases. In 1871 he obtained sixty blocks of dry country near Cobar but did not stock the area until 1877. In 1880 Morton and two sons tried north-east of the Torowoto Swamp, forty miles from the Queensland border. This venture was also defeated by drought and his sons died of rheumatic fever; of 30,000 sheep, 9000 were mustered and sold for 2s. 9d. each.

Despite tragedy and bankruptcy, Morton remained interested in Australia's development. In 1882 his article, 'Tyranny of Democracy in Australia' in the *Victorian Review*, pleaded for Federation of the colonies, and in 1884 he advocated separation of the Riverina from New South Wales. About 1886 he moved to Belair near Adelaide to live with his son William Lockhart, a Presbyterian minister. He died on 10 March 1898, survived by one of his four sons and his wife Mary Anne, née Stone, whom he had married in 1849.

A. Henderson (ed), *Australian families*, 1 (Melb, 1941); V&P (LA Vic), 1886, 1 (D3, D4); SMH, 11 July 1859; *Examiner* (Melb), 13 June 1863; *Argus*, 3 Nov 1864, 7 Feb, April, 1 May 1865, 2 Feb 1884, 4 Aug 1885, 20 Feb, 3 July 1886, 4 Nov 1892, 12 Mar 1898; *Australasian*, 9 Jan 1875, 1 Jan 1876, 12 May 1877; *Once a Month*, July 1884–June 1886.

J. ANN HONE

MOSMAN, HUGH (1843-1909), mine-owner, was born on 11 April 1843 at Mosman's Bay, Sydney, eldest son of Archibald Mosman [q.v.] and his wife Harriet, née Farquharson. Educated at The King's School, Parramatta, he was one of the many young men who, attracted to Queensland in 1860 by the pastoral boom, found themselves penniless after the slump of 1866 and contraction of the northern and western pastoral frontier. Like other broken squatters he turned to prospecting, basing himself on the newly-discovered Ravenswood field. With George Clarke and James Fraser, Mosman prospected the country west of Ravenswood late in December 1871. There his eleven-year-old Aboriginal servant, Jupiter, found promising traces of gold at a place which Mosman named Charters Tors (Towers) in honour of the mining warden, W. S. E. M. Charters. The find was reported in January 1872 and stimulated a rush which founded North Queensland's richest goldfield. Mosman's life was easy from that time onward. Between 1872 and 1886 he floated or participated in several reefing companies.

In 1882 Mosman lost his left forearm in a premature explosion of dynamite but the accident did not affect his activities. He was one of the social lions of Charters Towers and the main street was named after him. Although politically well connected (one sister married Sir Arthur Palmer and another Sir Thomas McIlwraith [qq.v.]) he kept out of public life until June 1891 when he accepted nomination to the Queensland Legislative Council. His speeches were few, conservative and unremarkable and he resigned in January 1905. His great enthusiasm was the turf and his highlight was the winning of the Queensland Turf Club Derby with Balfour in 1902. After

many months of illness his placid and comfortable life ended at Toowong on 15 November 1909. Unmarried, he left an estate of more than £70,000 to his relations. Jupiter, the discoverer of the riches of Charters Towers, was patriarch of the Charters Towers Aboriginal reserve when he died in 1945.

W. F. Morrison, *The Aldine history of Queensland*, 2 (Syd, 1888); W. Lees, *The goldfields of Queensland* (Brisb, 1899); *Port Denison Times*, Jan-Mar 1872; *Ravenswood Miner*, Jan-Mar 1872; *Brisbane Courier*, 23 Jan 1882, 16 Nov 1909.

G. C. BOLTON

MOSS, WILLIAM (1828-1891), Congregational minister and philanthropist, was born on 23 July 1828 at Farnham, Surrey, England, second son of George Moss and his wife Sarah Leah, née Turner. Though his parents had been Anglicans they attended the Farnham Independent Chapel and sent William to the local Nonconformist day school. With a passion for self-improvement he attended the Farnham Mechanics' Institute. By 1846 he had given his first public lecture and was a church member, superintendent of the Tilford Sunday school and a village preacher. Instructed in theology and homiletics by his pastor, Rev. John Fernie, he was appointed a 'preacher of the Gospel' by his church on 4 February 1848.

In 1850 Moss abandoned his plan of training for the ministry and sailed to Port Phillip in the *Countess of Yarborough* with the Browning family, whose sons he expected to tutor on their proposed station while acting as a local preacher. On arrival at Melbourne in August, he was engaged as a preacher by A. Morison [q.v.]; Browning decided to stay in Melbourne. Moss settled at Prahran where he continued his studies under Morison and Rev. Thomas Odell of West Melbourne. On 5 October 1852 Moss was ordained and inducted as pastor of the newly-constituted Independent Church at Prahran, the first ceremony of its kind in Victoria. The original chapel was the centre of social life in the village and gave its name to Chapel Street. Moss was a leading 'father' of the community and helped to found the Mechanics' Institute, the Prahran and South Yarra Ladies' Benevolent Society and the Prahran Town Mission of which he was secretary. An active voluntaryist, he took part in anti-state-aid demonstrations. In 1853-62 he was corresponding patron of the Prahran National school, and secretary of the local committee of common schools in 1862-72. Though he lost election to the Prahran Board of Advice in 1873 by six votes,

Moss

the result was considered a testimonial to his services to primary education despite contemporary resentment at clerical involvement in state schools. He continued his ministry at Prahran until October 1878 when he and his wife undertook superintendence of the Blind Asylum.

Moss took a leading role in denominational affairs. His itinerant labours had commenced in September 1851 when he visited the Ballarat diggings as 'a kind of chaplain' to a party of church members, and later with Rev. J. L. Poore [q.v.] he helped to start the Congregational Church in Ballarat. A tent mission in Windsor was begun in 1852. He took part in intercolonial conferences, served as secretary of the first Congregational Home Mission and was a founder of the Congregational Union and Mission of Victoria, becoming chairman in 1862. A founding committee member of the Congregational College in 1866, he was secretary of the Independent Ministers' Fraternal Association and the Victorian auxiliary of the London Missionary Society. From the 1860s his name was linked with the leading public charities in Victoria. With F. J. Rose he founded the Deaf and Dumb Institution in 1861-62 and was its secretary for thirty years. He was a committeeman, secretary and later superintendent of the Asylum and School for the Blind; he also founded the Adult Deaf and Dumb Mission in 1883-85.

Moss was described as straight and well-proportioned, 'fair in complexion, with large, deep, thoughtful blue eyes, gentle in manner, and soft in speech'. He had remarkable success in drawing the attention of governors and parliamentarians to his charities, partly by his own persuasiveness, partly through the support of influential Free-churchmen such as George Rolfe and F. J. Sargood. Moss was twice married: first, to Elizabeth, second daughter of Andrew McClure, by whom he had four sons and three daughters; and second, to Mary Eleanor, third daughter of S. R. Herdsman, by whom he had one son and three daughters. He died at his home in Malvern on 14 March 1891, survived by seven of his children.

T. W. H. Leavitt (ed), Australian representative men, 2nd ed (Melb, 1887); J. B. Cooper, The history of Prahran (Melb, 1912); J. H. Burchett, Utmost for the highest (Melb, 1964); Victorian Congregational Year Book, 1892; Age, 16 Mar 1891.   NIEL GUNSON

MOUBRAY, THOMAS (1825-1891), businessman and alderman, was born on 12 September 1825 at Ballintra, County Done-gal, Ireland, fourth and youngest son of William Mowbray, landowner of Scottish descent, and his wife Euphemia, née Teevan. After local education he went with his parents in 1842 to join his eldest brother Robert in New Zealand and thence to northern Van Diemen's Land. In 1848 Thomas went to Melbourne where he entered the softgoods business.

In 1853 the foundations for a prosperous business and personal wealth were laid when Moubray, Lush & Co., wholesale and retail drapers, outfitters, silk mercers, carpet and furniture warehousemen, was established with Thomas as senior partner. With larger premises in 1878 the firm was reconstituted as Moubray, Rowan & Hicks. Moubray retired from the firm in 1891. He was said to have 'never entered into a business speculation which did not turn out successful'. His involvement in many commercial ventures won him high repute in financial circles. From 1870 he was a director of the Commercial Bank of Australia Ltd and in 1881-91 chairman of the board, where 'his genial tact was responsible for the fact that during the whole period of his chairmanship there was not a single "division" at the board'. In 1869-74 and 1879-91 he was a director of the National Mutual Life Association and at different times the Union Trustee Co., vice-chairman of Goldsbrough, Mort [qq.v.] & Co. and a founding director of the Victoria Mutual Building and Investment Co. and of the St James Estate Co. He was largely responsible for the amalgamation in 1878 of Melbourne's three gas companies into the Metropolitan Gas Co. and was its deputy chairman for many years.

Although he rejected many offers of nomination to parliament he represented Lonsdale Ward in the Melbourne City Council as a councillor from 21 February 1865 and alderman from 28 April 1877. On 9 October 1868 he was unanimously elected mayor for a year. Apart from entertaining the duke of Edinburgh, his mayoral term was comparatively uneventful. He continued the works begun in 1867 by J. S. Butters [q.v.], such as the new Town Hall and the Western Market, laid down many miles of new streets, improved the cleansing and lighting, attempted to modernize buildings on the main streets and struggled with the government to secure more parklands and more assistance in combating the city's drainage and sewerage problems which were then extremely serious. To inform the citizens Moubray had the corporation by-laws published for sale as a pamphlet and completed his term without having to raise a loan. He also served the council for many years as chairman of the Public Works Committee, which carried out much of the administrative work; in 1877-79 he represented the council on the Harbor Trust of which he was chairman, and in 1891 on the new Melbourne and Metropolitan Board of Works, though ill health prevented him from playing an active part.

For some time Moubray was a member of the Early Closing Association which campaigned for shorter working hours for shop employees. With G. S. Coppin [q.v.] and others in 1869 he was a founding member of the Old Colonists' Association of Victoria and donated some homes to the old colonists' 'village'. He gave extensively and unostentatiously to many charities, especially hospitals. Of literary bent, he had a large knowledge of the British poets and contributed a series of articles to the *Age* which attracted attention. He was married on 3 December 1864 to the widow Emma Augusta Griffith, née Dry; though childless he contributed to the education and upbringing of several of his and his wife's relations. He was much respected for his business acumen and integrity. After months of ill health he died of valvular heart disease on 25 September 1891 at his home, Armadale, St Kilda Road, South Yarra.

Garryowen (E. Finn), *The chronicles of early Melbourne* (Melb, 1888); A. Sutherland et al, *Victoria and its metropolis*, 2 (Melb, 1888); I. Selby, *History of Melbourne* (Melb, 1924); National Mutual Life Assn of A'sia, *A century of life* (Melb, 1969); *Bankers' Mag of A'sia*, 5 (1891-92); *A'sian Insurance and Banking Record*, 19 Oct 1891; *Argus*, 5 Oct 1865, 26 Sept 1891; *Age*, 26 Sept 1891; Goldsbrough Mort & Co. records, Moubray estate, 2/655 (ANU Archives); Moubray letters and papers (held by family and author). Anthony R. Rainer

MOULTON, JAMES EGAN (1841-1909), Wesleyan Methodist missionary, was born on 4 January 1841 at North Shields, Northumberland, England, son of Rev. James Egan Moulton and his wife Catherine, née Fiddian. A member of a well-known Wesleyan Methodist family, he was educated at Kingswood School, Bath, but asthma prevented him from entering a university. He worked as a clerk in a shipping office before acceptance into the Wesleyan ministry in 1863. He sailed in the *Merrie England* and arrived at Sydney on 31 May. He was headmaster of Newington College until 1865 and soon had every place occupied, with many applications for the first vacancy.

Early in 1865 Moulton was appointed to Tonga and left Sydney in May. Next year he established a college to which King George Tupou gave his name and patronage. Under Moulton Tupou College succeeded

and had a profound influence on young Tongans training for the ministry and government positions. On 2 June 1877 he left Tonga for Sydney on his way to London where he worked on translations. He visited Sydney and Fiji in May-June 1880 before returning to Tonga. A dispute between Moulton and another missionary, S. W. Baker [q.v.], led to controversy which was probably the cause of Tupou establishing the Free Church of Tonga and leaving out the small Wesleyan nucleus. The cleavage had serious political, social and religious consequences. A deputation from the New South Wales and Queensland Conference found that members of the Wesleyan Church were cruelly persecuted and many Wesleyans exiled to Fiji. 'In a period of crisis [Moulton's] loyalty and fortitude won for him the respect and admiration of those from whom he differed'. Assured that his work would continue under Rev. George Brown [q.v.], Moulton left Tonga on 11 August 1888 for Suva and then to Sydney.

In 1893 Moulton was appointed president of the New South Wales Conference and in March succeeded Rev. Dr William Kelynack [q.v.] as president of Newington College. 'Within a few weeks he was utterly involved in the life and affairs of Newington — refuting charges in the Press that the College was in a "poor state", raising loans from banks and private persons'. By December the tide turned in Newington's favour. Moulton raised the subject of 'suitable arms and insignia for the college' in the council and 'the editorial of the *Newingtonian* demanded a school song'. In 1895-1906 he was chairman of the Tonga District and in 1902 completed his translation of the Bible from the original languages. His scholarship and sure knowledge of Tongan enabled him to give the islanders 'the finest literary expression of their own language'. The Moulton Bible, recently reprinted in the new official spelling, is 'more popular than ever'. His hymns are reputed to have had an almost greater influence than his Bible. 'He did not translate literally from the English but took Tongan ideas and developed them with the insight of true poetical genius'. He invented a tonic sol-fa system and introduced Tongan choirs to the great composers. He died at Lindfield on 9 May 1909 and was buried in Gore Hill cemetery. He was survived by his wife Emma, née Knight, whom he had married in Melbourne on 23 December 1864, and by three sons and three daughters. His estate was valued for probate at £1216.

A portrait of Moulton is in the chapel of Tupou College.

G. Brown, *George Brown . . . an autobiography* (Lond, 1908); J. W. Burton, *The call of the Pacific* (Lond, 1912); J. E. and W. F. Moulton, *Moulton of Tonga* (Lond, 1921); J. E. Carruthers, *Memories of an Australian ministry 1868-1921* (Lond, 1922); N. Rutherford, *Shirley Baker and the King of Tonga* (Melb, 1971); A'sian Wesleyan Methodist Church, *Minutes of the 13th NSW and Qld conference* (1886); Methodist Church of A'sia, *Minutes of the 9th NSW conference* (1910); Methodist Missionary Soc of A'sia, *Missionary Review*, Aug 1922; MS cat under J. E. Moulton (ML).

S. G. CLAUGHTON

MUECKE, CARL WILHELM LUDWIG (1815-1898), educationist, pastor and editor, was born on 16 July 1815 at Büden, near Magdeburg, Germany, son of a teacher. He studied classics and natural sciences in the Zerbst Gymnasium and the Freiberg School of Mining, and attended the Universities of Bonn and Berlin. In the 1840s an active educationist, he was provoking the wrath of the Prussian authorities by controversial articles, editing the *Pädagogische Jahrbücher* and a children's newspaper, directing the Norddeutscher Volksschriften-Verein, re-organizing schools, attending the National Education Commission in Frankfurt, and writing or editing some eight or more books for artisans, peasants and children in which up-to-date scientific and technological information was imparted in the form of simple stories. Several of these were reprinted up to 1879 and some translated into other languages. In 1847 the University of Jena, taking cognizance of these activities, awarded him a Ph.D. without examination or thesis. He took part in the 1848 revolution but its failure moved him to organize groups of like spirits interested in emigration. He sailed with his family from Hamburg and arrived at Port Adelaide on 7 August 1849.

After a brief spell of farming Muecke was invited to become pastor of the new Tabor Church in Tanunda; sectarianism or 'certain prevailing conditions', in the discreeter language of clergymen, 'made the organization of a third congregation in Tanunda, humanly speaking, unavoidable'. To Pastor Kavel's [q.v.] Old Lutherans, Muecke and his congregation were *Weltkinder* and even dangerous latitudinarians and blasphemers; more objectively, they were liberal. Besides the Tabor congregation Muecke served churches at Greenock, Schoenfeld, Daveyston and Wasleys. He resigned in 1869.

For forty years he was closely connected with the German press as newspaper proprietor, editor and journalist. His editorial policy, and that of M.P.F. Basedow, his son-in-law and partner in the *Tanunda Deutsche* (later *Australische*) *Zeitung*, differed from that of rival German papers in giving more space to colonial than to Fatherland affairs. A frequently expressed sentiment was that German immigrants were or should be Australian patriots but that this did not entail either pro-English or anti-German feeling. After 1870 pro-German sentiment was more strongly expressed along with a degree of republicanism.

Education was another preoccupation. In 1851 Muecke had applied in vain for the inspectorship of German schools in South Australia, but he was not discouraged. On his suggestion a German Teachers' Federation was established. He advocated the formation of an agricultural college and his well-informed pamphlet, *National Schools for South Australia* (Adelaide, 1866), in boldly rhetorical but not faultless English, on the desirability of a state school system, speaks of teachers' colleges and libraries, school inspections, the teaching of sciences and compulsory attendance after the centuries-old German model. Other writings reveal the scientist investigating the diseases of wheat. In 1878 the University of Adelaide awarded him an M.A. *ad eund*.

One of the best-known public figures of German birth in the colony, Muecke was reputed a good orator and lecturer as well as an indefatigable journalist. His views were those of a liberal and a patriot; an idealist in youth, he remained sanguine to his later years. He had married three times: first, to Emilie in Germany; second, to Caroline, sister of Richard Schomburgk [q.v.]; and third, on 10 November 1887 at Port Adelaide to Maria Gehrke who had arrived from Germany in 1882. He died at Hahndorf on 4 January 1898, survived by two of the three children of his first wife.

A. Lodewyckx, *Die Deutschen in Australien* (Stuttgart, 1932); PP (SA), 1868-69 (20); R. B. Walker, 'German-language press and people in South Australia, 1848-1900', *JRAHS*, 58 (1972); family papers.

D. C. MUECKE

MUELLER, BARON SIR FERDINAND JAKOB HEINRICH VON (1825-1896), botanist, was born on 30 June 1825 in Rostock, Schleswig-Holstein, only son of Frederick Mueller, commissioner of customs, and his wife Louise, née Mertens. After his parents died Mueller was apprenticed to a chemist in Husum and graduated in pharmacy in 1846. His extensive research into the vegetation of Schleswig-Holstein in 1840-47 and his impressive herbarium came to the notice of Professor Nolte of the University of Kiel; there he was awarded a Ph.D. for his thesis on *Capsella Bursa-pastoris*. Ill health persuaded him to seek a warmer climate. Dr J. Preiss [q.v.], newly returned from Western Australia, told him of its unique vegetation and recommended him to go to Australia. Mueller and his two sisters sailed from Bremen in the *Hermann von Beckerath*, arriving in Adelaide on 15 December 1847. Working as an assistant chemist, he used his spare time in investigating flora as far north as Lake Torrens. He contributed papers to the Linnean Society, London, the German *Linnea* and newspapers in Adelaide on his findings. He tried farming in the Bugle Ranges with F. E. H. W. Krichauff [q.v.] but soon left because it interfered with his botanical work.

In 1852 Mueller went to Melbourne and, on the recommendation of Sir William Hooker, with whom Mueller had corresponded, Lieut-Governor La Trobe appointed him government botanist in 1853. With J. Dallachy [q.v.] he visited Mount Buffalo and the Ovens River where he reported indications of gold. Alone he went to Mount Buller to observe the alpine vegetation and spent several weeks around Port Albert and Wilson's Promontory before returning to Melbourne. He estimated that he had collected specimens of over half the indigenous vegetation of Victoria. He discovered species earlier claimed to be found only in Tasmania and added new genera to the flora of Australia. He reported on the possible medicinal value of some plants in the treatment of consumption, rheumatism and scurvy, and emphasized the commercial value of the acacia for its wood, tannin and gum, and the Australian manna for its saccharine content. On a second expedition he travelled via the Grampians to the Darling and Murray junction and thence to Albury, Omeo and the Buchan district with increasing hardship and danger in difficult and often unexplored regions, finally reaching the mouth of the Snowy River. He sent duplicate specimens of all species to Hooker, 'the plants being so much more useful in Kew than in Australia'.

In 1854 Mueller was appointed a commissioner for the Melbourne Exhibition and spent much time organizing an exposition. He was also active in absorbing the Victorian Institute for the Advancement of Science into the Philosophical Society. In November he set off for the La Trobe and Avon River districts, where he predicted that the fertility of the soil would enable a large and prosperous population to settle. He climbed Mount Wellington, worked up the Dargo River, went to Mount Bogong and thence to Mount Kosciusko which he ascended on New Year's Day 1855. On his return to Melbourne he claimed that he had investigated 'almost completely the Alps flora of this continent'.

Mueller was appointed botanist to the North West Australia Expedition under A. C. Gregory [q.v.]. In July 1855 the party left Sydney in the *Monarch*. They called at Moreton Bay before sailing to the mouth of the Victoria River. They explored much country on their journey overland to Moreton Bay, travelling 5000 miles in sixteen months. Mueller had observed nearly 2000 species, of which some 800 were new to Australian botany. Soon after his return to Melbourne in January 1857 he was appointed director of the Botanical Gardens while still retaining his post as government botanist from which he had been given unpaid leave. He immediately arranged for the construction of an herbarium, contributed his own already extensive collection and began work on his *Fragmenta Phytographiae Australiae* which was published in twelve parts in 1858-82. As director of the gardens Mueller was responsible for exchanging seeds and plants with botanists throughout Australia as well as European and American herbaria.

The need for a comprehensive systematic survey of the botanical resources of Australia had long been recognized. Hooker and his son Joseph [q.v.] were convinced that the work could not be attempted without reference to the notes and specimens in the collections of Banks, Brown, Cunningham, Leichhardt [qq.v.] and others in Europe. As early as 1855 the Hookers had urged Mueller to return so that he could combine his wide field experience with the resources of these collections to produce a work on Australian flora, but Mueller insisted that the work be undertaken and completed in Australia. He had long hoped to write a flora of Australia and had compiled much material towards it, but with extreme reluctance he agreed to step down in favour of George Bentham [q.v.] whom he was to assist. *Flora Australiensis* appeared in seven volumes between 1863 and 1878. This comprehensive survey synthesized the isolated efforts of explorers and amateur and professional botanists throughout the colonies. It went close to Hooker's ideal of a work that 'should last, and . . . be a standard for all time'. In the preface of the first volume Bentham praised Mueller's zeal, talent and industry, but these words did little to sooth his professional pride and the wound never healed.

Among the first to take a scientific interest in Victorian forests, Mueller saw the dangers of indiscriminate clearing of land and advocated the establishment of local forest boards in an effort to provide timber for the future. He predicted the commercial value of Victorian timber in the manufacture of charcoal, gunpowder, tar, vinegar, spirits and potash. Specially recognizing the value of the eucalypt he had encouraged Joseph Bosisto [q.v.] in 1853 to distil eucalypt oil on a commercial scale, and was responsible for exporting eucalypt seeds to California, India, Algeria, Hong Kong and elsewhere, advocating their planting as a measure to combat malaria. Always sensible to the practical application of his scientific work, he brought great economic value to the settlers of Victoria, though he made no financial profit himself for the introduction of useful vegetation from other countries.

By 1868 Mueller was already answering criticism of his directorship of the gardens: 'no foundations exist . . . neither are statues erected . . . works of art we can call forth at pleasure, while time lost in forming the plantations cannot be regained'. Late in 1871 he lectured on the objects of a botanic garden but his efforts were in vain and in 1873 he was replaced as director by W. R. Guilfoyle [q.v.]. Mueller remained government botanist and suffered no pecuniary loss but felt the injustice of his dismissal from the gardens; he is reputed never to have entered them again.

An indefatigable worker, Mueller's correspondence sometimes reached 3000 letters a year; he published over 800 papers and major works on Australian botany and lectured on subjects ranging from rust in cereals and the culture of tea in Victoria to an historical treatise *On the advancement of the Natural Sciences through Ministers of the Christian Church.* He published *The Natural Capabilities of the Colony of Victoria* in 1875 and his *Select Plants Readily Eligible for Industrial Culture or Naturalization in Victoria* in 1876. Next year at the request of the Western Australian government he surveyed its forests and coast as far north as Shark Bay. His report, published in London in 1879, advocated independent timber resources for all countries and recommended that Western Australia establish a forest administration. In that year he also issued the first part of *The Native Plants of Victoria,* a work which was never completed, and the first decade of his *Eucalyptographia: A Descriptive Atlas of the Eucalypts of Australia and the adjoining Islands,* the tenth decade of which appeared in 1884. Part 1 of his *Systematic Census of Australian Plants* was published in 1882 and next year he was awarded the Clarke [q.v.] medal by the Royal Society of New South Wales. His two volumes of *Key to the System of Victorian Plants* were published in 1885-88.

Mueller's widespread interests included the exploration of New Guinea and Antarctica. He argued that Australia was responsible for the development of these land masses and published his *Descriptive notes on Papuan Plants* in 1875-90. He served on the first Australian Antarctic Exploration Committee and devoted much time to it in his last years. He contributed to discussions on acclimatization and continued to introduce fauna and flora to Australia. He also encouraged searches for the remains of Leichhardt's party and in 1865 organized the Ladies' Leichhardt Search Committee to raise funds.

Mueller had become chairman of the Philosophical Society in 1859. A fellow of the Linnean and Royal Societies in London, he was a founder of the Royal Society of Victoria and president of the (Royal) Geographical Society, Victorian Branch. He was also active in the Melbourne Liedertafel and the Turn Verein, and supported the Lutheran Church and its mission in central Australia. In 1861 he was appointed a hereditary baron by the King of Württemberg. He was made C.M.G. in 1868 and K.C.M.G. in 1869. He was awarded a royal medal of the Royal Society, London, in 1888 and won many European honours.

Soon after arriving in Adelaide Mueller had been naturalized. Though fiercely loyal to the British Crown, he was still a German and his European scientific contacts were of immense value to Australian science. He was largely responsible for the international recognition given to Australian scientific endeavour. Much of his work has never been superseded and is a measure of his lasting contribution to botany. He had little private life, his time, energy and finance being devoted to his work. He never married; though engaged to Euphemia Henderson in 1863 he gave reasons of ill health and pressure of work for breaking the engagement. Survived by a sister, he died on 10 October 1896 in South Yarra, Melbourne.

A. Lodewyckx, *Die Deutschen in Australien* (Stuttgart, 1932); M. Willis, *By their fruits* (Syd, 1949); C. Daley, 'The history of *Flora Australiensis*', *Vic Naturalist*, 44 (1927-28); J. H. Willis, 'Botanical science in Victoria 100 years ago', Roy Soc Vic, *Procs* 73-74 (1961); M. E. Hoare, 'Learned societies in Australia: the foundation years in Victoria, 1850-1860', Aust Academy of Science, *Records*, 1 (1967), no 2; L. A. Gilbert, Botanical investigation of New South Wales 1811-1880 (Ph.D. thesis, Univ New England, 1971).   DEIRDRE MORRIS

MULLAGH, JOHNNY (1841?-1891), Aboriginal cricketer, was born on Mullagh station, near Harrow, Victoria, and originally answered to 'Mullagh Johnny'. His Madimadi tribal name may have been Muarrinim; his romanticized portrait in the Harrow Mechanics' Institute suggests that he was part-European but neither surviving photographs nor contemporary testimony support this inference. He was a capable stockman and assisted with shearing, spending most of his life on J. B. Fitzgerald's Mullagh property or on David Edgar's Pine Hills station. He became a celebrity and local folk-lore is rich in anecdotes testifying to his popularity and undoubted strength of character. Since legends lack verification and either contain racist overtones or exude sentimental paternalism, they are best ignored.

About 1864 Mullagh and other Aboriginal station hands learned the rudiments of cricket from Edgar's schoolboy son and two young squatters, T. G. Hamilton and W. R. Hayman. In 1865 an Aboriginal team defeated a European one at Bringalbert station. The victors then challenged Western District clubs with much success, Mullagh emerging as the most versatile player. By September 1866 Hayman secured the coaching services of T. W. Wills [q.v.], financed through the Edenhope Club. Wills led an Aboriginal team on to the Melbourne Cricket Ground on Boxing Day and then with Hayman took the players on a financially disastrous tour to Sydney. Mullagh was one of the few successful players.

In 1867 Hayman, two financial backers and Charles Lawrence, a former Surrey all-rounder, regrouped the team, smuggled it out of the colony and conducted it efficiently on the first Australian cricket tour of England. Between 25 May and 17 October 1868 the thirteen Aboriginals captained by Lawrence played 47 matches in 40 centres, winning fourteen and losing the same number. Mullagh and Lawrence carried the burden of the tour, Mullagh playing in 45 matches.

Few cricketers better merited the title of all-rounder. At his best against fast bowling, Mullagh batted high in the order and completed 71 forceful innings, averaging 23.65 from 1698 runs (94 highest score). Underarm bowling was then optional but he favoured the round-arm delivery, with a 'free wristy style'. His 1877 overs included 831 maidens and numbered twice those delivered by any other Aboriginal. He is credited with 245 wickets for an average of 10, although he captured 257 wickets. In addition he often kept wickets. His performances won him a cup at Reading and sundry monetary presentations, but his great match was at Burton-upon-Trent: he top scored with 42, took 4 for 59, caught a fifth and as wicketkeeper stumped the other five. All matches were enlivened with athletics and displays of Aboriginal prowess; Mullagh was the star boomerang thrower. He also threw the cricket ball further than most challengers and cleared the high-jump bar at 5 ft. 3 ins.

Mullagh never played intercolonial cricket but he represented Victoria in 1879 against the All England 11, scoring 36. Until the 1890 season he played regularly with the Harrow Club, a member of the Murray Cup competition. His prowess apparently overcame racial barriers and he was widely respected. He died unmarried on 14 August 1891 in his camp at 'Johnny's dam' on Pine Hills station. He was buried in the Harrow cemetery, and the *Hamilton Spectator* sponsored a district subscription for an obelisk to his memory at the 'Mullagh oval' in Harrow. He must be rated as a player of class at a time when cricketing standards were at a low ebb.

J. C. Hamilton, *Pioneering days in Western Victoria* (Melb, 1913); D. J. Mulvaney, *Cricket walkabout* (Melb, 1967); *Hamilton Spectator*, 15, 20, 27 Aug, 1, 3 Sept 1891.

D. J. MULVANEY

MULLEN, SAMUEL (1828-1890), bookseller, was born on 27 November 1828 in Dublin, son of George Mullen, bookseller, and his wife Eliza, née Orson. Educated at Nuttgrove College and Trinity College, Dublin, he was indentured to an apothecary at 16. He disliked the work and was soon apprenticed to the booksellers, William Curry, Jun. & Co., where he met George Robertson [q.v.]. Mullen completed his apprenticeship in 1848, went to London and worked for John W. Parker & Son, where he met an apprentice, William Charles Rigby (1834-1913), who in 1859 started a bookshop in Adelaide.

At 24 Mullen decided to migrate and sailed for Melbourne in the *Great Britain*; Robertson was a fellow passenger. They arrived on 12 November 1852 and Mullen went to Apsley, near Hamilton, with an introduction to S. M. Baird of Mount Bute station. Next year he became first assistant to Robertson who had opened a bookshop in Melbourne. They adjusted to their new conditions and the business grew rapidly. To shorten the time between ordering and receiving stock Robertson decided in 1857 to open a London office and chose Mullen for the post. On 6 October 1855 at St Peter's Church, Melbourne, he had married Eliza Moss. With his wife and infant son he sailed in the *Essex* but in London found that Robertson had appointed his own brother. No explanation was made and the two never spoke to each other again, although they later published some books in conjunction.

Supported by some London publishers, Mullen planned to open a bookshop and library in Melbourne. He selected stock and returned to Victoria in 1859 with his family and brother William Lowell. He opened at 55 Collins Street East. Based on Mudie's of London, his library was the first of its kind in Australia. It contained serious works besides better-class fiction and with vice-regal patronage was an immediate success. The book department catered for the intellectual *élite* and became a popular meeting place. William organized a stationery section and Samuel was appointed a bookseller to the University of Melbourne. He had books in foreign languages besides the best English literature. Several of his assistants achieved distinction: Adam Graham Melville (1842-1921) took charge of the library in the 1860s; Leonard Slade (1859-1954) served in 1876-1939 and became a partner; Richard Powell Raymond (1843-1918) was later manager for Robertson; and J. R. G. Adams became librarian to the South Australian Public Library in 1896. In Slade's opinion the greatest bookman to enter the shop was Alfred Deakin. In the 1870s Mullen had warned his staff that he 'appears to be buying more books than he can afford', but Deakin always paid. Mullen moved in 1879 to larger premises at 31 Collins Street East.

Although he sponsored some important works, Mullen had no clear publishing policy. His authors were more pragmatical than creative and ranged from J. Bonwick to Bishop Moorhouse [qq.v.]. He published several textbooks at matriculation level and his Christmas cards of flower studies by Mrs Ellis Rowan in 1883 were claimed to be the first Australian prints by chromolithography. At the royal commission on tariffs in 1882 he opposed duties on school books and printing papers. An avowed free trader, he argued that local manufactures could best be encouraged by placing Victorian copyright works on the school list.

For some years Mullen suffered from a heart ailment. In Ocober 1889 he sold out to his brother William, A. G. Melville and L. Slade. At a farewell dinner given by fellow booksellers he expressed sympathy for the 'poor suffering dock labourers' on strike in England. He planned to spend two years abroad but died in London on 29 May 1890, leaving an estate of £14,900. Predeceased by his wife on 15 October 1868, he had married Wilhelmina, daughter of Dr J. J. Wild of Zurich, at St Luke's Church, Emerald Hill, on 17 September 1870. She survived him with a son and daughter, and four sons and two daughters of the first marriage.

As president of the Booksellers' Association, Mullen had supported the Early Closing Association and held office in the Protestant and Catholic Orphanages and the Austin and Children's Hospitals. Prominent in St Luke's Church, Emerald Hill, he had been a warden of St Paul's in the city. He was a founder of the Melbourne Chess Club, the Melbourne Shakespeare Society and the Mechanics' Institute at Emerald Hill, where he had lived, and was active in the move to open the National Gallery on Sundays. Mullen's was an institution. Marcus Clarke, Fergus Hume [qq.v.] and W. J. Turner wrote about it, and a visiting author in 1889 claimed that 'Half the respectable families in Melbourne belong to Mullen's'. In 1921 Melville and Mullen merged with George Robertson & Co. to form Robertson & Mullens.

H. M. Humphreys (ed), *Men of the time in Australia: Victorian series*, 2nd ed (Melb, 1882); J. H. Burchett, *Utmost for the highest* (Melb, 1964); J. Holroyd, *George Robertson of Melbourne* (Melb, 1968); G. Serle, *The rush to be rich* (Melb, 1971); V&P (LA Vic), 1883, 2nd S, 4 (50); A. G. Melville, 'The book trade in Australia since 1861', Lib Assn of A'sia, *Procs of Sydney meeting*, 1898; L. Slade, 'Melbourne's early booksellers', VHM, 15 (1935); *A'sian Sketcher*, 5 July 1879; *Illustrated London News*, 19 Jan 1889; *Leader* (Melb), 17 Aug 1889; *Argus*, 30 Oct 1889, 2 June 1890; *Age*, 2 June 1890; *Herald* (Melb), 26 Oct 1939. J. P. HOLROYD

MULLIGAN, JAMES VENTURE (1837-1907), prospector, was born on 13 February 1837 at Dumgoodland, County Down, Ireland, son of James Mulligan, farmer, and his wife Maria, née Lee. He later adopted his second name. On 25 February 1860 he sailed in the *Curling* for Victoria and landed in Melbourne on 10 June. After an abortive attempt to join the Burke and Wills [qq.v.] expedition he moved to New South Wales and settled in Armidale, where he opened a butcher's shop and learnt prospecting on the Peel River and other northern goldfields. In Queensland he joined the rushes to Gympie in 1867, Gilberton in 1871 and the Etheridge in 1873.

On 5 June Mulligan led a party of six from Georgetown to investigate a reported gold discovery by William Hann [q.v.]. Despite Aboriginal hostility he returned on 3 September with 102 ounces; after proclamation of the Palmer goldfield the party received £1000 reward in 1875. In 1874 he had led three more expeditions covering much country which later included the Hodgkinson goldfield. Though he found little gold his careful but determined leadership enhanced his repute among miners. On 29 April 1875 he led a government-sponsored expedition which passed the sites of Mareeba and Atherton, crossed the Herberton Range and discovered tin in the Wild River but found little gold. On 23 October he left Cooktown and returned on 13 March 1876 with sufficient gold to stimulate the Hodgkinson gold rush. As the Hodgkinson was mainly a reef field many disappointed prospectors blamed Mulligan.

In 1877 Mulligan settled at Thornborough on the Hodgkinson, running a store with his old mate, James Dowdall, but in 1879 the partners were declared insolvent. After paying a dividend of 1s. 10d., they were discharged in 1881. Mulligan returned to prospecting and was subsidized by the government in 1890 to prove the Palmer conglomerates. Though the gold was not payable he found antimony.

Widely respected for his bush skills and religious principles, Mulligan became a justice of the peace in 1894. In Brisbane on 5 November 1903 he was married by an Anglican minister to the 47-year-old widow Fanny Maria Buls, née Rolls. On 23 August 1907 he was fatally injured in trying to protect a woman against a drunkard and died next day in the hospital at Mount Molloy.

Mulligan enjoyed exploration as much as prospecting and was never secretive about his finds. His lively diaries, published regularly in the *Queenslander*, were republished in 1875 as *A guide to the Palmer River and Normanby goldfields*. His name is commemorated by Mount Mulligan, a plaque at Mareeba and the Mulligan Highway.

R. L. Jack, *Northmost Australia*, 1-2 (Lond, 1921); G. C. Bolton, *A thousand miles away* (Brisb, 1963); H. Holthouse, *River of gold* (Syd, 1967); V&P (LA Qld), 1874, 2, 755, 1876, 3, 395, 1891, 4, 241, 266; *Government Gazette* (Qld), 1879, 1, 796, 1417, 1881, 1, 45, 2, 533; G. Pike, 'James Venture Mulligan: prospector and explorer of the north' JRHSQ, 4 (1948-52), no 4; *Brisbane Courier*, 3 Sept 1873, 29 Mar, 24 Apr 1875, 27 May 1876; *Queenslander*, 15 Apr, 3 June 1876, 28 Mar, 4 Apr 1885; information from R. S. Mulligan, Armidale.

H. J. GIBBNEY

MUNRO, DAVID (1844-1898), engineer, speculator and contractor, was born in Kirkintilloch, Dumbartonshire, Scotland, son of John Munro, blacksmith, and his wife Esther, née Dunlop. The family and some near relations migrated to Victoria in 1854 in the *Tudor*. The adult males worked at Geelong for £90 a year with rations. John soon started business as a blacksmith and contractor in King Street, Melbourne, where his three sons joined him as they grew up. They won the contract for the Moorabool viaduct in Geelong in 1858 and as the colony's railways extended shared in many government contracts. By 1869 only David remained with his father, trading as John

Munro & Son. In September they filed a voluntary petition in insolvency, showing a deficit of £1419 from business losses. Their schedules showed that John Munro controlled all the assets while David owned only the £3 worth of clothes he wore in court, 'a very unsatisfactory Estate' according to the official assignee. After release from sequestration in February 1870 David apparently did not resume business with his father. In 1871 he married Sarah Elizabeth Sydenham.

David started his own engineering and machinery supply business, finally occupying land in Queen Street, a'Beckett Street, and Elizabeth Street, Melbourne. His trademark was a phoenix arising from the flames and his motto *Resurgam*. In the construction and railway boom of the 1870s and 1880s David Munro & Co. was one of the colony's biggest employers of labour. Two of his best works still carry traffic across the Yarra: Queens Bridge built on the site of the old Falls Bridge for £45,000 and opened in April 1890; and the new Princes Bridge built in 1888 for £137,000. His many railway contracts included the Fitzroy-Whittlesea line built for £100,000, and the Frankston-Crib Point line for £53,000. Munro sold every type of sawmilling, threshing and mining equipment, either for cash or on his new 'Purchasing Lease System'. His patented or improved machines were commonly used by selectors and included a post-boring machine, the 'Victory Self-adjusting Windmill' and portable engines using 'the colonial fire-box, the steam jacketted cylinder, the variable expansion gear, the sliding crank shaft bracket, the three-way force-pumps'. Like many capitalists he was harsh on his employees and in the temporary slump of 1887 cut their wages from 7s. to 6s. 6d. a day. Unmoved by protests he told the men that their union leaders were 'vermin to be squelched'.

Munro served as president of the Chamber of Manufactures, councillor of the National Agricultural Society and in 1881-83 on the royal commission on the tariff. He also developed close links with Thomas Bent [q.v.] after sharing with him the construction of the Nepean Road tramway. They were directors in the Brighton Gas Co. Ltd. In 1888 Bent and John Blyth [q.v.] suggested to Munro that he convert his business into a public company and offer shares on the stock exchanges. In return for his assets Munro received 40,000 shares with a face value of £5 paid up to £2 10s. each and 80,000 shares paid up to £1 each. Bent and Blyth each took up 10,000 partly-paid shares and persuaded the graziers W. and S. Kiddle to take thousands more. Munro plunged into the land boom with abandon, borrowing large sums on mortgage from the Bank of South Australia and Bank of Australasia and investing it in land for subdivision at Somerton, Canterbury and elsewhere. He bought several expensive acres in Kooyong and built a mansion. Under his wife's name, large sums were borrowed from the Mercantile Finance Co. Ltd for land speculation.

Munro floated the Caledonian Land Bank Ltd, its purpose the acquisition of his properties at Brighton and Canterbury. A meeting of shareholders early in 1889 claimed that he had sold the properties to the company at grossly inflated valuations. Munro offered to make good any loss, produced a bag of bank-notes and on the spot bought the shares of dissatisfied shareholders. Eleven days later a shareholders' committee of investigation asked Munro to buy all the remaining shares. He refused and wrote scornfully to the newspapers criticizing shareholders who sought 'to relieve themselves of their personal liability'. Nineteen days later he filed a voluntary petition in insolvency. While speculating in land he had continued as managing director of his engineering business on a five-year agreement. At the time of flotation he had about £500,000 worth of contracts in hand. Recommended by Bent and Blyth, he arranged a large overdraft with the City of Melbourne Bank to finance these contracts, but weaknesses in the land market led the bank to insist on Munro's resignation from the engineering works. Incompetent managers were appointed, many contracts ran late and the company suffered heavy loss. A shareholders' meeting on 5 April disclosed losses on contracts of £90,000.

In the land-boom collapse the value of shares in David Munro & Co. Ltd dropped almost to nothing as did the market price of his land. When a call of 5s. a share was made, Munro could not pay and had to forefeit his 120,000 shares. His personal estate showed debts of nearly £380,000 on bank overdrafts, calls on shares and sums owing to other land speculators. His wife also went through the Insolvency Court with debts in her name to land companies of a further £45,000. Six years later a Supreme Court investigation found grave irregularities in the City of Melbourne Bank's manipulations of his engineering works. Since the bank's manager, Colin Milne Longmuir, had disappeared at sea, no criminal charges were made and Munro was not recompensed for his losses. The Munros moved from their mansion to a small cottage in Parkville, where he died on 31 March 1898 from a haemorrhage and alcoholism. He was survived by his wife who died in 1914, three sons and two daughters.

H. M. Franklyn, *A glance at Australia in 1880* (Melb, 1881); A. Sutherland et al, *Victoria and its metropolis*, 2 (Melb, 1888); M. Cannon, *Land boom and bust* (Melb, 1972); *Melb Bulletin*, 24 Dec 1885; *Argus*, 9 Oct 1886, 21 July 1887, 6 Apr 1889; *A'sian Sketcher*, 27 Jan 1887; *Age*, 1, 12, 21 Feb, 12 Mar 1889; *Table Talk*, 22 Jan 1892; David Munro & Co. Ltd, file 1251 (VA).
                                        MICHAEL CANNON

MUNRO, JAMES (1832-1908), businessman, temperance leader and politician, was born on 7 January 1832 in Sutherlandshire, Scotland, son of Donald Munro, and his wife Georgina, née Mackey. Educated at Armadale village school, he was apprenticed in 1848 to the Edinburgh printing house of Constable & Co. and soon joined the total abstinence movement. In December 1853 he married Jane Macdonald, and in 1858 with his wife and three children, migrated to Melbourne, arriving in the *Champion of the Seas* on 7 November.

Munro was described as a 'rough tyke' in his early years. He was quick tempered and authoritarian but always 'easy to get on with if you let him have his own way'. With a strong voice and pronounced accent he was known for his invective when roused and a tendency to dance with rage, habits which endured and must have contrasted with his patriarchal appearance of tall, broad figure, massive head and flowing beard.

At first Munro followed his trade with Fergusson & Moore in Flinders Lane. In 1865 he started his own first and most successful enterprise, the Victoria Permanent Property Investment Building Society, remaining its executive secretary until pressured to resign in December 1881. This was the first building society to depart from the terminating principle and was adapted from Scottish examples. He became an acknowledged expert on building and friendly society management, and he began to buy land. He had a controlling interest in several companies in the 1860s and 1870s, including the Melbourne Woollen Mill Co. and the Victoria Permanent Fire Insurance Co. Throughout his public life Munro was criticized for the diversity of his interests and his inattention to detail in most of them. About 1870 he moved from the Prahran-South Yarra district where he had first settled, and at Gardiner joined the District Road Board and witnessed its transition to a shire, becoming president in 1872-73. He was appointed magistrate in December 1873. His bid for Dundas in the Legislative Assembly had failed in 1869 but in 1874 he became liberal member for North Melbourne and resigned from the shire council.

In 1876 Munro moved into his large but unpretentious house, Armadale, in Kooyong Road, Armadale, then Boundary Road, Toorak. He was already rich and respected for his social involvement. He was an earnest Sabbatarian and member of the board of management of the Toorak Presbyterian Church in 1878-92, an original board member of the Alfred Hospital in 1870-76 and auditor in 1876-85, and a vice-president of the reconstituted Caledonian Society of Melbourne. A member of every notable temperance organization, Munro's influence was greatest on four of them: the Independent Order of Rechabites where he had helped to found the Prahran branch (Perseverance Tent) in 1865 and held executive office at district headquarters for twenty years; the Melbourne Total Abstinence Society of which he was president in 1878-92; the Permissive Bill Association of 1871 and its successor the Victorian Alliance for the Suppression of the Liquor Traffic, over which he presided in 1881-92. Through the association Munro gained valuable political experience and won such repute in the 1870s that without much additional effort on his part temperance events polarized around him. He assumed the mantle of temperance champion as soon as he entered parliament. He was president of International Temperance Conferences in Melbourne in 1880 and 1888, after which he slipped from the temperance limelight.

A member of royal commissions on employment and tariff protection to which he was committed, Munro was largely responsible for the decision which led Victoria to stage the International Exhibition of 1880; its success must be attributed to the work by him and J. J. Casey [q.v.] as executive vice-presidents. Munro was also a commissioner for the 1888 Exhibition.

Munro's financial career entered a new phase in 1882 when he established the twin institutions of the Federal Bank and the Federal Building Society. For years he and his colleagues had deliberately attracted support on the basis of their respectability, one symbol of it being their coffee palaces. Munro had thousands of shares in the Federal, the Grand and the Victoria which competed with each other in Melbourne and the Broken Hill and Geelong Grand Coffee Palaces; he was a director of all but the last and all were in difficulties by 1890. In 1887 he created the Real Estate Mortgage and Deposit Bank to simplify his land transactions. The need for this should have warned him that his affairs were already out of control, but nothing had yet occurred to shake his reputation or confidence. He had shared in bargaining to ensure that railways expanded in the right directions. As well as suburban property, a country seat at Narbethong and directorates on numerous companies, he had acquired huge stations and leaseholds in the Northern Territory, Queensland and Western Australia. To pay for his investments he borrowed from the financial institutions which he controlled; in turn they absorbed overseas loans and the deposits of countless small investors, lent hundreds of thousands of pounds on insufficient security to a clique of Munro's friends and family, and borrowed from institutions operating on similar lines. Munro claimed to have had unencumbered personal assets of £240,000 in 1889; he had no difficulty in raising capital on a visit to Britain in 1890.

Possibly through association with Graham Berry [q.v.] in the Collingwood Observer, Munro entered politics as a Berry supporter. He was minister of public instruction in Berry's short-lived government of 1875. A consistent advocate of land and constitutional reform, Munro professed sympathy for the working classes but his political views were usually trimmed to his economic interests and occasionally to his morality. He wanted female suffrage partly because of its supposed influence on the temperance vote. He was admired for his electoral tactics in 1877 when he pursued his co-representative for North Melbourne, the publican John Curtain, into the new and pro-publican electorate of Carlton. When opponents prevented Munro from hiring a hall, he built his own within fourteen days for some £2500 and won the seat. He was a vice-president of the National Reform League and of the National Reform and Protection League. By 1879 he was out of sympathy with the radicals and tried to establish a new liberal corner with Casey. He lost his seat in 1880 but next year regained North Melbourne. After a second defeat in 1883, business and ill health kept him out of the assembly, in 1884 he half-heartedly challenged Dr J. G. Beaney [q.v.] for his Legislative Council seat, and in 1885 went abroad.

In 1886 Munro re-entered the assembly for the temperance stronghold of Geelong. Before the elections he formed the National Liberal League with James Mirams [q.v.] and others, and tried in vain to unite liberal factions against the Gillies [q.v.]-Deakin government. By 1889 Munro had emerged clearly as leader of the Opposition but he could not inspire personal loyalty and was politically insecure. He became premier and treasurer in November 1890 on his credit as a financier.

Frightened by government extravagance, the colony expected a financial miracle. Unluckily, Munro's political triumph coincided with collapse of his fortune. His term of office was undistinguished but he cannot be blamed for the administrative and economic crisis that he inherited. A scandal arose when the Voluntary Liquidation Act was passed on 3 December 1891. Its aim was to prevent mischievous speculators from forcing companies into compulsory liquidation against the will of the majority of shareholders. This met with general approval, but it also meant that a minority shareholder who suspected fraud had small chance of forcing a public inquiry into company affairs, and that a company seeking to evade official scrutiny could do so by winding up its affairs privately. Equally provocative, building societies were included so that they too could be liquidated without benefit of publicity. Munro did not initiate the legislation but as premier agreed to it. The Federal Building Society and the Real Estate Bank soon suspended payment and later went into voluntary liquidation.

Already shaken by the failure of the Constitution amendment bill introduced in September, Munro prepared to hand over the government to his deputy William Shiels. He arranged to replace Sir Graham Berry as agent-general in London but remained premier until the last possible moment. Shiels resisted public protest and a violent press campaign against Munro, who left for England in March 1892; he returned just before Christmas to face the consequences of failure. The Federal Bank gave up the struggle to survive in January 1893 and Munro filed his schedule in February.

Munro lacked originality and imagination. He did not question contemporary business standards or the nature of the boom conditions. Though not the worst of the speculators, his failure was more shocking because of his moral pretensions. A measure of his sincerity and his incompetence is that he gambled on the success of his own companies and lost. In looking after his family he involved most of its members in his disgrace. Forced to live with relatives in North Brighton, he was released by the Insolvency Court when it became clear that he could not pay any of his debts. He died on 25 February 1908 and was buried in the St Kilda cemetery beside his wife who had died in 1904. He was survived by four sons and three daughters of his eight children.

T. W. H. Leavitt (ed), *Australian representative men* (Melb, 1887); A. Sutherland et al, *Victoria and its metropolis*, 2 (Melb, 1888); International Temperance Convention, *Temperance in Australia* (Melb, 1889); J. B. Cooper, *A history of Malvern* (Melb, 1935); M. Cannon, *The land boomers* (Melb, 1966); *Table Talk*, 9 Oct 1891, 6 Oct 1893; *Age*, 4 Dec 1891, Jan-Feb 1892; *Argus*, Jan-Feb 1892; *Observer* (Collingwood), 5 Mar 1908; S. M. Ingham, Some aspects of Victorian liberalism 1880-1900 (M.A. thesis, Univ Melb, 1950); J. E. Parnaby, The economic and politicial development of Victoria, 1877-1881 (Ph.D. thesis, Univ Melb, 1951); R. J. Moore, Marvellous Melbourne: a social history of Melbourne in the eighties (M.A. thesis, Univ Melb, 1958); M. G. Finlayson, Victorian politics 1889-94 (M.A. thesis, Univ Melb, 1964); A. D. Milner, James Munro, banker, boomster, wowser and temperate (B.A. Hons thesis, Monash Univ, 1965); A. M. Mitchell, Temperance and the liquor question in later nineteenth century Victoria (M.A. thesis, Univ Melb, 1966); Liquidation and Insolvency records (VA). ANN M. MITCHELL

MURDOCH, WILLIAM LLOYD (1854-1911), cricketer, was born on 18 October 1854 at Sandhurst (Bendigo), Victoria, son of Gilbert Murdoch and his wife Susanna, née Fleigge. In the early 1860s he moved to New South Wales with his parents. He played for the Albert Cricket Club with F. R. Spofforth [q.v.] and from 1875 for New South Wales as wicket-keeper. In 1877 Spofforth refused to play against James Lillywhite's team in Melbourne when Murdoch was not selected. In that year he qualified as a solicitor and practised with his brother Gilbert.

In 1878 Murdoch toured England with D. Gregory's [q.v.] team as first wicket-keeper. Next year he became the first Australian to carry his bat through an innings in first-class cricket when he made 82 not out for New South Wales against Lord Harris's English team. When he was given run out in the second innings the crowd rushed the ground and Harris was struck several times and threatened to block any future tours of England. Murdoch captained Australian teams in England in 1880, 1882 and 1884 and each time headed the batting averages, but no longer kept wickets. In 1880 at the Oval in the only Test he backed himself to beat W. G. Grace's score of 152 and in the second innings made 153 not out; thereafter he wore on his watch-chain the sovereign he had won from Grace. Meanwhile in June 1879 the firm Murdoch & Murdoch was dissolved and in December William was bankrupted with debts of £775; his only asset was clothing valued at £10. The release of his estate in 1881 revealed that his share of the profits of the 1880 English tour had gone to his brother.

In 1882 Murdoch scored 321 for New South Wales against Victoria, the first Australian innings over 300. In 1884 his 211 at the Oval was the highest score by an Australian in any Test until 1903 and the highest for Australia against England until 1930. Short and plump with a stiff stance,

Murdoch was unexpectedly fast on his feet and best on a hard wicket. Using a very high grip he excelled at cuts and off-drives. On wet wickets he had good defence but few scoring shots. As captain in sixteen out of his eighteen Tests, he was a shrewd tactician and one of the earliest to change his field for different batsmen. Jovial and optimistic, he inspired confidence, comradeship and high morale.

On 8 December 1884 at Melbourne Murdoch married Jemima, daughter of J. B. Watson [q.v.], a mining magnate from Bendigo; their eldest son was born in 1886 at Cootamundra. Later they lived in Melbourne. In 1890 Murdoch was persuaded to lead one more team to England and again topped the averages. He settled in England and qualified for Sussex. In 1891-92 he toured South Africa and kept wickets for England in the first Test. In 1893-99 he captained Sussex and made six centuries; K. S. Ranjitsinhji had chosen to play for Sussex in order to have Murdoch as his captain. In his last years of first-class cricket he played for Grace's London County side and in 1904, his last season, made 104 for Gentlemen v. Players. Murdoch hit twenty-one centuries in first-class cricket including five double centuries. He scored 17,319 runs at an average of 26.64 and in Tests made 896 runs at an average of 32.

Murdoch enjoyed practical jokes, was an expert pigeon shooter and later an enthusiastic golfer. In 1893 he published a small manual, Cricket. In 1910 he visited Australia and died suddenly on 18 February 1911 at Melbourne while watching a Test match against South Africa. His body was embalmed and buried in the Kensal Green cemetery, London. He was survived by his wife, three sons and a daughter.

R. H. Lyttleton et al, Giants of the game (Lond, 1899); M. B. Hawke et al, The memorial biography of Dr. W. G. Grace (Lond, 1919); A. G. Moyes, A century of cricketers (Lond, 1950) and Australian batsmen (Syd, 1954); A. A. Thomson, Cricket: the great captains (Lond, 1965); Bulletin, 2 Apr, 7 May 1881; Parade, Oct 1962.

CHRISTOPHER MORRIS

MURNIN, MICHAEL EGAN (1814-1894), merchant and businessman, was born in Ireland, arrived in New South Wales about 1839 and began business as a merchant and commission agent. By the 1840s as owner of the 134-ton Bee he was shipping livestock to New Zealand and acting as the Sydney agent of an Auckland merchant and shipowner, John Sangster MacFarlane. He soon became part-owner of other trading vessels.

Business transactions from August 1844 to 1855 led to a dispute with MacFarlane who sued Murnin in the Supreme Court of New South Wales for alleged breaches of duty as an agent and damage to his credit. The complex suit, involving nineteen separate issues, was heard before Judge Dickinson [q.v.] and a special jury in April 1857. The court found against Murnin on the major issues and he was ordered to pay £3428 damages. His lawyers applied for a new trial but Murnin objected to the conditions and appealed to the Privy Council. In January 1860 MacFarlane petitioned the New South Wales parliament for action and payment. In March the Privy Council dismissed the case unheard for non prosequitur.

Murnin was a promoter and committee member of the Sydney Chamber of Commerce in 1851, a member of the first board of directors of the Royal Exchange in 1852 and one of the first directors and sometime chairman of the Australian Mutual Provident Society. He was a director and later chairman of the New South Wales Marine Assurance Co. and the Australian Joint Stock Bank, a director of the Sydney Insurance Co. and the Newcastle Wallsend Coal Co., and a trustee of the Mutual Building and Investment Society. Like many merchants he devoted some attention to charitable institutions; he was a director of the Sydney Infirmary and Dispensary and of the Home Visiting and Relief Society.

In 1865, after suffering heavy losses on his four runs in the Port Curtis District of Queensland, and on railway contracts, Murnin's liabilities amounted to £150,000 and he was forced to divide his available assets. In June the Australian Joint Stock Bank recovered a judgment in the Supreme Court against him for £1649 and on 6 March 1868 J. S. Mitchell, managing director of the bank, instituted bankruptcy proceedings against him. His liabilities were £61,418, of which £39,072 was secured, and his assets £39,350. After his discharge he carried on business until 1876 when he retired to live near Mittagong.

Though politically inactive, Murnin joined other conservatives on the general committee of the Constitutional Association in November 1860. He was a founder of the Union Club in 1857 and a member of the Royal Society of New South Wales from 1865. He had lived at first in Glebe and later at Mona, Darling Point, opposite St Mark's Church, and then at Burwood. Actively associated with the establishment of St Mark's, he was a churchwarden for many years. He was a lay member of the Church Society for the Diocese of Sydney and also a member of the New South Wales Auxiliary Bible Society. Predeceased by his first wife Catherine Arnold, he died aged 80 at his residence, Eisenfels, Nattai, near Mittagong, on 16 November 1894. He was survived by a son and three daughters of his second wife Grace Abbott, whom he had married in Sydney on 7 October 1847.

V&P (LA NSW), 1859-60, 2, 87; SMH, 14 Sept 1844, 16, 21 Apr 1857, 7 Mar, 1 Apr, 21 Oct 1868, 20 Nov 1894.   G. P. WALSH

MURPHY,   DANIEL   (1815-1907), Catholic archbishop, was born on 15 June 1815 at Belmont, County Cork, Ireland, son of Michael Murphy and his wife Mary, née McSweeney. Educated at a local seminary and Maynooth College, he was ordained priest on 9 June 1838. Refused permission to go to Australia with Dr W. Ullathorne [q.v.], he volunteered for missionary service under Dr John Fennelly, vicar-apostolic of Madras; he reached India in 1839 and was sent to Hyderabad. In 1845 Rome agreed to Fennelly's request for Murphy as his coadjutor bishop. Murphy went to Rome and thence to Ireland where he was consecrated on 11 October 1846 at Kinsale. Nominated vicar-apostolic of Hyderabad he served until 1864 when he resigned because of ill health and returned to Ireland.

Murphy was named bishop of Hobart Town and with his nephew Father Michael Beechinor as chaplain sailed for Melbourne in the Great Britain. He arrived at Hobart in April 1866 and was installed on 6 May. Despite opposition from his predecessor, Bishop R. W. Willson [q.v.], he was followed in October by another nephew Father Daniel Beechinor and by his sister Mother Superior Frances Murphy and four other Presentation Sisters. In 1867 Murphy authorized the first issue of the Tasmanian Catholic Standard, devoted to the defence of the Holy See, and began the fight to retain state aid. He organized massive petitions against the state aid commutation bill which received the royal assent in 1869. Instead of an annual grant of £3466 the Church was given £23,106 for permanent endowment. After the withdrawal of state aid to denominational schools he built up a system of education. In the early 1870s he strongly objected to the direct tax on Catholics for support of public schools. He fought to establish the Christian Brothers' St Virgil's College but it was not opened until 1911.

In 1869-71 Murphy attended the Vatican Council in Rome and voted for papal infallibility. In 1877 he appealed for funds to rebuild St Mary's Cathedral after its 'utter instability' had been exposed. In 1868-80 Daniel Beechinor had charge of

the cathedral and was succeeded by Father P. Gleeson, another of the bishop's nephews. After the shooting of the duke of Edinburgh in 1868 Murphy had tried to calm sectarian passions by preaching against Fenianism. In July 1879 when the Canadian lapsed priest, Charles Chiniquy, lectured in Hobart, Murphy was praised by Governor Weld for preventing bloodshed. He persuaded a large gathering of armed Catholics in the Domain not to march to the Town Hall which was guarded by Orangemen; instead they escorted the bishop home. In 1882 he made a pilgrimage to Jerusalem and visited Rome.

In 1888 Murphy celebrated his golden jubilee as a priest and the see of Hobart was made an archbishopric. On 12 May 1889 Cardinal Moran conferred the pallium on him. Autocratic, stubborn and devious, Murphy was opposed by fourteen of his twenty-two priests when he tried to have a bill passed giving him sole control of church property. He had four nephews who were priests in Tasmania and was often accused of nepotism. In 1892 he again visited Rome and tried to have Daniel Beechinor appointed coadjutor but after petitions to Rome from his priests Bishop Patrick Delaney was appointed in December 1893 to assist the ageing 'nephew-ridden' Murphy.

A fine horseman, Murphy was also an astronomer. In 1892 he impressed the Australasian Science Association Congress meeting in Hobart with his paper on solar phenomena and their effects and in 1895 addressed its Brisbane congress on the conservation of solar energy. Courteous and endowed with lively humour, he frequented Government House. In 1896 he celebrated his episcopal golden jubilee. He died at Low Head on the Tamar mouth on 29 December 1907 and was buried at Hobart.

P. F. Moran, History of the Catholic Church in Australasia (Syd, 1895); M. Beechinor, Memoir of Archbishop Murphy (Launceston, 1916); J. N. Molony, The Roman mould of the Australian Catholic Church (Melb, 1969); W. T. Southerwood, Planting a faith in Hobart (Hob, 1970); V&P (HA Tas), 1867 (19, 38), 1873 (79), 1875 (61); Australasian, 31 Oct 1896; Argus, 30 Dec 1907; CO 280/387.

MURPHY, SIR FRANCIS (1809-1891), pastoralist and parliamentarian, was born in Cork, Ireland, son of Francis Down Murphy, head of the Cork Convict Transport Department, and his wife Mary, née Morris. Educated for the medical profession in Cork, Trinity College, Dublin, and London (M.R.C.S., 1835), he migrated to Sydney in June 1836. Appointed by Governor Bourke colonial surgeon to the Bungonia district in

January 1837, Murphy abandoned his medical career after acquiring pastoral and agricultural interests in the area.

A successful farmer and prominent in local affairs, particularly as magistrate on the Goulburn bench for eight years, Murphy married Agnes, daughter of Dr David Reid [q.v.], in 1840. Six years later they moved to Port Phillip, following Agnes's brother David who had overlanded in 1838, and took over the Tarrawingee run on the Ovens River. At one stage running 13,000 sheep and employing 42 hands, Murphy worked Tarrawingee until at the first elections for the Legislative Council after separation he became member for the Murray district. When the council met in November 1851 he was elected chairman of committees, a post he relinquished in March 1853 to become president of the Central Roads Board. Tarrawingee was sold that year. Murphy lived with his family at Mayfield, a substantial house on the Yarra River at Collingwood. He stayed after the district became a noxious industrial suburb, not holding himself aloof but engaging in local roads, bridges and clean-air issues, and was a member of the East Collingwood Volunteer Rifles, eventually with the rank of major.

In the Legislative Council from 1851 to 1855 Murphy introduced useful pastoral legislation and was instrumental with others in preserving provision for National schools in Victoria. In 1854 he was on the committee which recommended government action on railways, and active in debates on the form of the new constitution to come into effect in 1856. His record as head of the Roads Department was mixed. Often accused of neglecting busy country routes in favour of little-used town roads, he was also praised as an efficient administrator who blended his patronage with integrity.

Murphy resigned from the Roads Board in November 1856 to take up the main role of his career in government, as Speaker of the Legislative Assembly. One of the oldest and most experienced members returned at the first elections under responsible government, he won the chair by 39 votes to 17 in a contest with C. J. Griffith [q.v.], who had stated his intention of joining in debate, while Murphy promised to take no part in accordance with English precedent. He was Speaker for fifteen years, holding the seat of Murray Boroughs until 1866 when he moved to the Grenville electorate, which he lost at the elections of 1871. He was a member of the 1861 royal commission on Burke and Wills [qq.v.], sat by invitation on the commission which in 1864 decided the site for the New Zealand capital, chaired the Industrial Exhibition Commission in 1866 and was on the royal commission on inter-

colonial legislation in 1870. In December 1871 he won a seat for Eastern Province in the Legislative Council, retiring in November 1876. At the same time he resigned as trustee of the Public Library and two years later from the Council of the University of Melbourne, of which he was a founding member.

Murphy was a conservative but during his years in the Legislative Assembly adopted no defined political stance; according to critics, he tended to support the stronger in any contest. Twice he gave substantial aid to the liberal cause. In 1861 his support during the election campaign for J. H. Brooke's [q.v.] proposal to make land available for small farms by issuing occupation licences had assisted the return of the radical Heales [q.v.] government. More importantly, Murphy's ruling as Speaker in 1865 that the combination of appropriation and tariff legislation was not a tack encouraged the constitutional deadlock which brought to a head conflict between the Houses of Parliament. At the election which followed in January 1866 the Opposition campaigned against him in Murray Boroughs, but he soon obtained ministerial aid in securing a new seat. Overall, however, Murphy more resembled a senior civil servant than a politician. Impartiality and unique experience partly explain his long tenure as Speaker at a time of extreme political and institutional fluidity. He was also firm and dignified in control of the House, helpful to members new to procedure, punctilious in attendance and manner. Members observed that he was alert throughout the most tedious debate, always politely interested, never resorting to 'ironical language'.

Murphy was well paid for his conscientiousness, for most of his term at £1500 a year. He was appointed K.B. in 1860. A pension of £1000 was proposed when he retired as Speaker in 1871, but reduced to a lump sum of £3000 under pressure from members who argued that he was not in need. Indeed his personal fortune was large. On the profits from his early pastoral speculations he accumulated extensive town property and other investments, often in association with Sir James Palmer [q.v.]. He became a director of the National Bank in 1863 but resigned in 1870 when as chairman of the board he was criticized for poor management of the bank's affairs.

Murphy visited Europe several times between 1876 and 1883 and then lived in retirement. Aged 82 he died on 30 March 1891 in Melbourne; after an Anglican service he was buried at Boroondara cemetery. He was survived by his wife, three sons and six daughters, among them Francis Reid, member of the Queensland Legislative

Assembly, Herbert Dyer, member of Mawson's Antarctic expedition 1912, and Frances Emma, wife of Herbert James Henty [q.v.].

G. Blainey, *Gold and paper* (Melb, 1958); G. Serle, *The golden age* (Melb, 1963); PD (Vic), 1856-71; *Argus*, Nov 1856, 31 Mar 1891; *Leader*, 24 May 1862; *Age*, Oct-Nov 1871.

MARGOT BEEVER

MURPHY, WILLIAM EMMETT (1841-1921), cabinet maker and trades hall official, was born on 12 May 1841 in Dublin, son of William Murphy, publican. Educated at the Christian Brothers' College, he was apprenticed at Liverpool to his uncle, a cabinet maker. In 1865 he migrated to Melbourne and became active in the Cabinet Makers' Association as one of its office-bearers. By 1877 he was secretary of the Trades Hall Committee which was then refusing to dabble in 'politics'. In 1882 the question of giving evidence to the factories and shops commission compelled the committee to reconsider its powers, and in June Murphy moved that the committee be reconstructed as the Trades Hall Council. He became its first secretary at a salary of £20. His main income seems to have been his pay as a sergeant of engineers.

As a Trades Hall official Murphy was energetic and successful. In 1882 he helped to organize and win the tailoresses' strike, becoming first secretary of their union. He also had a large part in the success of the bootmakers' strike in 1885. He often arranged private arbitration on disputes between the Employers' Union and trade unions. This method won him greatest success in 1886 after the Melbourne wharf labourers had been on strike for three weeks claiming an eight-hour day. As their advocate he won the case before a Board of Arbitration with Professor Kernot [q.v.] as president.

This triumph was not enough to protect Murphy from his enemies. In September 1886 he was removed from office as secretary and at a later council meeting some minor defalcations were alleged against him. His defence seems to have been successful and the matter was dropped. A more serious charge against him appears to have been his interference in the West Melbourne election to the detriment of the Liberal candidate. Long interested in parliamentary politics, he had become the secretary of the Anti-Chinese League in 1877 and a councillor in Graham Berry's [q.v.] National Reform and Protection League in 1878. As a delegate and secretary to the Trades Union Intercolonial Conference of 1884 he moved for a committee 'to watch over the legislative proceedings in all questions recommended by this Congress', and became one of its members. Next year in the Trades Hall Council he moved for the direct parliamentary representation of labour but withdrew after a three-night debate. In March 1886 he contested North Melbourne, losing by less than 200 votes. He tried again in 1889 but failed by only 60 votes.

By then Murphy had rejoined the Trades Hall Council, representing the Geelong Eight Hours' League; the council had agreed that his membership of the Chamber of Manufactures did not debar him. In 1886 he had become an auctioneer and estate agent, thus extending his functions as the secretary of the Operatives' Permanent Building Society, a post he had held while secretary of the Trades Hall Council. He still found time for its affairs and helped to organize the Tramways Union and its disastrous strike in 1888. In 1890 the council appointed him secretary of its Finance and Control Committee, which became responsible for managing the maritime strike in Melbourne and for schemes to deter potential strike-breakers and to employ strikers, but without success.

With the onset of depression Melbourne Trades Hall offered less scope for Murphy's energies, some of which he diverted to writing. Always interested in working men's education, he was a leading organizer of the fund required to match Francis Ormond's [q.v.] bequest in 1889 for a working men's college and was actively associated with it for twenty years. In 1888 he had largely contributed to *The History of Capital and Labour in all lands*, and in 1896 published in Melbourne the first volume of his *History of the Eight Hours' Movement*; the second followed in 1900. Although his private papers contain drafts for several articles and pamphlets he does not seem to have published them, and after 1890 his only office in the Trades Hall was that of trustee. In 1869 in Melbourne he had married Louisa Walsh. Survived by his wife, two sons and two of his three daughters, he died at Daylesford on 26 February 1921 and was buried in the Melbourne general cemetery.

Argus, 1 Mar 1921; W. E. Murphy papers (ML).

J. HAGAN

MURRAY, ANDREW (1813-1880), journalist, was born on 16 May 1813 in Kirkbean, Kirkcudbrightshire, Scotland, son of Rev. William Murray and his wife Marianne, née Bridges. Educated in Glasgow and at its university where in 1836 with a work on Oliver Cromwell he won the Peel Club's first prize essay, he arrived at Port Adelaide in January 1839. He formed the drapery business of Murray, Greig & Co., but it failed in November 1842. He became editor of the South(ern) Australian early in 1843 and its proprietor from 31 October 1844 to 19 August 1851. Opponents called it 'a tame rag . . . not worth the postage', but it was noted for mild editorials, general support of the government and catering for the wealthy pastoralists who disliked the *South Australian Register* for favouring small farmers. From 1845 Murray had also acted as government printer and at his office in Rundle Street issued many periodicals, the weekly government gazette and annual South Australian almanacs and directories. In January 1852 he founded the conservative *Adelaide Morning Chronicle* but sold it in May 1853. On 2 November 1841 he had married Jessie, sister of Catherine Spence [q.v.].

In 1852 they moved to Melbourne where Murray joined the *Argus* as its commercial editor and political writer. In the late 1850s he bought land at Boroondara, naming his house Balwyn from the Gaelic *bal* and the Saxon *wyn*, meaning 'the home of the vine'. Balwyn Road and district were named after it. First to grow vines there, he made wine and won prizes at the Geelong National Show of 1866 for both his white and red wines. On 2 October 1868 he was elected president of the Vinegrowers Association. Active in the district's affairs, he served as chairman of the Boroondara Roads Board in 1864-68 and helped to form a local committee under the 1866 Common Schools Act, becoming its chairman. The board flourished and he was able to gain such concessions as a fair proportion of the toll fees for the Richmond Bridge. He commanded the respect of his colleagues.

Murray's strongly decentralist attitude to government was reflected in his newspapers. Editor of the *Argus* in 1855-56, he then founded, owned and edited *Murray's Prices Current* in 1862-67 and *Bear's Circular and Rural Economist* in 1862-75 at his office at Bourke Street West. The *Economist* emphasized free trade and catered exclusively for the squatting, proprietary and agricultural interests. His editorials reiterated the hope that 'reason and England will prevail against democracy and America'. A staunch conservative in his attacks on pure democracy, he preferred local self-government ruled over by those he termed 'the respectable and educated classes'.

Murray had the disposition and manners of a gentleman and his regal air fitted him well as chairman of various committees. In 1874 he retired from publishing and lived at Boroondara until 1877 when he moved to Yarragon, Gippsland. He died there on 8 October 1880 of gastritis and was buried in the Presbyterian section of the Kew cemetery. He was survived by his wife, four sons and five daughters.

A portrait is in the Camberwell Town Hall.

D. Maclean, *Balwyn 1841-1941* (Melb, 1941); G. Pitt, *The press in South Australia, 1836 to 1850* (Adel, 1946); *SA News*, 15 May 1842; *South Bourke Standard*, 1861-73; *Australasian*, 3 Oct 1874, 9 Oct 1880; J. A. Allan, History of Camberwell (LaTL and Camberwell Public Lib).
D. CAMFIELD

MURRAY, DAVID (1829-1907), merchant and politician, was born on 28 December 1829 at Anstruther, Fife, Scotland, son of William Murray. He arrived in South Australia with his brother William in 1853 and they set up a retail drapery store in Gilbert Place, Adelaide. In 1855 they moved to larger premises in Grenfell Street where a wholesale department was added. In 1862 they turned entirely to wholesale trade and in 1866 moved to a site in King William Street. Next year they opened a clothing factory and later others for boots and shirts. In 1874 Murray opened an indent and merchandise department and in conjunction with the firm's London agency built up a large import and export business. For some years Murray's father acted as their buyer, financier and general agent in England. In 1886 the firm moved into an impressive new warehouse in Gawler Place; its five storeys cost £20,000 and contained, as part of Murray's policy, comfortable and modern amenities for the employees. In 1897 the firm became a limited liability company. Branches were opened in Melbourne, Brisbane, Sydney, Perth, Launceston, Rockhampton, Townsville and Broken Hill. Murray was senior partner of the firm until 1907.

In public affairs Murray was well known and respected. He represented East Adelaide in the House of Assembly from 28 March 1870 to 23 December 1871 and East Torrens from 27 March 1877 to 13 March 1878. Elected for Yatala on 25 April 1881 he was unseated on 28 June for charges of bribery. The case aroused sympathy for Murray and he was persuaded to stand again, winning the seat on 13 July. However, he was ruled ineligible for re-election by the House of Assembly's Committee of Privilege and on 18 August had to resign. In 1882 he was elected to the Legislative Council holding the seat till 1891. A terse and clear speaker, he had served as chief secretary in the Downer administration in 1886-87.

As an elder of the Flinders Street Presbyterian Church from 1858, Murray sought 'in a characteristically quiet and unostentatious way' to promote friendship between the denominations and often held informal gatherings of clergy in his home, St Andrews, North Adelaide. He was a founder of the Adelaide Young Men's Christian Association, its president in 1881-83 and a liberal provider of funds for its activities. In 1875 he was chairman of the League for the Education Act. An ardent lover of books, he read widely and his personal library contained many rare works. When the new building for the School of Mines and Industries was planned, Murray gave £500 for a library which was named after him; he attended the opening of the school in February 1903 and left £1000 in his will as a further contribution to the library. He provided libraries and reading rooms for his employees and left £4000 to the library and reading room of his birthplace. As an art collector and critic, he acted with others as a buyer on behalf of the Board of Governors of the Public Library. He also left £2000 to the Flinders Street Church and £5000 to the Presbyterian Church of South Australia, £3000 and all his prints and engravings to the library, and £2000 to found scholarships in the University of Adelaide where he had been elected to the council in 1887.

Murray enjoyed angling as a recreation and had a small property near Mylor on the Onkaparinga River where he grew fruit and hops by irrigation. On 9 May 1856 at North Adelaide he had married Rebecca, daughter of Thomas Godfrey of Dublin, Ireland. Their only child, a son, died in infancy. Business took Murray on eleven round trips between Australia and England. His wife often went with him and they finally settled in England in March 1900. She survived him when he died at his London home in Pembridge Square, Bayswater, on 6 January 1907. He left an estate worth £203,669.

H. T. Burgess (ed), *Cyclopedia of South Australia*, 1 (Adel, 1908); *Register* (Adel), 14, 15 July, 19 Aug 1881, 8 Feb 1886, 14 Feb 1900, 26 Feb 1903; *Observer* (Adel), 7 May 1887.

SALLY O'NEILL

MURRAY, JAMES (1828-1909), Roman Catholic bishop, was born on 25 March 1828 in County Wicklow, Ireland, son of James Murray, farmer, and his wife Catherine, née Doyle. Educated for the Church, he was sent at 16 by his great-uncle, archbishop of Dublin, to live at Propaganda College and study at the Urban University in Rome. There he became a protégé of Archbishop Cullen [q.v.]. In 1851

Murray was awarded a doctorate for theses on the authority of the Roman Pontiffs; ordained next year he returned to Ireland. After a short period of parish work he was Cullen's private secretary for eleven years. In 1865 Murray was appointed first resident bishop of Maitland, New South Wales. He and his cousin Matthew Quinn [q.v.], first bishop of Bathurst, were consecrated by Cullen on 14 November. With Quinn's brother James [q.v.], bishop of Brisbane, they formed the basis of a powerful Cullenite influence in the Australian Church.

Murray arrived in Sydney on 21 October 1866 with Quinn, nine priests and sixteen nuns to be greeted by great Irish celebrations; in the absence of Archbishop Polding [q.v.], they discomfited the Benedictines and embarrassed secular clergy. Murray made an immediate impact on his diocese which stretched from the coast near Newcastle to beyond the Darling and north almost to Brisbane, and was served by only six priests and a tiny community of nuns. Some of Murray's first actions emphasized the Cullenite connexion: he gave his friend and successor as Cullen's secretary, Patrick Moran, the title of vicar-general, and vigorously disputed with Polding over diocesan boundaries. For years Murray was virtually a bush missionary but by 1878 had built up his staff of priests to twenty-five, established convents at Maitland, Newcastle, Singleton, Tamworth and Gunnedah, and founded an orphanage, an institution for deaf girls, a boys' college and many denominational schools. By 1887, when his diocese was reduced to cover only the Hunter, Manning and Hastings valleys, he had reorganized his mission on a proper parish basis. Though his lack of financial acumen worried some of his senior clergy, his pastoral energies were striking. Five pastoral letters, several circulars to clergy, a general conference of priests, a number of sessions of 'in-service' training for young clergy and a round of episcopal visits were normal for a single year.

Murray greatly influenced the whole Australian Church. To him Polding's Benedictine régime was not only too English in outlook for the Irish who made up most of the colony's faithful but also inclined to be complaisant towards intellectual and social developments that Murray saw as hostile to religion. His peculiar mission was to stiffen the resistance of Australian Catholicism to secularist ideas and to strengthen Australian bonds with Rome. He wounded Polding with his criticism of the archdiocese's policy on mixed marriages, which was at variance with Roman practice but not with current canon law, and stressed the point at the 1869 Provincial Council. He forced Polding into stronger opposition than the archbishop favoured to the New South Wales Education Act of 1866 and with Matthew Quinn framed the council's decree on the subject. He and his supporters succeeded in opposing the appointment of Polding's protégé, S. J. A. Sheehy [q.v.], to a bishopric but failed to prevent Roger Vaughan [q.v.] from becoming coadjutor to the archbishop; Murray finally triumphed when Moran succeeded Vaughan in 1884 and the Plenary Council of 1885 radically reshaped the Church's discipline, particularly on mixed marriages. Murray did not attend the Vatican Council but was devoted to Pius IX and unswervingly supported the infallibility decree. His critical influence in developing a peculiarly Roman flavour in Australian Catholicism was emphasized by his introduction of the Redemptorists to Australia in 1881.

In his diocese Murray's charitable works made him popular with his people. He also strived to moderate sectarian bitterness which had been particularly severe in Maitland when he arrived, yet towards his clergy he was authoritarian, at times insensitive and always inclined to favouritism. He was a close adviser of Bishop Reynolds [q.v.] of Adelaide and the brothers Quinn in their dispute with the Josephite Order over episcopal jurisdiction.

Murray paid *ad limina* visits to Rome in 1871, 1881 and 1889. By the mid-1890s his health was deteriorating and in 1897 he chose his protégé, Patrick Vincent Dwyer, as coadjutor bishop, thereby ensuring that his pastoral policies would survive him. Despite an accident in 1903 he remained strictly as controller of his diocese and as elder statesman of the Church. He died at West Maitland on 9 July 1909 and was buried in the Catholic cemetery, Campbell's Hill.

H. Campbell, *The diocese of Maitland 1866-1966* (Maitland, 1966); J. N. Molony, *The Roman mould of the Australian Catholic Church* (Melb, 1969); W. G. McMinn, 'Bishop Murray and the pattern of Australian Catholicism', *J of Religious Hist*, Dec 1971; Moran papers (Roman Catholic Archives, Syd); Murray papers (Roman Catholic Diocesan Archives, Maitland).   W. G. McMINN

MURRAY, REGINALD AUGUSTUS FREDERICK (1846-1925), geologist, was born on 18 February 1846 in Scotland, eldest child of Virginius Murray (1817-1861) and his wife Elizabeth Alicia, née Poitier; his great-grandfather was John Murray, fourth earl of Dunmore. In 1852 his father, who had sold out from the army, migrated to Victoria, where he served as warden and

police magistrate on the goldfields; his wife and children followed in 1855.

Educated at home and in Melbourne at the Rev. T. P. Fenner's Collegiate School at South Yarra, Murray worked on a cattle run near Avoca and then had some success as a digger. In April 1862 he became field assistant to C. S. Wilkinson [q.v.] in the Victorian Geological Survey Department directed by his kinsman A. R. C. Selwyn [q.v.]. With Wilkinson Murray worked in the Bacchus Marsh and Ballan districts and in 1864 the Otway Ranges.

After passing the civil service examination, Murray was a junior assistant in the Geological Survey from 1865 to 1869 when the survey was disbanded on the grounds of economy. Meanwhile he had qualified as a mining surveyor and secured a post as mining surveyor and registrar for the Alexandra subdivision. In 1871 he returned to his former work as a geological surveyor under R. Brough Smyth [q.v.], secretary for mines. Murray was active in the Bendigo and Ballarat fields but from 1873 his main attention was devoted to extensive reconnaissance surveys of the rugged country of eastern and south-eastern Victoria in the course of which he suffered much hardship, once having to travel for six days without food. In Gippsland he worked partly with A. W. Howitt [q.v.]. Their reports are models of careful observation and probably the earliest accounts of regional geological studies in Australia to be supported by the techniques of microscopic petrography.

Murray returned briefly to mining and surveying after his dismissal on Black Wednesday, January 1878. Reappointed in May, he became in effect government geologist of Victoria in 1881 though not officially accorded that title for some years. The impressive list of publications issued by the Geological Survey in the next years testifies to a high state of activity despite Murray having the help of only one geological surveyor. He investigated the brown coal deposits that later proved important to Victoria's economy but, as administrative duties in Melbourne increased, his field-work was more and more restricted to brief inspections of mineral prospects.

Murray resigned from the civil service in 1897 to take up private geological practice. He visited Western Australia and then examined ore deposits at Lawn Hill, near Burketown, for the Queensland Silver Lead Mines Ltd, but opportunities for such consulting work were limited. When leaving the survey he had hoped to develop the brown coal deposits near Altona as a source of power for South Melbourne. This plan was frustrated when one of the promoters

Murray

absconded with funds raised for the work; Murray was among those severely embarrassed. In reduced circumstances he undertook examining for the Ballarat School of Mines and was occasionally given work by the Geological Survey of Victoria; his last report, *Bulletin* 38, was issued in 1916. His later years were spent in seclusion at Willow Grove on the Tanjil River in Gippsland. He was twice married: first, in 1869 to Jane Louisa Otway (1840-1887), daughter of Henry Ford; and second, in 1888 to Ethel (d. 1912), daughter of Thomas Thompson Bates. He died at Caulfield on 5 September 1925, survived by children of both marriages.

Murray was a notable pioneer of systematic geological exploration in Australia with a pragmatic attitude to geology. Although his experience was confined largely to Victoria he recognized the need for particular geological attention to be directed to the study of mineral deposits of economic importance throughout Australia. His presidential address to Section C of the Australasian Association for the Advancement of Science in Christchurch, New Zealand, in 1891 is devoted to this subject. In 1888 he had been elected fellow of the Geological Society of London; he was also prominent in the Geological Society of Australasia, and in 1898-99 was president of the Victoria Chamber of Mines. As well as producing many reports and maps, mainly in Victorian official publications, Murray wrote an important review, *Victoria. Geology and Physical Geography* (Melbourne, 1887; 2nd edition 1895), in which he displays a remarkable generosity in acknowledging the contributions of others and a dispassionate approach to his subject, rare among his contemporaries.

E. J. Dunn and D. J. Mahony, 'Biographical sketch of the founders of the geological survey of Victoria', Geological Survey Vic, *Bulletin*, 23 (1910), and for bibliog to 1899; *Argus*, 19 Sept 1925; information from Mrs Katrine E. A. Balfour, Geelong.   T. G. VALLANCE
                                    D. F. BRANAGAN

MURRAY, STUART (1837-1919), civil engineer and administrator, was born on 8 October 1837 in Dundee, Scotland, second son of James Murray, store-keeper, and his wife Jessie, née Simmers. Educated at Dundee High School, he studied engineering for two years at Madras College, St Andrews. Attracted by gold he went to Victoria in 1855 and continued his studies privately, qualifying with distinction as a land and mining surveyor, architect and civil engineer. After settling in Kyneton he practised these professions. For six years he was

government mining surveyor in Daylesford, and in the early 1880s shared in a contract to construct the St Arnaud-Donald railway but lost financially. He also surveyed mining leases, settlements in northern Victoria under the Land Acts and for the Water Conservancy Board under G. Gordon and A. Black [qq.v.]. He thus acquired valuable knowledge of the colony and a dedication to water conservation, sparked off by the sight of a settler's child crying for water in a dry summer.

The report by Gordon and Black was the basis of the 1881 Water Conservancy Act which established rural waterworks trusts for stock and domestic purposes. The largest project was the United Echuca and Waranga Waterworks Trust in 1882 with Murray as its engineer.

In 1884 Alfred Deakin appointed Murray secretary of the royal commission on water supply. It led to the epoch-making Irrigation Act of 1886 which restricted riparian rights of landowners by vesting in the Crown the sole right to the use and control of practically all surface waters, and provided for certain national works and for loans to trusts for promoting irrigation undertakings and for reorganization of the Water Supply Department, then attached to the Department of Mines. In reviewing reports of proposed irrigation schemes Murray recommended as essential to all planning of water resources a comprehensive system of river gaugings. Appointed engineer-in-chief of the new department in 1886, he introduced the system and put Victoria years ahead of European countries in this field and was later made *Chevalier du Mérite agricole* by the French government.

Under the new legislation ninety trusts were soon operating extensively but they ran into difficulties through the farmers' reluctance to pay for water. By 1899 a Relief Act had written off three-quarters of the trusts' liabilities, and in 1904 under the direction of George Swinburne, minister of water supply, new legislation was drafted and embodied in the 1905 Water Act. Control of irrigation development by local trusts was removed except for Mildura and centralized under a new instrumentality, the State Rivers and Water Supply Commission, set up under the Act which also, as urged by Murray, vested in the Crown the beds and banks of all streams despite opposition from landed interests. Although over retiring age he was appointed chairman of the new commission in 1906-08.

In 1886-1908 Murray had planned and supervised such major water conservancy works as the Goulburn-Waranga National Channel (Stuart Murray Canal), the upper Coliban reservoir supplying Bendigo, Laane-

322

coorie Weir on the Loddon, the Little Coliban reservoir supplying Kyneton, the storage basin on the Kow swamp, intake works from the Murray River and an outlet aqueduct known as the Macorna Channel; he also had charge of Geelong's water supply and was supervising engineer of the works subject to government control. His greatest work was the Goulburn Weir, of which he was co-designer, with the Waranga storage and its channels.

In 1902 as Victoria's delegate to the interstate royal commission on the River Murray he was mainly responsible for the monumental report outlining development of irrigation and navigation on the river system, thus providing a basis for the interstate agreement reached in 1915. In 1909 he advised the South Australian government on river improvement works and was consulted by the New South Wales government on Sydney's water supply and Burrinjuck reservoir.

Murray was said to have advised or been active in all his professions of mining surveying, land surveying, municipal and water supply engineering. He was a member of all four boards, the founding 'father' of the Victorian Institute of Surveyors in 1874, a member of the University of Melbourne's faculty of engineering and of the Institution of Civil Engineers, London. After retirement he was busy with public affairs in Kyneton and translated French works on engineering and viticulture. In 1859 he had married Elspeth Stott from Aberdeen; they had ten children. A lifelong Congregationalist, he died at his home, Mornington, Kyneton, on 12 April 1919 and was buried privately, survived by three daughters and by three sons, two of whom were surveyors in the Water Supply Department.

Murray had a keen analytic mind, an exceptional memory and capacity for work that allowed great attention to detail, with a sense of perspective which enabled him to see each problem as part of the whole. He knew that his stern, imperious ways did not inspire affection or popularity but his main concern was to achieve the practical goals set by his sense of public duty.

A. S. Kenyon, 'Stuart Murray and irrigation in Victoria', VHM, 10 (1925); Aust Surveyor, 1 Dec 1942; J. N. Churchyard, 'Pioneers of irrigation in Australia . . . Stuart Murray', Aqua, 8 (1956); Weekly Times (Melb), 12 June 1897; Australasian, 4 Dec 1897; Age, 14 Apr 1919; information from Mrs M. S. Edmanson, Bundanoon, NSW, and Mrs W. A. Downie, Ocean Grove, Vic.   VALERIE YULE

MURRAY-PRIOR, THOMAS LODGE (1819-1892), pastoralist and politician, was born on 13 November 1819 at Wells, Somerset, England, son of Thomas Murray-Prior, officer of Hussars at Waterloo, and his wife Elizabeth Catherine, née Skynner. Educated at Brussels under Rev. William Drury and in England by private tutors, he served in H.M.S. Donegal in 1837-38 but resigned and on 24 May 1839 left for Sydney. While acquiring colonial experience at Dalwood near Maitland he met Leichhardt [q.v.] and in June 1843 travelled with him to Moreton Bay. From August 1844 to 1850 he held Broomelton in the Logan District in partnership with Hugh Henry Robertson Aikman. On 3 September 1846 at Cecil Hills near Liverpool he married Matilda Harpur.

Murray-Prior sold Broomelton in September 1853 and in 1854 bought Hawkwood in the Burnett District. He lost 8000 sheep from scab and in 1858, worried by the massacre of the Fraser family at Hornet Bank station, he sold out and took up a banana plantation at Ormiston near Cleveland. In November 1864 he bought Maroon station in the Fassifern district where he settled. He failed to win election for East Moreton in 1860 and joined the public service as postal inspector in 1861 and as postmaster-general in 1862. When that office was transferred to the political arena he was nominated to the Legislative Council on 10 April 1866. He served as postmaster-general in the Herbert [q.v.] ministry from July to August 1866, under Mackenzie [q.v.] from August 1867 to November 1868 and Palmer [q.v.] from 1870 to 1874. In 1863 Rachel Henning [q.v.] had written, 'I suppose it does not require any great talent to be a Postmaster General. I hope not, for such a goose I have seldom seen. He talked incessantly and all his conversation consisted of pointless stories of which he himself was the hero'.

In November 1868 Murray-Prior's wife died and on 18 December 1872 in Sydney he married Nora Clarissa Barton, aunt of the poet A. B. Paterson. Murray-Prior died at Whytecliffe in the Nundah district on 31 December 1892, survived by seven of the eleven children of his first marriage and by seven of the eight children of his second. His eldest daughter Rosa Caroline (1851-1935) married Arthur Campbell Mackworth Praed in 1872 and won literary fame.

Described as suave, courtly and cultured, Murray-Prior collected pictures, some of which are in the Brisbane Art Gallery. He was noted for his strong loyalty to the throne probably because of his claim to be descended from the Emperor Charlemagne.

R. C. Praed, My Australian girlhood (Lond, 1902); M. J. Fox (ed), The history of Queensland, 1 (Brisb, 1909); The letters of Rachel Henning, D. Adams ed (Syd, 1963); M.

Aurousseau (ed), *The letters of F. W. Ludwig Leichhardt* (Cambridge, 1968); I. Hannah, 'The royal descent of the first postmaster-general of Queensland', *Qld GJ*, 55 (1953); E. C. Davies, 'Some reminiscences of early Queensland', *JRHSQ*, 6 (1959); *Brisbane Courier*, 2 Jan 1893; F. E. Lord, 'Brisbane's historic homes', *Queenslander*, 18 Sept 1930.   H. J. GIBBNEY

MURRAY SMITH; see SMITH, ROBERT MURRAY

MUSGRAVE, SIR ANTHONY (1828-1888), governor, was born on 17 November 1828 at Antigua, West Indies, son of Dr Anthony Musgrave, member of the island's House of Assembly and treasurer in 1824-52, and his wife Mary, née Sheriff. Educated in the West Indies, he became private secretary at 21 to the governor of the Leeward Islands. In 1851 he was admitted to the Inner Temple, London, but soon returned to Antigua where he served as treasury accountant in 1852-53 and colonial secretary in 1854-60. In 1853 he had married Christiana Elizabeth Byam; she died in 1858.

Musgrave was administrator of Nevis from October 1860 to April 1861, then of St Vincent and in May 1862 became lieut-governor. In 1864-69 he governed Newfoundland. At San Francisco on the way to his new charge in British Columbia he married Jeannie Lucinda Field by whom he had three sons. Instructed to bring British Columbia into the Canadian Union, he succeeded by insisting on construction of the Canadian Pacific Railway. He was transferred to Natal in 1872.

On 6 March 1873 Musgrave became governor of South Australia. In 1875 he was created K.C.M.G., lost a son, published his *Studies in Political Economy*, occasional economic articles in London journals and two pamphlets, and became a shareholder in the *Westminster Review*. The colony was booming but cursed by political instability with four changes of government in his four year term. His valedictory address in 1877 pointed out the folly of this system and urged stability.

After six years as governor of Jamaica, he became governor of Queensland on 21 July 1883. With Samuel Griffith, who became premier in November, he shared a deep enthusiasm for Australian Federation and a concern for the protection of primitive peoples. He ridiculed colonial fears of German influence in New Guinea and distrusted the motives of the sugar interests but accepted the establishment of a protectorate over southern New Guinea in 1884. He visited England in 1886 and planned to retire but in June 1888 Sir Thomas McIlwraith [q.v.], whom he detested, be-

came premier. The two soon clashed over the governor's right to unfettered exercise of the prerogative of mercy. Musgrave appealed to the Colonial Office, McIlwraith defied him and London supported the premier. A few weeks later Musgrave died, probably of angina pectoris, on 9 October 1888. The premier immediately pressed for a colonial voice in the selection of governors.

Musgrave was assessed by Sir William MacGregor as kind and honest, but 'falling a little behind the times in his conception of popular government'. He left an insurance policy for £3000 and a small Jamaican estate. He is often confused with his nephew Anthony who was his private secretary for years and became colonial secretary of British New Guinea.

V&P (LA Qld), 1886, 1, 679, 1889, 1, 601; I. D. McNaughtan, 'The case of Benjamin Kitt', *JRHSQ*, 4 (1951); B. Scott, *The governorship of Sir Anthony Musgrave, 1883-1888* (B.A. Hons thesis, Univ Qld, 1954); Griffith papers (Dixson Lib, Syd); Musgrave papers (NL); CO 13/129-135, 234/43-49.
                                                H. J. GIBBNEY

MUSGROVE, GEORGE (1854-1916), theatrical entrepreneur, was born on 21 January 1854 at Surbiton, England, son of Thomas John Watson Musgrove, accountant, and his wife Fanny, née Hodson, an operatic star loved by audiences and related to Myra Kemble [q.v.] and the Sarah Siddons. One sister married W. S. Lyster [q.v.] and another was a well-known London actress. George went to Victoria at 12 and after education at Flinders School, Geelong, Lyster gave him a post as treasurer. At All Saints Church, St Kilda, on 1 August 1874 he married Emily Fisk Knight.

In 1879 Musgrove visited London where theatrical circles were gripped by intense excitement; Gilbert & Sullivan had begun their popular operas. Musgrove had seen Williamson's [q.v.] successes in the 1870s and determined to better him. In December 1880 at Melbourne with the rights of Offenbach's *La Fille du Tambour Major* and a full company, Musgrove leased the Opera House. Christmas and the exhibition had drawn many visitors to Melbourne. The production was a sensation the like of which had never been seen. It swept audiences off their feet and ran for 101 nights.

Musgrove was a new sort of producer. Unlike the old actor-manager, he never played a part although he allegedly once dashed across the stage on roller skates. In 1882 a partnership was formed and Williamson, Garner and Musgrove became known as 'The Triumvirate'. They acquired theatres in Melbourne and Sydney, scoring successes. In the 1880s managers had remarkable material. They found real talent not only in imported artists but among the Australian born or trained players. In November 1883 with Nellie Stewart [q.v.] as the drummer boy, *Tambour Major* appeared in a Sydney theatre with the first use of public electric light. A tour of New Zealand with Gilbert & Sullivan operas followed in 1884. In 1884-85 the Comic Opera Company was formed, alternating light musicals with drama. Melbourne's Princess Theatre was rebuilt in 1886 and in 1887 *The Mikado* was produced in a benefit for Nellie Stewart before she sailed for London with Musgrove and his mother and aunt. They returned to Australia in August.

Friction dissolved the partnership in 1889 and Musgrove left for London where he had reverses. On return to Australia he managed a successful season of *Paul Jones* with Marion Burton and Nellie Stewart in leads. In December 1892 he and Williamson formed a new partnership which lasted for seven years. Musgrove spent much time in London. He introduced Nellie Stewart in *Blue Eyed Susan* at the Prince of Wales Theatre and at the Drury Lane in *Forty Thieves*. At first *The Belle of New York* failed in America but he imported the entire American cast including chorus girls whom he allegedly changed every fortnight and played it in 1897 to capacity houses at the Shaftesbury Theatre in London for two years. It was a consistent money-getter for a decade but he split with Williamson over sending it to Australia.

Musgrove continued on his own with dogged faith, boundless energy and imagination. After a show was chosen in London he sent most of the costumes and equipment to Australia. He carefully studied the taste of audiences before introducing new ideas. Sometimes brusque he was kind-hearted and always just and considerate to his players. His aim was good production; money was a secondary matter and he is said to have made and lost half a dozen fortunes. In 1900 he kept productions at the Shaftesbury in London and leased the Princess in Melbourne simultaneously for a season of grand opera. He opened with *Sweet Nell of Old Drury* with Nellie Stewart in 1902. In 1903 he presented Melba; in her first and most successful concert tour of Australia and New Zealand she was responsible for one of the finest all-round productions of opera ever heard in Australia. A tour of the United States in 1906 was disappointing but his company from Berlin in 1907 gave a fine season of grand opera to the Australian public, though the National Opera Company brought out in 1909 failed to please. In a 'smalls' tour of New Zealand with a full company headed by Nellie Stewart in 1910-11 they visited thirty-two towns in Maoriland and a tour of country towns in eastern Australia followed. Financial worries and ill health dogged his later years. In 1914 his career as a producer ended with *Madame Du Barry* at the King's Theatre in Melbourne. On his sixty-second birthday he died at his home in Sydney on 21 January 1916. He bequeathed six-tenths of his estate to Nellie Stewart and, after mention of several small legacies covering the balance, explained that he did not provide for his daughter Rose because against his often expressed wish and 'in defiance of her father's desires she adopted the stage as a profession and having done so she is providing for herself'.

N. Stewart, *My life's story* (Syd, 1923); P. McGuire et al, *The Australian theatre* (Melb, 1948); V. Tait, *A family of brothers* (Melb, 1971); *Australasian*, 16 Feb 1907; *Punch* (Melb), 5 Mar 1908, 25 Apr 1912; *SMH*, 22, 24 Jan 1916.
                                    JEAN GITTINS

N

NAIRN, WILLIAM EDWARD (1812-1869), public servant and politician, was born at Widcombe, Somerset, England, only son of Captain William Nairn [q.v.] and his wife Mary Ann. In January 1830 he entered Queen's College and until 1834 was a scholar at Lincoln College, Oxford (B.A., 1833). In London he met Alexander Maconochie [q.v.] who told him that Sir John Franklin was to replace Lieut-Governor Arthur in Van Diemen's Land. Nairn's father had bought a schooner for £500 in the Sandwich Islands and with a royal certificate sailed to Madras, Swan River and Hobart Town where the authorities refused to allow her to clear for any port except in the Sandwich Islands. In January 1836 William Edward wrote to Franklin who agreed to grant the schooner a licence for trade on the Tasmanian coast. With this experience Nairn sailed from Southampton in the *Fairlie* with Franklin's party and arrived at Hobart in February 1837.

Nairn was appointed clerk in the Colonial Secretary's Office in June but his diligent competence soon won him more important posts. On the voyage he had offered to serve on the Tasmanian Board of Education and in February 1839 Franklin appointed him as an Anglican member of the board in place of Captain Swanston [q.v.]. In October Nairn became its secretary, holding that office intermittently until 1847, and retained his seat on the board until 1858, when it was made a council; he served as its president until 1868. He had acted as clerk to the Executive and Legislative Councils in 1840 and as assistant colonial secretary and assistant police magistrate at Prosser's Plains in 1842. As assistant comptroller of the Convict Department in 1843, he had charge of the prisoners in Tasmania and Norfolk Island, was departmental registrar in 1855-56 and comptroller-general of convicts at a salary of £800 in 1859-68. He was also sheriff of Hobart in 1857-68.

Nairn had been elected unopposed for Meander to the Legislative Council and became its president in January 1856. When Tasmania was granted responsible government he again won Meander and in the first administration, led by W. T. N. Champ [q.v.], in November became minister without portfolio. The government fell in February 1857 but Nairn was re-elected for Meander and again in 1865 and continued as president of the Legislative Council. He was invited to sit on a dozen select committees of the House of Assembly. His up-rightness and urbanity eased the transaction of business with colleagues and those who served under him. In September 1868 he took sick leave but did not recover. He died at Hobart on 9 July 1869, survived by his wife Maria, née Swan, whom he had married on 26 April 1845 at St David's Church, and by three sons and five daughters. His estate of £2200 in Tasmania and £4400 in England was left to his widow.

V&P (HA Tas), 1859 (72), 1870 (13); *Mercury*, 10 July 1869; CSO 5/4/32, 206/5103, 22/18/1853, 50/12/1838, 13/1839, 25/1843, 27/1850 (TA).

NASH, JAMES (1834-1913), discoverer of the Gympie goldfield, was born on 5 September 1834 at Beanacre, Wiltshire, England, son of Michael Nash, farm labourer, and his wife Elizabeth, née Prosser. At 9 he left school for farm work and migrated to Sydney at 23. He alternated between labouring work and prospecting on various goldfields in New South Wales. Quiet and solitary he was an indefatigable walker: once he walked 600 miles to the Taloon diggings and returned unsuccessful.

Nash moved to Queensland in 1863, working at Calliope and Nanango. He found rich gold on an extended prospecting tour in 1867 near the Mary River, and his report on 16 October started 'one of the wildest rushes in Queensland history'. It has been called the salvation of the depressed colony: the Bank of Queensland had closed, a financially embarrassed government had stopped work on the Ipswich-Toowoomba railway and unemployed were marching the Brisbane streets. The government had offered £3000 reward for a payable new field, but the terms had not quite been met, and for his discovery of a field which was to produce gold worth £14,538,328, Nash was granted only £1000 after twelve months' debate. The field even lost the name 'Nashville' and became 'Gympie'. He and his brother won a further £7000 from their claims, but unwise investments in mining stock and an ill-fated drapery store, soon dissipated their winnings. In 1888 the government graciously made him Gympie's powder-magazine keeper at £100 a year, and after his death on 5 October 1913 granted an annual pension of £50 to his wife Catherine, née Murphy, whom he had married in 1869 at Maryborough; they had three sons and two daughters. Despite the government's forgetfulness, posterity has honoured him with a seven-ton granite block memorial fountain in Gympie's Park.

Alcazar Press, *Queensland, 1900* (Brisb, nd); A. L. Stumm and W. C. Woolgar, *Historical sketch of Gympie, 1867-1927* (Gympie, 1927); *Maryborough Chronicle*, 16, 30 Oct 1867; *Gympie Times*, 15 Sept 1896, 16 Oct 1917 jubilee supp.   JUNE STOODLEY

NATHAN, CHARLES (1816-1872), surgeon, was born in London, eldest child of Isaac Nathan [q.v.] and his first wife Rosetta, née Worthington (d. 1824). His father's cruelty and stepmother's indifference led him to run away at 13 and apprentice himself to an apothecary (L.S.A., 1837). He enrolled at Westminster Hospital School of Medicine and won scholarships throughout his four-year course. Graduating with honours, he began a practice in Belgrave Square, but decided to join his family in migrating to Sydney. Arriving in the *York* on 7 April 1841, he started a successful practice in Elizabeth Street North. In 1842 at Christ Church St Laurence, he married Emmeline Harriet, daughter of Henry Fisher, a prosperous wine merchant.

In 1845 Nathan was one of the original four doctors appointed to the new Sydney Infirmary and Dispensary. In June 1847 he and Dr Belisario [q.v.] administered the first anaesthetic in Australia. Bitterly attacked for this innovation in the *Australian Medical Journal*, Nathan was defended in an editorial in the *Sydney Morning Herald*. He encouraged the use of ether at the infirmary, particularly for manipulating congenital dislocation of the hip, but later preferred chloroform which he administered to his own wife in childbirth. An honorary F.R.C.S. in 1857, he was called when the duke of Edinburgh was wounded on 12 March 1868.

On his retirement from the infirmary in 1864 Nathan had become a consulting surgeon and later was also a consultant at St Vincent's Hospital. A founder of the New South Wales branch of the British Medical Association, he was also a foundation member of the Senate of the University of Sydney, an examiner in medicine and a fellow of St Paul's College. He was a member of the Medical Board of New South Wales in 1854-72 and a vice-chairman of the Australian Mutual Provident Society.

Nathan's baritone voice had been trained by his father, music being the family's greatest recreation. He was a foundation member of the Society for the Promotion of the Fine Arts in Australia and a member of the Sydney Philharmonic Society. A fervent Evangelical, he was a warden and trustee of St James's Church, King Street, and daily read a chapter from the New Testament in the original Greek which he had taught himself. Generous, kindly and tolerant, he died from heart disease at his home in Macquarie Street, Sydney, on 20 September 1872 and was buried in the Anglican section of the Camperdown cemetery. He was survived by his wife, four sons and eight daughters. His eldest daughter, Eliza Anne, married Sir Normand MacLaurin.

A portrait is held by his great-grandson, Charles Venour Nathan, Vaucluse.

V. Plarr, *Lives of the fellows of the Royal College of Surgeons* (Lond, 1930); C. Mackerras, *The Hebrew melodist* (Syd, 1963); N. J. Dunlop, 'An essay relating chiefly to anaesthetics and their introduction to Australia and Tasmania', *MJA*, 29 Jan 1927; D. Miller, 'The medical pioneers of St. Vincent's Hospital', *Syd Univ Post-graduate Cttee of Medicine, Bulletin*, 13 (1957), no 3; C. Kemp diary (ML); family letters and information.   CATHERINE MACKERRAS

NEILD, JAMES EDWARD (1824-1906), forensic pathologist, drama critic, medical editor and journalist, was born on 6 July 1824 at Doncaster, Yorkshire, England, son of James Neild and his wife Sarah, née Bilton. His father was educated for the English Church but espoused Wesleyanism; he was successively a schoolmaster, timber merchant (at the time of his son's birth) and brewer. As a child, Neild acquired an early knowledge of music, literature and art, showing such aptitude and enthusiasm for the latter that he wished to make it his career. However, at the behest of his mother he was apprenticed to his uncle, a prominent medical practitioner in Sheffield in 1842, spending five years in this work and in attending lectures and clinical practice at the infirmary. In 1847 he enrolled for the course in surgery at University College, London (L.S.A., 1848). After two years in general practice in Oulton, Yorkshire, he became house surgeon to the dispensary at Rochdale, near Manchester, where his insistence on using anaesthetics led to conflict with authority. However, on his resignation in 1853 he was presented with a suitably inscribed case of instruments by the board of governors and a certificate expressing the approval and confidence of the medical staff.

Neild had already shown evidence of the wide range of interests and delight in controversy which later characterized his life in Melbourne. He had been an occasional contributor, chiefly of verse, to various journals since he was 13. In Sheffield and London he haunted the art galleries and theatres, becoming a drama critic whilst in Sheffield and at Rochdale near the Manchester theatres. Politically 'very democratic', he refused, alone amongst his fellow students, to be sworn in as a special constable when in April 1848 the Chartists marched in London to present their petition; as a personal acquaintance of John Bright he was active in moves to repeal the Corn Laws.

In 1853 Neild, attracted by colonial gold, went to Australia as surgeon in the *Star of the East*, disembarking at Sydney. From Melbourne, a few weeks later, he walked to the Castlemaine diggings, where he combined medical practice with mining. He returned to Sydney to investigate a government post as medical officer at Grafton, which he declined because of its remoteness. Back in Melbourne, he entered the business of David Rutter Long, chemist and druggist. Early in 1855 he joined the general reporting staff of the newly-established *Age*, but in that year he and Long's eldest son took over the pharmaceutical business, trading as Long & Neild for six years. In this period he was theatrical critic to *My Note Book*, which he edited for a time, the *Examiner* and the *Argus*, writing as 'Christopher Sly'. Neild's name first appears on the medical register in 1856, but he did not begin medical practice in Melbourne until 1861. He was soon elected to the Medical Society of Victoria, on which he was to exercise a strong influence as an office-bearer over nearly twenty years; he was president in 1868. He proved a most competent librarian in 1863-66 and 1870-74 (an appointment he also held in the Royal Society of Victoria) and secretary in 1875-79, and diligently fulfilled the difficult task of editing the society's *Australian Medical Journal* in 1862-79 where his pen found adequate scope for controversy, either as editor or as 'Sinapis'. Indeed, it was an argument over the minutes and journal report of a meeting which precipitated his dramatic resignation of both positions.

Granted a degree by the University of Melbourne (M.D., 1864), Neild was appointed lecturer in forensic medicine against much opposition in the recently established medical school in 1865. He held this position until 1904, when his signal service was recognized by a special testimonial from the council. His increased medical activity in this period is reflected in some association with Professor G. B. Halford's [q.v.] researches, notably on snake-bite, but more particularly in an increasing volume of medico-legal work. Encouraged by the coroner, Dr Youl [q.v.], he acquired considerable experience and repute in forensic pathology, but a proposal to create the post of government pathologist, with

Neild as its first occupant, met with a mixed reception from the medical profession and was dropped. He was for a time acting coroner and city medical officer of health, an honorary physician to the Melbourne Benevolent Asylum and an assistant honorary medical officer at the Melbourne and Alfred Hospitals. In 1865, continuing his tireless work for his professional brethren, he helped to found the Medical Benevolent Association, of which he was honorary secretary, and in 1868 a short-lived Medico-Ethical Society. In 1879 with Dr Louis Henry and eight other doctors he established the Victorian Branch of the British Medical Association, holding the first meeting in his home; later he was honorary secretary and in 1882 president, and as Victorian correspondent he helped to establish its journal in New South Wales, the *Australasian Medical Gazette*. He played a major role in founding a branch of the St John Ambulance Association in Victoria, continuing as an examiner at least until 1897; he was enrolled as an honorary associate of the Grand Priory of the Order of the Hospital of St John of Jerusalem in England in 1895. He was the first president of the Victorian Eye and Ear Hospital, an appointment which he held until 1871.

Between 1865 and 1890 Neild, as 'Jacques' or later 'Tahite', was theatrical critic for the *Australasian*, in which role he exerted a forthright and profound influence; as an example, he claimed to have been the first to recognize the brilliance of Melba's voice, advising her to forsake her studies of the piano. As 'Cleofas', Neild published *On Literature and Fine Arts in Victoria* (1889), and a theatrical novel *A Bird in a Golden Cage, Christmas, 1867* (1867); two of his comediettas are said to have been successfully produced on the stage. He wrote numerous articles for the *Herald* and its associated publications, the Melbourne *Punch* and the *Weekly Review*, and for the *Victorian* as 'The Grumbler'. He was a founder of the Melbourne Shakespeare Society, of which he was president in 1890, and was partly responsible for developing a literary and art section in the Royal Society. In 1890 he was given a public testimonial at a formal gathering at the Princess Theatre presided over by his friend George Coppin [q.v.] in recognition of his many public services, particularly in relation to the theatre.

Neild's signed medical papers are few, perhaps the most valuable being those containing recollections of the early medical school, published in the *Australian Medical Journal* (1887) and *Speculum* (1892 and 1900). His lectures were punctuated by Shakespearian quotations and, of more interest than the formal matter, by illustrations from his extensive and varied personal experience. He contributed a paper on the advantages of burning the dead to the Royal Society of Victoria in 1874.

Keen-eyed and beetle-browed, Neild was 'short, natty' and very alert, 'always suggestive of a terrier saying "who said cats" '. He was described by Dr G. T. Howard as a 'versatile genius', probably the sanest and brainiest of a Bohemian clique including Marcus Clarke, G. G. McCrae, Dr Patrick Moloney, 'Orion' Horne, J. J. Shillinglaw, Henry Kendall and Adam Lindsay Gordon [qq.v.]. These and many actors and artists gathered at his home at 21 Spring Street regularly on Sunday afternoons, when the conversation was 'always spirited'. Neild was described as 'personally a delightful man, courteous and obliging . . . of wide reading and culture, but also a keen fighter for what he thought to be right . . . beloved by his friends, and most cordially hated by his particular enemies, of whom he has a good many'.

Neild died at his home on 17 August 1906. In 1857 he had married Susannah (1831-1918), daughter of D. R. Long. Nine children survived to adult life. Of three sons, Charles, an architect, was killed in World War I; Edwin died in 1949 leaving two daughters; and Joseph, who shared his father's interests in pathology, journalism, theatre and literature, died unmarried in 1949. Only two of the six daughters married. Most of the family records, collected by Dr Neild and his sons, have been lost.

A portrait is held by the St John Ambulance Association in Victoria, and a plaster likeness by the Medical Society of Victoria.

W. Johnston, 'Dr. James Edward Neild and the early history of the St. John Ambulance Association in Australia', MJA, 5 Oct 1963; Table Talk, 1 Aug 1890; Argus, 18 Aug 1906; F. Taylor, Notes on Dr James Edward Neild and his descendants, 8105 (LaT L); Neild papers (Medical Soc of Vic Museum).

BRYAN GANDEVIA

NETTLETON, CHARLES (1826-1902), photographer, was born in north England, son of George Nettleton. He arrived in Victoria in 1854 accompanied by his wife Emma, née Miles. In Melbourne he joined the studio of T. Duryea [q.v.] and Alexander McDonald and specialized in outdoor work. He carried his dark tent and equipment with him everywhere, a necessity in the days of the collodion process when plates had to be developed immediately after exposure. He became special photographer for the government and the Melbourne Corporation and is credited with having photographed the first Australian steam train when the private Melbourne-Sandridge (Port Melbourne) line was opened on 12 September 1854.

Nettleton systematically recorded Melbourne's growth from a small town to a metropolis. Every major public work was photographed including the water and sewerage system, bridges and viaducts, roads, wharves, diversion of the River Yarra and construction of the Botanical Gardens. His public buildings include the Town Hall, Houses of Parliament, Treasury, Royal Mint, Law Courts and Post Office and he also photographed theatres, churches, schools, banks, hospitals and markets. His collection of ships includes photographs of the Cutty Sark, and the Shenandoah. He photographed the troops sent to the Maori war in 1860, the artillery camp at Sunbury in 1866 as well as contingents for the Sudan campaign and the Boxer rising. The sharp delineation of his pictures taken at six seconds exposure was a credit to his skill.

Nettleton visited the goldfields and country towns, photographed forests and fern glades, and rushed to disaster areas. In 1861 he boarded the Great Britain to take pictures of the first English cricket team to come to Australia. During the Victorian visit of the duke of Edinburgh in 1867 he was appointed official photographer. He was police photographer for over twenty-five years and his portrait of Ned Kelly [q.v.], of which one print is still extant, is claimed to be the only genuine photograph of the outlaw. Nettleton had opened his own studio in 1858. His souvenir albums were the first of the type to be offered to the public. However, when the dry-plate came into general use in 1885 he knew that the new process offered opportunities that were beyond his scope. Five years later his studio was closed. His work had won recognition abroad. His first success was at the London Exhibition of 1862 and in 1867 he was honoured in Paris. He was not a great artist but a master technician.

Nettleton was an active member of the Collingwood Lodge of Freemasons and a match-winning player of the West Melbourne Bowling Club. Aged 76 he died on 4 January 1902, survived by his wife, seven daughters and three sons.

J. Cato, The story of the camera in Australia (Melb, 1955); Age, 6 Jan 1902; Argus, 6 Jan 1902.

JEAN GITTINS

NEUMAYER, GEORG BALTHASAR VON (1826-1909), scientist, magnetician, hydrographer, oceanographer and meteorologist, was born on 21 June 1826 in Kirchenbolanden, Bavarian Palatinate. Devoted to science, he studied at Munich University (Ph.D., 1849) and specialized thereafter as a magnetician, hydrographer, oceanographer and meteorologist, and became a disciple of the great American oceanographer, M. F. Maury.

The 1830s and 1840s had seen a great upsurge of activity in the investigation of the problems of terrestrial magnetism, and through this Neumayer became aware of the importance of polar exploration and was specially impressed by the work of Captain James Clark Ross. Realizing the need for field experience, he sailed before the mast to South America and acquired a mate's certificate. He then returned to Europe, obtained a chair in physics at Hamburg and later helped to carry out a magnetic survey of Bavaria under the direction of King Maximilian II.

Neumayer next decided to investigate the possibilities for field work and research in the southern hemisphere. Sailing before the mast again, he went to Sydney in 1852. For two years he worked as a miner at Bendigo, as a sailor on coastal ships and carrying out research at the Hobart Magnetic Observatory set up in 1840 by Captain Ross and J. H. Kay [q.v.]. Neumayer's observations and experiences convinced him that Australia provided valuable opportunities for scientific research, and in 1854 he returned to Germany determined to enlist support for organized work in his chosen subjects.

Backed by the scientist and geographer, Baron Friedrich Heinrich Alexander von Humboldt, Neumayer enlisted the interest and support of King Maximilian in his plan to set up a physical observatory in Melbourne to study terrestrial magnetic and related phenomena. Other support came from experts in the British Association and the Royal Society, and with £2000 worth of instruments and equipment from Maximilian, he sailed for Melbourne, arriving on 27 January 1857.

After gaining the interest and support of the press, the commercial community and local scientists, the government was approached on 15 June with a definite plan to set up the observatory on a site in the Botanic Gardens. The setting up of an astronomical observatory was then causing much agitation and a committee of the Philosophical Institute of Victoria, in a memorial to the government on 24 November, recommended that the two projects be set up together on a site at Royal Park. But Neumayer showed that this site was unsatisfactory for his purposes and, being denied the site in the Botanic Gardens, settled for one on Flagstaff Hill, using the existing Signal Station buildings. The government agreed on condition that he also carried out meteorological work. Unfortunately, it would not grant him all the needed funds but the German community helped him with a donation of £500.

By May 1858 both magnetic and meteorological observations were under way, and in time he was able to employ assistants and to set up a uniform system for meteorological work in the colony. In 1859 he received an increased government grant and took over control of all government meteorological stations. He also collected ships' logs, and provided advice to shipmasters on navigational problems. His most spectacular achievement, however, was the completion of a thorough magnetic survey of Victoria, carried out almost single-handed in 1858-64, travelling some 11,000 miles on foot or by pack-horse, and setting up 230 magnetic stations from sea-level to an altitude of 7200 feet. His report on this survey, published in 1869, gives an enlightening account of his travels and observations, including information on the development of the colony and on the pioneering personalities he met. As the Flagstaff Hill location became untenable due to near-by building developments, he was allowed in 1862 by the government to shift to the Botanic Gardens site, though only in conjunction with the establishment of the astronomical observatory then operating at Williamstown. By September the transfer was completed and he remained there until he returned to Germany in 1864 when his work was taken over by the government astronomer.

Neumayer's work in Victoria was facilitated by the growth of interest in scientific investigations that accompanied the rapid development of the colony during and after the gold discoveries of the mid-century. Curiously enough, he encountered a certain amount of prejudiced opposition, even in the colonial legislature. As a dedicated scientist, he was not discouraged by such pettiness, and entered whole-heartedly into the scientific life of the colony, to such effect that he was elected a councillor of the Royal Society of Victoria in 1859, a vice-president in 1860 and a life member in 1864. One important result of his work was the preparation of a register of icebergs reported in high latitudes along the great circle sailing routes between Europe and Australia, together with a route and average track chart for the guidance of mariners. He was also greatly interested in the exploration of the interior of Australia, particularly in the work and fate of Ludwig Leichhardt [q.v.], and in 1868 tried without success to organize a proper scientific expedition into the interior.

On returning to Germany Neumayer had such repute that in 1872 he was appointed hydrographer to the German Admiralty and from 1876 to 1903 was director of the Hamburg Oceanic Observatory. He never lost interest in the scientific exploration of the Antarctic region, reading papers on the subject to international geographical congresses and trying to organize expeditions. His efforts bore fruit when, as a result of growing international interest in the region, a German expedition worked there from 1901 to 1903.

Neumayer died at Neustadt on 24 May 1909 knowing that he had helped to stimulate the great revival of scientific interest in Antarctic exploration ushered in by the twentieth century. He was a fine example of the dedicated and many-sided scientist peculiar to the nineteenth century, and Victoria was fortunate to have had the benefit of his enthusiasm and talents when the first organized moves were being made to shape the community's cultural life.

A. Sutherland, *Victoria and its metropolis*, 1 (Melb, 1888); R. A. Swan, *Australia in the Antarctic* (Melb, 1961); M. E. Hoare, 'Learned societies in Australia: the foundation years in Victoria, 1850-1860', Aust Academy of Science, *Records*, 1 (1967), no 2.

R. A. SWAN

NEWBERY, JAMES COSMO (1843-1895), industrial chemist and public servant, was born on 28 June 1843 at Leghorn (Livorno), Italy, fourth son of William Boxer Newbery, and his wife Elizabeth, née Fraser. At an early age he went with his parents to Boston, America. He was appointed assistant to Josiah Parkins Cooke, professor of chemistry at Harvard University, and also studied at its Lawrence Scientific School (B.Sc., 1864). He went to London and briefly attended the Royal School of Mines where he won certificates in metallurgy and assaying. Selected analyst to the Geological Survey of Victoria under A. R. C. Selwyn [q.v.], he sailed for Melbourne and arrived in June 1865.

In 1869 the government decided to close the Geological Survey as an economy measure, but next year the new Industrial and Technological Museum was opened and Newbery became scientific superintendent, with the right of private practice. He vigorously developed the museum trustees' policy for technical education, and within a year courses were offered in chemistry, metallurgy, geology, physiology, astronomy and telegraphy. The training of Victoria's first apprentices in pharmacy was added

under the 1876 Act. These classes continued until the Working Men's College took them over in 1887. He also developed the museum's display and inquiry services very effectively.

Newbery continued as analyst to the Mines Department, although in January-April 1878 he was a victim of G. Berry's [q.v.] civil service retrenchments. With high repute as a consultant in mining technology, he served on many technical commissions. In 1890 an improved method of chlorination for gold extraction, worked out by Newbery and Vautin, achieved worldwide adoption and Newbery was recognized as an authority on gold amalgamation. His most far-reaching assignment was his mission to Germany in June 1891 with Victorian brown coal samples for firing and briquetting tests. In February 1892 he returned with details of the Lührig process which appeared to create far greater interest than brown coal.

Newbery's laboratory at the museum was enlarged in 1876 to cope with increasing duties which included student training and consultant services to the mining industry. He also collected food samples and analysed them for contaminants, thus laying the foundation for the 1905 Act for preventing adulterated foods. Newbery was also a member of the Central Board of Health. His scientific erudition and personal qualities led to his appointment as honorary superintendent of juries and awards for the 1880 International Exhibition in Melbourne. In 1881 he was appointed C.M.G.

On 15 December 1870 at St George's Church, Malvern, Newbery married Catherine Florence Maud, daughter of George Hodgkinson of Dorking, England. Unhappily he suffered spinal and chest injuries in the Windsor railway collision of 11 May 1887; although never fully recovered, he still carried out much important work. He died at his home in Hotham Street, East St Kilda, on 1 May 1895.

A portrait bust in marble by Percival Ball, commissioned by friends, is in the Science Museum, Melbourne.

Ure's *dictionary of arts, manufactures and mines*, supp to 7th ed (Lond, 1878); *A'sian Chemist and Druggist*, 113 (1885); E. J. Dunn and D. J. Mahony, 'Biographical sketch of the founders of the geological survey of Victoria', Vic Geological Survey, *Bulletin*, 23 (1910) and for publications; *Argus*, 26, 27 May 1882, 12 May 1887, 17 June 1891, 22, 24, 27 Feb 1892, 2 May, 14 June 1895; *Aust Mining Standard*, 25 June, 8 Oct 1890; *Australasian*, 13 June 1891, 27 Feb 1892; *Age*, 10 Oct 1899; J. C. Newbery, Application for museum post 1870 and Letter to chairman re assistance 1872 (VA).

R. H. FOWLER

NEWCASTLE-UNDER-LYME, HENRY PELHAM FIENNES PELHAM CLINTON, 5th DUKE (1811-1864), statesman, was born on 22 May 1811 at 39 Charles Street, Berkeley Square, London, eldest son of the 4th duke of Newcastle and his wife Georgina Elizabeth, née Mundy. Styled earl of Lincoln, he was educated at Eton in 1824-28 and Christ Church, Oxford (B.A., 1832; D.C.L., 1863); he was president of the Oxford Union in 1831 and formed a lifelong friendship with W. E. Gladstone. In 1832 he married Lady Susan Harriet Catherine Douglas, only daughter of the 10th duke of Hamilton, and through his father's interest represented South Nottinghamshire until 1846. In 1834-35 and 1841-45 he served in Peel's first two ministries and followed him when he split the Tories over the corn laws. Lincoln divorced his wife on 14 March 1850, suffered pecuniary embarrassment through estrangement from his father over politics and was depressed by the death of Peel. With Gladstone he mixed with the 'colonial reformers' and followed their general hostility to the policies of the third Earl Grey. Robert Lowe [q.v.] became a protégé of Lincoln and helped to shape his views on Australian questions. On 12 January 1851 he succeeded his father as duke of Newcastle.

In December 1852 Newcastle became secretary of state for war and the colonies under Lord Aberdeen. On 17 February 1853 he confirmed that no more convicts would be sent to eastern Australia and in an able speech in the House of Lords on 10 May defended the decision to send convicts to Western Australia. Newcastle had to interpret Grey's 1847 Order in Council which tried to settle the land demands of the squatters. Although dilatory at first, he supported Lieut-Governor La Trobe against the Victorian squatters who claimed leases for fixed periods of all the lands they already held as well as unconditional rights of pre-emption. In January 1853 he had confirmed Pakington's decision to allow the colonies full control of their runs and land revenue as soon as they had drawn up acceptable new constitutions with adequate civil lists, but did not stipulate that the upper houses of the new legislatures should be nominated not elected.

Newcastle recognized the importance of granting responsible government to every qualified colony before the boon was sought, because it had improved relations in Canada and reduced unnecessary burdens on the Colonial Office. On 4 August 1853 he wrote to Governor-General FitzRoy requiring that the new constitutions contain provisions for the introduction of responsible government. After his dispatch reached Sydney, the Legislative Council amended the constitution bill according to Newcastle's wishes. In July 1854 after the early disasters of the Crimean war, the offices of secretary of state for war and the colonies were separated. Imprudently Newcastle took the War Office, which was beyond his administrative abilities.

In 1859-64 Newcastle returned to the Colonial Office under Palmerston but introduced no fresh policies. In 1860 he allowed Tasmania to amend its Constitution to make the Upper House elective. Next year he mildly criticized his friend Governor Sir John Young in Sydney for 'swamping' his Legislative Council, thereby taking the viceregal office into politics and aiding the 'democratic cause'. Convinced that the navy was a bastion of imperial unity, Newcastle was cool towards Victorian projects for a colonial fleet. In 1863 he followed Grey's policy of reducing the imperial garrisons by making the colonies pay for their military forces. He continued to support responsible government and in a memorable letter to Governor Sir George Bowen declared that it should continue even if it led sometimes to bad government. A poor judge of men, Newcastle made some strange appointments in Australia. His most famous mistake was the appointment of Governor Sir Charles Hotham.

A keen Anglican, Newcastle followed Gladstone's advice in making episcopal appointments and in attempting to win parliamentary sanction for constitutional action by colonial Anglicanism. But Newcastle did not uphold denominational privilege; he took action on the Canadian clergy reserves and declined to interfere with the abolition of state aid to public worship in New South Wales.

Newcastle retired through ill health on 2 April 1864 and died at his family seat, Clumber Park, on 18 October. He had been lord lieutenant of Nottinghamshire since 1857 and was appointed K.G. in 1860. Succeeded by his eldest son Henry Pelham Alexander, he was survived by three other sons and his only daughter.

H. Martineau, *Biographical sketches* (Lond, 1888); J. Martineau, *The life of Henry Pelham, fifth duke of Newcastle* (Lond, 1908); J. M. Ward, *Earl Grey and the Australian colonies, 1846-1857* (Melb, 1958); A. G. L. Shaw, *Convicts and the colonies* (Lond, 1966); J. M. Ward, *Empire in the Antipodes* (Lond, 1966); B. A. Knox, 'Colonial influence on imperial policy, 1858-1866', *Hist Studies*, no 41, Nov 1963; J. M. Ward, 'The Australian policy of the duke of Newcastle, 1852-1854', *JRAHS*, 50 (1964); Newcastle papers (Univ Nottingham Archives).

JOHN M. WARD

NEWELL, JOHN (1849-1932), miner, businessman and politician, was born on 30 November 1849 at Listooder, County Down, Ireland, son of James Newell, farmer, and his wife Margaret, née McDowall. Educated at a National school, he spent seven years with a grocery firm in Belfast.

In 1872 Newell arrived at Brisbane in the *Gauntlet* to join an elder brother in mining at Stanthorpe; he left in 1876 for the Hodgkinson gold rush. Unsuccessful as a prospector, he returned to Brisbane, secured employment in a wholesale house and in 1877 was sent north to open a branch of the firm at Smithfield. The firm closed in 1878 and Newell went prospecting on the Palmer without success, then moved to the Tinaroo tin field where he joined forces with William Jack and two others. In 1879, guided by John Atherton [q.v.], the party prospected in the Herberton area and on 20 May 1880 located the lode which later became the Great Northern mine. Jack soon sold out to John Moffatt and established a store. In 1882 Newell joined him and on 21 January 1885 at Watsonville he married Jack's daughter Janet.

The firm of Jack & Newell expanded rapidly and branches were established throughout north Queensland. Newell became a justice of the peace in 1884, mayor of Herberton in 1888-89, chairman of the shire council and was active in many local societies. In 1896 he was elected to the Legislative Assembly for Woothakata, holding the seat until his resignation on 11 March 1902. Until 1921 he was a member of the Cairns Harbour Board. Predeceased by his wife, he died at Herberton on 29 July 1932 and was survived by two sons and two married daughters.

M. J. Fox (ed), *The history of Queensland*, 3 (Brisb, 1923); *Queenslander*, 4 Aug 1932.

H. J. GIBBNEY

NEWTON, FREDERICK ROBERT (1841-1926), schoolmaster and Anglican minister, was born at Nailsea, Somerset, England, eldest son of Robert Newton, timber merchant and contractor, and his wife Elizabeth, née Cox. He completed his education at Neuwied, Germany, and was confirmed at Coblenz in 1857. In the *Great Britain* he arrived at Sydney in 1858 to look for land for his parents who intended to migrate, but his mother died that year and he was appointed assistant master at Calder House School, Newtown, by J. F. Castle. In 1870 he taught mathematics at The New School (Eaglesfield) under W. J. Stephens [q.v.], but left in December to open a Church of England Grammar School at Grafton with

the rector, Rev. Josiah Spencer, in 1871. Newton visited the German church there as a lay reader and addressed the congregation in their native tongue. He also visited the Richmond River where his brother Walter Stephen had settled at Brockley, Wollongbar, in 1869. In 1875 he opened a private school for boys on his brother's property for a year.

Realizing the need for ministers in the vast parish of Casino which extended to the Queensland border, Newton devoted himself to parish work under Rev. W. H. Dunning and his successor. He assumed responsibility for the entire area in their absence. Made deacon in 1876 and ordained by Bishop Turner [q.v.] at Armidale in 1877, he became the first incumbent of the new parish of the Lower Richmond and Tweed with headquarters at Lismore. Often working without remuneration, he was constantly in the saddle visiting the scattered congregations. When Rev. Henry Porter took over the parish of Casino and the Upper Richmond in 1878 Newton made his first trip to the Tweed over the dangerous Nightcap route. In that year he also started a boys' school at Lismore with Robert Laverty. In 1880 when appointed rector at Wollombi in the Newcastle Diocese he brought Porter and Laverty with him and the school was continued until 1882. He returned to the Richmond in 1884 to conclude the financial arrangements of the churches he had partly endowed and then accepted a curacy at All Saints' Church, Parramatta.

In 1885-93 Newton was curate at Liverpool, Woolloongabba in Brisbane, Beaudesert, Beenleigh, and finally Gayndah. He continued his charitable work begun in 1876 by adopting Henry Newton (Wilkinson) as his own son at Grafton. Taking charge of the welfare and education of the three Dhalke boys, he found them employment with R. M. Collins [q.v.], a former pupil at Calder House School. Newton represented the Queensland government at the dedication of the memorial church for Albert Dhalke who had been murdered by cattle duffers. At the end of 1893 Henry Newton (B.A., Sydney, 1889; M.A., Oxford, 1893) returned from England where he had been ordained to work with his foster-father in the huge parish of Esk in Queensland. After relieving in the diocese of Brisbane Frederick Newton briefly returned to the Richmond to take charge of the parish of Coraki.

Newton became vicar at Nimbin, his last parish before retiring to live with his brother at Wollongbar. Unmarried and aged 84 he died there on 23 April 1926 and was buried in the Anglican cemetery. He had shunned

all churchly honours and given help whenever it was needed. A firm opponent of
sectarianism, he had exerted a wide influence in the frontier districts where he
worked. His adopted son became bishop of
Carpentaria in 1915 and of New Guinea in
1922; in 1938 he published a pamphlet, *The
Life Story of the Rev. Frederick Robert
Newton.*

R. L. Moxon, *Short history of the work of
the Anglican Church in the north coast districts of New South Wales* (Grafton, 1904);
A. F. Elkin, *The diocese of Newcastle* (Syd,
1955); V. J. V. Robinson, History of the
Anglican Church on the Richmond River
(Richmond River Hist Soc, Lismore).

LOUISE T. DALEY

NICHOLLS, CHARLES FREDERICK (b.
1826), mining consultant and journalist, and
HENRY RICHARD (1830-1912), newspaper
editor and author, were born in London, the
second and third sons of Henry Nicholls,
merchant, and his wife Ann Elizabeth, née
Bright. The brothers were educated at
London and Binfield, Berkshire. Their father,
a socialist and friend of many continental
revolutionaries, contributed to the *Leader,
Christian Socialist* and other papers, and in
1853-54 owned and edited the radical
Weekly Examiner. Under his influence,
Charles, who was training as an architect
and civil engineer, and Henry, who was
studying Latin, French and literature at the
Westminster Mechanics' Institute, became
ardent Chartists in 1848. Charles was
prominent in such movements as the Parliamentary Reform League and Henry contributed fiery verses. Later Henry lectured
and wrote articles for various papers,
especially the radical *Leader*.

Henry migrated to Melbourne in 1853,
and soon afterwards joined George Black,
another Chartist, in editing the anti-
government *Diggers' Advocate*. During the
licence troubles they sent a cart to Castlemaine draped with the tricolour and the
driver dressed in red. But their doctrinaire
internationalism was out of touch with the
inchoate local protest and the paper failed
in August 1854. Charles arrived in November and joined Henry at Ballarat. Welcomed
by the Eureka rebels, the brothers enrolled
at the stockade but left before the attack
because they were appalled by the lack of
discipline. After the tragedy they joined
J. B. Humffray [q.v.] in petitioning the
governor for an amnesty for the rebels and
fair dealing for the Ballarat population.
Charles chaired the committee which organized the first Eureka memorial pilgrimage,
was elected to the local (mining) court and

initiated the People's League to campaign
for legislation to allow mining on private
property. While vice-president of the league,
he was chiefly responsible for a united
approach to parliament by the goldfields'
communities. Like Henry, however, he found
the miners unsympathetic to plans for co-
operative company mining. He managed to
sway the members of the local court into
granting the first leases at Ballarat, but lost
his seat at the next elections. Henry had
already resigned from the court in 1855
when it refused to allow barristers to
appear.

The brothers moved to Creswick where
Henry mined and Charles, largely at his own
risk, floated the first co-operative company.
Dismayed by popular opposition, he campaigned vigorously for free enterprise and
capital investment. In England he had
written many articles on co-operation, but
following his Creswick experience he became critical of that great hope of the working man. After prospecting at Daylesford
Charles settled at Clunes, studied mining
techniques and joined the committee of 'outsiders' in their struggle with the Port Phillip
Co. In 1860 he was captain of a subsidized
prospecting party and in 1864 explored
Gippsland with another party. At that time
he was combining active mining with investment and company promotion. He worked
hard for legislative reform like the no-
liability clause in the 1864 Mining Act and
wrote many articles on the technical and
financial aspects of mining. His first major
mine promotion, north of Clunes, failed
despite efforts to place shares on the London
market. His general optimism was later
justified by success at Ballarat in 1880 when
he was prominent in securing Melbourne
capital for the Sir Garnet Wolseley Co. of
which he was chairman.

Charles was also interested in newspaper
ventures. He helped to float the short-lived
Leader at Ballarat in 1855 and in 1867-69
owned and edited the *Evening Star* at Melbourne. For about ten years he was Melbourne correspondent for his brother
Henry's *Ballarat Star*, for which he wrote
many articles on mining and electoral
reform. His *Democracy and Representation,*
a review of Thomas Hare's system of voting,
was published in book form in 1871. He
also wrote on general topics, especially
literature, agriculture and poultry-breeding.
He contested the Legislative Assembly seat
of Talbot in 1856 and North Gippsland in
1864 without success but remained active in
electoral affairs. In 1886 he bought land and
a hotel at Little River catering for sportsmen
in quest of game on the Werribee plains.

At St Kilda on 24 September 1870 Charles
had married Isabella Taylor with Congre-

gational ritual. The date and the place of his death are unknown.

Henry Nicholls acted as Creswick correspondent for the Ballarat *Times* before joining its staff in 1858. He became editor of the *Ballarat Star*, and was its sole proprietor from 1875 to 1880, when he took W. B. Withers [q.v.] and E. E. Campbell as partners until he sold out in 1883. The paper's policy was democratic and constitutionalist. Like many Chartists, Nicholls feared politics without principles, distrusted the voice of an uneducated population and detested men like C. E. Jones [q.v.], the demagogue go-getter. Nicholls used the term 'screech' to describe their shouting down of opponents. He published An *Essay in Politics in Verse* in 1867. In the Victorian constitutional crises of the 1860s and 1870s he gave qualified support to the Legislative Council, but called strongly for an end to faction and party. To him the 'great cause of Australian nationality' was social and not political and he deplored George Higinbotham's [q.v.] campaign against the Colonial Office. His idealistic concept of the national good was centred around education, on which he justified almost any expenditure, believing that poor children should aspire even to the universities. For adult education he advocated free libraries with a practical not classical emphasis and inter-library loans. He preached co-operation and welcomed government interference in righting social wrongs despite a basic belief in free enterprise. An investor and company director, he was nevertheless among the earliest to advocate company responsibility for mining accidents. In 1880 he stood impressively but in vain against Peter Lalor [q.v.] for the Legislative Assembly seat of Grant.

In 1883 Nicholls became editor of the Hobart *Mercury* where his themes remained the same. 'The interests of society are less carefully guarded than those of the individual', he claimed, and kept calling for public men to work in a 'lofty spirit' for Federation, for trade unions free of self-interest, for equality between the colonies and the mother country and for an intellectual life transcending class and creed. His liberalism derived from the study of history and humanity, not from 'dry formulas'. 'Great things are not going to be done by men who have not great ideas', he thundered, taking equally to task Tasmanian, mainland and British legislators. In the 1890s he called with fervour for the achievement of nationhood. Outspokenness took him to the High Court in 1911 for contempt of the Arbitration Court, but the (test) case was dismissed and he was honoured with a crowded reception at the Hobart Town Hall. As 'Henricus' he had, throughout his career, written significant articles for the *Argus* and *Australasian*, thereby becoming a national figure. He had also been president of the Hobart Club. With a leading article unfinished on his desk he died of pneumonia at his home in Battery Point on 13 August 1912 and was buried in Queenborough cemetery. Predeceased by his wife Ellen, née Minchin, whom he had married at Ballarat with Anglican rites on 9 June 1863, he was survived by two daughters and six sons. One of them, Herbert (1868-1940), became chief justice of Tasmania in 1914 and was appointed K.C.M.G. in 1927.

H. M. Humphreys (ed), *Men of the time in Australia: Victorian series*, 1st ed (Melb, 1878); W. B. Withers, *The history of Ballarat*, 2nd ed (Ballarat, 1887); *Mercury*, 14, 16 Aug 1912.

WESTON BATE

NICHOLS, GEORGE ROBERT (1809-1857), lawyer and politician, was born on 27 September 1809 in Sydney, second son of Isaac Nichols [q.v.] and his second wife Rosanna Abrahams, daughter of Esther Johnston [q.v.]. Educated in England in 1819-23, he returned in the *Thalia* in May 1823 and was articled to W. H. Moore [q.v.]. His duties included forming special juries and taxing costs and in 1831 Governor Darling alleged he was inefficient. At St James's Church on 23 March 1831 he married Eliza Boggs (d. 1835) and on 16 December 1837 he married Susannah Eliza Barnes. On 1 July 1833 he was the first native-born Australian admitted as a solicitor in New South Wales. Nichols opposed the division of the legal profession effected in November 1834. The Bar disputed his right to appear as an advocate at Quarter Sessions but the court made an exemption in his favour, although he could not appear in the Supreme Court. In 1857 D. H. Deniehy's [q.v.] bill to admit Nichols to the Bar lapsed after bitter opposition.

In 1830 Nichols strongly attacked the 'tyranny and oppression' of the colonial government and soon became active in radical politics and the 'Australian party' centred on W. C. Wentworth [q.v.]. After 1835 he was joint sub-secretary of the Australian Patriotic Association. William Bland [q.v.] was a close friend, and James Martin and Richard Driver [qq.v.] were protégés who served their articles with him. In the late 1830s Nichols's influence with the native-born group was increased by his purchase and editing of the *Australian*. He consolidated his forceful oratory, advocated self-government, denounced transportation and justified his self-description as 'a radical reformer'. In July 1842 he became insolvent with debts over £10,000 and could pay only 10s. in the £. A leading Freemason, he was solicitor to the commissioners of the City of Sydney in 1854-56, a member of the Parramatta District Council and a trustee of the Sydney Grammar School.

In July 1848 Nichols was elected to the Legislative Council for Northumberland Boroughs. By 1851 he had introduced twenty-three bills with success, sat on numerous select committees and had a hand in most of the other legislation passed. Re-elected in September, he argued that relief should be given from general revenue to the poor, the blind, the lame, the old and the infirm, and advocated law reform. He sought a revision of the Constitution to obtain 'true popular representative government' and counselled vigilance to ensure that transportation should not be renewed. In 1856 he won his old seat at the first responsible government elections after espousing certain legal reforms and a land system that would compensate squatters for surrendering arable land and prevent waste lands 'from falling into the hands of companies and capitalists'. He explained that illness had prevented him taking part in the debates on the constitution bill, which on the whole he approved. In the first ministry from 6 June to 25 August he was auditor-general and secretary for lands and works. H. W. Parker [q.v.] considered him as solicitor-general in the third ministry but his health 'rendered it utterly impossible'.

On 12 September 1857 he died of dropsy at his residence in York Street, survived by his third wife Eliza, née Smith, whom he had married at Scots Church on 14 July 1854, and by two sons. With Archbishop Polding [q.v.] leading the procession he was buried in the old cemetery; his remains were transferred about 1900 to the Anglican section of Rookwood. His estate was valued at £400 and a testimonial fund was arranged for his widow. Standing 6 ft. 3 ins., 'Bob' Nichols had a striking physical appearance and great personal charm. R. J. Flanagan [q.v.] wrote that 'among the native-born he perhaps occupied the second position in ... patriotism and ability', while the *Sydney Morning Herald*, noting the quality of his legislative record, described him as 'the earnest, eloquent and graceful advocate of all that was good ... and the stern, determined and resolute foe of anything approaching to bigotry or oppression'.

HRA (1), 16; J. Normington-Rawling, *Charles Harpur: an Australian* (Syd, 1962); M. Roe, *Quest for authority in eastern Australia 1835-1851* (Melb, 1965); J. M. Bennett (ed), *A history of the New South Wales Bar* (Syd, 1969); J. N. Molony, *An architect of freedom* (Canberra, 1973); A. Halloran, 'Some early legal celebrities', *JRAHS*, 10 (1924); *SMH*, 2 Sept 1840, 4, 22 July, 6 Aug, 21 Oct, 16 Dec 1842, 12, 13 July 1848, 20 Sept 1851, 24 Mar 1856, 14, 16 Mar, 27 Apr, 15 May 1857; *Australian*, 12 Jan 1841; S. A. Donaldson ministry letters (ML); G. R. Nichols, Letters from clients 1832-48 (ML); MS cat under G. R. Nichols (ML).

G. P. WALSH

NICHOLSON, GERMAIN (1814-1888), grocer, was born on 18 October 1814 in Lamplugh, Cumberland, England, son of William Nicholson, factory owner, and his wife Elinor, née Germain. Educated at a private school, he was apprenticed to a grocer and from 1835 was employed as house manager of Cornthwaite & Co., merchants of Liverpool. On 26 September 1841 at Liverpool he married Eleanor Joplin, and in October they sailed for Port Phillip in the *Arkwright*, arriving at Hobson's Bay on 7 January 1842. He had sold much merchandise on the voyage and, with the proceeds and other goods he had already sent out, he immediately established himself as an importing grocer and provision merchant in Melbourne. His brother Thomas arrived in the colony in 1843 and managed some of the business until he died on 16 December 1853.

In 1844 Nicholson bought the business and premises of Parker & Beadle in Elizabeth Street and by December had three business houses in full operation. He had problems of overstocking during the 1845 recession but when it ended he expanded rapidly, with branches in Melbourne and throughout Victoria by the time of the gold rushes. In the early 1850s he imported goods in huge quantities, anticipating the continued influx of population and later began exporting gold on a large scale. His trade dealings with England and the East were very successful and his best-known import was the first cargo of tea from Hankow to Australia.

Nicholson's speculation in land was also profitable. In 1843 he bought and sold a King Street property, the first of many town sites to bring him good returns. In 1850 he bought land at East St Kilda, where he built his family home, a pre-fabricated, two-storied house imported from California. He was a director of the Victorian Life and General Insurance Co. and in 1853 a founder of the Bank of Victoria, serving as a director until 1888. He was also a founder and director of the Melbourne and Hobson's Bay Railway Co.

A philanthropist, Nicholson contributed to the Ragged Schools and the Melbourne Protestant Orphan Asylum. He was a founder of the Church of England Grammar School in St Kilda Road and the first to donate £100 to the appeal for building (old)

St Paul's Church. He declined several times to enter politics, but was a magistrate for Melbourne and St Kilda from 1857. He had taken a leading role in the anti-transportation movement and in 1851 was one of the 'Thirty Patriots of Melbourne' who each subscribed 100 guineas for a deputation to plead their cause in England.

Nicholson was well known and admired for his commercial acumen and success as well as his generosity. He offered shelter in his warehouses to the hordes of immigrants arriving in Melbourne before they set off for the goldfields. His reputation as 'the poor man's friend' was said to have protected his goods from being stolen and allowed him to ride in the forest around Albert Park unmolested by bushrangers. He died on 22 November 1888 in the *Salazie* bound for England and was buried at sea. He was survived by his wife and their only child, a daughter.

A. Sutherland et al, *Victoria and its metropolis*, 2 (Melb, 1888); *Argus*, 3 Dec 1888; *Town and Country J*, 8 Dec 1888.

SUZANNE G. MELLOR

NICHOLSON, JOHN HENRY (1838-1923), teacher and writer, was born on 12 June 1838 at Lyme Regis, Dorset, England, eldest surviving son of John Nicholson, orientalist, theologian and linguist, and his wife Anne, née Waring. He was a nephew of Mark [q.v.] and William Nicholson, sponsor and friend of Leichhardt [q.v.]. Educated privately and at Croft House Academy, Brampton, Cumberland, he was sent at 16 on a sea voyage but left the ship on reaching New South Wales, where among various occupations he tried whaling and gold prospecting. After a brief return to England he settled in 1859 in Queensland, opening a private school at Toowoomba. Soon afterwards he moved to Warwick where he tutored until 1863 and then started another private school. On 3 March 1860 he had married German-born Anna Wagner; they had no children but adopted a daughter. In May 1865 he joined the Board of General Education and had charge of National schools at Nundah in 1865-68, Springsure in 1870-76 and Enoggera in 1877-85.

Between 1867 and 1878 he produced three small books of miscellaneous prose and verse, the first two under the pseudonyms of 'Tadberry Gilcobs' and 'Salathiel Doles'. These books were largely facetious and of little literary merit, the best of them being *The Opal Fever* (Brisbane, 1878). A volume of undistinguished verse in 1879 was followed by *The Adventures of Halek* (London, 1882), an allegory, inspired partly by *Pilgrim's Progress*, of a man's development from sinful worldliness to ideal goodness. Although it attracted much praise from some critics and went through further editions in Brisbane in 1896 and 1904, *Halek* was never a success and its sequel, *Almoni* (Brisbane, 1904), fared no better. Both works had fine sentiments and a dignified harmonious style but were too remote from everyday life to have much impact.

In April 1885 Nicholson resigned from the government service and in 1886-90 had a private school at Enoggera. Always somewhat eccentric and liable to bouts of melancholia, he spent most of 1891 in the mental hospital at Goodna. Thereafter he continued teaching, mostly privately and at Brisbane, although from September 1893 to December 1894 he was with the government as head teacher at Cambooya. In February 1898 he was appointed registrar of births, marriages and deaths at Nundah. In 1901 his wife died, and on 7 July 1905 he married another German, Anna Cordes, who had been attracted to him while making a translation of *Halek* and had come from California to join him. Three months after the marriage Nicholson was readmitted to the Goodna mental hospital and remained there except for occasional intervals until he died on 30 June 1923; he was survived by his wife and daughter.

Nicholson's other works included two plays, a humorous mathematical booklet, various prose and verse, and some popular patriotic songs. The English composer, John Ireland (1879-1962), was his nephew. His literary achievement was small but in his time, after J. B. Stephens [q.v.] and Essex Evans, he was one of the leading writers in Queensland.

V. Palmer, *Intimate portraits and other pieces*, H. P. Heseltine ed (Melb, 1969); C. Hamer, 'An Australian allegorist', *Biblionews*, July 1966; P. J. Roberts, John Henry 'Halek' Nicholson (B.A. Hons thesis, Univ Qld, 1971); Nicholson papers (Oxley Lib); Education Department records (QA); private information.

PHILIP J. ROBERTS

NICHOLSON, MARK (1818-1889), pastoralist, was born at Clifton, near Bristol, England, youngest son of Rev. Mark Nicholson (1770-1838), sometime fellow of Queen's College, Oxford (M.A., 1797), and president of Codrington College, Barbados, in 1801-21, and his wife Lucy, née Elcock, who came from a distinguished West Indian family.

Trained to the law, Nicholson never practised. Intending to prepare the way for others of his family, he sailed in the *Duchess of Kent*. Arriving at Port Phillip in June 1840, he took up a cattle run near Mount

Macedon with a relation, Dr Edmund Higgins, as partner. In 1845 Nicholson left it and took up Lake Wangoom as well as Cudgee and Mount Warrnambool with Craigieburn as an out-station. In that year he married his cousin Elizabeth Cobham, whose mother was a sister-in-law of Georgiana McCrae, G. W. Cole and Dr D. J. Thomas [qq.v.], thereby becoming connected with other prominent people in the formative years of the Port Phillip District. He had five sons and two daughters.

In 1848 Superintendent La Trobe asked Nicholson, Thomas Manifold [q.v.] and Henry Foster to become justices of the peace so that the new town of Warrnambool might have more influence in the Magistrates' Court at Belfast (Port Fairy). As prominent churchmen, Nicholson and Foster were requested by Bishop Perry [q.v.] to conduct services in the township until Dr Beamish became the incumbent in 1850. In 1853 Nicholson was elected, unknown to himself, to represent Belfast and Warrnambool in the Victorian Legislative Council, where his family connexions, G. W. Cole, J. Graham and W. C. Haines [qq.v.], were fellow members. He successfully moved for a survey of the ports of Belfast and Warrnambool. He was also responsible for the motion to provide funds in 1854 for a museum of natural history, now the National Museum of Victoria. He resigned in 1854 in order to return to England to educate his children.

Nicholson's brother, William Alleyne, was a patron of Ludwig Leichhardt [q.v.] and Mark's migration led Leichhardt to travel to Australia too. Because Leichhardt's ship carried him to Sydney, the two never met in Australia but they corresponded and three of Leichhardt's letters to Nicholson are in the Warrnambool Public Library. In 1843 he asked Leichhardt to superintend his western station but withdrew the offer because of the colony's financial troubles in which Nicholson was heavily involved. At Clifton he had been a pupil of Dr J. E. Bromby [q.v.] and was partly responsible for his becoming the first headmaster of Melbourne Church of England Grammar School in 1858. A nephew, J. H. Nicholson [q.v.], settled in Queensland.

Nicholson visited Victoria on business in 1859 and 1868, and in 1873 returned with his family to settle. In his 72nd year he died at his home, Waveney, near Warrnambool, on 27 October 1889. His generosity, charm and talent for friendship had won him a wide circle of friends.

A portrait is in the Warrnambool City Council Chambers.

M. Aurousseau (ed), *The letters of F. W. Ludwig Leichhardt* (Cambridge, 1968); C. E. Sayers, *By these we flourish* (Melb, 1969); R. M. Jukes (ed), Some Nicholson letters and papers (held by author).   R. M. JUKES

NICHOLSON, WILLIAM (1816-1865), merchant and politician, was born on 27 February 1816 at Whitehaven, Cumberland, England, son of Miles Nicholson, farmer, and his wife Hannah, née Dalziel. He migrated to Port Phillip in 1842 and started as a retail grocer in Melbourne. The business prospered and became W. Nicholson & Co., gradually extending its investments into farming and pastoral property. A foundation member of the Benefit Building Society in 1847 and the Bank of Victoria in 1852, he served both as a director. He was also connected with the Australian Fire and Life Insurance Co. and the Melbourne Exchange Co., and in 1859-60 was chairman of the Melbourne Chamber of Commerce.

In November 1848 Nicholson was elected unopposed for the La Trobe Ward in the Melbourne City Council. In 1850 he became an alderman and was mayor for a year from November. He resigned from the council in 1852, and in November was returned to the Legislative Council at a by-election for North Bourke; he held this seat until March 1856. He served on over twenty-five select committees, including that on the Constitution. Late in 1855 the council debated the electoral bills required by the Constitution and Nicholson indicated that he would move that 'any electoral act should be based upon the principle of voting by ballot'. On 18 December his motion was carried 33 to 25 against the Haines [q.v.] government. To the surprise of its supporters including Nicholson, Haines resigned and Nicholson, about to leave for England, was asked to form a government. His half-hearted attempts to do so were unsuccessful and on 29 December he withdrew and Haines was then reinstated. When the secret ballot came up again Nicholson agreed that it would not be a ministerial question. With strong support in matters of detail from Nicholson the provision for a secret ballot was passed by a majority of seven.

Nicholson has often been credited as 'Father of the Secret Ballot'. The claim is dubious. Vote by ballot had been one of the six points of the Charter and caused much agitation in Victoria during the 1850s; Nicholson was said to have twice opposed the ballot as then unnecessary. However, the main qualification to Nicholson's claim stems from his inability in 1855 and 1856 to go beyond a statement of principle. His ideas on the ballot were confused and devoid of any idea for making the ballot work. Haines's law officers refused to draft the clauses incorporating the ballot into the Electoral Act under the new Constitution so at a meeting of Nicholson's supporters, H. S. Chapman [q.v.] offered to do so; his drafting also overcame the problem of illiterates marking a ballot paper and reduced the risk of fraud while still protecting the voter's anonymity. Without Chapman's work the ballot may have been rejected by the council or if passed would have been discredited as unworkable; Chapman, therefore, must take at least equal credit with Nicholson as 'mid-wife to the ballot in Victoria'.

In 1853 Nicholson had been chairman of directors for the Hobson's Bay Railway Co. and as president of the Early Closing Association had some success in persuading shop-keepers to close at 7 instead of 8, but the movement withered. He left for England in March 1856 and returned to Victoria in July 1858. Fêted as a colonial reformer, he was, by his own account, invited to stand for parliament in any one of five constituencies, among them his home town. A few weeks after his return he was unsuccessful in a by-election for South Melbourne. In January 1859 at a by-election he won the seat of Murray in the Legislative Assembly; soon afterwards he transferred to the seat of Sand-ridge, which he held from October 1859 to August 1864. Within a year of his re-election Nicholson was premier and chief secretary, holding office from 27 October 1859 to 26 November 1860.

Rapid economic and constitutional changes in the colony had stirred aggressive individuals to covet power and to conflict with authority and among themselves. Land Conventionists had helped to put Nicholson in power but were not strong enough to capture the government. After much shuffling they persuaded other members to join the 'Corner' group which introduced such radical bills as the eight-hour day and payment of members. The land bill, intro-duced by James Service [q.v.] in November 1859, was designed to open land for free selection. This and other proposals see-sawed back and forth between the two Houses. The council returned the bill emasculated by a multitude of amendments. The assembly tried to restore the vital points but the council refused to budge. After public dis-turbances and two attempts by Nicholson to resign, the almost useless Act was passed in September 1860, leaving a pattern of con-flict between the two Houses for the next twenty years.

Nicholson suffered a severe illness in 1863 after which he was not active in politics. A further attack in January 1864 presaged his death at St Kilda on 10 March 1865. He was survived by his wife Sarah Burkitt, née Fairclough, and four sons.

Nicholson is remembered for his associ-ation with the passing of the secret ballot in 1855-56 and, less distinctly, for the struggle to secure the Nicholson Land Act of 1860. He was 'a plain plodding fellow'; good-natured, candid and self-confident, he took pleasure in his wealth and position and the knowledge that he was self-made. In many ways he was typical of the radical merchant of his day.

G. Serle, *The golden age* (Melb, 1963); E. Scott, 'The history of the Victorian ballot', *VHM*, 8 (1920); *Argus*, 10 Mar 1865.

PETER COOK

NICKLE, SIR ROBERT (1786-1855), army officer, was born on 12 August 1786 at sea, son of Robert Nicholl of the 17th Dragoons, who changed the spelling of his name. Educated at Edinburgh, he joined the Dur-ham Fencibles as an ensign and in 1798-99 served in the Irish rebellion. In 1804 he joined the 88th Regiment and in 1806 went to South America where he won distinction and was severely wounded. Captain on 1 June 1809, he served with his regiment in most of the Peninsular war, fighting in nine major actions, and at Toulouse was again wounded. He usually commanded the light company of the 88th. He was distinguished for generosity to a defeated opponent and was decorated for bravery. In 1814 he was wounded again in America. Promoted lieut-colonel in 1825, Nickle commanded the 30th Regiment in the West Indies in 1830 and was appointed K.H. In 1832-33 he ad-ministered the government of St Kitts. In 1838 he served in the Canadian rebellion and for his services was knighted in 1841. In 1848 he was promoted brevet colonel and in 1851 major-general.

In 1853 Nickle was appointed commander-in-chief of the military forces in the Aus-tralian colonies. After several false starts in the unlucky steamer *Australian* he travelled in the *Argo* and arrived at Sydney on 24 July. When gold was discovered in Victoria his headquarters were moved to Melbourne, where Nickle and his staff arrived on 6 August 1854.

After the disturbances at Ballarat in November Nickle sent reinforcements from Melbourne and accompanied by Colonel Edward Macarthur [q.v.] followed with a slower-moving force of infantry and artillery. He reached Ballarat on 6 December, three days after the storming of the Eureka stockade. Feelings were running high but Nickle moved amongst the diggers' tents without an escort. Though he deprecated the revolt he showed his disapproval of the actions which had caused it. Grievances were aired, tension subsided, arms were handed in, Nickle addressed a public meeting and martial law was repealed on 9 December. On the 19th he left Ballarat.

Early in 1855 Nickle's health deteriorated, perhaps because of his exertions in the heat of Ballarat. He applied for leave to return to England but died on 26 May at his residence, Upper Jolimont House. After a large service at St Peter's Church, Eastern Hill, he was buried in the Carlton cemetery. Predeceased by his first wife Elizabeth, daughter of William Dallas, whom he had married in 1818, he was survived by a son Robert and two daughters, and by his second wife, the widow of General Nesbit.

Nickle's courage, firmness and good judgment were combined with humanity, courtesy and a gentleness which earned him general liking and respect.

G. Serle, *The golden age* (Melb, 1963); *Argus*, 28 May 1855; *Herald* (Melb), 28 May 1855; *Age*, 29 May 1855; *Melb Mthly Mag*, June 1855.

RONALD McNICOLL

NICOLAY, CHARLES GRENFELL (1815-1897), clergyman, geographer and geologist, was born on 3 August 1815 at Cadogan Place, Chelsea, England, seventh child of Frederick Nicolay (d. 1817), Treasury clerk, and his wife Maria Georgina, née Granville. In 1841 he was made deacon by the bishop of Exeter and on 28 March licensed to a curacy at Tresco in the Scilly Isles. On 7 June he married Mary Ann, daughter of Henry Baldwin Raven; they had eight children.

In 1843-58 Nicolay was librarian of King's College, London, also acting as chaplain of the hospital and in 1854-58 lecturer in geography. On 7 June 1844 he had been priested by the bishop of London, and until 1866 was a fellow of the Royal Geographical Society. He also published many papers and books on geography, history and social matters. Perhaps his greatest achievement was in 1848 when he joined F. D. Maurice in founding Queen's College, London, the first institution for higher education of women in England. He served Queen's as dean, deputy-chairman, and professor of geography and ancient history until 1856 when he resigned because of dissension. He accepted appointment as chaplain to the British residents of Bahia, Brazil, and was elected a fellow of King's College, University of London, and an honorary fellow of Queen's.

The Church of St George in Bahia had been consecrated in 1857 by Bishop M. B. Hale [q.v.] on his way to take up his see in Perth; he also paid part of Nicolay's salary at Bahia. Nicolay remained in Brazil until he went on leave to England in 1867. Next year the subscribers to his church sought his resignation. Left without a charge until 1870, he was appointed chaplain at Geraldton in Western Australia.

Nicolay arrived at Fremantle in the *Lady Louisa* on 25 April. His immediate interest in the colony's affairs and resources impressed Governor Weld and F. P. Barlee [q.v.]. Soon after moving to Geraldton in June he recommended the establishment of an experimental coffee plantation as the climate seemed similar to those parts of Brazil where coffee flourished. In July Weld authorized the creation of a reserve west of the Moresby Range. There Nicolay planted coffee seed from Aden and later from Brazil but by December 1873 the experiment had failed and he recommended sale of the reserve. In July 1874 a syndicate bought the *Western Australian Times* and made him editor. He tried to combine his chaplaincy at Geraldton with his editorial duties in Perth but Hale made him resign from Geraldton. He was probably editor until 1875. In 1886-87 he wrote a series of editorials on European politics for the *Inquirer*.

For the government from December 1873 to May 1874 Nicolay had investigated the feasibility of cutting a canal between the coast and the lower reaches of the Swan River, thus making its deep part into the main harbour for Fremantle. He favoured the canal but it was rejected by a committee with other schemes. His role of editor and government adviser was scathingly criticized in the *Herald*. In 1875 he was commissioned to lead an expedition to investigate reports of coal in the Fitzgerald River near the south coast. Though condemned by the *Inquirer* for lack of qualifications, he appears to have led the expedition ably and showed that the area had no significant coal.

In 1876 Governor Robinson commissioned Nicolay to prepare a 'Handbook of Western Australia' for prospective migrants. The manuscript was completed in August 1877 but not published until 1880. He revised the work and in 1896 brought out a second edition, but it did not reach the standard of the first. In 1877 he had prepared a report for the Intelligence Branch of the War Office on the colony's defence organization. He was then acting as curate in the parish of Perth and as chaplain at the gaol. In 1878-93 he was chaplain at the Fremantle convict establishment. In 1880-82 he helped to teach divinity students at Bishop's College, Perth.

Nicolay was the founder of Western Australia's first public museum. In 1881 Robinson authorized him to begin a collection of rocks and minerals. Housed in the old guard-room at the convict establishment, the collection had several names and as the Geological Museum was transferred in 1889-90 to the old gaol building in Perth as the first part of the Western Australian Museum. In the 1880s he had advised the government on minerals sent in for examination and on the geology of the Guildford-Clackline railway route. In 1886 he prepared a circular on prospecting for gold and published *Some notes on the geology of Western Australia* and *Notes on the Aborigines of Western Australia* for the Colonial and Indian Exhibition. He also became involved in a dispute with E. T. Hardman [q.v.] over the incorrect labelling of some specimens deposited in the Geological Museum. Hardman was scathing in his criticism but Nicolay's reply was dignified: he had 'never assumed the character of an accomplished geologist' and his 'knowledge of geology, was, originally, such as was required for me as Professor of Physical Geography, the only one then in London'.

Nicolay was keen and sympathetic for Aboriginal welfare. His humanitarian views, ably expressed in the *Handbook*, were far more liberal than those of most contemporaries. In 1878 he was responsible for the governor setting aside an Aboriginal reserve of 50,000 acres in the upper Murchison area. In 1892-97 he served on the Aborigines Protection Board. Predeceased by his invalid wife on 31 January 1887, he died suddenly at Fremantle on 9 May 1897. Descendants still live in Western Australia.

Nicolay was talented but suffered through his lack of a university degree. He appears to have had no deep interest in the church but was a humanist with broad interests in science. Unhappily his quick temper antagonized some people, resulting in frequent conflicts which seriously influenced his career.

JRWAHS, 7 (1969); P. E. Playford and I. Pridmore, Reverend C. G. Nicolay—biographical data, file PR5382 (Battye Lib, Perth).

PHILLIP E. PLAYFORD
I. PRIDMORE

NICOLL, BRUCE BAIRD (1851-1904), shipowner and politician, was born on 3 October 1851 in Sydney, second son of George Robertson Nicoll (d. 1901), shipwright and shipowner, and his wife Sarah (d. 1897), née Baird. At 6 he went with his parents and brother George Wallace (1848-1906) to Scotland, where he was educated at Dundee. Returning to Sydney about 1864, he worked in his father's shipping office. He and his brother then started business as commission agents and shipowners and

from 1871 they ran the first regular and rapid passenger and cargo service to the northern rivers; it led to closer settlement and the growth of Lismore, Casino, Coraki and Ballina. After 1877 they began to build and import steamers at the rate of one a year. In twelve years they spent over £250,000 on about twenty steamships and wharfage and dockage facilities.

In evidence before the parliamentary standing committee on public works on 10 July 1889 Nicoll claimed that wrecks and repairs to steamers had cost him £22,500 in 1880-89. He estimated the value of the imports and exports of the Richmond River at about £1 million and the population increase from about 2000 to about 20,000. On dissolution of the partnership in the mid-1880s he concentrated on the Richmond River trade while his brother sent his ships to Coffs Harbour, Woolgoolga, Tweed River, Byron Bay and Brisbane as well as to the South Sea Islands and the New South Wales south coast. In the 1890s both brothers were absorbed by the North Coast Steam Navigation Co.

A protectionist, Nicoll was one of three representatives in 1889-94 for the Richmond in the Legislative Assembly; he favoured payment of members, an elective Upper House, the taxing of large estates, the proposed Grafton-Tweed railway and local public works. In October 1889 he represented Ballina at the first National Protection Conference in Sydney. Fluent and energetic, he concentrated on communications, land and marine matters and was a diligent local member. He was a republican, staunch federationist and president of the New South Wales branch of the Australian Natives' Association. On 5 June 1890 he told the assembly that Federation on the American model was desirable for economic and defence reasons and would mean 'intercolonial free trade and protection against the outside world'. He favoured Australian-born governors and the abolition of 'flimsy' and 'shoddy' imperial titles and honours. He also saw Asian immigration as 'a racial danger to the future of the Australian people'. In March 1892 he accused Sir Henry Parkes [q.v.] of putting Federation into the background 'to please the labor party'. President of the Corowa Conference in August 1893, he criticized Sir George Dibbs's [q.v.] Federation scheme of 1894 and was vice-president of the Bathurst Convention in 1896. He was also a founder and original shareholder of the *Australian Star*, the protectionists' organ.

A member of the Union and Reform Clubs, Nicoll was respected, popular and generous; in 1886 he had given £500 to assist the families of those lost in the *Ly-ee-*

Q

moon disaster. In December 1903 when alighting from a tram he was injured and his health began to fail; he died at his residence, Hillview, Boulevarde, Dulwich Hill, on 18 September 1904 and was buried in the Presbyterian cemetery, Rookwood. At the Presbyterian Church in Elizabeth Street, Sydney, he had married Jane Ann Zahel on 1 March 1873, and was survived by three sons.

George Wallace Nicoll died at his residence, Blink Bonnie, William Street, Canterbury, on 4 November 1906 and was buried in the Presbyterian cemetery, Rookwood. His estate was sworn for probate at £60,114. He was survived by two sons and a daughter of his first wife, Helen McDonald, and by his second wife Janet Constance (d. 1932), daughter of William Lewins, and by their five sons.

L. T. Daley, *Men and a river* (Melb, 1966); E. Digby (ed), *Australian men of mark*, 2 (Syd, 1889); V&P (LA NSW), 1889, 5, 516; SMH, 19 Feb 1889, 16 June 1890, 19, 20 Sept 1904, 5 Nov 1906; *Town and Country J*, 30 Mar 1889; *Argus*, 23, 25 Jan 1890.   G. P. WALSH

NICOLLE, EUGENE DOMINIQUE (1823-1909), refrigeration engineer, was born at Rouen, France, son of Pierre Nicolle, florist. His scientific training in Rouen was thorough and after experience with French and English engineering works he arrived in Australia in 1853. By 1855 he was practising as an engineer in Sydney and in New Zealand married Jane, née Williams, in 1859; their first child was born two years later in Sydney.

Nicolle was managing the Wilkinsons' sawmill in Sydney when his first ice-making patent was registered in 1861 in the names of himself and Richard Dawson. Next year Nicolle, Dawson and the Wilkinson brothers bought the Sydney Ice Co. from P. N. Russell and James Harrison [qq.v.] of Geelong with the franchise to use Harrison's machine in New South Wales. They moved the factory from George Street to land leased by Nicolle and Dawson in Paddington and began producing ice with Nicolle's machine in 1863. He had built an improved machine when the enthusiasm of Augustus Morris [q.v.] diverted him to designing refrigerating machinery for ships. Plans were prepared and a public meeting in 1866 unsuccessfully appealed for subscriptions to finance the construction and trial of a model. In the summer of 1866-67 Nicolle and Morris persuaded T. S. Mort [q.v.] that the scheme was practical.

With Mort's support at the renamed New South Wales Ice Co. Nicolle demonstrated in 1867 that with his machinery food could be frozen for long periods, thawed, cooked and eaten. A public subscription for a trial shipment of meat to England in 1868 proved premature as shipboard refrigeration posed problems not met on shore. Mort continued his support over the next ten years. In that time they designed, patented and produced a variety of refrigerating devices, including one for domestic use and another for making powdered milk, equipped a large cold-store at Darling Harbour in 1872, and produced refrigerated railway vans for meat and milk, but failed to develop a machine ideally suited to ships. The seven main apparatuses Nicolle constructed relied, successively, on systems based on ammonia absorption, air expansion, low pressure ammonia absorption and ammonia reabsorption. He was a pioneer in developing these heat exchange systems and the mechanical contrivances by which they were made effective.

In 1875 Nicolle sold Mort his interest in all their patents except one, together with the lease of the ice-works; Mort made them over to the newly-formed New South Wales Fresh Food and Ice Co., at the same time guaranteeing Nicolle a three-year appointment as consulting engineer. In 1877 the *Northam* sailed without the trial shipment of frozen meat financed by public subscription, but with the ineffective refrigerating equipment installed by Nicolle and the company. Next year his contract expired and Mort died. Nicolle went to England and France with his family and on the return voyage his wife died in 1879 and was buried in Adelaide. He retired to a 300-acre property he owned near Wollongong and remarried. He died on 23 November 1909 and was buried in the Anglican cemetery at Wollongong. He was survived by a son, twin daughters and a stepdaughter. His estate was sworn for probate at £18,000.

A. Barnard, *Visions and profits* (Melb, 1961); N. Selfe, 'A pioneer refrigerating engineer', *Ice and Refrigeration*, Apr 1899; J. Jervis, 'Notes on the lives of Augustus Morris and Eugene Dominique Nicolle', JRAHS, 34 (1948).
                                                  ALAN BARNARD

NIMMO, JOHN (1819-1904), surveyor, businessman and parliamentarian, was born on 20 October 1819 in Catrine, Ayrshire, Scotland, son of John Nimmo, mason, and his wife Janet, née McClure. Trained in Glasgow, he arrived at Melbourne in the *Abdallah* with his wife Catherine, née Kelly, in July 1853. He had some capital and is said to have set up in his own contracting business but the shipping lists show him as a grocer, and his first recorded actions involve the separation of Emerald Hill (South Melbourne) from the Melbourne City Council in May 1855. He was appointed collector of rates and inspector of lodging-houses and nuisances for Emerald Hill in September; the post was divided in May 1856 and he was surveyor and inspector until September 1863. His major business interests thereafter are obscure. He was in coffee and spice wholesaling for some years and then moved into big business, misplacing his confidence in James Mirams [q.v.] and joining the directorates of the Essendon Land Tramway and Investment Co. (later Essendon Land and Finance Association), the Federal Coffee Palace and the Premier Permanent Building Land and Investment Association; he was chairman of the last two.

Mirams probably exploited Nimmo's reputation for honesty. Like most of his contemporaries, Nimmo had been optimistic to the point of irresponsibility; however, it was his initial investigations that led to the collapse of the Premier Permanent in 1889. At the resulting trials for fraud and conspiracy in October-December 1890 his probity was not challenged; he said that he lost everything in the Premier Permanent and could not afford a barrister for his defence. He did not use any of his directorates for unethical private gain and did not go bankrupt.

Nimmo identified closely with Emerald Hill and was a popular figure. In 1867-76 he was a councillor and three times mayor in 1869-73. He was appointed a justice of the peace in 1868 and regularly attended the bench, gaining an early reputation for rash judgments born of inexperience. Admired for his declamatory skill, especially with Burns's poetry, he was president of the St Kilda (later Royal Alfred) Bowling Club, and a somewhat passive vice-president of such important temperance institutions as the Victorian Alliance for the Suppression of the Liquor Traffic, the Victorian Band of Hope Union and the International Temperance Conventions of 1880 and 1888. He was also a commissioner for the Melbourne International Exhibition of 1880. A tall man, cartoonists loved him for his flashing dark looks which they kept in a state of round-eyed surprise.

As the candidate of the National Reform and Protection League, Nimmo was elected to the Legislative Assembly in 1877, and for sixteen years remained at the head of successive polls for Emerald Hill (Albert Park after 1889). He was above all the voice of his locality but accepted his share of parliamentary duties and sat on three royal commissions and eight select committees. His reasonable advocacy was important to the

success of legislation to curb the retail trade in alcohol in the 1880s.

Nimmo was gazetted a commissioner of the Melbourne Harbor Trust in December 1878 and for seven years protected its interests in the House. In 1880 he introduced a Harbor Trust amendment bill and chaired the select committee appointed to consider it. The report in November recommended the widening of the Yarra and the trust's control of the new Princes Bridge, which Nimmo opened in October 1888 as minister of public works. He resigned from the trust when he accepted this office in the Gillies [q.v.]-Deakin government in February 1886; in March he received the complementary posts of commissioner of public works and vice-president of the Board of Land and Works, which put him in charge of water supply. This association and the longer one with the Harbor Trust have been a source of confusion for most early biographers.

Nimmo's elevation was not well received by conservatives or radicals and in June 1889 he was asked to resign. He remained a Deakinite and did not cross the floor in support of the no confidence motion which put James Munro [q.v.] in office in November 1890. Discouraged by business losses and his failure at the elections of April 1892, Nimmo returned to Catrine in 1894 and lived in retirement. Predeceased by his wife, he died on 11 March 1904; they had no children.

Garryowen (E. Finn), The chronicles of early Melbourne, 2 (Melb, 1888); A. Sutherland et al, Victoria and it metropolis, 2 (Melb, 1888); B. Hoare, Jubilee history of the Melbourne Harbor Trust (Melb, 1927); C. Daley, The history of South Melbourne (Melb, 1940); M. Cannon, The land boomers (Melb, 1966); Argus, Oct-Dec 1890, 21 Apr 1904; Age, 21 Apr 1892; Table Talk, 20 July 1894; J. E. Parnaby, The economic and political development of Victoria, 1877-1881 (Ph.D. thesis, Univ Melb, 1951); R. J. Moore, Marvellous Melbourne: a social history of Melbourne in the eighties (M.A. thesis, Univ Melb, 1958); M. G. Finlayson, Victorian politics 1889-94 (M.A. thesis, Univ Melb, 1964); A. M. Mitchell, Temperance and the liquor question in later nineteenth century Victoria (M.A. thesis, Univ Melb, 1966); Minute books 1855-63 (South Melbourne Council).   ANN M. MITCHELL

NOBELIUS, CARL AXEL (1851-1921), orchardist and nurseryman, was born on 19 June 1851 in Tampere, Finland, eldest child of Carl Petter Nobelius, horticulturist, and his wife Louisa Amalia. His parents were related to Alfred Bernhard Nobel (1833-1896) and had migrated to Finland from Gefle, Sweden.

Nobelius was trained in horticulture and in February 1871 arrived in Melbourne. He was employed first in the Toorak nurseries of Taylor & Sangster. Later he moved to the nurseries of Joseph Harris in South Yarra, a step that had consequences, because Harris was an important influence in forging close links between himself, Brunning [q.v.], Rimington, Cheeseman and Nobelius. Before 1900 these men were to control much of the nursery trade in Melbourne and were largely responsible for its successful combination of aggressive business drive, massive exports, strict quality control and restless inventiveness. Nobelius was tall and strong and had great energy. About 1884 he bought land near Emerald in the Dandenong Hills and for years went each Saturday afternoon by train to Narre Warren terminus and then walked sixteen miles to his land, where he cleared, cultivated and planted before walking back to catch the Sunday night train. By 1890 he had established his business at Emerald; fifty acres of orchard and nursery were under cultivation and he was doing well with raspberries and strawberries as well as hard fruit for the markets in Melbourne and Sydney. One handicap was the cost of carting his produce to Narre Warren by bullock drays, but he told the parliamentary standing committee on railways in 1898 that 'all these ranges ought to be planted with apples [which] are not suffering from the drought this year in the slightest'. In 1903 he was able to advertise a million trees for sale. By 1914 his 'Gembrook Nurseries' held two million stock trees, produced quantities of apples and pears, and conducted a huge export trade with other Australian States and overseas with New Zealand, South Africa, India, Japan, Europe and South America. The size of export is indicated by annual shipments of 400,000 tree stock to South Africa alone.

Nobelius's experimental skill and persistent advertising persuaded countless Australian country towns to line their streets with European shade trees and he made other contributions to Victorian horticulture, including a revival in the cultivation of flax. But the great heart of his business was the propagation and sale of fruit trees and fruit tree stock, augmented by a large apple and pear orchard which he established at Freshwater on the Tamar River in Tasmania.

The nurseries, which were run as a family business by Nobelius and four sons and which sometimes employed almost every wage-earner within reach, dominated the economic and social life of the Emerald-Gembrook district. The high period ended when the outbreak of World War I in August 1914 destroyed the export trade

and compelled contraction and reorganization, but in 1920 the nursery was said to be still the largest south of the equator. Nobelius died of pneumonia at his home in Emerald on 31 December 1921. Predeceased by his first wife Emily Jane, née Brightwell, whom he had married on 5 January 1877, he was survived by his second wife Mary Louise, née Holdsworth, and by five sons and three daughters. By direction of his will the nurseries and orchards were sold and the proceeds divided within the family. A son regained control of the central nursery and held it until 1955.

J. Lyng, *The Scandinavians in Australia* ... (Melb, 1939); Nettie Palmer, *The Dandenongs*, 2nd ed (Melb, 1953); H. Coulson, *Story of the Dandenongs, 1838-1958* (Melb, 1959); E. E. Pescott, 'The pioneers of horticulture in Victoria', VHM, 18 (1940).

R. F. ERICKSEN

NORMANBY, GEORGE AUGUSTUS CONSTANTINE PHIPPS, 2nd MARQUESS (1819-1890), governor, was born on 23 July 1819 in London, only son of the 1st marquess of Normanby and his wife Maria Lydell, daughter of Lord Ravensworth. Styled earl of Mulgrave he served in the Scots Fusilier Guards in 1838-46, represented Scarborough in 1847-50 and 1852-57 in parliament, was comptroller in 1851-52 and treasurer in 1853-58 of the Queen's household, and lieut-governor of Nova Scotia in 1858 until succeeding as marquess in 1863. He had been a privy councillor from 1851, and was appointed G.C.M.G. in 1877 and G.C.B. in 1885. In Yorkshire on 17 August 1844 he had married Laura (d. 1885), daughter of Captain Robert Russell, R.N.; they had four sons and three daughters.

Normanby was governor of Queensland in 1871-74, New Zealand in 1874-78 and Victoria in 1879-84. Despite his origins he saw himself as a career governor, possibly as his Yorkshire estates brought him no more than £7000 a year. In the colonies he was described as safe and sagacious, a moderate conservative who could be trusted to take the sting out of awkward situations and to blunt the energies of thrusting demagogues. His term in Queensland coincided mainly with A. H. Palmer's [q.v.] premiership which ended with narrow majorities but produced no major constitutional crises. Prosperity was returning and exploration renewed. The governor travelled widely and his titles were duly honoured in the naming of the Normanby and Mulgrave Rivers, electoral districts and various streets.

On transfer to Victoria in February 1879, Normanby found Graham Berry [q.v.] in power and the conservatives incensed at the preceding governor, Bowen, for allegedly favouring Berry in the controversy over the Legislative Council's powers. In 1880 Normanby granted dissolutions to Berry and his opponent Service [q.v.], but neither election returned the outgoing ministry or brought political stability. Irritated at Berry's tactics in overthrowing the Service ministry in June, Normanby refused to authorize a third election after Berry requested it in 1881. Instead the O'Loghlen [q.v.] ministry was commissioned and survived until granted a dissolution in 1883 when it was ousted by the Service-Berry coalition. In all these manoeuvres Normanby was an experienced interpreter of current constitutional practice and kept the Colonial Office's approval although his impartiality tended to bear harder on reformers than on conservatives.

Normanby was a 'whip' of no common order: at full gallop he habitually drove his coach through the back gate of Government House with only an inch or so to spare. He rarely missed an important race meeting. He also enjoyed the hospitality of such pastoralists as Sir Samuel Wilson and W. J. Clarke [qq.v.] whose baronetcy he recommended, but some called his own public entertaining 'plain and unassuming' while H. G. Turner [q.v.] wrote of his 'frigid parsimony'. Other landmarks of his governorship included the opening of the Melbourne International Exhibition in 1880 and the signing of Ned Kelly's [q.v.] death warrant.

His wife suffered from a heart disease and in January 1884 Normanby announced his resignation on the ground of her ill health and his own. In April they left for London where she died on 26 January 1885. 'Entirely altered', he visited Australia in 1887-88 and then settled at Brighton, Sussex. He died on 3 April 1890 and was buried in Yorkshire. Descendants of his third son live in Queensland.

H. G. Turner, *A history of the colony of Victoria*, 2 (Lond, 1904); J. Rutherford, *Sir George Grey* (Lond, 1961); *Graphic*, 29 July 1871; *A'sian Sketcher*, 18 Jan 1879; *Illustrated Aust News*, 21 Mar 1879, 16 Apr 1880; *Imperial Review* (Melb), June 1880; *Australasian*, 19 Jan 1884, 31 Jan 1885; *Argus*, 5 Apr 1890.

G. C. BOLTON

NORTH, JOHN BRITTY (1831-1917), stockbroker and mining agent, was born in Taunton, Somerset, England, son of John Britty North, merchant, and his wife Mary, née Willis. At 9 he moved to London with his parents and at 13 went to work for Self,

Coles & Co., warehousemen, and stayed for seven years. He reached Sydney in the barque *Senator* in February 1852.

In 1853 North visited London with £1000 to buy goods for North, Rutherford & Wilson, merchants, a partnership he joined that year. He returned to Sydney in the *Windsor* on 2 November with some of his family. In 1855 he left the firm before it was declared bankrupt in 1856 and North, who had contributed little capital, received a certificate of discharge in 1857. He probably spent five years in Queensland but by 1861 he was again working in New South Wales, first as a commercial traveller. Later he became a wholesale wine and spirits merchant, at first with G. S. Leathes & Co. and in 1864-67 on his own in Wynyard Street, Sydney. In 1867 he added the business of an auctioneer and commission agent and as J. B. North & Co. borrowed the price of his auctioneer's licence from his sister-in-law, Mrs Weynton.

In 1871 'heavy amounts paid for interest and the depression of the times' made North bankrupt again, but by 1872 he had discharged his debts, and twelve months after its foundation joined the Sydney Stock Exchange. In the 1870s with Robert Henry Reynolds, whom he later bought out, he began to mine for coal in the Jamieson Valley near Katoomba. Once, without machinery and with only a few men, he hauled a 4-cwt block of coal 1100 ft. up the slopes to exhibit it in Sydney where it secured for North a government contract. An exacting employer, North had over a hundred men at his Katoomba Coal Mine which in 1878 he registered as a company. It was awarded a certificate at the Sydney International Exhibition of 1879 for the excellent steaming qualities of its coal.

In 1880 North located a seam of the reddish purple kerosene shale at the Ruined Castle in the Jamieson Valley and in 1882 sent his manager to prospect it. North and his son John took up 1392 acres as mineral conditional purchases. In 1885 North bought £36,000 worth of equipment, formed the Katoomba Coal and Shale Co. Ltd and became managing director. To remove the shale he employed a Scottish engineer to build an elevated tramway 200 ft. high for two miles across the valley but it was a structural failure and the company went into voluntary liquidation in February 1892.

The tenacious North had reconstructed the Australian Kerosene Oil and Mineral Co. Ltd. It leased the Jamieson Valley property and worked it successfully with T. S. Mort's [q.v.] Glen Shale mine on the western side of the Megalong ridge, which North had bought in 1890. The two mines were linked by tunnels and continued to yield good quality shale until 1895. The 20,000 tons of shale exported, worth £4-£10 a ton, yielded up to a hundred gallons of oil to the ton. It was refined in Italy and shipped back to the colonies as kerosene. For some time coal lying above and below the shale was extracted but by 1897 it proved unprofitable and the mine was closed; all the machinery had been removed by 1903. After the mine closed North continued as a Pitt Street stockbroker and colliery agent for many mining companies with his sons John and Alfred as partners at different times. In 1917, although retired, North was governing director of Main Range Collieries & Estate Ltd and Alfred was chairman of the Stock Exchange.

Probably from commercial motives North actively promoted the growth of Katoomba, especially its development as a tourist resort. Chairman of the progress committee which achieved the incorporation of Katoomba in 1889, he served briefly as an alderman on the council. He was also a trustee of Katoomba, Leura, Banksia and Echo Parks. He died at his home, Lynton, Wahroonga, on 14 October 1917 and was buried in the Gore Hill cemetery beside his wife Clarissa Mary Hack (d. 1906), a niece of David Jones [q.v.]; they had married in 1855. A Nonconformist, he was survived by two sons and six daughters. His estate was sworn at £19,660 and the firm, J. & J. North, was still operating in 1973.

H. Wood et al, *Mineral products of New South Wales* (Syd, 1887); E. Digby (ed), *Australian men of mark*, 2 (Syd, 1889); J. E. Carne, *The kerosene shale deposits of New South Wales* (Syd, 1903); P. W. Spriggs, *Our Blue Mountains yesterdays* (Leura, 1962); J. R. Bennett, *The Katoomba coal mine* (Blue Mountains Hist Soc, Katoomba, 1972); V&P (LA NSW), 1879-80, 4, 327, 1887-88, 7, 296, 1888-89, 1, 46, 1889, 2, 91; *Shipping Gazette* (Syd), Feb 1852; *SMH*, 16 Oct 1917; *Blue Mountain Echo*, 26 Oct 1917; Bankruptcy files 3646, 10526, 10526/7 (NSWA); information from Mr D. A. and Dr A. L. North, Leura.

SUZANNE EDGAR

NORTON, ALBERT (1836-1914), pastoralist and politician, was born on 1 January 1836 in Sydney, eighth child of James Norton [q.v.] and his first wife Jane, née Mackenzie. Educated at Fred Wilkinson's school, Meads, near Ashfield, he left in 1852 to gain experience in grazing both as employee and partner in New England. He travelled with stock in the west of Victoria, New South Wales and Queensland, and in 1861 bought a station at Rodd's Bay near Port Curtis, where he settled and began to breed cattle, becoming a successful pastoralist.

Norton was defeated by Arthur Palmer [q.v.] for the Legislative Assembly seat of Port Curtis in 1866. In September 1867 he was called to the Legislative Council but resigned next May. Invited in 1878 to represent the Port Curtis District in the assembly after the Redistribution Act, he was elected unopposed. He supported Thomas McIlwraith [q.v.] particularly in the passing of Acts relating to divisional boards, the three million loan, licensing boards, local works loans, railway companies, preliminary immigration, settled districts pastoral leases and tramways. He gave strong support to the British India Co. mail contract via Torres Strait, which was later justified by its advantages to the colony. For eight months in 1883 he was secretary of public works and mines in McIlwraith's government and later supported him in Opposition. Norton was elected Speaker in June 1888 and served until defeated in April 1893. In August he was called to the Legislative Council, where he was chairman of committees in 1902-07 and held his seat until 1914.

Norton was a voracious reader in a wide variety of subjects. His speeches were noted for care in preparation and reliability in figures and references as well as relevance. Though his interests were mainly pastoral he also encouraged mining interests to develop the colony's mining resources. He opposed payment for members of parliament but when it was introduced he applied a large portion of his salary to establishing the School of Arts in Port Curtis, where he provided mineralogical lectures, and distributed the balance amongst schools in his district. A trustee of the Royal Society of Queensland, he contributed ten papers to its *Proceedings*. He was also a prolific writer both for the press and the *Antiquarian Gazette* in which he later related some of his early experiences at Leichhardt in New England and the western areas.

At Longford, Tasmania, on 12 February 1862 he had married Mary Elizabeth Ann Walker. She died on 10 March 1863, survived by one daughter. At Sydney in 1866 he married Harriet Maule Deacon; they had one son. In 1900 at Brisbane he married Amy Symes Barton who survived Norton when he died at Brisbane on 11 March 1914. He was buried in Toowong cemetery with Anglican rites.

Roy Soc Qld, Procs, 1914; *SMH*, 19 July 1906; *Brisbane Courier*, 12 Mar 1914.

NORTON, JAMES (1824-1906), solicitor, was born on 5 December 1824 in Sydney, eldest son of James Norton [q.v.] and his first wife Jane, née Mackenzie. He was educated at W. and W. T. Cape's [qq.v.] schools, Sydney College in 1835-39, by Rev. J. F. Walpole as tutor in 1840 and under Rev. Robert Forrest [q.v.] at Campbelltown in 1841. In 1842 he was articled to his father, admitted a solicitor on 2 July 1848 and joined his father as Norton & Son, later Norton, Son & Barker. On 1 June 1854 at Longford, Tasmania, he married Harriet Mary (d. 1860), daughter of deputy-commissary-general Thomas Walker [q.v.], and in 1859 bought Ecclesbourne, Double Bay. On 31 December 1862 he married Isabella, sister of Professor W. J. Stephens [q.v.]. A notary public from 1860, Norton became senior partner of his firm, Norton, Smith & Co., and solicitor to the University of Sydney from 1886. His clients included Sir Edward Macarthur [q.v.].

Norton was also a director of the Australian Gaslight Co., the North Shore Gas Co. and the Australian Joint Stock Bank, a fellow of St Paul's College in the University of Sydney from 1869, an alderman of Double Bay from 1873, an elected trustee of the Australian Museum in 1874-1906, and a trustee of Hyde, Phillip and Cook Parks from 1878 and chairman in 1894-1904. A trustee of the Free Public Library from 1878, he was its chairman in 1890-1906 and as D. S. Mitchell's [q.v.] legal adviser was greatly interested in the building of the Mitchell Library. In 1879 he became a trustee of the Zoological Station, Watson's Bay, and was president of the royal commission on the working of the Real Property Acts and on 7 October was nominated to the Legislative Council. A strong critic of the purity of Sydney's water supply, he advocated its filtering. On 2 May 1884 he became postmaster-general in Alexander Stuart's [q.v.] ministry, but Governor Loftus reported that although Norton was highly 'esteemed his appointment has not been favourably received by public opinion'. When the ministry fell in October 1885 he was criticized by the Daily Telegraph as a 'respectable incapable'.

A member of the Royal Society of New South Wales from 1873, Norton became a founder of the Linnean Society of New South Wales in 1875 and served on its council in 1878-79 and 1881-1906, as treasurer in 1882-97 and president in 1899 and 1900. An 'observer rather than a writer', he studied the indigenous flora and was an ardent horticulturist and vice-president of the Horticultural Society of New South Wales in the 1870s. He met informally with Stephens, R. D. FitzGerald [q.v.] and Edwin Daintree to compare their botanical collections. Norton was very proud of the 'trees and shrubs, especially those of indigenous species, which he cultivated in his fine old garden'. Each spring when his South African bulbs flowered at Ecclesbourne he had a garden party and delighted in his country estate at Springwood where he safeguarded the native plants and compiled a census of its flora. In June 1890 he read a paper on Australian Birds. Useful and Noxious to the conference of fruit-growers and vine-growers, which was published in its report. Earlier that year St Andrews University awarded him an honorary doctorate of laws. In 1891 he was elected a member of the Royal Geographical Society of Australia. He had a fine collection of Australian books and was a committee member of the Union Club.

Norton died at Ecclesbourne on 18 July 1906 and was buried in the Anglican section of Rookwood cemetery. He was survived by a son and two daughters of his first wife, and by his second wife and their son and daughter. His estate was sworn for probate at £43,000. FitzGerald named a rare Blue Mountain orchid Adenochilus Nortoni after him.

The Nortons of Sussex and New South Wales (Syd, 1912); Linnean Soc NSW, Procs, 32 (1907); J. H. Maiden, 'Records of Australian botanists', Roy Soc NSW, Procs, 42 (1908); SMH, 13 July 1906; C. H. Bertie, 'Pioneer families', Home, May 1933; MS cat (ML); CO 201/600, 603.   K. G. ALLARS*

O

OAKDEN, PERCY (1845-1917), architect and surveyor, was born at Launceston, Van Diemen's Land, second son of Philip Oakden [q.v.] and his wife Georgiana, née Cowie. Educated at Horton College, Ross, he was one of the first five to take the Tasmanian Council of Education's degree of Associate of Arts in 1860. He served his articles with Henry Hunter [q.v.] of Hobart in 1861-65. He then went to London and worked under Sir Matthew Digby Wyatt as well as attending Professor Thomas Hayter Lewis's lectures at University College and in 1867 winning the first award of the Donaldson silver medal. He also became an associate of the Royal Institute of British Architects.

Oakden went to Victoria in 1868 and practised for six years at Ballarat; as borough architect he was responsible in 1870 for modifying Lorenz's design for the town hall. He practised with J. H. Fox in 1869-72, his works including the large wooden St John's Presbyterian Church, Peel Street (1871), the Clunes Town Hall (1872) and in Melbourne the Congregational Church in Victoria Parade (1871-72, demolished), and the Wesleyan Church, Sydney Road, Brunswick (1872).

Oakden moved to Melbourne and on 1 January 1874 became the partner of Leonard Terry [q.v.] though the oeuvre of the partners remained largely distinct. The year after Terry died the firm published an illustrated work, What to Build and How to Build It (Melbourne, 1885), which can be seen not only as a promotional exercise but as Oakden's attempt to recast the firm's image on his own more progressive lines. The book advocated exposed brick walls (a characteristic of Oakden's work) which were to be made waterproof by means of a cavity, an extra thickness of brick or painted with silicate solutions; it also disparaged ornamental cast-iron work in favour of 'the Italian system of stone balconies and balconettes', preferred tiles as the roofing most appropriate to brick buildings and concrete as 'a splendid walling material' not yet used in the colony, and gave a brief account of pisé construction.

With their former pupil, Nahum Barnet, the partners in 1883 had won a competition for the design of the working men's college (Royal Melbourne Institute of Technology) and were jointly responsible for the first building in 1885-87; the La Trobe Street front and tower were later designed by Oakden, Addison & Kemp, and begun in 1891. Oakden probably had a large part in the competition design, and that for Allan [q.v.] & Co.'s building in Collins Street (1877; destroyed by fire, 1956), which was Gothic at the client's express request, but in the firm's other major works Oakden's personal contribution cannot be distinguished. It is apparent in many of the numerous church and school buildings, beginning with the Wesleyan Church in Nicholson Street, North Fitzroy (1874; attributed on stylistic grounds), and including state schools at King Street, West Melbourne, and at Wilson Street, Brighton (both 1875), the Church of England Girls Grammar School, South Yarra, and Wesleyan Churches at Dana and Lydiard Streets, Ballarat (1884), at Sackville Street, Collingwood (1886), and at Williams and Toorak Roads, Toorak (1887).

Oakden's buildings are characteristically of brown brick with cream, warm red and other brick dressings and patterns, often serrated about the arches, and are to some extent a Gothic equivalent of Joseph Reed's [q.v.] Lombardic Romanesque. He also worked in stone on two very personal commissions at Ross, Tasmania, a Wesleyan chapel and a new building for Horton College, and traces of Oakden's detailing can be seen in the bluestone St Matthew's Church of England, Prahran (1877-80). Some common characteristics of his work in both stone and brick are paired and multiple Gothic windows, decorated period tracery, stone corbels used to widen the base of gables in porches and bell-cotes, heavily moulded arches supported on slimmer shafts, octagonal towers and spires, and pierced quatrefoil parapets.

G. H. M. Addison had joined the firm in 1885 and took charge of a Brisbane branch while also supervising work at Perth and elsewhere; Henry H. Kemp joined in 1886, and in 1887 both were admitted to partnership as Oakden, Addison & Kemp. Their works included the Queen's Coffee Palace at Rathdowne and Victoria Streets, Carlton (1887; demolished), Queen's College in the University of Melbourne (1883-87) and the dining hall wing (1889-90), and in Collins Street the New Zealand Insurance Co.'s offices (1888). In conjunction with John Beswicke the firm designed the twelvestorey Australian Building, then Melbourne's tallest, in Elizabeth Street (1889), with Nathaniel Billing & Son the Y.M.C.A. building at Westwood Place and Bourke Street (1890), and with Lloyd Tayler [q.v.], Lambert & Sons' premises in Collins Street (1890).

Oakden's hand is probably evident in the

Y.M.C.A. building, its busy, clumsy Renaissance design recalling the Clunes Town Hall. The polychrome Gothic of the New Zealand Insurance building is directly related to the earlier Allan's building, but perhaps shows something of Kemp's as well as Oakden's hand. Oakden seems to have been responsible for the Tudor design of Queen's College and Wesleyan Churches, now in a style of less strident polychromy, at Albert Park (1890) and Male Street, Brighton (1891).

In 1892 the firm became Oakden & Kemp, but the practice dwindled in the depression. Kemp left for Sydney late in 1895 and the partnership dissolved next year. In 1901 Cedric H. Ballantyne, who had been Oakden's pupil and then his chief draftsman, joined him in a partnership which was responsible for the City Club, Lister House, the New Zealand Loan and Mercantile Agency Co.'s offices at the corner of Collins and King Streets, Champion's buildings and others.

Oakden was standing architect to the Fire Brigades Board and designed No. 2 Metropolitan Fire Station, was honorary treasurer and honorary architect to the Consumptive Hospital at Echuca, a life governor of the Melbourne Children's Hospital, a board member of the Y.M.C.A., and a deputy-grand master of the Grand Lodge of Freemasons. He was honorary director of architectural classes at the Working Men's College and at the University of Melbourne a member of the engineering faculty and coexaminer in architecture from 1906. He was a member of the Metropolitan Board of Works Inquiry Board. He was elected a fellow and councillor of the Royal Victorian Institute of Architects in 1890, vice-president in 1891-92 and president for 1892-93, 1896-97 and 1901. In 1902 at the Hobart meeting of the Australasian Association for the Advancement of Science he was president of Section H and read a paper on 'The relation of architecture to engineering'. In 1916 his health failed and he retired. He was a practising Wesleyan, a connexion which brought him many commissions, and within the profession was well liked and looked upon as a father figure. In his last years he lived at his home, Ambleside, Hampton Street, North Brighton. He died at Brighton on 25 November 1917, survived by his wife Cora Clara, née Glass, whom he had married in 1889; they had no children.

A. Sutherland et al, *Victoria and its metropolis*, 2 (Melb, 1888); J. Smith (ed), *Cyclopedia of Victoria*, 1 (Melb, 1903); *Scientific Australian*, 20 Mar 1900; Roy Vic Soc of Architects, J, Jan, May 1906, May 1909, May 1917, Jan 1918; *Mirror* (Melb), 25 Jan 1889; B. Echberg and J. Malina, Percy Oakden (B.Arch. report, Univ Melb, 1970).   MILES LEWIS

OAKES, GEORGE (1813-1881), pastoralist and politician, was born at Parramatta, eldest son of Rev. Francis Oakes, Wesleyan missionary, and his wife Rebecca (d. 1883), née Small. Educated by Rev. John Eyre [q.v.] and at Rev. Frederick Wilkinson's school, he early followed pastoral and agricultural pursuits and bought land within the nineteen counties in the 1840s with his brother Francis as partner. He lived near Goulburn for a time but made his headquarters at Parramatta, where he became a member of the District Council in 1842 and was active in getting a water supply for the town. He was on the committees of the local Benevolent Asylum and District Hospital.

A member of the Anti-transportation League, Oakes defeated William Macarthur [q.v.] in a bitter fight to represent Parramatta in the Legislative Council in 1848. *The Empire*, 5 September 1851, applauded the re-election of this 'earnest advocate for popular rights' who had not 'suffered himself to be wheedled or bounced out of the independent exercise of his own judgment', but warned him 'to turn his eyes from the pageantries of Government House'. In 1856-60 he represented Parramatta in the Legislative Assembly and supported the Cowper-Robertson [qq.v.] faction. Defeated in 1860, he was appointed to the Legislative Council on 10 May 1861 in an attempt to carry the land bills but was not sworn in as the president, Sir William Burton [q.v.], walked out. In June he 'absolutely' declined appointment to the reconstructed council as he could not accept the ministry's conditions of voting for an elective council and for the land bills.

Oakes continued to prosper. He had a house in Parramatta, an orangery with 2500 trees and an 'estate', Oak Park, 1907 acres in the counties of King and Georgiana. By 1854 he had three runs in the Wellington District amounting to over 100,000 acres and carrying 3000 cattle. By 1857 he had added another 46,000 acres and 4000 sheep. In the 1860s he held his runs in partnership with J. F. Josephson [q.v.] and by 1871 had five runs in the Bligh and Wellington Districts on which he paid £275 rent.

After his defeat in 1860 Oakes visited Europe for some years and became a regular 'habitué of the House of Commons'. In 1869 he was defeated for Parramatta after attacking the electoral activities of the local Protestant Political Association. A life member of the British and Foreign Bible Society, he affirmed his Protestantism but deplored the mixing of religion and politics.

In 1872 he won a by-election for East Sydney. One of the 'most embittered opponents' of Henry Parkes's [q.v.] government, he did not identify himself with the Opposition; without political friends he saw himself as head of a new 'party'. Parkes thought him a 'sneak' who was 'forever pretending to be the friend of some body of men, while . . . secretly endeavouring to discredit them'. In the 1870s Oakes was a director of the Australian Gaslight Co. and a councillor of the Agricultural Society of New South Wales. When in Sydney he lived at the Reform Club in Macquarie Street. He visited England again and was a New South Wales representative commissioner at the 1876 Paris and Philadelphia Exhibitions. On his return in 1879 he was appointed to the Legislative Council. In 1880 he was a commissioner for the Melbourne Exhibition.

On 10 August 1881 after leaving Parliament House Oakes was run over by a steam-tram and died in the Sydney Infirmary. He was buried in the Wesleyan section of the Parramatta cemetery. He was survived by his mother, reputedly the second child born in the colony, and by a son of his first wife Mary Ann, daughter of Rev. William Shelley [q.v.], whom he had married at St John's Church of England, Parramatta, on 25 May 1837. He was predeceased by his second wife Mary Anne Morrison, a widow whom he had married in Hobart Town on 30 April 1867. His goods were valued for probate at almost £50,000.

J. Jervis, 'A history of politics and politicians in Parramatta', Parramatta and District Hist Soc, J, 3 (1926); SMH, 29 Mar 1856, 13 July 1863, 2, 14 Dec 1869, 11, 12, 13 Aug 1881; Empire (Syd), 9 Apr 1856; Illustrated Sydney News, 17 Oct 1874; Bulletin, 20 Aug 1881; Cowper and Macarthur papers (ML); MS cat under Oakes (ML); Col Sec land letters (NSWA); CO 201/518; information from Miss M. Oakes, Mosman.

MARTHA RUTLEDGE

O'CONNELL, SIR MAURICE CHARLES (1812-1879), soldier, public servant and politician, was born on 13 January 1812 in Sydney, son of Maurice Charles Philip O'Connell [q.v.] and his wife Mary, daughter of Governor Bligh. He left for Ceylon with his parents in 1814 and in 1819 was sent to Europe for schooling. In 1828 he joined the 73rd Regiment at Gibraltar and Malta but in 1835 raised and led a regiment of Irish volunteers in the Spanish Carlist wars, rising to general of brigade in the British Auxiliary Legion. Before embarking for Spain he married Eliza Emily le Geyt at Jersey.

When the legion was disbanded O'Connell returned to England with several Spanish decorations and in June 1838 purchased a captaincy in the 28th Regiment. In that year his father was appointed to command the troops in New South Wales and on 6 December O'Connell junior arrived in the Fairlie as an assistant military secretary to his father. After the regiment sailed to India in 1842 he stayed in New South Wales and sold his commission in 1844. He failed in a first attempt to win a seat in the Legislative Council but represented Port Phillip from August 1845 to June 1848 and then became commissioner of crown lands for the Burnett District.

Early in 1854 O'Connell became government resident at the new Port Curtis settlement. In August 1855 the appointment was criticized in the Legislative Council and a select committee chaired by Henry Parkes [q.v.] decided that the office was unduly expensive, that a police magistrate would have done as well and that O'Connell was not particularly suited for such a post. The office was abolished and he again became commissioner of crown lands. He financed a party which found gold near Port Curtis and was reappointed as government resident to cope with the rush, allegedly created by his own too optimistic reports. While in Gladstone he acquired several squatting properties and developed a small copper-mine but in February 1860 his office was again abolished. He refused reappointment as commissioner of crown lands and for five years vainly pursued a campaign for compensation as far as the Colonial Office.

When the colony of Queensland was created in 1859 O'Connell was given command of the volunteers. He was also one of the first nominees to the Legislative Council and acted as minister without portfolio in the first Herbert [q.v.] ministry. When Sir Charles Nicholson [q.v.] resigned in August 1860 O'Connell became president of the council. He held the post until 1879 and acted ex officio as deputy to the governor four times. Knighthood had been proposed for him in 1864 but was not granted until 1868 when as administrator of the government he was host to the duke of Edinburgh. He died of cancer in Parliament House on 23 March 1879 leaving no children. His widow received a government pension.

R. Cannon (ed), Historical record of the Seventy-third Regiment (Lond, 1851); W. F. Morrison, The Aldine history of Queensland (Syd, 1888); J. F. Hogan, The Gladstone colony (Lond, 1898); V&P (LC NSW), 1855, 3, 915, 945, (LA NSW), 1858, 2, 855, 902, 989, (LA Qld), 1863 (2nd S), 180, 1864, 267, 1879 (2nd S), 1, 521; J. F. Campbell, 'Notes on the historical development of Macquarie Street south, 1810-1880', JRAHS, 23 (1937); Week, 2 June 1877; Queenslander, 29 Mar 1879; Town and Country

J, 29 Mar 1879; Archer, O'Connell and Piper papers (ML); MS and newspaper cats (ML); CO 234/7/8, 257, 11/134, 18/502, 20/5; WO 17/2328.

H. J. GIBBNEY

O'CONNOR, DANIEL (1844-1914), butcher, mining speculator and politician, was born on 13 September 1844 at Tipperary, Ireland, son of Patrick O'Connor, butcher, and his wife Margaret, née Honan. In 1854 he migrated with his parents to Sydney in the *Lord Hungerford*. After a few months schooling he worked in his father's shop. Despite long hours he read avidly, especially the speeches of British and Irish orators, and in 1858 began to frequent the Sydney School of Arts. In 1869 he studied classics and English literature at Sheridan Moore's [q.v.] City College. With his own butchering business by 1871 he had amassed fourteen houses and £7000 which he lost in five months' speculation in gold-mining shares in 1871-72, but he rehabilitated himself within seven years.

Active in the Catholic Association, O'Connor chaired the welcome to pardoned Fenian prisoners, and was founding chairman of the Catholic Truth Society in 1871. His 1876 campaign for Phillip Ward in the Sydney City Council was organized by such Irish Catholics as J. P. Garvan [q.v.] and his creditor Samuel Priestley but although his two opponents were prominent Orangemen he eschewed sectarianism. He represented the ward until 1885 except for a few months in 1879 when he was unseated after irregularities in his election. His uneven, florid oratory and warm personality soon gained him power in city politics.

In the Legislative Assembly O'Connor represented West Sydney, the main working-class electorate, from 1877 to 1891. He championed the campaign against Chinese immigration, the extension of municipal franchise and the payment of members of parliament. But he strongly opposed Henry Parkes's [q.v.] 1880 Public Instruction Act and was assailed by his fellow Catholic, John McElhone [q.v.]. Soon after a council meeting, O'Connor charged McElhone with truckling to Orangemen and received a black eye in the ensuing scuffle. Always prominent at St Patrick's Day banquets, O'Connor quietly helped to welcome William and John Redmond [q.v.] in 1883. In 1887 he finally obtained free rail travel for children attending denominational schools, and in 1888 led the movement that reinterred the remains of Daniel Deniehy [q.v.] in Waverley cemetery. He backed most sports, especially sculling, and supported the licensed victuallers and their wares.

O'Connor became postmaster-general in John Robertson's [q.v.] 1885 cabinet. He supported Parkes's 1887 ministry and joined his 1889 ministry as postmaster-general. With white beard, silk hat, frock coat and buttonhole, he cut a picturesque and popular figure, but was often chided by Parkes for slackness. The advent of the Labor Party and his campaign against a popular but bawdy journal, the *Dead Bird*, lost him his seat in the 1891 elections. Appointed to the Legislative Council he remained in office until October.

In 1887 O'Connor went into an auctioneering, mining and general agency with John Hurley [q.v.]. In 1892 O'Connor was declared bankrupt and resigned from the council. Reappointed in 1895 he resigned in 1898 to contest an assembly seat as a federal oppositionist. With protectionist support in a 1900 by-election he won Sydney-Phillip. He held the seat in the 1901 elections but next year was successfully sued by Paddy Crick, secretary for lands, for money Crick had given for O'Connor's campaign in exchange for a promise of support. In the 1904 elections O'Connor withdrew when he was not endorsed as a Liberal. Soon afterwards he started a world tour, lectured on Australia in England and Ireland and lost his belongings in the 1906 San Francisco earthquake. He lived quietly after his return and in 1913 was admitted to the Liverpool Asylum, where he died on 24 January 1914 of acute dysentery and heart failure; he was buried in the Catholic section of Waverley cemetery. In 1868 he had married Mary Carroll (d. 1899) and was survived by two of their seven children.

Ex-M.L.A., *Our present parliament, what it is worth* (Syd, c1886); P. Loveday and A. W. Martin, *Parliament factions and parties* (Melb, 1966); *Freeman's J* (Syd), 27 May, 29 July 1871, 24 Mar 1888; *SMH*, 22 Nov 1876, 26 Nov 1878, 28 Nov 1879, 27 May 1881, 25 Jan 1886, 12 June 1891, 26 Jan 1914; *Sydney Mail*, 7 Feb 1880; *Bulletin*, 2 Oct 1880, 28 Jan 1882; *Town and Country J*, 26 Mar 1887, 14 Sept 1895; *Daily Telegraph* (Syd), 23 June 1894, 30 June 1903; Parkes letters (ML); CO 201/595, 610.

MARK LYONS

O'CONNOR, JOSEPH GRAHAM (1839-1913), journalist, politician, was born at Dareen House, King's County, Ireland, son of Stephen O'Connor, tanner and currier, and his wife Ann, née Graham. At 2 he went with his parents to New South Wales. Educated by the Christian Brothers and at the Sydney College, he was apprenticed to a wood engraver and printer.

In the late 1850s O'Connor began business as an engraver and printer and in 1860 produced the short-lived *Sunbeam* for the Catholic Young Men's Society. In 1864 he joined W. B. Dalley, W. J. Macleay and J. J. Harpur [qq.v.] in bringing out the unsuccessful *Sydney Times*, devoted to 'the promotion of Australian literature and the advocacy and encouragement of native industry'. In 1867 he began the *Balmain Reporter*, one of the earliest suburban newspapers. His journalistic pursuits became more exclusively Irish and Catholic. In 1870-71 he edited and printed the *Catholic Association Reporter*. In 1876 he had debts of over £1400, sold his press and was not discharged from bankruptcy until 1884 after paying 3s. in the £. In 1877 he had begun the *Catholic Times* in opposition to the *Freeman's Journal*. In 1880 Archbishop Vaughan [q.v.] was dissatisfied with the *Freeman's* independent attitude and bought the *Catholic Times*, changing its name to the *Express*. In 1884 O'Connor took it over again and began the *Nation*, devoted to Irish news; he incorporated it in the *Express* in 1887. In 1890 debts forced him to close his last newspaper venture and his estate was again sequestered. He had supported his unprofitable newspapers with a mostly successful printing business, but in 1892 his friends had him appointed chief clerk on the Water and Sewerage Board at Newcastle, from which he retired in 1909.

As a youth O'Connor had helped to collect funds to relieve the 1858 Donegal famine victims and next year became an original member of the Celtic Association. In 1869-72 he was lay secretary of the Catholic Association, founded by Archbishop Polding [q.v.] in 1867 to support a separate system for Catholic schools. In the 1870s and 1880s he organized several concert tours of country districts to raise funds for the Church. Active in municipal politics with various Irish Catholic factions, he was auditor of the Sydney City Council in 1870-74. After several attempts he was elected in 1873 to the Legislative Assembly for Mudgee in the Catholic interest. Defeated in 1875, he lost again in 1880. O'Connor helped to organize the annual St Patrick's Day celebrations and did not eschew more controversial Irish causes: in 1866 he was treasurer of the Irish State Prisoners' Fund, organized to assist the dependants of Fenian prisoners in Ireland; in 1871 he helped to welcome Fenian prisoners released from Western Australia and in 1883 he was one of the few prominent Irish Catholics to welcome William and John Redmond [q.v.]. Affectionately known as 'old white hat' from the topper he invariably wore, he chaired their first Sydney meeting and was president of the local branch of the Irish National League. He remained close friends with the Redmonds and helped later Irish delegates.

At Sydney in 1861 O'Connor had married Mary Earl (d. 1903). He died of bronchitis at his Mayfield home on 22 July 1913 and was survived by a married daughter. The Irish Parliamentary Party contributed to a monument over his grave in Sandgate cemetery.

J. Shaw, *J. G. O'Connor; a short biography* (Newcastle, 1910); *Freeman's J*, 28 Apr 1866, 29 July 1871, 24 Feb 1883, 24 July 1913; *Empire* (Syd), 2 Dec 1867; *SMH*, 11 Dec 1868; *Bulletin*, 13 Nov 1880; M. Lyons, Aspects of sectarianism in New South Wales circa 1865-1880 (Ph.D. thesis, ANU, 1972); J. G. O'Connor papers (Irish National Assn, Syd); Insolvency files 12,756 and 2388 (NSWA).   MARK LYONS

O'CONNOR, MICHAEL (1829-1883), Catholic bishop, was born on 4 October 1829 in Dublin, son of John O'Connor and his wife Mary, née Murtagh. In 1845 with W. Kelly [q.v.] and T. Cahill he studied at Maynooth. Out of a class of seventy in his logic year (1847) he won first prize and was soon promoted to Dunboyne where the most distinguished students were sent; he won repute for integrity and scholarship, taking the chair of moral theology while a professor was ill. Ordained on 10 June 1854, he was soon given the important parish of Rathfarnham, through the patronage of Cardinal Cullen [q.v.]. He was noted for missionary work among the poor and for his affectionate and kindly way with subordinates.

On 31 March 1874 the suffragan diocese of Ballarat was created on Archbishop Goold's [q.v.] recommendation and on 17 May O'Connor was consecrated to the see by Cardinal Franchi in the Church of Propaganda, Rome, with Goold and Dean Moore [q.v.] attending. He arrived at Melbourne in the *Ceylon* on 18 December. With Goold he was drawn to St Patrick's by four white horses but Goold upstaged him as the bells pealed and a *Te Deum* was sung. In Ballarat he was drawn by four grey horses and installed bishop on 20 December, also to a *Te Deum*; he was then given a carriage and pair.

According to Moran, O'Connor 'seemed to be sent by Providence to grapple with the difficult problem' of Catholic education. For this reason he must have been preferred to the less gifted Dean Moore, who in welcome had stressed that religion was flourishing despite a hostile and dangerous system of education. O'Connor replied that they might as well deny the infant the care and protection of its mother as deprive it of religious education. He soon began a tour of his diocese, cogently persuading his flock to combat secularization. In 1875 his Lenten Pastoral opposed the divorce of religion and knowledge: the state's duty was not to educate but to enable parents to do so, and he could hardly suppose that the government was actuated by bad motives so much as ill-informed as to what Catholics wanted. He concluded that: 'Crime does not arise from ignorance of secular knowledge; it arises from the unsubdued passions of the wicked'. He entered into polemics in the *Courier*, but without acrimony.

O'Connor's rule was notable for building forty new churches and bringing in teachers such as the Loreto nuns from Rathfarnham, the Sisters of Mercy and the Christian Brothers. Most lavish was the splendid bluestone two-storied Bishop's Palace in Sturt Street West near Lake Wendouree. It stood in a twelve-acre park and cost £10,000. As Ballarat was suffering recessions, this clerical Keynesianism was appreciated by non-Catholics. In March 1881 he left for Europe to make his *ad liminem* and to recruit priests. His flock donated 1080 sovereigns. He had a private audience with Leo XIII, gave him £400, praised Australian Catholics and told him that all that was wrong in Australia was the state school system. Leo said that was a *maximum malum* and granted his request to put the diocese under the patronage of Mary Immaculate.

After eight months in Ireland O'Connor returned via America and was enthusiastically received. His popularity derived from his gentle disposition and the prestige which his scholarship lent to this Irish flock. Early in 1883 his health failed and on 14 February he died after a sudden haemorrhage of the lungs. The obituary in the *Star* was inserted on request; the *Courier* gave only six inches. However, he was esteemed by Protestants and a Methodist minister was at his graveside. His old Maynooth colleague, Fr Cahill, preached the panegyric and 'wept bitterly at the vault'.

P. F. Moran, *History of the Catholic Church in Australasia* (Syd, 1895); R. Fogarty, *Catholic education in Australia 1806-1950*, 2 (Melb, 1959); *Advocate* (Melb), 11 July, 19, 26 Dec 1874, 16 Jan, 6, 13, 20 Feb 1875, 17, 24 Feb 1883; *Ballarat Star*, 18, 21 Dec 1874, 2 Mar 1881, 15, 18 Feb 1883; *Illustrated Aust News*, 27 Jan, 14 June 1875; *Ballarat Courier*, 3 Feb 1875, 15 Feb 1883; *A'sian Sketcher*, 14 Mar 1883.

JAMES GRIFFIN

O'CONNOR, RICHARD (1810-1876), parliamentary officer, was born in March 1810 in County Cork, Ireland, eldest son of Arthur O'Connor of Mangan Castle,

Bandon, and his wife, née O'Neal. He arrived in Sydney on 15 April 1835 in the American brig *Black Warrior* from the Pacific Islands and New Zealand. From 8 June to 8 July he was an extra clerk to the Legislative and Executive Councils and from 12 January 1836 assistant clerk under William Macpherson, clerk of the councils from 1837. As town clerk from 7 September to 16 November 1842 he organized the elections for the first city council. With the establishment of the Legislative Council Library in 1843 he became librarian and published its first three catalogues.

On 15 May 1856 O'Connor became clerk of the new Legislative Assembly with a salary of £800 and relinquished the post of librarian to Walter McEvilly [q.v.]. With Macpherson he planned the staffing of both Houses. O'Connor applied his knowledge and experience to the assembly, drafting its standing orders, guiding its procedures and relations with the council. He acted as chairman for the assembly's first meeting which elected Daniel Cooper [q.v.] as Speaker. On 1 January 1860 he became clerk of the Legislative Council but the assembly refused to vote him an extra £100. In 1864 he was designated clerk of the parliaments and in 1868 produced the first edition of the *Parliamentary Handbook*.

About 1837 O'Connor had joined the Sydney Mechanics' School of Arts. In 1845 he was a member of the provisional committee of the Australian Clerks' Benevolent Society Fund. Active in establishing St John's College in the University of Sydney, he was a fellow in 1858-76. He was also a trustee of the Savings Bank of New South Wales from 1860, served on the management committee of the Roman Catholic Orphan School at Parramatta from 1861 and on the board of management of the Government Asylums for the Infirm and Destitute in 1862-72. He played the flute, concertina and guitar.

In June 1870 O'Connor wanted to retire because of age and failing health but continued in office until 31 March 1871 at the request of the council president, Sir Terence Murray [q.v.]. Dedicated, with a high sense of public service, O'Connor contributed much to the smooth functioning of parliamentary government. E. Deas Thomson [q.v.] among other associates testified to his zeal and ability. He died from heart disease at his home, Mary Ville, Glebe Point, on 27 June 1876 and was buried in the Catholic cemetery at Petersham. He was survived by his wife Mary, née Harnett, whom he had married at St Mary's Cathedral on 7 January 1845, and by two of their four sons and two of their six daughters. His goods were valued at £500. His son Richard

Edward, a faithful supporter of Edmund Barton and Federation, became an original High Court judge.

H. E. Maiden, *The history of local government in New South Wales* (Syd, 1966); *SMH*, 30 June 1876; LC letters (LC NSW); MS cat under O'Connor (ML).   L. A. JECKELN

ODDIE, JAMES (1824-1911), Ballarat pioneer, was born on 31 March 1824 at Clitheroe, Lancashire, England, eldest son of James Oddie, retired innkeeper, and his wife Margaret, née Hargreaves. Educated in Preston by a Congregational master and then at a Wesleyan Chapel school, he was apprenticed in a foundry at 15. On becoming a journeyman moulder, he worked for an engineering firm in Manchester. As a boy in Preston he had witnessed agitation for parliamentary reform and Chartist demonstrations, and as a member of the Moulders Club was involved in strikes for better conditions. In London by 1845 he worked in a foundry and on railway and shipbuilding projects. He married Rachel Riding in 1847. After seeing letters from J. D. Lang [q.v.] recommending settlement in Australia, he sailed with his wife and daughter in the *Larpent* and arrived in Geelong on 28 June 1849.

James conducted a foundry in Geelong until August 1851 when gold fever lured him to Buninyong. On 1 September he moved to Golden Point, Ballarat, where as a diggers representative he protested against the miners licences. He joined the rushes to Mount Alexander and Bendigo and after varying luck opened a store in 1853 at Smythesdale, where he was among the first to oppose the £50 store licence. He was probably the author of the pamphlet, *Laughing a Crime* (Melbourne, 1853). In 1854 he moved his store near the Eureka stockade, attended many protest meetings and witnessed what he described as 'the massacre of innocent diggers'. A friend and admirer of Peter Lalor [q.v.], he later erected his statue at the cost of £2200 in the main street of Ballarat.

James and his brother Thomas (b. 1830) set up as auctioneers in the new township. They acted as commission, house and estate agents, some well-known properties in the Western District passing through their hands. James also developed a money-lending agency which he later constituted a deposit bank with a cash deposit of some £250,000. By 1885, when he sold the building and business for £10,000 to a Melbourne bank, he was one of Ballarat's wealthiest citizens. However, in the 1890s he was financially crippled when the Mercantile Bank collapsed and his career as a philanthropist was seriously curtailed.

As first chairman of the Ballarat Municipal Council in 1856-58 he helped despite opposition to pioneer a scheme for piping water from Yuille's swamp to the city centre; his arguments for an improved water supply were reflected in the *Corn Stalk*, a monthly of which he and Thomas were proprietors. He also helped to secure land and a government grant for the Botanical Gardens. In January 1859 he failed by one vote to win re-election as a councillor for Ballarat West. Overwhelmed by defeat, he announced his retirement from public life but later took an important part in municipal affairs. He campaigned for increasing local government powers, was a member of the Benevolent Asylum Board in 1860-91, vice-president of the Alfred Hospital in 1869 and founder and patron of the Art Gallery in 1884.

A fellow of the Royal Geographical and Geological Societies of London, Oddie was zealous for technical education and science. A trustee of the School of Mines and vice-president of its council in 1881, he founded an associateship course. At his own cost he built and equipped the Mount Pleasant Observatory. He studied developments in the use of gas and electricity and was especially interested in the invention of the telephone. A Wesleyan Methodist, he helped to finance the building of the Lydiard Street Church, where he was Sunday school superintendent and a circuit steward. Favouring the National system of education, he was president of the managing committee of the Dana Street National school in the late 1850s and president of the Ballarat Anti-State Aid League. In 1875 he campaigned for greater lay representation in the Methodist Church and resigned from his local church, but later resumed active connexion with its affairs. Sabbatarian and lifelong abstainer, he was once described as 'the Dick Whittington of Ballarat'.

Predeceased by his first wife, their only daughter and in 1884 by his second wife Mary, née McCormack, Oddie died on 3 March 1911 without direct descendants. Small in stature and dignified in appearance, he had enterprise, initiative, definite principles and intense conviction. A devout Christian and a passionate democrat, he often clashed with others but was widely respected for his liberality.

W. B. Withers, *The history of Ballarat*, 2nd ed (Ballarat, 1887); H. Glenny, *Jottings and sketches* (Belfast, 1888); N. F. Spielvogel, *History of Ballarat* (Ballarat, 1935); *Spectator and Methodist Chronicle*, 11, 24 Dec 1875, 10 Mar 1911; *Ballarat Star*, 13, 14, 17 Jan 1859, 26, 31 July 1886, 19, 23 Apr 1890, 2 Sept 1909, 4 Mar

1911; *Ballarat Courier*, 4 Mar 1911; R. Howe, The Wesleyan Church in Victoria, 1885-1901: its ministry and membership (M.A. thesis, Univ Melb, 1965); Minute books 1856-59 (Ballarat Municipal Council); Circuit minute book 1858-63, Quarterly Meeting minutes 1853-76 (Wesley Methodist Church, Lydiard St, Ballarat); Oddie papers (held by Ballarat Hist Soc and Miss J. Oddie, Chepstowe, Vic).

G. A. ODDIE

O'DOHERTY, KEVIN IZOD (1823-1905), Irish nationalist and medical practitioner, was born on 7 September 1823 in Dublin and baptized two weeks later at the Roman Catholic Church of St Andrew, son of William Dougherty, solicitor, and his wife Ann, née McAvoy. He began to study in the Catholic School of Medicine in 1842 but in May 1848 became involved with the Young Ireland movement and as co-editor of the nationalist *Tribune* was sentenced to transportation for treason-felony at Dublin in August. He sailed in the *Mount Stewart Elphinstone* to Sydney and thence in the *Emma* to Hobart Town, arriving on 31 October 1849. Granted a ticket-of-leave, he was allowed to settle in the Oatlands District. He became manager of the dispensary in Hobart in November 1850 and in January 1851 was acting surgeon at St Mary's Hospital. In June 1853 he received a conditional pardon, which forbade residence in the United Kingdom, and went to live in Paris whence he made a secret visit to London to marry Mary Eva Kelly (1829-1910) on 23 August 1855. He received an unconditional pardon next year and returned to Dublin. He graduated as a fellow of the Royal College of Surgeons in June 1857 and set up practice.

O'Doherty returned to Victoria in 1860 and after a short stay in Geelong moved to Sydney and settled at Brisbane in 1865 where he became a leading physician. He was one of the first presidents of the Queensland Medical Society and carried out extensive honorary work at Catholic hospitals. A member for Brisbane in the Legislative Assembly in 1867-73, he had wide interests. In 1872 he was responsible for the first Health Act in Queensland and in 1875-77 gave evidence to many commissions on medical matters. In January 1868 he became one of the first trustees of the undenominational Brisbane Grammar School, but in 1874 declined to serve on the royal commission on education in protest at 'the proposed withdrawal of aid to non-vested schools'. He was a member of the Legislative Council in 1877-85 and as an opponent of the traffic in Kanakas sponsored the bill to stop their recruitment. A leading figure in

the Queensland Irish Association, he was elected president of the Irish Australian Convention held in Melbourne in 1883.

In 1886 O'Doherty was elected to the House of Commons as member for North Meath but resigned after the split in Parnell's party and returned to Brisbane. Unable to set up practice again, he was finally appointed secretary to the Central Board of Health and supervisor of the quarantine station. He died on 15 July 1905 at his home in Torwood, Brisbane, survived by his wife and one of his eight children. The Queensland Irish Association raised a monument over his grave in Toowong cemetery.

His wife was a poetess, known as 'Eva of the *"Nation"*,' and continued to write throughout her married life but her poems written in Queensland had a tone of sadness and a longing for Ireland. She published *Poems* (San Francisco, 1877) and a second edition at Dublin in 1909.

R. S. Browne, *A journalist's memories* (Brisb, 1927); J. H. Cullen, *Young Ireland in exile* (Dublin, 1928); H. A. Kellow, *Queensland poets* (Lond, 1930); T. J. Kiernan, *The Irish exiles in Australia* (Melb, 1954); V&P (LA Qld), 1875, 2, 295; O'Doherty papers (microfilm, ML, NL and Oxley Lib, Brisb); Ac no 2/363 (TA).

G. RUDE

O'DONOVAN, DENIS (1836-1911), scholar and librarian, was born on 23 August 1836 at Kinsale, Ireland, son of William O'Donovan and his wife Anne, née Crowley. According to his own account, he was educated in Ireland and France, achieving some fame while at school when he published articles and poems one of which was included in an Irish anthology. On completing his degree he toured Europe, attended lectures in Italy and returned to France as professor of modern languages and literature in the Collège des Hautes Etudes. In 1859 he published *Memories of Rome* for which he received a medal from Pope Pius IX and letters from the Queen of Spain and others. He had often written for *L'ami de la religion* and was for some time an editor. From 1864 he was in London for two years. O'Donovan moved to Melbourne in 1866 and ran a school at Emerald Hill in 1871-74. In 1871 and 1872 he had delivered lectures on industrial design which were published by the Melbourne Industrial and Technological Museum. On 1 May 1868 he married a widow, Aimée Besson, née Leroux; they had two sons and three daughters.

On 1 August 1874 O'Donovan was appointed librarian to the Queensland parliament and soon moved to Brisbane. He was able to do much for the library through the contacts that he maintained with the intellectual world of Europe and crowned his efforts in 1883 by the production of a printed analytical and classified catalogue which was a large advance on any such work done in Australia. He was honoured for his work by numerous European learned societies, received *la croix du chevalier de la légion d'honneur* and was appointed C.M.G. in 1894. He was a prominent member of Brisbane's Catholic community and as a leader of the agitation against Bishop James Quinn [q.v.] was publicly refused the sacraments on the bishop's instructions.

O'Donovan's wife died in 1892 and in June 1902 he retired from the library. He went to live in France but returned to Australia to visit a son settled in Perth and died on 30 April 1911 at Claremont, Western Australia.

C. W. Holgate, *An account of the chief libraries of Australia and Tasmania* (Lond, 1886); T. W. H. Leavitt (ed), *Australian representative men* (Melb, 1888); Alcazar Press, *Queensland, 1900* (Brisb, nd); PD (Qld), 1874, 8566; *West Australian*, 1 May 1911; *Brisbane Courier*, 5 May 1911; Box D5 (Roman Catholic Archives, Syd).   H. J. GIBBNEY

O'DONOVAN, JOHN (1836-1912), Catholic priest, was born on 6 November 1836 at Ballyvaden, County Waterford, Ireland, son of John O'Donovan, farmer, and his wife Mary, née Walshe. Educated at the Mount Melleray Monastery, Waterford, for two years and All Hallows College, Dublin, he was ordained on 24 June 1861. In September he sailed for Sydney, was wrecked in Bass Strait and arrived in January 1862. He took up duties at St Benedict's in February where he attracted attention as a preacher. In 1864-68 he was parish priest at Orange.

In October O'Donovan became parish priest at Mudgee; he was then an 'athlete of no mean character' and a noted horseman. In 1871 his assistant was Fr John Dunne who became bishop of Bathurst. O'Donovan planned imposing buildings and spent £16,000 on a Gothic stone church, St Mary's, which was blessed in 1876. He designed a substantial convent for the Mercy nuns who were introduced in 1875 and built churches in Gulgong, Rylstone, Wollar and other places. In 1896-97 he visited Ireland and Europe and was made a domestic prelate (monsignor) by the Pope. In 1903 he had a new bell for St Mary's cast in Dublin and next year raised the money for a new pipe organ by an art union and a play. He served

on the committee of the local hospital for many years. Well known as an orator in Sydney and a fellow of St John's College in the University of Sydney, he travelled widely to speak on such occasions as the consecration of Bishop Dunne at Brisbane in 1882.

In Mudgee O'Donovan maintained the state attributed to a parish priest in Ireland; his sister and later his niece, Annie Ita Halley, presided over his establishment, which included a Chinese cook and several maids; he also entertained local squatters in return for a day's shooting. Famous for his fine horses, he never opened a gate but rode straight over the fence. Henry Lawson wrote in 'A Fragment of an Autobiography', 'Father O'Donovan was a character and I liked him . . . [he] attended the Mudgee races, all three days, to look after the "big bhoys" of his flock whom [he] corrected on occasions with a buggy-whip. They say he always had a horse or two running, but this didn't prevent him from taking care of the boys'.

In 1911 O'Donovan celebrated his golden jubilee as a priest by erecting the spire on St Mary's and by a banquet, with the mayor as chairman, when he was given a fine 24 horse-power motor car, gold sleeve-links and ten Japanese pictures by the convent children. He died on 24 April 1912 and was buried in a vault in St Mary's. In his 44 years as parish priest he had performed 450 marriages and 2520 baptisms. He left £200 each to the Catholic school fund and the orphanage in Bathurst, his library to Fr O'Donnell in Gulgong, his guns to Dr Harvey Nickoll of Mudgee and the residue of his estate, sworn at £4144, to his niece.

A. W. Maher, *Mudgee Catholic centenary* (Mudgee, 1952); 'A fragment of autobiography', *The stories of Henry Lawson*, C. Mann ed (Syd, 1964); *Catholic Press*, 25 Apr 1912; *Freeman's J* (Syd), 25 Apr 1912; *Mudgee Guardian*, 25, 29 Apr 1912; Roman Catholic Archives (Bathurst and Syd).   C. J. DUFFY

O'FARRELL, HENRY JAMES (1833-1868), paranoic, was born at Arran Quay, Dublin, youngest child of William O'Farrell, butcher. The family moved to Liverpool, and left for Victoria, arriving early in 1841 at Melbourne where William (d. 1854) became a rate collector and later a land agent.

In 1843-47 O'Farrell boarded at David Boyd's school and in 1848-49 at St Francis's school. In 1850-52 he attended St Francis's seminary and received deacon's orders. In 1853-54 he was in Europe for further study but in 1855 had a dispute with Bishop Goold [q.v.] and was not ordained. He became a sheep farmer near Clunes. Later as partner of his cousin Joseph Kennedy he became a grain merchant at Ballarat. In 1864 in a libel suit his brother Peter lost repute as a leading solicitor and fled from Melbourne; soon afterwards Kennedy died of delirium tremens.

Depressed by these misfortunes, O'Farrell failed in speculations and fell into debt. He took to drink and brooded over his failure to become a priest. In January 1867 he suffered a serious mental breakdown, with bouts of delirium tremens, talking of plots to poison him, brandishing pistols and threatening to kill people. Two of his sisters took him to Melbourne. Back in Ballarat he collapsed again and suffered several epileptic fits but recovered and in April wrote to Bishop Sheil [q.v.] about preparing for ordination. In September he went to Sydney and stayed at Tierney's Currency Lass Hotel until asked to leave because of his strange behaviour. At the Clarendon Hotel from December he was sustained by money sent by his sister and was noticeably agitated whenever Fenianism was discussed. On 11 March 1868 he practised pistol shooting at Waverley and next day shot and wounded the duke of Edinburgh at Clontarf.

O'Farrell first claimed that he had acted on instructions from a band of Melbourne Fenians, but later retracted and stated that 'From continually thinking and talking of . . . "the wrongs of Ireland", I became excited and filled with enthusiasm for the subject, and it was then under the influence of those feelings that I attempted to perpetrate the deed for which I am now justly called upon to suffer'. Found guilty of attempted murder O'Farrell was hanged at Darlinghurst gaol on 21 April and buried in the Catholic section of Rookwood cemetery.

O'Farrell's fantasies about Fenianism and the state of Ireland reflected the effects of alcoholism on an unstable personality shaped in a morbid domestic and religious atmosphere. The social tension and political excitement generated by his unique crime made a fair trial impossible, but the duke's efforts to have O'Farrell's life spared support the view that the correct verdict would have been not guilty because of insanity. The incident was an important factor in intensifying the sectarianism latent in a colony with many Protestant and Catholic Irish concentrating on their native land rather than on their adopted country.

O'Farrell's brother, Peter, attempted to shoot Archbishop Goold [q.v.] on 21 August 1882 in Brighton, Victoria.

V&P (LA NSW), 1868, 1868-69, 715, 1869, 339; P. M. Cowburn, 'The attempted assassination of the Duke of Edinburgh, 1868', JRAHS, 55 (1969); D. I. McDonald, 'Henry James O'Farrell: "Fenian, or moonstruck miscreant"', Canberra & District Hist Soc, J, Sept 1970; M. Lyons, Aspects of sectarianism in New South Wales circa 1865-1880 (Ph.D. thesis, ANU, 1972).
                                    MARK LYONS
                                    BEDE NAIRN

OFFICER, CHARLES MYLES (1827-1904) and SUETONIUS HENRY (1830-1883), pastoralists, were born at Hall Green, New Norfolk, Van Diemen's Land, sons of Robert Officer [q.v.], and his wife Jamima, née Patterson. Charles was born on 14 July 1827 and Suetonius on 4 January 1830; they moved with the family to Hobart Town in 1835 and attended local schools until 1841 when they went to Scotland to the Edinburgh Academy. Charles had begun his medical studies and Suetonius had entered the Military Academy when in 1844 they were recalled to Van Diemen's Land.

Charles was trained in pastoral pursuits in the Bothwell district and for a time grew hops at New Norfolk. In 1848 he moved to the Wimmera in the Port Phillip District to his father's run, Mount Talbot, managed by his eldest brother Robert. In 1852 Charles went to the goldfields where he had little luck but enjoyed himself, and in 1854 with Suetonius took over the management of Mount Talbot. The run of 100 square miles was some of the best merino country in Victoria, with 15,000 sheep and 500 cattle. In 1856 the brothers took over the 25,000-acre Lingmer station acquired by their father in 1849. By 1859 they were able to buy Mount Talbot and continued as partners, though Suetonius soon went north to manage their Riverina holdings.

In 1866 Mount Talbot was thrown open for selection and Charles moved his family to Melbourne. Soon back at Mount Talbot he remained until 1873 when he moved permanently to live at Landcox, Brighton, instructing his land agent to buy the necessary sections of Mount Talbot as they came up for sale. He had trouble with various 'sharks' who bought lots crucial to the squatter and forced him to pay dearly for them. Officer finally gained freehold of 16,756 acres.

The political instability of 1878-79 worried Officer and only the inability to realize on his Victorian property prevented him from transferring to New South Wales where he had large interests. However, in 1880 he was persuaded to contest Dundas seat in the Legislative Assembly. Elected in the anti-Berry [q.v.] interest he supported the O'Loghlen [q.v.] ministry. In February 1883 Officer was returned unopposed and served on the royal commission on lunatic asylums in 1884-86. In that year he was again returned and continued to support the coalition ministries but was defeated in 1892. In his last term he had voted against the stock tax, was dissatisfied with the railway construction bill and helped to organize a group of forty dissatisfied country members.

Officer's business sense was highly valued and he was generally respected. He was one of the first directors of the Australian Frozen Meat Export Co. formed at meetings in 1879-80, chairman of the board of advice of Dalgety [q.v.] & Co. in 1885-94 and a director of the Trustees and Executors Association. He was a commissioner for Tasmania at the Melbourne International Exhibition of 1880 and treasurer for a decade of the Deaf and Dumb Asylum. A lieutenant in the Field Artillery Brigade, he was appointed aide-de-camp to Governor Loch in May 1887. A councillor of the Zoological and Acclimatisation Society for ten years and president in 1887, he was also a member of the Protection of Animals Society and of the Central Board for Protection of the Aborigines. He had learnt the language of the Mount Talbot tribe and was a justice of the peace. A Presbyterian, Officer supported the Ormond College scholarship fund for some years but in 1884 was unable to continue. The financial strain of acquiring the freehold of Mount Talbot and losses from drought on his West Darling holdings gave him a worrying time. On 25 June 1897 he was declared bankrupt in New South Wales.

Officer died at Landcox on 1 February 1904, predeceased by his first wife Christina Susannah, née Robertson, whom he had married on 24 January 1854, and by four of their eleven children. He was survived by his second wife Ellen Agnes, née Besnard, whom he had married on 28 November 1876, and by seven of their eight children.

Suetonius left the Wimmera in 1862 and bought the rights of Mellool station in the Riverina. He sold it and with Charles acquired Murray Downs, Willakool and the 998,000-acre Kallara station on the Darling River. On the river frontage of Murray Downs Suetonius installed pumps worked by horse, windmills and later steam, and irrigated large paddocks for lucerne and maize as well as orchards and groves of Jaffa oranges.

An avid reader, Suetonius had scientific interests. In November 1878 he read a paper to the Zoological and Acclimatisation Society of Victoria on the ostriches he had introduced at Murray Downs. He was also interested in astronomy and had a good telescope. A member of the Darling District Pastoral Association, a magistrate and a leader in the religious and philanthropic development of the Swan Hill district, he helped to finance the Presbyterian Church and at the school awarded prizes for scripture. On 13 December 1866 he had married Mary Lillias Rigg, daughter of Dr Adam Cairns [q.v.]; she laid the foundation stone of the Swan Hill Presbyterian Church and was its first organist. In 1881 Suetonius moved to Melbourne for the education of his four sons and two daughters. He bought Leighwood, Toorak, where after a long illness he died on 26 July 1883. He was widely mourned and left much of his pioneering irrigation unfinished. His estate was valued for probate at £59,000, of which he bequeathed some £8000 to twelve educational and philanthropic institutions.

A. Sutherland et al, Victoria and its metropolis, 2 (Melb, 1888); A. Henderson (ed), Early pioneer families of Victoria and Riverina (Melb, 1936); Riverine Herald, 26 Nov 1878; Australasian, 7 May 1887; Argus, 4 Feb 1904; Pastoral Review, 16 Feb 1904; Horsham Times, 26 Sept 1947; Armytage papers (LaT L); Letters (Ormond College Archives, Melb).

J. ANN HONE

OGILVIE, EDWARD DAVID STEWART (1814-1896), pastoralist, was born on 25 July 1814 at Tottenham, Middlesex, England, son of William Ogilvie, naval officer, and his wife Mary, née White. With free passages William sailed with his family in the convict ship Grenada for Sydney, arriving on 23 January 1825. He settled at Merton, a 2000-acre grant on the Upper Hunter, and later extended his holdings to the Liverpool Plains. Educated by his mother, Edward was soon working on his father's stations and later managed the sheep. In 1840, after the ex-convict Richard Craig had refused to let them join Dr John Dobie's [q.v.] party which he was guiding to the Clarence, Edward pushed on with his brother Frederick and an Aboriginal and reached the Clarence at Tabulum ahead of Craig. Downstream Edward took up fifty-six miles on both sides of the river and later named the runs Yulgilbar. On his return to Merton to collect their flocks he found an easier route by Tenterfield.

The two brothers and a 'new chum' C. G. Tindal [q.v.] settled at Yulgilbar. The Aboriginals were hostile but Edward became fluent in the local dialect and at a parley explained that he only wanted the grass and gave them complete hunting rights on his run including honey. They soon joined with Aboriginals in wrestling matches and races and found their 'sable friends no mean antagonists'. Ogilvie planted lucerne and clover and was soon making palatable wine.

In 1847 he was appointed a magistrate and bought an 'old edition of *Blackstone*'. However, Tindal told his father that Ogilvie 'like many good managers, is too fond of having everything done his own way'. By 1850 Yulgilbar was about 300 square miles and included Fairfield, a 100,000-acre cattle station in the mountains. When Ogilvie lost his European hands to the goldfields he employed Aboriginals and Chinese and negotiated with William Kirchner, consul for Austria, Hamburg and Prussia, to import German shepherds. In 1853 he started buying freehold blocks on his runs.

In August 1854 Ogilvie sailed for Europe; he described his experiences, visits to the war front in the Crimea and his enchantment with Florence in his *Diary of Travels in Three Quarters of the Globe*, which he published in London in 1856 under the pseudonym 'An Australian Squatter'. For two years he travelled widely buying stock and engaging German craftsmen for Yulgilbar. At Donnybrook Church near Dublin on 2 September 1858 he married Theodosia, daughter of Rev. William de Burgh. He returned with his wife in 1859. Next year the foundation stone for the 'Big House' was laid: completed in 1866 for a cost of £8000 it was built from local serpentine and sandstone round a courtyard with a crenellated roof and two towers. Ogilvie was his own architect.

In the 1860s Ogilvie found the country too wet for sheep and successfully switched to cattle. Unpopular in Grafton, he developed the new town of Lawrence and built his own wharf to facilitate shipping his cattle to Sydney. He was a director of the Clarence and Richmond Rivers' Steam Navigation Co. His business activities in Lawrence were managed by Thomas Bawden who later went bankrupt. Ogilvie had to pay despite Sir William Manning [q.v.] as counsel. In 1863-89 Ogilvie was a member of the Legislative Council where he contributed little. Increasingly quarrelsome, he fought with successive managers, and with the Department of Lands over boundaries, pursuing lawsuits against any who annoyed him. He took active measures to discourage selectors on Yulgilbar but could do little about the miners. An early member of the Australian Club, he was a founding member of the Linnean Society of New South Wales in 1875.

In late 1884 Ogilvie took his wife and eight daughters to England; Theodosia died on 23 March 1886 at Torquay. Fascinated by heraldry and his ancestry, he made several visits to Florence and became a close friend of the poet, Robert Browning. Ogilvie and his children were all musical. On 21 December 1890 he married Alicia Georgiana

Loftus Tottenham, whose sister was the wife of (Sir) Alexander Onslow [q.v.]. They lived at the Villa Margherita, Florence, and entertained in the grand manner. Threatened by the 1893 depression and banking crisis, they returned to Yulgilbar. Ogilvie died at Fernside, Bowral, on 25 January 1896 and was buried at Yulgilbar with Anglican rites. He was survived by two sons and eight daughters of his first wife and by his second wife. His estate was sworn for probate at nearly £116,000; he left Yulgilbar and a third of its income to his sixth daughter Mabel, wife of Charles Lillingston.

Portraits by Pietro Milani at Florence in 1859 and by Tom Roberts at Yulgilbar in December 1894 are held by Mrs Griselda Carson and in the Mitchell Library.

L. T. Daley, *Men and a river* (Melb, 1966); G. Farwell, *Squatter's castle* (Melb, 1973); Sel cttee on scab in sheep, V&P (LC NSW), 1854, 2; V&P (LA NSW), 1872-73, 1, 51, 1875-76, 2, 919, 1876-77, 3, 343, 1878-79, 1, 183, 1879-80, 5, 784; R. L. Dawson, 'Pioneering days in the Clarence River district', JRAHS, 20 (1934); SMH, 4 June 1842, 22 Jan 1923; *Town and Country J*, 15 July 1871; K. Bland, Notes about my grandparents (ML); M. Bundock, Memoir of E. D. S. Ogilvie, Clarence River Hist Soc records, 1 (ML); Tindal family letter-books and Yulgilbar station diaries (ML); Ogilvie family papers (Univ New England Archives).

MARTHA RUTLEDGE

OGILVY, ARTHUR JAMES (1834-1914), public servant, land reformer and author, was born on 15 April 1834 in Calcutta, son of James Balfour Ogilvy of the Bengal civil service and his wife Anne, née Kinloch; he was descended from the Ogilvies of Inverquharity, Forfarshire. He was educated in Calcutta and at Marlborough College, Wiltshire. After his parents died he sailed for Van Diemen's Land in June 1851 to join his uncle, Captain David Ogilvy, who had acquired a large property near Richmond. On a visit to England Arthur married Mary Camilla Letitia Needham on 8 August 1861 and took her to Tasmania. They lived near Richmond where in 1862 he became a justice of the peace and later a member of the Municipal Council. As secretary of the Richmond Reading Room and Library, he persuaded the government to place it in the old police watch-house. In May 1870 he applied in vain for the post of assistant clerk in the House of Assembly, but in November was appointed chief district constable for the Waterhouse goldfields near George Town and for Emu Bay, at Stanley in 1872 and briefly at Cam River. He resigned about July 1876 and in August he made an indenture with his wife to buy a home in New Town for her and the children while he lived at Inverquharity near Richmond. On 24 October his uncle died, leaving his estate to his wife Caroline Helena and Arthur. He accepted his share of the legacy 'never dreaming that there was any harm in it' but renounced it in 1879 after being 'enlightened' by reading Henry George's [q.v.], *Progress and Poverty*.

Ogilvy started his writings on economic and social problems with an article on 'National Character' in the *Sydney Quarterly Magazine* in 1886. Next year he began to issue tracts on the gospel of land nationalization and published *The Land* in Hobart and Adelaide; he also became founding president of the Tasmanian Land Nationalisation Society and ran its paper, *Land and Labour*. In 1888 he went to England, where as a vice-president of the parent society he lectured widely, wrote more tracts, corresponded with Gladstone and impressed many other notable people. On returning to Hobart Ogilvy was elected a fellow of the Royal Society on 17 November 1890 and read a paper, 'Can strikes really improve the condition of the masses?' In 1892 he published such tracts as *The Third Factor of Production and other Essays* and read to the economic and social science section of the Australasian Association for the Advancement of Science in Hobart a paper, 'Is capital the result of abstinence?' He published *The Cause of a [Financial] Crisis* in 1894 and for the Hobart *Mercury* wrote 'Labour v. Capital' in 1895 and 'The Appreciation of Gold' in 1897. In June 1896 he had chaired the conference which formed the Democratic League, forerunner of the Tasmanian Labor Party. When asked why he did not sit for parliament he said that he would inevitably introduce a land nationalization bill and when it was rejected would walk out.

By 1900 Ogilvy was turning away from the doctrines of Henry George and finding inconsistencies in single tax. Influenced by Alfred Russel Wallace, who had written an introduction to Ogilvy's *Colonists' pleas for Land Nationalisation* in 1892, he took up the study of evolution. He published *Elements of Darwinism* (London, 1901), in 1905 wrote a novel, *Sullivan & Co.*, and in 1907 published some poetry, *Charades, Acrostics and Epigrams*. In 1908 he read a paper on 'Altruism' to the Ethical Society in Hobart and in 1913 wrote *The Ape Man*. He died at Inverquharity on 30 June 1914; his last work, *Phases of the Land and Labour Questions*, appeared posthumously. He was survived by his son Kenneth (b. 1863), warden of Richmond, and by three daughters.

Clipper, 14 July 1896, 15, 22, 29 Oct 1904, 3 Apr 1908; *Daily Post* (Hob), 2 July 1914; *Mer-*cury, 2 July 1914; *Land Nationaliser*, Sept 1914; CSD 7/28/300, 39/664, 10/50/1090.

O'GRADY, MICHAEL (1824-1876), businessman, politician and Roman Catholic community leader, was born on 16 October 1824 at Frenchpark, County Roscommon, Ireland, son of James O'Grady and his wife Cecelia, née Giblon. As a young man he went to London where he became manager of an insurance office. In 1852 he attended a public dinner for C. G. Duffy [q.v], who was impressed by O'Grady's ability. The friendship begun in London was continued in Victoria when in 1855 he was sent by his company to establish a branch office in Australia. After six months in Sydney he decided to settle in Melbourne.

O'Grady was secretary of the People's Provident Assurance Society (later European Assurance Society) from 1856 until 1861 when his entry into politics led his London directors to require his resignation. He was managing director of the Australian Alliance Assurance Co. from its formation in July 1862 until 1876. He had been chairman of the Boroondara Road Board in 1858, a member of the Hawthorn Municipal Council in 1860-61 and mayor in 1870-71.

O'Grady had been elected for South Bourke to the Legislative Assembly in 1861-68 and was vice-president of the Board of Land and Works and commissioner of public works in the Sladen [q.v.] ministry from 6 May to 11 July 1868, though he failed to win the ministerial by-election. He was a representative of Villiers and Heytesbury in 1870-76, and under Duffy's ministry served again in public works from 17 June 1871 to 10 June 1872. Never prominent as a politician, O'Grady had been mainly interested in issues affecting Catholics. His parliamentary career coincided with the climax of debate on the education issue; he served on the Board of Education in 1867-72, regularly attended meetings of the Catholic Education Committee and actively opposed the 1872 Education Act. These were not his only services to Victoria's Irish Catholic community. In 1861 he aided tenant farmers evicted at Glenveagh, Donegal, by organizing a relief committee which brought many of the victims to Australia; at many other times he gave advice and practical help to Irish migrants. An active supporter of Catholic charities and a member of the 1870 royal commission on charitable institutions, he helped to found the weekly Catholic *Advocate* in 1868. For his services to the Catholic community he was created a knight of St Gregory by Pope Pius IX in 1871.

Genial and kind, O'Grady had ability and

integrity. One of Melbourne's most influential Catholic laymen, he was deeply attached to the land of his birth and the faith of his fathers, and by his generous public and private services to his countrymen and co-religionists he merited the description 'a typical true-hearted Celt'. On 5 January 1876 he died suddenly from a liver complaint at his home, Erinagh, Hawthorn. His funeral service was conducted by a score of priests and attended by a large crowd; the shops of Hawthorn were closed as a mark of respect during the funeral procession to Boroondara cemetery. Predeceased in 1874 by his wife Elizabeth Mary, née Reynolds, he was survived by five of their seven children. Although successful in business he left an estate valued at only £1750.

J. F. Hogan, *The Irish in Australia* (Melb, 1888); C. G. Duffy, *My life in two hemispheres*, 2 (Lond, 1898); P. S. Cleary, *Australia's debt to Irish nation-builders* (Syd, 1933); *Age*, 6 Jan 1876; *Advocate* (Melb), 8 Jan 1876; *Australasian*, 8 Jan 1876; M. Mullaly, Aspects of the Catholic viewpoint on education and its political consequences in Victoria, 1870-1881 (B.A. Hons thesis, Monash Univ, 1966).

JANICE BURNS WOODS

O'GRADY, THOMAS (1824-1890), contractor, was born on 21 December 1824 at Lusmagh, King's County, Ireland, son of Thomas O'Grady, farmer, and his wife Mary Ann. Trained as a journeyman carpenter, he worked at his trade in Ireland for some years. He eagerly attended evening classes and lectures in mechanical drawing, engineering, building and kindred subjects. In the early 1850s he moved to London where he was very successful as a builder and contractor. He migrated to Melbourne in 1854 and in December contracted to build Sir William à Beckett's [q.v.] residence. When it was completed he decided to remain in Victoria as a contractor. His major public works were the Melbourne gaol, the Lunatic Asylum at Ararat and in 1870-72, with Leggett & Noonan the fifty-six-mile railway from Essendon to Seymour.

In November 1868 he entered the Melbourne City Council for the South Ward and was alderman of the Victoria Ward in 1870-90; as mayor in 1872-73 he helped to initiate Hospital Sunday. From 1873 he was also chief magistrate and for years chairman of the council's public works and health committees. He was chairman of the Tramway Trust from its formation in 1884 until 1889 and in 1882-90 a member of the Melbourne Harbor Trust, serving as chairman in 1886-89. Though often approached by those wishing to nominate him for parliament he always refused, claiming that his

active contribution on the municipal level would then be lost. A commissioner for the Melbourne Exhibitions in 1880 and 1888, he was a trustee and director of several companies.

O'Grady was genial and privately liberal to the needy; as a chairman he had rare tact and controlling power. He died at Carlton on 28 April 1890, survived by his wife Catherine, née Goodwin, five sons and a daughter. Although brought up a Catholic and buried in the Melbourne general cemetery according to Catholic rites, he sent a son to Wesley College. His estate in Victoria was valued at £45,178 and in New South Wales at £4000; he left it to his family.

Age, 30 Apr 1890; *Carlton Gazette*, 2 May 1890.

SUZANNE G. MELLOR

O'HEA, TIMOTHY (1846-1874), Victoria Cross winner and explorer, was born in Bantry, County Cork, Ireland. He enlisted in the 1st battalion, the Prince Consort's Own Rifle Brigade, and went with his regiment to Canada during the Fenian troubles. On the night of 19 June 1866 a truck, loaded with gunpowder and attached to a passenger train carrying 800 German migrants, caught fire. O'Hea, one of four soldiers escorting the ammunition, gave the alarm and called for assistance in the Queen's name but was urged to stand back. He found a bucket, water and a ladder which he mounted nineteen times and single-handed put out the fire after nearly an hour. A military board recommended him for the Victoria Cross; he was gazetted on 1 January 1867. Recent changes in the regulations allowed the award to be made in peacetime and the usual inscription was changed to 'for conspicuous courage under circumstances of great danger'.

O'Hea left the army and went to New Zealand where he served in the mounted constabulary. He moved to Sydney in June 1874 and two days later begged to join Andrew Hume, who had been released from prison on a charge of horse-stealing to substantiate his claim that a survivor of the expedition of 1848 led by Leichhardt [q.v.] was living with Aboriginals in north-west Australia. F. E. Du Faur [q.v.] who had financed Hume arranged for O'Hea to join him at Maitland. They lingered on the way to south-west Queensland because of Hume's weakness for 'the cursed grog shops' and at Mungindi were joined by Lewis Thompson, an English ex-soldier. The party spent about six weeks at Thargomindah station owned by V. J. Dowling [q.v.], who was absent.

Growing impatient, the expedition did not wait for Dowling's return and left Nockatunga station on 1 November. Next day they headed for Cooper's Creek and camped at Graham's Creek, where Hume refused to allow O'Hea to fill the large water-bags. Unaware that Cooper's Creek after running north and south to Naccowlah suddenly turned west to the South Australian border, Hume travelled parallel with it. Despite desperate search they could find no water and after three days Hume decided to return to Graham's Creek. On 6 November O'Hea collapsed and Thompson left the others to seek water, which he found and staggered back to Nockatunga. A search party found Hume's body and O'Hea's was probably later found by Aboriginals. Thompson claimed that they 'were as fine companions as I have ever met'. Dowling told Du Faur that 'it seems inexplicable to me that an experienced bushman like Hume should have so mismanaged . . . I know that the risk run was unnecessary and unwise. The fact is simply this: Hume was over confident'.

O'Hea had left his V.C. with Du Faur's brother-in-law, who presented it to the Art Gallery of New South Wales where it was found in a drawer in 1950 and later given to Field-Marshal Lord Wilson, commander-in-chief of the Rifle Brigade, to be placed in the Regimental Museum, Winchester, England.

O'M. Creagh and E. M. Humphris (eds), *The V.C. and D.S.O.*, 1 (Lond, 1924); A. H. Chisholm, 'The V.C. of Timothy O'Hea', 1955); T. Dunbabin, 'Tim O'Hea's Canadian V.C.', *Citizen* (Ottawa), 10 Aug 1951; *Town and Country J*, 9 Jan, 6, 13, 20 Feb 1875; A. H. Chisholm, 'The V.C. of Timothy O'Hea', *SMH*, 25 Feb 1950; V. G. Dowling press contributions, Holdings 81 (ML).

A. H. CHISHOLM

O'KANE, THADEUS (1820-1890), newspaper editor, was born on 24 January 1820 and probably christened Timothy Joseph at Dingle, County Kerry, Ireland, son of Gregory O'Kane and his wife Johanna, née Fraimes. Educated at Maynooth College and intended for the priesthood, he turned to journalism in London, where he lived with the actress Margaret Matilda Augusta Morris and claimed to have married her on 2 October 1851; they had one son and four daughters. After a visit to Ireland, where he edited the *Kerry Star*, he returned to London and pursued his career in radical journalism. It seems clear that he was the T. J. O'Kane who in October 1863 sought a divorce from his wife for adultery with Lord Palmerston. In February 1864 he with-

drew the suit, and the case was dismissed as an attempt at extortion, no proof of marriage having been produced. Soon afterwards O'Kane adopted the name of Thadeus and sailed for Australia.

In 1865 O'Kane was a sub-editor on the *North Australian* at Ipswich and prominent in the Irish community. He then moved to Rockhampton where he taught in a private school and sub-edited the *Morning Bulletin* until 1872. From August 1873 to mid-1890 he edited the *Northern Miner* in Charters Towers, owning a half share by 1874 and sole interest after a successful libel action. He served as alderman in 1880-83 and 1884-87, and as a prominent member of the early Goldfields Committee, the Chamber of Commerce, and boards of the School of Arts, the state school and the hospital was largely responsible for establishing a local school of mines. However, he failed in parliamentary contests for Bowen in 1880 and for Charters Towers in 1883 and 1888. He died at Ipswich on 17 May 1890, survived by two daughters and a son, who succeeded him in the *Northern Miner*.

O'Kane was one of the most colourful, influential and hard-hitting figures in early Queensland journalism: he lost count of the libel actions he faced. In his own words, he had 'a warm temperament and strong passions', and was a staunch friend and a bitter enemy. He abhorred J. M. Macrossan [q.v.], editor of a rival paper, but was a persuasive advocate for such favourite interests as the Liberal Party, Roman Catholicism, separation, republicanism, Irish Home Rule, mining development and miners' safety. Once called 'the best Radical in North Queensland', he had a brand of paternalistic liberalism which, by his death, ceased to satisfy an increasingly radical mining community.

G. C. Bolton, *A thousand miles away* (Brisb, 1963); J. Ridley, *Lord Palmerston* (Lond, 1970); *The Times*, 27 Jan, 3, 5 Feb 1864; *Brisbane Courier*, 18 Feb 1865, 19 May 1890; *Boomerang* (Brisb), 21 Jan, 28 Apr, 5 May 1888; *Gympie Miner*, 21 May 1890; H. Bryan, The political career of John Murtagh Macrossan (M.A. thesis, Univ Qld, 1954); CO 234/12/.162.

JUNE STOODLEY
H. J. GIBBNEY

OLIVER, ALEXANDER (1832-1904), public servant, was born on 30 September 1832 in Sydney, son of Andrew Oliver, silk mercer, and his wife Mary Ann, née Kenyon. About 1830 his parents had left Manchester for the Swan River settlement, moved to New Zealand then settled in Sydney. His father died in 1841 and his mother married T. W. Smart [q.v.]. Educated at W. T.

Cape's, Henry Cary's [qq.v.] and George Taylor's schools, Alexander's career was interrupted when he lost his left arm in a shooting accident. In 1852 he matriculated and was one of the first twenty-four students at the University of Sydney (M.A., 1869). He worked as an articled clerk to Holden [q.v.] & McCarthy, solicitors. At 21 he went with his family to England and entered Exeter College, Oxford (B.A., 1860). Admitted to the Inner Temple in 1856 and called to the Bar on 17 November 1862, he practised as a barrister in England. On 30 June he had married Adelaide Beresford Gwyn. In 1864 they went to Sydney where in June she died; they had no children.

On 12 December Oliver was appointed examiner to the Council of Education and from 1 August 1865 was one of two parliamentary draftsmen at a salary of £250. He was secretary to the Law Reform Commission in 1870-72 and in 1883 with Sir Alfred Stephen [q.v.] published the *Criminal Law Manual, Comprising the Criminal Law Amendment Act of 1883*. In 1871 he joined Lieutenant Thomas Gowlland [q.v.] in the *Governor Blackall* on a successful search for the survivors of the shipwrecked brig *Maria*. Later he presented Gowlland with a testimonial in verse from the volunteers in the expedition. At St Mark's Church, Darling Point, he married Gowlland's sister, Eliza Celia, on 30 January 1875.

In 1873 Oliver became an elective trustee of the Australian Museum and from 1874 was examiner of titles under the Real Property Act at £800 a year as well as fees of about £100 as registrar of the Friendly Societies. On 1 June 1878 he was reappointed sole parliamentary draftsman at a salary of £1000. He served on the royal commission into the fisheries in 1880, presided over the Great International Fisheries Exhibition Commission in 1882 and was a commissioner of fisheries from 1885. He was also registrar of trade unions from 1882, a trustee of the Free Public Library from 1885, a fellow of the Senate of the University of Sydney, presided over the intoxicating drink inquiry commission in 1886 and was a member of the Civil Service Board in 1888-89.

A close friend and correspondent of leading figures, Oliver contributed many articles and letters to the newspapers, particularly the *Sydney Morning Herald* and *Australasian*, and spent most of his literary earnings on his library, reputed 'one of the best in private hands'. His catholic taste included the classics, theology, history, political economy, philosophy, science, sea poetry, novels and works by contemporary Australian writers. In 1887 he strongly supported Sir Henry Parkes's [q.v.] proposed

state house to commemorate the colony's centenary and was a member of the state house design board. Among many legal manuals he published three volumes of *Collection of Statutes of Practical Utility, Colonial and Imperial, in force in New South Wales* (Sydney, 1879-81).

In 1892-1904 Oliver was president of the Land Appeal Court at a salary of £2000. In addition to questions of land tenure and problems arising out of the Land Acts of 1884 and 1889, his tribunal also dealt with cases arising under legislation anent water rights and rabbit extermination. In (James) *Wilson* v. *Minister for Lands* which lasted from 1896 to 1901, the Land Appeal Court upheld the decision of the Local Land Board but the New South Wales Supreme Court reversed the decision and severely criticized the handling of the case. However, the Privy Council upheld the decision of the Land Appeal Court. Oliver's experience and travels helped him as royal commissioner on the federal capital; he published several reports on possible sites. Late in 1903 he was appointed royal commissioner to inquire into land holdings and land use in Norfolk Island, but never completed his report. On returning with his daughter the *Overlau* caught fire near Lord Howe Island; all the passengers were put ashore on 19 October and saw the ship explode. Oliver got 'rather tired of the monotony' while awaiting rescue because 'all our books have been devoured & nothing unread is available'.

A keen yachtsman, Oliver was a member of the Royal Sydney Yacht Squadron in the 1860s and sailed the 11-ton cutter *Vivandiere*; in 1897-1900 he was rear-commodore of the squadron and owned the auxiliary yacht *Antidote*. He was also interested in shooting. He died on 2 June 1904 at his home Shelcote, Neutral Bay. After a service at Christ Church St Laurence he was buried in the cemetery of St Thomas's Church, North Sydney. He was survived by his second wife, four sons and three of their five daughters. His estate was valued for probate at £5552; his library was sold and an art union of some of his possessions with 2500 one guinea tickets was held for the benefit of his widow. The prizes included the *Antidote*, piano, engravings and pictures, two of them by Julian Ashton.

Land Appeal Court Cases NSW, 3-14 (1893-1904); *NSW Law Reports*, 20 (1899), 104; *NSW State Reports*, 1 (1901), 177; A. Oliver papers (Univ Syd Archives); MS and printed cats (ML).
M. F. HARDIE

OLIVER, MAGGIE (1844-1892), actress, was born on 14 December 1844 in Sydney, daughter of Michael Walsh, blacksmith, and his wife Catherine, née Fitzgerald. Baptized a Catholic, she was married to John Edward King, banker, on 21 March 1869 by J. D. Lang [q.v.] at Scots Church; they were later divorced.

As Maggie Oliver, she had joined in 1862 the Redfern Dramatic Society in Sydney which claimed to stage plays 'of a high-class character'. Known for her excellence in Irish comic parts, she was later involved with a dramatic club which performed in a renovated iron building in Sussex Street and impressed audiences with her lively sense of comedy. Her favourite part was Paddy Miles in *The Limerick Boy*, which required some male impersonation. A fellow player, W. J. Holloway, suggested that she and other actors should turn professional and form a company to tour the goldfields and country towns. When Maggie and Holloway left the amateur stage is uncertain but in 1866 she was engaged as principal comedienne by the Princess Theatres of Forbes and Grenfell. On Boxing night she played Princess Negroni in *Lucretia Borgia* at Grenfell and also as Paddy Miles. Irish parts seem to have formed the main part of her repertoire and her experience as a touring comedy actress helped to develop the rapport with audiences that was to characterize her work.

By 1868 Maggie was performing at the Royal Victoria Theatre, Sydney, where the stage manager, John Bennett, described her as 'a really good girl and a capital actress'. Critics pointed to her ability to breathe life into even the most wooden of farcical parts. By 1869 she was well established as a character actress capable of changing her voice and appearance to an extraordinary degree; at Sydney's Theatre Royal she performed with Lingard, an actor specializing in the impersonation of famous historical figures. In a legitimate theatre world dominated by visiting stars acting in Shakespearian tragedies, a native Australian actress with Maggie's special talents had little room, so she joined the Theatre Royal Adelphi in Sydney, which concentrated on contemporary 'sensation-dramas' such as *Formosa* by Dion Boucicault [q.v.]. She became Australia's best-known Arrah in the title role of Boucicault's *Arrah Na Pogue*.

At the Adelphi in September 1871 Maggie met the West Indian actor, Morton Tavares; in his Queensland Theatre Co. she opened in Brisbane on 21 April 1874. Although she seems to have played extensively in Queensland, her appearances in Sydney, mostly at the Adelphi, received the consistent critical acclaim accorded to those whose worth is in no doubt. In 1875 she was associated with Australian playwright W. H. Cooper [q.v.] and Australian actors Charles and Clarrie Burford and Holloway. When she appeared as Audrey in Mrs Scott-Siddons's star presentation of *As You Like It* on 12 May 1876 her colonial birth was noted.

In later years Maggie often supported 'serious' actors such as George Darrell [q.v.] with what the *Sydney Morning Herald*, 4 March 1878, called 'low comedy'. She was also accepted as an important comic actress playing Irish parts, character roles of all kinds and even principal boys in Melbourne pantomime. Less was said of her skill than of her 'kindness and goodness in private life'. An old theatre critic writing in the *Sportsman*, 18 March 1908, recalled: 'It was her ill-fortune to marry, and, ill-mated, she was hurried to an early grave'. She won little notice after 1888 and when she died of cirrhosis of the liver at Sydney Hospital on 21 May 1892, the *Bulletin* described her as 'alone and quite forgotten'. She was buried in the Catholic section of Waverley cemetery.

Empire (Syd), 2 May, 8 Sept 1871; 'Stageland', *Evening News* (Syd), 4, 11 Jan, supp, 1902; 'Mummer's memoirs', *Sportsman* (Syd), 18 Mar, 1 Apr 1908; J. Palmer, The origin and development of dramatic art in Brisbane (Oxley Lib, Brisb); Qld miscellanies (Oxley Lib, Brisb).

HELEN M. VAN DER POORTEN

O'LOGHLEN, SIR BRYAN (1828-1905), politician, was born on 27 June 1828 in Dublin, third son of Michael O'Loghlen (1789-1842) and his wife Bidelia, daughter of Daniel Kelly of Dublin. The O'Loghlen family had been settled for centuries in County Clare. Michael was a distinguished lawyer who was elevated to the Irish bench in 1836 and appointed first baronet in 1838. He was the first Catholic since the 1688 revolution to be raised to a judicial office either in England or Ireland.

Bryan was educated at Oscott College, Birmingham. On 14 October 1845 he entered Trinity College, Dublin, where he took honours in classics and mathematics but left in 1847 to join the Young Ireland movement. Hoping to become a railway engineer he was articled in 1848 to T. Flanagan, an engineer of the Bolton, Blackburn and Clitheroe line. During the railway slump of 1849 he returned to Ireland and in 1850 gained farming experience on the family estate, Drumconora, County Clare. In 1851 he worked in a Swiss-German mercantile house in London. In 1852 he decided to read for the Bar and returned to Trinity College (B.A., 1856) and was called to the Irish Bar in Easter term. After five years on the Munster Circuit he arrived at Melbourne in January 1862 and was soon admitted to the local Bar. In April 1863 he was appointed a crown prosecutor and in the 1870s conducted some of the heaviest criminal cases in the metropolitan district. On 17 September 1863 he married Ella, third daughter of James Mackay Seward of Melbourne.

In 1876 O'Loghlen was appointed a land tax commissioner, but resigned to contest North Melbourne without success for the Liberal party in the election of May 1877. On 22 July he succeeded to the baronetcy when his elder brother died unmarried. Friends nominated O'Loghlen to succeed his brother as member for Clare in the House of Commons and, despite absence, he headed the poll. Meanwhile Graham Berry's [q.v.] Liberal ministry was in conflict with the Legislative Council, one of the issues being reform of the council itself. O'Loghlen's candidature for North Melbourne at the by-election on 4 February 1878 was deemed so crucial that the government proclaimed a half-holiday to facilitate a full poll. His opponent was J. G. Francis [q.v.], but O'Loghlen won by ninety votes. He joined the ministry without portfolio and on 7 March became attorney-general. In the ministerial election he again defeated Francis but with a reduced majority. For accepting an office of profit under the Crown, his seat at Westminster was declared vacant by the committee of elections of the House of Commons on 24 April 1879. From 27 December 1878 to 17 June 1879 he was acting premier during Berry's absence in London. However, he was one of the 'Berryites' to lose his seat in the election of February 1880. Next July he was returned for West Bourke in another general election.

O'Loghlen was not a member of Berry's third ministry formed in July 1880. Since 1877 Sir John O'Shanassy [q.v.] had tried to gain educational concessions for Catholics. In July 1880 Berry rejected his conditions for joining the ministry and offered the attorney-generalship to O'Loghlen but refused his terms of payment by results to Catholic schools. He therefore declined office in loyalty to his Church and to O'Shanassy with whom he had little in common save their Irish-Catholic background. Berry remained premier for eleven uneasy months, having to contend with opposition from Conservatives, O'Shanassy's small Catholic 'bloc' and Liberal malcontents. O'Loghlen and O'Shanassy pressed for an inquiry on Catholic educational grievances and criticized Berry's 'narrow-minded and bigoted liberalism'. Meanwhile the conflict over reform of the Legislative Council dragged on. Although Berry insisted on a solution on Liberal party terms, parliament and the electorate had wearied of the protracted struggle. Sensing this, O'Loghlen moved an amendment for a conference with the council which was carried by 75 votes to 5 on 15 June 1881. The agreed reform was on the lines proposed by the council. Conscious of the kudos gained from his initiative, O'Loghlen then carried a no confidence motion by 41 votes to 38. Invited to form a ministry, he planned to lead an administration of prominent Conservatives and discontented Liberals, but the Conservatives had decided to refuse his overtures and to force him to concede the premiership to Robert Murray Smith [q.v.]. This stratagem was nullified when Thomas Bent [q.v.] broke Conservative ranks and agreed to serve under O'Loghlen. With both sides of the House in disarray O'Loghlen became premier, attorney-general and treasurer on 9 July 1881, but lacked a majority. The Conservatives kept him in office to avoid another Berry administration. To his utter amazement O'Shanassy was offered neither the premiership nor a place in the ministry. Of this stop-gap administration Alfred Deakin wrote that 'never was there such a scratch team constituted in Victoria'.

After constitutional traumas O'Loghlen chose the apt slogan of 'peace, prosperity, progress', but imprisoned by an unstable political situation the record of the twenty-month ministry was unremarkable. Any prosperity was based to some extent on the return of good agricultural seasons. O'Loghlen kept his word that he knew little about finance. To court popularity the government sponsored a huge railway programme and then bungled a major overseas loan to partly finance it. A Water Conservation Act was passed. Reacting to mounting anti-Chinese agitation, the government reimposed a £10 poll tax and prohibited ships from bringing in more than one Chinese for every 100 tons of goods. A royal commission on education was established and submitted two conflicting reports in 1884; one favoured Catholic claims. The furore over the 'Grattan Address' of May 1882 gravely embarrassed O'Loghlen who dissociated himself from its militant sentiments on Anglo-Irish relations, and the resulting crisis nearly brought down the government. Early in 1883 he tried to improve his position by obtaining a dissolution on the ground that 'the existing House is divided into numerous sections of parties'. The election was a disaster for the government and O'Loghlen lost his seat, leaving office on 8 March.

O'Loghlen returned to the assembly in February 1888 after winning a by-election for Belfast (renamed Port Fairy in 1889). He gave a much-needed fillip to the weak opposition to the Duncan Gillies [q.v.]-Deakin administration. In July 1890 he moved the adjournment of the House to speak on behalf of the growing number of unemployed. He argued that the government should provide work for the unemployed, since 'no other body in the colony . . . could take this responsibility'. Later that year he was among those leaders who condemned the employers' refusal of an unconditional conference with the trade unions during the maritime strike; and he also claimed that employers would have to revise the old-fashioned concept of 'freedom of contract'. The strike committee of the Trades Hall Council thanked him for his forthright stand. In November he was prominent in moves to defeat the Gillies-Deakin government for its alleged mishandling of the strike emergency. He was not a member of the next two ministries but helped to lead the Opposition to William Shiels's government and was a force behind three motions of no confidence.

On 23 January 1893 J. B. Patterson [q.v.] became premier and O'Loghlen attorney-general. The government was beset by the depth of a grave depression and the associated collapse of a number of banks. O'Loghlen's most notable action as attorney-general was his decision to alter, and then abandon, the prosecution of directors of the Mercantile Bank which had closed its doors. The election of September 1894 swept the Patterson ministry from office. In 1895 O'Loghlen lost a by-election for South Carlton but in October 1897 he won the Port Fairy seat. He took little part in parliamentary proceedings and lost his seat in October 1900. In 1903 he was an unconvincing and unsuccessful candidate at the Senate election. In the early 1890s O'Loghlen had stressed the necessity of a democratic federal constitution and spoken strongly for provision of a double dissolution in any bicameral legislature. Yet he had combined this democratic bias with an extraordinary attitude of 'state rights' which included control of the tariff. He died at his home in St Kilda on 31 October 1905, survived by his wife who died on 9 June 1919, and by five sons and six daughters.

O'Loghlen had genuine liberal and even radical views, insisting that the advent of the Labor Party was 'a good thing for the country'. Narrow sectarian considerations were alien to his generous temperament: for a term he was president of the Royal Society; he was a loyal Catholic and staunch champion of the Irish nationalist cause. But for his Irish-Catholic background and a certain gentle and aristocratic indolence, he might have had more success in politics. A competent lawyer, he was appointed Q.C. in 1879 but refused a judgeship in 1879 and 1881 to remain in politics. He was honoured by the University of Melbourne (M.A., *ad eund*, 1879). A popular figure in and out of parliament, he was respected by political friend and foe alike.

M. Cannon, *The land boomers* (Melb, 1966); G. Serle, *The rush to be rich* (Melb, 1971); *Age*, 1 Nov 1905; G. R. Bartlett, Political organization and society in Victoria 1864-1883 (Ph.D. thesis, ANU, 1964).   S. M. INGHAM

O'MAHONY, TIMOTHY (1825-1892), Catholic bishop, was born on 17 November 1825 at Rathard, Aherla, County Cork, Ireland. He was educated for the priesthood at the Irish College in Rome with his cousins James and Matthew Quinn [qq.v.]. Ordained in 1849, he returned to Cork next year and became director of the Society for the Propagation of the Faith, involving himself in the education of the poor. He was consecrated bishop of Armidale on 30 November 1869 and attended the Vatican Council where he revealed strong papalist tendencies.

O'Mahony arrived at Sydney in 1871 and took possession of his see on 23 March. Friendly, hospitable and a bright conversationalist, he was preferred by Archbishop Vaughan [q.v.] to the other bishops. Finding a paucity of amenities, he started to provide suitable buildings in Armidale and made a visitation of his vast diocese. Involved in colonial church politics, he signed with his fellow Irish suffragans in 1873 a *post-factum* objection to Vaughan as Archbishop Polding's [q.v.] co-adjutor. Next year Vaughan referred to Propaganda serious charges against O'Mahony that had become widespread among the clergy and laity in the north. His jovial habits were interpreted as intemperance and a claim against him by a young woman about the paternity of her child became public knowledge. Later this charge was withdrawn and the author of the blackmail, a priest whom O'Mahony had trusted, was named. Edward Butler [q.v.] said that O'Mahony's indiscreet actions made him tremble to take the matter to court. However, ill-advised steps to control the rumours brought about the 'Armidale scandal'.

Vaughan was told by Rome to investigate the charges and was accused of bias in his selection of witnesses by Bishop James Quinn of Brisbane. Afraid for the prestige of the Irish bishops and scenting a conspiracy against them, Quinn sent Father George Dillon to Armidale to get evidence to clear O'Mahony from the charge of being 'a perpetual drunkard' and mounted a violent counter-attack in Australia and the Irish College. Quinn argued that the credibility of the anti-O'Mahony witnesses could be destroyed and that a conspiracy had been formed to get the bishop to compromise himself, but Rome accepted Vaughan's 1875 report in which he found the main charge unproven but recommended that O'Mahony resign and go to Rome.

Once such serious charges, whether true or false, had been made, O'Mahony had no choice but to resign with the burden of proving his own innocence. He submitted in 1878 and was appointed auxiliary bishop of Toronto, Canada. He died there on 8 September 1892 and was buried in a vault in St Paul's Church where he had been pastor.

P. F. Moran, *History of the Catholic Church in Australasia* (Syd, 1895); *Evening News* (Syd), 8 Dec 1876; *Glen Innes Examiner*, Dec 1876, Jan 1877; Propaganda College Archives (Rome); Roman Catholic Archives (Armidale and Syd).

C. J. DUFFY

O'NEILL, CHARLES GORDON (1828-1900), engineer and charity worker, was born in Glasgow, Scotland, son of John O'Neill, hotel proprietor, and his wife Mary, née Gallagher. He trained as an engineer in Glasgow and graduated as a member of the Institution of Civil Engineers and for some time was chief assistant in the Public Works Office, Glasgow. As a captain in the 3rd Lanarkshire Rifle Volunteers he made miniature targets for the better training of soldiers in rifle shooting. On graduation he had joined the Society of St Vincent de Paul, a society of Catholic laymen devoted to works of charity. He was secretary at Dumbarton in 1851 and by 1863 was president of the Superior Council of Glasgow and a member of the Council General in Paris. He resigned in August and went to New Zealand where he became in January 1864 surveyor to the Otago provincial government and later district engineer at Clutha. He laid out the town of Milton and supervised the construction of a bridge over the Clyde River in 1865. In the House of Representatives he held a seat for the Otago Goldfields District in 1866-70 and Thames in 1871-75. He became provincial engineer at Wellington and helped to survey a railway route between Wellington and Wairarapa. He planned and supervised the construction of Wellington's tramway system, and reported on water-supply systems for the Otago and Thames goldfields and for Auckland. His evidence at a commission of inquiry into an explosion on the Thames goldfield had helped to create an Inspection of Machinery Department in 1874. In Wellington he was active in the Society of St Vincent de Paul and in 1876 founded its first conference to be aggregated in New Zealand.

In 1881 O'Neill moved to Sydney and, with aid from the Marist Fathers, founded on 24 July the first conference of the Society of St Vincent de Paul in Australia to be firmly established at St Patrick's, Church Hill. On that day a preliminary meeting was held, resulting in the formation of a conference at St Francis's, Haymarket; by December four branches were established. Recognized as head of the society in Sydney because of his leadership and apostolic zeal, he became first president of the Particular Council of Sydney on 28 January 1884. His untiring energy in the visitation of conferences strengthened them and encouraged their members; by 1890 Sydney had twenty conferences and Braidwood one, and the first special work of the society, St Aloysius Home for Boys (St Vincent's Boys' Home, Westmead) was established in Surry Hills. He was also a member of the third order of St Francis and of the Total Abstinence Society.

On the tenth anniversary of the founding of the Society of St Vincent de Paul in Australia O'Neill was presented with an illuminated address. He resigned as president in July 1891 because of an impending lawsuit on the liquidation of the Northumberland Banking Co. Ltd of which he was a director. Acquitted of any misconduct, he remained active in the society. In Sydney he practised as an architect and engineer, and was a member of the Engineering Association of New South Wales in 1883-90. He supervised the construction of church and school buildings. In 1885 he had tendered for the construction of a tunnel under the harbour to North Sydney. After reporting on a proposed water-supply scheme for Temora, he gave evidence to a Legislative Assembly select committee in 1887 on the Broken Hill water-supply bill, asserting the practicability of pumping water from the River Darling.

In 1888 O'Neill was a vice-president of the Irish National League. Aged 72 O'Neill died in St Vincent's Hospital on 8 November 1900 and was buried in Rookwood cemetery. In 1961 his remains were removed to the society's burial plot for the destitute at Rookwood in company of those he served so well. A bachelor, his inseparable companion was his brother John (d. 1901).

G. H. Scholefield (ed), *A dictionary of New Zealand biography* (Wellington, 1940); *PD* (New Zealand), 1867-1875; *V&P* (LA NSW), 1887-88, 2, 877; *New Zealand Tablet*, 1873-1881; *Freeman's J* (Syd), 30 July 1881-12 July 1902; *SMH*, 26 Nov 1891, 2 Mar 1892, 9 Nov 1900; Council reports (St Vincent de Paul Soc, Syd).

C. J. FOLEY

ONSLOW, SIR ALEXANDER CAMPBELL (1842-1908), judge, was born on 17 July 1842 at Farnham, Surrey, England,

fourth son of Arthur Pooley Onslow, sometime surveyor of Customs at Sydney, and
his wife Rosa Roberta, daughter of
Alexander McLeay [q.v.]; his oldest brother
was Arthur Alexander Walton Onslow
[q.v.]. Educated at Westminster School and
Trinity College, Cambridge (B.A., 1864), he
was called to the Bar of the Inner Temple
in 1868. He practised on the Home Circuit
until 1878 when he was appointed attorney-
general of British Honduras, and on 4
February married Madeline Emma Loftus,
youngest daughter of Rev. Robert Loftus
Tottenham. In 1880 he was appointed
attorney-general of Western Australia.

Onslow arrived at Albany in December
1880 and was immediately taken ill; according to a contemporary he suffered a sun-
stroke while playing cricket. This illness
seems to have troubled him for most of his
life and is often offered as an explanation
for some of his later conduct. He early
showed himself as both indiscreet and ill-
tempered. His want of discretion appeared
in an association with Baron Gifford,
colonial secretary, and Sir Thomas Cockburn-Campbell [q.v.], editor of the West
Australian, in circumstances which led
Governor Robinson to suspect the formation
of a clique to oppose him. Robinson also
reported that Onslow was offensive to all
who differed from him and extremely
arrogant and dictatorial, so much so that in
1881 Robinson ceased all personal communication with him except in Executive
Council.

Onslow was appointed chief justice on 23
December 1882 but illness delayed him from
taking his seat until July 1883. His relations
with Governor Broome seem to have begun
amicably; Broome, applying for leave in
1884, thought that he would 'do well to
administer', adding 'he is a thorough gentleman and a nice fellow' though 'his temper
and judgment are perhaps not quite perfect'.
But in Broome's absence Onslow, yielding
to pressure from A. P. Hensman [q.v.],
showed him and John Forrest a letter
addressed to Broome by Lee Steere complaining of their conduct. Onslow seems to have
sensed the unfairness of Broome's action in
disclosing the letter to all other members
of the Executive Council; moreover, the
letter was thought to have been procured by
Broome as a tactical move in the conflict
between him and the Forrest group. But the
letter was marked 'Confidential', and Broome
was incensed by its disclosure, which he
described as 'a hanging matter'. He determined that Onslow should not again
administer the government and appointed
Malcolm Fraser [q.v.] administrator during
an absence in 1885; this was a particular
affront to Onslow's pride.

Conflict arose next over Broome's requests
for Onslow's advice as chief justice on
appeals for remission of sentences handed
down by the court. Onslow appears to have
taken a narrow but proper view of a Colonial
Office instruction on this subject and in
some instances to have returned the papers
with the governor's proposals without comment. But Broome appears to have wanted
more, because he sought either guidance or
to bend Onslow to his will. On the issue of
practice the Colonial Office upheld Onslow.
Unfortunately he had been indiscreet first
in detaining some papers pending a reply
from the Colonial Office despite Broome's
request for their return, and then in
ventilating the whole matter in letters to
the press, which among other things disclosed the contents of a confidential
Colonial Office dispatch. Broome used this
as an excuse to interdict Onslow from the
exercise of his office on 14 September 1887.
The action provoked protest from the
colony's anti-government forces, for whom
Onslow provided a rallying point. At least
twice the governor was burnt in effigy. The
Colonial Office chided Onslow for disclosing
confidential information but was unwilling
to confirm the interdict and recommended
removal of the suspension imposed by the
Executive Council in December 1887. Amid
great rejoicing Onslow returned to his seat
on the bench in May 1888.

The next move against him began six
months later. In October Charles Harper
[q.v.] and J. W. Hackett, proprietors of the
West Australian and the Western Mail,
petitioned the governor complaining of
Onslow's judicial conduct in openly exhibiting from the bench prejudice against the two
newspapers; as a result they were constantly
threatened with libel actions. Only four
specific instances were cited; a contempt
proceeding in 1883, and defamation actions
in 1885, 1887 and 1888, the last involving
Onslow's friend and supporter Hensman.
The governor in Executive Council held an
inquiry into the substance of the petition
at Government House in early January
1889. Onslow was obliged to defend himself
against the accusations and his brother
judge, E. A. Stone, was called to give
evidence. No conclusion was reached. In
March Broome asked to be allowed to send
all papers connected with the petition to the
Privy Council, without the Executive Council taking any action or even expressing an
opinion. The secretary of state refused to
act without a clear lead from either the
Executive or Legislative Council. The matter
was then passed to the Legislative Council
as 'the constitutional guardian of justice in
the community'. In April it adopted by 10
votes to 7 a series of resolutions which

declined to endorse all the petitioners' complaints, characterized some of Onslow's conduct as hasty and ill-considered, and recorded that 'peace and harmony cannot be hoped for so long as Mr. Onslow continues to occupy his present position'.

Onslow had begun his leave four days earlier, and in March 1890 accepted a twelve months' extension. Before it expired responsible government had been introduced, Robinson had again become governor and Onslow's old ally Forrest the first premier. Onslow returned in 1891 to the propitious accompaniment of a conciliatory editorial from the *West Australian* and a hearty welcome from Robinson and many friends. His last years in Western Australia passed without further turbulent incidents. The dormant commission to act as administrator was restored and he acted with distinction three times in the next ten years. He was appointed K.B. in 1895. Ill health forced his retirement in 1901, and he returned to England where he died on 20 October 1908.

An accurate impression of Onslow's character and his attributes as lawyer and judge is hard to make. For most of his stay in Western Australia he had an undefined illness which probably rendered his temper even more uncertain. He seems to have been quick to take offence and stand on his dignity, to oscillate between rigid adherence to the letter of the law in situations which called for flexibility, and to let his emotions get the better of his judgment, a tendency noted by the Privy Council in an appeal from one of Onslow's judgments. He seems to have discharged his official duties with common sense and competence, and though he was sometimes thought indiscreet and lacking in impartiality, his honour and integrity were never impugned. He was a faithful Anglican but his impulsive reaction against what he deemed humbug and hypocrisy led to conflicts with church authorities, notably in the Gribble [q.v.] affair. He had a 'magnificent bass voice' and with his wife was active in the colony's musical circles. Lady Onslow is said to have encouraged Percy Grainger (1882-1961).

P. J. Boyce, 'The governors of Western Australia under representative government, 1870-1890', *Univ Studies in History*, 4 (1961-62), no 1; V&P (LC WA), 1889, 1st S (4); *West Australian*, 8, 14 Sept, 5 Dec 1887, 12 May 1888, 15, 18 July 1891, 14 Feb 1901; *Inquirer*, 12, 14 Feb 1890; W. F. P. Heseltine, The movements for self-government in Western Australia from 1882-1890 (B.A. Hons thesis, Univ WA, 1950); CSO records, Governor's confidential dispatches and RWAHS records HS/264, 293 (Battye Lib, Perth).   E. K. BRAYBROOKE

ONSLOW, ARTHUR ALEXANDER WALTON (1833-1882), naval officer and politician, was born on 2 August 1833 at Trichinopoly, India, son of Arthur Pooley Onslow of the East India Co. and his wife Rosa Roberta, née McLeay. In 1838 he arrived at Sydney and lived with his grandfather Alexander McLeay [q.v.]. In 1841 he went to England with the widow of Colonel Dumaresq [q.v.] and rejoined his family including his brother Alexander Campbell Onslow [q.v.]. Educated in Surrey and Nottingham, he entered the navy in May 1847 as a midshipman in the *Howe*. He served with the Channel and Mediterranean Squadrons, and in the suppression of the slave trade on the west African coast. In 1852 he became a lieutenant. In the Baltic Squadron in the Crimean war he was at the bombardment of Sveaborg. In 1857-61 he was in the *Herald* in the survey of Shark Bay, Torres Strait and the Barrier Reef; returning to England he studied steam navigation, served in the Gulf of Mexico and the Mediterranean and became a commander in 1863. Taking sick leave, he went to Sydney in 1864 and with the rank of post captain retired from the navy in 1871. In 1874 he went with his cousin William Macleay [q.v.] in the *Chevert* to explore the New Guinea coast.

On 31 January 1867 at Camden Onslow married Elizabeth, only child of James Macarthur [q.v.] and his wife Emily, née Stone, and lived at Camden Park, Menangle. In 1869 he won the seat of Camden in the Legislative Assembly. At first he was said to be a follower of James Martin [q.v.], but was critical of his government in 1870-72, and took a similar stance towards Henry Parkes's [q.v.] 1872-75 ministry. In distributing his criticism of successive governments of John Robertson [q.v.] and Parkes for the rest of the 1870s Onslow emerged as a typical independent member of the pre-1891 New South Wales parliament, adept at obstructing business. Before his resignation in 1880 he had introduced only three bills but in 1873 was responsible for the royal commission into public charities that cleared charges against Lucy Osburn [q.v.]. Regarded as 'impetuous, but . . . a gentleman' he seasoned 'his speeches with quotations, some of them from old and quaint writers', but 'allow[ed] himself to be carried away by impulse . . . commencing an address reasonably enough, he will suddenly raise his voice into a fortissimo tone and bellow out a denunciation as if he were hailing the main top'. Parkes had him appointed to the Legislative Council in December 1880, 'proof that the government is not very particular with respect to appointing gentlemen who may be expected to support it'. In 1881 Dr G. Goode won a verdict of £1250 from him in a libel action.

Leaving goods valued at under £500, and survived by his wife, six sons and one of their two daughters, Onslow died of paralysis on 31 January 1882 and was buried at Camden Park.

His wife Elizabeth was born on 8 May 1840 at Camden Park. In 1892 she changed her name to Macarthur-Onslow. She inherited the bulk of the Macarthur estates and died on 2 August 1911 in England, leaving an estate sworn at £196,668.

NSW Law Reports, 2 (1881); SMH, 20 Feb 1871; Illustrated Sydney News, 30 May 1874; Town and Country J, 4 Feb 1882; newspaper cuttings vol 167 and MS cat (ML).

BEDE NAIRN

O'QUINN, JAMES; see QUINN

ORD, SIR HARRY ST GEORGE (1819-1885), soldier and governor, was born on 17 June 1819 at North Cray, Kent, England, son of Harry Gough Ord of the Royal Artillery and his wife Louisa, née Latham. Educated privately at Woolwich and at the Royal Military Academy, he was commissioned second lieutenant in the Royal Engineers in December 1837 and in turn stationed in Ireland, the West Indies, West Africa and Ascension. On 28 June 1846 in London he married Julia Graham, daughter of Admiral James Carpenter; they had three sons. In November 1855 Ord entered the colonial service, first as a special commissioner to the Gold Coast and then as lieut-governor of Dominica in 1857, governor of the Bermudas in 1861, special commissioner in West Africa during the Ashanti disturbances in 1864 and as first governor of the Straits Settlements in February 1867.

Ord served for six years in Singapore, where he curbed deficit financing and helped to promote colonial trade, seizing on opportunities offered by the opening of the Suez Canal in 1869 and increasing use of steamships, one of which he bought for his government. Most of the colonial revenue came from excise on opium and spirits. He used his influence to persuade the British to abandon their interests in Sumatra and helped to negotiate the Anglo-Dutch convention of 1871. Seemingly popular with unofficial members of the Legislative Council, he was suspected by the Straits Settlements Association founded in 1868. A court of inquiry was appointed soon after he left, following complaints in the House of Lords against his selfish administration of the Malay Peninsula.

His health impaired by tropical disease, Ord remained unemployed until offered the governorship of South Australia in April 1877. He refused but in November assumed office as lieut-governor and in January as governor of Western Australia. He had been appointed K.C.M.G. before taking office.

Agitation for responsible government was revived in the first Legislative Council session of Ord's administration. Although he opposed all such bids he recognized that economic grievances were feeding political discontent, especially delays in building the eastern railway to York, withdrawal of imperial convict grants and the obligatory use of crown agents for negotiating public loans and contracts. In the council Ord leaned heavily on two unofficial members, Maitland Brown and Sir Thomas Cockburn-Campbell [qq.v.], who used The West Australian to strengthen the governor's cause. By December 1878 Ord could report to the Colonial Office a government 'victory' in all but three of the colony's electoral divisions. Although little memorable legislation was added in Ord's term, the volume of bills was impressive, thirty-three having been passed in his last two months. A £200,000 loan for public works was also approved and work commenced on the Fremantle-Guildford railway, but the budget deficit increased. Though he suspended government-sponsored immigration, which seemed to swell the ranks of the unemployed, he agreed to a Legislative Council request for subsidized importation of Chinese coolies. Although his administration was free of serious public dispute, Ord quarrelled with Chief Justice Burt [q.v.] over certain court judgments.

Ord left the colony early in 1880 and retired on a maximum pension to Fornham House near Bury St Edmunds. He was appointed a G.C.M.G. in 1881 and died suddenly of heart disease at Homburg, Germany, on 20 August 1885. One of his three sons, Harry St George, settled in Australia.

PD (HL), 21 May, 6 July 1874; Inquirer, 26 Aug 1885; Ooi Swee Lee, The first colonial governor: Sir Harry Ord, 1867-1873 (B.A. Hons thesis, Univ Malaya, 1959); P. J. Boyce, The role of the governor in Western Australia, 1829-1890 (M.A. thesis, Univ WA, 1961).

PETER BOYCE

O'REILLY, CHRISTOPHER (1835-1910), farmer, mining engineer and politician, was born at Ballybeg, County Meath, Ireland, youngest son of Terence O'Reilly and his wife Anna, née Blundell; his first cousin was Bernard O'Reilly, Catholic bishop of Liverpool. Educated privately, Christopher went into commerce. In 1854 he migrated to Victoria and thence to Tasmania, where he farmed in the Huon District and worked as a mining engineer near Scottsdale in the north of the island.

In 1871 O'Reilly won the Kingborough seat after surviving a challenged election. He became commissioner for works and crown lands under Thomas Reibey [q.v.] in July 1876. Though not forceful in debates he was very knowledgeable on mining and agriculture. He submitted a scheme for the Mersey-Deloraine railway for £400,000 but the House of Assembly, preferring a property and income tax, rejected it and in August 1877 the government resigned. O'Reilly was appointed commissioner for works and lands under Dr W. L. Crowther [q.v.] but the Opposition was so strong that nothing could be done and in October 1879 the ministry was defeated by one vote. W. R. Giblin [q.v.] succeeded in forming a coalition with O'Reilly again commissioner. He was prominent in adding to the Statute Board and proposed the survey of a railway to Scottsdale and Fingal. His elaborate scheme for public works was passed by the assembly but modified by the Legislative Council and he resigned on 31 December 1882. In that year he was appointed a knight of St Gregory by Pope Leo XIII.

O'Reilly became stipendiary magistrate and coroner at Ringarooma, near Scottsdale, and later commissioner of the Court of Requests and Mines for the north-eastern districts of Tasmania. He retired from the public service in December 1903. In the Legislative Council he represented South Esk from May to December 1909. In his last electoral campaign he had an attack of bronchitis and could not throw it off. He had sold his estate, Brefney, Scottsdale, which he had bought in 1885, and moved to the home of his niece Mrs Catherine Blundell Dove in Longford. He died there on 11 January 1910 of cancer, leaving an estate of £3110. Among his many legacies he bequeathed his *Agnus Dei*, piano, cutlery and chinaware to his sister Helen and his insignia of knighthood with the jewelled sword and appurtenances to Mrs Dove. He left £1500 to the Sisters of Charity at St Joseph's Convent, £500 to the Launceston Catholic Mission, £550 for support of the Scottsdale Convent Poor Schools and £10 to the priest at Longford 'in payment for the offering of forty public masses for the repose of my soul'.

Cyclopedia of Tasmania (Hob, 1900); *Mercury*, 12 Jan 1910.

O'REILLY, JOHN BOYLE (1844-1890), author, editor and patriot, was born on 24 June 1844 in Drogheda, Ireland, second son of William David O'Reilly, master at the National school attached to the Netterville Institution for Widows and Orphans at Dowth Castle, and his wife Eliza, née Boyle. He was educated by his father, apprenticed at 11 as a compositor to the *Drogheda Argus* and at 15 joined the *Guardian* at Preston, Lancashire, where he became a reporter. Involved in the Fenian movement, he returned to Ireland in 1863, enlisted in the 10th Regiment and concentrated on persuading soldiers to join the revolutionary organization. Soon 'treasonable songs and ballads', learnt in his quarters, were sung throughout the regiment. His sedition was not suspected until he was betrayed in February 1866. Court-martialled on 27 June at the Royal Barracks, Dublin, he was convicted of having withheld knowledge of 'an intended mutiny', and was ordered to be shot on 9 July. This sentence was commuted to life imprisonment and later to twenty years penal servitude.

After two years in English prisons O'Reilly was transported with sixty-two other Irish ex-patriots in the *Hougoumont*, arriving in Western Australia on 10 January 1868. In his first weeks at the Convict Establishment in Fremantle he worked with the chaplain, Father Lynch, in the prison library. O'Reilly was transferred to a road party at Bunbury but was soon given clerical duties and entrusted to deliver the weekly report to the local convict depot. Befriended by the priest, Patrick McCabe, and a settler, James Maguire, O'Reilly planned to escape. Foiled in his first attempt, he hid on Maguire's farm until he could board the American whaler *Gazelle* on 18 February 1869. After narrowly escaping capture at Roderiquez Island, transferring to the American *Sapphire* at St Helena and joining the *Bombay* as a deck-hand at Liverpool, he arrived at Philadelphia on 23 November.

O'Reilly promptly became an American citizen and settled in Boston, working first as a journalist, then editor and in 1876 part-owner of the *Pilot*. A devout Catholic and ardent democrat, he advocated Home Rule for Ireland but now favoured constitutional reform rather than physical force and in the *Pilot* criticized the Fenian invasion of Canada in 1870. In 1875 he and others devised a daring scheme to rescue six Irish political prisoners still in Fremantle gaol. The plan involved the purchase of the American whaler *Catalpa*, which was sent to Bunbury to await the arrival of a whale-boat bringing the escapees from Fremantle. Nearly foiled by squally weather and a skirmish with the government ship, *Georgette*, the mission was successful and the Fenians reached New York safely on 19 August 1876.

O'Reilly was gregarious and always surrounded by a host of friends; he won repute in America as a poet and lecturer. Reminiscent of Western Australia, his novel *Moondyne* appeared in 1879; described as 'an idealistic extravaganza', it tells the story of an escaped convict who returned to the colony as comptroller-general of convicts to reform the penal system. In 1885 he was awarded an honorary doctorate of laws by the University of Notre Dame, Indiana. A fine athlete and canoeist, he compiled *Ethics of Boxing and Manly Sport* in 1888 and in 1889 edited *The Poetry and Song of Ireland*. A complete edition of his own poems was published posthumously by his wife in 1891.

O'Reilly had married Mary, daughter of John Murphy and his wife Jane, of Charlestown, Massachusetts, on 5 August 1872. On 10 August 1890 he died at Hull from an overdose of chloral which he normally took as a cure for insomnia. He was buried in Holyhood cemetery, Brookline, survived by his wife and four children.

A memorial was erected on the Boston Fenway and a bust is in the Catholic University, Washington.

J. J. Roche, *Life of John Boyle O'Reilly* (New York, 1891); *New Catholic Encyclopedia*, 10 (New York, 1967); *Western Mail* (Perth), 6 Jan 1938, 3 Sept 1953; *West Australian*, 21 June, 23 Aug, 20 Dec 1952; *Pilot* (Boston), 9 Mar 1968.

WENDY BIRMAN

O'REILLY, THOMAS (1819-1881), Anglican clergyman, was born at Douglas, Isle of Man, son of Thomas O'Reilly, Irish army officer, and his wife Susannah, née O'Brien. In the early 1840s he went to Sydney with his widowed mother and sister and was befriended by N. D. Stenhouse [q.v.]. Trained as a surveyor he worked in the Port Phillip District supplementing his income by gathering wattle bark. In 1847 he offered himself for the Anglican ministry. After training from Bishop Tyrrell's [q.v.] chaplain at Morpeth in the Newcastle diocese he was made deacon on 24 September 1848 and sent as curate to Rev. John Cross [q.v.] at Port Macquarie. He was ordained priest on 22 September 1850. At Port Macquarie on 15 December 1853 he married Gordina (d. 1860), daughter of Major Archibald Clunes Innes [q.v.]. When Cross died in 1858 O'Reilly became incumbent of St Thomas's. He had splendid physique and rowed many miles to visit his parishioners.

In 1861-64 O'Reilly was curate at St Philip's, Church Hill, Sydney. On 8 April 1863 he married Rosa Smith and next year was given charge of St Andrew's wooden pro-cathedral. He supervised the building of the new cathedral and increased the congregation from 150 to more than 700. In 1868 when the stone cathedral was consecrated he was appointed a canon and had charge of its parish. On 1 July 1869 he became incumbent of St Philip's. He installed new lights in the church at a cost of £133, added a large new schoolroom, and in 1871 managed to extract the parish registers for 1826-39 from H. Kerrison James [q.v.]. O'Reilly had much mechanical aptitude and 'built a first-rate boat for his boys with his own hands'; in 1874 when a new organ was bought for £885 he trusted no one else to carry the great pipes and built it into the organ chamber himself. In 1875 additions to the parsonage were completed for £1850.

A vigorous Protestant, O'Reilly was averse to ritual but eschewed Orangeism. He rigidly practised the fourth commandment and would allow nothing hot to be eaten in his home on Sundays, banned Monday's *Sydney Morning Herald* as it was printed on the Sabbath and walked to all Sunday appointments. Ardent, tender-hearted and a bold preacher 'in style a Boanerges', he denounced the liquor traffic and those engaged in it. Incensed by worldliness, he denounced horse-racing in the cathedral in the presence of the governor, Sir Hercules Robinson, who as a devotee of the sport vowed never to enter the cathedral again if O'Reilly was preaching.

In February 1879 ill health forced O'Reilly to take a year's leave and he visited the Isle of Man with his family. When he returned to St Philip's his health had not improved and he died aged 62 at Harborville, Parramatta, on 8 December 1881 and was buried in Rookwood cemetery. He was survived by two sons of his first wife, by his second wife, to whom he left his estate of £3000, and by their two sons and two daughters. Their second son Dowell Philip became a writer and member of the New South Wales Legislative Assembly. Dowell's daughter is the novelist Eleanor Dark.

A. Howison, *A short history of St Philip's Church* (Syd, 1910); A. B. Piddington, *Worshipful masters* (Syd, 1929); *Aust Churchman*, 22 Dec 1881; MS cat (ML).   NEIL O'REILLY

ORMOND, FRANCIS (1829-1889), grazier and philanthropist, was born on 23 November 1829 in Aberdeen, Scotland, only son of the three children of Francis Ormond (d. 1875), mariner, and his wife Isabella, née Essen. The family moved to Liverpool where

Francis had an elementary education at Tyzack's Academy. His father made several voyages to Australia and in command of the *John Bull* with free immigrants arrived at Melbourne in January 1840. On returning to England he bought the barque *Tuscan* and sailed for Port Phillip with his family. In the winter of 1843 he leased twenty acres at the site of Shelford on the River Leigh from the Clyde Co. for seven years, agreeing to improve the land and build a substantial inn. Known as Ormonds or the Settler's Arms, it was the first inn on the route from Geelong to Hamilton and prospered accordingly. As a stable-boy and book-keeper young Francis helped with the inn, gained much experience with livestock and learned to manage the sheep runs that his father acquired. In 1851 the 'Skipper' sold the inn and near Skipton bought some 30,000 acres of Borriyalloak station, which Francis managed until he took over the property in 1854. Renewed pastures after the 1851 bushfires, expanding goldfields markets and his skill in breeding stock and managing stations provided the basis for the wealth that he later poured into philanthropic ventures. Among other properties he acquired the 6000 acres of Banaal station adjoining Borriyalloak in 1861 and bought in 1881 a large section of James Balfour's [q.v.] 45,000-acre Round Hill station, calling his part Kirndeen, and later other properties in New South Wales. He seems to have had no investments apart from land and livestock.

On 26 November 1851 at Geelong Ormond married Ann, daughter of Dr George Greeves. By 1853 he was a territorial magistrate and by 1876 had joined the migration of successful squatters to city mansions. At Toorak he helped to found the Presbyterian Church and became an elder. On 6 July 1881 his wife died at their home, Ognez, Toorak; his memorial donation to St Paul's Cathedral in Melbourne enabled the completion of the central and western towers. On 1 October 1885 at the Presbyterian Church, Regent Square, London, he married Mary Irvine, daughter of Ebenezer Oliphant, a deceased grazier. Neither marriage had issue but the Ormonds adopted a boy and two girls, whom they carefully educated and took on world tours.

Ormond's earliest ventures in educational philanthropy were the provision of a Presbyterian theological scholarship in 1872 and the financing of printed sermons for rural distribution. His respect for education was closely associated with religion, morality and successful living. In 1877 he donated £300 to the appeal for a proposed Presbyterian college in the University of Melbourne for theological training and residence. Becoming involved in the scheme, he

had paid for the completed original building by 1881 and later made additions till over £112,000 (over £40,000 during his life) of his money was invested in Ormond College. Another special interest was the education of working men, and in England and on the Continent after 1860 Ormond took particular note of institutions for technical education. In 1881 he began his long struggle to found a technical institute in Melbourne, but his toil and doggedness did not succeed until the Working Men's College was founded in 1887. He contributed £20,500 to this project and as its chairman spent much anxiety and effort. He was also a contributor to the foundation of the Gordon Institute of Technology in Geelong. Music was another special interest. In 1882 he subscribed to the foundation of the Royal College of Music in London and in the 1880s tried to found a college of music in Melbourne; when other assistance was not forthcoming he gave £20,000 to found the Ormond chair of music at the university.

In 1882-89 Ormond was a representative of South-Western Province in the Victorian Legislative Council. At Skipton he had helped in 1855 to found an Agricultural and Pastoral Association which was later absorbed by the society at Ballarat. He was appointed to the royal commission on education in 1881-84; he refused to be its chairman because of his known advocacy of religious education in state schools but served on the commission, signing three reports. He encouraged appointment of the Technological Commission which in 1886-88 recommended the introduction of technical education to state schools. He was also chairman of the Council of the Presbyterian Ladies' College. On his fifth visit to Europe Ormond had a rapid physical breakdown ascribed to overwork and died at Pau, South France, on 5 May 1889. His body was sent to Melbourne and after a service at Scots Church and a large procession to Spencer Street was taken by train to Geelong where he was buried on 7 September. He was survived by his wife who died in 1925.

Ormond left an estate of nearly £2 million, three-quarters of it in Victoria and the rest in New South Wales. His will provided £5000 each to the Melbourne Hospital, the Benevolent Asylum, the Orphan Asylum, Deaf and Dumb Asylum, Blind Asylum (Ormond Hall), Sailors' Home, Alfred Hospital, Children's Hospital, Geelong Hospital, Geelong Orphans' Asylum, Ballarat Hospital, Ballarat Benevolent Asylum, and £1000 each to St George's Presbyterian Church, Geelong, and Toorak Presbyterian Church, in addition to his large educational bequests.

Proud of his achievement in rising from

stable-boy to wealthy Christian philanthropist, Ormond sometimes aroused the jealousy of other successful graziers. Liberal both in politics and religion, he tried to overcome those class divisions which appeared to threaten the colony he loved by educating the masses to enlightenment and consequent contentment, and by providing an example of social service to his wealthy peers.

A Melbourne suburb was named after him and Point Ormond after his father. Portraits are at Ormond College, a statue is in the Royal Melbourne Institute of Technology and a bust at the Gordon Institute, Geelong.

C. S. Ross, *Francis Ormond* (Melb, 1912); P. L. Brown, *Clyde Company papers*, 3-7 (1958-71); C. F. Macdonald, 'Francis Ormond', VHM, 19 (1941-42); D. Chambers, 'Francis Ormond', *Ormond Papers*, 1 (1965); *Australasian*, 11 May, 14 Sept, 21 Dec 1889.   DON CHAMBERS

ORTON, ARTHUR (1834-1898), presumed imposter, was born in Wapping, London, son of George Orton, butcher and purveyor of ships' stores. The business became quite prosperous, and young Arthur acquired basic literacy. In 1849 he joined the *Ocean*, trading to South America. Deserting at Valparaiso in June, he began a sojourn in up-country Chile, notably at Melipilla, where he was befriended by a family named Castro. He learned some Spanish and facility as a cattleman.

Orton returned to Wapping in 1851 and late next year boarded the *Middleton* bound for Hobart Town, where he disembarked and settled. Over the next two years and a half he worked for various butchers, for a while keeping a stall in the city's market. His letters homeward at this time show Orton as fond of dogs and children and affectionate towards his Wapping girl-friend. Other evidence suggests heavy drinking, and he appeared before the magistrates for minor trade malpractices.

Orton moved late in 1855 to Gippsland, working first on cattle stations. He subscribed to the Crimean patriotic appeal and read Mary Elizabeth Braddon's novels. His career then became obscure, but essentially it was an exemplar of the outback worker's life: gold-mining, mail-running, station work, tinged with hints of bushranging and even murder. This carried him through the Riverina to Wagga Wagga, where he settled as a butcher's help from early 1864 under the name of Thomas Castro. Such is the assumption of this article: subsequently Castro was to deny his identity as Orton.

At Wagga, if not before, Castro's character appears to have degenerated into boor-ishness, his affairs into chronic debt. In January 1865 he married Mary Ann Bryant, an illiterate second generation Australian, already a mother. Late that year, encouraged by a local solicitor, William Gibbes, he responded to world-wide advertisement seeking one Roger Tichborne, heir to an ancient Hampshire baronetcy. Roger (b. 1829) evidently had drowned off South America in 1854, but his mother refused to accept this, and hence the advertisements. Castro claimed to be Roger.

Consequently, 'the Claimant' (as the man is henceforth best called) returned to Britain late in 1866, to begin a period of fantasy. Apart from Roger's mother, the Tichborne family disputed the claim, which therefore prompted a civil action in 1871-72; this failed, and thereupon the Claimant was charged with perjury, finally being sentenced to fourteen years' gaol in March 1874 after another mammoth case. The balance of evidence was always against him, yet he showed remarkable tenacity. Drink, food and lechery helped to sustain him: his weight rose to twenty-seven stone. His very appearance seemed to change from that of a colonial rough to a debauched gentleman. He showed skill as a fly-fisherman and a pigeon-shot. When a popular movement developed in the Claimant's favour, he responded as a true demagogue. During the criminal trial he drew many brilliant cartoons.

Released from prison in October 1884, the Claimant argued his case before the public as a music-hall turn. Drink and women were still major interests, and in his last years he was kept by publicans and their clients. He died in London on 1 April 1898. By then he had recanted a 'confession' of his imposture, published in 1895, and a little doubt remains. His cause continued to be upheld by a daughter, eldest of four children borne him by his wife (d. 1926).

D. Woodruff, *The Tichborne claimant* (Lond, 1957).   MICHAEL ROE

OSBORNE, JOHN (1842-1908), Wesleyan minister, journalist and secretary, was born on 25 September 1842 at Wollongong, son of Robert Osborne, builder, and his wife Rebecca, née Musgrave. Educated at Wollongong, Osborne worked in a solicitor's office, entered the firm of John Bright and in Sydney joined Farmer [q.v.] & Co. as a clerk. He decided to join the Methodist ministry and after private study was received by the Wesleyan Methodist Conference in 1867 and sent as a missionary to Samoa, accompanied by his wife Elizabeth Wastell, whom he had married on 9 April.

Osborne was not a denominationalist at heart and disliked Wesleyan competition with the London Missionary Society in Samoa; at his own request he was transferred to Fiji in 1869 and Rotuma Island in 1870. After two years he returned to circuit work in New South Wales for his wife's health. He ministered at Adelong in 1873, Yass in 1874-76, Newtown in 1877-79 and Newcastle in 1880-82 and won repute as a topical preacher. In 1883 the conference appointed him to York Street, the mother church of colonial Methodism, hoping that Osborne's style would revive it.

At York Street Osborne introduced 'Sunday evening lectures for working men' and his liberal approach to Christianity soon increased his congregations but also disturbed conservative Wesleyans. His generous praise of the Roman Catholic archbishop of Sydney, Roger Vaughan [q.v.], in a sermon on charity provided the opportunity for the trustees of York Street to charge him with heresy. In July the district meeting accepted Osborne's professed adherence to Methodist standards but concluded that his presentation of Christian truth was 'so inexact' as to give the impression of error. Acquitted but enjoined to more discretion in the pulpit, Osborne found his reputation enhanced and ignored the committee's admonition. He offended again when he attended the Requiem Mass for Archbishop Vaughan, defended George Higinbotham's [q.v.] lecture on 'Science and Religion' and supported Charles Strong [q.v.] in Melbourne. In January 1884 before the conference could send him elsewhere he resigned from the Wesleyan ministry and the Methodist Church.

Osborne joined the editorial staff of the *Daily Telegraph* but still felt the urge to preach and in February started the *Christian Platform* ostensibly to combat free-thought. Most of the York Street congregation, including the choirmaster and organist, followed him. At first he identified himself with the 'Broad Church' party, which he believed transcended denominational barriers, and hoped to present a Christian option to secularism but spent more time attacking orthodox Christianity than free-thought. The *Christian Platform* lasted until August 1885; Osborne pleaded the pressure of professional duties but his following had declined. In December 1886 he failed to launch a new series of week-end evening lectures. By then he had announced himself a secularist and a convert from free trade to protection.

In March 1885 Osborne contested the Argyle by-election for the Legislative Assembly as a candidate for Alexander Stuart's [q.v.] government against Sir Henry Parkes [q.v.]. An enthusiast for the

dispatch of the Sudan contingent, he made Parkes's opposition to it the principal issue of the compaign. Parkes dismissed him as a 'decayed parson' but Osborne lost by only 42 votes. After a rowdy campaign in Newcastle, he was narrowly defeated for the third seat of Northumberland in the elections of February 1887. Soon after the Argyle by-election Osborne had joined the *Sydney Morning Herald* staff but in 1889 found more congenial work as a leader writer for the protectionist *Australian Star*; in 1890 he became its forthright editor, advancing his political views and attacking his opponents, especially Parkes and the free traders. This post largely fulfilled his political aspirations and in 1899 he left the *Star* to become secretary of the new Public Service Association of New South Wales and editor of the *Public Service Journal*. A capable organizer, he exercised a powerful influence in the formative years of the association and started its mutual provident fund.

After a year of ill health Osborne died at Double Bay from a heart attack on 1 September 1908, survived by his wife, four sons and three daughters. Despite his uncertain attitude to religion, he was given an Anglican burial in the South Head cemetery. His estate was sworn at £451.

J. E. Carruthers, *Memories of an Australian ministry 1868-1921* (Lond, 1922); J. E. Carruthers, *Lights in the southern sky* (Syd, 1924); A'sian Wesleyan Methodist Church, *Conference minutes* (1867-73), and *Minutes of the NSW and Qld Conference* (1874-84); *Protestant Standard*, 11 Dec 1886; *Public Service J* (Syd), 10 Sept 1908; *Bulletin*, 16 June 1883; *SMH*, 21 July 1883, 2 Sept 1908; *Aust Star* (Syd), 1 Sept 1908; *Daily Telegraph* (Syd), 2 Sept 1908; W. W. Phillips, Christianity and its defence in New South Wales circa 1880 to 1890 (Ph.D. thesis, ANU, 1969).   WALTER PHILLIPS

OSBORNE, JOHN WALTER (1828-1902), inventor, was born on 20 February 1828 in Ireland. Well educated in literature and the classics, he also experimented in electrical phenomena and invented a vibratory apparatus for relieving sufferers of nervous diseases. Listed as an engineer he sailed from Queenstown with his 21-year-old wife Anne in the *Peru* and arrived at Melbourne on Christmas Day 1852. On 1 March 1858 he joined the Magnetic Survey Department at a salary of £180 under the director, Dr George Neumayer [q.v.], who had established an observatory in Melbourne. On 1 March 1859 Osborne was appointed photolithographer in the Survey Department by the governor-in-council at a salary of £300 but continued his duties at the observatory.

On 1 September his appointment to the civil service became permanent.

The laborious work involved in making reduced plans of large maps caused difficulty in meeting the Survey Department's demand for land. On 1 August Osborne had begun to investigate the problem of transferring plans from a photographic negative directly on the lithographic stone. Encouraged in the project by Neumayer, Osborne arranged for a colleague to take over some of his work so that he could devote more time to experiment at the department. On 25 August he arrived at a solution to the problem: employing his process, reduced plans of 'country lots, parishes of Ravenswood and Mandurang', were printed and sold to the public on 3 September at 1s. each. With the new method, preparation was cut from six days to three hours; his discovery made photolithography commercially feasible and had an immense effect on the printing industry.

Osborne's process, which he immediately patented for Victoria, was the transfer of the image by a chemically-prepared negative imprinted by steam pressure directly on the lithographic stone. The Victorian government was ceded its free use. He was admitted a member of the Philosophical Institute of Victoria on 14 September. On the 17th he sent an account of his process to a friend in Ireland but was told that it had been anticipated in Europe. A later account in the London *Photographic Journal* was published in April 1860. At the Philosophical Institute on 30 November 1859 he had read a paper; it was illustrated with a map, the 1000th reduced copy of the original. An official description of the process was sent to England in May 1860.

Although accepted as an advance by technical circles in Europe Osborne's discovery was opposed by local lithographic draftsmen, engravers and even photographers, fearful of ruin to their callings. An independent board, appointed by the government in August to determine the originality and merits of the invention, recommended an immediate increase in Osborne's salary and, contingent upon the free use of the process being ceded in perpetuity to the Victorian government, he was granted £1000 in compensation.

In March Osborne was elected to the Council of the Royal Society of Victoria and in October appointed member of a committee to advise on the introduction of new animals and agricultural seeds into the colonies. He left Victoria in March 1862 to exploit his invention in Europe but found it already patented and in use. He went to the United States, where the rights for his process were secured by the American Photolithographic

Co., for which he appears to have worked in New York and Washington D.C. His many inventions attracted the attention of the Patent Office and he was employed for years by a firm of patent attorneys as an expert. He moved to San José, California, and drawn by the literary and scientific atmosphere at Stanford University retired to Palo Alto. He died there on 20 November 1902 of emphysema and was buried in Oak Hill cemetery. He was survived by his wife but had no children. News of his death reached Melbourne on 21 February 1903.

S. Kenyon, 'Photo-lithography — a Victorian invention', VHM, 11 (1926-28); V&P (LA Vic), 1860-61, 3 (11); *San Jose Daily Mercury*, 21 Nov 1902; *Argus*, 21 Feb 1903 information from Roy Soc Vic.   JEAN GITTINS

OSBORNE, PAT HILL (1832-1902), pastoralist, was born on 20 May 1832 at Marshall Mount, Dapto, New South Wales, second son of Henry Osborne [q.v.] and his wife Sarah Elizabeth, née Marshall. Educated in England, he returned to work on his father's scattered stations; in the 1850s he managed Brookong. On 27 January 1864 at Garley, near Reading, Berkshire, he married Elizabeth Jane (Jeanie), daughter of Major-General E. H. Atkinson. They returned to Lakelands, Dapto.

In November Osborne was asked to contest the Illawarra seat in the Legislative Assembly. He told his electors that he had 'no desire to enter Parliament unless as an independent member, totally unfettered by pledges' and maintained that the wealthy classes should contribute more to the revenue; yet the *Illawarra Mercury* taunted him with supporting James Martin's [q.v.] ministry. In December he won by a comfortable majority but proved an inactive member and resigned without explanation to his constituents on 4 August 1866 and again visited England.

In 1865 Osborne bought Currandooley on Lake George and told his wife that she would 'have to rough it a little'. A keen shot, he was impressed by 'no end of Wild Duck, Swans and a variety of other game'. Wild horses were on the station and he later introduced deer. In 1873 he built a mansion where they entertained governors, neighbours and English visitors. He continued with his brothers to have an interest in his father's stations and coal-mines in Illawarra and Maitland including the Osborne Wallsend colliery at Wollongong. He had mining leases of his own and speculated moderately in mining shares. In the 1870s and 1880s he bought and sold stations; in 1875 he acquired Orange Plains on the Bogan with his brother George whom he bought out in

1883. By 1902 in addition to Currandooley and Orange Plains he had Willeroo, Douro and Gundaroo and five other properties. He travelled widely to his scattered stations and Sydney. In 1888 he bought shearing machinery from F. Y. Wolseley [q.v.] but unfortunately when shearing came round in November 'the machinery was not working well'.

An energetic race-goer, he bred horses from his thoroughbred mares to carry his all-green colours at local southern meetings. With Acmena he won the Australian Jockey Club's Champagne Stakes and Oaks in 1894, and several good races in England. He visited England where he had an estate Karenza, near Cheltenham. About 1898 he raised a local contingent of the 1st Australian Horse. Its Easter encampment was on Currandooley, where Osborne provided free rations, transport and forage besides entertaining the officers at dinner. In 1899 his fifth son Lieutenant James Bunbery Nott went with the 1st Australian Horse to South Africa; he later married the American actress Maud Jefferies.

Pat Osborne died suddenly from uraemia at Currandooley on 17 October 1902 and was buried with Anglican rites. He was survived by his wife, four sons and five daughters to whom he left an estate valued for probate at over £225,000. His widow returned to London and entertained many Australian soldiers in World War I.

G. N. Griffiths, *Some southern homes of New South Wales* (Syd, 1952); V&P (LA NSW), 1880-81, 1, 141, 1881, 1, 29; P. J. B. Osborne, 'Some family history', Canberra and District Hist Soc, *Papers*, 1958; *Illawarra Mercury*, 22 Nov, 13 Dec 1864, 24 Aug, 4, 7, 14 Sept 1866; *Goulburn Herald*, 20 Oct 1902; SMH, 20 Oct 1902; *Sydney Mail*, 22 Oct 1902; Osborne family papers and press cuttings (held by H. P. G. Osborne, Currandooley, Bungendore).

EDGAR BEALE

OSBURN, LUCY (1835-1891), hospital nurse, was born on 10 May 1835 at Leeds, England, daughter of William Osburn, Egyptologist, and his wife Ann, née Rimington. She was well educated and 'mistress of several languages'. About 1857 she visited a cousin in the Middle East where her 'best loved occupation was breaking-in Arab horses on the Syrian plains'. Interested in nursing from childhood, she worked four months in the Kaiserwerth Hospital, Dusseldorf, and visited hospitals in Holland and Vienna. In 1866, against her family's wishes, she attended the Nightingale Training School attached to St Thomas's Hospital and worked in both men's and women's surgical, medical and accident wards. She left on 29 September 1867 and for three months studied midwifery at King's College Hospital.

After Henry Parkes [q.v.] appealed to Florence Nightingale for trained nurses for the Sydney Infirmary and Dispensary, Lucy was appointed lady superintendent at a salary of £150, and with five trained sisters including Haldane Turriff [q.v.] arrived in Sydney on 5 March 1868. Far from robust, she had an indomitable will and courage. Dark, pretty and slim, she enchanted Parkes by her 'bright ingenuous manner'. Within a week she was called on to supervise the nursing of the wounded duke of Edinburgh.

At the infirmary Miss Osburn's promised new quarters had not been started; the buildings were crumbling, verminous and malodorous from sewers running under them and the kitchens 'thick with grease'. She was opposed by the doctors and frustrated by the board, and from 26 April to 17 May ill with dysentery, but she made light of her difficulties in letters to Miss Nightingale.

By December Miss Osburn had trained sixteen nurses but made no headway with the house committee on the vermin problem. Desperately lonely, she wrote to Parkes 'I cannot tell what a relief I find in a little refined society'. Continually obstructed by the visiting surgeon, Alfred Roberts [q.v.], she was attacked in the Legislative Assembly by David Buchanan [q.v.] in 1870, abetted by the house committee. For worshipping at Christ Church St Laurence she was pilloried by the *Protestant Standard* and accused of bible-burning, but a subcommittee appointed by the directors cleared her. She was also plagued by the love affairs of her sisters, and some of them wanted her place.

In December, against advice, Miss Osburn agreed to remain at the infirmary subject to three months' notice on either side. In the 1873 royal commission on public charities Roberts claimed that Miss Nightingale had accused Lucy of 'having views of her own . . . beyond the Nightingale system'. Miss Osburn sought help from Parkes who wrote to Miss Nightingale, expressing his 'entire confidence' in the lady superintendent. In its first report the commission under W. C. Windeyer [q.v.] dealt with the Sydney Infirmary and roundly condemned the 'horrible' operating room, the stench and vermin and accused the committee of management of 'utter neglect' and 'interfering between the head of the nursing establishment and her nurses'. Miss Osburn was completely vindicated and the commission praised 'the vast improvement' in the nursing.

From 1874 matters improved slowly. Miss

Osburn's salary had been raised to £250 in 1873 and in all her troubles she had the unfailing support of Parkes and Lady Belmore. She became friends with the Macarthur [q.v.] and Windeyer families and with Lady Robinson and her daughters. In 1880 the Sydney Hospital Act abolished the infirmary's old name and set up new conditions of management.

In 1884 Miss Osburn resigned. Under intolerable conditions she had successfully established trained nursing on Nightingale principles in New South Wales. She returned to London and in 1886-88 worked as a district nurse among the sick poor in Bloomsbury and then became superintendent to the Southwark, Newington and Walworth District Nursing Association. In 1891 she visited her sister Ann's boarding school, Dunorlan, in Harrogate, where she died of diabetes on 22 December. Her estate in New South Wales was sworn for probate at £5553; she left £100 to Lucy, daughter of W. C. Windeyer.

J. F. Watson, History of the Sydney Hospital 1811-1911 (Syd, 1911); Z. Cope, Six disciples of Florence Nightingale (Lond, 1961); D. G. Bowd, Lucy Osburn (Windsor, 1968); F. MacDonnell, Miss Nightingale's young ladies (Syd, 1970); V&P (LA NSW), 1870, 2, 550, 1870-71, 1, 95, 108, 4, 129, 1873-74, 6, 32, 241, 257, 1882, 2, 1186; S. Pines, 'The first Australian hospital', International Nursing Review, 7 (1932); E. P. Evans, 'Nursing in Australia', International Nursing Review, 12 (1936); M. P. Susman, 'Lucy Osburn and her five Nightingale nurses', MJA, 1 May 1965; SMH, 2 Mar 1868, 19 Sept 1873; The Times, 25 Dec 1891; Nightingale papers (BM); Parkes letters (ML); MS cat (ML).   JOHN GRIFFITH

OSBURNE, RICHARD (1825-1895), journalist and historian, was born on 15 November 1825 in New South Wales, son of William Osburne, paymaster, and his wife Mary, née McLeod. He went to Melbourne in 1837 and two years later was apprenticed to general printing on J. P. Fawkner's [q.v.] Port Phillip Patriot and Melbourne Advertiser.

In 1847 Osburne moved to Warrnambool. He was correspondent for the Argus and Bell's Life in Sydney, ran a general store with his brother-in-law, J. M. Chisholm, and with John Wilkinson founded the Warrnambool Examiner in March 1851. The gold rush closed the paper and Osburne reluctantly moved to Forest Creek, near Castlemaine, where he ran a store with a nephew. In October 1853 Osburne resumed publication of the Examiner. He leased it to H. Laurie and W. Fairfax for five years from October 1867, and with his family temporarily moved to Melbourne. When Osburne resumed control of his paper, Laurie and Fairfax launched the Warrnambool Standard; another competitor was the short-lived Guardian. The 'father of the Warrnambool press' complained of disloyalty from friends and the public, and gave up his proprietorship at the end of 1880. In 1883 the Examiner was incorporated in the Standard.

In 1887 Osburne published The History of Warrnambool, Capital of the Western Ports of Victoria, from 1847 ... to the end of 1886. This detailed chronicle of local events is valuable beyond its purpose: it unconsciously emphasizes the dependence of pioneering communities on a few men of Osburne's stamp. He was closely associated with the founding of Aboriginal reserves, the mechanics' institute, the lending library, the hospital, the first Sunday school and St John's Presbyterian Church. He helped to establish a National school (favoured, Osburne said, by most country people while no church had the numbers to set up its own school). He was involved with a committee to press for district amenities, municipal council, bathing baths on the beach, cricket club, fire brigade, anglers' protection society, Shakespearian society and dramatic club, parliamentary debating club, building society, meat preserving company and a committee to promote exploration for gold in the Otway Ranges. He retired to Merri, Octavia Street, St Kilda, in 1882. He died of dysentery at Prahran on 16 January 1895. He had married Eliza Plummer in March 1854; they had five children.

A. Sutherland et al, Victoria and its metropolis, 2 (Melb, 1888); C. E. Sayers, By these we flourish (Melb, 1969).   JOHN BARRETT

O'SHANASSY, SIR JOHN (1818-1883), politician and businessman, was born at Ballinahow, near Thurles, County Tipperary, Ireland, son of John O'Shanassy, surveyor, and his wife Margaret, née Dwyer. His education was curtailed when his father died in 1831 and he was apprenticed to B. B. Armstrong, a Tipperary draper and wine and spirits merchant. In 1839 he married Margaret McDonnell of Thurles.

Deciding to follow a relation who had settled in Sydney, they sailed from Plymouth in the William Metcalf on 26 July. Arriving at Hobson's Bay on 15 November, they met Rev. Patrick Geoghegan [q.v.] who, impressed by O'Shanassy's intelligent manner and robust physique, dissuaded the migrants from proceeding to Sydney. O'Shanassy bought a small property, Windriet, near Western Port, but lack of capital, drought and low prices made him sell it and move to Melbourne where he opened a small drapery shop in Collins Street on 26 May 1845. Later he transferred to Elizabeth Street; for about ten years he was a successful draper, largely through his wife's shrewd business sense and perseverance.

O'Shanassy's political career began in 1846 when he won a by-election to become a member of the Melbourne Council. In November he was defeated at the council elections; as a Catholic he probably suffered from the ill feeling generated by the 'Orange' riots in Melbourne on 13 July. He soon became identified with popular agitations such as the separation movement and opposition to any revival of transportation and to the sale of crown lands to finance assisted immigration. After the separation of Victoria he was returned as a member for Melbourne at the first Legislative Council elections in September 1851. For five years he was the virtual leader of the opposition to the official and nominee elements and squatting interests that dominated the council. He then thought that the squatters should pay higher rents and taxes. In June 1852 he championed the miners' cause, urging the government to sell land near the goldfields for agricultural purposes. In 1853 he was one of the twelve members of a select committee on the goldfields which recommended a modification of the licence fee. In 1853-54 he served on a select committee to inquire into the best form of constitution for a colony on the threshold of responsible government. During the constitutional debates in the committee and later in the council, he attempted to modify the conservative attitudes of his opponents. A firm supporter of a bicameral legislature, he thought that the new Legislative Council should represent property but not excessively so. The committee recommended a property qualification of £10,000 freehold for legislative councillors, but finally O'Shanassy's proposal of £5000 was accepted. His suggestion of a six-year tenure for councillors who would retire by rotation every two years was overruled; he also claimed that the £1000 property qualification for the franchise was too high. Three of his proposals for the Legislative Assembly were defeated: a property qualification of £200 for electors, triennial parliaments and equal electoral districts. However, he opposed the ballot which was enacted early in 1856. He spoke strongly against the proposition that the Constitution could only be altered by the assent of two-thirds of the members of each chamber but later had the satisfaction of carrying an amendment for an absolute majority.

The growing tension between the government and the miners led to the establishment of a commission on the goldfields in November 1854. O'Shanassy was appointed one of the six commissioners, but before witnesses could be examined, the miners rebelled at Eureka. At a public meeting in Melbourne on 5 December 1854 he was one of the speakers who deplored the resort to arms and called on all classes to submit to law and order. From 18 December to 4 January 1855 the commissioners visited the main mining areas; on return to Melbourne they heard additional evidence and submitted their report in March. Their recommendations vindicated the miners' grievances. The report owed most to the deliberations of William Westgarth [q.v.] and the practical common sense of O'Shanassy who suggested the term 'miner's right' to combine a cheap licence fee with eligibility for the franchise. He also initiated the suggestion that the old Legislative Council should be enlarged by twelve members, eight representing the goldfields and four nominees.

By the mid-1850s O'Shanassy was a man of consequence in Melbourne. He was a founder and president (1845-51) of the St Patrick's Society, aiming to lift it above exclusively Irish-Catholic associations. For many years the leading lay Catholic, he pressed their educational claims on the Denominational Schools Board. He was one of the first trustees of the Public Library. His business activities prospered. He actively promoted some early building and land societies and in 1855 the Colonial Bank, popularly the 'Diggers' Bank', and was chairman of its directors until 1870. In 1853 he paid £1200 for sixteen acres in Camberwell; within a few years he had an imposing mansion, Tara, and a commanding view of the city. To the east, Burwood village rejoiced temporarily in the name of Ballyshanassy.

With the advent of responsible government O'Shanassy was a successful candidate for the two Legislative Assembly constituencies of Melbourne and Kilmore at the September 1856 elections. He chose to represent Kilmore and held the seat until December 1865. The first two parliaments in 1856-61 were characterized by political instability, faction and intrigue; no group in the assembly could command a secure majority despite six ministries. O'Shanassy sat in opposition to W. C. Haines's [q.v.] administration. One of his political allies was then C. G. Duffy [q.v.], a recent arrival. As a member of the 'Irish Catholic' group Duffy wished to reach an understanding with urban democrats and goldfields' representatives on the issue of liberalism against the conservatism of the landed interests. The abolition of the property qualification for members of the Legislative Assembly in 1856 was an outcome of that tentative alliance. Next year Haines lost office because of alleged misappropriation of immigration funds. O'Shanassy became premier on 11 March 1857. He tried to form a stable ministry by making overtures to centrist politicians in preference to any alliance with the 'left'. These manoeuvres were symptomatic of his growing conservatism. He formed his administration with difficulty but three members of his cabinet were defeated at the ministerial elections. After seven weeks of nominal power he was forced to give way to another Haines ministry on 24 April 1857. Although in opposition for almost a year he exerted much influence. He strongly supported the alteration of oaths of office from a religious form to one which required a simple oath or affirmation. He welcomed the government's reluctant concession of manhood suffrage for assembly elections but attacked the retention of the plural voting provisions. Early in 1858 the government yielded to the pressure for triennial parliaments.

In March the Haines ministry was defeated on the increase of members bill which also included the principle of equal electorates. O'Shanassy became premier for a second time on the 10th; he again sought a parliamentary majority by conciliating centrist politicians. In broad terms his ministry represented urban finance-capital. Owing to a pledge of the previous government, he was committed to raising a loan of £8 million for railway construction. Earlier loans had been raised through financial agents and through them from the British public. This time the agency was six local banks, members of the cabinet (including O'Shanassy) being directors of some of them. By this arrangement he won modest repute as a financier. In May the council rejected his electoral bill by two votes. Instead of seeking a dissolution on the issue of equal electorates he clung to office but in October accepted the council's amendments which, although permitting the assembly to be enlarged to seventy-eight members, negated the principle of the one vote one value. He confessed to second thoughts about equal electorates which ignored the elements of 'wealth, labour, land or intelligence'. An important decision of the ministry was to extend state aid to the Jewish religion. O'Shanassy's growing distaste for anything savouring of radicalism was attested by the resignation of Duffy, minister of lands, early in 1859. Duffy wanted sterner measures against the squatters and a system of generous deferred payments for small farmers. By contrast O'Shanassy advocated the sale of agricultural land near towns at a fixed

price of £1 an acre, the auction of better lands and the continuation of annual pastoral licences. He managed to retain office by lengthening the parliamentary recess that preceded the election in August. However, the ministry was defeated and O'Shanassy resigned on 27 October 1859 after losing a motion of no confidence in the assembly by 56 votes to 17.

In the second parliament O'Shanassy remained in opposition. At the election in August 1861 the premier, Richard Heales [q.v.], improved his position, yet within three months his ministry was defeated on the budget. O'Shanassy then formed his third, strongest and most successful ministry on 14 November. His former opponent, Haines, was treasurer and Duffy, minister of lands. All three were united in their determination to retain state aid for religion and denominational education but the tide in parliament and the electorates was turning against them. In 1862 they were forced to accede to the Common Schools Act which numbered the years of state-aided denominational education. The government's most ambitious project was the Crown Lands Act which aimed at opening up much agricultural land to selectors, but its clauses were too loosely drafted to prevent wholesale evasion of the law. Other notable measures were the Local Government Act and the Municipal Act Amendment Act. The government was responsible for two important administrative reforms: the Civil Service Act which classified salaries and set out principles for promotion; the Electoral Act Amendment Act abolished public nomination and imposed a deposit of £50 for candidates at assembly elections. One of its provisions appeared to place the ballot in jeopardy; O'Shanassy opposed the principle but denied that the offending clause was designed to subvert it. The purpose of the Distillation Act was to encourage the making of colonial spirits by means of a differential duty, and an Immigration Act was designed to attract skilled labourers from Europe to assist the wine industry. The ministry was defeated by twelve votes in the assembly over the estimates of revenue from pastoral runs and O'Shanassy resigned on 27 June 1863, little realizing that he would not hold office again. Until December 1865 he was the unofficial leader of the Opposition to James McCulloch's [q.v.] ministry. The government won a landslide victory at the election in August 1864, McCulloch having 53 supporters to the Opposition's 14. As a free trader and a firm upholder of the constitutional rights of the Legislative Council, O'Shanassy denounced the 'tacking' of the proposed customs duties to the appropriation bill in 1865. The restricted scope for political manoeuvre in the assembly and ill health were the main factors in his decision not to contest the election early in 1866. Meanwhile in 1862 he had joined the squatter ranks by buying the run Moira, 44,500 acres in the Riverina; later he held many pastoral licences in Queensland such as Berribone cattle station in 1873.

O'Shanassy decided to spend a year overseas. At a public dinner in Melbourne on 10 May 1866 he received a testimonial of £1500 and left in the *Great Britain* on the 16th. In Rome Pope Pius IX appointed him a knight of the Order of St Gregory in recognition of his services for Catholic education. In Tipperary he revisited childhood scenes and enjoyed the prestige of a migrant who had prospered in distant parts. In London the secretary of state for the colonies attended a banquet in his honour on 1 May 1867. He sailed in the *Great Britain* and arrived in Melbourne on 13 July.

O'Shanassy's absence abroad coincided with the greater part of the constitutional deadlock over the tariff and the Darling grant. He continued to support the stand of the Legislative Council, and was one of the ex-executive councillors who had signed a protest against the conduct of Governor Darling. Though jealous of the status of the Upper House he favoured some reduction of property qualifications for its members and electors. In May 1868 he was elected to the council for Central Province, and was returned unopposed in August 1872. He received honours appropriate to a conservative leader in the council: C.M.G. in 1870 and K.C.M.G. in 1874. In his new role O'Shanassy had mixed fortunes. He carried an important amendment to the land bill of 1869 which allowed selectors to convert their selections into freehold on easy terms, but opposed in vain the temporary introduction of payment of assembly members and the abolition of state aid to religion. His estrangement from Duffy provoked perhaps his greatest political miscalculation. Personal and political differences separated them and Duffy had replaced his former colleague as the leader of the Catholic interest in parliament. In 1871 Duffy became premier of a liberal ministry which included prominent radicals such as Graham Berry [q.v.]. In 1872 O'Shanassy was at pains to thwart and defeat the government; Duffy thought that his compatriot was one of his 'most vehement and vindictive opponents'. But Duffy's downfall in May cleared the way for the introduction of 'free, secular and compulsory' education which both had opposed.

O'Shanassy's pastoral interests proved to be a political embarrassment. In 1873 William Joachim selected 2880 acres of the Moira run on behalf of himself and his eight children. O'Shanassy disputed the legality of selection by minors; litigation in Sydney and before the Judicial Committee of the Privy Council decided the case substantially in Joachim's favour in 1876. Meanwhile Duffy had left for Europe and did not contest the election in 1874. Wishing to reassert himself as the leading Catholic politician, O'Shanassy resigned from the council in April and contested his old assembly seat of Kilmore. The sitting member, Lawrence Bourke, had obeyed O'Shanassy's orders to vote against Duffy in the crucial division which had defeated his government in 1872, but rejected his former leader and refused to retire in his favour. Duffy's supporters ran their own candidate, Thomas Hunt [q.v.], a Kilmore journalist and appropriately, from Tipperary. They referred constantly to the Joachim case in an electorate where the majority of voters were Catholic and pro-selector. Hunt won the seat. The local paper observed that O'Shanassy had 'changed [and] times have changed'. In January 1876 he suffered a similar humiliation at a by-election for Villiers and Heytesbury, Duffy's old seat. A minor consolation was his appointment in 1875 as chairman of the royal commission on volunteer forces.

O'Shanassy was returned to the Legislative Assembly for Belfast at the election of May 1877. His main aim was to retain state aid for non-government schools which would cease in 1878. However, his room for political manoeuvre was again limited. The Berry ministry (1877-80) had a huge majority and was committed to payment of members, reform of the council and a higher tariff which included a stock tax. O'Shanassy opposed all these measures and complained that the stock tax was unfair to squatters. In the grave constitutional deadlock between the two Houses, redress of Catholic grievances rated a low priority. On 24 September 1878 he introduced a bill to provide for the payment for instruction in sectarian schools according to secular results; early in December he withdrew it. He became a prominent activist in the Catholic Education Defence Association formed on 5 July 1879. At the election of February 1880 he campaigned against Berry on the education issue and embarked on a brief career of making and unmaking ministries. He found to his cost that he could help to destroy governments in evenly-divided assemblies but that he was not the 'king-maker' of the late 1850s who could form a ministry. After the election he and his seven Catholic supporters held the balance of power between Berry's 43 Liberals and James Service's [q.v.] 35 Conservatives. Berry's party was accordingly relegated to the Opposition and when the Service ministry took over in March 1880 they refused to consider Catholic claims and also fell. At the ensuing election O'Shanassy supported Berry who had promised to set up an education commission to examine Catholic grievances. After another Berry ministry was formed in August, the Liberal caucus agreed to the Education Commission on terms which satisfied the Catholic bishops. But O'Shanassy also sought power for himself, wanting either the premiership or at least equal status with Berry and the right to nominate three members of the ministry. For understandable reasons Berry did not agree and, ignoring his promises on education, remained in office for an uneasy year. Meanwhile Sir Bryan O'Loghlen [q.v.], a prominent Irish Catholic and a former 'Berryite', refused to join a ministry which was allegedly anti-Catholic, but his initiative resolved the impasse over reform of the council. In June 1881 he moved a successful motion of no confidence against Berry which O'Shanassy supported. In the contest for the spoils of victory O'Loghlen won: he formed a coalition ministry which did not include O'Shanassy. O'Loghlen, like Berry, did not want to share power with an aspiring but failing 'king-maker'; moreover their only common political ground was the education issue. During 1882 O'Shanassy was in impotent opposition. O'Loghlen appointed a royal commission whose tasks included the examination of the alleged educational grievances endured by Catholics. O'Shanassy objected to 'alleged'. He made his last important speech in June 1882 at the height of the furore over the 'Grattan Address' which he deplored. He said that he had warned its promoters not to import old-world loyalties into a new land and to remember that they should act as Australians in their adopted country. At the election in March 1883 he lost Belfast to a young Australian Catholic. No doubt his sentiments expressed in the campaign went against him: 'Young Australia indeed; time enough for young Australia to speak in twenty years' time'. It was ironical that he had alienated native-born Catholics and Irish Home Rule supporters by refusing to be associated with the visit of W. and J. Redmond [q.v.] just before he died on 5 May 1883. Predeceased by his eldest son, he was survived by his wife who died on 13 July 1887 and by two sons and three daughters. He had become affluent, his New South Wales properties alone being valued at £75,000 in 1885. It is likewise ironical that, in the wake of the 'Grattan Address' and Home Rule controversy, few were interested in erecting a monument to a man who had been thrice premier of the colony.

O'Shanassy's political mentor was Daniel O'Connell and, like the 'Liberator', he sought to preserve his limited programme of reform from the taint of radical innovations. Until 1863 he was able to enlist substantial support both in parliament and in the electorate; but for his identification with the Catholic community his political position might have been stronger. He then drew closer to the Conservatives when colonial liberalism sought further conquests and his business and pastoral interests made him less sympathetic to popular movements and more equivocal on land reform. However, the Conservatives saw scant profit from an alliance with a prominent leader of the Catholic laity. He also started to lose ground among some of his fellow Irish Catholics who rejected his politics despite his forthright stand on the education issue. His estrangement from the more democratic Duffy was symptomatic of a wider alienation. O'Shanassy's bustling ambition and a strong strain of egotism contributed to his growing isolation. He was partly successful in his determination to be nothing less than premier between 1857 and 1863, but his later terms were unacceptable and helped to sabotage the very cause closest to his heart. Yet he had qualities which attracted followers for some years. He had an impressive physique and undoubted intelligence. Conscious of his limited educational opportunities, he read widely but sometimes his speeches suffered from his untrained and unsystematic habits of study. On some matters he held enlightened views, particularly on the necessity of Federation and on the general role of Irish Catholics in a new country. When Melbourne was a village O'Shanassy was a practical and exemplary pioneer; in the hectic 1850s he was a vigorous politician who did not stint his energies in the public interest; and at his death he was entitled to a little of the credit for 'marvellous' Melbourne.

G. Serle, *The golden age* (Melb, 1963); W. H. Archer, 'Sir John O'Shanassy: a sketch', *Melbourne Review*, 8 (1883); *Argus*, 7 May 1883; G. R. Bartlett, Political organization and society in Victoria 1864-1883 (Ph.D. thesis, ANU, 1964); S. Dew, The Belfast electorate 1863-1883 (B.A. Hons thesis, Monash Univ, 1969).   S. M. INGHAM

OSTER, PHILIPP JACOB (1830-1897), Lutheran clergyman, was born on 16 February 1830 at Strasbourg, Alsace-Lorraine, son of Philippe Jacques Oster, Lutheran pastor, and his wife Sophie Emilie, née Stamm. His father moved to Metz, where he worked for the Society for the Propagation of the Gospel as a missionary to the Jews; in 1843 he accepted a call to minister to Lutheran congregations in Posen. In 1847 ill health compelled him to resign and, after medical advice that a warmer climate would improve his health, he accepted the invitation of Lutheran migrants to go to South Australia with them as their pastor. He sailed with his family in the *Gellert* on 29 August 1847, but on the voyage he died and was buried at sea on 28 October. A staunch defender of orthodox Christian beliefs he had been an outspoken opponent of the Prussian Church Union, and in 1830-45 published several pamphlets which won him repute as a theologian.

Philipp Jacob had been educated at Strasbourg and Metz, and in 1843-47 at the Friedrich Wilhelm Gymnasium at Posen, where he became friendly with Adolph Strempel [q.v.] who went with the Osters to South Australia. The *Gellert* arrived at Port Adelaide in December 1847. The two friends enrolled at Lobethal College to study under Pastor G. D. Fritzsche [q.v. Kavel] whose courses were designed to be equivalent to that of a theological faculty at a German university. Pioneering difficulties and strife within the congregations interrupted their work but after passing a preliminary examination in 1851 and matriculation in 1852, they studied theology, graduated and on 29 August 1855 were ordained.

Oster was naturalized and on 14 October he was installed as pastor of the Hoffnungsthal-Rosedale parish. For over forty-one years he faithfully served his parish and ministered to an increasing circle of congregations at Rowlands Flat, Lyndoch, Freeling, Pinkerton's Plains, Conconda, Dalkey (Balaclava) and Hummocks. In 1864 he was elected chairman of the committee which conducted negotiations with the Hermannsburg Mission Society in Hanover and in 1866-75 controlled the mission venture at Killalpaninna among the Dieri in central Australia. In 1856 he had been elected to the Council of the Evangelical Lutheran Church of Australia and was president in 1873-97. In 1882-93 he also represented the Church on the council which ran the Hermannsburg Mission on the Finke River amongst the Aranda Aboriginals. He was highly respected for his calm judgment and impartiality. His placid nature, deep insight, thorough knowledge and qualities of leadership stood him in good stead in many church and interchurch meetings. Not easily swayed from what he believed to be the right course, he was ever ready to search the Scriptures for the truth and then follow it without hesitation.

On 8 July 1857 Oster had married Amalie Emilie Rieger (d. 1918), who had migrated with her parents from Posen in 1847. Their first home was attached to the Hoffnungsthal Church. In 1863 they moved to Rosedale into a humble home which Oster had built. He died on 15 July 1897 and was buried in the Rosedale cemetery, survived by seven of their eleven children.

W. Iwan, *Um des Glaubens willen nach Australien* (Breslau, 1931); A. Brauer, *Under the Southern Cross* (Adel, 1956); *Lutherische Kirchenbote für Australien*, 24 (1897); *Lutheran Almanac* (Adel), 1955; Oster papers and Church records (Lutheran Church Archives, Adel); family information.

F. J. H. BLAESS*

O'SULLIVAN, PATRICK (1818-1904), politician, was born on 14 March 1818 at Castlemaine, Ireland, son of William O'Sullivan, soldier, and his wife Ellen, née Moriarty. He was well educated, joined the army and was on duty in London with his regiment at the coronation in 1837. On 2 January 1838 he was accused at Canterbury of assault with a bayonet, sentenced to fifteen years transportation and on 21 July arrived at Sydney in the *Bengal Merchant*. After working in Illawarra, he was given a ticket-of-leave on 20 February 1845 for the Windsor District. He began hawking, moved to Bathurst late in 1845 and in May 1847 to Ipswich, Queensland. There he settled as a store-keeper and received a conditional pardon on 20 October 1849. On 7 May 1851 he married Mary Real.

O'Sullivan became a successful businessman and landowner. He was elected for Ipswich to the Queensland Legislative Assembly on 10 May 1860 and held the seat till 30 May 1863. He represented West Moreton from 2 July 1867 to 28 September 1868, Burke from 22 August 1876 to 9 December 1878 and Stanley from 10 December 1878 to 23 August 1883 and from 23 May 1888 to 29 April 1893. In the role of comic Irishman expected of him, he was prone to Hibernian witticisms and to extravagant gestures like nominating a British statesman for the local parliament. However, the buffoon's mask concealed a keen political brain and a firm belief in closer settlement which made him at first an opponent of the squatter party and later a supporter of Sir Thomas McIlwraith [q.v.].

Although a fervent Catholic, O'Sullivan was capable of rejecting episcopal authority in a cause which he deemed good and in 1862 was almost excommunicated by Bishop James Quinn [q.v.] for supporting his own parish priest against the bishop's nominee in a dispute over church property. He was always prominent, however, in defending his church and his country when attacked. He died at Ipswich on 29 February 1904, survived by eight of his thirteen children. Three of his sons became lawyers; the eldest, Thomas, served in the Legislative Council and became attorney-general and a Supreme Court judge. O'Sullivan's grandson, Neil, became a Commonwealth minister and was knighted.

C. A. Bernays, *Queensland politics during sixty years* (Brisb, 1919); *North Australian*, 23 Apr 1861; *Brisbane Courier*, 28 Mar, 1 Apr, 23 July, 13 Aug 1862, 1, 2 Mar 1904; *Qld Times*, 1 Mar 1904; *Telegraph* (Brisb), 1 Mar 1904; *Catholic Press*, 3 Mar 1904; *Freeman's J* (Syd), 12 Mar 1904; Convict indents (NSWA); Land sale records SUR 4, 5 (QA); HO 27/55/343.

H. J. GIBBNEY

O'SULLIVAN, RICHARD (1840?-1880), journalist and newspaper proprietor, was born in Bantry, County Cork, Ireland, son of Daniel Sullivan. Educated in Dublin at St Xavier's College and the Catholic University (B.A., 1862), he was a brilliant student of English literature. He was drawn to journalism and worked on the Dublin *Nation* and *Weekly News* both owned and edited by his elder brother A. M. Sullivan, later a leading nationalist politician. Late in 1865 ill health forced him to migrate to a warmer climate. Arriving in Sydney, he found work with the *Freeman's Journal*, the organ of the colony's Irish Catholics. In December 1866 he became editor and part-proprietor.

Despite his youth O'Sullivan soon became a leading figure in Sydney's Irish community; he was devoted to ultramontanist Catholicism and the cause of Irish independence. From mid-1866 he penned fiercely anti-English leaders for the journal and gave the paper an Irish nationalist orientation which became more pronounced after he became editor. This coincided with the peak of Fenian activity in Ireland and England, and although O'Sullivan disagreed with the Fenians' methods he sympathized with their hatred of England and desire for Irish independence. To most colonists this seemed like sympathy with the movement and they viewed Irish Catholics with suspicion. O'Sullivan earned himself, his paper and most Catholics notoriety by the invective he directed at Henry Parkes [q.v.] and all supporters of the 1866 Public Schools Act. On 12 March 1868 the daily papers reported that at a meeting of the St Patrick's Day Regatta Committee O'Sullivan had boasted that he would never drink the loyal toast. Later that day the attempted assassination of the duke of Edinburgh at Clontarf by an Irishman calling himself a Fenian gave notoriety to O'Sullivan's declaration. A week later the premier, James Martin [q.v.], carried in one day a bill with seven clauses of the British Treason Felony Act of 1848 to which he added three of his own. Two of them were aimed directly at O'Sullivan and forbade the 'factious refusal to join in a loyal toast' and expressions of 'approval of persons suspected of being engaged in treasonable practices'. However, Martin's attempts to use it against O'Sullivan and the *Freeman's Journal* bogged down in technicalities.

O'Sullivan remained unrepentant. In early 1869 he clashed with some of his compatriots and fellow proprietors after sponsoring criticism of their cautious approach to the St Patrick's Day celebrations. They clashed again that year over his sponsoring of a fund to assist the Fenian prisoners released by the British government from captivity in Western Australia. When he organized a welcome for the ex-prisoners to be held at Clontarf, the Catholic authorities advised their flocks not to attend. O'Sullivan denounced this as clerical interference in non-religious matters and was dismissed by his co-proprietors. He sold his share in the paper and sailed for San Francisco, where in 1870 he became editor of the Irish Catholic *Monitor* and was admitted to the Bar. He died unmarried on 15 or 16 January 1880 of pneumonia.

H. Quigley, *The Irish race in California* (San Francisco, 1878); *Freeman's J* (Syd), 29 Dec 1866, 17 Apr, 20 Nov 1869, 3 Sept 1870; *Nation* (Dublin), 14 Feb 1880; *Express* (Syd), 21 Feb 1880; M. Lyons, Aspects of sectarianism in New South Wales circa 1865-1880 (Ph.D. thesis, ANU, 1972).   MARK LYONS

OWEN, ROBERT (1799-1878), solicitor, landholder, politician and judge, was born on 8 September 1799 at Tynemouth, England, second son of Robert Owen, sea captain, and his wife Sarah, née Hall. In 1813 his mother paid £110 as duty when Robert was articled as a clerk to William Webster, solicitor. On 20 April 1820 he was admitted an attorney in England where he practised. He married Jessie Thriepland, daughter of Lord Moncrieff (legal) of Fingask Castle, Perth; they had two sons and a daughter. About 1840 he decided to seek his fortune in Australia, bought a small schooner and, with his two sons, the elder aged only 13, sailed to Melbourne, where he remained for some months before moving to Sydney. Admitted a solicitor of the Supreme Court of New South Wales on 5 June 1841, he later became a partner in the legal firm of Carr, Roger & Owen, Sydney. In 1842 he was elected to the first Sydney City Council for Bourke Ward and was chosen one of the first six aldermen.

Owen became a large landholder in the Illawarra district where he bought Hyam's [q.v.] store, owned houses from Wollongong to Jamberoo, leased coal and mineral lands, and invested in collieries. In 1848 with John Pring he held Mangoplar, a large sheep station on the Murrumbidgee, until the partnership was dissolved in 1850 and his interest transferred to Pring. He also held in his own name two other properties in the Murrumbidgee District, Coppacumbalong and Lanyon (Bindoo or Bindar) of 16,000 acres each in the 1850s. A keen yachtsman and member of the Anniversary Regatta committee, he won the first-class yachts' race in 1848 with *Sylph*. In 1850 he also dissolved his legal partnership and sold his library of 1500 volumes before visiting England. After 1854 he lived at the Australian Club when in Sydney.

In 1858 Owen was elected to the Legislative Assembly for East Camden. He was chairman of committees and active in debates. In February 1859 his votes on resolutions on the reconstruction of ministerial departments were challenged on the ground that when voting he had already accepted appointment as a District Court judge. A select committee reported that the offer had been a month earlier and condemned his action as unconstitutional, but its report was not adopted by the House. The press however castigated Owen. On 1 March 1859 he became the first and only solicitor appointed a District Court judge and chairman of Quarter Sessions. While a judge he successfully advocated the use of Illawarra coal on government railways, personally travelling on a locomotive making the test.

Owen resigned from the bench on 30 June 1861 and lived in Wollongong. In 1868 he visited England and on his return was appointed on 8 December to the Legislative Council as government representative with a seat in John Robertson's [q.v.] ministry. In January 1870 Robertson made Owen's inability to conduct the government's affairs the excuse to ask Governor Belmore to appoint more councillors. Belmore reported that 'Owen's appointment last year was unfortunate, and that he is hardly equal to his position'. In August he resigned his office but retained his seat in the council until he died. He was also a trustee of the Free Public Library from March 1870 to November 1878.

Kind and courteous on the bench, Owen deeply regretted that he had never practised at the Bar. He died on 25 November at 88 Elizabeth Street, Sydney, and was buried in Rookwood cemetery. He was survived by a son of his first wife and by his second wife Mary Catherine, née Hogan, whom he married according to Catholic rites on 1 February 1854 at Wollongong, and by their two sons and three daughters. His goods were sworn for probate at £15,000.

HRA (1), 22; *Government Gazette* (NSW), 1 Mar 1859; SMH, 30 Mar, 5, 6, 7, 29 Apr 1859, 13 Mar 1875, 30 Nov 1878; *Illawarra Mercury*, 22 June 1915; Roll of barristers, X25 (NSWA); Articles of clerkship, CP 5/168/76 (PRO Lond); CO 201/548/288, 557/44.   H. T. E. HOLT

OWENS, JOHN DOWNES (1809-1866), medical practitioner and goldfields leader, was born in Shropshire, England, son of John Owens, surgeon, and his wife Martha, née Downes. He studied medicine and claimed membership in the Royal College of Surgeons in 1839 and a doctorate of medicine in 1840. In 1850 he sailed as surgeon in an immigrant ship for Sydney and Adelaide and after a short stay went to South America and then to California where he visited the goldfields. He returned to Sydney in the *Queen of Sheba* on 1 January 1852 and went to Melbourne and then Bendigo where as one of the first doctors he had a lucrative practice. In 1853 he practised in the Ovens District for a few months and, indignant over the shooting of a miner by a policeman, began to involve himself in miners' issues. The miners rallied round him and elected him their representative at the inquiry but it was never held.

At Melbourne in 1853 Owens presided at a meeting of the Colonial Reform Association on the land question and joined the deputation to La Trobe asking that squatters be given no privileges detrimental to the interests of the community. In Bendigo, where he again took up practice, he was a leader in the agitation for a reduction in the miners' licence fee, arguing that it be completely abolished. He was a spokesman for the miners in an interview with La Trobe from which he returned to Bendigo with government messages of conciliation. In January 1854 when the Bendigo miners were seeking representation in the legislature Owens and James Egan Wall were their delegates to the Legislative Council, where they asked to be heard on the new constitution bill.

In May Owens moved to Brighton where he bought land but a depression in values soon caused him financial loss and he went to Mount Blackwood where he had a successful practice. He contributed to the *Age* until December when he announced his plan to publish his own weekly journal. In December 1855 Hotham was at last persuaded to nominate him to the Legislative Council to represent the diggers. In March 1856 he retired from the council and patented a gold-washing machine which was found too uneconomical to run.

Owens was elected to the Legislative Assembly for the Loddon District from November 1856 to August 1859 and in August 1861 won a seat for Mandurang, holding it until he resigned in 1863, 'too consistent and high minded' to succeed in politics. He served on eight select committees, including that in 1858 on the Lunatic Asylum at Yarra Bend in which he was greatly interested. In that year during debates on the medical practitioners bill he asked many questions and moved that unqualified medical practitioners who had been practising since 1849 should be allowed to continue to do so. He was appointed acting health officer at Queenscliff in 1864, briefly resident surgeon at Pentridge gaol in 1865

and next year secretary of the royal commission on the Wine and Spirits Statute.

Owens died at Windsor on 26 November 1866 and was buried in St Kilda cemetery. His cousins E. and W. Anderson were chief mourners. Described by his obituarists as 'a persevering advocate of popular rights' and 'too honest for his material advancement' they claimed that he was not sufficiently recognized for his services to the colony.

A painting by Theodore K. King, showing Owens returning thanks on his first election, is in the Bendigo Art Gallery.

G. Serle, *The golden age* (Melb, 1963); *Government Gazette* (Vic), 14 Feb 1865; *Aust Medical J*, Dec 1866; *SMH*, 2 Jan 1852; *Argus*, 12 May, 8, 20, 28 Dec 1854, 27 Nov 1866; *Age*, 30 Dec 1854; *Illustrated Melb Post*, 24 Dec 1866; *Illustrated Aust News*, 27 Dec 1866; G. R. Quaife, The nature of political conflict in Victoria 1856-57 (M.A. thesis, Univ Melb, 1964).

ALLAN JOHNSTON

P

PACKER, CHARLES (STUART SHIP-LEY) SANDYS (1810-1883), musician, was born at Reading, Berkshire, England, son of Charles Packer and his wife Amelia, née Sandys. He was early enrolled at the Royal Academy of Music, London, where he studied composition, pianoforte and singing. He claimed that as a youth he had composed an opera to a libretto by Mary Russell Mitford and played piano duets with Queen Adelaide. His pupils included the daughters of Sir Robert Peel. At Middlesex on 19 May 1836 he married Eleanor Mary Theresa Grogan.

On 4 February 1839 Packer was sentenced to life transportation for forgery and in May 1840 arrived at Norfolk Island in the *Mangles*. Transferred to Hobart Town in September 1844, he was allowed to take pupils while still assigned and soon began to appear in concerts as a pianist and vocalist. After a conditional pardon in 1850 he leased a theatre. At Hobart on 21 August 1852 he went through a clandestine marriage ceremony with Mary Frances Moore, daughter of the proprietor of the *Hobart Town Guardian*, and the union was advertised a fortnight later after a second ceremony by a Roman Catholic priest had been halted. Soon afterwards he moved to Sydney where one of his compositions, *The City of Sydney Polka*, was published in 1854.

Critics assessed Packer as Sydney's most talented resident musician after he had appeared as organist to the Vocal Harmonic Society and as conductor in a brief opera season in 1859. His success appeared to be assured by the production on 9 April 1863 of the first part of an oratorio, the *Crown of Thorns, or Despair, Penitence and Pardon*. It was presented complete on 15 October but the inclusion of a vocal part for Christ was criticized and not repeated until 14 February 1880 as part of the musical programme of the Sydney International Exhibition.

Meanwhile Packer's fortunes were reversed when he was tried for bigamy. His defence counsel R. M. Isaacs [q.v.] sought to subpoena Governor Young, who claimed protection of the court. On 22 December 1863 he was sentenced to five years' hard labour. His appeal was dismissed when the Full Court found his first marriage proved and that he had the means of knowing his wife was alive. In Darlinghurst gaol he composed sacred music and organized a choir for church services, but when the murderer Henry Louis Bertrand entered the chapel in 1866 Packer refused to conduct the singing. On his release he resumed teaching and conducted the revival of the *Crown of Thorns* but returns from his work and teaching on a borrowed piano were meagre and he was soon impoverished. Although his musical compositions were said to be voluminous, few were published apart from the *Crown of Thorns* and in 1883 his setting of a New South Wales anthem, *Loyalty! or God Save our Queen*.

Packer died from lung congestion on 13 July and was buried in Waverley cemetery after an impressive ceremony by brass bands and a choir performing two of his compositions before a crowd estimated at 6000. He was survived by three daughters by Mary Frances Moore and by two sons and a daughter by Frances Mary Little, with whom he had formed a liaison in 1862. His nephew, Frederick Packer [q.v.], migrated to Tasmania.

Packer failed to form any lasting associations with musical organizations and his contribution to Australian music was negligible. His marital affairs kept him out of polite society and his attractive personality made him only an object of pity. His published works show that as a composer he was capable of writing satisfactorily in the clichés of the period.

F. C. Brewer, *The drama and music in New South Wales* (Syd, 1892); Cases at law, *Supreme Court Reports*, 3 (1864), p 40; *SMH*, 22 Dec 1863; *Illustrated Sydney News*, 4 Aug 1883; CO 201/530/24.   E. J. LEA-SCARLETT

PACKER, FREDERICK AUGUSTUS GOW (1839-1902), musician and civil servant, was born in Reading, England, eldest of twelve children of Frederick Alexander Packer, organist of Reading Abbey and an associate of the Royal Academy of Music, and his wife Augusta, also of that academy, daughter of the composer Nathaniel Gow and granddaughter of Neil Gow, described as Scotland's 'national musician'. Instructed by his parents, Packer sang and played the organ as a boy, gaining presentations to the choirs of St George's Chapel, Windsor, and the Chapel Royal, St James.

In 1852 the family migrated to Hobart Town. They settled at New Town and soon became prominent in the musical life of the colony. Packer followed his father not only as organist of St David's Cathedral, Hobart, but also as a teacher of music and as a composer who attained some eminence beyond the colony. The organ in the Hobart Town Hall was procured mainly through his efforts, as a result of which he became honorary city organist. Some of his songs became long-running hits in nineteenth-century Australia: he was called on to compose the Ode of Welcome and to conduct royal concerts when the duke of Edinburgh visited Australia; he composed commemorative pieces for science congresses and colonial exhibitions; his comedy operas had successful seasons; he was also renowned as a skilled pianist and a most sympathetic accompanist. On retiring from his official position he was encouraged by musical publishers to visit England to avail himself of the wider scope for publishing his compositions there. Other members of Packer's family also distinguished themselves in music, including his uncle, Charles Sandys Packer [q.v.], with whom he has sometimes been confused.

Packer was first appointed to the colonial civil service as chief operator in the telegraph office in 1859. After a short time as landing-waiter in the Customs Department in Launceston, he returned in 1862 to Hobart, where he served as clerk in several departments. He became chief clerk in the telegraph department in 1866 and superintendent of telegraphs in 1873. In 1878 he moved to the House of Assembly as assistant clerk and librarian, and was clerk of the House from 1882 till his retirement in 1894. He was twice married in Hobart: first, on 1 March 1869 to Marianne Chamberlain; and second, on 22 November 1890 to Clarice Octavia Allison. Packer moved in 1895 to Sydney and after long illness in the Parramatta Asylum died on 1 August 1902.

Several of his brothers became civil servants in Tasmania and Queensland, and two rose to permanent headships: in the Tasmanian Treasury and Public Works Departments. Sir Frank Packer of Consolidated Press, Sydney, is a grandnephew. The Tasmanian State Library has the scores of many of Packer's songs, both religious and secular.

Tasmanian Mail, 11 May 1895; *Mercury*, 2 Aug 1902.   R. L. WETTENHALL

PADBURY, WALTER (1820-1907), pastoralist, merchant and philanthropist, was born on 22 December 1820 at Stonesfield, Oxfordshire, England, second son of Thomas Padbury, small farmer, and his wife Ruth. With little schooling he sailed to Western Australia in the *Protector*, arriving at Fremantle on 25 February 1830 with his father who intended to send for his wife and other children. Unfortunately he died in July, leaving his son in the care of a married couple who also arrived in the *Protector*; they stole the money his father had left him and absconded.

Padbury worked around Perth and at 16 was employed as a shepherd by the Burges [q.v.] brothers of York for £10 a year; he stayed with them until 1842 when his wage was £40. He then went fencing, shearing and droving. He sold stock to butchers very profitably and brought his mother and the family to the colony. In April 1844 he married Charlotte, 18-year-old daughter of William Nairn [q.v.] and his wife Mary Ann.

In 1845 Padbury opened a butchery in Perth and by 1857 was able to buy Yathroo, a property which he gradually developed. He also established a flour-mill and gave his employees good wages and comfortable quarters. In 1863, stimulated by F. T. Gregory's [q.v.] report on his north-west expedition, Padbury bought the cutter *Mystery*, took up a station on the De Grey River and sent the first shipment of stock there. On 25 June at a public dinner in his honour he was congratulated by Governor J. S. Hampton for his enterprise. In 1866 he bought the *Emma* for the north-west trade; she was lost in 1867 with all on board. This loss and low wool prices forced him and his friends to abandon the area.

In 1865 Padbury bought the *Bridgetown* and traded profitably with India, Singapore and London. With William Thorley Loton he set up as W. Padbury & Co., general store-keepers, in Perth and Guildford. In 1874 they took delivery of the *Charlotte Padbury* which had been built for them at Falmouth. They acquired other ships, including the *Helena Mena* in 1876. Their shipping venture was very successful until about 1890 when competition became too keen and they withdrew. In 1898 Padbury started the Peerless Flour Mills Ltd at Guildford, a boon to farmers in the surrounding district. These mills still operate with a member of the family as director.

Padbury was long associated with the Agricultural Society and had early won its award for the best shepherd in the colony. He was elected president in 1875-76 and 1885, and vice-president in 1907. Active in public affairs he was first elected to the Perth City Council in 1864. He represented Swan River in the Legislative Council from December 1872 to January 1878 and in 1883 became a justice of the peace. In 1884 he became chairman of the Guildford Municipal Council and in 1887 the first mayor. In 1887-92 he served on the commission on agriculture. He had taken his wife to

England in 1878 hoping to retire there but found the climate too severe and returned to Western Australia in 1880, on the journey travelling widely in the United States and New Zealand. Charlotte died in February 1895, warmly remembered for her private and secret charity.

Padbury wrote many letters to the press on such subjects as protection versus free trade, immigration, land reforms, the jury system, overstocking of runs and education. He retained his interest in the north-west and his various farming properties and also gave much time to church work and charitable institutions. Through his generosity the Church of England established the diocese of Bunbury. He also contributed generously to the Parkerville Children's Home. He died on 18 April 1907 and was buried in the East Perth cemetery. With no heirs, he left legacies to relations and friends, and money in trust for the upkeep of St George's Cathedral. The balance of his estate, about £90,000, was to be divided between the diocesan trustees of the Church of England, the trustees of the Hospitals and Lunatic Asylums and the trustees of the Poor Houses. The money left to the latter is still held in trust; known as the Walter Padbury Bequest, it endures as a memorial to one of Western Australia's outstanding pioneers.

C. Cammilleri, 'Walter Padbury . . . pioneer pastoralist, merchant and philanthropist', JRWAHS, 7 (1971), pt 3, and for bibliog; Walter Padbury Bequest, Minutes, annual reports and Crown Law file 1043 (Battye Lib, Perth); Swan District Agr and Horticultural Soc, Annual report 1876 (Battye Lib, Perth).

CARA CAMMILLERI

PALING, WILLIAM HENRY (1825-1895), musician, merchant and philanthropist, was born on 1 September 1825 at Woerden, Netherlands, son of John Paling, pianoforte manufacturer. He was trained in music under Berthold Tours, a leading violin pedagogue, who favoured Paling as a pupil and made possible his appointment as violin teacher at the Academy in Rotterdam. In later advertisements he described himself as 'first violinist of the Royal Holland Academy' and as director of an academy of music in that country. He sailed for Sydney and arrived in 1853.

Paling attracted quick recognition as a music teacher and entrepreneur. He offered private tuition in both violin and piano, and was also a 'professor of music' at Springfield College, a ladies' boarding school founded at Darlinghurst by Lady Murray. From the same period dates the first W. H. Paling music warehouse at 83 Wynyard Square, 'an

unpretentious place, built of timber and galvanized iron, and surrounded by an uneven wooden fence'. As composer he issued his 'Sydney Railway Waltz' to commemorate the inauguration of the Sydney to Parramatta railway on 26 September 1855. Later that year he appeared in concerts as soloist in the Beriot concerto and in association with Edouard Boulanger, Flora Harris, Sara Flower and the Sydney Philharmonic Society; the most favoured venue was the concert room of the Royal Hotel. In November Paling announced the opening of a 'New South Wales Academy of Music — arranged on a continental system'. It was established at 5 Bligh Street although the notices were issued from Paling's residence at 66 Macquarie Street. He also inaugurated a Quartette and Glee Club for Gentlemen Amateurs, and a society, Erudito Musica, which first met in January 1856. In that year he assumed exclusive direction of the Academy of Music, took charge of piano classes at the School of Arts, appeared as organist with the Sydney Choral Society and conducted a Philharmonic Society concert.

The favourable economy of the golden years generated demand for imported European pianofortes and local topical sheet music. Paling obtained an agency from European pianoforte manufacturers and his commercial enterprises rapidly brought him affluence and influence. They also enabled him to combine concert promotion with his philanthropic aspirations; among the most spectacular was a vocal and instrumental concert on 12 April 1858 to raise funds for victims of the Indian mutiny. Such successful fund-raising concerts, mostly on behalf of local institutions including the Bent Street Library in 1860, increasingly absorbed Paling's energies. His own compositions then reflected not only the taste for topical programme titles but also acknowledged the fascination of the popular European virtuoso repertory in such work as the 'Fantasia for Violin on themes from Bellini's Norma' in 1858.

In 1864 Paling went to Europe to obtain new instruments and sheet music for sale in the colony. On his return he advertised in the Sydney Morning Herald, 7 June 1865, that friends and the public were invited to inspect his large and varied 'selections of Pianofortes from the best makers . . . being guided by many years' experience respecting the most suitable instruments for the climate'. He went to Europe again in 1870-71 and in 1884-85 when he made contact with the Austrian musician-entrepreneur Pietro Marich, who joined the company as his personal secretary, became general manager in 1888 and managing director in 1895. Expanding business compelled Paling to seek

S

larger premises than the original building in Wynyard Square. He acquired a site in Barrack Street, opened an extensive show-room at 352 George Street in 1875 and another in Ash Street in 1880. In 1883 he bought large premises at 356 George Street for £45,000 and reorganized the business as a limited liability company. In 1891 Paling moved to the company's present site at 338 George Street. He also established branches at Toowoomba in 1884, Brisbane in 1888 and Newcastle in 1892.

Paling's zest for civic and philanthropic activities won him many honorary public offices. He was made a justice of the peace in 1872 and regularly attended the bench in Sydney until unpaid justices of the peace were replaced by stipendiary magistrates. In 1879 he had become a founding director of the Mercantile Mutual Insurance Co. In 1880 he was elected a member of the Royal Society of New South Wales. He lived at Stanmore and was an alderman of Petersham Municipality in 1876-89 and mayor in 1881-82. In June 1886 he presented a clock for the tower of the local town hall, where it remained in service until the building was demolished in 1938. His far-sighted pre-occupation with questions of sanitation, health and hospital accommodation culminated in his presentation to the colony on 23 April 1888 of his 450-acre model farm Grasmere at Camden, valued at £20,000, to be used as a hospital for convalescents and incurables; he also donated £10,000 for the erection of suitable buildings. A public committee led by Sir Henry Parkes [q.v.] raised a further £15,000 for equipment and development at the Carrington Convalescent Hospital on the site.

Paling made his last trip to Europe in 1892 and in November 1894 returned in failing health. He died at Stanmore on 27 August 1895 and was buried in the Waverley cemetery. His first wife Mary Anne, née Maney, whom he had married at Norwich, England, died on 27 September 1877 and was buried in the old Balmain cemetery. At 53 he married the widow Anne Lake, née Leeder; neither union had any issue. His estate was valued for probate at £208,563 and was mostly left to his three stepsons.

Paling's brother, Richard John, also migrated to Sydney. He moved to Melbourne and ran a music store and importing agency from 1857 to 1886. He became a partner in his brother's firm and returned to Sydney; he died at Bondi on 6 March 1914 leaving an estate of £36,500.

W. A. Orchard, *Music in Australia* (Melb, 1952); E. Keane, *Music for a hundred years* (Syd, 1954).   ANDREW D. McCREDIE

PALMER, Sir ARTHUR HUNTER (1819-1898), pastoralist and politician, was born on 28 December 1819 in Armagh, Ireland, son of Arthur Palmer, naval lieutenant, and his wife Emily, née Hunter, of Dublin and Downpatrick. Educated at Youghal Grammar School and by a private tutor in Dublin, Palmer sailed in the *City of Edinburgh* and arrived at Sydney in 1838. In 1839 he worked on a property in the Illawarra district, probably as a jackeroo, and in 1840 became manager of the New England pastoral holdings of Henry Dangar [q.v.]. Increasingly involved in the affairs of the family, Palmer was entrusted with the care of all their properties and affairs while Dangar and his wife visited England in 1852. More than once Palmer mediated in disagreements between Dangar and his children. On his return in 1856 an agreement was drawn up making Palmer general manager of all the Dangar holdings, thereby enabling him to accumulate much capital and stock. Despite his worth to the family they refused him permission to marry Margaret Dangar in 1857. He did not press his claims and continued to manage the Dangar affairs until 1863 when the conditions of the agreement were fulfilled. From the profits Palmer had by then begun his own pastoral endeavours in Queensland.

After failing to obtain suitable land in the Mitchell District, Palmer leased thirteen runs totalling 900 square miles near the Belyando River in the South Kennedy District in 1863; he called his station Beaufort. According to C. A. Bernays [q.v.], Palmer gained his earliest experience in Queensland as a bullock-driver. This seems very unlikely; he did own bullock drays but only for use on his holdings and as a business enterprise. To improve his stock he bought rams at the Darling Downs Sheep Show in July 1864. Over the years he expanded Beaufort and speculated in other land holdings, but with the succession of financial crises, the application of land Acts to large stations and Palmer's troubles as a director of the Queensland National Bank, Beaufort passed from his possession in 1897.

Once established as a successful pastoralist, Palmer began to take an active part in local politics. In 1865 he acted as a magistrate in the Port Curtis District. By then he felt secure enough to contemplate marriage. He sought the hand of Cecilia, daughter of a close associate, Archibald Mosman [q.v.], for whose wife's marriage settlement in 1847 Palmer had been a trustee. Though he proposed to Cecilia in December 1863 and received parental approval, they were not married until 8 June 1865 in Sydney.

In 1866 Palmer was elected for Port Curtis to the Legislative Assembly and as expected aligned himself with the squatter party. After the Macalister [q.v.] government fell in 1867, Palmer became colonial secretary and secretary for public works under R. R. Mackenzie [q.v.]. In this 'political apprenticeship' Palmer proved his worth as an administrator. The ministry had come to power in difficult times, and Palmer initiated stringent economies in the government departments. Because of his affiliation with the squatter party and his retrenchment policy, he was bitterly criticized by the liberal faction, odium that he was to carry long into the next decade. The Mackenzie ministry fell in November 1868 and Palmer joined the Opposition.

When Charles Lilley's [q.v.] ministry fell in May 1870 Governor Blackall asked Palmer to take the reins of government. This request came as a complete surprise for he had arranged to retire from politics and leave Brisbane. The party he gathered around him was the best-organized and cohesive group that the colony had hitherto seen. Palmer was colonial secretary and premier, holding office until January 1874.

Even though his supporters were well integrated, Palmer cannot be said to have been instrumental in producing much legislation. The colony had no tradition of self-government and little awareness of parliamentary procedure. On the other hand, what the members lacked in experience they made up with zeal. Since the party system had not developed any close discipline, regionalism and private interest were rife. During his premiership general elections were held in September 1870, September 1871 and December 1873. The tactics adopted by the Liberal opposition made proceedings difficult for the government; public meetings, petitions to the governor, persistent attacks through the Brisbane press and deliberate absence from the House were among the methods employed by the Opposition. Because of the depressed economy in 1870 Palmer again adopted a retrenchment policy, an action far from popular with city dwellers. In 1871 the most significant issue was railway extension. The Opposition sought the completion of the Brisbane-Ipswich line while the government wanted to extend the railway to north Queensland. Later that year attention turned to electoral reform. However, by August 1872 a working compromise had been reached and important bills were passed. Most significant for Palmer was the Electoral Redistribution Act which divided the colony according to the proportion of adult males and allowed one member for each electorate, although it was probably responsible for shattering Palmer's majority in the next general election. Other successful bills dealt with the Brisbane-Ipswich railway, stimulus to European immigration, and a Homestead Areas Act which provided for the resumption of runs in the Darling Downs and the Moreton District to permit the increase of small-scale settlement on the land, then the most liberal land regulation in Australia. Permission was granted for floating a loan in England for public works and other government projects.

During the parliamentary recess from August 1872 to May 1873 Palmer revealed his growing liberalism by working on a bill for the complete reform of state education. Strangely enough, he was at one with Lilley, his staunchest political opponent, both believing that state education was the only form which government expenditure should support. He collaborated with Lilley in drafting the bill and as a private member introduced it on 3 June 1873. It recommended only one class of schools and one system of primary education, the administration of which was to be directly responsible to parliament under a ministry for education. The principle of free education was vital to Palmer. In this bill he proposed that, after free primary education, the students who passed examinations could proceed to free grammar schools and even to a free university. For Palmer, free education was also to be compulsory; 'he looked upon it as the first duty of the State—particularly in a colony like this, where every male adult possessed such large political privileges—to educate the inhabitants so that they might know how to value and avail themselves of these privileges'. This liberal stance lost Palmer much favour from his own party members, who preferred the church school system with state aid. The Roman Catholics and Anglicans vigorously opposed this system as they stood to lose all financial support from the state and no provision was made in the bill for religious instruction during school hours. It failed at the second reading with most of Palmer's colleagues voting against it and he resigned. The governor dissolved parliament to allow an enlarged House to be elected on the broader basis of the new Electoral Act.

The election resulted in leaving Palmer's party very much in the minority. When parliament assembled on 6 January 1874 Palmer was defeated and became leader of the Opposition. In 1875 Griffith introduced an education bill which Palmer claimed to be a conflation of the two bills he had prepared. He associated more and more with Thomas McIlwraith [q.v.], who increased control of Palmer's political party. In 1878 he retired as leader of the Opposition in favour of McIlwraith and was elected for North Brisbane; McIlwraith became premier and in January 1879 Palmer was appointed colonial secretary, secretary for public instruction and president of the Executive Council. In 1879 their affairs became further intermeshed by McIlwraith's marriage to Harriette Ann, sister of Palmer's wife. For a time in 1879-80 Palmer acted as premier while McIlwraith was in England negotiating an ambitious loan of £3 million for public works. This close association was to bring Palmer certain misfortunes when, for example, in 1880 Griffith accused Palmer and McIlwraith of owning shares in the shipping firm of McIlwraith, McEacharn & Co. which had been granted the contract to ship steel rails for Queensland railway construction. Both were exonerated from this scandal by a royal commission in 1881. Palmer was appointed K.C.M.G. In December he resigned from the assembly and was called to the Legislative Council. From 2 May to 6 November 1883 and from 9 October 1888 to 1 May 1889 he acted as administrator of the colony in the absence of the governor and from 15 November 1895 to 9 April 1896 was the first lieut-governor of the colony.

In 1885 his wife had died, leaving three sons and two of their four daughters. Palmer's last years were not easy. He had poor health and suffered much from arthritis. He was also involved in financial scandals in association with McIlwraith. Perhaps the most dramatic was the result of his directorship of the Queensland National Bank. Through a policy of careless loans and mismanagement E. R. Drury [q.v.], the general manager, over-extended the resources of the bank and in the financial crises of the early 1890s was forced to suspend payments. The new manager, Walter Varden Ralston, discovered the extent of the bank's insolvency, but in McIlwraith's absence Palmer had to face the public outcry as one of the old directors. The Supreme Court found Palmer and the other directors not guilty of collusion and they were acquitted of the charges. This decision cleared his name but was issued after he died on 19 March 1898 at his home, Eastern Grey, Toowong, Brisbane. He left an estate of £23,900.

E. Palmer, Early days in North Queensland (Syd, 1903); C. A. Bernays, Queensland politics during sixty years (Brisb, 1919); A. D. Fraser (ed), This century of ours (Syd, 1938); G. Blainey, Gold and paper: a history of the National Bank of Australasia Limited (Melb, 1958); D. K. Dignan, Sir Thomas McIlwraith: a political portrait (B.A. Hons thesis, Univ Qld, 1951); J. X. Jobson, A biography of Sir Arthur Hunter Palmer (B.A. Hons thesis, Univ Qld, 1961); Palmer-McIlwraith letters (Oxley Lib, Brisb).   J. X. JOBSON

PALMER, GEORGE EUGENE (1859-1910), cricketer, was born on 13 February 1859 at Mulwala, New South Wales, eldest child of David Bernard Palmer, poundkeeper, and his wife Mary, née Barry. Educated at Macgregor's school in Emerald Hill, Melbourne, he joined the 'Young Victoria' cricket club and through his bowling skill was invited to play with the South Melbourne club.

In December 1878 Palmer played for the Victorian 15 against the Australian 11 and against Lord Harris's English 11, taking 4 wickets for 72. In the same season when the Victorian 11 played Harris's team he took 6 for 64 off 34 overs and 3 for 30 off 20 overs. His reputation made, he toured England with the 1880 Australian side and in eleven-a-side games he took 80 wickets at an average of 11, second only to Spofforth [q.v.]. In the 1882 tour he took 138 averaging 12, 132 at 16 in 1884 and 106 at 22 in 1886. In first-class cricket he took 591 wickets at 17, including 78 in Test matches at 21, with best performances 7 for 68 at Sydney in 1882 and 7 for 65 at Melbourne in 1883. With a smooth action he bowled medium-paced off and leg cutters. Later his batting improved and in the 1886 tour he scored over 1000 runs. For Victoria he took 103 wickets at 17, and scored 558 runs averaging 21 with a top score of 77. He was one of the best Australian cricketers of the 1880s.

Popular with his team-mates and known as 'Joey', Palmer had a keen sense of humour and was well known for his practical jokes. He called W. G. Grace 'Fantail'. A knee injury in 1887 cut his active career short and he went to Launceston as coach and ground caretaker. On the death of his wife Lucinda, a sister of J. M. Blackham [q.v.], he returned to Victoria where he died of pneumonia at Benalla on 22 August 1910.

Age, 23 Aug 1910; SMH, 23 Aug 1910; Australasian, 27 Aug 1910.   IAN JOHNSON

PALMER, SIR JAMES FREDERICK (1803-1871), medical practitioner and politician, was born on 7 June 1803 at Great Torrington, Devon, England, fourth son of Rev. John Palmer, nephew of Sir Joshua Reynolds, and his wife Jane, daughter of William Johnson. He was articled to Dr John Gunning, surgeon-in-chief of the army, and in 1824 became a house surgeon at St George's Hospital (M.A.C.S., 1826). For some years he practised in London, living in Golden Square, and became senior surgeon at St James's Dispensary. In 1835-37 he edited in four volumes the work of the anatomist,

John Hunter, and became a fellow of the Royal Medical and Chirurgical Society. On 21 November 1831 he had married Isabella, third daughter of Dr Gunning, then inspector-general of hospitals.

Palmer twice contested vacancies for surgical appointments without success. Disappointed and annoyed by the second defeat, he determined to migrate. He arrived at Sydney with his wife in September 1840 and registered as a medical practitioner on 21 February 1842. He soon moved to Melbourne but set up as a cordial manufacturer and then as a wine merchant. In 1847-54 he held pastoral interests in common with James Henty and Francis Murphy [qq.v.]. He also became local chairman of directors of the Liverpool and London Fire and Life Assurance Co.

Palmer made his home at Richmond near the Yarra and soon established Palmer's Punt (near Hawthorn Bridge), thus making a steady income from the woodcarters of the Boroondara district. In 1851 largely at his instigation the punt was displaced by a wooden bridge. With prosperity he built a new house, Burwood, in Hawthorn near the bridge. The property was later bought by George Coppin [q.v.] and later still by Sir William McPherson (1865-1932); it became the Invergowrie Homecraft Hostel.

Palmer was mayor of Melbourne in 1845-46. In September 1848 he was elected one of the five to represent the Port Phillip District in the Legislative Council of New South Wales, but resigned in June 1849. In 1851 he was returned to the Victorian Legislative Council for the Western District seat of Normanby, Dundas and Follett and was elected first Speaker. He served on the select committee which drafted the Constitution in 1853 and on the committee that proposed the Act for creating the University of Melbourne. In 1856, having retained his office in the old council and having been elected for Western Province, he became first president of the new Legislative Council and in 1857 was knighted. He presided over the council until 1870 when he did not seek re-election.

Outside parliament Palmer was prominent in many fields. He was an original trustee of the Public Library and was associated with the Melbourne Hospital from the earliest proposals for its foundation. At a public meeting on 5 March 1845 he moved the motion that the hospital 'is hereby formed' and then served on its building and management committees. As mayor he delivered the main address when Sir Charles Hotham laid the foundation stone of the hospital. Palmer predicted that the hospital would become a centre of medical education and research which would benefit rich and poor

alike. He was vice-president in 1851-65 and president until ill health forced him to resign in 1870, but his association went far beyond that of a conventional office-bearer. In 1856 he unsuccessfully suggested an endowment of land for the hospital to cope with its serious financial problems.

Palmer was an active and devout Anglican layman, but in the field of education, where his contribution was important, he was identified with the National system. He was chairman of the Board of National Education while it lasted in 1851-62 and became chairman of the Board of Education in 1863. At the royal commission in 1866 he defended the 1862 educational compromise as the most satisfactory situation for the moment, argued that withdrawal of aid from church schools should be gradual and strongly defended the 'payment by results' system.

Palmer died at Burwood on 23 April 1871, leaving an estate worth some £13,000. His high repute rested on character and reliability. La Trobe in supporting the recommendation for a knighthood had described him as 'a gentleman by birth, education and profession. Sometimes he pulled against, more often for, but I always respected him as honest'. He was hard-hitting at times; one letter to Sir George Gipps was returned with the rebuke that it was 'couched in language studiously offensive'. To Westgarth [q.v.] he was an 'old Tory' but with 'just a trace of the oddly positive in him'. Though perhaps not of outstanding ability, his series of presidencies and the remarkable range of his activities indicate his tact, common sense, breadth of interest and earnestness of purpose.

Garryowen (E. Finn), The chronicles of early Melbourne (Melb, 1888); E. LaT. Armstrong, The book of the Public Library . . . 1856-1906 (Melb, 1906); J. A. Allan, 'The Red Lion Inn', VHM, 21 (1945-46); Argus, 24, 26, 27 Apr 1871.
ALAN GROSS*

PALMER, ROSINA MARTHA HOSANAH (1844-1932), singer, was born on 27 August 1844 in Hobart Town, eldest of five daughters of the Marchese Jerome Carandini di Sazano and his wife Madame Marie Carandini [q.v.], née Burgess.

Rosina's father was penniless and her mother became the family's mainstay by her tours as a singer, dominating the lives of all close to her. Before her daughters' voices matured she travelled widely to cities and country towns in Australia. Rosina first showed promise as a pianist but was early placed under the tutelage of F. A. Packer [q.v.] for singing lessons in Hobart. With her mother's determined ambitions behind her, and at the risk of destroying her youthful soprano voice, Rosina appeared at 14 as Adalgisa to her mother's Norma in that Bellini opera. From that day her mother encouraged her in nothing but singing. For some years she travelled up and down the country with her mother and later with her sisters giving concerts. In the 1860s they were known as the 'Carandini Family Troupe' and with other performers toured as far afield as India and California.

In Hobart on 8 November 1860 Rosina married Edward Hodson Palmer, cashier and later accountant in the Bank of Australasia. In 1866 they moved to Melbourne; she exchanged her mother's dominance for her husband's prudery and the duty of rearing a young family. The tours were replaced with concerts in the major cities; the operatic appearances ceased in favour of oratorio. When the duke of Edinburgh visited Melbourne he was so charmed by Rosina's singing that he promised to provide the means for her musical education by first-rate European masters, but nothing came of it. Though it was improper for a respectable matron to appear on the always-suspect opera stage, the poorly paid solo parts with the respectable Melbourne Philharmonic Society and the Liedertafels were socially acceptable.

In 1872 Rosina sang as a soprano in a travelling quartet with the American Mrs Cutter as contralto, E. A. Beaumont [q.v.] the blind tenor and S. Lamble as bass, visiting New Zealand and touring Australia. With Beaumont she became one of the two principal singers in the W. J. Turner series of popular concerts in the Exhibition Building in Melbourne. She was also the soprano soloist in the choir of Scots Church in 1880-1910. Her performances were legion and her income small, but fortunately she was allowed to go on singing because her husband's income was only a little larger. Economy won consent but not approval. She became a teacher in the end with an extensive following. When she sang with visiting celebrities she was always praised by them. Charles Santley (1834-1922) in particular regretted that she could not leave her family and sing in Europe, though later she visited America and sang for a notable teacher, Mancusi, who told her that he could teach her nothing more. She might have stayed but her mother was ill and she returned to Melbourne. Predeceased by her husband on 28 June 1928, she died at South Yarra on 16 June 1932, survived by a son and two daughters of her eight children.

Undoubtedly Rosina Palmer had gifts but, like so many talented contemporaries, the demands of her social position and her married state acted as a barrier against full development. Only women of the character of her mother could successfully break through the barricades of convention, compelling respect and admiration, pushing the weaker spirits of her daughters to the sticking point and finally marrying them off to titles and fortunes, all except Rosina.

Tasmanian Times, 29 Apr 1869; *Table Talk*, 22 Aug 1890; *Illustrated Sydney News*, 23 May 1891; *Australasian*, 12 May 1894, 31 Dec 1910; *Argus*, 8 Oct 1910, 17 June 1932; *Age*, 18 June 1932; Kenyon papers, P1735 (LaT L).
MAUREEN THERESE RADIC

PALMER, THOMAS McLEOD (1831-1915), pastoralist and dairy farmer, was born on 21 June 1831 in London, son of Frederick Palmer, an officer in the East India Co., and his wife Mary Eliza, née Wood. His father decided to try his luck in Australia and sailed with his wife and ten children in the *Barke Madra*, arriving in Van Diemen's Land in November 1838. Educated at Launceston Grammar School, Thomas worked for two years with the Launceston merchants, Marriott, Byars & Co. In February 1850 he left for the Californian goldfields and on the voyage learnt navigation and kept the second mate's watch. He had some success on the goldfields and helped to raise the Liberty Pole in San Francisco on 2 July 1850. He was drawn back to Australia by news of the gold discoveries but the return trip was interrupted as the ship was seized for debt at the Sandwich Islands. Palmer occupied his time by running a store and is reputed to have entered into an unsuccessful farming speculation with David Kalakua, future king of the islands.

On 22 May 1854 Palmer arrived in Sydney and overlanded to the Ovens River district. With a brother he took up Dederang station and for the next ten years had mixed success as a pastoralist. Cattle disease and low prices finally persuaded the brothers to sell. In 1863 Thomas moved to the Western District and bought Grassmere station, where the land was so fertile that he ran fifteen sheep to the acre. In 1872 he bought Tooram on the Hopkins River and began a dairy farm. While owned by Palmer it was one of the greatest dairy farms in Victoria. The 1150 acres, divided into paddocks by hawthorn hedges, were covered with rye, grass and clover. In good years the property carried 500 cows and Palmer's annual return was £8000. He also fattened pigs on the whey and the boiled-down meat of the calves, and had a bone-crushing mill.

At the end of 1882 Palmer imported twenty-eight Afghans to work on his farm. This step led to what one local newspaper described as a 'most unhappy mis-adventure'. He was evidently uneasy from the start about the experiment and carried a loaded revolver all day and slept with it within reach. When on 17 March 1883 a message came that the men were beating one of their number to death in the milking shed, Palmer rushed off with his gun and thoughts of the Indian mutiny in mind. His eyesight was poor and he seems to have lost his head and fired blindly into the milling men. Afterwards he took the greatest care of the wounded but one died. Palmer was tried for manslaughter at the Warrnambool Assize Court before Mr Justice Holroyd [q.v.] and successfully defended by Moles-worth and Gaunt [qq.v.]. The jury con-sidered he had had sufficient cause to fear for his life and the Western District rejoiced that 'an honoured and worthy citizen had escaped from a deadly peril'. Admittedly Palmer was impulsive but most people agreed that he would never wittingly injure any-one. Palmer got rid of his coolies after his acquittal.

Palmer, a justice of the peace, was on the Warrnambool Shire Council and its presi-dent for five years. He was first president of the Warrnambool Club. In 1873 he formed one of the deputation which presented J. G. Francis [q.v.] with Warrnambool's claims for the construction of a breakwater. In 1886 he was embroiled in the town's dispute over the site for the railway station. His stand was seen as an example of his 'pushing enterprise and quick grasp of business essentials'; less complimentary things were also said.

An operation on his eyes in September 1883 was successful but by 1890 failing sight and poor health forced Palmer to retire from active life and sell Tooram. Predeceased in 1888 by his wife Elizabeth, née Miller, he died on 31 July 1915, survived by one daughter and two sons.

T. W. H. Leavitt (ed), Australian represen-tative men (Melb, 1887); C. E. Sayers, Of many things: a history of Warrnambool Shire (Olinda, 1972); Warrnambool Standard, 20 Mar, 5 May 1883; Argus, 27 Dec 1884, 2 Aug 1915; Warrnambool Independent, 1 Apr 1886.

J. ANN HONE

PALMERSTON, CHRISTIE (1850?-1897), explorer and prospector, was baptized Cristofero Palmerston Carandini in Mel-bourne, probably son of Jerome Carandini and his wife Marie [q.v.], née Burgess. A North Queensland myth fathers him on Viscount Palmerston (1784-1865) who was 10,000 miles away at the appropriate time. Christie is said to have left Hobart as a youth to work on a station in the Broad Sound area of Queensland and thence to the Palmer gold rush in 1873-74; more likely he went to Queensland with his mother's con-cert party in 1870. He was certainly at the Hodgkinson rush of 1876, where he first made his name as a pathfinder. Cooktown merchants, fearing rivalry from the new port of Cairns as an outlet for the Hodgkinson trade, backed Palmerston and W. C. Little to cut a track in April 1877 from the gold-field to an even more convenient port at Island Point. Palmerston discovered a route along the Mowbray River, and this led to the founding of Port Douglas. Because of the rivalries between the mushroom ports of North Queensland for the hinterland traffic, Palmerston was often employed to cut tracks between the Atherton Tableland and the coast, mostly through difficult, precipi-tous and scrub-covered country. In July 1880 he connected Port Douglas with the newly-discovered Herberton tinfields. Late in 1882 he cut a track from Mourilyan Harbour (near Innisfail) to Herberton. In December 1884 he blazed a route from Herberton to the new South Johnstone diggings and in 1886 found gold on the upper Russell River but in no great quantity.

Respected as a consummate bushman, Palmerston was on unusually close terms with the Aboriginals whose allegiance he won by not interfering with their women and by his firmness and skill as a shot. He hated the Chinese alluvial diggers, with whom he carried on a running feud. In 1887 when the Russell gold rush proved dis-appointing he induced over 200 Chinese to go to the diggings, where with a posse of Aboriginals he prevented any Chinese from leaving for several months, while he levied tribute from all comers, sold provisions at exorbitant prices and beat up any malcon-tents. After this adventure he settled down in Townsville, where at St Joseph's Church on 6 December 1886 he married Teresa Rooney, a publican's daughter and violinist; they had one daughter who left descendants. Palmerston found town life dull and, after a brief spell as a Townsville publican, moved to Borneo and then to Malaya where he worked for the Straits Development Co. He contracted fever in the jungle and died at Kuala Pilah on 15 January 1897.

Probably because of his theatrical back-ground, Palmerston loved display and mystery-mongering. Yarns about his mysterious origins, hairbreadth escapes from death and hidden finds of gold proliferated around his name. Few records survive to indicate the truth about a hardy and skilful bushman who had rare insight into the life and habits of North Queensland Aboriginals in the first years of white contact.

G. C. Bolton, A thousand miles away (Brisb, 1963); F. Reid, 'Christy' Palmerston, North Queensland's super-bushman', Cummins & Campbell's Mthly Mag, Jan 1933; J. W. Collinson, 'Rise and decline of Port Douglas', JRHSQ, 4 (1948-52), pt 4; F. W. Woolston and F. S. Colliver, 'Christie Palmerston — a North Queensland pioneer, prospector and explorer', Qld Heritage, 1 (1967), no 7; W. S. Walsh, Report re assault case against Palmerston, 5 Dec 1887, CSO 9984/1887 (QA).

G. C. BOLTON

PANTON, JOSEPH ANDERSON (1831-1913), public servant, was born on 2 June 1831 at Knockiemil, Aberdeenshire, Scotland, son of John Panton of the Hudson's Bay service and his wife Alexina McKay, née Anderson. He was educated at the Scottish Naval and Military Academy, where he developed a keen interest in drawing, and at the University of Edinburgh, leaving without a degree. At the suggestion of his uncle, Colonel Joseph Anderson [q.v.], Panton migrated to Sydney in the Thomas Arbuthnot, arriving in March 1851, and went to the Port Phillip District. After farming briefly at Mangalore, he tried for gold without success at Mount Alexander and then applied to La Trobe for appointment as an officer in the gold escort. As he later told the story, 'The Lieutenant-Governor looked me up and down, and then remarked jocularly "This fellow seems too big for a trooper. Too heavy. It would be too severe on the horses. I think he would make a Commissioner".'

Panton was appointed assistant commissioner at Kangaroo Gully, near Bendigo, under J. E. N. Bull [q.v.] in 1852, senior assistant commissioner at Bendigo in 1853 and senior commissioner in 1854. He investigated the resentment against Chinese diggers and his recommendation for a Chinese protectorate was adopted by Governor Hotham in 1855. With Lachlan McLachlan [q.v.] he had handled the diggers' protest movement at Bendigo in 1853 with tact and conciliation. His administration was commended by the commission which inquired into affairs at the diggings after Eureka, though William Howitt [q.v.] described him as 'most inert'.

Panton left Bendigo in 1858 on leave without pay, but with high repute as warden, magistrate and protector of the Chinese, and for going far beyond his routine duties. He helped to organize the Melbourne Exhibition in 1854 with a preliminary exhibition at Bendigo, and was a commissioner for the Melbourne International Exhibition in 1880.

From Bendigo in 1858 Panton went to Scotland and then to Paris to study art with his friend Hubert de Castella [q.v.]. On his return he was appointed warden and magistrate at the Jamieson-Wood's Point and next at the Anderson's Creek goldfields. He then became magistrate at Heidelberg, where he found time to map the Yarra Valley, leaving his name at Panton Hills. Panton's Gap where the road to Ben Cairn and Donna Buang branches from the Don Road near Healesville derives its name from a small house he had there. He also named Donna Buang which he first called Mount Acland but renamed it after learning the Aboriginal name. From Heidelberg he was transferred to Geelong and moved to Melbourne as senior magistrate in 1874-1907. He regularly attended musical recitals and was very active in the Victorian Artists Association and the Victorian Academy of Art which developed into the Victorian Artists Society. A fellow of the Royal Geographical Society in London he was also vice-president of the Royal Geographical Society of Australasia, Victorian Branch.

At Bendigo Panton owned vineyards at Epsom and Huntly from which prize-winning wines were produced. He was a strong advocate of the development of a local wine industry as alluvial mining faded. At Epsom he had the land deeply trenched and filled with bones and bullocks' heads. Attracted by the outback, he took up leases in the outer districts of New South Wales and Western Australia. Friendship with the explorer, Ernest Giles [q.v.], possibly strengthened his interest. Panton later moved to a lease in the Northern Territory and took up land in the Kimberley District. He also foretold the discovery of gold in Western Australia. An enthusiastic yachtsman, he often spent his holidays sailing. 'Handsome and stand[ing] a good deal over six feet', he was a good conversationalist. On 5 December 1860 he had married Eleanor Margaret, daughter of Colonel John Fulton of the Bengal Native Infantry. In 1895 he declined the honour of knighthood but was appointed C.M.G. Predeceased by his wife, he died at St Kilda on 25 October 1913; although brought up in the Church of Scotland he was buried with Anglican rites. He was survived by two daughters, one of whom, Amy, was a well-known portrait painter.

W. Howitt, Land, labour, and gold (Lond, 1855); G. Mackay, The history of Bendigo (Melb, 1891); G. Fetherstonhaugh, After many days (Syd, 1918); F. de Castella, 'Early Victorian wine-growing', VHM, 19 (1941-42), no 76; Argus, 27 Oct 1913; Panton memoirs (LaT L).

ALAN GROSS*

PARKER, EDWARD STONE (1802-1865), assistant protector of Aboriginals and

Methodist preacher, was born on 17 May 1802 in London, son of Edward Stone Parker and his wife Mary. Apprenticed to a printer, he became a Sunday school teacher and a candidate for the Methodist ministry. He broke the conditions controlling probationers by marrying Mary Cook Woolmer in 1828. Suspended from the ministry, he turned to teaching. In 1838 he was in charge of a Methodist day school in Greater Queen Street, London, when the Colonial Office appointed him assistant protector of Aboriginals in the Port Phillip District, one of four to serve under G. A. Robinson [q.v.]. The protectors were to prevent conflict between black and white, teach the Aboriginals to cultivate the soil, promote their 'moral and religious improvement' and build 'suitable habitations'.

Parker sailed with his wife and six sons for Sydney and then moved to the Port Phillip District. In early 1839 he first attempted to contact the Aboriginals of the Loddon area. He travelled widely, collecting information about the Aboriginals and investigating clashes with settlers. He often found that complaints against Aboriginal 'depredations' were exaggerated but, when convinced that Aboriginals had been murdered, he was unable to obtain convictions in the courts. He held that the Aboriginals had a right to the 'soil and its indigenous production', and his attempts to intervene in cases where Aboriginals were ill-treated brought him into conflict with neighbouring squatters and station hands.

In 1841 Parker established the Aboriginal station of Larnebarramul (Jim Crow) at Franklinford in central Victoria. It flourished for a time: the white staff included a teacher and several free and assigned labourers; the protector's homestead was constructed among several out-buildings; and the presence of up to 200 Aboriginals gave the station the appearance of a populous village. But by 31 December 1848 the protectorate ended; only twenty or thirty Aboriginals were then on the station and only a handful had learnt to read and write or acquired a trade. Parker lived on at Franklinford, retaining his interest in the Aboriginals and farming some of Larnebarramul. The influx of population with the gold rushes reduced the few remaining Aboriginals to mendicants on the edge of the white community.

From his arrival in Port Phillip Parker was a leading layman and preacher in the colony's Methodist community. He served on the Council of the University of Melbourne in 1853, was a nominated member of the Legislative Council in 1854-55 and in 1857-62 an inspector for the Denominational Schools Board.

Parker was the most understanding of the Port Phillip Aboriginal protectors. He believed fervently that 'the permanent civilization of the savage is dependent on the influence of Christian instruction' and that the Aboriginals' failings were moral, not physical or mental. Above all his Christianity led him to believe in the common origin and brotherhood of all mankind. Perceptive and humane, he wrote to Robinson and La Trobe describing the plight of the Aboriginals and arguing for a more generous policy. Before government inquiries he testified that the Aboriginals would respond to education or opportunities to develop their land if they could see some advantage and not just in the interest of white intruders. Parker learnt the language and observed the customs of the Jajowurrong or Loddon Aboriginals. His lecture on 10 May 1854 to the John Knox Young Men's Association was published as *The Aborigines of Australia*. His writings preserved in the La Trobe Library are a valuable source of information about these people.

Parker's first wife had died in 1842; she had given birth to one daughter in Australia. He died on 27 April 1865 at Franklinford, survived by his second wife Hannah, née Edwards, whom he had married in 1843, and by ten children.

W. L. Blamires and J. B. Smith, *The early story of the Wesleyan Methodist Church in Victoria* (Melb, 1886); E. J. B. Foxcroft, *Australian native policy* (Melb, 1941); E. Morrison, *Early days in the Loddon Valley* (Daylesford, 1965); T. M. O'Connor, 'Edward Stone Parker: pioneer and protector', *Heritage*, 15 (1963); *Wesleyan Chronicle*, 20 July 1865.

H. N. NELSON

PARKER, SIR HENRY WATSON (1808-1881), civil servant and politician, was born on 1 June 1808 at Lewisham, England, fourth son of Thomas Watson Parker and his wife Mary, née Cornell. Educated privately by Dr Waite, he was prevented by delicate health from joining the army and was recommended to undertake sea travel. He entered the East India Co. and visited India, China and the Cape of Good Hope. He then toured France, Holland and Belgium, and was unemployed until 1837 when he was appointed private secretary to Governor Gipps. On 24 February 1838 with Gipps he reached Sydney in the *Upton Castle*. On 21 November 1843 his marriage to Emmeline Emily (d. 1888), youngest daughter of John Macarthur [q.v.], linked him to powerful and conservative colonial groups. He built a large house, Clovelly, at Watson's Bay.

Parker's 'precise and methodical mind' soon adjusted to the problems pressing on the governor from 1838 and he developed into a proficient and shrewd official. He was appointed to the Legislative Council on 11 May 1846 and was chairman of committees until 29 February 1856, at a salary of £250, raised to £500 on 1 January 1853. Parker performed his duties meticulously as imperial control of New South Wales gave way to responsible government, meanwhile 'cautiously, but in a progressive spirit, examining principles, and forming to himself a political creed'. In 1855 he was on a council committee that inquired into the powers and duties of the chief officers of the new executive government. On 29 March 1856 he won the seat of Parramatta at the first general election and in May was defeated as Speaker by one vote. In June the *Empire* reported that Parker 'pulls down the waist of his coat before commencing to speak, calls the attention of the Speaker by a sharp little cough [and] uses language as finely drawn and involuted as a cobweb', in contrast with the rugged candour of John Robertson [q.v.], a leader of the liberal reformers. On 5 August in the precincts of Parliament House he was attacked with a riding whip, but the affair was hushed up.

By October two ministries had fallen in the confusion caused by the parliamentarians' inexperience and their inchoate division into a conservative group, representing the officials of the old order and wealthy landholders, and a nascent liberal group speaking for city and country progressives. In an attempt to achieve some political stability by fusing the two groups Governor Denison commissioned Parker to form a ministry. Charles Cowper [q.v.], the Liberal leader, refused to join, but Stuart Donaldson [q.v.], the Conservative leader, agreed, and on 3 October Parker's cabinet was sworn in. The ministry included three officials of the old order and met with persistent opposition, but it lasted until 7 September 1857 and attempted to repair legislative deficiencies. In the 1856-57 session Parker carried four of the five public bills he introduced, including the Sydney Municipal Council Act. But his government fell on the electoral bill, amid indications that the liberals were gathering strength. In 1858 he was knighted and returned to England.

In 1848 Parker was a Crown trustee of the Australian Museum and an official trustee in 1856-57. He had fitted nicely into colonial society and politics in the pre-responsible government era, but his style was not suited to the novel kind of democratic government from 1856. His accession as premier that year reflected a fleeting period in which the new breed of politicians had not had time to emerge and the experience and status of colonial conservatives were attractive and useful to the governor. In England Parker lived at Stawell House in Richmond. In 1868 he opposed Gladstone at Greenwich. He was appointed K.C.M.G. in 1877. He was a commissioner for the Sydney and Melbourne Exhibitions in 1879 and 1880. Survived by his wife, he died on 2 February 1881. His estate was proved at under £140,000.

HRA (1), 25; H. Parkes, *Fifty years in the making of Australian history* (Lond, 1892); J. N. Molony, *An architect of freedom: John Hubert Plunkett* (Canberra, 1973); *Empire* (Syd), 8 Apr, 24 June, 6 Aug 1856; *The Times*, 5 Feb 1881; *Bulletin*, 9 Apr, 16 July 1881; CO 201/494.

BEDE NAIRN

PARKES, EDMUND SAMUEL (1834-1887), banker, was born on 11 July 1834 in Devon, England, son of Samuel Parkes and his wife Agnes, née Tozer. Educated in London, he acquired commercial knowledge when employed at an early age by a firm of ship-brokers. He then worked in the London and Westminster Bank where he was thoroughly trained in banking. He was later appointed one of the joint managers of the Alliance Bank of London. The liquidation of some difficult Australian business of the bank probably led to his appointment as inspector of the Bank of Australasia, the chairman of directors announcing the commission at a meeting of shareholders on 19 August 1867. By then Parkes was on his way to Melbourne where he had relations.

The Bank of Australasia, established in the 1830s, suffered contraction in the depression of the next decade but recovered during the gold rushes. Despite some local animosity Parkes quickly proved his worth. He was appointed general inspector in 1871 and superintendent in 1876, holding that office until 1887. He was one of the best-educated bankers of Victoria. His extensive knowledge of banking, based on his training and a big private library, was appreciated. His evidence to the royal commission on banking laws shows a clear grasp of the special needs for government influence on banking which was then not fully understood. The commission had been set up to investigate bank lending on mortgage security, especially by those banks whose charters had prohibited it. Parkes suggested that banks should be free to take whatever security they could get but that more frequent (later monthly) disclosures of their balance sheets should allow the public a better judgment of their performances. In effect he recommended more *laissez faire* in banking and less secrecy about the banks' financial conditions.

Parkes showed his familiarity with American and Continental banking when he suggested that the banks issue notes only after depositing government securities with the government auditors, thus making runs on the banks less frequent. In the 1880s the limited number of local issues by the Victorian government was probably as much to blame for the non-acceptance of Parkes's ideas on banking as his claim that in Victoria 'the public seem to have a contented mind'. Building societies continued to solicit funds from non-members on deposits and to lend on the security of long-term mortgage. Parkes's warnings against this practice were little heeded but the 1893 bank collapse would have been less severe had they been accepted.

Parkes was not only a master of management and finance; for a strict disciplinarian he had a 'large and tender heart'. An Anglican, he was, according to a later writer, 'the spiritual pillar of the Holy Trinity Church at Balaclava'. With his friend F. S. Grimwade [q.v.], he served on its first parochial committee. A window and reredos commemorate his activities in the church. At Penzance, Cornwall, he had married Nancy Penrose Lawry; they had four sons and six daughters. Predeceased by his wife, Parkes died after a railway accident between Prahran and Windsor on 11 May 1887 and was buried in St Kilda cemetery.

A. Sutherland et al, *Victoria and its metropolis* (Melb, 1888); J. B. Cooper, *The history of St. Kilda . . . 1840 to 1930* (Melb, 1931); S. J. Butlin, *Australia and New Zealand Bank* (Melb, 1961); V&P (LA Vic), 1887, 3 (65); Roy Soc Vic, *Procs*, 24 (1887); *A'sian Insurance and Banking Record*, 14 May 1887; family information.   RAOUL F. MIDDELMANN

PARKES, SIR HENRY (1815-1896), politician and journalist, was born on 27 May 1815 in Warwickshire, England, youngest of the seven children of Thomas Parks, tenant farmer on Stoneleigh Abbey Estate, and his wife Martha, née Faulconbridge. Forced off their farm in 1823 by debt, the Parkes family moved to Glamorganshire and about 1825 settled in Birmingham, where Thomas was a gardener and odd-job man. Henry's formal education was in his own words, 'very limited and imperfect'; he briefly attended Stoneleigh parish school and later joined the Birmingham Mechanics' Institute. Obliged as a boy to help in supporting the family, he worked as a road labourer and in a brickpit and rope-walk, before being apprenticed to John Holding, bone and ivory turner of Moseley Street.

Having served his articles, he began his own business in 1837. On 11 July 1836 at Edgbaston Parish Church he had married Clarinda, 23-year-old daughter of John Varney, butcher. They regularly attended Carr's Lane Independent Chapel under the formidable John Angell James, whose precepts and oratorical style left a permanent impress on Parkes. Another important Birmingham influence was Thomas Attwood's Political Union, which Parkes joined at 17. He heard Attwood, Scholefield and Edmunds orate at Newhall Hill, sported the union badge and in 1833 dedicated a poem on the wrongs of Poland to Attwood's son.

The business failed and in 1838 Parkes took Clarinda to London in search of better prospects. They survived a few weeks by pawning his tools, then determined to leave for New South Wales as bounty migrants. In March 1839 Hetherington's *Charter* published verses from Parkes as 'A Poet's Farewell', indignantly condemning a society through whose injustices 'men like this are compelled to seek the means of existence in a foreign wilderness'. Parkes assured his Birmingham family of his certainty of 'making my fortune and coming back to fetch all of you'. He and Clarinda sailed from Gravesend on 27 March 1839 in the *Strathfieldsaye*, their ears 'incessantly assailed by the coarse expressions and blasphemies' of other steerage passengers.

They reached Sydney on 25 July 1839 with a first surviving child born at sea two days earlier. Parkes found work as a labourer on Sir John Jamison's [q.v.] Regentville estate but after six months returned to Sydney to work in Thomas Burdekin's ironmongery and Peter Russell's [q.v.] brassfoundry. In 1840 he became a tide-waiter in the Customs Department, slowly bought tools and in 1845 set up in Hunter Street as an ivory turner and importer of fancy goods. Impressed by what seemed 'flattering prospects' of developing 'a respectable mercantile business', he opened branches in Maitland and Geelong, but both failed and by 1850 he was in financial difficulties, writing remorsefully to his wife of 'too culpable neglect of my business in Sydney'. He had by then become deeply involved in literary and political activities, attractions which highlighted the dullness of a business life.

Parkes's talents as a writer, extraordinary for one so lacking in formal education, developed quickly in the 1840s. He was briefly Sydney correspondent for the *Launceston Examiner*, and contributed occasional poems and articles on political and literary topics, sometimes under the pseudonym 'Faulconbridge', to the *Sydney Morning Herald*, the *Australasian Chronicle* and the *Atlas*. In 1842 he published by subscription a first book of verse, *Stolen Moments*. Through W. A. Duncan and Charles Harpur [qq.v.], his 'chief advisers on matters of intellectual resource and enquiry', he came to be associated with most of the colony's radical patriots. Discussion gave place in 1848 to action, when with J. K. Heydon [q.v.] he became organizing secretary of a tradesmen's committee which successfully promoted Robert Lowe [q.v.] for the City of Sydney seat in the Legislative Council. Later that year he joined radicals in the Constitutional Association which developed out of the Lowe committee to agitate for franchise extension and land reform. In his first public speech, made at the City Theatre in January 1849, Parkes advocated universal suffrage as the best guarantee that the people, 'growing in enlightenment', would avoid 'the excesses of Paris and Frankfurt'. His radicalism reached a brief apogee in April 1850 when Rev. J. D. Lang and J. R. Wilshire [qq.v.] established the Australian League to work for universal suffrage and transformation of the Australian colonies into a 'Great Federal Republic'. Parkes wrote to Lang to denounce the 'dung-hill aristocracy of Botany Bay' and to assert his eagerness to 'enrol in the league for the entire freedom and independence' of this 'land of my adoption and of my children's birth'. In July he worked as chief organizer and canvasser when Lang stood against J. R. Holden [q.v.] for a vacant Sydney seat in the Legislative Council. In this campaign Parkes joined the Chartist, David Blair [q.v.], to issue the *Representative: A Daily Journal of the Election* as a counter to the 'discreditable handbills' circulated by Lang's opponents. Lang won the seat but his league did not survive long and Parkes's republicanism soon evaporated. Daniel Deniehy [q.v.] told Lang that Parkes had 'too much, not of the Englishman *in* him, but of "*Englishmanism*" about him', to lend serious comfort to the republicans of New South Wales. But this was only part of the story; Parkes was already finding a more congenial cause in the liberal movement which by the early 1850s was becoming the most effective spearhead against the old colonial conservatives.

Parkes, who had been prominent in the great protest which greeted the convict ship *Hashemy* in 1849, eagerly dedicated his organizational talents to the Anti-transportation League and drifted easily into the liberal campaigns against the anti-democratic Electoral Act of 1851. Late in 1850 he found support to set up as editor-proprietor of the *Empire*, a newspaper destined to be the chief organ of mid-century liberalism and to serve as the rallying and reconciliation point for the sharpest radical and liberal

minds of the day. Critics of the existing system as diverse as C. G. Duffy, Edward Butler, James Martin, William Forster [qq.v.], Deniehy and Lang were contributors but Parkes was presiding genius. Full-time journalist and politician now, he abandoned shopkeeping for a happy reconciliation of desire and duty: the *Empire* allowed devotion to a political cause and promised steady economic support for a growing family. By 1853, deeply involved in organizing the Constitution Committee to oppose Wentworth's [q.v.] constitution bill, he was ready to seek a place in the Legislative Council. Failing at a by-election that year, he won Wentworth's old Sydney seat in 1854, defeating Charles Kemp [q.v.] in a contest generally seen as a trial of strength between liberals and conservatives over the constitutional issue. The radicals' acceptance of a frankly liberal Parkes as their candidate in place of Lang symbolized the merging in his person of radical and liberal movements. The liberal leader, Charles Cowper [q.v.], warmly welcomed him to the council as an opponent of 'Wentworthian and Thomsonian [q.v.] policy', and Parkes's election to the Chamber of Commerce signified his acceptance into the inner liberal group.

Parkes entered the council near its end: the constitutional proposals were under scrutiny in London and no longer a subject for effective local debate. Meanwhile the liberals' reformism was chiefly reflected in a range of inquiries instituted by the dying council into such matters as a nautical school for boys, the importation of Asiatic labour, the adulteration of food and the state of agriculture. In this work Parkes won repute as an assiduous and imaginative committeeman.

In March 1856 at the first Legislative Assembly established by the new Constitution, Parkes was one of the liberal bunch which carried all four seats in the premier Sydney City constituency. He supported Cowper in the complex manoeuvres of the first parliament until obliged in December to resign to give full attention to the *Empire*, then in serious financial difficulties. He re-entered parliament in January 1858 for the North Riding of Cumberland but in August had to resign for insolvency. The *Empire* had collapsed, ending his dream of using the paper as 'an independent power to vivify, elevate and direct the political life of the country' and leaving him 'to begin life afresh with a wife and five children to support, a name in a commercial sense ruined and a doubt of the practical character of my mind'. He survived bankruptcy proceedings, struggled on with the support of friends and the proceeds of occasional journalism and planned briefly to abandon politics for a legal career. But in June 1859 he was back in parliament to represent East Sydney.

Politics in the assembly had by then settled into a faction mould. Having in 1857 declared his independence of Cowper and John Robertson [q.v.], Parkes developed a personal following in the House and in 1859-60 emerged as critic and rival of the established liberal leadership. But economic insecurity made him vulnerable, and early in 1861 he accepted an invitation by Cowper to tour England with W. B. Dalley [q.v.] as government lecturer on emigration at a salary of £1000.

Parkes sailed in May, leaving his family in poverty on their rented farm at Werrington. In England he attended vigorously to his duties, though with limited success. Prevailing English sentiment was well expressed by Sir John Pakington, who declared at Parkes's meeting in Droitwich his unwillingness to see 'the pith of our English population seeking a home elsewhere'. Early in 1863 Parkes returned to Sydney in good spirits, his self-confidence strengthened by the kind attention he had received from government officials and such literary idols as Carlyle, Hughes and Cobden, and having established while in Birmingham a new fancy goods importing business which he hoped might in the next six years 'provide for the rest of our lives'.

An opportunity to return to parliament offered itself in August 1863 when J. B. Darvall [q.v.] sought ministerial re-election at East Maitland. Parkes opposed Darvall and lost the contest after a bitter campaign, but in January 1864 was returned at a by-election for Kiama, a seat he held until 1870. From late 1864 until early 1866 he opposed consecutive Martin and Cowper ministries, while steadily rebuilding his own faction. In 1865 Cowper tried without success to buy him off again, with offers first of the lucrative post of inspector of prisons, then of a portfolio in his ministry. By early 1866 Martin and Parkes were in private negotiation: successful censure of Cowper followed and Martin, commissioned to form a ministry, included Parkes, as colonial secretary, and two followers.

This coalition, scarcely more than a marriage of convenience, failed to develop a positive and unanimous programme. Its leaders differed on such basic issues as the tariff, state aid, electoral and land reform. Parkes was responsible for establishing the hulk *Vernon* as a nautical school for destitute boys, for an Act requiring the inspection of hospitals and for bringing to Sydney under Lucy Osburn [q.v.] nursing sisters trained by Florence Nightingale. But the government's support was uncertain and its ministers quarrelsome; its only major legislation in two years and a half of office, Parkes's 1866 Public Schools Act, passed the assembly with Opposition assistance. This measure was Parkes's first important contribution to education reform. Prompted by the high cost of competing national and denominational systems of education, it aimed at rationalizing expenditure by placing both under a Council of Education which was also to oversee teacher training and the content of secular lessons.

The measure aroused sectarian controversy which Parkes did little to assuage. It revived again in March 1868 when H. J. O'Farrell [q.v.] attempted to assassinate the visiting duke of Edinburgh. The government, alleging a Fenian plot, carried a savage Treason Felony Act suspending civil rights, but no conspiracy was discovered. In September Parkes resigned from the ministry in protest at its handling of a quarrel between the treasurer, Geoffrey Eagar [q.v.], and W. A. Duncan, collector of customs. Lacking Parkes's support, Martin's ministry fell within a month. Meanwhile in a speech at Kiama Parkes had alleged that he had evidence to prove O'Farrell had acted on Fenian orders and that one conspirator had been murdered when suspected of revealing the plot. While his move had obvious political purposes, Parkes's correspondence also shows that he was obsessed with fears for his own safety and a belief in Catholic ambitions to seize political hegemony. A select committee under W. J. Macleay [q.v.] found no proof of the allegations, but though Parkes rallied sectarian and factional support to have its report expunged from the records of the House, the 'Kiama ghost' long remained an embarrassment.

Parkes's financial difficulties had been mounting: his importing venture failed and in December 1870 he collapsed again into bankruptcy. He resigned his seat but soon assured his sister that he would be 're-elected to the Legislature whenever I choose to offer myself, and strange as it may seem two-thirds of the mercantile classes will vote for me. They have got a notion that I am wholly unfit for business, but the fittest of all men for Parliament'. He survived by borrowing from friends, working as a journalist and briefly acting as travelling agent for H. H. Hall [q.v.]. In January 1872 he was returned for Mudgee in time to help in ousting the Martin-Robertson coalition ministry. General elections in February-March confirmed Martin's defeat and after complex negotiations Parkes became premier for the first time. His achievement bore witness to the political arts of which he was now supreme master: besides his own followers the ministry included old Cowper-Robertson men and Butler, a barrister who had covertly engineered sectional Catholic support for Parkes at the election.

The ministry took office in May at a time of commercial prosperity. By December, thanks chiefly to the rising sale of public lands, the Treasury had a substantial surplus. Parkes embarked on vigorous development of public works, effected a downward revision of tariff schedules and negotiated an agreement with Victoria on free border trade. Though once 'bitten by the doctrine of fostering infant industries' Parkes had in 1861 learnt from Cobden the error of his ways: now as tariff reformer, he received a gold medal from the Cobden Club and established his image as high priest of free trade in New South Wales. He also won the confidence of Sir Hercules Robinson, a convinced free trader and experienced colonial governor, whose eagerness to discuss administrative and constitutional problems with cordiality and balance proved important for Parkes's development.

Despite favourable assembly majorities, the council mauled government bills to consolidate the criminal law and to redraw electoral boundaries. The governor refused a ministerial request for new appointments and the council threw out a bill which, with overwhelming assembly support, aimed to give the Upper House an elective component. Echoes of former constitutional battles brought Parkes kudos as an old liberal campaigner. He emerged less happily from another crisis which arose in 1873 when his attorney-general and personal friend, Butler, resigned in protest against his failure to honour an implied promise of the chief justiceship then vacant. Though correct in judging that Martin had superior claims to the post, Parkes extricated himself from the obligation to Butler without displaying the frankness of a gentleman or the sensitivity of a friend and colleague. His deviousness is understandable in the light of pressure from the Bar, of his instinct for intrigue, of his unease at Butler's unpredictability and of the danger of his ministry falling. The reputations of both men were not enhanced when Butler made public their correspondence. The unhappy consequence of the breach was more than personal since the Parkes-Butler alliance had effected a liberal-Catholic *rapprochement* full of promise for the colony's best interests.

After an assembly motion in November 1874 which condemned the handling of messages on the governor's response to petitions for and against the release of Frank Gardiner [q.v.], the ministry resigned in January 1875. Public passions muddied the constitutional issues at stake and the

ministry's defeat had resulted from a clever Opposition stratagem: the permanent significance of the case lay in calmer discussions between Robinson, Parkes and the Colonial Office leading to clearer definition of the responsibilities of ministers and governor in exercising the prerogative of pardon.

Parkes led the opposition to Robertson's ministry of 1875 and was premier from March to August 1877. By then politics had drifted into chaos. Of the faction leaders of the 1860s only Parkes and Robertson remained, but neither helped to readjust members' loyalties by developing distinctive policies; while both shuffled on major issues, a 'third party' was formed under J. S. Farrell [q.v.] and short-lived governments did little more than business essential to the conduct of administration. On 13 December 1878 Robertson resigned from parliament, hoping that 'the Assembly will naturally arrange itself into two parties'. Four days later a meeting of opposition members, mostly Robertson's followers, invited Parkes to become their leader. On 21 December he formed a new ministry with himself colonial secretary and Robertson, speedily appointed to the Upper House, vice-president of the Executive Council. 'It only remains to be hoped', wrote Governor Robinson dryly, 'that these gentlemen who have for nearly a quarter of a century assailed each other with such bitter political hostility will now work together harmoniously in the same cabinet'. But Parkes's claim that the coalition had been effected 'without any violation of principles' was substantially correct. The government, overwhelmingly supported in the assembly, passed appropriation and loan bills with an ease unknown to its predecessors. By late 1880 its Lands, Public Instruction and Electoral Acts had surpassed in importance any legislation for more than a decade. Elections in November enlarged the ministry's majority. Its 1881 Licensing Act regulated the liquor trade and established local option, for which the temperance movement had long clamoured. Chinese immigration was restricted and employers' liability for workmen's injuries extended. New public works were started, electoral boundaries revised and stipendiary magistrates set up.

The Public Instruction Act was for Parkes the ministry's most significant measure, an earnest of his deep conviction of the social necessity of equal educational opportunity. He had steadily defended the 1866 settlement against pressure from the Public School League and embattled Catholic and Anglican denominationalists until by the late 1870s administrative difficulties on the Council of Education, concern to spread scarce resources more widely and the alliance with Robertson led him to move in a way most practical politicians were coming to think inevitable. Archbishop Vaughan's [q.v.] 'audacious' attacks on National schools embittered the debate but did not prompt the 1880 legislation. Parkes correctly insisted that his bill was not anti-religious and tempered pragmatism with that liberal faith in 'freedom and equality' for which he had argued in his *Empire* days. Though he understood the Catholic position, he grieved at the separation of Catholic children from others with whom they would have to 'mix in later years', and his exhortations still echoed the simple colonial nativism of the 1840s and 1850s: 'let us be of whatever faith we may, let us still remember that we are above everything else free citizens of a free commonwealth'.

In December 1881 on medical advice Parkes began a holiday voyage, leaving Robertson as acting premier. He was accepted abroad, according to *The Times*, as 'the most commanding figure in Australian politics'. Hoping to further Australian interests, he secured commissions from all colonial governments except Victoria to represent, in the United States government and financial circles, their wish for support for the trans-Pacific steamship service and for a relaxation of import duties on wool. Though Parkes's speeches and talks on these matters had no perceptible effect on American policy he was treated everywhere with flattering attention which made his six weeks in America something of a personal triumph. He arrived in England in March 1882. His health was still poor but he found strength to become one of the social lions of the season: 'fortunately for me', he wrote, 'I can enjoy the Dinners because I have little exertion and new men of mark I constantly meet are of unfailing interest to me'. He was noticed by royalty, politicians, expatriate Australians, guilds and companies; he spoke at dinners, visited Birmingham as the mayor's guest, stayed three days with the Tennysons at Farringford, lunched at Brussels with the King and Queen of Belgium and at Potsdam spent a day as the special guest of Prince Frederick and his wife, eldest daughter of Queen Victoria. Invited by Lord Leigh he visited his birthplace, Stoneleigh, where he slept at the abbey and spoke to an assembly of village children in authoritative tones: 'you will not all rise to a position of power, honour, influence and responsibility such as that I now fill. But by resolving to discharge the duties of life, and in being of use and service in your day and generation, you will do far better than I have done'. He returned to Australia in August to be honoured at civic banquets in Melbourne and Sydney.

Parkes spoke to friends of new ministerial goals: to establish a comprehensive system of local government and make a vigorous attempt to federate the colonies. But on 16 November the government was defeated on Robertson's land bill and advised a dissolution. A general election proved unfavourable; Parkes lost the East Sydney seat but won Tenterfield and the government resigned on 4 January 1883. Its abrupt fall followed Robertson's refusal to recognize weaknesses in his 1861 land system. The governor, Lord Augustus Loftus, also noted that since his return Parkes had squandered the 'popularity and confidence he had previously enjoyed . . . had become dictatorial in his mode of action and overbearing in his manner, and whether intentionally or not had assumed a despotic tone which latterly became not only offensive to the Parliament but to the country'.

Loss of office dampened Parkes's zest for politics and loss of ministerial salary brought him financial problems: he returned to business and went to England as agent for a Sydney firm. Though absent from July 1883 to August 1884 he held the Tenterfield seat at the request of his constituents. In England a busy social round was punctuated by hard work on his own affairs. He addressed the Glasgow Chamber of Commerce and other public meetings in Scotland and was the moving spirit in founding the Australasian Investment Co., with its head office in Edinburgh and in Sydney a colonial board, on which he was to be prominent. He brought ivory goods home for sale and undertook to become Australasian representative of the engineering firm of Latimer, Clark, Muirhead & Co. After three months in the assembly as an ordinary Opposition member, he resigned on 3 November in protest at what he saw as the corrupt railway policy of Alexander Stuart's [q.v.] government. To a friend he also wrote that at 70 he was being forced by adversity 'to close a great career' to give all his time to improving his finances.

This self-imposed retirement ended when in March 1885 he attacked Dalley's decision to send colonial troops to the Sudan and contested the Argyle seat as the 'one way of constitutionally testing the opinion of the country'. Though his election by a narrow majority proved little, his principled and lucid approach to the Sudan affair did much, once jingoism abated, to reduce the government's prestige. In parliament he faced an expulsion move by enemies anxious to brand as a 'gross libel' his public assertion, made when resigning Tenterfield, that 'political character had almost disappeared from the proceedings of the Legislative Assembly'.

He survived and before the dissolution in October became the spearhead of a sustained Opposition attack on the government's alleged corruption.

In the elections Parkes contested St Leonards against G. R. Dibbs [q.v.] and won the seat after an acrimonious campaign. In the new parliament the government fell after announcing a large deficit resulting from economic recession and the collapse of land revenue following Stuart's land reforms. Robertson unwillingly formed a ministry in December but Parkes refused to join him. Robertson fell in February 1886 and Jennings [q.v.] took office, to struggle in a turbulent House to carry measures to meet the financial crisis. A group led by Parkes, alarmed by protectionist clamour out of doors, chose to interpret a proposed 5 per cent *ad valorem* tariff as 'sneaking in protection'. The climax to wild scenes in the assembly came at midnight on Saturday, 10 July, when after three days of continuous sitting Parkes led his followers out of the House, throwing on the table a written protest against the government's determination to sit on into the next day as a violation both of the Constitution and of the Sabbath.

When Jennings resigned in January 1887 Parkes formed his fourth ministry and went to the country with the slogan 'good government and commercial freedom'. He won a resounding victory, partly through his own energetic electioneering and partly through the work of the Free Trade Association of New South Wales which had taken charge of organizing the campaign. In the new parliament he led a majority whose dedication to the principle of free trade forced political divisions into a party-like mould and signalled the imminent end of the old faction system. For Parkes a ministerial salary compensated for the collapse of his commercial hopes in a third bankruptcy.

By 1889 the ministry had 'balanced' the budget, mildly reformed the tariff and amended the bankruptcy and criminal laws. Major reform of public works administration and railway management followed. In 1888 Parkes had responded to the Chinese immigration crisis with restrictive measures which defied imperial authority and nettled other colonial leaders anxious for concerted action. Given these successes, some mystery surrounds Parkes's virtual abdication of power in January 1889 when he 'courted defeat' by refusing to answer charges against the integrity of W. M. Fehon, appointed to the new Railway Commission. Parkes professed weariness in face of the Opposition's obstructive tactics; some supporters were disgruntled at his equivocal attitude to free trade and direct taxation, and his cabinet

was divided. Parkes was also under personal strain: he was still in financial difficulties; Clarinda had died on 2 February 1888; and his marriage at St Paul's Church of England, Redfern, on 6 February 1889 to Eleanor Dixon offended his family and provoked social censure.

Defeated on a snap adjournment division, Parkes resigned on 16 January. In protest William McMillan rallied the free traders who denied supply to the new Dibbs government and the House was dissolved. Narrowly victorious at the poll, the free trade party asked Parkes to resume leadership. In March he was back in office at the head of a reconstituted free trade ministry, and held office until October 1891, being dependent after June on support from the new Labor Party.

For Parkes, the principal departure of these years was the campaign which resulted in the Federation Conference and the Australasian Federal Convention of 1890-91. Though an advocate of colonial union for over thirty years, Parkes had shunned the Federal Council and puzzled federalists by seeking, largely at the prompting of Sir Alfred Stephen [q.v.], to alter the name of New South Wales to Australia. In January 1889 he had announced in Melbourne his readiness to join 'heart in hand' to promote true Federation, and in June warmed to a suggestion from the governor, Lord Carrington, that to confederate the colonies would be a 'glorious finish' to his life. He told his daughter that he had lost much of his 'former relish for parliamentary work' and was moved by 'repeated suggestions and invitations from the other colonies' to offer himself 'as leader in a great movement to federate on a solid basis all the colonies'. He sounded Duncan Gillies [q.v.] on the subject and in October employed Major-General Edwards's [q.v.] reports on defence as evidence of the urgent need for Federation. In that month, as a counter to Gillies's insistence that New South Wales join the Federal Council, he went to Brisbane to consult Queensland ministers and on his return journey delivered at Tenterfield a speech calling for a federal convention to devise 'a great national Government for all Australia'. The following Federal Conference and Convention owed much to the private negotiations of Lord Carrington yet were also personal diplomatic triumphs for Parkes and at the convention he was, according to Deakin, 'from first to last the Chief and leader'.

Political opportunism and the hope of strengthening his immediate position in New South Wales doubtless supported large-minded idealism in Parkes's commitment to Federation after 1889. But in Sydney the draft Constitution bill of 1891 divided free traders, was suspected by Labor and aroused little public enthusiasm. Meantime the maritime strike and its aftermath focussed attention on more urgent social issues. While the other colonies awaited a lead, Parkes failed to press the bill to an issue in his parliament, dallying lest opponents persuade the electors 'that we had consumed our time in the "fad" of federation . . . and had neglected the legislation so urgently required for the advancement of New South Wales'. He was also in poor physical shape to fight forlorn battles after injuries from a cab accident in 1890, though he continued to hold the reins of government firmly, as acting premier McMillan found in September when an injudicious reaction to the Circular Quay riots earned sharp censure from the premier. But another minister, J. H. Carruthers, feared that Parkes's health was 'gradually breaking and feebleness supervening his usual vigour'.

In October 1891 Parkes supported a motion to adjourn the debate on the recommittal of the coal mines regulation bill; the motion was not carried and he resigned leaving office with 'joyful satisfaction'. Though pressed to stay as free trade Opposition leader he refused. 'I am working on my book and ... resting from political turmoil', he told Carrington two months later. In June 1892 Parkes completed *Fifty Years in the Making of Australian History*, his great apologia, its vitality reflecting the wells of strength that were his. By 1893 'extremely well in bodily health', he toured Victoria in November to speak on Federation, dined and danced at Government House, and enjoyed the Derby with Sydney friends who invited him out in a 'brand new drag and four fine horses' : he 'climbed to a top seat with a young lady on each side of me and went to Flemington with a dash'. But his old political acumen did not accompany renewed physical strength. In 1894 he pettishly revealed his resentment of Reid's re-election as free trade leader and shocked friends by moving formal censure on the new government. Out of tune with Reid's fiscal and social reformism, he became obsessed with an ambition to head 'a new Party'. In the 1895 election he joined his old enemy Dibbs to form a shadowy 'Federal Party', which was labelled by the *Sydney Morning Herald* as 'an act of flagrant political immorality—an insult to the country'. In the Sydney-King electorate he challenged Reid, to fail after a vituperative campaign, which underlined his genuine concern for Federation but cruelly revealed his insensitiveness to the electorate's mood and the erosion by old age of his former powers. He unsuccessfully contested two other seats,

and his political career was at an end.

Parkes had been appointed K.C.M.G. in 1877 and G.C.M.G. in 1888. Lady Parkes, 'for whom I have paid so heavy a penalty and who has been such a true friend to me', died of cancer during the King campaign. He determined to retire to 'perfect privacy', but still spoke on Federation, hinted at another trip to England and rejoiced 'in better health than for many years past'. On 24 October 1895 he married Julia Lynch, but on 27 April 1896 died suddenly at his home Kenilworth, Annandale, of heart failure after an attack of pneumonia. He was reconciled on his deathbed to Reid and at his own wish was buried without pomp beside his first wife at Faulconbridge on the Blue Mountains. He was survived by his third wife and by five daughters and a son of the twelve children of his first marriage, and by four sons and a daughter of the second. The *Bulletin*, which had never spared him, carried a cartoon-epitaph which captured the momentary mood of the whole colony. Under the caption 'Finis', a young cornstalker, the 'Little Boy from Manly', with tear-filled eyes wistfully closed a great volume, on its spine the simple legend, 'Parkes'.

Largest figure of nineteenth century Australian politics, Parkes also remains the most enigmatic. In a celebrated obituary, William Astley [q.v.] saw him merely as a 'master of the art of seeming great'; more sensitively, Alfred Deakin felt 'there was in him the man he dressed himself to appear'. Deakin's instinct for the real Parkes has not in fact been bettered : 'though not rich or versatile, his personality was massive, durable and imposing, resting upon elementary qualities of human nature elevated by a strong mind. He was cast in the mould of a great man and though he suffered from numerous pettinesses, spites and failings, he was in himself a large-brained self-educated Titan whose natural field was found in Parliament and whose resources of character and intellect enabled him in his later years to overshadow all his contemporaries'. Parkes's papers add other dimensions which indicate a personality moulded over a long and changeful life by inner conflict, as he sought to reconcile deeply held principles, a mighty drive for self-realization and the compromises which were the price of success. Astley further sensed that his 'heart was . . . not in politics but in literature, in history and in art. There was a singular vein of sentiment in his nature which found no appropriate vent in his public existence . . . To see him handle a letter of Tennyson or Carlyle, or the simple autograph of Lincoln, was to receive a lesson in reverence. Books and other mementoes of the illustrious dead were to him the wine of life. And yet he was no scholar—scarcely even to be termed a student. As to his own place in literature, his poems are a byword'. Fate deprived him of easy paths to the preferred life of the 'choice spirit' (his phrase), through gentle birth, education, independence or business success, and the way of politics offered a sometimes unhappy alternative.

His vanity, craving for recognition and overbearing manner were the concomitants of a ruthless pursuit of personal success. Yet fiery integrity bit through in his scorn for the world's judgment of his marital and financial affairs and his inner resources provided resilience to weather crises which might have destroyed other men. While a remarkable instinct for political guile explains his ascendency in faction politics, he held tenaciously to important principles and prejudices. He was ever suspicious of the Church of Rome, steady in his concern to prevent cant depriving children of education, genuine in his wish to see justice achieved within the framework of a *laissez faire* system, dedicated to the idea of keeping Australian society racially homogeneous and sincere in his chosen role as guardian of constitutional proprieties. His probity and skill as an administrator cannot be seriously challenged, and his energy and self-sacrifice in tasks sincerely undertaken command profound respect.

Bearded after 1861, he was always physically impressive, though imposing rather than handsome. For studied oratory he had few peers among colonial contemporaries, despite his uncertainty about aspirates and a tendency towards affectation. He collected autographs, books and artistic bric-à-brac, and his friends were always intrigued by his choice menagerie of native wild animals. Though temperate, he enjoyed champagne and had, as William Walker [q.v.] had it, great faith in the virtue of gastronomy as a political force.

Parkes's other volumes of verse were *Murmurs of the Stream* (1857), *Studies in Rhyme* (1870), *The Beauteous Terrorist and other poems* (1885), *Fragmentary Thoughts* (1889) and *Sonnets and Other Verse* (1895). His other prose works include *Australian Views of England: eleven letters written in 1861 and 1862* (1869) and many political pamphlets. An *Emigrant's Home Letters* is an edited collection of his letters to his family in 1838-43, published in 1896 by his daughter Annie.

Portraits by Julian Ashton are in the National Memorial School of Arts, Tenterfield, and copies are in the Parliament Houses in Sydney and Canberra; by Tom Roberts in the National Gallery, Adelaide; by Mary Stoddard in the Legislative Council Chamber, Sydney; and by John Henry Chinner in the National Library of Australia. A bust by Nelson Illingworth is in the National Library and a bust by Theodora Cowen in the Art Gallery of New South Wales.

C. E. Lyne, *Life of Sir Henry Parkes* (Syd, 1896); W. Walker, *Recollections of Sir Henry Parkes* (Windsor, 1896); A. Deakin, *The federal story*, H. Brookes ed (Melb, 1944); A. W. Martin, *Henry Parkes* (Melb, 1964); P. Loveday and A. W. Martin, *Parliament factions and parties* (Melb, 1966); G. N. Hawker, *The parliament of New South Wales, 1856-1965* (Syd, 1971); A. W. Martin, 'Sir Henry Parkes, and public education in New South Wales', *Melbourne studies in education 1960-1961*, E. L. French ed (Melb, 1962); A. W. Martin, 'Henry Parkes and electoral manipulation, 1872-82', *Hist Studies*, no 31, Nov 1958; N. B. Nairn, 'The political mastery of Sir Henry Parkes', *JRAHS*, 53 (1967); M. Rutledge, 'Edward Butler and the chief justiceship, 1873', *Hist Studies*, no 50, Apr 1968; *Bulletin*, 9, 16 May 1896; *Daily Telegraph* (Syd), 28, 30 Apr 1896; *SMH*, 28 Apr 1896; J. A. Ryan, B. R. Wise: an Oxford liberal in the Freetrade Party of New South Wales (M.A. thesis, Univ Syd, 1964); M. Lyons, Aspects of sectarianism in New South Wales circa 1865-1880 (Ph.D. thesis, ANU, 1972); Carrington papers (by courtesy of Brigadier Llewellyn Palmer); J. D. Lang, Parkes and Windeyer papers (ML).   A. W. MARTIN

PARKIN, WILLIAM (1801-1889), businessman, politician and philanthropist, was born on 24 August 1801 at Glastonbury, Somerset, England. About 1838 he married Sarah May. With free passages he and his wife sailed for South Australia in the *Recovery* and arrived at Port Adelaide on 19 September 1839. He farmed briefly near Willunga and then opened a drapery in Hindley Street, Adelaide. Despite suffering in the 1840-43 depression he recovered and his business prospered. By 1856 he had moved into larger premises in Rundle Street with G. W. Chinner as his partner. He retired from business with a 'comfortable fortune' and devoted himself to politics. He was a representative of the City of Adelaide in the House of Assembly in 1860-62 and a member of the Legislative Council in 1866-77. Quiet and conscientious, he won repute for his 'quaint, humorous, but intelligent addresses'.

Parkin is best remembered as a philanthropist and benefactor of the South Australian Congregational Church. He was a prominent and generous member of Rev. T. Q. Stow's [q.v.] Church in Freeman Street, and later attended the Glenelg Congregational Church for twenty years. In 1876, after consultation with R. D. Hanson and John Brown [qq.v.], he founded the Parkin Trust for the training and maintenance of students for the Congregational ministry by a gift estimated at £10,000, £8000 of it in cash and 4160 acres worth £2000 near Palmerston in the Northern Territory. The trust was also to be used for building churches and schools, and supplying benefactions for the widows of ministers. In 1882 he established the 'Parkin Congregational Mission of South Australia' for maintaining missionaries in the less settled parts of South Australia, and for aiding twenty widows over 60, chosen by the governors as 'worthy of assistance' by giving them £5 each at Christmas. To provide for these purposes he gave his valuable property in Rundle Street. The Parkin Mission was duly incorporated on 24 October 1882.

Parkin had been prominent in many commercial concerns. He was one of the largest shareholders in the Wallaroo and Kadina Tramway Co. and a member of the syndicate which took over the *Advertiser* in 1864. He was not in the front rank of South Australian colonists, but his success in commerce and politics, and his support of religious and philanthropic activities were typical of the many Dissenters who prospered in the 'Paradise of Dissent'.

Predeceased by his wife on 23 March 1871, Parkin died at Plympton on 31 May 1889 and was widely mourned. He was buried in the family vault at West Terrace cemetery, survived by his second wife Ellen Stonehouse, whom he had married on 28 February 1872; he had no children. His estate of £22,550 was divided among his many relations, his church and benevolent societies. His home and nine acres at Plympton became the property of the trust when his widow moved to Glenelg a few years after his death. Two memorial windows were placed in the Glenelg Congregational Church, one by his wife and the other by the governors of the trust and mission that bear his name.

Parkin Theological College was opened in North Terrace, Kent Town, in 1910, but the decline of Congregationalism in South Australia led to the close of the college in 1969. Its few remaining students and large endowments were transferred to the Methodist Wesley College in Wayville, which now functions under the name of Parkin-Wesley College.

G. E. Loyau, *The representative men of South Australia* (Adel, 1883); J. J. Pascoe, *History of Adelaide and vicinity* (Adel, 1901); F. W. Cox and L. Robjohns, *Three-quarters of a century* (Adel, 1912); *Observer* (Adel), 1, 8 June 1889.

DIRK VAN DISSEL

PARRY, HENRY HUTTON (1826-1893), Anglican bishop, was born on 18 December 1826 in Antigua, second son of Thomas Parry, archdeacon of Antigua and from 1843 bishop of Barbados, and his wife Louisa, née Hutton. Educated at Rugby, he entered Balliol College, Oxford, (B.A., 1851; M.A., 1859), and the University of Durham (D.D. by diploma, 1876). As a curate and deacon he returned to the West Indies, was ordained priest in 1852 and in 1855-60 was tutor at Codrington College. In 1861 his father appointed Henry archdeacon and when ill health forced him to return to England, Henry became vicar-general of the diocese. Episcopal work was performed by neighbouring bishops until Henry was appointed coadjutor bishop to his father and was consecrated in England on 15 November 1868. His father died on 16 March 1870 and Henry became administrator and married Elizabeth Mary Thomas (d. 11 November 1877). In 1874 he returned on account of her health, becoming locum tenens at St Neot's, Huntingdonshire. In 1876 he accepted the offer of the Perth see from A. C. Tait, archbishop of Canterbury, who had chosen Parry despite the request of the Western Australian Church for a bishop with private means.

In his large and isolated diocese Parry's continuous problem was financial stability. At first the sources of income were the imperial grant, grants from such societies as S.P.C.K., S.P.G. and the Colonial and Continental Church Society and grants from the colonial government. None of these grants was permanent and in 1877 the imperial government warned that the colony would soon have to provide for itself. Throughout his episcopate Parry encouraged the development of three funds: the Sustentation Fund which was to maintain the ministrations of religion if colonial grants were withdrawn; the Diocesan Church Fund which was to provide ready money to meet emergencies; and the Building Fund which was to make loans without interest for new churches, schools and rectories. In appeals for money Parry always encouraged every member to make regular contributions, however small.

One of Parry's recurring difficulties was the provision of a worthy new cathedral. Public worship in Perth had been held since 1845 in St George's Church but it had become inadequate. Finance was the great problem but the Cathedral Fund was boosted in 1878 by a gift of £2000 from Sir Luke Leake [q.v.] whose widowed niece, Mary Suzanna, Parry married on 15 April 1879. Built of red brick and limestone, the cathedral was consecrated on 15 November 1888 by the primate, Bishop Barry [q.v.]. Its final cost was paid in 1891 when church land was sold for £5500.

In his annual reports to synod and in his

preaching Parry stressed the need for personal discipleship and church attendance. He encouraged Sunday schools and such societies as communicants' guilds, the Purity Society and the Church of England Temperance Society. To stimulate help from the laity, he was prepared to licence 'duly qualified' lay readers for areas without normal services. He also tried to recruit overseas clergy and find their stipends. He travelled widely throughout the diocese and in 1889 claimed that 'within a little over two years he had visited every parish in his diocese and confirmed 850 persons at different confirmations'. He was also concerned with events in the rest of the Church both in Australia and in England.

Parry had a lively interest in education but achieved little of permanent value in that field. Soon after his arrival he opened Bishop's Boys' College as a hostel under a resident clergyman so that religious education, then debarred from the high school, could be given out of school hours. He also hoped to train theological students as 'a first step towards a native Ministry for the Diocese'. Disturbed by the lack of religious training in government schools, he joined other ministers in September 1879 to have the Education Act amended to allow clergymen half an hour each week in these schools. In 1878 he announced to synod the establishment of a Girls' School and College including the names of a lady principal and a head teacher; they had twenty-six girls of whom six were boarders. By 1880 Bishop's College had fallen on hard times; the two theological students moved into Bishop's House and the buildings were rented to the Girls' College, which itself was closed in 1888 for lack of funds. In 1882 a commercial school had been established at Fremantle under the general management of the clergy of the parish and a committee. In 1885 Parry stressed the need for church primary schools in the colony's chief centres, for teacher training and for funds to aid religious instruction in government schools. In 1892 a Diocesan Board of Education was set up by Act of Synod.

Concerned about the Aboriginal population, Parry began early in 1878 to discuss the matter and by 1880 a committee was organized. In 1884 the governor reserved 150,000 acres in the Murchison and Gascoyne area, and Rev. John Gribble [q.v.] was invited to superintend the mission but within a year an acrimonious controversy was stirred up in the north and in Perth. Gribble left the diocese without leave and his clerical licence was revoked. The health of his successors forced them to withdraw and for want of funds the mission lapsed in January 1892.

The turning point of Parry's episcopate was in 1887. In 1885 he had been asked by synod to 'visit England and lay before the influential members of the Mother Church the needs of the colony'. On his return in 1887 he reported that his mission had failed financially, a disaster that compelled the Western Australian Church to depend upon itself. In 1888 a Diocesan Council replaced the Standing Committee for all the temporal affairs of the church. Synod also established 'The Diocesan Trustees', a corporation with perpetual succession and a common seal; all church lands were transferred to its care. A Diocesan Church Office was set up and in 1892 a secretary was appointed. For church extension a Diocesan Home Mission Society had been set up in 1890 with a central fund to provide for clergy and their maintenance in poor or newly-settled areas. The fund was to be maintained by a quarterly subscription of 1s. from each church member and an annual collection; an organizing chaplain was appointed in 1892.

After a short illness Parry died on 15 November 1893 on the silver jubilee of his consecration. He was survived by his second wife, by three of her children and by three from his first marriage.

Parry as bishop was described as saintly, scholarly and idealistic, traits which shaped his episcopate. From his arrival in the transition years that led to responsible government, the scope of his work was curtailed by primitive transport and stringent finance which were not ameliorated until the gold rush in the time of his successor. His main work was to strengthen church organization, but his primary interest was in the spiritual development of his people. Twenty more ecclesiastical buildings, increased local contributions, a team of clergy more than doubled, and the cathedral he built all stand as memorials of his work in Western Australia.

C. L. M. Hawtrey, *The availing struggle* (Perth, 1949); F. Alexander (ed), *Four bishops and their see* (Perth, 1957); *WA Catholic Record*, 1875-76, 1879-93; *Q Mag* (Diocese of Perth), 1889-93; L. W. Parry and M. L. R. Sanderson, 'The story of the building of St George's Cathedral 1880-1888', *West Aust Church News*, Dec 1930; *Inquirer*, 1875-76, 1879-93; *West Australian*, 1879-93; *Daily News* (Perth), 1882-93; *Western Mail*, 1885-93; Synod reports, 1877-93 (Perth Diocesan Registry); M. L. R. Sanderson, Short life of Henry Hutton Parry (held by author); Papers re West Indies period (SPG Lib, Lond); H. H. Parry, Diaries and letter-book, Diocese of Perth, 1877-86, 1888-93 (held by family), letters to dean of Perth 1886-87 (Battye Lib, Perth), papers and memoirs (held by M. L. R. Sanderson, Perth).

MARK HAYNES

PASCO, CRAWFORD ATCHISON DENMAN (1818-1898), naval officer and police magistrate, was born in Plymouth, England, youngest son of Rear-Admiral John Pasco and his wife Rebecca, née Penfold. As a lieutenant his father had signalled 'England expects every man will do his duty' at Trafalgar and later commanded Macquarie's escort to New South Wales and returned with Bligh to England.

At 12 Crawford entered the navy and as a midshipman was in H.M.S. Nimrod at the blockade of the Scheldt in 1832 and with the squadron on the Tagus in the Portuguese civil war and siege of Oporto in 1833. In 1834-37 he served in the Blonde and Satellite, stationed chiefly off Peru and Chile, where he witnessed the repercussions of revolutions and earthquakes. In 1838 he was appointed to the Britomart under Lieutenant Owen Stanley [q.v.] and sailed to Port Essington to prepare a settlement. In 1839 Pasco transferred to the Beagle. He served first under J. C. Wickham, then under J. L. Stokes [qq.v.], engaged in surveying parts of Australia's northern and western coasts, discovering in particular the Adelaide River, the future port of Darwin and the Victoria River. In 1842 he was temporarily transferred to the Vansittart for survey work in Bass Strait. On his return to England in 1843 Pasco was appointed to the Vestal, sailed via America to the Far East, South Africa, Van Diemen's Land and thence to Canton and Singapore with two million dollars, reparation from the Opium war. He sailed for Penang, subdued a rebellious rajah in Borneo, and then visited the Philippines.

Pasco was transferred to the paddle-steamer Vulture. In September 1846 he wrote to the editor of the Hong Kong Register suggesting that the Peninsular and Oriental Steam Navigation Co. might extend its mail steamer services from Singapore to Australia. The letter was republished in the Sydney Morning Herald and other Australian papers. Meanwhile Lieutenant Pasco continued survey work first of the Canton River and then of the Palawan Island area, where he renewed contact with Borneo rebels. After a severe illness in 1851 he was sent to England and given two years' leave. In 1852 with a free passage from the P. & O. Co. in the steamship Chusan on its inaugural voyage to Australia, he was a great help with the navigation, particularly compass deviation, and took the ship through Port Phillip Heads himself.

Pasco retired from the navy and settled in Victoria. He was appointed a police magistrate and helped to organize a greatly expanded water police force at Williamstown. He dealt mainly with deserting crews and was instrumental in having convicted sailors imprisoned in hulks instead of a Melbourne gaol. Appointed a visiting justice of the hulks, he clashed with their officers and after a board of inquiry was transferred to Swan Hill to his great chagrin in 1857. Pasco was later appointed to Maryborough, Port Albert and Alexandra with various subsidiary duties, and was finally dismissed with many other magistrates on 24 January 1878.

Pasco retired to Melbourne. There he became a founder member of the Victorian branch of the Geographical Society in 1884. At its inaugural meeting the presidential address by F. Mueller [q.v.] led to the formation, with the Royal Society, of the first Antarctic Exploration Committee; Pasco was made chairman. The committee was extremely active, particularly in 1886-93, encouraging support in Australia, Britain and Scandinavia from politicians, scientists, whalers, explorers and philanthropists.

Pasco was twice married: first, at Hobart on 21 September 1852 to Mary Elizabeth Emmett; and second, to Francis Emily, daughter of Dr Thomas Barker. In 1897 he published A Roving Commission, a vivid account of his naval life. He feared God and the Melbourne Club. He died on 18 February 1898 and was buried in St Kilda cemetery.

B. Cable, A hundred year history of the P. & O. (Lond, 1937); R. A. Swan, Australia in the Antarctic (Melb, 1961); V&P (LA Vic), 1862-63, 3 (11); Australasian, 3 July 1897; Argus, 21 Feb 1898.   MICHAEL T. MOORE

PASLEY, CHARLES (1824-1890), military engineer, was born on 14 November 1824 at Chatham, England, eldest son of General Sir Charles William Pasley, a leading military engineer, and his second wife Martha Matilda, née Roberts. Educated at the King's Grammar School, Rochester, and from 1840 the Royal Military Academy at Woolwich, he was commissioned in the Royal Engineers on 20 December 1843. He served in Britain until 1846, in Canada and then in Bermuda whence he returned to England because of sickness. From early 1851 he was on the staff of the Great Exhibition. In April 1853 he was appointed colonial engineer of Victoria. He reached Melbourne on 17 September. His department, hitherto undermanned and demoralized, soon busied itself with port improvements and with the building of barracks, court-houses and offices throughout the settled districts. His captaincy in the Royal Engineers was dated 17 February 1854.

When later that year unrest increased on the Ballarat goldfield, Pasley had no doubt that the situation was serious and offered his services to the commander-in-chief. On 28 November he reached the camp at Ballarat and took up duty as aide-de-camp to Captain Thomas of the 40th Regiment. He fully agreed with the firm measures taken by the authorities to bring matters to a head. In the assault on the Eureka stockade on 3 December Pasley commanded the skirmishers in the centre; after the place had been captured he was active in restraining soldiers from taking reprisals on the prisoners.

Pasley had been an official nominee in the old Legislative Council from October 1854 to November 1855 when the new Constitution was introduced. On 28 November he was appointed commissioner of public works in the ministry of W. C. Haines [q.v.], thus acting as both political and professional head of his department. Some major Melbourne works projects were begun in 1856, including Parliament House, Victoria Barracks, the gaol at Pentridge, the lunatic asylum at Kew and in 1857 the Customs House. Many of these buildings reflected Pasley's taste. He consistently favoured the use of local materials, and recognized the virtues of the Melbourne basalt or 'bluestone'. His efforts to encourage local designers were well known. Among many extraneous duties he was president of the Central Road Board, a commissioner of the Melbourne-Mount Alexander railway, a councillor of the Philosophical Institute, a vice-president of the Melbourne Philharmonic Society and first patron of the Victorian Institute of Architects.

Since the new Constitution provided for a wholly elected parliament, Pasley could only continue as a minister by winning a seat at the forthcoming election. His father had lent him money to help in buying a house as his property qualification. He stood for South Bourke in the Legislative Assembly. With a liberal policy he favoured measures to check the alienation of public lands by grazing interests and would have reserved from sale the land adjoining railway routes. He supported state aid to religion. He won the seat easily, but lost his ministerial status on 11 March 1857 when Haines was displaced by J. O'Shanassy [q.v.]; Pasley resigned his seat in July.

In 1858 Pasley was vice-president of the royal commission on the colony's defences, which adopted his proposal for Melbourne to be defended by batteries on Hobson's Bay rather than at Port Phillip Heads, because of the performance of the artillery then in service and the expense of manning forts at the heads. However, when rifled ordnance was introduced in 1859, he recommended the fortification of the heads. The chief Melbourne monuments to his last years in the department are the Treasury, by J. J. Clark [q.v.], and the General Post Office, which was completed after he left.

Late in 1859 the royal commission on the civil service, overruling Pasley's protest, recommended that the Public Works Department be headed by a non-professional. It was time for Pasley to go. He failed to obtain compensation for loss of office but was given leave on full pay to enable him to rejoin his corps and resume his military career. He was about to embark for England in July 1860 when news of a military reverse in New Zealand decided Major-General Pratt [q.v.] to take the field in person. Pasley, who had missed the Crimean war, could not pass by the chance of active service so close at hand. He offered his services and on 24 July embarked with General Pratt.

In Taranaki Pasley soon found himself employed as an engineer. In the attack on one of the Maori forts on the Kaihihi River on 11 October he was emplacing a heavy gun when the enemy opened a fusillade from concealed positions and he was severely wounded in the thigh. He was invalided to Melbourne in November. For his work in New Zealand he was promoted brevet major and mentioned in dispatches. His convalescence was prolonged but on 29 May 1861, after receiving many tributes, he sailed for England.

Rejoining his corps, Pasley was appointed commanding engineer at Gravesend. In 1864 he succeeded his former colleague, Major Andrew Clarke [q.v.], as special agent for Victoria, a part-time office largely concerned with advice on armaments and procurement of warlike stores. Pasley dealt not only with land armaments but with the equipment of H.M.V.S. Nelson, and with the design, construction and armament of the turret-ship Cerberus and its dispatch to Victoria. He filled this appointment for four years.

In October 1865 Pasley became superintending engineer of the naval dockyard at Chatham, which was about to undergo a major extension. He managed this project for eight years. In September 1873 he succeeded Clarke as director of works at the Admiralty. He held this office until September 1882 and was responsible for such important works as the entrance locks at Chatham Yard, dry docks at Devonport and Haulbowline, and the barracks and the Naval Engineering School at Keyham. In 1874 he was elected an associate member of the Council of the Institution of Civil Engineers. He retained his connexions with Victoria, and in July 1879 was appointed a commissioner for the Melbourne International Exhibition. In 1800-82 he acted as Victoria's agent-general and chairman of the Board of Advice in London. He was appointed a civil C.B. in April 1880, and in August 1881 on his retirement from the army he was promoted major-general. He died at his home, Bedford Park, Chiswick, on 11 November 1890. At Hampton, Middlesex, on 29 March 1864 he had married his cousin Charlotte Roberts, who survived him; they had no children.

Slight in stature, Pasley was self-effacing but contemporaries found him responsible, conscientious and sound in judgment; his gravity was tempered by a sense of humour so that he was liked as well as respected. However conventional in morals and behaviour, he was enterprising and original in his professional practice. While in charge of public works in Victoria he administered his department with skill, coping with wide fluctuations in financial appropriations, and he left his mark.

G. Serle, *The golden age* (Melb, 1963); J. Stokes, 'Major-General Charles Pasley, C.B.', *Roy Engineers J*, 2 Feb 1891; *Punch* (Melb), 6 Dec 1855, 12 June 1856; *Aust Builder and Railway Chronicle*, 30 Apr, 29 May, 26 June, 21 Aug 1856, 26 Jan 1861; *Argus*, 22 July, 18 Aug 1856, 25 July, 21 Nov 1860, 24 Jan, 11 May 1861; CO 309/22/58.   RONALD McNICOLL

PATERSON, JAMES (1826-1906), shipowner and coal merchant, was born on 17 July 1826 at Middlethird Farm, Galston, Ayrshire, Scotland, eldest son of Robert Paterson, farmer, and his wife Agnes, née Howie. Educated locally, he won the Highland Agricultural Society of Scotland prize for agricultural chemistry in 1845. He remained on the farm until he sailed from Liverpool in June 1852, arriving at Melbourne in October.

For five months Paterson was a successful gold-digger at Forest Creek, near Castlemaine, and then spent a lucrative year as a teamster, operating between Melbourne and Ballarat. Illness forced him to quit and on returning to Melbourne he established a coal-importing business in partnership with Edward Newbigin. James Paterson & Co. soon acquired a fleet of small sailing ships and continued with them even after the first steamer was bought in 1875. In the 1870s the firm became the largest coal importer in Melbourne and diversified into the bay towage business after buying two iron paddle steam tugs, an investment that remained important for the life of the company. Although Paterson was seen as a brusque martinet he was also considered to be fair and a shrewd businessman of undoubted probity.

Paterson's civic life was varied. He was elected to the Melbourne City Council and represented Lonsdale Ward from 1870 until 1885. He was mayor in 1876-77, and also worked hard to have the Eastern Market rebuilt; it was reopened in 1880. His influence was present again in maritime matters as a member of the Victorian Shipowners' Association from its inception in the mid-1860s and chairman in 1875. In addition he represented the shipowners at the inaugural meeting of the Melbourne Harbor Trust in April 1877. Moreover he was closely involved with the development of the port while a commissioner of the trust in 1877-79. He was also a member of the Marine Board of Victoria for some time. Other public offices included the royal commissions on low-lying lands in 1873, and the Paris Exhibition in 1878.

An active churchman, Paterson materially assisted in establishing the West Melbourne Presbyterian Church and was associated, especially in his later years, with Scots Church and the Hawthorn Presbyterian Church. He was always generous in his gifts not only to the church and its agencies but also to many other charitable and philanthropic institutions. His main sporting interest was horse-racing and for some time he served on the committee of the Victoria Racing Club. He was an owner-breeder of several fine thoroughbreds, the best known being Hymettus, and the successes of his stable included the Oaks, the Adelaide St Leger and two Caulfield Cups.

Paterson died on 6 November 1906, survived by his wife Mary Jane, née Forbes; they had no children. The nearest kin were nieces and nephews, of whom Henry Masterton was Paterson's chosen successor to control the business. His estate was valued for probate at about £300,000.

H. M. Humphreys (ed), *Men of the time in Australia: Victorian series*, 2nd ed (Melb, 1882); F. Doherty, *The Paterson story* (Melb, 1958); *Argus*, 10, 29 Nov 1906; *Age*, 12 Nov 1906.
                                          G. R. HENNING

PATERSON, JOHN FORD (1851-1912), artist, was born in Dundee, Scotland, son of John Ford Paterson and his wife Elizabeth, née Stewart. He studied at the Royal Scottish Academy Schools in Edinburgh where at 20 he exhibited his first painting. He migrated to Melbourne with others of his family in 1872 but in 1875 returned to Scotland to further his study of landscape painting. He was influenced by members of the 'Glasgow School' who were striving for new expression in art that was decorative and rejected the sentimental and photographic works that had long been popular. In the next nine years Paterson exhibited in Edinburgh, Glasgow, Liverpool and Manchester. He became well known in London where he frequented the Savage Club. In 1884 he returned to Australia where he remained except for a visit to Scotland in 1892.

Paterson renewed his friendship with Louis Buvelot [q.v.] whose *plein-air* methods suited the romantic Scot. He showed at the inaugural exhibition at Buxton's Gallery, but as a landscape painter he was not as successful as others in the Heidelberg group. His work was more romantic in mood and his sense of colour, draftsmanship and mystical feeling for the bush placed him among the important Australian artists of the nineteenth century. With such artists as Conder [q.v.] and Roberts he broke away from the Victorian Academy of Art to found the Australian Art Association. In 1888 these organizations amalgamated as the Victorian Artists' Society; Paterson was its president in 1902. At its winter exhibition in 1896 his 'Evening in the Bush' received excellent notices. It was exhibited in London in 1898 at the Australian Art Exhibition and with 'A Nocturne' was ecstatically praised. In 1900 his 'Bush Symphony' attracted attention when exhibited at the Old Court Studios in Melbourne and was bought by the National Gallery of Victoria.

Paterson often claimed that the Australian landscape had 'a new sensation to offer, a new beauty to explain . . . Whiles I think airt is a kind o' suggestiveness, a hint, a kind o' promise, something evanescent. 'Tis a kind of spirituality o' things I'm after. A dream picture that's real, an yet ye canna put your han' to it'. Lionel Lindsay called him 'a quaint essentially artistic character, but he filled a big enough place in the art of his day. His ideas were greater than their fulfilment'. With little interest in money he turned in bad times to poultry farming near Ringwood. Though retiring and careless in dress, he commented on art spontaneously and his popularity suggests an outgoing personality. The smoke nights at the 'Vic. Artists' were famed for his jovial Scottish airs, and he always brought the house down with his rendition of 'We are nae fu'.' Aged 62 he died suddenly on 1 July 1912 at his home in Queensberry Street, Carlton.

Paterson never married despite his old-world courtesy to the ladies. Notable contributions to Australian art and letters were made by his brother Hugh, whose daughters Esther and Betty were artists; a nephew, Louis Esson, was a poet and dramatist.

The Victorian Artists' Society holds an oil portrait by Bess Norris Tait and an ink sketch by Max Meldrum is privately owned. His work is represented in the galleries of

Australian capitals as well as the galleries in Bendigo, Castlemaine, Newcastle and Ballarat. On 24 September 1932 a retrospective exhibition in Melbourne won attractive reviews.

An elder brother, Charles Stewart Paterson, born on 5 January 1843 in Edinburgh, was apprenticed to the house-decorator, John Nesbit. As chief decorator for Dabies of Edinburgh he decorated and restored Ayrton Castle and other mansions. He arrived at Melbourne in 1872 and formed the firm of Paterson Bros, which later monopolized the decoration of wealthy homes and such public buildings as Government House, Melbourne Town Hall, the Parliamentary Library and the Prahran Public Library. In 1888 he built the Grosvenor Chambers in Collins Street East as an art centre at a cost of £9000. His wide interests included work in several institutions. He was a founder of the Working Men's College, serving as treasurer and in 1902 as president. He was active in the Juvenile Exhibition and Caledonian Society, and chairman of the Operatives' Building Society and the Queen's Coffee Palace Co. He also helped to make the Fern Tree Gully area a popular resort. After a long illness he died on 14 April 1917, survived by his wife Annie, née McFarlane, and by two sons and two daughters.

J. Smith (ed), *Cyclopedia of Victoria*, 1 (Melb, 1903); D. H. Skinner and J. Kroeger (eds), *Renniks Australian artists*, no 1 (Adel, 1968); G. H. Gill, '"The Vics": an historical record', *The gallery on Eastern Hill*, C. B. Christesen ed (Melb, 1970); *Table Talk*, 27 Apr 1888, 25 July 1901; *Illustrated Aust News*, 1 July 1896; *Review of Reviews for A'sia*, 20 Aug 1904; *Age*, 1 July 1912, 17 Apr 1917, 24 Sept 1932; *Argus*, 16 Apr 1917; L. Lindsay, 'J. Ford Paterson', *Art in Aust*, no 7 (1917); B. Burdett, 'John Ford Paterson', *Art in Aust*, 15 Aug 1933; family information.   MARJORIE J. TIPPING

PATON, JOHN (1834-1914), soldier and prison officer, was born in Stirling, Scotland, son of Matthew Paton, soldier, and his wife Isabella, née Bell. He enlisted in the Black Watch, but at the outbreak of the Crimean war volunteered in the Argyll and Sutherland Highlanders. He first saw active service twelve days after arriving in the Crimea in the battle of the Alma, September 1854. He then fought at Balaclava and served for about a year before Sebastopol. At the end of the war he returned to Scotland. In 1857 the regiment was on its way to China when it was diverted to India.

Paton saw active service in the mutiny and won the Victoria Cross at Lucknow on 16 November 1857, 'for distinguished personal gallantry . . . in proceeding round the Shah Nujjiff under an extremely heavy fire, discovering a breach in the opposite side, to which he afterwards conducted the Regiment, by which means that important position was taken'. He was voted his award by the non-commissioned officers of his regiment. In a later interview he emphasized his good fortune and recalled his fallen comrades: 'At Lucknow we had several hard fights in one day, but we pushed on to the besieged Residency and had [Sir Henry] Havelock out the next night together with the women and children. It was there I won the Cross. My bonnet was shot away and my pouch, also a button from the front of my coat, besides having the arm of my over-all torn by a bullet. Yet then, as afterwards, though always in the thick of it, I never received a scratch, although many and many a time, my beloved comrades dropped on either side of me'. Paton was certainly 'in the thick of it' in the first relief of Lucknow, the battle of Cawnpore, the second siege of Lucknow as well as storming many forts.

In 1861 Paton left the army and went to New South Wales where he joined the prison service on 28 May. He was chief warder at Port Macquarie for ten years from September 1865, chief gaoler at Deniliquin in 1875-88 where his wife acted as matron, and on 15 November 1888 he was appointed governor of Berrima gaol. On 1 July 1890 he succeeded Peter Herbert as governor at Goulburn gaol at a salary of £388. He retired from the prison service on 29 February 1896 and went to live in Sydney.

John Paton, 'Hero of Lucknow', died at his residence, Verona, 19 Prospect Road, Summer Hill, on 1 April 1914, survived by twin daughters of his first wife Mary Miller (d. 1869), whom he had married at Goulburn in 1866, and by his second wife Amelia Martha Crook Spurling (d. 1923), whom he had married in Sydney in 1872. He was buried with full military honours in the Church of England cemetery, Rookwood. His estate was sworn for probate at under £900.

A memorial is in St Andrew's Church of England, Summer Hill, where his Victoria Cross and campaign medals are preserved.

A. E. J. Cavendish, Am Reisimeid Chataich: the 93rd Sutherland Highlanders . . . 1799-1927 (Lond, 1928); O'M. Creagh and E. M. Humphris (eds), The V.C. and D.S.O., 1 (Lond, 1924); London Gazette, 24 Dec 1858; SMH, 16 Nov 1907, 2 Apr 1914; Goulburn Evening Penny Post, 2 Apr 1914.   G. P. WALSH

PATON, JOHN GIBSON (1824-1907), Presbyterian missionary, was born on 24 May 1824 at Kirkmahoe, Dumfriesshire, Scotland, eldest of eleven children of James Paton (d. 1868), a stocking manufacturer of Covenanting principles, and his wife Janet Jardine, née Rogerson (d. 1865). Educated in the parish school at Torthorwald where his family settled in 1829, he worked at various trades before migrating to Glasgow. On graduating from the Free Normal Seminary, he was briefly a relieving teacher in the Maryhill Free Church School and for some ten years an evangelist in the Glasgow City Mission. After spare-time study at the University of Glasgow, the Andersonian (Medical) College and the Reformed Presbyterian Divinity Hall he was licensed on 1 December 1857 as a preacher and on 23 March 1858 ordained as a minister and missionary to the southern New Hebrides.

On arrival at Aneityum on 29 August Paton was appointed to Port Resolution, Tanna, where he was settled on 5 November 1858. His stay was brief and tragic. In March 1859 his wife Mary Ann, née Robson, and infant son died of malaria, and Paton was incapacitated by the same disease for months. A general movement towards Christianity in 1860 was checked early in 1861 by a measles epidemic which carried off a third of the populace, and three devastating hurricanes reduced the remnant to starvation. The death from cerebral malaria on 21 January 1861 of Paton's young colleague, S. F. Johnston, and the martyrdom on 20 May of Rev. and Mrs G. N. Gordon on Erromanga further alienated the anti-Christian party. After the visit of H.M.S. Cordelia and Pelorus in June the situation deteriorated. On 18 January 1862 war broke out between the rival confederacies and Paton fled overland to Anuikaraka whence on 3 February he and the sickly missionary, J. W. Matheson, withdrew to Aneityum.

For lack of other work Paton was dispatched to Australia to raise funds for the mission and its new ship, Dayspring. His graphic description in the Chalmers Presbyterian Church, Sydney, of his supposed hairbreadth escape from cannibals won him many sympathizers. Its unwearied repetition in some 470 meetings in New South Wales, Victoria, South Australia and Tasmania and the hostility it occasionally evoked among the rougher elements made his name a household word. In May 1863 after two great farewell meetings in Melbourne and Sydney, which brought his receipts to £5000, he left for Scotland to recruit more missionaries and in 1864 was made moderator of the Reformed Presbyterian Church of Scotland. On his return to Sydney in January 1865 with his second wife Margaret, née Whitecross, he raised another £1700 to meet the running expenses of the Day-

413

T

spring; on a third visit in 1866 he secured permanent support for the ship by the Sabbath schools. His part in the controversial bombardment of Port Resolution by H.M.S. *Curacoa* in August 1865 had cost him many Sydney supporters. He therefore spent some months stirring up missionary enthusiasm in the newly-united Presbyterian Church of Victoria and was appointed its first missionary. Uneasy over returning to Tanna whose people refused to readmit him, he at last accepted appointment to Aniwa, which became nominally Christian by July 1867 and wholly so by 1872, when his wife's illness rendered his connexion with the island more tenuous.

At this stage Paton rapidly became an international figure. After the *Dayspring* was wrecked in 1873 he raised £3000 in Victoria and New Zealand for a new schooner, *Paragon*. In 1876-77 he toured Victoria in mission interests. In 1881 ill health forced his virtual retirement from the islands and he became general mission agent for the Victorian Church, in which post he continued to take a deep, if proprietary, interest in the New Hebrides mission and its ship. In 1884 he raised £6000 in Britain for an auxiliary steamship, in defiance of the mission synod and the Sydney *Dayspring* Board. On the rejection of his initiative in 1890 he hotly opposed the contract with Burns Philp & Co., acting for the Australasian United Steam Navigation Co., as harmful to mission interests. He forced the issue in Melbourne after his triumphal tour of the United States and Britain in 1892-94 when he announced the gift by his London committee of £1000 a year towards maintaining the new ship and handed over another £12,527 of his total proceeds of £25,432 for work in the New Hebrides. When the steamer was wrecked in 1896, he campaigned for yet another *Dayspring* but had to concede defeat.

Meanwhile Paton threw himself into the perennial debate on the future of the New Hebrides. A rabid opponent of the Melanesian 'slave trade', that chief bar to mission progress, he bombarded the Colonial Office with alleged recruiting irregularities. On an official visit to Queensland in 1886 he denounced a local Presbyterian proposal for a Kanaka mission as subversive of the cause. In 1890 he exacerbated local opinion, Presbyterian and otherwise, by bitter attacks on Griffith's plan to reopen the trade in 1892, thus associating himself, however innocently, with the rising sentiment for 'white Australia'. He also hotly opposed French ambitions in the New Hebrides, where in 1877 he had backed an abortive move by James Balfour [q.v.] to make a British protectorate. In March 1883 he informed Earl Derby of the French seizure of mission land at Vila; faced with new threats in June, he and Rev. D. Macdonald of Efate urged James Service [q.v.] to annex the group. He then vigorously supported Service's campaign to that end. On his return to Britain in 1884 Paton begged Gladstone to annex the Solomons and New Hebrides as well as New Guinea and devoted much time in 1885 to stirring up British public opinion on the issue. A member of a deputation of the Heathen Missions Committee to D. Gillies [q.v.] in March 1886, he was also to the fore in June after the landing of French troops at Efate and Malekula; at Gillies's request he wrote a lengthy account of British and Protestant interests there. In December, as moderator of the Victorian Church, he signed a petition for British annexation of his 'beloved islands'. In 1890, after a heated exchange with the New Hebrides Synod over their proposed relaxation of discriminatory legislation against British settlers, he took up Sir John Thurston's earlier proposal for an international ban on arms and liquor for native races. Lacking only American approval, he interviewed Presidents Cleveland and McKinley but had to wait ratification of the agreement until 1902.

In his last years Paton became a legend. He still visited the islands, notably in February 1899 when he gave the Aniwans their complete New Testament, but his main message was to the civilized world wherever he could speak of his work in the New Hebrides. Among his many publications his two-volumed *Autobiography* (London, 1889), compiled by his youngest brother James, ran to numerous editions and brought him new admirers in North America and above all in Britain, where the founding in 1891 of the interdenominational 'John G. Paton Fund' by his devoted friend A. K. Langridge of the British Post Office assured him continuing finance. Honorary Doctor of Divinity (Edinburgh, 1891), he was the idol of the thousands of all ages who flocked to hear him. Even in his last visit to the United States and Britain in 1899-1902 when illness limited his activities he addressed 820 meetings and collected another £13,014, bringing up a grand total of £80,000. On returning to Australia he went twice to the islands to visit or settle Paton Fund missionaries, notably one of his five sons, Frank Hume Lyall. After his wife died in May 1905 his excursions in Australia in aid of the mission rapidly undermined his strength. In Gippsland he had a recurrence of an internal disorder in 1906 and died in Melbourne on 28 January 1907. He was buried in the Boroondara cemetery.

A lifelong anti-smoker, teetotaller and

ardent Evangelical, Paton lacked some of the missionary flair of John Williams [q.v.] or John Geddie of Aneityum but as a propagandist he had no peer. If prone to exaggerate, he kept the New Hebrides issue before the public and helped to develop an Australian conscience; but for him the New Hebrides must have become wholly French. He also contributed much to the contemporary upsurge of missionary enthusiasm in the English-speaking world, which indeed may be said to have died with him.

R. Steel, *The New Hebrides and Christian missions* (Lond, 1880); M. W. Paton, *Letters and sketches from the New Hebrides*, James Paton ed (Lond, 1894); A. K. Langridge and F. H. L. Paton, *John G. Paton: later years and farewell* (Lond, 1910); D. A. Scarr, *Fragments of empire* (Canberra, 1967); P. O'Reilly, *Hébridais* (Paris, 1957); *Reformed Presbyterian Mag*, 1860-76; G. S. Parsonson, 'La mission presbytérienne des Nouvelles-Hébrides', *J de la Société des Océanistes*, Dec 1956; Presbyterian Church of Vic, Minutes of Heathen Missions C'ttee 1872-1907, Minutes of the New Hebrides Mission Synod 1857-1907 and John G. Paton Mission Fund quarterly jottings 1893-1907 (ML); Vic Premier's Dept records 86/2403.

G. S. PARSONSON

PATTERSON, Sir JAMES BROWN (1833-1895), butcher, auctioneer and politician, was born on 18 November 1833 at Alnwick, Northumberland, England, son of James Patterson, road contractor, and his wife Agnes, née Brown. He received an elementary education in Alnwick. He migrated to Melbourne in 1852 and tried the Forest Creek goldfield without success before taking up farming at Glenlyon near Daylesford. The demands of the goldfields led him to move into the cattle slaughtering business at Chewton in 1858. By 1870 he had become prosperous and prominent, though his early business methods later drew acidic comment from opponents who often professed wonder at the number of cattle alleged to have strayed into Patterson's yards. Much respected, he easily secured election to the local council and for four successive years was mayor of Chewton. In 1857 at Glenlyon he had married Anna Merrick Walton.

The family moved to Melbourne in 1870 and Patterson entered the booming real estate business with Robert Richardson; the partnership was dissolved and became Patterson & Son, later conducted by Patterson's nephews. After unsuccessful attempts in 1866 and 1868 he won a by-election in December 1870 to the Legislative Assembly for Castlemaine; he held the seat until 1895. His sharp, vigorous style drew public

attention and his association with the radical section led to office as commissioner for public works and vice-president of the Board of Land and Works in the first Berry [q.v.] ministry from 7 August to 20 October 1875. Patterson's reputation was made, however, in the second Berry Government from May 1877 to March 1880 when he was again in control of works. Though outspoken and uncompromising support for his administration was unremarkable, his Berry in his conflict with the Legislative Council in 1878 won Patterson unwarranted fame for wild radicalism, a reputation which he at first enjoyed and used but later carefully repudiated. In his third term of office from August 1880 to July 1881 under Berry he was vice-president of the Board of Land and Works and commissioner for railways; his administration of railways was efficient and remembered for his efforts to eliminate patronage from the department.

In 1884 Patterson went to England and returned to his birthplace where he addressed public meetings on the importance of the empire and its ties. Throughout his public life Patterson was an unremitting exponent of the imperial connexion and a formidable critic of those who questioned such ties. Later he was also a firm advocate of Federation of the Australian colonies. On his return to Victoria in 1885 he was in the Opposition until in April 1889 he joined those whom he had opposed and accepted office as commissioner for trade and customs in the Gillies [q.v.] government. He was also commissioner for public works and vice-president of the Board of Land and Works in June-September 1890 and postmaster-general in September-November. During the maritime strike he advocated a strong line against the strikers and spoke often of the need for determined action to promote law and order. In so doing he was only one among many, and he played no significant part in creation or implementation of government policy toward the strike, yet many were deceived and he was widely applauded first for stiffening and then directing the government's resolve. Alfred Deakin knew better and was among those who resented Patterson's acceptance and promotion of his own inflated role.

In 1891 after another visit to England Patterson was acknowledged the 'leader of the Opposition' in the assembly. His experience was considerable and his prestige was high. He enjoyed, as he had for many years, the support of David Syme [q.v.], editor of the influential *Age* and their relations were sufficiently close to give some credence to the frequent jibe from Patterson's opponents that he was 'Syme's puppet'. However, his standing was unimpaired and from 1891 he was often spoken of as a likely future premier. After the fall of the Shiels government on a vote of no confidence moved by Patterson, he was installed on 23 January 1893 as premier and chief secretary.

Patterson had great drive and evident ambition. The culmination of his career, however, proved disappointing. The establishment of his government coincided with the financial crisis of 1893 and his ministry could do little to rectify the position or alleviate conditions. His ministry took the full brunt of the criticism of those who suffered and lost in the crisis, and attempts to economize in government expenditure were bitterly resented. With his treasurer, G. D. Carter [q.v.], Patterson was denounced for suspended bank trading in a 'Bank Holiday' from 1 to 5 May 1893. By this action he and his ministry intended to avert what they believed and were advised was a likely total collapse of the banking system in Victoria. In this they were probably correct, but the immediate effect was to aggravate the prevailing disquiet and erode confidence in the economy and the government. To make matters worse he was known to be associated with several of the 'boomers' who had done so much to inflate the bubble which collapsed in 1893; although Patterson's personal integrity was not seriously questioned the association was damaging. David Syme was among those who withdrew their support.

The ministry was evidently doomed and the public discussed the likely composition of the next administration for some months before Patterson's government was defeated in August 1894. At the election in September his supporters fared badly and for the first and only time he was returned second in the poll, but the succeeding Turner ministry soon proved no more competent and Patterson's repute once again increased. He had waited expectantly: appointed K.C.M.G. he was mellower, the elder statesman, 'father of the House', and 'Leader of the Opposition'. He retained much of the bustle of his earlier days; his political cunning and adaptability were undiminished and his rough, direct speech in debate had softened only a little. He was an Orangeman throughout.

In politics as in life Patterson was completely self-made. He died suddenly of influenza at Murrumbeena on 30 October 1895. Aged 61 his wife had died after a long illness on 2 December 1894. Both were buried with Anglican rites in the Melbourne general cemetery, and survived by their only child, Rose Kaeppel, who inherited a life interest in Patterson's estate of £11,727.

A. Deakin, The crisis in Victorian politics, 1879-1881, J. A. La Nauze and R. M. Crawford eds (Melb, 1957); Age, 31 Oct 1895; Argus, 31 Oct 1895; Australasian, 2 Nov, 14 Dec 1895.

PETER COOK

PATTESON, JOHN COLERIDGE (1827-1871), Anglican bishop, was born on 1 April 1827 in London, elder son of Sir John Patteson, judge, and his second wife Frances Duke, daughter of James Coleridge of Ottery St Mary and niece of the poet. Brought up near his mother's relations, he began his education at Ottery St Mary. 'Coley' went to Eton in 1838-45 and Balliol College, Oxford (B.A., 1848; M.A., 1853; D.D., 1861). He had played cricket for Eton but refused to play for Oxford. After graduation he travelled in Europe and studied German, Hebrew and Arabic. Returning to Oxford, he was a fellow of Merton College in 1852-71. On 25 September 1853 he was made deacon and curate of Alphington, Devon, and on 24 September 1854 was ordained priest at Exeter Cathedral, but agreed to accompany Bishop G. A. Selwyn to New Zealand as a missionary.

In March 1855 Patteson sailed in the Duke of Portland and arrived at Auckland in July. For five years he sailed in the schooner Southern Cross on annual cruises among the islands and ran the mission's summer school at Kohimarama, Auckland. On 24 February 1861 at Auckland he was consecrated first bishop of Melanesia. A brilliant linguist, he later spoke twenty-three of the many Melanesian languages: finding them in groups, he printed grammars and vocabularies and translated some gospels into the Mota dialect. Each year he spent some months on Mota in the New Hebrides.

In March 1864 Patteson visited Australia. In Sydney he addressed a large meeting which pledged systematic support of the Melanesian Mission; the Anglican Churches agreed to meet the annual expenses of the Southern Cross. Patteson's gentleness made a deep impression and he became friendly with the families of Sir Alfred Stephen and T. S. Mort [qq.v.]. In Brisbane Patteson conferred with Governor Bowen about moving the mission school to Curtis Island. Patteson devoted to the mission his private fortune which included money inherited from his father and income from his Merton College fellowship. The mission also received support from the Eton Melanesian Society and his cousin Charlotte Yonge donated the proceeds from her novel The Daisy Chain. In 1865 Patteson again visited Sydney and the governor, Sir John Young, offered him a grant on Norfolk Island for his headquarters. Funds were raised by friends of the mission to buy more land. In 1867 the Melanesian Mission moved to Norfolk Island where it was called St Barnabas. In the milder climate the school could not only continue in the winter months but native foods such as yams could be grown. Patteson started bringing girls to the school to provide wives for his scholars. Dynamic and practical, he taught his scholars to speak English, play cricket and tend livestock.

The visits to the islands were becoming yearly more dangerous. In 1869 he wrote to Lady Stephen: 'the vessels which have been taking away S. Sea islanders for the Fiji & Queensland labour market have in some cases to my knowledge acted in a very sad miserable way. I have a good deal of moral, not perhaps strictly legal, evidence of treachery, violence etc. The effect is . . . to embitter the islanders against *any* white man whom they do not as yet know well to be their friend'. Patteson noted the depopulation of many islands and that unscrupulous traders used his name to entice natives aboard their ships. In July 1870 he told Bowen that 'it is the regulation rather than the suppression of the employment of native labourers that I advocate'. In an official memorandum he advocated the licensing of a few ships to transport the islanders; all others were to be treated as pirates and confiscated summarily when caught, and frigates were to cruise constantly among the islands. In January 1871 he made another appeal for imperial legislation on Pacific Island labour.

In April Patteson sailed to the islands in the *Southern Cross*. On 20 September he landed alone on Nukapu near Santa Cruz where he was clubbed to death in retribution for a recent outrage by blackbirders. In a canoe his body was taken to the *Southern Cross* and was buried at sea. Despite the plea of missionaries at Norfolk Island for no retribution Captain Markham of H.M.S. *Rosario* fired at and killed some natives. The Melanesian Mission continued to expand on Patteson's foundations while his life was a lasting inspiration to the Anglican Church in Australasia. Patteson's death led to the imperial Kidnapping Acts of 1872 and 1875 along the lines he had suggested.

C. M. Yonge, *Life of John Coleridge Patteson*, 2nd ed (Lond, 1874); W. E. Gladstone, *Gleanings of past years, 1843-78*, 2 (Lond, 1879); J. Gutch, *Martyr of the Islands* (Lond, 1971); *Sydney Mail*, 2 Apr 1864; *SMH*, 10 Oct 1865, 25 Mar, 6, 7, 15 Nov 1871; D. L. Hilliard, Protestant missions in the Solomon Islands 1849-1942 (Ph.D. thesis, ANU, 1966); P. Corris, Passage, port and plantation . . . Solomon Islands labour migration, 1870-1914 (Ph.D. thesis, ANU, 1970); J. C. Patteson papers in the Selwyn papers (Selwyn College, Cambridge,

and microfilm ANU); Stephen papers MS777 (ML); MS cats (ML); CO 201/552, 565.

MARTHA RUTLEDGE

PATTISON, WILLIAM (1830-1896), businessman, mine director and politician, was born on 23 May 1830 at Hobart Town, son of Joseph Pattison, baker, and his wife Mary, née Barnes. Educated in a private school at Bagdad, he began work at 12 on his father's farms near Glenorchy and Green Point. In 1846 he moved to Melbourne and after running a dairy at Fishermens Bend set up a butchery. In 1851 William went to the goldfields at Ballarat, Forest Creek and Bendigo. A successful miner he returned to Melbourne and with his brother Joseph opened a wholesale butchery, contracting to supply the government troops. In 1858 William was a representative of Bourke Ward in the Melbourne City Council but on 5 August 1859 the brothers were declared insolvent.

Pattison may have been in New Zealand for three years but in 1863 he opened a butcher's shop at Rockhampton, Queensland. He acquired near-by station property and soon became a prominent stock dealer and public figure, serving as alderman for several years, twice as mayor, as chairman of Gogango Divisional Board and president of the Chamber of Commerce. He was a member of the Rockhampton Jockey Club, the Hospital Board and the School of Arts. One of the original shareholders and later chairman of directors of the Mount Morgan gold-mine, he held 125,000 shares in 1866.

Pattison represented Blackall in the Legislative Assembly in 1886-88 and was senior member for Rockhampton in 1888-93. He was minister without portfolio in McIlwraith's [q.v.] government from 13 June to 30 November 1888 and colonial treasurer in the Morehead [q.v.] ministry to 19 November 1889 when he suddenly resigned, alleging that McIlwraith had broken a promise to relieve him of the Treasury. In reply McIlwraith accused Pattison of selling Mount Morgan shares to cabinet members to secure advantages for the company. Despite the ensuing scandal Pattison served as minister without portfolio till 12 August 1890 and retired from the assembly in May 1893.

Pattison was married twice: first, on 20 August 1855 in Melbourne to Helen Margaret Grant; and second, on 23 October 1878 in Rockhampton to Susan Annie Stephenson. He died at Rockhampton on 8 June 1896, survived by eight of his fourteen children.

Pattison's business career was successful apart from the disastrous 1888 crash in

Mount Morgan shares in which he had unwittingly involved several fellow politicians. His short and unhappy political career gave some truth to the claim that business success does not make a treasurer. The 'Mount Morganism' allegations, though unsubstantiated, upset him severely. Critics found him bumptious and domineering yet according to one opponent he had 'a heart like a bullock', always responsive to anyone in distress. His attempts in 1888 to bolster the market and save his friends (including some later critics) permanently embarrassed his finances.

E. J. T. Barton, *Jubilee history of Queensland* (Brisb, 1910); J. G. Pattison, '*Battler's' tales of early Rockhampton* (Melb, 1939); PD (Qld), 1889, 2206, 2603, 1890, 511, 546; *Telegraph* (Brisb), 10 May, 13-15 June, 30 Nov 1888, 17 Sept 1890; *Brisbane Courier*, 21 May, 13 June, 30 Nov 1888, 16 Sept, 19, 20 Nov, 2 Dec 1889, 5 Aug, 18 Sept 1890, 31 Mar 1893, 9 June 1896; D. K. Dignan, Sir Thomas McIlwraith: a political portrait (B.A. Hons thesis, Univ Qld, 1951); J. C. Vockler, Sir Samuel Walker Griffith (B.A. Hons thesis, Univ Qld, 1953); J. Stoodley, The Queensland gold-miner in the late nineteenth century (M.A. thesis, Univ Qld, 1964); B. G. Patterson, Secret history of Mount Morgan, and Mount Morgan 1853-1927 (Oxley Lib, Brisb); Palmer-McIlwraith papers (Oxley Lib, Brisb).   JUNE STOODLEY

PEACOCK, GEORGE (1824-1900), jam manufacturer, was born in Bath, England, son of John Peacock and his wife Margaret. He arrived at Hobart Town in 1850 and opened a grocery and fruit shop in Murray Street. In February 1856 he married a widow Margaret Pryde, née Tobin, at the Congregational Church, New Town.

By 1867 Peacock had become one of the first manufacturers of canned jam in the colonies. In 1870 he moved his factory to a large stone warehouse on the Old Wharf, Hobart, with copper pans and two boilers to supply the necessary steam for canning. Reputed a hard worker and disciplinarian by his factory hands, Peacock was also interested in their welfare. He conducted hymns and prayers before each day's work, strongly disapproved of blasphemy and dismissed any man who showed signs of drinking.

In 1880 Peacock decided to make jam in Sydney and opened the Produce Exchange in Sussex Street with his stepson H. J. Pryde as manager. He imported fruit from Tasmania despite continual difficulties over duty imposed on boiled fruit. Apple and pear pulp travelled well and was exempt from duty but berry fruit had to be boiled to stand the journey and was dutiable. In 1881 he was allowed to import parboiled fruit in cases, free of duty, but in September 1884 it was found that some fruit was being imported in open tubs and other containers on deck, in such condition that the inspector of nuisances often had to condemn the pulp as unfit for consumption. In 1886 he published a pamphlet, *What is Pulp Fruit? Should it be Dutiable?* In that year the assistant government analyst, W. M. Hamlet, examined a tin of Peacock's jam which was alleged to have poisoned a family of six. Tests showed no fault in the jam but an accumulation of organic matter swarming with bacteria of putrefaction at the angle between the bottom and sides of the tin. His son William changed the firm's name to the Australasian Jam Co. and tried to bribe Hamlet to give a favourable report on the jam. In a letter to the colonial secretary, G. R. Dibbs [q.v.], William claimed if the report were published it 'could mean nothing short of positive death to the firm's commercial existence'. During a debate in the Legislative Assembly on 22 July 1886 Dibbs went even further, saying that the bulk of the jam was made up of pumpkin, squash or rotten fruit with only a spoonful of fruit pulp to give the appropriate flavour. He was accused of persecuting the Peacock family and of favouring A. Hilder, the agent for another Tasmanian jam manufacturer, who had helped Dibbs during his election campaign for St Leonards. William later admitted having challenged Dibbs 'very temperately' but when Dibbs ignored the challenge he took the only course open of publicly accusing the colonial secretary of falsehood and cowardice, degrading to a minister of the Crown.

In 1882 George Peacock had experimented with canning fish and sent samples to every Australian capital. They were well received but he did not continue the supply because of the high cost of installing refrigeration. He retired in 1891 and the Hobart business was taken over by his son Ernest Alfred, the foreman Henry Jones and A. W. Palfreyman. He died at his home in Petersham on 29 April 1900, survived by his wife and eleven children. His estate in New South Wales was valued at £1151; his wife received the income from his estate which at her death was to be divided equally between her two unmarried daughters.

Cyclopedia of Tasmania, 1 (Hob, 1900); V&P (HA Tas), 1882 (132); PD (NSW), 1885-86, 3557, 3617, 5399; J. Reynolds, 'Sir Henry Jones, K.B.', PTHRA, Mar 1973; SMH, 30 Apr 1900; Peacock's jam, 4/868.3, 1885-86 (NSWA).

PEARCE, HENRY JOHN (1852-1920), professional sculler and master fisherman, was born in Hounslow on the River Thames, London, son of James Pearce, labourer, and his wife Ann, née Young. Best known as Harry, he migrated to Sydney in 1859 and worked on Thomas Playfair's [q.v.] butcher boats at £4 a week. He began competitive rowing in 1869 and in the 1870s rowed with Elias Laycock's four-oared crew which was seldom beaten. The champion Edward Trickett [q.v.] beat him in 1874.

Successful in light skiffs and heavy watermen's boats, the wiry, close-knit Pearce began to attract notice as a possible champion. On 1 January 1880 he defeated Richard Hickey in Newcastle and on 26 January won the *Sydney Morning Herald* trophy of a new cedar skiff in the watermen's skiff handicap at the New South Wales anniversary regatta, with 'strength but very little science'. In February he laid £100-£60 to row against Laycock over the championship course on the Parramatta River in equal watermen's skiffs. Rowing with 'a swing as regular as a clock's pendulum' Pearce won by twelve lengths. In July he was involved in a dispute over fouling William Trickett's boat on the Clarence River at Grafton. Sports columnists attacked Pearce but the local regatta committee exonerated him and upheld the umpire's decision, yet he had difficulty in arranging matches for some months. In 1881 he made a comeback at the Pyrmont regatta in January where his extraordinary performance in winning three races on the same day had never been equalled. He won the wager boats race, defeating W. Trickett, John Laycock and Power; then with J. Lynch he won the double sculls; with only time to change boats, he came out against fresh men in the watermen's race, carried top weight of 100 lbs and 'rowed his opponents down one after another'. Pearce was now seen as 'a fine piece of stuff', and 'the coming man for the championship of Australia'.

On 26 December Pearce beat William Beach [q.v.] carrying a 45 lb. weight in the boat. When E. Laycock returned to England in 1882 he took with him Pearce whom he considered 'second to none in the colony'. Supported by J. Davis and others, Pearce had to sell his boat to raise the fare but left on 3 March in the *Potosi*. At Putney, backed by Laycock, he was twice matched against England's second sculler, John Largan, but failed because he was overweight. Pearce amazed the English by demonstrating the prehensile toes from which his nickname 'Footy' derived : he could lift a 56 lb. weight with each foot and knock them together in the air. Deflated by their failures, Pearce and Laycock returned to Sydney on 30 August in the *Sorata* but on 30 December when Largan visited Sydney Pearce beat him

on the Parramatta River before huge crowds.

In 1884 Tom Clifford beat Pearce who now found himself too heavily handicapped to make competition worthwhile and retired. Out of 60 races he had won 25 and was placed in 9. He became one of the most eminent master fishermen and boatowners on the harbour.

A member of the Royal Order of Foresters and a highly respected trader at the Woolloomooloo markets, Pearce married Susan Rebecca Chamberlain in 1875; with five sons and seven daughters he founded a well-known family of sportsmen and fishermen. His son Harry was a sculling champion in his father's lifetime and Sydney a prominent footballer; his daughters Alice and Lily rowed successfully against a visiting Maori team in 1911. Aged 68 Pearce died on 31 July 1920 at Pearce Street, Double Bay, and was buried in the South Head cemetery with Anglican rites.

J. E. Tonkin (ed), *The English, Australian & American sporting calendar* (Syd, 1884); *Sydney Mail*, 'Aquatics', 31 Jan 1880-24 Feb 1883; *Town and Country J*, 'Aquatics', 31 Jan 1880-24 Sept 1881, 4, 11 Jan, 1 Feb 1911; *Sunday Sun*, 24 June 1906; *Australasian*, 31 July 1920; *SMH*, 2 Aug 1920; *Bulletin*, 5 Aug 1920.

SUZANNE EDGAR

PEARCE, SIMEON HENRY (1821-1886), civil servant and land agent, was born on 27 January 1821 at Randwick, Gloucestershire, England, son of James Pearce and his wife Elizabeth. He and his cousin Samuel arrived as bounty immigrants in Sydney on Christmas Day 1841 in the *Lady Clarke*. Their partnership as butchers was dissolved in March 1844 and Simeon was financed by the innkeeper James Thompson, whose eldest daughter Alice Isabella he married in January 1848. His brother James married in 1849 Thompson's youngest daughter and on her majority in 1852 each brother received £1300.

In September 1847 Simeon bought four acres of market garden on the heights above Coogee Bay, named them Randwick and in 1848 built Blenheim House. After repeated petitions to Sir Thomas Mitchell [q.v.] to preserve vegetation along the sandhills, he was appointed bailiff in August 1849 and in 1851-56 commissioner of crown lands in Sydney, when he warned of the danger to 'rising generations' of draining sewerage into the harbour. By 1854 with James he had bought 200 acres of land at both Manly and French's Forest, and over 200 acres in parcels around Randwick and St George which were subdivided and sold profitably after the promotion of Randwick as a fashionable residential area. In 1853 he had petitioned for a road from the city to Coogee, later surveyed it and became a commissioner of its trust; in March 1855 Isaac Nathan [q.v.] publicly denigrated his work.

Pearce campaigned strongly for Randwick's incorporation which was gazetted in February 1859 despite protests from Coogee residents. Nathan and other defeated candidates calumniated Pearce's election as inaugural mayor, and in April *Bell's Life in Sydney* published 'The Book of Simeon', a damaging exposé. He was again mayor in 1866-68 and 1882, and a magistrate from 1861. Pearce's chief opponent in the council's perpetual disputes over the allocation of funds was Charles Moore [q.v.]. To curtail development at Coogee Pearce failed in 1860 to divide the borough into wards each raising its funds internally but in 1867 stopped Coogee residents from seceding. In 1884 he resigned from the council after a paralytic stroke.

The first Anglican services were held in Pearce's house and in November 1857 he became a trustee of the first St Jude's Church. In 1856 Frederick Jones had bequeathed £3000 for an Anglican church at 'Big Coogee'; Pearce persuaded a trustee of the estate, Canon Allwood [q.v.], that since the drafting of the will Randwick had replaced Coogee as the area's name; in May 1861 Allwood laid the foundation stone of St Jude's, originally designed as a replica of the parish church at Randwick, Gloucestershire. Within a month Moore brought a restraining action in the Supreme Court; at first nonsuited on a technicality, he lost his appeal in July 1862 but court costs halved the bequest. As trustee of St Jude's cemetery Pearce was in 1864 involved in litigation over its drainage. He sat on Sydney Diocesan Synod in 1866-76. In 1868 he was appointed managing trustee of the Church of England portion and in 1871 secretary of the general Rookwood cemetery.

Pearce supported the building in 1856 of the Randwick Asylum for Destitute Children (Prince of Wales Hospital) and was a founding director and sometime president of its board but thought the children were too well treated. He was also a director of the Sydney Infirmary and Dispensary. In 1857 Pearce visited his birthplace and again in 1881. He died on 18 January 1886 after a second stroke, leaving an estate of £28,320 to his wife, two sons and four daughters. The west end windows of St Jude's Church were erected in 1889 as his memorial.

D. M. Cooper, *History of Randwick* (Syd, 1909); W. B. Lynch and F. A. Larcombe, *Randwick, 1859-1959* (Syd, 1959); SMH, 8 Mar 1855, 19 Jan 1886; *Bell's Life in Sydney*, 9 Apr 1859;
Pearce papers (ML); newspaper cat under Pearce (ML).   RUTH TEALE

PEARSE, WILLIAM SILAS (1838-1908), merchant, was born on 21 May 1838 at Fremantle, eldest son of William Pearse and his wife Susannah, née Glyde. Educated at local private schools, he embarked on a business career which included butchering, shipowning, importing and the development of the Western Australian leather industry. Prospering steadily, he moved into the pastoral industry in 1874 by dispatching a small private expedition to the Murchison, where with his brother and a managing partner he founded a sheep station, Meka. From 1881 he was a shareholder in three West Kimberley properties, Meda, Oobagooma and Liveringa. As befitted a solid citizen he held most local offices. A justice of the peace, fifteen years a councillor on the Fremantle Town Council and chairman in 1868-71, trustee of the Congregational Church and founding president in 1875 of the Fremantle Building Society, he was an elected representative for the Fremantle District in the Legislative Council in 1872-80 and 1884-90. After responsible government he represented North Fremantle in the Legislative Assembly from December 1890 to May 1895 as a reliable back-bencher, notable only for the brevity of his speeches. An early advocate of responsible government and a vigilant watchdog of Fremantle's interests, he favoured low tariffs on foodstuffs and careful financial management by government officials. He was useful on select committees but never held office.

On 23 April 1863 Pearse married Johannah, daughter of John Hawkes of Warwick, England. She died in 1891 and their only daughter next year. In 1893 he married his cousin Alice, widow of Edward Higham, a fellow Congregationalist and political associate. His only unexpected action was resignation from parliament in 1895 when he disposed of his business interests to his brother and lifelong partner, George (1839-1914), and went to England with his wife. He died of cancer on 30 December 1908 at Clifton, Bristol.

J. K. Ewers, *The western gateway* (Fremantle, 1948); *WA Bulletin*, 14 Apr 1888; D. H. Ford, The Pearse family of Western Australia, HS/PR 1487 (Battye Lib, Perth).
                                         G. C. BOLTON

PEARSON, CHARLES HENRY (1830-1894), historian, educationist, politician and journalist, was born on 7 September 1830 in Islington. London, fourth son and tenth child of John Norman Pearson (1787-1865), Anglican clergyman, and his wife Harriet, daughter of Richard Puller, merchant. He was educated at home by his father until 13, at Rugby and King's College, London, where he was much influenced by J. S. Brewer and F. D. Maurice, and at Oriel and Exeter Colleges, Oxford. Finding little stimulus in the formal Oxford teaching, he gave his best energies to the Union of which, despite his espousal of such minority causes as Christian Socialism, he was elected president in 1852-53. After graduating with first-class honours in *literae humaniores* he was elected a fellow of Oriel and began to study medicine. Forced to abandon these plans by a severe attack of pleurisy, he returned to the academic life and in 1855-64 was professor of modern history in King's College, London. In these years he worked on *The Early and Middle Ages of England* (1861), wrote for the London weeklies, travelled widely in Europe and studied the art and literature of the Italian Renaissance.

In 1864, suffering from 'sluggish liver' and depressed by Oxford's failure to appoint him to the Chichele professorship of history and by King's refusal to increase his modest salary, he took a year's unpaid leave and set off for South Australia, intending to invest in sheep. Finding that runs were about to be revalued, he bought a farm of about 640 acres near Mount Remarkable, only to experience the worst drought the colony had then known. Driven back to England in 1866, he defended the political stability of Australian democracy in *Essays on Reform*, arguing that 'the conservative apathy of men partially shut out from the world and, coming to believe that the trodden way is the best', was far more to be feared than 'any revolutionary fervour for sudden and great changes'. While lecturing in 1868 for the new North of England Council for Promoting the Higher Education of Women he brought out an enlarged two-volume edition of his *History of England*, supplemented in 1869 by his pioneering *Historical Maps of England, during the first thirteen Centuries*. In 1869-71, after a visit to the United States, he lectured in modern history at Cambridge, but eyestrain from poring over medieval manuscripts, a lack of good students and nostalgia for the dry climate and free life of the bush induced him to return to his colonial farm.

On 10 December 1872 at Gawler he married Edith, daughter of Philip Butler, an absentee visiting Yattalunga, his South Australian station. Pearson then had hopes of combining farming with a professorship in the embryo University of Adelaide but, as it was slow to open and his wife proved unable to bear the hot summer, he negotiated with the University of Melbourne for a lectureship in history and political economy. It proved a frustrating post, for although required to deliver eight lectures a week he was not permitted by the council to choose his own textbooks or even to plan his own courses. On 4 June 1874 he found some compensation by launching a university debating club which attracted such talented members as Alexander Sutherland, T. F. Bride [qq.v.], Alfred Deakin, William Shiels, H. B. Higgins and Theodore Fink. Subjects of current social and political interest were chosen and Pearson, who always chaired the debates until December, was often invited by the meeting to give his own views.

On 20 November Pearson had accepted the headmastership of a new 'Ladies' College in Connexion with the Presbyterian Church of Victoria', the first school in Australia to offer girls an education equivalent to that of the leading boys' schools. On 11 February 1875 in an inaugural lecture on 'The Higher Culture of Women' he predicted that the majority who chose to become housewives would increasingly find release from much traditional work through inventions like the sewing machine, and others, once equipped, would compete equally with men for 'the career open to talents'. As the University of Melbourne still refused to admit women, Pearson planned courses of lectures for the senior girls and also 'for the convenience of ladies who have left school, but desire to carry on their education, or of those who propose to go out as governesses'. As a secondary school the Ladies' College was an immediate success, the numbers rising from 60 in the first term to 170 in the fourth, but Melbourne had too few women with the basic schooling to sustain the lecture system.

Anonymous articles by Pearson in the New York *Nation* in 1875-76 reveal that he was becoming alarmed at developments in Victoria outside the field of education, in particular the accumulation of the colony's land by a few hundred proprietors, the failure of democracy to produce a stable two-party political system and the power of an undemocratically elected Upper House to frustrate the will of the majority. He found it symptomatic of Victorian politics that the most widely respected Liberal politician, George Higinbotham [q.v.], preferred 'the position of a free lance to that of leader of a party or lieutenant of an administration' and should withdraw from parliament. On 11 December 1876 Pearson lectured on 'The History of Taxation in England, and its Bearing upon Taxation in Victoria'. Allying himself with the *Age* and the more radical Liberals, he advocated a progressive tax on the unearned increment accruing to large landowners, a tax which should effectively limit the size of estates to 40,000 acres and thereby meet the chronic deficit in the colony's budget caused by the drying up of revenue from the sale of crown land. Although admitting that he believed in free trade 'as he believed in the rules of arithmetic', he thought it 'infinitely more important that the land tax should be put on a sound basis than that a few duties in the tariff should be struck off or diminished'.

Gratified by this speech, the organizers of the newly-founded National Reform and Protection League invited him to deliver one of two key addresses at its first 'monster meeting' in the Princess Theatre on 19 February 1877. Pearson accepted and in so doing immediately became, as Deakin wrote in 1900, 'a leading figure in one of the fiercest campaigns of party warfare waged within the Empire in this century'. The league was regarded by the pastoralists, bankers and merchants as the most serious challenge to their economic and political power since the granting of responsible government. Pearson seemed a class traitor: *Melbourne Punch* referred to 'Professor Pearson's alliance with the Communists'. Within days of the Princess Theatre meeting the principal of the Ladies' College, Rev. George Tait, had asked him to resign his headmastership on the ground that he was alienating the college's 'constituency'. Aware that his wife was expecting a second child and that he had no immediate alternative employment, Pearson countered with an offer to give up politics for the remainder of the contract, but Tait proving adamant he reluctantly agreed to resign within five months. On 1 March he accepted an invitation to stand for the electorate of Boroondara and persisted with his candidacy despite publication in the *Age* of a letter, signed by the head-masters of Melbourne's four leading boys' schools, four university professors and four lecturers, in which the signatories sincerely regretted that he had deemed it his duty to resign, expressed sorrow that 'anyone should forget that educators have by no means laid aside the duties of citizens in accepting educational work' and hoped 'that this calamity may be averted'. When an embarrassed Tait offered Pearson a new contract which would have reduced his income by at least 30 per cent he replied that he was not only pledged to his committee at Boroondara but would refuse such an offer in any circumstances.

While ready to make Pearson their 'lion' on the land question, the leaders of the National Reform and Protection League had not been prepared to offer a safe seat to an untried candidate who admitted to being a free trader, and in the elections of 11 May 1877 which gave the league president, Graham Berry [q.v.], a huge majority in the assembly, Pearson narrowly failed to carry Boroondara. A greater disappointment was Berry's failure to mention the progressive principle when outlining a new land tax, although a progressive tax had been league policy. At the next meeting of the league Pearson therefore seized the opportunity, when moving adoption of a report on the election, to remind members that the league had been working 'not to reward the personal popularity of any leader, however well merited; but to institute lasting measures of organic change', and went on to expound a long-term legislative programme which would realize the 'idea of a democratic community . . . perhaps fifty years hence'. The speech which followed exemplified his role as a 'colonizer' of new ideas, for his prophetic programme included not only a progressive tax on land but a complete system of free education, 'from the State School to the grammar school, and from the grammar school to the university', laws regulating overtime and the working conditions of women and children, limits on the 'importation of foreign immigrants to glut the labor market', the setting up of some form of state arbitration system, state insurance of taxpayers against old age and sickness and state aid to the unemployed. The repeated 'loud cheers' drawn from the audience demonstrated that he already had a large following among the league's rank and file as a radical intellectual. This popularity and the powerful support of the *Age*, which had regularly reported his speeches at length, must have helped to induce Berry to offer him appointment as a one-man royal commission to make 'suggestions for the thorough organization of the Education department, also drawing out a plan for connecting the national school system with the University'.

Pearson began his inquiries in July 1877 and presented his *Report on the State of Public Education in Victoria, and Suggestions as to the Best Means of Improving it* in March 1878 after inspecting seventy-two scattered state primary schools and every other educational institution of importance. Convinced that Victoria, with its limited area and resources, could only sustain a large population in the future if she followed New England, United States of America, and trained one of the most highly-skilled workforces in the world, and concerned that the democratic form of government should not fail through want of well-educated legislators and public servants, he placed much emphasis on the expansion of secondary and tertiary education. For training teachers he recommended a central college close to the university so that they could be educated 'not as a caste apart, but as men and women having a need for common culture with the members of other professions'. To encourage experienced country teachers to further their education, the new college should provide forty sets of rooms for students in residence. 'I know no greater mistake', he argued, 'than to suppose that man or woman can be over-educated for the position of teacher in a primary school'. To connect the state primary schools with the university he proposed that the state should assist good, existing 'middle class' schools which were struggling to survive in twelve large country towns, and should supplement these with new state co-educational 'high schools' in thirteen country districts and four city suburbs where private schools were non-existent or inadequate. In defence of this dual system he argued that 'a body of highly trained teachers should continue to work outside of State control, pursuing their own methods, and in some instances imparting knowledge which it might not lie within the State's province to impart'. At the summit of the educational pyramid the university should be more democratic and utilitarian. As he had been elected a member of the university council in January 1875 for five years he was able to press for university reforms, and at council meetings combined with M. H. Irving and Dr J. E. Bromby [qq.v.] to carry a radical draft bill 'To extend the Powers and Benefits of the University of Melbourne' which he later included in his report. Unfortunately the Berry government was more interested in saving than in spending money on education and few of Pearson's ideas were immediately adopted, but the report was widely read by educationists and provided a blue-print for the future.

On 7 June 1878 Pearson won an assembly by-election for the seat of Castlemaine, drawing from Deakin 'most hearty and sincere congratulations' and the assurance that 'with the exception of Mr. Higinbotham no public leader possesses such general confidence as you do'. Pearson was immediately recruited by the Berry government as chief adviser in its struggle to reform the Victorian Constitution. For over a year he had been arguing that deadlocks between the two Houses could best be resolved by a plebiscite of all assembly electors, as in Switzerland, and this device was incorporated in the reform bill which the assembly passed by 50 votes to 21. When it was rejected by the council the assembly voted £5000 to defray the costs of sending Berry, Pearson and H. H. Hayter [q.v.] to England on an 'embassy' to persuade the imperial

parliament to pass a bill which would enable the assembly to reform the Constitution without the agreement of the council. While in London from February to June 1879 Pearson published a pamphlet detailing the occasions on which the Victorian Upper House had obstructed the clearly expressed will of the people, wrote letters to *The Times*, contributed an article on 'Democracy in Victoria' to the *Fortnightly Review* and met many influential men. The weakness of his case was that no election had been won specifically on the bill, and this was seized on by Conservative colonial secretary, Hicks-Beach, who refused to contemplate any action by the imperial parliament until such an election had been held and won. Yet the embassy was not entirely fruitless for Hicks-Beach indirectly warned the council that persistent rejection of a 'reasonable' reform of the Constitution could invite the interference sought. Pearson enlisted the interest and sympathy of many prominent Liberals, but Berry confused the issue on his return to Victoria by abandoning the bill which had earlier been passed by a large majority in the assembly in favour of a new proposal for a nominated rather than elected council; finding nomineeism unpopular, he readopted the plebiscite for the elections of February 1880 but failed to win a majority. Disheartened but persistent, Pearson continued to work for reform and in 1881, after Berry had regained power, helped to negotiate a compromise Act which made the council more democratic but left its powers intact. The plebiscite, with which he had been so closely identified, had been abandoned, although the idea continued to find many supporters in Victoria and would eventually find its way into the Australian Constitution under the name of referendum.

In the third Berry ministry from August 1880 to July 1881 Pearson held the unsalaried office of minister without portfolio, on the understanding that as soon as convenient to the ministry he would be appointed Victorian agent-general in London. In the assembly he concerned himself with constitutional reform, with carrying an Act 'to amend the law relating to the University of Melbourne' which amongst other things guaranteed equal rights for women, and with a thorough reorganization of the Department of Industrial and Reformatory Schools, which involved boarding-out the 200 children housed in state Industrial Schools, the recruiting of two professional 'visiting agents' to supplement the work of volunteers in supervising the boarding-out system, and the appointment of a new departmental head. Both these campaigns sought to realize recommendations he had made as royal commissioner in 1877-78 and powerfully supported in a series of unsigned editorials in the *Age*. He had begun writing for the *Age* soon after his arrival in Melbourne in 1874 and from 1878 until he visited England in 1885 he probably earned up to £1000 a year from this source. An account book in his papers identifies some 650 articles written for the *Age* and its weekly, the *Leader*, from August 1880 to February 1884. When the editor fell sick in that year Pearson took over for several months.

Finding his services useful in the protracted search for a viable constitutional reform, Berry delayed appointing Pearson agent-general until his government was about to surrender office. Having criticized an earlier government for making last-minute appointments, Pearson now publicly refused on principle what must have been a most attractive post, thus relegating himself to the back benches. Appointed an honorary trustee of the Melbourne Public Library, Museums and National Gallery, he proposed to his colleagues on 4 May 1882 that they respond to the offer by Francis Ormond [q.v.] to donate £5000 to help found a Melbourne working men's college. Next day in an *Age* editorial he deprecated government inaction and appealed for immediate public support in raising the matching £5000 required by Ormond as a condition of his gift. This editorial in turn led the Trades Hall Committee to approach Ormond, who then organized a provisional council representing library, Trades Hall, university, government and subscribers. As honorary secretary of this council and as editorial writer, Pearson played a major role in raising funds for the first part of the building, reiterating his argument that Victoria's future prosperity would depend on the technical expertise of her working men.

In 1883 Pearson played the same dual role in campaigning for the Sunday opening of the Public Library, Museums and National Gallery. At a meeting of the trustees on 30 April he seconded a successful motion 'That the technological Museum and the Galleries be opened to the public on each Sunday during the Month of May from 1.30 to 5 p.m.'. Bitterly opposed by Sabbatarians but supported by a 'monster meeting' in the Town Hall chaired by Higinbotham, the trustees put the motion into effect and on the four Sundays in May some 18,902 visits were recorded. To parliament Pearson presented a petition of '38,150 inhabitants of Melbourne and the suburbs, in favour of opening the Public Library, National Gallery, and Museums on Sunday', and for the *Age* of 18 May he wrote a masterly satire on the Sabbatarians, but failed to muster a majority when the matter came to a division in the assembly; the promising experiment came to an end, not to be repeated for twenty-one years.

Pearson's *Age* editorials also sought to inform and shape opinion on questions that were Australian rather than Victorian in scope. He attacked the inhumanity of 'blackbirding', opposed the use of Chinese and Indian coolie labour in northern parts of the continent on the ground that Australia should have no second-class citizens, argued that the people of New Guinea would be better served if their country became a British Protectorate rather than an extension of Queensland, urged closer consultation between Britain and Australia about imperial strategies that could involve Australian troops, suggested the need for an Australian 'West Point' and warned that excessive government borrowing could lead to a disastrous depression. He supported equal rights for women in divorce and employment, and advocated state insurance schemes and state control of urban housing conditions.

In January 1886, with the imminent break-up of the Service [q.v.]-Berry coalition, Pearson and Deakin found themselves at political cross purposes. Pearson, as the most senior and experienced member of the Liberal caucus, recommended that the Liberals should seek to govern independently on their own platform, looking for support to organized labour. In contrast, Deakin urged that the coalition be continued in the interest of stable government. Deakin's policy prevailed, resulting in the formation of the Gillies [q.v.]-Deakin ministry which lasted until November 1890, the longest since responsible government in Victoria. Defeated in caucus, Pearson agreed to join the coalition as minister of education, partly because he doubtless felt himself better equipped for the post than any other member, and partly because, as he admitted later to Deakin, he needed the ministerial salary.

Pearson now enjoyed opportunities of realizing some of the recommendations he had made in his 1878 report. His greatest success lay in the field of scientific and technical education. In 1887 he gave the first lecture in the Melbourne Working Men's College and opened the Gordon Technical College in Geelong. In 1888, when the boom was reaching its height and Melbourne staged its great International Exhibition, he published a digest of the voluminous evidence taken by the 1881-84 British royal commission on technical instruction together with his reflections on its relevance to Victoria, and also chaired a special commission 'to inquire into the best method of promoting technical education'. His skilful advocacy led the government to raise the grant for the teaching of science and technology from £18,098 in 1887-88 to £44,304 in 1889-90, thereby enabling a rapid expansion of the new technical colleges and the building of new chemical, biological and mechanical laboratories in the university. Increased support was also given to the established Schools of Mines in Ballarat and Bendigo and to another new technical college in Castlemaine. However, he was not able to obtain the system of state high schools from which he had hoped so much in 1878 but had to content himself with the annual award of 200 scholarships for primary school children to proceed to independent secondary schools. He also expanded the state school curriculum to include more teaching of elementary science and Australian history and geography, and appointed an expert to lecture teachers on 'the Kindergarten system of instruction'. A major achievement was the building of a fine new teachers' college near the university with the residential accommodation for country teachers he had recommended in his report.

In 1889, after three years of agitation by state schoolteachers and after making extensive inquiries, Pearson finally overrode the recommendations of the majority of his inspectors and abolished the system of payment by results. He refused, however, to bow to the determined campaign by the National Scripture Education League to have undenominational Bible instruction given in state schools during school hours as in New South Wales, and successfully opposed a motion in the assembly which sought to introduce the principle of local option, arguing that Bible instruction would be offensive to the 20,000 Roman Catholic children in state schools and to the 600 Roman Catholic teachers, while constant local option contests would 'undo, to a great extent, the wholesome system of mutual toleration we have hitherto enjoyed'.

In letters written to his English friends George Goschen and James Bryce, Pearson made much of Australia's potential as an ally of Britain in any future war, prophesying that Australia could raise 400,000 to 560,000 men and would be prepared to send a significant proportion overseas. 'Where', he asked Bryce, 'could England recruit such another corps and what would not be the moral effect of such a *corps d'armée* emerging so to speak from the Southern Seas and disembarking at Calcutta or Bombay?' Proud of his realism, he took active steps to prepare young Victorians for such an imperial struggle. By 1890 some 13,740 state school children were taking military drill and about 2000 were being trained as cadets to form a 'reserve, from which the militia could be recruited in any emergency'.

With the fall of the Gillies-Deakin government in 1890 Pearson threw himself feverishly into writing his most significant book, *National Life and Character. A Forecast* (1893). Drawing on observations made in his travels, wide reading and knowledge of the Australasian colonies, he made two main predictions: first, that the so-called 'higher races of men, or those which are held to have attained the highest forms of civilisation' would in a few decades find themselves 'elbowed and hustled and perhaps even thrust aside' by peoples whom they had assumed to be innately servile; he made a particular point of China's potential, claiming that it only needed a dynamic new religion like Islam, the genius of a ruler like Peter the Great and modern European industrial techniques to become one of the world's most formidable powers; second, he concluded that in English-speaking and European countries the state would increasingly take over the traditional roles of family and church. 'We may imagine the State *crèche*, and the State doctor, and the State school, supplemented, it may be by State meals, and the child, already drilled by the State, passing out from school into the State work-shop.' Most people would live out meaningless lives in huge, orderly, dull cities. But such a degree of socialism would not remove national rivalries, and youths would be conscripted for service in large standing armies.

The book created a stir in London and Washington. Gladstone commended it and Theodore Roosevelt reviewed it, contesting some of its conclusions. It influenced Madison Grant who found in it a warning to the United States to keep her population as 'Nordic' as possible in order to withstand successfully the predicted pressure from the coloured races. In Australia it was quoted by Edmund Barton in defence of the exclusion of coloured migrants, and taken up as a sophisticated warning against what Deakin would call in 1908 'the Yellow Peril to Caucasian civilization creeds and politics'.

In August 1892, exhausted by writing his book and troubled by a persistent cough, Pearson sailed for England hoping that the voyage and a stay in Colombo would renew his health. Soon after his arrival in London he was offered by the Victorian premier, William Shiels, what he believed to be the permanent position of secretary to the agent-general at a salary of £850, but in January 1894 a new premier and old political rival, J. B. Patterson [q.v.], gave him notice that he was to be superannuated, claiming maliciously that he did no work.

Impoverished by losses in the Australian depression of the early 1890s Pearson worked on doggedly, his cough steadily worsening. He died on 29 May 1894 in the presence of his wife and three teenage daughters. Probate of his will on 18 July 1894 revealed a personal estate with a gross value of £511 14s. 4d.

Pearson was the outstanding intellectual of the Australian colonies. A democrat by conviction, he combined a Puritan determination in carrying reforms with a gentle manner and a scrupulous respect for the traditional rules and courtesies of public debate. Short-sightedness reinforced an impression of aloofness, but with his inner circle of such friends as J. G. Duffy, H. A. Strong [qq.v.] and G. Higinbotham he could be a warm and brilliant conversationalist. He took a particular interest in the careers of promising young native-born Australians, many of whom were influenced by his ideas in newspapers and journal articles, books and speeches. 'I can candidly assure you', wrote Deakin in 1892, 'that on summing up your colonial experiences you would need to throw into the credit side of the scale an immense amount of other men's actions & words of which you have really been the parent'.

W. Stebbing (ed), *Charles Henry Pearson ... memorials by himself, his wife, and his friends* (Lond, 1900); J. Tregenza, *Professor of democracy: the life and work of C. H. Pearson, 1830-1894* (Melb, 1968); J. Tregenza, 'The Pearson papers', *La Trobe Lib J*, Oct 1970.

JOHN M. TREGENZA

PEARSON, JOSIAH BROWN (1841-1895), scholar and divine, was baptized on 4 February 1842 at Chesterfield, Derbyshire, England, son of Benjamin Pearson, hatter, and his wife Sarah. Educated at Chesterfield Grammar School and St John's College, Cambridge (B.A., 1864; M.A., 1867; LL.M., 1871; LL.D., 1877; D.D., 1880), he took the only first in the moral sciences tripos and was Burney prizeman in 1864. A fellow of St John's in 1865-80, he was made deacon in 1865 and ordained priest in 1866. In addition to his college duties he held several curacies in Cambridge before becoming vicar of Horningsea in 1871-74 and of Newark in 1874-80 when he acted as commissary for Bishop Moorhouse [q.v.] in 1876-80. Pearson acted as lecturer to his college in moral science in 1864-71; in 1872 he was Hulsean lecturer, Ramsden preacher and Whitenell preacher. In 1872-74 he was a preacher at the Chapel Royal, where he won the attention of Disraeli. Though he published no major work he was recognized at Cam-

bridge as an outstanding intellectual; the British Museum Catalogue has ten entries after his name. He regularly attended the Discussion Club, originated by John Grote, Knightsbridge professor of moral theology.

Through the influence of a fellow member, Moorhouse, Pearson was elected on 4 September 1879 by the Newcastle Diocesan Synod as successor to Bishop Tyrrell [q.v.]. The election was notable as the first under the authority of regulations approved by the Diocesan Synod and by the Church of England in Australia and Tasmania; the choice was then approved by the Australian House of Bishops and a pattern was set for future episcopal elections. Pearson was consecrated in St Paul's Cathedral, London, on 1 May 1880 by Archbishop Benson of Canterbury and sailed for Melbourne in the *Potosi* with his wife Ellen, née Tallents, whom he had married in London on 10 February. The form of his election and the reputation of his scholarship attracted much public attention. After impressive welcomes in Melbourne and Sydney he was enthroned in Newcastle on 26 August and took up his residence at Morpeth.

Pearson's public addresses, especially to synod over which he presided faithfully, and his sermons were thoughtful and influential but his diocese was in financial difficulties and its organization gave little scope to episcopal initiative. Opposed to pew rents in principle, he held comprehensive views on church unity rather than uniformity and stressed that the church must retain its independence of the state. He strongly opposed legislation on divorce. A strong advocate of sound clerical education, he encouraged a higher standard of preaching among his clergy. In the general administration of his diocese he was popular and successful but could not achieve the parochial expansion he felt essential.

Increasingly despondent at his failures, he accepted in 1886 an offer from Moorhouse, then bishop of Manchester, of the vicarage of Blackburn with an assistant bishopric in the diocese, but fell ill, withdrew his acceptance and went on leave for a year to recuperate. He suffered such a severe mental breakdown that his mind was not clear enough until 18 June 1889 to complete his resignation from Newcastle. In 1893 he was sufficiently recovered to accept the small parish of Leck in North Lancashire, where he died on 10 March 1895 aged 54. He was survived by his wife who died in 1925.

The most distinguished scholar to serve as an Anglican bishop in Australia, Pearson was ill adapted to the almost frontier conditions of an Australian see with its wide distances, few clergy, no great cathedrals or academic centre, but with scattered churches of all sorts and sizes.

A. P. Elkin, *The diocese of Newcastle* (Syd, 1955); *Maitland Mercury*, 18 Mar 1895; *Guardian* (Syd), 20 Mar 1895; MS material (Newcastle Diocesan Registry).

J. J. AUCHMUTY

PEARSON, WILLIAM (1818-1893), pastoralist and politician, was born on 20 September 1818 at Hilton, Kilmany, Fife, Scotland, son of Captain Hugh Pearson, R.N., and his wife Helen, née Littlejohn. Educated at Edinburgh High School, he joined an American timber ship but deserted to join an East Indiaman, becoming third officer in 1838.

After his father died in 1839 William left the sea and in September 1840 sailed in the *John Cooper* from Greenock arriving at Adelaide in March 1841 and at Port Phillip in April. He left Melbourne for Gippsland in June, travelled to Omeo and the Mitchell River, where he stocked Lindenow station and in September took up in his mother's name 12,800 acres, near the junction of the Thomson and La Trobe Rivers, which he named Kilmany Park. It was transferred to his name in 1848 and by 1868 was converted to freehold, nearly all bought at auction. By 1882 it included over 14,500 acres. In 1848-51 in partnership with H. Reoch and F. Brodribb he held land at Hill End, Tanjil, Grass Hills and in 1872-76 Maryville, 22,900 acres on the La Trobe. Despite trouble with the Aboriginals, with whom he is reputed to have dealt severely, and the desertion of his men to the goldfields, Pearson's pastoralist interests prospered. In June 1865 the Long Tunnel Extended Gold Mining Co. at Walhalla was formed; he took 900 shares and was the largest shareholder. The original £5 shares rose to £212, earning dividends of £512 each during the forty years of the mine's operation.

In 1864 Pearson was elected to the Legislative Assembly for North Gippsland, defeating his opponent, the miners' candidate C. F. Nicholls [q.v.], by 223 votes to 211, on a platform of assisted immigration. He retained his seat in the 1866 elections but resigned before the introduction of salaries for members, a measure he opposed. In the Legislative Council he was a representative of Eastern Province in 1881 and Gippsland in 1882-93.

A horse-breeder and racing enthusiast, Pearson won his first race in 1842 at the Flooding Creek (Sale) race-course. Reputed to have won over 300 races, though never the Melbourne Cup, he bred over a hundred winning horses. A heavy gambler, he often put over £1000 on one of his horses in a steeplechase at Flemington or Caulfield. He was a member of the Victoria Racing Club Committee and the Victoria Amateur Turf Club. An accomplished horseman, he introduced one of the early packs of hounds to Victoria and with them hunted kangaroos and dingoes. Though of reputed aristocratic looks and stern demeanour, he was quick to react when he believed his honour questioned. In 1849 he was found guilty of aggravated assault and in 1867 lost his claim for damages in a libel suit over his methods of handicapping horses.

On a visit to Scotland Pearson had met Eliza Laura, daughter of H. J. Travers, formerly of the East India Co., and on 4 August 1859 they married at Grassdale, Gippsland. Pearson spent most of his last years at his home, Craigellachie, Orrong Road, East St Kilda, where after suffering for months with a heart disease he died on 10 August 1893. Predeceased by his two elder sons, he was survived by his wife, three sons and two daughters. His heir William was born on 25 June 1864 at Craigellachie. Educated at Geelong Grammar School, he travelled for two years with Bishop Green and on his return worked for his father at Kilmany Park. He acquired Bonegilla station near Wodonga and on his father's death moved to Kilmany Park. He was president of the North Gippsland Agricultural Society and of the Sale Turf Club. In 1896-1916 he represented Gippsland Province in the Legislative Council and for years was chairman of committees of the Anglican synod. He died at Kilmany Park on 31 March 1919, survived by his wife Sophie Emily, née Gooch, whom he had married on 2 July 1887, and by their son and two daughters.

A. Sutherland et al, *Victoria and its metropolis*, 2 (Melb, 1888); A. Henderson (ed), *Australian families*, 1 (Melb, 1941); R. A. Paull, *Old Walhalla* (Melb, 1963); V&P (LA Vic), 1867 (1st S), 1 (A17); *Argus*, 16 Oct 1849, 11 Aug 1893; *Australasian*, 2 Feb, 6, 16 Mar 1867, 12 Aug, 23 Sept 1893.   DEIRDRE MORRIS

PECK, JOHN MURRAY (1830-1903), coachline proprietor and auctioneer, was born on 26 January 1830 at Lebanon, New Hampshire, United States of America, third son of John Waters Peck and his wife Frances (Fanny), née Huntington. His ancestors had arrived at Boston in 1637 from England and helped to found New Haven, Connecticut. Brought up on his parents' farm, Peck joined Wells, Fargo & Co. In June 1853 he arrived at Melbourne in the *Eagle* and with Freeman Cobb [q.v.], James Swanton, and John B. Lamber soon founded a carrying company known as Cobb & Co., which was converted in December 1853 to coaching. Their first coach ran to Forest Creek (Castlemaine) and Bendigo on 30 January 1854. Peck and Swanton, expert drivers and horse-breakers, managed the road and acted as relief drivers.

The original Cobb & Co. partnership was dissolved in May 1856 and Peck returned to America, visiting Chicago and his home in Lebanon. In 1858 he returned to Victoria with eight new Concord coaches and a supply of harness. Four of these coaches could carry forty passengers each and had been built to Peck's design. To operate them on Cobb & Co.'s Bendigo line a syndicate known as the Victorian Stage Co. was formed in August 1858 with thirteen members including Peck. It was dissolved in 1860 and Peck managed the Bendigo route for new owners. In 1861 he lost most of his capital when an outbreak of scab ruined his speculation in sheep.

In 1862 Peck joined Dal Campbell & Co., stock and station agents, and soon became the leading auctioneer of fat cattle in Victoria. His voice could be heard for half a mile and as a good judge of stock he always drafted and classed the cattle he was to sell. His humour, stories and rapid sales made him popular with a wide clientele. His own firm was long Victorian agent for James Tyson [q.v.] and Sidney Kidman. He left Dal Campbell & Co. in 1870 and formed a partnership with William Hudson and T. R. Raynor; it was dissolved in 1887 when his son Harry Huntington joined him in forming J. M. Peck & Son. Another son R. O. (Dick) later joined the firm which in 1922 was acquired by the Australian Mercantile, Land and Finance Co. Ltd.

Tall and powerful, Peck had a great zest for life, a keen sense of duty and the flamboyance of the mid-century Yankee businessman. He was first president of the Associated Stock and Station Agents in 1888, a councillor of the Agricultural Society, a justice of the peace, a councillor of the Borough of Essendon and Flemington serving as mayor in 1872, and a vice-president of the Essendon Football Club, a member of the Australian Club and the Victoria Racing Club. Known as 'Honest John', he was proud of his home and garden. Though a Wesleyan, he was fond of dancing and supported the Essendon Quadrille Club. He lived at Mascoma, Ascot Vale, and later at Lebanon, Pascoe Vale, where he died on 19 November 1903. He was buried in the Broadmeadows cemetery, survived by his wife Louisa Ellen, née Roberts, whom he had married in 1859 at Geelong, and by their eight children. Streets in Essendon North and Ascot Vale are named after him.

His son, Harry Huntington, became a noted stock auctioneer and was author of *Memoirs of a Stockman* (Melbourne, 1942).

K. A. Austin, *The lights of Cobb and Co.* (Adel, 1967); W. A. Blair, A pioneer of coaching days (held by Mrs L. H. Earp); J. M. Peck papers (Cobb & Co. Transport Museum, Toowoomba, Qld); MS cat under L. H. Earp (LaT L); information from the Town Clerk, City of Essendon, and Mrs L. H. Earp, Glenrowan, Vic.

K. A. AUSTIN

PELL, MORRIS BIRKBECK (1827-1879), professor of mathematics, was born on 31 March 1827 at Albion, Illinois, United States of America, son of Gilbert Titus Pell and his wife Elizabeth, née Birkbeck. His maternal grandfather Morris Birkbeck (1783-1825), English social reformer, had founded the prairie settlement of Albion. Gilbert Titus joined it, prospered and in 1822-24 and 1828-39 was a member of the 'Convention Legislature' of Illinois. In 1835 the family separated and Mrs Pell took her children first to Poughkeepsie, New York, then to Plymouth, England, in 1841, where Morris attended the New Grammar School. On 11 March 1845 as a sizar he entered St John's College, Cambridge (B.A., 1849). A senior wrangler in mathematics and second Smith's prizeman, he was elected a fellow of St John's on 18 March 1850. On 17 February 1852 he married Julia, daughter of James Rusden, naval officer of Plymouth.

In 1852 Pell was chosen from twenty-six candidates as first professor of mathematics and natural philosophy in the University of Sydney at a salary of £825 with allowances and students' fees extra. On 16 March he sailed in the *Asiatic* with his wife, mother and two sisters, arriving at Sydney in July. Pell found the mathematical preparation of the university students low because of the poor state of secondary education. He developed courses in mathematics at pass and honours levels. The mathematical topics for the first bachelor of arts degree awarded by the university included arithmetic in all its branches, logarithms, algebra to quadratic equations and the first four books of Euclid. The subjects in his honours courses were more diversified and advanced as Pell kept in touch with the courses being offered in Cambridge, London and Edinburgh. They also reflected his own research interests: calculus of variations, probability, finite differences, differential geometry, optics and astronomy. He specialized in problems on mortality rates and life expectation. He published *Geometrical Illustrations of the Differential Calculus* for his students and won repute as a fine teacher.

In 1854 in evidence to a Legislative Council select committee on education Pell advocated the opening of a secular grammar school. In 1859 he testified to the Legislative Assembly select committees on the Sydney Grammar School and the University of Sydney on the composition of the senate, the adverse effect of clergy on enrolments, the new buildings, the value of liberal studies in the education of businessmen and squatters, and the beneficial effect of the university on secondary education. His evidence resulted in *ex officio* membership of the university senate for professors. He was a member of it in 1861-77 and after resignation was re-elected to the senate in 1878 by members of convocation.

Pell was chairman of a commission to inquire into the Surveyor-General's Department in 1855, a member of the commission on a fatal railway accident in 1858, chairman of the commission on methods of testing marine steam-boilers in 1868, the Hunter River Floods Commission in 1869-70, the board inquiring into the land titles branch of the Registrar-General's Department in 1870 and chairman of the Sydney City and Suburban Sewage and Health Board in 1875-77. Pell had been admitted to the Bar on 2 December 1863 and from 1872 was an examiner in law at the university. In 1854 he had become actuarial consultant to the Australian Mutual Provident Society and in 1870 was a director and consulting actuary of the Mutual Life Association of Australasia. He was connected with such business enterprises as mining, brickmaking, glassmaking and manufacturing fertilizers by crushing bones.

A member of the Philosophical Society from 1856, Pell served on its council in 1858. He was a member and secretary of the Royal Society of New South Wales from 1867 and a member of its council from 1869. In its *Transactions* he published papers 'On the Rates of Mortality and Expectation of Life in New South Wales' (1867) and 'On the Constitution of Matter' (1871). He also published in the *Journal* of the Institute of Actuaries, London, 'On the Distribution of Profits in Mutual Insurance Societies' (1869) and 'On the Institute of Actuaries' life tables' (1879) among other papers.

For many years almost crippled by an injury to his spine, Pell resigned in mid-1877 as professor of mathematics on a pension of £412 10s. He died of progressive paralysis on 7 May 1879 at Glebe and was buried in the Balmain cemetery. He was survived by his wife, five sons and three daughters. His goods were valued for probate at £4000, and he left an annuity of £80 to his estranged wife Julia, then residing in Tasmania, provided that she did not return to Sydney.

G. Flower, *History of the English settlement in Edwards County, Illinois*, E. B. Washburne ed (Chicago, 1882); H. E. Barff, *A short historical account of the University of Sydney . . . 1852-1902* (Syd, 1902); E. E. Sparks (ed), *The English settlement in the Illinois* (Lond, 1907); V&P (LC NSW), University of Sydney, 1853, 1; Sel cttee on education, Evidence, 1854, 2, (LA NSW), 1858, 1, 327, 3, 857, 1876-77, 1, 241; A.M.P. *Messenger*, Jan 1931.

I. S. TURNER

PENFOLD, CHRISTOPHER RAWSON (1811-1870), medical practitioner and vigneron, son of John Penfold, vicar of Steyning, Sussex, England, and his wife Charlotte June, née Brooks. Trained at St Bartholomew's Hospital, he practised medicine at Brighton in 1838-44. On 26 May 1835 he married Mary, only daughter of Thomas Holt, medical practitioner of Edmonton, London.

Penfold arrived in South Australia with his wife and daughter Georgina in the *Taglioni* on 18 June 1844 and took up land in the foothills of the Mount Lofty Ranges, about four miles from Adelaide. Before leaving England he had paid a deposit to the Colonial Land and Emigration Commission and soon after arrival paid Edmund Trimmer £1200 for land originally held by Robert Cook and William Ferguson. This property in the district of Magill consisted of 500 acres of 'the choicest land, 200 acres of which [were] under crops'. Within two years he was producing large quantities of grain 'without the smallest attempt at cultivation'.

Before sailing for South Australia, Penfold had obtained vine cuttings from the wine-growing districts of France and these had been carefully nutured until planting was possible. Believing that wine was a useful medicament, especially for the treatment of anaemia, he carefully selected a site for his vines to produce good quality red wines. A growing demand for his wine led to further development of the vineyard. Through the careful husbandry of Mary and a domestic servant, Ellen Timbrell, the output was gradually increased until in 1871 the stock on hand was 107,000 gallons, nearly one-eighth of the total production for South Australia in that year. At first Penfold restricted his output to wines of the port and sherry types but clarets and rieslings later became important.

Penfold had started medical practice soon after he arrived but, as the demands of his vineyard increased and his health began to fail, he had difficulty in meeting requests for his professional advice although he continued to practise until 1870. In 1859-63 he was gazetted a legally qualified medical practitioner, with responsibilities to attend inquests and conduct post-mortems as directed and to certify the mental condition of any person suspected of lunacy. He was also prominent in local government. Appointed to the Burnside District Council, he was elected its first chairman in 1856 but after a year resigned from the council. From 1863 he was a member of the vestry of St George's Church, Magill. After a long illness he died at his home, The Grange, on 25 March 1870, survived by his wife and only child. As his funeral cortège passed through the village to St George's Church flags were flown at half-mast and commercial houses closed their doors as a mark of respect to one who through 'the kindness of his disposition' had won many friends.

Mary continued to develop the vineyard assisted by Ellen Timbrell and later by Thomas Francis Hyland, a former member of the Victorian Civil Service who on 24 September 1862 had married Georgina. By 1881 a flourishing trade had been built up within Australia whilst a successful export market had been established in New Zealand. The family later extended its interests to Victoria and New South Wales. Mary Penfold died on 31 December 1895 and was buried beside her husband in St George's churchyard. Her property passed to Georgina Hyland and thence to her descendants who later adopted the name Penfold-Hyland.

Penfold's home is preserved as part of the Magill vineyard and a small portrait is in the cottage. He has been called 'the first scientific vigneron of Australia' but much of his success was the result of the patience and understanding of wine production which Mary had developed whilst her husband was busy in his profession.

S. A. Mills (ed), *Wine story of Australia* (Syd, 1908); Burnside Council, *Burnside, South Australia, 1856-1936* (Adel, 1936); E. Keane (ed), *The Penfold story* (Syd, 1951); A. Simon, *The wines, vineyards and vignerons of Australia* (Melb, 1966); M. Lake, *Vine and scalpel* (Brisb, 1967); E. Jolly, *The Penfold Cottage story* (Adel, nd); *Register* (Adel), 8 Aug 1844, 10 Jan 1846, 15, 28 Aug 1856, 5 Mar 1857, 28, 30 Mar 1870; C. R. Penfold notes (SAA); Penfold family papers (held by Mrs E. Jolly, Medindie, SA).
D. I. McDONALD

PEPPIN, GEORGE HALL (1800-1872), pastoralist and sheepbreeder, was born at Old Shute Farm, Dulverton, England, son of George Peppin, sheepbreeder who acquired some of George III's flock, and his wife Maria née Hall. In 1850 when farming was at a low ebb in England he sailed for Port Phillip in the *Ann Maria* with his wife Harriet, née Thompson, whom he had married in 1825, and two sons, GEORGE (1827-1876) and FREDERICK LOCH (1828-1911). By mid-1851 they were settled at Mimaluke near Mansfield and after years of fluctuating fortune sold out when scab and fluke destroyed their flock. In March 1858 Peppin & Sons bought from W. A. Brodribb [q.v.] South Wanganella station in the Riverina and its 8000 sheep for £10,000. They used the run for fattening sheep for the Melbourne market, and in 1859 when five shearers claimed that tents were insufficient accommodation, George junior successfully sued them.

In 1861 the Peppins, beaten by Riverina conditions, offered Wanganella for sale at Scott's Hotel in Melbourne but found no buyer. They decided to try again and continue their earlier attempts to breed a type of merino suitable to the area, a larger, more robust, stronger woolled sheep and with a bulky back to stand up to summer dust and heat. In 1864 Peppin & Sons exhibited six pens of sheep at the first Echuca Agricultural Show and were awarded four first prizes and one second. This success had been achieved by careful selection of 200 of their best ewes and 100 Rambouillet-sired stud ewes from Nicholas Chadwick of Canally, New South Wales, and mating them with Rambouillet and Negretti rams. In 1866 Peppin & Sons bought the Rambouillet ram, Emperor, who annually yielded twenty-five pounds of greasy or twelve pounds of scoured wool when such weights were almost unknown. They also bought two sons of Old Grimes, a famous Vermont ram, and acquired a few of the best Victorian rams but then bred only from their own sheep, experimenting on a small scale only 'and in such a way that they could do no permanent injury'. Peppin & Sons acquired the neighbouring properties of Morago and Boonoke. Wanganella was managed by George junior and his father and brother lived at Morago. G. H. Peppin died intestate on 16 April 1872 and was mourned as 'a fine old English gentleman'. He was buried in the Deniliquin cemetery with Presbyterian rites.

In 1874 the Peppin brothers formed a double stud selected by T. F. Cumming [q.v.]. They kept careful records of the yields of individual sheep and breeding was methodically conducted. At the Deniliquin show in July 1878 Peppin & Sons won the society's, Goldsbrough's [q.v.] and the president's prizes for sheep. Next year Wanganella sheep won first prize for the most valuable fleeces from six ewes at the Sydney International Exhibition.

George was a magistrate from 1859, regularly attending the Deniliquin bench and vice-president of the Riverine Association formed in 1863 to advocate separation from New South Wales. About 1873 he visited England and on his return the brothers decided to sell the runs. Before this could be done George died on 12 June 1876, survived by two sons and four daughters of his wife Maria, née Brown Smith.

In October 1878 Frederick sold Wanganella, South Boonoke and Long Plains with 28,168 sheep, 837 stud sheep, 200 cattle, 25 horses and 32,857 acres of freehold for £77,000 to Austin [q.v.] & Millear. North Boonoke station with 26,788 sheep, 290 cattle, 63 horses and 31,484 acres of freehold land was sold for £67,000 to F. S. Falkiner [q.v.] & J. R. Ross in November.

By 1877 with John Webber, Frederick had invested in thirty runs in the South Gregory District of Queensland. He lived in Melbourne where he was involved in the Australian Frozen Meat Export Co. and in 1880 advocated fitting up sailing ships to carry frozen meat to the English market. He was a councillor of the Royal Agricultural Society of Victoria and president in 1893-94, and a councillor of the Pastoralists' Association of Victoria and Southern Riverina. He helped to establish the Chamber of Agriculture and was on the original committee of the *Flock Book for British Breeds of Sheep in Victoria*. He bred Exmoor ponies and Jersey cattle on his farm at Epping which he sold in the mid-1880s. He visited England and on his return in 1888 bought Fernbank near Loch in South Gippsland, where he bred Southdown sheep and dairy Shorthorn cattle. On his Queensland stations 90,000 sheep and all the cattle died in the long drought, and in 1902 the banks took over the stations. A vice-president of the Federation League, he was a manager of the Alfred Hospital, a committee member of the Charity Organization Society and the Austin Hospital for Incurables, and a manager of the Leongatha Labour Colony. He died on 29 January 1911 and was survived by his wife Sarah Ellen Morgan, daughter of a London doctor, and by three sons and a daughter.

The Peppin sheep gained in popularity and predominate among the flocks of South Africa as well as in New Zealand and South America. In Australia over 60 per cent of merinos have Wanganella blood.

C. McIvor, *The history and development of sheep farming from antiquity to modern times* (Syd, 1893); H. M. Eastman, *Memoirs of a sheepman* (Deniliquin, 1953); J. F. Guthrie, *A world history of sheep and wool* (Melb, 1957); M. L. Kiddle, *Men of yesterday* (Melb, 1961); F. Clune, *Search for the golden fleece . . . the Peppin merino* (Syd, 1965); G. L. Buxton, *The Riverina 1861-1891* (Melb, 1967); *Riverine Herald*, 20 Apr 1872; *Pastoral Review*, 15 Dec 1909, 15 Feb 1911; *Argus*, 1 Feb 1911; George Peppin diary 1859 (ML); newspaper cuttings (ML).																	J. ANN HONE

PERKINS, PATRICK (1838-1901), brewer and politician, was born on 10 October 1838 at Cashel, County Tipperary, Ireland, second son of Thomas Perkins, farmer, and his wife Ellen, née Gooley. Educated at the local National school, he migrated to Victoria in 1855 with his family. Successful on the Ballarat and Bendigo goldfields, he and his brother Thomas (1841-1876) as partners acquired a share in the Reedy Creek mine for £8000 and later opened a store and brewing business at Castlemaine.

Perkins visited Queensland in 1866 and opened the Toowoomba Brewery in 1869. Its operations were extended to Brisbane, where 'Castlemaine XXXX' ale soon won repute and a large following. In 1876 he settled in Brisbane and became involved in real estate, mining, brewing and hotel speculations. In 1888 with McIlwraith and Morehead [qq.v.] he floated Perkins & Co., a large brewing and hotel business. Unlike others Perkins was astute and ruthless, and disposed of most of his shares before the firm struck financial difficulties. Retribution followed when he joined his political associates in speculating heavily in Mount Morgan shares (9104 in 1892) and hotel properties. By then his overdraft at the Queensland National Bank (£99,485) was one of the largest in the colony and the securities lodged were then worth scarcely half this debt. By 1898 he was even unable to pay an £8000 call on his 20 per cent share in R. M. Collins's [q.v.] and Thomas McIlwraith's North Australian Pastoral Co. In his last years he was almost impoverished.

Perkins had entered the Legislative Assembly on 1 May 1877 as member for Aubigny, a Darling Downs constituency. Unseated for election irregularities in 1884, he surprisingly won Cambooya in the Nationalist sweep of 1888. He wisely refrained from contesting that electorate in 1893 and was appointed on 23 May to the Legislative Council where he retained his seat until 1901.

Resembling McIlwraith in size and opinions if not in vision and intellect, Perkins aroused astonishment by becoming secretary of public lands in the first McIlwraith ministry from January 1879 to November 1883. As a minister he worked hard, relying on his under-secretary to save him from mistakes. His régime was unmarked by policy innovations but marred by his involvement in the Peak Downs affair when he allegedly reduced the price of crown lands in a transaction with his colleague Morehead. Although nothing was proved, the affair did little for Perkins's reputation, already blighted by inability to absorb criticism and by his fiery temperament and vituperative tongue. His flagrant abuse of electoral laws, effrontery and blatant cynicism made the Aubigny election of 1883 one of the most notorious in Queensland. After a violent and alcoholic diatribe against 'McIlwraith, Orangemen and Psalm-singers' at Toowoomba on 2 January 1888 Perkins forfeited not only his leader's 'sympathy but incurred his strongest disapproval'. The end of this warm and intimate friendship, combined with opposition from the Brisbane press, led to his exclusion from the new ministry. In the council he was more effective as a genial roads-and-bridges member of the old colonial school whose political actions became increasingly absorbed with preserving property and defeating reform. An agreeable and hearty companion but unrelenting to such enemies as W. H. Groom [q.v.], he left few impressions on the colony beyond his survival of three shipwrecks.

Perkins was an influential member of a small legal and business group of Roman Catholics who uneasily coexisted with the new Queensland mercantile establishment. He was given a dinner in May 1886 on the eve of his visit to Ireland. He died on 17 May 1901 at Hawthorn, Victoria. He left £250 to charities, £100 to Riverview College and the residue of his £4000 estate to his wife Mary Ellen, née Hickey, by whom he had four sons and four daughters.

C. A. Bernays, *Queensland politics during sixty years* (Brisb, 1919); V&P (LA Qld), 1883-84, 403; *Australasian*, 22 May 1886, 29 June 1901; *Boomerang* (Brisb), 7 Jan 1888; *Brisbane Courier*, 18 May 1901; McIlwraith papers (Oxley Lib, Brisb).   D. B. WATERSON

PERMEWAN, JOHN (1837-1904), carrier, was born in Penzance, Cornwall, England, son of John Permewan and his wife Grace, née Harvey. He arrived in Ballarat in the early 1850s and soon realized the potential of a carrying service by river and road. In 1854 Browne, Osborne & Co. started in Geelong as carriers and commission agents operating between Geelong and Ballarat; Permewan was an employee until 1861 when he became a partner. In that year Browne and Osborne formed separate companies; Browne, Sons & Co. lapsed, but T. Osborne & Co., with Permewan in association, carried on business until 1869. E. Hunt joined them in 1864 and in 1869 Permewan Hunt & Co. was formed. Hunt retired in 1876, J. E.

Wright replaced him and the company became Permewan Wright & Co. It became a limited company in 1879.

By then business had expanded dramatically both in volume and area covered. In July 1875 Permewan Hunt & Co. bought Coghill's and the Wagga Wagga Steam Navigation Co. and within six months had the largest share of the Echuca trade, having run smaller and hitherto effective agents out of business. From Echuca the company expanded up the Darling and Murrumbidgee Rivers, consolidating constantly and eliminating competition. By 1888 Permewan Wright had forty-eight branches in Victoria and New South Wales and agencies at almost every railway station; the network extended from Bourke on the Darling through all the principal towns on the Murray and Murrumbidgee, to Geelong and Melbourne. Their London agent, Pickford & Son, linked them to an extensive international trade. Their commission business meant that they sometimes had £50,000 advanced on goods, and the Collins Street three-storied bluestone warehouse was full of produce, especially colonial-grown tobacco and hops often stored for local manufacturers. The company pioneered 'express waggons' which could carry six tons and used teams of relief horses stationed along the roads. It also had two cargo and three passenger steamers constantly running between Geelong and Melbourne. In the 1890s when many agents, particularly river traders, were forced out of business, Permewan Wright & Co. continued and thereby were stronger than competitors after the depression.

John Permewan remained superintendent of the firm until failing health forced him to retire in 1902. He travelled constantly on train and coach through Victoria and New South Wales, seeming only to tire in his last years. He was interested in charities and his unfinished will, by which he had intended to give to charities, was carried out by his family. His only public post was a seat on the Ballarat Hospital Committee. Aged 67 he died at his home in Ballarat on 23 December 1904, survived by his wife Isabelle, née Towers, and by a son and a daughter.

A. Sutherland et al, *Victoria and its metropolis*, 2 (Melb, 1888); S. Priestley, *Echuca: a centenary history* (Brisb, 1965); *Traveller*, 1897; *Argus*, 25 Dec 1904.   SUZANNE G. MELLOR

PERRY, CHARLES (1807-1891), Church of England bishop, was born on 17 February 1807 in London, third son of John Perry, sheriff of Essex and wealthy owner of the

East India Docks at Blackwall, and his second wife Mary, sister of Richard Green, who became a partner and carried on the business after John Perry died in 1810.

Charles was educated in private schools at Clapham Common and Hackney and for four years at Harrow, where he played cricket against Eton. In 1824 he followed his brothers to Trinity College, Cambridge (B.A., 1828), graduating with first-class honours and as senior wrangler, seventh classic and first Smith's prizeman. In October 1829 he passed the examination which entitled him to a fellowship of the college. He had been admitted to the Inner Temple in 1828 but after two years and a half his health broke down. Forced to abandon legal studies, he returned to Trinity (M.A., 1831) at the invitation of William Whewell (master 1841-66) and was an assistant tutor in 1832-40.

The example which his mother had given him in simple Christian duty helped Charles considerably at this difficult stage of his life. At Trinity he was given a Bible by the students for attending chapel most often amongst the fellows of the college when the fellows themselves ordered attendance at chapel eight times a week instead of five. Perry's example was appreciated by the students who formed a 'Society for the Prevention of Cruelty to Undergraduates'. Through one of his pupils, Edward Hoare, Perry was introduced into an Evangelical circle which included Thomas Fowell Buxton and Joseph Gurney. The effect of this association was to settle his religious doubts and confirm his desire to be ordained. He became impressed by the duty of private judgment and subsequently seldom doubted the correctness of his doctrinal views. On 16 June 1833 he was made deacon at St Margaret's, Westminster, by the bishop of Gloucester and on 26 November 1836 ordained priest by the bishop of Ely.

Beside his academic work Perry developed a special pastoral interest in the growing area of Barnwell near Cambridge. Having bought the advowson of the living of St Andrew-the-Less, he began to develop it into a parish. Appointing as vicar a contemporary at Trinity College, Rev. Thomas Boodle, he encouraged and assisted the building of two other churches. Christ Church, Barnwell, was completed in 1839 and St Paul's, New Town, was opened in 1842 with Perry as assistant curate under Boodle. When the parish was divided in 1845 Perry became vicar of St Paul's. Meanwhile he had resigned as a fellow at Trinity and on 14 October 1841 married Frances, daughter of Samuel Cooper, a Hull merchant.

Perry's keen interest in developing theological education within the university and his active work on behalf of the Church Missionary Society brought him under notice, and when the secretary of state for the colonies was seeking a suitable candidate for the proposed diocese of Melbourne, Perry was nominated by Henry Venn, secretary of the C.M.S., and accepted by the bishop of London and the archbishop of Canterbury. On 29 June 1847 in Westminster Abbey, Archbishop Howley consecrated Charles Perry as bishop of Melbourne, William Tyrrell [q.v.] as bishop of Newcastle, Augustus Short [q.v.] as bishop of Adelaide and Robert Gray as bishop of Cape Town. The University of Cambridge had conferred the degree of D.D. (literas regius) on Perry in May.

The new bishop arrived with his wife in the clipper Stag at Melbourne on 23 January 1848 and was installed at St James's pro-Cathedral on the 28th. His letters patent designated Melbourne a city by virtue of being the seat of the bishop's see and defined his jurisdiction as 'bounded by a line drawn from Cape Howe to the nearest source of the River Murray, and by the course of that river, until it reaches the one hundred and forty-first parallel of East Longitude'. The population in this area was over 43,000, nearly half of whom were Anglicans; within eighteen months Perry had visited all the main centres. Disappointed at the ineffectiveness of the three colonial chaplains stationed at Melbourne, Geelong and Portland, Perry had to rely heavily on the three clergy and three lay readers who had accompanied him. Of these, Rev. H. B. Macartney [q.v.] was to prove his most trusted and able helper. The shortage of clergy was partly solved by appointing colonists who offered for ordination as lay readers under the superintendence of a clergyman until they had passed a qualifying examination. In the 1860s Perry's use of lay readers was severely criticized but in the early stages it was a valuable expedient in a diocese short of both men and money.

Perry's legal training made him appreciate that the ecclesiastical laws of England could not be applied in a colony where the Church of England was not 'established' and that clergy would be reluctant to serve in a diocese subject to the arbitrary will of the bishop. He also saw that the laity, unaccustomed to the necessity of supporting the clergy financially, could not be encouraged unless they had a proper share in appointing clergy to parishes and in the government of the Church. The practical needs of the diocese, coupled with a strong desire to divest himself of what he described as 'despotic power', led Perry to press for a revision of ecclesiastical law at the first opportunity.

After a conference and correspondence with his metropolitan, Bishop Broughton [q.v.], Perry had two bills introduced by his registrar, Henry Moor [q.v.], in the Legislative Council at Sydney in August 1850. The bills were designed to place clerical discipline on the same basis as that in England and to give the laity a distinct share in patronage. Local misunderstanding, denominational jealousy, hasty preparation and dislike of Moor led to withdrawal of the bills after a public meeting in Melbourne petitioned against them.

Two months later Perry was amongst the six Australasian bishops who met at Sydney 'to consult upon the various difficulties in which we are at present placed by the doubtful application to the Church in this province of the Ecclesiastical Laws now in force in England, and to suggest such measures as may seem to be most suitable for removing our present embarrassments'. The bishops were unanimous that the Church in Australia should be self-governing but were divided on the best way to achieve this aim. Perry believed that nothing short of an imperial Act could give the Church this right and was supported at this stage by Bishop Tyrrell. Bishop Selwyn of New Zealand and Bishop Short saw no legal barriers to drawing up a constitution on the basis of consensual compact, but no immediate action was taken beyond forwarding the minutes of the conference to the archbishop of Canterbury in the hope that the British government would provide a solution.

Feeling in church-state relationships was intense in 1850 because the Privy Council had overruled the ecclesiastical Court of Arches and pronounced that opinions on baptismal regeneration expressed by Rev. G. C. Gorham were consistent with the articles and formularies of the Church of England. At the Sydney conference Perry had incurred the displeasure of his fellow bishops by putting forward an independent statement on holy baptism doctrinally in sympathy with Gorham's opinions. This statement, coupled with Perry's insistence on the need for a constitution by legislative enactment, led him to be accused of 'Erastianism'. However, he was a strong contender for the voluntary principle and in his primary Charge to his clergy in 1852 he showed that his views on baptism were reached independently of any party. With Selwyn, Perry insisted strongly on the need for adequate lay representation in any future synods, and in mid-1851 he called an assembly of his clergy and lay representatives to discuss the minutes of the bishops' conference and to express their views on the desirability and mode of

synodical government. The assembly coincided with the separation of Victoria from New South Wales and Perry was able to obtain the unanimous support of the assembly for the Church of England in Victoria to begin to investigate ways and means of becoming self-governing. When Archbishop Sumner's colonial church regulation bill was rejected by the House of Commons in 1853, Perry asked William Stawell [q.v.] to draw up a bill based on this defeated measure but designed to apply exclusively to the Church of England in Victoria. The purpose of Sumner's bill had been to remove legal objections to any diocese drawing up its own constitution, and local sympathy for this principle was sufficient to enable Perry to obtain the support of a representative assembly of his own Church. He then had the bill passed by the Victorian Legislative Council in November 1854 and left immediately for England to plead in person for Royal assent. On 12 December 1855 Act 18 Vic. no 45 became law. In October 1856 he summoned the first legally authorized synod of the Church of England in the colonies. The Victoria Church Act became the model for other Australian diocesan constitutions and was cited in other colonial attempts to obtain synodical government.

Perry's episcopate coincided almost exactly with the transfer of educational responsibility from the church to the state in Victoria and when he left Melbourne in 1874 the church was receiving the final instalments of government assistance towards clerical stipends and church buildings. Perry did not favour the National schools, introduced to Port Phillip in 1848, because the teacher was forbidden by law to give any form of religious education and he did not believe that Christianity could be successfully imparted by a visiting instructor once a week. State aid to all denominations he described as 'a false and pernicious principle . . . stereotyping, so far as the State can do, every existing religious error'. In 1852 he told the select committee on education that state aid to denominational schools encouraged the establishment of rival schools in rural areas where the population was not sufficient for more than one. However, although he preferred the voluntary system, he would not oppose the majority of his fellow churchmen who believed the government grants for stipends, churches and vicarages, to be absolutely necessary; later he admitted that in the circumstances the Church of England could not have done without state aid.

A conflict between his views as an individual Christian and his official position as bishop, caused Perry to have difficulties in the field of government control of education. He recognized the practical necessity for the state to support elementary schools, especially in the gold rushes, but he did not believe that education should be altogether paid for by the government. Perry held that parents, not the state or the church, were primarily responsible for education. The government's responsibility, he said, was 'to take care that facilities for religious instruction are given in accordance with the tenets of the several parents and to confine its exertions to the secular instruction and moral education of the children', whilst the churches were to provide the religious instruction which the parents required. He was happy with a curriculum of religious instruction in primary schools on which all non-Roman Catholic churches could agree and believed that distinctive denominational principles should be reserved for secondary schools.

When National and denominational schools were brought under a single administration in 1862, Perry had no quarrel with the policy of the Common Schools' Board, provided that the property rights of his church were protected. He was even ready to allow voluntary combinations of churches to run a school and to provide religious instruction in areas where the population was not sufficient to justify more than one school. His liberal attitude brought him into conflict with the denominationalists on his own education committee. In 1867 he led a determined attack on Higinbotham's [q.v.] public instruction bill, embodying the recommendations of a royal commission that sectarian instruction in National schools and state aid to denominational education should be discontinued. Perry believed that such measures would foster an irreligious people and his opposition was largely responsible for Higinbotham withdrawing the bill. But the reprieve was only temporary and many Anglican day schools were closed after state aid to religion was abolished in 1872.

Perry's greatest contribution to education in Victoria was in the establishment of the Melbourne Diocesan Grammar School, begun under R. H. Budd [q.v.] in 1849, and the Geelong Grammar School which commenced under Rev. G. O. Vance [q.v.] in 1857. A warm admirer of the principles of Thomas Arnold, Perry believed that schools of this nature with a continuing tradition for sound learning and a religious education were best adapted for providing leaders in the community. He was personally responsible for the choice of Dr J. E. Bromby [q.v.] as headmaster of Melbourne Grammar School in 1858. In the field of tertiary education, the bishop was a foundation member of the Council of the University of Melbourne and a beginning had been made on Trinity College before he retired; he also gave 400 of his books to its library.

H. G. Turner's [q.v.] estimate of Perry as a pious but somewhat narrow-minded Evangelical, who was out of touch with contemporary thought, needs qualification. Certainly the bishop showed a marked antipathy to ritualism, partly because he believed it at variance with the literal sense of the Articles of the Church of England, partly because he saw ritualism as a danger to the unity of the diocese and the well-being of the Church. But as early as 1855 the five sermons which Perry preached before the University of Cambridge show that he was aware that scientific discoveries were challenging traditional interpretations of the Bible. In his numerous lectures delivered in the 1860s Perry acknowledged the need for scientific criticism to be met honestly. At the same time he remained confident that neither historical criticism nor scientific discoveries could ever demolish the essential truth of the Bible.

By the mid-1860s Perry saw that his diocese would soon need subdivision as the population continued to increase steadily after the spectacular immigrations to the goldfields in the 1850s. Reviewing the progress of the Church since 1851, the bishop told the Church Assembly in 1869 that in two decades the total number of clergy had increased to 113, whilst 162 churches and 75 parsonages had been built. State aid had supplied about a third of the cost of these buildings and clerical stipends, but an adequate maintenance for his clergy remained his most pressing concern; from his own pocket Perry more than once helped his clergy in distress. The creation of the bishopric of Ballarat was made possible in 1873 by appropriating capitation grants from the state to endow the new see.

On 26 February 1874 Perry and his wife sailed for England. He had been given the task of choosing a bishop for the new diocese in consultation with Sir William Stawell and the archbishop of Canterbury. Having chosen Rev. Samuel Thornton [q.v.], Perry wrote to Dean Macartney, the vicar-general, announcing his retirement. He agreed, however, to assist in finding a suitable successor and on 22 October 1876 Rev. James Moorhouse [q.v.] was consecrated as second bishop of Melbourne.

After the death of Bishop Selwyn Perry was appointed Prelate of the Order of St Michael and St George in the 1878 Queen's birthday honours list and at the invitation of Bishop Ollivant became a canon of Llandaff Cathedral. In retirement he was an active vice-president of the Church Missionary

Society and a committee member of both S.P.G. and S.P.C.K. Until 1883 he regularly attended the Church Congress, often speaking strongly for the Evangelical viewpoint. His greatest achievement in retirement was the foundation of the theological college, Ridley Hall, Cambridge, officially opened in 1881. By introducing the principle of doctrinal tests to which members of the council were expected to subscribe, Perry drew criticism upon the whole project from such eminent scholars as B. F. Westcott and J. B. Lightfoot, but as chairman of the council he justified this action as being necessary at a time when both ritualism and rationalism were distracting the Church.

Canon S. L. Chase, who served under Perry for many years in Melbourne, described the bishop as a man made up of many paradoxes, in whom an intensely affectionate nature hid itself under a crust of repelling severity and a confiding spirit under a veil of sternness and suspicion. Lacking the brilliance of personality to match the force of his intellect, Perry was often underestimated by his contemporaries. His refusal to compromise his doctrinal convictions made him unpopular with critics who did not always equally appreciate his readiness to sacrifice his own interests and his scrupulous attempts to be impartial. The *Argus* had often attacked his policies but described him as an antagonist whose courtesy freed arguments from bitterness and one whose life was a daily moral lesson to the community. His outstanding achievement was to obtain legal synodical government for the Church of England in Victoria and his greatest insight was the importance of the laity in the total organization and life of the Church. He died on 2 December 1891 and was buried in the family grave at Harlow, Essex. His wife died on the first anniversary of his death; they had no children. His probate in Australia was sworn at £33,000.

A portrait by Henry Weigall is in the La Trobe Library, Melbourne, and his personal copy was bequeathed to Ridley Hall, Cambridge.

G. Goodman, *The church in Victoria during the episcopate of ... Rev. Charles Perry* (Melb, 1892); R. Robson, *Ideas and institutions of Victorian Britain* (Lond, 1967); A. de Q. Robin, *Charles Perry, bishop of Melbourne* (Perth, 1967), and for bibliog; K. E. Dear, 'Bishop Perry and the rise of national education in Victoria, 1848-1873', *Melbourne studies in education*, E. L. French ed (Melb, 1965); A. de Q. Robin, 'Bishop Perry and lay representation in colonial synods', *J of Ecclesiastical Hist*, Apr 1964.   A. DE Q. ROBIN

PERSSE, DE BURGH FITZPATRICK (1840-1921), pioneer pastoralist and company director, was born on 25 September 1840 in Moyode Castle, County Galway, Ireland, youngest of the sixteen children of Burton Persse, twelve of them by his second wife Matilda, daughter of Henry Persse, of Roxborough. Through each parent he was a cousin of Augusta Persse, Lady Gregory, dramatist and *grande dame* of the Irish literary renaissance whose friend and collaborator, W. B. Yeats, described in his *Autobiographies* the feudal manner of life of the Galway Persses, a branch of the Northumberland Percys. De Burgh Persse grew up in the world of the Protestant ascendancy, and hunting and farming became abiding interests. At Cuba House School, Banagher, he showed intellectual promise and he read classics, mathematics, philosophy, science and medicine at Trinity College, Dublin (B.A., 1861). He was then commissioned lieutenant in the 22nd Regiment.

Adventurous by nature, he was inspired by Sir John Young and a visit to the 1862 International Exhibition in London to resign his commission and go to Queensland. He arrived at Brisbane in the *Golden City* on 6 March 1863 and went straight to the bush: first on an exploration for pastoral purposes to Arthur Downs, west of St Lawrence, and thence with Arthur McKenzie and 1000 head of cattle to stock May Downs, near Yalton, where they were probably the first white men. Reduced by fever and privations to a shadow, he returned to Brisbane to recuperate. After further experience at Tieryboo on the Condamine, he was appointed in 1864 to manage Tambourine and later Maroon stations for the Bank of Australasia, and was thus led to the Albert River district south of Brisbane, where in 1865 he bought Tabragalba, the station near Beaudesert which became his lifelong home. He was one of the first in Queensland to inoculate stock for pleuro-pneumonia. Having brought Tabragalba into sound working order, he left in 1870 for Ireland, where on 16 November 1871 he married his cousin Mary Persse, daughter of William Blair, of Cappa, Kilrush, County Clare. In July 1872 they sailed for Queensland, and in the next decade he extended his pastoral interests, after journeys into territory where he was sometimes the first white man, by founding Palpararra and Connemara on Farrar's Creek, Tally-ho on the Mayne, Buckingham Downs on the Wills and Lake De Burgh. His new properties were stocked with cattle of his own breeding from Tabragalba. Having established these and then sold them to John Costello [q.v.] and others, he acquired four stations in the Burnett, of which Hawkwood passed with Tabragalba to his elder son Charles Dudley (1874-1959), and Eidsvold to his son-in-law Fitzpierce Joyce.

In April 1878 Persse was elected by a large majority for Fassifern to the Queensland Legislative Assembly. Albeit a squatter he was regarded by many as 'a liberal and a man for the people' and by himself as 'a thoroughly independent member, tied to no party' and determined 'to advocate and support any views which he considered would be for the general welfare of the colony'. For five years he constantly rode the fifty miles from Tabragalba to Brisbane and made more than 150 speeches on many subjects, especially pastoral ones, the extension of railways and the treatment of Aboriginals, whom he had lived amongst and knew well. His views were always vigorous, commonsensical and humane. He resigned in September 1883 and after two years at Castle Lambert in Galway and five in Queensland, he spent nearly three years at Moyode Castle where he acted as head of the family and followed tradition by being high sheriff of Galway in 1890 and master of the County Galway hounds, the Blazers, in 1889-91.

Apart from visits to Ireland in 1900-02 and 1914-15, he spent the remainder of his life in Queensland, where he was active in public life at Beaudesert and president of the Agricultural and Pastoral Society and of the Jockey Club, and in Brisbane president of the Queensland Club in 1899-1900. From 1886 he had been a director of the Royal Bank of Queensland and from 1899 of the Queensland Meat Export and Agency Co., of which he was chairman in 1915 when it was divided into the Queensland Meat Export Co. and the Australian Stock Breeders' Co., retaining this position in both companies until 1921. In Singapore he established the Cold Storage Co. in 1903; he was also chairman of the Raub Australian Gold Mining Co. In most of these interests he was succeeded by his younger son, De Burgh Bannatyne Bentinck (1881-1947), who in 1909 married Fanny, fourth daughter of the Persses' friend and near neighbour R. M. Collins [q.v.]. Two grandsons, Dudley (son of Charles) and Robert, married daughters of William Collins [q.v.].

Always an ardent sportsman, Persse helped to introduce hunting in Queensland, and was president and trustee of the Queensland Turf Club, importing blood horses from Ireland and having some success on the antipodean turf at the same time as his nephew Atty Persse was at the height of his fame as an owner-trainer in England. Tabragalba became a splendid property with a lovely homestead and garden, a mecca for visitors, to which he and his wife brought the best

of their Anglo-Irish background—wit, charm, kindness, hospitality and spaciousness as well as a magic of their own. In their later years they were surrounded by grandchildren, and their descendants have remained close to one another and their Irish and English kin. Persse refused a knighthood. Autocratic but kindly, disliking half-measures but generous of time, money and affection, he rejoiced to share his interests with others, especially the young; perhaps his best service to Australia was as an unconscious educator and transmitter of civilization. He died at Southport on 17 February 1921, leaving an Australian estate valued at £91,709. He was survived by his wife (d. 1923) and five children, whose marriages had all strengthened the family's ties with Queensland.

M. J. Fox (ed), *The history of Queensland*, 1 (Brisb, 1919); C. W. Hughes, *A tale of two companies* (Syd, c1968); PD (Qld), 1878-82; *Brisbane Courier*, 11 Apr 1878, 30 Aug 1883, 4 July 1903, 18 Feb 1921; *Queenslander*, 4 July 1903; *Pastoral Review*, 15 Aug 1907, 16 Mar 1921; family information.

MICHAEL D. DE B. COLLINS PERSSE

PETER, JOHN (1812-1878), pastoralist, was born near Glasgow, Scotland, son of a prosperous farmer. His father offered a farm and flour-mill to dissuade him from migrating, but Peter was determined. At 20, with £50 for the return fare in his pocket, he sailed from Liverpool in the *Mail*, arriving at Sydney on 3 December 1832. Introduced to Alexander McLeay [q.v.], Peter accepted his offer as manager of his station at £40 a year with 1 per cent on the value of the wool clip in the first year and an additional 1 per cent thereafter. Ten days later he found the station littered with the bones of sheep dead from scab and starvation. In 1836 a severe catarrh epidemic reduced the flocks of most local settlers but Peter lost only a fifth of his sheep by providing plentiful supplies of rock salt. He decided to move to the Murrumbidgee District where he knew salt bush was prolific.

At Camden on 10 February 1837 Peter contracted an auspicious marriage with a widow, Mary Bourke, a native of Campbelltown. J. Gormly [q.v.] described Mrs Bourke as 'a capable station manager and one of the most active women among stock I have known'. Her first husband had left her the run, Gumly Gumly, for which Peter took out a licence in 1837 in addition to a ten-mile frontage on the Murrumbidgee for himself. For twelve years he managed the Macleays' properties as well as his own. He increased the quantity and quality of their

U

stock, sometimes surviving only on savings, through droughts, the depreciation of colonial produce in the early 1840s, labour shortages and a severe epidemic of Cumberland disease. When he left the Macleays', they gave him a thousand select ewes.

In 1854 after the gold discoveries the value of fat sheep rose from 5s. to 30s. and cattle from 15s. to £8-£10. With his wife's help, Peter accumulated vast pastoral holdings in the Murrumbidgee and Lachlan Districts. In 1848 he was licensee of Cuba, Gumly Gumly, Ugoble and Sandy Creek; by 1859 he had 15 runs in 3 districts and by 1866 had 17 runs totalling over 740,000 acres including Bungerra, Banandra, Gumly Gumly and 9 runs comprising Tubbo estate. In the 1860s in Queensland J. Peter & Co. held Thalberg and Winterbourne in the Port Curtis District and with George Macleay, Arthur Onslow [qq.v.], Andrew Bonar and William Onslow held Carnarvon and Consuelo in the Leichhardt District. He also owned properties on the Culgoa River near Bourke and at Broadmeadows near Melbourne. Although he did little rough work he closely supervised the detailed running of his enormous transactions, keeping a light carriage and good horses to travel quickly around the stations. Known as 'Big Peter', he was reputed to be one of the most progressive pastoralists in the Murrumbidgee area.

Peter was active in local affairs and the growth of Wagga Wagga. He was influential in agitating for the establishment of a Court of Petty Sessions there in 1847 and became one of the most regular of the local magistrates. He was also treasurer of the board appointed to build the National school and contributed handsomely in funds and pupils from his outlying stations. As president of the 1856 committee which later provided a hospital, he also gave liberally to the Mechanics' Institute and the Presbyterian Church.

In 1845 Peter bought three £5 shares in the South Australian Burra copper-mine which yielded fifteen dividends of 200 per cent each for the next five years. By the late 1850s he had become the wealthiest resident squatter in New South Wales. Retaining his colonial interests, he retired to Britain in the early 1860s. He took a house in Piccadilly and another in Suffolk, dividing his time between them and Glasgow with visits to Europe interspersed with splendid shooting parties in the Highlands for his friends. One of these, Roger Therry [q.v.], found him markedly generous with 'shrewdness of judgement and a persevering spirit'.

Childless, Peter provided liberally for his friends, family and the education of his nieces and nephews; his reputed income by

1866 was £40,000 a year. He died on 28 January 1878 at Torquay, leaving substantial legacies to his family and the charities with which he had been associated in Wagga Wagga. His goods were sworn at £65,000. His wife died on 23 September 1884 aged 73.

R. Therry, *Reminiscences of thirty years' residence in New South Wales and Victoria*, 2nd ed (Lond, 1863); J. Gormly, *Exploration and settlement in Australia* (Syd, 1921); R. B. Ronald, *The Riverina: people and properties* (Melb, 1960); K. Swan, *A history of Wagga Wagga* (Wagga Wagga, 1970); J. J. Baylis, 'The Murrumbidgee and Wagga Wagga', *JRAHS*, 13 (1927); *Sydney Herald*, 3 Dec 1832; *Australian*, 17 July 1838, supp; *Town and Country J*, 6 Apr 1878; D. Denholm, Some aspects of squatting in New South Wales and Queensland, 1847-1864 (Ph.D. thesis, ANU, 1972); Macarthur papers (ML).

PETHERICK, EDWARD AUGUSTUS (1847-1917), bookseller, publisher, bibliographer and book collector, was born on 6 March 1847 at Burnham, Somerset, England, eldest of nine surviving children of Peter John Petherick, stationer, and his wife Ann, née Press. The family sailed from Bristol in the *Kyle* and arrived at Melbourne in March 1853 with 400 books. Edward could read at 5 and while working for his father attended Alfred Brunton's School at Fitzroy part-time until 1860. On 11 August 1862 he joined the bookselling and stationery firm of George Robertson [q.v.], who was impressed by Edward's precocious knowledge of books and enthusiastic application to his duties. In spare time he acted as secretary to the Sunday school at the Oxford Street Congregational Church, Collingwood, and its Penny Savings Bank and Young Men's Society.

In 1870 Robertson chose Petherick to reorganize the London office. He soon transformed the branch and remained manager till 1877 when the possibility of Robertson's retirement required him to return. When Robertson decided to continue as the firm's head Petherick returned to the London office. The next years were probably the most fruitful and satisfying for Petherick. In 1865 he had begun to collect titles for a catalogue or bibliography of Australia but put it aside in 1870. In 1878 he wrote: 'the business of the London department being well organised, I took up the work again; but finding I could do little without the books, I began to collect them—as they came within my grasp, and the savings of a limited salary'. In 1882 he won public recognition as a bibliographer by publishing the *Catalogue of The York Gate Geographical and*

Colonial Library. Its success prompted William Silver to enlarge his collection with help from Petherick whom he commissioned to prepare a second edition sub-titled 'An index to the Literature of Geography, Maritime and Inland Discovery, Commerce and Colonisation'; it was published by John Murray in 1886. Assisted by his brother Harold, Petherick had worked for four years on the book which won immediate and wide acclaim. When Silver died in 1905 Petherick arranged the sale of the York Gate Library to the South Australian branch of the Royal Geographical Society of Australasia. With tireless industry, inexhaustible energy and bachelor freedom, he became involved with many learned societies and corporate activities from the Royal Geographical, Hakluyt and Linnean Societies to the Royal Colonial Institute and the Library Association, becoming a life member of them all. He also wrote numerous reviews, letters and articles, many of which were never published.

When Robertson retired, Petherick set up business in 1887 as the Colonial Booksellers' Agency at 33 Paternoster Row with a capital of £800, the backing of a number of publishers and the assistance of Australian banks as distributing branches in Sydney, Melbourne and Adelaide. By 1894 he had immensely influenced the content of reading on Australia. He also entered publishing, issuing quarterly the Colonial Book Circular and Bibliographical Record (later the Torch) and in 1889 launched his Collection of Favourite and Approved Authors. On 1 March 1892 in Dorset he married a widow Mary Agatha Skeats, née Annear, and next year visited Australia in connexion with his business.

In 1894 Petherick went bankrupt with debts of about £50,000. His book stocks were sold to E. W. Cole [q.v.] of Melbourne and his Collection of Favourite and Approved Authors was taken over by George Bell & Sons. With his wife's help he met his difficulties and she and a number of friends succeeded in saving his own collection of Australiana. Broken by his business failure, he became a cataloguer with Francis Edwards & Co. in 1895-1908 and produced a series of outstanding catalogues of Australasian material. As means permitted he continued his collecting and devoted much effort to complete his 'Bibliography of Australia and Polynesia'; he prepared a printed prospectus of it in 1898 but was unable to arrange publication.

In 1894 Petherick had approached Edward Braddon and Duncan Gillies [q.v.] with an offer to present his collection to 'Federated Australia', he to be appointed librarian of the collection at a nominal salary. The offer

was considered in December 1895 at a meeting of Australian agents-general who asked the Imperial Institute to house the collection. Although the institute was unable to co-operate Petherick clung to the idea of presenting the collection to the Australian people. When the Commonwealth came into being in 1901 he wrote on 15 March to Prime Minister Barton proposing that the collection be added temporarily to 'the High Commissioner's Office' in London with himself as its custodian and buyer for the Federal Parliamentary Library. His approach was premature and no action resulted. In 1908 he and his wife took the collection to Australia and soon negotiated with the Federal Parliament. Its Library Committee on 27 May 1909 recommended acquisition of the collection 'in consideration of an annuity of £500 a year: Mr Petherick to render during the currency of the annuity such services in the Commonwealth Library as the Committee may from time to time prescribe'. An agreement between the Pethericks and the Commonwealth was signed on 4 November, and was confirmed by the Petherick Collection Act of 1911.

In 1909-17 Petherick tended his collection with growing frustration, compensated only by appointment as C.M.G. in 1916. Apart from the casual recognition which Australians made of his overseas achievements he found himself in complete antipathy to the Commonwealth librarian, Arthur Wadsworth, under whom he worked. This disharmony was increased by Petherick's belief that his experience and knowledge as the foremost authority in the world on Australiana were being ignored. In this situation his bibliography came no nearer publication, except for some sections in the Victorian Historical Magazine in 1911 and 1912. Its 100,000 entries remain in manuscript, available for consultation in the National Library. Predeceased by his wife on 10 May 1915, Petherick died disappointed in Melbourne on 17 September 1917.

PD (Cwlth), 1910; C. McDonald papers MS40 (NL); Petherick papers MS41, MS760 and letter files (NL); Petherick bibliog of Aust and Polynesia (NL).   C. A. BURMESTER

PETRIE, JOHN (1822-1892), contractor and mayor, was born on 15 January 1822 at Edinburgh, eldest son of Andrew Petrie [q.v.] and his wife Mary, née Cuthbertson. He arrived in Sydney with his family in 1831 and was educated at J. D. Lang's [q.v.] school. In 1837 he went to Moreton Bay, where his father had been appointed clerk of works, and accompanied him on explorations to the west and north of Brisbane; he also became a champion oarsman.

After 'apprenticeship' in the family building and contracting business John assumed increasing responsibility for its management after his father's blindness in 1848 forced him to retire. John became sole proprietor and the firm was changed from Petrie & Son to John Petrie. The enviable repute for fine workmanship under his father was sustained by John. His skill can still be seen in many buildings in Brisbane, but he lacked his father's drive and business acumen. In 1882 Petrie's son, Andrew Lang, became manager of the reconstructed firm, John Petrie & Son. The business was then centred on cabinet making and joinery, brick and tile making and monumental masonry. The firm went bankrupt in 1894 during the depression; it later revived but confined its operations to monumental masonry.

Although Petrie seems to have had little interest in politics, he was public-spirited and held many important offices. He topped the poll in Brisbane's first municipal election in 1859 and was mayor three times by 1862. He twice resigned from the council in protest against what he deemed the high-handedness of the majority faction, but continued after re-election to serve as an alderman until 1867. As mayor he had welcomed the first governor of Queensland, Sir George Bowen, to Brisbane in 1859. Practical experience and common sense fitted Petrie for laying the sound foundations of municipal administration in Brisbane and for guiding the council in providing public works and services. Closely associated with the Enoggera Creek scheme while it was planned by the council, he later saw it constructed as a member of the Board of Water Works; as its chairman in 1875 he was a leader in implementing the Gold Creek project and planning of the Mount Crosby scheme. After serving as mayor, he had difficulty in 'playing second fiddle' and was prone to indulge in such manoeuvres as walking out of council meetings.

Petrie devoted much time to community welfare. For years he served on the management committee of the Brisbane Hospital and was chairman after 1885. He was also a member of the Board for Administering Outdoor Relief and the Central Board of Health. Appointed to the New South Wales Commission of the Peace in 1859, he remained a member of the Brisbane bench until 1892. He gave long service on the Brisbane Licensing Board and was often returning officer for the parliamentary electorate of Brisbane. A trustee of the Brisbane general cemetery and of Bowen Park and a ranger for protecting native birds on the Enoggera Water Reserve, he was a director of several building societies

and of the Queensland Steam Navigation Co. Elected to the North Brisbane School of Arts Committee in 1864 and 1866, he was also an enthusiastic member of the first Masonic lodge in Queensland.

In 1850 Petrie had married Jane Keith, daughter of Daniel McNaught of Dunbarton, Scotland, who became foreman of the Petrie building and contracting business after migrating to Brisbane. Of their five sons and five daughters, Andrew Lang was the eldest son and heir to the family business; he represented Toombul in the Legislative Assembly in 1893 and, apart from his insolvency in 1894, held the seat until 1926. John Petrie died on 8 December 1892. A staunch Presbyterian, he was an elder and worked with enthusiasm for building St Paul's Church. Integrity and long association with the city made him one of the best known citizens of Brisbane.

Portraits are in the Brisbane City Council and the Oxley Library.

W. F. Morrison, *The Aldine history of Queensland*, 2 (Syd, 1888); C. C. Petrie (ed), *Tom Petrie's reminiscences of early Queensland*, 1st ed (Brisb, 1904); G. Greenwood and J. Laverty, *Brisbane 1859-1959* (Brisb, 1959); J. Whiteley, Two families of early Brisbane (B.A. Hons thesis, Univ Qld, 1963); Municipal Council minutes, 1859-67 (Town Hall, Brisb).

JOHN LAVERTY

PETRIE, THOMAS (1831-1910), explorer, grazier and friend of Aboriginals, was born on 31 January 1831 in Edinburgh, third son of Andrew Petrie and brother of John [qq.v.]. He arrived with his parents at Sydney in the *Stirling Castle* in March 1831 and moved with them to Moreton Bay in 1837. Educated by a convict clerk, he was allowed to mix freely with Aboriginal children. He learnt to speak the Brisbane tribal dialect (Turrabul) and was encouraged to share in all their activities. At 14 he was taken on the triennial walkabout to the feast at the Bunya Range. Accepted by the Aboriginals as a friend, he was in constant demand as a messenger or companion for exploration expeditions. During journeys with his father he gathered a knowledge of surveying and bushcraft and an intimate acquaintance with the Brisbane district and its settlers.

In 1851 Petrie spent six months trying his luck on the Turon goldfields and for five years worked on various fields mainly in Victoria, 'finding only enough gold to make a ring'. After returning to Brisbane, in 1859 he married Elizabeth, daughter of James Campbell, hardware merchant. In the Pine Creek district on the Whiteside run he bought ten square miles which he called Murrumba (Good Place). Despite the fears of other white men he was helped by friendly Aboriginals to clear his land and construct his first buildings. He continued to explore widely, his main aim being the search for new timber areas and places for further settlement along the coast. In 1862 he was the first white man to climb Buderim Mountain, where he explored a stream that became known as Petrie's Creek. He marked a road from Cleveland to Eight Miles Plain so that his squatter friends could transport their wool. In 1868 he organized an Aboriginal welcome for the duke of Edinburgh.

When the Douglas [q.v.] ministry opened Queensland's first Aboriginal reserve on Bribie Island in 1877, Petrie became its chief adviser and overseer. The experiment was terminated next year by Palmer [q.v.] largely because Petrie's report on Aboriginal attitudes and activities was not encouraging. He played little part in politics but was a foundation member of both the Caboolture and Redcliffe divisional boards and for years returning officer for Moreton electorate.

Petrie died at Murrumba on 26 August 1910, survived by his wife who died aged 90 on 30 September 1926 and by two sons and five daughters of their nine children. Though Murrumba had been reduced to 3000 acres the family kept the property until 1952. In 1910 the name of the North Pine district was changed to Petrie in his honour and next year a free-stone monument was erected in the township and unveiled by Sir William MacGregor.

W. F. Morrison, *The Aldine history of Queensland*, 2 (Syd, 1888); C. C. Petrie (ed), *Tom Petrie's reminiscences of early Queensland*, 1st ed (Brisb, 1904); E. Foreman, *The history and adventures of a Queensland pioneer* (Brisb, 1928); T. Welsby, *Bribie, the basket maker* (Brisb, 1937); J. Whiteley, Two families of early Brisbane (B.A. Hons thesis, Univ Qld, 1963); N. C. Stewart, A history of the Pine Rivers Shire (B.A. Hons thesis, Univ Qld, 1970).   NOELINE HALL

PETTERD, WILLIAM FREDERICK (1849-1910), scientist and boot importer, was born on 13 July 1849 at Hobart Town, son of William Frederick Petterd, poulterer, and his wife Sarah, née Andrew. He early showed an ardent interest in natural history and as a boy he was asked so often to identify specimens of conchology and entomology that he decided to make collection his profession. By 1870 his ability as a collecting naturalist was widely recognized. In 1873 he joined a scientific exploration to collect geological specimens in the Solomon Islands and in 1875 the *Chevert* expedition fitted out by W. J. Macleay [q.v.] to New

Guinea. As a competent taxidermist he contributed many specimens to Macleay's collection. When the *Chevert* returned to Somerset Petterd was sick with fever and rheumatism, but he decided to join the party led by Octavius Stone, F.R.G.S., in an attempt to cross the peninsula of New Guinea from Port Moresby. Petterd found specimens of coleoptera and lepidoptera he had never seen before. The party returned to Cape York on 2 February 1876.

Petterd went to Hobart and worked in a boot shop. On 22 September 1877 according to the rites of the United Methodist Free Churches he married Harriet Rule. In 1880 they moved to Launceston and he opened his own boot and shoe business in Brisbane Street. He also started a rose garden and continued his horticultural experiments and other collections. He was elected a member of the Royal Society of Tasmania on 12 July 1881 after reading to the society his 'Monograph on the Land Shells of Tasmania' in November 1878 and additions in March 1879. With E. J. Higgins, he prepared papers for the society on a new cave-inhabiting spider (1881), three new helices from Australia (1882) and many other shells in the 1880s. In the next decade he turned to the study of geology, on which he published over a dozen papers, most of them with W. H. Twelvetrees who named Petterdite, a new kind of oxychloride of lead. After 1900 he returned to conchology but continued to write on minerals. Altogether he published over fifty papers and was elected a fellow of the Linnean Society of New South Wales and a corresponding member of the Zoological Society of London. In 1902 he was a vice-president of the geology and mineral section of the Hobart meeting of the Australasian Association for the Advancement of Science. He was then chairman of several mining companies and managing director of the Magnet Silver Mining Co.

Petterd had a first-rate laboratory at his home and an excellent library. Despite a retiring disposition he was a member of the Oddfellows Lodge for over thirty years. He had a huge circle of scientific friends and in conversation was intelligent and witty. An enthusiastic promoter of horticultural competitions, he did much to beautify gardens in Launceston. Meanwhile he continued to prosper as an importer of boots and shoes. Predeceased by his first wife, he died suddenly from heart failure at his home in Frankland Street, Launceston on 15 April 1910 and was given a large funeral. He was survived by his second wife Lucy, née Manning, whom he had married on 1 October 1890 at Launceston with Primitive Methodist rites. He left an estate of £11,542 bequeathing £400 to the two sons and two daughters of his first marriage, and the remainder to his wife and her two daughters. In 1893 he had revised his *Census of Tasmanian Shells*, and early in 1910 finished the revision of his *Catalogue of the Minerals of Tasmania*; listing some 20,000 species it was published after he died. His mineral collection, valued at £1212, was placed in charge of the Royal Society of Tasmania on loan for 999 years.

O. C. Stone, *A few months in New Guinea* (Lond, 1880); Roy Soc Tas, *Papers*, 1910; Linnean Soc NSW, *Procs*, 36 (1911); *Age* (Brisb), 3 Mar 1876; *Mercury*, 16 Apr 1910; *Examiner* (Launceston), 16 Apr 1910.

PHILLIPS, SAMUEL POLE (1819-1901), 'Squire' pastoralist, was born on 11 March 1819 at Culham, Oxfordshire, England, youngest son of John Phillips and his wife Anne Francis, née Shawe. Though educated for the Anglican ministry at Winchester College, he migrated in the *Montreal* to Western Australia, arriving in 1839. With Edward Hamersley, a relation by marriage, he bought land in the Toodyay Valley where he built his homestead, Culham.

Phillips was a director for the Toodyay District on the Western Australian Roads Trust in 1840-42 and 1847. Appointed a district magistrate in 1840 and a justice of the peace in 1855, he served for many years. In 1847 he married Sophia (1829-1902), eldest daughter of J. S. Roe [q.v.]; she was the first child born to any of the official party after the *Parmelia* arrived in 1829. Roe commemorated his son-in-law in Phillips River and Culham Inlet on his southern exploration in 1848-49.

Like most others Phillips faced ruin in the depressed years and talked of leaving the colony but when convicts arrived in 1850 his fortunes soon recovered. Hamersley & Co. with Lockier Burges as working partner, took up a vast cattle run on the Irwin River and next year overlanded cattle there. Phillips periodically visited the station but devoted most of his time to horse-breeding on his Toodyay runs. He was a founder of the Western Australian Turf Club in 1852 and the Newcastle Race Club in 1865. In his English drag and four fine horses he followed every race meeting and was noted for skilful driving and fearless riding. While on a visit to Adelaide in 1865 he was presented with a silver jug from the citizens and a silver medal from the Humane Society for riding into stormy seas to rescue drowning men from the immigrant ship *Electric*.

St Phillips's Church at Culham, opened on 19 July 1857, was begun in 1849 after a visit by his brother-in-law, Bishop Short

[q.v.], but work was suspended when the Phillipses visited England in 1853-55. They returned with two family friends and three thoroughbred stallions. The three men became partners in breeding horses for the lucrative India market. Phillips's already large pastoral leases north of Culham were extended beyond Bolgart Springs for several miles. The partnership broke up in 1858, and in the depressed 1870s Phillips had to relinquish many of his Toodyay pastoral leases.

Phillips led a very active public life. In 1857-72 he was a nominee in the Legislative Council. He was then elected to the Toodyay Roads Board in 1872-78 and 1881-83, mostly serving as chairman. He boasted that the roads from Perth to Culham were the best in the colony, but his high-handed methods lost him his seat. For short periods in 1876, 1878 and 1880 he acted as resident magistrate for the Toodyay District. Long accustomed to undisputed rule on the bench, he met his match in Octavius Burt, resident magistrate in 1880-84, and Phillips was obliged to apologize for his rudeness and offensive behaviour. He then retired from public life.

About 1880 his eldest son Samuel James (1855-1920) took over the management of his father's share of the company's property on the Irwin River. In 1883 he was elected to the Irwin Roads Board and sometimes chairman. In 1885 he was appointed a justice of the peace and represented Irwin in the Legislative Assembly in 1890-1904. In 1891 he had planned the town of Mingenew, the only privately surveyed townsite in the colony, when the Midland railway was built across his land. He died unmarried on 20 June 1920. The second son John Hugh (1860-1917) married Laura Lukin in 1881 and managed his father's properties in the Toodyay Valley.

Culham was always conducted in the best English county tradition and the 'Squire' continued to dominate the valley until he died on 13 June 1901. Over six feet tall and bearded to his chest, he had an imposing appearance. His abrupt manner and quick temper were offset by fondness for children, practical joking and generous hospitality. His hunts for kangaroo and wild cattle were featured in the *Illustrated London News* (1857). For years house parties were held in Toodyay Fair week, and at Easter in the 1890s a special train from Perth brought cricketers and supporters to the Culham cricket match and race meeting. In pampered old age, beset by gout, he was wheeled round Culham in a bathchair and sometimes driven in a low dogcart with his wife to call on neighbours. These he regarded as his tenants and they humoured him by springing to attention and pulling forelocks, an English custom scorned by the young folk but treasured by their elders. Despite his faults they recognized him as 'a gentleman born'.

Phillips, his wife and several of their nine children were buried at St Phillips's. Culham is still held by descendants, and incorporated in a wing of the old homestead is the original stone building in which the 'Squire' first lived.

J. T. Reilly, *Reminiscences of fifty years' residence in Western Australia* (Perth, 1903); A. T. Thomas, *History of Toodyay* (Perth, 1949); F. W. Gunning, *Lure of the north* (Perth, 1952); P. U. Henn (ed), *Wollaston's Albany journals* (Perth, 1954); R. Stephens, 'Mingenew story', *JRWAHS*, 5 (1959), pt 5; R Erickson, 'Early days at Bolgart', *JRWAHS*, 6 (1964), pt 3; *Northam Advertiser*, 13 June 1901; *Newcastle Herald* (WA), 11 Oct 1902; Sophia Phillips diary (ML); Toodyay records and Toodyay Roads Board minute books (Battye Lib, Perth).

RICA ERICKSON

PIDDINGTON, WILLIAM RICHMAN (1815-1887), bookseller and politician, was born in London, brought up in the book trade and worked in Edgely's Book Shop, Bond Street. In 1838 he migrated to New South Wales and farmed for a time on the Hunter. He returned to Sydney and in February 1848 joined W. A. Colman, bookseller of George Street. When the partnership was wound up after Colman's death fourteen months later, Piddington narrowly avoided bankruptcy and set up on his own. In 1853 he published *The Bushranger: A Play, and Other Poems* by Charles Harpur [q.v.].

Nurtured in the English radical politics of Joseph Hume, Piddington soon became active in public affairs. In June 1849 he had protested against the landing of convicts from the *Hashemy* and became a member of the council of the Anti-transportation League. He attacked proposals to introduce the British authors' bill (1850) which he feared would 'legalise the sale of piratic editions of British authors'. In 1851 he was elected to the Sydney City Council but soon found the council unworkable and resigned. Secretary of the New South Wales Constitution Committee, he regarded W. C. Wentworth's [q.v.] constitution bill as 'villainous', urged that it be 'burnt by the hand of the common hangman' and described his speeches as the 'ravings of a monomaniac'.

On the introduction of responsible government in 1856 Piddington campaigned for constitutional reform, the development of a rural railway system and the extension of local government but opposed the sale of land by auction and placing any further financial burden on the colony. He won the seat of Northumberland and Hunter and held it in the 1858 elections. He opposed the extension of the franchise to all adult males which he said would lead to 'a rabid and unbridled democracy'. He represented the Hawkesbury in 1859-77 and in 1859-60 was chairman of committees and later served on various standing and select committees. A friend of Henry Parkes [q.v.] Piddington wrote to him in 1862 that the current parliament was 'by far the worst House we have ever had—the most corrupt—the most lazy & useless'. He helped Parkes financially and 'played a good game at romps' with his children.

In the 1860s Piddington supported James Martin [q.v.], but although described by David Buchanan [q.v.] as 'a little, squat, burly piece of pompous vulgarity' who 'abandoned all his political opinions and turned Tory', he supported such liberal measures as Parkes's 1866 Education Act, opposed state aid for public worship as 'contrary to the spirit of Christianity' and contributed to the rebuilding of St Mary's Cathedral. A constant critic of successive colonial treasurers, he was apt 'in picking out discrepancies'. Fluent and agile in debate, he made effective use of quotations and irony. In 1867 and 1871 he was taunted with securing 'the exemption from duty of the imported printed books and periodicals in which he dealt'. In 1870 he refused to serve under the Martin-Robertson [q.v.] coalition as Martin would not agree to strong measures of retrenchment in the civil service. In May 1872 he became colonial treasurer under Parkes but his health broke down and he resigned office on 2 December. He was again treasurer in Parkes's short-lived 1877 ministry and lost his seat in the October elections. On 7 October 1879 he was appointed to the Legislative Council on Parkes's recommendation and was chairman of committees in 1885-87.

In 1850 Piddington had become a subscriber to the Australian Subscription Library and in 1865 served on its committee of management. He was a director of the Australasian Steam Navigation Co. and the Bank of New South Wales and a trustee of the Savings Bank of New South Wales. He remained a friend of Parkes and sent him the signature of Louis XIV. In the 1880s Piddington built a house at Mount Victoria. Unmarried he died on 25 November 1887 from obstruction of his bowels, a complaint he had suffered for thirty-eight years. He was buried in the Anglican section of Rookwood cemetery and his estate was valued for probate at over £12,000.

D. Buchanan, *Political portraits of some of the members of the parliament of New South Wales* (Syd, 1863); P. Loveday and A. W. Martin, *Parliament factions and parties* (Melb, 1966); P. Loveday, ' "Democracy" in New South Wales', *JRAHS*, 42 (1956-57), pt 4; *SMH*, 24 Feb 1848, 6 Apr 1849, 17, 21, 26, 27 Aug, 17 Sept 1850, 4, 11, 16, 18 Aug, 6 Sept 1853, 31 Jan, 27 Mar, 21 Apr, 29 Nov 1865, 17 Mar, 5 Dec 1866, 30 Sept 1867, 16, 18 Jan, 10 Feb, 27 Sept, 30 Nov 1869, 20 Feb 1871, 24 Jan, 3 Nov 1877, 26 Nov, 1 Dec 1887; *Empire* (Syd), 17 May 1856; *Town and Country J*, 15 June 1872; *Illustrated Sydney News*, 27 June 1874; Aust Subscription Lib, Procs of general meetings 1845-71 and minute books (ML); Parkes letters (ML); CO 201/569, 583, 584.

D. I. McDONALD

PIGDON, JOHN (1832-1903), building contractor and businessman, was born on 3 July 1832 at Linghissley, Northumberland, England, only son of James Pigdon and his wife Margaret, née Thompson. For more than six years he was apprenticed to a joiner in Newcastle upon Tyne. He migrated in the *Ottillia*, arriving at Melbourne on 10 October 1852. He soon established a building and contracting business. In 1857 he bought land at the first sale in the Carlton area; it became the site of a business that reached a pinnacle of excellence in the late 1880s. His notable buildings include St Jude's Church of England, Carlton (1866-70), the Registrar-General's Offices, Queen Street, Melbourne (1874-77), the Public Offices, Bendigo (first stage 1884-87) and the Roman Doric west façade of Parliament House, Melbourne (1885-92).

Pigdon's involvement in company affairs arose directly from his business: he was a founding director in 1874 and sometime chairman of the Melbourne Builders' Lime and Cement Co. Pty Ltd; chairman in 1899-1903 of Hoffman Patent Steam Brick Co. Pty Ltd; and first chairman in 1896-1903 of the Co-operative Brick Co. Pty Ltd, formed to rationalize production, and sale of bricks and related building materials manufactured by member companies.

Pigdon began his civic career in 1869 when he was persuaded to stand for Smith Ward of the Melbourne City Council. He won by over 100 votes and represented the ward until 1903, serving as an alderman from 1895. He was a member of its Public Works Committee and the chairman from 1898. On 9 November 1877 he became mayor for a year. In that office he presided at the opening of Queen Victoria Market early in the morning on 20 March 1878 and then entertained the market gardeners at breakfast; on 9 May he laid the foundation stone of the Eastern Market with the 'usual formalities', followed by *déjeuner* at the Council Chambers where 'many speeches were made, but politics were carefully eschewed'. He was appointed a commissioner for both the Sydney and Melbourne International Exhibitions held in 1879-80 and in 1880-81. Other public offices he held until 1903 were territorial magistrate (later justice of the peace) from 1874, trustee of Royal Park from 1881, commissioner of the Melbourne and Metropolitan Board of Works from 1891 and of the Melbourne Harbor Trust from 1898. In 1883 he contested the East Bourke Boroughs seat in the Legislative Assembly but lost to C. H. Pearson [q.v.]; in 1892 he stood for Carlton against F. H. Bromley and J. Gardiner on the platform 'against one man one vote' but Bromley won the seat. Pigdon Street, North Carlton, was named in his honour in 1885.

In 1857 Pigdon married Jane, born on 11 October 1835, daughter of John Clelland, superintendent of police, Wigtownshire, Scotland. She died on 11 July 1891; they had four sons and six daughters. Their second daughter Annie Isabel married George, fourth son of James Munro [q.v.]. Pigdon died suddenly on 24 October 1903 while on a visit to Bendigo; he was survived by three sons and five daughters. He held extensive land in Carlton and near-by suburbs from which all his children benefited. An Anglican, he was a churchwarden at St Jude's, Carlton, for thirty years from 1873 and a generous pew-holder; he contributed a stained glass window in memory of his wife.

H. M. Humphreys (ed), *Men of the time in Australia: Victorian series*, 1st ed (Melb, 1878); J. Smith (ed), *Cyclopedia of Victoria*, 1 (Melb, 1903); *Argus*, 19, 21 Mar, 10 May 1878, 9, 23 Feb 1883, 21 Apr, 28 May 1892, 26, 27 Oct 1903; Co-operative Brick Co. Pty Ltd papers, Hoffman Brick & Potteries Pty Ltd papers, Melbourne Builders' Lime and Cement Co. Pty Ltd papers (Univ Melb Archives); records (St Jude's Church, Carlton). JULIE MARGINSON

PIGUENIT, WILLIAM CHARLES (1836-1914), artist, was born on 27 August 1836 at Hobart Town and baptized on 23 September at St David's Church, eldest son of Frederick Le Geyt Piguenit (d. 1886), of Huguenot stock, and his wife Mary Ann, née Igglesden. For receiving government stores his father had been sentenced to transportation for fourteen years and arrived at Hobart in the *Royal George* on 8 October 1830. Mary Ann, a girl of good family, followed him and after they were married on 18 February 1833 she ran a school for young ladies. In 1836 Frederick was a clerk in the Convict Department and in 1842 received a free pardon.

Educated at Cambridge House Academy, William Charles received some lessons from Frank Dunnett, a Scottish painter, and was commended for his superior drawing, mapping and penmanship. On 24 September 1850 he was appointed a draftsman in the Survey Office. In 1867 he published six lithographic plates in *The Salmon Ponds and Vicinity, New Norfolk* (reprinted in the *Transactions* of the Australasian Association for the Advancement of Science, Hobart, 1892). In 1872 he resigned from the Survey Office to devote himself to landscape painting and in 1874 travelled on foot with J. R. Scott [q.v.] and R. M. Johnston to the Gordon River and painted the Arthur Range, Lake Pedder and Hell's Gates, but his paintings sold slowly until 1887 when J. W. Agnew [q.v.] persuaded the government to buy six of his works on the western highlands, now in the Hobart Art Gallery.

In 1875 Piguenit had moved to Sydney and contributed to exhibitions at the New South Wales Academy of Arts and held a one-man exhibition. In September he joined a group of artists at Grose Valley near Hartley Vale, where he had 'the first opportunity of illustrating our mountain scenery from the points where it can be studied to the best advantage, from the bottom of the gorges instead of the summit of the ranges'. In 1880 he settled at Lane Cove. An enthusiastic explorer, he travelled widely looking for natural scenery. He visited the Clarence River and the south coast of New South Wales and among other excursions went with James Sprent's [q.v.] party to the Tasmanian west coast and Lake St Clair in 1887.

In 1898 and 1900 Piguenit visited Europe and his work was included in the exhibition of Australian Art at the Grafton Galleries in London and the Paris Salon. In 1902 the New South Wales government commissioned him to paint Mount Kosciusko for £175 and £25 expenses. Unassuming and retiring, he shrank from controversy and quietly resigned from the Art Society of New South Wales when it split over the impressionist movement. The first Australian-born artist of note, he delighted in mountain scenery and often chose dramatic subjects for his painting. In 1901 one of his finest canvases, 'Thunderstorm on the Darling' won the Wynne prize, Sydney; he also won several gold medals for his careful and sensitive observation of nature.

Ten days after an appendix operation Piguenit died on 17 July 1914 at Hunter's Hill unmarried and was buried in the Field of Mars cemetery.

Bernard Smith, *Australian painting 1788-1960* (Melb, 1962); C. H. Currey, *Mount Wilson* (Syd, 1968); V&P (HA Tas), 1874 (54); *Colonial Times*, 21 Dec 1849; *Bulletin*, 21 May 1881; W. V. Legge, 'An appreciation of a Tasmanian artist', *Illustrated Tas Mail*, 6 May 1915; GO 1/34 /183, 1/76/240, 33/20/761.

PILLINGER, ALFRED THOMAS (1839-1899), landowner and politician, was born at Antill Ponds, near Oatlands, Van Diemen's Land, son of James Pillinger and his wife Sophia, née Peters. His father was born on Norfolk Island in 1806; the family went to Van Diemen's Land in 1808; he worked for William Kimberley who had taken up much land and ran a large herd of wild cattle in the unsettled areas. By 1830 James was overseer at Salt Pan Plains for Kimberley whose recommendation of Pillinger as 'sober, honest and industrious' won him a free grant of 320 acres near Oatlands. Pillinger then had 400 sheep, 30 cattle, 4 working bullocks and a mare. In 1831 he bought 500 adjoining acres and with help from Thomas Anstey [q.v.] was appointed poundkeeper at Kitty's Rivulet. In 1836 James was appointed division constable at Oatlands. He was married at St David's, Hobart Town, on 7 September.

Alfred was educated at private schools and Horton College in Ross and became enthusiastic for astronomy. He then worked for his father and soon won repute as an expert in farming and husbandry. With headquarters at his father's property, Millbrook, near Tunbridge, he acquired various other holdings totalling 15,000 acres and stocked them with cattle and merino sheep. Worried by the drain of young Tasmanians to the mainland, he told the select committee on immigration in 1865 that the island had at least a million unsettled acres fit for cultivation where newcomers could start with only £50 if they clubbed with neighbours for acquiring bullocks and equipment. To set an example, he continued to lease crown lands and redeem them from their wild state by fencing, building and road-making at his own cost. However, the 1872 Waste Lands Act limited these activities despite his petition to parliament.

Pillinger became a coroner and a territorial magistrate. Attracted by public affairs, he was elected a councillor of the Oatlands Municipality and became its warden in 1874. He resigned in 1876 when elected for Oatlands to the House of Assembly on 17 July. He was minister for land and works under

445

v

P. O. Fysh from October 1888 to August 1892 and under Sir Edward Braddon from April 1894 to May 1899. He travelled widely in Tasmania and acquired exceptional understanding of parliamentary practices and local government. Although no orator, he won the respect of all parties for his shrewd judgment, sincerity and good temper. He was generous in creating jobs for those out of work and supporting those in distress, especially old people. In his own electorate he advocated conservation at Lake Crescent to provide irrigation for the lowlands and prevent flooding.

Pillinger died in Hobart on 6 May 1899 and was survived by his wife Georgina, née Nichols, whom he had married on 15 April 1886 at Castra near Ulverstone, and by one son and three daughters. His public funeral was the largest until then in Hobart. Flags were flown at half-mast in the city and the crowded service in St David's Cathedral was conducted by an Anglican clergyman. At the graveside in Cornelian Bay cemetery a Wesleyan minister gave an address since Pillinger was reared and died as a Methodist.

Cyclopedia of Tasmania, 1 (Hob, 1900); A. McKay (ed), *Journals of the land commissioners for Van Diemen's Land, 1826-28* (Hob, 1962); V&P (HA Tas), 1865 (61), 1878 (70, 94), 1888-89 (124); *Examiner* (Launceston), 8 May 1899; *Mercury*, 8 May 1899.

PITMAN, JACOB (1810-1890), builder and architect, was born on 28 November 1810 at Trowbridge, Wiltshire, England, eldest son of Samuel Pitman, clothier, and his wife Maria, née Davis; a younger brother became Sir Isaac, the inventor of phonography. Jacob was apprenticed for seven years to a local builder and then worked in London for a building firm. After four months in the London training school of the British and Foreign Bible Society, he taught for a time at North Nibley, Gloucestershire, where on 31 December 1833 he married Emma Hooper.

Jacob applied for free passages to South Australia in November 1837 and sailed with his wife and two infants in the *Trusty*. On arrival at Holdfast Bay in May 1838 Pitman soon put his skills to use and found early prosperity. He wrote to his parents: 'I toil no harder than at Nibley and am 10 times better paid'. Established as a builder and architect in Rundle Street East, he could afford much investment in suburban and rural land. When depression hit the province in 1840 he stopped building and began to surrender his leased acres. With debts of £268 he was declared insolvent in October 1843. His discharge certificate was issued in March 1846 and by the 1850s he was busy building or supervising the construction of several bridges across the Torrens and the span across the Onkaparinga at Echunga.

Outside the building trade Pitman's achievements were to last longer. In the *Trusty* he had befriended William Holden who became a notable journalist in the colony and shared with him a deep commitment to religion. Pitman founded the first society of the New (Swedenborgian) Church in the southern hemisphere in Adelaide on 7 July 1844 and officiated as the society's minister until 1859. He was also responsible for introducing the 'stenographic soundhand' system of his brother Isaac into South Australia. In the *Trusty* James had brought the first hundred copies of his brother's first manual of 'phonography' (called shorthand from 1841) which he circulated among the colony's leaders. He continued his interest in this system and began teaching it in Adelaide in 1846 and later in Victoria and New South Wales. He claimed to have 'sown the first seed of phonography in the Australian colonies'. His friend Holden had shared his deep attachment to the New Church and was one of the first journalists to use phonography.

Pitman left South Australia about 1870 but returned briefly to become superintendent of public works at Mount Gambier. His wife died in Adelaide on 4 June 1881. At the New Church, Melbourne, on 1 January 1883 he married Catherine Mary Yates, widow of Paul Hayden. Pitman died in Camperdown, New South Wales, on 12 March 1890, survived by his second wife and by five of the nine children of his first marriage. He was buried in Rookwood cemetery, where above his grave is an epitaph in Isaac Pitman's reformed spelling, describing Jacob as an 'arkitekt' who 'introduist fonetik shorthand'.

A. Baker, *The life of Isaac Pitman* (Lond, 1919); D. Packham (ed), *The Australians of a branch of the Pitman family* (Lond, 1954); D. Pike, *Paradise of Dissent* (Melb, 1957); PP (LC SA), 1855-56 (21); *Observer* (Adel), 11 June 1859, 15, 22 Mar 1890; *Register* (Adel), 12, 16 Oct 1897; SMH, 20 June 1882; P. J. Jones, The history of commercial education in South Australia (M.A. thesis, Univ Adel, 1967); Pitman letters (held by Sir Isaac Pitman Pty Ltd, Carlton, Vic).   BRUCE MUIRDEN

PITT, GEORGE MATCHAM (1814-1896), stock and station agent, was born on 16 February 1814 at Richmond, New South Wales, son of Thomas Matcham Pitt (d. 1821), farmer and Hawkesbury pioneer, and his wife Eliza, née Laycock. He was a grandson of Mary Pitt, née Matcham, a connexion of Lord Nelson, who had arrived in December 1801 as a free settler in the *Canada* and received a 100-acre land grant at Mulgrave Place, Richmond, on 1 March 1802. Her daughters Susannah and Esther married William Faithful and James Wilshire [qq.v.]. Pitt was one of the first white men to explore the new country in the Gwydir District and in 1848 held the 72,000-acre Coorar station where he lived. In the 1850s he held Lower Gerawhey in the Wellington District and in the 1860s held five runs with Thomas Sullivan at Moree and later on the lower Macquarie.

In the early 1860s Pitt established a stock and station agency business with Sullivan; in 1870 it became G. M. Pitt & Son and in 1879 Pitt, Son & Badgery when Henry Septimus Badgery [q.v.] was admitted to partnership. In June 1888 a limited company with authorized capital of £100,000 was formed to acquire the firm's business for £40,000 and Pitt was chairman of the new company under the same style until 1896. At first Pitt had sold stock in private saleyards on the Western Road beyond Parramatta and at Homebush, Petersham and Annandale, but in February 1878 he told a Legislative Assembly committee that public yards, preferably at Homebush, were desirable to protect both the trade and the public. He also strongly opposed the country killing of meat for the Sydney market.

Pitt lived at Fairlight, Manly, for a time and later at North Sydney; he became an alderman of East St Leonards in 1878 and was mayor in 1879-83. Interested in politics, he often wrote short letters to the press on current issues. He was of the hardy stock of pioneers, with a breezy and genial disposition and reputedly 'a voice like thunder'. Largely self-educated, he had a good memory and read widely: Burns and Shakespeare were his favourite authors and he had the habit of clinching his arguments with apt quotations, especially from Burns. He was popular, generous to the poor, and in 1885 donated £100 to the Patriotic Fund for the Sudan contingent. He served on the council of the Agricultural Society of New South Wales.

Pitt died of chronic Bright's disease at his residence Holbrook, Carabella Street, North Sydney, on 12 October 1896 and was buried in St Peter's Church of England cemetery, Richmond. Probate of his estate was sworn at under £11,832. At Windsor on 22 September 1835 he had married Julia Johnson (1815-1886); of their nine sons and three daughters, six sons and a daughter survived him. A daughter, Julia Eliza, had married his partner H. S. Badgery in 1869.

V&P (LA NSW), 1877-78, 2, 849-852; SMH, 13, 14 Oct 1896; Town and Country J, 17 Oct 1896; MS cat under Pitt (ML).

G. P. WALSH

PLANT, EDMUND HARRIS THORNBURGH (1844-1926), mine-owner and politician, was born on 10 December 1844 at Nottingham, England, third son of C. Fredrick Plante, lace-thread manufacturer, and his wife Maria, née Nevill. The boys received a grammar-school education, but their father went bankrupt and at 12 Edmund left for America.

In 1861 Plant arrived penniless in Queensland, where he began work as a shepherd and at various station occupations before turning to gold prospecting at Peak Downs, then near Rockhampton (but finding no gold on Mount Morgan) and at Ravenswood. He and Thomas Jackson built Ravenswood's second crushing battery, and he thought of venturing on the Etheridge, but finally erected a mill instead at Charters Towers, where he had been one of the first to join the 1872 rush. He acquired interests in several gold mines there and on the Palmer, and in copper, tin and wolfram on other northern fields. He also bought cattle stations and a sugar land near Ingham, but his main centre was Charters Towers, where he and his brother became prominent businessmen, public and social figures.

A self-taught engineer and member of the Australian Institution of Mining Engineers, Plant initiated the system of treating pyrites tailings that helped to establish the field's prosperity, and is said to have been the first to install electricity there. Gaining great wealth, he became chairman of four mining companies and a member of several other directorates, as well as of such public bodies as the Chamber of Commerce and the Hospital Board, a founder and chairman of the Water Board, chairman of the Dalrymple Divisional Board for ten years, and a member of the Townsville Harbour Board. He also joined the London Chamber of Commerce, the Royal Colonial Institute and the London Art Society on a two-year visit to London in 1888. In July 1905 he was appointed to the Queensland Legislative Council, where he watched the interests of the north. As Charters Towers gold began to cut out, he helped to secure government aid for deep-testing with diamond drills; but the field was on the decline and with it his own fortunes, as 'game to the finish', he tried to stave off the inevitable, considering it his duty to put money back into the industry that had made him wealthy. Eventually his magnificent home Thornburgh, for long a centre of social life, was sold as a school, and he retired to his Ingham property and finally to Sandgate, where he died on 28 April 1926. He was survived by six children of his marriage in 1872 to Elizabeth Esther, sister of F. C. Hodel, Townsville's first building contractor.

Plant was a keen supporter of the National Party, but with quiet determination rather than heat or aggressiveness. In business he was a heavy, knowledgeable investor of much influence; in personality described as quiet, unassuming, rather solitary, he was a good listener, completely honest and well trusted, a loyal friend and without enemies, in success unostentatious, modest, tolerant and generous, and in adversity quiet and undismayed.

W. F. Morrison, *The Aldine history of Queensland*, 2 (Syd, 1888); M. J. Fox (ed), *The history of Queensland*, 3 (Brisb, 1923); G. C. Bolton, *A thousand miles away* (Brisb, 1963); *Northern Miner*, 4 Jan, 1 Dec 1886, 24 Feb 1890, 23 Mar 1903, 9 Feb 1925, 8 May 1926; *Brisbane Courier*, 29 Apr 1926; *North Qld Register*, 3 May 1926; *Sunday Mail* (Brisb), 2 July 1972.   JUNE STOODLEY

PLAYFAIR, (JOHN) THOMAS (1832-1893), butcher and ships' providore, was baptized on 12 February 1832 at Earl's Colne, Essex, England, eldest son of Thomas Playfair, tailor, and his wife Mary Anne, née Arnold. He joined the navy at 12 and served as a captain's and wardroom steward. In 1859 he arrived in H.M.S. *Pelorus* at Sydney, where he settled after his discharge. He became a partner of E. J. Bailey, a wholesale butcher. In 1860 Bailey & Co. had shops in South Head Road and Crown Street. By 1862 he had separately opened in lower George Street as a shipping butcher. From 1863 until the 1870s he remained in partnership with Bailey's widow as Bailey & Playfair. His own enterprise prospered. Windjammers then provided a lucrative market for salt and fresh beef and for live animals to be slaughtered at sea.

In 1875 Playfair was elected to the Sydney City Council for Gipps Ward which he represented unopposed until 1893. A good committeeman and vigorous reformer, he battled for a better city water supply, the demolition of slums and rookeries, and improved sanitation. He achieved the widening of George Street North and the establishment in 1882 of the Homebush sale-yards at a cost of £60,000. As mayor in 1885 his unannounced inspections played a part in maintaining the standard of public cleanliness which he had earlier helped to impose. In March 1889 he was elected to the Legislative Assembly as a member for West Sydney and as a free trade supporter of Sir Henry Parkes [q.v.]. With limited ability as a public speaker, he rarely spoke in the House. He was defeated in the 1891 elections.

Playfair was well known for his extensive charitable work especially for the Sydney Ragged School. He also helped the Boys' Brigade and the Sisters of St Joseph's Providence. 'Everyone who knew him went to Tom Playfair for advice or help in their hour of need'. John Bullish in appearance, he was described as a 'bluff, kindly, Saxon . . . generous, genuine and straight'.

Playfair was married twice: first, on 7 November 1860 to Ellen, daughter of Thomas Matheson of Woolloomooloo; second, at Scots Church on 26 February 1867 to Georgina Hope, his deceased wife's sister. Predeceased by both wives Playfair died at Sydney on 15 November 1893 and was buried in the Anglican section of Waverley cemetery. He was survived by two sons of his first wife and by a son and daughter of his second wife. His estate was valued for probate at over £33,000. He had acquired much real estate in the city and North Sydney. His second son Edmund inherited the business.

In his memory a fountain was erected at the Flemington sale-yards in May 1896 and in 1960 a plaque was placed on the doors of Holy Trinity Church, Millers Point. Playfair Street and Playfair Stairs had already been named after him.

Thomas Playfair Pty Ltd, *The Playfair story, 1860-1960* (Syd, 1960); *Bulletin*, 3 July 1880; *Daily Telegraph* (Syd), 16 Nov 1893; *SMH*, 16, 17 Nov 1893, 29 May 1896; *Illustrated Sydney News*, 18 Nov 1893; Syd Municipal Council, Minutes of cttee and council meetings, 1875-93 (ML).   ROSS DUNCAN

PLUMMER, ANDREW (1812-1901), medical practitioner and agriculturist, was born on 25 November 1812 at Dalkeith, Midlothian, Scotland, son of William Plummer, butcher, and his wife Sarah, née King. Educated for the medical profession at the University of Edinburgh (L.R.C.S., 1832; M.D., 1834), he practised in Edinburgh and probably London before he arrived in Victoria on 31 May 1853. In July he settled at Sandridge and 'at once got into an extensive and lucrative practice'. He also entered into public affairs and was elected chairman of the relief committee formed after the Sandridge fire in 1854; he was elected to the Melbourne City Council, and in 1862-64 served as mayor of Sandridge after it separated from the City of Melbourne. From 1854 Plummer held such appointments as magistrate, deputy-registrar of births and deaths, officer for celebrating marriages, electoral returning officer, public vaccinator and medical officer in charge of various prison and reformatory hulks and training ships in Hobson's Bay. He also joined the naval brigade of the Victorian Volunteer Force.

In December 1857 Plummer began to buy land at Gisborne and by 1880 owned 1089 acres on the edge of the township. At Wyabun Park in the 1870s he bred longwool sheep, particularly Lincolns, which he exhibited with success at local shows, but in the early 1880s disposed of his stud and concentrated on mixed farming. He was a member of the West Bourke and Kyneton Agricultural Societies, and the Gisborne Roads Board. In 1871 he was elected to the inaugural Council of the National Agricultural Society, and later became a trustee and was president in 1882 and 1884-90. Plummer's involvement with the National Agricultural Society in the 1880s, and his support for J. L. Dow [q.v.], led to further offices. In 1883-89 he was chairman of the Council of Agricultural Education, the Board of Agriculture and the board of inquiry on tuberculosis in cattle. He was a member of the royal commission on vegetable products and of five other commissions appointed to organize Victoria's representation at various international exhibitions.

With a friendly disposition and later a large white beard, Plummer was very popular. His energy and organizing ability enabled him to take part in public affairs as well as maintaining a large medical practice (M.D., Melb., ad eund., 1867). Wyabun Park, 'one of the fancy farms of the colony', was run by an overseer according to detailed written plans by Plummer. In Edinburgh he had married Mary Nairne Ker; they had a daughter and two sons: James Ker Beck who became mayor of Port Melbourne in 1885 and 1889, and William Andrew. When he migrated to Victoria Plummer left his wife and daughter behind. On 3 October 1871 at St James's pro-Cathedral he married Mary Jacques who came from Newton Barry, County Wexford. He died at his elder son's home in Port Melbourne on 22 July 1901 and was buried in the Anglican section of the Melbourne general cemetery.

W. Thomson, *Typhoid fever: its cause and extent in Melbourne*, 3rd ed (Melb, 1878); Land tax register, *Government Gazette* (Vic), 9 Dec 1880; National Agr Soc of Vic, J, 15 Jan 1886; *Mildura Cultivator*, 1888-89, centennial exhibition issue; *Argus*, 23 July 1901; *Gisborne Gazette*, 26 July 1901; K. P. J. Barley, A history of two Victorian farmers' organizations: the Royal Agricultural Society and the Chamber of Agriculture (M.Agr. Sc. thesis, Univ Melb, 1952).   L. J. PEEL

POHLMAN, ROBERT WILLIAMS (1811-1877), judge, was born in March 1811 in London, son of John George Pohlman and his wife Annie Hamilton, née Williams. After schooling he studied law, was called to the English Bar, admitted as advocate in Scotland in March 1839 and worked briefly in the civil service.

In October 1840 Pohlman arrived at Port Phillip and with his younger brother Frederick Roper and Henry Phillips bought the rights of Elephant Bridge (Darlington) station. Frederick shepherded the sheep and Robert read law books, but the experiment did not succeed and in 1841 they sold out and invested in Glenhope station in Dalhousie County with 17,500 acres and 10,000 sheep.

In April 1841 Pohlman was admitted to the colonial Bar; he practised until 1846 when appointed commissioner of Insolvency. In 1847 he became Redmond Barry's [q.v.] junior and in July 1851 was gazetted master in Equity. In 1852 he became commissioner of the Court of Requests for the City of Melbourne and County of Bourke, and then first County Court judge and chairman of Quarter Sessions for Victoria. In January 1853 he was mentioned in La Trobe's dispatches for believing that he had the necessary seniority and standing to take the chief justice's post while Sir William à Beckett [q.v.] was on leave. La Trobe implied that Pohlman lacked experience and had a peremptory manner.

In November 1851 Pohlman became a nominee in the Legislative Council, where he showed much independence, particularly on the select committee on education in 1852. In January 1855 he was elected unopposed for Ripon, Grenville and Polwarth, after resigning in October 1854 when Governor Hotham reproved him for irregularity in giving notice of a motion seeking a higher grant for education without first consulting the Executive Council. His political career ended in March 1856 after failing to win a seat for South-West Province.

As County Court judge and chairman of General Sessions Pohlman sat almost continuously. From April 1859 to April 1861 and from July to December 1871 he acted as judge of the Supreme Court. He refused to retire in the early 1870s because he was offered only a County Court judge's pension. Devoted to his judicial duties, he worked long hours. Some observers described him as sphinx-like but philanthropic with a kindly disposition. 'Garryowen' [q.v. Finn] admired his honesty and painstaking application and claimed that he 'dispensed more justice in greater quantity than a more perceptive and intelligent man could have done'. Others agreed that he imposed severe sentences such as ten years (three in chains) and three whippings of fifty lashes for a garrotter, who Pohlman piously hoped would reform in gaol and learn a trade.

Pohlman was active in many areas other than the law. He was founding chairman of the Denominational Board of Education from 1848 until it merged with the National Board after the Common Schools Act of 1862. As members of the royal commission into education of 1866, he and J. E. Bromby [q.v.] were no mere spokesmen for their Church, for they had independent minds. Early in the commission Pohlman proposed that no more land be granted to denominational schools. He missed only four of the fifty-two meetings of the commission over five months.

Pohlman's church activities as a senior layman varied. He welcomed Bishop Perry [q.v.] on his arrival, represented Trinity College in the Church of England Assembly, was engaged in denominational meetings and in building churches, offering the first cheque towards St Paul's Cathedral, Melbourne. Active in public charities, he had a long association with the Melbourne Hospital. He was guardian of the Port Phillip Orphan Immigration Committee, a devoted official of the Merri Creek Northcote Inebriates Home committee of management set up under the Inebriates Treatment Act of 1872. He exercised his judicial powers on anyone who through adulterants or bad brews worsened the liquor problem. He was president of the first Early Closing Association, and was long a councillor of the University of Melbourne. To 'Garryowen' he was 'a respected nonentity, esteemed by many and disliked by none'.

Pohlman died at his home in Punt Road, Richmond, on 6 December 1877 and was buried in the Melbourne general cemetery where he had long been a trustee. Predeceased by his first wife, he married about 1872 Mercy Clifton Bachelor by whom he had one daughter.

His brother Frederick Roper was appointed to the Kyneton magisterial bench in April 1856 and on 1 August 1859 became a warden of the goldfields. From October 1860 until March 1866 he was police magistrate at Maryborough and in July 1867 was transferred to Rutherglen.

Garryowen (E. Finn), *The chronicles of early Melbourne* (Melb, 1888); G. M. Dow, *George Higinbotham: church and state* (Melb, 1964); *Age*, 7 Dec 1877; *Melb Bulletin*, 28 Jan 1878; CO 309/13.   SUZANNE G. MELLOR

POORE, JOHN LEGG (1816-1867), Congregational minister, was born on 10 January 1816 at Carisbrooke, Isle of Wight, eldest son of Henry Poore, tradesman, and his wife Mary, née Snudden. Educated at Newport Grammar School and other schools till 15, he taught at schools in Rochester, Canterbury and Shrewsbury. From 1834 he studied for the Congregational ministry at Yeovil Academy and Highbury College and was ordained in October 1839. For fourteen years minister of Hope Chapel, Salford, and officer of the Lancashire Congregational Union, he became known for his Evangelical and ecumenical interests, his anti-Chartist teachings and his deputational work in England and Ireland on behalf of the London Missionary Society. Through Rev. Thomas Binney [q.v.] he had become interested in the work of the Colonial Missionary Society and was recommended by Binney to supervise the society's work in the Australasian colonies. With Rev. Richard Fletcher (d. 1861), also from Manchester, and Rev. Edwin Day (1814-1896), Poore arrived at Melbourne on 22 March 1854 in the *Thomas Fielden*.

In 1855 Poore and Fletcher convened the first intercolonial conference in Melbourne and worked for a common college, hymnbook and periodical for the denomination. Poore spent much of each year in Victoria, New South Wales, Tasmania and South Australia preaching and obtaining funds for the new Home Missionary and Chapel Building Societies. His visits to Western Australia in 1861 and New Zealand in 1863 aroused much interest in eastern Australia. In Victoria he established Congregational churches at Dunolly and Maryborough in 1859. Under his leadership twenty churches were formed in the colonies. In many ways he was the 'John Wesley of Congregationalism' in Australia, claiming that he was 'expected to ride like a trooper; preach as a man ought to preach; make speeches—grave, gay, inspiriting, money-getting; teach classes of maidens and theological students; and generally to do what nobody else likes to do, or will do'.

Poore also did deputational work for the British and Foreign Bible Society and with the support of Bishop Perry [q.v.] convened the Committee for Promoting the Evangelisation of the Chinese in 1855. However, his plans to bring the Polynesian missions under control of the Australian churches were not implemented. He visited England in 1857, 1858 and 1863 to recruit ministers and selected and sent out twenty-eight men including John Graham of Sydney, A. M. Henderson and A. Gosman [q.v.] of Melbourne.

Poore and Fletcher left their imprint on the organization of Australian Congregationalism: the structure of the colonial unions closely resembled that of Lancashire; the Congregational College of Victoria, opened in 1862, directly resulted from their efforts to establish an Australian denominational training centre; the Ministers' Provident Fund, largely financed by Henry Hopkins [q.v.] in 1863, was one of their plans to attract ministers to migrate; the *Southern Spectator* which Fletcher edited in 1857-59 was the first Congregational periodical; and their fostering of intercolonial activities induced Congregationalists early to support the idea of colonial Federation. Poore's writings on church and colonial affairs, sometimes under the pseudonym 'Vectis', were published in the *Sydney Morning Herald* and the Melbourne *Christian Times*.

In England in 1864 Poore was persuaded to become secretary of the Colonial Missionary Society and visited Canada in 1865. In 1866 he decided to resign from his Australian work and returned to Melbourne to wind up his affairs. He served as minister *pro tempore* at St Kilda. His wife Mary, younger daughter of Rev. Samuel Hillyard of Bedford, whom he had married on 6 August 1841, was on her way out to join him when he died on 27 March 1867 at his country home at Osborne, near Mornington; he was buried at St Kilda. Besides Fletcher, his closest Australian friends were John Fairfax of Sydney and T. Q. Stow of Adelaide [qq.v.].

J. Corbin, *Ever working, never resting* (Lond, 1874); A. Gosman et al, *The principles and history of Independency* (Melb, 1879); J. King, *Ten decades; the Australian centenary story of the London Missionary Society* (Lond, 1895); B. Nightingale, *The story of the Lancashire Congregational Union 1806-1906* (Manchester, 1906); *Argus*, 29 Mar 1867.   NIEL GUNSON

POTTIE, JOHN (1832?-1908), veterinary surgeon, was born at Old Kilpatrick, Dumbartonshire, Scotland, son of Michael Pottie, veterinary surgeon, and his wife Margaret, née McDougal. He trained at the Royal (Dick) Veterinary College in Edinburgh where he obtained the Highland and Agricultural Society's certificate and on 21 April 1858 was registered as a member of the Royal College of Veterinary Surgeons. After practising in Renfrew with a brother he arrived in Sydney about 1860 in charge of a valuable consignment of horses sent by the British government. He decided to settle in Sydney and by 1861 had set up a veterinary practice on the corner of Elizabeth and Bathurst Streets. Later John Pottie & Sons moved to 232 Castlereagh Street.

In November Pottie accompanied three commissioners on an inspection of cattle infected with pleuro-pneumonia. In

evidence to a Legislative Assembly select committee on the slaughter of cattle under the Cattle Disease Prevention Act he recommended the inoculation of all working bullocks. On 13 March 1862 at the Congregational Church, Woollahra, he married Eliza Allen (d. 1907) from Belfast. In that month he became an inspector of cattle for Sydney and next year also a sheep inspector. He was consulting veterinary surgeon to the government and often advised the chief inspector of stock; he was also veterinary surgeon to the New South Wales police. From the 1870s with the approval of the inspector-general of police he experimented with processed stock food and claimed that no police horses died from sickness. In 1890 he wrote to Parkes [q.v.] urging the use of his sheep-licks to control worm infestation. In 1894 he warned Parkes of the loss to the wool industry from internal worms and the destruction of native grasses and salt bush, and asked him to 'insist on the appointment of a competent gentleman to look after our grass preservation'.

In 1872 he had published *The Horse in Health: and its Diseases; Their Nature, Symptoms, and Treatment* and in 1886 *Pottie's Guide in Cases of Difficult Foaling and Calving*. In 1881 he was a founding member of the short-lived Australian Veterinary Medical Association. He advertised widely and practised until 1908. He also had an absorbing interest in astronomy. Pottie died from heart disease on 18 August at Pittwater Road, Manly, and was buried in the Waverley cemetery with Presbyterian rites. He was survived by three sons and two daughters. In 1973 John Pottie & Sons was managed by his grandson Bruce Pottie.

V&P (LA NSW), 1862, 5, 244; Parkes letters (ML); information from W. L. Hindmarsh, Aust Veterinary Assn, Syd, and J. Pottie & Sons, Syd.   J. C. BEARDWOOD

POTTINGER, SIR FREDERICK WILLIAM (1831-1865), police inspector, was born on 27 April 1831 in India, second son of Lieut-General Sir Henry Pottinger of the East India Co., and his wife Susanna Maria, née Cooke, of Dublin. Educated privately and in 1844-47 at Eton, Pottinger purchased a commission in the Grenadier Guards in 1850 and served in England until 1854. Active in social life, he lost much of his adoring mother's wealth on the racecourse. In 1856 he succeeded his father as second baronet and soon dissipated his inheritance. Forced by debt to leave England, he migrated to Sydney. After failing on the goldfields he joined the New South Wales police force as a mounted trooper. A superb horseman, he spent the next few years on the gold escort between Gundagai and Goulburn.

Probably because of conditions imposed by his family who still supported him with funds, Pottinger kept his title secret but in 1860 it was discovered by the inspector-general of police, John McLerie [q.v.], and promotion came rapidly. In November he became clerk of petty sessions at Dubbo and on 1 October 1861 assistant superintendent of the Southern Mounted Patrol. Although determined to succeed in his career he was involved in a drunken brawl at Young on 20-21 December 1861. Sued, he received a public rebuke from Charles Cowper [q.v.] for his 'highly discreditable' behaviour. Posted to the Lachlan, he proved himself an indefatigable but unlucky hunter of bushrangers.

Under the 1862 Police Regulation Act Pottinger was appointed an inspector of police for the Western District. The Act was bitterly criticized and Pottinger seen as a symbol of its defects. In April 1862 he arrested Ben Hall [q.v.] at Forbes on a charge of highway robbery, but he was acquitted. Soon afterwards Hall joined Frank Gardiner's [q.v.] gang which on 15 June 1862 robbed the Lachlan escort of some £14,000. Quick in pursuit, Pottinger remained on the trail for a month, and arrested two of the bushrangers. They escaped several days later in a gun battle but Pottinger recovered the stolen gold taken by the prisoners. Criticized for his failure to send an adequate guard with the escort and his return without prisoners, Pottinger was praised by others for his determination and endurance. On the night of 9 and 10 August Pottinger and a party of police surrounded the house of Gardiner's mistress, Kate Brown, but the bushranger escaped when Pottinger's pistol misfired. They arrested a young boy on suspicion of being an accomplice and allowed him to remain in the lock-up without comforts; his death in March 1863 from gaol fever further diminished Pottinger's reputation. On 27 September 1862 Pottinger had appeared before a Bathurst court on a charge of assault.

In February 1863 Pottinger attended the Sydney trials of the escort robbers; jostled by larrikins in the street he again became the subject of public notice. He also threatened J. J. Harpur [q.v.] with his whip for charges made against him in the Legislative Assembly. Meanwhile the bushrangers in his district became more active. He later captured Patrick Daley, but on 17 August 1864 failed to arrest Alpin McPherson [q.v.].

In May 1863 the inspector-general had directed the police to act on their own initiative. Early in January 1865 hoping to lure Hall and Dunn into the open, Pottinger rode in the Wowingragong races in breach of police regulations. Despite his justifiable claim that his action 'fully warranted the discretionary departure in point from the letter (tho' not the spirit)' of the regulation he was dismissed from the police force on 16 February 1865. Protest meetings against his dismissal were held on the diggings and in the towns, with petitions for his reappointment. On 5 March 1865 at Wascoe's Inn in the Blue Mountains on his way to Sydney to seek redress, Pottinger accidentally shot himself in the upper abdomen while boarding a moving coach. He recovered enough to be moved to the Victoria Club in Sydney where he died intestate on 9 April 1865. He was buried at St Jude's Anglican Church, Randwick.

Yass Courier, 26 Feb 1862; Empire (Syd), 26 Mar, 24 July, 4 Oct 1862, 28 Mar 1863; Lachlan Observer, 25 Oct 1862; SMH, 10, 12 Apr 1865; Bell's Life in Sydney, 15 Apr 1865; Burrangong Argus, 15 Apr 1865; Sydney Mail, 29 Apr 1865; Field (Lond), 22 May 1937; M. Brennan, Police history of the notorious bushrangers of New South Wales and Victoria (ML); boxes 4/544, 4/547 and Police special bundle 2/674.10 (NSWA).   P. A. SELTH

POUPINEL, FRANCOIS VICTOR (1815-1884), Marist Father, was born on 14 November 1815 at Vassy, Calvados, Normandy, France, son of Jacques Poupinel, watchmaker, and his wife Marie-Anne, née Vauthier. Brought up by his widowed mother and uncle, Abbé Vauthier, he left secondary school and entered the Bayeux seminary. His abilities were soon recognized when he joined the Marists at Lyon in August 1838. He took vows on 3 September 1839 and was ordained priest on 15 September. Within a year he was appointed secretary to the founder of the order, Jean-Claude Colin. Victor Poupinel also became procurator in France in charge of the Marist Pacific missions, a position of growing responsibility.

Colin and his successor Julien Favre were worried not only by the loss of lives of missionaries, but also by autocratic bishops under whom Marists suffered gross privations. In 1857 Favre negotiated with Bishop Pierre Marie Bataillon, then in Europe, for a rule to safeguard the Marists. Poupinel was appointed visitor-general of the missions to represent the missionaries. He reached Sydney in September 1857 and was warmly welcomed to Villa Maria by Fr J. L. Rocher [q.v.].

Based in Sydney for the next thirteen years Poupinel visited isolated missions in New Caledonia, New Zealand, Fiji, Samoa, Tonga and the islands of Rotuma, Wallis and Futuna. With fatherly concern for the missionaries he handled the prickly Bataillon with patient tact and negotiated transfers but resisted the bishop's wish to amalgamate Villa Maria with a college to train island priests. Poupinel visited Europe in 1862, and Rome adopted his recommendation to detach Fiji in 1863 and later Samoa from Bataillon's vicariate, yet the bishop was one of many who sought Poupinel's reappointment to the Pacific for a second term.

Within the Sydney archdiocese Poupinel found the Marists hampered by the suspicion of Archbishop Polding [q.v.]. In 1859 Abbot Gregory [q.v.] had explained to Poupinel that the archbishop's refusal to countenance a Marist secondary college for boys was to protect the ailing Benedictine school, Lyndhurst. Early in 1868 Polding reversed his stand and requested Poupinel for a college and a model school for teacher training. He sponsored the request to Favre; the negotiations did not lead to a Marist Fathers' college but instead brought the Marist Brothers to Australia in 1872, led by Ludovic Laboureyas [q.v.]. Under Poupinel's leadership the Marists in Australia became more confident. With his friendliness and knowledge of church procedures he helped people and several bishops referred priests in difficulties to him. The misunderstandings with Polding were gradually sorted out, and the symbol of complete acceptance by the archbishop came in 1868, not only with the offer of the college but, after Archdeacon McEncroe [q.v.] died, with the offer of his parish of St Patrick's, Church Hill, to Poupinel and the Marists. As first Marist parish priest of this cherished shrine, Poupinel named Joseph Monnier [q.v.].

In 1870 Poupinel left Australia to take up the post of assistant superior-general of the order, second to Favre. He died of fever on 10 July 1884 at Lyon and was buried in the cemetery of St Foy-les-Lyon. Poupinel had won the affection of all who knew him. He had an immense capacity for work and ability to valuate men and situations. His penetrating reports on Australia and the Pacific missions gave his superiors a sound basis for estimating situations, although they wisely left as much as possible to Poupinel's decisions. He conserved records methodically and his amply documented travels provide valuable historical material about the Pacific.

J. Hosie, The French Mission: an Australian base for the Marists in the Pacific to 1874 (M.A. Hons thesis, Macquarie Univ, 1971); Rocher, Monnier and Poupinel letters (Marist Archives, Rome, microfilm ML and NL).

JOHN HOSIE

POWELL, WALTER (1822-1868), businessman and Wesleyan layman, was born in May 1822 at Tottenham, Middlesex, England, son of a merchant. In 1823 the family left by free passage for Van Diemen's Land where Walter received a poor education in a small school run by his mother. In 1834 he began work as a clerk for a Launceston merchant, leaving after three years to work for an auctioneer. Through the influence of his employer he attended Wesleyan worship services and became a member of the denomination after a revival conducted at Launceston by Revs William Butters and John Eggleston [qq.v.]. On 4 March 1845 he married Anne Bell, his employer's daughter.

Powell left for Melbourne where he worked as a clerk. He was appointed a class leader at the Wesleyan chapel, Collins Street, and was also secretary of the Sabbath school at Brunswick Street, Fitzroy. In 1848 he visited England to order goods for establishing an ironmongering business in Victoria. On his return to Melbourne he joined in partnership with two other Wesleyans to form Whitney & Chambers, importers and retailers of hardware. The discovery of gold in the colony during 1851 and the consequent demand for goods made a fortune for the partners. Anxious to use his new-found wealth for the glory of God, Powell gave generous donations to the Wesleyans and to public charities, including the Wesleyan Immigrants' Home and the Melbourne Benevolent Home. Butters, chairman of the district, nominated Powell for most of the major Wesleyan committees and he became a member of the Financial District Meeting, the Education Committee, the Chapel Building Committee and the Wesleyan Grammar School Committee. In 1855 he helped Rev. Daniel Draper [q.v.] to establish a pension fund for clergymen and their wives.

During a visit to England in 1857 for business purposes, Powell ordered goods which were donated for a bazaar held to raise funds for the proposed grammar school. On his return to Melbourne, freedom from business commitments allowed him to devote even more time to church and public affairs. He resumed his committee responsibilities and was particularly enthusiastic for establishing the grammar school. He was organist and Sabbath school superintendent at the St Kilda Church and gave a generous donation for the building of a new chapel opened in

1858. He also gave books and money for opening a Wesleyan Book Depot.

In February 1860 Powell left Melbourne to live in London, where in 1861-68 he was a business partner of Henry Reed [q.v.], a Wesleyan from Launceston. Although Powell was superintendent of the Sabbath school at Bayswater, he continued to influence affairs in Victoria and sent donations to Wesley Church, Melbourne, and the churches at St Kilda and Launceston. He was critical of the long delay in the establishment of the grammar school and while Draper was visiting England he helped with the choice of a headmaster. A generous donation from Powell enabled the school (later Wesley College) to be opened in 1866. He died at Bayswater on 21 January 1868, survived by his wife and a daughter. In church and public affairs he had displayed the energy and quick decision of a self-made man. He was pietistic, public-spirited and enthusiastic for the extension of education.

J. C. Symons, *Life of the Rev. Daniel James Draper* (Lond, 1870); B. Gregory, *The thorough business man: memoirs of W. Powell* (Lond, 1871); *Wesleyan Chronicle*, 23 Feb 1868.

RENATE HOWE

POWER, HENRY (1820-1891), bushranger, also known as Johnson, was born at Waterford, Ireland. He was transported for seven years in 1840 for stealing a pair of shoes, and arrived at Hobart Town in the *Isabella* on 21 May 1842. He received a ticket-of-leave in November 1847 and certificate of freedom in September 1848, and then moved to the Port Phillip District. He became a horse-dealer at Geelong, but was attracted by the gold discoveries. Stopped by two troopers at Daisy Hill, near Maryborough, in March 1855 on suspicion of horse-stealing, he wounded one of the police. A week later he was arrested whilst attempting to cross the Murray River and was sentenced on 25 September 1855 to thirteen years on the roads.

Confined to the hulk *Success*, Johnson was implicated with Captain Melville [q.v.] and others in the murder of Owen Owens and John Turner on 22 October 1856, but was found not guilty. After two years and a half in the hulks, he was transferred to Pentridge stockade. As Power he escaped in 1862, and lived at Middle Creek in the Ovens District, where he was assisted by the Kelly, Quinn and Lloyd families. Arrested on a charge of horse-stealing, he was sentenced at Beechworth on 19 February 1864 to seven years on the roads.

Power again escaped from Pentridge on 16 February 1869. He was assisted briefly by Ned Kelly [q.v.], who was then 13, but the arrangement proved unsatisfactory and thereafter Power operated independently. He held up the mail-coach at Porepunkah on 7 May and another coach on the Longwood-Mansfield Road on the 22nd. These were the first of over a year's depredations, during which Power claimed to have committed over 600 robberies.

In September the Victorian government offered a reward of £200, soon increased to £500, for Power's arrest; as a result he moved to New South Wales. He soon returned to Victoria where police efforts to capture him proved fruitless until he was arrested on 5 June 1870 by Superintendents Nicolson and Hare, who with Sergeant Montford and a black tracker, surprised Power in his hide-out (Power's Lookout) overlooking the Quinn property on the King River. The police were led there by James Quinn, who received the reward of £500. Power was sentenced at Beechworth to fifteen-years hard labour on three counts of bushranging and was again held at Pentridge.

In 1877, after accounts of Power's ill health by the 'Vagabond' [q.v. J. S. James] in the *Argus*, he was released on the application of several women, including Lady Janet Clarke [q.v.]. He worked on the Clarke property at Sunbury until he became a guide of the hulk *Success* in 1891. His body was found in the Murray River; he died 'on or about 11 October 1891 . . . near Swan Hill from drowning . . . there is nothing to show how he came into the river'.

Power was a fearless and daring rider and bushman, but never killed police or his victims. He broke from prison several times, defied the police in the Ovens District for a decade and was finally convicted through an informer.

F. A. Hare, *The last of the bushrangers* (Lond, 1892); *Argus*, 3, 10 Mar 1877.

IAN F. McLAREN

POWNALL, WILLIAM HENRY (1834-1903), Anglican clergyman, was born at Manchester, England, son of William Pownall. In 1857 he was ordained deacon by the bishop of Victoria (Hong Kong) at Islington, London, and appointed chaplain to the Sailors' Mission at Shanghai, supported by the Colonial and Continental Church Society. With his wife Sarah, née Backett, he reached Shanghai on 3 June 1858 and, despite climatic effects on his health, worked faithfully with the European crews of the ships. He was ordained priest on 18 March 1860. After his wife died of cholera he returned to England with his three daughters on 24 November 1862.

Pownall renewed his friendship with Mesac Thomas [q.v.], secretary of the Colonial and Continental Church Society, and on Thomas's appointment as bishop of Goulburn in 1863, agreed to join him in New South Wales. In 1864 in London Pownall married Sarah Sophia Swayne. He reached Goulburn in June and at Lambing Flat held his first service on 14 August in a 'little iron room with mud floor, borrowed forms and dingy kerosene lamp'. The physical demands of his large parishes were exacting and sheer exhaustion often overcame him, but he created a vigorous church community. He laid the foundation stone of St John the Evangelist's Church, Young, on 21 March 1865 and next year added a schoolhouse. In the turbulent mining community he preached and expected high standards of spiritual life from his people and worked to improve their education by weekly lectures in English history. In 1867-69 by arrangement with the Sydney diocese he also held services on the new goldfield at Grenfell.

In January 1870 Pownall moved to the Tumut and Adelong district and with 'customary energy' built up church activities, completing the parsonage and encouraging the Adelong people to build a church. In 1872-93 he had charge of the parish of Wagga Wagga, where he was a member of the Hospital Board and interested in the Working Men's Association. His high standards led to differences of opinion with many citizens and his hard-hitting Evangelical principles were criticized and satirized by the press. As a parish priest he was loved and respected but an aggressive element in his personality did not help him to work harmoniously with church committees.

In January 1874 Pownall was appointed archdeacon of the western part of Goulburn diocese and one of three commissaries to administer the diocese when Bishop Thomas was absent in 1874-75. Despite the illness of his wife, Pownall ably handled the complex problems of the diocese. In 1874 he was granted the Lambeth B.A. degree and in 1884 made a canon of St Saviour's Cathedral, Goulburn. Although he found synods an 'abomination', he took a leading part in their affairs. In 1889 he was appointed vicar-general and took charge during Bishop Thomas's last illness until the consecration of William Chalmers [q.v.] in November 1892. In 1891 he had become dean of St Saviour's Cathedral and as registrar of the diocese in 1892-95 assisted Chalmers in the settlement of the cathedral dispute. He returned to Young in 1895 and when Chalmers died in November 1901 acted again as vicar-general. As acting registrar

with temporary charge of the parish of West Goulburn, he gave invaluable help to the incoming bishop, C. G. Barlow.

In September 1903 Pownall resigned from the Young parish but died of diabetes in Goulburn on 29 November and was buried at St Saviour's Cathedral. He was survived by two daughters of his first wife, and by his second wife and their two daughters. His estate was valued for probate at £3316.

Colonial and Continental Church Soc, *Annual report* (Lond, 1859-63); M. Thomas, Letter-book 1865-90 (St Mark's Inst of Theology, Canberra); W. H. Pownall, Letter-book 1874-78 (Church of England Diocesan Registry, Canberra).
                                            BARBARA THORN

PRATT, SIR THOMAS SIMSON (1797-1879), army officer, was the son of Captain James Pratt and his wife Anne, née Simson. Educated at the University of St Andrews, in 1814 as a volunteer, he accompanied his father in the 56th Regiment on the expedition to Holland; he was under fire before Merxem on the day his ensigncy in the 26th Foot, the Cameronians, was gazetted. He served in the Mediterranean and Ireland, gaining his captaincy in 1825, and India, whence he was returned sick to England. In 1827 he married Frances Agnes, second daughter of J. S. Cooper.

On learning that the 26th was ordered to China, Pratt rejoined it in Calcutta. In the first China campaign in 1840-42 he commanded the land forces at the assault and capture of the forts of Chuenpi on 7 January 1841, for which he was made a brevet lieut-colonel; and he took part in the attack on the Boca forts, guarding the approach to Canton, on 26 February. He commanded the Cameronians in the attacks on Canton in May 1841, in the night attack on Ningpo in October and at Chapu, Wusang, Shanghai and Chinkiang in 1842. In October 1841 he was appointed C.B. and from 1843 to 1855 he was deputy-adjutant-general of the forces in the Madras Presidency.

In October 1858 Pratt became a major-general, and next year was appointed to command the troops in the Australian colonies. He reached Melbourne on 8 January 1860. His command embraced New Zealand, so that when early in July news reached Melbourne of the serious reverses suffered by British troops in the Waitara district of Taranaki, he decided not only to send reinforcements but to direct operations in person. He sailed from Melbourne with his staff on 26 July, the centre of much public interest heightened by his only daughter's marriage to Governor Sir Henry Barkly.

Pratt's operations in Taranaki were circumspect. Wary of the unorthodox methods of the Maoris, he avoided his predecessors' mistake of fighting in the open, and reduced the Maori forts with minimum casualties by using earthworks to give covered approaches to the assaulting troops, a method advocated by Captain Pasley [q.v.]. Progress was slow and unspectacular, and Pratt was criticized by New Zealand settlers and Australian editors: he did miss opportunities of using bush fighters who could have met the Maoris on equal terms. The authorities in London had decided to separate the New Zealand command from that of the Australian forces and a new commander arrived early in 1861. By then the Taranaki revolt had been suppressed. Pratt returned to Victoria in April, to receive acclaim in military circles, votes of thanks in parliament and grudging acknowledgment in the press. Wider appreciation of his work soon followed. In July he was appointed K.C.B. for his services in New Zealand. He was publicly invested with the insignia by his son-in-law on 15 April 1862, the first such investiture in Australia.

Pratt was then in an unusually strong position. He sat in the Victorian Executive Council, and was prominent in the colony's affairs. He presided over the royal commission on the Burke and Wills [qq.v.] expedition. Foreseeing that imperial troops would inevitably be supplanted by locally-raised units, he advocated the grouping of the future forces of the several colonies under a unified command, however difficult this might be to achieve. He had little respect for the local volunteer forces, of which he was the nominal head, and his views led to cool relations with two successive treasurers, Verdon and Haines [qq.v.]. He was not unduly troubled by the short-comings of the volunteers because he believed that the only external danger which the Australian colonies faced was that of raids from the sea.

In 1863 it was decided to lower the status of the command and to move the headquarters to New Zealand. Pratt left Melbourne in April 1863. In England he was appointed colonel of the 37th (North Hampshire) Regiment. In May 1873 he was promoted general, and in October 1877 retired. He died in England on 2 February 1879.

Pratt's portrait in 1862, whiskered and heavy-jowled, is that of an orthodox soldier of his time, and is given the lie by his distinguished early record and ability to learn lessons late in life.

J. W. Fortescue, *History of the British Army*, 12-13 (Lond, 1927-30); J. Cowan. *History of the New Zealand wars*, 1-2 (Wellington, 1922);

V&P (LA Vic), 1862, 2 (97); *Argus*, 25 July 1860, 12 Apr 1861, 16 Apr 1862; *Illustrated Melb Post*, Feb, Apr 1862; *The Times*, 6 Feb 1879.
RONALD McNICOLL

PRICE WARUNG; *see* ASTLEY, WILLIAM

PRIMROSE, ARCHIBALD PHILIP, fifth EARL of ROSEBERY (1847-1929), statesman and author, was born on 7 May 1847 in London, elder son of Archibald Primrose and his wife Catherine Lucy Wilhelmina, daughter of Earl Stanhope. He was educated at Eton and Christ Church, Oxford, where after three years he was forced to choose between his race-horse Ladas and his degree; this most literate of future prime ministers unhesitatingly opted to retain the horse. On 4 March 1868 he had succeeded to the earldom and many Scottish properties. On 20 March 1878 he married Hannah de Rothschild, 'the richest heiress in England'.

In 1879 and 1880 Rosebery brilliantly managed Gladstone's first and second Midlothian campaigns and in 1881-83 reluctantly filled and readily vacated the undersecretaryship at the Home Office, an unglamorous apprenticeship that Gladstonian rigidity prescribed. In September 1883 he travelled via America and New Zealand with his wife to Australia and arrived in Sydney on 17 November. In the next nine weeks he visited Queensland, Victoria, Tasmania and South Australia, looking at outback stations, mines, vineyards and horse-races, and enjoying himself immensely. On the inevitable colonial banquet circuit he talked of the exciting destiny of the Liberal empire. The climax came at the Adelaide Town Hall on 18 January 1884. With the temperature oppressive and a town drunk in attendance, the statesman and orator turned prophet and presented the Australian colonies as a nation and in a happy and enduring phrase the empire itself as a 'Commonwealth of Nations'. He had bought real estate in Sydney and lost it in the 1892 crash, but never lost his deep interest in Australia.

On his return to Britain Rosebery managed Gladstone's third Midlothian campaign and with characteristic moodiness fenced with the prime minister over acceptance of full cabinet office, surrendering only when the ministry was *in extremis* by the fall of Khartoum and the death of Gordon. Rosebery followed Gladstone although unenthusiastic for Irish Home Rule, and became foreign secretary in Gladstone's third and fourth ministries. After nineteen months of conflict between Gladstonian 'little England-ism' and Roseberyite 'Liberal Imperialism' he became prime minister in March 1894 on Gladstone's final resignation.

The Rosebery ministry was almost a disaster. His wife had died in 1890 and he was plagued by insomnia, isolated in the overwhelmingly Tory House of Lords and harried by Sir William Harcourt, the Liberal leader in the Commons and spokesman for the 'little Englanders'. After sixteen months Rosebery was ready to take any plausible excuse for resignation and after another six-teen months as leader of a discomfited Opposition resigned that office too. He was approached by Edmund Barton who in 1900 led the delegation to watch the passage of the Commonwealth Constitution bill through the imperial parliament. Rosebery introduced the delegates to many influential Liberals, thereby helping to advance their case for leaving the bill unaltered.

Rosebery was nominal leader of the Liberal imperialists during the South African war. For a decade he remained a great figure in British politics but had become extra-ordinarily remote and dated by the time of his death on 21 May 1929.

R. O. A. Crewe-Milnes, *Lord Rosebery* (Lond, 1931); R. R. James, *Rosebery* (Lond, 1963).

D. D. CUTHBERT

PRING, RATCLIFFE (1825-1885), lawyer and politician, was born on 17 October 1825 at Crediton, Devon, England, second son of Thomas Pring, a landed solicitor and clerk of the peace in Devon, and his wife Anne, née Dunne. Educated at King Edward VI Grammar School at Crediton and Shrews-bury School, he studied law for one year in his father's office, two years with a con-veyancer and two more with a special pleader in London. In 1849 he was called to the Bar of the Inner Temple. He practised at the Quarter Sessions at Exeter but bronchial attacks decided him to migrate to Sydney in 1853. He practised on the Goul-burn, Moreton Bay and Bathurst circuits and in Sydney until the New South Wales government expanded the Moreton Bay judicial establishment. Pring was appointed resident crown prosecutor in March 1857 and in April settled in Brisbane. On the separation of the colony of Queensland he was immediately commissioned attorney-general.

Pring served as attorney-general under Herbert [q.v.] from 10 December 1859 to 30 August 1865 and from 21 July to August 1866; under Mackenzie [q.v.] from 15 August 1867 to 25 November 1868; under Lilley [q.v.] from 12 November 1869 to 3

May 1870; under Palmer [q.v.] from 2 January 1874 for six days; and under McIlwraith [q.v.] from 16 May 1879 to 4 June 1880 when Pring was not re-elected in the ministerial by-election but stayed in office without a seat in parliament. In 1875 S. W. Griffith considered Pring for solicitor-general but later denied the offer. Pring was a busy legislator, especially in the mid-1860s. His more important legislation was on court structure, criminal law and commercial practice. In 1862 he compiled the first two volumes of *Statutes in force in the colony of Queensland at the present time* and edited a third on the statutes passed in 1863-64. In the Legislative Assembly he represented Eastern Downs from 1860 to 1862 and served for thirteen months in the Legislative Council. He then represented Ipswich in the assembly from 1863 to 1866 when he unofficially led the Opposition and advocated the Ipswich-Brisbane railway. After defeat in the Ipswich election he was returned for the Burnett in 1867 and was again unofficial leader of the Opposition. He represented Brisbane North in 1870-72, Carnarvon in 1873-74, Brisbane in 1878, and Fortitude Valley in 1878-79.

Pring's reputation in politics was marked by controversies which partly arose from his personality: impulsive, vain, hasty in temper, strong in opinion and forcible in expression. In the 1860 select committee on the judicial establishment of Queensland he gave evidence which with his later official stand as attorney-general incensed the in-cumbent judge, Lutwyche [q.v.]. In 1861-62 a rancorous and personal dispute was carried on by the judge against Pring and the government. Pring then prosecuted T. P. Pugh [q.v.], editor of the *Courier*, for libel concerning the government's attitude towards Lutwyche's salary. Events in 1865 showed Pring's turbulent spirit. His zealous defence of a parliamentary colleague, John Gore Jones, for breach of privilege was attacked in the press as interference with the course of justice. Finally he resigned after a dispute with Herbert over drafting a bill, but the premier attributed the resignation to Pring's drunkenness and con-trary nature leading to cabinet clashes.

In 1871 Pring was appointed commissioner of goldfields, charged to visit them and suggest their future legislation. The appointment was an office of profit and his seat was declared vacant in April. In the subsequent election he was returned and despite a petition disputing the election was allowed to retain the seat. On 10 January 1872 he entered the Legislative Assembly quite drunk, used insulting language to opponents and assaulted C. G. H. C. Clark [q.v.] even trying to arrange a fight outside the House. Found guilty of contempt of parliament, he resigned his seat. He left for the country on legal business but the House persisted, finding him guilty of further contempt by failing to attend to explain his behaviour.

As a lawyer Pring was praised for his fluency and dogged ability in criminal law cases. He was very successful in prosecuting and defending criminals and at times acted as crown prosecutor on the Criminal Circuit. He was appointed Q.C. in 1868. In 1875 he was appointed a judge of the Central District Court but resigned next year to accept a large fee in defence of a prominent businessman. In July 1880 he acted as judge after Lutwyche died. Some lawyers and politicians criticized the appointment as a threat to the independence of the judiciary. The matter dropped when in November Pring was commissioned second puisne judge. On the full bench he was distinguished by the number of times he 'concurred' with the other judges, but his health was failing.

A keen horseman, Pring became president of the Valley Race Club and the Queensland Turf Club. His horse North Australian won during the visit of the duke of Edinburgh in 1868. He also joined the Queensland Volunteers. He had married Frances Pye in London about 1850; they had no children but two sisters came to Queensland, one being married to A. F. Matvieff, the other to A. V. Drury [q.v.]. After long illness Pring died on 25 March 1885 of cardiac asthma. Soon afterwards he was criticized in the press for profligacy and leaving his wife almost destitute. The government granted her a gratuity of £1000.

Qld Supreme Court reports, 1 (1860-68); C. A. Bernays, Queensland politics during sixty years (Brisb, 1919); R. S. Browne, A journalist's memories (Brisb, 1927); PD (Qld), 1859-85; V&P (LA Qld), 1860, 487, 1861, 343, 1869, 1, 621, 1871, 255; J. D. O'Hagan, 'Fragments of legal history in Queensland from 1853 onwards', JRHSQ, 5 (1954); Brisbane Courier, 28 June, 30 July, 8 Sept 1860, 4 July, 1, 2 Sept 1861, 26 June 1862, 14 Apr 1871, 11, 26, 27, 29 Jan 1872, 27, 30 Mar 1885; 5 Apr 1895, 29 Jan 1932; Australasian, 6, 13 July 1867; Our Paper, 8 Aug 1868; Queenslander, 28 May 1885; Qld Figaro, 19 Sept 1885; Herbert letter-book (Oxley Lib, Brisb); CO 234/1/119, 6/381, 13/243.

W. ROSS JOHNSTON

PUGH, THEOPHILUS PARSONS (1831-1896), journalist, politician and public servant, was born on 6 November 1831 on Turk's Island, Caicos Group, British West Indies, son of Rev. Theophilus Pugh, Wesleyan minister, and his wife Mary, née Parsons. Educated at Kingswood School,

Bristol, and Wesley College, Taunton, he was apprenticed to a printer and worked on several English newspapers. In June 1855 he migrated to Brisbane and for some months was correspondent for Henry Parkes's [q.v.] Empire. In 1855 he succeeded Arthur Sydney Lyon as editor of the Moreton Bay Free Press, the mouthpiece of the squatting interests and much more vituperative than the Courier. Pugh quarrelled with the anti-separation policy of the Free Press, and in 1859-61 was editor, printer and publisher of the Moreton Bay Courier.

A capable and fearless journalist, Pugh brought out the paper three times a week from January 1860. In June 1861 he brought it out 'without a day's notice' as a daily and changed the name to the Courier. Pugh's Moreton Bay Almanac appeared in 1858 as a single sheet and from 1859 as a book. In 1866 it was enlarged and issued as Pugh's Queensland Almanac and continued annually under various publishers until 1927.

As secretary of the Separation Committee from 1857 to 1859 Pugh had a notable part in achieving autonomy from New South Wales. In 1860 the Courier charged the government in Sydney with misappropriating revenue belonging to Queensland and in an article on 24 June headed 'Stop Thief' Pugh demanded that the money be returned rather than credited to the colony and appealed to Queenslanders to pay their accounts direct to their own Treasury.

Pugh became Queensland's first unofficial government printer: he issued the first Government Gazette from the jobbing office of the Courier and continued to print the Gazette until W. C. Bellbridge was officially appointed in 1863. As printer and publisher of the Courier he was prosecuted for a leading article allegedly libelling the Legislative Council as 'corrupt and unjust' for reducing the salary of Judge Lutwyche [q.v.]. Ironically the trial judge was Lutwyche himself who had probably helped to write the offending editorials in the Courier. The case was heard on 21 August 1861; the jury was absent only a few minutes and returned with a verdict of not guilty. An enthusiastic crowd chaired Pugh to the Sovereign Hotel. The excitement continued all night with fireworks, bonfires, public meetings and a subscription list to defray the Courier's expenses.

In May 1863 Pugh resigned from the Courier and in the same month published his Weekly Herald. W. Coote [q.v.] described it as 'a capital selection of colonial and English news, fairly written tales . . . and much space devoted to stock and to cotton cultivation', but Brisbane was not ready for such literature and after a few issues it became part of the Guardian Weekly. When the *Brisbane Herald* started on 1 October 1872 Pugh was its first editor.

Pugh was elected for Brisbane to the Legislative Assembly on 30 May 1863. Chairman of committees in 1867-68, he resigned his seat on 3 February 1869. In 1874 he entered the Queensland Public Service and was police magistrate at Goondiwindi, Rockhampton in 1878-81, Warwick 1883-86 and Bundaberg 1888-92. He was at Beenleigh in 1893 and in 1896 was acting police magistrate at Nanango. In 1889 at the royal commission on the sugar industry he sympathized with the Kanakas but in 1892 announced a change of heart and sneered at the attitude of the Labor Party leaders. He had a serious operation in Toowoomba and a week later died on 14 March 1896. He was married twice: first in 1855 to Annie Thompson Trundle, who died in 1866; and second, to Jane Montgomery, by whom he had six children.

C. A. Bernays, *Queensland politics during sixty years* (Brisb, 1919); V&P (LA Qld), 1860, 409, 1889, 4, 312; C. Lack, 'A century of Brisbane journalism', JRHSQ, 4 (1948-52); *Brisbane Courier*, 16 Mar 1896, 22 Mar 1926, supp; *Queenslander*, 7 Aug 1909; Griffith papers (Dixson Lib, Syd).   CLEM LACK*

PUMPKIN (1850?-1908), Aboriginal stockman of the Boontamurra tribe of the Cooper Creek district, west Queensland, was about 18 in 1868 when Patrick Durack [q.v.] established Thylungra station on a tributary of Cooper Creek. Pumpkin at once claimed Durack as his 'brother', a relationship he honoured for the rest of his life. Strongly built and quick to learn, Pumpkin interested himself keenly in all aspects of station work. A splendid rider and stockman, he soon acquired a useful knowledge of carpentry, building, fencing and gardening. He accompanied Patsy Durack and other family members on many droving and buggy trips throughout Queensland and New South Wales.

In 1885 when Patrick Durack left Thylungra to make his home in Brisbane, he gave Pumpkin a plant of horses but on principle refused to take him from his country. On his own initiative Pumpkin followed the family to the city and persuaded them that as a childless widower his responsibility lay with the two Durack sons who were then pioneering Argyle station on the Ord River. Accordingly in April 1887 he accompanied Patrick Durack by ship from Brisbane to East Kimberley, where he assumed a many-sided pioneering task from the building of homesteads and yards to stock-tailing, droving, horse-break-

ing and even tracking horse thieves. Although suspicious of the local tribes and suspected by them, he learned that Mrs Durack was coming to make her home at Argyle, and managed to negotiate with them for a young wife to help her in the house. This encouraged other Aboriginals to enter station employment and Pumpkin undertook the training of a number of local boys for station work. His pupils, all of whom bore the stamp of Pumpkin's own conscientiousness, included such outstanding station natives as Argyle Charlie, Ulysses and Boxer, the last a remarkable Queensland Aboriginal whom Pumpkin adopted as a child.

Pumpkin's grave at Argyle is marked by a memorial headstone:

Here lies Pumpkin, a member of the Boontamurra tribe of Cooper Creek, who from boyhood served Patrick Durack of Thylungra, W. Queensland, following his sons to the West in 1887 and rendering faithful service and devotion to the day of his death in 1908.

M. Durack, *Kings in grass castles* (Lond, 1959); M. P. Durack papers and journals 1886-1950 (Battye Lib, Perth).   MARY DURACK

PURVES, JAMES LIDDELL (1843-1910), lawyer and nationalist, was born on 23 August 1843 in Swanston Street, Melbourne, eldest son of James Purves and his wife Caroline. His father, an early Victorian colonist from Berwick-upon-Tweed, became an importer, race-horse breeder and owner of the station Toolgaroop near Western Port. Purves attended several Melbourne schools, including the Diocesan Grammar School, but his health was poor and he was sent to Europe in 1855 to complete his education. His diary of the voyage to London was later published as *A Young Australian's Log* (1856); it shows precocious powers of expression and observation. He continued his studies in Germany and Belgium, obtaining a good knowledge of German and French, and in King's College School, London. In 1861 he matriculated and entered Trinity College, Cambridge, to study medicine, but soon changed to law at Lincoln's Inn, London. For four years he studied, travelled widely on the Continent and at times supported himself by writing literary and documentary articles for several London journals and newspapers. In 1865 he was called to the Bar and, in December 1866 on his return to Melbourne, was admitted to the Victorian Bar.

This varied education produced quick intelligence, a fluent and often brilliant tongue, and great charm, his influence on colonial opinion and practice being based less on intellect than on personality and style. In the late 1860s he contributed a witty column, 'Talk of the Town', to the Melbourne *Herald*, and became co-editor of the *Australian Jurist*. His rapid rise in the legal profession showed a special flair for spectacular cases: in 1871 the defence of a client accused of stealing a fortune in gold coin; in the mid-1870s a gold-mining case involving suspected fraud; and in 1878 the defence of a respectable softgoods firm charged with smuggling by the protectionist Berry [q.v.] government. From the early 1880s he undertook a number of will and divorce cases, all closely reported in the press, and was briefed to appear in almost every important jury case. He was retained as standing counsel by a large number of public and private institutions, including the Victorian railways, in the defence of which he appeared in the long series of compensation cases arising out of the railway disasters of 1881 and of 1886, when he was appointed Q.C. and acknowledged as the leader of the Victorian Bar. A colleague later commented acidly that Purves was master of all trades and deficient only in law.

Certainly his success depended less on abstract legalities than on his ready grasp of technical skills such as surgery and mining, and on his ability to make disputed points clear to a jury by apt, homely and often humorous similes. His greatest contribution to forensic law in Victoria was the development of a unique style of cross-examination, a persistent and acute questioning by which a hostile witness could be led to prejudice his own case. Although privately a kindly man to whom many younger colleagues turned for assistance, Purves was notoriously brusque with witnesses, and when a doctor whose reputation he had impugned in court later knocked him into the gutter in Collins Street, public sympathy was not all with the lawyer.

Purves entered the Legislative Assembly in April 1872 as a free trader and constitutionalist for Mornington, and was soon known for his oratory. He was several times offered cabinet rank and regarded by some as a potential leader of the constitutionalists. A latent demagogue, Purves always admired Berry's powers of leadership. But his own talents inclined less to administration than to ideological debate; at the height of the constitutional crisis he once had to be forcibly rescued by friends from an attempt to sway a fiercely pro-Berry mob. In February 1880 he made an apparently quixotic decision to contest the working-class electorate of Footscray, was defeated and in July lost again in the Liberal strong-

hold of Maryborough and Talbot. He never stood for parliament again.

From the mid-1880s Purves's political talents were channelled through the Australian Natives' Association, which had been founded in 1871 as a friendly society and gradually extended its activities to include mutual improvement, debate and public demonstration on questions of national importance. Purves was not, as he and others often claimed, a founder of the association; he joined in 1872 but took no part in its affairs until 1884 when it began a series of protest meetings calling for British annexation in the Pacific. In his addresses to these meetings, and later as president of the A.N.A., Purves developed a vague and ardent vision of Australia's future greatness which he placed sometimes within a renewed British empire, sometimes in glorious independence. During his presidency separatist elements within the A.N.A. pushed him and the association to the forefront of opposition to the Imperial Federation League in Victoria, but his attempt to establish a New South Wales A.N.A. failed when the republican movement in Sydney rejected his position as one of dual loyalty, to Australia and empire both. 'Emperor' Purves's two years as president of the A.N.A. in 1888-90 were marked more by oratorical fireworks than constructive leadership, but they confirmed the association's reputation within Victoria as a publicist organization with some political influence. Purves's oratory aroused in many of the younger generation a strong sense of responsibility for their country's development and a rather populist awareness of their own ability to direct it.

In the early 1890s Purves successfully defended the *Age* in two libel cases, of which the most famous and politically significant, *Speight* v. *Syme*, carried a great load of involved technical evidence; its hearing took 98 days and an appeal of 86 days was also lost. In this decade Purves was sporadically active in the long effort to persuade Victorians of the advantages of Federation, though pressure of business, sickness and his usual impatience with routine meetings kept him from the leadership. He failed to gain a place on the Victorian delegation to the Federal Convention of 1897 but was prominent in the dramatic crusading and canvassing in the last days before the first federal referendum.

Purves was also prominent in Victorian sporting circles as an owner of fine racehorses, a champion shot, and a keen lawn-tennis player and yachtsman. In 1875 he had married Annie Lavinia, daughter of R. Grice [q.v.]; she died in childbirth, and in 1879 he married Eliza Emma, daughter of

W. A. Brodribb [q.v.]. He had one son by his first marriage and two sons and three daughters by the second. On his death on 24 November 1910 the Victorian Bar mourned a leader and inspiration, the A.N.A. its greatest prophet.

Melb Bulletin, 21 Apr 1882; *Table Talk*, 7 Apr 1887; *Age*, 25 Nov 1910; *Argus*, 25, 26 Nov 1910; *Imperial Review*, 49 (1911); J. E. Parnaby, The economic and political development of Victoria, 1877-1881 (Ph.D. thesis, Univ Melb, 1951); M. Aveling, A history of the Australian Natives' Association 1871-1900 (Ph. D. thesis, Monash Univ, 1970).   Marian Aveling

PURVES, WILLIAM (1811-1870), Presbyterian minister, was born on 26 July 1811 at Haddington, East Lothian, Scotland, son of William Purves, artificer. Educated at the parish school, he attended arts classes at the University of Edinburgh in 1827-28 and 1830-31 while studying for the ministry of the Church of Scotland. He was licensed by the Presbytery of Dunbar on 6 April 1836 and arrived at Sydney in 1839. Ordained by the Presbytery of Sydney on 14 December 1840, he was inducted minister at Port Macquarie, where he had the first church and manse built and ministered to settlers in the Hastings, Macleay and Manning Rivers districts. In 1844 the presbytery investigated rumours about him, possibly involving alcohol, but they proved unfounded and malicious. In 1846 after Rev. William McIntyre's [q.v.] defection Purves was appointed to gather the remnant which remained loyal to the church established at East Maitland. With success he built up the congregation which he linked with Largs.

Handsome and cultivated, Purves became an influential figure in wider church and public affairs. In 1850-70 he was a fellow of the first Senate of the University of Sydney. He also chaired the committee which led to the foundation of St Andrew's College. After a visit to Scotland in 1852 as delegate to the Church of Scotland Assembly he returned in 1854, having helped to recruit ministers for the colony. In 1861 he toured the Clarence and Richmond Rivers districts, where he established churches. An ardent advocate of unifying the Presbyterian Churches in Australia, he had published A *Statement of the Merits of the Controversy between the Church of Scotland and the Free Church of Scotland, with remarks on Union* (1854). In 1866 he became second moderator of the reunited New South Wales General Assembly.

Despite their friendly relations, Rev. J. D. Lang [q.v.] claimed that Purves used to 'scamper about the colony in his own private

and secular business' buying land in the Illawarra and New Zealand, a partnership in a store near Yass and looking after his sheep and cattle in Queensland. He also owned real estate in Sydney and Port Macquarie. On 31 December 1840 he had married Alison Inglis Adams, of Portobello, Scotland; she died on 27 September 1857. On 29 July 1859 he married Lucy (d. 1867), daughter of Robert Havens and widow of Thomas Hyndes, of Cheshunt House, Cumberland Place, Sydney.

Purves resigned his charge on 15 March 1870 and on 14 April sailed in the *Patriarch* with his daughter, planning a stay in Britain. He died at sea on 26 April, survived by two sons and a daughter by his first wife, to whom he left goods sworn for probate at £17,000. His second son John Mitchell (1847-1915) was a founder of the real estate business, Batt, Rodd & Purves, represented the Clarence in the Legislative Assembly in 1880-87, was mayor of North Sydney, esquire bedell of the University of Sydney and a founder of the Sydney Lancers.

A memorial is in St Stephen's Church, East Maitland, and a portrait in St Andrew's College.

J. Cameron, *Centenary history of the Presbyterian Church in New South Wales* (Syd, 1905); A. J. Eipper, *The history of the Port Macquarie Charge of the Presbyterian Church* (Port Macquarie, c1947); A. D. Gilchrist (ed), *John Dunmore Lang* (Melb, 1951); C. A. White, *The challenge of the years* (Syd, 1951); *Maitland Mercury*, 27 July 1857, 28 July, 6 Aug 1859; *SMH*, 5 Sept 1870; Presbyterian Church, Sydney Presbytery minutes from 1840, Hunter Presbytery registers for Maitland and Purves references (Hist Records Lib, Assembly Hall, Syd); information from Keeper of MSS, Univ Edinb, and A. J. Gray (Scone).   Alan Dougan

PURY, FREDERIC GUILLAUME DE; *see* De Pury

PUTTMANN, HERMANN (1811-1874), journalist, writer and editor, was born on 12 August 1811 in Elberfeld, son of Anton Püttmann, merchant, and his wife Helene Maria, née Angermund. He became an apprentice in a commercial firm, then matriculated at the Elberfeld Gymnasium and studied briefly at Freiburg University. He settled in Barmen and married Fanny Maurenbrecher (1813-1893); they had eleven children, born between 1835 and 1852. He became editor of the *Barmer Zeitung* in 1839 and was active in the artistic life of the Rhine Province, writing art and travel books: *Die Düsseldorfer Malerschule* (1839); *Der Kölner Dom* (1842); *Kunstschätze und*

Puttmann

Baudenkmäler am Rhein (1843); and a biography of Chatterton and a translation of his works in two volumes (1840).

Püttmann moved to Köln in 1842 and as editor of the *feuilleton* of the *Kölner Zeitung* he was in close contact with some outstanding German writers. He became involved in radical social movements and was dismissed from his position in November 1844. He migrated to Switzerland, but was expelled from Zürich and settled in Kreuzlingen (Lake Constance). By publishing a number of radical anthologies he came into contact with Marx, Engels and Heine, and became a central figure of revolutionary socialist German literature: *Deutsches Bürgerbuch*, 2 volumes (1845-1846); *Rheinische Jahrbücher zur gesellschaftlichen Reform*, 2 volumes (1845-1846); *Prometheus. Organ zur sozialen Reform* (1846); *Album. Originalpoesien von G. Weerth, . . . Freiligrath, Grün, Heine . . .* (1847). Some of these were published uncensored, some immediately banned by the police. Püttmann's own articles as well as some of his volumes of poetry (*Tscherkessenlieder*, 1841; *Dithmarschen-Lieder*, 1844; *Sociale Gedichte*, 1845; *Gedichte*, 1846) show a merging of elements of revolutionary radicalism, utopian socialism, compassionate sentimentality and German nationalism; this 'True Socialism' was attacked and ridiculed by Marx and Engels in 1846-47.

After the outbreak of the 1848 revolution Püttmann returned to Elberfeld after a short stay in Berlin, but could publish only two issues of his new radical socialist weekly, *Der Volksmann* (1849). After the defeat of the revolution he probably left Germany for a time but later returned to Elberfeld, where he established a successful art gallery in 1852. To escape political persecution he fled to London where he was Prince Albert's assistant librarian at Buckingham Palace in 1854.

Püttmann arrived at Hobart Town with his family in May 1855, visited Sydney and finally settled in Melbourne. He was soon active in the literary life of the German immigrants by publishing the Sydney-based monthly *Deutsche Monatschrift für Australien* with J. Kruse in 1859, the weekly *Melbourner Deutsche Zeitung* in 1859-60 first edited with W. A. Brahe and J. Kruse and then by Püttmann alone, the *Australische Monatzeitung* in 1860-61 and the weekly *Deutsche Zeitung* in 1861-62.

Püttmann learned typesetting and his short-lived monthly *Australische Monatzeitung für die Colonien und Deutschland* in February-July 1862 was printed and published by H. Püttmann & Co. in Fitzroy. After an account of Burke's [q.v.] expedition *Geschichte der Victorianischen*

Expedition zur Erforschung Australien's unter Burke's Leitung, 1862) he published an anthology of German humorous writings (*Demokritos: Bibliothek des lachenden Weltweisen,* 1862) and a *Deutsches Liederbuch für Australien* (1862) with popular and classical poetry, patriotic, drinking and Masonic songs, mainly intended for the use of the choir of the Melbourne German 'Turnverein' and of other German-Australian associations in which he was very active. A strange mixture of liberalism and German as well as Australian 'patriotism' is also evident in his well-documented *Gedenkbuch an den Deutsch-Französischen Krieg, 1870-71* (1871) as well as in *Püttmann's Australischer Kalender,* published yearly from 1867 till 1894, and continued by his son after Püttmann died on 24 December 1874 at his house in Richmond. Occasional references to Püttmann appear in the works and letters of Droste-Hülshoff, Engels, Heine, Hess, Marx and Weerth. His extensive personal papers and correspondence were lost by flooding of the cellar of his granddaughter's house.

Püttmann was survived by three sons and five daughters. One of his sons, Carl, became a well-known musician in Adelaide. Püttmann's work as a German-Australian public figure, writer and journalist was mainly continued by his eldest son, HERMANN WILHELM (1840-1914), the founder of the Association for German Schools (Deutscher Schulverein) of Victoria. He published volumes of poetry in English (*In Lengthening Shadows,* 1902) and in German (*In der Fremde: Dichtungen,* 1907), which also contain translations from English into German and from German and French into English, demonstrating a genuine interest in fostering intercultural relationships. Under the pseudonym 'Wayfarer', he wrote a humorous sketch of Melbourne life in rhymed couplets, *Pen and Pencil in Collins Street,* 1891. In 1864 he married Annabella Thomson (1843-1910); they had ten children and were survived by several daughters and grandchildren.

A. Lodewyckx, *Die Deutschen in Australien* (Stuttgart, 1932); M. Gilson and J. Zubrzycki, *The Foreign-language Press in Australia 1848-1964* (Canberra, 1967); F. Kool and W. Krause (eds), *Die frühen Sozialisten* (Olten Freiburg, 1967); M. Vester (ed), *Die Frühsozialisten, 1789-1848,* 2 (Reinbek, 1971); H. W. Püttmann, 'Zur Erinnerung an Hermann Püttmann', *Püttmann's Australischer Kalender* (Melb, 1876).

LESLIE BODI

PYE, JAMES (1801-1884), orchardist, was born at Toongabbie, New South Wales, son of John Pye, farmer, and his wife Mary. John had arrived in the convict ship *Britannia* in 1791 and about 1810 began to grow oranges at Seven Hills near Parramatta. James followed suit, gradually acquiring large orchards in the Field of Mars, near Ryde, and Seven Hills districts.

Pye became an authority on fruit-growing and also carried on some mixed farming. Giving evidence in December 1865 to a Legislative Assembly select committee on disease in fruit trees, he claimed that the current infection in orange trees was caused by 'a change in climate' and variable weather. Prominent in agricultural circles, he was a founding member of the Cumberland, Camden and Cook Agricultural Society in 1843, a founder of the Cumberland Agricultural Society in March 1857, and a vice-president, trustee and committee member of the Agricultural Society of New South Wales in the 1860s. In June 1870 his long informative letter on farming in the County of Cumberland was reprinted in the *Australian Town and Country Journal*; in it he also referred to the value and dignity of labour and the training of youth for useful trades and commented on contemporary social evils.

In 1856 at the first elections under responsible government Pye was elected to the Legislative Assembly as second member for Cumberland (North Riding). Under the headings of 'Progress' and 'Advance Australia' he favoured 'speedy settlement of the land', better communications and the promotion of education. Defeated for Parramatta in the general election of 1858 by George Oakes [q.v.], Pye appealed to the elections and qualifications committee, alleging that Oakes had influenced voters by threats and that £100 had been deposited in a bank to the credit of the Speaker of the House. The committee reported in May 1858 that Pye's allegations were not proved, but his petition was 'not frivolous or vexatious'. Pye then contented himself with local affairs; he was an alderman for Parramatta in 1862-84 and mayor in 1866-67. A member of the local National School Board he also fought hard to secure a water supply for the growing town of Parramatta. In February 1860 he had given evidence to the select committee on the condition of the working class and strongly criticized the attitude and character of the labouring classes in general and colonial-born workmen in particular; he claimed that 'not one in twenty' of the labouring classes were worth employing and though himself native-born stated: 'I never employed a native of the Colony—they will not work—they are very idle'.

Knocked from his horse by a runaway

horse and cart, he died of his injuries on 30 December 1884 at his residence, Rocky Hall, Parramatta. He was survived by his wife Elizabeth (d. 1895), and at least two sons and four daughters. He was buried in St John's cemetery at Parramatta. Probate of his estate was sworn at under £2300.

V&P (LA NSW), 1858, 1, 6, 839, 1859-60, 4, 1444, 1862, 5, 106; SMH, 7 Mar 1850, 16 Mar 1859, 30, 31 Dec 1884; *Town and Country J*, 18 June 1870, 10 Jan 1885; *Illustrated Sydney News*, 25 Nov 1871, 17 Jan 1885; Parkes letters A926 (ML).
                                               G. P. WALSH

PYKE, VINCENT (1827-1894), politician, public servant and writer, was born on 4 February 1827 at Shepton Mallet, Somerset, England, son of James Pyke, ironmonger. At Bristol in 1846 he married Frances Elizabeth Renwick. With his wife and two sons he migrated in the *Candahar*, arriving in South Australia on 1 December 1851. He walked to the Victorian goldfields and after mining for two years used the proceeds to open a store near Forest Creek (Castlemaine). Joined by his family, the business grew slowly and his political activity increased. He opposed the government's mining policy and in 1855 was elected one of the digger representatives in the enlarged Legislative Council. His extreme views led to accusations of communism but his advanced democracy brought some order and realism to the radical opposition and won him respect. The *Argus* applauded his election in 1856 to the new Legislative Assembly, proving 'that the possession of the most decided political sentiments is quite compatible with the spirit of the gentleman'. Unable to afford his unpaid seat, he resigned as a member for Castlemaine Boroughs in February 1857 to become an immigration agent in England under Hugh Childers [q.v.]. This hasty decision was motivated in part by his wish to return to Somerset but more by the prospect of future advancement. The decision was disastrous; he sold his store at a loss and embarked on the first ship out of Melbourne before the legislation creating his post had been passed. The government fell and its successor did not implement the office.

Stranded in England without income until part of his salary arrived to enable him to pay his debts, Pyke returned with his family to Victoria in 1858. From old political allies now in office, he sought a place in the public service and £600 for the money he had lost, but a select committee awarded him only £450. He had been appointed a warden and magistrate at Sandhurst in circumstances that the premier, John O'Shanassy [q.v.], refused to divulge in a later parliamentary inquiry. Pyke's eagerness to accept political honours was frustrated by the absence of a suitable vacancy in Castlemaine and he had to wait until late 1859 before winning re-election for that borough. It coincided with the fall of O'Shanassy's ministry and Pyke became commissioner of trade and customs and in September 1860 president of the Board of Land and Works under William Nicholson [q.v.]. He held his seat in the Legislative Assembly and in 1862 went with a parliamentary delegation to New Zealand.

In Dunedin Pyke accepted an offer from the Otago Provincial Government to be secretary and organizer of its goldfields department. When that office was abolished in 1867 he served as warden and resident magistrate for the Dunstan and Tuapeka District until 1873 when he was elected to the New Zealand House of Representatives for Wakatipu until 1875, Dunstan in 1876-90 and Tuapeka in 1893-94. A competent democrat he was above all a powerful journalist.

In Victoria Pyke had published a lecture on Australian exploration in 1861 and in New Zealand wrote two novels, *The Story of Wild Will Enderby* (1873) and *The Adventures of George Washington Pratt: A Story of the New Zealand Goldfields* (1874).

He published a volume of verses in 1881, *Handy Book of Local Government Law* (1882), *The History of the Early Gold Discoveries in Otago* (1887), *Gold Miner's Guide* (1892) and other works. He promoted railways, explored, was captain in the volunteers, a Freemason and grand master for Otago under the Scottish Constitution, started the *Southern Mercury* at Dunedin in 1874, edited the *Guardian* and the *Dunedin Punch*, and as a devout churchman often acted as a lay reader. An accomplished elocutionist and an entertaining lecturer, he won a prize from the Ayrshire Association for his story, 'Craigielinn', in 1884, and wrote a series on old identities in the *Tapanui Courier*. Though inflexibly just on the bench, he was generous to a fault and a genial companion, using his abilities without stint, but fortune eluded him. He died at Lawrence, Otago, from chronic nephritis and asthenia on 4 June 1894. He was survived by his wife, who died on 7 May 1898, and by four sons and a daughter.

E. H. McCormick, *New Zealand literature* (Lond, 1959); G. Serle, *The golden age* (Melb, 1963); A. H. McLintock (ed), *An encyclopaedia of New Zealand*, 2 (Wellington, 1966); *Argus*, 23-24 Feb 1857, 28 Feb 1888; *New Zealand Mail*, 8 June 1894.   G. R. QUAIFE

Q

QUICK, WILLIAM ABRAHAM (1820-1915), Wesleyan minister, was born on 3 March 1820 at Exeter, England, son of Abraham Quick, furrier, and his wife Abigail, née Biffen. After a brief elementary education he was employed as a solicitor's clerk. Through his mother's influence he became a Wesleyan local preacher and in 1841 was accepted as a probationer for the ministry and appointed to the Liskeard circuit, Cornwall. After ordination in 1842 he married Margaret Saturley and as missionaries they sailed for Freetown, Sierra Leone. Because of trying physical conditions Quick returned to England next year, and served in circuits in Cornwall, London and Glasgow.

In 1855 Quick was sent to New South Wales under the direction of the Missionary Committee, and after his arrival at Sydney in December was superintendent of circuits at Maitland and Newtown. In 1859 he was appointed president of Horton College, a Wesleyan secondary school at Ross, Tasmania, and theological tutor for Tasmanian ministerial probationers. While at the college he capably filled important administrative positions within the Church and was chairman of the Tasmanian District in 1861-71 and president of the Australasian Conference in 1866. In 1872 he resigned from Horton College, and conference appointed him to Wesley Church, Melbourne. He was superintendent of circuits at St Kilda, Ballarat East and Richmond until 1884.

Although lacking formal theological education, Quick read widely and was an independent thinker. In Victoria he was a controversial figure among the Wesleyans. At the 1874 conference he initiated debate on the conditions of church membership, advocating that the test be attendance at Holy Communion rather than the weekly class meeting. Opposition to this proposed alteration was led by Rev. John Watsford [q.v.] who feared that the change would open membership of the denomination to those without religious experience. A further organizational change stressed by Quick was the need for a city mission in Melbourne and he served on the committee responsible for the establishment of the Central Mission at Wesley Church in 1894. Convinced of the importance of an educated ministry in forming a more liberal and progressive denomination, he and Rev. Lorimer Fison [q.v.] advocated the improvement of theological education and selection of candidates for the ministry. In 1879 he was appointed to a committee to raise funds for the establishment of a Wesleyan College to be affiliated to the University of Melbourne. Despite ill health Quick devoted himself in 1882-83 to raising money. The eventual establishment of Queen's College with its improved arrangements for theological education was largely a result of his determination. He was president of the College Council in 1888-1908. Widely respected in both church and community, his last years were spent in retirement at Brighton, where illness and failing sight kept him bed-ridden until he died on 12 November 1915. He published several theological pamphlets and a book, *Methodism: A Parallel* (London, 1889).

A portrait is in Eakins Hall, Queen's College.

Illustrated Aust News, 10 Aug 1874; *Weekly Times* (Melb), 30 Mar 1901; *Spectator* (Melb), 19 Nov 1915; R. Howe, The Wesleyan Church in Victoria, 1855-1901: its ministry and membership (M.A. thesis, Univ Melb, 1965).

RENATE HOWE

QUINN, JAMES (1819-1881), Roman Catholic bishop, was born on 17 March 1819 at Rathbane, County Kildare, Ireland, son of Matthew Quinn, farmer, and his wife Mary, née Doyle. Educated at Kelly's School in Dublin, he was entered at the Irish College in Rome by his uncle, Fr John Doyle, and graduated in 1845 with a gold medal from Pope Pius IX. After ordination on 15 August 1847 he worked in a parish at Blackrock near Dublin, coping with a cholera epidemic. From 14 June 1850 he was president of St Laurence O'Toole Seminary. As confessor and director of the Sisters of Mercy he visited France in 1854 to investigate continental nursing practices, helped to organize the Mater Misericordiae Hospital, Dublin, and arranged to recruit nursing nuns for the Crimean war.

On 14 April 1859 Quinn was appointed bishop of Queensland. After visiting Europe to recruit clergy and nuns he sailed in the *Donald Mackay* and reached Brisbane on 12 March 1861. He found an enormous diocese, weak in personnel, physical resources and financially in debt. His first attempt to resolve the financial problem by demanding control of educational funds collected in Ipswich parish precipitated a long unedifying quarrel with the pioneer Fr McGinty and influential parishioners like

465

Patrick O'Sullivan [q.v.], a quarrel which set the tone for his episcopate.

With help from Mother Mary Vincent Whitty [q.v.] of the order of Mercy he made rapid progress in establishing a Catholic education system, but in alliance with the Anglican Bishop Tufnell [q.v.] sought without success in 1863-64 to divert the tendency towards secularism in education. Quinn's purchase of the *North Australian* at Ipswich as a propaganda organ in the campaign alienated both friends and enemies, particularly when he stubbornly denied any share in the paper, and increased his financial problems. In 1862, impressed by the possibilities of immigration legislation, Quinn founded his Queensland Immigration Society which brought out ten ships with about 6000 migrants, mainly Irish. The Hibernian flood immediately aroused sectarian hostility, fanned by an unguarded remark of the bishop that the colony might yet be called 'Quinn's land'; in 1864 the society was dissolved.

Quinn's conception of his episcopal position was exemplified in a statement during the quarrel with McGinty: 'I am a sacred person . . . anyone attacking my character commits a most gross and sacrilegious act'. Fired by this ideal, he sought to regulate even the smallest details of his diocese and made countless enemies in the process. He tampered with the internal rule of the Sisters of Mercy and in March 1865 replaced the popular Mother Mary as head of the order by a sycophant who called him 'Pater Noster'. In 1867 six priests withdrew from the diocese and complained to Rome. Despite Quinn's objections, they were permitted to move to the United States.

In 1869 Quinn left for the Vatican Council at Rome. He was elected to two minor commissions of the council, neither of which ever met, and saw something of the Italian attack on Rome. During the council recess he visited Ireland but his efforts to recruit priests for his diocese were foiled by wide circulation of his authoritarian reputation and he had to be content with Italians.

On his return to Brisbane in May 1872 Quinn, suffering from rheumatism, faced new problems. His Italian recruits, already at loggerheads with his administrator, Dr Cani [q.v.], had complained to Rome. Unlike Mother Mary Vincent Whitty, Mother Mary McKillop [q.v.], of the order of St Joseph, refused to submit to Quinn's demand for rigid episcopal control of the order and in 1875 her withdrawal of the order from Queensland aroused violent public controversy both within and without the church. In 1877 another group of dissident priests compiled and circulated a

Syllabus Accusationum of twenty-one charges against Quinn which included nepotism, intemperance and undue accumulation of land. The syllabus and a counter petition, the signatures to which were allegedly inspired by pressure from Quinn, were referred by Rome to Archbishop Vaughan [q.v.] for report. Between 1878 and 1880, Vaughan laboured mightily to find the truth through a personal mission by Sir John O'Shanassy [q.v.] in 1878 and what was virtually a system of espionage through prominent clerics and laymen. Before the matter was resolved, Quinn fell ill on the way to Hobart and died at Brisbane on 18 August 1881. In a fervour of Irish nationalism after the Daniel O'Connell centenary of 1875, he had taken to calling himself O'Quinn; his death was registered in that form.

Quinn's piety, zeal and energy had never been in doubt, but in his almost monarchical idea of the episcopal office he frequently lost sight of some of the fundamental principles of Christianity. Curiously, he was not bigoted and was often censured by other members of his church for undue familiarity with Protestants. He may have been guilty of nepotism but charges of intemperance and an enormous personal fortune were probably groundless. His will left all his possessions to the church.

Life and labours of the Right Rev. Dr. O'Quinn (Brisb, 1881); Tyr-Owen, *Obituary notice of . . . Dr. James O'Quinn* (Brisb, 1881); P. F. Moran, *History of the Catholic Church in Australasia* (Syd, 1895); J. N. Molony, *The Roman mould of the Australian Catholic Church* (Melb, 1969); P. J. O'Farrell, *Catholic Church in Australia, 1788-1967* (Melb, 1968), and *Documents in Australian Catholic history* (Lond, 1969); M. X. O'Donoghue, *Mother Vincent Whitty* (Melb, 1972); V&P (LA Qld), 1863, 1st S, 521, 1875, 2, 249; *Brisbane Courier*, 21 Aug 1862; *Town and Country J*, 20 Feb 1875, 27 Aug 1881; Y. M. McLay, *James Quinn: an historical introduction* (MA qualifying thesis, Univ Qld, 1970); Roman Catholic Archives, Box D (Syd); CO 234/11/231, 275, 12/162, 13/297.

H. J. GIBBNEY

QUINN, MATTHEW (1821-1885), Catholic bishop, was born on 29 May 1821 at Eadestown, County Kildare, Ireland, youngest son of Matthew Quinn and his wife Mary, née Doyle. Educated at a private classical school in Dublin, he entered Propaganda College, Rome, in 1837 to study for the priesthood and transferred on 4 September 1839 to the Pontifical Irish College whence he graduated with a doctorate of sacred theology in September 1845. He had been ordained priest in the

Church of St John Lateran, Rome, on 15 February and left Rome on 30 July 1847 for Hyderabad as a missionary with Bishop Daniel Murphy [q.v.]. Broken in health he returned to Ireland in 1853 and became vice-president of St Laurence O'Toole's Seminary, Dublin. In 1859 he succeeded his older brother James [q.v.] as president on the latter's appointment as bishop of Brisbane. In the next years he helped to raise an army of Irish volunteers to defend the Papal States and organized shiploads of Irish migrants for Queensland.

Appointed first Catholic bishop of Bathurst, Quinn was consecrated with his cousin James Murray [q.v.] in Dublin Cathedral on 14 November 1865 by Archbishop Cullen [q.v.]. In the *Empress* he arrived at Sydney in October 1866 and was installed at Bathurst on 1 November. His early dealings with Henry Parkes [q.v.] and the Council of Education over such matters as textbooks for use in denominational schools and the certification and payment of teachers convinced him that government aid for denominational education would not continue indefinitely. He determined to establish a system of Catholic schools principally run by religious orders. Such a system had been initiated in Adelaide under Bishop Sheil and Father Julian Tenison-Woods [qq.v.]. His zeal in founding schools led to a dispute with Mother Mary McKillop [q.v.] over the administration of the Sisters of St Joseph, and finally caused Quinn to found his own congregation of Sisters of St Joseph at Perthville. The dispute frustrated his efforts for many years to get a congregation of Brothers for the diocesan boys' schools, yet he persisted, assured bishops, clergy and laity of the necessity to Catholic schools to increase and preserve the faith, founded St Stanislaus' College, the St Charles Seminary and introduced the Vincentian

Fathers. He was effectively the leader of the New South Wales hierarchy and laity for much of his episcopate. When he came to the colony the aged Archbishop Polding [q.v.] was abroad and the Irish Catholics were opposed to the English Benedictinism that Polding had been trying to establish. Hence they looked to Quinn, the senior of four Irish suffragan bishops, to champion their cause. Though he deplored the extremes to which Irish nationalism at times led, he vainly opposed the appointment of R. Vaughan [q.v.], another English Benedictine as co-adjutor archbishop of Sydney in 1872.

From his position of influence and by the success of his own schools, Quinn won the support of his brother bishops, including Vaughan, and the laity for his policy. When the famous *Joint Pastoral of the Bishops of New South Wales* was issued in 1879, it merely confirmed what Quinn had long been doing and he could rightly claim 'The Archbishop wrote it, but every word of it was mine'. The *Pastoral* precipitated the 1880 Public Instruction Act which withdrew all aid from denominational schools in 1882. Quinn's policy, by then universally implemented in all dioceses, ensured that not one Catholic school in his diocese closed because of the withdrawal of aid. In 1883-84 Quinn visited Europe. He died on 16 January 1885 at St Stanislaus' College and was buried in the Bathurst Cathedral.

B. J. Sweeny, Bishop Matthew Quinn and the development of Catholic education in New South Wales, 1865-1885 (M.A. thesis, Univ Syd, 1968); M. Lyons, Aspects of sectarianism in New South Wales circa 1865-1880 (Ph.D. thesis, ANU, 1972).   BRIAN J. SWEENEY

QUONG TART; *see* MEI QUONG TART